P9-DJL-984

PSYCHOLOGISTS' DESK REFERENCE

Psychologists' Desk Reference

Third Edition

Editors

Gerald P. Koocher
John C. Norcross
Beverly A. Greene

Oxford University Press is a department of the University of Oxford.
It furthers the University's objective of excellence in research, scholarship,
and education by publishing worldwide.

Oxford New York
Auckland Cape Town Dar es Salaam Hong Kong Karachi
Kuala Lumpur Madrid Melbourne Mexico City Nairobi
New Delhi Shanghai Taipei Toronto

With offices in
Argentina Austria Brazil Chile Czech Republic France Greece
Guatemala Hungary Italy Japan Poland Portugal Singapore
South Korea Switzerland Thailand Turkey Ukraine Vietnam

Published in the United States of America by
Oxford University Press
198 Madison Avenue, New York, NY 10016

Library of Congress Cataloging-in-Publication Data
Psychologists' desk reference / edited by Gerald P. Koocher, John C. Norcross,
Beverly A. Greene.—Third edition.
pages cm
Includes bibliographical references and index.
ISBN 978-0-19-984549-1
1. Clinical psychology—Handbooks, manuals, etc. I. Koocher, Gerald P., editor of compilation. II. Norcross, John C.,
1957–editor of compilation. III. Greene, Beverly, editor of compilation.
RC467.2.P78 2013
616.89—dc23
2013006556

9 8 7 6 5 4 3 2 1
Printed in the United States of America
on acid-free paper

We dedicate this volume to

Robin C. Koocher

Nancy A. Caldwell

and

Margaret C. Charmoli, Ph.D.

CONTENTS

PREFACE

Welcome to the third edition of the *Psychologists' Desk Reference*. This book, fondly christened the *PsyDR*, is intended as an authoritative and indispensable companion of mental health practitioners of all theoretical orientations and professional disciplines. This volume compiles, organizes, and presents key guides and essential information that clinicians, from practicum students to seasoned practitioners, want on their desks. It contains assessment guidelines, diagnostic codes, test information, report checklists, practice principles, psychotherapy pointers, ethics refreshers, legal regulations, special-population materials, professional resources, practice management tips, and related data that all clinicians need at their fingertips.

When asked what the *Psychologists' Desk Reference* includes, we reply, "Everything essential but the tissue box." When asked who should purchase it, we reply, "Every clinician."

This new edition, this *PsyDR3*, features the following:

- Thoroughly revised chapters by the field's leaders
- Addition of 29 new chapters, now totaling 145
- Elimination of 17 chapters that readers deemed dated or of limited utility
- Book sections reorganized into a dozen smaller and more specific chunks, making topics easier to find
- Increased emphasis on evidence-based and research-supported practices
- Diversity built directly into individual entries (e.g., citing critical gender, race, ethnicity, age, or other diverse population variations) as well as into the entire volume

A brief history of the *Psychologists' Desk Reference* places our objectives and the revised contents into proper perspective. In 1994, we sent letters to directors of psychology training programs requesting their thoughts on the contents of such a desk reference. In 1995, we surveyed members of the American Psychological Association's (APA) Division of Clinical Psychology. Over 500 practicing psychologists responded to the question, "All clinicians seem to have a file in which they place useful checklists, guidelines, and summaries. If you had such a collection at your desk, what topics would you want in it?" In addition to providing hundreds of nominations and a healthy consensus on the contents, the vast majority agreed that a *Psychologists' Desk Reference* would be both a very practical and a very popular manual for the practicing clinician. In 1996 and 1997, we inventoried the desk contents of several colleagues and interviewed dozens of practitioners regarding their preferences for a functional desk reference.

The second edition in 2005 continued the years of sequential research and development.

The final page of the *Psychologists' Desk Reference* cordially invited readers to inform us of what they would like to be included in future editions. Many excellent ideas were offered in response. Published reviews of the two editions and a dozen reviewers secured by Oxford University Press further sharpened our focus. And if imitation is indeed the sincerest form of flattery, then we are flattered that the *Psychologists' Desk Reference* has spawned several imitators—not nearly as good as our volume, but imitators nonetheless. In sum, the project began with an ambitious idea, was sharpened by program directors' responses, was strengthened by nominations of clinical psychologists across the nation, and was shaped by field observation and collegial feedback.

The positive receptions to the earlier editions convinced us to vigorously maintain our original emphasis on a compact and user-friendly resource. In the words of one reviewer, "The coverage is broad but not superficial; it is comprehensive yet focused." As a consequence, all 145 contributions are concisely written, designed as practical summaries or thumbnail guides, without the obligatory introductory and concluding paragraphs. We chose only authors who possessed special expertise in particular subject areas and who manifested an ability to synthesize the material in 10 double-spaced manuscript pages. That is, these brief contributions are not an "about" chapter but a focused "how to" mini-chapter. The text is a combination of narrative text, numbered or bulleted points, tables, and checklists. The chapter titles are succinct and descriptive; subtitles were prohibited. The six to eight references accompanying each contribution are not intended as an exhaustive listing but, rather, as documentation of key sources for additional reading. In fact, they are titled "References and Readings" instead of the conventional "References."

The format of the *Psychologists' Desk Reference* contributes to its ease of use. This entails the following:

- A detailed table of contents
- A coherent organization into 12 parts, in which the chapters are arranged both chronologically (according to how a treatment or a consultation would proceed) and topically
- Running heads that identify the part number and title on the left-hand page and the chapter number and title on the right-hand page
- Cross-references within contributions to related chapters in the book

This volume is the culmination of lengthy labors and multitudinous contributions; in the best sense of the term, it has been a "group effort." Although we are, of course, ultimately responsible for the book, we genuinely hope that the *PsyDR3* does justice to all those who have assisted us.

From its inception, Joan Bossert, editor extraordinaire at Oxford University Press, nurtured the book. In selecting the contents, directors of training programs, members of APA's Division of Clinical Psychology, dozens of colleagues, and the editorial board of Oxford Textbooks in Clinical Psychology provided invaluable assistance. We appreciate the affirming evaluations and constructive suggestions of the reviewers of the previous editions, as we do the multiple colleagues who recommended new chapters that appear in this edition. More than 175 authors participated generously and adhered to a challenging writing format. These authors represent, in the words of another reviewer, "a veritable *Who's Who* in psychology." Dr. Sam S. Hill III contributed mightily to the editing of the first two editions. Not to be outdone, our partners, children, and friends endured our absences and preoccupations with grace. Finally, we acknowledge each other for the collaborative spirit and the interpersonal pleasures of coediting this volume. Both the process and the product have improved over the years.

Gerald P. Koocher, Ph.D.
Chestnut Hill, Massachusetts

John C. Norcross, Ph.D.
Clarks Summit, Pennsylvania

Beverly A. Greene, Ph.D.
Brooklyn, New York

ABOUT THE EDITORS

Gerald P. Koocher, Ph.D., ABPP, is professor of psychology and dean of the College of Science and Health at DePaul University in Chicago. He also serves as a senior lecturer at Harvard Medical School. He holds diplomas from the American Board of Professional Psychology in clinical, clinical child and adolescent, health, couple and family, and forensic psychology. Dr. Koocher formerly served as editor of the *Journal of Pediatric Psychology* and *The Clinical Psychologist*, and he currently serves on the editorial boards of several scholarly journals and edits the journal *Ethics & Behavior*. A past president of the Massachusetts and New England Psychological Associations as well as four divisions of the American Psychological Association (APA), he served as APA President in 2006. Dr. Koocher is the author or coauthor of more than 230 articles and chapters, in addition to 15 books. His text (with Patricia Keith-Spiegel) *Ethics in Psychology: Professional Standards and Cases* is the best-selling textbook in its field. He has won research grant support from federal and foundation sources totaling more than $4 million.

John C. Norcross, Ph.D., ABPP, is professor of psychology and distinguished university fellow at the University of Scranton, adjunct professor of psychiatry at SUNY Upstate Medical University, editor of the *Journal of Clinical Psychology: In Session*, and a clinical psychologist in part-time independent practice. Author of 300+ scholarly publications, Dr. Norcross has cowritten or edited 20 books, most recently *Psychotherapy Relationships That Work, Self-Help That Works, Clinician's Guide to Evidence-Based Practices in Mental Health, Insider's Guide to Graduate Programs in Clinical and Counseling Psychology*, and *Systems of Psychotherapy: A Transtheoretical Analysis*, now in its eighth edition. He has served on the editorial board of a dozen journals and has served as president of the APA Society of Clinical Psychology and the APA Division of Psychotherapy. Among Dr. Norcross's awards are the Pennsylvania Professor of the Year from the Carnegie Foundation, the Distinguished Career Contributions to Education and Training from the American Psychological Association, and election to the National Academies of Practice.

Beverly A. Greene, Ph.D., ABPP, is professor of psychology at St. John's University in New York and a practicing clinical psychologist in Brooklyn, New York. She is a fellow of seven divisions of the APA as well as an active member of the APA governance. Author of over 100 publications, Dr. Greene served as founding coeditor of the APA Society for the Psychological Study of Lesbian, Gay, Bisexual, and Transgender Issues Book Series, and she serves on the editorial boards of numerous scholarly journals. Twelve of her publications have received national awards that include APA Society for the Psychology of Women Psychotherapy with Women Research Award, Association for Women in Psychology Distinguished Publication Award, and Women of Color Psychologies Publication Award for their contributions to the psychological literature on women, women of color, sexual minorities, and African American families. She is also the recipient of numerous other national awards, including the Carolyn Wood Sherif Award and the APA Distinguished Contributions to Psychology in the Public Interest Senior Career Award. She most recently coedited *A Minyan of Women: Family Dynamics, Jewish Identity, and Psychotherapy Practice,* recipient of the 2012 Association for Women in Psychology's Jewish Women's Caucus Award for Scholarship.

CONTRIBUTORS

Stuart A. Anfang, M.D.
Department of Psychiatry, Tufts University School of Medicine, Springfield, MA
Department of Psychiatry, Baystate Medical Center, Springfield, MA

Paul S. Appelbaum, M.D.
Department of Psychiatry, Columbia University, New York, NY
Division of Law, Ethics, and Psychiatry, New York State Psychiatric Institute, New York, NY

Jennifer L. Bakalar, B.A.
Department of Medical & Clinical Psychology, Uniformed Services University of the Health Sciences

Robert W. Baker, M.D.
Neurosciences Research, Eli Lilly and Company, Indianapolis, IN

Rochelle Balter, Ph.D., J.D.
John Jay College of Criminal Justice, New York, NY

Jeffrey E. Barnett, Psy.D., ABPP
Department of Psychology, Loyola University Maryland, Baltimore, MD

Joseph K. Belanoff, M.D.
Corcept Therapeutics, Menlo Park, CA

Yossef S. Ben-Porath, Ph.D.
Department of Psychology, Kent State University, Kent, OH

Bruce E. Bennett, Ph.D.
Retired, American Psychological Association Insurance Trust, Rockville, MD

Guillermo Bernal, Ph.D.
Department of Psychology, University of Puerto Rico, Rio Piedras, Puerto Rico
Institute for Psychological Research, Montreal, QC

Jane Holmes Bernstein, Ph.D.
Department of Psychiatry, Boston Children's Hospital and Harvard Medical School, Boston, MA

Paula J. Biedenharn, Ph.D.
Department of Psychology, Aurora University, Aurora, IL

Sha'kema M. Blackmon, Ph.D.
Department of Counseling Psychology, University of Memphis, Memphis, TN

Christine Blasey, Ph.D.
Palo Alto University, Palo Alto, CA

Ryan W. Blazei, Ph.D.
Independent Practice, Cary, NC

Bruce Bongar, Ph.D, ABPP
Pacific Graduate School of Psychology, Palo Alto University, Palo Alto, CA
Department of Psychiatry and Behavioral Sciences, Stanford University School of Medicine, Stanford, CA

Richard R. Bootzin, Ph.D.
Departments of Psychology and Psychiatry, University of Arizona, Tucson, AZ
Insomnia Clinic, University Medical Center, University of Arizona, Tucson, AZ

Catherine Boutwell, M.A.
Department of Psychology, New School for Social Research, New York, NY

Stanley L. Brodsky, Ph.D.
Psychology Department, University of Alabama, Tuscaloosa, AL

Elizabeth Brondolo, Ph.D.
Department of Psychology, St. John's University, New York, NY

Lori A. Brotto, Ph.D.
Department of Obstetrics and Gynecology, University of British Columbia, Vancouver, B.C.

Laura S. Brown, Ph.D., ABPP
Fremont Community Therapy Project, Seattle, WA

Gary M. Burlingame, Ph.D.
Department of Psychology, Brigham Young University, Provo, UT

James N. Butcher, Ph.D.
Department of Psychology, University of Minnesota, Minneapolis, MN

Elise Caccappolo, Ph.D
Department of Neurology, Columbia University Medical Center, New York, NY

Linda F. Campbell, Ph.D.
Department of Psychology, University of Georgia, Athens, GA

Michael P. Carey, Ph.D.
Centers for Behavioral and Preventive Medicine, Miriam Hospital, Providence, RI
Brown University, Providence, RI

Brian D. Carpenter, Ph.D.
Department of Psychology, Washington University in St. Louis, St. Louis, MS

Kara Cattani, Ph.D.
Counseling and Psychological Services, Brigham Young University, Provo, UT

Dianne L. Chambless, Ph.D.
Department of Psychology, University of Pennsylvania, Philadelphia, PA

William F. Chaplin, Ph.D.
Department of Psychology, St. John's University, New York, NY

Lindsay Childress-Beatty, J.D., Ph.D.
Ethics Office, American Psychological Association, Washington, D.C.

Lillian Comas-Díaz, Ph.D.
George Washington University Department of Psychiatry and Behavioral Sciences, Washington, D.C.

Mary Connell, Ed.D.
Independent Practice, Fort Worth, TX

Christopher J. Correia, Ph.D.
Department of Psychology, Auburn University, Auburn, AL

Rebecca Coleman Curtis, Ph.D.
Derner Institute of Advanced Psychological Studies, Adelphi University, Garden City, NY

Priscilla Dass-Brailsford, EdD
Department of Psychiatry, Georgetown University, Washington, D.C.

Charles DeBattista, M.D.
Department of Psychiatry, Stanford University School of Medicine, Stanford, CA

Leonard R. Derogatis, Ph.D.
Maryland Center for Sexual Health, Lutherville, MD
Department of Psychiatry, Johns Hopkins University School of Medicine, Baltimore, MD

Robin M. Deutsch, Ph.D.
Center of Excellence for Children, Families and the Law, Massachusetts School of Professional Psychology, Newton, MA

Carlo C. DiClemente, Ph.D.
Department of Psychology, University of Maryland, Baltimore, MD

Raymond DiGiuseppe, Ph.D.
Department of Psychology, St. John's University, New York, NY
The Albert Ellis Institute, New York, NY

M. Robin DiMatteo, Ph.D.
Department of Psychology, University of California Riverside, Riverside, CA

Melanie M. Domenech Rodríguez, Ph.D.
Department of Psychology, Utah State University, Logan, UT

Joyce S. Dorado, Ph.D.
Department of Psychiatry, University of California, San Francisco, CA

Sari Edelstein, Ph.D., R.D.
School of Nursing and Health Sciences, Simmons College, Boston, MA

Spencer C. Evans, B.G.S.
Clinical Child Psychology Program, University of Kansas, Lawrence, KS

Sheila M. Eyberg, Ph.D., ABPP
Department of Clinical Psychology, University of Florida, Gainesville, FL

Carol A. Falender, Ph.D.
Department of Psychology, Pepperdine University, Los Angeles, CA
Department of Psychology, University of California Los Angeles, Los Angeles, CA

David Faust, Ph.D.
Department of Psychology, University of Rhode Island, Kingston, RI
Department of Psychiatry and Human Behavior, Alpert Medical School, Brown University, Providence, RI

Larry B. Feldman, M.D., ABPN
Department of Psychology, Lake Michigan College, Benton Harbor, MI

Daniel J. Fischer, M.Ed.
Department of Psychology, University of New Mexico, Albuquerque, NM
Center on Alcoholism, Substance Abuse, and Addictions, University of New Mexico, Albuquerque, NM

Douglas Flemons, Ph.D.
School of Humanities and Social Sciences, Nova Southeastern University, Ft. Lauderdale, FL

Elaine Orabona Foster, Ph.D., ABPP
Prescribing Psychologist, Lt Col (ret.) USAF

Kenneth France, Ph.D.
Department of Psychology, Shippensburg University, Shippensburg, PA
Warm Line, Carlisle, PA

Lilli Friedland, Ph.D., ABPP
Executive Advisors, Beverly Hills, CA

Patrick C. Friman, Ph.D., ABPP
Vice President of Behavioral Health, Boys Town, Omaha, NE
Clinical Professor of Pediatrics, UNMC, Omaha, NE

Marjan Ghahramanlou-Holloway, Ph.D.
Department of Medical & Clinical Psychology and Department of Psychiatry, Uniformed Services University of the Health Sciences, Bethesda, MD

Nathan D. Gillard, M.S.
Department of Psychology, University of North Texas, Denton, TX

Gerard A. Gioia, Ph.D.
Division of Pediatric Neuropsychology, Children's National Medical Center, Washington, D.C.
Departments of Pediatrics, Psychiatry and Behavioral Sciences, George Washington University, Washington, D.C.

Carol D. Goodheart, Ed.D.
Independent Practice, Princeton, NJ

Whitney L. Gore, B.A.
Department of Psychology, University of Kentucky, Lexington, KY

Thomas Graf, Ph.D.
Driscoll Children's Hospital, Corpus Christi, TX

John R. Graham, Ph.D., ABPP
Department of Psychology, Kent State University, Kent, OH

Roger L. Greene, Ph.D., ABPP
Pacific Graduate School of Psychology, Palo Alto University, Palo Alto, CA

John M. Grohol, Psy.D.
PsychCentral.com, Newburyport, MA

Seth Grossman, Psy.D.
College of Medicine, Florida International University, Miami, FL
Independent Practice, Ft. Lauderdale, FL

James D. Guy, Jr., Ph.D.
Headington Institute, Pasadena, CA

Erin P. Hambrick, M.A.
Clinical Child Psychology Program, University of Kansas, Lawrence, KS

Kristin A. Hancock, Ph.D
Clinical Psychology Program, College of Graduate and Professional Studies, John F. Kennedy University, Pleasant Hill, CA

Christopher G. Hawkey, M.A.
Department of Psychology and Neuroscience, University of Colorado at Boulder, Boulder, CO

Susan Heitler, Ph.D.
Independent Practice, Denver, CO

Nancie H. Herbold, Ed.D., R.D.
School of Nursing and Health Sciences, Simmons College, Boston, MA

Shirley Ann Higuchi, J.D.
District of Columbia Bar Association, Washington, D.C.
Practice Directorate, American Psychological Association, Washington, D.C.

Thomas P. Hogan, Ph.D.
Department of Psychology, University of Scranton, Scranton, PA

Korey K. Hood, Ph.D.
Department of Pediatrics, University of California, San Francisco, School of Medicine, San Francisco, CA

Peter K. Isquith, Ph.D., ABPP
Department of Psychiatry, Dartmouth Medical School, Hanover, NH

Rafael Javier, Ph.D., ABPP
Department of Psychology and Office of Postgraduate Professional Development Programs, St. John's University, Queens, NY

Ronn Johnson, Ph.D., ABPP
Clinical Mental Health Program, University of San Diego, San Diego, CA

Arthur E. Jongsma, Jr., Ph.D.
Psychological Consultants of Grand Rapids, MI

Betsy Kammerer, Ph.D.
Department of Psychiatry, Boston Children's Hospital and Harvard Medical School, Boston, MA

Rhonda S. Karg, Ph.D.
RTI International, Waltham, MA and Durham, NC

Christie P. Karpiak, Ph.D.
Department of Psychology, University of Scranton, Scranton, PA

Florence Kaslow, Ph.D., ABPP
Kaslow Associates, Palm Beach Gardens, FL
Graduate School of Psychology, Florida Institute of Technology, Melbourne, FL

Patricia Keith-Spiegel, Ph.D.
Department of Psychological Science, Ball State University, Muncie, IN

Brian A. Kiernan, MSSA, LICSW
School of Medicine and School of Social Work, University of Washington, Seattle, WA
Swedish Family Medicine-Cherry Hill, Seattle, WA

E. David Klonsky, Ph.D.
Department of Psychology, University of British Columbia, Vancouver, B.C.

Bob G. Knight, Ph.D.
Davis School of Gerontology & Department of Psychology, University of Southern California, Los Angeles, CA

Keely Kolmes, Psy.D.
Independent Practice, San Fransisco, CA

Kathleen B. Kortte, Ph.D., ABPP-CN/RP
Division of Rehabilitation Psychology and Neuropsychology, Department of Physical Medicine and Rehabilitation, the Johns Hopkins School of Medicine, Baltimore, MD

Kathryn Kuehnle, Ph.D.
Department of Psychology, University of South Florida, Florida Mental Health Institute Tampa, FL

Niketa Kumar, M.A., MS
Department of Psychology, St. John's University, New York, NY

Luciano L'Abate, Ph.D., ABPP
Department of Psychology, Georgia State University, Atlanta, GA

Nicholas Ladany, Ph.D.
School of Education and Counseling Psychology, Santa Clara University, Santa Clara, CA

Michael J. Lambert, Ph.D.
Department of Psychology, Brigham Young University, Provo, UT

Jay L. Lebow, Ph.D., ABPP
Family Institute at Northwestern University, Evanston, IL

Kenneth N. Levy, Ph.D.
Department of Psychology, Pennsylvania State University, State College, PA

Teresa A. Lillis, M.A.
Department of Psychology, University of Kansas, Lawrence, KS

John C. Linton, Ph.D., ABPP
Department of Behavioral Medicine, West Virginia University School of Medicine, Charleston, WV

Carla A. Lourenco, Psy.D.
Department of Psychiatry, University of Massachusetts Medical School, Worcester, MA

James L. Lukefahr, M.D.
Department of Pediatrics, University of Texas Health Science Center, San Antonio, TX

Don-David Lusterman, Ph.D., ABPP
Independent Practice, Baldwin, NY

Lauren A. Maggio, MS (LIS), MA
Department of Medicine, Stanford University Medical Center, Stanford, CA

Marlene M. Maheu, Ph.D.
TeleMental Health Institute Inc., Cheyenne, WY

Monica McGoldrick, LCSW, Ph.D. (hc)
The Multicultural Family Institute, Highland Park, NJ

Joseph McMenamin, M.D., J.D.
McGuireWoods LLP, Austin, TX
Department of Legal Medicine, Virginia Commonwealth University School of Medicine, Richmond, VA

Lauren Mednick, Ph.D.
Department of Psychiatry, Boston Children's Hospital and Harvard Medical School, Boston, MA

David Medoff, Ph.D.
Department of Psychology, Suffolk University, Boston, MA
Harvard Medical School, Boston, MA

Theodore Millon, Ph.D., D.Sc.
Institute for Advanced Studies in Personology and Psychopathology, Port Jervis, NY

Clifton W. Mitchell, Ph.D.
Department of Counseling and Human Services, East Tennessee State University, Johnson City, TN

Linda R. Mona, Ph.D.
Veterans Administration Healthcare System, Long Beach, CA

Theresa B. Moyers, Ph.D.
Department of Psychology, University of New Mexico, Albuquerque, NM
Center on Alcoholism, Substance Abuse, and Addictions, University of New Mexico, Albuquerque, NM

James A. Mulick, Ph.D.
Department of Pediatrics, The Ohio State University, Columbus, OH

James G. Murphy, Ph.D.
Department of Psychology, University of Memphis, Memphis, TN

Tess M.S. Neal, Ph.D.
Department of Psychiatry, University of Massachusetts Medical School, Worcester, MA

Aaron P. Nelson, Ph.D., ABPP
Departments of Psychiatry and Neurology, Center for Brain/Mind Medicine, Brigham and Women's Hospital and Harvard Medical School, Boston, MA

Eve-Lynn Nelson, Ph.D.
Department of Pediatrics, University of Kansas Medical Center, Kansas City, KS
Center for Telemedicine & Telehealth, University of Kansas Medical Center, Kansas City, KS

Melanie M. Nelson, Ph.D.
Department of Pediatrics, University of Oklahoma Health Sciences Center, Oklahoma City, OK

Alan C. Nessman, J.D.
Legal and Regulatory Affairs, Practice Directorate, American Psychological Association

Katherine C. Nordal, Ph.D
Practice Directorate, American Psychological Association, Washington, D.C.

Margaret O'Connor, Ph.D., ABPP
Department of Neurology, Harvard Medical School, Boston, MA
Cognitive Neurology Unit, Beth Israel Deaconess Medical Center, Boston, MA

Sueli S. Petry, Ph.D.
The Multicultural Family Institute, Highland Park, NJ
University of Medicine and Dentistry of NJ, Newark, NJ

Kenneth S. Pope, Ph.D., ABPP
Independent Practice, Norwalk, CT

James O. Prochaska, Ph.D.
Cancer Prevention Research Center, University of Rhode Island, Kingston, RI

Myron L. Pulier, M.D., DABPN(P)
Department of Psychiatry, UMDNJ-New Jersey Medical School, Newark, NJ

Stephen A. Ragusea, Psy.D., ABPP
Independent Practice, Key West, FL

Tayyab Rashid, Ph.D.
Health & Wellness Centre, University of Toronto Scarborough, Ontario, Canada

William J. Reed, M.D., F.A.A.P.
Developmental Behavioral Pediatrics, Driscoll Children's Hospital
Texas A&M Health Science Center, Corpus Christi, TX

Robert J. Resnick, Ph.D., ABPP
Department of Psychology, Randolph-Macon College, Ashland, VA

Celiane Rey-Casserly, Ph.D., ABPP
Department of Psychiatry, Boston Children's Hospital and Harvard Medical School, Boston, MA

Courtney E. Rice, Ph.D.
Department of Pediatrics, Nationwide Children's Hospital, Columbus, OH
Department of Pediatrics, Ohio State University, Athens, OH

P. Scott Richards, Ph.D.
Center for Change, Department of Psychology, Brigham Young University, Provo, UT

Ruth Roa-Navarrete, Psy.D., M.S.
Clinical Psychopharmacology, United States Air Force, Alliant International University, Niceville, FL

Michael C. Roberts, Ph.D., ABPP
Clinical Child Psychology Program, University of Kansas, Lawrence, KS

Sean M. Robinson, M.S., M.A.
Nova Southeastern University, Center for Psychological Studies, Ft. Lauderdale, FL

Richard Rogers, Ph.D., ABPP
Department of Psychology, University of North Texas, Denton, TX

Robert M. Roth, Ph.D.
Department of Psychiatry, Neuropsychology Program & Brain Imaging Laboratory, Dartmouth Medical School, Hanover, NH

Sylvain Roy, Ph.D.
Community Head Injury Resource Services of Toronto, Toronto, ON

Alice K. Rubenstein, Ed.D.
Monroe Psychotherapy & Consultation Center, Rochester, NY

Glenda M. Russell, Ph.D.
Counseling and Psychological Services, University of Colorado, Boulder, CO
Independent Practice, Boulder, CO

Colleen A. Ryan, M.D.
Department of Psychiatry, Child and Adolescent Psychiatry Inpatient Service, Boston Children's Hospital and Harvard Medical School, Boston, MA

Jeremy D. Safran, Ph.D.
Department of Psychology, New School for Social Research, New York, NY

Karen J. Saywitz, Ph.D.
Department of Psychiatry and Biobehavioral Sciences, UCLA, David Geffen School of Medicine, Los Angeles, CA

Alan F. Schatzberg, M.D.
Department of Psychiatry, Stanford University School of Medicine, Stanford, CA

Gary R. Schoener, M. Eq.
Walk-In Counseling Center, Minneapolis, MN

Carolyn S. Schroeder, Ph.D., ABPP
Clinical Child Psychology Program, University of Kansas, Lawrence, KS

Edward P. Shafranske, Ph.D., ABPP
Psychology Division, Graduate School of Education and Psychology, Pepperdine University, Los Angeles, CA

Kavita J. Shah, B.S.
Department of Psychology, University of Scranton, Scranton, PA

Allison J. Shale, Psy.D.
Department of Psychology, Loyola University, Maryland, Baltimore, MD

Kimberly Smith, Psy.D.
Cedars Sinai Medical Center, Department of Psychiatry and Behavioral Neurosciences, Los Angeles, CA

Linda Carter Sobell, Ph.D., ABPP
Center for Psychological Studies, Nova Southeastern University, Ft. Lauderdale, FL

Mark B. Sobell, Ph.D., ABPP
Nova Southeastern University, Ft. Lauderdale, FL

Lacey M. Sommers, B.A.
Pacific Graduate School of Psychology, Palo Alto University, Palo Alto, CA

Len Sperry, M.D., Ph.D., ABPP
Department of Mental Health Counseling at Florida Atlantic University, Boca Raton, FL
Department of Psychiatry and Behavioral Medicine, Medical College of Wisconsin, Milwaukee, WI

Sarah J. Sternlieb, B.A.
Department of Psychology, Suffolk University, Boston, MA

Jennifer Stroup, M.S.
Department of Psychology, Radford University, Radford, VA

Glenn R. Sullivan, Ph.D.
Department of Psychology, Virginia Military Institute, Lexington, VA

Susan M. Swearer, Ph.D.
Department of Psychology, University of Nebraska, Lincoln, NE

Andrew Tatarsky, Ph.D
Center for Optimal Living, New York, NY

Marilyn L. Tinsley, M.A.
Lane Medical Library, Stanford University Medical Center, Palo Alto, CA

Caroline Titcomb, M.A.
Department of Psychology, University of Alabama, Tuscaloosa, AL

Michael A. Tompkins, Ph.D.
San Francisco Bay Area Center for Cognitive Therapy, Oakland, CA
Department of Psychology, University of California, Berkeley, CA

Nhung T. Tran, M.D., FAAP
Department of Pediatrics, Texas A&M Health Science Center College of Medicine, Bryan, TX

Michael L. Trieu, M.D.
Psychiatry Inpatient Service, Boston Children's Hospital and Harvard Medical School, Boston, MA

Paula T. Trzepacz, M.D.
Neurosciences Research, Eli Lilly and Company, Indianapolis, IN
Department of Psychiatry, Indiana University School of Medicine, Indianapolis, IN

Peter A. Vanable, Ph.D.
Department of Psychology, Syracuse University, Syracuse, NY
Center for Health and Behavior, Syracuse University, Syracuse, NY

Leon VandeCreek, Ph.D., ABPP
School of Professional Psychology, Wright State University, Dayton, OH

Melba J. T. Vasquez, Ph.D., ABPP
Independent Practice, Austin, TX

Elizabeth M. Vera, Ph.D.
Counseling Psychology Program, Loyola University, Chicago, IL

Eric M. Vernberg, Ph.D., ABPP
Clinical Child Psychology Program, University of Kansas, Lawrence, KS

Steven Walfish, Ph.D.
The Practice Institute, Atlanta, GA

Bruce E. Wampold
Department of Counseling Psychology, University of Wisconsin, Madison, WI

Irving B. Weiner, Ph.D., ABPP
Department of Psychiatry and Neurosciences, University of South Florida, Tampa, FL

James L. Werth, Jr., Ph.D., ABPP
Department of Psychology, Radford University, Radford, VA

Judith C. White, M.S., LCSW
Independent Practice, New York, NY

Erica Whiting, M.S.
Department of Psychology, Radford University, Radford, VA

Thomas A. Widiger, Ph.D.
Department of Psychology, University of Kentucky, Lexington, KY

Arthur N. Wiens, Ph.D., ABPP
Department of Psychology, Oregon Health Sciences University, Portland, OR

Linda Wilmshurst, Ph.D., ABPP
Department of Psychology, Elon University, Elon, NC

Katie Witkiewitz, Ph.D.
Department of Psychology, University of New Mexico, Albuquerque, NM
Center on Alcoholism, Substance Abuse, and Addictions, Albuquerque, NM

Sean Woodland, B.S.
Department of Psychology, Brigham Young University, Provo, UT

Robert Henley Woody, Ph.D., Sc. D., J.D., ABPP, ABAP
Department of Psychology, University of Nebraska at Omaha, Omaha, NE

Victor J. Yalom, Ph.D.
Psychotherapy.net

Jeffery N. Younggren, Psy.D., ABPP
Department of Psychiatry and Biobehavioral Sciences, UCLA David Geffen School of Medicine, Los Angeles, CA

Brian A. Zaboski, B.S.
Department of Psychology, University of Scranton, Scranton, PA

Jeffrey Zimmerman, Ph.D., ABPP
The Practice Institute LLC, Chesire, CT

Edward Zuckerman, Ph.D.
Independent Practice, Greensburg, PA

PART I
Assessment and Diagnosis

1 LIFETIME PREVALENCE OF MENTAL DISORDERS IN THE GENERAL POPULATION

Christie P. Karpiak and Brian A. Zaboski

Table 1.1 summarizes the approximate lifetime prevalence rates of mental disorders in the general population. These rates will vary as a result of different sample compositions, assessment methods, and combinations of diagnostic categories. All sources report data from studies that utilized *DSM-IV* or *DSM-IV-TR* diagnostic criteria.

Eight data sources are presented in the table: the text revision of the fourth edition of the *Diagnostic and Statistical Manual of Mental Disorders* (*DSM-IV-TR*; American Psychiatric Association, 2000); the NIAAA National Epidemiologic Survey on Alcohol and Related Conditions (NESARC; Grant & Dawson, 2006); the National Survey of Children's Health (NSCH; Child and Adolescent Health Measurement Initiative, 2007); the National Survey on American Life (NSAL; Jackson et al., 2004); the National Latino and Asian-American Study (NLAAS; Alegría et al., 2004); the National Comorbidity Survey Replication-Adolescent Supplement (NCS-A; Merikangas et al., 2010); the National Comorbidity Survey Replication (NCSR; Kessler et al., 2005); and the World Health Organization World Mental Health Surveys (WMHS; Kessler & Ustun, 2008).

The *DSM-IV-TR* extracts its prevalence rates from various epidemiological and clinical studies reported in the literature. The next six sources are epidemiological surveys of large noninstitutionalized samples within the United States, and the final source is international in scope. The NESARC based its prevalence rates on structured face-to-face interviews in English or Spanish of more than 40,000 adults in the 50 states and Washington, DC. The NSCH, conducted every 4 years by the CDC's National Center for Health Statistics, is a telephone survey of parents conducted in English or Spanish on the health of children ages 0–17 years in the 50 states and Washington, DC. The 2007 study encompassed more than 90,000 children, and "lifetime" prevalence mental health information is reported for children through age 17.

The remaining data sources used versions of the same measure, an approach intended to facilitate comparison between the various demographic and international populations that were sampled. The WHO Composite International Diagnostic Interview is a structured measure that encompasses criteria from both the *International Classification of Diseases-10* and the *DSM-IV*. *DSM-IV* categories are reported here. The NSAL data come from face-to-face interviews of 6,082 adults, including 5,191 Black

TABLE 1.1. Lifetime Prevalence of Mental Disorders in the General Population

Disorder	*Diagnostic and Statistical Manual of Mental Disorders*, rev. 4th ed. (*DSM-IV-TR*)	National Epidemiological Survey on Alcohol and Related Conditions (NESARC)	National Survey of Children's Health (NCSH)	National Survey on American Life (NSAL) & National Latino & Asian-American Survey (NLAAS)	National Comorbidity Survey Replication-Adolescent (NCS-A)	National Comorbidity Survey Replication (NCS-R)	World Health Organization World Mental Health Survey (WMHS)
Any disorder					49.5%	46.4%	12.0%–39.3% Mdn. 26.0%
		51.2% White 36.7% Mex. American		30.5% African American 29.9% Latino 17.3% Asian American		47.6% White 43.7% Hispanic 38.5% Black	
Adjustment disorders	2.0%–8.0%						
Agoraphobia w/out panic					2.4% total	1.4% total	0.0–9.8% Mdn. 0.6%
				3.2% Latino 2.1% African American	3.4% of girls 1.4% of boys	1.6% women 1.1% men 2.7% Hispanic 2.4% White 2.3% Black	
Alcohol abuse		17.8% total				13.2% total	1.2%–13.5% Mdn. 6.7%
		24.6% of men 11.5% women 20.2% White 12.1% Mex. American		9.7% African American 5.9% Latino		19.6% men 7.5% women	
Alcohol dependence	15.0%	12.5% total				5.4% total	0.1%–4.1% Mdn. 1.5%
		17.4% men 8.0% women 13.7% White 9.8% Mex. American		4.3% Latino 3.7% African American			

Alcohol abuse/ dependence					6.4% total		
					7.0% of boys 5.8% of girls	15.0% Hispanic 13.4% White 9.5% Black	
Alzheimer's	0.8% of women 65y. 0.6% of men 65y. 14.0% of women 85y. 11.0% of men 85y. 25.0% of women 90y. 21.0% of men 90y.						
Anorexia nervosa							0.6% total
	0.5% of women 0.05% of men			0.2% Black total 0.1% women 0.2% men 0.1% Latino total 0.1% women 0.03% men		0.9% women 0.3% men	
Antisocial personality disorder		3.6% total 5.5% men 1.9% women				0.6%–1.0% total	
	3.0% of men 1.0% of women						
Anxiety disorder, any type			4.5% (2–17y)		31.9% (13–18y)	28.8% total	4.8%–25.3% Mdn. 13.7%
		18.3% White 12.2% Mex. American	4.8% boys 4.2% girls	15.3% Latino 9.8% Asian American	38.0% girls 26.1% boys	36.3% women 25.3% men 29.4% White 24.9% Hispanic 23.8% Black	
Attention- deficit/ hyperactivity disorder	3.0%–7.0%		9.5% total (4–17y)		8.7% total	8.1% total	0.9%–4.7% Mdn. 1.8%
			13.2% of boys 5.6% of girls		13.0% of boys 4.2% of girls	9.8% men 6.4% women	

(continued)

TABLE 1.1. Lifetime Prevalence of Mental Disorders in the General Population (*continued*)

Disorder	*Diagnostic and Statistical Manual of Mental Disorders*, rev. 4th ed. (*DSM-IV-TR*)	National Epidemiological Survey on Alcohol and Related Conditions (NESARC)	National Survey of Children's Health (NCSH)	National Survey on American Life (NSAL) & National Latino & Asian-American Survey (NLAAS)	National Comorbidity Survey Replication-Adolescent (NCS-A)	National Comorbidity Survey Replication (NCS-R)	World Health Organization World Mental Health Survey (WMHS)
Autistic disorder	0.02%–0.2%						
Autism spectrum disorder			1.1% total (3–17y) 1.7% of boys 0.4% of girls				
Avoidant personality disorder	0.5%–1.0%	2.4% total 2.8% of women 1.9% of men				5.2%	
Behavior or conduct disorder, any type			4.4% (2–17y) 5.9% of boys 2.8% of girls		19.6% (13–18y) 23.5% of boys 15.5% of girls		
Bipolar I/II					2.9% total 3.3% girls 2.6% boys	3.9% total 4.9% Black 4.3% Hispanic 3.2% White	0.1%–3.9% Mdn. 1.6%
Bipolar I	0.4%–1.6%	3.3% total 3.4% of women 3.2% of men				1.0% total 1.1% female 0.8% male	
Bipolar II	0.5%					1.1% total 1.3% female 0.9% male	
Binge eating disorder				1.7% Black total 2.4% women 0.8% men 1.9% Latino total 2.3% women 1.6% men		2.8% total 3.5% of women 2.0% of men	
Borderline personality disorder	2.0%	5.9% total 6.2% of women 5.6% of men				1.4%–1.6%	

Bulimia nervosa	0.1%–0.3% men 1.0%–3.0% women			1.5% Black total 1.9% women 1.0% men 1.6% Latino total 1.9% women 1.3% men		1.0% total 1.5% of women 0.5% of men	
Conduct disorder	<1.0–>10.0				6.8% total	9.5% total	0.2%–3.4% Mdn. 1.3%
					7.9% of boys 5.8% of girls	12.0% men 7.1% women	
Cyclothymia	0.4%–1.0%						
Delirium	0.4% ≥ 18 years ≥ 55 years						
Delusional disorder	0.5%–0.1%						
Dementia	1.4%–1.6% 65–69 years 16.0%–25.0% 85 years %>						
Dependent personality disorder		0.5% total 0.6% women 0.4% men				0.6%	
Depressive disorder, any type			3.7% (2–17y) 3.9% boys 3.5% girls	14.1% Latino total 19.1% Puerto Rican 16.2% Cuban American 12.8% Mexican American 14.4% Other Latino	11.7% (13–18y) 15.9% of girls 7.7% of boys		
Developmental delay, any type			4.8% (2–17y) 6.4% of boys 3.2% of girls				
Dissociative fugue	0.2%						
Dissociative identity D/O	Subject of controversy						
Drug abuse		7.7% total				7.9% total	0.5%–5.3% Mdn. 1.0%
		10.6% men		3.6% Latino		11.6% men	

(continued)

TABLE 1.1. Lifetime Prevalence of Mental Disorders in the General Population (*continued*)

Disorder	*Diagnostic and Statistical Manual of Mental Disorders*, rev. 4th ed. (*DSM-IV-TR*)	National Epidemiological Survey on Alcohol and Related Conditions (NESARC)	National Survey of Children's Health (NCSH)	National Survey on American Life (NSAL) & National Latino & Asian-American Survey (NLAAS)	National Comorbidity Survey Replication-Adolescent (NCS-A)	National Comorbidity Survey Replication (NCS-R)	World Health Organization World Mental Health Survey (WMHS)
		5.2% women 8.5% White 4.3% Mex. American		6.3% African American		4.8% women	
Drug dependence		2.6% total				3.0% total	0.0–2.2% Mdn. 0.5%
		3.3% men 2.0% women 2.7% White 1.8% Mex. American		2.5% African American 2.0% Latino			
Drug abuse/dependence					8.9% total 9.8% of boys 8.0% of girls	 9.1% Hispanic 7.9% White 6.3% Black	
Dysthymia	6.0%	4.9% total				2.5% total	0.1%–3.6% Mdn. 1.1%
		6.2% women 3.5% men 4.5% White 2.2% Mex. American		2.6% Latino total 4.2% Puerto Rican 4.0% Cuban American 2.4% Mexican American 2.0% Other Latino		3.1% women 1.8% men 4.3% White 3.5% Black 2.2% Hispanic	
Eating disorder, any type					2.7% total 3.8% of girls 1.5% of boys		
Encopresis	1.0% of 5-year-olds						
Enuresis	5.0%–10.0% of 5-year-olds 3.0%–5.0% of 10-year-olds 1.0% ≥ 15 years						

Gender identity disorder	0.003% of men 0.001% of women						
Generalized anxiety disorder	5.0%	4.1% total			2.2% total	5.7% total	0.1%–6.1% Mdn. 2.0%
		5.4% women 2.8% men 4.6% White 2.3% Mex. American		4.1% Latino total 7.3% Puerto Rican 5.4% Cuban American 3.7% Mexican American 3.3% African American 2.7% Caribbean Black	3.0% of girls 1.5% of boys	7.1% women 4.2% men 8.6% White 5.1% Black 4.8% Hispanic	
Histrionic personality disorder	2.0%–3.0%	1.8% total				0.0%	
		1.9% of men 1.8% of women					
Hypomania		2.4% total 2.5% of men 2.4% of women 2.3% White 2.2% Mex. American					
Impulse control disorder, any type						24.8% total	0.3%–9.6% Mdn. 4.4%
						28.6% men 21.6% women	
Intermittent explosive disorder						5.2% total	0.2%–4.7% Mdn. 1.9%
Learning disorder	2.0%–10.0% total 5.0% of students in public schools 4.0% reading d/o 1.0% math d/o		9.7% total 12.2% of boys 7.1% of girls				
Major depressive disorder		13.2% total				16.6% total	3.1%–21.0% Mdn. 10.3%
	10%–25% of women	17.1% women		15.2% Latino total		20.0% women	

(continued)

TABLE 1.1. Lifetime Prevalence of Mental Disorders in the General Population (*continued*)

Disorder	*Diagnostic and Statistical Manual of Mental Disorders*, rev. 4th ed. (*DSM-IV-TR*)	National Epidemiological Survey on Alcohol and Related Conditions (NESARC)	National Survey of Children's Health (NCSH)	National Survey on American Life (NSAL) & National Latino & Asian-American Survey (NLAAS)	National Comorbidity Survey Replication-Adolescent (NCS-A)	National Comorbidity Survey Replication (NCS-R)	World Health Organization World Mental Health Survey (WMHS)
	5%–12% of men	9.0% men 17.8% White 10.9% Mex. American		19.4% Puerto Rican 18.6% Cuban American 14.7% Mexican American 13.7% Other Latino 12.9% Caribbean Black 10.4% African American		12.8% men 17.9% White 13.5% Hispanic 10.8% Black	
Manic episode		3.6% total 3.7% of women 3.5% of men 3.2% White 2.8% Mex. American					
Mental retardation	1.0%						
Mood disorder, any type					14.3% total	20.8% total	3.3%–21.0% Mdn. 10.7%
				9.1% Asian American	18.3% of girls 10.5% of boys	24.9% women 17.5% men 21.9% White 18.3% Hispanic 16.0% Black	
Narcissistic personality disorder	<1.0%	6.2% total 7.7% of men 4.8% of women				<1.0%	
Narcolepsy	0.02%–0.16%						
Nonaffective psychosis (see also schizophrenia)						0.3%–1.5%	
Obsessive-compulsive disorder	2.5% of adults 1.0%–2.3% of children					1.6% total 2.6% women 1.0% of men	

Obsessive-compulsive personality disorder	1.0%	7.9% total 7.9% of men 7.9% of women			2.4% total	
Oppositional-defiant disorder	2.0%–16.0%			12.6% total 13.9% of boys 11.3% of girls	8.5% total 9.3% men 7.6% women	0.4%–3.1% Mdn. 1.2%
Panic disorder	1.0%–3.5%	4.4% total		2.3% total	4.7% total	0.2%–3.0% Mdn. 1.4%
		5.7% of women 2.9% of men 5.5% White 2.9% Mex. American	2.8% Latino total 4.9% Puerto Rican 2.7% Mexican American 2.5% Cuban American 4.1% Caribbean Black 3.5% African American	2.6% of girls 2.0% of boys	6.2% women 3.1% men 5.4% Hispanic 4.9% White 3.1% Black	
Paranoid personality disorder	0.2%–2.5%	4.4% total 5.0% of women 3.8% of men				2.3%
Pathological gambling	0.4%–3.4% adults in the United States, up to 7.0% of adults internationally, 2.8%–8.0% of teens/students	0.42%				0.6%
Personality disorder, any type		14.8%				9.1%–11.9%
Cluster A						5.7%
Cluster B						1.5%
Cluster C						6.0%
Posttraumatic stress disorder	8.0%	6.4% total		5.0% total	6.8% total	0.0–6.1% Mdn. 2.3%
		8.6% of women 4.1% of men	4.4% Latino total 6.8% Puerto Rican	8.0% of girls 2.3% of boys	9.7% women 3.6% men	

(continued)

TABLE 1.1. Lifetime Prevalence of Mental Disorders in the General Population (*continued*)

Disorder	*Diagnostic and Statistical Manual of Mental Disorders*, rev. 4th ed. (*DSM-IV-TR*)	National Epidemiological Survey on Alcohol and Related Conditions (NESARC)	National Survey of Children's Health (NCSH)	National Survey on American Life (NSAL) & National Latino & Asian-American Survey (NLAAS)	National Comorbidity Survey Replication-Adolescent (NCS-A)	National Comorbidity Survey Replication (NCS-R)	World Health Organization World Mental Health Survey (WMHS)
				4.3% Mexican American 4.1% Cuban American 9.1% African American 8.4% Caribbean Black		7.1% Black 6.8% White 5.9% Hispanic	
Schizophrenia	0.5%–1.5%						
Schizoid personality disorder		3.1% total					4.9%
		3.2% of men 3.1% of women					
Schizotypal personality disorder	3.0%	3.9% total 4.2% of men 3.7% of women					3.3%
Selective mutism	<1.0%						
Separation anxiety disorder	4.0% children and adolescents				7.6% total	5.2% total	0.3%–9.8% Mdn. 1.4%
					9.0% of girls 6.3% of boys	10.8% women 7.4% men	
Sleep terror disorder	Unknown						
Sleep terror episodes	1.0–6.0% of children <1.0% adults						
Sleepwalking disorder	1.0%–5.0% of children						
Sleepwalking episodes	10%–30% of children, 1%–7% of adults						
Social phobia	3.0%–13.0%	5.0% total			9.1% total	12.1% total	0.2%–9.5% Mdn. 2.5%
		5.7% women 4.2% men		7.5% Latino total 10.3% Puerto Rican	11.2% of girls 7.0% of boys	13.0% women 11.1% men	

		5.5% White 2.9% Mex. American		7.3% Mexican American 7.2% Cuban American 6.7% Other Latino 7.6% African American 6.0% Caribbean Black		12.6% white 10.8% Black 8.8% Hispanic	
Somatization disorder	0.2%–2.0% women <0.2% of men						
Specific phobia	7.2%–11.3%	9.4% total 12.4% women 6.2% men 9.8% White 7.1% Mex. American			19.3% total 22.1% of girls 16.7% of boys	12.5% total 15.8% women 8.9% men 13.1% Hispanic 12.5% White 11.7% Black	2.6%–12.5% Mdn. 7.1%
Stuttering	1.0% of children 0.8% of adolescents		6.1% total 8.4% of boys 3.8% of girls				
Substance abuse/ dependence, any type				 11.5% African American 4.0% Asian American	11.4% total 12.5% of boys 10.2% of girls	14.6% total 25.7% men 14.1% women 16.1% Hispanic 14.8% White 10.8% Black	3.05–15.0% Mdn. 6.8%
Tourette's disorder	0.05%–0.3% children 0.01%–0.02% adults 0.15% of girls		0.3% total (6–17y) 0.44% of boys				
Trichotillomania	0.6%						

Americans ages 18 years and older. The NLAAS data come from face-to-face interviews of 2,554 Latino and 2,095 Asian American respondents, with interviews conducted in the respondent's choice of one of five languages. The NCS-A reports data from face-to-face surveys of 10,123 13- to 18-year olds, and the NCS-R from face-to-face surveys of 9,282 English-speaking adults, ages 18 years and older.

The World Health Organization WMHS international prevalence estimates in the table are based on published data from participating countries. The data from the United States are found in the NCS-R column and are not included in the WMHS column in this table. Prevalence estimates of major categories (signified by the "any type" designation) are based on 16 countries: Colombia, Mexico, Nigeria, South Africa, Lebanon, Israel, Belgium, France, Germany, Italy, Netherlands, Spain, Ukraine, China, Japan, and New Zealand. Estimates for specific diagnoses are based on between 6 and 14 of these countries. The range and median prevalence estimates across contributing countries are provided.

References and Readings

Alegría, M., Takeuchi, D., Canino, G., Duan, N., Shrout, P., Meng, X-L.,...Gong, F. (2004). Considering context, place, and culture: The National Latino and Asian American Study. *International Journal of Methods in Psychiatric Research, 13,* 208–220.

Alegria, M., Mulvaney-Day, N., Torres, M., Polo, A., Cao, Z., & Canino, G. (2007). Prevalence of psychiatric disorders across Latino subgroups in the United States. *American Journal of Public Health, 97,* 68–75.

Alegria, M., Woo, M., Cao, Z., Torres, M., Meng, X., & Streigel-Moore, R. (2007). Prevalence and correlates of eating disorders in Latinos in the United States. *International Journal of Eating Disorders, 40,* S15–S21.

Alegria, M., Canino, G., Shrout, P. E., Woo, M., Duan, N., Vila, D.,...Meng, X-L. (2008). Prevalence of mental illness in immigrant and non-immigrant U.S. Latino groups. *American Journal of Psychiatry, 165*(3), 359–369.

Altarac, M., & Saroha, E. (2007). Lifetime prevalence of learning disability among US children. *Pediatrics, 119,* S77–S83.

American Psychiatric Association. (2000). *Diagnostic and statistical manual of mental disorders* (4th ed., text rev.). Washington, DC: Author.

Boyle, C. A. Boulet, S., Schieve, L. A., Cohen, R. A., Blumberg, S. J., Yeargin-Allsopp, M.,...Kogan, M. D. (2011). Trends in the prevalence of developmental disabilities in US children—1997–2008. *Pediatrics, 127,* 1034–1042.

Breslau, J., Aguilar-Gaxiola, S., Kendler, K. S., Su, M., Williams, D., & Kessler, R. C. (2006). Specifying race-ethnic differences in risk for psychiatric disorder in a US national sample. *Psychological Medicine, 36,* 57–68.

Broman, C. L., Neighbors, H. W., Delva, J., Torres, M., & Jackson, J. S. (2008). Prevalence of substance use disorders among African Americans and Caribbean blacks in the national survey of American life. *American Journal of Public Health, 98,* 1107–1114.

Centers for Disease Control and Prevention. (2009). Prevalence of diagnosed Tourette syndrome in persons aged 6–17 years—United States, 2007. *Morbidity and Mortality Weekly Report, 58,* 581–585.

Centers for Disease Control and Prevention. (2010). Increasing prevalence of parent-reported attention-deficit hyperactivity disorder among children—United States, 2003 and 2007. *Morbidity and Mortality Weekly Report, 59,* 1439–1443.

Child and Adolescent Health Measurement Initiative. (2007). *National Survey of Children's Health, 2007.* Retrieved July, 2011, from the Data Resource Center on Child and Adolescent Health Web site, www.nschdata.org.

Compton, W. M., Thomas, Y. F., Stinson, F. S., & Grant, B. F. (2007). Prevalence, correlates, disability, and comorbidity of DSM-IV drug abuse and dependence in the United States: Results from the national epidemiologic survey on alcohol and related conditions. *Archives of General Psychiatry, 64,* 566–576.

Falk, D. E., Yi, H., & Hilton, M. E. (2008). Age of onset and temporal sequencing of lifetime DSM-IV alcohol use disorders relative to comorbid mood and anxiety disorders. *Drug and Alcohol Dependence, 94,* 234–245.

Grant, B. F., Hasin, D. S., Stinson, F. S., Dawson, D. A., Chou, S. P., Ruan, W. J., & Pickering, R. P. (2004). Prevalence, correlates, and disability of personality disorders in the United States: Results from the national epidemiologic survey on alcohol and related conditions. *Journal of Clinical Psychiatry, 65,* 948–958.

Grant, B. F., Stinson, F. S., Hasin, D. S., Dawson, D. A., Chou, S. P., & Anderson, K. (2004). Immigration and lifetime prevalence of DSM-IV psychiatric disorders among mexican americans and non-hispanic whites in the united states. *Archives of General Psychiatry, 61*, 1226–1233.

Grant, B. F., Hasin. D. S., Blanco, C., Stinson, F. S., Chou, S. P., Goldstein, R. B.,...Huang, B. (2005). The epidemiology of social anxiety disorder in the United States: Results from the National Epidemiologic Survey on Alcohol and Related Conditions. *Journal of Clinical Psychiatry, 66*, 1351–1361.

Grant, B. F., Hasin, D. S., Stinson, F. S., Dawson, D. A., Ruan, W. J., Goldstein, R. B.,...Huang, B. (2005). Prevalence, correlates, comorbidity, and comparative disability of DSM-IV generalized anxiety disorder in the USA: Results from the National Epidemiologic Survey on Alcohol and Related Conditions. *Psychological Medicine, 35*, 1747–1759.

Grant, B. F., Stinson, F. S., Hasin, D. S., Dawson, D. A., Chou, S. P., Ruan, W. J., & Huang, B. (2005). Prevalence, correlates, and comorbidity of Bipolar I disorder and axis I and II disorders: Results from the National Epidemiologic Survey on Alcohol and Related Conditions. *Journal of Clinical Psychiatry, 66*, 1205–1215.

Grant, B. F., & Dawson, D. A. (2006). Introduction to the National Epidemiologic Survey on Alcohol and Related Conditions. *Alcohol Research and Health, 29*, 74–78.

Grant, B. F., Chou, S. P., Goldstein, R. B., Huang, B., Stinson, F. S., Saha, T.,...Ruan, W. J. (2008). Prevalence, correlates, disability, and comorbidity of DSM-IV borderline personality disorder: Results from the Wave 2 National Epidemiologic Survey on Alcohol and Related Conditions. *Journal of Clinical Psychiatry, 69*, 533–545.

Hasin, D. S., Goodwin, R. D., Stinson, F. S., & Grant, B. F. (2005). Epidemiology of major depressive disorder: Results from the National Epidemiologic Survey on Alcohol and Related Conditions. *Archives of General Psychiatry, 62*, 1097–1106.

Himle, J. A., Baser, R. E., Taylor, R. J., Campbell, R. D., & Jackson, J. S. (2009). Anxiety disorders among African Americans, blacks of Caribbean descent, and non-Hispanic whites in the United States. *Journal of Anxiety Disorders, 23*, 578–590.

Hudson, J. I., Hiripi, E., Pope, H. G., Jr., & Kessler, R. C. (2007). The prevalence and correlates of eating disorders in the national comorbidity survey replication. *Biological Psychiatry, 61*, 348–358.

Jackson, J. S., Torres, M., Caldwell, C. H., Neighbors, H. W., Nesse, R. M., Taylor, R. J.,...Williams, D. R. (2004). The National Survey of American Life: A study of racial, ethnic, and cultural influences on mental disorders and mental health. *International Journal of Methods in Psychiatric Research, 13*, 196–207.

Kessler, R. C., Berglund, P., Demler, O., Jin, R., Merikangas, K. R., & Walters, E. E. (2005). Lifetime prevalence and age-of-onset distributions of DSM-IV disorders in the National Comorbidity Survey Replication. *Archives of General Psychiatry, 62*, 593–602.

Kessler, R. C., Birnbaum, H., Demler, O., Falloon, I. R. H., Gagnon, E., Guyer, M.,...Wu, E. Q. (2005). The prevalence and correlates of non-affective psychosis in the National Comorbidity Survey Replication (NCS-R). *Biological Psychiatry, 58*, 668–676.

Kessler, R. C., & Ustun, T. B. (Eds.). (2008). *The WHO World Mental Health Surveys: Global perspectives on the epidemiology of mental disorder.* New York: Cambridge University Press.

Kessler, R. C. (n.d.). *NCSR (by sex and age)*. Retrieved July 18, 2011, from www.hcp.med.harvard.edu/ncs/ftpdir/table_ncsr_LTprevgenderxage.pdf

Kogan, M. D., Blumberg, S. J., Schieve, L. A., Boyle, C. A., Perrin, J. M., Ghandour, R. M.,...van Dyck, P. C. (2009). Prevalence of parent-reported diagnosis of autism spectrum disorder among children in the US, 2007. *Pediatrics, 124*, 1395–1403.

Lenzenweger, M. F., Lane, M. C., Loranger, A. W., & Kessler, R. C. (2007). DSM-IV personality disorders in the national comorbidity survey replication. *Biological Psychiatry, 62*, 553–564.

Merikangas, K. R., Akiskal, H. S., Angst, J., Greenberg, P. E., Hirschfeld, R. M. A., Petukhova, M., & Kessler, R. C. (2007). Lifetime and 12-month prevalence of bipolar spectrum disorder in the national comorbidity survey replication. *Archives of General Psychiatry, 64*, 543–552.

Merikangas, K. R., He, J., Burstein, M., Swanson, S. A., Avenevoli, S., Cui, L.,...Swendsen, J. (2010). Lifetime prevalence of mental disorders in U.S. Adolescents: Results from the National Comorbidity Survey Replication-Adolescent Supplement (NCS-A). *Journal of the American Academy of Child and Adolescent Psychiatry, 49*, 980–989.

National Survey of Children's Health Data Resource Center. Accessed 7/13/11. www.nschdata.org/DataQuery/SurveyQuestions.aspx

Ortega, A. N., Feldman, J. M., Canino, G., Steinman, K., & Alegria, M. (2006). Co-occurrence of mental and physical illness in U.S. Latinos. *Social Psychiatry and Psychiatric Epidemiology, 41*, 927–934.

Pietrzak, R. H., Goldstein, R. B., Southwick, S. M., & Grant, B. F. (2011). Prevalence and axis I comorbidity of full and partial posttraumatic stress disorder in the United States: Results from Wave 2 of the National Epidemiologic Survey on Alcohol and Related Conditions. *Journal of Anxiety Disorders, 25*, 456–465.

Pulay, A. J., Stinson, F. S., Dawson, D. A., Goldstein, R. B., Chou, S. P., Huang, B.,...Grant, B. F. (2009). Prevalence, correlates, disability, and comorbidity of DSM-IV schizotypal personality disorder: Results from the Wave 2 National Epidemiologic Survey on Alcohol and Related Conditions. *Primary Care Companion to the Journal of Clinical Psychiatry, 11*, 53–67.

Stinson, F. S., Dawson, D. A., Chou, S. P., Smith, S., Goldstein, R. B., Ruan, W. J., & Grant, B. F.. (2007). The epidemiology of DSM-IV specific phobia in the USA: Results from the National Epidemiologic Survey on Alcohol and Related Conditions. *Psychological Medicine, 37*, 1047–1059.

Stinson, F. S., Dawson, D. A., Goldstein, R. B., Chou, S. P., & Huang, B., Smith, S. M.,...Grant, B. F. (2008). Prevalence, correlates, disability, and comorbidity of DSM-IV narcissistic personality disorder: Results from the Wave 2 National Epidemiologic Survey on Alcohol and Related Conditions. *Journal of Clinical Psychiatry, 69*, 1033–1045.

Takeuchi, D., Hong, S., Gile, K., & Alegria, M. (2007). Developmental contexts and mental disorders among Asian Americans. *Research in Human Development, 4*, 1–19.

Takeuchi, D., Zane, N., Hong, S., Chae, D. H., Gong, F., Gee, G. C.,...Alegria, M. (2007). Immigration-related factors and mental disorders among Asian Americans. *American Journal of Public Health, 97*, 84–90.

Taylor, J. Y., Caldwell, C. H., Baser, R. E., Faison, N., & Jackson, J. S. (2007). Prevalence of eating disorders among blacks in the National Survey of American Life. *International Journal of Eating Disorders, 40*, S10–S14.

Williams, D. R., Gonzalez, H. M., Neighbors, H., Nesse, R., Abelson, J. M., Sweetman, J., & Jackson, J. S. (2007). Prevalence and distribution of major depressive disorder in African Americans, Caribbean blacks, and non-Hispanic whites: Results from the National Survey of American Life. *Archives of General Psychiatry, 64*, 305–315.

Williams, D. R., Haile, R., Gonzalez, H.M., Neighbors, H., Baser, R., & Jackson, J. S. (2007). The mental health of black Caribbean immigrants: Results from the National Survey of American Life. *American Journal of Public Health, 97*, 52–59.

Related Topics

Chapter 7, "Identifying and Assessing Alcohol, Drug, and Tobacco Use Disorders"

Chapter 10, "Using the *DSM-5* and *ICD-11* in Forensic and Clinical Applications with Children Across Racial and Ethnic Lines"

Chapter 13, "Using *the International Classification of Diseases* System (*ICD-10*)"

2 CONDUCTING A MENTAL STATUS EXAMINATION

Robert W. Baker and Paula T. Trzepacz

In conjunction with history taking, mental status examination (MSE) provides the database for psychiatric assessment and differential diagnosis. It comprises the observed and objective portion of the evaluation, along with results of laboratory and radiological testing. Although the MSE is part of a thorough physical examination, it is usually more comprehensive when performed by a psychiatrist or psychologist than when performed by other physicians. Except for the cognitive and language portions of the MSE, which usually are administered in a structured fashion, much of the MSE is semistructured, and information is obtained throughout an interview.

The following material describes a standard format for documenting the MSE, along with some advice for its performance. During assessments for follow-up, only particular portions of the MSE may be emphasized. This outline for the MSE has six sections and is derived from our textbook, *The Psychiatric Mental Status Examination*.

APPEARANCE, ATTITUDE, AND ACTIVITY

Appearance is ascertained by direct observation of physical characteristics. The following items should be considered:

- *Level of consciousness*: Normally patients are attentive and respond to stimuli; when this is not the case, the examiner may try to rouse the patient, such as by speaking loudly or shaking the patient's arm. "Hyperarousal" or "hypervigilance" is sometimes seen, such as in mania or stimulant intoxication. A decreased level of consciousness can be described in rough order of increasing severity with the following terms: drowsy, lethargic, obtunded, stuporous, and comatose. Delirious patients by definition have impaired consciousness, with a cardinal symptom of impaired attention.
- *Apparent age* is judged by vigor, mode of dress, mannerisms, and condition of hair and skin.
- *Position/posture* records where the patient is (e.g., in bed, on a chair, or on the floor) and pertinent abnormalities, such as the "waxy flexibility" of catatonia or the use of leather restraints.
- *Attire/grooming* is reported in nonjudgmental, descriptive terms, such as casually dressed, neat, clean, meticulously groomed, unshaven, disheveled, clothing torn, mismatched socks.
- *Abnormal physical traits* are noted, such as skin lesions or tattoos, body odor, sweating, amputations, and Down's syndrome facies.
- *Eye contact* can be described as "good" or "poor" or is described quantitatively (e.g., "made normal eye contact about half of the time").

Attitude describes the patient's approach to the interview:

- Degree and type of *cooperativeness*: Useful terms are cooperative/uncooperative, friendly, open, hostile, guarded, suspicious, or regressed.
- *Resistance*, if any, is noted here, such as "He refused to answer any questions about his family." Resistance may be nonverbal, such as avoiding eye contact, muteness, or fist shaking.

Activity describes physical movement. Five aspects to consider are as follows:

- *Voluntary movement* and its intensity: Increased movement is described directly (e.g., "He was pacing/fidgety/restless") or is labeled "psychomotor agitation." Decreased movement is localized (e.g., paresis or masked facies) or general, known as bradykinesia or (especially if mentation also is slowed or delayed) psychomotor retardation.
- *Involuntary movements* are observed at rest, during motion, and, if relevant, with provocative maneuvers, such as having the patient stand with eyes closed and arms outstretched. Tremors are regular or rhythmic. Resting tremor improves during action, whereas intention tremor is worst during the most demanding phase of an action. Chorea is sudden and irregular, while athetoid movements are irregular and writhing. Dystonias are sustained, like a muscle spasm.
- *Automatic movements* may appear spontaneously during partial seizures. Common examples are chewing, lip smacking, or clumsy limb movements. Movements may be more complex, such as walking or pulling at buttons, but purposeful action is not characteristic of automatism. Typically the patient has decreased alertness during automatic movement; if repetitive, automatisms usually are stereotyped; that is, the same movement is repeated.
- *Tics* are sudden, stereotyped, brief, abrupt, and sometimes (temporarily) consciously mitigated or suppressed. They may increase if topic matter is stressful. Most noticeable are facial tics, but other body areas can be affected, and tics can be verbal utterances, such as in Tourette's disorder.
- *Compulsions* may be reported by the patient or observed by the examiner. Screen by asking about repeated or undesired activities. Patients should recognize that the behavior is unreasonable, but they may become anxious if the action is resisted. Common compulsions include hand washing or checking (locks, stove, wallet, etc.).

MOOD AND AFFECT

Mood is a person's predominant feeling state at a given time. It is judged primarily by self-report but also by observation throughout the interview. Individuals with "alexithymia" have diminished awareness and inability to describe their mood state; nonverbal expression is inhibited. Listed next are six categories of mood states that are used to describe the predominant mood:

- *Normal*: calm, euthymic, pleasant, unremarkable
- *Angry*: belligerent, frustrated, hostile, irritable, sullen
- *Euphoric*: cheerful, elated, happy
- *Apathetic*: bland, dull
- *Dysphoric*: despondent, distraught, hopeless, overwhelmed, sad
- *Apprehensive*: anxious, fearful, frightened, panicky, tense, worried

Affect describes external manifestations of a person's emotional state. Unlike mood, description of affect is entirely objective, and affect is usually variable over the course of an interview, whereas mood usually is sustained for relatively longer periods. The following parameters of affect can be recorded:

- *Type* of affect: Types of affect seen during the interview are reported, using the same list of terms outlined for mood earlier.
- *Intensity* of affect: When increased, affect is described as "heightened" or "exaggerated"; reduced is "blunted"; no emotional expression is "flat" (flat affect has no intensity, range, or mobility).
- *Reactivity* of affect is assessed in the response to emotional cues from the examiner. Normally the examiner should see

reaction to very subtle cues, such as smiling or commiserating.

- *Range* of affect is measured in the variety of emotions expressed during an interview. Inability to express both happy and negative feelings is "restricted" affective range.
- *Appropriateness* or congruence of affect is monitored by comparing emotional expression to the subject matter. For example, the examiner should expect a frightened appearance when anyone is describing being pursued or poisoned by the CIA.
- *Mobility* is the changeability of affect. Rapidly changing affect, especially if precipitous and unprovoked, is "labile" or "volatile." Slowness in change of affective expression can be called "constricted" or "phlegmatic" affect; unchanging affect is "fixed" or "immobile."
- *Self-regulation of affect* refers to the ability of the person to exhibit control over one's emotional expression. The term *pseudobulbar affect* is used. Fast changes accompanied by incongruence to the situation often are associated with poor affective regulation and usually indicate an identifiable central nervous system abnormality. The person may or may not have insight into the problem.

SPEECH AND LANGUAGE

Careful examination can differentiate types of aphasia (demonstrated in Figure 4.2 and Table 4.2 of Trzepacz and Baker, 1993) or other language disorders. Major psychiatric disorders (e.g., mania) can affect speech or language. Eight speech and language parameters should be considered:

- *Fluency* is the initiation and flow of speech in conversation; its description is based on the smoothness of the speech rather than its communicativeness. Fluency is assessed in spontaneous speech, its initiation and maintenance, pauses between words, use of connectors, and grammatical correctness. Abnormalities include nonfluent aphasia, scanning, stuttering, and cluttering.
- *Comprehension*: Spoken and written comprehension is tested by increasingly complex commands (such as "open your mouth" and "touch your right ear with your left hand"). Deafness, paresis, or apraxia may falsely suggest impaired comprehension.
- *Repetition*: Tested by asking the patient to repeat words and phrases.
- *Naming*: Assessed by confronting with an object or picture and asking the patient for the name. Other approaches include requesting the patient to generate a list of words starting with a given letter or testing in nonvisual modalities (e.g., naming a small object by touch alone).
- *Writing*: Assessed by giving dictation and also by requesting spontaneous composition.
- *Reading*: Assessed by requesting patient to read aloud (visual impairment should be excluded).
- *Prosody*: Assessed by monitoring intonation, rate, rhythm, and musicality of speech and relationship of intonation to content of speech. With deficient prosody, speech is monotonous. Prosody underlies much of the emotional expressiveness of speech, such as sarcasm (e.g., consider the different ways to say "you're *really* smart"). Abnormally fast or slow speech is recorded here. Irrespective of rate, speech that is persistently difficult to interrupt is "pressured."
- *Quality of speech*: Assessed in pitch, volume, articulation, and amount. Articulation is tested with phrases like "no ifs, ands, or buts." Dysarthrias reduce clarity. Manics often speak loudly, and depressed individuals may speak softly, with prolonged latency and reduced spontaneity.

THOUGHT PROCESS, THOUGHT CONTENT, AND PERCEPTION

Thought process (or "form") is assessed in spontaneous communication and in answers to questions throughout the interview. It is evaluated orally or in written formats when patients cannot speak orally, such as when intubated. This part of the MSE is objective in that it is based on observation only, but it requires significant reflection and judgment by the clinician, such as "How clear was the communication?"; "Was I frequently confused by the patient?"; "Did he jump from subject to subject, or keep returning to one subject?"; "Did words or ideas keep coming 'out of the blue'?" The following two elements should be included in the MSE report:

- *Connectedness* of thought is how logically or smoothly statements and ideas flow from each other and how relevant answers are to questions. Decreased connectedness is described (in terms for increasing severity) as tangentiality, loosening of associations, or word salad. Circumstantiality is talking around a subject. Flight of ideas is quick and frequent tangentiality, usually with some obvious thread in meaning or word plays, and occurs most often in mania.
- *Peculiar thought processes*: neologisms, perseveration, clanging, or blocking.

Thought content also is described. Spontaneous speech is important, especially in identifying predominant themes, but it is helpful to specifically inquire about the following:

- *Delusions* may be clear-cut and spontaneously divulged or may appear only on questioning. For example, when persecutory psychosis is suspected, gentle probes such as "How safe do you feel?"; "How are people treating you?"; or "Do strangers seem to be noticing you?" may be revealing. Reality testing similarly can be assessed: "How certain are you of that?"; "What do you think is the reason for that?"; or "Do you think it could have been a coincidence?" Behavioral impact determines the severity or dangerousness of delusions. The type of delusion is recorded, such as persecutory, grandiose, referential, somatic, religious, or nihilistic.
- *Overvalued ideas* are illogical or objectively false beliefs, but compared with delusions they are held less tenaciously or with better recognition that they may be wrong.
- *Obsessions* are undesired and unpleasant ("ego-dystonic"); at times difficult to distinguish from delusions, obsessions are recognized by the patient as unreasonable or unwarranted. Ask about any ideas or thoughts that keep repeating; specifically query for common obsessions like losing control, doing something dangerous or embarrassing, or being contaminated by germs.
- *Rumination* is persistent mulling over of an unpleasant thought or theme.
- *Preoccupation* is an unduly prominent recurrent topic that is not a delusion or an obsession.
- *Suicidal ideation* may be expressed spontaneously; if not, probe directly by asking about thoughts of death and indirectly by discussing future plans. Questions about suicidality include "Have you thought about dying?"; "Would you be better off/happier/more comfortable dead?"; "Would you like to die?"; "Have you thought about killing yourself?"; "Are you going to kill yourself?" Other potentially relevant information includes intent, past suicidality, steps taken to settle affairs, means for suicide, alternatives to suicide, barriers to suicide, and so on.
- *Other violent ideas*: Self-harm ideation may be less severe than suicidality, such as laceration, mutilation, or intentional neglect. Ideation of violence to others can be of varying urgency and intensity (e.g., "I'd like to punch him" versus "I'd like to shoot him"). Some important issues are identification of a specific intended victim, availability of a weapon, and barriers to violent action.
- *Phobias*: Agoraphobia, social phobia, and relevant simple phobias are recorded here if the patient manifests such symptoms while being observed by the examiner.

Perceptual Abnormalities

- *Hallucinations* may be of any sensory modality, but auditory hallucinations are most characteristic of primary psychiatric illness. Helpful inquiries include asking whether people are talking about the patient, the patient hears voices without seeing anyone, or there has been communication from God or spirits. Auditory hallucinations may be behaviorally evident if the patient appears to talk to the unseen. Voices that talk to each other or make running commentary on the patient's behavior are particularly severe, but perhaps most important is the impact of hallucinations on behavior (e.g., obeying "command" hallucinations that require violence). Hallucinations of a visual, olfactory, tactile, or gustatory nature further raise suspicion of an identifiable organic etiology.

- *Other perceptual abnormalities* include illusions, derealization, depersonalization, déjà vu, and so on.

COGNITION

This section of the MSE describes higher cortical functions, such as the ability to use intellect, reason, attentiveness, logic, and memory. It is an important part of most screening exams and many follow-up exams, especially when neuropsychiatric dysfunction is likely. Some examination may be indirect, such as evaluating memory by discussion of past conversations, names of medicines, or last week's football game. Cognitive functions can be categorized into a number of main areas. Definitions vary, however, for different types of declarative memory. MSE usually does not include testing of procedural memory. Testing each of the following areas is a reasonable screen for cognitive impairment.

- *Orientation*: Orientation to time, place, and person usually are assessed. Disorientation to person is the best preserved, especially for recognizing oneself.
- *Attention and concentration*: Attentiveness or distractibility can be monitored in the interview itself or formally tested. Digit span is a measure of attention. Tests of concentration include backward recitation of months or weekdays, spelling backward, or serial subtraction. Trail Making Test Part A measures visual concentration.
- *Registration*: The capacity to immediately repeat a very short list of information, such as three to five words.
- *Short-term memory*: Memory over the course of a few minutes. Overlaps with what some term *working memory*. It can be saturated and is not permanent. A common approach is testing recollection of three unrelated items after 2–3 minutes. More detailed approaches include story recall, word list learning tasks, or testing other modalities such as visual memory.
- *Long-term memory*: More permanent memory stores that cannot be saturated. May be recent, such as days or weeks ago, or remote, such as years or decades ago. "Episodic" memory is personal and time tagged; a corroborative source is needed to exclude confabulation. "Semantic" memory tests general information, such as names of recent presidents.
- *Visuoconstructional ability*: Visuospatial abilities are necessary for everyday functions like driving or preparing a meal. Drawing or copying figures, such as a cube, intersecting pentagons, a clock, or a map of the state or country, or making a puzzle can test this function. Getting lost in a familiar environment can indicate visuospatial difficulties.
- *Executive functions*: These are higher level cognitive functions that include abstracting ability, planning ahead, and flexibly switching mental sets. Abstraction can be assessed in the interview through general conversation or by formal testing. For example, cognitively concrete individuals may respond literally to questions such as "What brought you to the hospital?" Formal testing includes identifying similarities between pairs of objects (e.g., table/chair, orange/apple, painting/poem) or meanings of well-known proverbs. Switching mental sets can be tested using Trail Making Test Part B or the Symbol Digit Test.

INSIGHT AND JUDGMENT

Insight is awareness of internal and external realities. Insight is impaired in many neuropsychiatric disorders, particularly when they affect prefrontal cortex function. For the MSE, assess the patient's recognition of illness, how it impacts other people, and the role of treatment.

- Assessment of *judgment* considers the ability to weigh different aspects of an issue. The examiner can discuss important past choices (marriage, work, retirement, big purchases) and recent choices (e.g., How did the patient come to clinical attention?) to demonstrate the degree of judgment used by the patient in decision making. Traditional tests for judgment (e.g., "What would you do if you found a stamped, unmailed envelope on the street?") are relatively insensitive.

- Insight and judgment are impacted by *defense mechanisms*. These are less frequently cited in mental status reports than in the past, but, if included, they belong here. One categorization of defense mechanisms is mature types: altruism, humor, sublimation, and suppression; neurotic types: repression, displacement, dissociation, reaction formation, and intellectualization; immature types: splitting, externalization, idealization, projection, and acting out; and psychotic types: denial and distortion.

References and Readings

American Psychiatric Association. (2000). *Diagnostic and statistical manual of mental disorders* (4th ed., text revision). Washington, DC: Author.

Campbell, R. J. (2004). *Psychiatric dictionary* (8th ed.). New York: Oxford University Press.

Cutting, J. (1990). *The right cerebral hemisphere and psychiatric disorders*. New York: Oxford University Press.

Kaplan, H. I., & Sadock, B. J. (1995). Psychiatric report, and typical signs and symptoms of psychiatric illness. In H. I. Kaplan & B. J. Sadock (Eds.), *Comprehensive textbook of psychiatry* (6th ed., pp. 531–544). Baltimore, MD: Williams & Wilkins.

Ovsiew, F. (2007). Bedside neuropsychiatry: Eliciting the clinical phenomena of neuropsychiatric illness. In S. C. Yudofsky & R. E. (Eds.), *American psychiatric publishing textbook of neuropsychiatry and behavioral neurosciences* (5th ed., pp. 137–187). Washington, DC: American Psychiatric Publishing.

Strauss, G. D. (1995). The psychiatric interview, history and mental status examination. In H. I. Kaplan & B. J. Sadock (Eds.), *Comprehensive textbook of psychiatry* (6th ed., pp. 521–531). Baltimore, MD: Williams & Wilkins.

Trzepacz, P. T., & Baker, R. W. (1993). *The psychiatric mental status examination*. New York: Oxford University Press.

Related Topics

Chapter 3, "Improving Diagnostic and Clinical Interviewing"

Chapter 4, "Increasing the Accuracy of Clinical Judgment"

Chapter 5, "Assessing Suicidal Risk"

3 IMPROVING DIAGNOSTIC AND CLINICAL INTERVIEWING

Rhonda S. Karg, Arthur N. Wiens, and Ryan W. Blazei

Clinical interviews are the foundation of assessment and diagnosis. First and foremost, the purpose of a clinical interview is to give clients the opportunity to present their unique perspectives on the reasons they have sought help. From the standpoint of the interviewer, the purposes of a clinical interview are to gather information about the client and his or her problems, to establish a relationship with the client that will facilitate assessment and treatment, and to direct the client in his or her search for relief. Toward these goals, the following list describes empirically supported and clinically tested guidelines to improve the efficacy and efficiency of interviews.

1. *Prepare for the interview:* Before the initial meeting, carefully review the referral request and other available data. Clients become understandably annoyed by being asked for information contained in the record and frequently feel slighted by interviewers who did not take the time to review their files. In a similar vein, interview preparation should involve becoming well informed regarding the problem areas presented by the client and symptoms that should be carefully assessed during the interview.

2. *Determine the purpose of the interview:* Before proceeding with an interview, the clinician should have a clear understanding of the objectives of the interview. For example, is the purpose to make a diagnosis, to plan treatment, to initiate psychotherapy, or all three? In other cases, the interview will accomplish more detailed objectives. For example, should the client be considered incompetent? Should this patient be released from the hospital? Along these lines, consider whether the priority should be sensitivity (to avoid false negatives) or specificity (to avoid false positives). Use this information to guide the depth and breadth of the interview and the selection of other assessment methods to complement your interview.

3. *Use structured or semistructured diagnostic interviews:* By ensuring coverage of critical areas of functioning and by standardizing the diagnostic assessment, structured and semistructured interviews enhance diagnostic reliability and validity. Examples of these include the Structured Clinical Interview for the *Diagnostic and Statistical Manual of Mental Disorders* (SCID-I and SCID-II; First, Spitzer, Gibbon, & Williams, 1996), the Schedule for Affective Disorders and Schizophrenia (SADS; Endicott & Spitzer, 1978), and the Composite International Diagnostic Interview (CIDI; World Health Organization, 1997).

4. *Administer screening instruments:* To increase efficiency and improve the accuracy of the clinical interview, administer psychometrically sound screening instruments immediately prior to the structured interview. Two of our favorites are the Psychiatric Diagnostic Screening Questionnaire (Zimmerman & Mattia, 2001) and the SCID Screen Patient Questionnaire (First et al., 1996).

5. *Convey the purpose and parameters of the interview:* Present the rationale for the interview and describe what information you expect the client (or other informant) to provide. The intent is to give the interviewee a "set" or an expectation of what will occur during the interview and why this time is important. Describe the amount of available time, the type of questions you will ask, the limits of privileged information, and to whom the interview findings may be reported. Solicit the client's goals and expectations for completing the interview. Monumental misunderstandings can occur when clinician and client are not "on the same page."

6. *Use a collaborative interview style:* Put two minds to work and explore problems *with* the client. A collaborative interview style not only helps build rapport but also sets the tone for working together during the course of treatment. By sharing the responsibilities of their assessment and treatment, clients gain a sense of control and are thereby more likely to adhere to recommendations and are less likely to complain if their progress is bumpy.

7. *Hear what the interviewee has to say:* Clients often express their appreciation that someone was willing to hear them. Give clients (or other informants) sufficient time to talk and tell their story in their own ways and words. Listen profoundly; devote 100% of yourself to the interview, hearing not only what the individual is saying (content) but also what meaning lies beneath the words (process and emotion). Truly listening to interviewees is vital to developing rapport and encourages the expression of valid diagnostic information.

8. *Include a comprehensive analysis of the problem behaviors:* Begin the functional analysis of behavior by probing for the three dimensions of problematic behavior: frequency (how often?), duration (how long?), and intensity (how severe?). Thoroughly examine the contexts in which the problem behaviors developed and in what contexts they are most likely to manifest themselves. For example, what was happening in the life of the person just prior to the onset of symptoms? What internal and external events appear to trigger or exacerbate the symptoms? What appears to strengthen or weaken the problem behaviors? Giving serious consideration to environmental or situational determinants can assist us in making a multiaxial diagnosis (particularly Axis IV, Psychosocial and Environmental Problems) and might reduce the chance of committing the fundamental attribution error.

9. *Include an assessment of character strengths:* As championed by Seligman and colleagues, the positive psychology movement calls for as much focus on strength as on weakness. Any interview should include a few moments on what works for the client, not only on what does not.

10. *Anchor verbal assessments with concrete behavioral terms:* Take pains to ensure that the client comprehends the content of the questions. Speak in terms he or she can understand. Rephrase questions using more concrete or lay terms to help clients grasp the underlying constructs. Provide examples of the symptoms (especially those that are denied) and solicit behavioral referents for the symptoms he or she endorses. Ask questions such as "Can you give me an example of what you mean when you say you are 'depressed'?" or "On a scale of 1–10, with '1' being 'No Desire to Live' and '10' being 'On Top of the World,' how would you rate your current mood?"

11. *Challenge inconsistent or dubious negative responses:* A number of strategies can be used to challenge questionable data. Our favorites are to (1) ask for more information, (2) use amplified reflection (e.g., "So there's *never* been a time when you drove after drinking any alcohol?"), (3) point out the inconsistency to the client (e.g., "Help me understand…"), or (4) normalize the experience (e.g., "Many people feel very upset when experiencing such a loss. How did you feel after your friend was killed?").

12. *Complement the interview with other assessment methods:* Clinicians who rely exclusively on the clinical interview are prone to miss important information. The comprehensiveness and validity of an interview are enhanced by the use of psychological testing, behavioral or situational observations, and collateral data from family or social reports. In fact, research consistently demonstrates that objective psychological testing (especially actuarially driven) should be used in practically all diagnostic interviews (e.g., Dawes, Faust, & Meehl, 1989; Meyer et al., 2001). A few of our favorites are the Minnesota Multiphasic Personality Inventory-2 Restructured Form, the Millon Clinical Multiaxial Inventory-III, and the Personality Assessment Inventory.

13. *Differentiate between skill and motivation:* Traditional interviews frequently confuse a person's skill and motivation. Ask yourself: Does the client have the skills to perform the behavior in question? If so, is he or she sufficiently motivated? What secondary gains are maintaining his or her behavior? While interrelated, the two have differing diagnostic and treatment implications and thus should be clearly delineated.

14. *Consider base rates of behaviors:* Base rates should guide, in part, the prediction of behaviors and the establishment of diagnostic decisions (Finn & Kamphuis, 1995). A corollary is to consider base rates when conducting the clinical interview. Acquire some knowledge of the frequencies of psychiatric symptoms and disorders in the population from which the client is drawn. For example, what is the base rate of committing suicide among older Caucasian males? Consult the extant literature on prevalence rates of psychiatric disorders across client characteristics, paying particular attention to those relevant to your professional setting.

15. *Avoid common interviewer biases:* Although formulating hypotheses is an integral component of interviews, one must guard against biases that might result in skewing information and in making incorrect decisions. As described by Meehl (1977), examples of such biases include a tendency to perceive people very unlike ourselves as being sick (the "sick-sick fallacy"), denying the diagnostic significance of an event because it has also happened to us (the "me-too fallacy"), and the idea that understanding clients' behaviors strips them of their significance (the "understanding-it-makes-it-normal fallacy"). Also be mindful of cultural differences that may interfere with establishing rapport and bias your follow-up probes and diagnostic impressions.

16. *Avoid common response biases:* Clinical interviewers can exhibit verbal and nonverbal cues that reveal their opinions or hypotheses about the client's behaviors. Mindfully demonstrate a nonjudgmental stance to help clients tell their story without concern that you are judging them, for better or for worse. Avoid leading questions and statements that may give the client hints about your judgment or hypotheses since these can lead to response biases. Instead, use open-ended questions and adopt a stance of innocent curiosity, asking clarifying questions even when you are fairly certain what the client is referencing.

17. *Tailor the interview to the client's characteristics:* Be mindful of the client's characteristics before, during, and after the interview. How does one proceed with a patient, a client, a student, an adult, a child, an inmate, a job applicant, a felon, or an athlete? How are interviews tailored for the client's cultural background; the motivated interviewee versus the reluctant interviewee; patients with different diagnoses; interviewees wishing to deceive?

18. *Delay reaching decisions while the interview is being conducted:* Research has generally shown that the most accurate clinical decision makers tend to arrive at their conclusions later than do less accurate clinicians (e.g., Elstein, Shulman, & Sprafka, 1978). The clinical implication of these findings is to reserve your diagnostic judgments until after the interview has been completed so that you are less susceptible to prematurely terminating data collection.

19. *Prepare for ending the interview:* Pause and silently review the information that you have collected. Have you met the objectives of the interview? Is there a part of the client's story that remains unclear to you? Do you need more information for differential diagnosis? Are you able to rate the client's functioning (Axis V) with confidence? If you are missing critical information, decide whether you can fill in the gaps during the current session or whether you will need to schedule a second interview with the client or a collateral informant.

20. *Provide a proper termination:* Anticipate the termination of the interview and prepare the client accordingly. Point out when time is running short (usually 5 to 10 minutes prior to ending the interview). One can combine this forewarning with a brief recapitulation, followed by eliciting the client's reactions to the interview and asking whether there is any additional topic he or she would like to discuss before ending. If applicable, communicate your diagnostic impressions and your treatment recommendations. End the interview with a concluding statement expressing your appreciation and your interest.

21. *Employ debiasing strategies:* Our natural tendency is to search for supporting evidence for our expectations. To help combat this bias, employ a disconfirmation strategy, hunting for information that will disprove initial impressions. What in this protocol disputes the evidence for, say, schizophrenia? Another debiasing strategy is to make yourself think about alternatives after you have generated an initial impression (Arkes, 1981). If we find ourselves unable to generate alternatives, it is time to seek consultation with colleagues. Again, we suggest using base rates and other objective means to help avoid biases and expectations.

22. *Seek supervision and consultation as needed:* Clinical interviews and diagnostic decisions are often complicated by unique and overlapping symptom presentations. Colleagues are a wellspring of information, insights, and perspectives that we may have otherwise failed to consider. Remember that peer supervision often benefits both those seeking and providing consultation, so do not hesitate to ask for help.

References and Readings

Arkes, H. R. (1981). Impediments to accurate clinical judgment and possible ways to minimize their impact. *Journal of Consulting and Clinical Psychology, 49*, 323–330.

Dawes, R. M., Faust, D., & Meehl, P. E. (1989). Clinical versus actuarial judgment. *Science, 243*, 1668–1674.

Elstein, A. S., Shulman, A. S., & Sprafka, S. A. (1978). *Medical problem solving: An analysis of clinical reasoning*. Cambridge, MA: Harvard University Press.

Endicott, J., & Spitzer, R. L. (1978). A diagnostic interview: The Schedule for Affective Disorders and Schizophrenia. *Archives of General Psychiatry, 35*, 837–844.

Finn, S. E., & Kamphuis, J. H. (1995). What a clinician needs to know about base rates. In J. N. Butcher (Ed.), *Clinical personality assessment* (pp. 224–235). New York: Oxford University Press.

First, M. B., Spitzer, R. L, Gibbon, M., & Williams, J. B. W (1996). *Structured Clinical Interview for DSM-IV Axis I Disorders, Clinician Version (SCID-CV)*. Washington, DC: American Psychiatric Press.

Meehl, P. E. (1977). Why I do not attend case conferences. In P. E. Meehl (Ed.), *Psychodiagnosis: Selected papers* (pp. 225–302). New York: Norton.

Meyer, G. J., Finn, S. E., Eyde, L. D., Kay, G. G., Moreland, K. L., Dies, R. R.,... Read, G. M. (2001). Psychological testing and psychological assessment: A review of evidence and issues. *American Psychologist, 56*, 128–165.

Wiens, A. N., & Brazil, P. J. (2000). Structured clinical interviews for adults. In G. Goldstein & M. Hersen (Eds.), *Handbook of psychological assessment* (pp. 108–125). New York: Pergamon.

World Health Organization. (1997). *Composite International Diagnostic Interview (CIDI), Version 2.1*. Geneva, Switzerland: Author.

Zimmerman, M., & Mattia, J. L. (2001). A self-report scale to help make psychiatric diagnoses: The Psychiatric Diagnostic Screening Questionnaire. *Archives of General Psychiatry, 58*, 787–794.

Related Topics

Chapter 2, "Conducting a Mental Status Examination"
Chapter 4, "Increasing the Accuracy of Clinical Judgment"
Chapter 8, "Interviewing Children's Caregivers"
Chapter 13, "Using the *International Classification of Diseases* System (*ICD-10*)"
Chapter 16, "Assessing Personality Disorders"

4 INCREASING THE ACCURACY OF CLINICAL JUDGMENT (AND THEREBY IMPROVING PATIENT CARE)

David Faust

Increased predictive accuracy improves clinical practice. Not only might patients seek guidance about the likelihood of various outcomes (e.g., "Am I in a relationship with a future?"), but intervention usually presumes prediction. Our interventions are guided by our formulations (predictions) about their effects and effectiveness. After all, we would not say, "Let's try this, although I don't have the slightest idea how well it's going to work, and who cares anyway, because what's going to happen next is of no concern," but rather, "I think what's most likely to help is ..." Similarly, therapeutic interpretation is guided by predicted impact or expected benefit.

There is much practical knowledge for increasing predictive accuracy, although mental health professionals may not get exposure to this information and methodology during their training. A few of the more important principles are conveyed in the "rules of thumb" that follow.

GO WITH THE MORE FREQUENT EVENT

Principle

Assume the evidence points about equally toward two alternatives and that the potential disadvantages of misidentifying both conditions or outcomes are about the same. Under such circumstances, you should guess that the more frequent of the two conditions is present. To the extent the frequency of the two conditions or outcomes varies, such a strategy will enhance predictive accuracy. In fact, not uncommonly, the frequency of an event (i.e., the base rate) is the single most predictive variable or useful piece of information.

Illustration

Suppose that Alzheimer's disease occurs about 10 times more often than Pick's disease and that the manifestations of these disorders, at least initially, are often very similar. If one guesses Alzheimer's disease every time, one will prove correct about 9 in 10 times. For example, if, across a series of 100 cases, there are 91 cases of Alzheimer's disease and 9 cases of Pick's disease, and if one guesses Alzheimer's every time, one will achieve a 91% accuracy rate.

Elaboration

This guide, as narrowly stated earlier, assumes that there is about equal evidence for the two conditions and roughly equal costs and benefits for both types of correct and incorrect judgments (i.e., correctly identifying Condition A versus missing Condition A; correctly identifying Condition B versus missing Condition B). Of course, such relatively clean examples are uncommon, and there is often an imbalance across one or both of these dimensions. This does not negate the underlying principle—that frequency data or base rates are often among the most important guides to decision making—but it does call for adjustments.

Suppose that a set of signs indicate posttraumatic stress disorder (PTSD) versus major depression (MD) at a 2:1 ratio, but that in the setting of application MD occurs four times more often than PTSD. Consequently, most individuals with the signs will still have MD. The 4:1 ratio (or base rate) favoring MD more than offsets the 2:1 ratio (of the signs) favoring PTSD. It is simply a matter of one indicator pointing to MD and the other to PTSD, with the former indicator possessing greater power or accuracy. However, there is a partial offset of the 4:1 ratio, and the base rate will not provide as strong an indicator of MD as it would were the sign neutral or not indicative of the alternative diagnosis. In essence, deviations from clean examples change the operating characteristics, although not the underlying principles, and call for certain steps to determine, for example, shifts in the relative probabilities of alternative outcomes.

It is difficult to make these adjustments impressionistically, especially as the differences among alternatives become less extreme. Fortunately one can make exact determinations using relatively simple formalisms (see Meehl & Rosen, 2006). One can also take steps to deal with gaps in information about frequencies or base rates, to incorporate the costs and benefits of different types of correct and incorrect decisions, to use base rates to estimate the likelihood of outcomes, and to combine diagnostic signs and indicators with base rates to determine likelihoods more accurately (see Faust & Ahern, 2012).

Summary of the First Principle

The frequency of a condition or event is often among the most useful, if not the single best, predictor of that event or outcome. Extremes illustrate this point: If something never occurs or always occurs, knowing this alone permits 100% predictive accuracy. Indeed, as events become more or less frequent, or more or less frequent than one another, we can achieve greater predictive accuracy by playing the base rates, that is, by guessing that the less frequent event will not occur or the more frequent event will occur. Under such circumstances, decision accuracy will sometimes increase 10-fold or more by utilizing base rates versus contrary diagnostic or predictive signs or indicators, even those that, in conditions of equal frequency, perform reasonably well.

INCLUDING A BAD PREDICTOR IS USUALLY MUCH WORSE THAN EXCLUDING A GOOD PREDICTOR

Principle

For reasons described later, mistakenly including a weak or invalid variable in the predictive mix often does considerably more harm than mistakenly overlooking or disregarding a good predictor. Therefore, in most situations, especially when other predictors of known value are available, if in doubt, exclude rather than include, that is, avoid incorporating additional variables into the decision process.

Explanation of Principle

We are commonly advised to integrate most or all the data, a strategy that flows from mistaken beliefs about validity and that will almost surely *decrease* overall accuracy. The misconception presumes that validity is cumulative and hence the more (data or predictors) the better. Authors of assessment texts may call for the integration of dozens, if not hundreds, of test scores and data points. Were validity strictly cumulative, then, if one could identify 15 predictors that each accounted for 10% of the variance, their combination would account for 150% of the variance! This does not hold true because predictors are often redundant or overlap with each other. Consequently, they do not carve out unique pieces of the predictive pie but rather re-cover the same ground. To illustrate, if we seek to obtain a proper physical description of a person and measure the person's weight in pounds and then in kilograms with trustworthy scales, the second measurement adds nothing new. We have only measured the same dimension twice. Similarly, two depression inventories may both measure essentially the same thing.

Starting with the first predictor (and for present purposes bypassing the issue of reliability), additional predictors enhance accuracy to the extent they are *both* valid and nonredundant. In many domains in clinical psychology, once one combines about three to five of the most valid and least redundant variables, adding a new variable often does little or nothing to increase predictive accuracy (owing to its redundancy), even if it has sound validity. However, including a weaker or invalid variable cannot help matters and will often decrease judgmental accuracy.

Suppose that sexual abuse has not occurred and that the three best predictors of abuse point in a negative direction. Three other variables, which, unfortunately and unbeknownst to the clinician, truly possess weak or poor validity, indicate otherwise. Clearly, if the weak predictors influence decision making, a correct conclusion might be overturned, and in the long run, the inclusion of weak or invalid variables will have a detrimental overall effect. More generally, one might keep in mind that the weaker a variable the more often it will disagree with the strongest variables.

Further Elaboration

A precise determination of shifts in predictive accuracy as variables are combined in different ways or are added or subtracted is very difficult to accomplish via observation, experience, or subjective methods. For example, even an astute observer will rarely get it exactly right when subjectively "calculating" the figure for shared variance or redundancy across two variables. Proper development of decision procedures through formal research includes analysis of predictive accuracy, level of redundancy, and the impact of adding new variables to the predictive mix. It is a tribute to human ingenuity that we have developed scientific and analytic methods that extend our cognitive reach, much as the telescope extended human senses.

Also contrary to common belief, the exact weighting of variables is often less important than selecting which variables to use and which to exclude. In many circumstances, weighting the relevant variables equally results in the same or similar predictive accuracy as optimal weighting, and the "optimal" weights derived in one situation are often relatively unstable across other situations, reducing their potential advantages (Dawes, Faust, & Meehl, 1989). All of these considerations lead to the same prescription: Identify (preferably through well-conducted research) the limited set of variables that are most valid and nonredundant and then act conservatively, that is, worry more about adding questionable variables to the mix than overlooking additional valid variables.

TO REDUCE RISK OF A BAD OUTCOME, START WITH THE *LEAST* LIKELY EVENT IN THE CHAIN OR SET

Principle and Explanation

When multiple events *all* must occur for something bad to happen, one can achieve the greatest proportionate reduction in risk by diminishing the probability of the *least* likely link. Consider the following example. Suppose two events (A and B) must take place for a bad outcome to occur. Suppose that the probability of Event A is .20 and Event B is .90, making the probability of the outcome .20 × .90 = .18. Now suppose that for practical reasons you can intervene with either A or B but not both, perhaps because of limited time or resources. Suppose further that you can decrease the probability of either variable by .10.

When attempting to reduce risk, intuition often leads us to focus disproportionately on the segment of the chain that appears most likely to occur. For example, if we are trying to avoid a suicide attempt, we might direct a good deal of our effort toward the most probable risk factor (e.g., access to a means). However, consider the consequences of this strategy using the hypothetical figures stated earlier. If I reduce Event B by .10, or from .90 to .80, the result is .20 × .80 = .16, or a minimal reduction in risk. In contrast, if I decrease A by .10, or from .20 to .10, the result is .10 × .90 = .09; that is, I have cut the risk in half.

Differences in proportionate impact can prove even more dramatic when the probability of the least likely event starts out rather low. For example, assume that the probability of A is .06, with B remaining at .90 (for a joint probability of .054), and we could reduce either A or B by .05. If we reduce B, the result is .06 × .85 = .051; but if we reduce A, it becomes .01 × .90 = .009. By correctly directing intervention, we go from a minimal change in risk to more than a five-fold reduction, or from about 1 in 20 to about 1 in 110. The obverse also holds and tends to align more closely with intuition: When one wants a positive outcome to occur, all other things being equal, bolster the least likely link in the chain.

Cautionary Note

Of critical importance, this principle of risk reduction assumes that *all* events in the set must occur for the event to occur. (Technically, one prefers the term *set* rather than *chain* because there is no need to assume a particular sequence.) Also, as with base rates, the conditions stated here (i.e., all other things being equal) often will not hold and adjustments will be needed (e.g., What if I can reduce A, the less frequent event, by .10 and B by .20?). However, a determination is usually simple because one need only multiply the probabilities of each variable by the others (i.e., A × B × C, etc.). The main point is that the tendency to focus time and effort on the most likely event is often misdirected as opposed to the more effective approach.

BEFORE DECIDING, GENERATE REASONS TO DECIDE OTHERWISE

Principle and Explanation

Merely generating reasons to decide otherwise, or actively considering or bringing to mind contrary evidence tends to counter a number of problematic judgment tendencies. For one, once we formulate hypotheses or tentative conclusions, we tend to look for possible confirming evidence more so than contrary evidence, or, given a certain mental set, supportive evidence may be more salient or noticeable. This may skew the evidence that is gathered or considered in favor of supportive evidence, resulting in premature termination of data collection, erroneous conclusions, and overconfidence. Active attempts to recognize and consider contrary evidence tend to rebalance the scales.

Further Explanation

Given the variability of human behavior over time and place, as well as error in our measuring devices, a plausible but false (or mainly false) conclusion will often still garner considerable supportive evidence. For example, even if one erroneously concludes that the patient's behavior leads to high levels of interpersonal conflict, thoroughly probing his or her history may well uncover multiple instances in which such problems occurred. If alternative or contrary evidence becomes more salient, we may overturn the false initial impression.

Confidence that is unduly inflated by the propensity to focus on one side of the coin, or evidence consistent with one's conclusions, can lead to many secondary, damaging judgment practices. For example, overconfidence is associated with tendencies to make unjustifiably extreme or risky predictions (e.g., "I know he won't commit murder when on parole"), to not gather important sources of information (because we believe we already know), and to not implement or learn the many useful methods that scientific research in decision making have uncovered.

PSYCHOLOGY HAS ANSWERED THE QUESTION OF HOW TO PREDICT MOST ACCURATELY

A massive body of literature exists on maximizing judgmental accuracy in psychology. Much of this literature might be reduced to a fundamental guideline: *Diagnostic and predictive accuracy is usually maximized by meticulous adherence to the best validated methods for gathering and interpreting information.* All else being equal, (a) formal or structured methods for gathering information versus less structured methods (e.g., formal tests versus free-form interviews) and (b) formal, scientifically based procedures for interpreting information versus subjective methods (e.g., statistical or actuarial methods versus impressionistic judgment) achieve greater overall accuracy (see Dawes, Faust, & Meehl, 1989; Grove, Zald, Lebow, Snitz, & Nelson, 2000). Meticulous application of these superior methods markedly increases the frequency with which clinicians achieve satisfactory or strong levels of predictive accuracy and markedly decreases the frequency of weak or poor performance levels (see Faust & Ahern, 2012). Such improved accuracy, especially over the life of a clinician, translates into major gains in patient welfare.

None of this is to argue for following formal procedures blindly or never deviating from validated or statistically based decision procedures. However, as research abundantly shows, one should not countervail the best supported procedures or outcomes too often or too freely because such a decision policy will very likely lead to more errors overall. As Einhorn (1986) cogently argued, one sometimes has to learn to live with a certain level of imperfection or error to make less error, lest our admirable intentions to do better inadvertently compound rather than reduce mistakes.

One often hears that few formal decision or interpretive procedures exist. This counterfactual belief tends to conflate the considerable but less voluminous body of studies comparing formal versus impressionistic judgment methods (which number in the hundreds) with studies on the development and evaluation of formal decision procedures or statistical methods (which number in the thousands). The comparative literature, which covers a broad array of decision tasks, shows that properly developed, formal decision methods almost always equal or exceed impressionistic methods and thus offer a superior overall method. Hence, in a predictive domain in which comparative studies have not been conducted, it is still a very good bet that formal methods will equal or surpass subjective methods and rather unlikely that the obverse will hold. Recognizing these odds, one can turn to the thousands of studies on the efficacy of formal or actuarial (statistical) decision methods, covering such matters as the identification of psychological disorders; the prediction of suicide, violent behavior, and reoffending; the diagnosis of brain disorders; and the selection of treatment modalities, and apply them productively to one's practice.

References and Readings

Arkes, H. R. (1981). Impediments to accurate clinical judgment and possible ways to minimize their impact. *Journal of Consulting and Clinical Psychology, 49,* 323–330.

Dawes, R. M., Faust, D., & Meehl, P. E. (1989). Clinical versus actuarial judgment. *Science, 43,* 1668–1674.

Einhorn, H. J. (1986). Accepting error to make less error. *Journal of Personality Assessment, 50,* 387–395.

Faust, D., & Ahern, D. C. (2012). Clinical judgment and prediction. In D. Faust, *Coping with psychiatric and psychological testimony* (6th ed., pp. 147–208). New York: Oxford University Press.

Grove, W.M., Zald, D. H., Lebow, B. S., Snitz, B. E., & Nelson, C. (2000). Clinical vs. mechanical prediction: A meta-analysis. *Psychological Assessment, 12,* 19–30.

Larrick, R. P. (2004). Debiasing. In D. J. Koehler & N. Harvey (Eds.), *Blackwell handbook of judgment and decision making* (pp. 316–337). Malden, MA: Blackwell.

Meehl, P. E. (1973). *Psychodiagnosis: Selected papers.* Minneapolis: University of Minnesota Press.

Meehl, P. E., & Rosen, A. (2006). Antecedent probability and the efficiency of psychometric signs, patterns, or cutting scores. In N. G. Waller, L. J. Yonce, W. M. Grove, D. Faust, & M. F. Lenzenweger (Eds.), *A Paul Meehl reader: Essays on the practice of scientific psychology* (pp. 213–236). Mahwah, NJ: Erlbaum.

Related Topics

Chapter 2, "Conducting a Mental Status Examination"

Chapter 3, "Improving Diagnostic and Clinical Interviewing"

Chapter 51, "Conducting Evaluations of Client Outcomes and Satisfactions"

5 ASSESSING SUICIDAL RISK

Kenneth S. Pope and Melba J. T. Vasquez

This chapter lists 22 risk factors for suicide, followed by seven important components of a valid, effective assessment of suicidal risk. Four qualifications apply when considering the following risk factors:

- The brief nature of this chapter allows mentioning these factors only in a very general way. Many exceptions may apply to the trends outlined here, and various factors may interact with one another to alter actual risk. Our purpose serves solely to call attention to some areas that clinicians should consider in assessing risk.
- This list presents a mere snapshot of some current trends. Emerging research continues to correct false assumptions and refine our understandings, as well as reflect changes. For example, some indications suggest an increase in the suicide rate for women, bringing it closer to that for men.

- This list is by no means comprehensive. It provides examples only of some of the kinds of factors statistically associated with suicide attempts or completed suicides.
- These factors may prove useful as general guidelines but cannot be applied in an unthinking, mechanical, conclusive manner. A given individual may rank in the lowest category of each of these factors and still commit suicide. These factors serve as aids to and not substitutes for a careful, comprehensive, and personal evaluation of a unique person's suicidal risk.

TWENTY-TWO RISK FACTORS

The following suicide risk factors are adapted from Pope and Vasquez (2011):

1. *Direct verbal warning.* A direct statement of intention to commit suicide is one of the most useful single predictors. Take any such statement seriously. Resist the temptation to reflexively dismiss such warnings as "a hysterical bid for attention," "a borderline manipulation," "a clear expression of negative transference," "an attempt to provoke the therapist," or "yet another grab for power in the interpersonal struggle with the therapist." It may be any or all of those and yet still indicate a serious risk of suicide.
2. *Plan.* The presence of a plan increases the risk. The more specific, detailed, lethal, and feasible the plan is, the greater the risk posed.
3. *Past attempts.* Most, and perhaps as many as 80% of, completed suicides are preceded by a prior attempt. found that the client group with the greatest suicidal rate were those who had entered into treatment with a history of at least one attempt.
4. *Indirect statements and behavioral signs.* People planning to end their lives may communicate their intent indirectly through their words and actions—for example, talking about "going away," speculating on what death would be like, giving away their most valued possessions, or acquiring lethal instruments.
5. *Depression.* The suicide rate for those with clinical depression is about 15–25 times greater than for the general population.
6. *Hopelessness.* The sense of hopelessness appears to be a key aspect of depression's link with suicidal risk.
7. *Intoxication.* Between one-fourth and one-third of all suicides are linked to alcohol as a contributing factor; a much higher percentage may be associated with the presence of alcohol (without clear indication of its contribution to the suicidal process and lethal outcome).
8. *Marital separation* (distinct from divorce). Wyder, Ward, and De Leo (2009) found that "[f]or both males and females separation created a risk of suicide at least four times higher than any other marital status. The risk was particularly high for males aged 15 to 24" (p. 208).
9. *Clinical syndromes.* People suffering from a distinct clinical syndrome such as schizophrenia, alcoholism and other substance abuse disorders, anxiety disorders, and mood disorders tend to be at much higher risk for suicide. Other clinical syndromes may also be associated with an increased risk.
10. *Sex.* The suicide rate for men is more than three times that for women. For youths, the rate is closer to four or five to one. The rate of suicide attempts for women is about two or three times that for men.
11. *Age.* A significant change occurred relatively recently in this category. In recent decades, the risk for suicide tended to increase over the adult life cycle. However, more recently suicide has peaked in middle age: "The highest rates of suicide by age group occurred among persons aged 45–54 years, 75–84 years, and 35–44 years (17.6, 16.4, and 16.3 per 100,000 population, respectively)" (Karch, Dahlberg, & Patel, 2010).
12. *Race.* Generally in the United States, American Indians, Alaskan Natives, and non-Hispanic Whites tend to have the highest suicide rates.
13. *Religion.* The suicide rates among Protestants tend to be higher than those among Jews and Catholics.

14. *Living alone*. The risk of suicide tends to be reduced if someone is not living alone, reduced even more if he or she is living with a spouse, and reduced even further if there are children.
15. *Bereavement*. When we lose someone we love or care about, statistically the risk of suicide goes up.
16. *Unemployment*. Unemployment tends to increase the risk for suicide.
17. *Health status*. Illness and somatic complaints are associated with increased suicidal risk, as are disturbances in patterns of sleeping and eating.
18. *Impulsivity*. Those with poor impulse control are at increased risk for taking their own lives.
19. *Rigid thinking*. Suicidal individuals often display a rigid, all-or-none way of thinking. A typical statement might be, "If I can't find a job by the end of the month, the only real alternative is suicide."
20. *Stressful events*. Excessive numbers of undesirable events with negative outcomes have been associated with increased suicidal risk.
21. *Release from hospitalization*. Hunt and colleagues' (2009) study of "Suicide in Recently Discharged Psychiatric Patients: A Case-Control Study" found that the "weeks after discharge...represent a critical period for suicide risk. Measures that could reduce risk include intensive and early community follow-up. Assessment of risk should include established risk factors as well as current mental state and there should be clear follow-up procedures for those who have self-discharged" (p. 443). Francis (2009) points out the relationship between suicidal risk and release from hospitalization may be complex when borderline personality disorder is at issue: "People with borderline personality disorder (BPD) are sometimes admitted to inpatient wards due to risk to themselves. However, recent research indicates inpatient settings are detrimental to BPD and can worsen symptoms (unless they are planned short stays). Staff are often too fearful...to release them if they are still expressing suicidal thoughts. If the presentation is not different (no major crises have occurred, no major losses made) then clinically indicated risk-taking is the recommended course of action" (p. 253).
22. *Lack of a sense of belonging*. Joiner's review of the research and his own studies led him to conclude that an unmet need to belong is a contributor to suicidal desire: "Suicidal individuals may experience interactions that do not satisfy their need to belong (e.g., relationships that are unpleasant, unstable, infrequent, or without proximity or may not feel connected to others and cared about)" (2005, p. 97).

CONDUCTING AN ADEQUATE ASSESSMENT

Even with an adequate knowledge of risk factors, assessing suicidal risk can be a stressful, difficult process for many of us. A patient's life may depend on an accurate assessment. Attending to the following issues can help insure a sound assessment.

- *The unspoken*. There can be times in psychotherapy when the possibility of suicide is the elephant in the room that neither therapist nor patient acknowledges. The myth that raising the topic of suicide with a patient may increase the likelihood that the patient will act on the idea is but one of the many factors that can lead therapists to avoid an explicit discussion. If we begin to suspect that the patient is actively avoiding the topic, might have concerns in that area, or could be at risk, exploring the issue sensitively, directly, and frankly can prove crucial.
- *Specifics*. If there are any indications of suicide risk, try to replace whatever is vague, abstract, or general with information that is as precise and specific as possible. For example, if the patient intends to commit suicide, is it at some unspecified place and time in the future or in a specific setting at a specific date and time of day? Does the intent include a plan? Is there a specific method (e.g., gun, pills, hanging), how likely lethal is the method and does the patient have access to the means or

already have the means in hand? Does the plan include physically injuring or killing another person (e.g., a murder-suicide)? Even if the patient does not intend to harm others, could the chosen method endanger others (e.g., jumping from an overpass into traffic).

- *Protective factors.* An adequate assessment includes protective factors. What cognitive-affective factors (e.g., attributional styles), personality traits, and social or environmental resources does the patient have that may be sources of resilience or serve as buffers against suicide? What is there that the patient cares about or feels connected to that can serve as a source of meaning, hope, comfort, or fulfillment? Is there a relative, neighbor, or pet whom the patient loves and for whom the patient has important responsibilities? Are there causes or projects to which the patient is devoted? Is the patient a member of a religious, civic, or other organization, club, institution, or group in which the patient can become more active and make a more meaningful and satisfying contribution? In some cases, particularly within the context of a strong therapeutic alliance, the presence of a contract (e.g., the patient promises not to commit suicide or not to commit suicide without first taking a set of specified steps such as meeting with the therapist to discuss it) can be a protective factor; however, sometimes contracts may be ineffective or even counterproductive. It is important to remember that even the presence of a contract and other buffering or protective factors does free the therapist from the responsibility of continuing to monitor suicide risk and to insure that the assessment remains current.
- *Ethical and legal responsibilities.* A patient's suicidal risk can, under certain circumstances, impose specific legal or ethical responsibilities on the psychotherapist. For example, statutes or case law may allow or require a therapist to breach confidentiality or take other reasonable steps to protect the patient. These legal standards differ from state to state and province to province. Psychologists need to know and understand the ethical and legal frameworks within their jurisdictions. Not only must the therapists be ready to act appropriately if the assessment triggers one of these duties, but in some instances the legal framework may be helpful in guiding the assessment. Moreover, therapists who do not understand clearly the possible legal consequences of the assessment (e.g., discretionary or mandatory breaching of confidentiality) will be unable to explain these possibilities to patients and obtain patients' informed consent for the assessment.
- *Cultural, religious, and other personal values.* Are there cultural, religious, or other personal values or issues that might make it difficult for either therapist or patient to address suicidal risk openly and adequately? For some, it may be hard to give voice to or listen empathically to suicidal impulses, intentions, or plans if suicide is considered a mortal sin. Sometimes therapists may be so uncomfortable with the prospect that a patient may commit suicide, so anxious about their own legal and professional duties, or so eager to intervene that they jump in with the equivalent of "but you can't do that! you have so much to live for!" before the patient has finished, giving the unintended message that they are unprepared to listen. Cultural differences can lead to misunderstandings, as can language barriers. In one instance, a patient for whom English was a second language was in distress as she talked to her doctor about taking sleeping pills to commit suicide. The doctor, for whom English was the sole language, talked with her about her situation, persuaded her to agree to a contact forbidding her from taking pills or using other means to end her life, thinking that to be sufficient. The doctor had misunderstood, believing that she was considering taking sleeping pills; however, she had been telling him that she had already taken the pills (Pope & Vasquez, 2011). It is best if both therapist and patient are fully fluent in the same language or dialect. If that is not feasible and if a translator is used, it should be someone who is unrelated to the patient and who is fully trained to translate in mental health settings. If a family member serves as translator, the patient may be reluctant to discuss suicide, feelings or concerns about that family member, and other sensitive topics frankly and openly.

- *Documentation.* The methods used to assess suicidal risk as well as the results should be carefully documented. If there is any significant risk of suicide at any point in therapy, the chart should show both that the risk was monitored on an ongoing basis (rather than mentioned once in the chart and never referred to again) as well as any interventions and the rationale for using those interventions. If a patient shows no substantial suicidal risk, some therapists find it useful to repeat something along the lines of "no evidence of suicidal risk" as part of each chart note. This form of documentation serves as a reminder to the therapist to continue to monitor suicidal risk (i.e., such a note should not be included unless the therapist has concluded, on the basis of an adequate assessment, that there is no evidence of suicidal risk) and documents that the therapist is addressing this area.
- *Continuing competence.* An adequate assessment of suicidal risk rests in part on the psychotherapist's competence to conduct the assessment. Even if we were not just competent but exceptionally skilled at one point in our careers, maintaining the ability to conduct a skilled, valid, and effective assessment is an active and continuing process. Staying abreast of new research, theory, and assessment methodologies is crucial.

References and Readings

Francis, R. D. (2009). *Ethics for psychologists* (2nd ed.) Chichester, England: BPS Blackwell/John Wiley.

Fraser, J. S., & Solovey, A. D. (2007). Self-harming and suicidal clients. In J. S. Fraser & A. D. Solovey (Eds.), *Second-order change in psychotherapy: The golden thread that unifies effective treatments* (pp. 245–270). Washington, DC: American Psychological Association.

Hunt, I. M., Kapur, N., Webb, R., Robinson, J., Burns, J., Shaw, J., & Appleby, L. (2009). Suicide in recently discharged psychiatric patients: A case-control study. *Psychological Medicine, 39,* 443–449.

Joiner, T. (2005). *Why people die by suicide.* Cambridge, MA: Harvard University Press.

Joiner, T. (2010). *Myths about suicide.* Cambridge, MA: Harvard University Press.

Karch, D. L., Dahlberg, L. L., & Patel, N. (2010, May 14). Surveillance for violent deaths—national violent death reporting system, 16 states, 2007. *CDC Morbidity and Mortality Weekly Report.* Retrieved January 2013, from www.cdc.gov/mmwr/preview/mmwrhtml/ss5904a1.htm

Pope, K. S., & Vasquez, M. J. T. (2011) *Ethics in psychotherapy and counseling: A practical guide* (4th ed.). New York: Wiley.

Wyder, M., Ward, P., & De Leo, D. (2009). Separation as a suicide risk factor. *Journal of Affective Disorders, 116,* 208–213.

Related Topics

Chapter 36, "Treating and Managing Care of the Suicidal Patient"

Chapter 37, "Intervening with Clients in Crisis"

Chapter 68, "Assessing and Treating Nonsuicidal Self-Injury"

Chapter 83, "Treating Veterans and Military Families"

6 ASSESSMENT OF MALINGERING ON PSYCHOLOGICAL MEASURES

Richard Rogers and Nathan D. Gillard

Psychologists vary considerably in their understanding of malingering and their sophistication at its detection. As a prelude to this synopsis, the standard definition of malingering is the deliberate fabrication or gross exaggeration of psychological or physical symptoms for some external goal. Critical decision points include (a) the deliberateness of the presentation (e.g., somatoform disorder vs. malingering), (b) the magnitude of the dissimulation (e.g., minor embellishment vs. gross exaggeration), and (c) the identification of the goal and its primary source (e.g., internal vs. external). Rogers (2008) provides a comprehensive resource for addressing these issues.

The focus of this synopsis is twofold. First, we address common misconceptions about malingering that are likely to influence professional practice. Second, we distill the empirical literature relative to the clinical detection of malingering. This distillation is necessarily selective and concentrates on the more robust clinical indicators for feigned mental disorders and cognitive impairment.

COMMON MISCONCEPTIONS

- *Because malingering is very infrequent, it should not be a cause of diagnostic concern:* There are two incorrect aspects of this misconception. First, research suggests malingering occurs in an appreciable percentage of cases, with variability across settings. Estimates range from 7%–8% in general clinical settings to 15%–17% in forensic criminal cases. The prevalence is likely even higher in personal injury (18%–33%) and neurological deficit cases (16%–26%), but these higher numbers often reflect faulty research designs. Variability can also be expected based on the nature of the claimed symptoms and the referral question. Likelihood aside, infrequency should not be equated with inconsequentiality—the social and monetary costs of misclassifications are enormous.
- *Because malingering is a global response style, it is easy to detect:* This premise is easily assailable. Psychological practice with veteran populations, for example, provides ample evidence of how some malingerers can become very targeted in their feigned posttraumatic stress disorder (PTSD). The implicit message of this misconception is that malingering is relatively easy to detect because of its obviousness. At least with feigned cognitive deficits, the available literature suggests that many simulators remain undetected, unless specific measures of malingering are employed.
- *If psychologists pay attention to* The Diagnostic and Statistical Manual of Mental Disorders (DSM-IV-TR) *indices, they are likely to be effective at identifying malingerers.* The *DSM-IV-TR* does not treat malingering as it does most diagnoses, instead classifying it as a "V code" indicating "other

conditions or problems that may be a focus of clinical attention." The indices for this classification do no function like the inclusion criteria found with most disorders; rather, they are intended merely to raise the index of suspicion. The *DSM-IV-TR* emphasis on criminality is largely unwarranted and may lead to misclassifications in both forensic (false-positives) and nonforensic (false-negatives) cases. As Rogers and Bender (2012) point out, treatment of malingering as a "diagnosis" is a fatal error that may result in a false-alarm rate in the range of 80%.

- *Inconsistencies are the hallmark of malingerers:* Although inconsistencies are found among many malingerers, the equating of inconsistencies with malingering is a grave error. For example, MMPI-2 research has demonstrated convincingly that inconsistent profiles may result from psychosis, inability to attend, and inadequate comprehension (Greene, 2008). Although malingerers tend to be inconsistent in their symptom presentation, a substantial minority of patients with genuine disorders are also markedly inconsistent. Depending on the prevalence rate for malingering in a particular setting, an inconsistent presentation may have a greater likelihood of being a genuinely disordered patient than a malingerer.
- *Test cut scores provide "laser accuracy" in determining response styles:* Clinicians often rely on single-point cut scores to classify feigning, without taking into account both classification errors and measurement errors. For scores within one standard error of measurement (SEM) of the cut score, the likelihood of misclassification typically exceeds 50% (Rogers, Gillard, Wooley, & Ross, 2012). Therefore, it is recommended that marginal cases (i.e., those within one SEM of the cut score) be classified as "indeterminate" and be investigated further.
- *Malingering precludes genuine disorders:* It is unlikely that most psychologists embrace this false dichotomy openly. However, our experience suggests that many clinical evaluations are concluded once malingering is determined and that most, if not all, symptoms are then viewed with great skepticism. Genuine and malingered symptoms are not mutually exclusive and neither offers any natural immunity to the other. Related to this point, malingering does not represent a homogeneous response style, but rather can be conceptualized based on severity, type, and clinical relevance. Malingering can range from exaggerations in the level of impairment to complete fabrication of symptoms.
- *Deceptive persons are likely to be malingerers:* The mislogic that "if you lie, you will malinger" should be apparent. While malingerers are deceptive persons, the obverse is not necessarily true. Within clinical or forensic settings, deception can be used for a variety of reasons. The sustained effort involved in successful feigning, the stigmatization of mental disorders, and the often severe penalties for detection are likely to militate against widespread malingering. Moreover, Ford, King, and Hollender (1988) cogently describe the numerous genuine disorders for which deception, but not malingering, is commonplace. Finally, some types of deception are, by their very nature, the polar opposite of malingering (e.g., denial of substance abuse).
- *Feigning measures indicate malingering:* When using validated feigning scales, it is essential that alternative explanations of feigning are investigated before any conclusions about malingering are warranted. Feigning scales cannot determine the underlying motivation. Alternatives include malingering, factitious disorder, and cases with elements of both that are often characterized as *dissimulation*. Assessments of possible motivations typically involve interviews, collateral sources, and reviews of clinical records.

ASSESSMENT OF FEIGNED MENTAL DISORDERS

The assessment of feigned psychopathology involves the use of well-validated measures in a multimethod evaluation. Because malingering is not a global response style, two important decisions must be implemented in the selection of measures. First, the detection strategies differ fundamentally across the three general domains of feigned mental disorders, feigned cognitive impairment, and feigned medical disorders. As a general guideline, detection strategies for feigned mental disorders measure *unlikely* or *amplified* symptoms. Second, the validation and purpose of a measure should not be ignored. For example, brief self-report measures are useful as screens; however, these measures lack the discriminability and extensive cross-validation to warrant their use in the determination of malingering (see Smith, 2008). For the domain of feigned mental disorders, the two best established measures are the MMPI-2 and the SIRS/SIRS-2. Each will be summarized separately.

The MMPI-2 is the most frequently used measure in forensic evaluations. A recent meta-analysis of the MMPI-2 and malingering (Rogers, Sewell, Martin, & Vitacco, 2003) underscored (a) its general usefulness in the evaluation of feigning but noted (b) its marked variability in optimum cutting scores. For example, Rogers et al. (2003) found feigning cut scores for F that ranged from 9 to 30. The recently published MMPI-2-RF provides a shorter test that may have psychometric advantages over the MMPI-2 for clinical interpretation. For the assessment of malingering, however, the handful of MMPI-2-RF published feigning studies have relied mostly on archival MMPI-2 data. Their results raise questions about the discriminability of MMPI-2-RF validity scales (Rogers & Bender, 2012). The following guidelines are proposed for the MMPI-2, although the general concepts apply to the MMPI-2-RF and other multiscale inventories:

1. Is the profile consistent? A random or inconsistent profile likely will be indistinguishable from a feigned profile on fake-bad indicators. One benchmark is to exclude inconsistent profiles with a VRIN >14.
2. Are the standard validity indicators extremely elevated? Patients with certain genuine disorders, such as schizophrenia or PTSD, often have very high elevations in the 80T range. To minimize false alarms, only extreme scores (e.g., F raw score >30) are likely to provide strong evidence of feigning. For any cut score, psychologists should consider too-close-to-call cases (e.g., ±1 SEM) as indeterminate.
3. Are specialized indicators markedly elevated? The best overall indicator of feigned mental disorders is the Fp raw score >9. A second useful indicator is Ds raw score >35.
4. Caution should be exercised in applying these results to minority populations. For instance, in nonclinical populations, African Americans and Hispanic Americans score higher on F than their European American counterparts. Importantly, Spanish-language and audio-taped MMPI-2 versions have not been validated for response styles, including feigned mental disorders.

The SIRS is a structured interview that has been extensively validated via simulation and known-groups designs with clinical, community, and correctional samples. The recently published SIRS-2 (Rogers, Sewell, & Gillard, 2010) utilizes data from more than 2,300 protocols. For continuity, the SIRS-2 retains the same primary scales but implements a more sophisticated decision model. The basic decision rule for feigning (≥3 scales in the probable feigning range or ≥1 scales in the definite range) is augmented by additional classification rules:

1. To minimize false alarms in severely impaired populations, the RS-Total scale was developed and validated.
2. To assist in classification of protocols with one or two scales in the probable feigning range, a Modified Total Index was developed to determine feigning or indeterminate cases.
3. To assess whether examinees were attempting to avoid the detection of feigning via disengagement from the SIRS-2 (e.g., very few affirmative responses), a Supplementary Scale Index was validated to classify suspected cases in the indeterminate-evaluate group.
4. To broaden the clinical usefulness of the SIRS-2, improvements included the addition of an Improbable Failure scale to screen for feigned cognitive impairment and empirically based interpretative guidelines for the Defensive Symptoms scale.

A Spanish SIRS-2 was translated, back-translated, and validated. In summary, the SIRS-2 is extensively validated for examinees feigning psychological impairment and mental disorders. For the domain of feigned cognitive impairment, other measures and detection strategies must be implemented. The next session addresses this important domain.

ASSESSMENT OF FEIGNED COGNITIVE IMPAIRMENT

Unlike the malingering of mental disorders, feigned cognitive impairment does not require the complex generation of believable symptoms and associated features that address onset and course of the simulated disorder. For the domain of feigned cognitive impairment, persons must decide intellectual or neuropsychological deficits they wish to simulate. They must then put forth a convincing effort as they fail test items measuring these deficits. To be effective, their day-to-day functioning should be consistent with their purported deficits. As noted, each feigning domain requires its own distinct detection strategies. Although the MMPI-2 is frequently recommended in neuropsychological consults where malingering is suspected, it lacks the appropriate detection strategies to be effective. Nonetheless, the MMPI-2 may be useful in those cases of global malingering when feigning encompasses both psychopathology and cognitive functioning.

Rogers (2008; Rogers & Bender, 2012) summarized detection strategies for feigned cognitive impairment. Importantly, most strategies are useful in screening for feigned impairment, but not for making the actual determination. The detection strategies include the following:

1. *Floor effect.* Some malingerers fail on exceptionally simple questions that even very impaired persons are able to answer correctly. For example, "Who is older, a mother or her child?" The most common use of the floor-effect strategy is found in the presentation of Rey's 15-Item Memory Test and on the Test of Memory Malingering (TOMM), both of which have only modest sensitivity.
2. *Performance curve.* Many malingerers do not take into account item difficulty. While they fail more difficult than easy items, the decline based on item difficulty is generally more gradual than found with genuine patients. Frederick (2003) has successfully applied this strategy to the Validity Indicator Profile (VIP). It has also been successfully applied to Ravens Progressive Matrices.
3. *Symptom validity testing (SVT).* Based on probability, some malingering cases can be identified based on performance worse than chance when given a large number of test items with equiprobable answers. The best validated measure for this purpose is the Portland Digit Recognition Test (PDRT). SVT is typically effective only with extreme forms of feigning.
4. *Magnitude of error.* Some malingerers are theorized to make very atypical mistakes, either in terms of gross errors or near misses, akin to the Ganser syndrome. It appears most malingers put little thought into *how* to answer incorrectly. This approach can be very effective (see Bender & Rogers, 2004).
6. *Inconsistent or atypical presentations.* Many clinicians believe that variable performance or an atypical pattern of test scores signifies malingering. Many factors argue against any facile conclusions: (a) no cutting scores are established for making this determination; (b) patients with genuine neuropsychological impairment often have variable performances; and (c) personality changes, as a result of brain injury, are likely to affect erratic performance.

In closing, determinations of malingering are complex, multimethod evaluations. Conclusions should never be based on a single symptom, scale, or measure. When data are inconclusive but suggestive of feigning, the response style may be described as "unreliable." Misclassifying a genuine patient as a malingerer may have devastating consequences to that individual's future treatment, financial well-being, and legal status. To misclassify a malingerer as a genuine patient may have grave consequences for other concerned parties (e.g., insurance companies, employers, or the criminal justice system). Psychologists shoulder a heavy professional responsibility in their efforts to minimize both types of misclassification in their assessment of malingering. They must base their findings on a comprehensive evaluation that utilizes well-validated measures that employ effective detection strategies for malingering and related response styles.

References and Readings

Bender, S. D., & Rogers, R. (2004). Detection of neurocognitive feigning: Development of a multi-strategy assessment. *Archives of Clinical Neuropsychology, 19*, 49–60.

Berry, D. T. R., Wetter, M. W., & Baer, R. A. (1995). Assessment of malingering. In J. N. Butcher (Ed.), *Clinical personality assessment: Practical approaches* (pp. 236–248). New York: Oxford University Press.

Ford, C. V., King, B. H., & Hollender, M. H. (1988). Lies and liars: Psychiatric aspects of prevarication. *American Journal of Psychiatry, 145*(5), 554–562.

Frederick, R. I. (2003). *The Validity Indicator Profile* (2nd ed.). Minneapolis, MN: National Computer Systems.

Greene, R. L. (2008). Malingering and defensiveness on the MMPI-2. In R. Rogers (Ed.), *Clinical assessment of malingering and deception* (3rd ed., pp. 159–181). New York: Guilford Press.

Rogers, R. (1990). Models of feigned mental illness. *Professional Psychology, 21*, 182–188.

Rogers, R. (Ed.). (2008). *Clinical assessment of malingering and deception* (3rd ed.). New York: Guilford Press.

Rogers, R., & Bender, S. D. (2012). Evaluation of malingering and related response styles. In R. K. Otto (Ed.), *Comprehensive handbook of psychology: Forensic psychology* (2nd ed., Vol. 11, pp. 517–540). New York: Wiley.

Rogers, R., Gillard, N. D., Wooley, C. N., & Ross, C. A. (2012). The detection of feigned disabilities: The effectiveness of the Personality Assessment Inventory in a traumatized inpatient sample. *Assessment, 19*(1), 77–88.

Rogers, R., Sewell, K. W., & Gillard, N. D. (2010). *Structured interview of reported symptoms* (2nd ed.) Professional manual. Lutz, FL: Psychological Assessment Resources.

Rogers, R., Sewell, K. W., Martin, M. A., & Vitacco, M. J. (2003). Detection of feigned mental disorders: A meta-analysis of the MMPI-2 and malingering. *Assessment, 10*, 160–177.

Slick, D. J., Sherman, E. M. S., & Iverson, G. L. (1999). Diagnostic criteria for malingered neurocognitive dysfunction: Proposed standards for clinical practice and research. *Clinical Neuropsychologist, 13*, 545–561.

Smith, G. P. (2008). Brief screening measures for the detection of feigned psychopathology. In R. Rogers (Ed.), *Clinical assessment of malingering and deception* (3rd ed., pp. 323–339). New York: Guilford Press.

Related Topics

Chapter 4, "Increasing the Accuracy of Clinical Judgment"

Chapter 21, "Assessing MMPI-2 Profile Validity"

7 IDENTIFYING AND ASSESSING ALCOHOL, DRUG, AND TOBACCO USE DISORDERS

Linda Carter Sobell, Mark B. Sobell, and Sean M. Robinson

This brief chapter contains two parts: (1) a summary of issues critical to conducting successful assessments, and (2) a review of clinically useful, user-friendly, and psychometrically sound measures for assessing alcohol, drug, and tobacco abuse.

1. *Value of an assessment:* Good assessments have numerous benefits: They serve as the basis for treatment planning and goal setting (e.g., determining intensity of treatment, assessing motivation to change, matching clients to treatments, identifying high-risk triggers); they help in formulating diagnoses; the results can be used to give clients feedback/advice about their past substance use and related behaviors, which can strengthen their motivation for change (Miller & Rollnick, 2002); and assessments can determine whether treatment is working (and, if not, help determine what the next step should be to modify the course of treatment, i.e., stepped care; Sobell & Sobell, 2011).

2. *Setting clients at ease:* Because there is a strong stigma related to substance use or any mental disorder (Wang et al., 2005), making the first call to a treatment program can be highly stressful. Similarly, arriving for the first appointment can provoke considerable anxiety. Individuals thinking of changing their alcohol, drug, or tobacco use have probably made a decision to seek treatment only after careful consideration and with some ambivalence. Thus, it is very important to set clients at ease by establishing rapport and being empathic and supportive. Because clients are often asked to complete several assessment instruments, it is important to gain their cooperation by explaining the nature of each instrument, why it is being used, and what feedback they might expect from the instrument. Early discussion of how long treatment will take and what treatment will entail will also help establish a solid therapeutic relationship.

3. *Self-reports of substance use are generally accurate:* Whether it is substance use or a mental disorder, most assessment and treatment information comes from clients' self-reports. Several studies have shown that individuals with substance disorders generally provide accurate self-reports of their substance use compared to other sources (e.g., biochemical measures, collateral reports; Babor, Steinberg, Anton, & Del Boca, 2000; Patrick et al., 1994; Sobell, Sobell, Connors, & Agrawal, 2003). One way to help ensure that clients provide accurate information is to inform clients that what is discussed in treatment is confidential and to explain the conditions under which confidentiality would have to be broken (e.g., child abuse). Because studies show that biochemical tests and collateral reports do not add sufficiently to self-report measurement accuracy to warrant their routine use, they should be used to complement rather than replace self-reports. An exception to valid self-reporting is when clients have been coerced into treatment (e.g., probation) or when they expect negative consequences for reports of substance use (Cook, Bernstein, & Andrews, 1997).

4. *Readiness to change:* Motivation is a state of readiness to change that not only fluctuates over time but that is also influenced by a therapist's behavior and treatment procedures (Miller & Rollnick, 2002). When clients enter treatment, it is important to evaluate their motivation for change. Thus, the assessment begins with a dialogue that is motivational in nature and is intended to express empathy and establish rapport. This, in turn, facilitates the development of a positive therapeutic relationship that is intended to enhance and maintain the client's motivation to change. Table 7.1 includes a measure, the Readiness to Change Ruler, which assesses a client's initial readiness for change, and a Decisional Balance exercise that can be used to enhance or strengthen a client's motivation for change. A key issue when treating clients who are assessed as not very committed to changing their substance use is to focus on increasing their motivation rather than on ways to achieve change.

5. *Motivational interviewing:* Motivational interviewing (MI) is a nonjudgmental, nonconfrontational, goal-directed and client-centered interviewing style that prompts clients to give voice to the need for change (Miller & Rollnick, 2002; also see Chapter 40). MI effectively minimizes resistance, a vital strategy when interviewing clients who are ambivalent about changing, as follows:

- *Express empathy:* Empathy can help health care professionals gain the acceptance and trust of clients and is associated with decreased client resistance and improved outcomes. A key way of expressing empathy is by *reflective listening,* in which the provider forms a reasonable guess about what the client has said and shares it with the client. Reflective listening also helps minimize resistance by validating what clients have said.

- *Manifest flexibility:* When health care professionals sense that clients are ambivalent or reluctant to discuss topics, it is important to "roll with resistance" by using reflective listening rather than confronting the resistance directly. It is also important to emphasize to clients that it is their choice whether a matter will be discussed.
- *Avoid confrontation and labeling:* Clients are generally reluctant to be labeled as "alcoholic" or "drug addict," especially when their problems are not severe (e.g., problem drinkers, cannabis users, nondaily cigarette smokers). Labeling should be avoided because it has no clinical advantage and because it has been associated with delaying or avoiding treatment (Wang et al., 2005). Asking people about their recent alcohol, drug, or tobacco use is more likely to get clients to engage in an open dialogue about their substance use versus asking them, "How many years have you had an alcohol, drug, or tobacco problem?"

6. *Severity of substance use disorders:* When evaluating a client's substance use, it is important to assess problem severity because such information is relevant to goal setting and treatment planning (Sobell & Sobell, 2011). Problem severity can be viewed as lying on a continuum ranging from mild (e.g., problem drinking, recreational drug use, nondaily cigarette use) to severe (e.g., chronic alcohol and drug use, physical dependence). Table 7.1 lists measures that can be used to evaluate alcohol, drug, and tobacco problem severity.

7. *Substance use history:* For all substance use disorders, including tobacco use, it is important to gather a profile of clients' psychoactive substance use (e.g., see DUHQ in Table 7.1). In addition, substance use patterns may change over the course of treatment (e.g., decreased or increased use of one drug, smoking cessation, or relapse). At least three issues are important when assessing polydrug use: (a) pharmacological synergism (a multiplicative effect of similarly acting drugs taken concurrently); (b) cross-tolerance (decreased effect of a drug due to previous or current heavy use of pharmacologically similar drugs); and (c) over half to three-quarters of individuals with substance disorders report smoking cigarettes (Lasser et al., 2000). Because it appears that continued smoking may serve as a trigger for relapse for some people attempting to change their drinking, the smoking behavior of individuals with substance use disorders should be a part of the assessment and treatment planning process.

8. *Psychiatric comorbidity:* There is a high prevalence of psychiatric comorbidity among persons with alcohol, drug, or tobacco use disorders. For example, about 50% of individuals with severe mental illness also have a substance use disorder (Kessler et al., 1996). As a consequence, diagnostic formulations with individuals who have a substance use disorders should assess (1) the extent and nature of the substance use problem; (2) the extent and nature of the psychiatric disorder; and (3) the extent and nature of the interaction between substance use and the psychiatric problems, including the temporal development of each disorder.

9. *Choosing assessment instruments:* When choosing an assessment instrument, health care professionals should consider the following questions: What purpose will it serve, is it clinically useful, and will it better inform the treatment of my client? Is it user friendly for clients (e.g., easy to complete, relevant)? How long does it take to administer and score, and for what time interval can information be collected (e.g., 1 month, 1 year)? What costs are involved, if any? The key question is: What will I learn from the instrument/measure that I will not otherwise know from a routine clinical interview?

TABLE 7.1. Psychometrically Sound and Clinically Useful Measures for Assessing Alcohol, Drug, and Tobacco Use

Adverse Consequences of Use/Problem Severity

Alcohol Use Disorders Identification Test (AUDIT): A 10-item, self-administered questionnaire addressing past and recent alcohol consumption and alcohol-related problems; identifies high-risk drinkers as well as those experiencing consequences. Scores range from 0 to 40; a score of 8 or greater is suggestive of an alcohol problem (available in several languages, including Spanish).[a,b,c]

Drug Use Disorders Identification Test (DUDIT): The DUDIT, an 11-item self-administered questionnaire screens individuals for drug problems, other than alcohol and tobacco. It was developed as an analogous instrument to the AUDIT. It collects information on frequency of drug use, drug-related problems, and drug dependence symptoms). Nine questions are scored on 5-point scales (0 to 4), and 2 on 3-point scales (0, 2, and 4). Scores range from 0 to 44, with a score of 8 or more suggestive of a drug problem.[d]

Drug Abuse Screening Test (DAST-10): The DAST-10, a 10-item self-administered measure of drug use consequences in the past 12 months, assesses drug problem severity. Scores range from 0 to 10; a score of 3 or more is suggestive of a drug problem (available in Spanish).[c,e]

Fagerström Tolerance Questionnaire (FTQ): The FTQ assesses severity of nicotine dependence. The 6-item version, Fagerström Test for Nicotine Dependence, is recommended for use in clinical practice. Scores range from 0 to 10 with higher scores reflective of higher nicotine dependence.[f]

Strength of Urges to Smoke (SUTS): The SUTS, a 6-item self-administered measure, assesses variables related to tobacco use (e.g., number of cigarettes smoked per day; time to the first cigarette, TTFC; strength of urges to smoke during a normal day). Higher scores suggest greater levels of nicotine dependence. While a single question, TTFC, has been shown to be highly predictive of nicotine dependence, the question on strength of urges has been found to be a good predictor of short-term success for quitting.[g]

Alcohol, Drug and Tobacco Use

Timeline Followback (TLFB): The TLFB uses memory aids to help people to recall their estimated daily alcohol, drug, or tobacco use for intervals ranging from 1 to 12 months prior to the interview. It can also be used during treatment as an advice/feedback tool to increase clients' motivation to change (available in several languages, including Spanish).[b,c,h,i]

Self-Monitoring (SM) Logs: SM logs ask clients to record aspects of their alcohol, drug, or tobacco use and urges to use during treatment (e.g., amount, frequency, mood, consequences). The logs have several clinical advantages, including identifying situations that pose a high risk of excessive substance use and providing feedback about changes in substance use (available in Spanish).[b,c,i]

Drug Use History Questionnaire (DUHQ): The DUHQ, a brief interviewer administered measure, captures lifetime and recent information (e.g., years used, route of administration, year last used, frequency of use) about the use of different drugs.[c,i,j]

High-Risk Triggers for Use

Brief Situational Confidence Questionnaire (BSCQ): The BSCQ, an 8-item self-report state measure of self-efficacy, was derived from the 100-item Situational Confidence Questionnaire. The BSCQ measures situation-specific self-efficacy (i.e., how confident people are at the present time that they would be able to resist the urge to drink heavily in eight major relapse categories).[b,c,i,k,l]

Brief Drug Taking Confidence Questionnaire (BDTCQ): The BDTCQ, an 8-item self-report global state measure of self-efficacy, was derived from the 50-item Drug-Taking Confidence Questionnaire. The brief DTCQ measures situation-specific self-efficacy applicable to resisting the urge to use drugs in specific situations.[b,c]

Motivation and Readiness to Change

Decisional Balance Exercise: The Decisional Balance exercise asks clients to evaluate their perceptions of the costs and benefits of continuing to use substances problematically versus changing; it is intended to make more salient the costs and benefits of changing and to identify obstacles to change.[c,i,l]

Readiness to Change Ruler (RCR): The RCR, a state measure, is a quick and easy way to determine clients' readiness to change during the assessment. Clients are asked where they are on a scale of 1 to 10 (1 = not ready to change to 10 = very ready to change). Depending on clients' readiness to change, discussions may take different directions. For example, for clients who are ambivalent (i.e., 4 to 6) the therapist can explore the pros and cons of changing.[c,i,l]

Note: Information and reviews about and/or copies of the measures can be found in the footnoted publications or Web site after each measure.

[a]Allen & Wilson, 2003.
[b]www.niaaa.nih.gov/publications/guide.htm.
[c]Sobell & Sobell, 2011.
[d]Voluse et al., 2011.
[e]Skinner, 1982.
[f]Heatherton, Kozlowski, Frecker, & Fagerström, 1991.
[g]Fidler, Shahab, & West, 2011.
[h]Sobell & Sobell, 2000.
[i]www.nova.edu/gsc/online_files.html.
[j]Sobell, Kwan, & Sobell, 1995.
[k]Breslin, Sobell, Sobell, & Agrawal, 2000.
[l]Substance Abuse and Mental Health Administration, 1999.
[m]Sklar & Turner, 1999.

There is no shortage of instruments, scales, and questionnaires for assessing individuals with alcohol, drug, and tobacco use disorders (for a review of instruments, see Allen & Wilson, 2003; Piper, McCarthy, & Baker, 2006; Rush, First, & Blacker, 2008). We have compiled a list of clinically useful measures for assessing alcohol, drug, and tobacco use disorders and a brief description of each measure in Table 7.1. These measures were selected because they are user friendly, require minimal time and resources, are psychometrically sound, whenever possible provide meaningful feedback to clients, and all are free to use.

References and Readings

Allen, J. P., & Wilson, V. (2003). *Assessing alcohol problems.* NIH Publication no. 03–3745. (2nd ed.). Rockville, MD: National Institute on Alcohol Abuse and Alcoholism.

Babor, T. F., Steinberg, K., Anton, R., & Del Boca, F. (2000). Talk is cheap: Measuring drinking outcomes in clinical trials. *Journal of Studies on Alcohol, 61*(1), 55–63.

Breslin, F. C., Sobell, L. C., Sobell, M. B., & Agrawal, S. (2000). A comparison of a brief and long version of the Situational Confidence Questionnaire. *Behaviour Research and Therapy, 38*(12), 1211–1220.

Cook, R. F., Bernstein, A. D., & Andrews, C. M. (1997). Assessing drug use in the workplace: A comparison of self-report, urinalysis, and hair analysis. In L. Harrison & A. Hughes (Eds.), *The validity of self-reported drug use: Improving the accuracy of survey estimates* NIDA Research Monograph 167. (pp. 247–272). Washington, DC: NIDA.

Fidler, J. A., Shahab, L., & West, R. (2011). Strength of urges to smoke as a measure of severity of cigarette dependence: Comparison with the Fagerström Test for Nicotine Dependence and its components. *Addiction, 106*(3), 631–638.

Heatherton, T. F., Kozlowski, L. T., Frecker, R. C., & Fagerström, K-O. (1991). The Fagerström Test for Nicotine Dependence: A revision of the Fagerström Tolerance Questionnaire. *British Journal of Addiction, 86*, 119–127.

Kessler, R. C., Nelson, C. B., McGonagle, K. A., Edlund, M. J., Frank, R. G., & Leaf, P. J. (1996). The epidemiology of co-occurring addictive and mental disorders: Implications for prevention and service utilization. *American Journal of Orthopsychiatry, 66*(1), 17–31.

Miller, W. R., & Rollnick, S. (2002). *Motivational interviewing: Preparing people to change* (2nd ed.). New York: Guilford.

Patrick, D. L., Cheadle, A., Thompson, D. C., Diehr, P., Koepsell, T., & Kinne, S. (1994). The validity of self-reported smoking: A review and meta-analysis. *American Journal of Public Health, 84*, 1086–1093.

Piper, M. E., McCarthy, D. E., & Baker, T. B. (2006). Assessing tobacco dependence: A guide to measure evaluation and selection. *Nicotine and Tobacco Research, 8*(3), 339–351.

Rush, A. J., First, M. B., Blacker, D., & American Psychiatric Association. (2008). *Handbook of psychiatric measures* (2nd ed.). Washington, DC: American Psychiatric Publishing.

Skinner, H. A. (1982). The Drug Abuse Screening Test. *Addictive Behaviors, 7*, 363–371.

Sklar, S. M., & Turner, N. E. (1999). A brief measure for the assessment of coping self-efficacy among alcohol and other drug users. *Addiction, 94*(5), 723–729.

Sobell, L. C., Kwan, E., & Sobell, M. B. (1995). Reliability of a Drug History Questionnaire (DHQ). *Addictive Behaviors, 20*(2), 233–241.

Sobell, L. C., & Sobell, M. B. (2000). Alcohol timeline followback (TLFB). In American Psychiatric Association (Ed.), *Handbook of psychiatric measures* (pp. 477–479). Washington, DC: American Psychiatric Association.

Sobell, L. C., & Sobell, M. B. (2011). *Group therapy with substance use disorders: A motivational cognitive-behavioral approach.* New York: Guilford Press.

Sobell, L. C., Sobell, M. B., Connors, G., & Agrawal, S. (2003). Is there one self-report drinking measure that is best for all seasons? *Alcoholism: Clinical and Experimental Research, 27*, 1661–1666.

Substance Abuse and Mental Health Administration. (1999). *Enhancing motivation for change in substance abuse treatment (Treatment Improvement Protocol Series).* Rockville, MD: US Department of Health and Human Services.

Voluse, A. C., Gioia, C. J., Sobell, L. C., Dum, M., Sobell, M. B., & Simco, E. R. (2012). Psychometric properties of the drug use disorders identification test (DUDIT) with substance abusers in outpatient and residential treatment. *Addictive Behaviors, 37*(1), 36–41.

Wang, P. S., Berglund, P., Olfson, M., Pincus, H. A., Wells, K. B., & Kessler, R. C. (2005). Failure and delay in initial treatment contact after first onset of mental disorders in the National Comorbidity Survey Replication. *Archives of General Psychiatry*, *62*(6), 603–613.

Related Topics

Chapter 3, "Improving Diagnostic and Clinical Interviewing"
Chapter 40, "Conducting Motivational Interviewing"
Chapter 93, "Common Drugs of Abuse and Their Effects"

8 INTERVIEWING CHILDREN'S CAREGIVERS

Carolyn S. Schroeder and Eve-Lynn Nelson

Parents, foster parents, or other guardians usually serve as the primary referral source when a child comes to the attention of a mental health professional. They have a unique knowledge and understanding of the child and thus are an integral part of the assessment and treatment process. During the initial interview with the parent(s), the information-gathering process begins, essential preliminary clinical decisions are made, and the parents become engaged in a collaborative working relationship with the therapist. A successful parent interview will ultimately determine treatment goals and their priority and will ensure that parents will cooperate in carrying out these goals.

Parent interviews can be highly structured or more open ended. Both methods have advantages and disadvantages. Structured interviews involve a prearranged set of questions asked in sequential order that usually focus on gathering information about a specific *Diagnostic and Statistical Manual of Mental Disorders* (*DSM*) or *International Classification of Diseases* (*ICD*) condition. Although providing a more standardized format, structured interviews generally give more global information about the existence of a disorder rather than specific details about a particular child, family, or peer group that are needed for planning an intervention program. An unstructured interview, on the other hand, allows the clinician more freedom to explore the nature and context of a particular problem, as well as the opportunity to investigate potential contributing factors, such as stimuli that may elicit the problem behaviors. Moreover, this type of interview allows the clinician to begin to delineate acceptable behavioral alternatives, as well as other potential problem areas for the child or family. Unstructured interviews, however, assume that the interviewer has the necessary knowledge about the nature of the specific presenting problem to guide the content and process of the interview. Some other problems with unstructured interviews include collecting information selectively, a lack of a systematic way to combine different types of information, and a tendency to make a judgment or diagnosis based on clinician familiarity or biases.

Given the limited psychometric support for structured interviews and the uniqueness of each child, family, and environment, we think the unstructured interview has more advantages than disadvantages over the structured interview format, and therefore we will focus on unstructured parent interviews.

One format for gathering and organizing information using an unstructured interview is called the Comprehensive Assessment-to-Intervention System (CAIS; Schroeder & Gordon, 2002). The CAIS focuses on the specifics of the behavior of concern and the characteristics of the child, family, and environment that potentially influence the behavior. Clinicians can use it in any setting, including primary care and telehealth contexts. It helps the interviewer decide which questions should be asked and ensures gathering essential information quickly and efficiently. Think of assessment as an ongoing process and recognize that the time required for the initial parent interview will depend on the nature and extent of the problem.

SETTING THE STAGE

Prior to interviewing parents, having them complete a general questionnaire about the child and family (see Schroeder & Gordon, 2002, for an example), as well as a rating scale that screens for problem behavior and compares the child's behavior to a normative sample, will prove helpful. Examples of useful, psychometrically sound behavior rating scales include the Behavior Assessment System for Children-2 (Reynolds & Kamphaus, 2004) and the Vanderbilt Behavior Rating Scale (Wolraich et al., 2003). Remember to consider the parent's preferred language and level of literacy in selecting and reviewing information/rating forms. Ask each parent to complete the selected behavior rating scale; if they have separated or divorced, each should be asked to complete a separate general parent questionnaire. When interviewing a guardian new to parenting the child, review the child's previous history first. The information gained from the completed questionnaires permits the clinician to generate preliminary hypotheses about the nature and causes of the problem, as well as to plan for and focus the parent interview.

Including both parents in the initial interview will prove useful, if they both actively participate in the child's life. If they are unable or unwilling to participate in a joint interview, make an attempt to interview them separately, even if only by telephone. Each parent brings his or her own perspective on the problem and will provide the clinician with information about his or her willingness to support the child's treatment. We routinely include preschool children in the initial parent interview, with age-appropriate toys and activities provided to keep the child occupied. Although some clinicians may find this difficult, we have discovered that the information discussed is rarely new to the child. Moreover, the opportunity to observe the child and the parent–child interaction firsthand far outweighs any disadvantages. If necessary, subsequent interviews can take place with the parents alone, to go over more sensitive information or to receive information or provide information to the parents without the distraction of a particularly disruptive child. We typically interview parents of school-age children alone, before seeing the child; and with adolescents include or exclude the adolescent from the first session with parents depending on the nature of the problem.

Interviewing parents becomes an interactive process that sets the tone for future intervention efforts. To promote collaboration, the interviewer must create an atmosphere that puts the parents at ease in discussing their child's problems and gives them some sense of optimism that the child's or family's life can improve as a result of professional help. Personal attributes of a good interviewer can set a positive tone. These include warmth, empathy, a sensitive and nonjudgmental approach that respects others' feelings and cultures, and an ability to keep the interview moving along in a smooth, purposeful fashion. The ability to listen carefully is also an essential skill. Listening helps parents focus on the problem, and reflecting or paraphrasing lets the parents know that they have been heard. Recognizing the parents' distress as they discuss areas of concern encourages them to share their fears and beliefs about the problem(s).

It will help to begin the interview by asking the parent about his or her understanding of and expectations for the meeting. This provides an opportunity to clarify any misconceptions about mental health services, explain the purpose of the interview (i.e., to get a better understanding of their concerns in order to help determine what, if any, intervention is necessary), and to briefly summarize what is already known about the situation. This also allows time to review information concerning consent to treatment and adherence to ethical-legal, HIPAA-compliant policies concerning privacy and confidentiality.

While important to get a thorough understanding of the nature and context of the problematic behavior, it is not possible or advisable to assess everything in the child or family's background. We recommend selective pursuit of particular topics. Working with children almost always involves an ongoing relationship with the parents; if a relevant area is missed initially, it will likely re-emerge for discussion in future meetings. Problems with parent interviews include inaccurate recall, conflicting perceptions of the child between parents, and a tendency to describe the child in unrealistically positive and precocious terms. Parents also may describe their child's behavior in excessively negative terms when they feel under personal stress (e.g., marital discord, depression). Focusing on the current situation—that is, current behavior, current child management techniques, and current family strengths and weaknesses—can help increase the reliability of parental reports.

COMPREHENSIVE ASSESSMENT-TO-INTERVENTION SYSTEM

A logical and systematic guide to assuring that information in important areas is gathered follows. The information does not have to emerge in any particular order, and although it may come forth during the parent interview, a variety of other sources and methods could be used (e.g., parent or teacher questionnaires, psychometric testing, observation of parent–child interaction). The CAIS will prove useful for complex cases, but it also provides a framework to assist the clinician in quickly gathering essential information for brief assessment cases.

Clarifying the Referral Question

Although the need to clarify the referral question seems obvious, its importance cannot be overemphasized. After the parent has described the problem, clinicians should make certain that they and the parent focus on the same problem. This can be done by simply reflecting what the parent has said: "It sounds like you have concerns about your child refusing to go to school, as well as the different ways you and your husband handle the situation." This gives the parent the opportunity to restate his or her concerns until a mutual understanding of the concerns is reached. In addition, note whether the parent's perception of the referral question differs from referral information from other sources, for example, primary care provider, school, or judicial system.

Determining the Social Context

A child is referred because someone is concerned. This does not necessarily mean that the child needs treatment or that the child's behavior is the problem. Consider: Who is concerned about the child? Why is this person concerned? Why is this person concerned now as opposed to some other time? The parents' affect in describing the problems is also significant. Do they feel overwhelmed, anxious, depressed, or nonchalant? Two mothers, for example, describe their 3-year-old daughters as being anxious and fearful. One mother presents as calm, in control of herself, and using good judgment in attempting to deal with the problem. The other mother, however, presents as extremely upset, fearful, and unable to view the problem objectively. Each of these parents will require a different focus for the assessment/intervention process.

The family's sociocultural characteristics can play an important role in the planning and implementation of a treatment program. Questions such as the following can help the clinician get a better understanding of the parent's perspective: What do you think has caused your child's problem? Why do you think it started when it did? How does the problem affect you or your child? How severe do you feel your child's problem is? Do you expect it will have a short- or long-term course? What kind of treatment do you think your child should receive? Who can help with the treatment? What are the most important results that you hope your child will receive from treatment? What is your greatest fear about your child? Asking the parents about their expectations, hopes, and fears in coming to a mental health professional helps in both gathering and interpreting the material, especially if the clinician's recommendations are contrary to the parents' expectations or confirm their worst fears. This information also can help the clinician develop a treatment program that is sensitive to sociocultural influences.

Assessing General Areas

Information about the characteristics of the child and the family is important in putting problems or concerns in perspective and determining the resources the family has or will need to carry out a successful intervention plan. Asking parents to briefly describe a typical day for their child (when he or she gets up; the morning, daily, and evening routines; when he or she goes to bed, etc.) usually gives a great deal of information about how the family and child functions, their stresses and limitations, and, in general, the context in which they live. Particular attention should focus on areas that represent significant change for the child versus a long-standing pattern. Focus on assessing the following key areas:

- *Developmental status.* Knowledge of the child's developmental status (physical/motor, cognitive, language, social, personality/emotional, psychosexual) allows the clinician to evaluate the child's behavior in comparison with that of other children of the same age or developmental level. Behavior considered a significant problem at one stage in development or at one age may qualify as normal at another. The clinician must assess whether the behavior of concern is less or more than one would expect of any child at that age and in that environment. A 3-year-old who wets the bed, for example, may qualify as "normal" for that age, whereas a 10-year-old who wets the bed has a significant problem. Behavior also changes over the course of development, and some problem behaviors change in the appropriate or desired direction without intervention.
- *Characteristics of parents and extended family.* Certain parent characteristics and parenting practices can facilitate or impede development, and such factors affect how parents view their children. For example, low parental tolerance, high expectations for child behavior, marital stress, parental psychopathology (e.g., depression), and family problems influence parents' perception of their child's behavior. Similarly, a mother's perception of her child's behavior correlates highly with the type of environmental interactions (positive or coercive) she has just experienced. The referring person may lack information about child development in general, may have emotional problems, or may feel under stress, all of which can distort their perception of the child's behavior. In addition, parenting styles, techniques, and models; marital status; and the presence of psychopathology in parents and other family members will prove especially important areas to assess, as will sibling relationships and the availability and use of social support.
- *Environment.* Recent stressful life events, socioeconomic status, and subculture norms and values can provide important information about the problems children experience and the intervention strategies that may prove most helpful. The child's environment provides context for the behavior and in some cases may prove a more appropriate focus for intervention than the behavior itself. The context can include very specific antecedents to the behavior (e.g., repeated commands, teasing, criticism, or hunger), socioeconomic status, or major events and losses, including a move, parental divorce, a death in the family, incarceration or deployment of a family member, loss of parent job, natural disaster, and a life-threatening or chronic illness. Clinicians should also assess for interpersonal violence, including both witnessing and experiencing all forms of

violence in the community and in the home (e.g., physical, sexual, or verbal abuse).

- *Consequences of the behavior.* How are the parents currently handling the behavior problem? What techniques have been tried in the past and how have these worked? What impact does the problem behavior have on the child, parents, and environment? What prognosis can we expect with and without treatment? Lack of careful assessment of the details usually leads to parents' responding to suggestions by saying, "Yes, but we've tried that and it doesn't work."
- *Medical/health status.* Gather information regarding prenatal history and early development, the family's history of medical or psychological problems, somatic complaints, acute and chronic illnesses of the child, hospitalizations and traumas, current health and medications (prescribed and over the counter), and substance abuse/use. Has the child recently seen a physician and received routine care?

Assessing Specific Areas

In addition to the general areas already mentioned, gather information on the specific behaviors or concerns, including (a) the persistence of the behavior (How long has it been going on?); (b) changes in behavior (Is the problem new behavior or a worsening?); (c) severity (Is the behavior very intense or dangerous or low level but "annoying"?); (d) frequency (Has the behavior occurred only once or twice or many times?); (e) situation specificity (Does the behavior occur only at home or in a variety of settings?); and (f) the scope of problem (Is the problem a discrete behavior or a diffuse set?).

Determining the Effects of the Problem

Who suffers as a result of the referral problem(s)? You may find the child's behavior bothers one parent, but not the other; or annoys the teacher, but not the parents. In other cases, although the behavior may interfere with some aspect of the child's development, parents may not see it as a problem, but without intervention it may lead to a poor outcome for the child. For example, a learning disability may not seem like a problem for the parents, but the child will likely suffer negative consequences in school if it goes unaddressed.

Determining Areas for Intervention

Intervention strategies will often follow naturally from the assessment, once assessment of the child's development and behavior and the emotional, physical, and sociocultural context in which he or she lives have been examined systematically. For example, interventions in the *developmental area* could include (a) teaching new responses; (b) providing appropriate stimulation; or (c) increasing or decreasing specific behaviors. In the *parental area,* one could (a) teach new parenting techniques; (b) focus on the emotional atmosphere in the home or school; (c) treat (or refer for treatment) marital problems or parent psychopathology; or (d) change parental expectations, attitudes, or beliefs. *Environmental* interventions might involve (a) changing the specific cues that elicit inappropriate behavior or prevent appropriate behavior from occurring; (b) focusing on the emotional atmosphere in the home by helping parents build support networks and deal with the stresses of daily life; (c) helping the child/family cope with life events such as a death; or (d) changing the physical environment where the problem behavior most often occurs. Focusing intervention on the *consequences of the behavior* might involve (a) changing the responses of the parents; (b) changing the responses of other significant adults such as teachers; or (c) changing the behavior of the child by focusing on a more appropriate payoff for the child (e.g., providing reinforcers). Intervening in the *medical/health* area may involve (a) referral for treatment of the cause of the problem (e.g., persistent ear infections) or (b) treating the effect of the problem (e.g., teaching relaxation skills to a child with cerebral palsy).

CLOSING THE INTERVIEW

Allow time at the end of the initial parent interview to summarize and integrate the information gathered. This lets the parents know that you have heard their concerns accurately and gives them feedback on your initial conceptualization of the problem. Provide an explanation for any additional information needed (e.g., school visit, behavioral rating scales, psychometric testing of the child, child interviews, further interviews with the parents, observations of parent–child interactions, medical evaluation) and discuss how to best gather it. If possible, discuss potential treatment strategies, as well as the estimated length of time and cost for that treatment. While it might not be possible to give all this information without further assessment, it is important that the parents have some understanding of the clinician's thoughts regarding treatment and a sense of hope that something can be done to help them and their child.

References and Readings

American Psychological Association Practice Central. (2009). *HIPAA: What you need to know now*. Retrieved January 2013, from www.apapracticecentral.org/business/hipaa/transaction-rule.pdf

Ecklund, K., & Johnson, W. B. (2007). Toward cultural competence in child intake assessments. *Professional Psychology: Research and Practice, 38*(4), 356–362.

Nelson, E., & Bui, T. (2010). Rural telepsychology services for children and adolescents. *Journal of Clinical Psychology, 66*(5), 490–501.

Reynolds, C. R., & Kamphaus, R. W. (2004). *BASC-2: Behavioral Assessment System for Children* (2nd ed.). Circle Pines, MN: American Guidance Services.

Romanelli, L. H., Landsverk, J., Levitt, J. M., Leslie, L. K., Hurley, M. M., Bellonci, C.,...Child Welfare-Mental Health Best Practices Group. (2009). Best practices for mental health in child welfare: Screening, assessment, and treatment guidelines. *Child Welfare, 88*(1), 163–188.

Sanders, L. M., Federico, S., Klass, P., Abrams, M. A., & Dreyer, B. (2009). Literacy and child health: A systematic review. *Archives of Pediatric and Adolescent Medicine, 163*(2), 131–140.

Schroeder, C. S., & Gordon, B. N. (2002). *Assessment and treatment of childhood problems: A clinician's guide* (2nd ed.). New York: Guilford Press.

Wolraich, M. L., Lambert W., Doffing, M. A., Bickman, L., Simmons, T., & Worley, K. (2003). Psychometric properties of the Vanderbilt ADHD diagnostic parent rating scale in a referred population. *Journal of Pediatric Psychology, 28*(8), 559–567.

Related Topics

Chapter 9, "Evaluating the Medical Components of Childhood Developmental and Behavioral Disorders"

Chapter 10, "Using the *DSM-5* and *ICD-11* in Forensic and Clinical Applications with Children Across Racial and Ethnic Lines"

Chapter 13, "Using the *International Classification of Diseases* System (*ICD-10*)"

Chapter 18, "Developmental Neuropsychological Assessment"

Chapter 85, "Principles of Treatment with the Behaviorally Disordered Child"

Chapter 88, "Interviewing Children About Sexual Abuse"

9 EVALUATING THE MEDICAL COMPONENTS OF CHILDHOOD DEVELOPMENTAL AND BEHAVIORAL DISORDERS

Nhung T. Tran and James L. Lukefahr

This chapter is designed to familiarize the psychologist with the medical evaluation of children with disordered development or behavior. The goals of a medical evaluation are to determine the etiology of the disordered development or behavior and assess for co-occurring conditions. The three components of a comprehensive medical evaluation (*medical history, physical examination,* and *laboratory studies*) will be described, with emphasis on those considerations pertinent to children with developmental or behavioral disorders.

MEDICAL HISTORY

The medical history and physical examination are the most important components of the medical evaluation of children with developmental or behavioral disorders. Findings by history and physical examination can help the clinician to narrow the list of possible etiologies and select the most appropriate laboratory studies to perform.

Birth History

- *Prenatal factors: Prematurity* (birth prior to 37 weeks of gestation) and *intrauterine growth restriction (IUGR)* are risk factors for developmental delays, cognitive and learning disabilities, and behavior disorders, especially attention-deficit/hyperactivity disorder (ADHD). Neurological outcome is directly related to the degree of prematurity and growth restriction. For example, there is a growing interest in and reports of autism spectrum disorders (ASD) in *very low birth weight* (defined as <1,500 grams) and *extremely low birth weight* infants (defined as <1,000 grams). *Small for gestational age* describes infants with weight, length, and/or head circumference below the 10th percentile but who may be constitutionally small. IUGR refers to SGA infants who did not achieve their genetically determined potential. IUGR strongly suggests the presence of an underlying pathological condition. A partial list of causes of IUGR is shown in Table 9.1.
- Congenital infections are a major contributor to infant morbidity and mortality. For example, congenital infection with *cytomegalovirus (CMV)* affects 1% of US newborns (about 40,000 infants every year). Most CMV-infected newborns are asymptomatic at birth. However, 6% have severe disease evident at birth, including IUGR, multiple organ involvement, and severe psychomotor retardation. Fourteen percent of CMV-infected infants who did not have

TABLE 9.1. Common Causes of Intrauterine Growth Retardation

Fetal
Chromosomal disorders (e.g., trisomy 13, 18, and 21)
Congenital fetal infection (e.g., toxoplasmosis, rubella, cytomegalovirus, herpes, human immunodeficiency virus, syphilis)
Congenital anomalies or malformation syndromes
Inborn errors of metabolism
Multiple gestation
Placental
Insufficiency (e.g., maternal preeclampsia)
Infection (chorioamnionitis)
Abnormal placentation (e.g., abruption, previa, accretia, infarction)
Maternal
Substance use (e.g., alcohol, drugs, tobacco)
Hypertension
Renal disease
Diabetes
Malnutrition

obvious disease at birth later develop vision and sensorineural hearing loss, making congenital CMV infection the most common cause of acquired deafness.

- *Fetal alcohol spectrum disorder (FASD)* affects an estimated 40,000 infants each year. However, the true prevalence is felt to be higher. *FASD* is an umbrella term used to describe the range of effects of prenatal alcohol exposure and the most common cause of preventable intellectual disability (formerly mental retardation). Children with *alcohol-related neurodevelopmental disorder (ARND)* have the brain dysfunction, including cognitive and behavioral impairments of prenatal alcohol exposure, but not the classic facial features and growth deficiency seen in *fetal alcohol syndrome.*
- *Perinatal factors:* Complications during labor and delivery cause fewer developmental and learning disabilities than was previously believed. However, infants with severe perinatal complications, such as premature infants and infants with severe congenital heart defects, are at risk for poor neurological outcomes if they sustain episodes of hypoxemia or intracerebral hemorrhage. Advances in neonatal intensive care have diminished the impact of *respiratory distress syndrome* (or *hyaline membrane disease*) on later development for most premature infants. *Neonatal hyperbilirubinemia* (or jaundice) is a common condition, reported to affect as many as 60% of all infants. Developmental sequelae occur primarily in infants who experience extremely high serum bilirubin levels or (more often) when the jaundice is a result of a severe perinatal illness.

Past Medical History

- *Chronic conditions:* Certain chronic conditions may result in developmental and/or behavioral impairments as an expression of the condition itself or the result of a treatment for the condition. Severe *congenital heart disease* may cause developmental delays due to the cerebral effects of chronic hypoxemia or co-occur as part of a genetic disorder. For example, *22q11 deletion syndrome* (which includes *velocardiofacial syndrome* and *DiGeorge syndrome*) is the most common cause of congenital heart disease, and often results in language, learning, and/or behavioral difficulties. It should be considered when a child presents with any combination of congenital heart defect, cleft palate (including submucosal), and characteristic facial features. Severe *chronic renal disease* can result in growth failure and developmental delays as a result of high levels of circulating toxic metabolic products. Children with *cancer* may experience cognitive impairments due to the malignancy itself or the toxic effects of treatment. *Epilepsy* can be idiopathic or the manifestation of an underlying brain lesion or malformation, or an *inborn error of metabolism*.
- *Other chronic conditions:* Certain chronic conditions may result in developmental and/or behavioral problems for other reasons. Severe *obesity* results in a variety of physical, psychosocial, emotional, and economic dysfunctions. The United States and other developed countries are experiencing an epidemic of obesity affecting children as well as adults, but the direct

neurological effects of obesity have not yet been fully elucidated. Frequent episodes of *asthma* may affect physical, emotional, and social development by preventing full participation in typical childhood activities or affecting school attendance. Adolescents with chronic conditions such as *diabetes, cystic fibrosis,* or *epilepsy* often rebel against their dependency on medical treatment regimens and refuse to comply, which may result in serious complications.

- *Recurrent illnesses:* Children with prolonged periods of mild conductive hearing loss due to *recurrent otitis media* in the first few years of life may sustain transient delays in speech and language development. However, recurrent otitis media is not a cause of moderate to profound speech and language delays or other lags in development. Recurrent severe bacterial illnesses such as pneumonia or meningitis may indicate the presence of an underlying immunological disorder.
- *Family history:* A three-generation pedigree can help identify heritable conditions. Examples of heritable genetic conditions with developmental-behavioral consequences include *tuberous sclerosis,* which is an autosomal dominant neurocutaneous disorder associated with seizures, intellectual disability and sometimes autism spectrum disorder, and *Fragile X syndrome.* The full mutation of Fragile X syndrome, which is X linked and thus affects males, is the most common cause of inherited intellectual and autism spectrum disorder. However, girls who are carriers for Fragile X syndrome can also have developmental delays, behavioral problems, and learning disabilities, but to a much lesser severity. Other conditions can also have familial occurrence patterns, such as *thyroid disease, collagen-vascular disease* (e.g., systemic lupus or juvenile rheumatoid arthritis), and *inflammatory bowel disease* (e.g., Crohn's disease). The clinician should inquire about heritable conditions known to occur within the family. In some cases, changes in behavior or school performance as a direct result of the illness or due to chronic pain may be the presenting symptom in the child. In recent years, there has been increased recognition of a hereditary or familial component in some behavioral disorders, such as ADHD, bipolar disorder, schizophrenia, anxiety disorders, and autism spectrum disorders. *Consanguinity* is a risk factor for autosomal recessive diseases.
- *Social history:* Physicians recognize the importance of psychosocial factors in disease states and are accustomed to exploring these concerns with parents of young children. *Child abuse and neglect* can exert severe negative consequences on the child's growth and emotional and developmental health. *Family disruption* such as domestic violence, divorce, and frequent moves can result in adjustment reactions involving increased anxiety and/or emotional and conduct problems. *Postpartum depression* and *maternal depression* are well-known risk factors for emotional and developmental health of infants and children, but they are often not detected in medical settings. Direct discussion of psychosocial issues with older children and adolescents during a single medical encounter can be difficult. A brief structured interview technique commonly utilized with adolescents is the *HEADSSS interview,* summarized in Table 9.2.

PHYSICAL EXAMINATION

Growth Parameters

Physicians routinely maintain *standardized growth charts* for their pediatric-aged patients. Growth charts allow comparison of a child's height (or length), weight, and head circumference to national norms for those growth parameters. As a rule, children whose height, weight, or head circumference is less than the 5th percentile or greater than the 95th percentile for age should undergo a thorough medical evaluation.

Disordered physical growth often accompanies developmental and behavioral disorders, especially ones that can cause significant

TABLE 9.2. The HEADSSS Psychosocial Interview Technique

H	Home environment (e.g., relations with parents and siblings)
E	Education/employment (e.g., school performance)
A	Activities (e.g., sports participation, after-school activity, peer relations)
D	Drug, alcohol, or tobacco use
S	Sexuality (e.g., is the patient sexually active; does he/she use condoms or contraception)
S	Suicide risk or symptoms of depression or other mental disorder
S	"Savagery" (e.g., violence or abuse in home environment or in neighborhood)

impairments. For example, children with *Prader-Willi syndrome* begin as infants who have *failure to thrive* and later develop *hyperphagia* and obesity in early childhood. This unique pattern of growth is readily captured on a growth chart. *Trisomy 21, Turner syndrome,* and *Williams syndrome* have well-characterized growth deficiency that has enabled the development of condition-specific growth charts.

Head circumference is particularly important in evaluating developmentally delayed children, since this growth parameter is closely correlated with brain growth. *Microcephaly* and *macrocephaly* are defined as head circumference less than 5th percentile and greater than the 95th percentile, respectively. For example, macrocephaly is a common finding in children with autism, believed to be due in part to dendritic disorganization of the cerebral cortex.

Body mass index (BMI) is the most widely accepted parameter for detecting and monitoring childhood obesity. The range of what constitutes a normal BMI varies significantly by age group. Standardized growth charts for plotting BMI are available and may allow for earlier detection of overweight and underweight status.

General Physical Examination

A thorough physical examination is needed to provide clues to an underlying cause for the child's developmental and behavioral disorder or to help direct laboratory testing. Special attention is given to finding dysmorphic features and the neurological examination. *Dysmorphic features* can be minor or major, and they occur as an isolated finding or as multiple findings. When they occur as multiple findings, the pattern may suggest a recognizable syndrome. For example, small palpebral fissures, thin upper lip, and long, smooth philtrum are the classic minor facial dysmorphisms in *fetal alcohol syndrome.* Serial evaluations of a patient can be useful in sorting out diagnostic suspicions. For example, the facial features of fetal alcohol syndrome may not be fully apparent in infants and toddlers and more apparent in later childhood. In addition to the growth parameters, some key features assessed on the physical examination may include the following:

- *Vital signs*: Temperature, blood pressure, pulse, respiratory rate
- *Head*: Shape and symmetry (e.g., abnormal in *craniosynostosis*), midface development
- *Eyes*: Appearance of pupils, lens, retina, orbit spacing (e.g., *hypotelorism* or *hypertelorism*), palpebral fissure length and inclination,
- *Ears*: Location, rotation, configuration, patency, middle ear, presence of ear pits or dimples
- *Nose*: Appearance
- *Mouth*: Upper lip volume, philtrum, vermilion border
- *Intraoral*: Palate, dentition (number, spacing, shape, enamel), tongue, uvula
- *Mandible*: Shape, size, position (e.g., *retrognathia* in Pierre-Robin Sequence); symmetry
- *Neck*: Posterior hair line, range of motion, redundant skin, webbing, presence of enlarged thyroid gland (goiter) or lymph nodes
- *Chest*: Shape, symmetry, location and appearance of nipples, presence of accessory nipples, symmetry of breath sounds
- *Cardiovascular*: Location of heart sounds (e.g., *levocardia* or *dextrocardia*), heart sounds, pulses
- *Abdomen*: General appearance (e.g., *truncal obesity* in Prader-Willi syndrome; *cachexia*

in malnutrition), umbilicus (e.g., *herniation* in congenital hypothyroidism), presence of organomegaly (e.g., *hepatomegaly* in inborn errors of metabolism), presence of masses
- *Genitalia*: Size (e.g., enlarged testes in Fragile X syndrome), appearance, palpation of testes (e.g., descended, undescended, or retractile), presence of ambiguity, presence of abnormal pigmentation (e.g., *penile freckling* in Bannayan-Rubalcava-Riley syndrome)
- *Back*: Symmetry, spine, hair pattern, presence of sinuses or hair tufts in intergluteal cleft (suggesting *occult spina bifida*)
- *Extremities*: Proportion, appearance, range of motion, presence of reduction of duplication of segments
- *Skin/nails*: Pigmentation (e.g., hypopigmented *ash-leaf spots* of tuberous sclerosis; hyperpigmented *acanthosis nigricans* associated with Type II diabetes); appearance of palmar, phalangeal, and flexion creases; presence of dimples or vascular lesions
- *Neurological*: Mental status; behaviors; cranial nerve function; muscle bulk, tone and strength; deep tendon reflexes; presence of persistent *primitive reflexes* (consistent with *cerebral palsy*); postural reflexes; cerebellar function (such as *stereognosis* and proprioception); coordination, including gait abnormalities; presence of involuntary movements

Vision and Hearing Testing

Accurate assessment of visual and auditory function should be performed in all children with developmental or behavioral disorders. Technology is available that permits such assessments even in newborns or children with severe cognitive or communication impairment.

Newborn hearing screening is required in most areas to screen for congenital hearing loss. Gestalt impression of a child's hearing status does not eliminate the possibility of mild or unilateral hearing loss. Therefore, hearing testing should be performed in children with developmental or behavioral disorders (especially language delays) to assess hearing sensitivity and evaluate for acquired hearing loss that may present later in infancy and childhood.

LABORATORY STUDIES

Table 9.3 provides a partial listing of laboratory tests that may be obtained during the evaluation of children with developmental or behavioral disorders.

Developmental disorders presenting in early infancy are usually more severe and warrant immediate evaluation for inborn errors of metabolism or congenital infection. Studies aimed at detecting infectious agents that may cause fetal injury include *cultures* or *antibody titers*. The timing of studies may be critical. For example, the diagnosis for congenital CMV is considered definitive by viral culture of body fluid (e.g., blood, urine, saliva, or cerebral spinal fluid) within the first 2 to 3 weeks of life. *X-rays* of the skull or extremities may detect metabolic, infectious, or immunologic damage to skeletal structures. *Head computed tomography (CT)* is indicated primarily in the evaluation of abnormal head size or shape for cranial anomalies, or suspected intracranial hemorrhage or increased intracranial pressure. *Brain magnetic resonance imaging (MRI)* is indicated when there is a suspicion of cerebral malformation or for supportive evidence of a congenital infection, such as *periventricular calcifications* in congenital CMV. A chromosomal *karyotype* is obtained to evaluate primarily for syndromes of aneuploidy (abnormal chromosome number) and rearrangement. Examples of syndromes of aneuploidy are Down syndrome, which is a complete or partial trisomy of chromosome 21, and Turner syndrome, which is a complete or partial absence of an X chromosome in girls. *Chromosomal microarray* is an advanced technology that is rapidly becoming a standard part of the genetic evaluation and may detect deletions and duplications of smaller size than those detectable by karyotype. Specific *DNA testing* for a variety of disorders with developmental or behavioral implications is available, such as for Fragile X syndrome, *Rett syndrome*, and *Duchenne muscular dystrophy*. Specific

TABLE 9.3. Selected Laboratory Tests and Their Indications in Evaluating Developmental or Behavioral Disorders

Laboratory Test	Indication
Amino acids, serum	Elevated in some inborn errors of metabolism
Ammonia, blood	Elevated in some inborn errors of metabolism
Antinuclear antibody (ANA), serum	Elevated in collagen-vascular diseases
Bilirubin, serum	Elevated in neonatal hyperbilirubinemia and in liver diseases
Chromosomal karyotype	Used to detect aneuploidy and rearrangements
Chromosomal microarray	Used to detect deletions and duplication
Creatinine, serum	Elevated in chronic renal diseases
DNA testing	Used to detect known genetic abnormalities for specific syndromes
Electrolytes, serum	Abnormal in some inborn errors of metabolism and renal diseases
Erythrocyte sedimentation rate (ESR), blood	Elevated in chronic inflammatory diseases
Gamma-glutamyltransferase (GGT), serum	Elevated in chronic liver diseases
Glucose, blood or serum	Abnormal in disorders of insulin (e.g., diabetes mellitus or congenital hypoinsulinemia) and in some inborn errors of metabolism
Glycosylated hemoglobin (hemoglobin A1C), serum	Elevated in poorly controlled diabetes mellitus
Hemoglobin electrophoresis, blood	Used to detect hemoglobinopathies (e.g., sickle-cell disease)
Lactate, blood	Elevated in some inborn errors of metabolism
Lead, blood	Elevated in chronic lead exposure
Organic acids, urine	Elevated in some inborn errors of metabolism
Thyroid function tests (thyroxine or T4, triiodothyronine or T3, thyroid-stimulating hormone, or TSH), serum	Abnormal in thyroid diseases
Transaminases (AST or SGOT; ALT or SGPT), serum	Elevated in acute or chronic liver diseases
Urea nitrogen (BUN), serum	Elevated in acute or chronic renal diseases
Very long-chain fatty acids	Elevated in some inborn errors of metabolism

DNA testing for other conditions is becoming increasingly available.

Laboratory studies of learning disabilities and behavioral disorders presenting later in childhood is usually not as extensive. For example, laboratory studies in a child with a long and relatively stable symptomatology such as reading disability or ADHD is usually not helpful. However, a child with acute changes in development, behavior, or physical health warrants immediate evaluation for a potentially treatable medical condition, such as *thyroid disease*, inborn errors of metabolism, or seizures. *Electroencephalography (EEG)*, typically along with a brain MRI, may be performed if a child's abnormal behaviors show a discrete episodic pattern suggestive of seizure activity. Otherwise, an EEG is not routinely indicated in the evaluation of learning and behavior problems.

References and Readings

Behrman, R. E., Kliegman, R. M., & Jenson, H. B. (Eds.). (2000). *Nelson textbook of pediatrics* (16th ed.). Philadelphia, PA: W. B. Saunders.

Brodsky, M., & Lombroso, P. J. (1998). Molecular mechanisms of developmental disorders. *Development and psychopathology, 10*(1), 1–20.

Levine, M. D., Carey, W. B., & Crocke, A. C. (Eds.). (1999). *Developmental-behavioral pediatrics*. (3rd ed.). Philadelphia, PA: W.B. Saunders.

Filipek, P. A., Accardo, P. J., Ashwal, S., Baranek, G. T., Cook, E. H., Jr., Dawson, G.,... Volkmar, F. R. (2000). Practice parameter: Screening and diagnosis of autism. Report of the Quality Standards Subcommittee of the American Academy of Neurology and the Child Neurology Society. *Neurology, 55*, 468–479.

Jones, K. L. (1997). *Smith's recognizable patterns of human malformation* (5th ed.). Philadelphia, PA: W. B. Saunders.

Moeschler, J. B., Shevell, M., & American Academy of Pediatrics Committee on Genetics. (2006). Clinical genetic evaluation of the child with mental retardation or developmental delays. *Pediatrics, 117*(6), 2305–2316.

Parker, S., & Zuckerman, B. S. (Eds.). (1995). *Behavioral and developmental pediatrics: A handbook for primary care*. Philadelphia, PA: Lippincott Williams & Wilkins.

Supplementary Material

Clinical Growth Charts, Center for Disease Control and Prevention: www.cdc.gov/growthcharts/

Practice Guidelines

Committee on Genetics. (2001). Health supervision for children with Down Syndrome. *Pediatrics, 107*(2), 442–449.

Filipek, P. A., Accardo, P. J., Ashwal, S., Baranek, G. T., Cook, E. H., Jr., Dawson, G., . . . Volkmar, F. R. (2000). Practice parameter: Screening and diagnosis of autism. Report of the Quality Standards Subcommittee of the American Academy of Neurology and the Child Neurology Society. *Neurology, 55*, 468–479.

Moeschler, J. B., Shevell, M., & American Academy of Pediatrics Committee on Genetics. (2006). Clinical genetic evaluation of the child with mental retardation or developmental delays. *Pediatrics, 117*(6), 2305–2316.

Resources for Professionals and Parents on Some More Common Syndromes Presenting With Developmental and Behavioral Disorders

Congenital Cytomegalovirus Foundation. www.congenitalcmv.org

The International 22q11 Deletion Syndrome Foundation, Inc. www.22q.org

National Down Syndrome Society. www.ndss.org

National Organization on Fetal Alcohol Syndrome. www.nofas.org

The National Fragile X Syndrome Foundation. www.nfxf.org

Tuberous Sclerosis Alliance. www.tsalliance.org

Related Topics

Chapter 8, "Interviewing Children's Caregivers"

Chapter 18, "Developmental Neuropsychological Assessment"

Chapter 85, "Principles of Treatment with the Behaviorally Disordered Child"

Chapter 86, "Helping Children Cope with Chronic Medical Illness"

Chapter 92, "Pediatric Psychopharmacology"

Chapter 95, "Medical Conditions That May Present as Psychological Disorders"

10 USING THE *DSM-5* AND *ICD-11* IN FORENSIC AND CLINICAL APPLICATIONS WITH CHILDREN ACROSS RACIAL AND ETHNIC LINES

Ronn Johnson

This chapter focuses on the appropriate use of the *Diagnostic and Statistical Manual of Mental Disorders* (*DSM*) and the *International Classification of Diseases* (*ICD*) diagnostic systems to fairly evaluate ethnoracially different children or adolescents. In addition, we address receiving culturally responsive clinical services or a fair criminal justice outcome when practitioners use the *DSM-5* or *ICD-11*. Like their predecessors, the forthcoming *DSM-5* and *ICD-11* will likely become the most widely used systems for classifying diverse behavioral disorders and mental health problems in clinical or forensic settings. A behavioral disorder can refer to one event or a pattern of events, past or present, that reflect poor judgment, thinking, and/or reasoning. Such disorders suggest vulnerability to stress and problematic functioning in the future. Although a mental disorder has no definition that specifies precise boundaries, several recognized professional sources purport to measure clinical signs (e.g., distress, dysfunction, dyscontrol, inflexibility, irrationality syndromal patterns). The *DSM* family of tools (*DSM-IV-TR* and *DSM-5*) and *ICD-11* are the most commonly used classification and diagnostic tools applied to children and adolescents across ethnoracial lines worldwide. The *ICD* and *DSM* have synchronized their systems to some degree, so that many categories are similar. Children or adults can be diagnosed with anxiety and mood disorders. The systems contain a wide-ranging category of anxiety disorders, which include posttraumatic stress disorder and obsessive-compulsive disorder, as well as various specific phobias and anxieties. The *DSM* and *ICD* include a distinct category of disorders with a typical onset during childhood and adolescence. For example, the prevalence of *DSM–IV* oppositional defiant disorder (ODD) was 3.9%, whereas the prevalence of *ICD-10* ODD was 5.4%. Moreover, children who met criteria for *ICD-10* ODD but not *DSM–IV* ODD demonstrated levels of impairment and comorbidity equal to children who fulfilled *DSM–IV* criteria for ODD. A frequent misconception is that classification of mental disorders classifies *people*, whereas this classification actually applies to *disorders* that people experience

All clinical or forensic tools have flaws. The authors of *DSM-5* and *ICD-11* are trying to craft diagnostic references for use worldwide. The *DSM-5* and *ICD-11* classification systems still rely upon assessment of behaviors and symptoms by qualified mental health professionals for work in specified clinical or forensic settings. A diagnosis of a mental disorder requires that a clinician decide whether a child or adolescent meets the criteria for one of the aforementioned classification systems. It is not unusual for children to present with several co-occurring disorders. In the United States, concerns have arisen about a spike in the diagnosis of bipolar disorder in children and adolescents. Diagnosis of children and adolescents in the United States is also impacted through the Individuals with Disabilities Education Act (IDEA), the federal law that safeguards children with disabilities. The process of diagnosis is also fraught with cultural and race-based controversy and considerable disagreement than spans over two centuries.

Cultural factors can impact the expression and interpretation of signs and symptoms. For example, practitioners commonly perpetuate dominant racial biases. For instance, African Americans have historically been disproportionately diagnosed with schizophrenia, as opposed to depression, when compared to Whites. Trierweiler et al. (2006) found that race of the practitioner (White vs. African American) can function as a critical decision-making variable in the diagnostic labels used. Ethically, the question of harm or malfeasance rises. Despite considerable attention to the importance of cultural and racial factors, some examiners using the *DSM-5* and *ICD-11* may operate with unexamined assumptions or inadequate training that fuel off-target use of these classification systems. Furthermore, the criticisms of the *DSM-5* and *ICD-11* are compounded by the perceptions of practitioners attempting to use them throughout the world. For example, there is a perception that violence in non-Western countries is routinely condoned.

The infusion of cultural considerations within the *DSM* and *ICD* occurs in a disjointed, uneven manner, largely because ethnoracial factors used in the diagnostic process vary—based upon the interaction among patient, environmental setting, and skill set of the mental health practitioner. One can argue that it is beyond the scope of the *DSM-5* or *ICD-11* to completely establish the role of culture within the diagnostic process, but it is nonetheless important to recognize and examine five central issues related to the use of the *DSM-5* and *ICD-11* with ethnoracial children across the world:

1. View culture and country of origin as a relevant factor when developing diagnostic impressions related to the mental illness in children. This requires significant effort because the *DSM-5* and *ICD-11* do not provide enough guidance in how to cogently integrate cultural influences with specific diagnostic questions with a global perspective. Arguments that such cultural concerns lie beyond the scope of these classification systems fail, since without sensitivity to cultural contexts any diagnosis is invalid.
2. Variability in the cultural competencies and resultant diagnostic decision making of clinicians working with ethnoracial minority children and adolescents makes interrater reliability an issue. Despite clear evidence that ethnoracial factors are important in competent clinical work, only within the past two decades have they emerged as a consistent topic within mainstream training programs.
3. Since cultural factors influence the way ethnoracially different children and adolescents present in clinical or forensic settings (e.g., patterns of cultural characteristics associated with behavior or shared meanings), cultural elements often relevant to the diagnosis demand consideration.
4. Applying the *DSM-5* and *ICD-11* in forensic and clinical contexts can be improved by prompting diverse practitioners to consider cultural and racial factors when using these classification systems.
5. The classification systems have explicit operational criteria for diagnosis of mental disorders. The process is filled with considerable worldwide criticisms (e.g., medicalization of the *DSM-5*) among a diverse group of mental health professionals, with the American Psychological Association and World Health Organization in the lead. Like previous editions, the *DSM-5* and *ICD* will have legitimate criticism lodged against them. The classification system is never complete but represents the aggregate professional thinking at the time of the manual

update. The *DSM-5* will introduce a dimensional feature.

A starting place for practitioners performing diagnostic work using the *DSM-5* and/or *ICD-11* with ethnoracially different children requires recognition of their differences. The issues summarized here do not exhaust the diverse content base necessary for working effectively with African American, Hispanic, or children from other nations or cultures but provide a basic guide.

- Culture generally refers to meanings held by members of a particular group. This includes their worldview, beliefs, ethics, values, and norms of conduct. These meanings must be understood and accounted for when formulating a diagnostic impression with each ethnic minority child or the diagnosis will be invalid.
- The practitioner will remain the largest source of error in the reliability and validity of *DSM-5* and *ICD-11* diagnosis with ethnoracially different children. Three factors associated with that error are discussed next.

  1. Transition distress refers to a child's reluctance or struggle to successfully move from one activity or setting to another. The clinician must competently assess the child's level of acculturation and the child's transition distress from the home culture to another cultural experience. To do so, the clinician must (at minimum) establish credibility with the child as well as with the adult caretakers and must conduct an appropriate interview addressing these issues.
  2. The practitioner must accept the client's language, socioeconomic status, and attitude toward mental health treatment as irrelevant to any psychopathology diagnosis.
  3. The clinician must also remain supremely aware of his or her impact on the interviewee. Unintentional discrimination by a clinician can affect the assessment data presented by ethnoracial patients.

- At times an operant cultural factor will impact use of the *DSM-5* or *ICD-11*. For example, in Mexico and Latin America, it is socially unacceptable to admit to a mental disorder; therefore, many people with a Mexican or Latin American cultural background will not disclose psychological symptoms to doctors. Instead, they will only report somatic symptoms—unless one uses their terminology—"ataque de nervios." In such a case, working with interpreters and being aware of multiple cultural identities would be important.
- The use of assessment tools to measure acculturation should be considered.
- The clinician must collect a culturally relevant history that includes an assessment of the child's racial identity. An informed examination of all the cultural influences on the child's identity may not be readily observable by the clinician, and some issues of racial identity development may contribute to a negative reaction to the clinician by the child. One preferred method of determining a child's racial identity development involves studying the various racial identity models. Unfortunately, this approach relies too heavily on the competencies that the clinician brings into the diagnostic process.
- The more mainstream the practitioner's own cultural identification, the more likely the practitioner will overlook certain salient cultural frameworks. Cultural sensitivity is not synonymous with cross-cultural competency. Cross-cultural training and requisite supervision are highly recommended for the practitioner working with an ethnic minority child.
- Finally, the practitioner's knowledge of ethnoracial oppression and rejection may offer a critical insight into the patient's response to the diagnostic process. For example, African Americans have historically been the targets of undesirable attributes or stereotypes (e.g., low intelligence, sexual prowess, criminal behaviors). African Americans also carry into the diagnostic process significant experiences of exploitation, discrimination, and generally bad treatment within the mental health service system. Consequently, many children are taught by adult caretakers to be wary of their disclosures to clinicians from

> other ethnoracial groups. The cultural will to protect and insulate children, passed on from generation to generation, is often perceived as service-related hostility.

It is only logical to presume those children's cultural expectations and experiences may cloud a clinician's ability to develop a more accurate diagnostic impression, so knowledge of those expectations and experiences is critical. A clinician from a cultural majority group may start to learn more about ethnoracial oppression and rejection through reading history and devoting part of the clinical interview to discussing racism experiences. Consultation with clinicians more conversant with the ethnoracial group of particular patients is also recommended.

FORENSIC WORK

The complexity and scope of clinical and forensic issues far exceed the space available in this chapter to discuss the uses of the *DSM-5* or *ICD-11* with ethnoracial children. The *DSM-IV-TR* states, "In most situations, the clinical diagnosis of a *DSM-IV* mental disorder is not sufficient to establish the existence for legal purposes of a mental order, mental disability, mental disease or mental defect" (American Psychological Association, 2000). These diagnostic systems have strong clinical support and have met *Daubert* challenges in legal proceedings as a result of a respectable number of articles in peer-reviewed scientific journals. One of the strengths of the *DSM-5* is the fact that it is empirically based on specified criteria for including certain disorders. It was developed in conjunction with the World Health Organization's publication of the 10th edition of the *ICD*. It is minimally sensitive to culturally relevant issues and represents a considerable improvement over the *DSM-IV-TR* in terms of cultural factors. Cultural considerations are now mentioned in a significant manner, in contrast to the scant allusion made to culture in the introductory sections of the *DSM-III-R*. In the *DSM-5*, descriptive sections accompany the criteria for many disorders on culture, age, and gender, reflecting an understanding of mental disorders in a context broader than their symptoms.

Extending this thinking, the practitioner can take the following steps to use the *DSM-5* and *ICD-11* more effectively with ethnoracial children and adolescents in clinical and forensic settings:

1. Practitioners should become as familiar as possible with the sections that specifically address childhood diagnostic issues. The *DSM-5* and *ICD-11* classification of disorders usually diagnosed in infancy, childhood, and adolescence is based on empirical findings and is developmentally relevant. For example, mental retardation, attention-deficit/hyperactivity disorder, stereotypic movement disorder, and other childhood-onset disorders may occur within the context of poverty, racial trauma, generational differences, immigration stress, and acculturation (Johnson, 1993), though they are not caused by cultural factors.
2. Practitioners must recognize that cultural conditions can have an impact on the presentation of these disorders. For example, an African American foster child was diagnosed as having ODD, but it was never disclosed that he had experienced several episodes of racial taunting by other riders on a school bus.
3. Understanding acculturation problems is key when an ethnic minority child comes to the attention of the psychologist. Acculturation reflects the extent to which ethnic minority children completely release, modify, and retain aspects of both their home environment and the mainstream culture. Acculturation occurs in at least two ways. External acculturation may be assessed through behavioral patterns (e.g., dress, language use). Internal acculturation involves the extent to which children articulate their experiences according to the home culture versus the more mainstream culture. There may in fact be no reportable difference. In this case, the child may feel less compelled to display a prescribed set of behaviors just to accommodate to the mainstream. On the

other hand, some children feel a need to display different sets of behavior due to some discomfort or other reasons. Diagnostically, the way the child presents under either of these conditions influences the clinical picture as assessed by the psychologist.

4. The practitioner should also recognize that diagnostically relevant behaviors might be cloaked by the child's stage of racial identity development. This may be important with biracial children who can have a more dichotomous racial identity. Some empirical evidence suggests that biracial children move through racial identity development in different ways than children from more racially homogeneous backgrounds.
5. The *DSM-5*'s appendixes should be utilized fully. While an appendix outline for cultural formulation and glossary of culture-bound syndromes examination appears to be most relevant to the issues being addressed here, each appendix has the potential to influence the effective use of the *DSM-5* and *ICD-11* with ethnoracial children. These appendices require the clinician to proactively use culture as a factor in the diagnostic process.

TREATMENT PLANNING

In a cautionary statement, the *DSM* warns practitioners that the manual is not intended to encompass all mental health conditions. Unfortunately, information available from the *DSM* may prove irrelevant for the development of treatment plans for ethnic minority children. Historically, the *DSM* has engendered considerable criticism for its ethnocentricity. Many of its diagnostic criteria have limited cross-cultural utility, and diagnosis with the *DSM-5* or *ICD-11* relies on clinicians who too often do not have adequate cross-cultural training. In addition, the tools or methods typically used to arrive at a *DSM* or *ICD* diagnosis for ethnoracially different populations are inadequate. The complexity and scope of clinical and forensic issues far exceed the space available in this chapter to discuss the uses of the *DSM-5* or *ICD-11* with ethnoracially different children. The brief cases provided here are offered to sensitize practitioners and researchers to the exhaustive list of clinical factors that should be used with these diagnostic tools.

Providing a diagnosis for a child with a diverse background is quite challenging due to faulty assumptions that can occur while observing the child, especially during occasions when the examiner is unfamiliar with the culture. For example, Hispanic parents tend to report lower rates of autism than parents of other groups. The Center for Disease Control and Prevention reached the conclusion that children with autism in Hispanic families may be underdiagnosed. This example is but one that reinforces the need to determine factors that complicate the diagnostic and treatment process for children and adolescents of Hispanic families. Similar cultural misunderstandings likely exponentially increase misdiagnosis for children worldwide.

A decision tree framework does allow a culturally skilled practitioner to inject culturally relevant questions at appropriate decision points before arriving at a diagnostic formulation for a clinical or forensic application where it may be required. For instance, one of the question points for clarifying an anxiety diagnosis regards determining the onset of anxiety concerning attachment figures. Some Hispanic girls are brought up to rely on and value a close-knit family. In their case, it is culturally appropriate to experience some distress when placed in situations away from the immediate family (e.g., distant sleepover or leaving home to attend college). The culturally informed clinician will question whether the distress represents a true anxiety disorder or more simply a culturally appropriate response to separation. Cultural influences on pathology and defined culturally based syndromes are provided. It also presents cultural issues salient to diagnosis (e.g., cultural identity, cultural explanations of the individual's illness) and encourages the clinician to generate narrative summaries for these same categories. The brevity of this section might erroneously lead some clinicians to believe there is little to know regarding cultural issues, but the intent is clearly the opposite. It makes passing mention of indigenous clinicians' capability of formulating their own diagnostic systems for some of the more commonly occurring North American idioms of distress (e.g., anorexia nervosa, dissociative disorders). Johnson (1993) has shown that some single-entity disorders (e.g., posttraumatic stress disorder) may be sorted into several subcategories, such as racial trauma or racial encounter distress disorder. Other extensions of appendices include consideration of certain ethnoracial factors such as cultural will in assigning a global adaptive functioning rating on Axis V.

The *DSM-5* and *ICD-11*'s attempts to be culturally appropriate make them reasonably responsive to practical clinical and forensic issues while allowing room for culturally competent practice. This chapter was guided by an assumption that cultural patterns affect the presentation of psychopathology and the diagnostic process. A culturally relevant diagnosis is at the heart of effective therapeutic interventions and outcome assessment. Communication between clinicians is enhanced when practitioners can share treatment information that includes cultural nuances.

A culturally competent practitioner needs to clearly identify the subtle interactions between the child, the practitioner, and the *DSM-5* and *ICD-11* in order to yield the most useful assessment for a clinical or forensic outcome. Quintana, Castilllo, and Zamarripa (2000) offer cultural and linguistic competencies an assessing clinician should possess. It is also worth noting that some practitioners have serious doubts about the presumptions within the *DSM-5* and *ICD-11*. Others might argue the need to extend the *DSM-5* axes and *ICD-11* axes to include identification of cultural and gender factors. The deficit challenges the practitioner to independently study the behavior of children and adolescents from diverse backgrounds across the world.

The increased alignment of *DSM* and *ICD* codes creates significant clinical and forensic implications for responding to the diverse mental health issues associated with children and adolescents. For example, international studies found that untreated mental health problems in young people lead to a range of poor outcomes, including poor educational attainment, family dysfunction, poor physical health, crime, and antisocial behavior (Rutter & Smith 1995). A well-defined research program is needed to rationalize a cultural axis with practical utility or scientific validation.

Our world is culturally and ethnically diverse, and psychologists must be adequately prepared to deliver services to all in either clinical or forensic settings. There are important cultural differences with implications for our work. The World Health Organization promotes a universalistic perspective on psychiatric disorders. Some may argue that the forthcoming *DSM-5* and *ICD-11* classification systems may constrain the ability to achieve a culturally relevant diagnosis for children and adolescents. Nonetheless, developing culturally responsive diagnostic approaches in work with children in clinical or forensic settings is a noteworthy objective. Efforts by researchers and practitioners to perfect diagnostic systems move us closer to a consistent foundation for valid assessment by those working with children in diverse settings. Better diagnoses in turn will facilitate evidence-based treatments to help children and adolescents across the world.

References and Readings

American Psychiatric Association. (2000). *Diagnostic and statistical manual of mental disorders* (4th ed., text rev.). Washington, DC: Author.

Johnson, R. (1993). Clinical issues in the use of the DSM-III with African American children: A diagnostic paradigm. *Journal of Black Psychology, 19,* 447–460.

Locke, D. C. (1992). *Increasing multicultural understanding: A comprehensive model.* NewburyPark, CA: Sage.

Quintana, S. M., Castilllo, E. M., & Zamarripa, M. X. (2000). Assessment of ethnic and linguistic minority children. In S. Shapiro & T. R. Kratchochwill (Eds.), *Behavioral assessment in schools: Theory, research and clinical foundations* (2nd ed., pp. 435–463). New York: Guilford Press.

Rutter, M., & Smith, D. J. (1995). Psychosocial disorders in young people: Time trends and their causes. Chichester, England: Wiley.

Trierweiler, S. J., Neighbors, H. W., Munday, C., Thompson, E. E., Jackson, J. S., & Binion, V. J. (2006). Differences in patterns of symptom attribution in diagnosing schizophrenia between African American and non-African

American clinicians. *American Journal of Orthopsychiatry*, 76(2), 154–160.

WHO World Mental Health Survey Consortium. (2004). Prevalence, severity, and unmet need for treatment of mental disorders in the World Health Organization World Mental Health Surveys. In *International statistical classification of diseases and related health problems* (2nd ed., 10th rev., p. 1208). Geneva, Switzerland: WHO.

Related Topics

Chapter 3, "Improving Diagnostic and Clinical Interviewing"
Chapter 13, "Using the *International Classification of Diseases* System (*ICD-10*)"
Chapter 69, "When English Is Not the First Language: Psychotherapeutic Considerations"
Chapter 64, "Tailoring Treatment to the Patient's Race and Ethnicity"

11 ASSESSING STRENGTHS IN CLINICAL PRACTICE

Tayyab Rashid

Human beings are unique in their ability to contemplate themselves. They can recall the past vividly, interpret the present intelligently, and predict the future. This remarkable ability, however, is characterized by negativity. Humans are probably hard-wired to sharply attend, select, discern, and remember weaknesses more clearly than strengths. Evidence supports that humans are more risk aversive than gain sensitive (Kahneman & Tversky, 1984). Evolution has conditioned humans in such a way that they are more adept at processing grudges than gratitude, competition than cooperation, criticism than praising, and hubris than humility. When humans encounter challenges, they are more likely to recall shortcomings, failures, and setbacks—their own and those of others—and when they do it persistently, they often experience psychological distress.

Positive Psychology has made concerted empirical efforts to advance the science that build strengths, in addition to undoing symptoms and stress. Most prominent among these efforts is the field of character strengths, which includes capacities of cognition, affect, volition, and behavior. They are the basic psychological ingredients that enable us to act in ways that contribute to our well-being and that of others.

Christopher Peterson and Martin Seligman (2004) spearheaded the first systematic effort in psychology to classify core human strengths, acknowledging that character strengths are morally desired traits of human existence but at the same time descriptive traits open to empirical examination. Table 11.1 presents brief descriptions of 24 core character strengths, which are subsumed under six broader categories called virtues.

Assessing strengths along symptoms is critical for balanced, comprehensive practice with the underlying goal that psychotherapy is as much about cultivation of wellness as it is about alleviation of distress. Clients seeking psychotherapy do not just want less worry or anxiety; they also want to be happy, fulfilled, and satisfied. Psychotherapy is also a place

TABLE 11.1. VIA Classification of Virtues and Character Strengths

Virtue	Character Strengths
Wisdom	**Creativity**: Originality; adaptive; ingenuity **Curiosity**: Interest; novelty seeking; exploration; openness to experience **Judgment**: Critical thinking; thinking things through; open-minded **Love of learning**: Mastering new skills and topics; systematically adding to knowledge **Perspective**: Wisdom; providing wise counsel; taking the big-picture view
Courage	**Bravery**: Valor; not shrinking from fear; speaking up for what's right **Perseverance**: Persistence; industry; finishing what one starts **Honesty**: Authenticity; integrity **Zest**: Vitality; enthusiasm; vigor; energy; feeling alive and activated
Humanity	**Love**: Both loving and being loved; valuing close relations with others **Kindness**: Generosity; nurturance; care; compassion; altruism; "niceness" **Social intelligence**: Emotional intelligence; aware of the motives/feelings of self/others, knowing what makes other people tick
Justice	**Teamwork**: Citizenship; social responsibility; loyalty **Fairness**: Just; not letting feelings bias decisions about others **Leadership**: Organizing group activities; encouraging a group to get things done
Temperance	**Forgiveness**: Mercy; accepting others' shortcomings; giving people a second chance **Humility**: Modesty; letting one's accomplishments speak for themselves **Prudence**: Careful; cautious; not taking undue risks **Self-regulation**: Self-control; disciplined; managing impulses and emotions

Source: Peterson & Seligman, 2004. Reprinted with permission of the VIA Institute.

for exploration of strengths. Focusing on clients' strengths can initiate and maintain positive feedback circuits that potentially foster the therapeutic alliance, augment the clients' receptiveness, and support the implementation of adaptive coping strategies (Flückiger, Franz, Grosse, & Willutzki, 2009).

Following are some reasons for assessing strengths in clinical practice:

- *Repairing or fixing weakness does not necessarily make clients stronger.* The traditional assumption in psychotherapy that alleviation of symptoms will make clients happier understates the evidence which supports that being symptom-free is not synonymous with fulfillment and flourishing.
- *Using strengths helps to reinterpret and reframe problems adaptively.* Using strengths increases clients' self-efficacy and confidence in ways focusing on weakness cannot. Being aware of strengths, in addition to weaknesses, helps clients to reinterpret and reframe problems from a strengths perspective rather than from a deficits perspective.
- *Fixing weakness does not necessarily cultivate happiness.* Much like weaknesses require fixing, strengths require nurturance. Fixing weakness yields remediation, while strengths nurturance produces growth and, most likely, greater happiness.
- *Strength awareness builds a cumulative advantage.* Evidence shows that people who are aware of their strengths can build self-confidence at a young age and tend to reap a "cumulative advantage" that continues to grow over a lifetime (Judge & Hurst, 2008). The broaden-and-build theory of positive emotions (Fredrickson, 2001) applied to clinical practice argues that strengths broaden the repertoire of action potentials in the present and build resources in the future.
- *Using strengths to promote resilience.* Knowing and using strengths in good times helps clients to learn strategies to use during tough times. Being aware of and using strengths not only promotes resilience but also prepares clients to encounter challenges adaptively.
- *Using strengths to find balance in daily interactions and manage relational challenges.* A balanced therapeutic approach to sour interactions will focus equally on criticism as well on complements, on eliciting and

savoring positive memories as well as recalling resentments, on self-centeredness as well as empathy. This balance will likely lessen interpersonal tension and create opportunities to adaptively adjust these interactions.

ASSESSMENT METHODS

Strengths in clinical practice are mostly assessed through self-report measures (e.g., *Values in Action Survey-Inventory of Strengths* [VIA-IS], *Strengths Finder, Realise 2*). It entails clients completing a free online measure (mostly *VIA-IS*; www.viacharacter.org). Their top-five scores are regarded as signature strengths, which are those strengths that an individual self-consciously owns and celebrates, and for which he or she feels a sense of ownership and authenticity (e.g., "This is the real me"). The individual feels excited while displaying these signature strengths, learns quickly as they are practiced, feels more invigorated than exhausted when using them, and creates and pursues projects that revolve around them. Generally, top-five VIA-IS scores are regarded as clients' signature strengths. Clients are then asked to find new ways to use their signature strengths.

Reliance on this approach, although useful in a nonclinical setting, may not meet critical clinical needs. For example, exclusive focus on top-ranked strength scores could give an inadvertent message to clients that weaknesses and deficits, which are equally real and inevitable, do not deserve clinical attention. Clinicians can obtain a deeper understanding of their client's strengths through feedback reports on various strengths measures. For example, Values in Action Institute www.viacharacter.org) currently offers two comprehensive reports on VIA. First, *VIA Me* is an 18-page report with description of signature strengths, related activities, quotes, benefit statement, and an overview of one's middle and lower strengths. Those who already have completed the VIA can also obtain this report. Second, *VIA Pro* is a 24-page report that includes various graphic representations of signature strengths with raw score averages for each of them, research findings about signature strengths, underuse and overuse of strengths, and a graphic description of one's signature strengths on a continuum of head/heart and self/others. Also included in the report is a comprehensive list of behavioral exercises for using and further building each of the 24 strengths. VIA also offers shorter versions for adults and youth.

An alternative is a dynamic strength assessment. In this approach (Table 11.2), the client is provided with a sheet of brief descriptions (approximately 20–25 words per strength) of core strengths, without their titles. I use the Values in Action classification model (Peterson & Seligman, 2004). The client is asked to identify (*not rank*) up to five strengths that best illustrate her or her personality. Identical collateral data are collected from a loved one. The client is then provided descriptions with titles to give strengths names and specific contexts. The client is asked to share memories, experiences, real-life stories, anecdotes, accomplishments, and skills that illustrate development and use these strengths. Then the client is asked to complete the self-report measure of strengths (e.g., *Values in Action—Inventory of Strengths*; Peterson & Seligman, 2004). This leads to discussion of all strengths identified

TABLE 11.2. Dynamic Strength Assessment: A Sample

	Strength	Self	Other	VIA	Tonic/ Phasic	Under/ Over	Desired	Composite
1	Appreciation of beauty							
2	Authenticity and honesty							
3	Bravery and valor							
4	Creativity							
5	Curiosity							

thus far, in terms of their usage, which could be *tonic* (kindness is displayed in nearly all situations) or *phasic* (kindness is displayed only at work but not at home, fairness only in few situations, or teamwork only with preferred group). The client can also identify underuse or overuse of strengths (e.g., underuse of kindness in close relationships, or overuse of curiosity about sports or fashion but not in close relationships, assuming that one has completely figured out his or her partner). After exploring such nuances and subtleties of strengths, the client is asked to identify five desired strengths, which could be deployed adaptively to solve presenting concerns. Each column is independent, and each cell is marked with X to denote corresponding strength. All the Xs across rows are summed to derive a composite. The top-five strength scores across rows are generally regarded as signature strengths.

Another approach to assess clients' strengths is by means of the clinical interview. Flückiger and colleagues (2009) have used the clinical interview to elicit clients' strengths in the therapeutic process. Following are several of their resource activation questions that can be readily incorporated into a Life History Questionnaire or clinical interview in routine practice:

- What do you enjoy most? Please describe your most enjoyable experiences.
- What are you good at? Please describe experiences that brought out the best in you.
- What are your inspirations for the future?
- What makes a satisfying day for you?
- What experiences give you a sense of authenticity?
- Please describe a time when you felt "the real you."

Clinicians can incorporate strengths in the therapeutic process by reflecting upon the following questions:

- Which specific strengths of your clients can facilitate their therapeutic progress and how can you assess these strengths?
- Do you view clients primarily as individuals entangled in persistent negative emotions and experiences, which obviously stand out more in treatment, or do you also view clients as capable of exploring and developing their strengths?
- Do you view strengths as potential buffers against psychological distress?
- Finally, do you consciously and deliberately make efforts to elicit and incorporate strengths in the therapeutic process?

References and Readings

Flückiger, C., Caspar,, F. H., Grosse, M., & Willutzki, U. (2009). Working with patients strengths: A microprocess approach, *Psychotherapy Research, 19*, 213–223

Fredrickson, B. (2001). The role of positive emotions in positive psychology: The broaden-and-build theory of positive emotions. *American Psychologist, 56*, 218–226.

Judge, T. A., & Hurst, C. (2008). How the rich (and happy) get richer (and happier): Relationship of core self-evaluations to trajectories in attaining work success. *Journal of Applied Psychology, 93*, 849–863.

Kahneman, D., & Tversky, A. (1984). Choices, values, and frames. *American Psychologist, 39*, 341–350.

Peterson, C., & Seligman, M. E. P. (2004). *Character strengths and virtues: A handbook and classification*. New York: Oxford University Press.

Schwartz, B., & Sharpe, K. E. (2006). Practical wisdom: Aristotle meets positive psychology. *Journal of Happiness Studies, 7*, 377–395.

Seligman, M. E. P. (2002). *Authentic happiness: Using the new positive psychology to realize your potential for lasting fulfillment*. New York: Free Press.

Related Topics

Chapter 3, "Improving Diagnostic and Clinical Interviewing"

Chapter 4, "Increasing the Accuracy of Clinical Judgment"

Chapter 32, "Compendium of Treatment Adaptations"

12 EVALUATING DEMENTIA

Elise Caccappolo

Dementia is not a disease in and of itself; rather, it is a diagnostic classification that refers to a significant decline in intellectual functioning that causes impairment in social and occupational functioning. The reduction in intellectual functioning is acquired; that is, it must represent a decline from a previous level of functioning, which differentiates dementia from congenital mental retardation. It is also persistent, which distinguishes dementia from delirium. Finally, the intellectual dysfunction of dementia affects multiple areas of cognition, in contrast to focal deficits such as aphasia caused by specific neurological lesions.

The methods and criteria used to evaluate dementia vary with the definition of dementia used. The American Psychiatric Association's fourth edition of the *Diagnostic and Statistical Manual of Mental Disorders* (*DSM-IV*, 2000) provides diagnostic criteria for the clinical syndrome of dementia as well as more specific criteria for diagnosing Alzheimer's disease and vascular dementia. The National Institute on Aging-Alzheimer's Association (NIA-AA) criteria for diagnosing possible or probable Alzheimer's disease are more commonly used for research purposes and require neuropsychological assessment. Various consensus groups have developed diagnostic criteria for other, less common forms of dementia, including frontotemporal dementia (FTD; Neary et al., 1998) and dementia with Lewy bodies (DLB; McKeith et al., 1996).

The *DSM-IV* criteria requires the presence of impaired memory plus impairment in at least one other cognitive domain, including aphasia (language impairment), agnosia (perceptual impairment), apraxia (impaired motor programming), or executive functioning. These clinical criteria are imperfect, however, as memory is not always impaired in dementia, particularly in nonamnestic dementias and dementia that occurs in the early stages of a disease. In addition, more recent definitions of dementia require impairment in three or more cognitive domains so as to decrease the likelihood of misdiagnosing dementia, i.e. committing false positive errors.

CLINICAL INTERVIEW

The evaluation of dementia requires a careful history, including a detailed clinical interview. The patient may very well be unaware of the extent of his or her level of impairment. Subsequently, information should be obtained from both the patient and a reliable collateral source such as a caregiver or knowledgeable family member. When possible, it is helpful to interview the informant separately so as to obtain information that may not have been voluntarily reported in the presence of the patient. The informant's information should be compared to that given by the patient to determine the patient's level of awareness or denial of symptoms. The interview can offer information about the onset and time course of cognitive and behavioral symptoms. Identifying the mode of onset of cognitive change is often difficult for the patient or family members to determine with certainty. Cognitive changes may come to the awareness of others following a "trigger" event. Physical trauma such as surgery, dehydration, or infection, or psychological trauma such as the death of a loved one or a move from familiar living arrangements may unmask symptoms that were previously unnoticed, leading family members to believe that the onset of cognitive decline was acute. In many situations, the death of a spouse uncovers a patient's cognitive and functional limitations as it becomes clear that the spouse, whether intentionally or not, compensated for the patient's deficits. Determining the course of the cognitive decline is also important: Is it progressive, stepwise, or fluctuating? A progressive course is typical of most neurodegenerative diseases such as Alzheimer's disease, while a stepwise course is usually more characteristic of a vascular etiology. Often, family members will report fluctuating levels of cognitive performance. A detailed analysis of this type of course is necessary in order to rule out specific types of dementia, such as DLB, for which alternating levels of arousal represent a primary clinical feature. To investigate whether the course is fluctuating, caregivers may be asked, "Does the patient have good days and bad days?" If so, it is helpful to explore whether there is a pattern to the fluctuations; that is, does the patient perform worse when sleep deprived? The interview also offers the opportunity to assess for any recent changes in the patient's lifestyle that may contribute to cognitive decline. For example, has the patient's living situation changed? Has his or her social network or support system been altered? Patients in the early stages of dementia often present with typical cognitive symptoms, and directed questioning can be used to obtain specific examples of such features. Positive responses to questions such as "Do you misplace items more frequently than in the past?" or "Do you frequently forget appointments?" suggest short-term memory impairment. Language functioning can be explored by inquiring as to whether the patient experiences word-finding difficulty or has experienced a change in his or her ability to complete a sentence while speaking. Visuospatial impairment may manifest as difficulty with finding one's way when driving or walking in unfamiliar places. Reports of difficulty following group conversations or understanding jokes may suggest executive dysfunction.

In addition to cognitive decline, dementia is also associated with mood and behavioral changes. Frequently, patients experiencing cognitive change may appear withdrawn or less interested in social interactions. Whether this alteration reflects the effects of emotional distress such as depression is often unclear to the caregiver. Patients who are cognitively impaired may seem isolative, particularly in large social situations, because they are unable to follow the flow of conversation. They may exhibit a "delay" in terms of responding to portions of earlier conversations as opposed to staying on topic. Less frequently, patients exhibit psychiatric symptoms, including hallucinations or delusions of persecution, particularly as the level of dementia severity increases. Patients and caregivers may not offer specific examples of psychotic behavior, which necessitates careful but sensitive probing about the existence of symptoms through directed questions. In addition to being asked about the presence of visual or auditory hallucinations, for example, "Do you ever see things that are not there, such as people, animals, or insects?" patients can be asked whether they ever feel a "phantom presence" or believe that someone is in the room with them. This line of questioning is especially useful when assessing patients with parkinsonism, who may experience "feeling of presence" or "phantom boarder" delusions. Oftentimes patients will accuse caregivers of infidelity. Given the sensitivity of the topic, the informant can be asked this question privately.

An assessment of functional status is necessary when evaluating a patient for dementia. Questions about activities of daily living (ADLs) should be asked to assess for changes in the patient's ability to care for himself or herself. One way to do this is to ask the caregiver whether there are specific tasks or activities that the patient is unable to perform as well as he or she did before the onset of cognitive and/ or behavioral symptoms. Questions about the patient's abilities should be posed to assess instrumental (IADLs). For example, is the patient able to manage his or her own finances; specifically, has the patient forgotten to pay bills on time or paid some bills twice? Has the patient made errors when balancing the checkbook? Can the patient make change for a purchase or calculate the tip on a bill? Does the patient require assistance to manage his or her medication regimen? Is the patient driving and, if so, has the quality of his or her driving skill changed? Has he or she become lost or disoriented while walking, driving, or using public transportation? Basic ADLs should also be assessed: Is there any change in hygiene; for example, does the patient require reminders to bathe, groom, or change clothes? Inquiries about social and leisure activities should also be asked: Is the patient reading as much as he or she did in the past? If so, what is being read? Has the patient switched from reading novels and books to reading the newspaper or magazines? Often, dementia patients will read shorter articles, either in newspapers, magazines, or online as opposed to books due to the fact that they may be unable to recall what was previously read in a book. Similarly, patients with dementia frequently lose interest in watching movies due to their difficulty in following the plotline or remembering who characters are. A patient may explain this disinterest in reading or viewing movies by stating that he or she finds them to be boring or uninteresting. This same reasoning is also often used when the patient is confronted with his or her tendency to forget recent conversations; that is, the patient may rationalize that he or she only recalls information that he or she is interested in.

A thorough medical and psychiatric history should be obtained to identify any conditions that can affect one's mental status. A review of the patient's past neurological history should include questions about prior head injuries, stroke, tumors, and seizures. A more general medical history is also necessary given that disturbances of endocrine function, such as a thyroid disorder, vitamin deficiencies such as low B12 levels, or metabolic disorders can affect cognitive functioning. It is important to obtain a full list of prescription and over-the-counter medications to assess the possibility that adverse effects which may result from accidental overdoses or poor compliance with medication regimens may be mistaken for dementia. Information regarding current and past use of alcohol and drugs should be obtained, as well as family history of dementia or other neurological disease. Visual acuity and hearing should be assessed to rule out a visual or hearing problem. Psychiatric conditions such as depression often mimic dementia. Previously referred to as "pseudodementia," the cognitive changes associated with depression represent a substantial percentage of patients who present for evaluation. Obtaining a developmental history is important to rule out any preexisting conditions such as perceptual problems, learning disabilities, or attentional disorders.

NEUROPSYCHOLOGICAL ASSESSMENT

Formal neuropsychological testing that uses standardized tests with appropriate normative data provides objective data on cognitive functioning, which assists in making a diagnosis. A comprehensive neuropsychological evaluation should assess all cognitive domains, including memory, language, visuospatial functioning, attention and executive functioning, sensory and motor functioning, and emotional functioning. One of the more difficult aspects of diagnosing dementia is determining whether the current level of intellectual function represents a definitive decline from previous levels. Unless patients have undergone baseline testing prior to the onset of cognitive changes, such as IQ testing while in school, it is often challenging to establish an accurate estimate of premorbid intellectual functioning. Therefore, information obtained from the clinical interview should include demographic and historical data such as education level (including the quality of education received), socioeconomic status, and occupational history. The patient's cultural background and primary language are also relevant to the evaluation. On neuropsychological testing, premorbid intellectual functioning can be estimated using single-word reading tests (e.g., National Adult Reading Test [NART], Wechsler Test of Adult Reading [WTAR]) that correlate highly with general intellectual functioning but are fairly immune to cognitive changes, as well as subtests on the Wechsler Adult Intelligence Scale

(WAIS; Information subtest) that are also considered relatively resistant to cognitive change. Caution should be taken when using such measures with ethnic and racial minorities, however, as they may underestimate premorbid functioning with groups. Finally, a full assessment of emotional functioning, including personality measures where necessary, should be obtained to rule out the effects of psychiatric symptoms such as anxiety and/or depression on cognitive performance.

References and Readings

American Psychiatric Association. (2000). *The diagnostic and statistical manual of mental disorders* (4th ed.). Washington, DC: American Psychiatric Publishing.

McKeith, I. G., Galasko, D., Kosaka, K., Perry, E. K., Dickson, D. W., & Hansen, L. A. (1996). Consensus guidelines for the clinical and pathologic diagnosis of dementia and Lewy bodies (DLB): Report of the consortium on DLB international workshop. *Neurology, 47*, 1113–1124.

McKhann, G., Knopman, D. S., Chertknow, H., Hyman, B. T., Jack, C. R., Kawas, C. H., ... Phelps, C. H. (2011). The diagnosis of dementia due to Alzheimer's disease: Recommendations from the National Institute on Aging-Alzheimer's Association workgroups on diagnostic guidelines for Alzheimer's disease. *Alzheimer's & Dementia, 7*, 263–269.

Neary, D., Snowden, J. S., Gustafson, L., Passant, U., Stuss, D., Black, S., ... Benson, D. F. (1998). Frontotemporal lobar degeneration: A consensus on clinical diagnostic criteria. *Neurology, 51*, 1546–1554.

Related Topics

Chapter 9, "Evaluating the Medical Components of Childhood Developmental and Behavioral Disorders"
Chapter 17, "Adult Neuropsychological Assessment"
Chapter 18, "Developmental Neuropsychological Assessment"
Chapter 19, "Assessment and Intervention for Executive Dysfunction"
Chapter 20, "Assessing and Managing Concussion"
Chapter 58, "Practicing Psychotherapy with Adults Who Have Cognitive Impairments"

13 USING THE *INTERNATIONAL CLASSIFICATION OF DISEASES* SYSTEM (*ICD-10*)

Michael C. Roberts and Spencer C. Evans

The *International Classification of Diseases* (*ICD*) is the standard diagnostic classification system used throughout the world for the diagnosis, treatment, and reporting of human disease and health problems, including mental and behavioral disorders. By providing a common diagnostic language, this global standard enhances the comparability and consistency of health information and statistics across countries (Reed, 2010). Developed, published, and maintained by the World Health Organization (WHO), the *ICD* is based on scientific data and sophisticated conceptual models of disease. In this classification system, medical and mental health conditions are organized in a comprehensive taxonomy and coding system, in which each disease or disorder entity is identified by a unique diagnostic code. These codes are used not only to aggregate health statistics (e.g., morbidity, mortality), but in some countries, such as the United States, they also direct the reimbursement of health care. At present, the *ICD* is in its 10th edition and revisions are currently under way for *ICD-11*.

The *ICD* system is used by a wide variety of users (e.g., medical, mental health, and public health professionals; government agencies; researchers) for diverse purposes (e.g., primary and mental health care; professional training and education; research investigations; public health activities) and in myriad settings around the world (e.g., hospitals and clinics; government agencies; research laboratories; insurance providers). Such extensive and varied usage promotes common definitions, criteria, and language for improved communication and statistical reporting. However, this also presents various challenges, such as cultural, linguistic, economic, and professional differences that must be accommodated. Toward this end, the WHO has developed three different adaptations of the *ICD-10* Mental and Behavioral Disorders classification system, each uniquely tailored for applications in mental health care, primary care, and research. Furthermore, the *ICD-10* system has been published in 42 languages and is available in a variety of formats (e.g., CD-ROMs, books). Many of these publications and their supporting materials (e.g., training manuals) can be downloaded free of charge from the WHO Web site (WHO, 2011), and the print versions are available for sale with reduced prices offered for low-income countries. Moreover, individual countries and regions are permitted to develop their own adaptations to increase cultural validity, for example, by including culture-specific diagnoses (e.g., the Latin American Guide for Psychiatric Diagnosis).

Although clinicians throughout most of the world use the mental and behavioral diagnostic codes in the *ICD*, American mental health professionals nominally rely on the *Diagnostic and Statistical Manual of Mental Disorders* (*DSM*). The *DSM* is currently in its fourth edition, text revision, and is published by the American Psychiatric Association (APA, 2000). However, the official US diagnostic system for mental illness is the *ICD*, even if US psychologists and psychiatrists ostensibly rely on the *DSM* in professional practice. That is, *DSM* diagnoses must be recoded or translated via computerized "crosswalks" into *ICD* codes for third-party billing, reimbursement, and official communication of incidence and prevalence of mental and behavioral disorders for governmental disease databases. For example, the *ICD* is required for Medicare claims by federal regulation and mandated by HIPAA for electronic information transfer. Additionally, even though the *ICD-10* is the current and most widely used edition of the *ICD* system, US health care still relies upon the *ICD-9-CM* (an American clinical modification of the *ICD-9*, developed and maintained by the National Center for Health Statistics; Centers for Disease Control and Prevention [CDC], 2011) for most clinical, billing, and reporting purposes. The United States is scheduled to convert to the *ICD-10-CM* beginning on October 1, 2014. Just as American health care will be transitioning to the *ICD-10* and the *DSM-5* (and any potential compatibility problems between the two), most of the rest of the world will be preparing for the *ICD-11*, which is expected to be published in 2015. One important implication for professional psychology is that practitioners will likely use the *DSM-5* and/or the *ICD-11* for diagnosis, treatment, training, and research; yet any diagnoses made according to those systems will have to be translated to the soon-to-be-outdated *ICD-10* coding system for billing and health reporting. Given the complexities of these classification systems within American health care, as well as the major transitions that occur over the next few years, psychologists will want to become familiar with the structure, content, and usage of the *ICD-10*.

CONTENT AND ORGANIZATION

The *ICD-10* is comprised of 22 chapters, each designated to a different category of human disease or health problem. Within this system, each diagnosis corresponds with a three- to five-character alphanumeric code of the form *A12.34*, which not only identifies the diagnosis but also represents how that diagnosis is classified within the *ICD-10* system. This code begins with a prefix letter (indicating a broad disease or disorder grouping), followed by a two-digit numeric code (indicating a disorder category), which is sometimes followed by a decimal with one or two numerals after it (indicating particular diagnoses and features). In the *ICD-10* system, all psychological conditions are contained in Chapter V: Mental and Behavioral Disorders (coded with the prefix *F*), which is subdivided into 10 different blocks of major mental disorder categories, grouped based on syndrome similarity (see Table 13.1). These higher order groupings (e.g., *F30-F39: Mood [affective] disorders*) are comprised of particular diagnostic categories (e.g., *F32: Depressive episode*), which are further subdivided based on features such as severity, course, and symptoms (e.g., *F32.11: Moderate depressive episode with somatic syndrome*).

TABLE 13.1. Organization of *ICD-10* and Chapter V: Mental and Behavioral Disorders

F00–F09	Organic, including symptomatic, mental disorders
F10–F19	Mental and behavioral disorders due to psychoactive substance use
F20–F29	Schizophrenia, schizotypal, and delusional disorders
F30–F39	Mood [affective] disorders
F40–F48	Neurotic, stress-related, and somatoform disorders
F50–F59	Behavioural syndromes associated with physiological disturbances and physical factors
F60–F69	Disorders of adult personality and behaviour
F70–F79	Mental retardation
F80–F89	Disorders of psychological development
F90–F98	Behavioral and emotional disorders with onset usually occurring in childhood and adolescence
F99	Unspecified mental disorder

Source: Adapted from the *International Classification of Diseases and Related Health Problems*, 10th revision, by the World Health Organization. Retrieved from apps.who.int/classifications/apps/icd/icd10online/

For each mental disorder, and for some groups of disorders, a clinical description and a set of diagnostic guidelines are provided. The description elucidates its clinical features, including both primary features and those which are commonly associated, but not essential for diagnosis. Diagnostic guidelines provide the clinician with general criteria about the number, type, balance, and duration of symptoms that would typically represent a particular diagnosis. These descriptions and guidelines are phrased so as to facilitate consistency and reliability across settings, while also retaining enough flexibility to take clinical judgment into consideration. Underlying the descriptions and diagnostic guidelines for each individual disorder is the broader definition of a mental disorder, which the *ICD-10* defines as "a clinically recognizable set of symptoms or behavior associated in most cases with distress and with interference with personal functions" (WHO, 2011).

More complex diseases have more complicated definitions. The codes for mental and behavioral disorders are intricate because of the complexities of dysfunction, in addition to differing theoretical models about human behavior, cultural presentations, and nuances. There are also unique considerations that apply to particular blocks of disorders. For example, child diagnoses (*F90-F98*), which are largely influenced and defined by developmental processes, often have age criteria and developmental considerations in their descriptions and diagnostic guidelines. As another example, substance use disorders (*F10-F19*) are arranged such that the same diagnosis (e.g., *F1x.26: Dependence syndrome, episodic use*) can be applied across different substances (e.g., alcohol [*F10.26*], opioids [*F11.26*], or cannabinoids [*F12.26*]).

As an example, in the diagnostic category *F20: Schizophrenia*, the description begins by stating that the schizophrenic disorders

> are characterized in general by fundamental and characteristic distortions of thinking and perception, and affects that are inappropriate or blunted. Clear

consciousness and intellectual capacity are usually maintained although certain cognitive deficits may evolve in the course of time. The most important psychopathological phenomena include thought echo; thought insertion or withdrawal; thought broadcasting; delusional perception and delusions of control; influence or passivity; hallucinatory voices commenting or discussing the patient in the third person; thought disorders and negative symptoms. (WHO, 2011)

This description also presents the typical course of schizophrenic disorders, as well as diagnostic procedures concerning comorbid symptoms, mental disorders, or physical diseases. Within this diagnostic category, more specific types of schizophrenia are also classified, such as *F20.0: Paranoid schizophrenia,* which is characterized by "relatively stable, often paranoid delusions, usually accompanied by hallucinations, particularly of the auditory variety, and perceptual disturbances. Disturbances of affect, volition and speech, and catatonic symptoms, are either absent or relatively inconspicuous" (WHO, 2011).

An example of a diagnostic category in childhood and adolescence block is the *Conduct disorders* (*F91*) where the characteristic symptoms of "a repetitive and persistent pattern of dissocial, aggressive, and defiant conduct" might be coded into *Conduct disorders confined to a family content* (*F91.0*); *Unsocialized conduct disorder* (*F91.1*); *Socialized conduct disorder* (*F91.2*); or *Oppositional defiant disorder* (*F91.3*), which has the distinctive features of "a pattern of persistently negativistic, hostile, defiant, provocative, and disruptive behavior, which is clearly outside the normal range of behavior for a child of the same age in the same sociocultural context, and which does not include the more serious violations of the rights of others" and is typically diagnosed prior to 9 or 10 years of age (WHO, 2011).

DSM AND *ICD*

The alternative mental health classification system similar to the *ICD-10* Mental and Behavioral Codes is the *DSM-IV-TR*. Although the *DSM* and *ICD* systems share many general similarities in structure, format, and content, there are several noteworthy differences between the two diagnostic classification systems, which may create some problems or confusion. First, the *ICD* and *DSM* may use different terminologies to refer to the same disorders (e.g., "attention-deficit/hyperactivity disorder" in the *DSM* is labeled "hyperkinetic disorder" in the *ICD*). Second, the same disorder often has slightly different diagnostic criteria in each system, or states similar criteria in a different manner. In this regard, the *ICD* tends to have more flexible and general *diagnostic guidelines,* whereas the *DSM* employs more strictly and categorically defined *diagnostic criteria*. Similarly, the *ICD-10* differentiates between what constitutes a "confident" diagnosis (i.e., meeting all the requisite criteria) versus one that is "probable," "provisional," or "tentative" (i.e., meeting some of the criteria, or in need of more information); the *DSM-IV-TR* does not make such distinctions. Third, there are differences in the organizing structure of the two systems. The *DSM* is organized into five axes, with all the psychological disorders grouped according to symptom similarity under Axes I and II. Similarly, in the *ICD,* all mental and behavioral disorders are contained in Chapter V, in which disorders are grouped into blocks. Most of these higher order groupings are similar across the two systems, for example, mood disorders and personality disorders. However, in some groupings, there are major nosological differences across the two systems. For example, the *DSM-IV-TR* separates *Anxiety Disorders* and *Somatoform Disorders,* whereas the *ICD-10* contains both within one block: *Neurotic, stress-related, and somatoform disorders* (*F40-F48*). At the lower order organization level similar differences arise. This can create situations in which diagnoses are difficult to find for a clinician trained on a different system.

Finally, many of the differences between the *DSM* and *ICD* can be elucidated by the differences between the sponsoring organizations, the APA and the WHO. The APA is a national professional organization of American psychiatrists that publishes the *DSM* as a proprietary venture. Consequently, the usage of the *DSM* is limited to countries and settings heavily influenced by the training and traditions of mental health care in the United States. And even within most of those settings, *DSM* codes must be translated into *ICD* codes for the purposes noted earlier. The *DSM* has been criticized for its American-centric cultural bias, lacking sensitivity and validity with persons of non-Western backgrounds. In contrast, the WHO is a global, nonprofit organization that maintains the *ICD* as a central component of its public health mission. The WHO has involved the international community in the mental health disciplines in all aspects of development, implementation, and evaluation of the *ICD*. The resulting product is a diagnostic classification system published in numerous languages, formats, and adaptations tailored to the unique needs of the diverse populations and applications that rely upon it. The *ICD* is also far more expansive than the *DSM*; in the *ICD* framework, mental illness is embedded within a comprehensive taxonomy of all human illness, disease, and health problems. Furthermore, the *ICD* is at the core of what is known as the "WHO Family of International Classifications," which also includes (a) the International Classification of Functioning, Disability, and Health and (b) the International Classification of Health Interventions.

FUTURE DIRECTIONS

The *ICD-10* began development in 1983, was approved by the WHO member nations in 1990, and the final version was published in 1992. The revision process is now well under way in preparation for the *ICD-11*, with an anticipated publication date of 2015. This process has been a global, multidisciplinary, multilingual effort, involving input from international agencies, nongovernmental organizations, and representatives from 193 countries within the WHO. It has involved formative research and summative/evaluative field trials, all with a clear emphasis on increasing clinical utility for practitioners. Details on the processes of the *ICD* revision are posted online (WHO, 2011). With each subsequent revision, the *DSM* and *ICD* have moved toward harmonization. At present, both systems are used as necessary tools in the diagnosis and treatment of mental illness with the official US government preference for the *ICD*.

Over time, it has been hoped that the classification systems would improve validity and reliability of diagnoses through reliance on significant advances in biopsychosocial research findings. Yet in the current revisions of the *ICD* and *DSM*, this does not appear likely, so the WHO revision process for all chapters in the *ICD* has emphasized improving the clinical utility of its systems as the way to improve diagnosis and treatment. Reed (2010) stated that "the clinical utility of a classification construct or category for mental and behavioral disorders depends on (a) its value in *communicating* (e.g., among practitioners, patients, families, administrators); (b) its *implementation characteristics* in clinical practice, including its goodness of fit (i.e., accuracy of description), its ease of use and the time required to use it (i.e., feasibility); and (c) its usefulness in *selecting interventions* and in making *clinical management* decisions" (p. 461).

There are many further identified issues pertaining to these classification systems that have yet to be resolved. Some of the major ones include (a) whether developmental discontinuity exists between particular childhood and adult disorders and how diagnostic criteria should be tailored for different ages (e.g., childhood conduct disorders and adult personality disorders, childhood and adult depression); (b) whether disorders and criteria are culturally universal and comprehensive enough to capture the diversity of symptom presentations in the various contexts; (c) whether a categorical or dimensional approach to the assessment and diagnosis of psychopathology (or some combination of the two) is more valid, reliable, and useful in clinical settings; (d) how clinically useful are the classification systems to the various users and stakeholders, and how to improve that clinical utility; (e) how to solve the problem of excessive comorbidity; (f) how best to arrange and format the diagnostic criteria, categories, and overall organization of the disorders within a diagnostic system; and (g) whether particular diagnoses should be included or excluded, as well as how they should be defined.

References and Readings

American Psychiatric Association. (2000). *Diagnostic and statistical manual of mental disorders* (4th ed., text rev.). Washington, DC: Author.

Center for Disease Control and Prevention: National Center for Health Statistics. (2011). *Classification of diseases, functioning, and disability*. Retrieved January 2013, from www.cdc.gov/nchs/icd.htm

Centers for Medicare and Medicaid Services. (2011). *ICD-10*. Retrieved January 2013, from www.cms.gov/ICD10/

International Advisory Group for the Revision of ICD-10 Mental and Behavioural Disorders. (2011). A conceptual framework for the revision of the ICD-10 classification of mental and behavioural disorders. *World Psychiatry, 10*, 86–892.

Reed, G. M. (2010). Toward ICD-11: Improving the clinical utility of WHO's International Classification of Mental Disorders. *Professional Psychology: Research and Practice, 41*, 457–464.

World Health Organization. (2011). *ICD-10 online: Current version (2007)* and *ICD-10 classification of mental* and *behavioural disorders: Clinical descriptions and diagnostic guidelines.* Retrieved January 2013, from www.who.int/classifications/icd/en/

Related Topics

Chapter 1, "Lifetime Prevalence of Mental Disorders in the General Population"

Chapter 3, "Improving Diagnostic and Clinical Interviewing"

Chapter 10, "Using the *DSM-5* and *ICD-11* in Forensic and Clinical Applications with Children Across Racial and Ethnic Lines"

14 TAKING A CLIENT'S SEXUAL HISTORY

Judith C. White

WHY ASK DIFFICULT QUESTIONS?

Many clinicians do not routinely explore clients' sexual histories. Therapists too often assume that taking a client's sexual history is not necessary unless a client's presenting problems are of an explicitly sexual nature. Without training in this area many have apprehension about how, when, and what to ask (Risen, 1995; Wiederman & Sansone, 1999). Material in the sexual history may hold important information about the client that goes beyond simply the client's sexual experiences. Such histories give us information about how people experience themselves and the quality of their relationships. It may also give us information about hidden trauma that otherwise would go unmentioned.

WHO SHOULD WE ASK AND WHEN?

Clinicians should explore the sexual history of every client, both individuals and couples of every age. This exploration can take place during the assessment phase at the outset of therapy or during the course of therapy when a positive working alliance has been established. Clients who present with sexual complaints usually expect to be asked questions about their sexual history and their current sexual experiences; however, clients who do not present with a sexual complaint may not appreciate the relevance of questions about sexual behavior and may find such questions intrusive. For the latter clients it is appropriate to focus initially on the presenting complaint. Some clinicians may choose to ask some questions about sexuality as a part of the initial assessment. Others might choose to delay taking this aspect of the patient's history until they have developed a positive working alliance with the patient. When working with a couple, a therapist may decide to take each person's history separately. Some couples may have been very open with each other about their histories and therefore the therapist may take the history with both partners present. However, it is usually helpful to meet individually with each partner since there are some aspects of sexuality that may feel emotionally charged and unknown to the partner (e.g., fantasy life, masturbation, sex outside the relationship). When therapists ask questions about sexuality, they communicate the importance of sexuality to the client and the acceptability of discussing such material. If the therapist initiates the discussion, doing so can make it easier for the client to raise sexual concerns during therapy. Questions about the client's sexual history may naturally flow during the initial phase. Many clients enter therapy with problems in their relationships and in that context may volunteer information about those relationships. At these opportunistic junctures, the therapist can inquire about whether the relationship was sexual and whether it felt satisfying to the client. The therapist can also ask the client to elaborate on why the experience felt satisfying or not.

HOW TO ASK

Two general approaches apply to taking a client's sexual history. In one approach, questions are designed to explore current sexual functioning followed by history taking. In another approach questions explore the historical development of a sexual self to the present sexual adaptation. When clients present with concerns regarding their current sexual functioning, this can become a starting point to assist the client in describing specific concerns. For example, men may experience difficulty in getting and sustaining erections or have problems with rapid ejaculation. Women may report painful intercourse or lack of desire. However, clients who feel uncomfortable talking about their current sexual experience may feel more at ease talking about their adolescent sexual development. It is helpful to begin with general, nonthreatening, open-ended questions, such as:

- May I ask you some questions about your sexuality?
- Are you sexually active?
- Have you been sexually active with anyone in the last 6 months?

Always use gender-neutral language to convey our understanding of the diversity of sexual orientation. We never presume that a client is heterosexual or that the client has not had sexual experiences with members of the same sex. Similarly, we do not assume that the client has been sexual at all.

Questions for Couples

- Do you and/or your partner have any sexual concerns?
- How would you describe your sexual relationship?

Questions Designed to Explore a Client's Early Sexual History

- What is your earliest memory of sexual feelings?
- How was sexuality talked about in your family?
- How was nudity handled in your family?

One of the most effective ways of asking a client or couple to share their sexual history is to consider asking clients to tell their "sexual story" (Risen, 2003). Sexual stories include both the historical narrative (i.e., the development of sexual identity and the accumulation of sexual experiences) and a current expression in thoughts, feelings, and behaviors (Risen, 2003).

Helping Clients Tell Their Sexual Story

Sexual Behavior

Although most clients may be used to *behaving* sexually, they may be less familiar with talking to someone about it. Many individuals may have engaged in joking about their sexuality with friends but have rarely had a serious discussion about their sexual feelings or their behavior. As such, they may need assistance in learning how to talk about their sexuality and develop comfort with this aspect of themselves. Some clients may use street or colloquial language to describe their experiences and may display great ignorance about the human body. It may be helpful for the therapist to use the same language as the client initially, as this may help the client to feel more at ease. Gradually, you can introduce the client to more accurate anatomical terms and descriptors.

While it is important to inquire about the sexual history of all clients, special sensitivity may be needed with members of religious groups who deem some sexual practices, such as sexual behavior prior to marriage, unacceptable or sinful. Members of these groups may feel that just talking about their sexual fantasies or behavior is sacrilegious and therefore off limits for exploration in therapy. Such clients may express curiosity or concern about the therapist's religious beliefs or absence of such beliefs. Responses should be managed in the same way as most other client requests for personal disclosures. The therapist should elicit the client's curiosity about why this is an issue as well as the multiple meanings of the client's interest. Some clients who currently practice abstinence may have been sexually active previously, while others may date and engage in sexual practices other than intercourse. Therefore, it is important to ask specific questions, albeit with sensitivity, about what specific sexual behaviors are practiced. Clients from these religious or cultural groups may also experience considerable guilt if they engage in sexual practices forbidden by that group. Refusing to speak about such behaviors can represent their way of maintaining their denial of any transgressions.

For example, a married woman who has not had sex with her husband for 10 years maintains that she has no sexual desire and that she has not had sex with anyone else. Her therapist noticed that the client would cancel appointments after these issues were raised in sessions. Exploration of the missed appointments revealed that the client was having sex outside of her marriage. The client felt she had violated the teachings of her church and was afraid that the therapist would condemn her as she condemned herself. Therapists use their knowledge of the dimensions of sexuality to both encourage and guide the client in the telling of the client's sexual story. Risen (2003) observes that sexual expression or sexual behavior is the outcome of the interweaving of identity, function, and relational meaning and that each of these components is multifaceted and complex. Therefore, the therapist must explore each entity separately.

Sexual Identity

Sexual identity is a category that includes both gender identity and sexual orientation (Risen, 2003). Gender identity refers to where the individual psychologically experiences himself or herself on the spectrum of what is considered masculinity and femininity in the individual's culture. Sexual orientation is defined by the biological sex of the person an individual is erotically attracted to. "The term 'transgender experience' is currently used to refer to the many different ways individuals may experience a gender identity outside of the simple categories of male or female" (Carroll, 2007, p. 479). Transgender individuals include transvestites and transsexuals. The term *transvestite* describes men or women who cross-dress temporarily or permanently (Pfafflin, 2003). Individuals who are preoccupied with the desire to live as the other sex and feel very uncomfortable with their biological sex may wish to pass as the other sex or change their biological sex via the use of hormones and surgical interventions. Such individuals are referred to as transsexual, and they may experience great distress, social isolation, stigma, and rejection. They may seek therapy to help them with these feelings and for rejection by family members and peers leading to isolation, as well as the squeal of the stigma and discrimination they encounter. For others, therapy may constitute a formal medical prerequisite for any surgical interventions to alter their sex, as well as after such interventions have occurred to adjust to the change.

A larger group of people experience a subjective sense of inadequacy about their gender presentation. Men may complain about not being masculine "enough" and women may complain about not being feminine "enough." Dissatisfaction with their bodies may be expressed, for men, in the belief that their penis is too small or that their voice is too high. For women this dissatisfaction may be expressed in the belief that their breasts are either too small or too big, or that they are too fat. Concerns about whether one's body image is feminine enough is often a source of conflict for women of color since the mainstream media still portrays feminine beauty as white, young, tall, and thin. These beliefs may cause these individuals a great deal of emotional distress and can prompt them to seek psychotherapy services for that distress or may be an underlying factor in other complaints. These feelings of inadequacy about gender presentation may be expressed behaviorally in emotional distress, social isolation, and avoidance of romantic and sexual contact (Risen, 2003).

The therapist can explore a client's feelings about his or her gender identity by asking the following questions as historical narrative:

- Can you tell me about the feelings you experienced when you began to menstruate?
- How old were you when your breasts began to develop?
- Was this about the same age range as your peers or different?
- Who prepared you for menstruation?
- How did your parents react to this change?
- How did you react to this change?

Responses will also help the therapist learn about a young woman's relationship with her parents, especially her mother and possibly her peers.

- How did you feel when you had your first ejaculation or wet dream?
- When did your voice start to change and when did you start to grow pubic and facial hair?
- Did anyone prepare you for these changes in your body?
- Were these changes in keeping with your peer group?

Responses can indicate whether normative maturational changes were welcome or felt alien to the client and may be important to explore further.

- How do you feel about your body now?
- What do you like about your body?
- What don't you like about your body?
- If you could change something about your body, what might that be?
- How do you feel with members of your sex?
- With members of the other sex?

Sexual Orientation

There are three ways to define sexual orientation: behavior, fantasy, and self-identification (Maurice, 1999). For the most part we think of people as lesbian, gay, bisexual, or heterosexual; however, these are reductionistic categories and do not capture the complexity of sexuality. Clients may have sexual feelings, fantasies, and behavior toward people of the same sex as well as people of the other sex. It is important to explore a client's sexual behavior, fantasies, and self-identification to gain a richer understanding of their sexual orientation. Kinsey maintained that human beings have the capacity to be sexual in behavior or fantasy with people of the same sex or different sex during their life span (Iasenza, 2010). Sexual orientation is not fixed and may vary during the life span for some individuals. Kinsey's work has been criticized because he assumed that sexual attraction and sexual behavior were congruent. However,

Iasenza (2010) argues that they are not necessarily congruent. A woman may engage in sex with men but fantasize primarily about sex with women and vice versa.

Other researchers have described sexual orientation as being more complex than Kinsey's research suggested; however, that is beyond the scope of this discussion. The interested reader may refer to Iasenza (2010).

As therapists, we must inquire about fantasies as well as behavior with all partners. We must also frame questions about partners or potential partners in sex-neutral terms. For example, you might ask: Can you describe your first sexual experience rather than who was your first boyfriend/girlfriend? The therapist may make reference to the Kinsey scale and ask a client whether she or he has had any same-sex fantasies or experiences. Making reference to the continuum of sexual orientation may make the client feel less ill at ease if he or she is having same-sex fantasies or relationships and experiences guilt or stigma about doing so.

Sexual Functioning

There are different models of human sexual response. These models influence how we conceptualize healthy sexual functioning and how we take a sexual history (Iasenza, 2010). A brief summary of the technical terms of sexuality and the varying models of sexual response are presented:

Sexual desire refers to the interest in being sexual and is subjective.

Sexual arousal, on the other hand, is a physiological experience that can be measured and is indicated by vaginal lubrication for females and erection for males in conjunction with a subjective experience of sexual excitement.

Orgasm is represented by rhythmic contractions as well as the subjective experience of pleasure at the peak of sexual excitement. Male orgasm and ejaculation are not the same, although they may occur simultaneously.

Masters and Johnson in the 1950s and 1960s conceptualized the human sexual response cycle (HSRC) consisting of four phases: excitement, plateau, orgasm, and resolution. At the time, the HSRC was a great contribution, as it provided a conceptual model and a sex therapy model. In the context of this model, human sexuality is understood as something that can be studied and that by doing so, people can learn to improve their sexual functioning. However, the HSRC has been criticized for being a linear model with a genital orgasm focus (Iasenza, 2010).

In the 1970s Helen Singer Kaplan added sexual desire to the first phase of the HSRC. Many patients, especially women, present with lack of sexual desire. Kaplan significantly contributed to the field of sex therapy by designing an integrated model of sex therapy. Kaplan, a psychoanalyst and a sex therapist, understood sexual dysfunctions as the outgrowth of psychological, biological, and relational factors (Bartlik, Rosenfeld, & Beaton, 2005).

Joanne Loulan (1984) conceptualized a nonlinear female sexual response cycle that began with willingness, followed by desire, excitement, engorgement, and orgasm-pleasure. The uniqueness of this model was that it included the person's subjective experience of sexual response, the experience of pleasure and not just the physical response of orgasm and ejaculation. Moreover, it emphasized that a person can decide to have sex. The process of decision making in sexuality is especially important in working with people who experience problems with sexual desire (Iasenza, 2010).

More recent researchers emphasize different models based on biological sex. Rosemary Basson maintains that the Masters-Johnson-Kaplan model of HSR is a male linear model that has described a circular model of female sexual response which includes the following: reasons for initiating sex, willingness to be responsive, subjective arousal, arousal and responsive desire, and sexual/emotional satisfaction. In contrast to earlier models, Basson maintains that arousal may come before desire. This is a revolutionary idea since earlier models of sexual response indicated that desire preceded arousal (Iasenza, 2010).

It is important for the therapist to recognize which model or models of human sexual response guides the history-taking process because this will shape the kinds of questions that you ask and your understanding of what is normative. All models suggest that sexual dysfunction can occur at any stage of a given model. For example, a person can refuse to engage in partner sex because he or she is unwilling to be sexual, not always because he or she is unable to do so (Willingness-Loulan's model). A person may not reach orgasm (Masters-Johnson/Kaplan). A woman who experiences sexual pleasure but does not reach orgasm might be seen as having a sexual dysfunction given the model of Masters and Johnson, but her experience could be seen as acceptable and possibly normative given the Loulan and Basson model.

The pattern of the sexual dysfunction is important to explore. Lifelong sexual problems are viewed as primary dysfunctions. Sexual dysfunctions that occur later in life are considered secondary or acquired dysfunctions. If a person experiences a sexual dysfunction in all situations, it is considered global dysfunction while dysfunction in specific situations is considered situational.

Whatever model of human sexual response one uses, the therapist should ask questions about each phase of the sexual response cycle to understand the functioning or dysfunction of each phase. The sexual status exam, introduced by Helen Singer Kaplan, is one means of gaining a more thorough description of an individual or couple's sexual experience and sexual function/dysfunction. The therapist asks the client to describe his or her last sexual experience as if they were both participating in and watching a video of the experience. The client is asked to reveal feelings, thoughts, behavior, and a very detailed account of what happened before, during, and after the sexual encounter (Bartlik et al., 2005).

Sexual histories should also include questions relevant to sexual health such as:

- Have you ever been diagnosed with a sexually transmitted disease?
- How are you practicing safe sex?
- Have you experienced any health issues that would affect your reproductive system?
- Has anyone ever forced you to have sex or be sexual in ways that you did not want to engage in? (Bartlik et al., 2005).

Relational Meaning of Sexual Behavior

People have partner sex for many reasons. The exploration of a client's motivation for having partner sex will reveal more information about the client and his or her relationship with his or her partner. A significant number of people may have sex to demonstrate or enhance love/affection/closeness to another. However, there are some people who may decide to have partner sex to avoid closeness or to express hostility. For example, a man who has been opposed to his wife's attendance at law school may demand sex the night before her final law school exams (Risen, 2003).

Challenges to Taking Sexual Histories

A challenge to taking a sexual history includes the therapist and client's lack of knowledge about the meanings of sexuality in a client's life and the therapist's lack of knowledge about healthy sexual functioning and dysfunction. However, sexuality is an important aspect of being human that influences our identity as well as how we relate to others. Furthermore, sexual problems may be a cause or consequence of emotional or psychological distress (Wiederman & Sansone, 1999, p. 312).

Sexuality, like race and ethnicity, is a topic that people can have intense feelings about and thus can stimulate intense emotion. This is true for both client and therapist. Therapists can respond to their discomfort by avoiding initiating exploration into these areas. In addition, a significant number of psychology doctoral programs and internships fail to provide adequate training in human sexuality (Wiederman & Sansone, 1999). Such training would involve course work in human sexuality and sexual dysfunction as well as practice in taking a sexual history.

Research has demonstrated that the therapist's personal attitudes and values about sexuality, as well as his or her relative comfort with sexual content, affects his or her ability to take a sexual history (Maurice, 1999; Wiederman & Sansone, 1999). Practicing sexual history taking or talking about one's sexual history with a colleague or friend (of both sexes and diverse sexual orientations) can increase the therapist's level of comfort with sexual history taking. Despite this, both the therapist and the client may experience some level of arousal during such conversations over time. Rehearsal may help the therapist become more comfortable with experiencing these feelings. If a client reports feelings of sexual arousal during the interview, depending on the client and his or her history, it can be helpful for the therapist to emphasize that they are engaged in talking about sexual activity and normalize the client's feelings in response to such disclosures and discussions. However, the therapist could acknowledge that while such discussions might stimulate sexual feelings, it would be unethical and inappropriate to act on these feelings. The therapist may also feel reluctant to explore sexual content, fearing that it might remind the therapist of his or her own unresolved sexual issues (Risen, 1995). For example, a therapist who has decided to abstain from sex may avoid talking about a client's sex history because to do so would stimulate uncomfortable feelings for the therapist.

References and Readings

Bartlik, B. D., Rosenfeld, S., & Beaton, C. (2005). Assessment of sexual functioning: Sexual history taking for health care practitioners. *Epilepsy and Behavior, 7*, SI5–S21.

Carroll, R. (2007). Gender dysphoria and transgender experiences. In S. R. Leiblum (Ed.), *Principles and practice of sex therapy* (pp. 477–508). New York: Guilford Press.

Iasenza, S. (2010). What is queer about sex? Expanding sexual frames in theory and practice. *Family Process, 49*(3), 291–308.

Loulan, J. (1984). *Lesbian Sex*. Midway, FL: Spinsters Ink Books.

Maurice, W. L. (1999). Sexual medicine in primary care. St. Louis, MO: Mosby.

Pfafflin, F. (2003) Understanding transgendered phenomena. In S. B. Levine (Ed.), *Handbook of clinical sexuality for mental health professionals* (pp. 291–310). New York: Routledge.

Risen, C. (1995) A guide to taking a sexual history. *Psychiatric Clinics of North America, 18*(1), 39–53.

Risen, C. (2003). Listening to sexual stories. In S. B. Levine (Ed.), *Handbook of clinical sexuality for mental health professionals* (pp. 3–19). New York: Routledge.

Wiederman, M. W., & Sansone, R. A. (1999). Sexuality training for professional psychologists: A national survey of training directors of doctoral programs and predoctoral internships. *Professional Psychology Research and Practice, 30*(3), 312–317.

Related Topics

Chapter 43, "Diagnosis, Assessment, and Treatment of Female Sexual Dysfunctions"

Chapter 44, "Diagnosis, Assessment, and Treatment of Male Sexual Dysfunctions"

Chapter 49, "Managing Sexual Feelings for Patients in Psychotherapy"

Chapter 70, "Understanding Sexuality in the Context of Disability"

15 SCREENING FOR SEXUAL OFFENDER RISK

David Medoff and Sarah J. Sternlieb

The comprehensive evaluation of sexual offender risk involves a multisource, multimethod detailed clinical assessment that synthesizes data regarding risk, protective factors, clinical findings, functional capacities, and aspects of both external containment variables and intervention needs. This chapter focuses more specifically on the process and content of *screening* for sexual offender risk and does not address all elements of a comprehensive evaluation.

THE CONTEXT OF SCREENING

Screening for sexual offender risk requires specialized training, education, and experience beyond that typically derived from clinical training. This is because assessment of this kind is by definition a forensic endeavor, as the nature of the phenomenon in question crosses into both clinical and legal domains. Although some screenings may occur in the absence of immediate legal involvement, such as those occurring in schools or other settings wherein legal charges are not considered, the *potential* for criminal charges exists in every case. Therefore, ethical and legal precautions must be taken when engaging in this type of screening.

Additional need for precaution stems from the interface of the complex legal implications of such cases and access to specific data required for competent risk assessment. That is, the legal rights and protections afforded to individuals are often at odds with the acquisition of risk assessment interview data, and care must be taken to avoid the inadvertent disclosure of self-incriminating information. Thus, professionals conducting sexual offender screenings are ethically required to be knowledgeable of the larger legal context in which they are engaged. Determining the legal context of the referral is the first essential step in performing such a screening, as this will dictate how the clinician should proceed by determining both the identity of the client per se (e.g., evaluation subject, attorney, school) and specific details regarding ownership and control of any potential findings.

Other essential knowledge involves the distinction between confidentiality and privilege, and the local laws governing them. The second step in conducting a sexual offender screening therefore involves the provision of a full informed consent, including disclosure of the nature and purpose of the screening as well as warnings regarding confidentiality and privilege. After providing a complete informed consent, the process of screening for sexual offender risk can begin.

THE PROCESS OF SCREENING

Combining Evidence-Based and Clinical Factors

Screening for sexual offender risk involves collecting information from various sources, analyzing acquired data, and formulating a risk estimate based on the balance of weight allotted to known risk factors and clinical considerations. Reliance on empirically supported factors of risk enhances the accuracy of risk estimates, although clinically derived factors have also been shown to be useful in this regard. Nevertheless, use of evidence-based factors anchors the clinical screening process to the most relevant data, and current best practice for screening sexual offender risk involves combining empirically derived variables with clinical assessment to form estimates of risk based on structured professional judgment (e.g., Craig, Beech, & Harkins, 2009; Witt, Dattilio, & Bradford, 2011). This is accomplished through combining the use of actuarial risk assessment tools or other empirically guided interview measures with broader based information derived from clinical interviewing and third-party sources. Such an amalgamation of data from these varied sources capitalizes on both the empirical foundation of established research and the practical and dynamic strengths of clinical assessment.

Evidence-Based Factors of Risk

A core of empirically established risk factors has been identified in the professional literature, most of which are included in a variety of published actuarial and physiologic assessment measures used for the estimate of sexual offender risk in adults (Hanson & Morton-Bourgon, 2005; Thornton & Laws, 2009). Although no fully validated actuarial tool exists for use with adolescents, one such instrument is in the process of being validated and several structured empirically guided interview measures serve the purpose of providing focused clinical inquiry composed of evidence-based variables.

Competent screening for sexual offender risk involves analysis of both static and dynamic factors that can be obtained from multiple assessment methods, including record review (e.g., police reports, victim witness statements), use of actuarial instruments or structured clinical interview tools, clinical interview, and contact with collateral sources of information (e.g., treatment providers, primary care clinicians, parents). Static factors are stable in nature and remain unchanged over time, such as victim characteristics, including age and gender of a victim, and the existence of one or more prior victims. Dynamic factors, on the other hand, change over time and include variables such as substance abuse status, degree of sexual preoccupation, and quality of social supports.

Several static variables are among the most well-established empirically supported risk factors, including the following:

- One or more prior victim
- Any sexual assault of a child under the age of 12 years and/or 4 years younger than the offender
- Any male victim
- Any unrelated or stranger victim
- Commission of an offense in a public place
- History of combined contact and noncontact sexual offenses
- Young offender age between 18 and 25 years (adults only)
- Antisocial personality features

Several dynamic risk factors are also empirically supported and include the following:

- Deviant sexual interest and/or arousal
- Sexual deviancy, including cognitive distortions (e.g., concepts about children, distorted attitudes regarding coercive sex and/or child sexual abuse)
- Sexual preoccupation
- Social isolation, lack of intimate peer relationships
- Problems in self-regulation

Clinically Derived Factors of Risk

In addition to the empirically supported factors described earlier, other factors routinely included in screening for sexual offender risk are clinically based and, although not currently benefitting from the authority of scientific support, can add value to risk assessment estimates. Many of these factors are contained in the structured empirically guided interview tools available for assessing recidivism risk among juvenile sexual offenders and have been described previously in a more comprehensive context (Medoff & Kinscherff, 2006). These variables can be organized into three categories that span a wide breadth of behavioral and historical factors, characteristics of the offender, and elements of the offense itself.

Behavioral and historical factors cover a diverse range of variables, including a history of nonsexual delinquent behavior, residential instability, marginal employment, discontinuation or termination of sex-offender-specific treatment, any sexual offense following completion of sex-offender-specific treatment, commission of a sexual offense while under court-sponsored or other supervision, and other criminal or antisocial conduct such as rule violations and school suspensions or expulsions.

Several clinically based offender characteristics are also of interest in screening for sexual offender risk and include deficits in impulse and/or anger control, emerging or established paraphilias (e.g., deviant sexual fantasy, possession of paraphilic pornography), severe substance abuse, and lack of motivation for change.

Relevant clinically derived offense characteristics include the selection of particularly vulnerable victims (e.g., very young, developmentally delayed, psychiatrically impaired), disproportionate use of force to achieve victim compliance (weapon use, threat of violence, drugging the victim), indications of planning and/or predatory behavior, lack of deterrence under conditions that might ordinarily inhibit misconduct, and evidence of gratuitous violence (e.g., violence beyond that necessary to effectuate the offense).

Structured Instruments

Several physiologic measures of sexual arousal and/or interest exist but remain somewhat controversial. These include the penile plethysmograph, several attention and reaction time measures based on sexual content-induced delay (SCID), choice reaction time (CRT) instruments, and viewing time (VT) procedures (Thornton & Laws, 2009). These tools are typically employed in more specialized assessments and are not generally necessary for screening of sexual offender risk.

Measures for Use with Adults

Actuarial risk assessment involves the statistical prediction of risk based on empirically supported factors derived from scientific research. These measures typically contain several items that are coded by well-defined scoring rules based on information obtained from a thorough record review. Actuarial tools produce a classification of risk typically ranging from "low" to "high" and utilize predictor variables that have been validated against a predefined outcome (i.e., the commission of a sexual offense). These tools function with fixed decision rules to reduce measurement error generated by unstructured clinical judgment and are objective instruments based on samples of individuals typically either charged or convicted of a sexual offense. Actuarial measures therefore estimate the risk of *recidivism*, the likelihood of committing a second sexual offense following an initial sexual offense, and are generally limited for use with subjects who have an existing sexual offense conviction or charge (Langton et al., 2007). While several of these tools have demonstrated stronger predictive validity than methods involving pure clinical judgment (Hanson & Morton-Bourgon, 2009), they have also been criticized for their overreliance on static variables, their estimate of risk based on nomothetic versus idiographic data, and their limited use of potentially critical dynamic risk factors (e.g., Craig, Browne, Stringer, & Hogue, 2008; Witt, Dattilio, & Bradford, 2011).

The Static-99 is among the most widely used actuarial measure in sex offender risk assessment. The Static-99 demonstrates moderate predictive validity for both sexual and violent recidivism of adult male offenders. This tool shows an overall higher degree of accuracy when compared to similar measures and evidences significant predictive accuracy for sexual and/or violent recidivism in child molesters. The Static-99 has also shown moderate levels of accuracy for sexual recidivism among intrafamilial (incest) offenders.

The Sex Offender Risk Appraisal Guide (SORAG) assesses both violence and sexual risk of recidivism among adult sex offenders and has moderate psychometric properties. This actuarial instrument shows moderate to high predictive validity for sexual recidivism among intrafamilial offenders and adequately predicts sexual and/or violent reoffending in extrafamilial child molesters. The SORAG lacks consistent predictive validity of risk for rapists and noncontact sexual offenders.

The Rapid Risk Assessment of Sexual Offense Recidivism (RRASOR) assesses risk of sexual reoffense among adult males and has demonstrated efficacy in accurately predicting sexual and violent offense recidivism, particularly among child molesters. It shows moderate accuracy with samples of intrafamilial offenders but less utility in the assessment of rapists or noncontact sexual offenders.

The Minnesota Sex Offender Screening Tool, third edition (MnSOST-3) is the newest version of its predecessor. The MnSOST-3 differs from other adult actuarial tools in that it provides for the adjustment of risk estimates based on the offender's supervision status in the community. It has been developed with a contemporary sample and shows moderate psychometric properties, although it has not been extensively validated to date.

The Sexual Violence Ris-20 (SVR-20) is a nonactuarial 20-item checklist of empirically supported risk factors for sexual violence. It is designed to structure and focus the risk assessment process and involves the coding of items based on their presence or absence as well as any recent changes in their status. The SVR-20 targets information across three domains, including psychosocial adjustment, sexual offenses, and future plans. It does not generate a specific score but rather informs structured professional judgment in generating estimates of risk.

Instruments for Use with Juveniles

The Estimate of Risk of Adolescent Sexual Offense Recidivism, second edition (ERASOR-2) is a structured risk assessment tool designed for use with adolescents. The ERASOR-2 utilizes both static and dynamic variables based on 25 empirically derived risk factors that tap into five categories, including sexual interests, historical sexual assaults, psychosocial functioning, family/environmental functioning, and treatment. While research has clearly established these 25 factors as related to sexual offense recidivism in juveniles, the ERASOR-2 has not to date developed a scientifically based manner in which to calculate a specific algorithm for combining these factors. Therefore, this instrument is typically used as one source among others in generating structured professional judgment regarding the estimate of risk.

The Juvenile Sex Offender Assessment Protocol, second edition (J-SOAP-II) is a structured interview instrument that assesses risk for sexual offending in adolescents. The JSOAP-II is not an actuarial instrument but remains widely used in structuring clinical inquiry across four domains, including sexual drive/preoccupation, impulsive/antisocial behavior, intervention items, and community stability/adjustment. Similar to the ERASOR-2, the J-SOAP-II is typically used to empirically anchor estimates of risk based on structured professional judgment.

The Juvenile Sexual Offense Recidivism Risk Assessment Tool, second edition (JSORRAT-II) is the only fully actuarial measure available for use with juveniles. The JSORRAT-II contains 12 items that address a range of variables, including victim and offense characteristics as well as treatment, supervision, and school-based factors. It is designed to be completed based on a thorough case record review and has shown strong predictive accuracy with limited samples. The JSORATT-II has not been extensively validated, however, and the authors caution its use in making forensic decisions for populations differing from its specific development samples.

Screening for sexual offender risk requires specialized training and begins with a complete understanding of the referral context, particularly with regard to potential legal implications. Initiation of the screening process involves the provision of a full informed consent and includes specific agreement as to the ownership and control over highly sensitive information that could be self-incriminating.

Current best practice requires a mixed multisource, multimethod screening process utilizing empirically based instruments and/or risk factors with clinically derived variables. In this way, information from record review, clinical interview, and third-party sources is combined to exploit the evidence-based foundation of established research in addition to the practical and dynamic strengths of clinical assessment. Together, this facilitates the development of structured professional judgment in formulating sound estimates of risk.

References and Readings

Craig, L. A., Beech, A. R., & Harkins, L. (2009). The predictive accuracy of risk factors and frameworks. In A. R. Beech, L. A. Craig, & K. D. Browne (Eds.), *Assessment and treatment of sexual offenders: A handbook* (pp. 51–74). West Sussex, England: Wiley-Blackwell.

Craig, L. A., Browne, K. D., Stringer, I., & Hogue, T. E. (2008). Sexual reconviction rates in the United Kingdom and actuarial risk estimates. *Child Abuse and Neglect, 32*, 121–138.

Hanson, R. K., & Morton-Bourgon, K. E. (2005). The characteristics of persistent sexual offenders: A meta-analysis of recidivism studies. *Journal of Consulting and Clinical Psychology, 73*(6), 1154–1163.

Hanson, R. K., & Morton-Bourgon, K. E. (2009). The accuracy of recidivism risk assessments for sexual offenders: A meta-analysis of 118 prediction studies. *Psychological Assessment, 21*, 1–21.

Langton, C. M., Barbaree, H. E., Seto, M. C., Peacock, E. J., Harkins, L., & Hansen, K. T. (2007). Actuarial assessment of risk for reoffense among adult sex offenders: Evaluating the predictive accuracy of the Static-2002 and five other instruments. *Criminal Justice and Behavior, 34*, 37–59.

Medoff, D., & Kinscherff, R. (2006). Forensic evaluation of juvenile sexual offenders. In S. N. Sparta & G. P. Koocher (Eds.), *Forensic mental health assessment of children and adolescents* (pp. 342–364). New York: Oxford University Press.

Thornton, D., & Laws, D. R. (2009). *Cognitive approaches to the assessment of sexual interest in sexual offenders*. West Sussex, England: Wiley-Blackwell.

Witt, P. H., Dattilio, F. M., & Bradford, J. M. W. (2011). Sex offender evaluations. In E. Y. Drogin, F. M. Dattilio, R. L. Sadoff, & T. G. Gutheil (Eds.), *Handbook of forensic assessment: Psychological and psychiatric perspectives* (pp. 97–117). Hoboken, NJ: Wiley.

Related Topics

Chapter 3, "Improving Diagnostic and Clinical Interviewing"

Chapter 4, "Increasing the Accuracy of Clinical Judgment"

16 ASSESSING PERSONALITY DISORDERS

Whitney L. Gore and Thomas A. Widiger

To assess personality disorders validly, an integrated approach must be utilized. The general strategy recommended herein is a two-step process: (1) administer a self-report inventory to gain information about the potential presence of particular maladaptive personality traits, and (2) administer a semistructured interview to verify and document the presence of these traits (Widiger, 2002). This integrated process is suggested because of the unique strengths and weaknesses present in both self-report inventories and semistructured interviews.

Although clinical practitioners tend to prefer the use of an unstructured interview to diagnose personality disorders, research suggests that there are a number of advantages to semistructured interviews (Widiger & Boyd, 2009). For example, the use of unstructured clinical interviews does not ensure that all of the necessary or important criteria are considered (Garb, 2005). Without this structure, research suggests that personality disorders tend to be diagnosed hierarchically, with clinicians understandably neglecting to assess for additional symptoms once they conclude that a particular personality disorder is present. Personality disorder diagnoses based on unstructured clinical interviews also tend to be not as reliable as those based on semistructured interviews (Widiger & Boyd, 2009). Finally, unstructured diagnostic interviews are relatively more prone to gender and cultural biases (Garb, 2005). In contrast, semistructured interviews provide documentation that a more comprehensive and objective assessment has taken place, as the clinician is compelled to assess systematically each diagnostic criterion with a standard set of inquiries. This documentation is especially useful in specific clinical situations where the validity of the assessment may be questioned (e.g., forensic assessments). In addition, the manuals for semistructured interviews often provide information to aid the clinician in understanding the rationale for diagnoses, interpreting inconsistent symptomatology, and for distinguishing between diagnoses.

Although the use of a semistructured interview is preferred, clinicians are understandably reluctant to administer an entire semistructured interview due to time considerations. A systematic semistructured assessment for all of the personality disorders within the American Psychiatric Association's diagnostic manual will typically require 2 hours, which is quite unrealistic for general clinical practice. Therefore, it is recommended that the clinician first administer a self-report inventory in order to identify which personality disorders are potentially present and which may be ignored with minimal risk. The initial administration of a self-report inventory is also useful in minimizing potential assumptions or biases. For example, it is not uncommon for clinicians (and researchers) to be biased in favor of histrionic personality traits, and against antisocial, in female patients (Widiger & Boyd, 2009). No such bias assumption will be present within a self-report inventory (albeit some self-report inventories have been shown to have their own specific assessment biases, an issue discussed further later). Following the administration of the self-report inventory, the clinician can administer only a small part of a semistructured interview, focusing only on the personality disorders identified as present by the self-report inventory, thereby saving considerable time.

It is possible that abbreviated personality disorder screening measures could be initially administered, but a complete self-report inventory designed to yield a comprehensive assessment is preferable. The savings in time that an abbreviated measure would provide does not appear to offset the benefits of administering a well-validated self-report measure that offers a more complete and thorough assessment. In addition, self-report inventories often include validity scales which can detect patient biases, response sets, and distortions (e.g., Millon Clinical Multiaxial Inventory-III [MCMI-III], Minnesota Multiphasic Personality Inventory-2 [MMPI-2]). These validity scales can be valuable assets because existing semistructured interviews for personality disorders do not assess for malingering and deception.

There are a few potential limitations to the use of self-report measures as a screening tool. One potential issue is the possibility of false-negative assessments (i.e., wrongly concluding that the disorder is absent). However, while such errors may occur, research suggests that far more false-positives than false-negatives are found through the use of self-report measures. Furthermore, a key feature of many of the personality disorders involves significant distortions of the self (Millon, 2011). Therefore, obtaining self-reported assessment information from persons suffering from a distorted sense of self may at times not yield the most accurate report (Oltmanns & Turkheimer, 2009; Widiger & Samuel, 2005).

FEATURES OF PERSONALITY DISORDER ASSESSMENT INSTRUMENTS

A variety of both self-report measures and semistructured interviews have been developed to assess personality disorders. Some of the strengths and weaknesses of the available measures are summarized here. For a more extensive review of such measures, see Millon (2011, Widiger and Boyd (2009), or Widiger (2002).

Reliability

Overall, semistructured interviews have been shown to obtain good interrater reliability. Most personality disorder instruments obtain good test-retest reliability, with one exception being the MCMI-III which obtains only adequate test-retest reliability (Widiger & Boyd, 2009).

Convergence

There are currently five alternative semistructured interviews for the assessment of personality disorders, but only limited research on their convergence (i.e., Diagnostic Interview for Personality Disorders [DIPD], International Personality Disorder Examination [IPDE], Personality Disorder Interview-IV [PDI-IV],

Structured Clinical Interview for *DSM-IV* Axis II Personality Disorders [SCID-II], and Structured Interview for *DSM-IV* Personality Disorders; see Widiger & Boyd, 2009). One study found that the IPDE and the SCID-II yield disparate results, although the median agreement rates between the two interviews did not differ significantly from results found with semistructured interviews for Axis I disorders.

Much more research has been conducted evaluating the convergence between semistructured interviews and self-report measures as well as the convergence among self-report measures. Research indicates that assessments with increased structure obtain higher convergent validity. Therefore, self-report inventories show a great deal of convergence.

FURTHER CONSIDERATIONS

Differentiating between Axis I and Axis II

Diagnostic assessments are necessary at the outset of treatment; however, it can be most difficult precisely at this time to adequately distinguish between Axis I pathology (e.g., mood and anxiety disorders) and personality pathology. When persons are seeking treatment they are typically in crisis or are experiencing severe levels of distress, anxiety, or depression. These acute symptoms will interfere with the way they would normally describe their typical way of thinking, feeling, behaving, and relating to others, which can interfere substantially with an accurate personality disorder assessment. Self-report measures are especially prone to this problem, tending to sharply overdiagnose personality disorders at the beginning of treatment. One way to determine whether a personality disorder was present prior to the current Axis I disorder is to document its presence back to late adolescence or young adulthood via a semistructured interview.

Personality disorder assessment measures vary tremendously in the extent to which they focus on age of onset of personality pathology. For example, many self-report measures (e.g., Schedule for Nonadaptive and Adaptive Personality [SNAP]) simply inquire about current symptoms or problems, whereas semistructured interviews more frequently assess for age of onset, although the requirements of some are more liberal than others. For example, the IPDE requires that only one diagnostic criterion be present since the age of 25, the SCID-II requires the presence of each criterion over a period of 5 years, and the DIPD focuses on the 2 years prior to the assessment (contributing to considerable overdiagnosis within clinical settings). The PDI-IV does not require the documentation of the presence of diagnostic criteria in young adulthood, although it does encourage the consideration of age of onset.

Inaccuracy in Self-Report Responses

At times, self-report measures and semistructured interviews have been criticized for the direct way in which criteria are assessed. While it is evident that some items seem to rely on the honesty and insight of the respondent, some questions included in semistructured interviews are more open-ended. They also consider the information derived from observations of the patient. Interviewers will also clarify or follow up on responses. However, it is possible that some respondents (e.g., forensic clients or prisoners) may be so uncooperative that it is necessary to seek out other sources of information. For example, the Psychopathy Checklist-Revised (PCL-R) relies heavily on the use of inmates' criminal records for information (Widiger & Boyd, 2009). However, these records are not available in most general clinical settings. In place of such supplementary information, informant reports can be very helpful (e.g., interviews with close friends and/or relatives). While some research suggests that self-reports are more valid and some suggests that informant reports are more valid, in general research has found that both sources of information add uniquely valid information (Oltmanns & Turkheimer, 2009).

Gender

Most of the personality disorders have differential sex prevalence rates, some of which have been questionable (Widiger & Boyd, 2009).

Historically, the potential gender bias present in personality disorder diagnosis has been a very controversial topic. Researchers have looked for the source of gender bias in the wording of diagnostic criteria (e.g., Do the criteria tend to favor one gender over another?), diagnostic thresholds (e.g., Is the level of impairment necessary for respective personality disorders lower for those disorders that occur more often in women?), clinical presentation, research sampling (e.g., Is the research on antisocial largely confined to men?), respondent presentation (e.g., Are men less willing to acknowledge dependent personality traits?), and items within self-report inventories. Some studies have also indicated that the failure of clinicians to systematically assess the diagnostic criteria has contributed to increased diagnoses of histrionic personality disorder in women.

It is important to be aware that some self-report inventories have provided gender-biased assessments. This can occur when measures contain gender-related items that are keyed in an adaptive rather than maladaptive direction. For example, items assessing for confidence can identify narcissistic persons and items assessing for gregariousness can identify histrionic persons within clinical settings in which these personality disorders are present. However, these kinds of items will overdiagnose respective personality disorders in settings with minimal personality disorder pathology (e.g., university counseling centers and custody dispute assessments). Furthermore, many of these items are closely associated with gender, thereby providing an overdiagnosis in one sex more than the other (e.g., an overdiagnosis of narcissism in men and histrionic in women). These concerns are particularly evident in the case of the histrionic, dependent, narcissistic, and obsessive-compulsive personality disorder scales of the MCMI-III and the MMPI-2 (Widiger & Boyd, 2009).

Culture and Ethnicity

There has been surprisingly little research on how culture and ethnicity may affect the diagnosis or assessment of personality disorders, even though one might expect variance across cultural and ethnic groups. For example, the World Health Organization's international classification of personality disorders does not even recognize narcissistic personality disorder. It is also evident that members of the dominant ethnic and cultural group write the items included in self-report inventories, whose meaning may not be preserved when applied to minority groups (e.g., items that assess feelings of being followed or inappropriately harassed). Before self-report inventories or interpretations of assessments are altered to apply to more varied ethnic and cultural groups, there needs to be more research on the mechanisms of cultural or ethnic group differences. This body of literature is relatively nascent and has focused predominantly on finding group differences rather than explaining them. For example, studies have found that African Americans score significantly higher on paranoid personality disorder scales. One possible sociocultural explanation for suspiciousness, cynicism, and distrust within an African American population, however, could be a history of cultural racial discrimination (Widiger & Boyd, 2009).

Despite the relative dearth of research on how culture and ethnicity affect personality disorder assessment, a potential advantage of both self-report measures and semistructured interviews is that the questions asked do not vary based on the race of the respondent. This may not be the case when unstructured assessments are administered (Garb, 2005).

References and Readings

Garb, H. N. (2005). Clinical judgment and decision making. *Annual Review of Clinical Psychology, 1*, 65–89.

Millon, T. (2011). *Disorders of personality. Introducing a DSM/ICD spectrum from normal to abnormal* (3rd ed.). New York: Wiley.

Oltmanns, T. F., & Turkheimer, E. (2009). Person perception and personality pathology. *Current Directions in Psychological Science, 18*, 32–36.

Widiger, T. A. (2002). Personality disorders. In M. M. Antony & D. H. Barlow (Eds.), *Handbook of assessment, treatment planning, and outcome for psychological disorders* (pp. 453–480). New York: Guilford Press.

Widiger, T. A., & Boyd, S. E. (2009). Personality disorder assessment instruments. In J. N. Butcher (Ed.), *Oxford handbook of personality assessment* (pp. 336–363). New York: Oxford University Press.

Widiger, T. A., & Samuel, D. B. (2005). Evidence based assessment of personality disorders. *Psychological Assessment, 17*, 278–287.

Related Topics

Chapter 1, "Lifetime Prevalence of Mental Disorders in the General Population"

Chapter 3, "Improving Diagnostic and Clinical Interviewing"

PART II
Psychological Testing

17 ADULT NEUROPSYCHOLOGICAL ASSESSMENT

Aaron P. Nelson and Margaret O'Connor

GENERAL CONSIDERATIONS

Fundamental Assumptions of Clinical Neuropsychological Assessment

1. It is possible to make valid inferences regarding the integrity of the brain through the observation of behavior. Such inferences require a firm grasp of brain–behavior relationships and characteristic neurobehavioral syndromes.
2. Observable behavior is frequently the most sensitive manifestation of brain pathology.
3. A neuropsychological test is simply one means of eliciting a sample of behavior, under standardized conditions, which is then to be observed and analyzed.
4. Test performance and "real-life" behavior are imperfectly correlated. Proceed with caution in using test data to predict behavior.
5. Most behaviors are multifactorial and depend on a complex interplay of cognitive, perceptual, emotional, and environmental factors.
6. Most neuropsychological tests are multifactorial and depend on a confluence of cognitive and perceptual functions for their performance.
7. As with any psychological intervention, the neuropsychological evaluation should proceed in a sensitive manner and with explicit communications regarding the use of clinical information.
8. A dynamic developmental life span perspective is critical in the evaluation of each patient.
9. All behavior should be viewed within a sociocultural context.

Uses of Neuropsychological Assessment

1. Neuropsychological assessment is indicated for questions of differential diagnosis and prognosis.
2. Neuropsychological assessment should be considered in the setting of a deterioration in neuropsychological status or when there is a history of neurological disease, injury, or developmental abnormality affecting cerebral functions.
3. Neuropsychological assessment is used to clarify the significance of known or suspected pathology for "real-life" functioning in everyday activity, relationships, education, and work.
4. Neuropsychological assessment provides information relevant to management, rehabilitation, and treatment planning for identified cognitive problems.
5. Baseline (pretreatment) status and measurement of treatment response (e.g., medication, neurosurgery, behavioral intervention, electroconvulsive therapy) can be monitored with serial neuropsychological testing.

6. Neuropsychological consultation is frequently critical in determination of legal/forensic issues, including need for guardianship, neuropsychological damages, criminal responsibility, and competence to stand trial.
7. Neuropsychological research investigations enhance the understanding of brain–behavior relationships and neurobehavioral syndromes. These studies are of tremendous value to the understanding of neurological disease and normal brain function.
8. Specialized applications include determination of viability for functional neurosurgery (Parkinson's disease), presurgical functional lateralization in patients who are to undergo epilepsy surgery (i.e., Wada testing), and intraoperative cortical mapping.
9. Neuropsychological testing has become central to evaluation of sports concussion and return-to-play decisions.

Approach to Neuropsychological Evaluation

1. Evaluation should be individually tailored to each patient.
2. Test data are viewed from both qualitative and quantitative perspectives.
3. Assessment proceeds in a hypothesis-testing manner. Tests are selected to answer specific questions, some of which emerge during the evaluation process.
4. Standardized tests can be modified to test limits and produce richer qualitative data.
5. Task performance is analyzed to determine component processes, with the goal of identification of dissociations between such processes.
6. The most pertinent normative data are used to analyze test scores with regard to salient demographic variables, including age, gender, ethnicity, and educational level.
7. Because typical neuropsychological assessments include a large number of individual tests, a small percentage of abnormal (i.e., impaired) scores may be obtained on the basis of chance alone; these may be spurious findings.

CLINICAL METHOD

Referral Question

The chief complaint and presenting problems are reviewed to produce a clear description of their onset and course, as well as information regarding the medical and social context in which the problem(s) emerged. The patient's overall understanding of his or her current circumstances and the reason for the consultation are sought.

History

Information is obtained from a variety of sources, including the patient's self-report, observations of family members or close friends, medical records, and prior evaluations from academic or work situations. Information is obtained regarding the following:

1. Developmental background, including circumstances of gestation, birth/delivery acquisition of developmental milestones, and early socialization skills
2. Social development, including major autobiographical events and relationships (a three-generational genogram is highly useful in gaining relevant family information)
3. Past medical history, including illnesses, injuries, surgeries, medications, hospitalizations, substance abuse, and relevant familial medical history
4. Psychiatric history, including hospitalizations, medications, and outpatient treatment
5. Educational background, including early school experiences and academic performance during high school, college, postgraduate study, and other educational and technical training
6. Vocational history, including work performance, work satisfaction, and relationships with supervisors and coworkers
7. Current functional level with regard to basic and instrumental activities of daily living, recreational interests, and hobbies
8. Review of systems, including quality of sleep, appetite, libido, physical activity, and pain

9. Assessment of effort has become a key component for all cases. Reduced effort can be observed in severe depression, pain, apathy, frank malingering, and failure to attain an appropriate "test-taking attitude." Individuals from divergent cultural backgrounds may have a different "set" or attitude toward the overall assessment enterprise. Effort can be assessed through the use of dedicated freestanding tests, embedded measures, and consideration of performance in the context of known functional status.

Behavioral Observation

Physical appearance is inspected, including symmetry of gross anatomic features, facial expression, manner of dress, and attention to personal hygiene. The patient is asked specific questions regarding unusual sensory or motor symptoms. Affect and mood are assessed with respect to range and modulation of felt/expressed emotions and their congruence with concurrent ideation and the contemporaneous situation. Interpersonal comportment is assessed in the context of the interview. Does the patient's behavior reflect a normal awareness of self and other in interaction? The patient's motivation and compliance with examination requests, instructions, and test procedures are observed with respect to the validity of test findings.

Domains of Neuropsychological Function

A sufficiently broad range of neuropsychological functions is evaluated using tests and other assessment techniques.

1. *General intellectual ability.* Intelligence encompasses a broad array of capacities, many of which are not directly assessed in the traditional clinical setting. The estimate of general intellectual ability is based on both formal assessment methods and a survey of demographic factors and life accomplishments. Particular care must be exercised in the evaluation of patients from varying educational and sociocultural backgrounds. In cases of known or suspected impairment, premorbid ability is surmised from performance on measures presumed less sensitive to cerebral dysfunction (i.e., vocabulary), so-called best performance methods, educational/professional accomplishment, avocational interests and pursuits, and demographic variables. The level of general ability provides a reference point from which to view performance on other measures.
2. *Sensation and perception.* It is important to establish to what degree primary sensation and perception are intact prior to initiation of testing. Significant impairment of sensory function (auditory, visual, kinesthetic) is usually obvious and points to a need for specialized assessment procedures. Unusual or abnormal gustatory and olfactory experiences should be sought through direct questioning. Simple auditory function can be assessed by finger-rub stimuli to each ear. Vision is examined with tests of acuity, tracking, scanning, depth perception, color perception, and attention/neglect for visual field quadrants. Kinesthetic perception is assessed with tests of graphesthesia and stereognosis. Double simultaneous stimulation can be used in auditory, visual, and kinesthetic modalities to determine whether hemiextinction occurs.
3. *Motor functions.* Naturalistic observations of the patient's gait and upper- and lower-extremity coordination are an important part of the motor examination. Hand preference should be assessed through either direct inquiry or a formal handedness questionnaire. Motor speed, dexterity, and programming are tested with timed tasks, some of which involve repetition of a specific motor act (e.g., finger tapping, peg placement) and others of which involve more complex movements (e.g., finger sequencing, sequential hand positions). Manual grasp strength can be assessed with a hand dynamometer. Various forms of verbally guided movement or praxis are examined.
4. *Attention/concentration.* The capacity to selectively maintain and shift attentional

focus forms the basis of all cognitive activity. Evaluation of attention includes observations of a broad array of interrelated behaviors. General level of arousal or alertness is determined through clinical observation. An appraisal is made of the extent to which environmental or diurnal factors modify arousal. Attentional functions are assessed in both auditory/acoustic and visual modalities. Attention span is measured by determining the number of unrelated "bits" of information that can be held on line at a given moment in time. Sustained attention is assessed with tests that require the patient to maintain focused attention over longer periods. Selective attention is measured with tasks requiring the patient to shift focus from one event to another. Resistance to interference is assessed with tasks requiring the patient to inhibit overlearned responses or other distractions that could undermine a desired response.

5. *Executive functions.* Executive functions comprise the capacity of the patient to produce cognitive behavior in a planned, organized, and situationally responsive manner. The assessment of executive functions is accomplished in an ongoing fashion through observation of the patient's approach to all types of tests and via his or her comportment within the consultation. Although few tests assess these functions directly or specifically, the clinician looks for evidence of flexibility versus perseveration, initiation versus abulia, self-awareness versus obliviousness, planfulness versus impulsivity, and capacity to assume an abstract attitude versus concreteness.
6. *Learning and memory.* The assessment of memory function is perhaps the most complex endeavor of the neuropsychological examination. Memory is assessed with respect to time of initial exposure (anterograde vs. retrograde), modality of presentation (acoustic vs. visual), material (linguistic vs. figural), and locus of reference (personal vs. nonpersonal). The evaluation of memory should include measures that allow the neuropsychologist to parse out the component processes (encoding, consolidation, retrieval) entailed in the acquisition and later recall of information. To this end, measures are used to assess performance with respect to length of interval between exposure and demand for recall (none vs. short vs. long delay) and extent of facilitation required to demonstrate retention (free recall vs. recognition). The assessment of retrograde memory function poses a special problem insofar as it is difficult to know with certainty what information was contained at one time in the remote memory of a particular patient. Although a number of formal tests can be used for this purpose, we also assess this aspect through asking for personal information that presumably is or had been well known at one time by the patient (e.g., names of family members, places of prior employment).
7. *Language.* Language is the medium through which much of the neuropsychological examination is accomplished. Language function is assessed both opportunistically, as during the interview, and via formal test instruments. Conversational speech is observed with respect to fluency, articulation, and prosody. The patient's capacity to respond to interview questions and test instructions provides an informal index of receptive language ability or comprehension. Visual confrontation naming is carefully assessed so that word-finding problems and paraphasic errors may be elicited. Repetition is measured with phrases of varying length and phonemic complexity. Auditory comprehension is evaluated by asking the patient questions that vary in length and grammatical complexity. Reading measures include identification of individual letters, common words, irregularly spelled words, and nonwords, as well as measures of reading speed and comprehension. Spelling can be assessed in both visual and auditory modalities. A narrative handwriting sample can be obtained by instructing the patient to describe a standard stimulus scene.
8. *Visuospatial functions.* After basic visuoperceptual status is established, the assessment of visuospatial function commences with the evaluation of the spatial distribution of

visual attention. Visual neglect is examined by way of tasks entailing scanning across all quadrants of visual space. Left/right orientation can be assessed by having the patient point to specific body parts on himself or herself or the examiner. Topographic orientation can be tested in most patients by instructing them to indicate well-known locales on a blank map. Graphic reproduction of designs and assembly of patterns using sticks, blocks, or other media are used to assess visual organization and constructional abilities.

9. *Psychological factors and emotion.* Standardized measures of mood, personality, and psychopathology can be used to explore the role of these issues in the patient's presentation and diagnosis. It is important to note, however, that neurological and other medical conditions can skew performance on certain personality tests; hence, interpretation must take this into account through the use of "correction" methods where available and in exercising caution in drawing diagnostic conclusions.

Diagnostic Formulation

Data from the history, observation, and testing of the patient are analyzed collectively to produce a concise understanding of the patient's symptoms and neuropsychological diagnosis. A configuration of abilities and limitations is developed and used both diagnostically and as a framework for the elucidation of goals for treatment. When possible, the diagnostic formulation should identify the neuropathological factors giving rise to the patient's clinical presentation, including underlying anatomy and disease process.

RECOMMENDATIONS AND FEEDBACK

Consultation concludes with feedback, in which findings and recommendations are reviewed with relevant individuals (e.g., referring physician, patient, family, treatment team members). A variety of treatment plans may be advised, including pharmacological intervention, psychiatric consultation, psychotherapy, vocational guidance, and cognitive-behavioral remediation. Recommendations should be pragmatic and individually tailored to each patient's specific needs. Strategies for optimizing performance in personal, educational, and occupational spheres are identified and discussed in lay language that the patient and family member can comprehend. Where possible, specific behaviorally based suggestions are made for remediation of identified problems. Further clinical evaluations and other neurodiagnostic procedures are suggested when appropriate in order to provide more information relevant to differential diagnosis, response to treatment, and functional status over time. Appropriate neuropsychological follow-up is also arranged.

References and Readings

American Academy of Clinical Neuropsychology. (2011). Position papers. Retrieved January 2013, from theaacn.org/position_papers

Heilman, K., & Valenstein, E. (Eds.) (2011). *Clinical neuropsychology* (5th ed.). New York: Oxford University Press.

Kaplan, E. (1988). A process approach to neuropsychological assessment. In T. Boll & B. Bryant (Eds.), *Clinical neuropsychology and brain function: Research, measurement, and practice* (pp. 129–167). Washington, DC: American Psychological Association.

Lezak, M., Howieson, D., Bigler, E., & Tranel, D. *Neuropsychological assessment* (5th ed.). New York: Oxford University Press.

Manly, J. J. (2008). Cultural issues in cultural neuropsychology: Profit from diversity. *Neuropsychological Review, 18,* 179–183.

Mesulam, M. M. (Ed.). (2000). *Principles of behavioral neurology* (2nd ed.). Philadelphia, PA: F. A. Davis.

Morgan, J. E., & Ricker, J. H. (2008). *Textbook of clinical neuropsychology.* London: Taylor and Francis.

National Association of Neuropsychology. (2011). Position papers. Retrieved March 19, 2013 from: www.nanonline.org/nan/Research___Publications/Position_Papers/NAN/_Research_Publications/Position_Papers.aspx?hkey=71602191-716a-4375-8eb8-4b4e6a071e3a

Schretlen, D. J., Munro, C. A., Anthony, J. C., & Pearlson, G. D. (2003). Examining the range of normal intra-individual variability in neuropsychological test performance. *Journal of the International Neuropsychological Society, 9*, 864–870.

Snyder, P. J., Nussbaum, P. D., & Robins, D. L. (2006). *Clinical neuropsychology: A pocket handbook for assessment* (2nd ed.). Washington, DC: American Psychological Association.

Related Topics

Chapter 12, "Evaluating Dementia"
Chapter 19, "Assessment and Intervention for Executive Dysfunction"
Chapter 20, "Assessing and Managing Concussion"
Chapter 58, "Practicing Psychotherapy with Adults Who Have Cognitive Impairments"

18 DEVELOPMENTAL NEUROPSYCHOLOGICAL ASSESSMENT

Jane Holmes Bernstein, Betsy Kammerer, and Celiane Rey-Casserly

FUNDAMENTAL ASSUMPTIONS OF NEUROPSYCHOLOGICAL ASSESSMENT OF CHILDREN

Clinical assessment in neuropsychology requires extracting diagnostic meaning from an individual's history, observations of behavior, and performance on targeted tests with the goal of optimizing adaptive functioning.

In evaluating behavior the clinician must bring to bear knowledge of the neuroanatomic circuitry supporting behavior, strategies for elucidating relevant brain–behavior relationships, and understanding of environmental and cultural influences on the functioning of the individual child. The developmentally framed analysis of behavior entails an understanding of trajectories of behavioral change through childhood/adolescence and of the dynamic changes that occur in the neural circuitry that supports behavior.

At all points in development observed behavior is a function of the interaction of the brain with the environment—from fundamental genetic processes to the complex epigenetic interactions of personal experience and cultural variables that shape the neural circuitry and the individual. The neuropsychologist must analyze both neurological and psychological (behavioral) variables and must situate these within a wider social context, requiring sensitivity to issues of culture, language, and diversity.

BASIC ASSUMPTIONS OF DEVELOPMENTAL ANALYSIS

Development implies a dynamic interaction between an organism and its environment. The principles at the core of a developmental neuropsychological (NP) analysis of behavior are those of the developmental sciences: structure, context, process, and experience. In the developing child the contribution of brain to observed behavior cannot be meaningfully assessed without reference to the child's developmental course, maturational status, immediate environmental demands, and wider sociocultural context. Knowledge of normal development and its variation is a prerequisite for all developmental analysis.

A perturbation of the brain at any point in time is necessarily incorporated into the subsequent developmental course. Both neurological and behavioral development will proceed in a different fashion around the new brain organization.

A brain insult will have differential impact on behavioral outcome as a function of the developmental status of the disrupted brain system at the time of the insult.

The behaviors (symptoms) that prompt referral occur in the context of the expected competencies of the child at a given developmental stage. Thus, the same underlying neuropsychological problem will be manifest in different ways at different points in development. Over time, the intersection of brain difference and change means that the child is at risk for failure to acquire new skills at all developmental levels.

INDICATIONS FOR NEUROPSYCHOLOGICAL ASSESSMENT

In contrast to adults, children with suspected neuropsychological problems undergo frequent psychological and/or educational testing. Overtesting thus becomes of serious concern. Clinicians should carefully review referral questions. In many instances NP consultation, rather than comprehensive NP assessment, is indicated. NP assessment should be considered under the following circumstances:

- Unexpected failure to meet environmental demands in academic or psychosocial contexts
- Lack of adequate explanation for presenting behavior, or insufficient information to guide intervention planning, subsequent to psychological, psychiatric, psychoeducational, or multidisciplinary assessment
- Change in behavior in the context of known/suspected neurological disorders, systemic disorders and/or treatment regimens with potential central nervous system impact, degenerative/metabolic/genetic disorders, and disorders associated with structural central nervous system abnormalities
- Need to clarify the relationship of behavioral change to specific medical/neurological/psychiatric diagnoses or to specific neural substrates
- Need for baseline profile and ongoing monitoring of neurobehavioral status to track recovery, effects of treatment, and/or the impact of developmental change on behavioral function
- Measurement of change in clinical research with neurological, psychiatric, and psychological populations

NP assessment provides important information to aid in the better understanding and management of behavioral consequences of childhood disorders (e.g., disruptions of executive capacities in spina bifida, prematurity, or attentional disorders; behavioral late effects in treated brain tumor and leukemias; the impact of seizure activity and/or medications in epilepsy) and of neuropsychological contributions to specific behavioral conditions (e.g., psychiatric disorders such as schizophrenia, obsessive-compulsive disorder, Tourette's syndrome; language processing in reading disorders; the interplay of social and cognitive factors in outcomes of traumatic brain injury; deficits in processing socially relevant information).

NP services are typically provided in the form of the following:

(a) Comprehensive individual assessments (outpatient)
(b) Consultation—to educational, psychiatric, social work, medicine, and rehabilitation professionals—including review of records, analysis of behavioral data, application of neurologically relevant information to everyday settings (home, school), and assistance in diagnostic formulation and intervention strategies

(c) Inpatient assessment or consultation to localize function (seizures), monitor behavioral change in the intraoperative setting, and document behavioral functioning in patients with altered mental status
(d) Forensic evaluation to provide a comprehensive description of cognitive functioning and psychosocial adjustment to address future risks/needs or document damage in forensic situations.

DIAGNOSIS IN NEUROPSYCHOLOGY

Diagnosis in neuropsychology is based on a formal assessment strategy that is ideally formulated as an experiment with an *N* of 1, theoretically driven, with hypotheses that are systematically tested and with a design and methodology that include appropriate controls for variability and bias. The expert clinician selects relevant evidence from a diverse knowledge base, entailing a multimethod approach to tap an appropriate range of behavioral domains. The strategy both addresses the referral questions and is framed within the biopsychosocial context of the child's life. It incorporates adaptive competence, emotional well-being, and functional processing style, as well as cognitive and academic abilities. The strategy integrates the vertical dimension of development with the horizontal dimension of the child's current neurobehavioral repertoire. Relevant diagnostic data are analyzed in the context of known neuroanatomic circuitry that underlies adaptive behavior and of the child's unique sociocultural context. Brain–behavior relationships are derived from integration of data from a detailed history of the individual and his or her symptoms, closely observed/reported behavioral reactions/responses in ecologically valid settings, and structured behavioral observations and levels of performance on selected psychological tests.

The diagnostic formulation is the basis for referencing the child's profile to categories of neurological, psychological, and/or educational disorders. These categories can be framed in terms of neuropsychological or neurodevelopmental variables, specific psychological (cognitive, perceptual, information processing, motivational) factors, primary academic deficits, and/or specific nosological schemes (e.g., *DSM, ICD*). The diagnostic formulation is the basis for determination of *risk* (prediction of future response to expectable challenges, both psychosocial and intellectual) and for the design and implementation of the *comprehensive, individualized management strategy* that addresses the pattern of risks faced by *this* child in *this* family with *this* history, *this* profile of skills, and *these* goals (both short and long term).

In NP assessment, behavioral domains are the units of analysis. These can be organized and labeled differently by clinicians with differing theoretical perspectives. What they have in common is that they are sufficiently wide-ranging to address both the behavioral repertoire of the individual being assessed and the referral question(s). Domains include the following:

- Regulatory and goal-directed *executive capacities* (arousal, attention, motivation, memory, learning, mood, affect, emotion, reasoning, planning, decision making, monitoring, initiating, sustaining, inhibiting, and shifting abilities)
- *Skills and knowledge bases* (sensory and perceptual processing in [primarily] visual and auditory modalities, motor capacities, communicative competence, social cognition, linguistic processing, speech functions, spatial cognition)
- *Achievement* (academic skills, adaptive functioning, social comportment, societal adjustment)

The neuropsychologist derives relevant data from personal interviews, the child's history, observations of behavior, and psychological test performance. The history is typically obtained from interviews of the child, parent(s)/guardian(s), and relevant professionals; medical/educational records; and questionnaires/rating scales. The goal is to determine the *child's heritage* (genetic, medical, socioeconomic, cultural, educational) derived from the family history and to assess the *child's ability to take advantage of this heritage* (the child's developmental, medical, psychological, and educational history). Systematic interviewing provides critical information about the social competencies of the child with peers and adults in different settings, as well as the attributions given by others as to the nature and source of the child's presenting difficulties.

Observational data are derived from examination of the child's appearance and behavior, questionnaire/interview information obtained from people familiar with the child in nonclinical contexts, direct observation of the child–parent interaction, analysis of the examiner–child dyad, and observation of the child's behavior and problem-solving style under specific performance demands.

Tests provide *psychometric* data relating level of performance to that of same-age peers; *behavioral* data (behaviors elicited under different problem-solving demands, problem-solving strategies for reaching solutions); and *task analysis* data (complexity of task demands, allocation of resources, systemic relationships in task/situation). They tap specific aspects of behavioral function and are constructed according to sound psychometric principles, administered rigorously, and scored according to standard guidelines. Their normative data should be up to date, reliable, valid, and appropriate in terms of age and/or cultural or language group for the population under study. Population-based standardized psychological test instruments are an important component of a comprehensive NP assessment protocol. They comprise a measure of general mental/cognitive abilities, appropriate to the child's age and general competency, that provides a context of general ability against which specific neuropsychologically relevant skills and weaknesses can be evaluated. Additional tests are selected to address other behavioral domains and provide more detailed analysis of specific psychological processes. These may have population-based or research-based norms. The latter typically have less extensive normative bases but can target specific skills more precisely.

Analysis of performance on psychological tests presents the clinician with a complex challenge. No test measures just one thing. All behavior, including test responses, is the result of a complex interaction of motivational/emotional, motor and sensory capacities, and perceptual, cognitive, and executive variables. Test performance varies in response to contextual factors, including the nature of the test setting, rapport with the clinician, age of the child, test format/materials, and test construction/scoring criteria. No test can be rendered so objective that the interaction between child and examiner is eliminated as an important source of diagnostic information. Test performance is also influenced by a child's prior experience with test procedures and attitudes, and the cultural values ascribed to the testing activity and its purpose. It can be undermined by lack of effort/motivation, by emotional distress, and by physiological factors (lack of sleep, inadequate nutrition).

COMMUNICATION OF FINDINGS

A clinical assessment is essentially worthless if the findings are not communicated effectively to the people responsible for the child's care and development. The neuropsychologist communicates findings by means of an *informing* (or *feedback*) *session* and *written report*. These are both necessary and complementary. In the informing session the clinician's responsibility is not only to communicate the clinical findings but also to explore and explain their meaning and relevance for the child's ongoing adaptive functioning since intervention/treatment goals that lack meaning for patients/families are often not followed. The session also provides an opportunity for parents to discuss and reframe their understanding of the child with the goals of empowering them in their support of the child in the future. The report provides details of the assessment process, the meaning of behavioral observations, the scores derived from standardized measures, the diagnostic formulation, and the management plan and recommendations.

The goal of the informing session and the report is to educate the child, parents/guardians, and teachers/other professionals about the nature of children's neurobehavioral development in general; to explain how brain–behavior relationships in children are examined in the evaluation; to normalize this child's NP performance by situating it in the larger context of neurobehavioral development; to relate observed behaviors to the specific medical/neurological condition (where relevant); and to demonstrate the relationship of the diagnostic formulation to the management plan proposed. The written report summarizes relevant history, observations, and test findings organized so that the import of the findings is clear; integrates the findings into a clear diagnostic statement (not a list of performances on individual tests or of what the child can and cannot do); discusses the relationship of the diagnostic formulation to the child's real-world adaptive functioning; addresses the referral question specifically; references the findings to the medical/neurological condition where relevant (noting specifically when data are, or are not, consistent with a known disorder and locus); identifies areas of concern (risks) based on or referenced to the diagnostic statement; and outlines the management plan and recommendations to maximize the child's functioning in the real-world contexts of family, school, and society at large.

THE MANAGEMENT PLAN

A management plan has two important components: *education* and *recommendations*. The neuropsychologist educates the child, parents/guardians, and other involved professionals in several ways: describing/explaining neurobehavioral development in children; relating this child's performance to that of other children (with and without a similar diagnosis); and providing detailed information about this child's individual style, expectable risks (both short- and long-term), and educational and psychosocial/emotional needs. The clinician will also address issues of medical and psychological health, as well as development and achievement in academic/vocational and psychosocial spheres.

Recommendations respond to the specific risks that the child faces now and in the future; are tailored to different contexts as necessary; provide general guidelines for maximizing behavioral adjustment in both social and academic settings; foster specific cognitive, social, and academic skills; and address psychosocial development and emotional well-being. They include specific interventions involving accommodations, compensatory strategies, remedial instruction, rehabilitation programming, and/or assistive technologies, as well as referral for additional services/evaluation from medical, psychological, physical, and/or educational-vocational specialists as indicated.

FUTURE DIRECTIONS

Neuropsychological evaluation of the developing child will be increasingly informed by advances in understanding complex interactions among genetic risk factors, development, and medical conditions. Future research that compares developmental trajectories across conditions and evaluates the impact of neuropsychologically informed interventions will expand the evidence base for practice in this specialty.

References and Readings

Baron, I. S. (2003). *Neuropsychological evaluation of the child*. New York: Oxford University Press.

Bernstein, J. H. (2000). Developmental neuropsychological assessment. In K. O. Yeates, M. D. Ris, & H. G. Taylor (Eds.), *Pediatric neuropsychology: Research, theory, and practice* (pp. 401–422). New York: Guilford Press.

Donders, J., & Hunter, S. J. (Eds.). (2010). *Principles and practice of lifespan developmental neuropsychology*. Cambridge, England: Cambridge University Press.

Farmer, J. E., Kanne, S. M., Grissom, M., Kemp, S., Frank, R. G., Rosenthal, M., & Caplan, B. (2010). Pediatric neuropsychology in medical rehabilitation settings. In R. G. Frank, M. Rosenthal, & B. Caplan (Eds.), *Handbook of rehabilitation psychology* (2nd ed., pp. 315–328). Washington, DC: American Psychological Association.

Koziol, L. F., & Budding, D. E. (2009). *Subcortical structures and cognition. Implications for neuropsychological assessment*. New York: Springer.

Mash, E. J., & Hunsley, J. (2005). Evidence-based assessment of child and adolescent disorders. *Journal of Clinical Child and Adolescent Psychology*, *34*(3), 362–379.
Morgan, J. E., & Ricker, J. H. (Eds.). (2008). *Textbook of clinical neuropsychology*. London: Taylor & Francis.
Stiles, J. (2008). *The fundamentals of brain development. Integrating nature and nurture*. Cambridge, MA: Harvard University Press.
Yeates, K. O., Ris, M. D., Taylor, H. G., & Pennington, B. F. (Eds.). (2010). *Pediatric neuropsychology: Research, theory, and practice* (2nd ed.). New York: Guilford Press.

Related Topics

Chapter 8, "Interviewing Children's Caregivers"
Chapter 9, "Evaluating the Medical Components of Childhood Developmental and Behavioral Disorders"
Chapter 10, "Using the *DSM-5* and *ICD-11* in Forensic and Clinical Applications with Children Across Racial and Ethnic Lines"

19 ASSESSMENT AND INTERVENTION FOR EXECUTIVE DYSFUNCTION

Robert M. Roth, Peter K. Isquith, and Gerard A. Gioia

Executive functions are interrelated control processes involved in the selection, initiation, execution, and monitoring of cognitive functioning, as well as aspects of motor and sensory functioning. They are self-regulatory functions that organize and direct cognitive activity, emotional responses, and overt behaviors. They may also be described as the orchestration of basic cognitive processes during goal-oriented problem solving, differentiating "basic" cognitive functions from "executive" cognitive control functions. In this metaphor, the executive serves as the conductor of the orchestra by making intentional decisions regarding the final output of the music and recruiting the necessary components in reaching the intended goal. The "instruments" are the domain-specific functions, such as language, visual/nonverbal reasoning, memory, sensory inputs, and motor outputs. The specific cognitive processes subsumed under the "executive" umbrella are a matter of continued debate. Nonetheless, processes commonly considered under the rubric of executive functions include the following:

- *Inhibit*: Ability to not act on an impulse, stop one's own activity at the proper time, and suppress distracting information from interfering with ongoing mental or behavioral activity
- *Shift (also referred to as set shifting, mental flexibility, or cognitive flexibility)*: Move

flexibly from one situation, activity, or aspect of a problem to another as the situation demands
- *Emotional control*: Control one's emotional response as appropriate to the situation or stressor; maintain an optimal level of arousal
- *Initiate*: Begin a task or activity without requiring external prompting
- *Working memory*: Hold information actively in mind over time
- *Sustain*: Stay with or stick to an activity for an age-appropriate amount of time
- *Plan*: Anticipate future events, set goals, and develop appropriate steps ahead of time
- *Organize*: Establish or maintain order in information, an activity, or a place; carry out tasks in a systematic manner
- *Self-monitor*: Check on one's own actions during or shortly after finishing a task to assure accuracy and appropriate attainment of goal; awareness of one's cognitive, physical, and emotional abilities or state; awareness of effects of our behavior on others
- *Problem solving*: Ability to think abstractly and form or develop concepts necessary to achieve a goal

Individuals with executive dysfunction can exhibit a broad range of problems such as acting inappropriately due to difficulty inhibiting impulses, quickly losing track of what they are thinking or doing, making poor financial or other personal decisions, or having considerable difficulty getting started on tasks. Difficulties with executive functions are often manifested in more than one specific cognitive domain, such that inhibitory control deficits can be expressed as verbal disinhibition, behavioral impulsivity, attentional distractibility, emotional reactivity, or social inappropriateness.

NEURAL BASIS OF EXECUTIVE FUNCTIONS AND OTHER CONTRIBUTING FACTORS

Historically, executive functions have been closely associated with the integrity of the frontal lobes. Much of the evidence supporting a role for the frontal lobes in executive functions has come from studies of patients with acquired focal damage to this brain region (Stuss & Knight, 2002). More recently, studies using advanced brain imaging techniques such as positron emission tomography (PET) and functional magnetic resonance imaging (fMRI) have shown that the frontal lobes play an intimate role in executive functions (Roth, Randolph, Koven, & Isquith, 2006). However, neuroimaging studies have also clearly shown that executive functions are not subserved by the frontal lobes alone, but rather by distributed neural circuitry that includes other cortical regions such as the temporal and parietal lobes, subcortical structures such as the hippocampus and basal ganglia, and the cerebellum. Studies of patients with acquired focal lesions in nonfrontal brain regions such as the basal ganglia have also provided further support for a distributed circuitry model of executive functions. Furthermore, there is increasing evidence that disruption of white matter pathways connecting frontal cortex to other brain regions can be associated with poor executive control. Thus, damage to any given component of this circuitry, including connectivity between certain regions, may result in executive dysfunction.

Executive functions are mediated by a number of neurochemicals, particularly dopamine, serotonin, and norepinephrine (Robbins, 2000). Roles for other neurochemicals such as glutamate, acetylcholine, and GABA are being increasingly investigated. Disruption of one or more of these neurochemical systems may in part account for executive dysfunction in conditions where there is no obvious structural brain damage.

Individual differences in executive functions have been associated with variations in age, brain structure such as volume or thickness of particular regions, genetic polymorphisms (e.g., catechol O-methyltransferase), and several personality characteristics (Braver, Cole, & Yarkoni, 2010). A variety of environmental factors such as parenting style, psychosocial stress, exercise, caffeine use, and medications (e.g., stimulants, certain anticonvulsants) have been shown to impact on the integrity of executive functions. Transient factors may also affect performance on tests of executive function and the ability to successfully use executive functions in everyday life, including sleep, fatigue, mood, and level of motivation among others.

It is important to note that there is no "executive function disorder." Rather, executive dysfunction may be seen in association with a wide variety of disorders, including the following:

- Attention-deficit/hyperactivity disorder (ADHD)
- Autism spectrum disorders
- Tourette's syndrome
- Learning disabilities
- Traumatic brain injury
- Epilepsy
- Brain tumors
- Multiple sclerosis and other disorders affecting white matter connectivity
- Parkinson's disease, Huntington's disease, and other movement disorders
- Alzheimer's disease and other dementias
- Psychiatric disorders such as schizophrenia, major depressive disorder, obsessive-compulsive disorder (OCD), and bipolar disorder
- Alcoholism and substance abuse disorders

The precise nature of the executive dysfunction observed in such conditions varies. For example, some disorders have been commonly, but not exclusively, associated with deficits in inhibitory control (e.g., ADHD-Combined type, OCD), while others appear to involve prominent deficits in working memory (e.g., ADHD-Inattentive type, schizophrenia, multiple sclerosis). Residual executive dysfunction may be observed in several disorders even when other symptoms are largely resolved (e.g., major depression, bipolar disorder, schizophrenia). In addition, evidence indicates that subtle problems with executive functions may be present prior to the onset of some conditions, and are present in at least a subset of the unaffected biological relatives of persons with some disorders (e.g., schizophrenia, alcoholism). It should be noted, however, that not all individuals with a given disorder demonstrate problems with executive functions on evaluation. For example, some children and adults with ADHD may show age-appropriate executive functions on performance-based measures (i.e., putative "tests" of executive function), despite several of the symptoms of the disorder listed in well-established formal diagnostic criteria (e.g., impulsivity, difficulty with organization) corresponding relatively well with executive dysfunction.

ASSESSMENT OF EXECUTIVE DYSFUNCTION

Numerous measures have been designed to assess executive function. Some of the most commonly employed performance measures are the Wisconsin Card Sorting Test, the Stroop Color-Word Interference Test, Verbal Fluency tests, Tower tasks (e.g., Tower of London, Tower of Hanoi), and Trail Making tests (Strauss, Sherman, & Spreen, 2006). Establishing that an individual has executive dysfunction usually includes not only such psychometric tests but also a clinical interview and behavioral observations, at times supplemented by reports from informants familiar with the individual. Confirming that executive dysfunction is present also requires that problems in the basic or domain-specific cognitive, sensory, and motor functions be ruled out as accounting for the appearance of executive dysfunction. These include basic attention, language, visuospatial skills, sensory inputs (e.g., hearing, vision), peripheral motor function, and learning and memory.

Assessment of executive function is thus complicated. It is difficult to tease apart deficits in executive from domain-specific functions, given that most neuropsychological instruments are multifactorial in nature. Furthermore, the highly structured testing setting may provide the organization, guidance, and cuing necessary for optimal performance on measures of executive function, which would generally not be available in naturalistic settings. Many measures of executive function are also susceptible to practice effects. That is, once a person figures out how to successfully complete the task, he or she often performs much better on repeat testing or on similar tasks. This is consistent with evidence that executive dysfunction is more readily observed when patients are faced with novel tasks or stimuli, rather than familiar or routine tasks. Despite these limitations, performance measures of executive function can be useful in discriminating between clinical and healthy samples, and exhibit good sensitivity but not necessarily high specificity for specific disorders (Pennington & Ozonoff, 1996).

One concern expressed with regard to more traditional performance-based measures of executive function has been their somewhat limited relationship to functioning in the everyday environment. Increased attention has therefore been devoted to the development of instruments with greater ecological validity, that is, showing a significant predictive relationship between scores on the instrument and a patient's behavior in "real-world" settings (Gioia, Kenworthy, & Isquith, 2010). Such measures of executive function include the following:

- Performance tests that require patients to complete "real-world" type tasks in the laboratory, such as the Test of Everyday Attention (TEA), Test of Everyday Attention for Children (TEA-Ch), and the Behavioral Assessment of the Dysexecutive Syndrome (BADS)
- Structured clinician rating scales such as the Frontal Behavioral Inventory
- Patient and/or informant completed questionnaires such as the Behavior Rating Inventory of Executive Function (BRIEF), Dysexecutive Questionnaire (DEX), and Frontal Systems Behavioral Scale (FrSBe)

There is evidence suggesting that both poor performance on performance-based measures, to some extent, and rating scales of executive function are associated with outcome variables such as academic and occupational functioning. In clinical practice, an assessment approach combining performance-based measures and rating scales may be the most fruitful in providing the most comprehensive understanding of a patient's level of functioning and factors that contribute to difficulties in everyday life.

INTERVENTION FOR EXECUTIVE DYSFUNCTION

An understanding of the executive components of an individual's functioning can lead to targeted pharmacological, behavioral, cognitive, or other therapeutic interventions. Although study findings have varied, in part due to differences in methods and study populations, improvement of executive functions may be observed with computerized training, noncomputerized games, exercise, mindfulness training, use of compensatory strategies, as well as with environmental modifications (e.g., reducing distractions). Interventions may be specifically targeted toward one area of executive functions, such as antecedent management for children with inhibitory control deficits, or may be more programmatic, such as comprehensive cognitive rehabilitation programs (Ylvisaker & Feeney, 2009). A systematic review of treatment studies for executive function deficits following brain injury found sufficient evidence from randomized clinical trials to recommend metacognitive strategy instruction (MSI) methods as a practice standard (Kennedy et al., 2008).

An executive system intervention focus is possible in many settings, including classroom and occupational settings, therapy, social/recreational milieus, and in the home. Ylvisaker and Feeney (2009) articulated key elements of collaborative problem solving interventions (e.g., MSI) in the everyday world of the individual, including the following:

- *Goal setting*: An initial decision about or choice of a goal to pursue (What do I need to accomplish?)
- *Self-awareness of strengths/weaknesses*: Recognition of one's stronger and weaker abilities, and a decision about how easy or difficult it will be to accomplish the goal (How easy or difficult is this task/goal? Have I done this type of task before?)
- *Organization/planning*: Development of an organized plan (What materials do we need? Who will do what? In what order do we need to do these things? How long will it take?)

- *Flexibility/strategy use*: As complications or obstructions arise, planned (e.g., staff members ensure that problems arise) or unplanned coaching of the students in flexible problem solving/strategic thinking (e.g., When/if a problem arises, what other ways should I think about to reach the goal? Should I ask for assistance?)
- *Monitoring*: A review of the goal, plan, and accomplishments at the end (e.g., How did I do?)
- *Summarizing*: What worked and what did not; what was easy and what was difficult and why

For individuals just starting to learn executive control behaviors, young children, or individuals with extreme executive dysfunction, the focus of intervention often needs to be more externalized or environmental, such as organizing and structuring the external environment for them, and cuing strategies and behavioral routines. They often need help to know when and how to apply the appropriate problem-solving behavioral routine. Direct rewards and positive incentives may be necessary to motivate the individual to attend to and practice new behavioral routines. A scaffolding approach may be particularly helpful, whereby an individual is provided with supports (e.g., cues) to help him or her complete relatively easy tasks that then become gradually more demanding as competence and self-confidence develop. Cognitive and/or behavioral strategies (e.g., self-talk, ways to improve organization and reduce distractions) may be provided to help the individual develop independence. Supports are then gradually faded as a function of the individual's increasing autonomy.

References and Readings

Anderson, V., Jacobs, R., & Anderson, P. J. (2008). *Executive functions and the frontal lobes: A lifespan perspective*. New York: Psychology Press.

Braver, T. S., Cole, M. W., & Yarkoni, T. (2010). Vive les differences! Individual variation in neural mechanisms of executive control. *Current Opinion in Neurobiology, 20*(2), 242–250.

Gioia, G., Kenworthy, L., & Isquith, P. K. (2010). Executive function in the real world: BRIEF lessons from Mark Ylvisaker. *Journal of Head Trauma Rehabilitation, 25*(6), 433–439.

Kennedy, M. R. T., Coelho, C., Turkstra, L., Ylvisaker, M., Moore Sohlberg, M., Yorkston, K.,...Kan, P-F. (2008). Intervention for executive functions after traumatic brain injury: A systematic review, meta-analysis and clinical recommendations. *Neuropsychological Rehabilitation, 18*(3), 257–299.

Pennington, B. F., & Ozonoff, S. (1996). Executive functions and developmental psychopathology. *Journal of Child Psychology and Psychiatry and Allied Disciplines, 37*(1), 51–87.

Robbins, T. W. (2000). Chemical neuromodulation of frontal-executive functions in humans and other animals. *Experimental Brain Research, 133*(1), 130–138.

Roth, R. M., Randolph, J. J., Koven, N. S., & Isquith, P. K. (2006). Neural substrates of executive functions: Insights from functional neuroimaging. In J. R. Dupri (Ed.), *Focus on neuropsychology research* (pp. 1–36). New York: Nova Science.

Strauss, E., Sherman, E. M. S., & Spreen, O. (2006). *A compendium of neuropsychological tests* (3rd ed.). New York: Oxford University Press.

Stuss, D. T., & Knight, R. T. (2002). *Principles of frontal lobe function*. New York: Oxford University Press.

Ylvisaker, M., & Feeney, T. (2009). Apprenticeship in self-regulation: Supports and interventions for individuals with self-regulatory impairments. *Developmental Neurorehabilitation, 12*(5), 370–379.

Related Topics

Chapter 9, "Evaluating the Medical Components of Childhood Developmental and Behavioral Disorders"

Chapter 12, "Evaluating Dementia"

Chapter 17, "Adult Neuropsychological Assessment"

Chapter 20, "Assessing and Managing Concussion"

Chapter 58, "Practicing Psychotherapy with Adults Who Have Cognitive Impairments"

20 ASSESSING AND MANAGING CONCUSSION

Gerard A. Gioia

Injury to the brain can have both obvious and subtle consequences for an individual's daily functioning at school, at work, at home, or in his or her social life. A concussion is a type of mild traumatic brain injury that has gained significant attention over the past 10 years with a better understanding of its functional effects. The Centers for Disease Control and Prevention (CDC, 2007) defines concussion as a complex pathophysiologic process affecting the brain, induced by traumatic biomechanical forces secondary to direct or indirect forces to the head. The blow to the head or body results in significant movement of the brain with shear strain disrupting its function due to changes in neurometabolism and neurotransmission. This disturbance of brain function is typically associated with normal head computed tomography and magnetic resonance imaging findings, as concussion does not typically result in structural damage to the brain tissue or blood vessels. A constellation of physical, cognitive, emotional, and sleep symptoms ensues, infrequently involving loss of consciousness (less than 10%–20%). The duration of these symptoms can vary widely from minutes to months, and even longer in a small number of cases.

By virtue of their training in behavioral and cognitive assessment, psychologists (clinical, neuro-, school) are well suited to assist in assessment and management of this injury. As a foundation, the clinician must possess appropriate knowledge of concussions and associated symptom domains. An approach to the assessment and management of concussion, using the Acute Concussion Evaluation (ACE) and ACE Care Plan, is presented to assist the clinician.

EVALUATING CONCUSSION

Individuals may present for evaluation early (days to weeks) or later (months to years) following the injury. Typically, early postinjury evaluation focuses on acute symptom assessment while later evaluation would additionally assess the progression of symptoms over time and other intervening activities or treatments that may have influenced the persistence of symptoms. In most cases, recovery is relatively rapid, with symptoms resolving for most individuals within a few weeks to a few months. A small minority of individuals exhibit persisting symptoms and/or neurocognitive changes.

A thorough understanding of injury characteristics and the type and severity of postconcussion symptoms in the context of the individual's preinjury history is fundamental to the concussion evaluation. The job of the clinician is to determine whether there is new onset of symptoms, exacerbation of preexisting symptoms, or both. Understanding the individual's developmental, medical, family, educational, and psychological history is critical to delineating the postinjury versus preinjury symptoms as there can be a tendency to overascribe symptoms to the injury. The evaluation of a concussion can be further complicated as many symptoms of concussion are also common to those of other medical or psychiatric conditions (e.g., posttraumatic stress disorder, depression, attention-deficit/hyperactivity disorder, headache). Determining the temporal proximity to the injury is an important aspect of the evaluation.

The concussion evaluation focuses on (1) defining injury characteristics, (2) identifying symptom status and neuropsychological dysfunction, (3) establishing the reported symptoms as greater than preinjury status, and (4) determining effects on the individual's life (e.g., school, work, home, social). To assist the clinician's assessment, Drs. Gioia and Collins developed the Acute Concussion Evaluation (ACE; see Appendix) to provide a systematic, evidence-based protocol to assess children and adults with known or suspected concussions. The ACE can be found online in the CDC's "Heads Up: Brain Injury in Your Practice" toolkit (www.cdc.gov/concussion). The ACE Symptom Checklist can be used for initial identification and to serially track symptom recovery over time. The ACE is appropriate for patients in which concussion is clearly indicated (e.g., loss of consciousness or change in mental status, confusion, or amnesia) and where concussion is suspected (e.g., forcible blow to the head or body with functional changes). A description of the ACE protocol follows.

DEFINING INJURY CHARACTERISTICS

Injury description. Assess how the injury occurred, type of force, and location on the head or body where the force (blow) was received. The force to the head may be indirect, such as with an individual being struck in the body resulting in the head accelerating forward and then backward quickly (e.g., whiplash).

Cause. The cause of the injury can help to estimate the force of the blow that was sustained. Generally, the greater the force, the more significant the symptoms. Symptoms associated with a relatively light force, however, may indicate increased vulnerability to concussion, or the presence of other physical or psychological factors contributing to symptom presentation.

Amnesia (retrograde, anterograde). Determine whether amnesia (memory loss) has occurred for events before the injury (retrograde) or after the injury (anterograde) and attempt to determine the length of time of memory dysfunction. Anterograde amnesia is also referred to as posttraumatic amnesia (PTA).

Loss of consciousness (LOC). Inquire whether LOC occurred or was observed and the estimated length of time the patient lost consciousness.

Early signs observed by others. Ask those who know the patient (parent, spouse, friend, etc.) about observed signs of the concussion early after the injury.

Seizures. Inquire whether seizures were observed (although this is uncommon).

ASSESSMENT OF POSTCONCUSSION SYMPTOMS

Symptom assessment. The ACE Symptom Checklist assesses symptoms reported by the patient (and/or parent or other informant, if necessary) in each of the four symptom areas: physical, cognitive, emotional, and sleep. As symptoms can be present prior to the injury (e.g., inattention, headaches), assess any *changes* from typical presentation. Any Total Symptom Score greater than "0" indicates the presence of postinjury symptoms.

Exertion. Symptoms often worsen or reemerge with exertional activity, which is important information for management recommendations. Assess any worsening of symptoms with physical activity (e.g., running, climbing stairs, bike riding) and/or cognitive activity (e.g., academic studies, multitasking at work, reading, or other tasks requiring focused concentration).

Overall "difference" rating. The ACE contains an overall 0–6 rating from the patient (and/or parent or informant) regarding his or her overall perceived change from their preinjury status. This rating is helpful in summarizing the overall impact of the symptoms.

HISTORICAL FACTORS THAT MAY PROLONG RECOVERY

The follow risk factors have been associated with a longer period of recovery from a concussion. Their assessment can be helpful to frame the recovery process.

Concussion history. Assess history of prior concussions, including the duration of symptoms for each injury. The effects of multiple concussions may be cumulative, especially if there is insufficient recovery time between injuries. A sign of increasing vulnerability is that less biomechanical force results in subsequent concussion.

Headache history. Assess personal and family history of treatment for chronic headaches (migraines in particular).

Developmental/school history. Assess for a history of learning disabilities, attention-deficit/hyperactivity disorder, or other developmental disorders.

Psychiatric history. Assess for history of depression, anxiety, and sleep disorder.

TREATING/MANAGING CONCUSSION

With a full definition of the concussion and its symptom manifestations, individualized management planning can proceed. The general psychologist who is less experienced with ongoing management should consider referring to a concussion specialist for management. In addition, referral for focused neuropsychological assessment should be considered when symptoms persist or assisting return to risk activities. Brief test batteries (computerized or abbreviated paper and pencil) have been validated for assessment and tracking of recovery. Testing can also be helpful in developing treatment strategies and to assist the process of return to safe sports participation, school, or work. Referral for more comprehensive neuropsychological assessment should be considered if symptoms persist beyond expectations.

The foundation to concussion treatment is managed rest with individualized management of physical and cognitive exertional activity. A basic treatment assumption is that symptom exacerbation or reemergence in the wake of physical or cognitive activity is a signal that the brain's dysfunctional neurometabolism is being pushed beyond its tolerable limits. Therefore, in guiding recovery, the therapeutic goal is to manage cognitive and physical activity at a level that is tolerable, that is, does not exacerbate or cause the reemergence of symptoms. The ACE Care Plan, also available on the CDC Web site, was developed to guide clinicians' management.

The presence of any postconcussion symptoms or cognitive impairment dictates that patients must not return to high-risk activities (e.g., sports, physical education, high-speed activities). Only when symptoms resolve should a patient slowly and gradually return to his or her daily cognitive and physical activities. Children and adolescents will need the help of their parents, teachers, and other adults to assist with their recovery. Symptom management involves all aspects of the patient's life, including home life, school, work, and social-recreational activities.

Daily Home/Community Activities

In developing an appropriate treatment plan with the patient, the clinician defines the typical schedule and types of activities at home and in the community. Patients should be advised to get adequate sleep at night and to take daytime naps or rest breaks when significant fatigue is experienced. Teach the patient that the return or exacerbation of symptoms is a guide to the level of activity that is safe and tolerable, limiting physical and cognitive exertion accordingly. Physical activity to be managed might include PE, sports practices, weight training, running, exercising, and heavy lifting. Cognitive activities to be managed might include heavy concentration, memory, reasoning, reading, or writing (e.g., homework, classwork, computer or other electronic screens, job-related mental activity). As symptoms decrease, patients may return to their regular activities gradually. Return to high-risk activities such as driving or operating heavy machinery must be carefully considered, especially if the patient has problems with attention, processing speed, or reaction time.

Return to School

The school team (e.g., teacher(s), the school nurse, psychologist/counselor, and administrator) should be informed of the student's injury, symptoms, and cognitive deficits with active efforts to put the appropriate supports in place for the student. School personnel should be advised to monitor for increased problems paying attention/concentrating, problems remembering/learning new information, longer time required to complete tasks, increased symptoms (e.g., headache, fatigue) during schoolwork, and greater irritability/less tolerance for stressors. Symptomatic students will require active supports and accommodations in school. Students with prolonged symptoms (i.e., longer than several weeks) may require special accommodations and services, such as those provided under a Section 504 Plan. As symptoms decrease, and/or as cognitive test results show improvement, patients may return to their regular activities gradually. The School Version of the ACE Care Plan was developed to assist management of cognitive tasks to accommodate the student's tolerance. Students who fatigue easily may benefit from regular rest breaks in the school nurse's office. Students with neurocognitive deficits in attention or concentration may benefit from breaking down larger assignments into smaller tasks or lightening of the workload. Other supports include time off from school (e.g., first several days post injury), shortened day, shortened classes, and scheduled rest breaks during the day. Students may also need allowances for extended time to complete coursework/assignments and tests, as well as a reduced workload and no significant testing while symptomatic. Symptom status should be monitored periodically to modify the types and intensity of the academic supports across recovery.

Return to Work

Similar to school, return-to-work planning (see Work Version of ACE Care Plan) should be based upon careful evaluation of symptoms and cognitive status. Employers/work supervisors should be informed of the employees' injury, symptoms, and cognitive deficits with an active effort to put the appropriate supports in place. To help expedite recovery, patients initially will need to reduce both physical and cognitive exertion. Repeated evaluation of symptom status is recommended to help guide the level of management. Until a full recovery is achieved, individuals may need the following supports: schedule considerations such as a shortened work day, allowance for breaks during work when symptoms increase, and reduced task assignments and responsibilities. Safety considerations while symptomatic also should be given, including no driving, heavy lifting/work with machinery, and no heights due to risk of dizziness and balance problems.

Return to Play (Sports and Recreation)

For persons of any age who participate in competitive or recreational activities, avoiding reinjury or prolonging recovery is a central management goal. Collision sports require special management to ensure full recovery prior to their return to play. As a fundamental tenet of sports concussion management, an individual should never return to competitive sport or recreational activities while experiencing any lingering or persisting concussion symptoms, including PE class, sports practices and games, and other high-risk/high-exertion activities such as running, bike riding, skateboarding, climbing trees, jumping from heights, playful wrestling, and so on. The individual must be completely symptom free at rest and with physical exertion (e.g., sprints, noncontact aerobic activity) and cognitive exertion (e.g., studying, schoolwork) prior to return to sports or recreational activities. As articulated by the international Concussion in Sport Group (McCrory et al., 2009), return to play should occur gradually and systematically with medical supervision, monitoring for symptoms, balance, and cognitive function during each stage of increased exertion.

Psychologists can actively participate in the evaluation and management of concussions (mild traumatic brain injury). They should develop a working understanding of the injury and its clinical manifestations. Individualized evaluation requires the clinician to define the characteristics of the injury, conduct a full assessement of postconcussion symptoms, and define any risk history that may modify recovery. Treatment involves active management of daily activities. The Acute Concussion Evaluation (ACE) and ACE Care Plan can assist the psychologist in this endeavor.

References and Readings

Centers for Disease Control and Prevention (CDC), National Center for Injury Prevention and Control. (2007). *Heads up: Brain injury in your practice*. Atlanta, GA: Author.

Gioia, G. A., & Collins, M. W. (2006). *Acute concussion evaluation*. Retrieved January 2013, from www.cdc.gov/concussion/headsup/pdf/ACE-a.pdf

Gioia, G. A., Collins, M. W., & Isquith, P. K. (2008). Improving identification and diagnosis of mild TBI with evidence: Psychometric support for the acute concussion evaluation (ACE). *Journal of Head Trauma Rehabilitation, 23,* 230–242.

Giza, C. C., & Hovda, D. A. (2001). The neurometabolic cascade of concussion. *Journal of Athletic Training, 36,* 228–235.

Halstead, M. E., Walters, K. D., & The Council on Sports Medicine and Fitness. (2010). Sport-related concussion in children and adolescents. *Pediatrics, 126,* 597–615.

McCrea, M. (2007). *Mild traumatic brain injury and postconcussion syndrome*. New York: Oxford University Press.

McCrory, P., Meeuwisse, W., Johnston, K., Dvorak, J., Aubry, M., Molloy, M., & Cantu, R. (2009). Consensus Statement on Concussion in Sport: The 3rd International Conference held in Zurich, November, 2008. *British Journal of Sports Medicine, 43,* i76–i84.

Sady, M. D., Vaughan, C. G., & Gioia, G. A. (2011). School and the concussed youth: Recommendations for concussion education and management. *Physical Medicine and Rehabilitation Clinics of North America, 22,* 701–719.

Related Topics

Chapter 12, "Evaluating Dementia"

Chapter 17, "Adult Neuropsychological Assessment"

Chapter 19, "Assessment and Intervention for Executive Dysfunction"

Chapter 58, "Practicing Psychotherapy with Adults Who Have Cognitive Impairments"

APPENDIX: ACUTE CONCUSSION EVALUATION (ACE)

ACUTE CONCUSSION EVALUATION (ACE)
PHYSICIAN/CLINICIAN OFFICE VERSION

Gerard Gioia, PhD[1] & Micky Collins, PhD[2]
[1]Children's National Medical Center
[2]University of Pittsburgh Medical Center

Patient Name:____________________
DOB: ____________ Age:____________
Date:____________ ID/MR#____________

A. Injury Characteristics **Date/Time of Injury________________ Reporter: __Patient __Parent __Spouse __Other________**

1. Injury Description ____

1a. Is there evidence of a forcible blow to the head (direct or indirect)? __Yes __No __Unknown
1b. Is there evidence of intracranial injury or skull fracture? __Yes __No __Unknown
1c. Location of Impact: __Frontal __Lft Temporal __Rt Temporal __Lft Parietal __Rt Parietal __Occipital__Neck__Indirect Force
2. **Cause:** __ MVC __Pedestrian-MVC __Fall __Assault __Sports (*specify*) ____________Other____________
3. **Amnesia Before (Retrograde)** Are there any events just BEFORE the injury that you/ person has no memory of (even brief)? __ Yes __No Duration
4. **Amnesia After (Anterograde)** Are there any events just AFTER the injury that you/ person has no memory of (even brief)? __ Yes __No Duration
5. **Loss of Consciousness:** Did you/ person lose consciousness? __ Yes __No Duration
6. **EARLY SIGNS:** __Appears dazed or stunned __Is confused about events __Answers questions slowly __Repeats Questions __Forgetful (recent info)
7. **Seizures:** Were seizures observed? No__ Yes__ Detail ____________________

B. Symptom Check List* Since the injury, has the person experienced any of these symptoms any more than usual today or in the past day?
Indicate presence of each symptom (0 =No, 1=Yes). **Lovell & Collins, 1998 JHTR*

PHYSICAL (10)		COGNITIVE (4)		SLEEP (4)	
Headache	0 1	Feeling mentally foggy	0 1	Drowsiness	0 1
Nausea	0 1	Feeling slowed down	0 1	Sleeping less than usual	0 1 N/A
Vomiting	0 1	Difficulty concentrating	0 1	Sleeping more than usual	0 1 N/A
Balance problems	0 1	Difficulty remembering	0 1	Trouble falling asleep	0 1 N/A
Dizziness	0 1	**COGNITIVE Total (0-4)** ____		**SLEEP Total (0-4)** ____	
Visual problems	0 1	**EMOTIONAL (4)**			
Fatigue	0 1	Irritability	0 1		
Sensitivity to light	0 1	Sadness	0 1		
Sensitivity to noise	0 1	More emotional	0 1		
Numbness/Tingling	0 1	Nervousness	0 1		
PHYSICAL Total (0-10) ____		**EMOTIONAL Total (0-4)** ____			
(Add Physical, Cognitive, Emotion, Sleep totals) Total Symptom Score (0-22)			____		

Exertion: Do these symptoms worsen with:
Physical Activity __Yes __No __N/A
Cognitive Activity __Yes __No __N/A

Overall Rating: How different is the person acting compared to his/her usual self? (circle)
Normal 0 1 2 3 4 5 6 Very Different

C. Risk Factors for Protracted Recovery ***(check all that apply)***

Concussion History? Y__ N__	√	Headache History? Y__ N__	√	Developmental History	√	Psychiatric History
Previous # 1 2 3 4 5 6+		Prior treatment for headache		Learning disabilities		Anxiety
Longest symptom duration Days__ Weeks__ Months__ Years__		History of migraine headache __ Personal __ Family________		Attention-Deficit/ Hyperactivity Disorder		Depression Sleep disorder
If multiple concussions, less force caused reinjury? Yes__ No__		________		Other developmental disorder______		Other psychiatric disorder ______

List other comorbid medical disorders or medication usage (e.g., hypothyroid, seizures)____________

D. RED FLAGS for acute emergency management: Refer to the emergency department with sudden onset of any of the following:
*** Headaches that worsen * Looks very drowsy/ can't be awakened * Can't recognize people or places * Neck pain**
*** Seizures * Repeated vomiting * Increasing confusion or irritability * Unusual behavioral change**
*** Focal neurologic signs * Slurred speech * Weakness or numbness in arms/legs * Change in state of consciousness**

E. Diagnosis (ICD): __Concussion w/o LOC 850.0 __Concussion w/ LOC 850.1 __Concussion (Unspecified) 850.9 __Other (854) ________
__No diagnosis

F. Follow-Up Action Plan **Complete *ACE Care Plan* and provide copy to patient/family.**
___ **No Follow-Up Needed**
___ **Physician/Clinician Office Monitoring** : Date of next follow-up____________
___ **Referral:**
___ Neuropsychological Testing
___ Physician: Neurosurgery___ Neurology___ Sports Medicine___ Physiatrist___ Psychiatrist___ Other ____________
___ Emergency Department

ACE Completed by:____________________

This form is part of the "Heads Up: Brain Injury in Your Practice" tool kit developed by the Centers for Disease Control and Prevention (CDC).

21 ASSESSING MMPI-2 PROFILE VALIDITY

James N. Butcher

The most important step in the Minnesota Multiphasic Personality Inventory-2 (MMPI-2) profile interpretation involves the initial determination of whether the profile contains valid, useful, and relevant information about the client's personality and clinical problems. A number of indices available on the MMPI-2 aid the clinician in determining whether the client's item responses provide key personality information or simply reflect response sets or deceptive motivational patterns to fend off the assessor as to the client's true feelings and motivations. This brief introduction to assessing MMPI-2 profile validity will provide the following: a summary of each of the useful response indices contained on the MMPI-2, a strategy for evaluating the validity indices, and key references for the information presented.

RESPONSE INDICES

Cannot Say Score

This index simply reflects the number of omitted items in the record and is used as an index of cooperativeness. If the item omissions occur at the end of the booklet (beyond item 370), the validity and clinical scales may be interpreted, but the supplemental and MMPI-2 content scales should not be interpreted. The content of omitted items often provides interesting information about the client's problems. If the individual has omitted more than 10 items, the MMPI-2 scales should be evaluated to determine the percentage of omitted items that appear on a particular scale. For example, a large number of items could appear on a particular scale, thereby reducing its value as a personality measure. If the person has omitted more than 30 items, the response record is probably insufficient for interpretation, particularly if the omissions fall within the first 370 items.

The L Scale

The L scale measures cooperativeness and willingness to endorse faults or problems. Individuals who score high on this scale ($T > 60$) have presented an overly favorable picture of themselves. If the L score is greater than 65, the individual has claimed virtue not found among people in general. The L scale proves particularly valuable in situations such as personnel screening or forensic cases because many individuals assessed in these settings try to put their best foot forward and present themselves as "better" adjusted than they really are.

The K Scale

The K scale was developed as a measure of test defensiveness and as a correction for the tendency to deny problems. The profiles of persons who respond defensively on the MMPI-2 are adjusted to offset their reluctance to endorse problems by correcting for the defensiveness. Five MMPI scales include corrections by adding a determined amount of the K score to the scale scores of Hs, Pd, Pt, Sc, and Ma. The K scale appeared to operate for MMPI-2 normative subjects much as it did for the original MMPI subjects. Consequently, the K weights originally derived for the MMPI stayed the same in the MMPI-2. In the MMPI-2, both K corrected and non-K corrected profiles can be obtained for psychologists interested in using non-K corrected scores.

The S Scale or Superlative Self-Description Scale

The S scale is an empirical measure developed by contrasting individuals who took the MMPI-2 in an employment selection situation from the normative sample. Applicants usually prove defensive when assessed in an employment screening context. Even well-educated individuals who apply for a highly desirable job tend to approach the MMPI-2 items with a cognitive mindset to convince the psychologist that they have a sound mind, high responsibility, strong moral values, and great capacity to work effectively with others. In their efforts to perform well on personality evaluation, applicants tend to deny psychological symptoms, aggressively disclaim moral flaws, and assert themselves as responsible people who get along extremely well with others and have the ability to compromise in interpersonal situations for the good of safety. In addition, they report being responsible and optimistic about the future, and they assert that they have a degree of good adjustment that most normals do not. In sum, they present themselves in a superlative manner, claiming superiority to the average person in terms of their mental health and morality. The five subscales contained on the S scale are described as follows: Beliefs in Human Goodness, Serenity, Contentment with Life, Patience/Denial of Irritability and Anger, and Denial of Moral Flaws.

The F Scale

The F scale is an infrequency scale that is sensitive to extreme or exaggerated problem endorsement. The items on this scale include very rare or bizarre symptoms. Individuals who endorse a lot of these items tend to exaggerate symptoms on the MMPI-2. High F responding frequently occurs in individuals with a mindset to convince professionals that they need to have psychological services. This motivational pattern also occurs among individuals with a need to claim problems in order to influence the court in some forensic cases, where the appearance of mental illness might benefit a defendant. High-ranging F scores can raise several possible interpretations: The profile could be invalid because the client became confused or disoriented or got mixed up in responding. The F scale is also elevated in random response records. High F scores also occur among clients who malinger or producing exaggerated responding in order to falsely claim mental illness, as in mental disability claim cases.

The $F_{(B)}$ Scale

The $F_{(B)}$ scale, or Back F scale, was developed for the revised version of the MMPI to detect possible deviant responding to items located toward the end of the item pool. Some subjects may modify their approach to the items partway through the item pool and answer in a random or unselective manner. Since the items on the F scale occur earlier in the test, before item number 370, the F scale will not detect deviant response patterns occurring later in the booklet. The 40-item $F_{(B)}$ scale was developed following the same method as for the original F scale, that is, by including items that had low endorsement percentages in the normal population. Suggested interpretations of the $F_{(B)}$ scale include the following considerations: If the F scale is above T = 90, no additional interpretation of $F_{(B)}$ is indicated, since the clinical and validity scales remain invalid by F scale criteria; if the T score of the F scale is valid (i.e., below a T = 89), and the $F_{(B)}$ is below T = 70, then a valid response approach is indicated throughout the booklet and no additional interpretation is needed; or if the T score of the F scale is valid (i.e., below a T = 89), and the $F_{(B)}$ is above a T = 90 (i.e., if the original F scale is valid and the individual has dissimulated on the later part of the booklet), then an interpretation of $F_{(B)}$ is needed. In this case, interpretation of the clinical and validity scales is possible; however, interpretation of scales such as the content scales, which require valid response to the later appearing items, should be deferred.

The $F_{(P)}$ Scale

The Psychopathology Infrequency Scale $F_{(P)}$ was developed to assess infrequent responding in psychiatric settings. This scale proves valuable in appraising the tendency for some people to exaggerate mental health symptoms in the context of patients with genuine psychological disorder. A high score on $F_{(P)}$, for example, above a T score of 80, indicates that the individual has endorsed more bizarre item content than even inpatient psychiatric cases endorse.

TRIN and VRIN

Two inconsistency scales for determining profile validity have been included in the MMPI-2. These scales are based on the analysis of the individual's response to the items in a consistent or inconsistent manner. The first scale, True Response Inconsistency (TRIN), is made up of 20 pairs of items in which a combination of two true or two false responses qualifies as semantically inconsistent—for example, a pair of items that contain content that cannot logically be answered in the same direction if the subject has responded consistently to the content.

TRIN can aid in the interpretation of scores on L and K, since the former is made up entirely of items that are keyed false and the latter is made up of items all but one of which is keyed false. Thus, an individual who inconsistently responds "false" to MMPI-2 pairs of items that contain opposite content will have elevated scores on scales L and K that do not reflect intentional misrepresentation or defensiveness. An individual whose TRIN score indicates inconsistent "true" responding will have deflated scores on L and K that do not reflect a particularly honest response pattern or lack of ego resources.

The Variable Response Inconsistency (VRIN) scale may help interpret a high score on F. VRIN is made up of 49 pairs (true-false; false-true; true-true; false-false) of patterns. The scale is scored by summing the number of inconsistent responses. A high F in conjunction with a low to moderate VRIN score rules out the possibility that the F score reflects random responding.

A Controversial Malingering Scale to Avoid

MMPI-2 users should remain aware of a problem validity scale that was developed for use in personal injury litigation to detect "malingering" of claims but has been more broadly expanded for use in all settings in which the MMPI-2 is used. The test publisher recently changed the name of the Fake Bad Scale to Symptom Validity Scale to avoid the disparaging term "fake bad" as a result of recent controversy over its use. The scale is the Lees-Haley Fake Bad Scale (FBS) published in 1991 by Lees-Haley, Fox, and Glenn. One major problem with the scale is that it contains a substantial number of items that assess actual physical problems or stress-related symptoms. Thus, the scale has a high proportion of false negatives (i.e., It classifies a high number of people who have actual physical or mental health problems as "malingering."). As a result of this high classification error rate, a number of court cases have seen use of the scale excluded as evidence because of the likelihood of misclassifying patients with genuine problems as "malingering" (see references dealing with the FBS controversy).

VALIDITY ASSESSMENT GUIDELINES

The following guidelines or strategies are recommended for determining the interpretability of profiles:

Clues to non-content-oriented responding

- High Cannot Say's (≥ 10)
  Noncompliance
- Preponderance of T or F
  Careless or devious omissions
- VRIN greater than 80
  Inconsistency

- TRIN greater than 80
  "Yea-saying" or "Nay-saying" (depending on whether the score is TRIN [T] or TRIN [F])

Indicants of defensive self-presentation

1. Overly positive self-presentation, leading to a somewhat attenuated record, if any, of these conditions, is present
   - Cannot Say between 5 and 29
   - L over 60 but less than 65
   - K over 60 but less than 69
   - S over 65
2. Likely invalid MMPI-2 because of test defensiveness if any of the following conditions are present:
   - Cannot Say greater than 30
   - L greater than 66
   - K greater than 70
   - S greater than 70

Indicators of exaggerated responding and malingering of symptoms

1. Excessive symptom claiming
   - F (infrequency) greater than 90
   - $F_{(B)}$ greater than 90
   - $F_{(P)}$ greater than 80
2. Possibly exaggerated-invalid range
   - F greater than 100
   - $F_{(B)}$ greater than 10
   - $F_{(P)}$ greater than 90
3. Likely malingering
   - F greater than 109, with VRIN less than or equal to 79
   - $F_{(B)}$ greater than 109, with VRIN less than or equal to 79
   - VRIN less than 79, with VRIN less than or equal to 79
   - $F_{(P)}$ greater than 100, with VRIN less than or equal to 79

References and Readings

Butcher, J. N. (2011). *A beginner's guide to the MMPI-2* (3rd ed.). Washington, DC: American Psychological Association.

Butcher, J. N., Arbisi, P. A., Atlis, M., & McNulty, J. (2003). The construct validity of the Lees-Haley Fake Bad Scale (FBS): Does this scale measure malingering and feigned emotional distress? *Archives of Clinical Neuropsychiatry, 18,* 473–485.

Butcher, J. N., Gass, C. S., Cumella, E., Kally, Z., & Williams, C. L. (2008). Potential for bias in MMPI-2 assessments using the Fake Bad Scale (FBS). *Psychological Injury and the Law, 1,* 191–209.

Butcher, J. N., & Han, K. (1995). Development of an MMPI-2 scale to assess the presentation of self in a superlative manner: The S scale. In J. N. Butcher & C. D. Spielberger (Eds.), *Advances in personality assessment* (Vol. 10, pp. 25–50). Hillsdale, NJ: Erlbaum.

Gass, C. S., Williams, C. L., Cumella, E., Butcher, J. N., & Kally, Z. (2010). Ambiguous measures of unknown constructs: The MMPI-2 Fake Bad Scale (aka Symptom Validity Scale, FBS, FBS-r). *Psychological Injury and the Law,* ePub ahead of print. doi: 10.1007/s12207-009-9063-2.

Lees-Haley, P. R., English, L. T., & Glenn, W. J. (1991). A Fake Bad Scale on the MMPI-2 for personal injury claimants. *Psychological Reports, 68,* 203–210.

Wetter, W, Baer, R. A., Berry, D. T, Smith, G. T, & Larsen, L. (1992). Sensitivity of MMPI-2 validity scales to random responding and malingering. *Psychological Assessment, 4,* 369–374.

Williams, C. L., Butcher, J. N., Gass, C. S., Cumella, E., & Kally, Z. (2009). Inaccuracies about the MMPI-2 fake bad scale in the reply by Ben-Porath, Greve, Bianchini, and Kaufmann (2009). *Psychological Injury and Law, 2,* 182–197.

Related Topics

Chapter 22, "Interpreting Clinical Scale Scores on the MMPI-2"

Chapter 23, "Interpreting Supplementary Scales of the MMPI-2"

Chapter 26, "Interpreting Test Scores and Their Percentile Equivalents"

22 INTERPRETING CLINICAL SCALE SCORES ON THE MMPI-2

John R. Graham

This chapter provides descriptive information for each Minnesota Multiphasic Personality Inventory-2 (MMPI-2) clinical scale. The information is based on a large body of empirical research. The most usual practice is to consider T scores above 65 as high scores; however, the higher scores are, the more likely it is that the descriptive information will apply. Limited and conflicting data concerning the meaning of low scores indicate that they should not be interpreted for most clinical scales. Exceptions are Scale 5 (Masculinity-Femininity) and Scale 0 (Social Introversion). These two scales are basically unidimensional with low scores indicating the opposite of high scores. Descriptors presented here should be treated as hypotheses that should be validated using information from other MMPI-2 scales, other tests, and nontest sources (e.g., behavioral observation, interview, history).

SCALE 1 (HYPOCHONDRIASIS)

- Scale 1 originally was developed to identify patients manifesting symptoms associated with hypochondriasis. The syndrome is characterized by preoccupation with the body and concomitant fears of illness and disease.
- Scale 1 is the most homogeneous and unidimensional clinical scale. All of the items deal with somatic concerns or with general physical competence. Patients with bona fide physical problems typically show somewhat elevated T scores on Scale 1 (approximately 60). Elderly individuals tend to produce Scale 1 scores that are slightly more elevated than those of adults in general, probably reflecting the declining health typically associated with aging.
- Persons with high scores on Scale 1 typically present with somatic complaints that may include chronic pain, headaches, and gastrointestinal discomfort. They view their problems as being medical in nature, seek medical treatment for their symptoms, and resist psychological interpretations. They tend to be quite self-centered and demanding of attention and support from others.

SCALE 2 (DEPRESSION)

- Scale 2 originally was developed to assess symptomatic depression. The primary characteristics of depression are poor morale, lack of hope in the future, and a general dissatisfaction with one's life situation. Many of the items in the scale deal with aspects of depression such as denial of happiness and personal worth, psychomotor retardation, withdrawal, and lack of interest in one's surroundings.
- Scale 2 is an excellent index of discomfort and dissatisfaction with one's life situation. Whereas highly elevated scores on this scale suggest clinical depression, more moderate scores tend to be indicative of a general

attitude or lifestyle characterized by poor morale and lack of social involvement.
- Scale 2 scores are related to age, with elderly persons typically scoring approximately 5–10 T-score points higher than the mean for the total MMPI-2 normative sample. Some individuals who have recently been hospitalized or incarcerated tend to show moderate elevations on Scale 2 that reflect dissatisfaction with current circumstances rather than clinical depression.

SCALE 3 (HYSTERIA)

- This scale was developed to identify patients who were utilizing hysterical reactions to stress situations. The hysterical syndrome is characterized by involuntary psychogenic loss or disorder of function.
- Some of the items in Scale 3 deal with a general denial of physical health and a variety of rather specific somatic complaints, including heart or chest pain, nausea and vomiting, fitful sleep, and headaches. Other items involve a general denial of psychological or emotional problems and of discomfort in social situations.
- It is important to take into account the level of scores on Scale 3. Whereas marked elevations (T > 80) may be indicative of a pathological condition characterized by classical hysterical symptoms, moderate levels are associated with characteristics that are consistent with hysterical disorders but do not include the classical hysterical symptoms. As with Scale 1, patients with bona fide medical problems for whom there is no indication of psychological components to the conditions tend to obtain T scores of about 60 on this scale.
- High scorers on Scale 3 may react to stress and avoid responsibility by developing physical symptoms. They display a marked lack of insight concerning the possible underlying causes of their symptoms. They are likely to see their symptoms as medical in nature, and they want to be treated medically. They tend to be immature psychologically and expect a great deal of attention and affection from others.

SCALE 4 (PSYCHOPATHIC DEVIATE)

- Scale 4 was developed to identify patients diagnosed as having a psychopathic personality, asocial or amoral type. Whereas persons in the original criterion group were characterized in their everyday behavior by such delinquent acts as lying, stealing, sexual promiscuity, excessive drinking, and the like, no major criminal types were included.
- The items in Scale 4 cover a wide array of topics, including difficulties with authorities, family problems, delinquency, sexual problems, and absence of satisfaction in life. Scores on Scale 4 tend to be related to age, with younger people scoring slightly higher than older people.
- One way of conceptualizing what Scale 4 assesses is to think of it as a measure of rebelliousness, with higher scores indicating rebellion and lower scores indicating acceptance of authority and the status quo. The highest scorers on the scale rebel by acting out in antisocial and criminal ways; moderately high scorers may be rebellious but may express the rebellion in more socially acceptable ways; and low scorers may be overly conventional and accepting of authority.
- High scorers on Scale 4 tend to be psychologically immature and impulsive. They are easily bored and tend to seek out excitement and stimulation. They accept little responsibility for their own problems. They make good first impressions, but relationships tend to be superficial and unrewarding.

SCALE 5 (MASCULINITY-FEMININITY)

- Scale 5 originally was developed by Hathaway and McKinley to identify homosexual invert males. The test authors identified only a very small number of items that differentiated homosexual from heterosexual men. Thus, items were added to the scale if they differentiated between men and women in the standardization sample. Items from an earlier interest test were also added to the scale.
- The test authors attempted, without success, to develop a corresponding scale for

identifying "sexual inversion" in women. As a result, Scale 5 has been used for both men and women. Fifty-two of the items are keyed in the same direction for both genders, whereas four items, all dealing with frankly sexual content, are keyed in opposite directions for men and women. After obtaining raw scores, T-score conversions are reversed for the sexes so that high raw scores for men yield high T scores, whereas high raw scores for women yield low T scores. The result is that high T scores for both sexes are indicative of deviation from one's own sex.

- Although a few of the items in Scale 5 have clear sexual content, most items are not sexual in nature, instead covering a diversity of topics, including work and recreational interests, worries and fears, excessive sensitivity, and family relationships.
- For men, high T scores indicate persons who tend not to have stereotypically masculine interests (e.g., sports, mechanics), and low T scores indicate persons who describe stereotypically masculine interests and activities. For women, high T scores indicate persons who do not describe stereotypically feminine interests and who are described as assertive and competitive. Low T scores for women indicate persons who describe traditionally feminine interests (e.g., cooking, child rearing). More educated women with low scores on Scale 5 present as more androgynous in interests and activities.

SCALE 6 (PARANOIA)

- Scale 6 originally was developed to identify patients who were judged to have paranoid symptoms such as ideas of reference, feelings of persecution, grandiose self-concepts, suspiciousness, excessive sensitivity, and rigid opinions and attitudes. Although some of the items in the scale deal with frankly psychotic behaviors (e.g., excessive suspiciousness, ideas of reference, delusions of persecution, grandiosity), many items cover such diverse topics as sensitivity, cynicism, asocial behavior, excessive moral virtue, and complaints about other people.
- The higher the score on Scale 6, the more likely it is that frankly psychotic symptoms will be present. Modest elevations (T = 60–70) suggest characteristics that are consistent with a paranoid orientation but do not necessarily indicate psychosis. Elevated scores at all levels indicate persons who are excessively sensitive and overly responsive to the opinions of others. High scorers may feel that they are getting a raw deal from life, and they tend to blame others for their problems. High scorers tend to be seen by others as suspicious and guarded and as exhibiting hostility and resentment.

SCALE 7 (PSYCHASTHENIA)

- Scale 7 originally was developed to measure the general symptomatic pattern labeled psychasthenia. Among currently popular diagnostic categories, the obsessive-compulsive disorder is closest to the original meaning of the psychasthenia label. Such persons have thinking characterized by excessive doubts, compulsions, obsessions, and unreasonable fears.
- Some items in Scale 7 deal with uncontrollable or obsessive thoughts, feelings of fear and/or anxiety, and doubts about one's own ability. Unhappiness, physical complaints, and difficulties in concentration also are represented in the scale.
- High scores on Scale 7 indicate a great deal of psychological discomfort and turmoil. High scorers tend to feel anxious, tense, and agitated. They may experience difficulties with concentration and memory, and decision making. They are lacking in self-confidence and often feel unhappy, sad, and pessimistic. They do not cope well with stress, often overreacting to even minor problems.
- High scorers on Scale 7 tend to be neat, orderly, and organized. They are seen by others as reliable and dependable and as capable of forming meaningful relationships.

SCALE 8 (SCHIZOPHRENIA)

- Scale 8 was developed to identify patients with diagnoses of schizophrenia. This category included a heterogeneous group of disorders characterized by disturbances of thinking, mood, and behavior. Misinterpretations of reality, delusions, and hallucinations may be present. Ambivalent or constricted emotional responsiveness is common. Behavior may be withdrawn, aggressive, or bizarre.

- Some items in Scale 8 deal with such frankly psychotic symptoms such as bizarre mentation, peculiarities of perception, delusions of persecution, and hallucinations. Other items deal with social alienation, poor family relationships, sexual concerns, and difficulties with impulse control.
- Very high scores on Scale 8 are suggestive of a psychotic disorder. Confusion, disorganization, and disorientation may be present. Unusual thoughts or attitudes, sometimes even delusional in nature, and extremely poor judgment may be evident. High scorers often feel as if they are not part of their social environments, and they may feel alienated, misunderstood, and unaccepted by peers. Consideration should be given to consultation concerning appropriateness of psychotropic medication and a structured treatment setting.
- Persons who are feeling demoralized and depressed may obtain relatively high scores on Scale 8. Some elevations on the scale can be accounted for by persons who are reporting a large number of unusual experiences, feelings, and perceptions related to the use of prescription and nonprescription drugs, especially amphetamines. Also, some persons with disorders such as epilepsy, stroke, or closed-head injury endorse sensory and cognitive items, leading to high scores on Scale 8.

SCALE 9 (HYPOMANIA)

- Scale 9 originally was developed to identify psychiatric patients manifesting hypomanic symptoms. Hypomania is characterized by elevated mood, accelerated speech and motor activity, irritability, flight of ideas, and brief periods of depression.
- Some of the items in Scale 9 deal specifically with features of hypomanic disturbance (e.g., activity level, excitability, irritability, grandiosity). Other items cover topics such as family relationships, moral values and attitudes, and physical or bodily concerns.
- Scores on Scale 9 are related to age. Younger people (e.g., college students) typically obtain scores in a T-score range of 50–60. For elderly people, Scale 9 T scores slightly below 50 are common.
- Scale 9 can be viewed as a measure of psychological and physical energy, with high scorers having excessive energy. When Scale 9 scores are high, one expects that characteristics suggested by other aspects of the profile will be acted out. For example, high scores on Scale 4 suggest asocial or antisocial tendencies. If Scale 9 is elevated along with Scale 4, these tendencies are more likely to be expressed overtly in behavior.
- High scores on Scale 9 may be indicative of a manic episode. Persons with such scores are likely to show excessive, purposeless activity and accelerated speech; they may have delusions of grandeur; and they are emotionally labile. Unrealistic self-appraisal may be present. High scorers may be involved in many activities, but they do not use energy wisely and often do not see projects through to completion. They often create good first impressions, but relationships tend to be rather superficial and not very rewarding.

SCALE 0 (SOCIAL INTROVERSION)

- Scale 0 was designed to assess a person's tendency to withdraw from social contacts and responsibilities. Items were selected by contrasting high and low scorers on the Social Introversion-Extroversion Scale of the Minnesota T-S-E Inventory. Scores on Scale 0 are quite stable over extended periods.
- High scorers on Scale 0 are insecure and uncomfortable in social situations. They tend to be shy, timid, and retiring. They are more comfortable by themselves or with a few close friends. They are quite concerned about what others think about them and are likely to be troubled about their lack of

involvement with other people. Low scorers on Scale 0 tend to be much the opposite of high scorers. They are socially extraverted, self-confident, and comfortable in social situations.

References and Readings

Butcher, J. N., Graham, J. R., Ben-Porath, Y. S., Tellegen, A., Dahlstrom, W. G., & Kaemmer, B. (2001). *Minnesota Multiphasic Personality Inventory-2 (MMPI-2): Manual for administration, scoring, and interpretation*. Minneapolis: University of Minnesota Press.

Graham, J. R. (2012). MMPI-2: *Assessing personality and psychopathology* (5th ed.). New York: Oxford University Press.

Graham, J. R., Ben-Porath, Y. S., & McNulty J. L. (1999). *MMPI-2 correlates for outpatient community mental health settings*. Minneapolis: University of Minnesota Press.

Related Topics

Chapter 21, "Assessing MMPI-2 Profile Validity"
Chapter 23, "Interpreting Supplementary Scales of the MMPI-2"
Chapter 24, "Understanding and Using the MMPI-2-RF"

23 INTERPRETING SUPPLEMENTARY SCALES OF THE MMPI-2

Roger L. Greene and Lacey M. Sommers

This overview of the MMPI-2 supplementary scales will be organized into four groupings of scales: generalized emotional distress scales (Welsh Anxiety [A], College Maladjustment [Mt], and Post Traumatic Stress Disorder–Keane [PK]); control/inhibition and dyscontrol/dysinhibition scales (Welsh Repression [R], Hostility [Ho], and MacAndrew Alcoholism–Revised [MAC-R]); alcohol/drug scales (MacAndrew Alcoholism–Revised [MAC-R], Addiction Admission [AAS], Addiction Potential [APS], and Common Alcohol Logistic–Revised [CAL-R]); and the Personality Psychopathology Five scales (PSY-5: Harkness, McNulty, & Ben-Porath, 2002). Given the limited amount of space, the less frequently used supplementary scales covering general personality dimensions (Dominance [Do], Over-Controlled Hostility [O-H]; Social Responsibility [Re]) and gender role scales (Gender Role–Feminine [GF] and Gender Role–Masculine [GM]) will *not* be discussed. Information on all of these supplementary scales can be found in Friedman, Lewak, Nichols, and Webb (2001), Graham (2006), and Greene (2011). Clinicians should keep in mind that a general style for individuals to maximize or minimize their reported symptoms will have a significant impact on the elevation, or lack thereof, for all of the MMPI-2 supplementary scales, as well as the standard validity and clinical scales and content scales. It will be assumed in discussing the supplementary scales that individuals have endorsed the items in an accurate manner.

GENERALIZED EMOTIONAL DISTRESS SCALES

Factor-analytic studies of the MMPI-2 clinical scales have consistently identified two factors that are variously labeled and interpreted. The first factor is generally acknowledged to be a measure of generalized emotional distress and negative affectivity, and Welsh developed his Anxiety (A) scale to measure this factor. The major content areas in the Welsh Anxiety (A) scale are (1) problems in attention and concentration; (2) negative emotional tone and dysphoria; (3) lack of energy and pessimism; (4) negative self-evaluation and hypersensitivity; and (5) obsessions and ruminations. There are 10 to 20 other scales in the MMPI-2 that measure this factor of generalized emotional distress and negative affectivity, all of which have high positive correlations with the A scale: the clinical scales 7 (Pt: .95) and 8 (Sc: .90); the content scales Work Interference (WRK: .93), Depression (DEP: .92), Anxiety (ANX: .90), Obsessions (OBS: .89), and Low Self-Esteem (LSE: .87); the restructured clinical (RC) scales Demoralization (RCD: .94) and Dysfunctional Negative Emotions (RC7: .90) and the supplementary scales Post Traumatic Stress Disorder–Keane (PK: .93), College Maladjustment (Mt: .93), and Marital Distress Scale (MDS: .79). There also are a number of MMPI-2 scales that have high negative correlations with the A scale and as such are simply inverted measures of generalized distress: Ego Strength (Es: −.83) and K (Correction: −.79). All of these scales can be characterized as generalized measures of emotional distress with little or no specificity despite the name of the scale, and there are little empirical data to support any distinctions among them.

CONTROL/INHIBITION AND DYSCONTROL/DYSINHIBITION SCALES

The second factor identified in these factor-analytic studies of the MMPI-2 clinical scales is a measure of control and inhibition, and Welsh developed his Repression (R) scale to measure this factor. The major content areas in the Welsh Repression (R) scale are the denial and suppression of and/or constriction and inhibition of interests *either positive or negative* in (1) health and physical symptoms; (2) emotionality, violence, and activity; (3) family and relationship problems; (4) social dominance and social participation; and (5) personal and vocational pursuits. There are 5 to 10 other scales in the MMPI-2 that measure this factor of control and inhibition, but the pattern of correlations with the R scale is much more variable and smaller than found with the A scale: the clinical Scale 9 (Ma: .43), the content scale Antisocial Practices (ASP: .36), the restructured clinical (RC) scale Hypomanic Activation (RC9: .60), the supplementary scales MacAndrew Alcoholism–Revised (MAC-R: .50) and Social Responsibility (Re: .38), and the PSY-5 scales Aggression (AGGR: .49) and Disconstraint (DISC: .43). The specific correlates of the second factor will be a function of the scale that is used to define it, but it is evident that this group of MMPI-2 scales is characterized by significant dyscontrol or dysinhibition associated with acting out or externalization of psychopathology.

Conjoint interpretations of the first two factors of the MMPI-2 (generalized emotional distress and control/inhibition) provide a succinct approach for how individuals are coping with the behaviors and symptoms that led them to treatment (see Greene, 2011, Table 7.5, p. 269). The A scale provides a quick estimate of how much generalized emotional distress the individual is experiencing, and the R scale indicates whether the individual is trying to inhibit or control the expression of this distress. It is particularly noteworthy in a clinical setting when the A scale is not elevated (T < 50) because it signifies that the individual is not experiencing any distress about the behaviors and symptoms that usually leads someone else to refer them to treatment. Similarly low scores (T < 45) on the R scale suggest that the individual has no coping skills or abilities to control or inhibit the overt expression of their distress. When one of these two scales is elevated significantly and the other scale is unusually low, clinicians should give serious consideration to the hypothesis that the individual is maximizing (A > 75; R < 45) or minimizing (A < 45; R > 60) his or her report of psychopathology. It is particularly pathognomonic when both the A and R scales are low (T < 50), a pattern that is seen in chronic, ego syntonic psychopathology.

ALCOHOL AND DRUG SCALES

The alcohol and drug scales on the MMPI-2 can be easily subdivided into rationally derived, or direct, measures (Addiction Admission [AAS] and Common Alcohol Logistic–Revised [CAL-R]) and empirically derived, or indirect, measures (MacAndrew Alcoholism–Revised [MAC-R] and Addiction Potential [APS]). These four alcohol and drug scales contain 111 different items, 96 of which are found on only one of the four scales. These different methodologies yielded very different item groupings on these four scales that can be seen in the low positive correlations among them: MAC-R with AAS .48, APS .29, and CAL-R .32; and AAS with APS .34; CAL-R .46. Consequently, the manifestations of alcohol and drug abuse will differ in specific individuals depending upon which scale is elevated.

The MAC-R scale is best conceptualized as a general personality dimension. Individuals who produced elevated scores (T scores > 64) on the MAC-R scale are described as being impulsive, risk taking, and sensation seeking, and they frequently have a propensity to abuse alcohol and/or stimulating drugs. They are uninhibited, sociable individuals who appear to use repression and religion in an attempt to control their rebellious, delinquent impulses. They also are described as having a high energy level, having shallow interpersonal relationships, and being generally psychologically maladjusted. Low scorers (T scores < 45) are described as being depressed, inhibited, overcontrolled individuals, who also may abuse substances, but in a different manner. If they abuse substances, they will prefer alcohol or sedating drugs. Once the MAC-R scale is understood as a general personality dimension for risk taking versus risk avoiding, the fact that mean scores vary drastically by codetype makes sense. For example, in men, the mean T score on the MAC-R scale in a 4-9/9-4 (risk-taking) codetype is 63.4 and in a 2-0/0-2 (risk-avoiding) codetype is 42.5 (see Greene, 2011, Appendix A), a difference of over two standard deviations. There are a number of issues that must be kept in mind when interpreting the MAC-R scale: Men score about 2 raw-score points higher than women across most samples, which indicates that different cutting scores are necessary by gender; there is not a single, optimal cutting score with raw scores anywhere from 24 to 29 being used in different studies; cutting scores appear to be influenced by a number of factors, so clinicians need to begin to determine empirically the best cutting score for their specific treatment facility to optimize the percentage of clients correctly classified as substance abusers; clinicians need to be very cautious in using the MAC-R scale in non-White ethnic groups, if it is used at all; classification accuracy decreases when clinicians are trying to discriminate between substance abusers and non-substance-abusing, clinical clients, which is a frequent differential diagnosis; classification accuracy may be unacceptably low in medical samples; and the MAC scale is a general measure of substance abuse that is not specific to alcoholism.

The Addiction Potential Scale (APS) consists of 39 items that differentiated among groups of male and female substance-abuse patients, normal individuals, and clinical clients. Individuals with elevated (T > 64) scores on the APS scale are generally distressed and upset, as well as angry and resentful. They also are concerned about what others think of them, a concern that is not evident in individuals who elevate the MAC-R scale. Low scorers (T < 45) on the APS describe themselves in relatively positive terms. They are not distressed or angry. If they are abusing substances, they either are not experiencing or not reporting any negative consequences. The APS scale appears to be more accurate at discriminating between substance-abuse clients and clinical clients than is the MAC-R scale. The APS scale also tends to be less gender biased than the MAC-R scale and to be less codetype sensitive. For example, in men, the mean T score on APS in a 4-9/9-4 codetype is 55.9

and in a 2-0/0-2 codetype is 48.5 (see Greene, 2011, Appendix A), a difference slightly over one-half of a standard deviation.

The Addiction Admission Scale (AAS) consists of 13 items, 9 of which are directly related to the use of alcohol and drugs. Clinicians should review the clinical history and background of any individual who elevates the AAS scale (T > 64) because of the explicit nature of the items and the fact that four or more of these items have been endorsed in the deviant direction to produce this elevation. The AAS scale typically performs better at identifying individuals who are abusing substances than less direct measures such as the APS and MAC-R scales, even though the items are face valid, allowing individuals not to report the substance abuse if they desire to do so. Weed, Butcher, and Ben-Porath (1995) have provided a thorough review of all MMPI-2 measures of substance abuse.

The Common Alcohol Logistic (CAL) scale because was developed out of concern that existing MMPI alcohol scales lacked adequate positive predictive power given the low base rate or prevalence of alcohol-related problems in general medical settings. Gottesman and Prescott (1989) raised similar concerns about the MAC-R scale in clinical clients. The 33 items for the CAL scale were identified and the item weights were assigned by using logistic regression in large samples of alcoholic clients, medical clients, and normal individuals. Malinchoc, Offord, Colligan, and Morse (1994) revised the CAL scale for the MMPI-2 by dropping the six items on the CAL scale that were not retained on the MMPI-2. They recomputed the item weights using logistic regression on similar groups of patients, and the resulting 27 items became the CAL-R scale that is appropriate for use with either the MMPI or MMPI-2. They did not use the MMPI-2 item pool in this revision, so it remains to be seen whether any of the new MMPI-2 items, particularly the items asking about alcohol and drug abuse, would have been selected for inclusion on the scale. High scorers (T scores of 65 or higher) on the Common Alcohol Logistic–Revised (CAL-R) scale have used alcohol excessively and they feel alienated from others and members of their family. They do not report physical symptoms as a consequence of their use of alcohol. The CAL-R scale appears to be particularly useful to identify substance abuse in medical settings, no doubt reflecting the context in which the scale was developed.

Although the focus of this section is on alcohol and drug scales, it is important to note that there are a number of specific MMPI-2 items related to alcohol and drug use (264, 489, 511, 544) that warrant further inquiry any time they are endorsed in the deviant direction. Most of these items are phrased in the past tense so the clinician cannot assume without inquiry whether the alcohol and drug use is a current or past event.

PERSONALITY PSYCHOPATHOLOGY FIVE SCALES

Harkness and McNulty created a five-factor model called the Personality Psychopathology Five (PSY-5) to aid in the description of normal personality and to complement the diagnosis of personality disorders. Using replicated rational selection, Harkness and McNulty identified five factors within 60 descriptors of normal and abnormal human behavior: Aggressiveness (AGGR), Psychoticism (PSYC), Disconstraint (DISC), Negative Emotionality/Neuroticism (NEGE), and Introversion/Low Positive Emotionality (INTR) (cf. Harkness, McNulty, Ben-Porath, & Graham, 2002). The AGGR scale assesses offensive aggression and possibly the enjoyment of dominating, frightening, and controlling others, and the lack of regard for social rules and conventions. The PSYC scale assesses the cognitive ability of the individual to model the external, objective world in an accurate manner. Persons who are low on the PSYC construct can realize that their model is not working and accommodate or revise the model to fit their environment. Although the PSYC scale has its largest correlations with Scales 8 (Schizophrenia [Sc]: .78) and Bizarre Mentation (BIZ: .90), it appears to be measuring a general distress factor, much like the NEGE scale. The DISC scale assesses a dimension from rule following versus rule breaking and criminality. The DISC scale is not correlated to most of the other MMPI-2 scales and, thus, would appear to have the potential to contribute additional information when interpreting the MMPI-2. The largest correlations of the DISC scale are with Scales 9 (Hypomania [Ma]: .40), MacAndrew Alcoholism–Revised (MAC-R: .51), Addiction Admission (AAS: .52), and Antisocial Practices (ASP: .57). The NEGE scale assesses a broad affective disposition to experience negative emotions focusing on anxiety and nervousness. The NEGE scale is another of the numerous markers for the first factor of general distress and negative emotionality on the MMPI-2. The INTR construct assesses a broad disposition to experience negative affects and to avoid social experiences. Although the INTR scale generally has its largest correlations with MMPI-2 markers for the first factor, the INTR scale is a measure of anhedonia that is suggestive of rather serious psychopathology. Such an interpretation of the INTR scale is particularly likely when the NEGE scale is not elevated significantly.

The PSY-5 scales are another potential source of information for the clinician in interpreting the MMPI-2 profile. Research that demonstrates their usefulness in patients with personality disorder diagnoses is needed. Until such information is available clinicians are cautioned to interpret them very conservatively.

The MMPI-2 supplementary scales should be scored and interpreted routinely as a valuable source of additional information that is not readily available in the standard validity and clinical scales or the content scales. For example, the conjoint interpretation of the A and R scales provides a quick insight into how individuals are experiencing and coping with their psychopathology that brought them to treatment. In addition, the information on alcohol and drug use can only be inferred indirectly from the MMPI-2 clinical and content scales, while this information is available both directly and indirectly in the supplementary scales. The information provided by the supplementary scales is invaluable in the treatment-planning process.

References and Readings

Friedman, A. F., Lewak, R., Nichols, D. S., & Webb, J. T. (2001). *Psychological assessment with the MMPI-2*. Mahwah, NJ: Erlbaum.

Gottesman, I. I., & Prescott, C. A. (1989). Abuses of the MacAndrew MMPI alcoholism scale: A critical review. *Clinical Psychology Review, 9,* 223–242.

Graham, J. R. (2006). *MMPI-2: Assessing personality and psychopathology* (4th ed.). New York: Oxford University Press.

Greene, R. L. (2011). *The MMPI-2: An interpretive manual* (3rd ed.). Boston, MA: Allyn & Bacon.

Harkness, A. R., McNulty, J. L., Ben-Porath, Y. S., & Graham, J. R. (2002). *MMPI-2 Personality Psychopathology Five (PSY-5) scales: Gaining an overview for case conceptualization and treatment planning*. Minneapolis: University of Minnesota Press.

Malinchoc, M., Offord, K. P., Colligan, R. C, & Morse, R. M. (1994). The common alcohol logistic–revised scale (CAL-R): A revised alcoholism scale for the MMPI and MMPI-2. *Journal of Clinical Psychology, 50,* 436–445.

Weed, N. C., Butcher, J. N., & Ben-Porath, Y. S. (1995). MMPI-2 measures of substance abuse. In J. N. Butcher & C. D. Spielberger (Eds.), *Advances in personality assessment* (Vol. 10, pp. 121–145). Hillsdale, NJ: Erlbaum.

Related Topics

Chapter 21, "Assessing MMPI-2 Profile Validity"

Chapter 22, "Interpreting Clinical Scale Scores on the MMPI-2"

Chapter 24, "Understanding and Using the MMPI-2-RF"

24 UNDERSTANDING AND USING THE MMPI-2-RF

Yossef S. Ben-Porath

The MMPI-2-RF (Restructured From) is a 338-item self-report measure of personality and psychopathology. Its items are a subset of the 567-item MMPI-2. The MMPI-2-RF norms are based on the MMPI-2 normative sample. The test is intended, and has been validated, for use in mental health, medical, forensic, correctional, and personnel screening evaluations.

A need to revise and modernize the MMPI/MMPI-2 *Clinical Scales* has been recognized for several decades (c.f., Butcher, 1972). The primary challenges encountered when using these scales involved excessive correlations between them, which limited their discriminant validity, and substantial content heterogeneity within the scales, which limited their convergent validity. Alternative interpretive approaches, focusing on code types, subscales, and supplementary scales, were devised to provide ad hoc solutions to these challenges.

In the early 1990s, Professor Auke Tellegen, of the University of Minnesota, initiated a project designed to address the psychometric shortcomings of the Clinical Scales directly. This research produced the *MMPI-2 Restructured Clinical (RC) Scales* (Tellegen et al., 2003), which were added to the MMPI-2 as supplementary sources of information. The RC Scales also served as the starting point for developing a restructured version of the entire inventory, published in 2008 as the *MMPI-2 Restructured Form* (MMPI-2-RF; Ben-Porath & Tellegen, 2008/2011; Tellegen & Ben-Porath, 2008/2011).

THE MMPI-2-RF SCALES

The MMPI-2-RF is made up of 51 scales, listed and described briefly in Table 24.1. The scales are divided into the following six sets:

1. *Validity Scales.* Nine MMPI-2-RF scales are measures of protocol validity, designed to alert the interpreter to various threats to the validity of an individual test protocol. They include measures of inconsistent responding, overreporting, and underreporting, which constitute the major threats to the validity of self-report measures of personality and psychopathology.

   The remaining 42 "substantive" scales are divided into five sets and organized in a hierarchical framework.
2. *Higher Order Scales.* At the broadest level of measurement the three Higher Order (H-O) Scales, Emotional/Internalizing Dysfunction (EID), Thought Dysfunction (THD), and Behavioral/Externalizing Dysfunction (BXD), indicate, respectively, whether and to what extent a test taker is likely experiencing problems in the domains of mood, thought processes, and behavior.
3. *Restructured Clinical Scales.* At the second tier of measurement, the nine RC Scales, carried over identically from the MMPI-2, provide an indication of the individual's standing on the nine psychological constructs identified by Tellegen et al. (2003)

as major distinctive core components of the original MMPI Clinical Scales.

4. *Specific Problems Scales.* The most narrowly focused MMPI-2-RF measures are the 23 Specific Problems (SP) Scales, which are subdivided into indicators of somatic and cognitive complaints, internalizing difficulties, externalizing behaviors, and interpersonal functioning. Some SP Scales focus on facets of RC Scales; however, they are not subscales and can be interpreted regardless of the test taker's standing on higher level MMPI-2-RF measures.
5. *Interest Scales.* The two Interest Scales were derived from the original MMPI Masculinity/Femininity scale, which has long been recognized as having two distinctive dimensions labeled Aesthetic/Literary Interests and Mechanical/Physical Interests on the MMPI-2-RF. In clinical assessments, low scores on these scales are found in individuals who for reasons such as severe depression have lost interest in, and have become withdrawn from, their environment.
6. *Personality Psychopathology Five (PSY-5) Scales.* The MMPI-2-RF PSY-5 Scales are revised versions of similarly labeled MMPI-2 scales, designed to provide a dimensional perspective on features of personality pathology (i.e., Axis II). They are based on a model of personality psychopathology developed and introduced by Allan Harkness and John McNulty, who also revised the MMPI-2 versions of these scales for the MMPI-2-RF.

ADMINISTERING AND SCORING THE MMPI-2-RF

The MMPI-2-RF can be administered with a booklet and answer sheet or by computer. The former mode typically requires 35 to 50 minutes, whereas computer (or "on-screen") administration can typically be accomplished in 25 to 35 minutes. In addition to requiring less time, on-screen administration of the MMPI-2-RF has the advantage of having the test taker enter her or his responses directly into the scoring software that is available for the instrument.

The MMPI-2-RF can be scored by hand or by computer. The former requires the use of special answer sheets, scoring templates, and profiles for reporting the test results and typically takes an experienced user (or assistant) 25 to 30 minutes to accomplish. The primary advantage of hand scoring is that it costs less than computer scoring, although when taking into account the professional or clerical time required to score the 51 scales of the test, this apparent advantage is less consequential. The primary disadvantage of hand scoring is that it is an error-prone process.

Automated or computer scoring can be accomplished either with software installed on the user's computer or by mailing the answer sheet to the distributor. The latter has the disadvantages of a higher cost, requiring additional time for mailing back and forth with the distributor, and reducing the customization options available when the MMPI-2-RF is scored on the user's computer. When scoring the MMPI-2-RF locally by computer, users have the option to include any of the available *Comparison Groups* along with the test taker's results. Comparison group data printed in a report include means and standard deviations of the selected comparison group printed and plotted along with the test taker's results and item response frequencies reported for the selected comparison group. Available standard comparison groups include ones made up of individuals assessed in traditional mental health settings (outpatient and inpatient), a substance abuse treatment setting, medical settings (e.g., candidates for bariatric surgery or spine surgery/spinal cord implants), forensic evaluations (civil and criminal), a correctional setting, and several types of personnel screening assessments. Users who have at least 200 valid cases stored on their local system can create and incorporate MMPI-2-RF findings from custom comparison groups.

Two software-based reports are available for the MMPI-2-RF at this time. The *Score Report* includes all the scale scores as well as information about noteworthy item-level responses. The *Interpretive Report* includes all of the elements of the Score Report as well as a computer-generated interpretation

TABLE 24.1. The MMPI-2-RF Scales

Validity Scales
VRIN-r *Variable Response Inconsistency*—Random responding
TRIN-r *True Response Inconsistency*—Fixed responding
F-r *Infrequent Responses*—Responses infrequent in the general population
Fp-r *Infrequent Psychopathology Responses*—Responses infrequent in psychiatric populations
Fs *Infrequent Somatic Responses*—Somatic complaints infrequent in medical patient populations
FBS-r *Symptom Validity*—Somatic and cognitive complaints associated at high levels with overreporting
RBS *Response Bias Scale*—Exaggerated memory complaints
L-r *Uncommon Virtues*—Rarely claimed moral attributes or activities
K-r *Adjustment Validity*—Avowals of good psychological adjustment associated at high levels with underreporting

Higher-Order (H-O) Scales
EID *Emotional/Internalizing Dysfunction*—Problems associated with mood and affect
THD *Thought Dysfunction*—Problems associated with disordered thinking
BXD *Behavioral/Externalizing Dysfunction*—Problems associated with undercontrolled behavior

Restructured Clinical (RC) Scales
RCd *Demoralization*—General unhappiness and dissatisfaction
RC1 *Somatic Complaints*—Diffuse physical health complaints
RC2 *Low Positive Emotions*—Lack of positive emotional responsiveness
RC3 *Cynicism*—Non-self-referential beliefs expressing distrust and a generally low opinion of others
RC4 *Antisocial Behavior*—Rule breaking and irresponsible behavior
RC6 *Ideas of Persecution*—Self-referential beliefs that others pose a threat
RC7 *Dysfunctional Negative Emotions*—Maladaptive anxiety, anger, irritability
RC8 *Aberrant Experiences*—Unusual perceptions or thoughts
RC9 *Hypomanic Activation*—Overactivation, aggression, impulsivity, and grandiosity

Specific Problems (SP) Scales
Somatic/Cognitive Scales
MLS *Malaise*—Overall sense of physical debilitation, poor health
GIC *Gastrointestinal Complaints*—Nausea, recurring upset stomach, and poor appetite
HPC *Head Pain Complaints*—Head and neck pain
NUC *Neurological Complaints*—Dizziness, weakness, paralysis, loss of balance, etc.
COG *Cognitive Complaints*—Memory problems, difficulties concentrating

Internalizing Scales
SUI *Suicidal/Death Ideation*—Direct reports of suicidal ideation and recent suicide attempts
HLP *Helplessness/Hopelessness*—Belief that goals cannot be reached or problems solved
SFD *Self-Doubt*—Lack of confidence, feelings of uselessness
NFC *Inefficacy*—Belief that one is indecisive and inefficacious
STW *Stress/Worry*—Preoccupation with disappointments, difficulty with time pressure
AXY *Anxiety*—Pervasive anxiety, frights, frequent nightmares
ANP *Anger Proneness*—Becoming easily angered, impatient with others
BRF *Behavior-Restricting Fears*—Fears that significantly inhibit normal activities
MSF *Multiple Specific Fears*—Fears of blood, fire, thunder, etc.

Externalizing Scales
JCP *Juvenile Conduct Problems*—Difficulties at school and at home, stealing
SUB *Substance Abuse*—Current and past misuse of alcohol and drugs
AGG *Aggression*—Physically aggressive, violent behavior
ACT *Activation*—Heightened excitation and energy level

Interpersonal Scales
FML *Family Problems*—Conflictual family relationships
IPP *Interpersonal Passivity*—Being unassertive and submissive
SAV *Social Avoidance*—Avoiding or not enjoying social events
SHY *Shyness*—Bashful, prone to feel inhibited and anxious around others
DSF *Disaffiliativeness*—Disliking people and being around them

Interest Scales
AES *Aesthetic-Literary Interests*—Literature, music, the theater
MEC *Mechanical-Physical Interests*—Fixing and building things, the outdoors, sports

Personality Psychopathology Five (PSY-5) Scales
AGGR-r *Aggressiveness-Revised*—Instrumental, goal-directed aggression
PSYC-r *Psychoticism-Revised*—Disconnection from reality
DISC-r *Disconstraint-Revised*—Undercontrolled behavior
NEGE-r *Negative Emotionality/Neuroticism-Revised*—Anxiety, insecurity, worry, and fear
INTR-r *Introversion/Low Positive Emotionality-Revised*—Social disengagement and anhedonia

of the results. All statements included in the interpretive report are annotated, indicating which scale(s) generated them, whether they are based on empirical correlates, test responses (i.e., item content), or are inferences of the report authors. For statements identified as being based on empirical correlates, references are provided to the literature where the empirical data supporting them can be found. Ben-Porath and Tellegen (2011) provide detailed descriptions of the two software-based MMPI-2-RF reports as well as instructions on how to interface with the software to generate customized reports.

INTERPRETING THE MMPI-2-RF

Ben-Porath and Tellegen (2008/2011) provide detailed interpretive guidelines for the MMPI-2-RF. Users who follow these guidelines should generate reasonably similar interpretations of the same test protocol, a feature of the test that is particularly helpful in forensic assessments and other types of evaluations where inter-interpreter agreement is important.

The guidelines include a recommended structure for organizing an MMPI-2-RF interpretation and interpretive recommendations of each of the 51 scales of the inventory. For the nine validity indicators the guidelines indicate the types of threats suggested at different score levels, possible reasons why a test taker may score at that level, and the implications for interpreting the protocol. In some cases, the guidelines indicate that the test protocol is invalid and uninterruptable. In other cases, the guidelines raise concerns about the possible impact of inconsistent responding, overreporting, or underreporting on the interpretability of scores on the substantive scales of the test.

In cases where the validity scale scores indicate that the protocol is interpretable, the guidelines call for organizing an interpretation of scores on the substantive following a structure anchored by the H-O scales. A process for generating the interpretive statements is described, and for each scale, both content-based statements and statements linked to empirical correlates are identified. The latter are based on empirical findings reported in the *MMPI-2-RF Technical Manual* (Tellegen & Ben-Porath, 2008/2011) and a growing body of publications that can be found at the publisher's Web site (see University of Minnesota Press under *For More Information* at the end of this chapter). For most of the substantive scales, the interpretive guidelines include diagnostic and treatment considerations. Additional guidance on how to interpret scores on the MMPI-2-RF is provided by Ben-Porath (2012) and Graham (2011).

APPLICATIONS OF THE MMPI-2-RF

In mental health settings the MMPI-2-RF is used primarily in differential diagnostic and treatment planning evaluations. Examples of use of the inventory in medical settings include presurgical assessments of candidates for weight-loss surgery, spine surgery, or spinal cord stimulator implants. In forensic settings the test is used in both criminal and civil proceedings, in cases where the individual's psychological functioning is at issue. In the correctional system the instrument is used at intake to identify mental health needs, during the course of an inmate's incarceration on a referral basis, and, in some jurisdictions, prerelease as part of the re-entry planning process. In personnel screening evaluations the MMPI-2-RF is used to assess candidates for public safety and other high-risk positions (e.g., clergy candidates) as part of an assessment designed to screen out individuals who are psychologically unfit for these positions.

AUTHOR'S NOTE

The author is a paid consultant to the MMPI-2-RF publisher, the University of Minnesota, and distributor, Pearson, and as co-author of the test he receives royalties on MMPI-2-RF sales.

References and Readings

Ben-Porath, Y. S. (2012). *Interpreting the MMPI-2-RF*. Minneapolis: University of Minnesota Press.

Ben-Porath, Y. S., & Tellegen, A. (2008/2011). *MMPI-2-RF (Minnesota Multiphasic Personality Inventory-2 Restructured Form): Manual for administration, scoring, and interpretation*. Minneapolis: University of Minnesota Press.

Ben-Porath, Y. S., & Tellegen, A. (2011). *MMPI-2-RF (Minnesota Multiphasic Personality Inventory-2 Restructured Form): User's guide for reports* (2nd ed.). Minneapolis: University of Minnesota Press.

Butcher, J. N. (1972). *Objective personality assessment: Changing perspectives*. Oxford, England: Academic Press.

Graham, J. R. (2011). *MMPI-2: Assessing personality and psychopathology* (5th ed.). New York: Oxford University Press.

Tellegen, A., & Ben-Porath, Y. S. (2008/2011). *MMPI-2-RF (Minnesota Multiphasic Personality Inventory-2 restructured form): Technical manual*. Minneapolis: University of Minnesota Press.

Tellegen, A., Ben-Porath, Y. S., McNulty, J. L., Arbisi, P. A., Graham, J. R., & Kaemmer, B. (2003). *MMPI-2 restructured clinical (RC) scales: Development, validation, and interpretation*. Minneapolis: University of Minnesota Press.

University of Minnesota Press. (2012). *MMPI-2-References*. Retrieved January 2013, from www.upress.umn.edu/test-division/MMPI-2-RF/mmpi-2-rf-references

Related Topics

Chapter 21, "Assessing MMPI-2 Profile Validity"

Chapter 22, "Interpreting Clinical Scale Scores on the MMPI-2"

Chapter 23, "Interpreting Supplementary Scales of the MMPI-2"

25 INTERPRETING THE FAMILY OF MILLON CLINICAL INVENTORIES

Seth Grossman and Theodore Millon

Psychological instruments are particularly informative when generated via a comprehensive theory of personality or psychopathology and coordinated with the official diagnostic system (*Diagnostic and Statistical Manual of Mental Disorders* [*DSM*]). All of the instruments of the Millon Inventories are theory based and provide a contextual view not only of both Axis I and Axis II but also of treatment-oriented trait domains. In this chapter, we present an overview of this family of instruments, beginning with the Millon Clinical Multiaxial Inventory-III (MCMI-III), the most established of the instruments; its primary personality scales provide a template for interpreting the other instruments. We then provide a brief overview of the four other clinically oriented Millon Inventories: Millon Adolescent Clinical Inventory (MACI), Millon Pre-Adolescent Inventory (M-PACI),

TABLE 25.1. A Cross-Comparison of Millon Inventories Personality Scales

Scale	MCMI-III	MACI	MCCI	MBMD	M-PACI*
1	Schizoid	Introversive	Introversive	Introversive	—
2A	Avoidant	Inhibited	Inhibited	Inhibited	(5) Inhibited
2B	Depressive	Doleful	Dejected	Dejected	—
3	Dependent	Submissive	Needy	Cooperative	(4) Submissive
4	Histrionic	Dramatizing	Sociable	Sociable	(2) Outgoing
5	Narcissistic	Egotistic	Confident	Confident	(1) Confident
6A	Antisocial	Unruly	Unruly	Nonconforming	(6) Unruly
6B	Sadistic	Forceful	—	Forceful	—
7	Compulsive	Conforming	Conscientious	Respectful	(3) Conforming
8A	Negativistic	Oppositional	Oppositional	Oppositional	—
8B	Masochistic	Self-demeaning	Denigrated	Denigrated	—
S	Schizotypal	—	—	—	—
C (9)	Borderline	Borderline tendency	Borderline	—	(7) Unstable
P	Paranoid	—	—	—	—

*The M-PACI Emerging Personality Pattern Scales follow a different numbering sequence in order to group together adaptive versus maladaptive patterns.

Millon Behavioral Medicine Diagnostic (MBMD), and Millon College Counseling Inventory (MCCI).

Table 25.1 summarizes the hallmark personality scales of each of the Millon Clinical Inventories. Following next is a list of the traits characterizing the prototypal personality scales.

MILLON PERSONALITY SCALE CHARACTERISTICS

Fourteen personality scales are utilized in the Millon Inventories (MCMI-III is the only instrument that utilizes all of the personality scales). These are based on a theoretical schema that parallels the *DSM-IV*; revisions in line with the *DSM-5* are currently under way.

- ***Scale 1.*** *Introversive/Schizoid.* This scale typifies persons who are unemotional, apathetic, listless, distant, and asocial. Affectionate needs and feelings are minimal. They are deficient in the capacity to experience both joy and sadness. They do not avoid others but are indifferent to the possibilities inherent in social relationships.
- ***Scale 2A.*** *Inhibited/Avoidant.* High scorers on this scale are shy and ill at ease with others. They would like to be close to others, but they have learned that it is better to keep their distance. Although they often feel lonely, they avoid close interpersonal contact, fearing rejection and humiliation.
- ***Scale 2B.*** *Dejected/Depressive.* These individuals characteristically exhibit a doleful and gloomy mood, perhaps since childhood. Their outlook on life is brooding and pessimistic. Most are prone to feelings of guilt and remorse, viewing themselves as inadequate or even worthless.
- ***Scale 3.*** *Submissive/Dependent.* High scorers on this scale show a softheartedness, sentimentality, and kindliness in relationships with others. Reluctant to assert themselves, they avoid taking initiative or assuming leadership roles. Many exhibit clinging behavior and fear separation, typically downplaying their achievements and underestimating their abilities.
- ***Scale 4.*** *Sociable/Histrionic.* High scorers on this scale tend to be talkative, charming, and frequently exhibitionistic and emotionally expressive. They seek stimulating experiences and excitement, often and usually are bored with routine and long-standing relationships.
- ***Scale 5.*** *Confident/Narcissistic.* These persons appear self-assured and confident in their abilities and are often seen by others as self-centered and egocentric. They take

others for granted, are often arrogant and exploitive, and do not concern themselves with the needs of others.

- ***Scale 6A.*** *Unruly/Antisocial.* This pattern is typified by impulsivity and a disregard for societal norms, often resisting culturally acceptable standards of behavior. Some display a pervasively rebellious attitude that brings them into conflict with legal authorities.
- ***Scale 6.*** *Forceful/Sadistic.* High scorers on this scale are strong willed and tough minded, tending to dominate and abuse others. They are often blunt and unkind, tending to be impatient with the problems or weaknesses of others.
- ***Scale 7.*** *Respectful/Compulsive.* These persons are serious minded, efficient, conforming, respectful, and rule conscious. They try to do the "right" and "proper" things, tending to keep their emotions in check and are overcontrolled and tense, preferring to live their lives in an orderly and well-planned fashion.
- ***Scale 8A.*** *Oppositional/Negativistic.* High scorers tend to be discontented, sullen, and passive-aggressive. They may be pleasant one moment but become hostile and irritable the next. They are often confused and contrite about their moodiness but are unable to control their labile emotions.
- ***Scale 8.*** *Denigrated/Masochistic.* These persons tend to be their own worst enemies, acting in self-defeating ways, at times seeming content to suffer. Many undermine others' efforts to help them, often denying themselves pleasure and sabotaging their own efforts at success.
- ***Scale S.*** *Eccentric/Schizotypal.* Persons matching this prototype appear odd, peculiar, and disconnected from their environment. Some act aloof and withdrawn evincing "magical" thinking; others appear anxiously fretful, responding primarily to troubling internal thoughts.
- ***Scale C or 9.*** *Unstable/Borderline.* High scorers on this scale are conflicted and ambivalent, exhibit marked affective instabilities, erratic interpersonal relationships, behavioral capriciousness, impulsive hostility, have a fear of abandonment, and engage in self-destructive actions.
- ***Scale P.*** *Suspicious/Paranoid.* These persons tend to be extremely guarded, disposed to see only the ill will of others. They tend to be querulous, immovable in their thoughts, and vigilant in their actions.

Most of these prototypal scales and their variants appear on each of the inventories; they serve as a contextual lens through which all other scales should be viewed. The configuration of these personality scales provides clinical depth in efforts to understand Axis I disorders and symptomatology (MCMI, MACI, MCCI), the health issues of medical patients (MBMD), and the expressed concerns of youngsters (MACI, M-PACI, MCCI).

All Millon Inventories use actuarial base rate (BR) score transformations. BR scores are calculated to reflect the actual patient frequency of a particular disorder (rather than equalizing them as done with conventional T scores). Thus, more patients will get a high score on a depression scale than on a sadistic scale because more patients are depressed than they are sadistic. These not only provide a basis for selecting optimal diagnostic cutting lines but also help ensure that the frequencies of scale-generated diagnoses coincide with actual patient prevalence rates.

MILLON CLINICAL MULTIAXIAL INVENTORY (MCMI-III)

The MCMI-III (Millon, Millon, Davis, & Grossman, 2009) is an adult clinical personality and psychopathology measure consisting of 14 of the prototypal *DSM-III*, *DSM-III-R*, and *DSM-IV* personality categories, 42 personality facet scales, 10 *DSM* clinical syndrome categories, and 5 modifier scales.

The *first section* of the inventory comprises five modifying indices (V: Validity, W: Inconsistency, X: Disclosure, Y: Desirability, and Z: Debasement); these identify distorting tendencies in clients' responses and are used to gauge not only overall validity but to inform the clinician as to the patient's style of approaching the test, for example, overcomplaining, self-protective. The next *two* sections constitute the 14 personality scales. The first of these sections (1–8B) appraises the moderately severe personality pathologies, ranging from the Schizoid to the Self-Defeating (Masochistic) scales; the second section (scales S, C, and P) represents the most severe personality pathologies: the Schizotypal, Borderline, and Paranoid. The final two sections cover a broad spectrum of Axis I disorders, ranging from the moderate clinical syndromes (e.g., anxiety, dysthymia, alcohol, drug abuse) to those of greater severity (e.g., thought disorder, major depression) The division between personality and clinical disorder scales parallels the original *DSM-III* multiaxial model and has important interpretive implications.

Following the main profile page of the MCMI-III are two pages covering the 42 Grossman Facet Scales. These scales represent a trait-oriented breakdown of the primary personality scales (1–8B and S, C, P) along theoretically derived and treatment-guiding purposes. Each primary personality scale is broken down into three subscales, each representing the three most salient personality facets of the possible eight personality domains that characterize each personality pattern (Millon, 2011). The eight domains are Expressive Acts, Interpersonal Conduct, Self-Image, Cognitive Style, Intrapsychic Content, Intrapsychic Dynamics, Intrapsychic Architecture, and Mood/Temperament. These treatment-guiding domains also correspond to the major classes of psychotherapies (cognitive-behavioral therapy, interpersonal, psychodynamic, etc.). A similar set of facet scales are also to be found on the Millon Adolescent Clinical Inventory (MACI).

A principal goal in constructing the MCMI-III was to keep the total number of items small enough to encourage use in diverse diagnostic and treatment settings yet large enough to permit the assessment of a wide range of clinically relevant behaviors. At 175 items, the final form is shorter than comparable instruments. Potentially objectionable items were screened out, and terminology was geared to an eighth-grade reading level. Most clients can complete the MCMI-III in 20–30 minutes, thereby minimizing fatigue and resistance. Answer choices (true and false) are printed next to each of the 175 item statements on the paper/pencil forms; items appear individually on the screen in computer administration.

Clinicians interpreting the MCMI-III should bear in mind that the richness and accuracy of all self-report measures are enhanced when their findings are viewed in the context of other clinical sources and data, such as demographic background, biographical history, and other clinical features. The personality traits and clinical features characterizing each scale should be briefly reviewed before analyzing profile configurations. Configural interpretation is a deductive synthesis achieved by refining, blending, and integrating the separate characteristics tapped by each scale and enhanced by a greater understanding and application of the underlying theory. The accuracy of such interpretations further depends on the meaning and significance of the individual scales composing the profile, rather than simply labeling patients and fitting them into procrustean diagnostic categories.

A basic separation should be made in the initial phase of interpretation between those scales pertaining to the basic clinical personality pattern (1–8B), those pointing to the presence of severe Axis II personality pathology (S, C, and P), those signifying moderate Axis I clinical syndromes (A–R), and those indicating a severe clinical state (SS, CC, and PP). Interpreting clinicians should progress by dividing the profile into a series of subsections, focusing initially on the significant scale elevations and profile patterns within each section. Once this is completed, the clinician can proceed to integrate each subsection. Retzlaff (1995) suggests the following stepwise approach with each section building on the prior: Modifying Indices, Severe Personality Pathology, Clinical Personality Patterns, Severe Syndromes, and Clinical Syndromes.

Many psychologists use the computer program (available from PsychCorp/Pearson Assessments) that administers the test and then generates MCMI-III profile scores and interpretive narratives, integrating both the personologic and symptomatic features of the patient. Interpretives are drawn from both scale score elevations and profile configurations, and are based both on actuarial research findings and the MCMI-III's theoretical schema, as well as the current *DSM-IV* and in the forthcoming *DSM-5*. The Interpretive Report employs a multiaxial framework and summarizes findings along its several axes: Clinical Syndrome, Personality Disorder, Psychosocial Stressors, and Therapeutic Implications.

Research on the judged validity of the reports indicate that they are appraised highly accurate in about 55%–65% of all cases; are considered as both useful and clinically informative in about another 25%–30% of cases; and seem off target or appreciably in error about 10%–15% of the time. These positive figures are 7–8 times greater than are random diagnostic assignments or chance (Millon, Millon, Davis, & Grossman, 2009). The MCMI-III is appropriate for use in a variety of inpatient and outpatient settings, as well as in forensic applications and correctional institutions (for which it has a separate normative group and interpretive report). It is not, however, a general personality instrument to be used for "normal" populations, for which the MIPS inventory would be most appropriate.

MILLON ADOLESCENT CLINICAL INVENTORY (MACI)

The MACI (Millon, Millon, Davis, & Grossman, 2006) is a 160-item, 31-scale, self-report inventory designed specifically to assess clinically troubled and/or justice-involved adolescents, their personalities, areas of concern, as well as current Axis I clinical syndromes. The Expressed Concerns scales of the MACI assess teenagers' attitudes regarding significant developmental problems, while the Personality and Clinical Syndromes scales reflect significant areas of pathological feelings and thoughts, as well as problematic behaviors that require professional attention.

Twelve of the fourteen personality prototypes of the MCMI are included in the MACI; Schizotypal and Paranoid scales are not represented; "Borderline Tendency" is included to represent early signs of borderline personality disorder. Seven clinical scales, ranging from Eating Dysfunction to Suicidal Tendency, capture important Axis I issues. The MACI also includes eight Expressed Concerns scales in which troubled adolescents can report problematic concerns of life (e.g., peer security, family discord, childhood abuse).

The MACI was constructed with four distinct adolescent normative groups divided by age and gender. The instrument can be completed by most adolescents in approximately 20 minutes. Configural interpretation of the MACI is essentially similar to that of the MCMI-III, proceeding from single-scale to configural syntheses, with appropriate integration of auxiliary data and background from aforementioned theoretical and empirical publications. Computerized administration/scoring and interpretation are available from Pearson/PsychCorp.

MILLON PREADOLESCENT CLINICAL INVENTORY (M-PACI)

Experience with the MACI, and a need expressed by many users for a similar multidimensional self-report measure of the challenges of 9- to 12-year-olds, led to the decision to develop the M-PACI (Millon, Tringone, Millon, & Grossman, 2005). This new inventory consists of 97 true/false items that generate 14 clinical scales across two diagnostic sets: Emerging Personality Patterns and Current Clinical Signs, as well as two response validity indicators; all test items were written at a third-grade reading level. Scale results are reported as a BR score to reflect the relative prevalence of the characteristics they measure. (It should be noted that the M-PACI utilizes a personality scale numbering system that is slightly different from the other Millon Inventories.) The inventory was kept to under 100 items, so that most 9- to 12-year-olds could complete the M-PACI in 20 minutes or less.

The M-PACI is adept at capturing a broad range of psychological concerns that are common among 9- to 12-year-olds. It may be used in many clinical, justice, and educational settings, inclusive of inpatient and outpatient facilities, as well as independent practices and school settings. As with other Millon Inventories, personality-oriented and syndrome-driven scales are printed on a single profile page in order to highlight the interaction and relatedness of the person and his or her symptomatology; expressions of anxiety or depression, for example, will be interpreted differently for different emerging personalities. Administration, scoring, and interpreting the M-PACI inventory can be beneficial at many points during the assessment and treatment process: as part of the initial clinical assessment, to gauge progress and reevaluate issues during the course of treatment, and as a treatment outcome measure.

MILLON BEHAVIORAL MEDICINE DIAGNOSTIC (MBMD)

The MBMD (Millon, Antoni, Millon, Minor, & Grossman, 2006) was developed to provide health care personnel with psychological information useful to treat the "whole patient." It is a 165-item, self-report inventory with 29 clinical scales (e.g., Coping Style and Stress Moderator sections), three response pattern scales, one validity indicator, and six Negative Health Habits indicators (e.g., smoking, drug use). It is designed to assess psychological factors that can influence the course of treatment for medical patients. For example, the Coping Style Indicator section may be seen as adaptive-range variants of Axis II personality patterns; the Psychiatric Indications section covers similar constructs as the Clinical Syndromes (Axis I sections) on other Millon Inventories. Much as Axis I and II are best understood in context; so, too, are section domains such as Treatment Prognostics (e.g., Medication abuse and Problematic compliance).

The MBMD seeks to understand the attitudes, behavior, and concerns of medical patients, especially those in which psychosocial factors may play a role in the course of the disease and treatment outcome. Many studies at diverse hospital settings (Millon & Bloom, 2008) have shown that patients who are assessed via the MBMD and who receive behavioral interventions require fewer medical services than those who do not; furthermore, integrating behavioral assessment and treatment into a patient's care significantly reduces health care costs and ultimately enhances patient work productivity, adherence to regimens, and receptivity and response to treatment.

In addition to the hallmark sections of the Millon Inventories Reports, the MBMD Interpretive Report adds a one-page Healthcare Provider Summary containing the essential assessment findings and treatment recommendations for health care providers other than clinically sophisticated psychologists. Notable also are interpretive checklists for *special normative comparison medical populations*, those scheduled for *Bariatric Surgery*, and those planned for two variants of *Pain Treatment*.

MILLON COLLEGE COUNSELING INVENTORY (MCCI)

The MCCI (Millon, Strack, Millon, & Grossman, 2006) is a multidimensional self-report inventory designed to serve the staff of college counseling centers that are increasingly overwhelmed with more troubled students than ever (e.g., more students with learning disabilities, pharmacologic history, and serious psychological disorders).

The MCCI consists of 150 items and has 32 profile scales grouped into three sets similar to the MACI: Personality Styles (e.g., dejected, needy, oppositional), Expressed Concerns (e.g., peer alienation, financial burdens, spiritual doubts), and Clinical Signs (e.g., suicidal tendencies, eating disorders, drug abuse). Scores on these scales are reported as BR scores scaled to reflect the relative prevalence of the characteristics they measure. In addition to the clinical scales, there are four Response Tendencies scales, similar to most Millon Inventories, as well as numerous Noteworthy Response measures.

The MCCI, like all Millon Inventories, provides a comprehensive coverage of diverse college students' psychological issues.

Furthermore, the MCCI extends beyond the most prevalent psychological symptoms in college students and contextualizes their relationships within the person, his or her symptoms, and his or her current reported concerns. As with all Millon inventories, the MCCI can furnish the college counselor with a quick computer-based interpretive report.

The MCCI was normed only on students who have sought therapy at college counseling centers. Those who experience or display severe levels of distress are often referred elsewhere. These realities are reflected in the instrument's scales; thus, one of the basic personality patterns (6B: Aggressive/Sadistic), as well as two of the more severe personality variants (S: Schizotypal, and P: Paranoid) are not represented in the development norm groups and hence are not included in the MCCI.

References and Readings

Millon, T. (2011). *Disorders of personality: Introducing a DSM/ICD spectrum from normal to abnormal* (3rd ed.). Hoboken, NJ: Wiley.

Millon, T., Antoni, M., Millon, C., Minor, S., & Grossman, S. (2006). *Millon behavioral medicine diagnostic manual*. Minneapolis, MN: Pearson Assessments.

Millon, T., & Bloom, C. (Eds.). (2008). *The Millon inventories: A practitioner's guide to personalized clinical assessment*. New York: Guilford Press.

Millon, T., & Grossman, S.D. (2007). *Resolving difficult clinical syndromes: A personalized psychotherapy approach*. Hoboken, NJ: Wiley.

Millon, T., Grossman, S. D., Millon, C., Meagher, S., & Ramnath, R. D. (2004). *Personality disorders in modern life* (2nd ed.). Hoboken, NJ: Wiley.

Millon, T., Millon, C., Davis, R. D., & Grossman, S. D. (2006). *Millon adolescent clinical inventory manual*. Minneapolis, MN: Pearson Assessments.

Millon, T., Millon, C., Davis, R. D., & Grossman, S. D. (2009). *Millon clinical multiaxial inventory-III manual*. Minneapolis, MN: Pearson Assessments.

Millon, T., Strack, S., Millon, C., & Grossman, S.D. (2006). *Millon college counseling inventory manual*. Minneapolis, MN: Pearson Assessments.

Millon, T., Tringone, R., Millon, C., & Grossman, S. D. (2005). *Millon pre-adolescent clinical inventory manual*. Minneapolis, MN: Pearson Assessments.

Retzlaff, P. (Ed.). (1995). *Tactical psychotherapy of the personality disorders: An MCMI-III based approach*. Boston: Allyn & Bacon.

Related Topics

Chapter 29, "Assessing the Quality of a Psychological Testing Report"

26 INTERPRETING TEST SCORES AND THEIR PERCENTILE EQUIVALENTS

Thomas P. Hogan

Interpretation of psychological and educational tests typically depends on the use of converted or normed scores. This entry defines types of scores commonly used for such interpretation. Figure 26.1 and Table 26.1 show the relationships among many of these normed scores. Figure 26.1 illustrates the equivalence of the various scores based on the normal curve. The figure has insufficient resolution for making conversions among

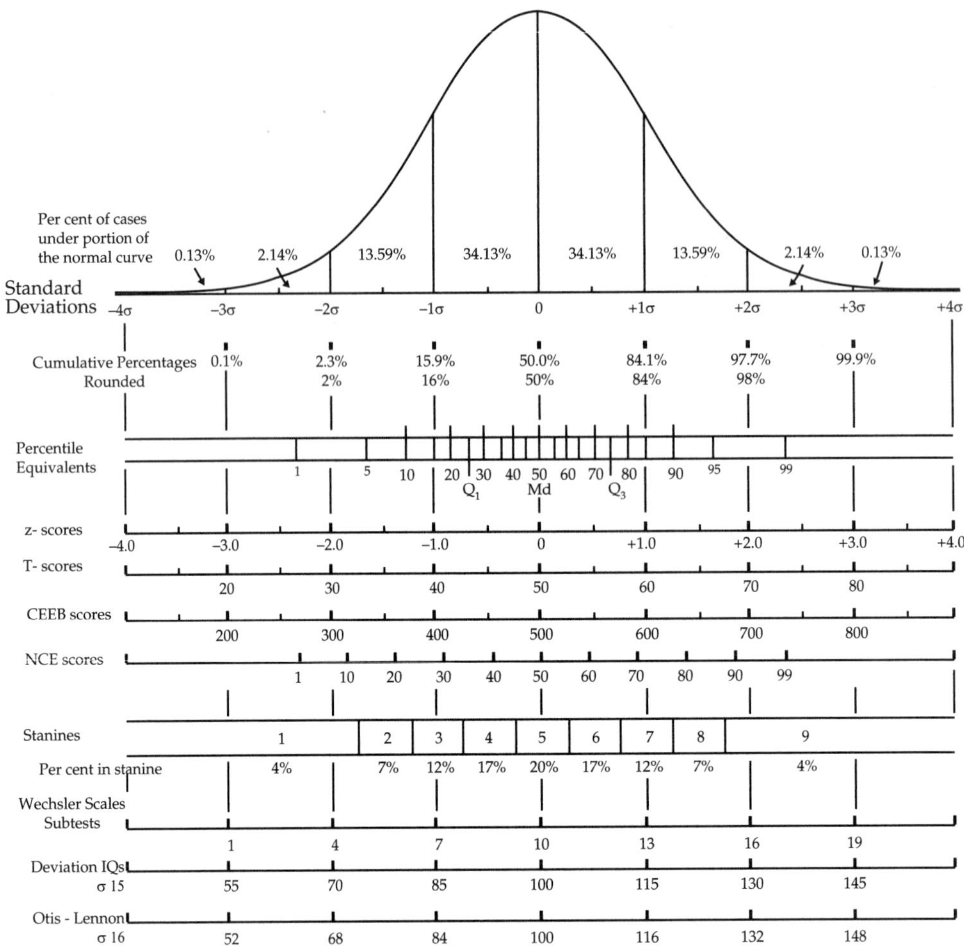

FIGURE 26.1. Equivalence of several types of norms in the normal curve. (Reprinted by permission of the Psychological Corporation from Seashore, n.d.)

the scores for practical or clinical purposes. However, Table 26.1 allows for such conversions. The table is constructed with percentile ranks as the reference columns on the left and right. The body of the table shows conversions to several types of scores, each of which is defined in the following text. Slightly different values might be entered for any particular percentile depending on how one rounds the entries or reads up or down for points covering multiple scores. This is particularly true at the extremes of the distribution.

Figure 26.1 and Table 26.1 treat the equivalence of different score modes, not the equivalence of different standardization groups. Scores from tests standardized on different groups cannot be equated simply by using the equivalencies illustrated here. It should also be noted that some tests may have independently determined norms for two different score modes (e.g., in standard scores and in percentiles); if the norms are independently determined, they will not correspond exactly with the equivalencies given here. For example, SAT uses a standard score system fixed at one point in time but also provides percentile systems that change from year to year, yielding the anomalous situation where a standard score of 500 may correspond to the 60th percentile.

TABLE 26.1. Percentile Equivalents of Several Standard Score Systems

Percentile	Stanine	NCE	IQ (15)	W Sub	T Score	SAT	Z Score	Percentile
99	9	99	133	17	73	730	2.33	99
98	9	93	130	16	70	700	2.05	98
97	9	90	129		69	690	1.88	97
96	9	87	127		68	680	1.75	96
95	8	85	125	15	66	660	1.65	95
94	8	83	123				1.56	94
93	8	81	122		65	650	1.48	93
92	8	80	121		64	640	1.40	92
91	8	78	120				1.34	91
90	8	77	119	14	63	630	1.28	90
89	8	76					1.23	89
88	7	75	118		62	620	1.18	88
87	7	74	117				1.13	87
86	7	73	116		61	610	1.08	86
85	7	72					1.04	85
84	7	71	115	13	60	600	.99	84
83	7	70					.95	83
82	7	69	114		59	590	.92	82
81	7	68	113				.88	81
80	7	68					.84	80
79	7	67	112		58	580	.81	79
78	7	66					.77	78
77	7	66	111				.74	77
76	6	65			57	570	.71	76
75	6	64	110	12			.67	75
74	6	64					.64	74
73	6	63	109		56	560	.61	73
72	6	62					.58	72
71	6	62					.55	71
70	6	61	108				.52	70
69	6	60			55	550	.50	69
68	6	60	107				.47	68
67	6	59					.44	67
66	6	59	106		54	540	.41	66
65	6	58					.38	65
64	6	58					.36	64
63	6	57	105	11			.33	63
62	6	56			53	530	.31	62
61	6	56	104				.28	61
60	6	55					.25	60
59	5	55					.23	59
58	5	54	103		52	520	.20	58
57	5	54					.18	57
56	5	53					.15	56
55	5	53	102				.13	55
54	5	52			51	510	.10	54
53	5	52	101				.08	53
52	5	51					.05	52
51	5	50					.02	51
50	5	50	100	10	50	500	.00	50
49	5	50					−.02	49
48	5	49					−.05	48
47	5	48	99				−.08	47
46	5	48			49	490	−.10	46
45	5	47	98				−.13	45

(continued)

TABLE 26.1. Percentile Equivalents of Several Standard Score Systems (*continued*)

Percentile	Stanine	NCE	IQ (15)	W Sub	T Score	SAT	Z Score	Percentile
44	5	47					–.15	44
43	5	46					–.18	43
42	5	46	97		48	480	–.20	42
41	5	45					–.23	41
40	5	45					–.25	40
39	4	44	96				–.28	39
38	4	44			47	470	–.31	38
37	4	43	95				–.33	37
36	4	42					–.36	36
35	4	42					–.38	35
34	4	41	94		46	460	–.41	34
33	4	41					–.44	33
32	4	40	93				–.47	32
31	4	40			45	450	–.50	31
30	4	39	92				–.52	30
29	4	38					–.55	29
28	4	38					–.58	28
27	4	37	91		44	440	–.61	27
26	4	36					–.64	26
25	4	36	90	8			–.67	25
24	4	35			43	430	–.71	24
23	4	34	89				–.74	23
22	3	34					–.77	22
21	3	33	88		42	420	–.81	21
20	3	32					–.84	20
19	3	32	87				–.88	19
18	3	31	86		41	410	–.92	18
17	3	30					–.95	17
16	3	29	85	7	40	400	–.99	16
15	3	28					–1.04	15
14	3	27	84		39	390	–1.08	14
13	3	26	83				–1.13	13
12	3	25	82		38	380	–1.18	12
11	3	24					–1.23	11
10	2	23	81	6	37	370	–1.28	10
9	2	22	80				–1.34	9
8	2	20	79		36	360	–1.40	8
7	2	19	78		35	650	–1.48	7
6	2	17	77				–1.56	6
5	2	15	76	5	34	340	–1.65	5
4	2	13	74		32	320	–1.75	4
3	1	10	72		31	310	–1.88	3
2	1	7	70	4	29	290	–2.05	2
1	1	1	67	3	27	270	–2.33	1

Notes: IQ (15) is for IQ tests with $M = 100$ and $SD = 15$, such as Wechsler Index scores and Full Scale IQ. W Sub is for Wechsler subtests and Stanford-Binet (5th ed.) subtests, where $M = 10$ and $SD = 3$. SAT covers any of the several tests that use $M = 500$ and $SD = 100$; these scores are usually reported to two significant digits (i.e., with the farthest right digit always 0), and that is how they are presented here.

STANDARD SCORES

Standard scores constitute one of the most frequently used types of norms. Standard scores convert raw scores into a system with an arbitrarily chosen mean and standard deviation. Although the standard score mean and standard deviation are "arbitrarily" chosen, they are selected to yield round numbers such as 50 and 10 or 500 and 100.

Standard scores may be either linear or nonlinear transformations of the raw scores.

It will usually not be apparent from a table of standard score norms whether they are linear or nonlinear; the test manual (or publisher) must be consulted for this purpose. Nonlinear transformations are used either to yield normal distributions or to approximate an equal interval scale (as in Thurstone scaling). When used for this latter purpose, particularly in connection with multilevel tests, the standard scores are sometimes called *scaled scores*, and they usually do not have a readily interpretable framework.

COMMON STANDARD SCORE SYSTEMS

The following are commonly used standard score systems. In these descriptions, *M* = mean and *SD* = standard deviation.

IQs. The IQ scores on most contemporary intelligence tests are standard scores with *M* = 100 and *SD* = 15, based on age groupings in the standardization sample. One needs to verify in a test manual the SD used since a few tests still use *SD* = 16.

T scores. T scores (sometimes called McCall's T scores) are standard scores with *M* = 50 and *SD* = 10. *T* scores are frequently used with personality tests, such as the MMPI-2 and NEO PI.

Wechsler subtests. Wechsler subtests use standard scores with *M* = 10 and *SD* = 3.

SAT scores. The SAT I (formerly, Scholastic Assessment Test) Critical Reading (formerly Verbal), Mathematics, and Writing Tests; the SAT II (subject tests); and the Graduate Management Admissions Tests (GMAT) all use standard score systems with *M* = 500 and *SD* = 100. In determining total scores for these tests (e.g., SAT Total), means are additive but *SD*s are not. Hence, the mean for SAT Total (Critical Reading + Mathematics + Writing) is 1500, but the *SD* is not 300; it is less than 300, since the tests being added are not perfectly correlated. Up until August 2011, the Graduate Record Examination (GRE) Verbal and Quantitative scores also used the *M* = 500, *SD* = 100 scale, but after that date these tests adopted a standard score scale ranging from 130 to 170.

Stanford-Binet, fifth edition (SB5). The fifth edition of the Stanford-Binet Intelligence Scale (2003) now uses the same score systems as the Wechsler scales: *M* = 100 and *SD* = 15 for total score; *M* = 10 and *SD* = 3 for subtests. It must be emphasized that this convergence in numerical values between SB5 and Wechsler scales does not mean their scores are directly comparable, because the two tests have different normative bases.

Other tests. The ACT (American College Test) uses a score scale ranging from 1 to 36, with *M* = 16 for high school students and *M* = 19 for college-bound students and *SD* = 5. The LSAT (Law School Admission Test) has *M* = 150 and *SD* = 10.

Stanines. Stanines (a contraction of standard-nine) are standard scores with *M* = 5 and *SD* = 2 (approximately), thus dividing the distribution into nine intervals (1–9), with stanines 2–8 spanning equal distances (each stanine covers ½ *SD*) on the base of the normal curve. Stanines are usually determined from their percentile equivalents, thus normalizing the resulting distribution. Stanines are frequently used with achievement tests and group-administered ability tests but are not used much outside these types of tests.

Stens. Stens (a contraction of standard-ten) are standard scores that span the normal curve with 10 units and with *M* = 5.5 and *SD* = 2; each sten covers ½ *SD*.

Z scores. Z scores are standard scores with *M* = 0 and *SD* = 1. These scores are used frequently in statistical work but virtually never for practical reporting of test results.

Normal curve equivalents. Normal curve equivalents (NCEs) are a type of standard score designed to match the percentile scale at points 1, 50, and 99. Thus, an NCE of 1 equals a percentile of 1, an NCE of 50 equals a percentile of 50, and an NCE of 99 equals a percentile of 99. The NCE scale divides the base of the normal curve into equal units between percentiles of 1 and 99. Using these criteria, NCEs work out to have *M* = 50 and *SD* = 21.06. NCEs were designed for use in federally funded programs in elementary and secondary schools and are used almost exclusively in that context.

PERCENTILES AND PERCENTILE RANKS

Percentiles and percentile ranks are among the most commonly used normed scores for all types of tests. A *percentile* is a point in the distribution at or below which the given percentage of cases falls. A *percentile rank* is the position of a particular score in the distribution expressed as a ranking in a group of 100. There is a fine, technical distinction between percentiles and percentile ranks, but the terms are often used interchangeably without harm.

Quartiles, quintiles, and deciles are offshoots of the percentile system, dividing the distribution of scores into quarters, fifths, and tenths, respectively. Unfortunately, there is no uniformity in designating the top and bottom portions of each of these divisions. For example, the "second" quartile may be either the second from the bottom (25th–49th percentiles) or the second from the top (50th–74th percentiles). Hence, special care is needed on this point when communicating results in any of these systems.

AGE/GRADE EQUIVALENTS

Age and grade equivalents are normed scores, but they are very different in important respects from standard scores and percentiles. Hence, they cannot be represented conveniently in Figure 26.1 or in Table 26.1.

An *age equivalent* score converts a raw score into an age—usually years and months—corresponding to the typical (usually median) raw score attained by a specified group. The specified group is ordinarily defined within a fairly narrow age range (e.g., in 3-month intervals in the standardization group). Age equivalents are used almost exclusively with tests of mental ability, in which case they are referred to as *mental ages*. However, they are also used with anthropometric measurements (e.g., height and weight) for infants and children.

Grade equivalents convert raw scores into a grade in school that is typical for the students at that grade level. "Typical" is usually defined as the median performance of students at a grade level. The grade equivalent (GE) is ordinarily given in school year and 10th of a year, in which the 10ths correspond roughly to the months specified below. Exact definitions of 10ths may vary by half months from one test series to another. Levels above grade 12.9 are sometimes given a nonnumerical descriptor such as PHS for "post–high school."

One of the peculiarities of age and grade

Sept.	Oct.	Nov.	Dec.	Jan.
.0	.1	.2	.3	.4
Feb.	Mar.	Apr.	May	June
.5	.6	.7	.8	.9

equivalents is that their standard deviations are not equal across different age and grade levels. It is this feature that prevents them from being charted in Figure 26.1. Generally the standard deviations increase with successively higher age or grade levels.

OTHER SCORES

Proficiency levels. Recent trends in educational assessment require the reporting of scores in proficiency levels. The most common designations are advanced, proficient, basic, and below basic. Cutoffs between levels are determined judgmentally usually by panels of educators and laypersons and are not comparable from one application (e.g., test area or state) to another.

Theta. An increasing number of tests utilize item response theory (IRT) for test development. The most immediate output from such a test is a theta score, representing position on the underlying trait. Theta scores usually range from approximately −6.0 to +6.0. For ordinary use, theta is converted into one of the familiar normed scores described earlier. Rudner (1998) provides a useful, online demonstration of theta scores operating in a computer adaptive test.

Code types. Several tests, including the MMPI-2 and Strong Interest Inventory, report scores as code types, which begin with some type of normed score and then place the normed scores in rank order. Code type scores typically identify the two or three highest scores, regardless of their actual values.

References and Readings

ERICAE. (2013). *Clearinghouse on assessment and evaluation*. Retrieved May 2, 2013, from ericae.net/testcol.htm

Hogan, T. P. (2013). *Psychological testing: A practical introduction* (3rd ed.). New York: Wiley.

Rudner, L. M. (1998). *An on-line, interactive, computer adaptive testing tutorial*. Retrieved, from EdRes.org/scripts/cat

Seashore, H. G. (n.d.). *Test Service Notebook 148: Methods of expressing test scores*. San Antonio, TX: Psychological Corporation.

Related Topics

Chapter 3, "Improving Diagnostic and Clinical Interviewing"

Chapter 21, "Assessing MMPI-2 Profile Validity"

Chapter 29, "Assessing the Quality of a Psychological Testing Report"

Chapter 131, "Understanding Statistics in the Research Literature"

27 LOCATING INFORMATION ABOUT PSYCHOLOGICAL TESTS AND MEASURES

Thomas P. Hogan

Tests are essential in the work of many psychologists. New tests and revisions of older tests now appear at an astonishing rate. It is impossible to be familiar with all of them or even a significant fraction of them. Hence, it is important to be competent in acquiring information about the many tests that one may encounter. This chapter presents an overview of five categories of sources of information about psychological and psychoeducational tests.

ELECTRONIC LISTINGS

Here are two exceptionally useful tools for obtaining information about tests through the World Wide Web:

1. ETS Test Link at www.ets.org/test_link/find_tests/
2. Buros Center for Testing at buros.org

The Educational Testing Service (ETS) Test Link is the database that contains information on over 25,000 tests in the ETS Test Collection (the physical collection). The database provides descriptive information about a test, such as author, publisher, scores, and number of items. It can be searched by test title, author, or subject descriptor (e.g., "anxiety"). The descriptive information does not provide a critical review of the test.

The Buros site, home for the Buros Center for Testing (formerly Buros Institute of Mental Measurements), provides searches for test reviews and several other sources of information. Some reviews can be downloaded directly from the site for a fee. See the following text for further information about the reviews.

The American Psychological Association (2013) recently launched PsycTESTS (www.apa.org/pubs/databases/psyctests/) as a new database about tests and measures. It intends to include full text of the tests. The source is too new to evaluate its usefulness.

Health and Psychosocial Instruments (HaPI) is a database of instruments compiled by Behavioral Measurement Database Services. HaPI is available through Ovid Technologies (www.ovid.com).

SYSTEMATIC REVIEWS

Two published sources provide professional reviews of tests: the *Mental Measurements Yearbooks* (*MMY*) and *Test Critiques* (*TC*). Both limit themselves to commercially available tests published in English. Both are updated every few years, providing reviews of new or revised tests. These two sources are the only ones that give thorough, professional reviews of a wide variety of tests.

The *Eighteenth Mental Measurements Yearbook* (Spies, Carlson, & Geisinger, 2010) is the most recent in the classic series of reviews sometimes referred to as *MMY*, or "Buros," after Oscar K. Buros, who compiled and published the first volume in 1938. The *MMY* series is now prepared by the Buros Center for Testing and published by the University of Nebraska Press. Historically, new editions of *MMY* appeared every 3 to 5 years, but new editions are now projected to appear every 18 to 20 months, thus precluding the need for interedition supplements. Each new yearbook contains references to reviews in earlier yearbooks.

MMY reviews for the ninth (1985) through the most recent volumes are also available on CD-ROM from SilverPlatter (SilverPlatter Information, 718-769-2599 or 800-343-0064); this source is available online in many academic libraries, allowing access without a fee. As noted earlier, individual reviews may be downloaded (for a fee) from the Buros Web site.

The second source of systematic reviews is *Test Critiques* (Keyser, 2004). This series is now available in 11 volumes, the first having been issued in 1984. Each volume of *TC* covers about 100 tests. In comparison with *MMY*, *TC* limits itself to more widely used tests and the reviews are somewhat longer, although covering the same basic points. Like *MMY*, each new *TC* volume contains a systematic listing of reviews contained in earlier volumes. *TC*, published by Pro-Ed (800-897-3202,www.proedinc.com), is not available in electronic format. The publisher does not currently plan to issue new volumes of *TC*.

COMPREHENSIVE LISTINGS

Several sources give comprehensive, hard-copy listings of tests. Generally, these sources provide basic information about the tests (e.g., target ages, publishers, types of scores) but refrain from giving evaluative comments. These sources are most helpful for two purposes. First, if one needs to know what tests are available for a particular purpose, these listings will provide an initial pool of possibilities for more detailed review. Second, if one knows the name of a test but nothing else about it, information in these listings will provide a brief description of the test and its source. Currently, there is much overlap between these comprehensive listings in hard copy and the electronic lists described earlier.

The venerable series known as *Tests in Print* is now in its eighth edition: *Tests in Print-VIII* (Murphy, Geisinger, Spies, & Carlson, 2011). Usually referred to as *TIP*, the current edition contains entries for several thousand tests. *TIP* attempts to include all tests that are commercially available in English. The first edition appeared in 1961, and new editions now appear about every 3–5 years. The Buros Institute (see earlier for contact information) prepares *TIP*.

Tests: A Comprehensive Reference for Assessments in Psychology, Education, and Business, 6th edition (Maddox, 2008), is a continuing series, first appearing in 1983, by the same publisher as *Test Critiques*. This source presents, for the three areas identified in the title, lists of approximately 3,000 tests from over 150 publishers. Each entry includes the age/grade range for the test, purpose, format and timing, type of scoring, publisher, cost, and a brief description of the test structure and content. (See *Test Critiques* for contact information.)

The ETS Test Collection referenced earlier under Electronic Listings also provides *Tests in Microfiche* (TIM), a microfiche collection of unpublished instruments and *Test Bibliographies* on selected topics. TIM began phase-out in 2005, with its contents gradually converted to downloadable PDF files from the ETS Store (www.ets.org/test_link/order/).

The *Directory of Unpublished Experimental Mental Measures* (Goldman & Mitchell, 2008) is a multivolume effort published by the American Psychological Association. As suggested by the title, the work concentrates exclusively on tests that are not available from regular publishers but appear in journal articles. Each volume includes information (name, purpose, source, format, timing, etc.) for several thousand tests in a wide variety of areas based on searching over 30 journals.

PUBLISHERS' CATALOGS

All the major test publishers produce catalogs listing their products. The publisher's catalog is the best source of information about the most recent editions of a test, including variations such as large-print editions and foreign language versions; costs of materials and scoring; types of scoring services; and ancillary materials. Publishers typically issue catalogs annually or semiannually; more conveniently, all publishers maintain electronic, Web-based versions of their catalogs. Publishers' representatives, either in the field or in the home office, are also an important source of information, especially about new products and services. A call to a publisher's representative can often save hours of searching for information about a price or scoring service. Publishers' catalogs are not good sources of information about the quality of tests; understandably, the publisher will cast one of its tests only in the most favorable light. For contact information for major test publishers, go to the Association of Test Publishers Web site (www.testpublishers.org) or enter the publisher's name in your favorite search engine to access the catalog.

OTHER TEST USERS

Finally, a valuable but often overlooked source of information about tests is other users of tests. Experienced colleagues can be especially helpful in identifying the tests widely used in a particular field and the peculiarities of certain tests. In effect, colleagues can provide brief, informal versions of the lengthier reviews one would find in the formal sources cited in this chapter.

References and Readings

American Psychological Association. (2013). *PsycTESTS*. Retrieved May 2, 2013, from www.apa.org/pubs/databases/psyctests/

Buros Center for Testing. (2013). Retrieved May 2, 2013 from http://buros.org

Educational Testing Service. (2011). *Find a test*. Retrieved May 2, 2013, from www.ets.org/test_link/find_tests/

Goldman, B. A., & Mitchell, D. F. (2008). *Directory of unpublished experimental mental measures* (Vol. 9). Washington, DC: American Psychological Association.

Keyser, D. J. (Ed.). (2004). *Test critiques* (Vol. 11). Austin, TX: Pro-Ed.

Maddox, T. (2008). *Tests: A comprehensive reference for assessments in psychology, education, and business* (6th ed.). Austin, TX: Pro-Ed.

Murphy, L. L., Geisinger, K. F., Spies, R. A., & Carlson, J. F. (Eds.). (2011). *Tests in Print VIII*. Lincoln: University of Nebraska Press.

Spies, R. A., Carlson, J. F., & Geisinger, K. F. (Eds.). (2010). *The eighteenth mental measurements yearbook*. Lincoln: University of Nebraska Press.

Related Topics

Chapter 16, "Assessing Personality Disorders"

Chapter 26, "Interpreting Test Scores and Their Percentile Equivalents"

Chapter 29, "Assessing the Quality of a Psychological Testing Report"

28 APPLYING RORSCHACH ASSESSMENT

Irving B. Weiner

The Rorschach Inkblot Method (RIM) is a relatively unstructured, performance-based personality instrument that provides dependable information on how people perceive and think about events; experience and express emotion; manage stress; and view themselves, other people, and social situations. By providing this information, Rorschach assessment facilitates decisions that are based at least in part on these personality characteristics. As an unstructured performance-based measure, moreover, the RIM frequently obtains information beyond what can be learned from self-report measures, and it is a difficult measure to fake. This chapter delineates the differences between performance-based and self-report measures that account for the utility of Rorschach assessment and identifies decision-making instances in clinical practice, forensic cases, and organizational settings in which the RIM is particularly likely to contribute incremental validity and resist impression management.

PERFORMANCE-BASED AND SELF-REPORT MEASURES

Self-report methods measure psychological characteristics in a relatively direct manner and provide data consisting of what people are able and willing to say about themselves. Whereas most individuals are well aware of many of their attitudes, affects, and action tendencies, they are only partially or not at all aware of some aspects of what they are like and how they tend to behave. Along with this limitation on what people can self-report, they may also be motivated for various reasons to withhold information about themselves or create a false impression, as in attempting to feign psychological disorder or present a deceptively positive picture of their attributes. Performance-based instruments, by contrast, are relatively indirect measures in which psychological characteristics are inferred not from what people say about themselves, but from how they deal with various tasks, such as reporting what an inkblot might be. Accordingly, the data obtained with performance-based measures are not limited to what people are able and willing to self-report; rather, these data are relatively independent of a person's level of self-awareness and his or her commitment to being forthcoming and truthful.

As a relatively unstructured assessment instrument, moreover, the RIM presents people with an ambiguous test stimuli and minimal guidance in how they are expected to respond to them. The RIM consequently differs from self-report instruments in the extent to which its intent and purposes are apparent, and respondents must consequently give their answers to these two types of tests at different levels of conscious awareness of what their responses might signify. The indirect and unstructured nature of Rorschach assessment can often result in its obtaining information about personality characteristics in addition to or different from what is identified by self-reports, especially with respect to a person's underlying dispositions to think, feel, and behave in certain ways. Relative uncertainty about what their responses may signify makes it more difficult for respondents to give misleading impressions of themselves on the RIM than on self-report measures, which is often an important consideration in forensic cases and organizational settings.

CLINICAL PRACTICE

Rorschach assessment is most clearly indicated in clinical practice when decisions depend in part on an individual's level of personality integration and his or her personality style. With respect to personality integration, evidence of an underlying psychotic process or emerging schizophrenia spectrum disorder has substantial implications for the extent to which a person should receive primarily supportive treatment and whether this treatment can be provided adequately on an outpatient basis. As key factors in making these decisions, the RIM provides quantitative indices of disordered thinking (elevated *WSum6*) and impaired reality testing (elevated *X-%*) that cannot readily be generated with other assessment methods and that contribute incremental validity to the identification of psychotic dysfunction.

With respect to other assessment methods, self-report measures capture manifest symptoms of psychotic disorder that an individual has recognized and is not hesitant to admit, but they lack the sensitivity of the RIM to instances of illogical reasoning and inaccurate perception that people have not recognized in themselves or are reluctant to disclose. In diagnostic interviews subtle signs of serious underlying or emerging disorder may be fleeting in an initial session and difficult to confirm even after several additional interviews—by which time a delay in instituting supportive management may result in decompensation that could have been avoided. With this consideration in mind, the time required to complete an initial Rorschach evaluation when there is a possibility of emerging or underlying psychotic disorganization is likely to be well worth sparing a patient from becoming increasingly distressed during a drawn-out diagnostic interview.

As for personality style, Rorschach assessment can contribute otherwise unavailable or inconclusive information that helps therapists tailor their treatment strategies to meet the needs and preferences of individual patients. For example, the Rorschach *EB* (Experience Balance) is a sensitive index of whether people favor a primarily ideational and reflective style of solving problems and making decisions (an introversive *EB*) or a primarily expressive and action-oriented style of coping with experience (an extratensive *EB*). The implications of this Rorschach finding for treatment planning derive from research suggesting that persons with an externalizing coping style are more likely to benefit from symptom focused than from interpersonallyfocused treatment strategies, whereas the opposite treatment response characterizes persons with an internalizing coping style.

With similar implications for treatment planning, the Rorschach *HVI* (Hypervigilance Index) effectively identifies underlying interpersonal suspiciousness, mistrust, and distaste for intimacy, and research findings indicate that people who are interpersonally aversive in these ways respond less well to directive forms of therapy than to treatments that de-emphasize therapist authority and guidance. Having such information available initially can help therapists avoid instituting a treatment approach ill suited to a patient's personality style and not recognizing this faulty treatment planning decision until after a period of patient disgruntlement or unresponsiveness, or even a premature termination.

FORENSIC CASES

In forensic cases the sensitivity of the RIM to underlying disorder and its resistance to impression management can provide useful and otherwise unavailable information in criminal, personal injury, and child custody litigations. The most common psycholegal questions in criminal cases concern whether defendants are competent to proceed to trial and whether they should be held responsible for their actions at the time of an alleged offense. As defined in legal terms, neither competence nor criminal responsibility is a personality characteristic. However, the previously mentioned Rorschach indices of being out of touch with reality or being thought disordered, both of which may emerge when such impairments are not self-recognized or self-reported, can help explain to the court why certain defendants are unable to appreciate the nature of the charges against them (a legal criterion for incompetence) or were not able to recognize the wrongfulness of their conduct (a legal criterion for insanity).

As for resistance to impression management, persons charged with crimes are more likely than patients evaluated in clinical practice to feign disorder—or "fake bad"—as a way of trying to escape or minimize punishment. However, even if they have read about or been coached in "crazy things" to say about the inkblots, people find it difficult to give a consistent and convincing Rorschach protocol with elevations on *X-%* and *WSum6*—unless they are in fact seriously disturbed. Instead, criminal defendants attempting to fake bad on the RIM typically go too far; that is, they report and elaborate deviant responses to an extent rarely seen except in people who have a long history of being treated for severe mental illness and whose disturbance has been overt and obvious as well to family, friends, teachers, and coworkers. The co-occurrence of a very high *X-%* and a very large *WSum6* in a criminal defendant with little or no prior history of blatant and readily apparent psychological disturbance can be a compelling clue to malingering in individuals whose currently strange behavior and bizarre self-reports have been misleading examiners to regard them as seriously disturbed.

In personal injury cases, the type of psychic harm most commonly claimed is an anxiety or posttraumatic stress disorder (PTSD). Persons claiming psychic injury are known at times to manufacture or exaggerate symptoms of distress, and in some of these instances a relatively unremarkable Rorschach protocol provides compelling evidence of otherwise undetected malingering persons with PTSD who are re-experiencing stressful events and who are in a state of mental and physical hyperarousal typically self-report these symptoms and also produce Rorschach protocols that are flooded with indications of anxiety and discomfort, including (a) evidence of substantial subjectively felt distress (large *D-minus* and *Adjusted D-minus* scores); (b) signs of intrusive worries about being helpless in the face of forces outside their control (numerous *m* responses); and (c) frequent response contents reflecting concerns about bodily integrity and vulnerability to harm (as measured by the *Trauma Content Index*, which is based on the percentage of Aggression, Anatomy, Blood, Morbid, and Sex responses in a record).

Should individuals who complain of marked re-experiencing and hyperarousal give an average-length unguarded Rorschach protocol in which the *D*-score is not negative (< 0), *m* are infrequent (< 2), and the *Trauma Content Index* is less than .25, it is likely that they are exaggerating their symptom complaints. In some instances, an anxiety or stress disorder is characterized not by re-experiencing and hyperarousal, but by defensive avoidance, in which case people tend to give guarded Rorschach protocols with fewer than average responses and a high percentage of unrevealing pure form (*F*) responses. However, persons who are attempting to malinger PTSD rarely choose defensive avoidance as their way of doing so, and a guarded Rorschach protocol is accordingly unlikely to have any implications for impression management.

In child custody cases, psychological assessment may be complicated not by efforts to appear disturbed or dysfunctional, as may occur in criminal and personal injury cases, but instead by the understandable motivation of litigating parents to put their best food forward—in other words, to fake good—and give a deceptively positive impression of their attributes and abilities. On the MMPI, which is the most frequently used self-report inventory in child custody evaluations, attempting to make a positive impression commonly leads to elevations on the L, K, and S validity scales together with normal-range scores on the clinical scales. This MMPI pattern alerts examiners to the likelihood of a fake-good protocol, but it rarely provides information about the nature and extent of any underlying psychopathology or maladaptive personality characteristics likely to interfere with a person's being an effective parent.

Persons being assessed with the RIM may elect to give a guarded record with few responses and a high percentage of pure form answers. However, such guarded Rorschach protocols constitute limited cooperation with the evaluation process, much as would leaving numerous MMPI items blank or declining to answer interview questions, and behaving in this way does not serve the purposes of someone who is trying to make a good impression.

For respondents who are not being guarded, the relatively unstructured nature of the RIM makes it as difficult to give a convincing fake-good protocol as it is to give a convincing fake-bad one. The record is likely to show notable inconsistencies and reveal underlying disorders that might not otherwise have been detected, and it may identify personality characteristics that typically limit a person's ability to provide constructive parenting. Chief among these are (a) the interpersonal aversiveness and distaste for intimacy captured by the previously mentioned hypervigilance index; (b) minimal interest in collaborative relationships, as suggested by the absence of cooperative responses (COP = 0); and (c) limited empathic capacity, as identified by frequent inaccurate perception of human figures (*M-* > 1).

ORGANIZATIONAL SETTINGS

In organizational settings, personality assessment is commonly utilized to assist in selecting and evaluating personnel. Personnel selection and evaluation may involve determining whether a job applicant is suited for a particular position in an organization, or it may consist of assessing whether a current employee should be promoted to a more senior or responsible position. Both types of decision often call for identifying personality characteristics that are likely to enhance or interfere with performance in the particular position and then measuring the level of these personality characteristics in individuals under consideration.

As in litigating for custody of their children, being considered for employment or promotion usually motivates people to attempt to give a good impression of their personality strengths. Because Rorschach assessment is an indirect and relatively unstructured procedure that provides information beyond what people are able and willing to say about themselves, it can help identify critical job-related personality characteristics that might not otherwise come to light. Suppose, for example, that contrary to outward appearances in a person attempting to make a good impression, Rorschach findings of a low *Afr* and *H* < *Hd* + *(H)* + *(Hd)* point to emotional withdrawal and social discomfort. This person would probably not be a good fit for a position in sales or public relations that calls for extensive and persuasive interaction with people. Among persons being considered for hire as an air traffic controller or a nuclear power plant supervisor, Rorschach indications of minimal coping capacities and limited ability to remain calm and exercise good judgment in stressful situations (low *EA*, *D* < *0*, low *XA%*) can help avoid hiring a person ill suited to handle the demands of this position. As a third example, the RIM provides indices of behavioral passivity (*p* > *a* + 1) and painstaking care in coming to conclusions (*Zd* > +3.0) that might not be apparent from how people present and describe themselves and that would caution against appointing or promoting a person to a position of leadership requiring initiative and rapid decision making.

Personnel evaluations may also involve assessing the current fitness for duty of individuals whose ability to function in their work has become impaired by psychological disorder or substance abuse. Individuals being assessed for this purpose, especially impaired professionals, are commonly eager to make the best possible impression and be cleared to return to their jobs or practices. In some instances, however, particularly if they are receiving substantial sick leave or unemployment compensation, people may aim to convince assessors, employers, and third-party payers that they are not sufficiently recovered from their psychological difficulties to return to work. As in the previously mentioned instances in which people being assessed may be motivated to feign disorder or present a deceptively positive picture of their personality characteristics, Rorschach findings can play an important role in these fitness-for-duty evaluations by contributing incremental validity in the assessment of psychological disorder and being relatively resistant to impression management.

References and Readings

Del Giudice, M. J. (2010). What might this be? Rediscovering the Rorschach as a tool for personnel selection in organizations. *Journal of Personality Assessment, 92*, 78–90.

Erard, R. E. (2005). What the Rorschach can contribute to child custody and parenting time evaluations. *Journal of Child Custody, 2*, 119–142.

Gacono, C. B., & Evans, F. B. (Eds.). (2009). *Handbook of forensic Rorschach psychology*. New York: Routledge.

Huprich, S. K. (Ed.). (2006). *Rorschach assessment of the personality disorders*. Mahwah, NJ: Erlbaum.

Kleiger, J. H. (1999). *Disordered thinking and the Rorschach*. Hillsdale, NJ: Analytic Press.

Norcross, J. D. (Ed.). (2011). *Psychotherapy relationships that* work (2nd ed.). New York: Oxford University Press.

Society for Personality Assessment. (2005). The status of the Rorschach in clinical and forensic practice: An official statement by the Board of Trustees of the Society for Personality Assessment. *Journal of Personality Assessment, 85*, 219–237.

Weiner, I. B. (2003). *Principles of Rorschach interpretation* (2nd ed.). Mahwah, NJ: Erlbaum.

Weiner, I. B., & Meyer, G. J. (2009). Personality assessment with the Rorschach inkblot method. In J. N. Butcher (Ed.), *Oxford handbook of personality assessment* (pp. 277–298). New York: Oxford University Press.

Related Topics

Chapter 21, "Assessing MMPI-2 Profile Validity"

Chapter 29, "Assessing the Quality of a Psychological Testing Report"

29 ASSESSING THE QUALITY OF A PSYCHOLOGICAL TESTING REPORT

Gerald P. Koocher and Celiane Rey-Casserly

The summary provided in Table 29.1 describes key points that should be addressed in conducting any psychological assessment for which a report is prepared.

TABLE 29.1. Key Points for Conducting a Psychological Assessment

Criterion	Quality Indicators
Referral questions and context	• Does the report explain the reason for referral and state the assessment questions to be addressed? • Does the report note that the client or legal guardian was informed about the purpose of and agreed to the assessment? • Is the relevant psychological ecology of the client mentioned (e.g., recently divorced, facing criminal charges, candidate for employment)? • If the evaluation is being undertaken at the request of a third party (e.g., a court, an employer, or a school), does the examiner note that the client was informed of the limits of confidentiality and whether a release was obtained?
Current status/behavioral observations	• Has the examiner described the client's behavior like during the interview, especially with respect to any aspects that might relate to the referral questions or the validity of the testing (e.g., mood, ability to form rapport, concentration, mannerisms, medication side effects, language problems, cooperation, phenotype, or physical handicaps)? • Has the examiner described any deviations from standard testing administration or procedures?
Listing of instruments used	• Is a complete list (without jargon or abbreviations) of the tests administered presented, including the dates administered? • Does the report explain the nature of any unusual instruments or test procedures used? • If more than one set of norms or test forms exists for any given instrument, does the psychologist indicate which forms or norms were used?
Reliability and validity	• Does the psychologist comment specifically on whether the test results in the present circumstances can be regarded as reasonably accurate (e.g., the test administration was valid and the client fully cooperative)? • If mediating factors apply, are these discussed in terms of reliability and validity implications? • Are the tests used valid for assessing the aspects of the client's abilities in question? This should be a special focus of attention if the instrument used is nonstandard or is being used in a nonstandard manner.
Data presentation	• Are scores presented and explained for each of the tests used? (If an integrated narrative or description is presented, does it report on all the aspects assessed, such as intellectual functioning, personality structure, etc.?) • Are the meanings of the test results explained in terms of the referral questions asked? • Are examples or illustrations included if relevant? • Are technical terms and jargon avoided? • Does the report note whether the pattern of scores (e.g., variability in measuring similar attributes across instruments) is a consistent or heterogeneous one? • For IQ testing, are subtest scatter and discrepancy scores mentioned? • For personality testing, does the psychologist discuss self-esteem, interpersonal relations, emotional reactivity, defensive style, and areas of focal concern?
Summary	• If a summary is presented, does it err by surprising the reader with material not mentioned earlier in the report? • Is it overly redundant?
Recommendations	• If recommendations are made, do these flow logically from the test results mentioned and discussed earlier? • Do the recommendations mention all relevant points raised as initial referral questions?
Diagnosis	• If a diagnosis is requested or if differential diagnosis was a referral question, does the report specifically address this point?
Authentication	• Is the report signed by the individual(s) who conducted the evaluation? • Are the credentials/title of each person noted (e.g., Mary Smith, Ph.D., Staff Psychologist, or John Doe, M.S., Psychology Intern)? • If the examiner is unlicensed or a trainee, is the report cosigned by a qualified licensed supervisor?
Feedback	• Is a copy of the report sent to the person who made the referral? • Is some mechanism in place for providing feedback to the client, consistent with the context of testing and original agreement with the client?

References and Readings

American Psychological Association. (1993). Record keeping guidelines. *American Psychologist, 48,* 308–310.

American Psychological Association. (2012). *Joint standards for educational and psychological testing.* Retrieved January 2013, from www.apa.org/science/programs/testing/standards.aspx

American Psychological Association, American Educational Research Association, & National Council on Measurement in Education. (1998). *Standards for educational and psychological testing.* Washington, DC: American Psychological Association.

American Psychological Association, Testing and Assessment. (n. d.). Resource site. Retrieved from www.apa.org/science/programs/testing/index.aspx

Assessment of Competency Benchmarks Work Group. (2007). *Assessment of competency benchmarks work group: A developmental model for defining and measuring competence in professional psychology.* Washington, D.C.: American Psychological Association.

Buros Institute of Mental Measurements. (2011). *Buros center for testing.* Retrieved January 2013, from www.unl.edu/buros

Eyde, L. D., Robertson, & G. J., Krug, (2009). *Responsible test use: Case studies for assessing human behavior.* Washington, DC: American Psychological Association.

Koocher, G. P., & Keith-Spiegel, P. C. (2008). *Ethics in psychology and the mental health professions: Professional standards and cases* (3rd ed.). New York: Oxford University Press.

Rey-Casserly, C., & Koocher, G. P. (2012). Ethical issues in psychological assessment. In J. R. Graham & J. A. Naglieri (Eds.), *Handbook of psychology: Assessment psychology* (2nd ed., Vol. 10, pp. 295–330). Hoboken, NJ: Wiley.

Related Topics

Chapter 105, "Defending Against Legal (Malpractice and Licensing) Complaints"
Chapter 110, "Understanding Special Education Law"
Chapter 125, "Prototype Mental Health Records"
Chapter 127, "Elements of Authorization Forms to Release or Request Client's Records"

PART III
Individual Adult Treatment

30 COMPENDIUM OF PSYCHOTHERAPY TREATMENT MANUALS

Michael J. Lambert

The earliest treatment manuals were developed in the 1960s to provide operational definitions of treatment parameters for psychotherapy research. By utilizing manuals in clinical trials, researchers can reduce variability among psychotherapists in what they do by assuring their adherence as well as their competence in the treatment under investigation. Manuals have also been used to train and guide novice therapists, and more recently as a means of helping therapists deliver empirically supported treatments and evidence-based treatments. Manuals often provide the foundational structure and treatment guidelines for certification in specific treatment methods (along with didactic workshops with practice and supervision). Manuals have finally found a place in routine care.

Manuals vary in quality and coverage. The clinician might assess the value of a manual based on six criteria: (a) presentation of the main principles behind the techniques of that psychotherapy; (b) description of etiology and/or assessment approaches needed to understand the disorder of interest; (c) specifically delineated description of treatment program (e.g., session by session, step by step, phases); (d) concrete examples of each technical principle/treatment method; (e) scales to guide independent judges in evaluating sessions to determine the degree of conformity to the manual; (f) and sufficient attention to cultural concerns that might contribute to or interfere with treatment.

In clinical practice, manuals have several advantages. Manuals provide a succinct theoretical framework for treatment of a specific disorder, concrete descriptions of therapeutic techniques, session-by-session guidelines, and case examples of appropriate applications. The increased precision in detailing treatment techniques has generated enthusiasm among training programs, internships, third-party payors, and service settings, such as community mental health centers and the Veterans Administration.

However, others have expressed concerns over the use of treatment manuals in clinical practice. Among these concerns are the degree to which the individual rather than the disorder is the focus of treatment, and the complexity of presenting problems such that multiple problems are presented without the strict inclusion/exclusion criteria used in clinical trials. In addition, the emergence of more salient problems as the treatment progresses is not uncommon. Questions regarding treatment efficacy of the manual-based therapy have been raised (Lambert & Ogles, 1988). Both overadherence (the degree to which some therapists are not flexible when working from a manual) and underadherence to the manual (the degree to which some therapists modify procedures in clinical practice) are disconcerting (Addis, 1997). Finally, serious questions have been raised that most manual-based therapies tend to neglect relationship factors (Norcross, 2011) and do not lend themselves to integrative approaches.

In light of the possible advantages afforded by treatment manuals and with due consideration of their tradeoffs, my colleagues and I provided a list of useful manuals (Lambert, 2004) in the second edition of this *Psychologists' Desk Reference*. However, it is no longer possible or desirable to do so. There are now far too many available manuals and effective alternative approaches to list all the possibilities. Moreover, search engines permit the interested clinician to locate and obtain manuals that are specific to the disorder of concern and treatment type under consideration.

In searching for psychotherapy manuals, it makes sense to turn to lists of evidence-based treatments and treatment guidelines. A manualized treatment that has been shown to be effective compared to no treatment, placebo, and alternative treatments such as treatment-as-usual would be preferable to assuming that a manual must be based on empirical evidence. There are also a variety of edited books with contributions from experts who have studied empirically supported treatments. Barlow's (2013) is exemplary in this regard, as it provides numerous manuals for many common adult disorders as well as other resource material. Unfortunately, it does not attempt to capture many treatments outside of cognitive-behavioral interventions.

Here are five online means of locating and obtaining psychotherapy treatment manuals:

(1) *www.psychologicaltreatments.org* This compilation of evidence-based treatments from the Society for Clinical Psychology (APA Division 12) includes manuals for research-supported treatments for particular disorders.

(2) *www.nationalregistry.samhsa.gov* The Substance Abuse and Mental Health Services Administration offers the National Register for Evidence-based Programs and Practices. It has developed its own standards of evidence and provides details of the nature of the manual-based treatments as well as their readiness for dissemination, costs, and the like.

(3) *ucoll.fdu.edu/apa/lnksinter.html* This Web site encompasses more than 30 federal, state, professional, and university sites that enumerate evidence-based interventions. It has provided an active and ever-expanding Web-based site that regularly evaluates and adds new treatment options.

(4) *www.thecochranelibrary.com* and *guidance.nice.org.uk/* These two information resources identify and synthesize randomized clinical trials in mental health and the addictions. In so doing, they typically cite the treatment manuals used in any given study and thus offer direct leads to locating those manuals.

(5) *www.google.com* If one googles "psychotherapy treatment manuals," hundreds of connections are immediately available. However, one becomes immediately aware that variability in the quality of manuals is extreme and that manuals are provided that have never been employed in research studies or that the treatment advocated has any empirical evidence whatsoever. Searching for manuals in general through this procedure is destined to be time consuming and frustrating, but searching for a particular manual by its exact title is likely to bear fruit.

At this stage of scientific development it is fair to say that hundreds of manuals exist, that they can prove valuable resources in implementing effective psychotherapies, but just because a manual exists does not mean that its use has been validated. New manuals appear at a rapid rate, and older manuals are frequently updated, making it difficult to keep up with new developments.

References and Readings

Addis, M. E. (1997). Evaluating the treatment manuals as a means of disseminating empirically validated psychotherapies. *Clinical Psychology: Science and Practice, 4*, 1–11.

Barlow, D. H. (Ed.). (2013). *Clinical handbook of psychological disorders: A step-by-step treatment manual* (5th ed.). New York: Guilford Press.

Lambert, M. J. (2004). *Bergin and Garfield's handbook of psychotherapy and behavior change* (5th ed.). New York: Wiley.

Lambert, M. J., & Ogles, B. M. (1988). Treatment manuals: Problems and promise. *Journal of Integrative and Eclectic Psychotherapy, 7*, 187–205.

Norcross, J. C. (Ed.). (2011). *Psychotherapy relationships that work.* (2nd ed.) New York: Oxford University Press.

Related Topics

Chapter 31, "Compendium of Empirically Supported Treatments"
Chapter 32, "Compendium of Treatment Adaptations"
Chapter 33, "Compendium of Evidence-Based Therapy Relationships"

31 COMPENDIUM OF EMPIRICALLY SUPPORTED TREATMENTS

Dianne L. Chambless and E. David Klonsky

Beginning in 1993, the Society of Clinical Psychology (Division 12 of the American Psychological Association) has sponsored an endeavor to identify empirically supported psychological interventions and to publicize their existence to clinical psychologists, training programs, and consumers (Task Force on Promotion and Dissemination of Psychological Procedures, 1995). The goals are to serve the public and the profession by (1) helping psychologists and training programs readily identify promising treatments upon which their training efforts might, in part, be focused; (2) aiding psychologists in practice by providing data to support their choice of psychological interventions and the efficacy of their treatment in order to make their services available and to obtain reimbursement for them; and (3) providing information for the public about evidence-based psychotherapies. This effort is akin to movements within American psychiatry and medicine in Britain (e.g., Straus, Glasziou, Richardson, & Haynes, 2011) to foster evidence-based practice by educating clinicians about the research base for practice and provides a large part of the research basis for the evidence-based practice in psychology endorsed by the American Psychological Association (APA Presidential Task Force, 2006). Within clinical psychology, this work may be seen as a logical extension of the Boulder model of scientist-practitioner training and of the clinical science model of training.

A succession of Division 12 task forces have constructed and elaborated lists of empirically supported treatments (ESTs, initially called *empirically validated therapies*) for adults and children. Other professional groups have joined in this effort. These lists are necessarily incomplete: Not all treatments have yet been reviewed, and new evidence for treatments emerges monthly.

Recognizing the need for an easily updatable and accessible source of information, in 2008 the Society launched a Web site on research-supported psychological treatments, at www.div12.org/PsychologicalTreatments/index.html (and also accessible via the address www.PsychologicalTreatments.org). The Web site aims to be an informational resource rather than an exhaustive list of empirically supported treatments. For each treatment, the Web site describes (a) the nature of research evidence, (b) clinical resources such as manuals and relevant books, and (c) training opportunities. The Division 12 Web site is focused on problems of adults. The Association for Behavioral and Cognitive Therapies and Division 53 of APA (Society of Clinical Child and Adolescent Psychology) have banded together to create a Web site focused on treatment of younger patients, which has EST information for consumers and professionals: www.abct.org/sccap/. In addition, the National Institute for Health and Clinical Excellence in the United Kingdom posts comprehensive evaluation reports on their Web site, although to date the number of reports on psychotherapy is small (guidance.nice.org.uk/Topic/MentalHealthBehavioural).

These are not the only groups to create EST lists. Chambless and Ollendick (2001) compiled the work of eight major efforts to identify ESTs conducted in the United States or Great Britain. They found extensive agreement across the reports by the eight groups, indicating that reliable evaluations of what treatments may be considered empirically supported are possible.

In Tables 31.1 and 31.2, we present a list of ESTs as summarized by Chambless and Ollendick (2001) augmented with treatments more recently included on the Divisions 12 and 53 Web sites. Treatments are listed in one of two columns according to the quantity and quality of evidence as to their efficacy. Where work groups differed in their evaluation of the level of evidence for a given treatment, we have listed the treatment according to the most positive evaluation.

A number of factors need to be taken into account in using these lists. First, the task forces have concentrated on specific treatments for specific psychological problems. That psychotherapy in general is beneficial for the average adult psychotherapy client is well known. The lists of ESTs represent an attempt to provide more focused information. Second, the task forces have followed a number of decision rules in determining what constitutes sufficient evidence for listing a treatment. Decisions are largely based upon randomized controlled studies that passed muster for methodological soundness, and the preponderance of the data across studies must have been positive (Chambless & Hollon, 1998). Third, broad generic labels (e.g., cognitive-behavior therapy) may be misleading. Readers should check the original sources to determine the precise treatment procedures used in studies providing efficacy evidence. Fourth, the absence of a treatment from the lists does not mean it is ineffective. It may or may not be. No listing may simply reflect a dearth of research data or the possibility that the treatment has not yet been formally reviewed for inclusion in the list. Finally, as more evidence on a treatment accrues, initial evaluations of a treatment's efficacy may be reconsidered and the categorization of a treatment downgraded. For this reason, we encourage the use of the Web sites to check on the most recent results.

The EST projects have been lauded and condemned. Those who favor ESTs frequently argue that training in specific psychological interventions is meaningful—that is, that there are important outcome differences among approaches to psychotherapy and among approaches for different disorders. Those who believe that individual difference variables (e.g., characteristics of the client, the therapist, or the particular therapeutic relationship) are of the utmost importance in treatment outcome find EST lists less useful, as do those who believe that psychologists are not yet able to define clients' problems or our interventions in terms meaningful enough to allow fruitful matching of treatments to target problems. Indeed, there is still debate about the relative importance of symptom relief (the major, although not the sole focus of EST evidence) versus less well-specified goals like personal growth, and whether the most important changes clients make in experiential and psychodynamic therapies can be reliably assessed.

Reactions to the EST lists also probably differ as a function of viewing the identification of evidence-based treatments as a support or a threat to clinical practice. The

TABLE 31.1. Empirically Supported Therapies for Adults: Summary Across Work Groups

	Well Established	Probably Efficacious
Anxiety and Stress		
Agoraphobia/panic disorder with agoraphobia	CBT; exposure	Couples communication training as adjunct to exposure; partner-assisted CBT
Blood injury phobia		Applied tension
Generalized anxiety disorder	Applied relaxation; CBT	
Geriatric anxiety		Relaxation
Obsessive-compulsive disorder	Exposure and response prevention; cognitive therapy	Family-assisted ERP and relaxation; Relapse prevention
Panic disorder	Applied relaxation; CBT	Exposure; panic-focused psychodynamic therapy
Posttraumatic stress disorder	Exposure; cognitive processing therapy; EMDR; Seeking Safety; Stress inoculation; Stress inoculation combined with cognitive therapy and exposure	
Public speaking anxiety	CBT; CBT plus exposure	Systematic desensitization
Social anxiety/phobia	CBT; CBT plus exposure	Systematic desensitization; Exposure
Specific phobia	Exposure	Systematic desensitization
Stress	Stress inoculation	
Chemical Abuse and Dependence		
General substance and alcohol abuse or dependence	Motivational interviewing	
Alcohol abuse and dependence	Behavioral couples therapy; motivational interview	Behavioral marital therapy and disulfiram; Community reinforcement; Cue exposure; Cue exposure therapy and urge coping skills; moderate drinking (Web application); Prize-based contingency management; Social skills training with inpatient treatment
Benzodiazepine withdrawal for panic disorder		CBT
Cocaine abuse/dependence		Behavior therapy; CBT relapse prevention; prize-based contingency management
Mixed methadone and cocaine abuse/dependence	Prize-based contingency management	
Opiate dependence		Behavior therapy (reinforcement); Brief dynamic therapy; Cognitive therapy
Depression		
Bipolar disorder		CBT for medication adherence; Psychoeducation
Geriatric depression	Behavior therapy; Brief dynamic therapy; CBT; Psychoeducation; Reminiscence therapy (mild to moderate only)	Interpersonal therapy; Problem-solving therapy

(*continued*)

TABLE 31.1. Empirically Supported Therapies for Adults: Summary Across Work Groups (*continued*)

	Well Established	Probably Efficacious
Major depression	Behavior therapy/behavioral activation; Behavioral marital therapy (for MDD conjoint with marital distress); cognitive behavioral analysis system of psychotherapy; cognitive therapy; CBT; Interpersonal therapy; problem-solving therapy; self-management/ self-control therapy	Brief dynamic therapy; emotion-focused therapy (process-experiential); reminiscence/life review therapy; self-system therapy
Health Problems		
Anorexia	Family-based therapy (for patients <19 years old)	Behavior therapy; Behavioral family systems therapy; Cognitive therapy
Binge-eating disorder	CBT; interpersonal therapy	Comprehensive behavioral weight loss program
Bulimia	CBT; interpersonal therapy	Family-based treatment
Chemotherapy side effects (for cancer patients)		Progressive muscle relaxation with or without guided imagery
Chronic pain (heterogeneous)	Multicomponent CBT (for fibromyalgia and rheumatologic pain)	Acceptance and commitment therapy; CBT with physical therapy; EMG biofeedback; Operant behavior therapy
Chronic pain (back)	CBT	Operant behavior therapy
Headache	Behavior therapy; CBT	
Idiopathic pain		CBT
Irritable bowel syndrome		Cognitive therapy; Hypnotherapy; Multicomponent CBT
Migraine		EMG biofeedback and relaxation; Thermal biofeedback and relaxation training
Obesity	Behavioral weight-loss treatment	Hypnosis with CBT
Raynaud's		Thermal biofeedback
Rheumatic disease pain	Multicomponent CBT	
Sickle cell disease pain		Multicomponent cognitive therapy
Smoking cessation	Multicomponent CBT with relapse prevention	Group CBT; Scheduled reduced smoking with multicomponent behavior therapy
Somatoform pain disorders		CBT
Marital Discord	Behavioral marital therapy	CBT; Cognitive therapy; Emotion-focused couples therapy (no more than moderately distressed); Insight-oriented marital therapy; Systematic therapy
Sexual Dysfunction		
Erectile dysfunction		Behavior therapy aimed at reducing sexual anxiety and improving communication; CBT aimed at reducing sexual anxiety and improving communication
Female hypoactive sexual desire		Hurlbert's combined therapy; Zimmer's combined sex and marital therapy

(*continued*)

TABLE 31.1. Empirically Supported Therapies for Adults: Summary Across Work Groups (*continued*)

	Well Established	Probably Efficacious
Female orgasmic disorder/ dysfunction		Behavioral marital therapy with Masters and Johnson's therapy; Masters and Johnson's sex therapy; Sexual skills training
Vaginismus		Exposure-based behavior therapy
Other		
Avoidant personality disorder		Exposure; social skills training
Borderline personality disorder	Dialectical behavior therapy	Schema-focused therapy; transference-focused therapy
Body dysmorphic disorder		CBT
Dementia	Behavioral interventions applied at environmental level for behavior problems	Memory and cognitive training for slowing cognitive decline; reality orientation
Geriatric caregivers		Psychoeducation; psychosocial interventions
Paraphilias/sex offenders		Behavior therapy
Schizophrenia and other severe mental illness	Assertive community treatment; behavior therapy and social learning/ token economy programs; Behavioral family therapy; CBT; cognitive remediation; family psychoeducation; Social learning/token economy programs; Social skills training; Supportive long-term family therapy; supported employment; Training in community living program	Cognitive adaptation training; family systems therapy; illness management and recovery; supportive group therapy; supported employment
Sleep disorders	CBT; paradoxical intention; relaxation training; sleep restriction therapy; stimulus control therapy	Biofeedback (electromyograph)
Unwanted habits		Habit reversal and control techniques

Notes: Different work groups have used different labels for treatment with higher and lower levels of evidence. The labels used here are the most common. ESTs as summarized by Chambless and Ollendick (2001) augmented with treatments more recently included on the Divisions 12 and 53 Web sites. CBT, cognitive-behavioral therapy; ERP, exposure and response prevention; MDD, major depressive disorder.

great majority of ESTs identified to date are behavioral or cognitive-behavioral in nature, reflecting the greater research activity of psychotherapy outcome researchers of that orientation. Perhaps as a result, psychodynamic practitioners have proved to hold less favorable views of ESTs than cognitive-behavioral practitioners in our research. Some non-CBT practitioners have expressed fear that their access to third-party payments will be reduced because they do not practice treatments on the list. Other clinicians have found that they can draw on the list to promote the efficacy and desirability of their treatment plans. To some degree, this particular controversy also centers on the best ways to react to the escalating demands for more efficient use of health care dollars.

Finally, research indicates that the EST movement displeases practicing psychologists to the degree that they see the promotion of manualized efficacious treatments as denigrating the importance of the therapeutic relationship and minimizing the benefits of their clinical experience as a guide to treatment decisions. Other psychologists see no reason that manual-based treatments cannot be flexibly used as best for a particular client and conducted in the context of a strong therapeutic alliance.

TABLE 31.2. Empirically Supported Therapies for Children and Adolescents: Summary Across Work Groups

	Well Established	Probably/Possibly Efficacious
ADHD	Behavioral parent training; behavior modification in classroom; behavioral peer interventions	
Anxiety Disorders		
General anxiety disorders (separation anxiety, avoidant disorder, overanxious disorder)		Individual CBT; CBT and family AMT; group CBT; group CBT with parents; the Coping Cat; individual CBT with parents; individual CBT with cognitive parent training; group CBT with parental AMT for anxious parents; family CBT; parent group CBT; group CBT with parents + Internet
Obsessive-compulsive disorder		Individual CBT; individual CBT + sertraline; family-focused CBT; group family-focused CBT
Phobias	Participant modeling; rapid exposure (school phobia); reinforced practice	CBT; filmed modeling; imaginal desensitization; in vivo desensitization; live modeling; CBT for school refusal with parent/teacher training; parent/teacher training for school refusal; emotive imagery for darkness phobia; in vivo behavioral exposures with EMDR for spider phobia; exposures plus contingency management for specific phobia; exposures plus self-control for specific phobia; one-session exposure treatment for specific phobia; one-session exposure treatment with parents for specific phobia
PTSD	Trauma-focused CBT	School-based CBT; group CBT; CBT for PTSD; resilient peer treatment; child-centered therapy; EMDR; family therapy; child–parent psychotherapy
Social phobia		Family-focused individual CBT; social effectiveness training; the Coping Cat
Autism, early	Lovaas's method	
Bipolar Disorder		Family-focused treatment for adolescents; multifamily psychoeducation; child-focused CBT; family-focused CBT; individual family psychoeducation; dialectical behavior therapy (adolescents)

(continued)

TABLE 31.2. Empirically Supported Therapies for Adults: Summary Across Work Groups (*continued*)

	Well Established	Probably/Possibly Efficacious
Conduct Disorder and Oppositional Defiant Disorder	CBT; cognitive problem-solving skills; functional family therapy; multisystemic therapy; parent training based on *Living with Children* (children and adolescents); videotape-modeling parent training	Anger control training with stress inoculation (adolescents); anger coping therapy (children); assertiveness training; delinquency prevention program; parent–child interaction therapy; problem-solving skills training; rational emotive therapy; time-out plus signal seat treatment; manualized behavior management programs; *Helping the Noncompliant Child; Triple P* (Positive Parenting Program) — standard individual treatment; enhanced; *Incredible Years* — parent training; child training; parent–child interaction therapy; problem-solving skills training (standard; plus practice; plus parent management training); group assertiveness training (counselor-led; peer-led); multidimensional treatment foster care; group anger control training; *Reaching Educators, Children, and Parents (RECAP);* manualized behavior management programs; *Triple P* (Positive Parenting Program) — standard group treatment; *First Step to Success Program; Self-administered Treatment, plus Signal Seat*
Depression		
Depression, children	CBT group, child only; CBT child group plus parent component	School-based group CBT; Penn Prevention Program (PPP), including culturally relevant modifications as seen in the Penn Optimism Program (POP); self-control therapy; behavior therapy
Depression, adolescents	CBT group, adolescent only; individual interpersonal therapy	Adolescent CBT group, plus parent component; individual CBT; individual CBT, plus parent/family component; *Adolescents Coping with Depression (CWD-A); Interpersonal Therapy for Depressed Adolescents (IPT-A)*
Distress Due to Medical Procedures (mainly for cancer)	CBT	
Eating Disorders		
Anorexia nervosa (adolescents)	Family therapy for anorexia nervosa	Psychoanalytic therapy for anorexia nervosa; Cash's body image therapy, plus virtual reality
Bulimia (adolescents)		Guided self-care for binge-eating in bulimia nervosa; family therapy for bulimia nervosa
Enuresis and Encopresis	Behavior modification	
Obesity	Behavior therapy	

(*continued*)

TABLE 31.2. Empirically Supported Therapies for Adults: Summary Across Work Groups (*continued*)

	Well Established	Probably/Possibly Efficacious
Psychophysiological Disorder	Family therapy	
Pervasive Developmental Disorders, Undesirable Behavior In	Contingency management	
Recurrent Abdominal Pain		CBT
Recurrent Headache	Relaxation/self-hypnosis	Thermal biofeedback
Substance Abuse (Adolescents)	Group CBT; multidimensional family therapy; functional family therapy	Brief strategic family therapy; behavioral family therapy; multisystemic therapy; individual CBT; transitional family therapy; strength-oriented family therapy; Minnesota Model 12 Step

Notes: Different work groups have used different labels for treatment with higher and lower levels of evidence. The labels used here are the most common. ADHD, attention-deficit/hyperactivity disorder; CBT, cognitive-behavioral therapy; PTSD, posttraumatic stress disorder.

However controversial, the EST movement has gained sufficient credence that some didactic instruction and clinical supervision in ESTs are now specified in APA's *Guidelines and Principles for Accreditation of Programs in Professional Psychology* for both internships and doctoral training programs. Thus, future generations of students will have exposure to one or more evidence-based treatments. Research indicates that graduate school training in the research basis of psychotherapy is related to later positive attitudes towards ESTs, making it likely that in the coming years practitioners will find ESTs less controversial.

References and Readings

APA Presidential Task Force. (2006). Evidence-based practice in psychology. *American Psychologist, 61*, 271–285.

Chambless, D. L., & Hollon, S. D. (1998). Defining empirically supported therapies. *Journal of Consulting and Clinical Psychology, 66*, 7–18.

Chambless, D. L., & Ollendick, T. H. (2001). Empirically supported psychological interventions: Controversies and evidence. In S. T. Fiske, D. L. Schacter, & C. Zahn-Waxler (Eds.), *Annual Review of Psychology* (Vol. 52, pp. 685–716). Palo Alto, CA: Annual Reviews.

Straus, S. E., Glasziou, P., Richardson, W. S., & Haynes, B. R. (2011). *Evidence-based medicine: How to practice and teach it* (4th ed.). Edinburgh, Scotland: Elsevier/Churchill Livingstone.

Task Force on Promotion and Dissemination of Psychological Procedures. (1995). Training in and dissemination of empirically-validated psychological treatments: Report and recommendations. *The Clinical Psychologist, 48*(1), 3–23.

Related Topics

Chapter 30, "Compendium of Psychotherapy Treatment Manuals"
Chapter 32, "Compendium of Treatment Adapatations"
Chapter 33, "Compendium of Evidence-Based Therapy Relationships"
Chapter 72, "Locating the Best Research Evidence for Evidence-Based Practice"

32 COMPENDIUM OF TREATMENT ADAPTATIONS

John C. Norcross and Bruce E. Wampold

Psychotherapists have long advocated tailoring or adapting the treatment to the individuality of the patient and the singularity of the situation. Every psychotherapist recognizes that what may work for one person may not work for another; we embrace the individual difference maxim of "Different strokes for different folks." This matching process has been accorded different names: adaptation, responsiveness, attunement, tailoring, matchmaking, customization, prescriptionism, and individualization. However, the goal is identical: to increase treatment effectiveness by tailoring it to the person.

The most widely discussed and used means of adapting treatment has been to match a particular treatment to the patient's disorder. A patient presenting with, say, a specific anxiety disorder might be matched with cognitive-behavioral therapy, the most researched form of psychotherapy for anxiety. Such matching is certainly useful for select disorders; some psychotherapies make better marriages with some mental health disorders. But only matching disorder to treatment in this way is incomplete and not always effective (Wampold, 2001). As Sir William Osler, father of modern medicine, said: "It is sometimes much more important to know what sort of a patient has a disease than what sort of disease a patient has." The research demonstrates that it is indeed frequently effective to match psychotherapy to the entire person—not only to his or her disorder.

In this chapter, we summarize the meta-analytic research and clinical practices on effectively adapting psychotherapy to the individual patient. The research reveals evidence for six effective means of tailoring psychotherapy to transdiagnostic patient features.

REACTANCE LEVEL

Reactance refers to being easily provoked and responding oppositionally to external demands. Think of this personality trait along a defiance–compliance continuum: Some people tend to respond defiantly to authority figures and power, while others tend to respond in more compliant, easygoing ways. A meta-analysis of 12 select studies (1,102 patients) revealed a medium to large effect size (d = .76) for matching therapist directiveness to patient reactance (Beutler, Harwood, Michelson, Song, & Holman, 2011). High-reactance patients benefit more from self-control methods and less structured treatments. Low-reactance clients, on the other hand, benefit more from therapist directiveness, explicit guidance, and more structured treatments.

All other things being equal, trait-like resistance serves as indicators for patients who respond to directive treatments. Thus, psychotherapists are advised to assess their patients' reactance level, avoid stimulating patient's reactance in session, and match their degree of directiveness to patient reactance. In select instances, client resistance to a treatment may well be the result of mismatch; for example, a structured treatment used with a patient with a high level of reactance. Skilled therapists systematically vary their degree of directiveness to enhance treatment results and to prevent dropouts. Finally, as with all of these matches to patient characteristics, beware matching the degree of directiveness to the *psychotherapist's* reactance level; this frequently surfaces among neophyte therapists who unwittingly project their own personality structure onto clients.

STAGES OF CHANGE

Patients enter psychotherapy with varying readiness to change or what researchers have called stages of change. Some minimize or deny their problems (precontemplation stage), some acknowledge their problems but are not yet ready to modify them (contemplation stage), while others are ready and eager to alter their problems immediately (action stage). A patient's stage of change reliably predicts the success of psychotherapy. In a meta-analysis of 39 studies involving 8,238 patients, those clients starting treatment in the precontemplation stage did not fare nearly as well as those starting in the contemplation or action stage ($d = .46$; Norcross, Krebs, & Prochaska, 2011). Another meta-analysis of 47 different studies showed large effect sizes ($d = .70$–$.80$) for matching treatment methods to the different stages of change (Rosen, 2000). Specifically, consciousness-raising and emotion-generating methods (traditionally associated with psychodynamic, experiential, and cognitive therapies) are most effective in helping people move from contemplation, while skills training and more behavioral methods (traditionally associated with behavioral, exposure, and solution-focused therapies) are most effective for those in the action stage.

Clinically, psychotherapists can assess a client's stage of change and avoid treating everyone as though he or she is in the action stage. Optimally tailor the treatment to the client's stage and then move realistically from one stage to another. Perhaps most important, avoid stage-mismatching wherein the therapist and client are literally not on the same page. Disparate systems of psychotherapy will prove effective when differentially embedded in the stages of change. (See Chapter 34 on "Applying the Stages of Change" for more details.)

PREFERENCES

Psychotherapy can also be profitably matched in many cases to the patient's preferences in terms of the desired treatment modality (e.g., psychotherapy, medication), therapy method (e.g., psychodynamic, cognitive-behavioral, experiential), treatment format (individual, family, group), therapist characteristic (e.g., age, gender, religion), and treatment length (brief, medium, or long). A meta-analysis of 35 studies that compared the treatment success of clients matched to their preferences versus clients who were not matched found that clients receiving their preferences did significantly better ($d = .31$) and were a third less likely to drop out of psychotherapy prematurely (Swift, Callahan, & Vollmer, 2011).

Psychotherapists can recognize that desires and needs are not universal across patients and accordingly assess client preferences at the beginning of treatment. It is recommended that therapists reduce barriers that might prevent clients from expressing their preferences directly, such as dearth of information about treatment options or a belief that it would be impudent or disrespectful to discuss preferences with a doctor. It is the wise and evidence-based psychotherapist who explicitly accommodates the client's strong preferences whenever ethically and practically possible. Even when the therapist believes that a client's preferences will not prove best, share these concerns in session so that treatment decisions can be made collaboratively and transparently.

CULTURE

Evidence-based practice integrates the best available research with clinical expertise in the context of patient characteristics, culture, and preferences (American Psychological Association, 2006). A meta-analysis of 65 studies, entailing 8,620 clients, evaluated the impact of culturally adapted therapies vs. traditional (nonadapted) therapies. The results showed a definite advantage ($d = .46$) in favor of ethnic/racial clients receiving culturally adapted treatments (Smith, Rodríguez, & Bernal, 2011; see also Benish, Quintana, & Wampold, 2011).

In practice, patients will probably benefit when psychotherapists align treatment with their clients' cultural backgrounds. Whenever possible, conduct psychotherapy in the client's preferred language as this emerged as one of the strongest means of adapting treatment to culture. Professionals and clients can adapt psychotherapy to culture in various and multiple ways, such as incorporating cultural content/values into treatment, matching clients with therapists of similar ethnicity/race, and adapting the explanation to fit the client's belief about his or her problems. The greater number of these components incorporated, the more effective the treatment. In addition, the meta-analysis suggests that the therapist's visible, genuine efforts to align treatment to culture may count as much as the specific procedures undertaken to do so.

COPING STYLE

Another patient trait concerns coping style: how we characteristically respond to new or problematic situations in our lives. Some people tend to habitually withdraw or blame themselves (internalizers), some tend to regularly lash out or act out (externalizers), and of course, others are in the middle and use a balanced coping style. A meta-analysis of 12 studies (1,291 patients) found medium effect sizes ($d = .55$) for matching the therapist's method to the patient coping style (Beutler, Harwood, Kimpara, Verdirame, & Blau, 2011). In other words, patient coping style is a robust moderator of treatment outcome.

In practice, the research suggests assessing each patient's predominant coping style in the interest of treatment planning. Match the focus of treatment to that coping style: interpersonal and insight-oriented treatments tend to be more effective among internalizing patients, while symptom-focused and skill-building treatments tend to be more effective among externalizing patients. Even with internalizing patients, the research highlights the value in beginning treatment with symptom-reducing, pathology-stabilizing methods and then switching to more indirect, insight-oriented approaches. Psychotherapists can select among several treatment methods that fit patient personalities and preferences.

RELIGION/SPIRITUALITY

Some patients enter psychotherapy with a definite interest in incorporating their religious beliefs or spiritual values into the work. Many research studies have investigated whether these religious or spiritual-accommodative therapies work as well as, or better than, their secular counterparts. A meta-analysis of 46 studies, involving 3,290 clients, found that patients receiving such therapies experienced equivalent if not superior progress (Worthington, Hook, Davis, & McDaniel, 2011). When examining the most rigorous studies, in which the religious-accommodative therapies and alternative therapies shared the same theoretical orientation and treatment duration, there were no significant differences in the mental health outcomes between the treatments. However, patients receiving the religious or spiritual-accommodative therapies progressed significantly better ($d = .33$) in their spiritual outcomes than patients receiving secular therapies.

Religious and spiritual (R/S) psychotherapies perform as well if not outperform alternate psychotherapies on both psychological and spiritual outcomes. They are valid options for clients seeking or desiring them. At the same time, adding R/S to an established secular treatment does not reliably improve psychological outcomes over and above the effects of the secular treatment. But R/S therapies do offer spiritual benefits that are not usually present in secular therapies; thus, for patient and contexts where spiritual outcomes are highly valued, R/S therapies may be considered a treatment of choice. Such is particularly likely for highly religious patients.

OTHER POSSIBILITIES

Two more patient dimensions—outcome expectations (Constantino, Glass, Arnkoff, Ametrano, & Smith, 2011) and attachment style (Levy, Ellison, Scott, & Bernecker, 2011)—are related to treatment outcome. More optimistic and more securely attached patients reap greater benefits from psychotherapy, compared to patients manifesting pessimistic expectations and anxious attachment. However, we do not yet have as much or as compelling research on how to adapt psychotherapy specifically to client expectations and attachment. With empirical confidence, we can recommend that psychotherapists assess these patient dimensions, glean from the results of those assessments as to how the patient is likely to respond to treatment and the therapist, and work assiduously to cultivate more positive expectations and secure attachments. Research indicates that patient expectations and attachment style can be modified during treatment, which also suggests that such changes can be properly viewed as proximal treatment outcomes, not only as predictive or moderator variables.

The effectiveness of psychotherapy can be demonstrably improved by tailoring psychotherapy to one or more of these six transdiagnostic patient characteristics: reactance level, stage of change, preferences, culture, coping style, and religion/spirituality. Psychotherapists can create a new, responsive psychotherapy for each distinctive patient and singular situation—in addition to his or her disorder (Norcross & Wampold, 2011).

References and Readings

American Psychological Association Task Force on Evidence-Based Practice. (2006). Evidence-based practice in psychology. *American Psychologist, 61*, 271–285.

Beutler, L. E., Harwood, M. T., Kimpara, S., Verdirame, D., & Blau, K. (2011). Coping style. In J. C. Norcross (Ed.), *Psychotherapy relationships that work* (2nd ed., pp. 336–353). New York: Oxford University Press.

Beutler, L. E., Harwood, T. M., Michelson, A., Song, X., & Holman, J. (2011). Reactance/resistance level. In J. C. Norcross (Ed.), *Psychotherapy relationships that work* (2nd ed., pp. 261–278). New York: Oxford University Press.

Constantino, M., Glass, C. R., Arnkoff, D. B., Ametrano, R. M., & Smith, J. Z. (2011). Expectations. In J. C. Norcross (Ed.), *Psychotherapy relationships that work* (2nd ed., pp. 354–376). New York: Oxford University Press.

Levy, K. N., Ellison, W. D., Scott, L. N., & Bernecker, S. L. (2011) Attachment style. In J. C. Norcross (Ed.), *Psychotherapy relationships that work* (2nd ed., pp. 377–401). New York: Oxford University Press.

Norcross, J. C, Krebs, P., & Prochaska, J. O. (2011). Stages of change. In J. C. Norcross (Ed.), *Psychotherapy relationships that work* (2nd ed., pp. 279–300). New York: Oxford University Press.

Rosen, C. S. (2000). Is the sequencing of change processes by stage consistent across health problems? A meta-analysis. *Health Psychology, 19*(6), 593–604.

Smith, T. B., Rodríguez, M. D., & Bernal, G. (2011). Culture. In J. C. Norcross (Ed.), *Psychotherapy relationships that work* (2nd ed., pp. 316–335). New York: Oxford University Press.

Swift, J. K., Callahan, J. L., & Vollmer, B. M. (2011). Preferences. In J. C. Norcross (Ed.), *Psychotherapy relationships that work* (2nd ed., pp. 301–315). New York: Oxford University Press.

Wampold, B. E. (2001). *The great psychotherapy debate: Models, methods, and findings.* Mahwah, NJ: Erlbaum.

Worthington, E. L., Jr., Hook, J. N., Davis, D. E., & McDaniel, M. A. (2011). Religion and spirituality. In J. C. Norcross (Ed.), *Psychotherapy relationships that work* (2nd ed., pp. 402–419). New York: Oxford University Press.

Related Topics

Chapter 11, "Assessing Strengths in Clinical Practice"

Chapter 31, "Compendium of Empirically Supported Treatments"

Chapter 33, "Compendium of Evidence-Based Therapy Relationships"

Chapter 34, "Applying the Stages of Change"

Chapter 64, "Tailoring Treatment to the Patient's Race and Ethnicity"

33 COMPENDIUM OF EVIDENCE-BASED THERAPY RELATIONSHIPS

John C. Norcross and Michael J. Lambert

The American Psychological Association's Division of Psychotherapy and Division of Clinical Psychology jointly sponsored a task force to identify and disseminate what works in the therapy relationship (Norcross, 2011). The task force commissioned a series of original meta-analyses to investigate the association between elements of the therapy relationship and treatment effectiveness. Paralleling the notion of evidence-based *treatments of choice,* the meta-analytic results provide evidence-based *relationships of choice.*

Looking at four decades of research, the task force concluded the following:

- The therapy relationship makes substantial and consistent contributions to patient success in all types of psychotherapy studied.
- The relationship accounts for why clients improve (or fail to improve) as much as or more than the particular treatment method.
- Efforts to promulgate best practices or evidence-based practices (EBPs) without including therapy relationship variables are clinically incomplete and potentially misleading.
- The relationship acts in concert with treatment methods, patient characteristics, and practitioner qualities in determining outcome. A comprehensive understanding of effective psychotherapy will consider all these determinants and their optimal combinations.

In this chapter, we summarize 11 evidence-based elements of the therapy relationship primarily provided by the psychotherapist. (A twelfth element, repairing ruptures in the alliance, is covered in Chapter 52.) We define each therapist relational behavior in theoretically neutral language, review the results of the meta-analysis between that relationship element and treatment outcome, and then highlight the resultant therapeutic practices, in terms of both the therapist's contribution and the client's perspective.

Alliance in individual psychotherapy. The alliance is an emergent quality of partnership and mutual collaboration between therapist and client, built principally on a positive emotional bond between therapist and client and their ability to agree on the goals of treatment and to reach a mutual consensus on the tasks. A meta-analysis of 201 studies, involving over 14,000 patients, found an effect size (ES) of $r = .275$ (Horvath, Del Re, Flückiger, & Symonds, 2011). The magnitude of this relation accounts for roughly 8% of the total variance in therapy outcomes.

The research suggests that the development and maintenance of a good alliance is essential for the success of psychotherapy, regardless of the type of treatment. The ability of the therapist to bring the client's needs, expectations, and abilities into a therapeutic plan is important in building that alliance.

Because the therapist and client often judge the quality of the alliance differently, active monitoring of the alliance from the client's point of view throughout therapy is recommended. Responding nondefensively to a client's hostility or negativity is critical to establishing and maintaining a strong alliance.

Alliance in child and adolescent psychotherapy. As in the adult research, the alliance in youth treatment is characterized as a collaborative bond between client and therapist. But here the psychotherapist typically established two alliances: one with the youth and one with the parent or guardian. A meta-analysis of 29 studies with 2,202 youth clients and 892 parents was conducted to estimate the association between alliance and outcome in youth therapy (Shirk & Karver, 2011). The effect size was .19, both between the therapist and the youth as well as between the therapist and the parent/guardian.

Alliances with both youth and their parents predict positive treatment outcomes. Thus, therapists need to attend to the development of multiple alliances, not just to the alliance with the youth. A solid alliance with the parent may be critical for treatment continuation in particular. Alliance formation is not simply an early treatment task; it is a recurrent task. Maintaining a positive alliance over time predicts successful outcomes as well.

Alliance in couple and family therapy. Just as in individual therapy, the alliance in couple and family therapy (CFT) involves the creation of a strong emotional bond as well as negotiation of goals and tasks with the therapist. However, family members often vary in the degree to which they like and agree with the therapist about treatment goals and tasks. Thus, a unique characteristic of CFT is that at any point in treatment there are multiple alliances interacting systemically.

Friedlander and colleagues (2011) conducted a meta-analysis of 24 studies (7 couples, 17 family studies; 1,461 clients) in which CFT alliances were used to predict treatment retention, improvement midtreatment, and/or final outcomes. The effect size was $r = .26$, indicating that the alliance accounted for a substantial proportion of variance in CFT retention and outcome. According to conventional benchmarks, an r of .26 ($d = .53$) is a medium effect size in the behavioral sciences; the success rate increases from 37% to 63% in low- versus high-alliance cases.

The resultant implication is that therapists need to be aware of what is going on within the family system while monitoring the personal bond and agreement on goals and tasks with each individual family member. The shared sense of purpose within the family, an essential dimension of the CFT alliance, involves establishing overarching systemic goals (e.g., "It sounds like what the two of you want is a relationship in which you feel both connected and that you can sometimes do your own thing") rather than competing, first-order, individual goals (i.e., "I want him to stop watching sports on TV every Saturday"). Another important aspect of CFT alliances is the degree to which family members feel safe and comfortable with each other in the therapeutic context. Creating a safe space is critical, particularly early on in therapy, but doing so requires caution. A therapist who allies too strongly with a resistant adolescent may unwittingly damage the alliance with the parents, particularly when the latter are expecting the teen to change but are not expecting to be personally challenged by the therapist.

Cohesion in group therapy. Cohesion describes therapeutic relationships in group psychotherapy and has two dimensions: relationship *structure* and relationship *quality*. *Structure* refers to the direction of the relationship. In describing direction, vertical cohesion refers to a group member's perception of the group leader's competence, genuineness, and warmth. Horizontal cohesion describes a group member's relationship with other group members and with the group as a whole. The *quality* of the group relationships is defined by how members feel with their leader and with other members (positive bond), by the tasks and goals of the group (positive work), and also the empathic failure with the leader and conflict in the group (negative relationship).

A meta-analysis of 40 studies, composed of 3,323 patients, was conducted on the association between cohesion and the success of group psychotherapy (Burlingame, McClendon, & Alonso, 2011). The overall effect size was a moderate *r* of .25. This indicates that, as cohesion levels increase in groups, client outcomes improve and psychological symptoms decrease. This correlation was found for therapy groups across different settings (inpatient and outpatient) and diagnostic classifications.

In practice, group leaders should strive to foster cohesion in its multiple manifestations. Group leaders emphasizing member interaction, irrespective of theoretical orientation, achieve higher cohesion-outcome links than groups without this emphasis. Thus, it is important to encourage member interaction. In addition, cohesion is strongest when a group lasts more than 12 sessions and is composed of 5 to 9 members. Group cohesion thus requires time to build. And younger group members tend to experience the largest outcome changes when cohesion is present within their groups. Fostering cohesion will be particularly useful for those working in college counseling centers and with adolescent populations.

Empathy. Much of the research continues to follow Carl Rogers's definition of empathy as the therapist's sensitive ability and willingness to understand the client's thoughts, feelings, and struggles from the client's point of view and communicate that understanding to the patient. A meta-analysis examined the association between therapist empathy and treatment outcome (Elliott, Bohart, Watson, & Greenberg, 2011). The analysis of 57 studies, representing 3,599 clients and 224 separate effects, resulted in an overall ES of .30, a medium effect, between therapist empathy and client success (suggesting a success rate of 57% compared to 43% for higher versus lower empathy). Empathy predicted treatment outcome consistently across different theoretical orientations (e.g., CBT, humanistic) and was strongest for client-rated empathy.

These results indicate that psychotherapists should make efforts to understand their client's experiences and to demonstrate this understanding through responses that address the client's needs as the client perceives them. Empathic therapists do not parrot clients' words back or reflect only the content of those words; instead, they understand clients' overall goals and moment-to-moment experiences. Such empathic responses can take many forms, including straightforward responses that convey understanding of the meaning of experience but also responses that support the client's perspective, that try to bring the client's experience to life using evocative language, or that aim at what is implicit but not yet expressed in words. Prioritize the client's experience of empathy as it best predicts treatment retention and success.

Goal consensus. At the beginning of treatment, psychotherapists and clients outline the conditions of their work together. Agreement about the nature of the problem for which the client is seeking help, goals for treatment, and the way that the two parties will work together to achieve these goals are the essence of *goal consensus*.

A meta-analysis was undertaken to address how patient–therapist goal consensus relates to psychotherapy outcome (Tryon & Winograd, 2011). The goal consensus-outcome meta-analysis—based on 15 studies with a total sample of 1,302—yielded an overall effect size of .34. This substantial result reflects the meaningful positive outcomes that are associated with higher agreement between therapists and clients about the aims of treatment and how to accomplish such aims.

The results argue that therapists and clients who begin psychotherapy by agreeing on treatment goals and the ways they will go about reaching them together will have the better outcomes. Therapists who push their own agenda instead of listening to what patients say and formulate interventions without their input will have poorer outcomes.

Collaboration. To help clients fulfill mutual treatment goals, professionals and patients should function as a team. *Collaboration* represents the active process of their cooperation in this endeavor.

The collaboration-outcome meta-analysis—based on 19 studies involving 2,260 patients—yielded an overall effect size of .33 (Tryon & Winograd, 2011). As with goal consensus, this result suggests that patient well-being is considerably enhanced with a better collaborative relationship. Good treatment entails valuing clients' contributions throughout psychotherapy by respectfully requesting their feedback, insights, reflections, and elaborations. Finally, clients need to recognize the important role they play in achieving goal consensus and collaboration with mental health professionals.

Positive regard/affirmation. Carl Rogers's (1951, p. 20) notion of positive regard is embodied in two questions he posed: "Do we tend to treat individuals as persons of worth, or do we subtly devaluate them by our attitudes and behavior? Is our philosophy one in which respect for the individual is uppermost?" This caring attitude has most often been termed *positive regard,* but early studies and theoretical writings preferred the phrase *nonpossessive warmth.*

To investigate the association between the therapist's positive regard and treatment outcome, Farber and Doolin (2011) performed a meta-analysis of 18 studies. The overall effect size among these studies was $r = .27$, indicating that positive regard has a moderate association with therapeutic outcomes. Only 2 of the 18 studies had negative effect sizes. Thus, like many other relational factors, positive regard appears to be a significant but hardly an exhaustive part of the process-outcome equation. The results indicated that as the percentage of racial/ethnic minorities increases in a study, the overall effect size also increases.

The provision of positive regard is strongly indicated in practice. At a minimum, it "sets the stage" for other beneficial treatment methods. Positive regard may be especially useful when a nonminority therapist is working with a racial/ethnic minority client. It appears to be important that therapists ensure that their positive feelings toward their clients are communicated to them. For many, if not most clients, the conviction that "my therapist really cares about me" likely serves a critical function, especially in times of stress and exposure of negative feelings.

Congruence/genuineness. Congruence or genuineness refers to a therapist's relational quality with two facets: a mindful genuineness and a capacity to conscientiously communicate his or her experience to the client. Congruence is thus both a personal characteristic (intrapersonal) of the therapist, as well as an experiential quality of the therapy relationship (interpersonal).

A meta-analysis was conducted on the relation between therapist congruence and treatment outcome in 16 studies involving 863 clients (Kolden, Klein, Wang, & Austin, 2011). The overall effect size for congruence with outcome was .24, a small to medium-sized effect, accounting for about 6% of the variance in outcome.

In practice, psychotherapists can embrace the idea of striving for congruence with their clients. This involves acceptance of and receptivity to the client as well as a willingness to use this information in conversation. An effective therapist *models* congruence. This may involve self-disclosure as well as sharing of thoughts and feelings, opinions, pointed questions, and feedback regarding client behavior. Congruent responses are honest; they are not disrespectful, overly intellectualized, or insincere. Moreover, a congruent therapist *communicates* acceptance and the possibility of engaging in a genuine relationship, something not easily expected from others in clients' lives. As with all of these relational elements, therapists can discern the differing needs and preferences that their clients have for congruence. Effective therapists will tailor their congruence style according to client characteristics (e.g., culture, age, education).

Collecting client feedback. In this relational behavior, the therapist systematically monitors a client's mental health vital signs through the use of standardized scales and expected treatment response. Results of this monitoring are then fed back in real time to the therapist and discussed in session with the client. Several well-developed feedback systems are in operation, including the Outcome Questionnaire measures and the Partners for Change Outcome Measurement System.

Lambert and Shimokawa (2011) conducted a meta-analysis to estimate the impact of feedback methods on treatment outcomes. The meta-analysis contained nine studies that examined the effectiveness of these two popular but distinct feedback methods. Results of the meta-analysis showed overall effect sizes between .23 and .33. When client feedback with warning signals for at-risk therapy were combined with decision support tools for such cases, the effect sizes reached .70. Rates of patient deterioration in psychotherapy were cut by two-thirds and positive outcomes doubled under such circumstances.

Accordingly, patients are better off when practitioners routinely monitor patients' ongoing mental health functioning. Such monitoring leads to increased opportunities to repair alliance ruptures, enhance motivation, attend to client social support, and reduce premature termination. Systematic feedback is especially useful in helping clinicians identify the possible failure of ongoing treatment and collaborating with the client in restoring positive outcomes. Feedback systems that rely on client self-reports of functioning and particularly negative change during treatment can compensate for a therapist's limited ability to accurately detect client worsening in psychotherapy. Effective use of these methods requires therapists to be aware of those situations in which clients feel it may be in their interest to understate (or overstate) their problems and produce inaccurate ratings on feedback systems.

Managing countertransference. Countertransference (CT) is a psychotherapist's internal and external negative reactions to a client, presumably influenced by the therapist's personal vulnerabilities and unresolved conflicts. Hayes, Gelso, and Hummel (2011) located 27 studies involving a total of 1,152 patients that investigated CT, CT management, and client outcome. The overall association of CT with treatment outcome in these studies was negative but small, $r = -.16$. On the other hand, the association of CT management to treatment outcome was positive and large, $r = .56$; that is, better management of therapist negative feelings led to 63% of the clients being better off versus 37% when CT is poorly managed.

As translated into practice, psychotherapists' unresolved inner conflicts seem to be related to the likelihood of antitherapeutic effects of CT, which in turn are associated with poorer client outcomes. Psychotherapists acting out of their CT can be harmful, and it appears wise for therapists to work at preventing such acting out. Therapists are encouraged to resolve their personal conflicts through self-reflection, personal therapy, clinical supervision, or all three. Insofar as CT management facilitates positive treatment outcomes, therapists are urged to manage internal CT reactions in ways that prevent them from being manifested behaviorally in session.

SUMMARY

Researchers cannot study all of these relationship behaviors simultaneously, and it is obvious that there is considerable overlap in these constructs and in the amount of variance they account for in psychotherapy. At the same time, it is demonstrably true that these relationship behaviors are important predictors and contributors to psychotherapy success that can be learned and, in most cases, taught.

References and Readings

Burlingame, G., McClendon, D. T., & Alonso, J. (2011). Group cohesion. In J. C. Norcross (Ed.), *Psychotherapy relationships that work* (2nd ed., pp. 110–131). New York: Oxford University Press.

Elliott, R., Bohart, A. C., Watson, J. C., & Greenberg, L. S. (2011). Empathy. In J. C. Norcross (Ed.), *Psychotherapy relationships that work* (2nd ed., pp. 132–152). New York: Oxford University Press.

Farber, B. A., & Doolin, E. M. (2011). Positive regard. In J. C. Norcross (Ed.), *Psychotherapy relationships that work* (2nd ed., pp. 168–186). New York: Oxford University Press.

Friedlander, M. L., Escudero, V., Heatherington, L., & Diamond, G. M. (2011). Alliance in couple and family therapy. In J. C. Norcross (Ed.), *Psychotherapy relationships that work*. (2nd ed., pp. 92–109). New York: Oxford University Press.

Hayes, J., Gelso, C., & Hummel, A. (2011). Managing countertransference. In J. C. Norcross (Ed.), *Psychotherapy relationships that work* (2nd ed., pp. 239–259). New York: Oxford University Press.

Horvath, A. O., Del Re, A., Flückiger, C., & Symonds, D. (2011). Alliance in individual psychotherapy. In J. C. Norcross (Ed.), *Psychotherapy relationships that work* (2nd ed., pp. 25–69). New York: Oxford University Press.

Kolden, G. G., Klein, M. H., Wang, C., & Austin, S. B. (2011). Congruence/genuineness. In J. C. Norcross (Ed.), *Psychotherapy relationships that work* (2nd ed., pp. 187–202). New York: Oxford University.

Lambert, M. J., & Shimokawa, K. (2011). Collecting client feedback. In J. C. Norcross (Ed.), *Psychotherapy relationships that work* (2nd ed., pp. 203–223). New York: Oxford University Press.

Norcross, J. C. (Ed.). (2011). *Psychotherapy relationships that work* (2nd ed.). New York: Oxford University Press.

Rogers, C. R. (1951). *Client-centered therapy*. Boston, MA: Houghton Mifflin.

Shirk, S. R., & Karver, M. (2011). Alliance in child and adolescent therapy. In J. C. Norcross (Ed.), *Psychotherapy relationships that work* (2nd ed., pp. 70–91). New York: Oxford University Press.

Tryon, G. S., & Winograd, G. (2011). Goal consensus and collaboration. In J. C. Norcross (Ed.), *Psychotherapy relationships that work* (2nd ed., pp. 153–167). New York: Oxford University Press.

Related Topics

Chapter 31, "Compendium of Empirically Supported Treatments"
Chapter 34, "Applying the Stages of Change"
Chapter 40, "Conducting Motivational Interviewing"
Chapter 52, "Repairing Ruptures in the Therapeutic Alliance"
Chapter 53, "Reducing Resistance in Psychotherapy"

34 APPLYING THE STAGES OF CHANGE

James O. Prochaska, John C. Norcross, and Carlo C. DiClemente

Over the past 30 years our research has focused on the structure that underlies both self-initiated and treatment-facilitated behavior change (see DiClemente, 2006; Norcross, Krebs, & Prochaska, 2011; Prochaska & Norcross, 2013). From a transtheoretical perspective, this chapter summarizes prescriptive and proscriptive guidelines for improving treatment based on the client's stage of change.

THE STAGES

1. *Precontemplation* is the stage at which there is no intention to change behavior in the foreseeable future. Most individuals in this stage are unaware or underaware of their problems. Families, friends, neighbors, or employers, however, are often well aware that the precontemplators have problems. When precontemplators present for psychotherapy, they often do so because of pressure from others. Usually they feel coerced into changing by spouses who threaten to leave, employers who threaten to dismiss them, parents who threaten to disown them, or courts who threaten to punish them.

There are multiple ways to measure the stages of change. In our studies employing the discrete categorization measurement of stages of change, we ask whether the individual is seriously intending to change the problem behavior in the near future, typically within the next 6 months. If not, he or she is classified as a precontemplator. Even precontemplators can wish to change, but this is quite different from intending or seriously considering change. Items that are used to identify precontemplation on the continuous stage of change measure include the following: "As far as I'm concerned, I don't have any problems that need changing" and "I guess I have faults, but there's nothing that I really need to change." Resistance to recognizing or modifying a problem is the hallmark of precontemplation.

2. *Contemplation* is the stage in which people are aware that a problem exists and are seriously thinking about overcoming it, but they have not yet made a commitment to take action. People can remain stuck in the contemplation stage for long periods. In one study of self-changers, we followed a group of 200 smokers in the contemplation stage for 2 years. The modal response of this group was to remain in the contemplation stage for the entire 2 years of the project without ever moving to significant action.

Contemplators struggle with their positive evaluations of their dysfunctional behavior and the amount of effort, energy, and loss it will cost to overcome it. On discrete measures, individuals who state that they are seriously considering changing their behavior in the next 6 months are classified as contemplators. On the continuous measure, these individuals endorse such items as "I have a problem and I really think I should work on it" and "I've been thinking that I might want to change something about myself." Serious consideration of problem resolution is the central element of contemplation.

3. *Preparation* is a stage that combines intention and behavioral criteria. Individuals in this stage are intending to take action in the next month and have unsuccessfully taken action in the past year. As a group, individuals who are prepared for action report small behavioral changes, such as smoking five fewer cigarettes or delaying their first cigarette of the day for 30 minutes longer than precontemplators or contemplators. Although they have reduced their problem behaviors, individuals in the preparation stage have not yet reached a criterion for effective action, such as abstinence from smoking or alcohol abuse. They are intending, however, to take such action in the very near future. On the continuous measure, they score high on both the contemplation and action scales.

4. *Action* is the stage in which individuals modify their behavior, experiences, and/or environment in order to overcome their problems. Action involves the most overt behavioral changes and requires considerable commitment of time and energy. Behavioral changes in the action stage tend to be most visible and externally recognized. Individuals are classified in the action stage if they have successfully altered the dysfunctional behavior for a period from 1 day to 6 months. On the continuous measure, individuals in the action stage endorse statements like "I am really working hard to change" and "Anyone can talk about changing; I am actually doing something about it." They score high on the action scale and lower on the other scales. Modification of the target behavior to an acceptable criterion and concerted overt efforts to change are the hallmarks of action.

5. *Maintenance* is the stage in which people work to prevent relapse and consolidate the gains attained during action. For addictive behaviors, this stage extends from 6 months to an indeterminate period past the initial action. For some behaviors, maintenance can be considered to last a lifetime. Remaining free of the addictive behavior and consistently engaging in a new incompatible behavior for more than 6 months are the criteria for the maintenance stage. On the continuous measure, representative maintenance items are "I may need a boost right now to help me maintain the changes I've already made" and "I'm here to prevent myself from having a relapse of my problem." Stabilizing behavior change and avoiding relapse are the hallmarks of maintenance.

However, change is not a linear progression through the stages; rather, most clients move through the stages of change in a *spiral pattern*. People progress from contemplation to preparation to action to maintenance, but most individuals will relapse. During relapse, individuals regress to an earlier stage. Some relapsers feel like failures—embarrassed, ashamed, and guilty. These individuals become demoralized and resist thinking about behavior change. As a result, they return to the precontemplation stage and can remain there for various periods of time. Approximately 15% of relapsers in our self-change research regressed to the precontemplation stage. Fortunately, most—85% or so—move back to the contemplation stage and eventually back into preparation and action.

PRACTICE RECOMMENDATIONS

1. *Assess the client's stage of change.* Probably the most obvious and direct implication is the need to assess the stage of a client's readiness for change and to tailor interventions accordingly. Stages of change can be ascertained by multiple means, of which three self-report methods will be described here.

A first and most efficient method is to ask the patient a simple series of questions to identify his or her stage—for example, "Do you think behavior X is a problem for you now?" (if yes, then contemplation, preparation, or action stage; if no, then maintenance or precontemplation stage) and "When do you intend to change behavior X?" (if some day or not soon, then contemplation stage; if in the next month, then preparation; if now, then the action stage). A second method is to assess the stage from a series of mutually exclusive questions, and a third is a continuous measure that yields separate scales for precontemplation, contemplation, action, and maintenance.

2. *Beware treating all patients as though they are in action.* Professionals frequently design excellent action-oriented treatment and self-help programs, but then are disappointed when only a small percentage of people register or when large numbers drop out of the program after registering. The vast majority of people are not in the action stage. Aggregating across studies and populations, we estimate that 20% are prepared for action, approximately 35% to 40% are in the contemplation stage, and 40% to 45% in the precontemplation stage. Thus, professionals approaching patients and settings only with action-oriented programs are likely to underserve or misserve the majority of their target population.

3. *Assist clients in moving one stage at a time.* If clients progress from one stage to the next during the first month of treatment, they can double their chances of taking action in the next 6 months. Among smokers, for example, of the precontemplators who were still in precontemplation at 1-month follow-up, only 3% took action by 6 months. For the precontemplators who progressed to contemplation at 1 month, 7% took action by 6 months. Similarly, of the contemplators who remained in contemplation at 1 month, only 20% took action by 6 months. At 1 month, 41% of the contemplators who progressed to the preparation stage attempted to quit by 6 months. These data indicate that treatments designed to help people progress just one stage in a month may double the chances of participants taking action on their own in the near future.

4. *Recognize that clients in the action stage are far more likely to achieve better and quicker outcomes.* The amount of progress clients make during treatment tends to be a function of their pretreatment stage of change (Norcross, Krebs, & Prochaska, 2011). For example, an intensive action- and maintenance-oriented smoking cessation program for cardiac patients achieved success for 22% of precontemplators, 43% of contemplators, and 76% of those in action or prepared for action at the start of the study were not smoking 6 months later. This repeated finding has direct implications for selecting and prioritizing treatment goals.

5. *Facilitate the insight-action crossover.* Patients in successful treatment evidence steady progression on the stages of change. Patients entering therapy are often in the contemplation or preparation stage. In the midst of treatment, patients typically cross over from contemplation into action. Patients who remain in treatment progress from being prepared for action to taking action over time. That is, they shift from thinking about their problems to doing things to overcome them. Lowered precontemplation scores also indicate that, as engagement in therapy increases, patients reduce their defensiveness and resistance. The progression from contemplation to action is postulated to be essential for beneficial outcome regardless of whether the treatment is action oriented or insight oriented.

6. *Anticipate recycling.* Most self-changers and psychotherapy patients will recycle several times through the stages before achieving long-term maintenance. Accordingly, intervention programs and professionals expecting people to progress linearly through the stages are likely to gather disappointing results. Be prepared to include relapse prevention in treatment, anticipate the probability of recycling patients, and minimize therapist guilt and patient shame over recycling.

7. *Conceptualize change as processes, not specific techniques.* Literally hundreds of specific psychotherapeutic techniques have been advanced; however, a small and finite set of change processes or strategies underlie these multitudinous techniques.

Change processes are covert and overt activities that individuals engage in when they attempt to modify problem behaviors. Each process is a broad category encompassing multiple techniques, methods, and interventions traditionally associated with disparate theoretical orientations. These change processes can be used within therapy sessions, between therapy sessions, or without therapy sessions.

The processes of change represent an intermediate level of abstraction between meta-theoretical assumptions and specific techniques spawned by those theories. While there are 500-plus ostensibly different psychotherapies, we have been able to identify only 12 different processes of change based on principal components analysis.

Table 34.1 presents the eight processes receiving the most theoretical and empirical support in our work, along with their definitions and representative examples of specific interventions. A common and finite set of change processes has been repeatedly identified across diverse disorders.

8. *Do the right things (processes) at the right time (stages).* Thirty years of research in behavioral medicine, self-change, and psychotherapy converge in showing that different processes of change are differentially effective in certain stages of change; a meta-analysis of

TABLE 34.1. Titles, Definitions, and Representative Interventions of Eight Processes of Change

Process	Definition: Interventions
1. Consciousness raising	Increasing information about self and problem: observations; confrontations; interpretations; feedback; bibliotherapy
2. Self-reevaluation	Assessing how one feels and thinks about oneself with respect to a problem: value clarification; imagery; corrective emotional experience
3. Emotional arousal (or dramatic relief)	Experiencing and expressing feelings about one's problems and solutions: psychodrama; grieving losses; role playing; journaling
4. Social liberation	Increasing alternatives for nonproblem behaviors available in society: advocating for rights of repressed; empowering; policy interventions
5. Self-liberation	Choosing and committing to act or belief in ability to change: decision-making therapy; New Year's resolutions; logotherapy techniques; commitment-enhancing techniques
6. Counterconditioning	Substituting alternatives for anxiety related behaviors: relaxation; desensitization; assertion; cognitive restructuring
7. Stimulus control	Avoiding or countering stimuli that elicit problem behaviors: restructuring one's environment (e.g., removing alcohol or fattening foods); avoiding high-risk cues; fading techniques
8. Contingency management	Rewarding oneself or being rewarded by others for making changes: contingency contracts; overt and covert reinforcement; self-reward

Source: Adapted from Prochaska, DiClemente, & Norcross, 1992.

47 studies (Rosen, 2000) found effect sizes of .70 and .80 for the use of different change processes in the stages. In general terms, change processes traditionally associated with the experiential, cognitive, and psychoanalytic persuasions are most useful during the earlier precontemplation and contemplation stages. Change processes traditionally associated with the existential and behavioral traditions, by contrast, are most useful during action and maintenance.

In the transtheoretical model, particular change processes will be optimally applied at each stage of change. During the precontemplation stage, individuals use the change processes significantly less than people in any of the other stages. Precontemplators process less information about their problems, devote less time and energy to reevaluating themselves, and experience fewer emotional reactions to the negative aspects of their problems. In therapy, these are the most resistant or the least active clients.

Individuals in the contemplation stage are most open to consciousness-raising techniques, such as observations, confrontations, and interpretations, and are much more likely to use bibliotherapy and other educational techniques. Contemplators also profitably employ emotional arousal, which raises emotions and leads to a lowering of negative affect when the person changes. As individuals became more conscious of themselves and the nature of their problems, they are more likely to reevaluate their values, problems, and themselves both affectively and cognitively.

Both movement from precontemplation to contemplation and movement through the contemplation stage entail increased use of cognitive, affective, and evaluative processes of change. Some of these changes continue during the preparation stage. In addition, individuals in preparation begin to take small steps toward action.

During the action stage, people use higher levels of self-liberation or willpower. They increasingly believe that they have the autonomy to change their lives in key ways. Successful action also entails effective use of behavioral processes, such as counterconditioning and stimulus control, in order to modify the conditional stimuli that frequently prompt relapse. Contingency management also comes into frequent use here.

Successful maintenance builds on each of the processes that came before. Specific preparation for maintenance entails an assessment of the conditions under which a person would be likely to relapse and development of alternative responses for coping with such conditions without resorting to self-defeating defenses and pathological responses. Continuing to apply counterconditioning, stimulus control, and contingency management is most effective when based on the conviction that maintaining change supports a sense of self that is highly valued by oneself and significant others.

9. *Prescribe stage-matched "relationships of choice" as well as "treatments of choice."* Psychotherapists seek to customize or tailor their interpersonal stance to different patients. One way to conceptualize the matter, paralleling the notion of "treatments of choice" in terms of techniques, is how clinicians determine therapeutic "relationships of choice" in terms of interpersonal stances (Norcross, 2011).

The research and clinical consensus on the therapist's stance at different stages can be characterized as follows. With precontemplators often the role is like that of a nurturing parent joining with the resistant youngster who is both drawn to and repelled by the prospects of becoming more independent. With contemplators, the therapist role is akin to a Socratic teacher who encourages clients to achieve their own insights and ideas into their condition. With clients who are in the preparation stage, the stance is more like that of an experienced coach who has been through many crucial matches and can provide a fine game plan or can review the person's own action plan. With clients who are progressing into action and maintenance, the psychotherapist becomes more of a consultant who is available to provide expert advice and support when action is not progressing as smoothly as expected.

10. *Avoid mismatching stages and processes.* A person's stage of change provides proscriptive as well as prescriptive information on treatments of choice. Action-oriented therapies may be quite effective with individuals who are in the preparation or action stages. These same programs may be ineffective or detrimental, however, with individuals in the precontemplation or contemplation stages.

We have observed two frequent mismatches. First, some therapists rely primarily on change processes most indicated for the contemplation stage—consciousness raising, self-reevaluation—while they are moving into the action stage. They try to modify behaviors by becoming more aware, a common criticism of classical psychoanalysis: Insight alone does not necessarily bring about behavior change. Second, other therapists rely primarily on change processes most indicated for the action stage—contingency management, stimulus control, counterconditioning—without the requisite awareness, decision making, and readiness provided in the contemplation and preparation stages. They try to modify behavior without awareness, a common criticism of radical behaviorism: Overt action without insight is likely to lead to temporary change.

11. *Think complementarily.* Competing systems of psychotherapy have promulgated purportedly rival processes of change. However, ostensibly contradictory processes become complementary when embedded in the stages of change. Our research has consistently documented that ordinary people in their natural environments and psychotherapists in their consultation rooms can be remarkably effective in synthesizing powerful change processes across the stages of change.

References and Readings

DiClemente, C. C. (2006). *Addiction and change.* New York: Guilford Press.

Norcross, J. C. (Ed.). (2011). *Psychotherapy relationships that work* (2nd ed.). New York: Oxford University Press.

Norcross, J. C., Krebs, P. M., & Prochaska, J. O. (2011). Stages of change. *Journal of Clinical Psychology, 67,* 143–154.

Prochaska, J. O., DiClemente, C. C., & Norcross, J. C. (1992). In search of how people change: Applications to addictive behaviors. *American Psychologist, 47,* 1102–1114.

Prochaska, J. O., Norcross, J. C., & DiClemente, C. C. (1995). *Changing for good.* New York: Avon.

Prochaska, J. O., & Norcross, J. C. (2013). *Systems of psychotherapy: A transtheoretical analysis* (8th ed.). Pacific Grove, CA: Brooks/Cole.

Rosen, C. S. (2000). Is the sequencing of change processes by stage consistent across health problems? A meta-analysis. *Health Psychology, 19,* 593–604.

University of Rhode Island, Cancer Prevention Research Center. (n.d.).Retrieved January 2013, from www.uri.edu/research/cprc/

Valasquez, M. M., Maurer, G., Crouch, C., & DiClemente, C. C. (2001). *Group treatment for substance abuse: A stages-of-change therapy manual.* New York: Guilford Press.

Related Topics

Chapter 32, "Compendium of Treatment Adaptations"
Chapter 40, "Conducting Motivational Interviewing"

35 ENHANCING PATIENT ADHERENCE TO TREATMENT

M. Robin DiMatteo

Adherence (also called *compliance*) refers to the success of a client/patient in implementing the recommendations of a health care professional for the prevention or management of health conditions. More simply, adherence refers to "cooperation with therapy." Health professionals are often frustrated by noncompliance, such as when their patients fail to take medication as prescribed, or test their blood glucose levels only sporadically, or make misguided health care choices based on the recommendations of friends or television commercials instead of the advice of their providers. Consumers may be nonadherent because they forget or misunderstand the regimen, fail to apply the necessary effort, or ignore the prescribed treatment altogether because they do not believe it is worth the trouble. Even patients who are very committed to a regimen might find it too difficult and beyond their resources.

Herewith are a dozen evidence-based methods for improving patient adherence to treatment.

1. *Assess adherence.* The first step in achieving adherence involves assessing it correctly, an endeavor that can be surprisingly challenging. Determining whether patients have been using their cognitive therapy techniques or have taken their antidepressant requires trust and open communication. The behavioral challenges that patients face might be difficult for them to acknowledge. Clinicians should not assume that all their patients are adherent; likely many of them are not (see item 4). A clinician should offer clients a safe atmosphere in which to disclose adherence difficulties and a supportive context in which to respond to straightforward questions about adherence. Researchers and clinicians often use other means as well—counting remaining pills, weighing the contents of canisters such as inhalers, and asking family members—but direct communication with patients about their adherence remains the best way to determine what patients are doing.

2. *Adopt an open and collaborative relationship regarding the regimen.* A therapeutic relationship that fosters adherence is built with the patient through active listening, a nonjudgmental attitude, and empathy (see Chapter 33). These elements of care are best conveyed through positive and supportive verbal messages and nonverbal cues involving facial expressions, body orientation and attention, and vocal tone. A therapeutic relationship that allows both honest discussion about adherence difficulties and a commitment to working together to overcome them has the greatest chance of success. Although patients are often not eager to tell their health professionals about the many factors that might interfere with their adherence, the clinician should strive toward open communication that offers a view of the treatment picture from the patient's point of view. Sometimes the client has no idea what the health professional is talking about (but nods his or her head in agreement anyway). Patients can do only what they understand and they need to feel safe enough to ask questions.

3. *Do not equate adherence with outcome.* It is critically important not to confuse treatment outcomes with adherence. Adherence is behavior; it might be highly related to outcome, but the two are not equal. If the clinical picture is confusing and the patient is not exhibiting the predicted clinical response, it is certainly possible that nonadherence is the reason. However, while striving to assess adherence accurately (see item 1), the clinician should explore the possibility that the treatment is not working. Needless to say, the success of the treatment depends upon the fit and efficacy of the treatment regimen.

4. *Understand the prevalence.* The prevalence of nonadherence depends upon the type of disorder and on the complexity of the treatment regimen. Across hundreds of studies, adherence rates average from 20% to about 50%, with the highest level of adherence occurring when the disease is considered serious and adherence is essential to survival (e.g., HIV disease, cancer), and when the intervention has immediate and obvious effects (e.g., reduction in pain/distress in arthritis and gastrointestinal disorders). Adherence tends to be considerably lower for the treatment of such conditions as diabetes, where care can be complex and limiting, and patients do not necessarily feel better when they adhere. In pharmacotherapy for mental disorders, adherence to medication tends to be lower in the context of difficult side effects or the absence of obvious benefits and higher when medications make people feel better. The clinician should be aware of the potential for nonadherence when treatment is not immediately or obviously helpful in relieving patient suffering.

5. *Address the patient's views of effectiveness.* Adherence is not necessarily positively correlated with the objective efficacy of treatment. A patient's subjective assessment of the effectiveness of his or her treatment is a better predictor of that patient's adherence. Clinicians should be thorough in communicating to patients the value of their treatment regimen and should make clear the expected benefits of adhering. Clinicians should also strive to understand their patients' beliefs about the regimen; while nonadherence might make little sense to the clinician, it is often viewed by the patient as a perfectly rational choice. An honest conversation about what the patient has heard and believes about the treatment will help to determine whether the patient is committed to the treatment or remains unconvinced that the regimen is worthy of the time and trouble it demands. Patients tend to follow only treatments they believe in. Sometimes, unfortunately, television advertisements and neighbors' opinions make more sense to the client than those of the health care professional.

6. *Understand the patient's practical reasons for nonadherence.* Health care is likely a small part of a patient's everyday life. What makes sense to "commit to" in the office might be quite difficult to implement at home, where competing demands of work and family jeopardize adherence. Patients usually allocate their limited resources as well as they can. Every treatment regimen should be tailored as much as possible to fit into the patient's life. Often, there are practical challenges to patient adherence that need to be addressed and overcome, whether they involve complex lifestyle choices and self-care routines for medical conditions, the control of thoughts and behaviors using psychological methods, or the management of mental conditions with medication. Patients can only do what they are able to do, and clinicians can only help their patients if they know what challenges they are facing.

7. *Use written communication.* Misunderstanding and forgetting are common in treatment. Immediately post visit, as many as 50% of patients cannot accurately report what their health professionals have told them during the office visit. The clinician should consistently check what the patient has understood, reinforcing essential messages. The clinician should offer written instructions and explain them carefully to the patient; the patient's understanding should be ascertained.

8. *Encourage patient involvement.* Clinicians should encourage their patients to be actively involved in their care, to voice concerns, and to state preferences for their care outcomes. Patients' participation enhances their sense of control and meaning in the face of illness and may facilitate disease management. Offering opportunities for patient involvement conveys respect. A client who is encouraged to try medication to manage anxiety should have the opportunity to discuss with the clinician the various options for treatment and to chart a plan for evaluating its effects.

9. *Incorporate cultural beliefs.* Many patients have their own personally or culturally based explanations for their illness, which, if understood by the health professional, can help patients follow their treatment regimens. Adherence requires the patient's belief in his or her susceptibility to a serious health threat and belief that a treatment is effective and offers sufficient benefit given its costs in time, money, and difficulty. The cultural context in which the patient lives can exert considerable influence on his or her health beliefs. While it might be easier for the clinician to understand a patient's beliefs if that patient and the clinician have identical ethnic backgrounds, any differences in education, economic status, and social network may present additional challenges to full understanding between them. Clinicians should devote effort to understanding the cultural beliefs and practices of their patients, through training courses and/or community contacts.

10. *Build in social support.* Many studies show that there is a profound impact of both practical and emotional support on patient adherence, and the role of clinicians in helping patients to garner and maintain such support is central. Patients' marital status or their living with others is not nearly as important as their having available supportive and helpful others who care about them. The cohesiveness of patients' families can strongly support their adherence, while family conflict can seriously jeopardize it. The clinician should determine what practical and emotional support is available to the patient and should regularly be attuned to, and screen for, family conflict that can derail a patient's attempts to adhere to the treatment regimen. When appropriate, working with the family to foster a patient's treatment adherence may be an important addition to the care of the patient.

11. *Screen for depression.* Depression in medical patients is strongly linked to nonadherence to medical treatments; the risk of medical nonadherence is significantly higher among depressed patients than among those who are not depressed. Adherence to mental health care for depression is also problematic, as the condition itself can introduce barriers to adherence. Depressed patients are at increased risk of nonadherence because of the hopelessness, interference in constructive thinking and planning, and withdrawal from social support that can accompany depression. Patients receiving psychological or pharmacological treatment for depression may need particular attention and supportive care to adhere, and clinicians should always screen for depression in medical patients.

12. *Attend to risk factors for nonadherence.* In addition to depression, certain patient factors predispose patients toward nonadherence. Compared with the positive role of family support and the negative effects of mood disorders, demographic factors are not strong predictors of adherence. Some demographic factors do have a moderate effect on adherence, however, and should be noted by clinicians. There is a trend for adolescents to be less adherent than younger pediatric patients, and a trend for lower adherence among individuals in middle age (probably because of competing demands) and advanced older age (probably because of cognitive deficits). The relationship between education and adherence is stronger in the care of chronic illness than acute illness, likely due to the necessity for complex self-care for chronic illness.

In summary, adherence is *unlikely* to be fostered by lecturing patients that they have a serious condition, that treatment is good for them, or that the health professional knows best and should be obeyed. Rather, clinicians should build partnerships with their patients, learn about and respect their perspectives on the illness, understand their expectations for health care outcomes, and relate to them in an empathic and compassionate manner. Good communication and satisfying relationships with patients increase clinicians' professional job satisfaction, and reduce the impact of job stress; professionals' job satisfaction in turn improves patients' adherence to treatment.

References and Readings

DiMatteo, M. R., Lepper, H. S., & Croghan, T. W. (2000). Depression is a risk factor for noncompliance with medical treatment: A meta-analysis of the effects of anxiety and depression on patient adherence. *Archives of Internal Medicine, 160,* 2101–2107.

DiMatteo, M. R., Haskard-Zolnierek, K. B., & Martin, L. R. (2012). Improving patient adherence: A three-factor model to guide practice. *Health Psychology Review, 6*(1), 74–91.

Grenard, J. L., Munjas, B. A., Adams, J. L., Suttorp, M., Maglione, M., McGlynn, R., & Gellad, W. F. (2011). Depression and medication adherence in the treatment of chronic diseases in the United States: A meta-analysis. *Journal of General Internal Medicine,* ePub ahead of print. doi: 10.1007/s11606-011-1704-y

Haskard-Zolnierek, K. B., & DiMatteo, M. R. . (2009). Physician communication and patient adherence to treatment: A meta-analysis. *Medical Care, 47*(8), 826–834.

Martin, L., Haskard-Zolnierek, K. B., & DiMatteo, M. R. (2010). *Health behavior change and treatment adherence: Evidence-based guidelines for improving healthcare.* New York: Oxford University Press.

Morisky, D. E, & DiMatteo, M. R. (2011). Improving the measurement of self-reported medication nonadherence: Response to authors. *Journal of Clinical Epidemiology, 64*(3), 255–263.

Zygmunt, A., Olfson, M., Boyer, C. A., & Mechanic, D. (2002). Interventions to improve medication adherence in schizophrenia. *American Journal of Psychiatry, 159,* 1653–1664.

Related Topics

Chapter 50, "Improving Completion of Therapeutic Homework"

Chapter 53, "Reducing Resistance in Psychotherapy"

36 TREATING AND MANAGING CARE OF THE SUICIDAL PATIENT

Bruce Bongar and Glenn R. Sullivan

Patient suicide is a real occupational hazard for clinicians involved in direct patient care. Suicide is the most frequently encountered of all mental health emergencies. The "suicide-free" practice in which only nonsuicidal patients are treated is a phantasm born of denial and incompetence. Psychologists who believe that none of the adult patients in their caseloads are at elevated risk for suicide or have had past suicidal crises should reconsider the quality of their suicide risk assessments.

Outpatient management is the most common treatment modality for suicidal patients. Hospitalization of even acutely suicidal patients can be difficult to accomplish, and in any case it does little to address the underlying, chronic issues that often contribute to suicidal crises. It is not possible to completely "screen out" potentially suicidal patients from a practice or agency. It is unethical and unprofessional to abandon patients who have revealed suicidal thoughts or behavior. We believe that the assessment and treatment of suicidal patients should be a core competency of practicing psychologists.

GENERAL PRINCIPLES

The mental health professional's assessment and treatment efforts represent an opportunity to translate knowledge (albeit incomplete) of elevated risk factors into a plan of action (Bongar & Sullivan, 2013). The management plan for patients who are at an elevated risk for suicide should ameliorate those risk factors that are most foreseeably likely to result in suicide or self-harm. Several general principles that apply across broad diagnostic and demographic categories should guide the treatment of patients at elevated risk for suicide:

- The most basic principle is that, because most suicide victims take their own lives or harm themselves in the midst of a psychiatric episode, it is critical to perform a proper diagnostic assessment and to design a collaborative management/treatment plan that addresses the acute and chronic symptoms associated with the identified psychiatric disorders. More than 90% of adult suicide victims meet diagnostic criteria for a mental illness at the time of their deaths.
- Diagnostic categories in which suicide risk is elevated include major depressive disorder, bipolar disorder, schizophrenia (especially during the first years of the illness), and alcohol or other substance use disorders. The only major *DSM* diagnostic category is which suicide risk is not generally elevated, compared to the general population, is mental retardation. Antisocial personality disorder and borderline personality disorder are Axis II disorders that are associated with high suicide risk.
- Special precautions must be taken when assessing and treating patients who present with chronic suicidal ideation and behavior (i.e., where the clinician takes repeated calculated risks in not hospitalizing). The clinician must weigh the short-term benefits of hospitalization against the long-term goals of treating the chronic condition in an outpatient environment. Patients who repeatedly engage in nonfatal deliberate self-harm represent a significant suicide risk (Nock, 2010). For decades, these patients—who demonstrate severe psychopathology—had often been dismissed as "attention seekers."
- Involve the patient's family and support network to maximize adherence to the treatment plan. However, the psychologist must first ascertain the presence or absence of toxic interpersonal matrices in the family.
- Consult with the patient's other health care providers, including his or her primary care physician, medical specialists, psychiatrist, and so on. Obtain treatment records from these providers and from all past therapists. Discuss with medical providers the possible interaction between mental illness and the patient's physical disorders.
- Focus on the provision of hope, particularly to new-onset patients. Consider administrating Linehan's *Reasons for Living Inventory* as a means of strengthening the patient's desire to live. Review evidence-based, cognitive-behavioral interventions for decreasing hopelessness.
- Because the availability of firearms, especially handguns, plays such a prominent role as the "method of choice" for many completed suicides, the psychologist should assiduously assess the presence of, access to, and knowledge the patient has about this highly lethal means. This also necessitates carefully thinking through the patient's entire life environment and how the patient spends each day, so as to determine proactively the presence of any potentially lethal means (e.g., the hoarding of pills; access to poisons; or whether the patient has a means in mind, such as hanging, jumping from a particular building, or driving the car off the road). Furthermore, it is worth mentioning again that the psychologist must not hesitate to contact others in the patient's life and enlist their support in the treatment plan.
- Continuously monitor indications for voluntary or involuntary psychiatric hospitalization. Periodically, and at every significant treatment juncture, the psychologist should record his or her rationale for continuing

outpatient treatment and not hospitalizing the patient. The decision process should be clearly stated, with acknowledgement of both the risks and benefits of outpatient care versus hospitalization.

- Clinicians must assess their own technical proficiencies, as well as their emotional tolerance levels for the intense demands required in treating suicidal patients. The mental health professional who is called upon to treat the suicidal patient needs to have already evaluated the strengths and limitations of his or her own training, education, and experience in the treatment of specific patient populations in specific clinical settings.
- Meticulously document every aspect of the patient's care. This procedure should be regarded not as a mere formality, nor as a means of limiting liability in the event of tragedy. Superior charting contributes to superior patient care. To do the best you can for a patient, it is necessary for your assessments, treatment plans, progress notes, records of contacts with collateral informants, and so on to be thorough, well reasoned, and clearly articulated.
- When treating suicidal patients, routinely consult with other mental health professionals, including senior colleagues.

All of our assessment and management activities also should include a specific evaluation of the patient's competency to participate in management and treatment decisions, including the patient's ability to form a therapeutic alliance (Bongar & Sullivan, 2013). An essential element in strengthening this alliance is the use of informed consent—that is, patients have the right to participate actively in making decisions about their care. Clinicians need to directly and continuously evaluate the quality of this special relationship—to understand that the quality of this collaborative alliance is inextricably part of any successful treatment/management plan.

RISK ASSESSMENT AND MANAGEMENT

The consultation model operationalized by Bongar and Sullivan (2013) seeks to optimize clinical, legal, and ethical standards of care for suicidal patients. The model first emphasizes the importance of developing a strong therapeutic alliance, facilitated via informed consent procedures at treatment initiation. The informed consent procedure should begin an ongoing process of information-giving and collaboration with the client. By involving patients and their families, when appropriate, as collaborative risk management partners, cooperation with treatment is improved, the protective net is widened, responses to treatment are more closely monitored, and the quality of available data is improved.

Second, the model emphasizes the importance of routinely seeking professional consultations from colleagues, particularly ones who are senior clinicians or have forensic expertise. These consultants should be retained professionally and given sufficient information to provide reasonable advice, and their advice should be carefully recorded in the psychologist's records. This written record is necessary in order for the consultation to be legally recognized and unquestioned.

Although the following list of discussion points is not exhaustive, it does suggest the sort of specific questions that could be discussed with a consultant when treating the suicidal patient. These include reviewing the following:

1. The overall management of the case, specific treatment issues, uncertainties in the assessment of elevated risk or in diagnosis. This can include a review of the mental status examination, history, information from significant others, the results of any psychological tests and data from risk estimators, suicide lethality scales, and so on; also, a review of the psychologist's formulation of the patient's *DSM* diagnosis.
2. The patient's competency to participate in treatment decisions, along with an assessment of the quality of the therapeutic alliance and the patient's particular response to the psychologist and to the course of treatment (e.g., intense negative or positive transference).

3. The psychologist's own feelings about the progress of treatment and feelings toward the patient (e.g., the psychologist's own feelings of fear, incompetency, anxiety, helplessness, or even anger) and any therapeutic reactions such as negative countertransference or therapist burnout.
4. The advisability of using medication or need for additional medical evaluation (e.g., any uncertainties as to organicity or neurological complications); also, a request for a re-evaluation of any current medications that the patient is taking (e.g., effectiveness, medication adherence, side effects, polypharmacy).
5. The indications and contraindications for hospitalization; a review of available community crisis intervention resources for the patient with few psychosocial supports; day treatment options; emergency and backup arrangements and resources; and planning for the psychologist's absences.
6. Indications and contraindications for family and group treatment; indications and contraindications for other types of psychotherapy and somatic interventions; questions on the status of and progress in the integration of multiple therapeutic techniques.
7. The psychologist's assessment criteria for evaluating dangerousness and imminence (e.g., Does the consultant agree with the clinician's assessment of the level of perturbation and lethality?); review of specifics of patient's feelings of despair, depression, hopelessness, impulsivity, cognitive constriction, and impulses toward cessation.
8. The issues of informed consent and confidentiality, and the adequacy of all current documentation on the case (e.g., intake notes, progress notes, utilization reviews, family meetings, supervisor notes, telephone contacts).
9. Whether the consultant agrees with the psychologist's current risk-benefit analysis and management plan in particular. Does the consultant agree that the dual issues of foreseeability and the need to take affirmative precautions have been adequately addressed?

SUMMARY GUIDELINES

We believe that the following steps constitute a set of standards that will ensure the highest level of care for suicidal patients.

1. *Evaluation and assessment.* For each patient seen as part of a clinician's professional practice activities, there must be an initial evaluation and assessment, regular ongoing clinical evaluations and case reviews, consultation reports and supervision reports (where indicated), and a formal treatment plan. All of these activities need to demonstrate specifically a solid understanding of the significant factors used to assess elevated risk of suicide and how to manage such risk—with a documented understanding of the prognosis for the success (or possible paths to failure) of subsequent outpatient (or inpatient) treatment or case disposition.
2. *Documentation.* Clinicians must be aware of the vital importance of the written case record. In cases of malpractice, courts and juries often have been observed to operate on the simplistic principle that "if it isn't written down, it didn't happen" (no matter what the subsequent testimony or elaboration of the defendant maintains). Defensive clinical notes, written after the fact, may help somewhat in damage control, but there is no substitute for a timely, thoughtful, and complete chart record that demonstrates (through clear and well-written assessment, review, and treatment notes) a knowledge of the epidemiology, risk factors, and treatment literature for the suicidal patient. Such a case record should also include (where possible) a formal informed consent for treatment, formal assessment of competence, and a documentation of confidentiality considerations (e.g., that limits were explained at the start of any treatment).
3. *Information on previous treatment.* Clinicians must obtain, whenever possible, all previous treatment records and consult with past psychotherapists.
4. *Consultation on present clinical circumstances.* Clinicians should routinely obtain consultation and/or supervision (or make

referrals) on all cases where suicide risk is determined to be even moderate and after a patient suicide or serious suicide attempt. They also should obtain consultation and/or supervision on (or refer) cases that are outside their documented training, education, or experience, as well as when they are unsure of the best avenue for initiating or continuing treatment. The principle that two perspectives are better than one should guide the clinician in moments of clinical uncertainty.

5. *Sensitivity to medical issues.* Clinicians should be knowledgeable about the effects of psychotropic medication and make appropriate referrals for a medication evaluation. If the clinician decides that a medication consultation is not indicated in the present instance, he or she should thoroughly document the reasoning for this decision in the written case record. Where appropriate, the patient (and, when it is indicated, the patient's family or significant others) also should be included in this decision-making process.
6. *Knowledge of community resources.* Clinicians who see suicidal patients should have access to the full armamentarium of resources for voluntary and involuntary hospital admissions, day treatment, 24-hour emergency backup, and crisis centers. This access can be direct or indirect (through an ongoing collaborative relationship with a psychologist or psychiatrist colleague).
7. *Consideration of the effect on self and others.* If a patient succeeds in committing suicide (or makes a serious suicide attempt), clinicians should be aware not only of their legal responsibilities (e.g., they must notify their insurance carrier in a timely fashion) but, more important, of the immediate clinical necessity of attending to both the needs of the bereaved survivors and to the clinician's own emotional needs. (The clinician must acknowledge that it is both normal and difficult to work through feelings about a patient's death or near-death and that he or she, having lost a patient to suicide, is also a suicide survivor.) The concern should be for the living. After consultation with a knowledgeable colleague and an attorney, immediate clinical outreach to the survivors is not only sensitive and concerned clinical care, but in helping the survivors to deal with the catastrophic aftermath via an effective clinical postvention effort, the clinician is also practicing effective risk management.
8. *Awareness of diversity and multicultural considerations.* Clinicians must be cognizant of the current evidence on diversity and multicultural assessment, management, and treatment considerations in working with suicidal patients, and take affirmative steps to ensure that they have the requisite knowledge, training, experience, and clinical resources to work with both ethnic minority and LGBTQ patients (i.e., "one size does not fit all").
9. *Special populations.* Clinicians must be cognizant of the current evidence on working with special populations (e.g., veterans and active duty military personnel, older adults, children and adolescents, etc.) with regard to assessment, management, and treatment considerations in working with suicidal patients, and take affirmative steps to ensure that they have the requisite knowledge, training, experience, and clinical resources to work with specific special populations.
10. *Preventative preparation.* Most important, clinicians must be cognizant of the above standards and take affirmative steps to ensure that they have the requisite knowledge, training, experience, and clinical resources prior to accepting high-risk patients into their professional care. This requires that all of these mechanisms be in place before the onset of any suicidal crisis.

References and Readings

Bongar, B., Maris, R. W., Berman, A. L., & Litman, R. E . (1992). Outpatient standards of care and the suicidal patient. *Suicide and Life Threatening Behaviors, 22,* 453–478.

Bongar, B., & Sullivan, G. R. (2013). *The suicidal patient: Clinical and legal standards of care* (3rd ed.). Washington, DC: American Psychological Association.

Brown, G. K., Ten Have, T., Henriques, G. R., Xie, S. X., Hollander, J. E., & Beck, A. T. (2005). Cognitive therapy for the prevention of suicide attempts: A randomized controlled trial. *Journal of the American Medical Association, 294*, 563–570.

Jobes, D. A. (2006). *Managing suicidal risk: A collaborative approach.* New York: Guilford Press.

Maltsberger, J. T., & Goldblatt, M. J. (Eds.). (1996). *Essential papers on suicide.* New York: New York University Press.

Nock, M. K. (2010). Self-injury. *Annual Review of Clinical Psychology, 6*, 339–363.

Shneidman, E. S. (1999). *The suicidal mind.* New York: Oxford University Press.

Related Topics

Chapter 5, "Assessing Suicidal Risk"
Chapter 37, "Intervening with Clients in Crisis"
Chapter 106, "Minimizing Your Legal Liability Risk Following Adverse Events or Patient Threats"

37 INTERVENING WITH CLIENTS IN CRISIS

Kenneth France

A crisis exists when a person's usual coping methods fail to successfully handle current pressures and the individual feels overwhelmed by seemingly unresolvable difficulties. Finding oneself in crisis usually results in new coping efforts, which may include actions such as contacting a psychologist. A person reaching out in this way is desperate for an end to the stress and is likely to welcome the professional's crisis assistance (Halpern, 1973). Together they work in a problem-solving alliance that draws on the client's knowledge and experience to forge the beginnings of an adaptive resolution. Empirical research has demonstrated that crisis intervention can result in client benefits such as decreased anxiety, depression, confusion, anger, and helplessness, as well as improved performance in career and family roles (France, 2007). Here are 10 recommendations, based on controlled research and clinical experience, for intervening effectively with clients presenting in crisis.

1. *Distinguish between crisis intervention and emergency mental health intervention:* Crisis intervention is appropriate if the person is in crisis and is able to participate in logical problem solving. Emergency mental health intervention is necessary when active guidance and assertive decision making by the psychologist are required to decrease imminent danger. Making the right choice between these two options is crucial. Individuals in crisis who are simply told what to do often fail to implement the suggestion. Consequently, emergency mental health intervention is inappropriate for most persons in crisis. Likewise, problem solving does not work with someone who is incapable of rational decision making. Thus, crisis intervention is doomed to failure with such individuals.

2. *Make the most of the time you have:* In a 50-minute session, you must make an early decision as to whether you should employ crisis intervention or emergency mental health intervention. If emergency mental health intervention is your choice, then the session's activities may involve the following: determining appropriate diagnoses; surveying previous treatment; exploring suicidal/homicidal danger, availability of support, and level of cooperation; and securing necessary authorizations from service gatekeepers. When you choose crisis intervention, there may be exploration relating to danger and suicide lethality, but the majority of the time will be spent in collaborative problem solving.

3. *Conduct a suicide lethality assessment:* Both in crisis intervention and in emergency mental health intervention, it is appropriate to ask whether the client has been thinking about suicide. An affirmative response to this question necessitates further examination. If you believe there is an ongoing risk of suicide, you may want to examine the following five factors that have been shown to increase the probability of suicide: the existence of a plan for suicide that is specific, available, and deadly (or the person believes is deadly); the person feeling hopeless, depressed, or that one is a burden on others; past suicide attempts by the client (although most people who die by suicide kill themselves on the first attempt) and past attempts or completed suicide by close relatives or friends; a recent upsurge in difficulties experienced by the client; and significant object loss associated with the current crisis (France, 2007).

4. *Decide whether to support outpatient therapy or hospitalization:* Bengelsdorf and colleagues (1984) developed the Crisis Triage Rating Scale to assist clinicians in deciding whether a person needs outpatient or inpatient services. The evaluator assigns scores for dangerousness, support, and cooperation, then adds the numbers together. Bengelsdorf and his colleagues believe that a total score of 9 or lower suggests a need for hospitalization, whereas a score of 10 or higher tends to indicate outpatient services as being appropriate. The scale's scoring criteria are described next.

DANGEROUSNESS

1. Threats of suicidal or homicidal behavior, a recent dangerous attempt, or unpredictable violence
2. Threats of suicidal or homicidal behavior or a recent dangerous attempt, but sometimes views such ideas and actions as unacceptable, or past violence but no current problems
3. Ambivalence associated with life-threatening thoughts, a "suicide attempt" not intended to end in death, or impulse control that is inconsistent
4. Some ongoing or past life-threatening behavior or ideas but clearly wants to control such behavior and is able to do so
5. No life-threatening ideas or actions and no history of problems with impulse control

SUPPORT

1. Inadequate support from family members, friends, and community resources
2. Possible support but effect is likely to be small
3. Appropriate support possibly developed but with difficulty
4. Appropriate support possibly developed, but some components may not be reliable
5. Access to appropriate support

COOPERATION

1. Unwilling or unable to cooperate
2. Little appreciation or understanding of ongoing intervention efforts
3. Passively accepts intervention efforts
4. Ambivalence or limited motivation regarding intervention efforts
5. Actively requests outpatient services and wants to productively participate in therapy

5. *Set realistic goals:* The minimum goal in crisis intervention is restoration of the previous level of functioning. The optimal goal is for the crisis to become a learning experience that leaves the person better able to cope with future pressures. Positive outcomes are more likely when intervention is immediately available. Although the response from the psychologist is an active one, all efforts recognize and use the client's abilities. As a secondary prevention activity, crisis intervention catches the difficulties in their early stages, thereby decreasing the episode's duration and severity. Such progress is brought about by engaging the individual in a problem-solving process.

6. *Enhance problem solving.* The central endeavor in crisis intervention is problem solving. Although there are many approaches to this activity, one strategy is to think of it as involving three phases: exploring thoughts and feelings, considering alternatives, and developing a plan (France, 2007). And while a variety of communication styles can be effective, the use of reflection, along with a judicious number of open-ended questions, tends to be beneficial. (Open questions usually begin with the word *what* or *how*. Reflection involves using new words to summarize central ideas and emotions communicated by the other person.)

7. *Explore patient's thoughts and feelings.* During this phase of problem solving, the task is for the client and the psychologist to develop a joint understanding of the issues confronting the person and the emotions associated with those topics. Specific events should be discussed in conjunction with the related feelings, so that a shared view develops as to how the crisis came about and what has been happening. As long as new material continues to emerge, the exploration phase should continue. It ends with agreement on three areas: the nature of the distressing circumstances, how the person is feeling about them, and what changes the individual desires.

8. *Consider alternatives.* Once there is a mutual understanding, the interaction moves to deciding what to do about them. The goal of this phase is to identify and consider two or three solid options. One tactic for generating these possibilities is to explore three questions: What has the client already tried? What has the client thought about doing? And, right now as you are talking, what other ideas can the client generate? (Only after strongly pulling for options from the client is it advisable for the crisis intervener to make a suggestion.) When exploring a promising possibility, have the client consider the likely positive and negative consequences associated with that option. This phase ends with agreement on an approach, or a combination of approaches, that can become the person's plan.

9. *Develop a plan.* The one absolute requirement of an initial crisis intervention contact is the development of a plan that has four characteristics. The plan is collaboratively created rather than dictated by the psychologist (Deci & Ryan, 1987); it focuses on current issues, and there are aspects of it that the client can begin working on the same day or the next day; it involves specific tasks that have been thought through; and it is likely, not just possible, that the individual will carry out those tasks. Once a negotiated, present-focused, concrete, and realistic plan has been developed, the client should review its major components. Clarify any misunderstandings or ambiguities that become apparent and arrange a subsequent contact.

10. *Engage in follow-up contact.* The initial activity of a subsequent contact is to review the client's efforts in implementing the plan. Successes should be highlighted, and difficulties should be identified. Negotiate necessary modifications in existing components of the plan, and engage in problem solving with regard to important issues that still need to be addressed.

References and Readings

Bengelsdorf, H., Levy, L. E., Emerson, R. L., & Barile, F. A. (1984). A Crisis Triage Rating Scale: Brief dispositional assessment of patients at risk for hospitalization. *Journal of Nervous and Mental Disease, 172*, 424–430.

Deci, E. L., & Ryan, R. M. (1987). The support of autonomy and the control of behavior. *Journal of Personality and Social Psychology, 53*, 1024–1037.

France, K. (2007). *Crisis intervention: A handbook of immediate person-to-person help* (5th ed.). Springfield, IL: Charles C Thomas.

Halpern, H. A. (1973). Crisis theory: A definitional study. *Community Mental Health Journal, 9*, 342–349.

Related Topics

Chapter 5, "Assessing Suicidal Risk"

Chapter 36, "Treating and Managing Care of the Suicidal Patient"

Chapter 106, "Minimizing Your Legal Liability Risk Following Adverse Events or Patient Threats"

38 TREATING BORDERLINE PERSONALITY DISORDER

Kenneth N. Levy

Borderline personality disorder (BPD) is a highly prevalent, chronic, and debilitating disorder characterized by emotional lability, impulsivity, interpersonal dysfunction, angry outbursts, and suicidality. Prevalence rates in the general population range from 0.4% to 5.9%, with a rate of 2%–3% being most typical. Prevalence in outpatient samples range from 10% to 20% and are about 20% to 25% in inpatient samples.

BPD is frequently comorbid with other disorders such as depression, bipolar disorder, anxiety disorders, posttraumatic stress disorder, eating disorders, substance abuse, and other personality disorders. This pattern of comorbidity is often referred to as *complex comorbidity* because of the number of comorbid diagnoses and the pattern that includes both internalizing and externalizing disorders. In addition to representing common comorbidities, differential diagnosis from these disorders is important. One especially complicated differential diagnosis is bipolar disorder, particularly bipolar II.

BPD has historically been thought to be difficult to treat, with patients frequently not adhering to treatment recommendations, using services chaotically, and repeatedly dropping out of treatment. Many clinicians are intimidated by the prospect of treating BPD patients and are pessimistic about the outcome of treatment. Psychotherapists treating patients with BPD have displayed high levels of burnout and have been known to be prone to enactments and even engagement in iatrogenic behaviors. However, controlled trials strongly suggest that, contrary to popular belief, BPD is a treatable disorder.

Below are 12 evidence-based principles and recommendations from the burgeoning research literature on the treatment of BPD over the last 20 plus years:

1. Evidence suggests that clinicians may not recognize and do not diagnose personality disorders in ordinary clinical practice. Fully 74% of patients in a study for BPD had previously been misdiagnosed despite an average of 10 years since their first psychiatric encounters (Meyerson, 2009). The most common false-positive diagnoses were bipolar disorder, depression, and anxiety disorders. Left to their own judgments, clinicians diagnosed BPD in 0.4% of almost 500 patients seen, compared to 14.4% by structured interview (Zimmerman & Mattia, 1999). Providing clinicians with the findings from the structured interviews significantly increased the likelihood of the BPD diagnosis from 0.4% to 9.5%. These findings suggest that training in, and use of, structured assessments (e.g., structured interviews) are important for identifying BPD, which in turn has strong clinical utility for treatment planning. Clinicians who do not use structured assessments are likely to miss many cases of BPD, which can result in incomplete treatment.

2. Given that BPD is commonly comorbid with several disorders, whenever a clinician determines that a patient meets criteria for one of these disorders (major depression, bipolar disorder, an anxiety disorder, posttraumatic stress disorder, or a substance use disorder), it is incumbent upon them to assess whether there is a comorbid BPD diagnosis because it will likely affect the course and treatment of the disorder. Likewise, complex comorbidity and/or a history of being diagnosed with various psychological disorders suggest clinicians should formally assess for BPD.

3. When comorbid, BPD negatively affects the course of these disorders and the efficacy of otherwise efficacious treatments of these disorders. For example, bipolar patients with comorbid BPD are less likely to be employed, use more medications, and have increased rates of alcohol and substance use disorders, show poorer treatment response, and have significantly worse interepisode functioning. Interestingly, a comorbid bipolar disorder does not affect the course or outcome for BPD patients (Gunderson et al., 2006). Additionally, a number of studies have now found that improvements in BPD were often followed by improvements in major depressive disorder but that improvements in major depressive disorder were not followed by improvements in BPD (Gunderson et al., 2004; Klein & Schwartz, 2002; Links et al., 1995).

4. Although common comorbidities (e.g., major depression) may require simultaneous treatment with BPD, it is important not to assume that treatment of these conditions will result in the remission of BPD and privilege those treatments to the neglect of treating BPD. The evidence strongly suggests the contrary.

5. Psychotherapists should typically share the results of their diagnostic assessment with the BPD patients. Studies have found that mental health professionals report difficulty disclosing BPD diagnoses. This can often be anxiety provoking for the therapists who might fear the patient's response. However, many patients with BPD suspect that they may have BPD and/or may learn their diagnosis from secondary sources (e.g., other treaters, bills, insurance documents, medical records). It is usually best to have an open and sensitive discussion with the patient about the nature of his or her difficulties and how best to proceed in treatment. Doing so is typically part of setting the treatment frame and agreeing on therapy goals.

6. There are now several treatments—deriving from both the cognitive-behavioral and psychodynamic traditions—that have shown efficacy in randomized controlled trials and are now available to clinicians and their patients. These treatments include dialectical behavior therapy (DBT; Linehan et al., 2006), mentalization based therapy (MBT; Bateman & Fonagy, 2010), schema focused psychotherapy (SFPT; Gisen-Bloo et al., 2006), transference focused psychotherapy (TFP; Clarkin et al., 2007; Levy et al., 2006), dynamic deconstructive psychotherapy (DDP; Gregory & Remen 2008), and a number of versions of supportive-dynamic psychotherapies. There is also a number of short-term psychoeducational, cognitive-behavioral-therapy-base d or skill-based groups designed to be used as adjunctively that show promise, particularly STEPPS (Blum et al., 2008). Thus, practitioners and patients have a range of options across a number of orientations available to them. Although DBT has been tested in more randomized controlled trials than the other treatments, findings from both direct comparisons and meta-analytic studies are clear that there are a number of equally good treatments available to patients with BPD and that there is no credible evidence that any one treatment is significantly better than any other.

7. It is important that clinicians who treat individuals with BPD have training in one or more of the empirically supported treatments and employ evidence-based principles deriving from these treatments. These empirically supported treatments all represent modifications of standard psychodynamic (PDT) or cognitive-behavioral therapy (CBT) treatments and tend to integrate aspects of different traditions. Additionally, the evidence suggests that standard unmodified PDT and CBT are not effective for individuals with BPD.

8. Despite positive findings from randomized controlled trials, only about half the patients in treatment respond regardless of treatment. Additionally, although many patients have shown symptomatic improvement and even diagnostic remission, they still experienced significant social and functional impairments (e.g., Skodol et al., 2005). Thus, a significant portion of individuals receiving an efficacious treatment are not improving, and these individuals might be better served in different treatments. Additionally, given the heterogeneity of BPD, having different treatment options is important because it is unlikely that any one treatment will be useful for all patients.

9. Medications appear useful as adjunctive in the treatment of BPD but are generally not thought to be sufficient by themselves. The frequent targets are three symptom domains of mood, thought process, and impulsivity. However, polypharmacotherpay has been associated with a number of untoward effects, including paradoxical side effects, adverse events, iatrogenic symptoms, and negative health outcomes such as obesity and diabetes (being on three or more psychotropic medications is a greater risk factor for obesity than a family history of obesity or a sedentary lifestyle). Additionally, prescribed medications are often used in drug overdoses. There is some evidence for the superiority of monopharmacotherpay with BPD patients and for selecting medications based on tolerability and safety rather than symptom picture (see Zanarini, 2004). Additionally, some randomized controlled trials have convincingly shown that you can decrease medication use and obtain efficacy for psychotherapy (Bateman & Fonagy, 1999, 2008; Linehan et al., 1991).

10. Considering the commonalities across the empirically supported treatments allows us to derive a number of important strategies, tactics, and techniques for treating BPD:

- Provide a structured, coherent, and explicit treatment that makes sense to both the clinician and the patient and identifies a hierarchy for priorities in treatment. Such a structure provides guidance to the therapist during times of intense affect and provides the patient with a sense of containment.
- Consider being in supervision or intervision to protect against burnout, implicit collusions with the patient, therapist acting out, and engagement in iatrogenic behaviors.
- Pay particular attention to and be explicit about the treatment frame (or contract), including the rationale for the treatment, patient and therapist responsibilities, and explicit instructions for handling emergencies. The need for an explicit frame is common to all treatments of BPD.
- Develop the treatment frame and priorities collaboratively so not to be experienced as an imposition by the patient. Therapists should be attentive for signs of acquiescence by the patient as it does not represent a true agreement. Likewise, it is important for therapists not to acquiesce as they contain expertise relevant to helping the patient. Developing a truly collaborative frame may take a number of sessions and require occasional revisiting.
- Emphasize explicitly the treatment frame or contract. Many aspects of treatment may not be explicit or as well articulated in the patient's mind as is often the case with healthier patients. Patients should be clear about what is expected of them, realistic goals, and potential treatment interfering behaviors or events. Setting a solid frame is part of providing a safe haven for the patient to explore his or her difficulties and for the therapist to work within. The absence of a treatment frame potentially licenses the patient to engage in treatment-interfering behaviors and/or acting-out behaviors.
- Explore difficulties that have arisen in past treatments because they can provide important indicators of the kinds of difficulties that might arise in your treatment with the patient (e.g., lateness, missed sessions, feeling that the therapist is trying to control the patient).
- Assess the nature of interpersonal relating between the patient with past therapists and significant others (particularly around the patient's most problematic behaviors—for example, self-injury) as these dynamics can

guide the current treatment. For example, if the patient tends to feel controlled by others and often responds to this feeling by not talking in session or withholding important information from the therapist or others in his or her life, which in turn leads to a crisis, it will be important to discuss the likelihood of this happening in the new therapy and come to some collaborative agreement about how to structure the therapy to address this issue.

- Avoid rigidity in setting the contract (e.g., prohibiting behaviors such as self-injury). Rather, it is important that the patient can agree with the therapist that reducing certain behaviors would be a treatment goal and setting up conditions that facilitate the patient bringing up such feelings and minimizing the likelihood of it occurring. Setting up a rigid frame or coming to a premature agreement about the frame is associated with early dropout.
- Make special efforts to attend to and manage the therapeutic relationship, which will prove more variable with patients diagnosed with BPD and attend to that variability to provide them with clues to the patient's mental states. Positive and negative alliances should be discussed with the patient.
- Consider the addition of a group component to individual sessions. The added value of a group component is unclear; however, research strongly suggests that all aspects of treatment, adjunctive or otherwise, including medications, need to be well coordinated and require collaboration among the various professionals. In this regard, treatments provided within an agency or organization appears to be more effective than treatments across organizations—most likely a result of better communication between treaters.

11. Because BPD is a chronic disorder that has developed over many years, it will most likely require a longer term treatment that meets at least weekly. All the efficacious treatments for BPD are a multiyear process (although most have only examined efficacy after 1 year of treatment). These treatments tend to be intense, meeting for 2 to 5 hours a week.
12. BPD is a heterogeneous disorder. Only about 50% of patients respond to any of these treatments, and treatment responses, while clinically significant, are nonetheless incomplete. Hence, it is recommended that communities have several of the evidence-based treatments available to patients and that therapist consider obtaining expertise in more than one evidence-based therapies.

References and Readings

Bateman, A. W., & Fonagy, P. (2006). *Mentalization-based treatment for borderline personality disorder: A practical guide*. Oxford, England: Oxford University Press.

Clarkin, J. F., Yeomans, F. E., & Kernberg, O. F. (2006). *Psychodynamic treatment of borderline personality organization*. Arlington, VA: American Psychiatric Publishing.

Gregory, R. J., & Remen, A. L. (2008). A manual-based psychodynamic therapy for treatment-resistant borderline personality disorder. *Psychotherapy: Theory, Research, Practice, Training, 45*, 15–27.

Kellogg, S., & Young, J. (2006). Schema therapy for borderline personality disorder. *Journal of Clinical Psychology, 62*, 445–458.

Leichsenring, F., & Leibing, E . (2003). The effectiveness of psychodynamic therapy and cognitive behavior therapy in the treatment of personality disorders: A meta-analysis. *American Journal of Psychiatry, 160*, 1223–1232.

Linehan, M. M. (1993). *Cognitive-behavioral treatment of borderline personality disorder*. New York: Guilford Press.

Paris, J., Gunderson, J., & Weinberg, I . (2007). The interface between borderline personality disorder and bipolar spectrum disorders. *Comprehensive Psychiatry, 48*, 145–154.

Related Topic

Chapter 16, "Assessing Personality Disorders"

39 TREATING RELUCTANT AND INVOLUNTARY CLIENTS

Stanley L. Brodsky and Caroline Titcomb

Therapists working with involuntary clients should not ignore their own role in thwarting change in their clients. Therapists who externalize responsibility to the client for therapeutic failure will reify negative judgments of the client. If therapists offer counseling for reluctant and involuntary clients from the same frame of reference as they do for eager, voluntary clients, they set up themselves and their clients for frustration.

When working with reluctant or coerced clients, a treatment provider's common reactions to difficult clients—distancing oneself, impatience, anger, fear, excessive expectations—may become magnified (Brodsky, 2011). Involuntary clients often do not view therapists as expert or trustworthy, nor do they provide the customary positive feedback to therapists. Many therapists take this lack of appreciation personally and feel threatened or incapable. Confrontational demands by therapists for clients to give up their reluctance and do their part may ensue. Clients may put forth a façade of the motivated patient to mask their reluctance. Therapists should pay special attention to both of these tendencies—on the part of the therapist and the client—to address threat and frustration as foreground issues.

FALSE ASSUMPTIONS AND PERCEIVED ROLES

False Assumption 1: All Involuntary Clients Need Therapy

The beginning point in approaching treatment of these clients is awareness of working assumptions regarding the referral. Often agencies do not know exactly why they have referred a client beyond something "being wrong" with the client. It is incorrectly concluded by many clinicians that being a defendant or offender is prima facie evidence of need for psychotherapy. Our alternative advice is that the therapist should ascertain the reason for a coercive referral, the treatment aims, the referrer's anticipation of success, the time constraints, the legal or familial frames of reference, and the influences of the client's situation. Without clarifying and redefining the referral, therapists become engaged in a vague plan of "just doing therapy."

False Assumption 2: Change Can Only be Measured One Way

Most therapists are aware of Prochaska and Norcross's (2001) six stages of readiness for change. This dimensional model posits a *precontemplation* stage in which clients are unaware of their need to change or are so fearful that they are resistant to change. Specific therapeutic techniques that address ambivalence toward change, such as motivational interviewing, are becoming more common. However, the approaches imparted by these and other experts remain foreign or difficult to master for many practitioners.

It is likely that missing the therapeutic focus espoused by such techniques—getting the client to the contemplation stage of change—is holding therapists back. Simply put, therapists often have their eye on the wrong prize. Some reluctant clients will never fully participate in counseling; for them, quick termination of the treatment may be the decision of choice. For a few clients, the reluctance becomes transformed into active participation and the treatment itself becomes a productive venture. The productive outcome does not have to be the therapeutic goal at the onset. For most coerced clients, the better goal is to move clients from a stance of hesitation or aversion to therapy into consideration of therapy and openness to change.

False Assumption 3: Insight Must Precede Progress

Working under this assumption, therapists are likely to label clients not wanting to change as unreachable, particularly those suffering with an addiction (Parhar, Wormith, Derkzen, & Beauregard, 2008). However, this reluctance is common to many therapy clients and should not be used as an excuse for slow progress when working with coerced clients. In particular with sexual, violent, or other high-risk offenders, mandated treatment may be necessary for developing intrinsically motivated change.

Role of the Therapist

Involuntary or institutionalized clients often experience their therapists as a primary point of contact—the persons upon whom clients believe they can rely or use in a system of limited resources and freedoms. While this affiliation may promote a therapeutic bond, it also creates a paradox in which the therapist becomes the most likely individual for the client to manipulate. Some involuntary clients will appear to comply with treatment just to receive attention or gain an ally on their side. Therapists should not hold the suspect motivation for therapy against the client, but they should remain focused on moving the client forward in treatment.

LEVERAGE AND PERSPECTIVE IN THE THERAPEUTIC CONTEXT

Therapy as an Aversive Contingency for Inappropriate Behavior

If the treatment itself is a negative experience for clients, it can be used as an aversive stimulus following undesirable behavior. While it may seem counterintuitive for therapists to conceptualize their work as an "aversive stimulus," just such motivation for avoiding treatment may in fact lead to progress, particularly with antisocial youthful offenders. In family therapy and in institutionalized mental health settings, anecdotal reports have indicated that clients' problem behaviors have diminished or disappeared with the promise that therapy attendance would no longer be required.

Leverage and Coercion

Law violators are the most frequent category of reluctant client, often explicitly coerced to enter psychotherapy as a condition of their case disposition or proof of progress. Resistance may be followed by legal consequences. As professional helpers, therapists do not like to consider themselves as part of this coercive force. Therapists may be classified as falling on a continuum from system professional to system challenger, depending on the extent to which they accept the referring agency's aims. They need to define their stances and consider client versus agency responsibilities, coercion effects, and other values implicit in treatment activities.

Therapists should not isolate themselves from the context in which they provide services. It is generally accurate to assume that the majority of involuntary clients would not enter therapy on their own volition. Therapists may benefit from conceding their influence and conceptualizing the intervention as leverage rather than coercion (Brodsky, 2011). Leverage—in the form of money, housing, criminal sanctions, outpatient commitment—is not uncommon to therapeutic relationship and has been shown to increase treatment retention and outcome (McNiel, Gormley, & Binder, 2008). Informed therapists avoid conceptualizing therapy only as forced, but instead also frame it as an opportunity for clients to gain leverage over their situation. While the consequences for individuals who refuse mandated therapy are undesirable, so may be traditional therapists' ideas of treating involuntary clients. At this stage, the goal is for the therapist and the client to accept therapy as the best available alternative.

Perceived Coercion

An early step is to explore each client's perception of coercion within the therapy context. Many people who are coerced into treatment do not view themselves that way and assert that they would have entered into treatment without external pressure. Moreover, a formal mandate to attend therapy does not automatically equate with clients' reluctance for change. Presenting problems, personalities, and treatment needs should be identified for each client. Therapists who anticipate the stereotypically defensive "problem client" may be setting the stage for opposition that otherwise may not have been present (Brodsky, 2011, p. 21).

Cultural Sensitivity

All psychotherapy has implicit values. Therapists need to be sensitive to imposing values on clients. They should not assume an understanding of the views that contribute to a client's perception of being coerced, needing treatment, or wanting change. Therapists should make the social values with which one is practicing explicit to the client, as well as considering clients' ethnicity, race, gender, and social class in case conceptualization. For example, a member of a social class may see traditionally viewed involuntary pressures (e.g., criminal sanctions) as culturally expected and, subsequently, be more likely to be aware of mandated treatment. Opposition to therapy may be rooted in the clients' perceived differences from the therapists. Lower- and upper-class populations may each feel threatened in different ways. However, research has suggested that culturally "cognitive similarities" may trump tangible dissimilarities between therapist and client (Zane et al., 2005, p. 582). Becoming aware of and acknowledging clients' cultural perspectives helps bridge gaps between therapist and client. Moreover, effective therapists consider contextual factors (e.g., lack of resources), that may influence clients' responses. The development of collaborative relationships with community resources (e.g., housing services, welfare) may improve the client's more proximal environment and the therapeutic context.

Right to Refuse Treatment

All clients' right to decline treatment, as well as to choose treatment knowledgeably, should be respected. Still, the choice to refuse treatment should be an informed one, particularly when there are institutional, occupational, or familial consequences of not entering therapy. Therapists ensure that clients understand available treatment alternatives, how long therapy lasts and how well it works, the nature of therapeutic procedures, and the assumption of client self-determination. Contracts with clients and outlines of information to be given to clients have been gathered in Bersoff (2008).

The Low Trust–High Control Dilemma

With voluntary clients, the customary therapeutic relationship is characterized by high trust and little effort to control the other's behaviors. With confined populations and clients pressured to enter therapy, mutual distrust of motives is often accompanied by the therapist having considerable control over client living conditions, privileges, and release. The result is a role conflict between helping and "supervising." The typical trust and rapport can become displaced by fear of manipulation and excessive control measures, which themselves are antagonistic to good treatment. The resolution of these dilemmas lies in explicit delineation of limits and confidentiality among the treatment provider, the client, and the referring agency, as well as clear separation of therapeutic roles from evaluative and organizational roles.

ADJUSTING THERAPEUTIC TECHNIQUE

Errors in Technique

When the criterion for success is reduced recidivism, many approaches traditionally used with low-risk offenders have little payoff. Vaguely targeted, nonintensive therapy seems to fail. For instance, insight-oriented therapies and group therapies with individuals with diagnosed antisocial features in particular, are associated with higher rates of future crime. When offered to such individuals, preferred interventions specifically address behaviors that provide relapse prevention training.

Unconditional Neutral Regard

In working with defiant clients, often the traditional tendering of unconditional positive regard is not possible. Consider, instead, the benefits of working from an "unconditional neutral regard" angle (Brodsky, 2011, p. 128). This framework is realistic, allows for therapeutic growth toward developing more genuine earned regard, and permits therapists freedom for spontaneity and more natural responses to inflexible clients.

The Hostile and Abrasive Client

There is a significant difference between clients who are generally resistant to change and those who actively and fiercely resist the therapy process itself. Hostile and abrasive clients have a special knack for irritating others. They are adept at jabbing at the vulnerabilities of others, their therapists included. Therapists react to this often subtle prodding when they find themselves getting annoyed without apparent good reason. Abrasive individuals defend against their high need for intimacy by mobilizing their fear of closeness (Wepman & Donovan, 1984). Clients who criticize their therapist's tone of voice, appearance, work, or background succeed when the therapist rejects them. The appropriate intervention is to directly confront the clients' vulnerability, which may afford the clients enough latitude to lower their guard, perhaps enough to make room for a genuine therapeutic exchange. By being treated as a whole person rather than just a "hostile client," clients' views of themselves may broaden as well.

Avoid Taking a Backseat

Therapy with reluctant or defensive clients fails when therapists (a) passively accept problematic aspects of the client's behavior and attitudes, such as evasiveness and negativism; (b) fail to address deficiencies in the therapeutic relationship; or (c) present destructive or poorly timed interventions. Effective therapists do not sit back in their office armchairs, cloaked with the fundamental attribution error, and designate the client as the problem instead of aspects of the therapeutic context as the problem (Morrow & Deidan, 1992). A passive therapist is likely to breed a stagnant therapeutic environment, in which the client may rightly be frustrated with the involuntary nature of the treatment and with the treatment provider. Successful therapists should be aware of the tendency to attribute angry insubordination to clients and, instead, should pay special attention to timing, specificity of focus, and their own active and directive involvement in therapy.

Using Resistance

When clients actively resist involvement and change, therapists should not be in direct opposition. They should consider aiming at second-order change so that clients accept in an oppositional way the view therapists would originally have wanted. Thus, one can ask resistant clients, "Why should you change?" or instruct clients to "go slow." In the same spirit, one might tell a distrustful client to never trust the therapy fully. These procedures are posited by several therapeutic techniques (e.g., "rolling with resistance" in motivational interviewing) and may be conceptualized as explicitly "honoring the client's resistance" by co-opting clients' cognitive space.

Avoid Asking Questions

Traditional forms of therapeutic listening, reflection, and asking open-ended questions are likely to fail when working with reluctant clients. Therapy is foreign to most involuntary clients, but interrogation is not. Peppering reluctant clients with questions will arm their defenses more. Asking "why" is a particularly ineffective strategy with defiant clients. An interrogative therapist is likely to receive disingenuous, resentful, or acquiescent answers. Moreover, therapists often already know the answers to the questions (e.g., why a particular client is being reluctant, why he or she is so angry and keeps acting out, or why a treatment referral was mandated). Asking *why* invites the client into an insincere exchange, one that may further alienate the client or extenuate the client's oppositional emotions.

Alternatives to Asking Questions

When traditional, nondirective therapeutic techniques are shelved, alternative methods must be introduced to fill the gap. Helpful therapists will provide directive feedback regarding clients' therapeutic exchanges and problems. Therapists may restate possible questions in an alternative and constructive format. Instead of asking "Why are you so angry?" they will state "You are so angry that it gets in your way. It's a lousy way to live." These therapists are not afraid to use humor and spontaneity when appropriate or to engage the client in a high level of activity. Engaging activities may include role playing and presenting therapeutic choices to the client (e.g., "We can decide to work on your anger in therapy now, or we can choose to set it aside until the moment seems right to get into this"). Other useful alternatives to asking questions are presented next.

Objective Self-Awareness

This phenomenon, as first described by Duval and Wicklund, has powerful implications for reluctant clients. When clients are encouraged to listen in at treatment meetings about their cases and discussions of their therapeutic progress, as well as to read reports and notes written about them, they become, in effect, outside observers of themselves. As a result, they become intrigued and even motivated. This principle can be used by sharing with clients the videotapes or audiotapes of sessions, ongoing therapy records, and discussions of their dynamics and progress (Brodsky, 2011).

Life Skills Enhancement

In this alternative to conventional open-ended therapies, efforts focus on enhancement of life skills. The interventions are offered as brief, closed-ended courses that are based on a published curriculum. Each unit of instruction attends to narrowly defined areas of functioning, such as conflict management, human sexuality, assertiveness training, and fairness awareness. The short courses have scheduled beginnings and endings, the use of pass or fail criteria, and the advance identification of specific treatment content.

Behavioral Rehearsal

Involuntary and reluctant clients often exist in a world in which they do not speak quite the same language or act the same way as much of law-abiding society. Behavioral rehearsal of important events in these clients' lives (e.g., parole hearings, treatment team meetings, interpersonal disputes) can assist in bridging the gap between the reluctant client's way of communicating and that of the broader and socially accepted patterns. Because outside parties typically hold power over involuntary clients, this exercise serves to increase clients' sense of mastery and influence over their situation while also teaching adaptive communication and life skills. Just motivating clients to rehearse such activities may generalize to further therapeutic growth.

Session Modifications

Do not get overly discouraged early on. Research suggests that little to no relationship exists between first-session events and eventual therapeutic outcome, but that a strong relationship exists between third-session events and outcome. By that time, clients may became involved, and that involvement can make a difference. Thus, the therapist should set up contracts or trial therapy agreements for three or four sessions at the outset of therapy. Furthermore, avoid becoming entrained by the 50-minute therapy hour and the belief that "good" clients should find 50-minute sessions desirable as well. As a beginning point for future use with difficult clients, experiment with very short or long sessions.

Concrete Changes

Client reluctance may come from frustration with an insight-oriented approach to therapy when clients could benefit from a more tangible, problem-solving approach. Giving clients immediate and concrete coping methods yields good motivation to continue in therapy (e.g., teaching diaphragmatic breathing and relaxation techniques in response to anxiety, or improving sleep problems), particularly in institutionalized settings. Concrete changes that visibly improve clients' interpersonal or emotional functioning may provide a tangible foundation upon which to build, or it may be enough to achieve in its own right.

References and Readings

Bersoff, D. N. (Ed.). (2008). *Ethical conflicts in psychology* (4th ed.). Washington, DC: American Psychological Association.

Brodsky, S. L. (2011). *Therapy with coerced and reluctant clients*. Washington, DC: American Psychological Association Books.

McNiel, D. E., Gormley, B., & Binder, R. L. (2008, August). *Leverage, the treatment relationship, and treatment participation*. Paper presented at the Annual Meeting of the American Psychological Association, Boston, MA.

Morrow, K. A., & Deidan, C. T. (1992). Bias in counseling process: How to recognize and avoid it. *Journal of Counseling and Development, 70*, 571–577.

Parhar, K. K., Wormith, J. S., Derkzen, D. M., & Beauregard, A. M. (2008). Offender coercion in treatment: A meta-analysis of effectiveness. *Criminal Justice and Behavior, 35*, 1109–1135.

Prochaska, J. O., & Norcross, J. C. (2001). Stages of change. *Psychotherapy Theory, Research, Practice, Training, 38*, 443–448.

Wepman, B. J., & Donovan, M. W. (1984). Abrasive-ness: Descriptive and dynamic issues. *Psychotherapy Patient, 1*, 11–20.

Zane, N. W., Sue, S., Chang, J., Huang, L., Huang, J., Lowe, S., ... Lee, E. (2005). Beyond ethnic match: Effects of client-therapist cognitive match in problem perception, coping orientation, and therapy goals on treatment outcomes. *Journal of Community Psychology, 33*, 569–585.

Related Topics

Chapter 52, "Repairing Ruptures in the Therapeutic Alliance"
Chapter 53, "Reducing Resistance in Psychotherapy"
Chapter 87, "Engaging the Reluctant Adolescent"

40 CONDUCTING MOTIVATIONAL INTERVIEWING

Theresa B. Moyers and Daniel J. Fischer

Clinicians are usually trained in how to work with people who want to change, but they are less often prepared to help people want to change. People, even those seeking treatment, are often ambivalent about change: They want it, and they do not. When the idea of change is advised by the clinician, this ambivalence is often expressed by the client as resistance. Motivational interviewing (MI) was designed specifically to help clinicians work with clients who are less ready for change. Originally developed to address substance use disorders, it is now used to enhance motivation for change in a wide array of health behaviors.

MI is a client-centered, yet directive method for evoking intrinsic motivation to change (Miller & Rollnick, 2002). Ambivalence is understood as a normal stage in the process of change, and MI seeks to resolve ambivalence in the direction of commitment to change. For clients who perceive little or no need for change, the initial goal of MI is usually to develop discrepancy (ambivalence) that is then resolved toward change. MI is a complex and unfolding process—a way of being with, and behaving toward, a client who is contemplating change.

MI should not be misunderstood as client-centered therapy, or decisional balance, or cognitive-behavioral therapy. Nor is it simply a technique for tricking clients into changing. Furthermore, it is not always the best treatment approach; if a client is already motivated toward the proposed change, then it is likely that another empirically supported treatment is more appropriate.

Over the past 20 years, research into MI has resulted in more than 300 randomized clinical trials. MI has been adapted as an effective behavioral intervention for a wide variety of target behaviors, ranging far beyond its original use as an intervention for problematic drinking. Summaries of outcome research on MI (Lundahl, Kunz, Brownell, Tollefson, & Burke, 2010) suggest that MI is useful at various points along the treatment continuum, whenever ambivalence is prominent. MI has been found to be an effective intervention across diverse cultural groups.

FOUR GUIDING PRINCIPLES

MI is not a technique so much as a method of psychotherapy. The underling spirit of MI is collaborative, evocative, and respectful of client autonomy (Miller & Rollnick, 2002). The collaborative aspect involves a companionable partnership of client and counselor, de-emphasizing power differentials. The therapist avoids an expert or authoritarian role, instead regarding clients as experts on themselves. Information and advice are provided when requested, but primary emphasis is on evoking the client's own intrinsic motivation for change and perspectives on how to achieve it. The clients' autonomy and ability to choose their own life course are prized.

Four principles guide the practice of MI:

1. *Express empathy.* MI is heavily rooted in a client-centered style of counseling, as formulated by Carl Rogers and his associates. Therapeutic empathy, acceptance, and respect are communicated through the use of reflective listening to attain accurate understanding of the client's own perspectives. Accurate empathy is a foundational skill, without which MI proficiency cannot be achieved.
2. *Develop discrepancy.* The MI therapist helps clients to recognize the discrepancy between their current behavior and their important goals or values. This is done primarily by having the client, rather than the therapist, give voice to the reasons for change. Clients literally talk themselves into changing.
3. *Roll with resistance.* "Resistance" is understood simply as clients voicing the status quo side of their ambivalence. The therapist avoids arguing, pushing against, or confronting such resistance, which only tends to entrench it. Instead, the therapist responds in ways that diffuse resistance and direct the client back toward intrinsic motivation for change.
4. *Support self-efficacy.* Finally, the therapist actively conveys the message that the client is capable of change. The client is the expert in solving the problem, and the therapist draws upon his or her own particular strengths and resources. The motivational interviewer is a consultant, offering options that clients may not have considered from a broad menu of change strategies, and particularly eliciting clients' own ideas.

TWO PHASES OF MOTIVATIONAL INTERVIEWING

It is helpful to think of MI as occurring in two phases. The first phase focuses on *evoking intrinsic motivation* by having the client give voice to *change talk*—in essence, arguments for change. Four types of change talk are distinguishable, memorable by the acronym DARN:

- *Desire.* Why and in what ways does the client *want* to change?
- *Ability.* Why and how would the client be *able* to change, should she choose to do so?
- *Reasons.* What are some reasons for change, from the client's perspective?
- *Need.* Why and in what ways is it *important* for the client to make a change?

Giving voice to such change talk moves the client along toward voicing *commitment to change*, which is the focus of the second phase of MI. Timing is important here. The therapist needs a sense for when the client is developing the intention to change, and at this point shifts toward evoking a specific plan for implementing change, and commitment to carry it out. If the therapist shifts prematurely to phase two, resistance occurs and the therapist returns to phase one strategies for further evoking intrinsic motivation.

OARS AND THE DIRECTIVE ASPECT

Four specific skills are particularly emphasized for fostering client safety, acceptance, and change, represented by the acronym OARS:

1. *Open questions.* The psychotherapist asks open-ended questions intended to evoke change talk (desire, ability, reasons, need). Relatedly, the therapist avoids asking questions the answer to which would be arguments for the status quo (e.g., "Why haven't you...?" or "What keeps you from...?"). With a well-crafted open question, the answer is change talk.
2. *Affirmation.* The therapist emphasizes and affirms the client's strengths, efforts, abilities, and steps in the right direction.
3. *Reflective listening.* Again, the Rogerian skill of accurate empathy is crucial, manifest in skillful reflective listening that helps the client to continue exploring and experiencing the current dilemma.
4. *Summaries.* As the client offers arguments for change, the therapist provides periodic summaries in which change-talk statements are drawn together. In essence, the

therapist collects each change-talk theme like a flower, and then offers them back to the client in ever larger bouquets.

These skills are used in a directive manner to promote and reinforce change talk. The therapist first and foremost evokes clients' own motivations for change. Clients, of course, hear themselves voice these arguments for change. Next, they hear the therapist affirm and reflect their change talk, in essence emphasizing and reinforcing it. Then they hear their change statements yet again, collected into summaries.

In essence, MI involves the selective and strategic use of OARS with the goal that clients will talk themselves into change. The therapist asks *particular* open questions, *selectively* reflects change talk, affirms movement in the hoped-for direction, and *selectively* summarizes the clients' own motivations for change. It is here that MI evolves from Rogers's conception of client-centered therapy as nondirective, by providing specific guidelines for strategically responding in a directive manner in order to evoke the client's own arguments for change. An analogy for MI is that of ballroom dancing: One moves smoothly with the partner, but he or she is also leading in a particular direction.

THERAPEUTIC USES OF MOTIVATIONAL INTERVIEWING

Consider a client who is having trouble managing his diabetes. In a first scenario, MI could be used as a prelude to treatment in order to enhance client motivation for change. Our example patient may be reluctant to engage in diabetes treatment, monitoring his diet, or engaging in more regular exercise. A psychologist might use MI to explore the client's ambivalence toward engaging in treatment and ultimately may use MI to build the client's own intrinsic motivation toward changing his behavior. Clinical trials indicate that an initial session at the beginning of treatment can enhance retention, adherence, and motivation for treatment. When added to other treatment approaches, MI appears to have a synergistic effect on outcomes.

Second, MI has been used as a stand-alone brief intervention. Our example patient may present himself at an emergency department for medical care. In this setting, MI could be as a brief intervention, conducting a brief and client-centered conversation that is directed toward changing client behaviors in favor of more effective diabetes management such as better monitoring of glucose levels or more stringent adherence to medication management. A single session of MI has been found to be effective in triggering significant change relative to no treatment or placement on a waiting list. MI has also been used for opportunistic interventions, where a problem is detected for which the person was not initially seeking help. For example, patients seeking health care can be screened for alcohol abuse, and MI can be used as a brief intervention within the context of primary health care.

Third, MI can be integrated with other treatments. The style of MI can be used by the clinician even when the specific focus on reducing ambivalence is no longer necessary. Maintaining the supportive-directive style of MI may help to minimize client resistance or renew a flagging commitment to ongoing treatment. It is not uncommon to encounter ambivalence and resistance later in treatment, as it progresses and new challenges are encountered. In the diabetic example, the clinician can augment ongoing treatment with an MI-style intervention when the client is drifting from monitoring glucose levels or adherence to prescribed medications. As ambivalence resolves and resistance fades, the clinician returns to the intended therapeutic approach, dancing back and forth between the elements of MI and other methods.

References and Readings

Center on Alcoholism, Substance Abuse, and Addictions (CASAA). (n.d.). *Motivational interviewing*. Retrieved January 2013, from casaa.unm.edu/mi.html

Glynn, L. H., & Moyers, T. B. (2010). Chasing change talk: The clinician's role in evoking client language about change. *Journal of Substance Abuse Treatment, 39*(1), 65–70.

Lundahl, B. W., Kunz, C., Brownell, C., Tollefson, D., & Burke, B. L. (2010). A meta-analysis of motivational interviewing: Twenty-five years of empirical studies. *Research on Social Work Practice, 20*(2), 137–160.

Miller, W. R., & Rollnick, S. (2002). *Motivational interviewing: Preparing people for change* (2nd ed.). New York: Guilford Press.

Miller, W. R., Yahne, C. E., Moyers, T. B., Martinez, J., & Pirritano, M. (2004). A randomized trial of methods to help clinicians learn motivational interviewing. *Journal of Consulting and Clinical Psychology, 72*(6), 1050–1062.

Miller, W. R., Zweban, A., DiClemente, C. C., & Rychtarik, R. (1992). *Motivational enhancement therapy manual: A clinical research guide for therapists treating individuals with alcohol abuse and dependence.* (Project MATCH Monograph Series: Volume 2). Rockville, MD: National Institute on Alcohol Abuse and Alcoholism.

Motivational Interviewing. *Resources for clinicians, researchers, and trainers.* Retrieved 2013 from www.motivationalinteriew.org

Moyers, T. B., Martin, T., Houck, J. M., Christopher, P. J., & Tonigan, J. S. (2009). From in-session behaviors to drinking outcomes: A causal chain for motivational interviewing. *Journal of Consulting and Clinical Psychology, 77*(6), 1113–1124.

Related Topics

Chapter 31, "Compendium of Empirically Supported Treatments"
Chapter 34, "Applying the Stages of Change"
Chapter 53, "Reducing Resistance in Psychotherapy"

41 ASSESSING AND TREATING ATTENTION-DEFICIT/HYPERACTIVITY DISORDER

Robert J. Resnick

Attention-deficit/hyperactivity disorder (ADHD) is a neurobehavioral disorder and the most frequent reason children access health care. Incidence is such that each classroom is likely to have two children with ADHD. This disorder is not outgrown in adolescence. It is estimated that 5%–8% of children have ADHD and almost two-thirds have persistent symptoms of ADHD into adulthood. Boys outnumber girls by about 3–4 to 1, and they may present in different ways. Boys tend to be more externalizing and aggressive, whereas girls tend to be more internalizing with more difficulties showing emotion. Girls with ADHD also tend to be more talkative and overly social as well as being less assertive compared to boys with ADHD. Minorities tend to be underdiagnosed and, when diagnosed, treatment options tend to be less aggressive. However, response to pharmacological and behavioral interventions is equally robust between genders and among minorities when education, single-parent status, and public assistance are statistically controlled. ADHD has a significant genetic and inherited etiology, and poor parenting, chaotic homes, diet, allergies, and/or inadequate educational environments are not causative. However, any of these factors may exacerbate ADHD symptoms.

The *Diagnostic and Statistical Manual of Mental Disorders*, Fifth edition (*DSM-5*; American Psychiatric Association, 2013) posits two primary symptom clusters: impulsivity-hyperactivity and inattention. The diagnostic rubrics are attention-deficit/hyperactivity disorder: predominantly inattentive type (there is no hyperactivity of significance); attention-deficit/hyperactivity disorder: predominantly hyperactive-impulsive type; attention-deficit/hyperactivity disorder: combined type (incorporating both clusters); and attention-deficit/hyperactivity disorder: not otherwise specified, for individuals who exhibit symptoms of ADHD but do not meet full criteria. For adolescents and adults who currently have symptoms but no longer meet full criteria, the notation "in partial remission" can be added. Onset of symptoms occurs before age 7, lasts at least 6 months, and is observed in more than one setting (e.g., home, school, church, work, neighborhood, day care). Symptoms must be at an age-inappropriate level, with significant impairment in social, occupational, or academic functioning. *DSM-5*, will include an additional diagnosis of *Inattentive Presentation (restrictive)* that emphasizes symptoms of inattention and only two symptoms of hyperactivity-impulsivity in the past 6 months. Age of onset of symptoms is raised to 12 years.

Appropriate "rule outs" need to be considered as they can mimic or mask ADHD or mask symptoms. In children and adolescents, mood disorders (especially bipolar), anxiety, autism and other developmental disorders, intellectual retardation, hearing loss, and poor vision should be considered, ruled out, or included as a comorbid. Similarly, seizure disorders (especially brief but frequent seizures known as "absence" and petit mal) need to be eliminated as well. Because of the nature of the symptoms and their behavioral sequelae, conduct disorders and oppositional defiant disorders are common comorbid conditions. Similarly, many children will also be diagnosed with ADHD and learning disabilities. Some patients will be learning disabled because of the ADHD, and, in others, the learning disability is a parallel process. The former type of learning disability shows more improvement with treatment of the ADHD than the latter. Sleep disorders, both onset and maintenance, are common that exacerbate ADHD symptoms.

With adults, depressive disorders as well as bipolar disorders can present as ADHD. Anxiety disorders, schizophrenia, borderline and schizotypal personality disorders, intellectual retardation, and learning disabilities may also mask as ADHD. It would be unusual for an adult to have had a seizure undiagnosed since childhood. Women are more likely to present with depression, which may mask comorbid ADHD. Academic and vocational underachievement, multiple marriages, and problems in social relationships should raise the question of ADHD. Disorganization, procrastination, problems handling everyday stress, moodiness, and hair-trigger temper, usually with quick offset, are often symptoms of ADHD. Older adolescents and adults frequently have alcohol and substance abuse issues.

THE EVALUATION

- *Executive functions.* Assessment of each patient should include (a) working memory, (b) self-regulation, (c) internalization of speech (self-talk), and (d) reconstitution (behavioral self-analysis and synthesis; see Barkley, 1997 for further discussion). Behavioral disinhibition and lack of *sustained* attention are considered hallmarks of ADHD.
- *History.* A rigorous psychological, developmental, academic, and social history must be taken. Include employment and educational history for adults.
- *School records.* A complete copy of school records, including report cards, achievement tests, teacher/school commentaries, and special services/special education testing along with individualized educational plans (IEPs), should be obtained. These provide an

invaluable view of the person over time in school. For older children, look for a downward spiral of grades, especially starting in third or fourth grade and again upon entering middle and/or high school.

- *Teacher ratings.* Teacher rating scales are helpful at baseline and treatment points. They are commercially available (www.ADDwarehouse.com).
- *Parent ratings.* Parents should fill out ratings separately because they, like teachers, frequently have different thresholds of tolerance for the child's behavior (www.ADDwarehouse.com)
- *Computerized assessments.* These measure inattention, distractibility, and impulsivity. Continuous performance tests are the most common and are commercially available (e.g., Conner's Continuous Performance Test; see www.ADDwarehouse.com).
- *Mental status exam.* Observe the person for ADHD symptoms and behaviors while ruling out other diagnoses by appropriate questioning/observation.
- The World Health Organization publishes an adult ADHD self-rating scale that is quite helpful.
- In adults, information from spouse/significant other or employer is often useful.
- It is not uncommon for ADHD patients, of any age, to minimize symptom and associated problems.

TREATMENT

School-Age Children

- Thorough explanation to parents and child of the nature of ADHD, including etiology, treatment, and outcome. Significant understanding of ADHD by family and child is imperative. Empower parents to become advocates. Help them help their child by making the world more ADHD friendly.
- High-protein, low-carbohydrate breakfast may reduce expression of ADHD symptoms and improve performance in school.
- School-based behavioral strategies to ensure homework, class work, and school participation are at an acceptable level. Strategies are also aimed at increasing compliance (on task) and decreasing inappropriate and frequently aggressive behaviors. Referral to the school system for special education screening and evaluation may be necessary so that the ADHD child can be identified as qualifying for special education services. Academic tutoring may also be helpful.
- Home-based behavioral interventions similar to the end points in school (i.e., ensuring completion and turning in of all schoolwork); additional intervention around household chores, siblings, and play/recreation. The goal again is to increase compliance with rules in the household and community by increasing patient's capacity to be aware of and apply rule-governed behavior. Parental skills training may be necessary.
- Behavioral treatment objectives: The goal of interventions is to provide structure (environment more ADHD compatible) and specific, measurable endpoints of interventions.
- Stimulant medication is first-tier drug of choice (differences in brands mostly related to absorption rate and half-life) and most often used in conjunction with the aforementioned strategies. Second-tier pharmacological agents can be used as well (i.e., antidepressants, antihypertensives). Antihypertensives may be used alone or in conjunction with stimulants. Other nonstimulant drugs are available (e.g., atomoxetine, modafinil) and may be helpful on a case-by-case basis. Clear treatment endpoints for medication management should be established.
- Individual therapy around issues of ADHD and/or comorbid features. Therapy may be intermittent over time. Long-term therapy for ADHD is not effective.
- Connect family to local, state, and national parents' support group, such as Children and Adults with Attention Deficit Disorder (CHADD) at www.chadd.org, Attention Deficit Disorders Association (ADDA) at www.adddelete.org, and *Additude* magazine at www.additudemag.com.

- Bibliotherapy for child and parents. Connect them to ADD Warehouse (800-233-9273)/ www.ADDwarehouse.com for free catalog.

Adults (and Teens, as Appropriate)

- Thorough explanation of the life course of the ADHD to adult and significant other. More effective to do this at same time.
- Cognitive and behavioral interventions at home and at work to decrease disorganization, inattention, and distractibility.
- Use of prompts and reminders place in iphones, Blackberry, and so on. Use post-it notes and/or daily organizers such as the Franklin Planner.
- Focused trial on stimulant medication or other pharmacological agents. Not as effective as use with children. Clear end points of medication trial should be delineated.
- Individual psychotherapy, as needed, for issues around ADHD and/or other comorbid conditions. Therapy often intermittent over time as stressors change.
- Marital/couples/partners psychotherapy focusing on the relationship and ways of coping with ADHD within that relationship.
- Bibliotherapy to augment understanding, intervention skills, work, and interpersonal relationships.
- Provide information about CHADD(.org) and/or ADDA(.org); the two national support groups who can segue to state and local chapters.
- ADHD coaching: regular, if not daily contact, with ADHD patient to ensure goals for day and tasks are completed with a supportive pep talk.

EMERGING TREATMENTS FOR ATTENTION-DEFICIT/HYPERACTIVITY DISORDER FOR ALL AGES

Neurofeedback

Neurofeedback provides immediate feedback regarding attention and focus; the training, when successful, generalizes to daily activities, increasing attention and reducing distraction. Course of treatment is 40–50 sessions twice weekly then once weekly. Clinician needs specialized training and equipment.

Cognitive Retraining

Cognitive retraining requires additional training for the clinician and specialized equipment. Training is, after initial consultations with the patient, completed at home with support from provider via Internet, and, if necessary, office consultation. Effective treatment improves access to working memory and reduces cognitive deficits. Has intrinsic interest, similar to neurofeedback, because of the "computer game" environment.

FEDERAL LAW AND ATTENTION-DEFICIT/ HYPERACTIVITY DISORDER

A number of federal statutes have a bearing on treatment of ADHD, and therefore, outcome. A school-age population with ADHD may be affected by Section 504 of the Rehabilitation Act of 1973 and the Individuals With Disabilities Education Act of 1975 (IDEA), which was reauthorized in 2004. Both can require specific interventions when a school-age person has been identified as having ADHD. A person at any age with ADHD may have legal standing under the Americans with Disabilities Act (ADA) of 1990 if education or employment, as a "major life activity," is "substantially limited."

In conclusion, there is no one treatment fits all. Treatment of ADHD, at any age, is most often multimodal, identifying those components that best work and support each other. Aligned in this manner, treatments tend to reinforce each other, leading to the most favorable outcomes.

References and Readings

American Academy of Child and Adolescent Psychiatry. (2007). Practice parameter for the assessment and treatment of children and adolescents with attention-deficit/hyperactivity disorder. *Journal of the American Academy of Child and Adolescent Psychiatry, 46,* 894–916.

American Psychiatric Association. (2013). *Diagnostic and statistical manual of mental disorders* (5th ed.). Washington, DC: Author.

Arns, M., De Ridder, S. Strehl, U., Bretekerm N, & Coenen, A. (2009). Efficacy of neurofeedback treatment in ADHD: The effects on inattention, impulsivity and hyperactivity: A meta-analysis. *Clinical EEG and Neuroscience, 40,* 180–189.

Arnold, E. L., Elliot, M., Sachs, L., Bird, H., Kraemer, H. C., Wells, K.,...Wigal, T. (2003). Effects of ethnicity on treatment attendance, stimulant response/dose, and 14-month outcome in ADHD. *Journal of Consulting and Clinical Psychology, 71,* 713–727.

Barkley, R. A. (1997). Behavioral inhibition, sustained attention, and executive functions: Constructing a unifying theory of ADHD. *Psychological Bulletin, 121,* 65–94.

Barkley, R. A. (2006). *Attention-deficit/hyperactivity disorder: A handbook for diagnosis and treatment* (3rd ed.). New York: Guilford Press.

Barkley, R. A. (2010). *Attention deficit hyperactivity disorder in adults.* Burlington, MA: Jones and Bartlett Publisher.

Nadeau, K. G., & Quinn, P.O. (2002) *Understanding women with AD/HD.* Silver Springs, MD: Vantage Books.

Related Topics

Chapter 85, "Principles of Treatment the Behaviorally Disordered Child"

Chapter 87, "Engaging the Reluctant Adolescent"

42 ASSESSMENT AND TREATMENT OF ANGER AS A CLINICAL PROBLEM

Raymond DiGiuseppe

Despite the fact that no official diagnostic category exists for an anger disorder in the *Diagnostic and Statistical Manual of Mental Disorders*, fourth edition, text revision (*DSM IV-TR*; American Psychiatric Association, 2000), clinicians report seeing as many angry clients as they do clients with depression and anxiety problems (Lachmund, DiGiuseppe, & Fuller, 2005; Posternak & Zimmerman, 2002). The failure to have a diagnostic model to understand anger seems to lead clinicians to overdiagnose clients presenting with anger problems and to categorize clients with disorders such as personality disorders or organic brain syndrome when no symptoms appear to support these disorders. It is possible that the presence of anger elicits the clinician's fear of aggression that leads to choosing more pathological diagnoses than can be supported. The first rule of practice is not to overdiagnose and present a more pessimistic impression of the client than is warranted. DiGiuseppe and Tafrate (2007) have proposed criteria for an anger regulation and expression disorder with three subtypes. These include a predominately subjective type, which represents holding one's anger in with few aggressive outbursts; a predominately expressive type, which represents a person who may have average degrees of trait anger but who explodes with aggression when he or she experiences anger; and a combined type.

Eckhardt, Norlander, and Deffenbacher (2004) noted that anger assessment instruments fail to present a unified model of anger as a clinical problem. They differ widely on which characteristics of anger they sample to include. Thus, the choice of which assessment instrument to use can result in very different information about a client. Many scales lack clear theoretical foundations and fail to specify how they define anger and which characteristics of anger they are sampling and why. The characteristics and purpose of many anger scales are unspecified. Many scales fail to specify whether they assess anger as a basic emotion/personality trait that is normally distributed or as a form of psychopathology or clinical problem. Clinicians should carefully select anger instruments that have a clear definition of anger as a clinical problem, and sample widely among the characteristics of anger such as anger triggers, cognitions, phenomenology, motives, and behaviors. The scale should have good psychometric characteristics, and the items should have been developed to be appropriate for diverse cultural and age groups.

Because anger is a multivariate construct, clinicians should use instruments that include many dimensions of anger. In such scales, the reliance on total scores of the psychometric instrument could be deceiving. Total scale scores could be in the normal range while the client has significant problems on several components of anger such as resentment, rumination, or revenge. Some clients can have average trait anger, but when they get angry they are vicious and sarcastic. Others could have modest elevations of a trait or total anger scale and an external expression of anger yet experience serious anger-in with brooding and rumination.

Several reviews of anger treatments have appeared (DiGiuseppe & Tafrate, 2007). Most of the empirical literature supports the effectiveness of cognitive-behavioral interventions. The most widely supported anger treatments included (a) relaxation training; (b) cognitive restructuring as proposed by Beck's cognitive therapy, Ellis's rational emotive behavior therapy, Nezu and Nezu's social problem solving therapy, and the Seligman reattribution model; (c) exposure interventions where clients learn new response to anger triggers; and (d) rehearsal of new positive behaviors to resolve conflict. Limited research supports mindfulness meditation, a Buddhist intervention, and Yalom's process-oriented or experiential group therapy. No outcome studies exist to draw upon to evaluate the effectiveness of therapies based on other theoretical orientations.

Anger treatments are equally effective for all populations that have been studied. Most of the research studies report that change is of a large magnitude. However, the magnitude of change is less than for anxiety and depressive disorders. Most likely, we cannot treat anger as successfully as we do other emotional problems, and we still need new creative interventions.

Several important topics have been left out of understanding of anger and the assessment and treatment models, and the field could increase its effectiveness if these topics were incorporated into clinical practice. These topics influence the therapeutic alliance with angry clients, and clinicians should attend to them carefully.

One characteristic of anger that permeates all areas of clinical practice is the desire for change. Humans all over the globe have little desire to change or control their experience of anger. The only emotion that people are less likely to want to change is joy (Scherer & Wallbott, 1994). This feature of anger poses the greatest problem for practitioners. Angry clients do not come for therapy; they come for supervision. They want us to consult with them about how to change the people who anger them. People in general evaluate the consequence of their anger as trivial and not harmful to their targets or victims. They see themselves as victims and believe that their reactions are justified and reasonable (Pinker, 2011).

Because angry clients often do not see their anger as a target for change, they might not store the information about their anger together. Their lack of insight on the damage they have done to others and to their interpersonal relations often leads angry clients to fail to develop a self-schema concerning their angry reactions. As a result, open-ended questions often fail to access important information about the frequency, intensity, and triggers of their anger or about the behavioral reactions that their anger sets in motion. Because of these assessment problems, clinicians could use some type of more structured assessment. This could take the form of more structured interview questions or self-report inventories, and interviews with significant others.

Angry clients often arrive for treatment in a precontemplative stage of change, and the agreement on the goal to change their anger is at best ambivalent. Most of the empirically based interventions for anger rely on action-stage interventions and begin with the assumption that the client wants to change. Perhaps clinicians had best assume that the client's goal to change his or her anger is weak, fragile, or absent. Therapy could start with motivational enhancement interventions that strengthen the desire to change before going on to other interventions. Several characteristics of anger suggest topics to explore during the motivational enhancement work. External attributions for blame and justification because one has been hurt are two of the cognitive hallmarks of anger. Failure to take responsibility for one's emotions is another. Motivational enhancement interventions appear to be the first line of interventions (DiGiuseppe & Tafrate, 2007).

Because angry clients believe that their anger was justified and that they are victims of another person's transgression, active interventions can easily have the result of the client feeling invalidated. Sometimes angry clients can accuse the therapist of siding with their enemies. It is important to validate the angry client's sense of being a victim and focusing on the existential choice of how he or she will respond to an unfair or unjust world. Therapists can easily become trapped into pointing out that the client's retaliation was much more severe than the transgression against them. Clients usually fail to perceive their retaliation as excessive and usually perceive themselves as justified. People will rate their anger as positive if they accomplish their angry motives, even if the motives are destructive or selfish. A discussion of the relative levels of retaliation interaction is likely to lead to invalidation and a rupture in the therapeutic alliance. It is best to acknowledge that the client perceives his or her self as a victim and focus on the different reactions the client can chose to react to the transgression, as well as the benefits of each. This approach is less threatening and less invalidating than challenging the client's exaggerated thoughts about the antagonist who triggered the anger.

Another characteristic of anger that could threaten the therapeutic alliance concerns empathy. People usually fail to elicit empathy from others when they experience anger (Palfai & Hart, 1997). No one likes to hug a porcupine. Because psychotherapists are people too, they often fail to experience empathy for and can have difficulty expressing empathy toward their angry clients. One can identify and reflect the angry client's desires and feelings without approving of them.

Angry clients often want to express their anger and believe that it is good and healthy for them to do so. Overwhelming evidence contradicts this common assumption (Olatunji, Lohr, & Bushman, 2007). Cathartic expression only reinforces the person's probability of having an anger response to a trigger associated with the episodes. Clinicians should discourage cathartic expression and help clients develop and practice new calm responses to their anger triggers.

Researchers have reported large magnitudes of change on physiological measures, self and other reports of positive and assertive behaviors, and with self and significant others' ratings of aggressive behavior. Eighty percent of all published and nonpublished research studies employed group therapy. We would speculate that the majority of practitioners treating anger problems work in correctional facilities, substance programs, hospitals, residential centers, and schools and regularly employ a group format. Our review of anger treatments (see DiGiuseppe & Tafrate, 2007) indicated that the group therapy format had significantly lower effect sizes than individual therapy intervention on measures of aggression. Group and individual anger interventions are equally effective on measures of anger, assertion, and physiology. However, aggression is an important dependent variable. What is it about group therapy that facilitates less change for aggression? A number of angry clients starting an anger management group at one time can easily reinforce each other for antisocial and aggressive attitudes. Clinicians should take strong efforts to avoid and interfere with social reinforcement of antisocial attitudes and behaviors such as these.

Revenge is a strong motive often associated with anger. Interestingly, the psychological community has rarely included revenge in content sampled in anger assessment instruments or in the empirically supported treatments for anger. The scientific research shows that revenge is a strong component of anger and the presence of this motive predicts aggressive behaviors. Revenge appears to be very reinforcing and areas of the brain associated with reward are active when people contemplate it. This suggests that the reinforcement of revenge plays an important role in the regulation of anger. No consensus has emerged on how to intervene to reduce someone's desire for revenge. Clinicians can use models of intervention designed for other positively reinforcing behaviors such as drug and alcohol abuse. Recently there has been an interest in forgiveness as a form of therapy to counteract revenge. A growing literature appears to support the effectiveness of forgiveness interventions.

Anger has long been thought to be an impulsive emotion. However, impulsivity does lead to an increase in impulsive behavior, and anger episodes last longer than all other emotion episodes (Scherer & Wallbott, 1994) in all cultures that have been studied. This suggests that anger involves a good deal of rumination. Also, anger rumination is very highly correlated with anger impulsivity. Perhaps that rumination about transgressions leads to anger and the desire for revenge. As the rumination persists, a person's self-control to inhibit his or her aggressive impulses is taxed and the self-control is depleted, leading to the phenomenology of an uncontrollable response (DiGiuseppe & Tafrate, 2007). Perhaps more interventions could focus on the rumination of angry clients rather than their impulsivity.

It is helpful to distinguish between two types of anger triggers (Robins & Novaco, 1999). The first are immediate or proximal stimuli that trigger immediate experiences of anger. Most clients report being very much aware of the immediate proximal cues to their anger, and therapy usually starts with teaching clients new cognitive-behavioral responses to such cues. However, many if not most angry clients have distal issues about which they are angry. Usually there are some resentments over past events about which the client ruminates. These distal or past resentments set the stage for the way clients interpret their world. The client may have resentment about specific and discrete abuse experiences, a history of ongoing abuse, or he or she may be an "injustice collector," who can recount a litany of ways he or she has been cheated by the world. The anger triggered by distal experiences seems to lower the clients' threshold for anger episodes and makes them more sensitive to proximal triggers. Clients often deny that their proximal triggered anger episodes have anything to do with the distal issues. They often do not wish to work on the anger and resentment associated with the distant issue. However, after they have learned some coping strategies to better cope with the proximal issues, they become more open to exploring the anger that seethes from these distal resentments. Clinical experience suggests that more than half of those clients presenting with anger problems have such resentments. Most therapy manuals used in therapeutic outcome studies focus on teaching new reactions to the proximal stimuli and fail to focus on the distal resentments.

Anger-in and anger-out are often considered orthogonal, independent aspects of anger. However, this does not seem to be the case. Anger-in scores seem to have an accelerating exponential effect on anger-out scores. Thus, the more a person holds his or her anger in, the higher the probability that a person will express his or her anger with some type of outwardly expressed aggression. When angry clients experience anger-in, they are annoyed by another person's behavior and make no mention of it. They sometimes engage in mind reading and think that the other person should know how they feel and what they do not like and fix it. They usually fail to assertively speak up. Therefore, the conflict goes unresolved. Angry clients are often very unassertive. They fail to speak up about an unpleasant event. After a long period of mind reading and no resolution, their anger and frustration increases and their urge to aggress grows. Then they explode. Teaching assertiveness is an important component of anger treatment. This provides the client a new skill to negotiate conflict. A problem, however, is that the angry client can demand that his or her assertiveness obliges the other person to comply; and of course no such guarantees of compliance exist. Angry clients can often learn assertiveness and say the word correctly. Anger is one of the most paralinguistically expressive emotions. Although their words may be mannerly, clients may still communicate anger in their tone or gesture. It is important that these aspects of communication receive adequate attention in the rehearsal of assertive responses.

References and Readings

American Psychiatric Association. (2000). *Diagnostic and statistical manual* (4th ed., text rev.). Washington, DC: Author.

DiGiuseppe, R., & Tafrate, R. (2007). *Understanding anger disorders*. New York: Oxford University Press.

Eckhardt, C., Norlander, B., & Deffenbacher, J . (2004). The assessment of anger and hostility: A critical review. *Aggression and Violent Behavior, 9*(1), 17–43.

Lachmund, E., DiGiuseppe, R., & Fuller, J. R. (2005). Clinicians' diagnosis of a case with anger problems. *Journal of Psychiatric Research, 39*(4), 439–447.

Olatunji, B. O., Lohr, J. M., & Bushman, B. J. (2007). The pseudopsychology of venting in the treatment of anger: Implications and alternatives for mental health practice. In T. A. Cavell & K. T. Malcolm (Eds.), *Anger, aggression and interventions for interpersonal violence* (pp. 119–141). Mahwah, NJ: Erlbaum.

Palfai, T. P., & Hart, K. E . (1997). Anger coping styles and perceived social support. *Journal of Social Psychology, 137*, 405–411.

Pinker, S. (2011). *The better angels of our nature*. New York: Viking.

Posternak, M. A., & Zimmerman, M. (2002). Anger and aggression in psychiatric outpatients. *Journal of Clinical Psychiatry, 63*(8), 665–672.

Robins, S., & Novaco, R . (1999). A systems conceptualization and treatment of anger. *Journal of Clinical Psychology, 55*, 325–337.

Scherer, K. R., & Wallbott, H. G. (1994). Evidence for the universality and cultural variation of differential emotional response patterns. *Journal of Personality and Social Psychology, 67*(1), 55–65.

Related Topics

Chapter 106, "Minimizing Your Legal Liability Risk Following Adverse Events or Patient Threats"

Chapter 118, "Assessing and Responding to Aggressive and Threatening Clients"

43 DIAGNOSIS, ASSESSMENT, AND TREATMENT OF FEMALE SEXUAL DYSFUNCTIONS

Leonard R. Derogatis and Lori A. Brotto

Female sexual dysfunctions (FSDs) as represented in the *Diagnostic and Statistical Manual of Mental Disorders*, fourth edition, text revision (*DSM-IV-TR*; American Psychiatric Association, 2000) consist of four categories of disorders: *sexual desire disorders, sexual arousal disorders, orgasmic disorders*, and *pain disorders*. Because of the relative centrality and prevalence of the first three classes of these disorders, and space limitations, we focus here on desire, arousal, and orgasmic disorders. We will devote minimal attention beyond enumeration and description to the pain disorders (i.e., dyspareunia and vaginismus), since assessment of these conditions is often principally conducted by physicians and other nonpsychologist health professionals. For these classes of disorders we will briefly review the following:

- Diagnostic criteria (including anticipated *DSM-5* changes)
- Risk factors
- Prevalence data
- Psychological interventions
- Pharmacological interventions and devices

HYPOACTIVE SEXUAL DESIRE DISORDER

Diagnostic Criteria

Hypoactive sexual desire disorder (HSDD) is defined in the *DSM-IV-TR* as a condition in which the individual presents with the following:

1. Persistently or recurrently deficient (or absent) sexual fantasies and desire for sexual activity. The judgment of deficiency or absence is made by the clinician, taking into account factors that affect sexual functioning, such as age and the context of the person's life.
2. The disturbance causes marked personal distress or interpersonal difficulty.
3. The sexual dysfunction is not better accounted for by another Axis I disorder (except another sexual dysfunction) and is not due exclusively to the direct physiologic effects of a substance (e.g., a drug of abuse, a medication) or a general medical condition.

Subtypes may be "lifelong" or "acquired" and "generalized" or "situational." It should be appreciated that these subtypes can be applied with all *DSM-IV* FSD diagnostic categories.

Anticipated *DSM-5* Revisions

In recognition of the long-standing dissatisfaction with the reliance of the sexual dysfunctions on Masters and Johnson's linear human sexual response cycle, because of the high degree of overlap between symptoms of low desire and problematic sexual arousal, and in recognition of the heterogeneity in how women experience sexual desire, the *DSM-5* sexual dysfunctions subworkgroup has proposed significantly revising HSDD for women. This proposal suggests that an individual meet at least three of six criteria; it includes objective frequency and duration criteria, and it introduces a list of specifiers that allow the clinician to estimate correlates of the condition. Sexual interest/arousal disorder (SIAD) is thus proposed as follows (www.dsm5.org), with the additional criterion that it must cause clinically significant distress or impairment:

A. Lack of sexual interest/arousal of at least 6 months duration as manifested by at least three of the following indicators:

1) Absent/reduced frequency or intensity of interest in sexual activity
2) Absent/reduced frequency or intensity of sexual/erotic thoughts or fantasies
3) Absence or reduced frequency of initiation of sexual activity and is typically unreceptive to a partner's attempts to initiate
4) Absent/reduced frequency or intensity of sexual excitement/pleasure during sexual activity on most sexual encounters
5) Sexual interest/arousal is absent or infrequently elicited by any internal or external sexual/erotic cues (e.g., written, verbal, visual, etc.)
6) Absent/reduced frequency or intensity of genital and/or nongenital sensations during sexual activity on most sexual encounters

Considerable debate surrounds this proposed disorder focusing on validity and reliability. Feminist critiques center on the broad pathologizing inherent to making a sexual dysfunction diagnosis.

Risk Factors

The known major risk factors for HSDD include age, relationship problems, depression, antidepressant medications, thyroid disorders, diabetes, cardiovascular disorders, and lower urinary tract syndromes. These factors generally represent major risks for the majority of FSDs.

Prevalence of Hypoactive Sexual Desire Disorder

The majority of early prevalence research on HSDD did not measure concomitant personal distress (an essential diagnostic criterion) and so reported rates of *low sexual desire* only. In a very comprehensive recent epidemiological study, termed the PRESIDE study, Shiffren, Monz, Russo, Segretti, and Johannes (2008) reported on a sample of 31,581 women aged 18 years and older and observed a prevalence of 9.5% for HSDD (i.e., low desire plus distress).

Psychological Interventions

Unfortunately there have been very few psychological treatment outcome studies focusing specifically on low desire. Earlier studies examined heterogeneous groups of women (and men) and found that behaviorally focused treatments (e.g., sensate focus) led to improvements in 57% of women with the primary complaint of low desire. More recent studies have examined cognitive-behavioral therapy (CBT); however, one uncontrolled study found that only 33% of women with low desire found the treatment helpful (McCabe, 2001), and another study that administered CBT to couples in group format found that 74% of women found the program helpful compared to a waitlist control group (Trudel et al., 2001). Most recently, mindfulness-based CBT, known as the third wave in the evolution of behavior-based therapies, has been adapted and tested among women with HSDD. One uncontrolled trial showed that a four-session mindfulness-based CBT group treatment for women with HSDD significantly improved sexual desire and mood (Brotto, Basson, & Luria, 2008). Clearly more research examining the efficacy of psychological interventions for low desire is needed in the context of randomized controlled trials.

Pharmacological Interventions and Devices

Although there are a number of investigational pharmacological agents currently being evaluated in Phase-II and Phase-III clinical trials, at the moment there are no FDA-approved drugs marketed for the treatment of HSDD in the United States. Those drugs that are administered for the condition are prescribed "off label." Principal among the off-label drugs used to treat HSDD is *testosterone*, administered as a transdermal gel or cream. Clinicians either prescribe men's testosterone products at greatly reduced doses or write prescriptions filled by compounding pharmacists who make up less potent personalized versions of *testosterone* specifically for women. The efficacy of transdermal testosterone prescribed in this manner is approximately 60%–65%. Other agents such as bupropion (i.e., Wellbutrin, an antidepressant) and various PDE_5 inhibitors, for example, sildenafil (i.e., Viagra), have also been tried with inconsistent results in women with HSDD.

FEMALE SEXUAL AROUSAL DISORDER

Diagnostic Criteria

Female sexual arousal disorder (FSAD) is defined as follows:

1) Persistent or recurrent inability to attain, or to maintain until completion of the sexual activity, an adequate lubrication-swelling response of sexual excitement.
2) The disturbance causes marked distress or interpersonal difficulty.
3) The dysfunction is not better accounted for by another Axis I disorder (except another sexual dysfunction) and is not due exclusively to the direct physiological effects of a substance or a general medical condition.

Anticipated *DSM-5* Revisions

The central feature of the *DSM-IV-TR* definition of FSAD is an inadequate lubrication-swelling response. However, because this symptom is rarely the presenting complaint among women seeking treatment in sex therapy clinics, there is a proposal to remove FSAD from the *DSM-5*. In its place, the symptom of reduced genital and/or nongenital sensations is proposed for inclusion in the proposed diagnostic criteria of SIAD.

Prevalence of Female Sexual Arousal Disorder

The PRESIDE study observed a prevalence rate of 5.1% for FSAD (arousal dysfunction plus distress).

Psychological Interventions

Controlled trials of psychological interventions that target FSAD do not exist, as there has been a predominant focus on testing pharmacological interventions for this condition. However, one uncontrolled trial of a mindfulness-based CBT administered to gynecologic cancer survivors with the primary complaint of FSAD found a significant improvement in self-reported sexual arousal and a marginal improvement in genital arousal as measured by a vaginal photoplethysmograph (Brotto et al., 2008). Another pilot study that compared a brief CBT intervention with a brief mindfulness intervention for women with sexual arousal difficulties associated with a history of childhood sexual abuse found that those women randomized to the mindfulness group had a significant increase in concordance between genital and subjective sexual arousal compared to women in the CBT group, though both treatments resulted in a significant reduction in sexual distress (Brotto, Seal, & Rellini, 2012).

Pharmacological Interventions and Devices

Although a series of clinical trials have been completed with a number of drugs in the treatment of FSAD, consistent positive results have been elusive. Several smaller studies have demonstrated efficacy with sildenafil, but these findings have not been confirmed in large-scale, randomized, double-blind trials. Alprostadil, a dopamine agonist, has also been utilized as a topical agent with arousal disorders but has failed to show a consistent clinical response. A vacuum device known as the EROS clitoral therapy device has shown some efficacy for FSAD and has been approved by the FDA for the treatment of this condition. The EROS device has been shown to provide benefit to select subgroups of women with FSAD, but it does not appear to afford a robust response in general.

FEMALE ORGASMIC DISORDER

Diagnostic Criteria

Female orgasmic disorder (FOD) is described as follows:

1. A persistent or recurrent delay in, or absence of, orgasm following a normal sexual excitement phase. The clinician should make the diagnosis with the awareness that women exhibit wide variability in their capacity for orgasmic response, and taking into account age, sexual experience, and the adequacy of the sexual stimulation she receives.
2. The disturbance causes marked personal distress or interpersonal difficulty.
3. The orgasmic dysfunction is not better accounted for by another Axis I disorder (except another sexual dysfunction) and is not due exclusively to the direct physiological effects of a substance (e.g., a drug of abuse or medication) or a general medical condition.

Anticipated *DSM-5* Revisions

Some women describe a distressing change in the quality of their orgasms such that orgasms still occur, albeit with markedly reduced intensity. The proposal for *DSM-5* recommends considering female orgasmic disorder when at least one of the two following symptoms is present for at least 6 months and is experienced on most occasions of sexual activity:

1. Marked delay in, marked infrequency, or absence of, orgasm
2. Markedly reduced intensity of orgasmic sensation

Prevalence of Female Orgasmic Disorder

The PRESIDE study observed a prevalence rate of 4.6% for FOD (orgasmic disorder with concomitant distress).

Psychological Interventions

There have been no new data on the efficacy of psychological interventions for FOD since 1997. Prior to then, directed masturbation was established as an effective treatment for lifelong anorgasmia, and, when combined with sex education, anxiety reduction, and CBT, remains a first-line treatment approach for lifelong FOD.

Pharmacological Interventions and Devices

As is true with the other categories of female sexual dysfunction, there are no FDA-approved drugs available to treat FOD in the United States. Several agents have reportedly shown some degree of success off label, in particular, sildenafil and buspirone (i.e., Buspar; Nurnberg et al., 2008). However, randomized, controlled clinical trials remain to be done with these drugs to demonstrate safety and efficacy. Some newer investigational agents have also shown promise in recent trials, such as bremelanotide, a novel melanocortin agonist (Ishak, Bokarius, Jeffrey, Davis, & Bahkta, 2010).

DYSPAREUNIA

Diagnostic Criteria

Dyspareunia is defined as follows:

1. Genital pain most commonly associated with sexual intercourse, although it may also be experienced before or after coitus. Intensity of the pain may range from mild to sharp.
2. The disturbance must cause marked distress or interpersonal difficulty.
3. The disturbance is not caused exclusively by vaginismus or lack of lubrication and is not better accounted for by another Axis I disorder (except for another sexual dysfunction), and it is not due exclusively to a substance (e.g., drug of abuse, medication) or a general medical condition.

VAGINISMUS

Diagnostic Criteria

The essential diagnostic features of vaginismus are as follows:

1. A persistent or recurrent involuntary contraction of the perineal muscles surrounding the outer one-third of the vagina when vaginal penetration with penis, finger, tampon, or speculum is attempted.
2. The disturbance causes distress or interpersonal difficulty.
3. The disturbance is not better accounted for by another Axis I disorder (except another sexual dysfunction) and is not due exclusively to the direct physiological effects of a general medical condition.

References and Readings

American Psychiatric Association. (2000). *Diagnostic and statistical manual of mental disorders* (4th ed., text rev.). Washington, DC: Author.

Brotto, L. A., Basson, R., & Luria, M. (2008). A mindfulness-based group psychoeducational intervention targeting sexual arousal disorders in women. *Journal of Sexual Medicine, 5*, 1646–1659.

Brotto, L. A., Goff, B., Lentz, G. M., Swisher, E., Tamimi, H., & Van Blarcom, A. (2008). A psychoeducational intervention for sexual dysfunction in women with gynecological cancer. *Archives of Sexual Behavior, 37*(2), 317–329.

Brotto, L. A., Seal, B. N., & Rellini, A. H. (2012). Pilot study of a brief cognitive behavioral versus mindfulness-based intervention for women with sexual distress and a history of childhood sexual abuse. *Journal of Sex and Marital Therapy, 38*(1), 1–27.

Ishak, W. W., Bokarius, A., Jeffrey, J. K., Davis, M. C., & Bahkta, Y. (2010). Disorders of orgasm in women: A literature review of etiology and current treatments. *Journal of Sexual Medicine, 7*, 3254–3268.

McCabe, M. P. (2001). Evaluation of a cognitive behavior therapy program for people with

sexual dysfunction. *Journal of Sex and Marital Therapy, 27*, 259–271.
Nurnberg, H. G., Hensley, P. L., Heiman, J. R., Croft, H. A., DeBattista, C., & Paine, S. (2008). Sildenafil treatment of women with antidepressant-associated sexual dysfunction: A randomized, controlled trial. *Journal of the American Medical Association, 300*(4), 395–404.
Shiffren, J. L., Monz, B. U., Russo, P. A., Segretti, A., & Johannes, C. B. (2008). Sexual problems and distress in United States women. *Obstetrics and Gynecology, 112*, 970–978.
Trudel, G., Marchand, A., Ravart, M., Aubin, S., Turgeon, L., & Fortier, P. (2001). The effect of a cognitive-behavioral group treatment program on hypoactive sexual desire in women. *Sexual and Relationship Therapy, 16*(2), 145–164.

Related Topics

Chapter 14, "Taking a Client's Sexual History"
Chapter 44, "Diagnosis, Assessment, and Treatment of Male Sexual Dysfunctions"
Chapter 49, "Managing Sexual Feelings for Patients in Psychotherapy"
Chapter 70, "Understanding Sexuality in the Context of Disability"

44 DIAGNOSIS, ASSESSMENT, AND TREATMENT OF MALE SEXUAL DYSFUNCTIONS

Leonard R. Derogatis and Lori A. Brotto

The categories of male sexual dysfunctions as represented in the American Psychiatric Association's *Diagnostic and Statistical Manual of Mental Disorders*, fourth edition, text revision (*DSM-IV-TR*) basically consist of three categories of disorders: *sexual desire disorders, sexual arousal disorders*, and two major classes of *orgasmic disorder: premature ejaculation* and *male orgasmic disorder.* Men also experience pain and other genitourinary conditions; however, because these conditions are, for the most part, medical disorders, we limit our focus to conditions involving low desire, problems with arousal (erectile dysfunction), and orgasmic difficulties. For each class of disorder we briefly review the following:

- Diagnostic criteria (including anticipated *DSM-5* changes, if any)
- Risk factors
- Prevalence data
- Psychological interventions
- Pharmacological interventions and devices

HYPOACTIVE SEXUAL DESIRE DISORDER

Diagnostic Criteria

Hypoactive sexual desire disorder (HSDD) is defined in the *DSM-IV-TR* as a condition exemplified by the following:

1. Persistently or recurrently deficient (or absent) sexual fantasies and desire for

sexual activity. The judgment of deficiency or absence is made by the clinician, taking into account factors that affect sexual functioning, such as age and the context of the person's life.
2. The disturbance causes marked personal distress or interpersonal difficulty.
3. The sexual dysfunction is not better accounted for by another Axis I disorder (except another sexual dysfunction) and is not due exclusively to the direct physiologic effects of a substance (e.g., a drug of abuse, a medication) or a general medical condition. Subtypes may be "lifelong" or "acquired" and "generalized" or "situational."

Note that unlike research on HSDD in women, which is abundant, very little research on HSDD in men exists. For some time many experts have believed this condition a chimera, essentially nonexistent, with apparent cases resulting from hypogonadism (low testosterone), clinical depression, or a secondary response to another sexual dysfunction like erectile dysfunction. Recently, however, a study describing the first controlled comparisons of HSDD in men as a distinct sexual dysfunction was reported. Participants were screened for serum testosterone levels, erectile dysfunction, and depressive symptoms, rendering the HSDD subsample essentially free of these confounding conditions. The study found statistically significant and clinically meaningful differences on measures of sexual desire, sex-related personal distress, and levels of sexual activity in those men who received a *DSM-IV*-based diagnosis of HSDD versus those who did not (Derogatis et al., 2012).

Anticipated *DSM-5* Revisions (If Any)

A thorough review of the literature on sexual desire in men concluded that there are likely more within-sex differences than between-sex differences when comparing the experience of sexual desire in men and women (Brotto, 2010). In particular, men, like women, describe a bidirectional relationship between sexual desire and arousal along with a variety of sexual and nonsexual triggers that elicit their sexual desire. However, due to the lack of sufficient evidence to warrant a change in the diagnosis of low desire for men, it is highly unlikely that HSDD for men will undergo any significant revision for *DSM-5* (www.dsm5.org).

Risk Factors

The risk factors for HSDD in men are not well known, but the condition can be *lifelong*, which implies constitutional factors, or *acquired* after a period of normal functioning. The etiology of cases of acquired low desire can be unclear because of a host of factors, including numerous medical problems, medications (e.g., SSRI antidepressants), relationship difficulties, the presence of erectile dysfunction, or sexual orientation conflicts.

Prevalence of Hypoactive Sexual Desire Disorder

The majority of prevalence research on HSDD in men has not measured concomitant personal distress (an essential diagnostic criterion) and often did not screen patients for hypogonadism or depression. In the past two decades no epidemiological research assessing HSDD in men has appeared in print; as a result, the rates reported address *low sexual desire* only. These studies report prevalence rates of low desire in the mid-teens (Derogatis et al., 2012). Based on these data, our best current estimate is that HSDD in men has a prevalence rate of approximately 5% or less.

Psychological Interventions

In the past decade not a single published study has examined the efficacy of a psychological treatment for HSDD in men. Sex therapists generally report that treatment of low desire is more difficult than treatment of arousal and orgasm disorders. A single uncontrolled study that has never been replicated examined behavior therapy and sensate focus over 7 weeks and found that 63% of the 90 men enrolled with HSDD had a significant improvement, defined by a single self-report item addressing whether the couple believed they had improved. Clinical evidence suggests that cognitive-behavioral and mindfulness-based therapies have an important role to play in treatment of low desire in men (as they do in women); however, they await empirical testing.

Pharmacological Interventions and Devices

As indicated earlier, most earlier research did not screen for depression, drug, or disease-induced confounds in men with low sexual desire, so we do not have a clear picture of the efficacy of pharmacological treatments for HSDD in men. Ample evidence shows that testosterone, administered either transdermally or through intramuscular injection, is highly efficacious with hypogonadal men, but we do not have a reliable estimate of its efficacy in true cases of HSDD. Likewise, low sexual desire due to medical conditions or drugs can often be remediated by treatment of the primary condition; however, sexual dysfunction due to a general medical condition is the more appropriate diagnosis in this case.

MALE ERECTILE DISORDER/ERECTILE DYSFUNCTION

Diagnostic Criteria

Male erectile disorder (ED) is defined as follows:

1. A persistent or recurrent inability to attain or maintain until completion of the sexual activity, an adequate erection.
2. The disturbance causes marked distress or interpersonal difficulty.
3. The dysfunction is not better accounted for by another Axis I disorder (except another sexual dysfunction) and is not due exclusively to the direct physiological effects of a substance or a general medical condition.

Anticipated *DSM-5* Revisions (If Any)

Two proposed changes to ED are under consideration for *DSM-5* (Segraves, 2010a; www.dsm5.org). One recommendation would include decreased erectile rigidity as a criterion in recognition of the finding that failure to obtain or maintain an erection is not the only clinical manifestation of ED. A second recommendation would introduce a 6-month duration criterion whereby short-term difficulties in erectile function would not lead to a formal diagnosis. Although treatment would not necessarily be withheld, requiring a 6-month duration avoids pathologizing short-term adaptive changes in sexual functioning.

Risk Factors

A number of well-established risk factors for ED include age, diabetes, depression, antidepressant use, antihypertensive use, hypertension, cardiovascular disease, and prostate disease.

Prevalence of Erectile Disorder

Burnett (2007) describes ED as the most thoroughly studied sexual dysfunction in epidemiological research and reports the overall adult male prevalence rate ranges from 10% to 20%, with most studies reporting rates closer to the latter figure. In addition, it is clear that rates increase dramatically with age, exemplified by data from the Massachusetts Male Aging Study, which showed prevalence of ED rising from 8% among 40 year olds to 40% among men aged 70.

Psychological Interventions

Psychological approaches to ED involve a variety of techniques borrowed from cognitive-behavioral therapy (to reduce anxiety and challenge irrational thoughts), sensate focus, couples therapy, masturbation training, and psychodynamic treatment (Montorsi et al., 2010). More commonly, psychological treatments are combined with PDE_5 inhibitors given that medications alone may restore the erection but not necessarily sexual intercourse or sexual satisfaction in a couple. In a randomized comparison of sildenafil versus sildenafil plus couples sex therapy in 44 couples, whereas both treatments significantly improved erectile function, the combined group led to significantly reduced cognitive biases in men, and a significant improvement in most domains of the female partner's sexual functioning. Treatment satisfaction was also significantly greater in the combined group.

Pharmacological Interventions and Devices

A popular paradigm used in ED management is termed the "Process of Care Model." The core of this approach to treatment uses a stepwise methodology combining processes, actions, and outcomes in optimizing treatment of the ED patient. This paradigm, which was first formalized in the late 1990s, reflects a strategy of staged therapeutic approaches as first-, second- and third- line interventions, ranging from patient education and psychological counseling/sex therapy, through oral and other pharmacological treatments, to third-line surgical interventions (Hatzichristou et al., 2010). Assessing specific elements of the model independently, treatment with PDE_5 inhibitors (e.g., sildenafil) has probably become the most popular treatment option, with a success rate of approximately 65%. Direct intracorporal injection with vasodilators (e.g., alprostadil, papaverine, or phentolamine) also has a high success rate (70%–90%), both with individual drugs and combinations, but it has the obvious downside of penile self-injection and possible scarring at the injection site. Other drugs and several devices also exist for the treatment of ED, but they are less often utilized.

MALE ORGASMIC DISORDER

Diagnostic Criteria

Male orgasmic disorder is described as follows:

1. A persistent or recurrent delay in, or absence of, orgasm following a normal sexual excitement phase. The clinician should make the diagnosis taking into account the patient's age and the adequacy of the sexual stimulation in terms of focus, intensity, and duration.
2. The disturbance causes marked personal distress or interpersonal difficulty.
3. The orgasmic dysfunction is not better accounted for by another Axis I disorder (except another sexual dysfunction) and is not due exclusively to the direct physiological effects of a substance (e.g., a drug of abuse or medication) or a general medical condition.

Anticipated *DSM-5* Revisions (If Any)

Consistent with conventional usage among experts in the field, there is a proposed name change to this condition to "delayed ejaculation." The presence of delay in orgasm or marked infrequency/absence of orgasm will be moved to separate criteria to facilitate diagnostic precision. Like the other sexual dysfunctions, there is a recommended 6-month duration to meet criteria (Segraves, 2010b).

Risk Factors

The risk factors for male orgasmic disorder can best be categorized in two broad groups: medical/pharmacologic and intrapsychic/interpersonal. In the former category are spinal cord and sympathetic nerve damage, pelvic surgery (e.g., prostatectomy), diabetic and alcohol-related neuropathies, thyroid disorders, and antidepressant and antihypertensive medications. The psychological risk factors are less well understood and tend to share reduced capacity for sexual arousal as a common denominator. This inhibition can result from intrapsychic conflicts or relationship-based interpersonal conflicts that constrain the capacity for high sexual arousal.

Prevalence of Male Orgasmic Disorder

Establishing the prevalence of male orgasmic disorder is complicated by the fact that there is no agreed-upon standard for length of delay before assuming clinical status. Even so, this is probably a relatively rare condition, with a recent international study reporting rates from 1.1% to 2.7% (Segraves, 2010b).

Psychological Interventions

Almost no literature exists on the psychological treatment of men with this condition. However, it is generally well accepted that counseling aimed at exploring factors contributing to the delayed orgasm is a crucial first step in treatment (Montorsi et al., 2010).

Pharmacological Interventions

If evidence suggests that the individual's orgasmic disorder arises from a remediable medical condition (e.g., thyroid disorder) or a specific pharmacologic agent (e.g., SSRI), then appropriate treatment or adjustments to a patient's drug regimen can often effectively treat the condition. Psychological conflict-based cases are less likely to respond to pharmacological interventions and are more likely to require psychotherapeutic treatment.

PREMATURE EJACULATION

Diagnostic Criteria

The essential clinical features of premature ejaculation (PE) are as follows:

1. The persistent and recurrent onset of orgasm and ejaculation with minimal sexual stimulation before, on, or shortly after penetration and before the person wishes it.
2. The disturbance must cause marked distress or interpersonal difficulty.
3. The disturbance is not caused exclusively by the direct effects of a substance (e.g., drug of abuse, medication).

In recent years increasing levels of dissatisfaction have developed concerning the *DSM-IV* definition of PE. The current definition is not evidence based, specific operational criteria are absent, and it places great reliance on the diagnostic judgment of the clinician. The International Society of Sexual Medicine (ISSM) convened a panel of experts in 2007 who proposed a new definition for lifelong PE. The ISSM definition characterizes the disorder as "ejaculation which always or nearly always occurs prior to or within about one minute of vaginal penetration, and involves the inability to delay ejaculation on all or almost all vaginal penetrations, with attendant negative personal consequences such as distress, bother, or frustration and/or the avoidance of sexual intimacy" (Althof et al., 2010, p. 2952).

Anticipated *DSM-5* Revisions (If Any)

In agreement with the proposed changes to PE by the ISSM committee, the proposal for *DSM-5* has this condition defined monothetically as a "persistent or recurrent pattern of ejaculation occurring during partnered sexual activity within approximately one minute of beginning of sexual activity and before the person wishes it" and that the symptom is experienced for at least 6 months and takes place on most occasions of sexual activity (Segraves, 2010c). Because of concerns about potentially pejorative connotations with the term "premature," it has been proposed that this condition be renamed "early ejaculation" for *DSM-5*.

Risk Factors

The number of putative risk factors for PE is very large, including psychological (e.g., performance anxiety), medical (e.g., prostatitis), pharmacologic (e.g., citalopram), genetic (e.g., diathesis hypothesis), and neurobiological (e.g., serotonernergic neurotransmission) elements. In addition, PE frequently develops as a secondary condition to primary erectile dysfunction (estimated 30%–50% of ED patients).

Prevalence of Premature Ejaculation

We lack reliable evidence of the prevalence of lifelong and acquired PE, in large measure because of the variety of different definitions of PE and the fact that different methods of collecting prevalence data (e.g., self-report vs. population-based vs. clinician judgment) have a decided effect on the rates reported. In their review, Althof et al. (2010) cite rates ranging from 30% (self-report) to 3% (population based).

Psychological Interventions

No controlled trials of a psychological treatment for PE exist; however, well-accepted practices among experts show effectiveness of cognitive-behavioral techniques that increase a man's sense of control to delay orgasm. Both the "stop-start" technique (i.e., temporarily ceasing sexual stimulation) and the "squeeze" technique (i.e., squeezing the frenulum of the penis) have been utilized for the past four decades in the treatment of PE along with other psychological strategies aimed at improving the man's self-confidence sexually, reducing anxiety, resolving interpersonal issues, and increasing couple communication. Unfortunately, however, long-term maintenance of gains remains a problem in this area. As with ED, experts tend to favor a combined treatment approach that integrates psychological and pharmacological aspects.

Pharmacological Interventions and Devices

Pharmacologic interventions for PE basically involve two classes of drugs: *SSRI antidepressants* and *topical anesthetics.* In addition, the tricyclic antidepressant clomipramine has been used very effectively with PE. These agents block axonal reuptake of serotonin from the synaptic cleft, resulting in enhanced 5-HT neurotransmission. These drugs can be used off label on demand, or off label via daily dosing. Drugs like paroxetine (Paxil) 10–40 mg, sertraline (Zoloft) 50–200 mg, and fluoxetine (Prozac) 20–40 mg have proven very effective in this regard. Benefits are usually seen within 5 to 10 days of treatment but may require up to 3 weeks. On-demand treatment initiated 3 to 6 hours before intercourse has shown a less robust therapeutic response than daily dosing but remains moderately effective. A limitation of the pharmacological approach is that PE returns if the drug is discontinued.

In addition, the use of topical anesthetics like prilocaine and lidocaine has a long history in PE. These topical drugs, in cream or gel form, have been shown to be moderately effective in treating PE; however, they can produce significant penile hypoanesthesia and vaginal numbness.

References and Readings

Althof, S. E., Abdo, C. H., Dean, J., Hackett, G., McCabe, M., McMahon, C. G.,...Tan, H. M. (2010). International Society for Sexual Medicine's guidelines for the diagnosis and treatment of premature ejaculation. *Journal of Sexual Medicine, 7,* 2947–2969.

Brotto, L. A. (2010). The DSM diagnostic criteria for hypoactive sexual desire disorder in men. *Journal of Sexual Medicine, 7,* 2015–2030.

Burnett, A. L., (2007). Evaluation and management of erectile dysfunction. In M. Campbell & P. Walsh (Eds.), *Urology* (9th ed., pp. 721–748). Philadelphia, PA: Saunders.

Derogatis, L. R., Rosen, R. C., Goldstein, I., Werenburg, B., Kempthorne-Rawson, J., & Sand, M. (2012). Characterization of hypoactive sexual desire disorder (HSDD) in men. *Journal of Sexual Medicine, 9*(3), 812–820.

Hatzichristou, D. G., Rosen, R. C., Derogatis, L. R. Low, W. Y., Meuleman, E. J., Sadovsky, R., & Symonds, T. (2010). Recommendations for the clinical evaluation of men and women with sexual dysfunction. *Journal of Sexual Medicine, 7,* 337–348.

Montorsi, F., Adaikan, G., Becher, E., Giuliano, F., Khoury, S., Lue, T. F.,...Wasserman, M. (2010). Summary of the recommendations on sexual dysfunctions in men. *Journal of Sexual Medicine, 7,* 3572–3588.

Segraves, R. T. (2010a). Considerations for diagnostic criteria for erectile disorder in DSM-V. *Journal of Sexual Medicine, 7,* 654–660.

Segraves, R. T. (2010b). Considerations for a better definition of male orgasmic disorder in DSM-5. *Journal of Sexual Medicine, 7,* 690–695.

Segraves, R. T. (2010c). Considerations for an evidence-based definition of premature ejaculation in the DSM-V. *Journal of Sexual Medicine, 7,* 672–679.

Related Topics

Chapter 14, "Taking a Client's Sexual History"

Chapter 43, "Diagnosis, Assessment, and Treatment of Female Sexual Dysfunctions"

Chapter 49, "Managing Sexual Feelings for Patients in Psychotherapy"

Chapter 70, "Understanding Sexuality in the Context of Disability"

45 WORKING WITH PATIENTS AT RISK FOR HIV AND OTHER SEXUALLY TRANSMITTED DISEASES

Michael P. Carey and Peter A. Vanable

Epidemiologic data from the Centers for Disease Control and Prevention confirm that the acquired immunodeficiency syndrome (AIDS) can affect anyone who comes into contact with the human immunodeficiency virus (HIV). Although AIDS was originally thought to be a disease that affected only gay men, AIDS affects women as well as men and does not discriminate among persons on the basis of sexual orientation, gender, or race. In the United States, more than 1 million people are currently living with HIV. Since the beginning of the AIDS epidemic, an estimated 600,000 people with AIDS have died in the United States. However, while AIDS remains a leading cause of death among young adults, effective treatments are now available that allow many who are infected with HIV (often referred to as HIV positive or HIV+) to live long, productive lives, provided they are able to take their medications as prescribed.

Neither cure nor vaccine exists for HIV and AIDS; thus, behavioral avoidance of the virus provides the only protection against infection. For people who are HIV positive, sustained health requires close adherence to HIV medications and avoidance of harmful health behaviors (e.g., high-risk sexual behavior, substance abuse). Psychologists should know the basics of HIV transmission and prevention to evaluate clients for their risk of infection and to provide risk reduction counseling when indicated. Further, psychologists should be equipped to work with HIV-positive clients and should be aware of the major stressors and challenges clients face in living with HIV.

This chapter provides an overview of four areas necessary for effective and ethical practice. First, we summarize the key information regarding HIV transmission. Second, we provide guidelines for efficiently screening HIV risk in a time-efficient manner. Third, we offer guidance on counseling clients regarding risk reduction. Fourth, we mention the central coping challenges and psychological treatment needs of persons living with HIV.

HIV TRANSMISSION

HIV is a fluid-borne agent. What this means is that, unlike tuberculosis or other airborne infectious agents, HIV is not spread through sneezing, coughing, sharing eating utensils, or other forms of casual contact. For HIV transmission to occur, an infected person's blood, semen, vaginal secretions, or breast milk must enter the bloodstream of another person. The two most common routes of transmission are *unprotected vaginal or anal sexual intercourse* with an infected partner; and *sharing unsterilized needles* (most commonly in the context of recreational drug use) with an infected person.

ASSESSMENT OF RISK

Careful listening serves as the cornerstone of the assessment process. Some clients may freely offer their concerns about HIV-related risk as a reason for psychotherapy. Despite the importance of sexual health, not all health professionals are comfortable discussing sexual topics. It is not uncommon for clients to report that they had tried previously to discuss sexual concerns with a health care professional but were met with avoidance, embarrassment, or apparent lack of interest; as a result, the clients did not pursue their concerns. Thus, the first guideline is to be open to clients' self-disclosures regarding sex, drug use, and other risk behaviors and to be aware of subtle messages you might convey to discourage the disclosure of such material.

Even when a therapist is open to client disclosure of such topics, many clients will be reluctant to independently raise their concerns regarding sexual or other risk behaviors. In these cases, the therapist will need to actively assess the client's risk in a sensitive and efficient manner. Assessment of risk should take place after a client and therapist have established rapport and the therapist has assured the client of confidentiality. Specific risk assessment should always begin with an appropriate introduction for the client. During this time, the reasons for asking questions about sexual and other socially sensitive behaviors should be provided. For example, one might say that a standard practice is to inquire about risk for HIV just as one routinely inquires about suicidal ideation, personal safety, and other important matters. Although sensitivity is advised, it is also important to ask questions in a direct fashion, without apology or hesitancy (Kinsey, Pomeroy, & Martin, 1948). If the clinician appears embarrassed about or unsure of the appropriateness of the questions, a client may sense this and provide incomplete or ambiguous responses. After the introductory remarks, the client can be invited to ask any questions he or she might have.

When assessing sexual behavior, we find it helpful to adopt certain assumptions to encourage honest disclosure (Wincze & Carey, 2001). These assumptions reflect the preferred direction of error. For example, we assume a low level of understanding on the part of the client and convey information in a clear, concrete manner. Other useful assumptions include the notions that clients will be embarrassed about and have difficulty discussing sexual matters, clients will not understand medical terminology, and they will be misinformed about HIV and AIDS. As the clinician learns more about the client, these assumptions are adjusted.

Depending on the client and the context, it may be useful to sequence the inquiry from the least to the most threatening questions. Thus, questions about receipt of blood transfusions might precede questions regarding needle sharing or sexual behavior. Experience in the assessment of sexual behavior also suggests that it can be helpful to place the "burden of denial" on the client (Kinsey et al., 1948). That is, rather than ask whether a client has engaged in a particular activity, the clinician might ask the patient how many times he or she has engaged in it. Use of this strategy will depend on the nature of the relationship with the client.

Given these process considerations, the content of the risk screening follows the transmission categories identified earlier. We advise inquiring about each of the following domains and pursuing follow-up questions as appropriate.

1. "When were you last tested to determine if you are infected with HIV (the virus that causes AIDS)? What were the results of that test?" Knowledge of the date of the test is important for the determination of subsequent risk activity. Because of the window period (i.e., the amount of time between exposure to and infection with the virus, and the development of antibodies detectable with serological tests), one should assess risk behavior going back at least 6 months prior to the most recent antibody

test. If a client discloses that he or she is infected with HIV, you will need to address the many health, relationship, and social consequences associated with HIV disease.

2. "Since your last HIV antibody test, with how many *men* have you had sex (oral, anal, or vaginal)? Did you always use condoms when having sex? If yes, did you use condoms during *every* penetrative contact, including oral sex? Did you always use *latex* (or *polyurethane*) condoms? Have any of your male partners had sex with other men?" Experts agree that anal sex confers more risk than vaginal sex, and that both are much more risky than oral sex. Experts disagree regarding the probability of HIV transmission through oral sex, although this vector of transmission has been demonstrated in some epidemiologic studies. Experts agree that latex condoms protect against HIV only when used consistently and correctly with all partners.
3. "Since your last HIV antibody test, with how many *women* have you had sex (oral, anal, or vaginal)? Did you always use condoms or other barrier protection (e.g., dental dam) when having sex?" Transmission of HIV from an infected woman is less likely than from an infected male, but some risk is still involved.
4. "How many times have you shared or borrowed a needle, or used another person's works (e.g., cotton, corker, cooker), to prepare or inject drugs? Did you disinfect the needle prior to reusing it? If so, how did you do this?" Contaminated needles are responsible for the second-largest number of infections in the United States. Although needles can be properly disinfected (e.g., by flushing with a bleach solution two or more times), they are typically shared without cleaning or after improper cleaning.
5. "Have you ever had sex with a person who used injection drugs?" All else being equal, injection drug users (IDUs) are more likely to be infected with HIV than are non-IDUs.
6. "Have you ever had a sexual partner whom you knew or suspected was HIV positive? If so, did you always use condoms when you had sex?" Having a partner known to be infected with HIV introduces the greatest risk of infection.
7. "Are you at all concerned that you might have been infected with the virus?" This leaves the door open for people who may not have felt comfortable responding to the earlier questions.

RISK REDUCTION COUNSELING

Three levels of intervention can be considered dependent on the circumstances. First, if a client reports that he or she has engaged in any high-risk activity (e.g., unprotected intercourse), it may be appropriate to encourage the client to seek testing for HIV. Early detection of infection can help clients to obtain preventive medical care, as well as psychosocial services. Knowledge of serostatus may enhance motivation for risk reduction practices in order to avoid infecting others.

Clients who express concern despite apparent low risk may also be advised to consider testing. Clients who have been abstinent or those who strongly believe themselves to have been in a mutually monogamous sexual relationship with an HIV-negative partner and have never shared an injection drug needle can be reassured and counseled to maintain low risk. Information about HIV-antibody testing is available from numerous sources, including American Red Cross chapters and local health departments.

Two types of testing are available: With *confidential* testing, the results are recorded in the client's medical files and may be disclosed to those with legal access to records; with *anonymous* testing, a code number is given when blood is drawn, and this number must be presented by the client to receive the results. The client's name is not associated with test results. Many states offer anonymous and/or confidential tests without charge. Although sites that offer HIV testing are required to provide pretest and posttest counseling, psychotherapists should be prepared to supplement such counseling, regardless of the outcome.

A second level of intervention involves simple education. If a client is misinformed about the basics of HIV and AIDS or has questions about transmission and prevention of HIV infection, most psychologists should be able to help immediately. If a client has been involved in risky sexual or drug-use practices, he or she should be advised promptly and specifically which behaviors enhance risk and what preventive action can be taken to reduce risk for infection. An at-risk client may require more than simple education, however.

The third level of intervention involves the provision of intensive risk reduction counseling. Intervention programs have been developed that are well grounded in psychological theory and have been evaluated in clinical trials with many populations (Carey, Scott-Sheldon, & Vanable, 2012). An excellent example of such a program is Kelly's (1995); his readable manual provides a step-by-step guide for implementing a research-supported risk reduction program. Psychologists can also refer to the sources cited herein and can call local, state, and national hot lines to learn of additional resources (e.g., National AIDS Hotline at 800-342-AIDS; National AIDS Hotline TTY/TDD service at 800-243-7889; and National AIDS Information Clearinghouse at 800-458-5231).

COUNSELING INDIVIDUALS WHO ARE HIV POSITIVE

It is common for men and women who are HIV positive to seek mental health treatment. Patients often experience acute distress following diagnosis, as well as more sustained difficulties stemming from the challenges of coping with a life-threatening, highly stigmatized illness. Improved treatments for HIV have provided much reason for optimism; however, not all patients experience sustained viral suppression. Maintaining optimal health requires strict adherence to demanding medication regimens that often carry serious side effects and a lifelong commitment to medical care.

Within this context, patients can often benefit from a focused stress management intervention for assistance in coping with both disease-specific and general life stressors (Brown & Vanable, 2008; Scott-Sheldon, Kalichman, Carey, & Fielder, 2008). Brief interventions are beneficial for patients who are experiencing minor adjustment difficulties. However, HIV patients often present with more severe adjustment difficulties that require longer term treatment. Major mood disorders (especially depression) and co-occurring substance abuse disorders are common and can contribute to disease management difficulties. As such, treatment often requires a multimodal approach to address the full spectrum of coping difficulties.

Because medication adherence is vital to long-term survival, treatment should always include an assessment of whether patients are experiencing adherence difficulties. Adherence difficulties are often exacerbated by stressful life contexts and mental health difficulties. As such, a flexible treatment approach is typically warranted, emphasizing the application of pragmatic behavioral strategies for improving medication adherence (e.g., the use of multiple reminders, daily pill boxes) in combination with treatment that is tailored to address other presenting concerns.

Clients may experience social rejection from family and friends because of their HIV diagnosis. In addition, because of stigmatization and concerns about disease transmission, HIV poses challenges for forming and maintaining intimate relationships. As such, therapy often focuses in part on the development of strategies for enhancing patients' social support. Because disclosure to family, friends, coworkers, and partners can incur risks (e.g., stigmatization) as well as benefits (e.g., increased social support), psychologists can play a vital role in assisting clients with difficult decisions regarding whom to disclose their HIV status to.

Finally, psychologists should be available to assist patients with the challenges of maintaining safer sexual practices. Most HIV-positive clients are well informed about HIV prevention basics and seek to avoid transmitting the virus to others. Nonetheless, patients may not realize that unprotected sex with other HIV-positive partners poses health risks because of the possibility of sexually transmitted disease coinfection and, less commonly, transmission of drug-resistant strains of HIV. A minority of patients may also experience difficulties in negotiating condom use with uninfected partners or partners of unknown serostatus. Reasons for such difficulties are varied but could involve problems with concurrent substance abuse, pressure from partners to have unprotected sex, and desires for greater intimacy with long-term partners. Psychologists should provide nonjudgmental support of patients' efforts to avoid sexual risk behavior.

References and Readings

Brown, J. L., & Vanable, P. A. (2008). Cognitive-behavioral stress management interventions for persons living with HIV: A review and critique of the literature. *Annals of Behavioral Medicine, 35,* 26–40.

Carey, M. P. (1999). Prevention of HIV infection through changes in sexual behavior. *American Journal of Health Promotion, 14,* 104–111.

Carey, M. P., Scott-Sheldon, L. A. J., & Vanable, P. A. (2012). HIV/AIDS. In I. B. Weiner, A. M. Nezu, C. M. Nezu, & P. A. Geller (Eds.), *Handbook of psychology, Vol. 9. Health psychology* (2nd ed.). New York: Wiley.

Kalichman, S. C. (1995). *Understanding AIDS: A guide for mental health professionals.* Washington, DC: American Psychological Association.

Kalichman, S. C. (2010). *Positive prevention: Reducing HIV transmission among people living with HIV/AIDS.* New York: Springer.

Kelly, J. A. (1995). *Changing HIV risk behavior: Practical strategies.* New York: Guilford Press.

Kinsey, A. C., Pomeroy, W. B., & Martin, C. E. (1948). *Sexual behavior in the human male.* Philadelphia, PA: Saunders.

Scott-Sheldon, L. A. J., Kalichman, S. C., Carey, M. P., & Fielder, R. L. (2008). Stress management improves mental health and quality of life in adults with HIV: A meta-analysis of randomized controlled trials, 1990 to 2006. *Health Psychology, 27,* 129–139.

Wincze, J. P., & Carey, M. P. (2001). *Sexual dysfunction: A guide for assessment and treatment* (2nd ed.). New York: Guilford Press.

Related Topic

Chapter 35, "Enhancing Patient Adherence to Treatment"

Chapter 62, "Counseling People Living with HIV"

46 TREATING WOMEN IN PSYCHOTHERAPY

Laura S. Brown

Women are a diverse, complex group, varying from one another on almost every dimension, including culture, ethnicity, sexual orientation, age and age cohort, disability, and religious or spiritual affiliation (Brown, 1994, 2009). A search of the phrase "psychotherapy with women" on the Web site of a popular online bookseller yielded 50 entries on topics ranging from psychotherapy with older women to psychotherapy with women in prison to spiritual issues for women in psychotherapy; in other words, women parsed along almost every variable and life circumstance.

Women can enter the psychotherapy process with any set of problems and distress, although certain diagnoses, such as major depression, eating disorders, and posttraumatic stress, are found at higher rates among women than among men, and others, such as sociopathy and the paraphilias, are found at markedly lower rates (Ballou & Brown, 2002; Society for the Psychology of Women and Society for Counseling Psychology, 2007). Women enter therapy individually, in heterosexual or same-sex couples, in their roles as parents, as caregivers of their own parents, and as workers. They are seen in inpatient and residential settings, in substance abuse treatment programs, and in growing numbers in treatment for violent offenders. How, then, can such a diverse, complex group be addressed by one set of recommendations for psychotherapy?

The answer, of course, is that no one set of norms and rules will cover all bases for psychotherapy with all women. Nonetheless, the therapist undertaking work with women clients can find a rich body of information about issues to consider when the client is a woman, be she a second-generation Asian American lesbian police officer or a Euro-American heterosexual full-time homemaker or a methamphetamine-addicted survivor of complex trauma living in a women's correctional facility.

In the early 1970s, the publication of the classic study by Broverman and her colleagues, which served as the impetus for the APA Task Force on Sex Bias and Sex Role Stereotyping in Psychotherapy (American Psychological Association, 1978), alerted the discipline of psychology to the pervasive presence of gender-based biases in psychotherapy with women. These biases were found to affect all aspects of training and practice in psychotherapy, and to adversely affect the quality of treatment received by women (Brodsky & Hare-Mustin, 1980). Such bias has diminished, but not entirely retreated, even as the numbers of women receiving doctoral degrees in professional psychology outpace those awarded to men.

Several specific issues were first identified during this initial period. These included the following :

- Androcentric biases in the construction of disorder and normalcy, with tendencies toward overrepresentation of feminine gendered behaviors and ways of being in constructions of disorder, and failures to interrogate how constructions of gender for men might be equally predisposing toward disordered ways of being.
- Lack of attention to the interaction between individual and social context in both diagnostic formulation and treatment planning.
- Sexist power dynamics in the psychotherapeutic relationship in which the therapist mirrored and transmitted nonconscious biases toward women clients.
- Lack of adequate scientific foundation for psychological practice with women, and overreliance on data derived solely from narrow, Euro-American, middle-class, heterosexual, and clinical, rather than diverse, general population-based samples.

In response to these emerging data, feminists within psychology began to conduct research, both on the psychology of women in general, and on psychotherapy with women in specific. This led to the initial development of a set of guidelines for psychotherapy with women, which were first published in 1986 (Fitzgerald & Nutt, 1986), were revised and updated in 1996, and under the newest title, *Guidelines for Psychological Practice with Girls and Women*, were updated again and adopted in 2007 (Society for the Psychology of Women and Society for Counseling Psychology, 2007). This most recent version of the guidelines has incorporated material on the diversity of women's and girls' intersectionalities of identities. The document is divided into three thematic sections: *Diversity, social context, and power*; *Professional responsibility*; and *Practice applications.* Because this most recent iteration is founded on a strong evidence base, and contains a thorough review of psychological science about women, girls, and gender, psychotherapists working with female clients of any age and in any setting should attempt to be informed in their practice by these guidelines which, while not enforceable, set the aspirational bar for the most effective work with more than half the human population, and considerably more than half of those entering psychotherapy. A brief review of those guidelines follows.

THEME ONE: DIVERSITY, SOCIAL CONTEXT, AND POWER

Guideline 1: Psychologists strive to be aware of the effects of socialization, stereotyping, and unique life events on the development of girls and women across diverse cultural groups.

Guideline 2: Psychologists are encouraged to recognize and utilize information about oppression, privilege, and identity development as they may affect girls and women.

Guideline 3: Psychologists strive to understand the impact of bias and discrimination upon the physical and mental health of those with whom they work.

THEME TWO: PROFESSIONAL RESPONSIBILITY

Guideline 4: Psychologists strive to use gender and culturally sensitive, affirming practices in providing services to girls and women.

Guideline 5: Psychologists are encouraged to recognize how their socialization, attitudes, and knowledge about gender may affect their practice with girls and women.

THEME THREE: PRACTICE APPLICATIONS

Guideline 6: Psychologists are encouraged to employ interventions and approaches that have been found to be effective in the treatment of issues of concern to girls and women.

Guideline 7: Psychologists strive to foster therapeutic relationships and practices that promote initiative, empowerment, and expanded alternatives and choices for girls and women.

Guideline 8: Psychologists strive to provide appropriate, unbiased assessments and diagnoses in their work with women and girls.

Guideline 9: Psychologists strive to consider the problems of girls and women in their sociopolitical context.

Guideline 10: Psychologists strive to acquaint themselves with and utilize relevant mental health, education, and community resources for girls and women.

Guideline 11: Psychologists are encouraged to understand and work to change institutional and systemic bias that may impact girls and women.

IMPLICATIONS FOR PRACTICE

What does it mean to put guidelines such as these into actual practice? First, the practicing psychologist needs to be cognizant of the emerging research on women, girls, and issues of gender. This can be construed as insuring the competency necessary for ethical practice with women and girls. As the empirical and clinical literature on treatment with women is continuously growing, and as attempts to replicate earlier findings are consistently leading to new information and disconfirmation of prior beliefs, it is important for the practicing psychologist to remain current. Journals such as *Psychology of Women Quarterly*, *Women and Therapy*, or *Journal of Feminist Family Therapy* are examples of sources useful for empirical and clinical information. Continuing education coursework on psychotherapy practice with women and girls that is tailored to a clinician's specific work is also imperative to maintain current knowledge and competent, evidence-based practice. One of the critiques that have been raised by a variety of writers on psychotherapy and gender has concerned the inattention to how gender affects the effectiveness and efficacy of a number of increasingly popular therapies whose evidence base has emerged through randomized clinical trials. Because research on women continues to argue for a greater emphasis on relational factors for many, although not all, women, psychotherapists working with women are particularly advised to acquaint themselves with the application of evidence-based psychotherapy relationship variables.

Second, the practicing psychologist needs to become acquainted with the range of women's diversity. Women clients from one cultural, social, or age group should not be assumed to be similar to or predictive of women clients from different groups. Psychologists who focus on specific groups of women, such as women of color (Comas-Diaz & Greene, 1994), women with disabilities (Asch & Fine, 1988), lesbian or bisexual women (Falco, 1991; Firestein, 1996), or Jewish women (Siegel & Cole, 1991) to name a few such groups, need to become familiar with scholarship pertaining specifically to that group. Health psychologists working with women must acquaint themselves with information both on gender-specific women's health concerns such as reproductive system and breast cancer or infertility, as well as medical disorders occurring at higher rates in women such as certain autoimmune diseases and fibromyalgia. Sports psychologists working with women athletes must deepen their knowledge of the special concerns of women in sports, including issues of body image, disordered eating, and sexual misconduct by coaches. Psychologists working in military settings must learn about military sexual trauma and the stressors inherent in parenting while deployed. All psychologists working with complex trauma populations must attend to the manner in which gender affects risk for and informs response to complex trauma. Child clinical psychologists need to attend to the gendered components of girls' development, to research on sexualization of girls, and the manners in which normative gendered issues can create risk factors for distress and/or disorder.

At the level of psychological assessment, psychologists need to carefully read manuals to determine whether tests were constructed with an adequate and representative sample of diverse groups of women. Care should be taken in the use of computerized interpretations of standardized tests, since many of these interpretations contain sexist assumptions and fail to take context into account. Women survivors of violence have been shown to be especially at risk for misdiagnosis when cookbook approaches or blind interpretations of testing are used. When gender role identification is assessed by an instrument, the psychologist needs to learn whether being inappropriately conceptualized as a continuous variable running from masculinity to femininity or whether, consistent with scholarship, it is constructed as two separate continuous variables of masculinity and femininity. When a women's fitness for parenting is being assessed, care must be taken that standards not be higher for her than for a male partner, and that a woman's reasonable anger at an abusive partner is not interpreted as per se evidence that she is unable to regulate affect. Psychological evaluations in forensic matters where issues of gender harassment or discrimination are being raised must demonstrate familiarity with the research on women's test performance in those situations, and interpretations must account for the effects of insidious trauma, microaggression, and betrayal trauma, all of which have been identified as common variables present in women's experiences of discrimination and maltreatment.

When women or girls are being offered psychotherapy or counseling, the psychologist attends carefully to issues of power dynamics in the therapy relationship (Ballou, Hill, & West, 2008; Brown, 1994, 2009; Mirkin, 1994; Worell & Remer, 1992) and to the development of therapeutic strategies that empower the female client. Models for gender-aware psychotherapy with women can be found in almost every major theoretical orientation, including psychodynamic, family systems, and cognitive behavioral. Feminist practice, an integrative, technically eclectic theory, offers a paradigm specifically constructed around issues of gender and power (Brown, 1994, 2009). Feminist practice emphasizes the development of an egalitarian relationship between therapist and client, attention to social and political context, and careful analysis of and attention to gender and power issues, both in the problems brought to therapy, and in the therapeutic relationship itself.

Whether a psychologist adopts an explicitly feminist treatment model, therapists working with women and girls are most likely to be effective when they intentionally integrate knowledge of gender and the intersection of a client's diverse identities at the location of gender, into treatment planning and the psychotherapy process. Psychologists conducting therapy with women clients should become conversant on norms of women's psychological development (Jordan, Kaplan, Miller, Stiver, & Surrey, 1991), female sexuality, and women's experiences in relationships and the workplace.

Women and men therapists alike can work effectively with women when gender is taken explicitly into account from the very inception of the professional relationship. Even when clients do not themselves punctuate gender, a diagnostic formulation that integrates the realities of gender socialization and gendered experiences for women within the context of diverse and intersecting identities will lead to greater precision in the assessment of the nature of a client's problems, more accurate empathy, and more empowerment of the client herself.

References and Readings

American Psychological Association. (1978). Guidelines for psychotherapy with women: Report of the Task Force on Sex Bias and Sex-Role Stereotyping in Psychotherapy. *American Psychologist, 33*, 1122–1123.

Asch, A., & Fine, M. (Eds.). (1988). *Women with disabilities*. Philadelphia, PA: Temple University Press.

Ballou, M., & Brown, L. S. (Eds.). (2002). *Rethinking mental health and disorder: Feminist perspectives*. New York: Guilford Press.

Ballou, M., Hill, M., & West, C. (Eds.). (2008). *Feminist therapy theory and practice*. New York: Springer.

Brodsky, A. M., & Hare-Mustin, R. (Eds). (1980). *Women and psychotherapy: An assessment of research and practice*. New York: Guilford Press.

Brown, L. S. (1994). *Subversive dialogues: Theory in feminist therapy*. New York: Basic Books.

Brown, L. S. (2009). *Feminist Therapy*. Washington, DC: American Psychological Association Press.

Comas-Diaz, L., & Greene, B. (Eds.). (1994). *Women of color: Integrating ethnic and gender identities in psychotherapy*. New York: Guilford Press.

Falco, K. (1991). *Psychotherapy with lesbian clients: Theory into practice*. New York: Brunner/Mazel.

Firestein, B . (Ed.). (1996). *Bisexuality: The psychology and politics of an invisible minority*. Thousand Oaks, CA: Sage.

Fitzgerald, L. F., & Nutt, R. (1986). The Division 17 principles concerning the counseling/psychotherapy of women: Rationale and implementation. *The Counseling Psychologist, 14*, 180–216.

Jordan, J., Kaplan, A., Miller, J. B., Stiver, I., & Surrey, J. (Eds.). (1991). *Women's growth in connection: Writings from the Stone Center*. New York: Guilford Press.

Mirkin, M. P. (1994). *Women in context: Toward a feminist reconstruction of psychotherapy*. New York: Guilford Press.

Siegel, R. J., & Cole, E. (Eds.). (1991). *Jewish women in therapy: Seen but not heard*. New York: Haworth.

Society for the Psychology of Women and Society for Counseling Psychology. (2007). *Guidelines for psychological practice with girls and women*. Retrieved April 2011, from www.apa.org/practice/guidelines/girls-and-women.pdf

Worell, J. K., & Remer, P. (1992). *Feminist perspectives in therapy: An empowerment model for women*. New York: Wiley.

Related Topic

Chapter 43, "Diagnosis, Assessment, and Treatment of Female Sexual Dysfunctions"

47 PSYCHOTHERAPY WITH LESBIAN, GAY, AND BISEXUAL CLIENTS

Kristin A. Hancock

In many instances, the presenting problems of lesbian, gay, and bisexual (LGB) clients in psychotherapy are no different than those presented by heterosexual clients. The one factor that complicates and, in some cases, exacerbates these problems is *stigma*. People with nonheterosexual orientations are subject to societal disapproval and negative attitudes and/or pejorative religious beliefs as well as the prejudice, discrimination, and violence that can accompany such attitudes and beliefs. LGB individuals continue to live with stigma or the prospect of it each and every day. In providing mental health services to LGB individuals, it is essential that this context and its effects be taken into account.

STIGMA: WITHOUT AND WITHIN

Despite the progress made regarding the rights, benefits, and privileges of LGB people (and perhaps because of it), the national debate about the right of LGB individuals to marry their same-sex partners has resurrected negative myths and stereotypes.

It is important for therapists to realize that the sociopolitical context can significantly impact the mental health and well-being of their LGB clients. Discrimination and victimization have been shown to be associated with significant psychological distress. The kind and degree of societal stigma with which LGB people contend may include negative attitudes about their sexuality, their adherence to gender norms, their families, and their relationships. When same-sex relationships become the subject of political campaigns, the experience and impact of stigma can intensify. Rostosky, Riggle, Horne, and Miller (2009) found increased psychological distress—particularly depressive symptoms—in states that had passed anti-gay marriage amendments. The authors also found that the negative impact was not due to preexisting conditions in their participants and that individuals may experience negative effects for some time—beyond the particular campaign period. For therapists who work with LGB clients during and after such tumultuous times, it may be helpful to assist the client by (1) validating his or her experience; (2) employing approaches that monitor and avoid internalization of the negative messages put forth in the media and elsewhere in the client's environment; and (3) reframing these experiences in a manner that empowers the client (Rostosky, Riggle, Horne, & Miller, 2009).

In addition, LGB individuals endure homophobic messages from some conservative religious groups and/or individuals (some of whom may be family of origin members). The conflicts that surface for those LGB individuals whose religious beliefs play a primary role in how they view themselves and behave in the world can be profound when those religious beliefs or the way they are interpreted condemn lesbian and gay sexual orientations. While religion and spirituality can mean different things to different people, Haldeman (2004) observes that "religious affiliation can serve as a central, organizing aspect of identity that the individual cannot relinquish, even at the price of sexual orientation" (p. 694). When working with individuals who are struggling with questions of sexual orientation in the face of conservative religious beliefs, it is essential to create a safe and respectful environment for the client to explore these issues without leading or directing the client to any particular decision. Rather, the therapeutic relationship should afford the client the space and safety to examine his or her experiences, feelings, and values and develop his or her own solution (Haldeman, 2004). It is important to note that efforts to change sexual orientation are generally considered ineffective and possibly even harmful (American Psychological Association, 2011). The therapist's obligation is to provide accurate information and assist the client by exploring sources of bias and a client's internalized prejudice that can impact the client's self-esteem. It is also important to note that many major religious traditions are supportive of LGB people and can provide an affirmative community to clients (American Psychological Association, 2011).

Generally speaking, therapists are urged to conduct a thorough evaluation of the client's history with regard to stigma—in its obvious and more subtle forms. It is also essential to evaluate the way in which any negative attitudes or instances of discrimination impact the client. When stigma is internalized, it can create and/or exacerbate problems with self-esteem, depression, anxiety, physical health, relationship quality, support systems, and job performance (Szymanski, Kashubek-West, & Meyer, 2008). Therapists working to address internalized stigma should create a safe and supportive interpersonal environment; consider the use of stress reduction techniques when appropriate; help the client to develop personal and social support resources; address the effects of trauma associated with discrimination and victimization; and support the client's capacity to confront stigma (American Psychological Association, 2011).

IDENTITY DEVELOPMENT ("COMING OUT")

Psychotherapy with an LGB client can be affected by the extent to which that client has accepted his or her sexual orientation. A number of identity development models have been presented (cf. Ritter & Terndrup, 2002) to assist therapists in the exploration of this process. The process generally involves several phases. In the first phase, the individual develops an awareness of nonheterosexual attraction and struggles with its meaning in light of any internalized negative attitudes and beliefs about homosexuality. The extent to which the individual struggles depends upon numerous intrapersonal (e.g., self-esteem or religious beliefs) and environmental/contextual factors (e.g., attitudes of family of origin and friends, prior experiences with LGB people or institutional homophobia). As noted earlier, some contextual factors can intensify an already difficult journey. Another phase (which may or may not begin during the first phase described earlier) involves the exploration of one's nonheterosexual orientation. Often this includes first relationships, coming out to others (i.e., friends, family, coworkers), and interactions with the LGB community. Finally, the last phase addresses the integration of one's LGB identity. In this phase, the person's nonheterosexual orientation becomes another part of the self without dissonance or distress from the internalization of stigma. Still, therapists should keep in mind that experiencing discrimination or victimization because of one's nonheterosexual orientation can retraumatize or, at the very least, resensitize a person to stigma and result in considerable psychological distress at any point in the life span.

The identity development process for bisexual individuals is rendered more complicated by the attitudes toward bisexuality on the part of heterosexual individuals, lesbians and gay men, and even some mental health providers who question the validity of bisexuality as a bona fide sexual orientation (Ritter & Terndrup, 2002). It is therefore important for therapists to respect the unique challenges individuals face as they come to terms with a bisexual orientation. Individuals may begin to address a bisexual orientation having come from heterosexual, lesbian, or gay relationships. The complexity of the challenges bisexual people experience should also be considered—particularly those that involve nontraditional relationship structures (American Psychological Association, 2011).

INTERSECTIONALITY

Greene (2007) notes the ease with which therapists focus upon a single aspect of identity—especially a stigmatized aspect of identity—without considering the interactions among this identity and others (which may be privileged or similarly devalued). "The tendency for a clinician or researcher to launch an exclusive focus on gender, sexual orientation, or ethnicity with no sense of the ways that they overlap or interact can be a serious hindrance to an understanding of these phenomena and to the therapy process" (Greene, 2007, p. 52). The task of the therapist is to understand the intersections of identities—not just the identities themselves. It is important to consider stigmatized and privileged aspects of identity as they connect and interact within the individual and between individuals. It is also useful to keep in mind that stigma impacts individuals to varying degrees. Greene (2007) reminds us that members of stigmatized groups may not readily identify the ways in which they are privileged. For instance, a White lesbian may have some difficulty acknowledging racist behavior or negative attitudes about bisexual individuals; an African American gay man may have some difficulty acknowledging sexist behavior.

Well-intended therapists have sometimes made the mistake of approaching their work with LGB clients with the attitude that says "we're all really alike" as people. Such a perspective ignores or denies the culturally unique life experiences of the individual—including the ways in which stigma and privilege have affected him or her. While this approach may provide temporary comfort to the therapist, it is likely to hinder understanding of the client. Similarly, an overemphasis of any single aspect of identity ignores or denies other aspects of identity and context. Therapists are urged to respect and pursue the various aspects of self as they relate to a client's nonheterosexual orientation.

THE ROLE OF THE THERAPIST

There is no denying the importance of the therapist in working with LGB clients. Certainly, the attitudes of the therapist toward nonheterosexual relationships is of the utmost importance. Negative attitudes on the part of the therapist can adversely impact both the assessment and treatment of LGB clients. These attitudes may be explicit or they can be implicit and even unconscious. Negative attitudes may be the result of a particular therapist's views, religious or political beliefs; however, they may also be a function of the education and training that therapist has received. A heterosexist perspective has permeated the language, psychological theories, and interventions in psychology (American Psychological Association, 2011). Whatever the source, negative attitudes and behavior on the part of the therapist continue to be a challenge in the competent treatment of LGB clients.

Despite the fact that lesbian and gay sexual orientations per se are no longer viewed as indicators of mental illness, some therapists may persist in attributing a client's presenting problems to his or her nonheterosexual orientation (Garnets, Hancock, Cochran, Goodchilds, & Peplau, 1991; Shelton & Delgado-Romero, 2011). Therapists also pathologize clients more subtly by assuming that the client needs additional therapy or lecturing clients about the difficulties of being LGB (Shelton & Delgado-Romero, 2011). Therapists have also avoided or minimized sexual orientation or overemphasized it when working with LGB clients (American Psychological Association, 2011; Shelton & Delgado-Romero, 2011). Some therapists may overidentify with their LGB clients (e.g., referring to their own LGB family member or, in the case of LGB therapists, assuming a client's conflicts are the same as their own) in an effort to minimize the discomfort of difference.

It is clearly essential that therapists take the time to evaluate their own attitudes, feelings, and beliefs about nonheterosexual orientations and LGB people (American Psychological Association, 2011). Greene (2007) recommends that therapists reflect upon their own identities and experiences with privilege and stigma and how these might relate to the identities and experiences of the client. She also encourages the therapist to consider the impact of difference upon his or her practice with a particular client and to develop a greater tolerance for the anxiety that often surfaces with difference—particularly that associated with power and privilege.

A therapist also needs to consider whether his or her education, training, and supervised experience have adequately prepared him or her to work affirmatively with LGB clients. If not, he or she should consider an appropriate referral or, at the very least, pursue professional consultation and additional education and training.

For optimal assessment and treatment of LGB clients, there needs to be an ongoing self-assessment for explicit and implicit bias. Where biases are explicit, therapists are ethically required to take steps to eliminate the effects of these biases in their work with LGB clients. When biases are more implicit or unconscious, they are more difficult to identify. Nevertheless, they can have a profound effect on the work. Research suggests that a combination of motivation and personal contact may significantly impact implicit or unconscious bias (Lemm, 2006).

References and Readings

American Psychological Association. (2011, August 29). Guidelines for psychological practice with lesbian, gay, and bisexual clients. *American Psychologist*. ePub ahead of print, doi: 10.1037/a0024659

Garnets, L. D., Hancock, K. A., Cochran, S. D., Goodchilds, J., & Peplau, L. A. (1991). Issues in psychotherapy with lesbians and gay men: A survey of psychologists. *American Psychologist, 46*, 964–972.

Greene, B. (2007). How difference makes a difference. In J. Muran (Ed.), *Dialogues on difference: Studies of diversity in therapeutic relationship* (pp. 47–63). Washington, DC: American Psychological Association.

Haldeman, D. C. (2004). When sexual and religious orientation collide: Considerations in working with conflicted same-sex attracted male clients. *Counseling Psychologist, 32*, 691–715.

Lemm, K. M. (2006). Positive associations among interpersonal contact, motivation, and explicit and implicit attitudes towards gay men. *Journal of Homosexuality, 51*, 79–99.

Ritter, K. Y., & Terndrup, A. I. (2002). *Handbook of affirmative psychotherapy with lesbians and gay men*. New York: Guilford Press.

Rostosky, S. S., Riggle, E. D. B., Horne, S. G., & Miller, A. D. (2009). Marriage amendments and psychological distress in lesbian, gay, and bisexual (LGB) adults. *Journal of Counseling Psychology, 56*, 56–66.

Shelton, K., & Delgado-Romero, E. A. (2011). Sexual orientation microaggressions: The experience of lesbian, gay, bisexual, and queer clients in psychotherapy. *Journal of Counseling Psychology, 58*, 210–221.

Szymanski, D., Kashubek-West, S., & Meyer, J. (2008). Internalized heterosexism: A historical and theoretical overview. *Counseling Psychologist, 36*, 510–524.

Related Topic

Chapter 64, "Tailoring Treatment to the Patient's Race and Ethnicity"

48 PRACTICING PSYCHOTHERAPY WITH OLDER ADULTS

Brian D. Carpenter and Bob G. Knight

CASE FORMULATION

When seeing any older adult for treatment, an initial task of therapy is to create a picture of the older adult, including the individual's life span developmental history, the social and environmental context in which the person lives, current physical and cognitive status, strengths and ways of functioning in the world, and the nature of the problem that has brought the person to treatment. This picture can be conceptualized in any of several ways: for instance, as building a model of the person, as describing the individual's characteristic defense mechanisms, or as identifying preferred coping styles. Whatever the framework, clinicians should be prepared that older adults, given their life span, are likely to have a lengthy, complex, and multifaceted personal history to take into account when developing a case formulation.

COHORT AND CULTURE

The identity of older adults in treatment will inevitably reflect the historical time during which they matured. Working with people at different ages, from different historical cohorts, is similar in many ways to working with clients from different cultural contexts. In both cases the therapist must be mindful of cohort- and culture-bound assumptions and stereotypes; differences in word use, values, and social norms; and the unique historical epoch and experiences that have shaped a person. Cohorts and cultures can also interact in the sense that earlier-born older adults may have a specific and strong sense of ethnic identity with regard to ethnicities that are no longer identified as separate or disadvantaged, for example, Irish or Italian. Likewise, generational differences in country of origin, timing of immigration to the United States, and subsequent acculturation deserve exploration. Finally, some older adults have different experience with and expectations about psychotherapy than younger clients.

EPIDEMIOLOGY OF DISORDER

Other than the dementias, the prevalence of psychological disorders is lower in older adults than in people of other ages. This statement flies in the face of stereotypes of old age as inevitably depressing or anxiety provoking. In fact, most older adults have sufficient psychological resilience that they do not develop new disorders in response to the transitions and life stressors that accompany aging. Nonetheless, depression and other disorders may be quite prevalent in older adults with comorbid medical and cognitive disorders, in both inpatient and outpatient medical care settings, and among those living in nursing homes. Delirium is another common clinical issue, particularly in inpatient settings. Likewise, rates of subsyndromal, yet clinically significant, psychological distress are quite high among older adults and deserve attention. Though base rates for drug and alcohol, eating, and sexual disorders are low in older adults, therapist stereotypes about older adults should not preclude thorough investigation. It is also worth noting that some disorders may present with a pattern of symptoms that look different than what is typically reported in younger clients, and an awareness of those differences can aid accurate diagnosis.

AGE OF ONSET

Early in the assessment, a key question is whether the current problem is a new situation altogether or a continuation, recurrence, or exacerbation of a previous problem. This consideration influences both inferences about etiology and choices about treatment. For a recurring problem, what worked before may be a place to start to address the current issue, and knowing what has been tried in the past and has not worked can save time in treatment planning.

DIFFERENTIAL DIAGNOSIS

Older adults typically have multiple problems. These may include emotional distress, cognitive impairment, chronic physical conditions, and changes in social network or environmental context, all of which exist in a complex, interactive system. One common differential diagnostic distinction is between depression and dementia (and delirium, in inpatient settings); indeed, one frequent referral question concerns the explanation for perceived changes in memory. A systematic way to consider differential diagnosis is through a decision tree: first, whether the pattern of functioning reflects normal aging versus some pathological process; second, whether the pathology is due to emotional distress, neuropathological changes (e.g., Alzheimer's disease, Parkinson's disease), physiological dysfunction (e.g., nutrient deficiency, medication interaction), or a combination thereof; and third, what aspects of the problem are reversible. Sometimes following a case over time is the most certain way of distinguishing among assessment hypotheses. Collaboration on diagnostic clarification with a neuropsychologist and medical provider also may be helpful.

ASSESSMENT

Psychological assessment with older adults frequently requires a working knowledge of neuropsychological assessment, as well as the use of personality and emotional assessment techniques with appropriate age norms. Simple screening devices, such as mental status examinations and brief scales to measure depression and anxiety, can be helpful in day-to-day practice if their limitations are understood (see Lichtenberg, 2010.) At times it may be necessary to use instruments for which there are no norms for older adults, and again, the limitations of those scales should be kept in mind.

EMERGENCIES

Often older adults get to a mental health professional only if there is some emergency, whether financial, psychiatric, or physical. In such instances, the therapist must first resolve the emergency and only then deal with the psychological circumstances.

SUICIDE

Of all age, gender, and ethnic groups, older White males are at highest risk for suicide. This reflects the fact that the ratio of suicide attempts to suicide completions is lower in this group. In addition, depression, substance abuse, and psychosis are associated with higher risk for suicide among all older adults. Older clients can, and do, make distinctions among not wanting to live, wanting to die, and wanting to kill themselves.

While society debates the legality of rational suicide and assisted suicide, psychologists must be alert to those whose suicidal impulses are motivated by psychological distress.

FAMILY

The family constitutes the primary social context of older adults. When older adults decline physically or cognitively, their health-related dependencies and needs for assistance have radiating effects on the family. In turn, families are themselves likely to vary a great deal in their structure, the range of support they can and want to provide to older adults, and what older adults are willing to accept from them. Indeed, the diversity of families will likely expand in the decades ahead, as blended families, single-parent households, same-sex partnerships, and other family structures become more commonplace. Regardless of this diversity, with appropriate consent of the older patient, treatment can include other family members or focus on the family unit, as in Quall's Caregiver Family Therapy (Qualls, 2008).

END-OF-LIFE CARE

Grief work is an inevitable part of psychotherapy with older adults, as they face their own mortality and as their friends and family members die. Psychologists can support patients and families in end-of-life care at a number of different junctures: after serious medical illness is diagnosed, during advanced illness and the dying process, and after the death of a patient, with bereaved survivors. This work is conducted in a range of settings, including outpatient medical clinics, hospitals, palliative care and hospice programs, and nursing homes.

SPECTRUM OF INTERVENTIONS

As different theoretical approaches to psychotherapy have emerged, each has been applied to older adults—for example, psychoanalysis, behavior modification, interpersonal therapy, and cognitive therapy. Some forms of treatment, such as structured life review, have emerged specifically for this population. Knowledge about developmental processes in later life (e.g., cognitive changes, emotion regulation, social engagement) has been used to inform intervention and should be considered regardless of the particular approach to treatment that is used. Research has shown that older adults respond well to a variety of forms of psychotherapy. Evidence-based interventions include cognitive-behavioral, brief psychodynamic, and interpersonal therapies for the treatment of depression, anxiety, sleep disturbance, disruptive behaviors in dementia, schizophrenia, and distress in family caregivers. (The empirical evidence for treating a number of disorders is summarized in a special section of *Psychology and Aging*, Volume 22, 2007.) Likewise, cognitive training techniques, behavior modification strategies, and environmental modifications have some utility in improving the functional abilities of cognitively impaired older adults. Finally, reminiscence and life review are effective on their own and as elements of other therapies. Across therapies, some modifications to usual treatment may be beneficial to accommodate sensory changes (e.g., reduced hearing), cognitive limits (e.g., slower speed of processing), physical impairments (e.g., chronic pain), and the unique setting of practice (e.g., conducting psychotherapy in a shared hospital room).

RELATIONSHIP ISSUES

There are potential differences in the therapeutic relationship when the client is older than the therapist. Older clients confront the therapist with aging issues in an "off time" way—that is, the therapist faces aging, illness, disability, and death before these issues have necessarily arisen in the therapist's own life. Older clients may remind the therapist of older relatives and elicit countertransferential reactions related to parents and grandparents. Likewise, therapists may have stereotypes about the elderly and expect their older clients to be boring, unattractive, asexual, or resistant to change. Biases also may influence diagnosis, as when therapists interpret the same symptoms as reflecting a cognitive disorder in an older person but depression in a younger client. At the same time, older clients may doubt the competence and expertise of a younger therapist.

INTERFACE WITH MEDICAL CARE SYSTEM

Older adults with mental health problems often come to the attention first of various nonspecialists. Consequently, psychologists who treat older adults must be prepared to work in interdisciplinary contexts and to collaborate with other professionals in primary care, rehabilitation, acute care, long-term care, and senior centers. Moreover, they must be informed about the reimbursement system (e.g., private insurance, Medicare, Medicaid) and become advocates for making the system responsive to their clients.

WHEN TO REFER TO A SPECIALIST OR TO SEEK MORE TRAINING IN CLINICAL GEROPSYCHOLOGY

When older clients have problems similar to younger clients and there is no reason to suspect a dementing illness, psychotherapy with older adults is similar to therapy with younger adults. As assessment issues become more complex and subtle, such as needing to disentangle multiple possible causes of symptoms, more specialized knowledge is needed. Practitioners who plan to work in an age-segregated environment (e.g., nursing homes) or desire to conduct more specialized treatments with older adults need training in clinical geropsychology (Knight, Karel, Hinrichsen, Qualls, & Duffy, 2009). Continuing education in clinical geropsychology can be found through the American Psychological Association, sponsored by Section 2 (Clinical Geropsychology) of Division 12 (Society of Clinical Psychology), or by Division 20 (Adult Development and Aging), by the Council of Professional Geropsychology Training Programs, by the Gerontological Society of America at its annual meeting, through state and local psychological associations, and through some universities and medical centers.

References and Readings

American Psychological Association. (2004). Guidelines for psychological practice with older adults. *American Psychologist, 59*(4), 236–260.

American Psychological Association, Committee on Aging. (2009). *Multicultural competency in geropsychology*. Washington, DC: American Psychological Association.

Gallagher-Thompson, D., Steffen, A. M., & Thompson, L. W. (Eds.). (2008). *Handbook of behavioral and cognitive therapies with older adults*. New York: Springer.

Knight, B. G. (2004). *Psychotherapy with older adults* (3rd ed.). Thousand Oaks, CA: Sage.

Knight, B. G., Karel, M. J., Hinrichsen, G. A., Qualls, S. H., & Duffy, M. (2009). Pikes Peak Model for training in professional geropsychology. *American Psychologist, 64*(3), 205–214.

Laidlaw, K., & Knight, B. G. (Eds.). (2008). *Handbook of emotional disorders in later life: Assessment and treatment*. New York: Oxford University Press.

Lichtenberg, P. A. (Ed.). (2010). *Handbook of assessment in clinical gerontology* (2nd ed.). San Diego, CA: Academic Press.

Qualls, S. H. (2008). Caregiving family therapy. In K. Laidlaw & B. Knight (Eds.), *Handbook of emotional disorders in later life: Assessment and treatment* (pp. 183–209). Oxford, England: Oxford University Press.

Related Topics

Chapter 36, "Treating and Managing Care of the Suicidal Patient"

Chapter 143, "Consulting on End-of-Life Decisions"

49 MANAGING SEXUAL FEELINGS FOR PATIENTS IN PSYCHOTHERAPY

Kenneth S. Pope

Experiencing unexpected, intense, or reciprocated sexual attraction to a patient can throw even the most well-trained and experienced among us off balance. At such times, it can be helpful to remind ourselves of some basics:

- Experiencing sexual feelings toward patients is a normal experience for psychotherapists (Ladany, Friedlander, & Nelson, 2005; Pope, Keith-Speigel, & Tabachnick, 1986; Pope, Sonne, & Holroyd, 1993; Rodolfa et al., 1994). The fact that the therapist is experiencing sexual feelings for a patient should never be a basis for the therapist or anyone else to reflexively assume that there is something wrong with the therapist or the therapy.
- Sexual feelings for a patient can make themselves felt in many ways. Surveys indicate that some therapists become sexually aroused in the presence of the patient, some experience sexual fantasies about the patient, and some fantasize about the patient when engaging in sex with someone else.
- Although sexual attraction to patients is a common and normal occurrence, surveys suggest that a substantial majority of therapists are uncomfortable with the feelings (e.g., feeling guilty, anxious, or confused). If we are uneasy when our attraction to a patient pulls our attention away from our work helping the patient, this too is a normal occurrence.
- In some cases, sexual feelings may make us uneasy because we sometimes confuse them with sexual involvement with patients. The normal experience of sexual attraction to a patient gains a form of "guilt by association." Distinguishing clearly between the two is a basic step in addressing both areas ethically and effectively.
- The surveys also suggest that for many of us, education and training on this topic have been inadequate. Some students may have been blamed, criticized, penalized directly or indirectly, or made to feel uncomfortable simply for disclosing sexual feelings for a patient. The challenge for those of us whose education and training in this area were insufficient (or actively unhelpful) is to take steps to overcome and compensate for our incomplete education.
- We may experience sexual feelings for a patient in ways and at times that are unexpected, awkward, baffling, and embarrassing. Although we cannot control when and how feelings occur, we can control our actions, making sure that our sexual feelings never lead to sexual involvement with the client, and that they do not interfere with the welfare of the patient, the treatment plan, and our professional responsibilities.

RECOGNIZING ATTRACTION IN DISGUISE

It can be *relatively* easier to manage even the most intense attraction to a patient when we are fully aware of it. Unfortunately, in some instance therapists recognize that they have sexual feelings for a patient only after weeks or months have passed. Meanwhile, the attraction may have had profound influences on the therapy and patient.

Therapists who have been slow in recognizing their own sexual attraction to a patient have later identified a number of ways in which their attraction found expression. Alertness to these disguised expressions of attraction can help us recognize it promptly. It is important to emphasize that some of these patterns can have other causes. However, it is worth paying attention to each and asking whether it is possible that it reflects attraction to the patient.

Here are some common ways in which unacknowledged sexual attraction to a patient sometimes finds expression:

- Scheduling the patient at the end of the day in order to spend time together in casual conversation while walking out with him or her
- Repeatedly letting that patient's sessions run long
- Letting therapy sessions drift farther and farther away from the treatment plan, the clinical needs of the patient, and the patient's healing, growth, or improvement
- Shifting the main focus of discussion in therapy sessions from the patient to the therapist
- Pressuring the patient to talk about sexual behavior, feelings, or fantasies
- Making repeated comments about the patient's appearance unrelated to legitimate therapeutic purposes
- Censoring comments about the treatment made to supervisors or consultants
- Censoring what goes into the therapy notes
- Becoming preoccupied or obsessed with that patient
- Daydreaming about the patient
- Having unbidden or intrusive thoughts about the patient when engaging in sexual activities
- Experiencing sexual fantasies about the patient
- Anticipating (or hastening) termination when the therapist believes he or she will be free to start spending more time with the patient, sharing meals, going to movies together, and so on.

TAKING CARE OF OURSELVES, OUR VULNERABILITIES, AND THE UNEXPECTED

Self-care, which includes self-awareness—and acting on that self-awareness—of both our strengths and our vulnerabilities is a key professional responsibility and is particularly important in this area (see, e.g., the sections on creating strategies for self-care on pp. 69–77, ethics in real life on pp. 6–15, and *emotional competence for psychotherapy* on pp. 62–68 in Pope & Vasquez, 2011).

Our work as psychotherapists can challenge our resources and resilience. Managed care policies at odds with patient safety or needs, worries about covering our office expenses, an endless tide of paperwork, urgent phone calls to return in the brief break between sessions, an absence of new patients, insurance companies putting us on hold before explaining that once again they are unable to find the forms we submitted long ago, unpleasant interactions with colleagues—these are but a few aspects of our work that can leave us harried, drained, or even burnt out.

Not only the work itself but also our personal lives can serve as a source of stress and depletion. A fraying marriage, the death of a loved one, an aging parent who requires increasing care, a doctor telling us we have a potentially life-threatening disease, and increasing difficulty covering the rent or mortgage are the kinds of events that can sometimes prevent a therapist from bringing adequate energy, attention, judgment, enthusiasm, alertness, and mindful awareness to work.

Neglecting self-care in our personal and professional lives can leave us prone to serious misjudgment and missteps, particularly in this area. We may begin looking to a patient for the excitement, attention, admiration, companionship, support, love, meaning, or fulfillment that is missing from our current lives. We may even begin to tell ourselves that the patient can fulfill our fantasy of an idealized romance. We may see the patient as an opportunity for acting on sexual impulses and desires whose expression remains blocked elsewhere in our lives. A sexual relationship with a patient may seem to us our last or only hope for escape or at least distraction from the stress, pain, or emptiness of our lives.

ASSURING CLEAR COMMUNICATION

We communicate sexual attraction and other sexual feelings nonverbally as well as verbally. The way we look at someone, how close we sit or stand, the amount of attention we devote, how closely we listen, whether and how we engage in touching, the giving of a gift—these are a few ways that can sometimes communicate sexual attraction. They can also sometimes serve as pathways of miscommunication.

Attending carefully to these pathways of communication and miscommunication can prevent countless missteps. A patient may, for example, misinterpret our sustained eye contact, careful listening, and smiles. We may misinterpret a patient's body language, gift, clothing, or hug at the end of a session. It is important to remain aware that sustained eye contact, a gift, a touch, and other behaviors can have sharply different meanings in different cultures. It is equally significant that the differences between individuals within a culture can be greater than the differences between cultures. Our judgments, understandings, and communications are informed and enriched by remaining aware of culture and other contexts but must be based on the two unique individuals—therapist and patient (Pope & Vasquez, 2011).

AVOIDING MISHANDLED ATTRACTION

It is an unfortunate reality that some therapists mishandle their attraction, violating the patient's trust, their own clinical responsibilities, and a basic and long-standing ethical prohibition (Maroda, 2010; Norris, Gutheil, & Strasburger, 2003; Pope & Vasquez, 2011). Exploiting the patient in this way may cause profound, pervasive, and lasting harm. Awareness of the common patterns of mishandling sexual attraction to a patient can help protect us from mismanaging our sexual feelings.

Here are 10 of the most common scenarios (see the section on sexual relationships with clients on pp. 209–234 of Pope & Vasquez, 2011):

- *True love.* The therapist romanticizes his or her sexual attraction, emotional desires, and personal wishes into a supposedly unique, exalted, and transcendent expression of "true love" and uses rationalizations to discount, disparage, or deny clinical, ethical, and professional responsibilities to the patient and to do no harm.
- *It just got out of hand.* The therapist fails to give adequate attention, care, and respect to the emotional closeness that can develop in therapy.
- *Time out.* The therapist acts as if the therapeutic relationship and the therapist's clinical, ethical, and professional duties to the patient disappeared between scheduled sessions or outside the therapist's office.
- *Role trading.* The therapist slips into the role of "patient" and both the actual therapist and actual patient begin attending to the wants and needs of the therapist.
- *Sex therapy.* Therapist begins sex with the patient under the guise of helping him or her with a sexual problem, describing the therapist–patient sexual involvement as a legitimate and valid treatment for sexual dysfunction.
- *As if....* Therapist treats the positive feelings that patients often develop for therapists (and which some psychodynamic theoretical orientations term *positive transference*) as if it were not the result of the therapeutic situation.
- *Svengali.* Therapist creates, nurtures, and exploits an exaggerated dependence on the part of the patient.
- *Drugs.* Therapist uses legal or illegal substances (e.g., cocaine, alcohol) to make it possible to engage in sex with the patient.
- *Rape.* Therapist uses actual or threatened physical strength, violence, blackmail (e.g., misuse of what the patient has told the therapist as part of the treatment with the

understanding that it would remain confidential and legally privileged), extortion, or intimidation to force the patient's submission.

- *Hold me.* Therapist exploits patient's desire for nonerotic physical contact and/or emotional intimacy as well as the possible confusion between erotic and nonerotic contact or intimacy.

These are only a few of the most common patterns of therapists' mishandling sexual feelings. Many instances do not fit into these general categories.

CONDUCTING A QUICK AUDIT

All of us have blind spots, can make mistakes, and are capable of deceiving ourselves. Asking ourselves the following questions (some of which are adapted from Pope, Sonne, & Holroyd, 1993) from time to time may make us aware that we are misreading a situation, overlooking something important, or heading down a wrong path. This kind of quick audit can put us in a position to prevent missteps or, if necessary, to take corrective action. None of these items per se indicates that anything is wrong, only that further exploration may be helpful.

- How, if at all, am I aware of this patient's sexuality?
- Does it seem that either I or the patient is actively avoiding mentioning a particular topic that might be related to sexual issues? If so, what?
- Am I sexually aroused or having sexual thoughts during any part of my sessions with this patient?
- Am I doing anything significantly different with this patient than I do with my other patients, something that seems out of character for me? If so, is it possible that my behavior is related in any way to sexual feelings?
- Is everything I am doing with this patient consistent with the patient's welfare and the principle "first, do no harm"?
- Is everything I am doing with this patient consistent with the patient's informed consent?
- Is any aspect of what I am doing with this patient primarily for my enjoyment?
- Is there anything that is important enough to be documented that I am actively avoiding putting in the patient's chart?
- Is there anything happening in therapy or any thoughts or feelings I am having about this patient that are making me uncomfortable?
- Am I doing anything that this patient might consider seductive or sexually inappropriate?
- Am I doing anything with this patient that a reasonable third-party might consider seductive or sexually inappropriate?

KNOWING WHEN WE NEED HELP

One of the most reliable steps to prevent mismanaging sexual feelings is to ask for help when we need it. Some who have mismanaged sexual feelings later reflected that they simply blocked out the awareness of the implications of their acts. Others have regretted failing to recognize where their actions were taking them. Still others have said that they recognized that what they were doing was wrong or at least realized it at some level and yet did not pay enough attention, did not act to slow or stop themselves, and allowed themselves to drift into trouble. A common thread in so many of these cases is that the therapist did not seek help and make use of it.

If the results of our self-audit or other paths to self-awareness lead us to realize or even just suspect that we are not doing our best work in this area, that we are missing or misunderstanding something important, or that we may be at risk for mismanaging sexual feelings, we may feel an understandable sense of embarrassment and even a tendency to isolate ourselves. *Particularly* at these times, reaching out for help can not only improve the situation but sometimes prevent disasters for our patients and ourselves.

For some, talking over the situation with a trusted colleague can be helpful. Formal consultation can provide a fresh and independent perspective, new ideas, useful questions, and needed support. For others, seeking formal supervision is the best route. Sometimes a therapist's reaction to a patient reflects the therapist's unresolved issues, self-defeating behavior patterns, a sense of being overwhelmed, or other more personal dynamics, and the therapist may find entering or reentering psychotherapy helpful.

Asking for help when we need it is an important professional responsibility. Feeling that we need help, like feeling attracted to a patient, does not mean that that something is wrong with us, that we are poor therapists. It only means that we are human and willing to admit it.

References and Readings

Ladany, N., Friedlander, M. L., & Nelson, M. L. (2005). Managing sexual attraction: Talking about sex in supervision. In N. Ladany, M. L. Friedlander, & M. L. Nelson (Eds.), *Critical events in psychotherapy supervision: An interpersonal approach* (pp. 127–153). Washington, DC: American Psychological Association

Maroda, K. J. (2010). *Psychodynamic techniques: Working with emotion in the therapeutic relationship*. New York: Guilford Press.

Norris, D. M., Gutheil, T. G., & Strasburger, L. H. (2003). This couldn't happen to me: Boundary problems and sexual misconduct in the psychotherapy relationship. *Psychiatric Services, 54*(4), 517–522.

Pope, K., Keith-Speigel, P., & Tabachnick, B. (1986). Sexual attraction to clients: The human therapist and the (sometimes) inhuman training system. *American Psychologist, 41*, 147–158.

Pope, K. S., Sonne, J. L., & Greene, B. (2006). Therapists' sexual arousals, attractions, and fantasies. In K. S. Pope, J. L. Sonne, & B. Greene (Eds.), *What therapists don't talk about and why: Understanding taboos that hurt us and our clients* (pp. 27–41). Washington, DC: American Psychological Association.

Pope, K. S., Sonne, J. L., & Holroyd, J. (1993). *Sexual feelings in psychotherapy: Explorations for therapists and therapists-in-training*. Washington, DC: American Psychological Association.

Pope, K. S., & Vasquez, M. J. T. (2011) *Ethics in psychotherapy and counseling: A practical guide* (4th ed.). New York: John Wiley.

Rodolfa, E., Hall, T., Holms, V., Davena, A., Komatz, D., Antunez, M., & Hall, A. (1994). The management of sexual feelings in therapy. *Professional Psychology: Research and Practice, 25*, 168–172.

Related Topic

Chapter 109, "Recognizing, Assisting, and Reporting the Impaired Psychologist"

50 IMPROVING COMPLETION OF THERAPEUTIC HOMEWORK

Michael A. Tompkins

Improving homework compliance begins with careful attention to how homework assignments are structured and implemented, as psychotherapists have far more control over the nature of homework assignments than they do over a client's psychological variables that influence homework compliance. This chapter demonstrates how psychotherapists can exercise care when setting up homework and maintain a manner with clients that (all things being equal) is likely to enhance clients' compliance with homework assignments.

This chapter presents 10 evidence-based means to improve compliance with psychotherapy homework.

- *Make the homework assignment doable.* Doable homework assignments are concrete, specific, and appropriate to the client's current skill level. Concrete and specific homework assignments are easier to carry out than vague assignments (Levy & Shelton, 1990) and include details about when, where, with whom, for how long, and using what materials. A concrete and specific homework assignment might read, "Sit down at your desk at 9 a.m., Monday through Friday, and work on your dissertation for 10 minutes each day; use pencil and paper; disconnect the telephone before beginning to write; and, after you have written for 10 minutes, reward yourself by reading the sports section of the morning newspaper." In contrast, a vague homework assignment might read, "Work a little on your dissertation every day."
- *Consider the client's level of functioning.* A depressed client who spends the bulk of his day in bed is not likely to hike all day Saturday with friends, even though he thinks he should be able to do this because he did it in the past. To assess whether a homework assignment is realistic, ask two questions: (1) Is the client already doing the homework assignment (or some variation of the assignment) and how difficult is it? and (2) Has the client done the homework assignment (or some variation of it) in the past, how long ago was that, and how difficult was it then? Therapists can ask clients to rate the difficulty or discomfort of the task on a 10-point scale (where 10 is most difficult or uncomfortable). As a rule, it is best when beginning treatment to start with homework that clients do already 30% of the time or more. For example, a client who sought treatment to become more assertive identified several types of people with whom she had trouble being assertive, ranked in order of the percentage of time she was assertive with that type of person. She and her therapist decided that at first she would focus on increasing her assertiveness with a coworker she liked and with whom she was able to be assertive 40% of the time.
- *Give a clear rationale for the homework assignment.* Clients are more likely to complete a homework assignment if they understand how doing it will help them accomplish their treatment goals. If the client's goal is to become less depressed, then it must make sense to the client how a particular homework assignment will help him or her feel less depressed. A homework rationale can be quite simple: "We've agreed that when you're doing certain activities, like having lunch with a friend, you feel less depressed. How about if we schedule several activities like that this week?"

Do not assign therapeatic assignments homework if the client has not understood and accepted its rationale. Clients who reject a homework rationale may be less open to change (Addis & Jacobson, 2000); perhaps because they are hopeless about anything helping, they have clear beliefs about what will and will not help them solve their problems that the therapist has not explored, or they do not understand the reason for doing it. To check whether a client has accepted the homework rationale, therapists can ask, "Do you understand why I'm suggesting you schedule activities this week?" Or "To what degree does the homework match your ideas about what is important to change to solve your problem? (on a scale of from 0 to 10, where 10 means the homework completely matches with your ideas about what needs to change)?"

- *Collaborate in creating homework.* Initially, the therapist provides the rationale for homework. However, over time and particularly when the therapist asks the client to repeat an assignment, the therapist can ask clients about the underlying reason: "Grace, why do you think it might be a good idea for you to write down what you eat during the day and whether you binge or not?" Not only does this encourage clients to take greater responsibility for designing and implementing their homework assignments, but also it is a good check that the client understands the homework rationale.

Collaboration between therapist and client when designing and implementing homework offers several advantages. First, clients who have input into homework may perceive themselves as having greater control of the assignment itself. This may lessen their anxiety and thereby increase the likelihood that the client will try the assignment. Second, when the therapist and client successfully work through a misunderstanding or disagreement to set up homework, this process strengthens the therapeutic relationship. Third, clients usually understand more fully than their therapists what is or is not a useful homework assignment and what difficulties may arise. At times, clients may suggest a homework assignment that seems unrelated to the focus of the therapy or to the client's treatment goals. Rather than dismissing the assignment, therapists can explore the client's rationale for the assignment, perhaps soliciting the advantages and disadvantages of this homework assignment over another one the therapist suggests. Sometimes, after each contributes an idea for a homework assignment, it may be necessary for the client and therapist briefly to negotiate a mutually agreeable homework assignment. Successful negotiations such as this can strengthen the therapeutic alliance and thereby foster greater motivation to try this and future homework assignments.

- *Make a homework backup plan.* Spend some time during the session anticipating potential homework obstacles and making a backup plan to handle them. For example, Josh, a depressed software engineer, agreed to call Philip, a friend, later in the day to invite him to go to for a jog. At the agreed-upon time, Josh dutifully called Philip, but when he heard a busy signal, he hung up the telephone and did not try again. Had Josh and his therapist planned how Josh would handle this situation if it arose (e.g., who would Josh call if he could not reach Philip), Josh might have completed his homework assignment.
- *Uncover homework obstacles.* Therapists can ask their clients directly: "Do you see any obstacles that would make it hard for you to carry out the assignment?" Therapists can ask clients whether they have tried similar homework assignments in the past and, if so, how they turned out. What problems did they encounter? Watch for clients who hesitate or are uncertain: "I think that I can handle that if it happens," or who quickly dismiss the therapist's concerns: "No, there won't be any problem." Ask these clients how they would handle a typical homework problem and see whether the solution is appropriate and doable given the client's current level of functioning. Or ask clients to rate the likelihood (0 to 100%, where 100% is highly likely) that they will do the homework as agreed. Low numbers can alert therapists to potential homework obstacles. Therapists can then explore with clients why they believe they may not do the homework and alter the homework assignment or plan a different assignment altogether, such as monitoring the problem the client is not ready to tackle.

Therapists can use covert rehearsal (Beck, 1995) to identify obstacles to completing homework assignments. In covert rehearsal, the therapist asks the client to imagine going through all the steps involved in completing the homework assignment, talking aloud to the therapist, who listens for potential obstacles. For example, Christine, a depressed child care worker who also worked nights and weekends as a waitress, seldom found time to go out with friends or to do anything fun. She agreed to take a bubble bath as a pleasurable activity to improve her mood and decrease her stress level. During covert rehearsal, Christine imagined, aloud, each step of the process. As she imagined reaching for the bubble bath, she remembered that she had run out of bubble bath several weeks ago. Christine and her therapist then discussed how and when she would go to the grocery store to buy bubble bath, and this task became her homework assignment. Had Christine not rehearsed her homework assignment beforehand, she might have thrown up her hands and gone to bed when she encountered the empty bubble-bath bottle.

- *Make a set of written homework instructions.* Many clients will remember the details of a homework assignment and follow through with what they have agreed to do. However, it is usually better to formalize these agreements with a set of written instructions (Shelton & Ackerman, 1974). Written homework serves as a record of what the client has agreed to do, which can circumvent misunderstandings and disagreements that erode the therapeutic alliance. At the minimum, written homework instructions describe exactly what the client will do (e.g., "Call Julio Thursday at 7 p.m. and invite him to the ballgame this Saturday") and what they will do (e.g., "If Julio can't attend the ballgame, then call Bob, then George, then Frank") if they run into problems (Tompkins, 2004).

- *Practice the homework assignment in session.* Although it is useful for clients to practice in session every homework before they try it on their own, there are times when in-session homework practice is particularly warranted: (1) when clients lack the necessary skill and knowledge; (2) when clients try a skill or response for the first time; and (3) when clients are to perform an assignment in the presence of strong emotion.

In-session practice enables therapists to observe whether their clients can complete the homework as devised. Paul, a depressed and recently divorced civil engineer, wanted to start dating again and agreed to a homework assignment in which he would introduce himself to a woman at the company Christmas party. Paul assured the therapist he knew how to handle this kind of situation, but the therapist was not so confident. At the therapist's urging, however, Paul agreed to role-play the planned interaction. Paul began his introduction by staring at the floor while mumbling under his breath, "Hi, I don't suppose you're interested in talking to me." After feedback from his therapist, Peter agreed that he would benefit from further skills training before he attempted this particular assignment.

In-session practice is particularly helpful when therapists anticipate that clients will have to perform homework in the presence of intense negative affect, such as fear, anger, guilt, or shame. For example, Katherine, a depressed young human resource manager, sought treatment because she had a difficult relationship with her mother, who often arrived unannounced at her apartment and would look through her drawers and listen to the messages on her telephone answering machine. Katherine was quite anxious about dating or inviting men to her apartment for fear that her mother would appear at the door. As a step toward greater assertiveness with her mother, Katherine agreed to tell her that she could not speak to her right then when she called that evening, as was her routine. Katherine practiced the homework assignment while the therapist played the role of her mother. Katherine did well until her therapist began to whine and tell her that she was an ungrateful and spiteful daughter; when she heard this, Katherine burst into tears. The therapist stopped the role-play and praised Katherine for hanging in there as long she did and reviewed with her the rationale for the homework. The therapist and Katherine then developed a set of adaptive responses she was to read through to help her better tolerate her feelings of guilt. With more practice, Katherine could hold her ground in the role-plays with her therapist and in interactions with her mother.

- *Be curious and consistent when setting up and reviewing homework.* Therapists are important reinforcers of client behavior and, as such, it is essential that they maintain a manner when speaking with their clients that increases the likelihood that the client will complete the homework (Tompkins, 2003).

Curiosity rather than rigid certainty avoids assumptions that can lead to misunderstandings that derail attempts to set up or review homework. Clients always have more information about what contributed to an unsuccessful homework assignment than their therapists, and a curious stance recognizes and takes advantage of this fact. A curious stance encourages clients to become curious about the homework themselves, including the obstacles they encounter or may encounter and their role in homework noncompliance. Last, and perhaps most important, curious therapists shift the responsibility for solving homework compliance problems to clients. Overly responsible therapists suggest, "Try this next time," while curious therapists probe, "Tell me what you might try next time." Curious therapists start any discussion of potential homework assignments by asking the client, "Perhaps you have an idea for a homework assignment that would help you with this problem?"

Consistently reinforce all pro-homework behavior. When clients say, "I thought about what I learned from the homework on my drive here today" or "Perhaps I could try a little tougher exposure assignment this week," nod, smile, and praise them. Similarly, avoid reinforcing homework noncompliance. Avoid saying, "That's okay," "No problem," "No big deal," when it's not, or "Better luck next time," when luck had nothing to do with it. When clients complete homework assignments, congratulate them and chat for a few minutes (if they enjoy chatting) to reinforce homework compliance. Take care that the praise is appropriate to the effort and is not overblown or exaggerated. When clients fail to do homework, respond in a neutral but curious manner and focus on identifying problems that may have contributed to homework noncompliance. If the homework was not completed (or attempted), set aside the entire session to review why the homework was not done, once again, as someone who is curious and puzzled by this turn of events. Did we make the homework too difficult? Were the homework instructions unclear? Did some unanticipated problem arise?

- *Reward client effort and partial successes.* When clients attempt the homework and some part of it was successful, focus on that part and praise their efforts: "Although we agreed that you would walk 5 minutes three times this week, you walked 5 minutes one day. Congratulations for walking 5 minutes that one day." Then, negotiate with the clients any modifications to their homework assignments so that they can do a bit more next time and reassign: "Now, let's take a look at how we can help you meet your goal of 5 minutes each day. What do you say?" However, if a client continues to fail to complete homework assignments, consider breaking future assignments into smaller doable pieces. In that way, the therapist can reinforce the client for completing the entire homework assignment, even if it is smaller. Take care that clients do not interpret the therapist's efforts to shape approximations to the desired homework to mean that the therapists accept incomplete homework. The goal of rewarding small steps is to have clients always complete their homework consistently and as agreed upon.

The 10 strategies presented here assume that clinicians can improve homework and its success through careful attention to how they set up and review such assignments. To that end, I encourage therapists to consider first whether they have done what they can do to improve homework before assuming that clients fail to do homework because of their psychopathology. However, when clients consistently fail to complete the homework they have agreed to do, client factors come to the fore and therapists then address homework noncompliance as they would manage any other client behavior that interferes with client progress and treatment success. In these instances, therapists benefit from a case formulation that explains why a particular client at a particular point in therapy might fail to complete his or her homework, as well as the psychological, interpersonal, and behavioral problems for which the individual has sought treatment in the first place (Tompkins, 1999).

References and Readings

Addis, M. E., & Jacobson, N. S. (2000). A closer look at the treatment rationale and homework compliance in cognitive-behavioral therapy for depression. *Cognitive Therapy and Research, 24,* 313–326.

Beck, J. S. (1995). *Cognitive therapy: Basics and beyond.* New York: Guilford Press.

Levy, R. L., & Shelton, J. L. (1990). Tasks in brief therapy. In R. A. Wells & V. J. Giannetti (Eds.), *Handbook of brief psychotherapies* (pp. 145–163). New York: Plenum.

Shelton, J. L., & Ackerman, J. M. (1974). *Homework in counseling and psychotherapy.* Springfield, IL: Charles C. Thomas.

Tompkins, M. A. (1999). Using a case formulation to manage treatment nonresponse. *Journal of Cognitive Psychotherapy, 13,* 317–330.

Tompkins, M. A. (2002). Guidelines for enhancing homework compliance. *Journal of Clinical Psychology, 58,* 565–576.

Tompkins, M. A . (2003). Effective homework. In R. L. Leahy (Ed.), *Overcoming roadblocks in cognitive therapy* (pp. 49–66). New York: Guilford Press.

Tompkins, M. A. (2004). *Using homework in psychotherapy: Strategies, guidelines, and forms.* New York: Guilford Press.

Related Topics

Chapter 35, "Enhancing Patient Adherence to Treatment"
Chapter 53, "Reducing Resistance in Psychotherapy"
Chapter 100, "Recommended Homework during Psychotherapy with Couples and Individuals"

51 CONDUCTING EVALUATIONS OF CLIENT OUTCOMES AND SATISFACTIONS

Michael J. Lambert and Kara Cattani

Psychotherapists have a scientific and ethical responsibility to learn whether they are providing effective services. Outcome assessment lets clinicians know whether individual clients are deteriorating, remaining unchanged, or recovering and can thereby improve the effectiveness of treatment. Although more and more psychotherapists are employing outcome measures in their practices, most clinicians do not yet objectively assess treatment outcome (Hatfield & Ogles, 2007).

Patient-focused research, a movement toward measuring the effects of therapy on individual clients, provides a strategy to enhance client outcomes. This strategy involves using session-by-session outcome to inform individual therapy in real time. The measured outcome allows clinicians increased awareness about client welfare and progress. Through such monitoring, for instance, the clinician has access to information about what seems to be changing or not changing in psychotherapy. This type of feedback enhances clinician performance and improves client outcome (Shimokawa, Lambert, & Smart, 2010).

This chapter summarizes recommended methods to (1) select potentially useful measures, (2) collect outcome and satisfaction data as a practical matter, and (3) use those data to enhance routine practice.

SELECTING POTENTIALLY USEFUL MEASURES

The following principles attempt to strike a balance between what is practical for the everyday clinician and what is scientifically necessary in order to obtain useful outcome data.

1. *Make sure the measure covers broad, yet crucial, content areas.* The three broad areas to be assessed are the subjective state of the client (intrapersonal functioning, including behavior, affect, and cognition), the state of the client's intimate relationships (interpersonal functioning), and the state of the individual's participation in the community (social role performance). Both symptomatic change and functioning are important, if not essential, targets for outcome assessment. A compendium of measures has been edited by Maruish (2004).
2. *Select a brief self-report measure.* Most clinicians assessing client outcome are using brief self-report measures. Outcome measures have been developed that can be completed by the client, a parent/spouse, the therapist, or an independent judge. However, because it is usually feasible to obtain only one perspective, in the case of an adult, a self-report measure is ideal and in the case of a child/adolescent, a parent-report measure is recommended. Additionally, it should be kept in mind that instruments and methods useful for diagnostic purposes and treatment planning are typically unsuitable for the purpose of measuring patient change (Vermeersch, Lambert, & Burlingame, 2000). Symptom-focused measures are most likely to reflect improvement and are therefore highly recommended. Literally hundreds of measures are available for use. We recommend the Brief Symptom Inventory (www.pearsonassessments.com/tests/bsi.htm), a shortened version of the Symptom Checklist-90-R that focuses on a wide variety of symptoms. The Short Form-36 Health Survey (www.sf-36.org) is also a promising measure for adults. The Outcome Questionnaire-45 (www.oqmeasures.com) is growing in popularity. It measures symptoms, interpersonal functioning, social role performance, and quality of life, and it has been shown to be sensitive to treatment effects. For children, the Ohio Youth Problems, Functioning, and Satisfaction Scales (www.mh.state.oh.us/what-we-do/protect-and-monitor/consumer-outcomes/instruments/index.shtml) and the Youth Outcome Questionnaire (www.oqmeasures.com/) appear to be especially promising because they are relatively short, sensitive to change, and available in parent-, self-, and other-report formats.
3. *Select measures that can detect clinically meaningful change.* Methods have been developed to set standards for clinically meaningful client change (Jacobson & Truax, 1991). The clinical significance methodology provides for the calculation of two specific statistical indexes: a cutoff point between normal and dysfunctional samples and an evaluation of the reliability of the change score. These indexes provide specific cut scores for interpreting the importance of observed scores and some existing measures provide such guidelines. When they are not available, however, the clinician can consult the work of Jacobson for the formulas for establishing a cutoff score, as well as a reliable change index.
4. *Use caution if you tailor the change criteria to the individual in therapy.* Tailoring change criteria with individualized goals for a particular patient has been advocated because it is likely to provide evidence for efficacy. The use of individualized change measures enables the therapist to assess change from an idiographic and multifaceted perspective, which is consistent with the wide range of problems presented by an individual (e.g., Persons, 2007). However, such change criteria are often poorly defined and subjective in nature. The amount of change reflected by such measures is often overly dependent on the therapist's judgments. On the other hand, in difficult-to-treat individuals, idiographic change criteria may be a necessary addition to standardized outcome measures. Such individuals abound in residential, geriatric, severely mentally ill, or neuropsychologically impaired populations that may be atypically responsive or appear to be nonresponsive on standard measures.

COLLECTING OUTCOME DATA IN A PRACTICAL MANNER

Practical concerns in routine practice demand that outcome assessment be painless and resource effective (i.e., minimize demands such as money, time, or energy). Brief self-report measures that can be completed in 5–10 minutes are recommended. A measure that can be easily administered and scored by computer or clerical staff is preferable. Some computer-based measures provide the practitioner with graphs that depict patient change over time. This visual depiction of change over time is easy to read and is immediately available once the measure is complete.

Once a measure is selected, it is best to have it completed prior to a session. For instance, clients complete the questionnaire when they arrive for their appointment and are waiting for the clinician. Ideally, this data will be gathered prior to every therapy session. This ensures that there will be at least one measure of change, provided that the client has a second appointment. Since many patients improve rapidly, and most attend few sessions, delaying the second assessment is likely to result in underestimating treatment benefits or failing to gather any outcome data.

USING OUTCOME DATA TO ENHANCE ROUTINE PRACTICE

The initial assessment can be used to (1) determine the client's incoming symptom severity and forming an opinion about expected length of treatment, (2) highlight possible target symptoms seen at the individual item level, and (3) identify particular strengths that might be capitalized on. For example, the measure(s) you select will have several "critical" items that you may want to routinely examine (e.g., "I have thoughts of ending my life"; "I have people around me that I can turn to for support").

The most important aspect of tracking change after the initial assessment (i.e., assessing outcomes on a session-by-session basis) is assessing whether client scores tend to increase, stay the same, or decrease in relation to the intake score. Research demonstrates that early positive response to treatment foretells final success, while negative change foretells final failure (Haas, Hill, Lambert, & Morrell, 2002). In any case, until the client's functioning is within the normal range, some kind of treatment is generally needed. As mentioned previously, measures are available that graphically display client data across time or sessions. Many clinicians find this helpful as it facilitates the visualization of score changes and general trends. If a client's scores worsen after beginning treatment, then the clinician can consider the causes and possibly modify treatment (e.g., more frequent sessions, medication referral, change in treatment focus). On the other hand, if the client's scores indicate improvement and a return to normal functioning, the focus of treatment could shift to preparing the client for termination and maintenance. The specific details of what to do in individual cases vary and are up to the treating clinician and the client.

One might ask how much a client's score needs to change in order to be considered meaningful. Although clinicians can try to rely on personal methods of detecting significant change, standardized methods are available to better serve clinicians and clients. As already noted, these methods operationalize meaningful change so clinicians can know how much a client's score must change in order to be considered clinically significant. If a client's score changes by at least the amount of the Reliable Change Index (RCI; individually calculated for the particular instrument being used), then the client is considered to have reliably changed, becoming symptomatically worse or better.

However, reliable change by itself cannot be equated with recovery. For example, a client's score may change in the amount of the RCI and still be in the dysfunctional range. If, however, a client's score (1) moves from the dysfunctional range to the functional range and (2) the amount of change is equal to or greater than the RCI, then the client is considered to have made clinically significant improvement, sometimes labeled recovery. Cutoff scores and reliable change indices (RCIs) for some of the most commonly used measures, such as the SCL-90R, BDI, and CBCL, are available free of charge (see Ogles, Lambert, & Fields, 2002).

Another way to use session-by-session data to enhance treatment outcome is to compare a client's treatment response to a typical or expected treatment response. By comparing a client's symptom course to the average symptom course among others that have the same initial assessment score, a clinician can know whether a client is progressing as "expected." Although this method is more specific than relying on RCIs and cutoff scores, it is not yet readily available for most outcome measures. Nevertheless, such data help to inform clinicians if the client is responding faster or slower than similar clients. Psychotherapy research investigating this method is promising and will probably become widely available for use in routine practice. The interested reader can consult other sources (Lambert et al., 2002; Ogles et al., 2002). This research demonstrates that feedback to therapists about potential treatment failure (based on client deviations from expected treatment response) improves outcomes and reduces deterioration for the 20%–30% of clients who are at risk for treatment failure (Lambert, 2010).

References and Readings

Haas, E., Hill, R., Lambert, M. J., & Morrell, B. (2002). Do early responders to psychotherapy maintain treatment gains? *Journal of Clinical Psychology, 58,* 1157–1172.

Hatfield, D. R., & Ogles, B. M. (2007). Why some clinicians use outcome measures and others do not. *Administration and Policy in Mental Health and Mental Health Services Research, 34,* 283–291.

Jacobson, N. S., & Truax, P. (1991). Clinical significance: A statistical approach to defining meaningful change in psychotherapy research. *Journal of Consulting and Clinical Psychology, 59,* 12–19.

Lambert, M. J. (2010). *Prevention of treatment failure: The use of measuring, monitoring, and feedback in clinical practice.* Washington, DC: American Psychological Association.

Lambert, M. J., Whipple, J. L., Bishop, M. J., Vermeersch, D. A., Gray G. V, & Finch, A. E. (2002). Comparison of empirically-derived methods for identifying patients at risk for treatment failure. *Clinical Psychology and Psychotherapy, 9,* 149–164.

Maruish, M. E. (2004). *The use of psychological testing for treatment planning and outcomes assessment* (3rd ed.). Mahwah, NJ: Erlbaum.

Ogles, B. M., Lambert, M. J., & Fields, S. A. (2002). *Essentials of outcome assessment.* New York: Wiley.

Persons, J. B. (2007). Psychotherapists collect data during routine clinical work that can contribute to knowledge about mechanisms of change in psychotherapy. *Clinical Psychology: Science and Practice, 14,* 244–246.

Shimokawa, K., Lambert, M. J., & Smart, D. W. (2010). Enhancing treatment outcome of patients at risk of treatment failure: Meta-analytic and mega-analytic review of a psychotherapy quality assurance system. *Journal of Consulting and Clinical Psychology, 78,* 298–311.

Vermeersch, D. A., Lambert, M. J., & Burlingame, G. M. (2000). Outcome questionnaire: Item sensitivity to change. *Journal of Personality Assessment, 74,* 242–261.

Related Topics

Chapter 27, "Locating Information about Psychological Tests and Measures"

Chapter 33, "Compendium of Evidence-Based Therapy Relationships"

52 REPAIRING RUPTURES IN THE THERAPEUTIC ALLIANCE

Jeremy D. Safran and Catherine Boutwell

Given the large body of evidence demonstrating that a considerable proportion of patients fail to remain in or benefit from psychotherapy (Wierzbicki & Pekarik, 1993), it is critical to identify those who are at risk for treatment dropout or poor outcome and to develop ways of improving the likelihood that they will complete psychotherapy and benefit from it.

Research has consistently shown that a strong or improving therapeutic alliance contributes to positive treatment outcome, regardless of treatment modality (Horvath, Del Re, Flückiger, & Symonds, 2011). Similarly, there is ample evidence that weakened alliances are correlated with unilateral termination (Samstag et al., 1998). These findings suggest that the process of recognizing and addressing alliance ruptures and negative therapeutic process can be important for many patients who are at risk for treatment failure.

In two meta-analyses, Safran, Muran, and Eubanks-Carter (2011) found that rupture-resolution episodes and alliance-focused training play meaningful roles in patient treatment and outcome. One meta-analysis of three studies showed that the presence of rupture-repair episodes over the course of therapy was related to good outcome. A second meta-analysis of eight studies investigating rupture resolution training/supervision revealed that deliberate focus on the therapeutic alliance and management of alliance ruptures in training/supervision is a small but statistically significant component in patient improvement. While it is difficult to draw definitive conclusions due to several limitations (see Safran et al., 2011), these studies highlight the importance of the therapist's ability to effectively discuss and explore alliance ruptures.

Research evidence suggests common principles in resolving alliance ruptures (e.g., Foreman & Marmar, 1985; Safran & Muran, 2000; Safran et al., 2011; Safran, Muran, Samstag, & Stevens, 2002). These are as follows:

1. Therapists should be aware that patients often have negative feelings about the treatment or the therapeutic relationship, which they are reluctant to broach for fear of the therapist's reactions. It is thus important for therapists to be attuned to subtle indications of ruptures in the alliance and to take the initiative in exploring what is transpiring in the relationship when they suspect that a rupture has occurred.
2. Patients profit from expressing their negative feelings about treatment to the therapist should they emerge or to assert their perspective on what is going on when it differs from the therapist's.
3. When this takes place, therapists should attempt to respond in an open and nondefensive fashion and to accept responsibility for their contribution to the interaction.

4. There is some evidence to suggest that the process of exploring patient fears and expectations that make it difficult for them to assert their negative feelings about treatment may contribute to the process of resolving the alliance rupture.

THERAPEUTIC METACOMMUNICATION

In addition to these principles, the literature suggests the value of skillful therapeutic metacommunication as a tool for resolving alliance ruptures (Safran & Muran, 2000). Alliance ruptures take place when both patient and therapist unwittingly contribute to a maladaptive interpersonal cycle that is being enacted by the two of them. Metacommunication consists of treating this cycle as the focus of collaborative exploration.

Key features of metacommunication in this context are that (a) there is an intensive focus on the here and now of the therapeutic relationship, (b) there is an ongoing collaborative exploration of both patients' and therapists' contributions to the interaction, (c) there is an emphasis on the in-depth exploration of the nuances of patients' experience in context of the therapeutic relationship (and a cautiousness about inferring generalized relational patterns), (d) the relational meaning of interventions (i.e., the idiosyncratic way in which each patient construes the therapist's intervention) is as important as the content of the intervention, and (e) intensive use is made of therapist self-disclosure and collaborative exploration of what is taking place in the therapeutic relationship for purposes of understanding and unhooking from the cycle.

The therapist's task when engaging in this type of exploration is to identify his or her own feelings and use them as a point of departure for collaborative exploration. Different forms of exploration are possible. The therapist may provide patients with feedback about their impact on him or her. For example, "I feel cautious with you…as if I'm walking on eggshells" or "I feel like it's difficult to make contact with you. On one hand, the things you're talking about really seem important. But on the other, there's a subtle level at which it's difficult for me to feel you," or "I feel judged by you." Such feedback can help the patient begin to see his or her own contribution to the rupture. It can also pave the way for the exploration of the patient's inner experience. For example, the therapist can add, "Does this feedback make any sense to you? Do you have any awareness of judging me?" This can help the patient begin to articulate a critical attitude that he or she has not been fully aware of, thus allowing the therapist to work through the alliance rupture with the patient. It is often useful for therapists to pinpoint specific instances of patients' eliciting actions. For example, "I feel dismissed or closed out by you, and I think it may be related to the way in which you tend not to pause and reflect in a way that suggests you're considering what I'm saying."

Next we describe specific principles for enhancing therapeutic metacommunication:

1. *Explore with skillful tentativeness and emphasize one's own subjectivity.* Therapists should communicate observations in a tentative and exploratory fashion. The message at both explicit and implicit levels ideally invites patients to engage in a collaborative attempt to understand what is taking place, rather than conveying information with objective status. It is also important for therapists to emphasize the subjectivity of their perceptions since this encourages patients to use therapists' observations as a stimulus for self-exploration rather than to react to them either positively or negatively as authoritative statements.

2. *Do not assume a parallel with other relationships.* Therapists should be wary of prematurely attempting to establish a link between the configuration enacted in the therapeutic relationship and other relationships in the patient's life. Attempts to make links of this type (while useful in some contexts) can be experienced by patients as blaming and can also serve a defensive function for therapists. Instead, the focus should be on exploring patients' internal experience and actions in a nuanced fashion, as they emerge in the here and now.

3. *Ground all formulations in awareness of one's feelings and accept responsibility for one's own contributions.* All observations should attempt to take into account what the therapist is feeling. Failure to do so increases the risk of a distorted understanding that is influenced by factors that are out of awareness. It is critical for therapists to take responsibility for their own contributions to the interaction. We are always contributing to the interaction in ways that are not fully in awareness, and a key task consists of clarifying the nature of this contribution in an ongoing fashion.

In some situations, the process of explicitly acknowledging responsibility for one's contributions to patients can be a particularly potent method. First, this process can help patients become aware of unconscious or semiconscious feelings that they have difficulty articulating. For example, acknowledging that one has been critical can help patients to articulate their feelings of hurt and resentment. Second, by validating the patient's perceptions of the therapist's actions, the therapist can reduce his or her need for defensiveness.

4. *Start where you are.* Collaborative exploration of the therapeutic relationship should take into account feelings, intuitions, and observations that are emerging for the therapist at the moment. What was true one session may not be true the next, and what was true one moment may change the next. Two therapists will react differently to the same patient, and each therapist must begin by making use of his or her own unique experience. For example, while a third-party observer may adopt an empathic response toward an aggressive patient, the therapist embedded in the interaction with that patient may have difficulty doing so. Therapists cannot conceptually manipulate themselves into an empathic stance they do not feel. They must begin by fully accepting and working with their own subjective reactions.

5. *Focus on the concrete, specific, and here and now of the relationship.* Whenever possible, questions, observations, and comments should focus on concrete instances in the here and now rather than on generalizations. This promotes experiential awareness rather than abstract, intellectualized speculation. For example, "I experience you as pulling away from me right now. Do you have any awareness of doing this?"

6. *Track patients' responsiveness to all interventions.* Therapists should carefully monitor the impact of their methods and statements. Do they seem to facilitate the process or perpetuate the rupture? If therapists sense that an intervention has not been facilitative, they should explore the way it has been experienced by the patient. For example, "How did it feel when I said that to you?" or "I'm not sure I know what's going on for you right now. I'm wondering if you might have felt criticized by what I said?" Exploring the patient's construal of an intervention that has failed can play a critical role in refining therapists' understanding of both the enacted configuration and the patient's inner world. This helps therapists to refine their therapy in a way that ultimately will lead to the resolution of the alliance rupture.

7. *Collaborative exploration of the therapeutic relationship and unhooking take place at the same time.* It is not necessary for therapists to have a clear formulation prior to metacommunicating. In fact, the process of thinking out loud about the interaction often helps therapists to unhook from the very configuration being discussed. Moreover, the process of telling patients about an aspect of one's conflictual experience can free therapists to see the situation more clearly.

8. *Remember that exploring what is occurring in the relationship can function as a new enactment.* For example, the therapist articulates a growing intuition that the patient is withdrawing and says, "It feels to me like I'm trying to pull teeth." In response, the patient withdraws further. In this way an already occurring enactment of therapist pursuit and patient withdrawal becomes further intensified. It is critical to track the quality of patients' responsiveness to statements and to explore their experience of what is and what is not facilitative. Does the intervention deepen the patient's self-exploration or lead to defensiveness or superficial compliance? The process of exploring the ways in which patients experience the treatment and the clinician helps to refine the understanding of the vicious cycle and to resolve the alliance rupture.

References and Readings

Foreman, S. A., & Marmar, C. R. (1985). Therapist actions that address initially poor therapeutic alliances in psychotherapy. *American Journal of Psychiatry, 142*, 922–926.

Horvath, A. O., Del Re, A. C., Flückiger, C., & Symonds, D. (2011). Alliance in individual psychotherapy. In J. C. Norcross (Ed.), *Psychotherapy relationships that work* (2nd ed., pp. 25–69). New York: Oxford University Press.

Lambert, M. J., & Bergin, A. E. (1994). The effectiveness of psychotherapy. In A. E. Bergin & S. L. Garfield (Eds.), *Handbook of psychotherapy and behavior change* (4th ed., pp. 143–189). New York: Wiley.

Safran, J. D., & Muran, J. C. (2000). *Negotiating the therapeutic alliance: A relational treatment guide*. New York: Guilford Press.

Safran, J. D., Muran, J. C., & Eubanks-Carter, C. (2011). Repairing alliance ruptures. In J. C. Norcross (Ed.), *Psychotherapy relationships that work* (2nd ed., pp. 224–238). New York: Oxford University Press.

Safran, J. D., Muran, J. C., Samstag, L. W., & Stevens, C. (2002). Repairing the alliance ruptures. In J. C. Norcross (Ed.), *Psychotherapy relationships that work* (pp. 235–254). New York: Oxford University Press.

Samstag, L. W., Batchelder, S. T., Muran, J. C., Safran, J. D., & Winston, A. (1998). Early identification of treatment failures in short-term psychotherapy: An assessment of therapeutic alliance and interpersonal behavior. *Journal of Psychotherapy Practice and Research, 7*, 126–143.

Wierzbicki, M., & Pekarik, G. (1993). A meta-analysis of psychotherapy dropout. *Professional Psychology: Research and Practice, 24*, 190–195.

Related Topics

Chapter 33, "Compendium of Evidence-Based Therapy Relationships"

Chapter 51, "Conducting Evaluations of Client Outcomes and Satisfactions"

Chapter 53, "Reducing Resistance in Psychotherapy"

53 REDUCING RESISTANCE IN PSYCHOTHERAPY

Clifton W. Mitchell

Historically, resistance in psychotherapy has been conceptualized as "residing" within clients. Such perspectives likely grew from early Freudian definitions that characterized resistance as clients' efforts to repress anxiety-provoking memories and insights (Otani, 1989) or as disputing the therapist's interpretations of their problems.

Alternatively, in the last half century resistance has frequently been conceptualized as a result of a negative interpersonal dynamic *between* the therapist and the client. Or, as Strong and Matross (1973, p. 26) state, "Resistance is defined as psychological forces aroused in the client that restrain acceptance of influence (acceptance of the counselor's suggestion) and are generated by the way the suggestion is stated and by the characteristics of the counselor stating it." From this perspective, the psychotherapist co-creates a mutual communication pattern that hinders treatment and that promotes resistance. This perspective empowers therapists to prevent and minimize resistance through adjustments in their interaction style by remaining aware of what they may be doing that promotes resistance and by developing alternative responses. This chapter presents ideas for managing psychological resistance by disrupting typical therapeutic interaction patterns and replacing them with interaction styles that resolve resistance.

1. *Do the unexpected.* A foundational principle in managing resistance is to strive to disrupt clients' common patterns of thinking, feeling, and behaving. This is first begun by responding in an unexpected manner and avoiding socially typical responses. Clients who have talked to non–mental health professionals (and some professionals) have likely heard the standard "how-to-fix-your-situation" advice. Frequently, this advice is not well received. Typical responses beget typical reactions, and typical reactions keep clients stuck in their situation. This is one reason why brief therapists assert that problems are maintained by solutions that are ineffective (Walter & Peller, 1992). Clinicians' typical responses are likely to be incorporated into established, ineffective solutions. The more we respond in a typical manner, the more likely we are to become part of the system that maintains resistance and problems.

To avoid the pitfalls of typical responses and the resistance that follows, you can avoid typical verbal and nonverbal responses. In doing this, you surprise clients, confound their anticipation of your response, and begin disrupting the patterns that are inherent to their thinking and problems.

The unexpected does not have to be complex. The better techniques taught in training programs are unexpected by most clients. The empathic response, the absence of criticism, the nonjudgmental posture, and the response that has the appearance of puzzlement or agreement out of sync with common rebuttals are examples of unexpected responses that potentially disrupt client patterns.

2. *Slow the pace.* When resistance is encountered, the prevailing urge is to increase the pace of the session and break through the resistance. This is a classic mistake. Instead, slow the pace. Make sure that each statement by the client is fully addressed and processed in detail.

To slow the pace, increase the space between your words and increase your use of silence. This does two things: It creates pressure to fill the space and it provides time to think and feel (Gerber, 1986). Most resistant clients avoid both of these tasks. Yet it is the pressure to fill the space as well as the time to think and feel that leads clients to doing their work. The real therapeutic work is done in the time between the words, during the quiet moments when new perspectives are examined and embraced. Another subtle benefit of slowing the pace is that it provides a few extra moments for clients' defenses to dissipate. When you try to progress too fast, you often move into a position of attempting to do the work yourself and, thus, hinder the change process.

Yet another benefit of slowing the pace is that it keeps the therapeutic tension within clients and does not place the therapeutic tension between clients and you (Mitchell, 2010). Increasing the therapeutic tension between you and clients is typically unhelpful because it tends to amplify resistance. The therapeutic tension should be within clients as they face their inner struggles. Slowing the pace does not mean to become passive and slow the therapeutic work. To the contrary, *slowing the pace typically intensifies the therapeutic work.* You slow the pace in order to focus on and magnify clients' internal struggles and search for answers. Resistance is overcome with an emphasis on direction, not speed.

3. *Focus on details.* Much of what appears to be resistance is a failure to acquire enough information about the richness of clients' worlds in order to increase understanding of why clients are responding as they are and to increase junctures at which interventions can be implemented (Mitchell, 2010). By assessing details you show genuine concern and respect for the client and are more likely to get to the crux of the conflicts. Broad, general discussions are rarely productive. "The devil is in the details" is more than a bit of folk wisdom; details are essential for solution creation and resistance management. Another benefit from a heightened attention to details is that choices emerge. Details create choices because, with every detail, options become more evident to clients. If a client feels that not enough options are available, you do not have enough details about that client's world.

4. *Avoid logic and excessive direct guidance.* Despite the masses of information regarding the dangers of harmful, unhealthy behaviors, people continue to do them. Information and logic alone rarely compel change and therapists who rely on them as motivators for change frequently meet frustration. If people changed because of logic, no one would smoke, no one would drink, and everyone would exercise. This is not to say that logic is unimportant to some aspects of change; however, when you closely examine the underlying forces that actually move people to change you discover that people most often change because they have *emotionally compelling* reasons to change (Mitchell, 2010). This is particularly true with reluctant, involuntary clients. With reluctant clients, direct guidance and logic often increase resistance and, as such, are less effective and can waste time. Instead, focus on discovering the underlying component of change that arouses the most emotional reaction in clients. Once discovered, construct a dialogue that keeps clients in touch with this emotion as a motivator. In this manner motivation for change comes from within clients and resistance is resolved (Miller & Rollnick, 2002).

5. *Increase empathic responding.* Too often empathy is seen as a tool to build rapport only. As a result, therapists may discount and limit the consistent use of empathy once rapport has been established. The logic here is something like, "Now that I have rapport, I will build a case for change." Such an approach is a mistake that can increase what appears to be resistance.

Empathy gets clients in touch with their emotionally compelling reasons for change. A well-worded empathic response always includes at least one reference to the specific emotion that the client is experiencing at the moment. The more resistant the client appears, the more empathic statements are needed to tap into internal motivations for change. For most resistant clients, logic without an underlying emotional impact is just talk. Failure to consistently include empathic statements in psychotherapy inevitably makes the task of overcoming clients' ambivalence to change more difficult and results in clients being wrongly labeled as resistant (Miller & Rollnick, 2002).

6. *Avoid responding from an expert position.* Clients enter therapy with a host of problems and you often become certain that your knowledge will be beneficial. As a consequence, you begin suggesting solutions to clients. To your dismay, resistant clients reject your suggestions and you start hearing "Yes, but ..." responses. Often, you become frustrated with the clients' rejection of your suggestions and begin labeling clients as resistant. "Yes but ..." responses are a signal that the current therapeutic interaction is not working. In such situations, the more knowledge you present about solutions, the greater the likelihood you will encounter what appears to be resistance.

The way out is to reverse the paradox—become curious, naïve, and puzzled. The reason behind this is that the more of an expert you become, the more you provide the needed ingredient to create resistance—that is, someone or something to argue against. The more naïve and puzzled you become, the less the client has to resist against. In addition, your expertise may result in clients losing the sense of freedom needed to explore possibilities on their own and willingly embrace change.

Moving to a position of naiveté and unknowing is sometimes difficult because your suggestions would likely benefit clients. However, it is not how much you know or how much you want to help that matters. What matters is the relationship between you and your clients at any particular moment. If clients are rejecting your suggestions, they are signaling that they are not "buying" what you are "selling." When this occurs, stop selling and return to gathering information about what clients might accept. Resistance is created when there is a mismatch between the method of delivering influence and clients' current propensity to accept the method by which the influence is delivered (Mitchell, 2010).

If clients are motivated and cooperative, and you have a good idea, by all means tell them. If they accept your suggestions and try them, move forward. Yet, if they are reluctant to accept your suggestions, become naïve. As a general rule, the more resistant the client, the less you know; the more motivated the client, the more you know (Mitchell, 2010).

7. *Accommodate client preferences.* Matching client preferences in psychotherapy has been shown to reduce dropout rates by about a third and improve treatment outcomes (Swift, Callahan, & Vollmer, 2011). Thus, it is recommended that therapists assess client preferences in initial meetings and periodically throughout the treatment process. Preferences are typically assessed through directly asking clients; however, written descriptions, rating scales, and surveys can also be used.

It is important to create an environment where clients can openly express preferences as they may be reluctant to state them for a number of reasons, including a lack of information about options, distrust in the system or therapist, and a low readiness to change. Accommodating preferences whenever clinically and ethically possible reduces resistance. Even when preferences cannot be accommodated, genuine efforts to discuss and address them can also prove beneficial in reducing resistance.

8. *Establish mutual goals.* One of the primary therapist errors that create resistance is failure to establish mutually agreed-upon goals. The key word here is *mutually*. Clients, particularly resistant clients, should be active participants in goal establishment. People do not resist what they want; they resist what they do not want and what is imposed upon them. If we start by first seeking what clients want, we build a foundation for mutually agreed-upon goals.

The centrality of mutual goals appears at two levels. First, there is agreement on the overall goal of treatment—what would constitute a successful outcome. Second, there is agreement between the client and therapist on the momentary goal within the session. Do the client and therapist agree that what is being done in that session is important to a successful outcome? Clients who do not view the content and tasks as important are likely to "resist."

9. *Deal with fears surrounding goals first.* Some people come to therapy because they realized that the probable solutions to their problems terrify them (Walter & Peller, 1992). This is common with clients in the contemplation stage. In cases where fear of change is considerable, focusing too strongly on goals may *increase* fear and *slow* progress. Instead, first focus on the fear before moving to discussions of actions to take. Therapists may inadvertently create "resistance" because the therapeutic interaction is mistimed and unaligned with clients' predominant apprehensions and readiness to change.

10. *Funnel problems to a particular person, place, and time.* At a seminar, David Burns stated that you are most helpful when the problem is defined at a level of clarity that includes a specific person, place, and time. Until this clarity and specificity are reached, clients may appear resistant; however, the underlying barrier to change may be that the problem is unmanageable because it is too broadly and vaguely defined. The problem has not been funneled down to the point where the client perceives that something can be usefully accomplished.

11. *Avoid early confrontation.* Although there is a place for negative feedback in psychotherapy, the research consistently shows that an early confrontive style tends to backfire. If you confront too early in the process, it tends to prove counterproductive and promote resistance.

There are two fundamental reasons to avoid early confrontation. First, the right to confront must be earned over time. Confrontation that occurs before a critical level of respect is achieved can increase resistance because it provides clients a strong stimulus to resist against. Second, rarely are the presenting problems the "actual" or "real" conflicts. To effectively deal with resistance, deeper problems need to be discovered and processed. Confrontation should be delayed until deeper concerns are revealed or until it is clear that genuine concerns are being discussed.

12. *Use paradox when appropriate.* Paradox is particularly useful for resistant clients because it alters resistive behavior without directly confronting it. Often defined as prescribing the symptom or giving clients permission to continue or increase unwanted behavior, paradoxical techniques have the therapeutic advantage of placing clients in a bind where the more they resist, the more they comply with therapists' suggestions. The benefit of paradoxical approaches is that they utilize the resistant behavior as a tool to promote therapeutic movement. A more subtle benefit is that therapists are conveying confidence that clients will make wise decisions about what to do when they see the consequences of their behavior from a magnified perspective. Thus, with the use of paradox, resistance is circumvented and a healthy independence is reinforced.

13. *Change your treatment approach.* Regardless of the client's preferences, if you have been working from a particular theoretical approach and it has proved ineffective, change. It is often difficult to predict which treatment or format will work with individual clients. Sometimes the approach that initially appears to fit with a particular client is the opposite of what works.

Some therapists are unwilling to accept that their favorite approach is not applicable for certain patients and circumstances. Those who continue with ineffective practices are resistant therapists; sadly, this is sometimes characterized as client resistance.

14. *Openly discuss clients' and your resistance.* When little has been accomplished and clients' resistance has become the elephant in the room, it can be beneficial to directly discuss their resistance with them (Ellis, 2004). Such a discussion will include acknowledgement of your own contributions to resistance, as resistance occurs only within the context of a relationship or a system (Miller & Rollnick, 2002). It is unlikely clients will directly address their own resistance openly; thus, therapists will likely have to take the lead in this discussion.

Addressing your contributions to the resistance is unexpected, leads to a productive focus on the therapeutic relationship, and models taking responsibility for actions contributing to the lack of progress (Mitchell, 2010). This, in turn, opens the door for a direct discussion of clients' resistance, which frequently leads to an explication, if not resolution, of the core conflicts.

References and Readings

Ellis, A. (2004). Methods to reduce and counter resistance in psychotherapy. In G. P. Koocher, J. C. Norcross, & S. S Hill (Eds.), *Psychologists' desk reference* (2nd ed., pp. 212–215). New York: Oxford University Press.

Gerber, S. K. (1986). *Responsive therapy: A systematic approach to counseling skills.* New York: Human Sciences Press.

Miller, W. R., & Rollnick, S. (2002). *Motivational interviewing: Preparing people for change* (2nd ed.). New York: Guilford Press.

Mitchell, C. W. (2010). *Effective techniques for dealing with highly resistant clients* (2nd ed.). Johnson City, TN: Clifton Mitchell Publishing.

Otani, A. (1989). Resistance management techniques of Milton H. Erickson, MD: An application to nonhypnotic mental health counseling. *Journal of Mental Health Counseling, 11,* 325–334.

Strong, S. R., & Matross, R. P. (1973). Change process in counseling and psychotherapy. *Journal of Counseling Psychology, 20,* 25–37.

Swift, J. K., Callahan, J. L., & Vollmer, B. M. (2011). Preferences. In J. C. Norcross (Ed.), *Psychotherapy relationships that work* (2nd ed., pp. 301–315). New York: Oxford University Press.

Walter, J. L., & Peller, J. E. (1992). *Becoming solution-focused in brief therapy.* New York: Brunner/Mazel.

Related Topics

Chapter 32, "Compendium of Treatment Adaptations"

Chapter 39, "Treating Reluctant and Involuntary Clients"

Chapter 40, "Conducting Motivational Interviewing"

Chapter 52, "Repairing Ruptures in the Therapeutic Alliance"

54 IMPLEMENTING STIMULUS CONTROL THERAPY FOR INSOMNIA

Richard R. Bootzin

The following constitute the stimulus control therapy instructions (Bootzin, 1972; Bootzin & Epstein, 2011):

1. Lie down intending to go to sleep only when you are sleepy.
2. Do not use your bed for anything except sleep—that is, do not read, watch television, eat, or worry in bed. Sexual activity is the only exception to this rule. On such occasions, the instructions are to be followed afterward when you intend to go to sleep.
3. If you find yourself unable to fall asleep, get up and go into another room. Stay up as long as you wish and then return to the bedroom to sleep. Although we do not want you to watch the clock, we want you to get out of bed if you do not fall asleep immediately. Remember the goal is to associate your bed with falling asleep *quickly*! If you are in bed more than about 10 minutes without falling asleep and have not gotten up, you are not following this instruction.
4. If you still cannot fall asleep, repeat Step 3. Do this as often as is necessary throughout the night.
5. Set your alarm and get up at the same time every morning irrespective of how much sleep you got during the night. This will help your body acquire a consistent sleep rhythm.
6. Do not nap during the day.

The focus of the instructions is primarily on sleep onset. For sleep maintenance problems, the instructions are to be followed after awakening when the patient has difficulty falling back to sleep. Although stimulus control instructions appear simple and straightforward, compliance is better if the instructions are discussed individually and a rationale is provided for each instruction (Bootzin & Epstein, 2000; Bootzin & Perlis, 2011; Bootzin, Smith, Franzen, & Shapiro, 2010).

- *Instruction 1.* The goal of this instruction is to help individuals with insomnia become more sensitive to internal cues of sleepiness so that they will be more likely to fall asleep quickly when they go to bed. This instruction should be viewed as an aspirational goal to be achieved gradually, rather than as an imperative to be started immediately. Becoming sensitive to internal cues of sleepiness aids in determining an appropriate time to go to bed based on sleepiness, not on the clock.
- *Instruction 2.* The goals here are to have activities that are associated with arousal occur elsewhere and to break up patterns that are associated with disturbed sleep. Often individuals with insomnia engage in activities in bed that interfere with falling asleep, such as reading, watching television, using computers or going on the Internet,

talking on the phone, text-messaging, worrying about the day's events, and so forth. If bedtime is the only time those with insomnia have for thinking about the day's events and planning the next day, they should spend some quiet time doing that in another room before they go to bed. Many people who do not have insomnia read or listen to music in bed without problems. This is not the case for insomniacs, however. This instruction is used to help those who have sleep problems establish new routines to facilitate sleep onset.

- *Instructions 3 and 4.* In order to associate the bed with sleep and disassociate it from the frustration and arousal of not being able to sleep, individuals with insomnia are instructed to get out of bed after about 10 minutes (20 minutes for those over 60 years old). This is also a means of coping with insomnia. Getting out of bed to engage in other activities when unable to sleep strengthens a perception of control over insomnia. This helps make the problem less distressing and more manageable.

There are several important matters to discuss with the patient to insure that the instruction to get out of bed is successfully implemented. First, how long should someone with insomnia wait before getting out of bed? The instructions place a premium on getting out of bed quickly. However, many individuals become anxious and they constantly watch the clock to check how long they have been in bed. To avoid that, patients are typically instructed to turn the face of the clock away from them so that clock checking does not occur. They are instructed instead to use an estimate of how long they have been in bed without falling asleep.

Second, once out of bed, how long should individuals stay awake and what should they do? A good rule of thumb is that patients should stay out of bed long enough to feel that they would successfully fall asleep if they returned to bed. Generally, this means staying awake 15 minutes of more before returning to bed. As for what individuals should do during this time, patients are encouraged to do something relaxing and enjoyable that does not involve bright light. This includes reading with a reading light, listening to music, watching television from a distance of at least 8 feet, meditating or doing relaxation instructions, and so forth. Bright light in the middle of the night will make it harder to establish a consistent sleep-wake circadian rhythm. Patients are discouraged from doing work or going on a computer when they cannot sleep. These activities are usually arousing and the light from a computer monitor when sitting close to it is brighter than most people realize.

- *Instruction 5.* Individuals with insomnia often have irregular sleep rhythms because they try to make up for poor sleep by sleeping late or by napping the next day. Keeping a consistent wake time helps develop consistent sleep rhythms and reduces daytime sleepiness. At the beginning of treatment, maintaining a consistent wake time may result in sleep deprivation after a night of insomnia. Sleep deprivation makes it more likely that patients will fall asleep quickly the following night, strengthening the cues of the bed and bedroom for sleep.
- Often insomniacs will want to follow a different sleeping schedule on weekends or nights off than they do during the workweek. It is important to have as consistent a schedule as possible, 7 nights a week. The goal is to reduce variability to no more than 1 hour in wake time on days off compared to wake time on work or school days. It may be necessary to approach that goal gradually over a few weeks, using successive approximations, if the deviations are large as is often observed in adolescents and college students.
- *Instruction 6.* The rationale for this instruction about not napping is to ensure that individuals with insomnia do not disrupt their sleep patterns by irregular napping. This instruction also aims to prevent losing the advantage of the previous night's sleep loss in increasing the likelihood of faster sleep onset the following night. For elderly insomniacs who feel that they need to nap, a daily late afternoon nap of less than 30 minutes, or the use of 20 to 30 minutes

of relaxation as a nap substitute, is recommended. Consistent late afternoon naps have the advantage of providing additional energy for evening activities for older adults.

Cognitive-behavioral treatments for insomnia, including stimulus control therapy, are primarily self-management treatments. The treatments are carried out by the patients at home. Consequently, adherence may be a problem. Most adherence problems can be solved by direct discussion. A common problem is the disturbance of the spouses' sleep when insomniacs get out of bed. Clinician discussions with the spouses are often helpful in ensuring full cooperation.

During the winter in cold climates, some patients may be reluctant to leave the warmth of their beds. Suggestions for keeping warm robes near the beds and keeping an additional room warm throughout the night, along with encouragement to try to follow instructions, are usually effective in promoting adherence.

Stimulus control therapy has been evaluated either as a single-component treatment or as part of multicomponent interventions with adolescents, adults, and the elderly. Reviews of outcome studies (e.g., Morin et al., 2006) have found that stimulus control therapy constitutes one of the most effective, single-component, psychological or behavioral treatments for insomnia. In an evidence-based practice parameters update report of 1999 practice guidelines published by the American Academy of Sleep Medicine (Morgenthaler et al., 2006, p. 1417), stimulus control therapy continued to be listed as meeting the highest practice standard as an "effective and recommended therapy in the treatment of chronic insomnia."

In recent years, multicomponent treatments (e.g., cognitive-behavioral therapy for insomnia, CBT-I) have been evaluated more frequently than single-component treatments.

CBT-I typically includes stimulus control therapy as one of the components along with sleep restriction therapy, sleep hygiene and education, and in some implementations, relaxation or meditation and/or cognitive therapy (Bootzin & Epstein, 2011). Multicomponent treatment lends itself well to clinical settings in which patients with diverse comorbid and insomnia symptoms are seen.

References and Readings

Bootzin, R. R. (1972). A stimulus control treatment for insomnia. *American Psychological Association Proceedings*, 395–396.

Bootzin, R. R., & Epstein, D. R. (2000). Stimulus control instructions. In K. L. Lichstein & C. M. Morin (Eds.), *Treatment of late-life insomnia* (pp. 167–184). Thousand Oaks, CA: Sage.

Bootzin, R. R., & Epstein, D. R. (2011). Understanding and treating insomnia. *Annual Review of Clinical Psychology, 7*, 435–458.

Bootzin, R. R., & Perlis, M. L. (2011). Stimulus control therapy. In M. Perlis, M. Aloia, & B. Kuhn (Eds.), *Behavioral treatments for sleep disorders* (pp. 21–30). New York: Academic Press.

Bootzin, R. R., Smith, L. J., Franzen, P. L., & Shapiro, S. L. (2010). Stimulus control therapy. In M. J. Sateia & D. J. Buysse (Eds.), *Insomnia: Diagnosis and treatment* (pp. 268–276). Essex, UK: Informa Healthcare.

Morgenthaler, T., Kramer, M., Alessi, C., Friedman, L., Boehlecke, B., Brown, T., ... Swick, T. (2006). Practice parameters for the psychological and behavioral treatment of insomnia: An update. An American Academy of Sleep Medicine Report. *Sleep, 29*, 1415–1419.

Morin, C. M., Bootzin, R. R., Buysse, D. J., Edinger, J. D., Espie, C., & Lichstein, K. L. (2006). Psychological and behavioral treatment of insomnia: Update of the recent evidence (1998–2004). *Sleep, 29*, 1398–1414.

Related Topics

Chapter 31, "Compendium of Empirically Supported Treatments"

Chapter 56, "Using Hypnosis to Invite Relaxation"

55 TERMINATING PSYCHOTHERAPY

Oren Shefet and Rebecca Coleman Curtis

The ending of the therapeutic endeavor is not an epilogue or an afterthought to a successful treatment, but rather a stage unto itself. It is a complex process that should be handled with delicacy and care (Fox, 1993; Tyson, 1996). This is the stage where the client and therapist may observe the work they have done and assess it together, consolidate its achievements, and come to terms with its shortcomings. This is also the stage in which many clients can work through traumas and fears surrounding separation, abandonment, and bereavement, as well as rise to the challenge of qualities such as independence and freedom. Unlike previous stages of therapy, mistakes and shortcomings that occur cannot be identified or remedied. Gains that have not been consolidated may deteriorate without further intervention. Abandonment fears that have not been worked through may hinder future independence and leave the client with an unsatisfied resolution.

THE TIMING OF TERMINATIONS

In most therapies it is the client who sets the therapeutic goals, and thus clients are in the best position to know whether the mission set for the therapeutic endeavor has been accomplished. Common goals include symptom relief and the increased ability to handle life problems on one's own. In psychodynamic therapies common goals also include increased affect tolerance (Curtis, 2002) and the resolution of transference. The ability to lead a satisfactory life outside of institutions or the ability to work and sustain relationships may also be useful measures. A complementary termination criterion is the lack of therapeutic benefits.

Termination should be considered when the client and therapist both agree that the therapy, while not accomplishing its goals, has low probability of advancing further. That may be due to a failure in alliance formation, an insurmountable therapeutic impasse, or a continuous reduction in the momentum of work and the motivation for therapy. Another instance in which the therapeutic endeavor must come to an end is in the case of treatment interruptions. In this category, we can include the emergence of an unavoidable multiple relationship, relocation of client or therapist, change in work settings of therapist, and so on. In the latter two reasons for termination, the focus may involve coming to terms with the disappointment of a therapy that ended before goals have been achieved. The therapist should aim for a successful referral, rather than the ending of all therapeutic contact. Arriving at the decision that the time has come to end the therapy is difficult not only for the client but also for the therapist (Curtis, 2002). Therapists may avoid discussing or initiating terminations for their own reasons, rather than their clients' interests.

SETTING THE TERMINATION DATE

Clients often seek to set the termination in conjunction with another date, either a major life event such as a wedding or graduation, or a minor one such as a vacation or a holiday. Sometimes clients may choose such a minor event as a way of avoiding their feelings and of minimizing the importance of the relationship ending. Therapists are advised to clarify those reasons with their clients and encourage them to choose a date that will stand on its own for the therapy's end.

Announcing the end of the treatment and ending the treatment in the same session is ill advised. Such a pace does not allow either the client or the therapist to deal with the difficult emotions the termination may bring about and can prevent coming to terms successfully with the treatment and its ending.

There are two possible termination strategies: time-limited terminations and spaced terminations. In timed-limited terminations, sessions occur in the same regularity as before, until the final session, when they stop. In spaced terminations the session frequency is gradually lessened, with the final session perhaps a month or more after the one before it. While some orientations weigh toward the choice of one or the other, the choice between the two will ultimately rest on the needs of the client.

Time-limited terminations imply to the client that the therapy is complete. Spaced terminations, on the other hand, imply that this is a test. The therapist and the client enter a process of lessening the therapy, which can be hastened or slowed, as needed. The client and therapist may feel that the termination is an option, which may or may not come into being.

CLIENTS' REACTIONS TO THE TERMINATION

Clients vary in their reactions to the termination. Some may react with profound anxiety and despair, some may be joyous at their "graduation," and others may not feel much at all. Pleasant emotions surrounding the termination may include a sense of relief from the financial burden and time pressures surrounding psychotherapy, pride at the accomplishments of therapy, joy, a sense of agency and independence, and hopefulness about the future (Tyson, 1996).

The client may also harbor negative emotions, including anger, sadness, and hopelessness. Fox (1993) conceptualized a possible series of emotions based on the stages of mourning as delineated by Kübler-Ross for death. In the first stage—denial—clients may ignore the coming termination, deny any feelings about it, or make relatively few attempts to approach the subject. It is the therapist's task to encourage clients supportively but persistently to ponder consciously the ending and its meaning. In the second stage—anger—the client may feel abandoned by the therapist, accuse the therapist of being uncaring or hostile, or devalue the gains made in the treatment. It is recommended to explore this negative reaction as one does any other, and contain the negative feelings in the therapist it may create. In the third stage—bargaining—the client may attempt to find the means of prolonging the therapeutic relationship. Common strategies are finding new problems or symptoms to work on or relapsing into symptoms that were previously resolved in the therapy. If those symptoms are especially severe, the therapist should reconsider the termination, even at the price of appearing inconsistent or unresolved (Tyson, 1996). A less pathological bargaining tactic is attempting to prolong the relationship, in fantasy or reality, by other means, such as planning to write an article with the therapist or talking about striking a posttermination friendship with him. In the fourth stage, depression, the client may feel the helplessness at stopping the coming end and obsess about it. The therapist should assist in working through these emotions. In the fifth stage, acceptance, the client will come to terms with the termination and be able to separate. It is important to emphasize that not all clients will go through these stages, and not necessarily within this order.

Tyson (1996) observed that the severity of abandonment felt by clients may reflect not only the ending of the therapeutic relationship but also of previous endings that were left unresolved. When the therapist is experienced as rejecting, it may lead to rage against the therapist combined with deep feelings of helplessness and loss. This is not a detriment to the therapy but rather a gain, because it allows the client and the therapist to work through those archaic fears before the termination of therapy. When strong erotic feelings develop in therapy, the client may experience the termination as a repeated rejection of an unfulfilled love. Clients may experience jealousy of their therapists' other clients, their families, colleagues, or friends. It is the therapist's role, at this point, to help the client renounce the unrealistic fantasy and come to terms with the loss. Idealization and devaluation may also occur. It is the therapist's duty to help the client develop a more realistic attitude toward the therapy and therapist in order to be able to separate appropriately.

When clients claim to be feeling "nothing at all," especially in a long-term therapy, it may be an indication that they truly are neutral about the subject, an indication of denial of the termination's reality, or an indication of avoidance of affects and affective communication. Thus, clinical judgment is necessary to decide whether therapists should reinforce the realities of the ending, encourage exploration of covered emotions, or let the client remain in an uninvolved state.

A prevalent client reaction is the preemptive strike. In this case the client either proposes the termination before the therapist can do so or terminates without allowing the therapist enough time to react. It is not uncommon to hear about clients ceasing to show when termination is first mentioned as a possibility. The positive aspect of such a behavior is the transformation of the clients into active players in the termination drama, a role that allows them to acquire and keep a sense of agency and control. The therapist should prevent such a preemptive strike while commending the client for an active stance, if possible.

THE TERMINATION TASKS

The therapist needs to help the client consolidate the gains made in therapy. The client and therapist ask themselves where the clients were when they started the therapy, where they are now, and how did change occur. Thus, they may review the client's mental state, her relationships, her attainment of life goals, and any other criteria that the therapy aimed at improving. Some specific ways that therapists can encourage such an assessment include reviewing counseling notes written early in the therapeutic process, soliciting the opinions of important others in the client's life, and using standardized outcome measures. One of the most important achievements of a well-executed review will be gaining a realistic insight into the therapeutic outcomes, including what has been gained, as well as the ways in which the therapy fell short.

A client who identified his accomplishments in treatment is more ready to transfer them to his life outside of the therapy. Ideally, this process has already begun before the termination has been discussed. Some have gone a step further and suggested the creation of a termination and transfer ritual to assist in the generalization task.

The use of a future-oriented perspective can be helpful for the client at this point. Therapists can ask clients how they will recognize instances in which they may use their newly found skills in the future, the challenges of doing so, and ways of overcoming them. They may empower the client by stating their true confidence in the client's ability to overcome future problems, and such a display of confidence may serve as a self-fulfilling prophecy.

As the therapy is ending, clients may experience an increased sense of freedom to voice their discontent, their disappointment, and their sense of failure. Therapists may feel apprehensive about dwelling on those failures. Therapists can remind clients that the failure belongs to the therapy and not to the client. The therapist should also help the client understand that therapies are almost never entirely successful or unsuccessful, and that the existence of areas of lack of progress does not negate the progress made. The therapist may suggest to the client other therapeutic modalities which might help in the problems that have not been resolved.

Termination, aside from a necessary stage in treatment, is also a loss. The separation anxiety and fears of abandonment that are evident to some degree in any client will be triggered by the termination. The process of working through involves the encouragement of expression and understanding of the affects triggered by the upcoming separation. It is the therapist's task, at this time, to contain any negative reaction that may emerge. Understanding the losses, and separating fantasy from reality, is crucial.

Therapists, who may have relied a good deal on a positive relationship and positive fantasies, may now encourage a more realistic view of the relationship and themselves. The termination should, by the end of exploration, be construed as the realistic ending of treatment, rather than abandonment. Therapists who up until that point may have relied on a "blank slate" position may introduce more of their real personality into the relationship (Curtis, 2002). Self-disclosures and a more active stance in therapy may encourage clients to see themselves as equal members in the dyad, leading to a sense of empowerment.

Preparations should be made for the possibility of relapse, and arrangements should be decided on concerning future contact. The therapist and client should review possible warning signs of a relapse and the steps with which clients may counter it if they perceive those signs. Those steps may include the resumption of therapy. The distinction between relapse and failure should be made explicit, to reduce hopelessness and self-blame.

Clients and therapists should also decide upon the possibility of posttherapeutic contact, calls, and e-mails and whether the client should expect a reply. Any arrangement may work as long as it is made explicit. Many therapists have been advised, however, not to respond to e-mails for ethical and legal reasons and clients should be told of this if it is the case. Curtis (2002) informs her clients that she would be happy to hear from them in the future, as it leads not only to the client's well-being but also to the therapist's ability to learn about the therapy and its impact. Therapists may wish to ask the client what was helpful and not helpful. The termination is obviously especially difficult for clients who have experienced significant loss previously in their lives. Mann (1973) devised a short-term therapy focused on the termination from the very beginning, thus dealing with loss as the central issue.

SPECIAL CONSIDERATIONS FOR CHILD THERAPY

Many family therapists, of course, think that it is preferable not to identify a child as the client who needs to change, whereas others think that there are circumstances when a child will benefit from an individual relationship with a therapist.

In child therapy the client often is conceptualized not only as suffering from specific symptoms but also as lagging in development. An important criterion for termination is the resumption of development and the overcoming of the developmental gap. Viewed in this way, the termination is a beginning of a new stage in the child's life.

Children who have suffered losses, such as that of a parental figure due to death or divorce, are confronted with another loss. In these cases, the therapy should be geared toward its end from the first session. The therapist is advised to encourage verbalizations of reactions toward termination even when the termination is not imminent.

The wish to hear about the client's progress after the therapy has been completed is a more prevalent and accepted practice in child therapies. As the child continues to grow and encounter new developmental challenges, therapists should make themselves available for therapy or referral assistance in the future.

Nonintensive therapy for children with severe emotional disorders has been found to most often result in no improvement or worsening of symptoms compared to longer, more intensive psychoanalytic treatment (Fonagy & Target, 1996). It may be that the loss of the therapist in nonintensive therapies is one of the factors contributing to this cautionary finding.

PREMATURE TERMINATION

Almost half of all therapy cases end in premature termination. In light of this high rate, premature termination might be considered a normative ending of therapy, albeit an undesirable one. This should be kept in mind with children where the child's caregivers, through their financial control and their emotional power over the child, are in a unique position to terminate the therapy prematurely.

Joyce et al. (2007) summarized and categorized the following list of risk factors: (1) client factors: minority ethnicity, low education, low social economic status, unmet expectations from therapy, lack of readiness to change, and highly developed ability to create positive interpersonal relationships; (2) therapist factors: lack of theoretical knowledge and lack of technical skills; (3) administrative factors: long waiting list, inadequate client preparation, lack of a predefined time limit for the therapy, and noncompliance with institutional demands; and (4) interactive factors: an initial impression of the therapist as lacking in warmth, empathy, or respect; lack of agreement concerning the problem dealt with in therapy or its cause; weak therapeutic alliance; or differences of opinions concerning the therapy.

The most common reasons for terminating prematurely are not finding the therapy helpful anymore, goals being met, not understanding the therapist, wanting a different experience, not liking what the therapist said, and not liking the therapist. Clients who have an anxiety or substance abuse disorder are more likely to end therapy without the therapist's agreement.

In the treatment, the therapist should be mindful of the working alliance at all times. When a negative reaction arises, as is apt to happen especially in long-term engagements, the therapist should encourage clients to express their negative emotions, rather than act-out on them by leaving. When a premature termination occurs, therapists should take measures to benefit both clients and themselves. If the client dropped out of therapy, the therapist should not just silently accept it, as that implies the therapist's agreement. Rather, the therapist should attempt to contact the client by phone, or if that fails, by letter. The letter should minimally include an assessment of the client's state at the time of last contact, recommendations for after care (medication, psychotherapy, etc.), an offer to resume treatment in the future, and an offer to assist in referral to another provider. For their own professional education, therapists should examine the therapy and understand to the best of their ability the reasons for the termination.

ETHICAL GUIDELINES FOR TERMINATIONS

The American Psychological Association's Ethics Code provides ethical guidelines for termination. Psychologists should not end therapy with clients who are currently in need of treatment (i.e., abandonment of clients). This rule was precluded from the APA's code of ethics due to the difficulty of clearly defining it. On the other hand, therapists are under the obligation to terminate therapy when therapeutic goals have been met, when it is clear that the client no longer benefits from therapy, or when the client is harmed by therapy. The first two conditions are clear. The third should include not only situations of negative therapeutic effect but also cases of increased dependence and unjustifiable financial expenditures of the client. The ethical code also allows for the possibility of termination being forced on the therapeutic dyad by external events. These include the death of the therapist or a change in the therapist's work status (illness, relocation, change of employment). Termination of therapy due to changes in the client's ability to engage in treatment (e.g., physical illness, relocation, etc.) is mentioned briefly but is not permitted directly. A special provision in the APA code allows therapists to terminate treatment with clients if they are threatened or otherwise endangered by either the client or a person with whom the client holds a relationship. Such a termination should be made in the way that is least harmful to the client while preserving the safety of the therapist. The APA's ethical code states that pretermination counseling is required unless the therapist is in danger or a third-party ceases to pay. Therapists should make "reasonable efforts" to ensure the client's continued treatment after death, injury, or illness of the therapist.

More extensive surveys of the termination process are available (Joyce, Piper, Ogrodniczuk, & Klein, 2007; O'Donohue & Cucciare, 2007; Salberg, 2010).

References and Readings

Curtis, R. (2002). Termination from a psychoanalytic perspective. *Journal of Psychotherapy Integration, 12*, 350–357.

Fonagy, P., & Target, M. (1996). Predictors of outcome in child psychoanalysis: A retrospective study of 763 cases at The Anna Freud Centre. *Journal of the American Psychoanalytic Association, 44*, 27–77.

Fox, R. (1993). *Elements of the helping process: A guide for clinicians*. New York: Haworth Press.

Joyce, A. S., Piper, W. E., Ogrodniczuk, J. S., & Klein, R. H. (2007). *Termination in psychotherapy: A psychodynamic model or processes and outcomes*. Washington, DC: American Psychological Association.

Mann., J. (1973). *Time-limited psychotherapy*. Cambridge, MA: Harvard University Press.

O'Donohue, W. T., & Cucciare, M. (2007). *Terminating psychotherapy: A clinician's guide*. New York: Routledge.

Salberg, J. (2010). *Good enough endings: Breaks, interruptions, and terminations from a contemporary relational perspectives*. New York: Routledge.

Tyson, P. (1996). Termination of psychoanalysis and psychotherapy. In E. Nersessian & G. K. Richard (Ed.), *Textbook of psychoanalysis* (pp. 501–524). Washington, DC: American Psychiatric Press.

Related Topic

Chapter 73, "Preventing Relapse"

56 USING HYPNOSIS TO INVITE RELAXATION

Douglas Flemons

As you have no doubt discovered during anxious or stressful times, purposefully trying to relax is like trying to fall asleep or trying to have fun. The expended effort undermines the intended goal. Any time your clients pit their conscious will against their racing thoughts or uptight bodies, trying to compel themselves to unwind or let go, they initiate a battle they can only lose. Their thoughts refuse to slow down and their bodies stay tense, leaving them feeling frustrated and defeated.

Relaxation cannot be dictated; it must be invited to develop, which is where hypnosis comes in. Bridging the chasm between mind and body, hypnosis offers your clients a wonderfully effective means to relax their efforts at relaxing, opening the possibility for nonvolitional change. In this chapter, I will provide some guidelines and illustrations for how to incorporate hypnosis into your practice, but for that discussion to make sense, I first need to talk a bit about the differences between conscious awareness and hypnotic experience.

UNDERSTANDING HYPNOSIS

In the everyday process of consciously perceiving stuff, you typically distinguish yourself as an observer, separate from what you observe. When the object of your perception lies outside of you, and particularly when it is somehow unpleasant, you tend to experience a self-other split between you and it. You insulate yourself from the annoying song blasting from the radio, the threatening clouds forming on the horizon, the rank odor emanating from the locker at the gym. But this same division between observer and observed also gets evoked when you are perceiving yourself, especially when you do not like what you are noticing, for example, the damn itch on your legs, the cold nausea that has been gripping you as tonight's speech looms ever closer, or the troubling memory that keeps popping up at inopportune times.

In everyday awareness, you often stay one step (or more) removed from your surroundings and your experience, as if there were an invisible wall erected between your "Observing-I" and the rest of the world, including the rest of *you*—your body, your thoughts, your emotions. This is the experiential source not only of alienation but also of the Cartesian mind-body split.

During hypnosis and related activities of engagement, such as meditation, prayer, reading, making love, playing sports, watching movies, and playing or listening to music, the invisible wall disperses, allowing the insular separateness of your Observing-I to dissolve. This accounts for the nonvolitional character of hypnotic experience (Flemons, 2002). As your sense of self moves from outside to inside your experience, facilitating the emergence and merging of an embodied mind and mindful body, no insular Observing-I remains to claim ownership of, or responsibility for, the arm that is levitating, the numbness that is spreading, or the warm heaviness that is increasing. As a result, these and other hypnotic phenomena seem to "just happen." Such an environment is ideal for your clients to learn how to relax without trying, without expending any conscious effort.

INVITING HYPNOSIS, INVITING RELAXATION

Over the years, clients have told me stories of other hypnotherapists they have seen who, when it came time to do hypnosis, put on their glasses and read a scripted induction, read a few scripted therapeutic stories, and read some scripted directives. Good hypnotic technique requires something quite different. Rather than focusing on a bunch of words on a page, you must be focused on your clients, attuned to, and in sync with, their experience. Of course, if you are going to work this way, you have to know what to do with your clients' responses to what you say and how you say it. Following are suggestions for how to put into practice a client-focused approach to hypnotically invited relaxation.

1. *Communicate your empathic understanding.* The best way to begin helping your clients change their relationship with themselves, facilitating a shift in their internal boundaries and the development of relaxation, is to help them change their relationship with you and their surroundings. Hypnosis does not begin when you start delivering an "induction"; it begins when your clients start trusting that you have a good handle on the intricacies of their experience. You help them relax into this trust by proving that you deserve it, by empathically communicating your understanding of the details and emotional nuances of their experience.

CLIENT: ...and by then I'm so stressed out that when it comes time to go to sleep, all I can do is lay there and replay what happened during the day, over and over.

THERAPIST: It's bad enough that you have to go through it the first time during the day, but then to have to live through it again and again, instead of drifting off to sleep: I bet you just want to scream.

CLIENT: Exactly. I do.

You know that you are connecting well with your clients when they are agreeing with your empathic statements. This is the rapport you need to move forward.

2. *Use permissive words, inviting possibilities.* Imagine walking into a bank and having the manager say, in a commanding tone, "You will open an account right now and deposit your money into it. I will count backwards from 10 to 1, and as I do, you will find yourself signing your name on these forms, and you will give me all your money: 10, 9, 8,..." You'd head straight for the door, right? Well, your clients are no different. What many therapists regard as resistance, I view as clients' healthy reluctance to go along with a course of action that, for whatever reason, does not fit for them (Flemons, 2002). My reluctance would certainly be heightened if a therapist were to start ordering me around:

THERAPIST: Now I want you to just relax as you look at me and listen to my voice. As I count backwards from 10 to 1, you will find yourself unable to look away from me, as if I were at the end of a dark tunnel and you could see nothing else. Soon that darkness will envelop you and your eyes will close all the way as you completely relax.

Yuk! Forget looking through a tunnel—I would be looking at the therapist through the office window, shaking my head as I headed back to my car. Rather than issuing directives, you will be much better off offering suggestions and possibilities, phrasing them with permissive words (O'Hanlon & Martin, 1992):

THERAPIST: I *don't know* if you'll be more comfortable closing your eyes or keeping them open. If they stay open for awhile, they *might* want to rest somewhere as I talk. You *can* listen to what I'm saying or you *can* let your mind wander; either is fine. Certainly there's *no need* to pay attention, or to try to make something happen or to try to help me out.

3. *Utilize what the surroundings and your clients offer up.* Is your office too bright or warm or cold for you to do hypnosis? Are the seats too uncomfortable? Are the walls too thin to block out the sounds of traffic, voices, phones, and plumbing? Are your clients too uptight to let go? Are they too intent on maintaining control to experience hypnosis? It makes sense that you would entertain such concerns, but if you approach hypnosis as an opportunity for utilization (Erickson, 1980), you can see each of these apparent roadblocks as possibilities for furthering hypnosis and relaxation.

THERAPIST: You can allow the sunshine streaming in through the window to shed light [utilizing the amount of light in the room to make a metaphorical statement about gaining understanding] on how you can feel so uptight, the temperature in the room helping you, perhaps, to warm you to the realization that warm light is light, that the lightness of warm air, the warmth of light air, takes it up, up, up [utilizing the too-warm room as part of a metaphorical expression ("to warm up to something") that suggests positive feelings, and to indirectly explore possibilities of developing sensations of lightness]. And I wonder just how high up, just how light, that feeling of being uptight can take you [utilizing being "uptight" as helpful in creating this movement up], like an updraft, perhaps accompanied by a developing sense, somewhere, probably not yet in your shoulders, maybe somewhere else already warming up to the possibility [again utilizing the temperature in the room] of sinking comfortably down, like water, aided by gravity, moving down through pipes [utilizing the sound of a toilet flushing], effortlessly moving along with nothing getting in the way.

No need to bother trying to help me out, as the cars and trucks out there, also rushing in their own way, speed by, and you can effortlessly follow the sound of their movement, rushing ahead of rush hour [utilizing the sound of traffic]. And what a rush it can be for it to slowly dawn on you, like the light of dawn (utilizing puns to change meanings], that the pace outside can be nicely complemented by the pace inside, that their zooming out can remind you how to more easily float in, like floating in the silence between each of the rings of the telephone. Such a relief that brief silence is [utilizing the incessant ringing of a telephone] more appreciated because of the lovely way in contrasts with the rings on either side of it, before and after it, and that voice out there answering, giving you the freedom to question [utilizing a voice answering the phone to move to the idea of questioning], going round and round, wondering what to make of hypnosis, knowing that you can question both before and after you experience it, wondering how your body is able to perfectly monitor and control your experience, just as it does when you're sleeping or otherwise occupied in some absorbing activity.

4. *Offer both-and suggestions.* If you think of contrasts—relaxed/tense; slow/fast; up/down—as exclusive opposites, you will assume that securing the desirable side of any distinction requires the elimination of the other. But if you treat contrasts as compatible and mutually important, as I did in the earlier example, then one side of a contrast can coexist with, or be the conduit to, the other. Rather than lecturing my clients about this, I tell stories or vignettes that allow them to vicariously experience the ideas. For example, if a client's thoughts are racing, I might offer a vignette or story that acknowledges the restless speed of the client's thinking as an ideal means for potentiating its complement:

THERAPIST: Wolves protect themselves by continually patrolling the perimeter of their territory, but if all of the wolves in a pack were to patrol all the time, none of them would get any rest. So they take turns. Part of the pack keeps moving, always moving, along the edge of their territory, making sure everything is safe and secure, while the rest are able, in the center, to rest deeply, relaxing and sleeping. Why not allow part of you to continue patrolling the perimeter of your awareness, ensuring that everything is safe and secure, while the rest of you rests deeply and comfortably?

A both-and approach to offering suggestions helps you not presume that quiet, calm thoughts are a necessary precursor for hypnosis, and it helps clients not to have to try to slow down their thinking or breathing. Hypnosis makes it unnecessary for them to be at odds with themselves. Here are some more both-and contrasts I sometimes offer, allowing clients to experience something new without having to first not experience something else. Notice how the juxtaposition of stories creates a both-and relationship among my descriptions.

THERAPIST: Isn't it fascinating how you can be zipping along in a car at 80 mph and yet feel like you're going 20? How is it that something so fast can feel so slow? Your thoughts can race on ahead or alongside or just behind me. I have a friend who, when we walk together, is always a half-step in front of me, and another, a former competitive ski racer, who always skis a half a breath in front of himself, staying on the leading edge of himself, effortlessly careening down the mountain, taking all the time he needs to ever…so slowly…carve…each screeching turn.

5. *Bring forth small shifts, rather than dramatic transformations.* I grew up in Canada, where I gained a lot of experience freeing cars from snow banks. When a vehicle is stranded, you rock it forward and back, while the driver alternates between hitting the gas and engaging the clutch. The goal is not instantaneous liberation but a process of ever-increasing trajectories of change.

You will enjoy greater success if you adopt the same attitude in helping clients. For example, instead of directly trying to get their shoulders to relax, help them discover that one of their fingers feels a little numb. A small change in sensation there can be the first step to an ever-so-slightly bigger change somewhere else, resulting, after awhile, in the shoulders letting go of their tension.

6. *Offer interactive relaxation (via weird body conversations).* Many hypnotherapists offer their clients some form of progressive (sometimes called Jacobson) relaxation, which involves purposefully contracting and then releasing different muscle groups for 10 or 15 seconds at a time. Other clinicians combine this with deep breathing techniques, timing exhalations with the releasing of tension. Still others offer guided imagery, taking clients to a vividly described beach or alpine meadow, or some other potentially relaxing setting, offering suggestions for enjoying the surroundings and relaxing into the experience.

Although these can all prove helpful, I, for the reasons I outlined earlier, invariably take a less directive path. I ask clients to find a place in their body that feels especially tense, and I get them to describe the sensations there with as much detail as possible. I then have them go in search of a relaxed place—some part of them that is comfortable or numb or so relaxed that they have not even noticed it for a while—and ask what they are able to describe about it, too. Then I provide a rationale for why it would make sense for the two areas to get into a kind of developing "conversation," each one sharing some important information with the other. As we proceed, I frequently check in on what is changing and then fold that into what I say next.

THERAPIST: Okay, so you feel the tension most in your shoulders, like a sharp, radiating ache?

CLIENT: Yes.

THERAPIST: And your right thigh feels warm and comfortable—almost asleep.

CLIENT: Pretty much, yeah.

THERAPIST: Great. You know, just as your lungs and heart work together to deliver oxygen to the cells throughout your body, they also coordinate with each other in the extraction and transportation of carbon dioxide from your body into the atmosphere. At a smaller level, the various cells of your immune system communicate with each other about intruders and, based on this shared information, they coordinate an appropriate response. So your body knows a lot about how to communicate within and between organs and systems, and it does this without your having to consciously understand how it happens.

So as you sit there and listen to me, why shouldn't your shoulders get into a body conversation with your right thigh? You can listen to me or think about whatever comes to mind, confident that your shoulders and your thigh can communicate in a way that you and I could never understand. But as your thigh keys into the sharp radiating tension there in your shoulders, it might learn something about how to allow sensations to radiate outward. If pain can radiate, why not comfort? I don't know how the muscles there in your thigh have figured out so brilliantly how to become so easily warm and loose, but your shoulders might as well get in on the secret. Let's let them get into a body conversation of sorts while you tell me what you're noticing.

7. *Practice extemporaneous collaboration.* Just as it is useful to encourage different parts of your clients' bodies to get into conversation with each other, it is vitally important for you to stay in touch with your clients as you help them develop their hypnotic ability. Watching their nonverbal responses to your suggestions will keep you partially apprised of what they are currently experiencing, but if you can get them to tell you in words, do it. Then base your next suggestion on the information you have just received.

THERAPIST: What's happening now?

CLIENT: My right hand is warm and soft, but my shoulders are still tight.

THERAPIST: Great. Your right hand was first off the mark in adopting some important understanding from your thigh. And we didn't even know it was listening! So now I don't know if your thigh will continue to help your hand develop that sensation while it engages in contact with your shoulders or whether your hand will serve as an intermediary of some sort. Could be that your hand passes along the information to your shoulders, maybe directly, or maybe by way of some other body part.... Let's let things continue, and let's see if your shoulders get in on the action at this point, or if some other part will first.

8. *Teach self-hypnosis and self-reliance.* The hypnosis sessions you offer in your office may be all your clients require to change how they have been orienting to the stresses in their lives. Nevertheless, by teaching them how to do self-hypnosis, you will give them the skill to invite relaxation on their own. I suggest to clients that since all hypnosis is, in a way, self-hypnosis, they, having already experienced it in my office, know almost everything they need to know in order to practice on their own.

THERAPIST: Find a comfortable place to sit or lie down at home, in your office, or wherever, and begin by noticing external and then more and more internal things or events that grab your attention, sounds and sights before and after you close your eyes; the sound and feel of your breathing; sensations on your skin; thoughts and feelings; smells or tastes; and so on. Devote one breath to each thing you notice, silently naming it in time with your exhalations: "The dog barking…birds chirping…jaw tense…the kids arguing downstairs…tight shoulders…the fan clicking…left hand heavy…waves of color…" The more you practice, the easier it will be for you to invite yourself into hypnosis, not needing to try to make anything happen, not needing to try to relax.

If clients attempt to give themselves suggestions in the midst of self-hypnosis, they will reinvoke the split between the Observing-I (a.k.a. the Bossing-Around-I) and the rest of the self, and the hypnotic experience will be interrupted. To help them avoid this problem, I suggest, passing along an idea of Milton Erickson's, that they begin each self-hypnosis time by posing a question to themselves—for example, "I wonder how my body will find its way into relaxation?"—and then let that wondering hover around them as they proceed with noticing their experience.

9. *Trust yourself.* If you are just getting started with hypnosis, you might feel inclined, despite my earlier cautions, to use some of my examples as scripts for use with your clients. I suggest instead that you study them closely for the logic informing them, explore diverse examples of other hypnotic work, and then work interactively and extemporaneously with your clients as you develop your own style.

10. *Get training.* Check with your state licensing board to find out whether you must obtain approved training in hypnosis prior to employing it in your practice. Even if there is no regulation to this effect in place, I highly recommend getting hands-on experience and supervision so you can keep your hypnotic work within the boundaries of your clinical knowledge and competence. Workshops are regularly offered by several professional organizations, including the American Society of Clinical Hypnosis, the Society for Clinical and Experimental Hypnosis, and the Milton H. Erickson Foundation (see below for Web site URLs), and some offer certification. Your state licensing board may also have a list of approved workshop providers in your area.

References and Readings

American Society of Clinical Hypnosis. (n.d.). Retrieved January 2013, from www.asch.net

Erickson, M. H. (1980). Further clinical techniques of hypnosis: Utilization techniques. In E. L. Rossi (Ed.), *The collected papers of Milton H. Erickson* (Vol. 1, pp. 177–205). New York: Irvington.

Flemons, D. (2002). *Of one mind.* New York: W. W. Norton.

Flemons, D. (n.d). Hypnosis and hypnotherapy. Retrieved 2013 from contextconsultants.com/clinicians-hypnosis-hypnotherapy

Lynn, S. J., Rhue, J. W., & Kirsch, I. (Eds.). (2010). *Handbook of clinical hypnosis* (2nd ed.). Washington, DC: American Psychological Association.

Milton H. Erickson Foundation. (n.d.). Retrieved January 2013, from www.erickson-foundation.org

O'Hanlon, W. H., & Martin, M. (1992). *Solution-oriented hypnosis: An Ericksonian approach.* New York: W. W. Norton.

Society for Clinical and Experimental Hypnosis. (n.d.). Home page. Retrieved 2011 from www.sceh.ush

Whalley, M. (n.d.). *Hypnosis and suggestion: Exploring the science behind hypnosis.* Retrieved 2011 from www.hypnosisandsuggestion.org

Related Topic

Chapter 31, "Compendium of Empirically Supported Treatments"

57 WORKING WITH THE RELIGIOUSLY COMMITTED CLIENT

P. Scott Richards

Large numbers of people believe in and are devoutly committed to their faith. For example, Gallup polls have consistently found that more than 90% of Americans profess belief in God and approximately 60% are members of a church. In light of these statistics, it is evident that most psychotherapists will work with religiously committed clients during their careers. But if they are not adequately prepared, psychotherapists may find it particularly challenging to work effectively with them.

There is evidence that religiously committed people from diverse traditions, including many Buddhists, Christians, Jews, Muslims, and Hindus, have unfavorable views of the mainstream, secular mental health professions and a distrust of psychotherapy (Richards & Bergin, 2000). These fears are rooted in an awareness of the reality that many psychologists during the past century have endorsed anti-religious, hedonistic, and atheistic values that conflict with those of traditional religious communities (Bergin, 1980).

Psychotherapists can increase their competency to work with religiously committed clients by reading books on the psychology and sociology of religion; canvassing literature about religion and spirituality in mainstream mental health journals; taking a workshop or class on religion and mental health and spiritual issues in psychotherapy; reading books or taking a class on world religions; acquiring specialized knowledge about religious traditions that they frequently encounter in therapy; seeking supervision or consultation from colleagues when they first work with a client from a particular religious tradition; and seeking supervision or consultation when they first begin using religious and spiritual interventions (Richards & Bergin, 2000).

Accommodating clients' religious and spiritual beliefs into psychotherapy and adapting treatment to those beliefs have been shown to enhance the efficacy and acceptability of mental health treatment (e.g., Worthington, Hook, Davis, McDaniel, 2011). Following are a series of therapeutic guidelines, culled from both the research evidence and clinical experience, designed to do just that.

THERAPEUTIC GUIDELINES

- *Develop multicultural spiritual sensitivity.* Psychotherapists with good multicultural skills are aware of their own religious and spiritual heritage and are sensitive to how they could impact their work with clients from different religious and spiritual traditions. They are capable of communicating interest, understanding, and respect to clients who have spiritual beliefs that differ from their own. They seek to learn more about the spiritual beliefs and cultures of clients with whom they work. They make efforts to establish trusting relationships with members and leaders in their clients' religious communities and seek to draw upon these sources of social support when it seems appropriate. They use spiritual resources and interventions in harmony with their clients' beliefs when it appears that these could help their clients cope and change (Richards & Bergin, 2000).

- *Select a spiritually oriented treatment.* Psychotherapists may wish to select a spiritually oriented treatment consistent with their own worldview and values to help guide their work with religiously committed clients. A large number of spiritually oriented therapies have been developed during the past couple of decades that affirm the importance of spirituality in therapeutic change. Buddhist, Hindu, Christian, Jewish, Muslim, and ecumenical theistic approaches have been proposed. Some scholars have also incorporated spiritual perspectives and interventions into cognitive, interpersonal, humanistic, multicultural, psychodynamic, and transpersonal psychologies (Richards & Bergin, 2000; Sperry & Shafranske, 2005). There is growing empirical evidence that with religiously committed clients, spiritually oriented psychotherapies are as effective, and sometimes more effective, than secular treatments (Richards & Worthington, 2010).
- *Prepare spiritually for psychotherapy sessions.* Psychotherapists incorporating spirituality into treatment may find they are more effective if they engage in personal spiritual preparation. Several research studies provide evidence that some psychotherapists prepare spiritually for sessions by praying, meditating, contemplating, or by engaging in other spiritual practices consistent with their beliefs that help them to be spiritually attuned.
- *Establish a spiritually safe environment.* Psychotherapists should explicitly let their clients know it is permissible to explore religious and spiritual topics should they so desire, and that their religious beliefs will not a priori be viewed as pathological. Therapists can do this in the written informed consent documents they give clients at the beginning of treatment and/or they can do so verbally during the course of therapy.
- *Respect other values and worldviews.* Psychotherapists should deal with religious differences and value conflicts with clients in a respectful and tolerant manner. Differences in religious affiliation and disagreements about specific religious doctrines or moral behaviors can threaten the therapeutic alliance if they are disclosed prematurely or addressed inappropriately. When such value conflicts become salient during therapy, it is important for therapists to openly acknowledge their values, while also explicitly affirming clients' rights to differ from them without having their intelligence or morality questioned. Psychotherapists should also openly discuss with clients whether the belief or value conflict is so threatening that referral is advisable.
- *Conduct a spiritual assessment.* Psychotherapists can include questions about clients' religious and spiritual backgrounds on an intake questionnaire. During the initial phase of the assessment process, therapists may wish to collect only information that will help them understand whether their clients' religious background may be relevant to their presenting problems and treatment planning (Richards & Bergin, 2005). Asking the following questions may help in making such a determination: (a) Is the client willing to discuss religious and spiritual topics during treatment? If not, this must be respected, although the issue may be returned to if new information warrants it. (b) What is the client's current religious-spiritual affiliation, if any? How important is this affiliation to the client? (c) How orthodox and devout is the client? (d) Does the client believe his or her spiritual beliefs and lifestyle are contributing to his or her presenting problems and concerns in any way? (e) Does the client have any religious and spiritual concerns and needs? (f) Is the client willing to participate in spiritual interventions if it appears that they may be helpful? (g) Does the client perceive that his or her religious and spiritual beliefs and/or community are a

potential source of strength and assistance? If it seems relevant, more in-depth spiritual assessment questions can then be pursued. Gathering information and seeking clarifications about clients' spirituality may be needed throughout the course of treatment.

- *Learn the language of clients' spirituality.* As psychotherapists conduct a religious and spiritual assessment, they can begin to understand a client's language of spirituality (Berrett, Hardman, & Richards, 2010). There are a number of spiritual themes that seem to be universal in the human family that can help clinicians and clients find common ground for understanding one another's spiritual language. These themes include love, faith, suffering, death and loss, meaning and purpose, responsibility, repentance, forgiveness, gratitude, belonging, congruence, honesty, family, community, enlightenment, transcendence, and the quest for a relationship with a higher power or Creator. These can be talked about and can help expand psychotherapists' understanding of their clients' spirituality as well as clients' understanding of their own spirituality.
- *Set appropriate spiritual therapy goals.* Spiritual goals that may be appropriate for psychotherapy, depending on the clients' unique concerns: (a) examine and better understand what impact clients' spiritual beliefs exert on their presenting problems and their lives; (b) identify and use the spiritual resources in clients' lives to assist them in their efforts to heal and change; (c) examine and resolve spiritual concerns that are pertinent to clients' disorders; and (d) examine how clients feel about their spiritual well-being and, if they desire, help them determine how they can continue their quest for spiritual growth (Richards & Bergin, 2005).
- *Create a space for spiritual awareness and experiences.* Psychotherapists can create an environment that gives clients the opportunity to recognize and affirm spiritual insights, impressions, and experiences (Griffith & Griffith, 2002; Richards & Bergin, 2005), that occur both within and outside of the therapy hour.
- *Appropriately use spiritual resources and interventions.* Religious and spiritual practices can both prevent problems and promote healing where problems have occurred. Examples of spiritual interventions include praying for clients, encouraging clients to pray, discussing theological concepts, making reference to scriptures, using spiritual relaxation and imagery techniques, encouraging repentance and forgiveness, helping clients live congruently with their spiritual values, self-disclosing spiritual beliefs or experiences, consulting with religious leaders, and recommending spiritual bibliotherapy (Plante, 2009; Richards & Bergin, 2005). Most of these spiritual interventions are actually practices that have been engaged in for centuries by religious believers.
- *Consult with clergy and other pastoral professionals.* Clergy and other pastoral professionals, such as clinical chaplains and pastoral counselors, can often be of assistance in helping clients more fully access the financial, social, and spiritual resources of their religious communities during treatment. Collaborative relationships can also help psychologists keep their role boundaries clear so that they do not engage in ecclesiastical functions that are more appropriately performed by clergy (Richards & Bergin, 2005). Clients can be asked if they would like to sign a release and provide contact information for their clergy person so that their psychologist can consult or refer if indicated.

References and Readings

Bergin, A. E. (1980). Psychotherapy and religious values. *Journal of Consulting and Clinical Psychology, 48,* 75–105.

Berrett, M. E ., Hardman, R. K., & Richards, P. S. (2010). The role of spirituality in eating disorder treatment and recovery. In M. Maine, B. H. McGilley, & D. W. Bunnell (Eds.), *Special issues in the treatment of eating disorders* (pp. 367–385). Burlington, MA: Elsevier.

Griffith, J. L., & Griffith, M. E. (2002). *Encountering the sacred in psychotherapy: How to talk with people about their spiritual lives.* New York: Guilford Press.

Plante, T. G. (2009). *Spiritual practices in psychotherapy: Thirteen tools for enhancing psychological health*. Washington, DC: American Psychological Association.

Richards, P. S., & Bergin, A. E. (Eds.). (2000). *Handbook of psychotherapy and religious diversity*. Washington, DC: American Psychological Association.

Richards, P. S., & Bergin, A. E. (2005). *A spiritual strategy for counseling and psychotherapy* (2nd ed.). Washington, DC: American Psychological Association.

Richards, P. S., & Worthington, E. L., Jr. (2010). The need for evidence-based, spiritually oriented psychotherapies. *Professional Psychology: Research and Practice, 41*, 363–370.

Sperry, L., & Shafranske, E. P. (Eds.). (2005). *Spiritually oriented psychotherapy*. Washington, DC: American Psychological Association.

Worthington, E. L., Jr., Hook, J. N., Davis, D. E., & McDaniel, M. A. (2011). Religion and spirituality. In J. C. Norcross (Ed.), *Psychotherapy relationships that work* (2nd ed., pp. 402–421). New York: Oxford University Press.

58 PRACTICING PSYCHOTHERAPY WITH ADULTS WHO HAVE COGNITIVE IMPAIRMENTS

Kathleen B. Kortte

Psychotherapy is a dynamic process that is facilitated by full engagement of the individual who sought out or was referred for psychotherapeutic services. However, full engagement could be hindered for individuals who have compromised cognitive functioning secondary to any number of neuropathologies or developmental or aging processes. Modification of the therapeutic process can ensure that these individuals are afforded the opportunity to fully benefit from such services despite the presence of more limited cognitive resources. Additionally, quite frequently these individuals experience distress characterized by anxiety and frustration, as well as other emotions and feelings of inadequacy related to the impairments in their abilities and functioning and the impact on their daily life. Thus, the individual may present to services with issues related to loss, changes in sense of self, learned dependency, and other such topics. By adapting the psychotherapeutic process and being mindful of some of the main presenting issues, the therapeutic relationship and process can be facilitated and be quite effective for helping an individual with cognitive impairments to improve his or her daily life functioning.

THERAPEUTIC ENGAGEMENT

An essential variable in most types of interventions is *engagement* of the individual in the process, and psychotherapeutic interventions are no different. As proposed by Lequerica and Kortte (2010), engagement occurs through effortful involvement in a task or process in which the level of engagement can be influenced by aspects of the person and/or by the environment. In general, the person by environmental factors that contribute to engagement are the same in all therapeutic relationships; however, attention to these factors when working with individuals with cognitive impairments will enhance true engagement in the process and enhance the potential for successful outcomes in this population specifically. Without full engagement, the individual may attend the therapy session without truly investing in the process and thus benefitting from it.

Therapeutic engagement is a multifaceted construct that has been hypothesized to include the perceived need for treatment, perceived self-efficacy for making change occur, expectancies for a successful outcome from treatment, and willingness to attend the appointments (i.e., showing up; Lequerica & Kortte, 2010). Part of the psychotherapeutic process initially should be to partner with the individual to understand his or her thoughts and beliefs about his or her needs for intervention and attitudes toward therapy and the ability to make changes. Exploring these thoughts and beliefs will assist the psychotherapist in tailoring interventions to assist the individual in understanding the need for interventions and enhancing his or her perceptions about being able to make positive behavioral changes and reach goals. Through this process, the individual is more likely to show up and engage in discussion and skill development to address the key issues.

STRUCTURING AND ACCOMMODATING IN THE THERAPEUTIC ENVIRONMENT

Conscious attention to the therapeutic environment can facilitate maximal engagement through structural modifications that will accommodate the needs of individuals with cognitive impairments. Given that psychotherapy is bound in communication between an individual and a psychotherapist, the therapeutic environment must support effective communication. Additionally, psychotherapy is geared toward helping the individual with cognitive impairments understand and cope with reality (Prigatano, 1999), and thus the cognitive domains of attention, memory, and executive functioning are foundational. For some individuals, their ability to communicate, process information, and incorporate past learning has been hindered by cognitive impairments. These disabilities do not mean that these individuals cannot benefit from psychotherapy; rather, it means that the environment and process needs to be modified to accommodate so they can engage fully. Outlined in Table 58.1 are recommendations for modifying the typical structure of the physical environment and session format to facilitate engagement of the individual. These modifications can reduce the impact of distractibility, fatigue, and poor memory encoding, which are all common cognitive impairments. In addition, simple accommodations built into the therapeutic process will assist the individual in carrying-over information from session to session, following through on "homework" assignments, comprehending and communicating more complex ideas, and adopting new skills. See Table 58.2 for recommendations for accommodating for cognitive impairments in the therapeutic environment. The overarching goal of these accommodations is to reduce the processing the brain on its own has to do (e.g., recalling, conceptualizing, visualizing) by providing the information in a written or visual form. For an in-depth discussion of adapting the psychotherapy process and environment to work with individuals with cognitive impairments, see Langer, Laatsch, and Lewis (1999) and Lawton and

TABLE 58.1. Structuring the Therapeutic Environment

- Ensuring environment has low stimulation (low light, low background noise)
- Minimizing visual and auditory distractions in therapy room
- Meeting the individual more frequently and/or for shorter therapy sessions
- Holding sessions at the individual's best time of day (i.e., best energy level)
- Promoting consistency by meeting at the same time of day, the same time each week, and by having a set structure to the therapeutic sessions
- Planning for longer duration of treatment given the potential for a slower learning curve

TABLE 58.2. Accommodating in the Therapeutic Environment

- Taking written notes either by or for the individual
- Using visual aids to communicate points (e.g., drawings, pictures, diagrams, checklists)
- Using rating or scaling techniques to anchor changes in subjective experiences
- Using session agendas created by the individual based upon his or her goals to structure session discussion
- Allowing for audio- or videotaping of sessions so that the individual can review material at home
- For individuals with communication impairments, allowing for the use of communication boards and electronic equipment so that the individual can communicate more easily
- Using role-playing to reinforce use of new coping and behavioral skills
- Using nontechnical terms and avoiding clinical jargon will reduce the chance for confusion
- Using multimodal learning approaches so that the individual has exposure to information in multiple ways (i.e., hear it, say it, write it, read it, use/apply it)
- Summarizing main points throughout the session will facilitate learning
- Ending all sessions with a verbal summary of what was learned and what are next steps (individual summarizes and psychotherapist acknowledges and modifies as needed)

Rubinstein (2000); and for greater discussion on how to facilitate learning in a therapeutic environment for individuals with cognitive impairments (or actually for everyone!), see Sohlberg and Turkstra (2011).

CLINICAL FOCUS FOR INTERVENTIONS

The focus of psychotherapy with individuals with cognitive impairments depends on many factors, including, etiology, age at onset, constellation and extent of impairments, and the level of impact of the neurobehavioral and cognitive impairments on functioning. A central feature of psychotherapy that cuts across diagnostic groups is the development of a therapeutic alliance (Prigatano, 1999). Because many individuals with cognitive impairments are referred by others, including family members, community agencies, or medical professionals, the individual may have a limited appreciation of the reason for psychotherapy. As noted earlier, one of the key elements to facilitate engagement is the individual believing that intervention is needed. Development of a strong therapeutic relationship will allow the psychotherapist to explore the need for intervention services with the individual regardless of the initial source of the referral. Matching to the individual's treatment needs and his or her priorities or goals will help to maximize engagement in the therapeutic process. Initial goals focus on developing the collaborative relationship necessary to improve awareness of self and behavior. The alliance and the contextual information specific to the individual's brain functioning provides the basis for tailoring psychotherapy to guide the person's behavior and adjustment to life.

One of the most challenging aspects of working with individuals with cognitive impairments is the potential for limited awareness of the changes in their cognitive and behavioral functioning. However, to some extent this is a matter of degree because awareness of oneself and monitoring of our own behavior is a challenge for every human being. Individuals with cognitive impairment have the potential of having greater challenges in being psychologically minded, monitoring their own behavior, learning from past mistakes, and recognizing areas of weakness or deficit secondary to their neurologic dysfunction. One goal of the therapeutic process is to facilitate the individual's understanding of maladaptive, ineffective, or inefficient behaviors that he or she may not even be aware of as problematic. Given that it is difficult to tease out whether the ineffective behaviors are new or have always been part of the individual's behavior repertoire, the psychotherapist is encouraged to consider the person as he or she presents for interventions and explore how that individual can maximize life functioning by capitalizing on strengths and minimizing or compensating for weaknesses rather than worry about the etiology of the problems per se. The goal for interventions is for the individual to improve his or her understanding of his or her own functioning and learn skills for engaging in life appropriately and effectively. For a summary discussion of impaired awareness with a suggested theoretical model, see Toglia and Kirk (2000).

In addition to impaired awareness, presenting issues of loss, poor self-esteem, reduced feelings of personal control, and issues of learned dependency are quite common for individuals with cognitive impairments. Creating a safe, nonthreatening, accepting, and trusting environment is critical to decrease anxiety and facilitate discussion of very sensitive topics. Psychotherapeutic approaches focus on goals of providing an environment for emotional outlet, enhancement of self-esteem and role functioning, minimizing psychological and behavior problems, and increasing coping skills (see Langer, Laatsch, & Lewis, 1999; Lawton & Rubinstein, 2000). Quite frequently family/caregivers are integrated into the therapeutic process to ensure that they are provided with guidance on how to appropriately support their loved one emotionally as well as functionally with daily life task completion as needed (Lawton & Rubinstein, 2000; Prigatano, 1999). There is a strong need to develop a shared understanding between the family and the individual with cognitive impairment about situations in which assistance is needed and when assistance hinders personal growth, feelings of self-sufficiency and self-esteem, and positive feelings for the relationship. As stated by Prigatano (1999), the goal of psychotherapy is to teach individuals to learn to behave in their own best interests, not selfish interests, and this goal applies just as well to family members. By encouraging everyone to partner together with the ultimate goal of improving life engagement, the engagement of the individual with cognitive impairments as well as the family members is enhanced. This process is, of course, delicate because quite often family members have so strongly adopted the caregiving role that they have difficulty recognizing how they can get their own needs met without feeling that they are neglecting the needs of their loved one. However, if each person learns the skills to enhance his or her own well-being, then the burden of care is reduced and the feeling of mutual appreciation enhanced.

GROUP PSYCHOTHERAPY

Structured group interventions can provide another avenue for facilitating adaptive change in individuals with cognitive impairments. Given the social and emotional aspects of cognitive impairments, there are abundant opportunities for the individual to benefit from the interactions with peers within the safe and structured setting. Group psychotherapy provides opportunities for receiving feedback for self-evaluation, sharing of compensatory strategies for cognitive and social skill deficits, comparison of strengths and limitations, and facilitating interpersonal dynamics of feeling helpful to and accepted by others (Langer et al., 1999). Typically this modality of treatment when used with individuals with cognitive impairments is focused on rebuilding basic social skills (e.g., eye voice volume, listening skills, and body language) and providing practice for managing emotional reactions through structured activities (e.g., modeling, role playing, and educational presentations). The goals parallel those of individual treatment modalities for this population, including improving emotional stability, social interaction skills, problem-solving skills, self-monitoring, self-acceptance, and awareness.

METATHERAPEUTIC FACTORS

When the psychotherapist has more limited experience in working with persons with disability, there are some additional issues to consider when undertaking psychotherapy with individuals with cognitive impairments. The therapist must guard against the bias that individuals with cognitive impairments are permanently disabled and will not benefit from psychotherapy because behavior change is not possible. It is well demonstrated that individuals with these deficits may benefit from psychotherapy and behavior change techniques to improve psychosocial function. And there are no data or rationale that the nonspecific factors of the psychotherapeutic relationship are any different or less important for achieving positive outcomes.

The psychotherapist should also be mindful of personal biases and assumptions in order to better avoid subscribing to a moral or medical model of disability. Such a model may bias the psychotherapist toward viewing persons with impairments as innately disabled or as individuals with shameful conditions, leading the psychotherapist to assume a paternalistic role (Olkin, 1999). Whereas adopting a more social or minority model, in which the disability is viewed as occurring at the interface of the person and his or her environment, may encourage the psychotherapist to be aware of the strengths and abilities of the individual and to focus on the individual's interpersonal and physical environment as key targets for intervention (Olkin, 1999).

After extensive experience with individuals with impairments in cognitive functioning, Prigatano (1999) proposed that "psychotherapy is about achieving a greater understanding of one's self and one's behavior" (p. 205). Through greater personal understanding and growth, an individual can learn to value and capitalize on his or her strengths and compensate and/or adapt to weaknesses. The psychotherapeutic process can facilitate the individual understanding the reasons that problems arise in his or her life and how to cope, adjust, adapt, and/or compensate. These are the overarching goals of psychotherapy regardless of the nature of the individual's cognitive functioning. Psychotherapy can be very helpful for individuals with cognitive impairments and, thus, psychotherapists can facilitate their engagement by appropriately structuring the therapeutic environment and process so that everyone can benefit.

References and Readings

Langer, K. G., Laatsch, L., & Lewis, L. (Eds.). (1999). Psychotherapeutic interventions for adults with brain injury or stroke: A clinician's treatment resource. Madison, CT: International Universities Press.

Lawton, M. P., & Rubinstein, R. L. (Eds.). (2000). *Interventions in dementia care: Toward improving quality of life*. New York: Springer.

Lequerica A. H., & Kortte, K. B. (2010). Therapeutic engagement: A proposed model of engagement in medical rehabilitation. *American Journal of Physical Medicine and Rehabilitation, 89*(5), 415–422.

Olkin, R. (1999). *What psychotherapists should know about disability*. New York: Guilford Press.

Prigatano, G. P. (1999). *Principles of neuropsychological rehabilitation*. New York: Oxford University Press.

Rusin, M. J., & Uomoto, J. M. (2010). Psychotherapeutic Interventions. In R. G. Frank, M. Rosenthal, & B. Caplan (Eds.), *Handbook of rehabilitation psychology* (pp. 359–371). Washington, DC: American Psychological Association.

Sohlberg, M. M., & Turkstra, L. S. (2011). The learning Context: Beyond Practice. In M. M. Sohlberg & L. S. Turkstra (Eds.), *Optimizing cognitive rehabilitation* (pp. 49–64). New York: Guilford Press.

Toglia, J., & Kirk, U. (2000). Understanding awareness deficits following brain injury. *NeuroRehabilitation, 15*, 57–70.

Related Topics

Chapter 12, "Evaluating Dementia"
Chapter 17, "Adult Neuropsychological Assessment"
Chapter 19, "Assessment and Intervention for Executive Dysfunction"
Chapter 20, "Assessing and Managing Concussion"

59 SELECTING A TREATMENT FORMAT

Larry B. Feldman

Psychotherapy begins with engagement, assessment, and treatment planning. A critical part of this process is the therapist's recommendation of a treatment format—individual, couple/family, group, or a combination of two or more of these formats. Selecting the right treatment format(s) can make a significant difference in the outcome of therapy. The format is the context in which treatment takes place; the right format facilitates the work, whereas the wrong format can derail the therapeutic process. In order to make an informed recommendation, the therapist needs to have a clear understanding of:

- The strengths and limitations of each format
- The benefits and potential complications of combining two or more formats
- The likelihood that a particular format would provide the most effective treatment for the particular problems being presented by this/these particular individual(s)
- The goals of therapy
- Patient preferences and resistances
- Efficiency of treatment
- New information that emerges as therapy progresses that suggests a need for changing the treatment format or adding an additional format

STRENGTHS AND LIMITATIONS OF THE FORMATS

Individual therapy provides a particularly valuable context for assessing cognitive and emotional problems and strengths, for establishing a one-to-one therapeutic alliance, and for promoting cognitive and emotional change. Couple and family therapy provide particularly valuable contexts for assessing couple and family interactional problems and strengths, for establishing a therapeutic alliance with couples and families, and for promoting couple and family interactional change. Group therapy provides a particularly valuable context for assessing individual behavior in a group context, for allowing patients to establish a therapeutic alliance not only with the therapist but also with a group of peers, and for promoting change processes facilitated by positive group interactions.

The limitations of each format reflect the strengths of the others. In individual therapy, the therapist cannot benefit from family members' observations of the patient's behavior outside of treatment, cannot directly observe the patient's interactions with family or group members, cannot establish an alliance with others who could potentially promote (or impede) positive change, and cannot directly facilitate interactional changes between the patient and family or group members. In couple/family and group therapy, the therapist cannot observe the patient outside of the context of the family or group, cannot establish an exclusively one-to-one therapeutic alliance, and cannot focus his or her attention exclusively on promoting individual change.

BENEFITS AND COMPLICATIONS OF COMBINING FORMATS

In some instances, a single format is sufficient to achieve the therapeutic objectives. In other instances, a combination of two or more formats is more likely to produce the desired results. When multiple formats are utilized, treatment in each format may either be conducted by different therapists or by the same therapist. Each approach has advantages and disadvantages (Feldman & Feldman, 2005). When two or more therapists are involved, good communication and collaboration between the different therapists is essential.

The major benefits of combining two or more formats are that the strengths of each can be utilized to promote therapeutic change and that the limitations of each can be countered by the strengths of the other(s).

Different treatment formats can be combined in either a concurrent or sequential structure. In a concurrent structure, therapy in each format may take place at the same time (e.g., individual therapy conducted by one therapist, group or family therapy conducted by another therapist) or, especially if one therapist is conducting therapy in both formats, they may alternate with each other (e.g., one or more individual sessions alternating with one or more family or group sessions). In a sequential structure, therapy is conducted in one format for a period of time, followed by therapy in another format (e.g., individual therapy for 3 months followed by group therapy for 3 months).

The major potential complications of a combined approach are that confidentiality can sometimes be difficult to manage and that the work in one format can sometimes complicate the work in the other(s). Careful attention to the process of establishing and maintaining a therapeutic structure can increase the benefits and diminish the potential complications of combining therapeutic formats (Feldman & Feldman, 2005).

PRESENTING PROBLEMS AND PROBLEM SEVERITY

When the presenting problems focus on a child or adolescent, family therapy is indicated, either alone or in combination with individual or group therapy. When couple dysfunction (conflict, lack of intimacy, etc.) is the initial complaint, couple therapy, alone or combined with individual or group therapy, should be part of the treatment plan. When the presenting problems are individually focused symptoms in an adult (e.g., anxiety, depression, addiction), individual therapy is indicated, either as the sole treatment or in combination with couple or group therapy. When the presenting problems are individual or interactional symptoms in a child, adolescent, or adult that have been shown to benefit from group therapy (e.g., eating disorders, alcohol or drug abuse, anger management), this format is indicated, either alone or in combination with individual or couple/family treatment. Table 59.1 summarizes many of these and subsequent selection criteria.

Some examples of problems that are likely to benefit from a combination of treatment formats include the following:

- Agoraphobia, which is often most effectively treated with a combination of individual and couple therapy

TABLE 59.1. Selection Criteria for Format: Individual, Couple/Family, and Group

Individual	Couple/Family	Group
1. Symptomatic adult 2. Symptomatic child or adolescent	1. Symptomatic child or adolescent 2. Relationship problems are presented as such 3. Adult symptoms are predominantly within the couple/family situation	1. Patient's problems are interpersonal, both outside and inside family situations. 2. Patient presents with problems that fit the focus of specialized groups (e.g., eating disorders, alcohol or drug abuse, anger management)

- Borderline personality disorder, which is often most effectively treated with a combination of individual and group therapy
- Alcohol addiction, which is often best treated with a combination of individual, couple, and group treatment

The *Diagnostic and Statistical Manual of Mental Disorders* (*DSM*) Axis V diagnosis, or General Assessment of Functioning (GAF), may be of particular importance in choosing a treatment format. Independent of the particular Axis I (and Axis II) diagnosis, the relative level of the GAF score may relate to the nature and process of differential treatment planning. In several contexts it has been suggested that relatively healthy individuals (those with GAF scores roughly between 100 and 70) are most likely to respond to most formats of therapeutic intervention. At the other end of the spectrum, those patients with severe and chronic difficulties (with GAF scores of roughly 30 to 0) may improve relatively little from most interventions without the assistance of significant others. This suggests that a couple/family and/or group format of treatment, either alone or in combination with individual therapy, would provide the most effective therapeutic intervention for patients with more severe and chronic problems.

The areas of problem expression provide important guidelines for the selection of a treatment format(s). In planning treatment, the therapist needs to assess the context(s) in which the presenting problems occur. For example, is the presenting problem hostility in a 43-year-old male who has this problem with his wife but not in social and work situations? Or, alternately, is he hostile in multiple environments in his life? In the former situation, couple therapy is indicated, either alone or in combination with individual therapy. In the latter situation, individual therapy is indicated, and couple and/or group therapy might be considered as additional possibilities.

GOALS OF THERAPY

The ultimate goals of therapy are alleviation of the presenting problems and improvement in overall psychological and interactional functioning. Intermediate, or mediating goals, are those that must be reached in order to achieve the final goals. The nature and extent of these mediating goals provide guidelines for treatment format recommendations. For example, if the therapist believes that insight about cognitive and emotional processes is an essential mediating goal, individual therapy is indicated. If positive changes in couple communication are needed, couple therapy is likely to be helpful. When improved interactions with peers are a necessary intermediate goal, group therapy might be recommended.

PATIENT PREFERENCES AND RESISTANCES

Couples who request conjoint treatment have a different conceptualization of the problem than a married individual who calls for individual treatment. The family that sends an adolescent for individual treatment is different from the family that together seeks assistance in dealing with the teenager's acting out. These patient preferences for a particular treatment format should be given serious consideration by the therapist, as both clinical experience and controlled research attest to their value in planning treatment (Swift, Callahan, & Vollmer, 2011). The old adage "meet the patient where he/she is" applies to individuals, couples, and families. Whenever possible, therapy should begin in the format that the patient requests. That does not mean, however, that the therapist should not suggest particular ways of structuring the therapy, along with an explanation for why that structure would be helpful. For example, when a parent calls to refer a young adolescent for individual therapy, the therapist may agree to meet with the adolescent individually but recommend an initial meeting with the adolescent and the parent(s) in order to make a more comprehensive assessment and treatment plan.

In addition to assessing patient preferences, the therapist is advised to assess patient resistances to particular formats. Some individuals enter therapy with a clearly expressed resistance; the therapist needs to be mindful of that resistance. For example, if a woman requests individual therapy to deal with marital problems and states: "We tried couple therapy and it didn't work—I'm not interested in doing that again," the therapist should probably begin with an individual session and, as part of the initial evaluation, assess the patient's experience with couple therapy. If the patient continues to express strong resistance to that format, the best approach is to proceed with individual therapy. If, at a later point in time, the therapist believes that couple therapy would provide significant benefits as an adjunct to the individual format, he or she can use the strength of the now-established therapeutic alliance to support a recommendation of this additional format.

TREATMENT EFFICIENCY

Psychologists increasingly function in a managed care world that emphasizes treatment efficiency. While this should never be the primary determinant of a treatment format (treatment efficacy should be), these realities must be given consideration. For example, if an individual with anger control problems can be as effectively treated in group therapy as in individual therapy, group therapy should be the recommended format based on treatment efficiency. Similarly, family therapy is more efficient than individual therapy because multiple individuals are treated at the same time. When family therapy or group therapy is combined with individual therapy, individual sessions should be limited to the minimum number needed for treatment efficacy.

CHANGING THE FORMAT OR ADDING AN ADDITIONAL FORMAT

As treatment progresses, the therapist may recommend a change, or addition, to the therapeutic format, based on new information about the nature or intensity of the problems, patient preferences and resistances, or the goals of the therapy. For example:

- A couple originally being seen together for conjoint therapy is so conflictual during the sessions that little progress is being made. The therapist adds individual sessions for both spouses as a way of helping them develop a more productive problem-solving process.
- An individual being seen for an anxiety disorder reveals that he and his partner have an intensely dysfunctional relationship. The therapist recommends couple therapy in addition to the patient's individual treatment.
- During the course of individual treatment for depression, a patient reveals a long-standing problem with alcohol. The therapist recommends adding an alcohol treatment group, in addition to the individual therapy.
- A patient with social phobia begins with individual treatment. When his anxiety has been reduced enough for him to benefit from group therapy, that format is added.

When adding a new format during ongoing treatment, the psychotherapist needs to decide whether it would be best to recommend that a different therapist conduct the new format, or whether it would be better for both formats to be conducted by the same therapist. Each approach has advantages and disadvantages, and the scant research on the topic offers no conclusive guidance. Thus, the decision should be predicated on the therapist's experience, comfort working in multiple formats, confidentiality dynamics, and the patient's preferences and resistances to a one-therapist or two-therapist structure.

References and Readings

Clarkin, J. F. (2005). Differential therapeutics. In J. C. Norcross & M. R. Goldfried (Eds.), *Handbook of psychotherapy integration* (2nd ed., pp. 343–361). New York: Oxford University Press.

Feldman, L. B. (1992) *Integrating individual and family therapy*. New York: Brunner-Mazel.

Feldman, L. B., & Feldman, S.L. (2005). Integrating therapeutic modalities. In J. C. Norcross & M. R. Goldfried (Eds.), *Handbook of psychotherapy integration* (2nd ed., pp. 362–381). New York: Oxford University Press

Pinsof, W. M. (1995). *Integrative problem-centered therapy*. New York: Basic.

Swift, J. K., Callahan, J. L., & Vollmer, B. M., (2011). Preferences. In J. C. Norcross (Ed.), *Psychotherapy relationships that work* (2nd ed., pp. 301–315). New York: Oxford University Press.

Related Topics

Chapter 30, "Compendium of Psychotherapy Treatment Manuals"
Chapter 74, "Recruiting, Selecting, and Preparing Patients for Interpersonal Group Psychotherapy"
Chapter 76, "Conducting Couple and Family Therapy"
Chapter 79, "Conducting Psychoeducational Groups"

60 TREATING THE EFFECTS OF PSYCHOLOGICAL TRAUMA

Laura S. Brown

Psychological trauma is an endemic phenomenon in human lives. Depending on how the data are collected, as many as 70% of general-population samples endorse having had at least one lifetime exposure to a highly traumatic event, such as an assault, serious accident, or natural disaster. When other types of trauma, such as microaggressions or insidious trauma, betrayal trauma, and systemic trauma of oppression, are factored into the equation, the omnipresent nature of trauma becomes more apparent. Despite this, most psychologists are poorly prepared to think about or address trauma in their clients' lives, frequently misinterpreting presentations of distress or behavioral dysfunction as evidence of other variables. While only around 20% of those people exposed to the classic *Diagnostic and Statistical Manual of Mental Disorders* (*DSM*) Criterion A stressor are likely to develop posttraumatic stress disorder (Briere & Scott, 2006), the bulk of the remaining 80% are not distress-free. They experience depression, anxiety, increased problems of chronic pain and illness, dissociative phenomena, and problems of affect regulation, trust, and interpersonal effectiveness.

Additionally, trauma occurs through the lens of individuals' multiple and intersecting identities, and it is frequently woven into that fabric. Many cultures that have historically been targets of colonization, discrimination, and other forms of systemic oppression have been described by some authors as embodying trauma in their norms and symbols, what has been referred to by some authors as a postcolonial syndrome. In these cultures, being a member of the group means that one has either direct exposure to some kind of trauma or is only a few generations away from it. Victims of hate crimes, including sexual assault, a gendered hate crime, frequently have the introject of trauma in those aspects of identities that were the location of the traumatic stressor (Brown, 2008). Psychologists working with members of target groups may, consequently, know of the historical trauma but fail to understand how its presence in the emotional ecology of the individual may be an important risk factor for presenting problems.

WHAT IS TRAUMA?

The version of the *DSM* in use at the time of writing defines a trauma as witnessing or experiencing an event that is, or is perceived to be, a threat to life or safety, or that of others. Other forms of trauma that have been identified as possible causes of posttraumatic symptoms include insidious trauma, also known as microaggression. These traumata consist of repeated, lower level, symbolically threatening events common in the life experiences of members of target groups. Trauma can also take the form of interpersonal betrayal; recent research has indicated that betrayal is a more potent risk factor for posttraumatic stress disorder (PTSD) than is life threat. Betrayal traumas are especially likely to occur in relationships of care, trust, and dependency. Other forms of trauma that have been identified are systemic traumata, such as oppression and discrimination, or postcolonial trauma, which represents traumagenic changes to cultures and systems arising from colonization and cultural genocide. Postcolonial trauma represents a type of intergenerational trauma, in which offspring of the traumatized individual experience the effects of the family member's trauma exposure.

ALWAYS ASK ABOUT TRAUMA

An important component of treating posttraumatic phenomena is routinely including questions about a wide range of trauma exposures in each and every intake interview, no matter what the setting or the official presenting problem. Some considerations to take into account include the following:

- Ask questions about trauma in both specific, yes/no formats and in open-ended formats.
- Consider the kind of trauma you are asking about; if you ask someone "Have you ever been raped?" and the person's definition of rape does not include sexual assault by an acquaintance, the person will say "no." It is better to ask about interpersonal violence in more general terms, for example, "Have you ever had an experience where someone forced, coerced, or tricked you into having sex?" Or "Have you ever had sexual experiences that were scary or confusing?"
- Do not expect a new client to fill you in on all of his or her trauma history immediately, especially sexual and other intimate, interpersonal trauma. There is shame attached to these traumas. Asking the question opens the door; the client knows you are willing to hear about it and are interested.
- Similarly, do not assume that men have no sexual assault trauma. Gendered assumptions about kinds of trauma exposures create avoidable errors of omitted data collection.
- Include questions about family history of trauma exposure. Ask about family members' experiences of immigration, war, and poverty. Frequently these will not be coded as traumas by the person or their family. Be aware that many trauma survivors do not discuss their traumatic experiences, but their families, particularly their children, may experience intergenerational effects of the trauma.

FORMAL PSYCHOLOGICAL ASSESSMENT

There are several testing instruments developed specifically to assess the range of posttraumatic symptoms. Additionally, common posttraumatic response patterns have been identified on general psychological assessment instruments. Tests developed specifically to assess for trauma sequelae include the Trauma Symptom Inventory and Trauma Symptom Inventory-2, the Multiscale Dissociation Inventory, the Cognitive Distortions Inventory, and the Post-Traumatic Diagnostic Scale. Research is available indicating common posttrauma profiles on the MMPI-2 and the Personality Assessment Inventory. Additionally, a robust and growing literature on trauma responses to the Rorschach is now available. Common posttraumatic presentations on tests of cognitive function have also been identified.

There are also a number of well-accepted, evidence-based interview schedules for PTSD and related posttraumatic presentations. These include the CAPS (Clinician Administered PTSD Scale) and the SCID-D (Structured

Clinical Interview for Dissociation). Information about the CAPS and other measures of PTSD can be found on the Web site of the National Centers for PTSD of the Veterans' Healthcare Administration.

COMMON POSTTRAUMATIC PRESENTATIONS

Several disorders have trauma exposure as their most prominent risk factor. These include PTSD, acute stress disorder, dissociative identity disorder, and somatoform disorders, better known within the trauma studies field as types of somatoform dissociation. When a client presents with the symptoms of these disorders, it is reasonable to assume a history of trauma exposure. Other problems with trauma as a prominent risk factor include chronic pain, depression, substance abuse disorders, disordered eating, and anxiety disorders. Borderline personality disorder has been shown to have neglect and abuse as co-occurring prominent risk factors; in the field of trauma psychology, a borderline personality disorder presentation has been reconceptualized as complex traumatic stress.

This nonexhaustive list of problems for which trauma is known to be a contributory factor illustrates two things. First, posttraumatic problems can be identified in a very broad spectrum of psychological problems. Second, there is no one treatment for posttraumatic difficulties because of this very wide range. Nonetheless, a number of specific, evidence-based treatments for trauma sequelae have been developed and should be considered by psychologists working with trauma survivors.

THE THREE-PHASE MODEL

No matter what specific interventions a therapist uses, best practice with trauma survivors suggests the application of a three-phase model of treatment. Clients will not necessarily move through these phases in a linear fashion. Nonetheless, trauma treatment is more likely to be effective if conducted using this framework as a guide.

The first phase of treatment focuses on safety, stabilization, and containment. This phase may be relatively brief for an individual who was functioning adequately and had good internal and psychosocial resources prior to trauma; it can constitute the bulk of treatment for persons with complex trauma, who are often very impaired in these domains and often live in unsafe contexts. The second phase of treatment is trauma processing or resolution, in which the experiences of trauma are remembered, grieved about, and metabolized, and trauma-specific symptoms such as intrusive images, nightmares, flashbacks, avoidant behaviors, and heightened arousal are targeted and reduced or eliminated. The final component of trauma treatment involves the integration of the trauma experience in the survivor's identity narratives. This last phase of trauma therapy addresses the existential and spiritual challenges that frequently arise in the wake of trauma, as well as attends to acceptance of the fact of trauma in the individual's life story. Reconnection with the healed self, with community, and with a sense of meaning are focuses of this third phase.

The most important take-home message of the three-phase model is that specific focus on trauma experiences should, when feasible, not proceed until the client is moderately skilled at containment and self-care. Too-early confrontation with trauma material, particularly in those individuals with a complex trauma history, has often been destabilizing and deleterious.

EVIDENCE-BASED TREATMENTS FOR POSTTRAUMA SEQUELAE

Using a broad definition of evidence-based treatment that includes not only specific interventions but also therapist, client, and relationships variables allows for the identification of very wide ranges of both trauma-specific and trauma-informed approaches to treatment. Research on psychotherapy relationship variables indicates that the presence of effective therapist empathy and a strong working alliance are particularly salient with those clients who have problems of trust, which is frequently characteristic of trauma survivors. Therapists' capacities to tolerate and relate effectively to strong affect and treatment-avoidant and therapy-interfering behaviors are evidence-based components of the emotional competence that therapists working with a trauma survivor population should bring to the table.

Specific interventions for posttraumatic symptoms fall into several categories. These include stabilization and containment strategies, exposure therapies, cognitive therapies, and eye movement desensitization reprocessing (EMDR).

Exposure therapies for trauma treatment reflect an emphasis on the anxiety and fear components of trauma response. Prolonged exposure is one of the best-known evidence-based exposure therapies for trauma, and it has been shown to be highly effective with survivors of adult-onset trauma. Recently, virtual reality exposure therapies have been introduced in settings treating individuals with combat trauma and have been found to be a powerful extension of the general exposure treatment model.

Cognitive therapies for trauma treatment, like other cognitive therapies, emphasize transforming problematic cognitions and appraisals of self, others, and the world that are common for trauma survivors. Cognitive processing therapy (CPT) and trauma-informed cognitive-behavioral therapy (T-CBT) are among the cognitive models with the strongest evidence base for their effectiveness. CPT has been found effective working with survivors of sexual assault and domestic violence, and T-CBT is now being routinely utilized in the US Veterans' Healthcare Administration to treat survivors of both combat and military sexual traumas.

EMDR was developed by Shapiro specifically for the treatment of trauma. It involves having a client call up an image of the trauma, relate it to a problematic cognition and bodily experiences of distress, and then complete repeated sets of dichotic stimulation, using either side-to-side eye movements, light touch to either side, or tones in alternate ears. While its mechanisms of action have been hotly debated since it was first proposed, several decades of research have demonstrated its effectiveness both for the treatment of intrusive symptoms and also for the development of self-soothing skills.

TREATMENTS FOR COMPLEX TRAUMA

Because complex trauma affects so many components of an individual's functioning, treatments for it focus not only on the reduction of specific posttrauma symptoms such as intrusive images but also on emotion regulation, self-care and self-soothing, reduction of self-inflicted violence and suicidality, and existential concerns. Stabilization and containment treatment models include dialectical behavior therapy skills training, skills training for affective and interpersonal regulation/narrative storytelling, trauma resolution integration program, and mindfulness-based approaches such as acceptance and commitment therapy.

WHAT ABOUT DEBRIEFING?

The notion that debriefing trauma-exposed individuals immediately after the trauma came into vogue in the 1980s, with the introduction of a variety of interventions, such as Critical Incident Stress Management, aimed initially at first responders, such as firefighters and law enforcement personnel, and subsequently at individuals involved in disasters. Debriefing's effectiveness came into question over time and was at one point critiqued as possibly increasing rates of posttrauma symptoms in debriefed individuals rather than otherwise. The most recent findings on various debriefing interventions suggest that they are overall neutral in their effect at best. While some individuals with particular vulnerabilities may benefit from acute intervention at or around the time of a trauma exposure, no evidence supports the value of immediate posttrauma debriefing interventions.

OTHER THERAPEUTIC INTERVENTIONS

In addition to those therapies that specifically target posttraumatic symptoms, systems-oriented therapies, such as couples and family therapies, have been found to be helpful, given the impact of trauma on the interpersonal environment of the trauma survivor. This is especially true when the trauma survivor is a child. Although children benefit from the full range of trauma-focused psychotherapies, their family systems often experience direct and indirect impacts of the child's trauma, with parental guilt, shame, and feelings of helplessness to have protected the child undermining normative parent–child relationships. In couples, sexual and emotionally intimate relating (sexual and emotional intimacy) are likely to be affected when one person is suffering from posttraumatic symptoms. Individual therapy for the nonsurvivor partner, as well as couples treatment to address the effects of the trauma on relational dynamics, can increase emotional safety and improve the quality of emotional resources available to the survivor her/himself.

Finally, the range of complementary and alternative therapies has been shown to be helpful in the treatment of posttraumatic symptoms. Dance/movement therapies, art and other expressive therapies, involvement in martial arts, yoga, tai chi, and other centering practices have all been shown to be valuable adjuncts to psychotherapy. Psychotropic medications, primarily in the selective serotonin re-uptake inhibitor family and the mood stabilizers, have been shown to be helpful in alleviating some symptoms of posttraumatic stress. However, the data for psychopharmacological treatments as stand-alone interventions are not strong.

Ultimately, the choice of treatments for trauma must reflect the clinician's careful evaluation of the individual client's emotional resources, the developmental aspects of the trauma, and the issues of culture and intersecting identities that are woven into the trauma experience. There is no one-size-fits-all treatment for posttraumatic symptoms. Emotional competence and self-care on the part of the therapist are boundary conditions for effective trauma treatment.

References and Readings

American Psychological Association, Division of Trauma Psychology. (n.d.). *Division 56*. Retrieved January 2013, from www.apatraumadivision.org

Baldwin, D. (n.d.). *David Baldwin's trauma information pages*. Retrieved January 2013, from www.trauma-pages.com

Briere, J., & Scott, C. (2006) *Principles of trauma therapy: A guide to symptoms, evaluation, and treatment*. Thousand Oaks, CA: Sage.

Brown, L. S. (2008). *Cultural competence in trauma therapy: Beyond the flashback*. Washington, DC: American Psychological Association.

Courtois, C. A., & Ford, J. (Eds.). (2009). *Complex traumatic stress disorders: An evidence-based guide*. New York: Guilford, Press.

Foa, E. B., Keane, T., Friedman, M., & Cohen, J. (Eds.). (2010). *Effective treatments for PTSD: Practice guidelines from the International Society for Traumatic Stress Studies* (2nd ed.). New York: Guilford Press.

Gold, S. N. (2000). *Not trauma alone. Therapy for child abuse survivors in family and social context*. Philadelphia, PA: Brunner-Routledge.

Herman, J. L. (1992). *Trauma and recovery*. New York: Basic Books.

International Society for the Study of Trauma and Dissociation. (n.d.). Retrieved January 2013, from www.isst-d.org

International Society for Traumatic Stress Studies. (n.d.). Retrieved January 2013, from www.istss.org

National Center for PTSD. (n.d.). Retrieved January 2013, from www.ptsd.va.gov/

Sidran Foundation. (n.d.). Retrieved January 2013, from www.sidran.org

Related Topics

Chapter 61, "Working with Patients Who Have Been Sexually Abused by Previous Therapists and Clergy"

Chapter 64, "Tailoring Treatment to the Patient's Race and Ethnicity"

Chapter 89, "Treatment of Child Sexual Abuse"

Chapter 106, "Minimizing Your Legal Liability Risk Following Adverse Events or Patient Threats"

61 WORKING WITH PATIENTS WHO HAVE BEEN SEXUALLY ABUSED BY PREVIOUS THERAPISTS AND CLERGY

Kenneth S. Pope

Therapists who encounter patients reporting sexual activity with a prior therapist, priest, minister, rabbi, or other clergy can face complex challenges. Patients may be unaware of standards prohibiting therapists or clergy from engaging in such activities. They may believe that the sexual involvement was a legitimate psychotherapeutic or religious practice. They may expect the subsequent therapist to engage in the same practice or feel certain that the subsequent therapist will feel disgust and contempt because they are too confused, too sexual, too angry, or too crazy. They may feel that no one will believe them.

The previous paragraph's key word is *may*. None of those beliefs, expectations, or feelings is rare among patients who have been sexually involved within a therapeutic or religious relationship. These common reactions are understandable responses to the therapist's or clergy's decision to betray the trust and responsibilities inherent in the relationship. But each patient is unique. A patient may experience none of the common reactions. Though this chapter emphasizes the importance of adequate preparation, the preparation should not lead to preconceptions that screen out or distort new information. We must draw on only that which is relevant for a particular patient.

The material that follows in this chapter begins with 10 steps to ensure adequate preparation, followed by sections on common therapist reactions that can undermine therapy and common patient reactions to sex in religious or therapeutic relationships.

PREPARATION

Adequate preparation includes the following:

- *Know the ethical prohibitions and related professional standards.* Therapists need to be familiar with the formal standards governing the patient's previous therapist or clergy.
- *Clarify that the prohibition and ethical standards impose requirements on the therapist or clergy rather than the patient.* Therapists or clergy who engage in prohibited sexual involvement often try to shift the responsibility to the patient or parishioner: It was the patient or parishioner who seduced the therapist or clergy; the parishioner's clothing and behavior made him or her impossible to resist; the patient's condition (e.g., borderline, suicidal) was so stressful that it impaired the therapist's or clergy's decision-making ability or willpower; and so on.

Clinicians knowledgeable in this area are well aware that a significant fraction of sexual misconduct instances are initiated by the patient. Such initiation empirically encompasses the full realm of human interaction from innuendo to overt requests, demands, threats, and blackmail, even to the threat of suicide. Subject to no code, patients are free to demand, request, and threaten as they wish. These behaviors are suitable for therapeutic exploration; the therapist alone bears the blame for acting on these behaviors, since axiomatically only the therapist can be blameworthy (Gutheil & Gabbard, 1993, p. 518).

- *Avoid intrusive advocacy.* While the responsibility for avoiding sexual involvement in therapeutic or religious relationships always falls solely on the therapist or clergy, in subsequent therapy it is the patient alone who decides what steps, if any, to take to address the prior sexual involvement. Subsequent therapists may believe that they know what the best or right course is for the patient. Therapists may believe, for example, that the patient must file a complaint so that the offending therapist or clergy will be prevented from abusing others, so that the patient can stop being a victim, or so that the patient can be made whole from a civil suit. Or the therapist may believe that the prior therapist or clergy does not deserve to face a formal complaint and sanctions, that the patient's claims will not hold up under cross-examination, or that the patient is too psychologically fragile to press a complaint. Such therapists may spend time and effort persuading, pressuring, or manipulating the patient into following the course that the therapist believes is right though it is not what the patient wants to do. Such *intrusive advocacy* (Pope, 1994, p. 116) runs counter to the therapist's responsibilities, does not accord with freely given informed consent, and undermines the therapy.
- *Know the legal standards and any reporting obligations.* Legislation, administrative regulations, and case law vary from jurisdiction to jurisdiction. Therapists need to know whether the sexual involvement is subject to civil, criminal, or administrative (e.g., licensing board) laws or regulations in the relevant jurisdiction. Is the subsequent treating therapist obligated to report such sexual involvement to any board or agency?
- *Recognize sexual involvement in a religious or therapeutic relationship that involves minors as child abuse.* Sometimes the framework of sexual activity within a religious or therapeutic relationship can make us slow to realize that if the sexual activity includes a minor, the child abuse reporting laws apply. Depending on the jurisdiction, these laws tend to specify a deadline of only a few days before a formal report must be made.
- *Do not overlook the possibility of pregnancy.* Although sex in the context of religious or therapeutic relationships tends to be discussed in ethical, legal, and psychological terms, under certain circumstances pregnancy can result. An adequate assessment includes whether the sexual involvement produced pregnancy and, if so, whether there was miscarriage, abortion, or birth.
- *Do not overlook the possibility of sexually transmitted diseases (STDs).* An adequate assessment also includes whether the patient became infected with one or more STDs, such as the human immunodeficiency virus as a result of sexual involvement with the therapist or clergy, and the current status of the disease(s).
- *Know the research and professional literature in this area.* Part of competence in any area of assessment and treatment is knowledge of the accumulated research and theory. Resources in this area include Firestone, Moulden, and Wexler (2009), Foote (2007), Pope (1994), Pope and Vasquez (2011), and "Sexual Issues in Psychology Training & Practice: Links to Articles, Books, and Abstracts" at kspope.com/sexiss/index.php
- *Know the common scenarios of sexual involvement in therapeutic or religious relationships.* Ten of the most common—True Love; It Just Got Out of Hand; Time Out; Role Trading; Sex Therapy; As If...; Svengali; Drugs; Rape; Hold Me (Pope, 1994; Pope & Vasquez, 2011)—are described in Chapter 49 in this volume.
- *Know the self-help and other adjunctive resources.* Some patients may benefit from

being in contact with other survivors of therapeutic or religious abuse. Organizations like SNAP (Survivors Network of those Abused by Priests) at www.snapnetwork.org offers support groups in over 60 cities along with other services to people who have been sexually abused by clergy in the Catholic, Greek Orthodox, Presbyterian, and other religious organizations.

COMMON THERAPIST REACTIONS THAT CAN UNDERMINE THERAPY

The following common reactions are adapted from Pope, Sonne, and Holroyd (1993), Pope (1994), and Pope and Vasquez (2011):

- *Unfounded disbelief and denial.* Many allegations of sex with a prior therapist can seem improbable at best. Perhaps the patient has said many things that later turned out to be untrue. Or has an ax to grind for other reasons against a priest. Or accuses a highly regarded therapist known for scrupulous integrity. Or has spoken positively about the minister many times without mentioning sexual involvement. Or is revealing for the first time to anyone events that supposedly happened decades ago when the patient was a young child. We ourselves may be motivated to dismiss the allegations. Perhaps the accused is a good friend, a source of needed referrals, a mentor, or someone who is powerful and vindictive. Living in a small community can magnify these dynamics.
- *Premature certainty that it happened.* Patient characteristics, context, and our own cognitive tendencies can push us just as hard in the opposite direction: Rather than quickly dismiss a patient's allegations as untrue, we leap to the conclusion that not only did the sexual involvement occur but that it occurred exactly as the patient described. This unfounded assumption can prevent useful exploration, close our minds to information that does not fit our preconceptions, and undermine the therapy.
- *Making the patient fit the textbook.* Some therapists may reassure the patient that they understand the patient's reaction to sex with a therapist or clergy—"You must have felt terrible!"; "He really shattered your trust, didn't he!"; "You must have wondered what was going on when she suddenly kissed you!"—even before they know what the patient's reaction was. Therapists may have read about common reactions, or they may be imagining how they themselves might feel in such a situation, or may simply be trying to reassure the patient. We undermine the therapy if we tell patients how they felt rather than listening to them.
- *Blaming the patient for the abuse.* Some therapists may point to the patient's clothing, makeup, behavior, and similar factors to encourage the patient to accept full responsibility for causing the sexual involvement and the blame for its negative consequences. They may emphasize that the patient did not resist and in fact continued to meet with the clergy or prior therapist. However, the long-standing ethical and legal prohibitions set standards for the behavior of the therapist or clergy rather than the client, and it is the therapist or clergy who is responsible for maintaining ethical and legal behavior, regardless of clothing, makeup, behavior, and other factors.
- *Sexual reactions to the patient.* Research studies have tended to show that sexual feelings for patients often bring discomfort, evoking guilt, anxiety, or confusion. The context of working with a patient who has already engaged in a sexual relationship with a therapist or clergy can intensify these reactions. Chapter 49 in this volume provides additional information about recognizing and managing these feelings.
- *Discomfort at the lack of privacy or need to testify.* Some patients who have been sexually involved with a prior therapist or clergy choose to press criminal charges, file a civil suit, or lodge a formal complaint with a licensing board or ethics committee. Under certain circumstances the therapist may be required to report instances of therapist–patient sexual involvement in

some jurisdictions. Some therapists, particularly those without forensic experience, feel uncomfortable that what is discussed in psychotherapy will not remain confidential, that their notes as well as the raw data for any assessments may be subpoenaed, and that they themselves may have to testify as fact witnesses in deposition and court.

- *Vicarious helplessness.* Those who have been sexually exploited by a therapist, priest, rabbi, minister, or other clergy can encounter countless challenges when turning to the courts for justice. The defense attorney may probe into the most intimate and private aspects of the patient's life, trying to gather information to establish or suggest that the patient has been sexually promiscuous, has engaged in sexual activities that some might condemn, has not always been scrupulously truthful, has not always shown exemplary character, is faking any apparent harm that resulted from the sexual involvement, is vindictive and attempting to profit at the expense of someone who only tried to help the patient, and so on. It is not uncommon for therapists to feel a vicarious helplessness as the defendant and defense attorney attack and attempt to discredit the patient.

COMMON REACTIONS TO SEX IN THERAPEUTIC OR RELIGIOUS RELATIONSHIPS

The following material is adapted from Pope (1994) and Pope and Vasquez (2011):

- *Ambivalence.* Extreme ambivalence as a result of sexual involvement with a therapist can virtually paralyze a patient. On one hand, they may want to break the taboo of silence (sometimes accompanied with threats) imposed by the prior therapist or clergy, to speak frankly about what happened to them, to seek justice from the courts, to file a complaint to prevent the abusive therapist from exploiting others, or to use therapy to heal and move on with their lives. On the other hand, they may feel that they must protect the perpetrator at all costs, that the abuser was a good person who sacrificed much to help them. The abuser may have convinced them that he or she was the only one who ever loved them or found them desirable.
- *Cognitive dysfunction.* Many people who have been sexually involved within a therapeutic or religious relationship experience interference with attention, memory, and concentration. Unbidden thoughts, intrusive images, flashbacks, memory fragments, or nightmares can afflict them. In some cases the pattern of consequences may resemble posttraumatic stress disorder.
- *Emotional lability.* Just as sexual abuse by therapist or clergy can disrupt a person's characteristic ways of thinking and produce cognitive dysfunction, the abuse can also disrupt the person's characteristic ways of feeling and produce emotional lability. The sudden shifts in emotion can seem disconnected from the current situation. Unpredictable and out of control, the patient's emotions are not familiar to the patient but seem strange, alien, and sometimes frightening.
- *Emptiness and isolation.* Sex abuse in a therapeutic or religious relationship can make some people feel as if they had been robbed of their sense of self or as if their self had been completely hollowed out. This emptiness can make them feel permanently cut off from other people, unable to form or feel a bond with others. Elma Pálos offered a vivid description of this sense of emptiness and isolation. Pálos had been the therapy patient and sexual partner of Sándor Ferenczi. Pálos's mother had also been the therapy patient and sexual partner of Ferenczi. She wrote in 1912: "This being alone that now awaits me will be stronger than I; I feel almost as if everything will freeze inside me.... If I am alone, I will cease to exist" (cited in Pope, 1994).
- *Irrational guilt.* Intense, persistent, irrational guilt may plague the patient. The guilt is irrational because it is in all instances the therapist's or clergy's duty to avoid engaging in abuse.
- *Impaired ability to trust.* When therapists or clergy intentionally and knowingly violate

someone's trust, as they do when they decide to sexually abuse the person, the effects on the person's ability to trust can be profound, pervasive, and lasting. This consequence of therapeutic or religious abuse can be one of the most effective barriers to treatment and one of the most difficult challenges for the therapist.

- *Increased suicide risk.* As a group, people who have been sexually involved in a therapeutic relationship may have significantly increased risk of both suicide attempts and completed suicides when compared with the general population and other groups of patients. For example, research published in peer-reviewed journals suggests that about 14% will make at least one attempt at suicide and that about one in every hundred patients who have been sexually involved with a therapist commit suicide (Pope, 1994).
- *Role reversal and boundary confusion.* Abusive therapists and clergy violate both roles and boundaries, shifting focus from the needs of the person they are supposed to help to meeting their own sexual and other desires at the expense of the other person. Part of the work of the subsequent therapy may be clarifying roles and restoring appropriate boundaries.

References and Readings

Firestone, P., Moulden, H. M., & Wexler, A. F. (2009). Clerics who commit sexual offenses: Offender, offense, and victim characteristics. *Journal of Child Sexual Abuse: Research, Treatment, and Program Innovations for Victims, Survivors, and Offenders, 18*(4), 442–454.

Foote, W. E. (2007). Psychological evaluation and testimony in cases of clergy and teacher sex abuse. In A. M. Goldstein (Ed.), *Forensic psychology: Emerging topics and expanding roles* (pp. 571–604). Hoboken, NJ: Wiley.

Gutheil, T. G., & Gabbard, G. O. (1993). Concept of boundaries in clinical practice: Theoretical and risk-management dimensions. *American Journal of Psychiatry, 150*, 188–196.

Pope, K. S. (1994). *Sexual involvement with therapists: Patient assessment, subsequent therapy, forensics.* Washington, DC: American Psychological Association.

Pope, K. S., Sonne, J. L., & Greene , B. (2006). *What therapists don't talk about and why: Understanding taboos that hurt us and our clients.* Washington, DC: American Psychological Association.

Pope, K. S., Sonne, J. L., & Holroyd, J. (1993). *Sexual feelings in psychotherapy: Explorations for therapists and therapists-in-training.* Washington, DC: American Psychological Association.

Pope, K. S., & Vasquez, M. J. T. (2011). *Ethics in psychotherapy and counseling: A practical guide* (4th ed.). Hoboken, NJ: Wiley.

Sexual Issues in Psychology Training and Practice. Retrieved January 2013, from kspope.com/sexiss/index.php

Related Topics

Chapter 60, "Treating the Effects of Psychological Trauma"

Chapter 89, "Treatment of Child Sexual Abuse"

Chapter 106, "Minimizing Your Legal Liability Risk Following Adverse Events or Patient Threats"

62 COUNSELING PEOPLE LIVING WITH HIV

Priscilla Dass-Brailsford

People living with human immunodeficiency virus (PLWH), like most people dealing with a life-threatening illness, are apprehensive about becoming ill and possibly dying as a result of their illness. However, there are many aspects of an HIV diagnosis that make it unique and different from other chronic illnesses. Counselors working with PLWH must have an appreciation of these differences in order to effectively help clients seeking help.

FEELINGS OF LOSS

An HIV diagnosis can be traumatic and triggers a series of losses. Some losses are experienced immediately, at the time of diagnosis, in loss of physical health, sexual freedom, and a normal life span. Others are experienced as feared losses in normal cognitive functioning, financial security, social support, and independence. Thus, the adjustment process after learning about an HIV-positive diagnosis can be conceptualized as adjusting to and coping with loss.

As PLWH confront their own feelings about losses due to an HIV-positive diagnosis, unresolved feelings related to past losses are also likely to emerge, especially if these losses have been ignored in the past. However, an HIV diagnosis can sometimes give PLWH the impetus to address past issues and this can then serve to improve their ability to cope with current circumstances. Discussing the impact of prior life events on a person's ability to deal with a major loss is an important goal of psychotherapy.

A person's loss of control over the course of illness is another important area of therapeutic focus. PLWH may feel helpless and hopeless in the face of an HIV diagnosis as they anticipate a disruption in their bodies and overall lives; they may have a sense of being out of control. Counselors who work with PLWH may observe clients with a defeatist attitude; an important therapeutic goal, in such cases, is to encourage and empower clients to play a larger role in their own health care. For example, a few specific areas in which PLWH can control their lives and which can result in a positive impact upon their physical health and well-being include diet, exercise, safe sexual behavior, compliance with medical appointments and recommended medical treatment, accessing social support, goal setting, and seeking psychotherapy.

Once issues of control are explored in psychotherapy, clients may feel better prepared to work at improving their day-to-day functioning. This discussion best takes place in the context of an empathic acknowledgment by the counselor of the many ways in which aspects of the PLWH's life are truly out of control. For some clients spirituality plays a central role in how they interpret and manage their illness. Counselors must be prepared to work with clients who may have such needs so that they can adequately support them (Holt, Houg, & Romano, 1999).

STRESS, STIGMA, AND UNCERTAINTY

Although great advances have been made in the medical treatment of HIV, and PLWH are now able to live longer, an HIV diagnosis generates an enormous amount of stress and uncertainty for clients. These stressors are multiplied by prevailing stigma toward those diagnosed with HIV; it is an illness that is inherently stigmatizing (Herek, Capitanio, & Widamin, 2002). Common psychological problems and symptoms emerge from underlying feelings of shame, stigmatization, humiliation, guilt, embarrassment, fear, and anger about being diagnosed and living with HIV/AIDS. Negative social consequences of a positive HIV diagnosis exacerbate these feelings and may result in violence, anxiety, depression, and discrimination in housing and employment. The astute counselor is aware of these stressors and prepared to support the client appropriately. Questions about the course of HIV illness, planning for the future, other responsibilities (e.g., child care), and uncertainty about how long one is likely to live are some of the uncertainties likely to surface. Since HIV is a chronic illness, it is important to address issues of denial that are always likely to emerge; identifying and addressing specific barriers to care ensures that clients remain treatment adherent (Naar-King et al., 2007). Thus, psychotherapy with PLWH involves not only helping them to accept the illness and adjust to its uncertainty but to follow a health care plan that keeps viral loads low.

Moreover, it is common for PLWH to assume that everything they feel, physically and emotionally, is related to the HIV infection. Headaches, stomach aches, fatigue, and depression are sometimes erroneously attributed to HIV. Psychoeducation can play a valuable role in increasing awareness about the illness and help differentiate between what is HIV related and what is not. Information about HIV minimizes uncertainty, while a lack of information or incorrect information can cause unnecessary distress.

The stress of living with HIV is likely to cause a disruption in self-functioning. Some individuals have the necessary resources to manage this disruption, but others can benefit from assistance while they are going through the adjustment process. PLWH who seek psychotherapy are a selective few who respond to feelings of distress by appropriately initiating contact with a psychotherapist or exhibiting behavior that leads to counseling. Self-referred clients are likely to express a sense of urgency and a motivation to resolve certain issues prior to becoming severely ill and/or dying. Sometimes, as a result of an HIV diagnosis, clients are motivated to use psychotherapy to change aspects of their lives they may otherwise have ignored, for example, a past sexual abuse history or relational issues. An HIV diagnosis can shed new meaning to previously disregarded aspects of life.

IDENTITY CHALLENGES

Identity is influenced by one's experiences in the world and is made up of the various aspects of the self to which one attributes meaning and significance. For PLWH, having an HIV diagnosis is likely to cause a major change in self-identity. The stigma associated with HIV derives primarily from the assumption that PLWH are assumed to be at fault because of their own behavior (sexuality, substance abuse, etc.). In addition, the association of this illness to already stigmatized minorities exacerbates the problem for these groups. PWLH are aware of societal rejection of their illness and internalize negative feelings about being HIV positive. Loss of self-esteem and a devalued sense of self are likely to result. Counselors must be sensitive to these changes in self-image and have an understanding of how stigmatization, rejection, and discrimination may compromise a client's ability to seek and receive quality care. A vital goal of counseling PLWH involves healing loss of self-worth and restoring integrity and strengthening self-identity. The more a counselor expresses accurate empathy and develops the ability to reflectively clarify and amplify a client's experiences, the more a client feels listened to, and understood. This increases the likelihood of clients sharing sensitive life experiences.

Acceptance of one's identity as a PLWH is a developmental process that takes place at several levels: first, acceptance of illness; second, disclosing illness to family members; and, third, informing the wider society of friends, and colleagues about one's illness. Self-stigma is likely to be most strongly felt early in diagnosis, and a key therapeutic task is to work through these negative feelings about the self and to accept one's illness.

One of the major challenges facing PWLH is with whom to share their diagnosis and how and when to do so. Widespread fear and discrimination against PLWH makes it difficult to acknowledge membership in this group. This challenge is intensified for PLWH who are also lesbian or gay since negative experiences of "coming out" influence their willingness to share their HIV status. For those who have not "come out," the problem is compounded and there is fear that a double disclosure will result in rejection and loss of relationships (Weiss, 1997). However, the difficulty many HIV-positive persons have in sharing their HIV serostatus with others limits their ability to derive much-needed social support. Although disclosure has been associated with higher self-esteem, PLWH should be guided to make decisions about disclosure carefully, cautiously, and rationally (Dworkin & Pincu, 1993). Premature or inappropriate disclosure can result in engendering stress rather than support.

Because of the demands of the illness, it is not unusual that being HIV positive becomes a central aspect of PLWH's identity. This is often reflected in how PLWH refer to themselves as being "HIV" rather than "HIV positive." While this may be a mere speech abbreviation, it also indicates the heightened degree to which PLWH perceive the self as defined by the virus. Examining the language used by PLWH as they talk about their illness is one way to explore how the subjective experience of being HIV positive may differ from the experience of having other life-threatening illnesses.

ISSUES OF SEXUALITY

HIV is often associated with sexuality and an immoral lifestyle; blaming the victim is a common societal response. More so than with other illnesses, HIV is associated with sexuality and of having played an active role in acquiring one's illness. Being HIV positive is linked to past sexual behavior; feelings of guilt, shame, and self-loathing are likely to emerge and the HIV diagnosis may be perceived as a deserved punishment. After finding out about an HIV diagnosis, PLWH are aware that they are capable of infecting others through sexual relations. PLWH often encounter messages, some subtle, some quite direct, that they should stop having sexual relations due to their ability to infect others with the virus. This can often result in problems with sexual interest. Yet it can be quite difficult for PLWH to discuss their problems in sexual functioning with others, and in psychotherapy. For psychotherapy to be successful, PLWH must feel that the counselor accepts him or her as a sexual being and is responsive to concerns regarding sexual functioning no differently than concerns about other areas of functioning.

For PLWH who are also lesbian or gay, sexuality is at the core of the experience of being HIV infected. Attention to sexuality in psychotherapy with HIV-infected lesbian or gay clients is likely to impact adaptation beyond the domain of sexual functioning. Addressing the client's feelings about sexuality can identify past unresolved conflicts (feelings about becoming HIV infected) and present concerns (feelings about living with HIV illness).

Similar to persons diagnosed with cancer, an HIV diagnosis may lead to a search for meaning. Clarifying with the client the specific threats and losses posed by the HIV infection sharpens understanding of the psychological stress experienced. It can restore a sense of order and purpose to life. While the illness does not always have a clear and profound meaning for every PLWH, the process of exploring the possible meaning of the illness can serve as an anchor. It allows the illness to become part of the self and one's history and identity, rather than something foreign and intrusive, fostering acceptance, rather than rejection of the illness. The goal in psychotherapy is to help clients find a way to integrate their diagnosis into the fabric of who they are so that they can live wholly, neither defined by nor disavowing of an HIV diagnosis.

CULTURAL CONCERNS

The dynamics of adjusting to an HIV diagnosis exist beyond the individual, intrapsychic level; the cultural and subcultural context also plays an essential role. People who have considerable coping resources and support are likely to deal with an HIV diagnosis very differently from those with fewer resources. Clients from a lower social class are more likely to be members of minority groups and to have considerable difference in the typical life experiences than people from higher income groups in terms of major life stressors (Wyatt et al., 2002). For low-income clients, life stressors are likely to be more chronic. There is a less clear beginning or end to stress; it may be viewed as part of daily life and the expectation that it will continue to be so may be prevalent. Typical daily stresses, including lack of money for adequate food, clothing, housing, and medical care; living in an environment where violence and crime are prevalent; and feeling discriminated against and victimized by society based on belonging to a minority group, are exacerbated with an HIV diagnosis. Stress is familiar to them, and thus HIV illness is viewed as one more thing to cope with in the midst of many other major life stresses as opposed to the one negative stress which has intruded on an otherwise relatively stress-free life. The therapist's appreciation of the way in which stress is experienced in the client's social setting can strengthen an empathic connection with the client.

WHAT TREATMENT TO OFFER

Co-occurring psychological difficulties commonly emerge after an HIV diagnosis (Farber, 2009). Common psychiatric disorders experienced by PLWH include mood disorders, psychotic disorders, anxiety disorders, adjustment disorders, personality disorders, and sleep disorders, any of which may have been present prior to and/or following the HIV diagnosis. Moreover, depending on the individual's viral load, CD4 count, and the presence of opportunistic infections, a person's mental health becomes vulnerable to changes in his or her medical condition.

Whether an individual develops mental health problems as a result of an HIV diagnosis is mediated by a range of factors that includes the number of current life stressors, coping strategies, availability of social support, and personal characteristics. A careful and thorough assessment and evaluation is critical when working with PLWH. There are several areas that need in-depth understanding when developing an appropriate treatment plan. These areas include preexisting mental health/substance abuse, current intimate relationships, family and peer relationships, social support, work status and satisfaction, current health status, and other responsibilities (parenting, elder care, etc.). An assessment of these factors and how they contribute to presenting concerns is central in treatment planning (Rubenstein & Sorrentino, 2008).

Psychotherapy is a critically important and effective resource that can help ameliorate HIV-associated distress, improve coping, and enhance well-being. Counseling people living with HIV must be informed by a full range of approaches that include a focus on psychological processes, behavioral skills, and the dynamics of sexual interactions and relationships. Theories of behavioral change should be attentive to the psychological factors that may interact with disease management to affect behavior (Fisher & Fisher, 2000). A focus on HIV-related information and risk reduction has to be mediated by the use of specific behavioral skills, such as condom negotiation with a sexual partner and the ability to apply a condom correctly. Such behavioral skills support a well-informed client motivated to modify his or her sexual risk behavior.

Clinicians who are committed to working with PLWH need to be knowledgeable and updated on HIV issues in order to best support their clients. This is a rapidly changing field and clinicians must keep abreast of emerging information. Information changes almost daily in terms of the conceptualization of the illness, medications and treatment recommended, and the social and political climate surrounding the illness. It is also vital that the counselor exercise flexibility and has an appreciation of the experiential world of PLWH. Ideally, the counselor creates a treatment setting that optimizes the client's freedom to explore feelings about his or her HIV infection; such an atmosphere is unencumbered by the therapist's opinions and values. Before beginning psychotherapy, the therapist should conduct a diagnostic assessment to determine whether psychotherapy is indeed indicated and, if so, what form of therapy would be most helpful for a particular client.

Treatment goals should be established as early on as possible in collaboration with the client. Aside from individual psychotherapy, other recommended treatments might involve group therapy for people dealing with similar issues, couples or family therapy, and/or pharmacotherapy. Counseling is aimed at helping individuals achieve an uncomplicated adjustment to living with a chronic illness and can serve to reduce any significant road blocks that may interfere with the adjustment process. It may involve psychoeducation concerning the adjustment process, assistance with problem solving, facilitation of the expression of emotions, advice about unique concerns, and guidance in decision making during challenging times. For some clients, psychoeducation and the development of coping skills may not be sufficient in managing their HIV illness. Personality, developmental, or emotional issues that are unresolved prior to the HIV-positive diagnosis and current circumstances may complicate their adjustment process.

A distinction can be made between various forms of psychotherapy: from the most supportive to the most insight-oriented and exploratory approaches. Supportive therapy primarily focuses on symptoms and behavioral change through the support of the clients' own and environmental resources. In contrast, psychodynamic-oriented psychotherapy involves making connections between current relationships and aspects of early upbringing. When psychotherapy is indicated, the counselor should be aware that unique issues can arise in the treatment due to the client's physical illness. These issues include missed appointments due to illness, feelings evoked by a client coming to sessions while ill, and the change in the relationship that occurs as a result of visiting clients who are hospitalized. This can often lead to meeting family members and partners, and interacting with clients in a manner that differs from being in the therapist's office.

CONCLUSION

Adjustment to being HIV positive is conceptualized as an ongoing process of confrontation with loss, uncertainty, and acceptance. Interventions offered to PLWH range from psychoeducation and supportive therapy to more insight-oriented therapies. The client's acceptance of his or her illness is shaped and colored by the degree and manner in which the diagnosis is integrated into one's identity. Sexuality is one core theme in psychotherapy with PLWH. It often plays a prominent role in triggering past unresolved conflicts as well as present concerns for which the client seeks therapy. Addressing the meaning that being HIV positive has for the client in therapy can promote acceptance of the illness and a cohesiveness of self. Cultural and subcultural differences in how life stress is experienced must also be taken into account in order to fully appreciate a client's concerns.

References and Readings

American Psychiatric Association. (2000). Practice guideline for the treatment of patients with HIV/AIDS. *Supplement to the American Journal of Psychiatry*, *157*(11), 1–62.

Dworkin, S. H., & Pincu, L. (1993). Counseling in the era of AIDS. *Journal of Counseling and Development*, *71*, 275–281.

Farber, E. W. (2009). Existentially informed HIV-related psychotherapy. *Psychotherapy Theory, Research, Practice, Training*, *46*(3), 336–349.

Fisher, J. D., & Fisher, W. A. (2000). Theoretical approaches in HIV risk behaviors. In J. L.Peterson & R. J. DiClemente (Eds.), *Handbook of HIV prevention* (pp. 3–49). New York: Kluwer Academic/Plenum.

Health Resources and Services Administration. (2001). Mental illness and HIV disease. *HRSA Care Action, January*, 1–5.

Herek, G. M., Capitanio, J. P., & Widamin, K. F. (2002). HIV-related stigma and knowledge in the United States: Prevalence and trends, 1991–1999. *American Journal of Public Health, 92*, 371–377.

Holt, J. L., Houg, B., & Romano, J. L. (1999). Spiritual wellness for clients with HIV/AIDS: Review of counseling issues. *Journal of Counseling and Development, 77*(2), 160–170.

Naar-King, S., Green-Jones, M., Wright, K., Outlaw, A., Wang, B., & Liu, H. (2007). Ancillary services and retention of youth in HIV care. AIDS Care, 19, 248–251. *AIDS Education and Prevention, 23*(6), 521–532.

Rubenstein, D., & Sorrentino, D. (2008). Psychotherapy with HIV/AIDS patients: Assessment and treatment plan development. *American Journal of Psychotherapy, 62*(4), 365–375.

Weiss, J. J. (1997). Psychotherapy with HIV-positive gay men: A psychodynamic perspective. *American Journal of Psychotherapy, 51*(1), 31–44.

Wyatt, G. E., Myers, H. F., Williams, J. K., Ramirez Kitchen, C., Loeb, T.,... Presley, N. (2002). Does a history of trauma contribute to HIV risk for women of color? Implications for prevention and policy. *American Journal of Public Health, 92*(4), 660–665.

Related Topic

Chapter 45, "Working With Patients at Risk for HIV and other Sexually Transmitted Diseases"

63 TREATING BIPOLAR SPECTRUM DISORDERS

Elizabeth Brondolo

Bipolar spectrum disorders (BSDs) are cycling mood disorders, including bipolar I, bipolar II, and cyclothymia. Although not all investigators agree, recurrent depression may also be considered a cycling mood disorder. BSDs are disorders of the brain, with interactive effects on the autonomic, neuroendocrine, and immune systems. BSDs are characterized by clinically significant problems in mood regulation, behavioral control, information processing, and stress reactivity and recovery. These disorders can present acute threats to the health and safety of the patient and contribute to impairments in social and occupational functioning and quality of life. Appropriate management of BSDs can lead to substantial improvements in health and functioning.

Depending on the severity of the condition, the treatment regimen can include medical interventions (e.g., medication, electroconvulsive therapy); psychotherapies at an individual, group, and/or family level; and occupational, cognitive, or social rehabilitation programs. Treatment planning requires an understanding of the biological, psychological, and social/environmental forces that influence the development and course of the disorder. Good outcomes require effective collaboration among the service providers and between these providers and the patient and his or her support network. Psychologists can play a key role in treatment, coordinating the network of services and using analytic and alliance-building skills to clarify the diagnosis, optimize treatment, and help the patient maintain hope.

DIFFERENTIAL DIAGNOSIS

BSDs vary in the degree to which the patients experience full or subthreshold manic or mixed or depressive episodes. Manic episodes are characterized by increased motivational drive, activity, energy, libido, and perceived self-worth, as well as a decreased need for sleep and a decreased perception of risk. In contrast, depressive episodes are characterized by a depletion of motivational drive, energy, libido, pleasure, and sense of self-worth, and an increased perception of threat. In depression, there may also be episodes of insomnia or hypersomnia and alterations in appetite. Mixed states include elements of both manic and depressive episodes. Despite the occurrence of manic episodes, most patients with bipolar disorder spend the majority of their time (up to 80%) exhibiting symptoms of a depressive state.

BSD is more common than many practitioners recognize. Population-based studies suggest that from 6% to 9% of the population suffers from a BSD. About 1%–2% of the population meets criteria for a diagnosis of bipolar I. Misdiagnosis is a common problem. For example, earlier studies suggested that as many as 50% of individuals with BSD had been previously diagnosed with major depressive disorder.

BSD can be difficult to diagnose because symptoms associated with the disorder can all appear to be an aspect of personality, a response to treatment, or a change in circumstances. For example, patients typically consider their level of energy or risk aversion to be a function of temperament or personality. This is particularly the case if others in their family have similar characteristics (i.e., "We are all high energy").

When a patient with symptoms of depression is treated with an antidepressant, a subsequent increase in energy, self-esteem, and motivation can appear to be evidence of improvement. It may take several weeks to determine whether the changes in mood and behavior actually are a function of a switch to hypomania. Mixed states can be particularly difficult to identify, since the combination of hypomanic and depressive symptoms can take several forms. For example, individuals may present with agitation and extreme irritability accompanied by dysphoria; severe psychomotor retardation accompanied by highly repetitive or racing intrusive thoughts; or a bristling irritability or interpersonal sensitivity combined with severe impairments in concentration.

It can also be difficult to recognize BSD or to identify symptoms of BSD in the context of other comorbid conditions. More than 70% of patients with BSD have comorbid conditions, with anxiety disorders among the most common of comorbid conditions. The energy of hypomania can fuel the anxiety-related symptoms, increasing their prominence and severity and masking other aspects of bipolar disorder. Substance abuse is very common among patients with BSD, making it difficult to determine whether the symptom presentation reflects BSD or the effects of acute or persistent substance use. In some cases, manic and depressive episodes can be accompanied by frank psychosis, particularly when the episodes are untreated, prolonged, or severe. In these cases the patient can be misdiagnosed with a primary diagnosis of a psychotic disorder such as schizophrenia.

Obtaining accurate information to establish a diagnosis can be difficult since it is often not possible to rely on the patient's or even a family member's reports. BSD-related impairments in frontal lobe functioning, particularly those associated with acute episodes of illness, may impair the ability to reliably self-report. The severity of a negative mood can alter the patient's ability to recall past episodes of hypomania or even mania. Symptoms of a mixed state can look and feel like depression, making it difficult to recognize underlying hypomania.

A diagnosis of BSD (or the decision to rule out the diagnosis of BSD) should remain provisional for a period of time, since months may need to pass before the pattern of cycling moods becomes apparent. In the absence of classic and observed signs of mania, careful observation and recording over a period of time are required to confirm this diagnosis. The psychologist's skills in observation, analysis, and careful documentation of symptoms (i.e., changes in mood, energy, irritability, pace and quality of thinking, intrusive thoughts, interpersonal sensitivity, sleep, appetite, motivation) can provide information critical to confirm or disconfirm the diagnosis.

NEUROBIOLOGY

Research on the genetic determinants of BSD suggests that these conditions are likely to be a function of variations in multiple genes and/or the interactive effects of these genes. These variations may result in disruptions in a number of different neurobiological pathways, including those involved in sleep, energy, motivation, mood, stress reactivity, and motor function, and a range of underlying cognitive processes. Environmental circumstances, including stress exposures, have been demonstrated to influence gene expression and affect the degree to which genetic variations have functional importance.

Therefore, rather than thinking of bipolar disorder as a single homogeneous syndrome, it can be useful to recognize that individuals with bipolar disorder may possess one or more different underlying traits or characteristics with observable manifestations (i.e., endophenotypes). These characteristics contribute to the overall symptom picture that is recognized as bipolar disorder. The difficulties in functioning that are associated with some of these underlying characteristics may require treatment, even if the individual does not possess all the characteristics associated with a more classic bipolar symptom presentation.

A clear understanding of the underlying neurobiology permits the clinician to identify potential underlying causes for particular symptoms and to identify the appropriate range of interventions that are required for effective symptom control and personal development. For example, the functional difficulties shown by some patients (e.g., failure to initiate a job search or to get to work on time) are often driven by problems in self-awareness and self-regulation. These difficulties in self-regulation reflect underlying impairments in the ability to tolerate negative affect, delay gratification, direct the focus of attention, and/or to manipulate and organize the information needed to develop and follow a step-by-step plan to achieve the goal, among other capabilities.

The types of strategies used to improve self-regulation depend on the factors that drive the deficits in self-regulation. The underlying capabilities in the regulation of attention, emotion, and behavior and associated cognitive process develop over time. They are subserved at least partly by the frontal lobes.

In patients who do not show evidence of brain disorders such as BSD, the psychologist may suspect that these self-regulatory failures are a function of inadequate or inappropriate training. Since many self-regulatory skills are acquired early in life in the context of relationships, deficits in self-regulation may develop as a result of exposure to poor learning environments (e.g., a dysfunctional family environment or other adverse conditions). In these cases, the psychologist might use the context of the psychotherapeutic relationship to offer psychoeducational and supportive interventions that help the patient to develop the capabilities necessary for independent self-regulation.

However, for patients with BSD, the problems in self-regulation are often driven by disruptions in underlying neurobiological systems that govern diurnal rhythms, reward, mood, and cognition. These difficulties may overwhelm the patient's ability to engage in or benefit from many of the attentional, cognitive, and motivational processes subserved by the frontal lobe and that normally govern goal-directed behavior. For example, difficulties getting out of bed may reflect problems in the length of the sleep/wake cycle, in the experience of pleasure or reward in response to the day's activities, or in the ability to direct the focus of attention or meet the cognitive demands of the day. These disruptions raise substantial barriers to the effective exercise of self-regulation. These barriers can often be addressed, but they must be recognized as separate from deficits in motivation and/or emotional and behavioral control that come from inadequate or harmful learning environments or impaired attachments.

For the overall treatment to be effective, specific interventions to address or compensate for these underlying neurobiological dysfunctions must be incorporated into the protocols. Treatment approaches that fail to consider the ways in which underlying neurobiological abnormalities affect self-regulation can have significant side effects. They can lead patients and their families to assume that defects in learning or attitude (i.e., defects of character or morality) account for the patient's difficulties in functioning. This can promote stigmatization and self-stigmatization that can, in and of themselves, increase symptoms and further impair functioning. To illustrate these issues, we will examine three major areas of functioning that require consideration in the treatment of bipolar disorder.

PROBLEMS IN SLEEP, ENERGY, AND AROUSAL

A growing body of evidence has documented a relationship between bipolar disorder and variations in the genes that govern biological or circadian rhythms. Daily biological rhythms or circadian rhythms are regulated by an internal circadian clock. This central clock resides in the suprachiasmatic nucleus (SCN) of the hypothalamus. The activities of the "clock" are triggered by ambient light hitting the retina, as well as other external (environmental) and internal (e.g., hormonal) factors. The clock regulates rhythms, in part through direct and indirect effects on gene expression throughout the systems of the body. In turn, these actions regulate the duration of the circadian cycle, the onset of sleepiness and wakefulness, fluctuations in body temperature and appetite, and the release of a wide range of hormones, among other factors.

On a daily basis, alterations in circadian rhythms can leave patients feeling depleted of energy or without the metabolic resources needed to face the demands of the day. Patients can feel "jet-lagged" because the internal cues that regulate sleep and wakefulness and arousal are out of sync with the demands of the environment. Problems with the length of the circadian rhythm can make it difficult for patients to keep to a steady schedule, despite being motivated to do so. They may dread potentially stressful encounters or taking new vocational or social risks because they know that without reliable and sustained sleep they will be unable to recover adequately from the previous day's stressors. Circadian cycles also permit us to feel "in sync" with other people when our nonverbal communications of energy and alertness are synchronous. The subjective experience of dysregulation in systems that control energy and wakefulness can impair feelings of social connection.

PROBLEMS IN MOOD LEVEL AND REGULATION

Although the evidence is not fully consistent, there are data suggesting that BSDs are associated with a range of variations in the genes and the processes of gene expression which govern the release and modulation of norepinephrine, dopamine, and serotonin and other neurotransmitters. Variations in the genes that regulate circadian rhythms also affect neurotransmitter synthesis, release, and modulation. Effects on neurotransmitter release and regulation are manifest in highly labile (i.e., changeable) moods or in negative or positive mood states that are too intense or too prolonged in response to environmental triggers.

Emotions interact with the processes that direct our attention, fuel persistence, facilitate the storage and retrieval of memories, and evaluate and organize information. Therefore, dysregulations in the biological systems that govern emotional regulation can have substantial downstream effects on motivation and self-perception. Disruptions in the functioning of neurotransmitter systems may also result in heightened or sustained emotional and physiological activation in response to stress. Heightened stress reactivity can impair the ability to switch the focus of attention, making it more difficult for patients to stop ruminating about stressful events, and consequently prolong stress exposure.

PROBLEMS IN INFORMATION PROCESSING

Although cognitive impairments are not included in the diagnostic criteria for BSD, the condition is associated with a range of difficulties in information processing, including deficits in working memory and executive function. Some individuals may exhibit cognitive difficulties primarily during acute episodes, but there is also evidence of persistent difficulties between episodes, and potentially even prior to the onset of acute illness. These cognitive impairments can be primary drivers of disability.

Deficits in working memory are expressed as limitations in the amount of information the individual is able to manipulate at any one time. Deficits in executive functioning include difficulties in planning, organizing, or sequencing, among other skills. As a consequence, routine multistep tasks (i.e., paying bills, cooking dinner, following medication regimens) may require a level of effort that is much greater than would be required for unaffected individuals. Without a clear understanding of the types of underlying cognitive problems and the barriers these problems create, individuals and their families may assume the person has difficulties in motivation or character. This misunderstanding can be exacerbated if the individual's cognitive performance fluctuates depending on the mood cycle.

TREATMENT

Psychopharmacological interventions are critical to the success of treatment. The medication regimens used to treat BSD are often complex because it is necessary to address multiple neurobiological pathways. Patients may require one or more medications (or other medical treatments) to stabilize mood, address symptoms of anxiety and/or depression, improve attention or memory, decrease psychosis, and control the side effects of other medications.

Psychologists can play a crucial role in maximizing the benefits and minimizing the risks of the medications. The detailed analysis of signs, symptoms, and problems in functioning can help the patient and psychopharmacologist identify targets for treatment and evaluate the effects of the treatment. For example, psychologists can work with patients to determine whether a particular impairment in functioning reflects difficulties with the cognitive demands of the task, deficits in sustained energy or activation, a lack of interest or pleasure, social anxiety, defensive avoidance, or other factors. The choice of medications and psychotherapeutic interventions will depend on the drivers of the symptoms and the functional difficulties. Psychologists also act as educators helping patients, their families, and their physicians develop a common vocabulary to describe the symptoms. Accurate and frequent feedback from the psychologist and patient to the psychopharmacologist is crucial to the effective management of BSD.

Psychologists can also draw on empirically validated therapies for BSD to improve functioning. The therapies include interpersonal and social rhythms therapy, which provides guidance for stabilizing diurnal cycles and decreasing the effects of impairments in circadian regulation on daily life, among other interventions. Family therapy for BSD, another empirically validated approach, works to help reduce exposure to family stress and increase the patient's ability to re-regulate in response to interpersonal conflict. A wide variety of cognitive-behavioral approaches can help patients address issues related to symptoms management and treatment adherence.

THE THERAPEUTIC ALLIANCE

The symptoms of BSD are painful and disorienting. The experience of psychic pain is similar to and as intense as physical pain, and people feel ashamed of being unable to tolerate this pain. Psychologists can use their analytic skills to clarify the nature of the distress, identify triggers, and obtain additional acute treatment (i.e., medication or hospitalization) as necessary. More frequent contact may be required during acute episodes. Many people with BSD respond well to medical intervention and are able to recover fairly rapidly. A proportion of patients whose symptoms are more severe or who do not readily respond to medication can be shocked to realize they have a chronic illness that can impair functioning and independence for a prolonged period. The relationship with the therapist can provide the type of trust and care that can help individuals become more self-accepting, regain hope and faith, and begin to develop and achieve new life goals.

References and Readings

Akiskal, H. S., & Benazzi, F. (2006). The DSM-IV and ICD-10 categories of recurrent (major) depressive and bipolar II disorders: Evidence that they lie on a dimensional spectrum. *Journal of Affective Disorders, 92*(1), 45–54.

Artashez, P., Fargian, S., Levi, A., Yeghiyan, M., Gasparyan, K., Weizman, M.,... Poyurovsky, M. (2006). Obsessive-compulsive disorder in bipolar disorder patients with first manic episode. *Journal of Affective Disorders, 94*, 151–156.

Basco, M. R., McDonald, N., Merlock, M., Rush, A. J., & Wright, J. H. (2004). *A cognitive-behavioral approach to treatment of bipolar I disorder*. Washington, DC: American Psychiatric Publishing.

Brondolo, E., & Amador, X. (2008). *Break the bipolar cycle: A day-to-day guide to recovery*. New York: McGraw-Hill.

Flint, J., Greenspan, R. J., & Kendler, K. S. (2010). *How genes influence behavior*. Oxford, England: Oxford University Press.

Frank, E., Swartz, H. A., Johnson, S. L., & Leahy, R. L. (2004). *Interpersonal and social rhythm therapy*. New York: Guilford Press.

Frank, E., Kupfer, D. J., Thase, M. E., Mallinger, A. G., Swartz, H. A., Eagiolini, A. M.,... Monk, T. (2005). Two-year outcomes for interpersonal and social rhythm therapy in individuals with bipolar I disorder. *Archives of General Psychiatry, 62*(9), 996–1004.

Goodwin, F. K., & Jamison, K. R. (2007). *Manic-depressive illness: Bipolar and recurrent depression* (2nd ed.). New York: Oxford University Press.

Johnson, S. L., & Leahy, R. L. (2004). *Psychological treatment of bipolar disorder*. New York: Guilford Press.

Judd, L. L., & Akiskal, H. S. (2003). The prevalence and disability of bipolar spectrum disorders in the U.S. population: Re-analysis of the ECA database taking into account subthreshold cases. *Journal of Affective Disorders, 73*(1–2), 123–131.

Li, X., Frye, M. A., & Shelton, R. C. (2012). Review of pharmacological treatment in mood disorders and future directions for drug development. *Neuropsychopharmacology Reviews, 37*(1), 1–25.

Miklowitz, D. J., Akiskal, H. S., & Tohen, M. (2006). *Psychosocial interventions in bipolar disorders: Rationale and effectiveness*. Hoboken, NJ: Wiley.

National Institutes of Health. (n.d.). www.nimh.nih.gov/healthinformation/bipolarmenu.cfm

National Institutes of Health. (n.d.). www.nimh.nih.gov/publicat/NIMHmedicate.pdf

Walter, G., Taylor, A., Porter, R., Mulder, R. T., & Berk, M. (2009). Clinical practice recommendations for bipolar disorder. *Acta Psychiatrica Scandinavica, 119*(Suppl. 439), 27–46.

64 TAILORING TREATMENT TO THE PATIENT'S RACE AND ETHNICITY

Guillermo Bernal and Melanie M. Domenech Rodríguez

There is strong consensus at present that ethnic minorities have been underserved in mental health. To address these health disparities, scholars have been asked to address cultural competence of practitioners and the applicability of evidence-based treatments. Cultural adaptations pertain to treatments yet require practitioners to be culturally competent. We define cultural adaptations as "the systematic modification of an evidence-based treatment (EBT) or intervention protocol to consider language, culture, and context in such a way that it is compatible with the client's cultural patterns, meanings, and values" (Bernal, Jimenéz-Chafey, & Domenech Rodríguez, 2009, p. 362). We review the rationale, conceptual frameworks, and evidence supporting the use of cultural adaptation models. We also provide guidelines for cultural adaptations and recommendation for future directions.

RATIONALE

There are solid reasons rooted in science and practice to utilize cultural adaptations in implementing EBTs. From a science perspective, EBTs are presumed to be ecologically valid for the groups on which they were developed and tested but may not be for other racial and ethnic groups. A careful conceptualization of commonalities across theories of psychotherapy (Ford & Urban, 1998) reveals three primary components that can be understood as underlying assumptions, mechanisms of change, and intervention techniques associated with a theory. There is ample evidence of differences in worldviews, values, beliefs about health and illness, and specific behaviors across cultural groups that could call into question any or all of the three common components of psychotherapies. In the absence of evidence supporting the use of EBTs across ethnic and cultural groups, we advocate for the use of "the best available evidence" (American Psychological Association [APA], 2006) in engaging cultural adaptations, which can in turn be documented and tested to establish the much-needed verification of treatment utility.

From a practice perspective, psychotherapy is assumed to be a cultural phenomenon that emerged in a particular historical context and has evolved over time. Psychotherapy has been adapted since it was born in the late 19th century, morphing in structure (couch, chair, phone, Internet), format (individual, groups, family, networks), intensity (multiple times per week, weekly, biweekly; changes to the 60-minute hour), and in content (e.g., from an id-based to ego-base psychology as psychoanalysis crossed the Atlantic). In the United States, Carl Rogers Americanized psychoanalysis by retaining key elements (e.g., focus on the therapy relationship) but adapting others to be more culturally attuned to middle-class US values (e.g., present oriented, focused on personal growth and actualization). A historical perspective would suggest that we have been adapting psychotherapy since its inception (see Chapter 1, Bernal & Domenech Rodríguez, 2012).

Early clinical experiences documented by ethnic minority psychologists led to questions regarding the utility of contemporary psychotherapy models with diverse populations. The challenges of engagement, retention, and outcomes led to calls on the need for "sensitivity," "relevance," and later "competence" in working with clients of a different race and ethnicity. The emergence of an ethnic minority psychology, later a multicultural psychology in the United States, the changing demographics of the population, and the lack of treatment outcome studies on diverse populations coalesced to further question the generalizability of the efficacy studies with racial and ethnic groups. These findings were of tremendous relevance given the literature on common factors (Norcross, 2011). These show that the psychotherapeutic relationship is critical to success regardless of underlying assumptions, stated theories, and specific techniques of a treatment.

In its most current form, evidence-based psychological practice calls for combining the best research evidence with competent expertise in delivering treatments, in the context of patient characteristics (APA, 2006). As such, cultural adaptations work to thoughtfully and systematically transport conventional models of EBTs to other cultural and linguistic groups, taking into account research approaches (e.g., gathering observations) and the most up-to-date findings in treatment application to ethnic and culturally diverse populations, while acknowledging the critical importance of clinician characteristics (e.g., cultural competence).

CONCEPTUAL FRAMEWORKS

There are 12 published cultural adaptation models identified in a systematic review (see Chapter 2, Bernal & Domenech Rodríguez, 2012) with more models surely waiting to be identified. Cultural adaptation models published since the mid-1990s appear to have been developed in relative isolation. For example, 8 of the 12 models were published between 2004 and 2006, suggesting that authors were working in parallel to help define their needs in attempting to reach racial and ethnic minorities. This body of work now provides us with the opportunity to cull the commonality in recommendations from these experts. There are a number of similarities across models that lend credibility to the recommendations for cultural adaptations. Chief among the recommendations, stated or implied in the models, is to follow a *systematic and rigorous process* that includes *documentation* and *evaluation* of the cultural adaptations. Most of these models also share two important attributes; they advocate for the use of *multiple/flexible methods* to gather information, and they specify that the cultural adaptation *process is iterative*, that is, adjustments are to be expected in the process of making adaptations.

The systematic procedures laid out across models vary in the way they prioritize particular actions; however, there is a great deal of consensus on the importance of *learning from important stakeholders* in treatment delivery. These stakeholders can be key community members, agency leaders, or specific individuals (e.g., clients, treatment providers). In addition, authors call for *maximizing existing knowledge*, pointing to the particular importance of culturally relevant variables (e.g., acculturative stress, discrimination, immigration, spirituality, cultural values) that may be, or may exert their influence upon, predictors, mediators/moderators, and outcomes. Indeed, cultural adaptations models are broadly concerned with modifications to the process and content of treatments that can support increased *engagement*, *acceptability*, and/or *outcomes* of treatments.

Many of the cultural adaptation models advance the need for addressing *ecological validity* of EBTs, that is, the alignment of the treatment with the client's cultural experience, language, and context. To that effect, some models point to common roots in Bronfenbrenner's ecological systems theory and Roger's diffusion of innovation theory. Many also consider *treatment provider characteristics* as central to the success of the cultural adaptation process. What specific characteristics are explicitly stated within models vary (e.g., collaborative approach, ethnic or language matching).

EVIDENCE

There is now strong evidence for the benefits of culturally adapting treatments. Several narrative reviews and four meta-analyses on the effectiveness of cultural adaptations have been published. Here we review the most recent reports published in 2011. In one study of 65 clinical trials with 8,620 clients, cultural adaptations were superior to the treatments that did not explicitly incorporate culture (Smith, Domenech Rodríguez, & Bernal, 2011). A medium effect size (d = .46) showed that clients receiving culturally adapted treatments had better outcomes. Those treatments that included a variety of cultural adaptations tended to be more effective than those with fewer adaptations, and those treatments that were attuned to client outcome goals and those that involved cultural metaphors tended to be more effective in contrast to other treatments. Another meta-analysis of 59 clinical trials with 1,242 clients directly compared culturally adapted to an unadapted or conventional psychotherapy (Benish, Quintana, & Wampold, 2011). An effect size (d = .32) showed that culturally adapted treatments were again superior to the unadapted ones. Outcome differences for the culturally adapted treatments were moderated by the explanatory model of the illness myth that is fundamentally cultural.

CULTURAL ADAPTATION GUIDELINES

We advance the thesis that the cultural adaptation process begins with the selection of a treatment. A treatment is selected based on relevance to the presenting concern and the fit of the underlying assumptions, stated theory, and associated techniques with the values, beliefs, and practices of the ethnic and cultural group population for which it is needed. Once a treatment is selected, the next question is: Are cultural adaptations needed? Answers will vary depending on whether the EBT (1) targets the appropriate mechanisms for good outcomes in the population of interest, (2) is itself acceptable to the population of interest, (3) has acceptable related treatment procedures (e.g., evaluation procedures), and (4) is sufficiently flexible to coordinate "fidelity" and "fit." In addition to these considerations and during this initial phase, it is critical to examine the availability of the EBT to practitioners in the field. Some EBTs require intense training to reach competent delivery standards and the time and financial resources required place them out of practical reach for treatment providers.

If cultural adaptations are warranted, we recommend that a systematic framework be followed, that all adaptations are carefully documented, and that outcomes are evaluated as much as possible. More specifically, we recommend involving the target population as much as possible. There are exemplars in the literature for how to do this, such as giving potential clients the manual procedures and gathering their impressions of their utility, acceptability, and relevance. We also recommend involving treatment providers with expertise in the particular ethnic and cultural group. The existing literature is rich and decade reviews and meta-analyses can be useful ways for practitioners in particular to get the most up-to-date findings in a manageable time frame. We advocate for thoughtful planning incorporating all these sources of knowledge prior to delivering a culturally adapted intervention. We also advocate for frequent checks on the impact of the treatment. In research this can be done by way of pilot tests prior to a large trial. In private practice this can be achieved via frequent and brief evaluations (e.g., peer observations, self-report, client reports).

Finally, we recommend those engaging in cultural adaptations of EBTs to carefully consider specific details of delivery such as format (e.g., group, individual), participants (i.e., Who should participate in treatment?), packaging (e.g., psychoeducation, psychotherapy), and location (e.g., school, therapy office, home visit). Other sources of support may also help in the evaluation process and associated iterations, such as regular peer consultation groups or a community advisory board.

CONCLUSIONS

There is a strong rationale for adaptations, models to follow, and evidence of positive impact. We are in an excellent position to take the next "big steps" to advance the field. The commonalities across models suggest an opportunity for convergence so that efforts can be directed at testing the cultural adaptation process (e.g., Which parts of the process yield the most powerful information?), types (e.g., Which adaptations yield the most benefit?), and utility (e.g., How can researchers and practitioners make cultural adaptation models more relevant for use in applied practice?). Another pressing need in the literature now concerns examples of culturally adapted treatments wherein researchers and practitioners alike can observe examples of the recommendations put into practice (e.g., What is an example of a "context" adaptation to an EBT?).

References and Readings

American Psychological Association. (2006). Evidence-based practice in psychology. *American Psychologist, 61*, 271–285.

Benish, S. G., Quintana, S., & Wampold, B. E. (2011). Culturally adapted psychotherapy and the legitimacy of myth: A direct-comparison meta-analysis. *Journal of Counseling Psychology, 58*, 279–289.

Bernal, G., Jiménez-Chafey, M. I., & Domenech Rodríguez, M. M. (2009). Cultural adaptation of treatments: A resource for considering culture in evidence-based practice. *Professional Psychology: Research and Practice, 40*, 361–368.

Bernal, G., & Domenech Rodríguez, M. M. (2012). *Cultural adaptations: Tools for evidence-based practice with diverse populations*. Washington, DC: American Psychological Association.

Ford, D. H., & Urban, H. B. (1998). *Contemporary models of psychotherapy: A comparative analysis* (2nd ed.). Hoboken, NJ: Wiley.

Norcross, J. C. (2011). *Psychotherapy relationships that work: Evidence-based responsiveness* (2nd ed.). New York & London: Oxford University Press.

Smith, T. D., Domenech Rodríguez, M. M., & Bernal, G. (2011). Culture. *Journal of Clinical Psychology, 67*, 166–175.

Whaley, A. L., & Davis, K. E. (2007). Cultural competence and evidence-based practice in mental health services: A complementary perspective. *American Psychologist, 62*, 563–574.

Related Topics

Chapter 10, "Using the *DSM-5* and *ICD-11* in Forensic and Clinical Applications with Children Across Racial and Ethnic Lines"

Chapter 69, "When English Is Not the First Language: Psychotherapeutic Considerations"

65 CONSIDERATIONS IN TREATING PEOPLE WITH DISABILITIES

Rochelle Balter

At any time, up to 20% of the US population, approximately 49 million people, report having a physical or sensory disability (CDC, 2009). These numbers only reflect those noninstitutionalized adults who do not have emotional disabilities. The percentage increases when we look at individuals over 65 years of age (CDC, 2009). Given these statistics, most psychologists will likely have one or more individuals with disabilities in their practices. These statistics also suggest that among their able-bodied clients, one or more may acquire a disability. However, since many disabilities are invisible and often not included in research samples or psychotherapy treatment groups, little information or training exists for those who treat people with disabilities.

This discussion will be limited to clients with physical (i.e., paralysis, weakness, and neurological issues, including traumatic brain injury and spinal cord injury) and sensory (i.e., blindness and visual impairment, deafness and hearing problems) disabilities.

DEFINING DISABILITY

The currently accepted definition of *disability* that appears in the Americans with Disabilities Act (1990) describes it "as a physical or mental impairment that substantially limits one or more major life activities of an individual." Major life activities include self-care tasks and manual tasks, seeing, hearing, eating, ambulation, speech, cognitive activities (thinking), communicating, and working. The amended ADA (ADAAA) also includes dysfunctional bodily processes in its definition of major life activities. The systems listed include, but are not limited to, problems with the immune system, digestive system, and neurological, brain, respiratory, and circulatory systems. An impairment that substantially limits one major life activity need not limit other major life activities in order to be considered a disability (ADAAA, 2008).

The ADA declared individuals with disabilities as a discrete and insular minority that has been subjected to a history of discrimination similar to other minority groups. An impairment may be readily apparent to observers or invisible (e.g., heart disease, respiratory problems, or diabetes). People with disabilities are a heterogeneous group. Individuals with similar diagnoses may have very different functional levels and appear very different to observers. For example, people with emphysema may show no symptoms or may need to carry an oxygen supply and nose piece; people with spinal cord injuries may use an electric wheelchair, walk with crutches, or simply demonstrate an awkward gait.

FACTORS THAT INFLUENCE HOW DISABILITY IS PERCEIVED

Consider the following factors when treating individuals with disabilities.

Time of Onset of the Disability

Individuals who are born with a disability often have a very different experience from those with adolescent or adult onset because the disabling condition will vary the person's developmental trajectory. When the disability occurs at birth or early in life, the child often undergoes treatment, may spend periods of time in rehabilitation facilities, and learns to play roles designated by parents and the system to earn approval. Those who develop disabilities in adolescence or early adulthood may need to deal with thwarted dreams, interrupted goals, reevaluating life's possibilities, and sometimes having to lose independence temporarily or permanently. Since the individual has already begun to experience independence, the transition to the adulthood period can prove difficult. When onset occurs during adulthood, a major upheaval typically follows. Those who develop disabilities after retirement age (incidence of disability increases after age 75) may be more familiar with the adaptive process if they have seen friends go through it, or they may become depressed and feel hopeless if they see the acquired disability as an end to life as they know it.

The Mechanism or Type of Onset May also Serve as a Defining Factor

If onset occurs at birth or in infancy, parental stress, care burdens, and attachment issues (i.e., the infant with a disability is difficult to hold or comfort) may lead to problematic parenting issues and potential abuse or neglect. If the disability results from an accident in adolescence or adulthood, adapting to the sudden life change, role reversals, and loss of status that occur are life changing. If the onset is due to a chronic condition with the possibility of a loss of overall function (e.g., multiple sclerosis or Parkinson's disease) even though the progression of disabilities is anticipated, a wide range of emotional responses to this reality can follow. If the onset flows from illness or degenerative causes in older individuals, a sense of hopelessness and anger may develop. The reactions are not often predictable. Each individual may react differently to the incurred disability. Healthy aging may be accompanied by aches and pains, but these do not necessarily indicate impending disability. However, when disability becomes a factor, if accompanied by depression and feelings of hopelessness, these feelings should become a focus of professional mental health treatment.

GENDER, RACE, ETHNICITY, AND SEXUAL ORIENTATION

Disability does not discriminate, occurring in both sexes, all ethnoracial groups, and among all sexual orientations. Women and men who acquire disabilities often find themselves treated and regarded differently. Women face more discrimination based on disability than men. They have a higher unemployment rate, lower salaries when hired in similar positions, and are offered lesser positions than males with disabilities. Women with disabilities are often subjected to higher rates of domestic violence and other abuses than women without a disability and more frequently than men who have a disability. Among individuals who identify with more than one minority group, or multiple minorities, there may be a hierarchy of identities. There may be both inter-identity and intra-identity conflicts depending upon how one's primary identity group regards the other minority group the client belongs to. The client's racial identification group may not welcome ethnically similar individuals, if they are gay or lesbian. The group in question might also feel similarly about the client's disability status. Sexual orientation may remain covert and when disability is invisible, it too can be hidden depending on group pressures. In some ethnic groups a disability may be regarded as a matter for families to handle privately, whereas other groups may offer assistance or actually reject those with disabilities outright.

SOCIAL, CULTURAL, AND RELIGIOUS FACTORS

Many cultural and religious groups have unique ways of viewing disability. In some cultures, the individual with the disability is viewed as dependent and in need of care and protection. This may interfere with the individual's desire for autonomy and a "normal life." The protective attitude may also change family dynamics in a number of negative ways with caretakers feeling resentment toward their new obligations and other family members feeling ignored and marginalized. Such attitudes may result not only in anger directed toward the person with the disability but also anger from that individual regarding how she or he now feels treated.

Religion has historically regarded certain physical conditions as representing punishment for past sins and as engendering shame. If people with a disability believe that their present situation is deserved, it may prevent them from engaging in activities needed to maintain health and safety. If the family attends a church that believes in healing services and laying on of hands, and, if the client is not healed, family problems may emerge regarding sin and blame. Such individuals with disabilities may realize that hard work will be involved in adapting to their conditions and may reject family religious values, leading to further problems.

EDUCATION AND PROFESSION/WORK ENVIRONMENT

Individuals who experience a disability as an adult (depending on the functional limitations that accompany the condition) may have to change their professions, return to school to retrain, or learn to cope with new conditions in their workplace. Those who experience spinal cord injuries and who previously engaged in physically active work may need to change fields, whereas those who did computer programming or accounting may simply need some reasonable accommodations. Individuals who lived alone before becoming disabled may no longer find this possible or may require personal assistants. If the newly disabled person was the head of a household or the primary wage earner, this role may now be taken by other family members, with resulting role reversals triggering a loss of self-worth.

MISCONCEPTIONS REGARDING DISABILITY

Physical and sensory disabilities often impact only one body part or system. Therefore, it is inaccurate to look at the total person as "disabled." Ideally, the therapist will view such clients as persons "with a disability," since the disability does not define the client's personhood. Clients with disabilities often have excellent health and should not be treated as ill. A person who is deaf or hard of hearing, or blind or visually impaired may have better general health than the therapist. Having a paralyzed limb or a missing limb is not an indication of one's general health or cognitive abilities. Sadly, many in our society believe that those who use wheelchairs or walkers are also probably hard of hearing or likely to have mental retardation. Health and mental health professionals tend to raise their voice volume when addressing clients with disabilities or speak to them in simpler language. This can be a hurtful error. Many people who use assistive devices have above average intelligence. If a client with a disability comes to see a psychologist and has a personal assistant or aide with her or him, it does not mean that the aide should be included in the therapeutic process or asked questions about the client. When this happens, as it often does, it feels demeaning to the client and may hinder forging a successful therapeutic relationship.

THEORIES OF DISABILITY

The first model of disability was the "moral model" that defined the disability as caused by a moral lapse or sin. In this model the cause was attributed to the individual as mentioned in the Bible. Punishments were imposed for these supposed sins, including banishment and stoning. The problem was seen as inherent to the individual.

The "medical model" views disability as a disease process that needs to be treated and cured. Patients are expected to overcome their problems and match their behavior to those in the dominant culture who are nondisabled. This model also sees the disability as inherent in the individual.

The "social model" holds that society is responsible for the problems that people with physical and/or sensory disabilities encounter and society has the responsibility for correcting these inequalities (Olkin, 2002). This model is becoming more accepted than the moral and medical models, but it too may lead to cognitive distortions, client anger, an unrealistic sense of entitlement, and an inability to deal with daily problems, which may involve medical treatment.

No matter which of these models the therapist subscribes to, one must use caution not to impose the therapist's chosen model on the client.

PREPARING TO SEE CLIENTS WITH PHYSICAL/ SENSORY DISABILITIES

The therapist should take a number of thoughtful steps before seeing a client with a disability. One of the most basic steps is to insure that both the psychologist's office and other services are accessible to the individual. Stairs (even one or two steps), narrow doorways, and small bathrooms are not welcoming spaces to wheelchair users. Those who are deaf may need an interpreter to benefit from services. One must address these issues before attempting to see the client. Therapists will also need to supply information on whether guide dogs and service animals are allowed in their offices.

The therapist also needs to be emotionally and ideologically accessible. Before seeing a client with a disability, professionals should acquaint themselves with information on the client's disability type in general and then preferably should check their own attitudes regarding the disability in question. This inventory should include whether the therapist feels fearful about any aspect of working with the client, whether the therapist has any stereotypic beliefs about groups that share the client's disability (e.g., all people who are blind need to be addressed loudly using simple words), or any preconceived issues that might interfere with the therapist's ability to clearly hear the client's issues. These ideas and emotions may involve a feeling of hopelessness about helping the client; feelings of pity for the client or family; or the idea that the person with the disability by virtue of having the disability is somehow flawed, which leads the psychologist to feel helpless in the face of what seems like overwhelming odds. If this were to occur, the psychologist should probably refer the client to someone else.

TREATING CLIENTS WITH DISABILITIES

Psychologists from any theoretical orientation have the ability to treat clients with disabilities, unless there is a specific capability that the client needs to have in the approach being used. Clients with disabilities are an underserved population and a heterogeneous cohort on which little research has been performed. There presently are no evidence-based approaches focused on clients with disabilities or with disability-related issues.

The first step in treating a client with a disability is the same as treating someone who is not disabled (i.e., determining the presenting problem). Clients with disabilities often see a psychologist for help with problems of daily living, relationship difficulties, performance anxiety, and other problems that are unrelated to their disabilities. The disability is not always the problem or even a part of the problem. However, if the psychologist identifies a nonexistent problem, the client may become docile and leave therapy, rather than standing up to an authority figure. Since clients with disabilities have often been/are involved in medical treatment, they have learned not to defend themselves for fear of losing services and necessary benefits.

It is often helpful for the psychologist to use an active listening and supportive approach during the first few therapy sessions. This helps the client to adapt to the new situation and to see the psychologist as someone who will assist the client to change rather than as just another expert/authority figure. The supportive stance will also help the therapist to see the patient's world through the patient's eyes (Balter, 1997).

It is sometimes difficult for nondisabled psychologists to truly hear and understand what the patient is relating because it is often foreign to the therapist's experiences. The therapist, no matter what her or his theoretical orientation might be, needs to listen carefully to the patient's narrative concerning her or his life and to collect extensive data before diagnosing the patient or challenging the client about the reality of her or his world. Establishing a trusting, nonjudgmental, and safe environment in which the client may reveal beliefs that may initially sound different, but on further exploration turn out to describe a very different world, is important in facilitating client change.

Such clients may also present with problems that may involve disability status, but they may not be aware of it. In this eventuality, the psychologist needs to gather data to present to the client, indicating why the psychologist believes that disability is part of the problem. To accomplish such a task, the psychologist may need to use the client's own verbalizations and what the client has said about those who do not have disabilities and how they cope. The psychologist may have to set up such a situation and ask the client whether she or he were not disabled, would the problem still be a problem and how would the individual handle it.

The client may also present with problems that are definitely disability related. These require exploration in depth and the client should be reassured that the problem is believable and does not make the perceiver see her or him as "crazy." In this situation, the psychologist needs to allow the client to act as expert on her or his disability and world. The client can then be given the responsibility for explaining her or his universe to the psychologist. Using open-ended questions and respectful listening will be valuable in establishing a trusting relationship with the client. In this instance it is also valuable to ascertain where the client is in the adaptation process when she or he comes to the psychologist.

If the person has a fairly new traumatic brain injury such as a stroke, she or he has probably been treated in a rehabilitation program. During such a program, which usually lasts a number of weeks, the client is probably reacting with denial and disbelief to what has happened in her or his life. Near the end of the rehabilitation process, the patient is just beginning to experience emotions connected with life changes she or he is facing but is not yet quite ready to confront the consequences of the disability. If this patient comes for outpatient treatment, the psychologist will need to work on coping skills and gathering community resources for the client. This type of problem is seen with returning injured military veterans.

If the individual with the disability has recovered and the problem seems to be "outside" of the client, in society, using a socio-therapeutic approach may be of use. This would validate the client's beliefs about the major culture without conferring victim status (Balter, 1997, 2012). Using data collection methods, including thought diaries, narratives, role plays, administering repeated mood state measures (e.g., the Beck Depression Inventory), and frequency of event diaries to gather data, will help the therapist to gauge attitude and behavioral change. As with all therapies, the client and therapist negotiate goals. Since clients can only work on changing themselves, and not others, goals may need to be renegotiated to teaching the client how to cope with other peoples' beliefs without incorporating them and to accommodate to the beliefs of important people in their lives without upsetting themselves or adopting their unworkable beliefs.

A psychoeducational approach often works well with clients who have disabilities, since it is focused, respectful, and easy for clients to adapt to. Based on psychotherapy integration models, almost any psychotherapeutic school of thought can adapt techniques and exercises utilized in other approaches. All approaches will work if marked by respect, empathy, and a sense of working with and fully hearing the client with a disability.

References and Readings

Americans with Disabilities Amendments Act. Secs 1201 et Seq., 42 U.S.C.A. (PL 110-325) (2008)

Balter, R. (1997). Using REBT with clients with disabilities. In J. Yankura & W. Dryden (Eds.), *Special applications of REBT: A therapist's casebook* (pp. 69–100). New York: Springer.

Balter, R. (2012). Using cognitive-behavioral therapy with clients who identify with more than one minority group: Can one size fit all? In R. Nettles & R. Balter (Eds.), *Multiple minority identities: Applications for practice, research and training* (pp. 117–140) New York: Springer.

Center for Disease Control (2009). *MMWR Weekly, 58*(16), 421–426.

Mona, L., Romesser-Sechnet, J., Cameron, R., & Cardenas, V. (2006). Cognitive-behavioral therapy an people with disabilities. In P. Hays & G. Iwamasa (Eds.), *Culturally responsive cognitive behavioral therapy: Assessment, practice and supervision* (pp. 199–222). Washington, DC: American Psychiatric Association.

Olkin, R. (2002). Could you hold the door for me? Including disability in diversity. *Cultural Diversity and Ethnic Minority Psychology, 8*(2), 130–137.

Related Topics

Chapter 70, "Understanding Sexuality in the Context of Disability"

Chapter 71, "Helping Patients Cope with Chronic Medical Illness"

66 PRACTICING HARM REDUCTION

Andrew Tatarsky

Harm reduction (HR) is a philosophy and a set of methods geared toward reducing the harms associated with risky behavior and improving the quality of life of the individual and the community. David Purchase, an early American harm reductionist, "suggested that harm reduction is more of an attitude than a fixed set of rules or regulations…a humanitarian stance that accepts the inherent dignity of human life and facilitates the ability to 'see oneself in the eyes of the other'" (Marlatt, 1998, p. 6).

HR emerged in response to the limitations of the traditional "abstinence-only" addiction treatments (Denning & Little, 2011; Marlatt, 1998; Tatarsky, 2007). It is an alternative paradigm for reducing the harms associated with substance use and other potentially risky behavior. Its emphasis on "starting where the person is" facilitates treatment matching and the therapeutic alliance and, thus, has increased effectiveness of treatments for a broad spectrum of problems. HR is also a human rights movement in that it asserts that members of stigmatized populations deserve the same respect, understanding, and care that the rest of society gets.

Harm reduction methods are generally considered to be strategies for working with clients who are not ready, willing, or able to embrace complete abstinence. There is much peer-reviewed, controlled trial research to support the efficacy of harm reduction with a wide variety of clients and disorders (Marlatt, Larimer, & Witkiewitz, 2012).

PRINCIPLES OF HARM REDUCTION

1. *Risky behavior has always and will always be part of the human repertoire.* Efforts to eradicate risky behavior have always failed. HR shifts the focus to helping people find ways to reduce the negative consequences of engaging in risk behavior.
2. *All reductions in drug-related harm are seen as successes.* Harm exists on a continuum of severity. HR seeks to help modify behavior along the continuum toward reduced risk. HR rejects abstinence as a necessary commitment to enter treatment or the only acceptable goal and, instead, recognizes any reduction of harm as valuable to the individual user and to society. This shift in focus opens the door to the whole range of ways that drug-related harm can be reduced, including safer methods of using, switching to safer substances, reducing, and abstaining. Small incremental positive changes are seen as steps in the right direction. Small steps, which build self-efficacy, are often integrated before next steps are possible. This is generally how behavior change happens.
3. *Meet the patient as an individual.* This principle reflects the fact that substance users and others who engage in risky behavior are widely diverse groups that vary on every psychosocial variable and, therefore, their patterns of use and the meanings that these behaviors have to them will vary accordingly. The clinical implication is that effective treatment must be individually tailored to each patient's unique characteristics.
4. *Meet the person where the person is.* HR has been called "compassionate pragmatism" (Marlatt, 1998) because it pragmatically acknowledges that people always have used potentially harmful substances and engage in risky behavior and that effective interventions must address drug users where they are. Compassionate understanding of the user is necessary to guide the development of interventions that will be both effective and acceptable to the person. Concretely, the treatment must embrace the goals and motivation the patient comes with. This enables the possibility of collaboration between patient and provider in the development of methods, decision making, and therapeutic relationships. Thus, the form, direction, and timing of the treatment can emerge out of collaboration rather than predetermined ways that are likely to derail treatment (Tatarsky & Marlatt, 2010).
5. *The patient's strengths can be mobilized in the service of treatment.* Patients come with many strengths that can be identified and supported in the service of their growth: the part of them that wants to feel better brings energy and motivation to change; the self-reflective part supports learning about the nature of the struggle and suffering; the adventurous, curious, and risk-taking qualities can support trying something new in the service of positive change.
6. *Do not hold a commitment to abstinence or other preconceived notions as preconditions for treatment before knowing the person.* Decisions about what people need or what treatment should be will prove most effective if they emerge out of an understanding of the patient and what the patient wants.
7. *Develop a collaborative relationship with the patient.* Collaboration between consumers and professionals in choosing interventions and designing programs has been central to HR. This is consistent with a number of contemporary therapeutic approaches such as motivational interviewing, humanistic therapy, cognitive-behavioral therapy, and relational psychoanalysis. Since the clinician cannot know what is best for the patient, she supports the patient in the discovery and clarification of what the patient needs.
8. *Destigmatize substance use and substance users.* People who use mood-altering substances or engage in risky behavior tend to be stigmatized in our culture. Stigma, the marginalizing of a group of people by labeling them as different and stereotyping them, dehumanizes, impedes understanding, and derails relationships. Clinicians must be alert to stigma as a social countertransference that can interfere with the therapeutic alliance. Stigma in patients can contribute to despair and self-hate and interfere with

their hopefulness. Stigma in institutions often is reflected in policies that are countertherapeutic, such as clinics that will not offer psychotherapy to patients who use drugs.

9. *People engage in risky behavior for a wide variety of reasons.* Most harm reductionists understand these behaviors in the context of the whole person in his or her social context (Denning, 2000; Tatarsky & Kellogg, 2010). These behaviors also take on multiple positive and negative meanings that are expressed by behavior: self-care, self-soothing, coping, self-medication, interpersonal expression, self-sabotage, group membership, and identity, to name a few. These variables interact in ways that are unique to each person. An accurate understanding of this interaction guides the design of effective interventions.
9. *The stages of change can guide HR work.* The stages acknowledge that the vast majority of humans engaging in risky behavior are not in the action stage; much work is required before people make a decision to change (see Chapter 34, this volume). The stages provide a rationale and structure to HR approaches.

METHODS OF HARM REDUCTION

- *Capitalize on the therapeutic alliance.* The therapeutic alliance is the expression of the HR principle of starting where the patient is. It has been found to be one of the most important contributors to treatment success (Norcross, 2011). The alliance is based on an agreement between patient and therapist on goals, consensus on tasks, and the quality of the bond between them. Thus, the patient's motivation and goals throughout the treatment are the basis for the alliance. The therapist's preconceived agenda for the patient is understood as countertransference that must be identified as potentially contaminating the therapist's capacity to listen. Alliance ruptures may be repaired if the therapist is alert to negative affect in the patient and willing to inquire with openness to owning her contribution to the rupture (see Chapter 52, this volume).
- *View the therapeutic relationship as a healing agent.* The therapeutic relationship is negotiated by therapist and patient as the therapist attempts to meet the patient with empathy and respect and offer aspects of herself to the patient in accord with the patient's needs. This creates safety and support for the patient's self-reflection, integration of self-management skills, and the possibility of reworking the patient's relational difficulties in the therapeutic relationship.
- *Build skills for self-regulation and positive change.* Risky behavior often reflects difficulties in self-regulation related to a failure to integrate these capacities in early relationships. Curiosity motivates self-reflection and learning. The therapist's genuine curiosity about the patient and empathic inquiry invite the patient to be curious. Teaching cognitive and behavioral skills for observing oneself (mindfulness) and regulating affective experience are often critical to the patient for making use of therapy and effectively modifying problematic behavior. These skills enable the patient to get in the driver's seat of the behavior change process. They are brought together in "urge-surfing" (Bowen, Chawla, & Marlatt, 2010). Bringing nonjudgmental awareness to the urge and sitting with the urge with slow, deep breathing enables reflection and a consideration of the meaning of the urge and safer, more satisfying alternative choices. These skills can be learned in the therapeutic process and can be taught in skills groups that focus on mindfulness and breathing techniques. Yoga and meditation also support these skills.
- *Treat assessment as part of treatment.* Assessment is not separate from treatment proper. The assessment and feedback process in the early sessions can promote the patient's self-awareness of the severity and multiple meanings of the problem behavior and co-occurring problems. Motivation to change emerges from this deepening self-awareness.
- *Unwrap the urge.* To the extent that the urge to engage in problematic behavior expresses meanings (feelings, needs, and wishes) that are out of awareness, the urge must be unwrapped to reveal them so they can be expressed in less potentially harmful,

more self-caring ways. This is accomplished by encouraging the patient to surf the urge and reflect on it. One might suggest that the patient ask questions such as: What thoughts, feelings, or images come to mind? What does the urge want? Does the urge have a story to tell? What part of you is expressing itself through the urge?

- *Embrace ambivalence.* To the extent that risky behavior expresses vital aspects of the person and significant functions, the patient is likely to be ambivalent about changing. The ambivalence must be accepted, respected, and clarified in order for a consideration of new ways to address what is expressed in the ambivalence. Inviting the patient to talk about both sides of the ambivalence invites the conflict into the therapy and enables a consideration of new resolutions to the dilemma. This process also promotes the experience of being a more integrated self in the presence of an other.
- *Set HR goals.* Clarification of risk and ambivalence about change make it possible to consider positive goals. Offering the patient choice of goals has been empirically shown to increase retention in therapy and positive outcomes (Marlatt, 1998). Whatever positive goal the patient is motivated to pursue is the starting point for treatment: safer use (e.g., opiate substitution treatment), reduced use, moderation, abstinence, or a goal unrelated to the problem behavior. "Any positive change" translates therapeutically into whatever small or large goal the patient is ready to pursue. Small changes build self-efficacy and build toward larger changes.
- *Personalize planning for working toward change.* Based on the assessment of the various domains related to the problem behavior, its meaning, the patient's goals, and the stage of change, a personalized plan can be developed.
- *Use the Ideal Use Plan exercise to clarify goals and planning to achieve them.* In this exercise the patient is asked to consider what might be one's ideal relationship to the problem behavior, one that maximizes the benefits and minimizes the costs. This will include the amount, frequency, and intensity of the behavior as well as changes in one's self-care, self-management, and lifestyle that will support the desired change. The Plan is a work in progress that can be implemented as an ongoing experiment with results leading to modifications in the direction of reduced cost and increased benefit.

References and Readings

Denning, P., & Little, J. (2011). *Practicing harm reduction psychotherapy: An alternative approach to the addictions* (2nd ed.). New York: Guilford Press.

Kellogg, S. (2003). On "gradualism" and the building of the harm reduction-abstinence continuum. *Journal of Substance Abuse Treatment, 25,* 241–247.

Marlatt, A, Larimer, M., & Witkiewitz, K. (2012). *Harm reduction: Pragmatic strategies for managing high risk behaviors* (2nd ed.). New York: Guilford Press.

Norcross, J. C. (Ed.). (2011). *Psychotherapy relationships that work* (2nd ed.). New York: Oxford University Press.

Rotgers, F., Kern, M., & Hoetzel, R. (2002). *Responsible drinking: A moderation management approach for problem drinkers.* Oakland, CA: New Harbinger.

Tatarsky, A. (2003). Harm reduction psychotherapy: Extending the reach of traditional treatment. *Journal of Substance Abuse Treatment, 25,* 249–256.

Tatarsky, A. (2007). *Harm reduction psychotherapy: A new treatment for drug and alcohol problems.* Northvale, NJ: Jason Aronson.

Tatarsky, A., & Kellogg, S. (2010). Integrative harm reduction psychotherapy: A case of substance use, multiple trauma and suicidality. *Journal of Clinical Psychology: In Session, 66,* 123–135.

Related Topics

Chapter 33, "Compendium of Evidence-Based Therapy Relationships"

Chapter 34, "Applying the Stages of Change"

Chapter 40, "Conducting Motivational Interviewing"

Chapter 52, "Repairing Ruptures in the Therapeutic Alliance"

Chapter 70, "Understanding Sexuality in the Context of Disability"

67 THERAPY WITH VICTIMS OF HATE CRIMES

Glenda M. Russell and Christopher G. Hawkey

In psychotherapy with victims of hate crimes, therapists should keep in mind the importance of the psychological, in contrast to the legal, definition of what constitutes such a crime. In the legal domain, the central question is whether harassment or assault meets the legal threshold for a hate crime (if, indeed, hate crime statutes cover a particular incident in a particular locale and apply to the identity group membership on the basis of which a person has been targeted). For purposes of assessment and therapy, the victim's psychological reality takes precedence over legal definitions. People in social groups that are targeted for significantly negative treatment may be psychologically impacted regardless of whether the action meets the legal criteria for a hate crime.

All victims of hate crimes are members of one or more stigmatized groups. However, while all such groups are subject to prejudice and discrimination, the specific nature of maltreatment varies among groups. In their work with hate crime victims, therapists need to have a working knowledge of both a client's group and the nature of the stigma directed against that group.

ASSESSMENT

Standard Clinical Assessment

During intake evaluation and ongoing clinical assessment, the therapist should assess not only those domains germane to a standard clinical intake but also domains associated with hate crime victimization. It is important to systematically screen clients across *The Diagnostic and Statistical Manual of Mental Disorders*, fourth edition (*DSM-IV*) diagnostic categories and to thoroughly evaluate and diagnose current and past symptomology. This can provide important information for conceptualizing a client's reaction to experiencing a hate crime and specify empirically supported treatment (EST) options. At minimum, the intake evaluation should include a reliable and valid measure of pathology such as the Structured Clinical Interview for *DSM* (SCID-I) for the evaluation of Axis I clinical disorders. The SCID-II (or similar measure) may be used to evaluate the presence of Axis II personality disorders if the evaluator deems it clinically necessary.

The unstructured clinical interview should include at minimum personal and family psychiatric history, medical history, and social and occupational functioning. Finally, ongoing evaluation throughout treatment should be used to evaluate fluctuations in symptoms and treatment efficacy. Measures commonly used to assess symptoms in this way include the Beck Depression Inventory, Hamilton Rating Scale for Depression, and Beck Anxiety Inventory. Myriad measures exist for the ongoing assessment of various other symptom domains, and these should be used where appropriate.

It is important for clinicians to be aware that members of marginalized populations experience more frequent (and oftentimes more psychologically impactful) traumas than the general population. Furthermore, victims of hate traumas commonly find themselves surrounded by truly threatening stimuli. Developing a working knowledge of the types of traumas most commonly experienced by members of a given client's group will facilitate a more thorough evaluation.

Trauma Assessment

The evaluation of trauma experiences and posttraumatic stress disorder (PTSD) symptoms is critical in clients presenting in the aftermath of having been targeted by a hate crime. Thoroughly documenting past, current, and ongoing sources of hate trauma, including pretrauma and posttrauma functioning, will provide an optimal basis for conceptualizing clients' symptoms and structuring their treatment.

One of the most commonly used assessments of traumatic experiences and PTSD symptoms is the SCID-I PTSD module. Administering this module as part of the standard SCID-I assessment battery provides a straightforward framework for identifying past traumatic experiences and evaluating the type and severity of subsequent symptoms. A similar measure, the Clinician-Administered PTSD Scale (CAPS), combines a Life Events Checklist (LEC) with an in-depth clinical interview aimed at assessing the severity and impact of a client's PTSD symptoms. The CAPS can also be used to systematically evaluate fluctuations in symptomology over the course of treatment as described earlier.

Group Membership Assessment

Given the importance of careful structuring of assessment and treatment around the unique aspects of clients' group memberships, it is necessary to also evaluate the extent to which they identify with that group. The measures used to evaluate such membership are as diverse as the groups they intend to measure. It is important to assess the extent to which a client is integrated into the group, has social support from the group, and perhaps experiences internalized oppression due to group membership.

TREATMENT

Given the relative dearth of research on treatments for the victims of hate crimes, little can be said about clinical practices that have been empirically supported for this population. The following recommendations represent a sampling of therapeutic strategies that have demonstrated efficacy for the treatment of related populations or symptoms.

The treatment progression outlined here is designed with a number of considerations in mind. First, clients presenting for the treatment of symptoms associated with hate crimes will vary in severity, type, and duration of symptoms. Thus, the development of a graded and progressive treatment approach provides the clinician with a framework that can be tailored to meet the needs of the client without prematurely employing strategies that may increase the likelihood of early termination. Simple psychoeducation regarding the nature of responses to traumatic experiences and activation of clients' social support-seeking behaviors may suffice for less severe cases. However, clients who are experiencing many symptoms or symptoms of greater severity or longer duration may benefit from the addition of skills training, cognitive reframing, and/or exposure techniques.

Second, not all symptoms observed in such clients will be "pathological" in nature. Educating clients about normative and nonnormative responses to trauma and helping them engage social support in strategic ways is often adequate. Similarly, teaching them skills to effectively engage with others, regulate their own emotions, and tolerate posttrauma mood fluctuations provides knowledge and skills that can benefit virtually anyone. These modules of treatment assume only that a client lacks or should be reminded of a set of specific information and skills. The goal in the opening three modules of treatment is not to change anything about clients; it is to enable clients to be more effective in their use of knowledge and skills.

Psychoeducation

Psychoeducation is a key component of many ESTs. While the effectiveness of psychoeducation as a stand-alone treatment has received mixed empirical support, many ESTs provide psychoeducation as a major component of their treatment packages. Our perspective is that providing pychoeducation about a client's symptoms and functioning can help to normalize their experience, provide a cognitive and behavioral framework for understanding their symptoms, and shed light on the multiple therapeutic alternatives available.

Although there are many forms of psychoeducation, we propose that psychoeducation for victims of hate crimes might include two specific foci. The first involves giving basic information about the impact of a hate crime. This description can be used in part to contextualize whatever symptoms the client is experiencing, a move that often reduces the client's concerns about their significance. The second focus entails identifying the context of social stigma that makes hate crimes a reality and help clients to make sense of this stigma and its impact on clients' lives. This discussion ideally includes information about how the client's group membership may impart special risks and also special opportunities.

Social Support–Based Behavioral Activation

Hate crimes, by definition, are social events. Pathological trauma responses, by definition, are avoidant reactions. Taken together, these observations imply the unique functioning of avoidance subsequent to experiencing a hate crime and highlight the importance of monitoring clients' social behaviors. Experiencing a hate crime can often lead to avoidance of the perpetrating member's group, the victim's own group, or even society at large. Helping clients to understand the genesis of their social deactivation, sharing resources for support within their community, and providing a systematic, safe behavioral activation plan can help clients increase their mood-enhancing experiences while helping them challenge their potentially overgeneralized avoidant strategies.

Behavioral Activation (BA), an empirically supported treatment developed for depression, is one model for structuring such an intervention. More recent efforts have also begun to explore BA's effectiveness with PTSD populations with some success. Given that this is a highly tolerable treatment and is well matched to address the symptoms commonly experienced by survivors of hate crimes, we suggest using its targeted and graded methods of activation to help clients re-engage their environments.

Skills Training

Once the therapist has conducted a thorough evaluation and provided psychoeducation and social support–based behavioral activation, it is often useful to address skills deficits in a variety of domains. According to the Dialectical Behavior Therapy model, clients' symptoms are exacerbated by skills deficits in interpersonal effectiveness, emotion regulation, distress tolerance, and mindfulness. Capitalizing on this framework, the therapist can give clients concrete skills that they can use to further enlist social support, understand and regulate their emotions, get through painful experiences without resorting to dysfunctional behaviors, and cultivate the ability to access and act from a wise mind state. These can be particularly important skills for those who have survived a hate trauma and continue to suffer from the symptoms of that experience.

Cognitive Therapy

Many clients will experience substantial improvement from careful assessment, psychoeducation, and skills training alone. However, for some clients, especially for those who have been multiply traumatized, intervening at the level of cognition can facilitate a more complete and enduring treatment effect.

Cognitive therapies involve identifying distorted thoughts and generating more adaptive, logical, and empirical alternatives. This approach can be particularly effective for clients who have employed overgeneralized or extreme cognitions after a traumatic event. Helping clients to understand the faulty nature of such distorted thoughts and aiding them in generating more realistic alternatives can provide them with the cognitive flexibility to adaptively distinguish dangerous from safe stimuli, which aids in the reduction of maladaptive avoidance behaviors.

HATE CRIME–SPECIFIC CONSIDERATIONS

In addition to these more general considerations, there are issues related specifically to the treatment of hate crimes that warrant therapists' attention. Taken as a group, these issues have received limited empirical support but considerable professional consensus.

Safety

It is widely recognized that establishing safety is a necessary foundation for improvement from varied forms of harassment and assault. In the case of violations rooted in the victim's identity or group membership, however, it is very difficult to establish absolute safety because the social stigma that gave rise to or facilitated a hate crime persists as an ongoing reality. It is therefore necessary for hate crime victims to work on concrete ways to reduce the potential for further abuse while simultaneously coming to terms with the reality of being a potential target of social violence.

It is critical that clients recognize that their abuse stemmed not from their identity or group membership but from the social stigma attached to that identity. This framing allows victims to differentiate themselves as persons from the social stigma that undergirded their victimization. The framing also underscores the fact that blame for the victimization rests not with the targets or their group but with the perpetrator and the form of social stigma that influenced the perpetrator's behavior.

Even as victims need to accurately understand where the blame lies, they also need to strategize ways to minimize the chances that they will be revictimized. The failure to consider such strategies courts the risk of the victim's feeling entirely powerless in the face of social stigma. The particular strategies that hate crime victims might use will be influenced by whether their stigma is readily visible to or is concealable from potential perpetrators. Visible stigmas render individuals obvious to would-be perpetrators and thus unable to avoid them. Concealable stigmas, on the other hand, may allow individuals to hide from would-be perpetrators, but they also carry the dangers of the denial of one's identity and avoidance of contact with one's community and the benefits that frequently ensue from such contact. Therapy with hate crime victims may return reiteratively to these concerns from its earliest to its final stages.

Clients' Sense of Group Membership

A related issue for hate crime victims is assessing and addressing the impact that the experience has had on the victims' sense of themselves as members of particular identity groups. At the most obvious level, the danger is that clients' identity or group membership will become associated with the negative experience of a hate crime. Factors that are important in making this assessment are the pre-crime level of identity development, positive contact with other members of the client's ingroup identity community, and the nature of the client's relationship with members of the outgroup.

Individuals' pre-crime levels of identity development will be a factor in what they feel and how much exploration of their feelings makes sense. People with a strong preexisting sense of identity may have a better foundation for working with such feelings. For victims who have not devoted much prior cognitive and affective attention to being a member of a stigmatized group, these explorations may require slower going and more time.

Feelings About Perpetrators/ Perpetrator Group

Clients who have been the victims of crimes often have strong ideas and feelings about their perpetrators. Such attitudes can be expected to be magnified when the victimization was rooted in the client's identity/group membership. Not only do victims need to work with their feelings about the individual perpetrator, they often need to consider their thoughts and feelings about the perpetrator as a de facto representative of a group of people who usually hold more social power and prestige than do members of the victims' own groups.

It is not unusual for clients to contend with fear and with resentment and anger about perpetrators and "their" groups. The therapy needs to allow room for the expression of such emotions as well as for the exploration of maladaptive behaviors in relation to the perpetrator's group(s). Therapists need to make room for and legitimize these feelings and behaviors even as they help clients to move beyond a position that keeps them immersed in these feelings. Very intense and ongoing affective ties to perpetrators reduce not only clients' comfort level but also their own experiences of themselves as separate agents of their own lives.

The framing of hate crimes as rooted in social stigma allows clients to recognize the essential unfairness of their victimization while moving beyond the intense affective ties to individual perpetrators and their groups. Exploring with clients their own ability to trust themselves, both as individuals and as members of a stigmatized group, serves as an important antidote to the sense of powerlessness and anger that are frequently aspects of their reactions.

Group Differences in the Therapy Relationship

When working with victims of hate crimes, it is often important to frankly acknowledge differences in group membership between the client and therapist. Therapists must be simultaneously willing to be educated by clients about their experiences and to take responsibility for learning about clients' groups. Therapists who are not members of the clients' targeted group may bear the brunt of the anger and fear that clients feel toward the perpetrator. In such cases, therapists can use clients' expressions of anger and fear to help clients to make sense of and work through these feelings.

Involvement in the Legal System

In some cases, clients will have made the decision to report a hate crime to the police. In other cases, clients may call on the therapist to help them to think through decisions around reporting. Familiarity with local police climate and practices will be helpful in this process. In general, clients want to make decisions that increase their sense of their own agency and behavioral options. Clients should consider that involvement with legal systems may be frustrating and postpone their healing as well as contribute to a sense of efficacy in the face of a violation.

References and Readings

Barlow, D. H. (2008). *Clinical handbook of psychological disorders: A step-by-step treatment manual* (4th ed.). New York: Guilford Press.

Bradlet, R., Greene, J., Russ, E., Dutra, L., & Westen, D. (2005). A multidimensional meta-analysis of psychotherapy for PTSD. *American Journal of Psychiatry, 162*, 214–227.

Dunbar, E. (2001). Counseling practices to ameliorate the effects of discrimination and hate events: Toward a systematic approach to assessment and intervention. *Counseling Psychologist, 29*, 281–310.

Garnets, L., Herek, G. M., & Levy, B. (1990). Violence and victimization of lesbians and gay men: Mental health consequences. *Journal of Interpersonal Violence, 5*, 366–383.

Kaysen, D., Lostutter, T. W., & Goines, M. A. (2005). Cognitive processing therapy for acute stress disorder resulting from an anti-gay assault. *Cognitive and Behavioral Practice, 12*, 278–289.

Related Topics

Chapter 47, "Psychotherapy with Lesbian, Gay, and Bisexual Clients"

Chapter 64, "Tailoring Treatment to the Patient's Race and Ethnicity"

68 ASSESSING AND TREATING NONSUICIDAL SELF-INJURY

E. David Klonsky

Nonsuicidal self-injury (NSSI) refers to the intentional destruction of one's body tissue without suicidal intent and for purposes not socially sanctioned. Other terms sometimes used synonymously with NSSI include self-mutilation and deliberate self-harm; however, because the former is often considered pejorative and the latter does not specify nonsuicidal intent, they have come to be used less frequently.

In clinical populations, the most common forms of NSSI are skin cutting, followed by burning and banging/hitting body parts (Klonsky & Muehlenkamp, 2007). Additional methods include needle sticking, interfering with wound healing, scratching, and rubbing against rough surfaces; most self-injurers have utilized more than one method.

However, not all types of self-damaging behaviors are regarded as NSSI. Behaviors associated with substance disorders (e.g., drug and alcohol abuse) and eating disorders (e.g., binging and purging) are not typically regarded as NSSI because the resulting tissue damage is not intentional. Body piercings and tattoos are also not typically regarded as NSSI when they are socially sanctioned forms of artistic or self-expression.

In *The Diagnostic and Statistical Manual of Mental Disorders*, fourth edition (*DSM-IV*), NSSI appears only once, as a symptom of a larger disorder (i.e., borderline personality disorder [BPD]). But as of the date of this writing, the American Psychiatric Association has proposed that NSSI be classified as its own diagnostic entity in the DSM-5 appendix for future study and consideration (www.DSM5.org, retrieved November 1, 2011). The rationale for this potential change is that NSSI has been documented to frequently occur outside a diagnosis of BPD and to be independently associated with clinically significant distress and impairment. A further aim is to help clinicians better distinguish between NSSI and attempted suicide.

PREVALENCE, DEMOGRAPHICS, AND CHARACTERISTICS

NSSI occurs most often among adolescents. Age of onset is typically between the ages of 12 and 14 years, although NSSI begins after age 18 in about one-third of cases. Whereas approximately 6% of adults report having self-injured at least once (Klonsky, 2011), this rate is higher, about 14%–17%, among adolescents and young adults. This pattern suggests that NSSI has become more common in recent years.

Although it is commonly believed that NSSI is more common among women/girls than men/boys, large studies of community populations do not find gender differences in rates of NSSI. However, there do appear to be gender differences regarding forms of NSSI. Specifically, women more often engaged in skin cutting, whereas men more often engaged in burning and self-hitting. There may also be a relationship between NSSI and ethnicity. In some (but not all studies) Caucasians appear more likely to self-injure than non-Caucasians. Finally, rates of NSSI appear to be disproportionately high among those who identify as bisexual or report being unsure about their sexual orientation.

There is considerable diagnostic heterogeneity among those who self-injure, and the presence of NSSI does not imply the presence of any particular mental disorder. At the same time, two psychological features appear to characterize those who repeatedly engage in the behavior.

1. *Negative emotionality*. People who self-injure tend to experience more frequent and intense negative emotions—including depression, anxiety, and anger—than non-injurers. Self-injurers also have difficulty being aware of and expressing their emotions. For these individuals, NSSI temporarily alleviates and provides relief from overwhelming negative emotions.
2. *Self-criticism (or self-derogation)*. Studies often find that measures of self-criticism, self-derogation, and low self-esteem are elevated among individuals who engage in NSSI. Slightly more than half of self-injurers report that the act of self-injuring is, in part, an act of self-directed anger or punishment.

ASSESSMENT AND TREATMENT

- *Understand the motivations.* The most common motivation for NSSI is affect regulation (Klonsky, 2007). Typically, episodes of NSSI are preceded by overwhelming negative emotions such as anxiety, anger, depression, and self-derogation, and the performance of NSSI is associated with reduced negative affect and an increased sense of calm and relief. Next to affect regulation, the most commonly reported motivation is self-punishment. Across numerous studies, approximately half of self-injurers endorse reasons such as "to express anger at myself" and "to punish myself." Less common motivations for NSSI include influencing others, coping with suicidal thoughts, ending episodes of dissociation/derealization, and excitement seeking.
- *Ensure good rapport.* Although the topic of NSSI can be private and sensitive, psychologists should not shy away from discussing and asking questions about NSSI, particularly given its high and perhaps increasing prevalence. It is important that psychologists manage reactions, such as disgust or disdain, that could damage rapport and client trust. Adopting a stance of "respectful curiosity" may help psychologists inquire about NSSI in a manner that maximizes rapport and client comfort.
- *Assess thoroughly.* Treatment planning should include thorough and systematic assessment of the NSSI, including the behavior's onset, frequency, medical severity, motivations, antecedents, consequences, and relation (if any) to suicidal ideation, plans, and attempts. Many valid and comprehensive instruments have been developed to assess the topography of NSSI (e.g., Nock et al., 2007) and motivations for NSSI (e.g., Klonsky & Glenn, 2009).
- *Consider the level of care.* A key choice that therapists must make is the level of treatment (e.g., outpatient vs. inpatient vs. no treatment with careful monitoring). NSSI confers increased risk for suicidal thoughts and behaviors. In cases where suicidal ideation is severe, inpatient treatment may be warranted to ensure client safety. If suicidal intent is absent or minimal, less aggressive approaches such as outpatient treatment are likely to be most appropriate and therapeutic. Notably, because most of the 14% to17% of adolescents and young adults reporting NSSI have engaged in the behavior only once or twice, some who self-injure may not require formal treatment as long as a parent or guardian can monitor for future instances of NSSI and related psychological distress.
- *Treat carefully.* There are no research-supported treatments for NSSI yet. However, much has been learned from treatment studies of populations in which NSSI is common.

In general, treatments emphasizing functional assessment, problem solving, and emotion regulation appear to be most effective for treating NSSI (Klonsky, Muehlenkamp, Lewis, & Walsh, 2011). Specific approaches that appear to be well suited to the treatment of NSSI include dialectical behavior therapy, motivational interviewing, problem-solving therapy, cognitive-behavioral therapy, and functional assessment.

- *Distinguish between NSSI and suicide attempt.* It was not uncommon for NSSI to be mistaken for or regarded as a failed suicide attempt. However, NSSI and suicide attempts have different motivations, and NSSI does not typically result in life-threatening tissue damage (Klonsky & Muehlenkamp, 2007; Klonsky et al., 2011). Confusing NSSI for a suicide attempt can have a number of harmful consequences, including inappropriate hospitalization. Involuntary or inappropriate hospitalization can severely damage a client's ability to trust his or her parents, loved ones, and therapist. Therefore, when NSSI does not result in medically severe tissue damage and is not accompanied by severe suicidal ideation, it is essential to avoid unnecessary and potentially iatrogenic hospitalizations.
- *Attend to heightened risk for suicidal behaviors.* At the same time, in some studies 50% or more of self-injurers have attempted suicide at least once, and there is increasing evidence that NSSI may be second only to suicidal ideation in conferring risk for a suicide attempt (Klonsky et al., 2011). One interpretation of this relationship is that NSSI confers "double trouble" for suicide risk. Some risk factors, such as depression or hopelessness, only indicate risk for suicidal desire, where as other risk factors, such as fearlessness about death, only increase risk for suicide capability. Because NSSI is associated both with increased negative emotions and habituation to self-inflicted violence, NSSI is relatively unique in that it confers risk *both* for suicidal thoughts and for acting on those thoughts. In sum, NSSI and attempted suicide are distinguishable phenomena, but NSSI confers heightened risk for suicidal thoughts and behaviors. Therefore, when NSSI is a presenting problem, psychologists should conduct a careful assessment of suicide risk and plan treatment accordingly.
- *Avoid misconceptions.* It is sometimes assumed that NSSI is a sure sign of BPD, a manifestation of childhood sexual abuse (CSA), or an attempt to manipulate others or get attention. Numerous studies have shown that clinically significant NSSI often occurs outside a diagnosis of BPD. That said, a positive relationship between presence of NSSI and BPD symptoms has been documented in numerous studies. This relationship is probably best understood as being due to the presence of elevated negative emotionality and emotion dysregulation in both conditions. Careful diagnostic assessment is required on a case-by-case basis, as an improper diagnosis of BPD could harm case conceptualization and treatment planning.

  Regarding CSA, a meta-analysis of more than 40 studies found that the association between NSSI and CSA is positive but relatively small (Klonsky & Moyer, 2008). Many people who engage in NSSI do not have histories of CSA, and many individuals with histories of CSA do not develop NSSI. Therefore, the evidence views CSA as one potential contributor of NSSI but not as its primary cause. At the same time, for some individuals CSA can contribute to the development of negative emotions and self-criticism that, in turn, can lead to NSSI.

Finally, there are indeed occasions in which NSSI is used for manipulative or attention-seeking purposes, but this is more the exception than the rule. Because NSSI can elicit strong reactions from others, it is easy to assume that the NSSI was performed for the purpose of eliciting such reactions. However, dozens of studies make clear that NSSI is most often a private act performed to cope with overwhelmingly negative and often self-critical emotions. Moreover, many who self-injure experience guilt or shame and concern that others will misunderstand or judge them.

Thus, a careful and open-minded approach to assessment and treatment is essential for establishing and maintaining rapport as well as accurate case conceptualization and effective treatment.

References and Readings

Klonsky, E. D. (2007). The functions of deliberate self-injury: A review of the evidence. *Clinical Psychology Review, 27*, 226–239.

Klonsky, E. D., & Glenn, C. R. (2009). Assessing the functions of non-suicidal self-injury: Psychometric properties of the Inventory of Statements About Self-injury (ISAS). *Journal of Psychopathology and Behavioral Assessment, 31*, 215–219.

Klonsky, E. D., & Moyer, A. (2008). Childhood sexual abuse and non-suicidal self-injury: Meta-analysis. *British Journal of Psychiatry, 192*, 166–170.

Klonsky, E. D., & Muehlenkamp, J. J. (2007). Self-injury: A research review for the practitioner. *Journal of Clinical Psychology: In Session, 63*, 1045–1056.

Klonsky, E. D., Muehlenkamp, J. J., Lewis, S., & Walsh, B. (2011). *Non-suicidal self-injury*. Cambridge, MA: Hogrefe.

Nock, M. K. (2009). *Non-suicidal self-injury: Origins, assessment, and treatment*. Washington, DC: American Psychological Association.

Nock, M. K., Holmberg, E. B., Photos, V. I., & Michel, B. D. (2007). Self-injurious thoughts and behaviors interview: Development, reliability, and validity in an adolescent sample. *Psychological Assessment, 19*, 309–317.

Nock, M. K., & Prinstein, M. J. (2004). A functional approach to the assessment of self-mutilative behavior. *Journal of Consulting and Clinical Psychology, 72*, 885–890.

Related Topics

Chapter 5, "Assessing Suicidal Risk"

Chapter 36, "Treating and Managing Care of the Suicidal Patient"

Chapter 60, "Treating the Effects of Psychological Trauma"

69 CONDUCTING PSYCHOTHERAPY WITH CLIENTS WHEN ENGLISH IS NOT THE FIRST LANGUAGE

Rafael Javier and Lillian Comas-Díaz

When providing psychological evaluations and/or treating individuals for whom English is not the first language, there are a number of important considerations to keep in mind:

1. Determine the level of linguistic proficiency in the second language as well as the first language, if possible.
2. Determine the level of comfort to process and communicate personal and emotionally laden information in the language of the evaluation/treatment.
3. Determine the level of cultural familiarity of the host society normally associated with levels of bilingualism.
4. Determine the level of emotional difficulty with which the individual is afflicted

(i.e., depression, schizophrenia, bipolar disorder).

We know that language is intimately involved in all aspects of cognitive and emotional development and the individual develops his or her language in relationship with his or her cultural environment and important individuals in his or her life. Once developed, language is involved in the organization and categorization of a variety of experiences the individual has throughout his or her life, from the initial stage of cognitive/emotional development to the latest stages of his or her development. It is this involvement that allows language to be implicated in the nature and quality of the different memories that are developed throughout life and thus determine the quality of a variety of learning experiences we have. Included in this process is the development of one's personality, self concept, personal identity, coping mechanism, and so on, where language is intimately involved. Psychologists make use of this quality of language to assess levels of cognitive functioning of individuals as well as the nature and quality of emotional development through the use of different psychological instruments (i.e., structured interviews, psychological tests, etc.) (Flanagan, McGrew, & Ortiz, 2000). When conducting psychotherapy with individuals for whom English is not the first language, the work of the psychologist in this regard becomes more complicated. Another complication to consider is the fact that language function could become greatly compromised under conditions of high emotional stress (resulting in depression, anxiety, posttraumatic stress disorder, etc.) and environmental toxicity (e.g., lead poisoning) (Needleman, Schell, Bellinger, Leviton, & Allred, 1990), and thus likely to affect the nature and quality of evaluation/treatment when under these conditions.

UNIQUE QUALITIES OF BILINGUALS

We know that those individuals for whom English is not the first language can develop different proficiency in the second language and that this proficiency has major implications for the processing of information and for learning in the second language, not to mention the ability to communicate important personal needs/emotions in the second language. Thus, one cannot expect that those who have developed a very rudimentary knowledge of the second language to function at the same level as those who have developed a much higher proficiency in the second language. In the psychological literature, these different kinds of bilingual individuals have been described as belonging to different bilingual groups. Because of the distinctive manner of these groups, their proficiency tends to have an effect on their ability to function well in their different environments (e.g., school, employment, relationships, ability to communicate emotions, etc.).

Clients who have a rudimentary knowledge of the second language have been referred to in the literature as "subordinate bilingual," as they tend to think and organize their experience in the first language and have acquired only a sufficient (but limited) vocabulary to maintain the most rudimentary of communication in the second language. This is characteristic of recent immigrants or immigrants who, despite the years in the host country, have not developed a proficiency in the second language for whatever reason. By contrast, those who acquire a good degree of proficiency in the second language are referred to as "coordinate bilingual" or "balanced bilingual." This latter group of bilinguals is considered "the true bilingual" because he or she is able to process information and function well in both languages. Normally, these bilinguals are more likely to have learned the second language early in life but after the first language was already established in the brain. When both languages are learned at the same time, the two languages may be organized in the same parts of the brain and hence a "compound bilingual organization" is more likely to have developed. The bottom line is that even when speaking both languages proficiently, there may be certain information that remains language specific. This is particularly the case with information that has emotional significance that tends to become organized around the language in which it happened.

Misdiagnoses and treatment failures that are a result of inadequate exploration of linguistic and cultural issues are not uncommon. This may occur even when interpreters are utilized if they are not appropriately trained.

FACTORS TO CONSIDER IN EVALUATING AND TREATING BILINGUAL INDIVIDUALS

There is some evidence from a number of neurolinguistic and psycholinguistic studies that confirm the idea that the brain/mind of the bilingual operates differently than the monolingual mind and that "how" the languages are learned, "when" they are learned, and the "level of proficiency" will determine the nature and extent to which certain information is accessible in one or the other language or both. These differences in accessibility are particularly evident with emotionally laden information; that is, it is more likely to remain language specific. However, it is also evident with other cognitive information, such as mathematical skills and so on. This bilingual phenomenon, as well as the often accompanying bicultural phenomenon, has been found to have serious implications for learning and school performance/literacy (Bialystok & Cummins, 2000) and for diagnostic complications (Marcos, Alpert, Urcuyo, & Kesselman, 1973). With regard to psychological evaluations, even in the so-called nonverbal tests, this phenomenon may still lead to inaccurate diagnostic impressions of what is really wrong/right with the individuals, particularly the diagnosis of learning disability (Flanagan et al., 2000). To this we should add the work of Robert Sternberg (1988), who strongly emphasized the importance of considering unique factors within individuals when utilizing intelligence tests to assess intelligence, particularly in individuals coming from different cultures and linguistic backgrounds.

BILINGUALISM AND ACCULTURATION

If language is a transmitter of culture, what is the relationship between language and acculturation for bilingual clients? Due to their fluency in English, many bilingual clients may present in therapy as highly acculturated. However, these individuals may identify more with their culture and language of origin, as opposed to their host culture (Valdez, 2000). To illustrate, in reviewing research findings on language and acculturation, Ruiz (2007) concluded that language is more important than ethnicity in determining Latinos' utilization of mental health services. Spanish-English bilingual clients, for example, may not be able to communicate their emotions effectively in psychotherapy when English is the language of treatment.

According to Meadow (1982), once the psychotherapist develops a positive relationship, the bilingual client is able to communicate and participate in therapy. However, to enhance their cultural competence with bilingual clients, psychotherapists need to familiarize themselves with psycholinguistic concepts and their effect on psychotherapy. Some of these concepts include code switching, or the facility to switch from formal to informal speech and vice versa (Weinreich, 1953). Moreover, most bilingual bicultural individuals have multiple cultural meaning systems and can shift between frames in response to the cues in the environment. Notwithstanding this ability, bilinguals experience a cost in language switching, leading to active inhibition or suppression of their stronger competitor language (Meuter & Allport, 1999). Following this analysis, emotional intensity displayed in therapy could potentially enhance such suppression. Hence, we suggest that monolingual therapists do not fully understand the experiences of bilingual clients. To bridge this gap, therapists must become cognizant of psycholinguistic dynamics present in psychotherapy with bilingual patients.

In yet another example, research findings suggest that bilingual bicultural individuals incorporate two cultures and develop culture-specific mental frameworks that activate different aspects of their identities (Luna, Ringberg, & Peracchio (2008). Consequently, clinicians need to be familiar with this phenomenon and address this issue in psychotherapy. Following are some suggestions for psychotherapists working with bilingual bicultural clients:

- Facilitate bilingual clients' examination of their repressed experiences in their non-English language.
- Foster bilingual client's ability to tap into their original culture. For example, use guided imagery to "listen" to relatives in their native language to identify the feelings that emerge (Guarnaccia & Rodriguez, 1996).

Acknowledge that bilingual bicultural clients may have "two identities," according to the language they speak (Luna, Ringberg, & Peracchio, 2008).

SELECTING PROPER METHODS OF EVALUATION

There is currently a movement in evaluation that calls for the need to consider instruments that are sensitive to the individual linguistic and cultural characteristics of clients when working with culturally and linguistically diverse populations. This includes the seminal work of Giuseppe Costantino and his colleagues in THEMAS (tell me a story) (Costantino & Malgady, 1983), the work of Dawn Flanagan and colleagues (2000), and others. These latter authors suggest a breakdown of different psychological instruments to evaluate cognitive function in terms of different levels (high, medium, and low) of cultural and linguistic demands. Flanagan and colleagues have suggested a cross-battery approach to assessment as the best practice to be able to capture the unique quality of the individual being evaluated. In Table 69.1 we have included an example of the types of different psychological tests and subtests Flanagan et al. identified as requiring high linguistic demands and different levels of cultural demands from the individual (the reader should review the work of Flanagan et al. for a more comprehensive understanding of the different tests and the different linguistic and cultural demands).

TABLE 69.1. Partial Listing of Linguistic and Cultural Loadings of Test Instrument

Subtest	Test Instrument	Age (years)
High Linguistic Demands and Cultural Loading		
• Similarities	Wechslers	3–74
• Vocabulary	Wechslers	3–74
• Information	Wechslers	3–74
• Comprehension	Wechslers	3–74
• Listening comprehension	WJ-R	4–85+
• Oral comprehension	WJ-III	4–85+
• Verbal comprehension	WJ-III	2–85+
• General information	WJ-III	2–85+
High Linguistic Demands and Moderate Cultural Loading		
• Incomplete words	WJ-R/III	2–85+
• Sound blending	WJ-R/III	4–85+
• Memory for words	WJ-R	4–85+
• Auditory attention	WJ-III	4–85+
• Decision speed	WJ-III	4–85+
High Linguistic Demands and Low Cultural Loading		
• Concept formation	WJ-R/III	4–85+
• Analysis synthesis	WJ-R/III	4–85+
• Auditory working memory	WJ-III	4–85+
• Pair cancellation	WJ-III	4–85+

IMPORTANT QUESTIONS TO CONSIDER WHEN WORKING WITH BILINGUAL/BICULTURAL INDIVIDUALS

We are suggesting that any evaluation/treatment of psychological functioning should include a series of questions that attempt to capture all aspects of the individual's experience with respect to language acquisition. We suggest the following questions:

Questions Regarding Level of Linguistic Proficiency/Cultural Competencies

- At what age did the subject learn the second language?
- In what language and cultural context did the subject have early schooling?
- How long has the subject been in the linguistic/cultural context of the language of the evaluation?
- What level of proficiency (in reading, writing, speaking, and thinking?) has the subject reached in the second language?
- What level of cognitive/scholastic achievement proficiency did the subject reach in the native language?

- What language does the subject use for intellectual/school-related material?
- In what language does the subject dream?
- In what language does the subject think?
- What language does the subject prefer when upset or dealing with emotions?
- What language is used with whom, for what, and under what conditions?
- What level of professional accomplishment did the subject reach in the country of origin?

Questions Regarding Basic Medical/Developmental History

- When did the subject reach the basic developmental milestones (i.e., walking, language, etc.)? This is particularly important in children.
- Was there any history of trauma, illnesses, and so on that could have affected the subject's cognitive and linguistic development? Is there a history of lead intoxication and other contaminants? Again, this is particularly important in children.

References and Readings

Bialystok, E., & Cummins, J. (2000). Language, cognition and education of bilingual children. In E. Bialystok (Ed.), *Language processing in bilingual children* (pp. 222–232). Cambridge, England: Cambridge University Press.

Costantino, G., & Malgady, R. G. (1983). Verbal fluency of Hispanic, black and white children on TAT and TEMAS, a new thematic apperception test. *Hispanic Journal of Behavioral Sciences, 5*, 199–206.

Flanagan, D. P., McGrew, K. S., & Ortiz, S. O. (2000). *The Wechsler intelligence scales and Gf-Gc theory: A contemporary approach of interpretation*. Boston, MA: Allyn & Bacon.

Guarnaccia, P. J., & Rodriguez, O. (1996). Concepts of culture and their role in the development of culturally competent mental health services. *Hispanic Journal of Behavioral Sciences, 18*, 419–443.

Javier, R. A. (2007). *The bilingual mind: Thinking, feeling and speaking in two languages*. New York: Springer

Luna, D., Ringberg, T., & Peracchio, L. A. (2008). One individual, two identities: Frame-switching among biculturals. *Journal of Consumer Research, 35*(2), 279–293.

Marcos, L. R., Alpert, M., Urcuyo, L., & Kesselman, M. (1973). The effect of interview language on the evaluation of psychopathology in Spanish-American schizophrenic patients. *American Journal of Psychiatry, 130*, 540–553.

Meadow, A. (1982). Psychopathology, psychotherapy, and the Mexican American patient. In E. E. Jones & S. J. Korchin (Eds.), *Minority mental health* (pp. 552–570). Washington, DC: American Psychological Association.

Meuter, R. F., & Allport, A. (1999). Bilingual language switching in naming: Asymmetrical costs of language selection. *Journal of Memory and Language, 40*(1), 25–40.

Needleman, H. L., Schell, A., Bellinger, D., Leviton, A., & Allred, E. N. (1990). The long-term effects of exposure to low doses of lead in childhood: An 11year follow-up report. *New England Journal of Medicine, 322*, 83–88.

Ruiz, P. (2007). Spanish, English and mental health (editorial). *American Journal of Psychiatry, 164*, 1133–1135.

Sternberg, R. A. (1988). *The triarchic mind. A new theory of human intelligence*. New York: Viking.

Valdez, J. N. (2000). Psychotherapy with bicultural Hispanic clients. *Psychotherapy, 37*(3), 240–246.

Weinreich, U. (1953). *Languages in contact*. The Hague, The Netherlands: Mouton.

Related Topic

Chapter 64, "Tailoring Treatment to the Patient's Race and Ethnicity"

70 UNDERSTANDING SEXUALITY IN THE CONTEXT OF DISABILITY

Linda R. Mona and Kimberly Smith

Psychologists have begun to reframe the experience of disability as a socially constructed status, rather than simply a medical condition. As this shift has occurred, people with disabilities (PWDs) are increasingly understood to be enabled or disabled as a function of the environments they inhabit and are increasingly recognized as multifaceted individuals with the same complement of needs and desires that nondisabled individuals possess. Along with that recognition comes an awareness that PWDs are neither asexual or a collection of medical problems and functions. A person's identity is also integrated into one's sexuality, as disability is integral to individual identity and is not static. Finally, disability is a collective minority cultural identity. Likewise a broad definition of sexuality to include individuals' identification as PWD, sensuality, and sexual activity is consistent with a holistic conceptualization of the intersectionality of multiple roles and behaviors that form the sexual lives of PWDs. Broadened definitions of disability and sexuality serve to foster inclusiveness and empower PWDs from diverse backgrounds.

COMMON ISSUES IN SEXUALITY AND DISABILITY

The sexual lives of PWDs are influenced by societal messages and definitions of attractiveness. For men with disabilities, issues with masculinity, sexual assertiveness, and/or sexual competence often arise. Specifically, traditional male gender-related concepts of being strong and virile are often challenged among men with disabilities. Similarly, gender expectations of women with disabilities may be difficult as societal norms of attractiveness and gender-related expectations are mismatched with body variations. The degree to which PWDs ascribe to nondisabled gender or sexual societal norms impacts their internal definitions and perceptions of disability and sexuality. Additionally, environmental and impairment-specific barriers (e.g., inaccessible physical environment to engage in physical sexual activity, person with restricted hand mobility navigating condom usage) play an important role in satisfying sexual expression among PWDs.

CULTURE, DIVERSITY, AND SEXUALITY AMONG PEOPLE WITH DISABILITIES

The social/minority model of disability acknowledges the unique cultural experiences of PWDs and is bound by four common factors: fortification against oppression, unification, commitment, and recruitment. Like any cultural group, disability culture has an established set of ideals (e.g., acceptance of human differences, willingness to accept help and assume interdependence, appreciation for the absurd, etc.) that influence the sexual identities and sexual health of its community members.

Lesbian, gay, bisexual, transgender, and queer (LGBTQ)–identified PWDs may experience disability identity differently within the context of sexual minority status. LGBT PWDs may struggle to find a place for themselves, break out of social isolation, find intimate partners, and learn to embrace their own bodies and sexual orientation. Living with the social challenges of stigma, prejudice, and discrimination creates a hostile and stressful social environment. That environment potentiates societal effects that impact short- and long-term physical and mental health. People of color living with disabilities also face more than one obstacle and certainly multifaceted social stigma when color and disability are intertwined in one individual. Social determinants such as education, income, and poverty interplay in a complex interaction that impacts PWDs on an individual and group level.

ADAPTIVE SEXUAL ACTIVITY

Sexual activity among PWDs may require more planning compared to nondisabled people. A willingness to expand the sexual repertoire beyond a limited focus on genitally focused sexual behavior increases PWDs' range of opportunities for sexual pleasure. This usually can be accomplished by defining sexual intimacy as mutual or solo pleasure and enjoyment expressed through any sensual activity (e.g., eye gazing, hand holding, kissing, touching oneself or a partner, penile-vaginal intercourse, anal intercourse, incorporating sexual products to assist with pleasure, watching erotic films). Additionally, a willingness to experiment, alone and/or with a partner, may help PWDs connect with their sensuality and sexuality. Experimenting with varying touches and sensations on the body can help further broaden the idea of what sexuality and intimacy means. The disability experience can challenge one's existing sexual belief system by requiring individuals to think more broadly about what may and may not be available to them as physical sexual options.

BARRIERS TO SEXUAL EXPRESSION

The following barriers to sexual expression should be explored by clinicians within the context of a caring, empathic, and nonjudgmental environment:

- *Beliefs about sexuality.* Many PWDs describe feeling neutral about sex, not feeling fully sexual, having sex minimized or dismissed by family and friends, and understanding that society in general may think they should not seek out intimate relationships. Invalidation of the sexual self may result in mistaken beliefs about the self and others, and it may inhibit seeking and attaining fulfilling sexual and intimate experiences.
- *Sexual self-esteem.* Global self-esteem (i.e., broad sense of self-value) among PWDs may or may not be significantly related to sexual self-esteem, defined as the value placed on one's self as a sexual being and partner. Assessing the degree to which PWDs internalize nondisabled heterosexual societal beliefs about sexuality and empowering awareness of potential sources of internalized beliefs and subsequent self-limiting behaviors may be an initial step toward reclaiming their sexuality and building a healthy sexual self-esteem.
- *Accessibility concerns.* PWDs are more vulnerable to physical, sexual, and emotional abuse compared to nondisabled people. Concerns specific to dating and sexual relationships include being left in the middle of a romantic date without adequate transportation, being able to count on continuing to receive general caregiving from a partner if a rift occurs in the intimate relationship, and staying with a partner even though emotionally abuse is continual because the PWD has no other accessible housing option or is financially supported by this partner.
- *Mobility.* Many PWDs experience limitations in mobility that must be accounted for

in order to promote overall sexual well-being. Spasticity, mobility limitations, joint contractures, and body areas hypersensitive to touch are among the conditions that may affect mobility when engaging in sexual activity. Experimenting with varied sexual positions expands the sexual repertoire and identifies opportunities for optimal pleasure for PWDs. If a person is physically unable to engage in masturbation or partner sex because of mobility limitations, personal assistance services (PAS; e.g., caregiving) might be utilized. PAS refers to having another person assist with solo or partner sexual expression. This is a broad controversial topic that may or may not surface clinically but providers should be aware that sexual behavior could be limited by mobility restrictions.

- *Pain.* PWDs may experience pain during sexual activities stemming from organic or nonorganic difficulties, or a combination of the two. Using prescribed pain medication 20 minutes prior to sexual activity may assist with increased pleasure and enjoyment. Pain within the context of sexual activity can be managed by scheduling sexual activities when symptoms are not occurring, experimenting with sexual positions and activities that minimize pain, and communicating with a partner regarding what does and does not cause pain, as well as engaging in other erotic activities that do not necessitate movement of painful body areas.
- *Concern about physical appearance.* Negative body image and devaluation of disabled bodies can occur among both men and women with disabilities. The internalization of ableist societal standards of attractiveness and desirability may also affect how PWDs view potential partners. Among heterosexual PWDs recent literature notes women with disabilities sometimes expressed a preference for young, athletic, good-looking, nondisabled male partners. Similarly, men with disabilities expressed a preference for nondisabled, younger, attractive women who appeared physically fit. Psychologists can explore these findings within the context of internalized ableism.
- *Access to partners.* There may be perceived or real logistical challenges in meeting potential partners. Meeting potential partners through the Internet is a common method of meeting interested individuals. Discussing disability early in the relationship, understanding how the body functions, and talking directly with partners about disability functions and limitation regarding sexual activity are key factors a PWDs may address during the course of a relationship. Finally, discussing partner-related stigma aids in alleviating communication difficulties and the fear of rejection.

POSITIVE SEXUAL EXPRESSION

An affirming environment that promotes medical, physical, and psychological safety empowers PWDs to engage in positive sexual expression. Participating in Tantric sex, an ancient practice of sexual intimacy that combines spirituality and physical contact, works toward de-emphasizing the goal of physiological orgasm and promotes the idea of being fully emotionally, physically, and spiritually present. Furthermore, PWDs are moved beyond physical and cognitive limitations and boundaries, while simultaneously sharing this positive sexual energy with their partner.

Ergonomically shaped sex toys, feathers, and remote-control vibrating devices can be useful in enhancing the sexual experiences of people who have mobility difficulties. In some cases, PAS can be incorporated into sexual activities to facilitate a sexual encounter. This facilitation may take the form of helping PWDs undress, providing aid in positioning for both partner sex and masturbation, or assisting with direct physical stimulation. Additionally, cushion wedges, sex swings, and body slings can be integrated into the sexual lives of PWDs to aid with varying levels of mobility.

SEX-POSITIVE TREATMENT APPROACHES

The National Institute on Disability and Rehabilitation Research's New Paradigm of

Disability incorporates a philosophy that focuses on well-being, wholeness, and thriving as it relates to all aspects of PWDs. This conceptualization of disability is applicable to sexual identity and physical intimacy in that access to and the promotion of positive sexuality can be viewed as a fundamental right for PWDs. In turn, psychologists are called to explore diagnosis and treatment that promotes full access to sexually fulfilling lives as defined by clients/patients.

There is a question of efficacy and appropriateness of evidence-based practices (EBPs), (i.e., the integration of the best research evidence with clinical expertise and patient values) with diverse populations. Most EBPs are designed for and validated on European American populations. The beliefs, values, or customs of people from diverse backgrounds, including PWDs, may not be accounted for with EBPs, which directly impacts the psychotherapy process and dilutes the efficacy of EBPs. Cultural adaptations of EBPs are recommended when working with diverse populations. As there is no guideline for adapting interventions with any particular diverse population, clinical judgment and cultural attunement to working with PWDs will play a role in interventions. Disability-specific values assessment is also vital when conceptualizing treatment.

Disability affirmative therapy (DAT) is a culturally centered, integrative framework that articulates an explicitly disability-positive orientation. DAT may complement traditional cognitive-behavioral treatments. In addition, third-wave cognitive-behavioral treatments that have begun to explicitly integrate mindfulness techniques, a present-focus orientation, and acceptance of a wide range of emotional experiences may be useful, as may feminist therapies and a range of sex therapies.

CLINICAL CONSIDERATIONS

Common reasons for seeking sexual health and reproductive treatment for PWDs include (1) feeling asexual and undesirable, (2) how and where to find partners, (3) disclosure of disability status, (4) sexual functioning, (5) body appearance, (6) sexual positioning/how the body works, (7) communication barriers, (8) bowel and bladder issues, and (9) fertility. When treating a PWD, in the beginning of treatment it is appropriate to establish rapport, ask about the nature of the disability, remain open to diverse perspectives, and keep in mind differences based upon privacy, control and rigidity, and family issues. Additionally, establishing trustworthiness and providing a safe and supportive environment will serve to facilitate clinical efficacy. It should be noted, when working clinically with PWDs, it is helpful to do the following:

- Participate in regular self-assessment around personal beliefs about disability, injury, and/or illness.
- Participate in regular self-assessment around personal beliefs about sexuality and specific thoughts or biases that are held around the sexual expression of PWDs.
- Clarify sexual concerns and do not assume that disability is a central part of the presenting issue.
- Explore values and beliefs as indicated in the assessment.
- Reflect the client's/patient's language.
- Normalize and validate concerns regarding environmental, medical, and social issues.
- Be mindful of ableist language (e.g., using words like "lame" to describe something negative, "emotionally crippled" to describe negative emotions, or the word "retarded" to describe oneself or someone else in a pejorative manner).
- Remember that the disability experience exists within the context of family or other social networks. Provide treatment within this cultural context and to what degree this network is important to the presenting individual.
- Provide information and specific suggestions, including hope for success (e.g., role model, other patients) to clients/patients with disabilities. If warranted, use Web-based information and books to supplement treatment.

By broadening the definition of sexuality among PWDs, psychologists are better prepared to deliver culturally competent care on this under-discussed topic. Clinicians are called to increase their assessment and treatment approaches to include a comprehensive evaluation of sexuality within the context of disability and offer treatment and resources that are aimed at enhancing the sexual well-being of this community. The meaning of sexual relationships and sexual behaviors is affected by multiple intersecting ideologies. Accordingly, the meaning of disability is also reliant upon personal, spiritual, and moral systems. Given that belief systems connect and clash in the therapeutic relationship, clinicians are asked to engage in ongoing self-assessment when providing services to PWDs. This self-assessment integrates critical awareness of personal biases, knowledge and respect for the core values, shared history and customs of PWDs, and the development of skills to meaningfully interact with PWDs in an empathic manner and being able to weave their cultural and personal context into therapeutic interventions.

AUTHOR'S NOTE

There is extensive literature based on the sexual lives of people with intellectual disabilities. This entry focuses exclusively on the sexual lives of people with physical disabilities given the unique social and physical factors that affect this community.

References and Readings

American Psychological Association. (2011). *Guidelines for assessment of and interventions with persons with disabilities.* Retrieved May 10, 2011 from: www.apa.org/pi/disability/resources/assessment-disabilities.pdf

Mona, L. R. (2003). Sexual options for people with disabilities: Using personal assistance services for sexual expression. In M. E. Banks & E. Kaschak (Eds.), *Women with visible and invisible disabilities: Multiple intersections, multiple issues, multiple therapies* (pp. 211–222). Gloucestershire, England: Hawthorn Press.

Mona, L. R., Cameron, R. P., Goldwaser, G., Miller, A. R., Syme, M. L., & Fraley, S. S. (2009). Prescription for pleasure: Exploring sex-positive approaches in women with spinal cord injury. *Topics in Spinal Cord Injury and Rehabilitation, 15,* 15–28.

Mona, L. R., & Gardos, P. S. (2000). Disabled sexual partners. In L. T. Szuchman & F. Muscarella's (Eds.), *Psychological perspectives on human sexuality* (pp. 309–354). New York: Wiley.

National Institute on Disability and Rehabilitation Research. (1999). *NIDRR long-range plan.* Washington, DC: Office of Special Education and Rehabilitative Services.

Olkin, R. (1999). *What psychotherapists should know about disability.* New York: Guilford Press.

Related Topics

Chapter 14, "Taking a Client's Sexual History"

Chapter 43, "Diagnosis, Assessment, and Treatment of Female Sexual Dysfunctions"

Chapter 44, "Diagnosis, Assessment, and Treatment of Male Sexual Dysfunctions"

Chapter 65, "Considerations in Treating People with Disabilities"

71 HELPING PATIENTS COPE WITH CHRONIC MEDICAL ILLNESS

Carol D. Goodheart and Korey K. Hood

Chronic illnesses are now the primary cause of disability and death in the United States, a change from the acute conditions of the past. By 2020, the number of Americans with a chronic illness will likely increase to 164 million (www.healthypeople.gov). The chronic illnesses form a spectrum of diseases; they may be life threatening, progressive, manageable, unpredictable, or of known or unknown etiology. Such illnesses include cancer, cardiovascular disease, diabetes, asthma, arthritis, HIV disease, Alzheimer's disease, postviral syndromes, and gastrointestinal disorders, among many others.

Behavior, genetics, and the environment interact to produce or prevent disease. Once disease is present, behavior, cognition, emotion, and interpersonal dynamics can all affect symptoms. The application of psychological interventions to patients with a chronic illness can improve behavioral management, mental health functioning, health outcomes, and result in reductions in medical service use. The following summary highlights the key elements in the psychological treatment of adults coping with a chronic illness.

Many models of psychological intervention during illness exist, with variations according to theoretical orientation, population, setting, and emphasis. Among the diverse approaches, however, there are common themes for the clinician (Goodheart & Lansing, 1997).

1. *Obtain medical information.* Clinicians need not become medical experts, but they must obtain sufficient background to understand the choices, treatments, and experiences of the adult with a chronic illness. Collaboration with the patient's health care provider can produce information on the *o*utcome, *p*rocess, *e*tiology, and management *n*eeds of a particular disease (the acronym OPEN makes the list easy to remember). Other important medical resources are available online, through medical reference libraries, and specific disease organizations such as the American Cancer Society, the American Diabetes Association, and the American Heart Association. *The Merck Manual of Diagnosis and Therapy* (Porter, 2011) provides a medical overview of most conditions a clinician will encounter and is searchable at www.merck.com/pubs/mmanual/. Perhaps the most valuable and comprehensive source of online medical information is the National Institutes of Health (NIH) home page for health information (www.health.nih.gov/). It is possible to search most health topics at this site and to gain access to MEDLINEplus, which is a health database maintained by NIH's National Library of Medicine, available in English and Spanish, and Healthfinder, a health resource maintained by the Department of Health and Human Services. Links are provided for clinical studies, drug information, library references, special programs, and other health agencies.

2. *Assess response to illness and psychological status.* The adult's capacity to cope with illness is affected by premorbid personality organization, life stage roles and tasks, maturational development, internal resources such as temperament and intelligence, and external resources such as socioeconomic status, family support, and level of access to health care. One can evaluate these factors through clinical interview and, in some situations, through specific standardized assessment measures/scales for depression, anxiety, somatization, hostility, or other relevant indices. The cultural context is also critical to assess as individuals vary widely in the meaning they make of their illnesses, whether it is the cause, severity, or stigma associated with the illness. These perceptions will factor in to the patient's beliefs about how the illness can be treated, the importance of treatment, and the ability to cope with illness management.

3. *Integrate theoretical orientation and illness.* Cross-fertilization between and among differing schools of psychological theory often occurs when clinicians work with chronically ill adults. Dynamic clinicians add behavioral and educational components; cognitive clinicians add inferred self- and relational components; family systems, feminist theory, humanistic, and eclectic clinicians add to the diversity. In general, clinicians tend to borrow from other clinicians' attitudes and techniques. Regardless of orientation, the focus on coping with illness is enhanced when clinicians understand the patient's global mastery-competence level and how the patient manages reality, affect, and anxiety, interpersonal relationships, and cognitive functions. Evidence-based approaches typically include a biopsychosocial model of understanding and intervention, an interdisciplinary collaborative approach to health care, and are appropriate for community practice and medical settings. A key reference guide is *Clinical Health Psychology in Medical Settings: A Practitioner's Guidebook* (Belar & Deardorff, 1995). Furthermore, the Chronic Care Model (www.improvingchroniccare.org/) drives approaches to chronic illness management from a health care standpoint and offers a critical perspective on providing care within the broader system of the patient.

4. *Consider pathways, desired outcomes, and competing needs.* Across a host of chronic illnesses, psychological functioning is associated with health outcomes, often through the path of illness management. Clinicians mindful of the demands of chronic illness management can assist patients in selecting both psychologically based outcomes (e.g., improved coping) as well as health outcomes (e.g., better disease management) and determine the best order to address them in treatment. For example, disease management may not improve until more adaptive coping is achieved and barriers to effective disease management are addressed simultaneously given the nature of the barriers (e.g., diminished motivation for better health).

Furthermore, adults with chronic illness vary in their willingness or ability to make use of the strategies, at times due to comorbid or competing areas of need. Problems that can complicate illness management and coping include isolation, losses and dependency, fear of death, confines of illness, and lack of familiarity with medical culture. In addition, loss of key roles and autonomy and control, disruption of plans, assault on self-image and self-esteem, and distressing emotions are all critical areas to assess and address with these interventions.

5. *Offer a menu of interventions.* The selection of interventions is based on the changing needs and capacities of the chronically ill adult and the knowledge and skills of the clinician. Interventions may be directed toward prevention of further illness (e.g., smoking cessation, weight control); toward screening for disease (e.g., decreasing the avoidance of warranted HIV testing or mammograms); or toward management of disease. The following interventions can improve the patient's ability to cope with the illness and manage it effectively:

- *Focused psychotherapy.* A time-limited approach to problem solving, based on biopsychosocial stressors and resources. Building general and illness-specific problem solving strategies promotes health and quality of life outcomes.

- *Decision making.* Helping adults arrive at the best decisions for their personal circumstances from among the medical choices they are given.
- *Medical symptom reduction.* Helping adults decrease pain, lessen side effects of treatments (e.g., anticipatory nausea associated with chemotherapy), or decrease frequency or intensity of acute episodes (e.g., incidents of asthma exacerbation).
- *Treatment adherence.* Helping adults develop motivation and overcome barriers to maintaining adherence to prescribed medical treatment regimens.
- *Stress and pain reduction.* Helping adults learn techniques of progressive relaxation, hypnosis, biofeedback, visualization, meditation, or focused breathing.
- *Interpersonal techniques.* Helping adults learn new or improved skills for communication, assertion, and conflict resolution with medical personnel, family, partners, employers, coworkers, and friends.
- *Adaptation.* Helping adults make quality of life adjustments to an altered reality due to the losses of illness, effects of medications, aftereffects of medical treatments, or disability.
- *Crisis management.* Helping adults mobilize internal and external supportive resources to regain control, for use when the patient is flooded with affect and overwhelmed by anxiety and when the patient's ability to cope on his or her own is compromised.
- *Anger management.* Helping adults control anger through the use of shame reduction, guided imagery, anger arousal combined with relaxation, and through improved self-efficacy in communication and problem solving.
- *Nonverbal psychotherapeutic techniques.* Helping adults express affect and experience through art therapy, sand play, or movement therapy. Rarely used alone, these visual, tactile, motile techniques are particularly useful in adults with learning disabilities, posttraumatic stress disorder, or a blocked, regressed, dissociated, or concrete state of functioning.
- *Family involvement.* Helping the caregivers, partners, and family members of adults with chronic illness by conjoint treatments and the development of coping and support structures within the home care system.
- *Support for self-disease management.* Helping adults contribute to their own well-being through self-selected adjunctive activities (e.g., personal illness diaries, exercise and nutrition programs [within limits of medical recommendations], religious and spiritual participation, humorous tapes and books).
- *Referral.* Helping adults decrease their isolation and increase the support network available to them through disease support groups and community services.
- *Handling uncertainty and fear of death.* Helping adults with the anxiety and depression that often accompany disease progression. The primary technique for death anxiety is to listen fully, which may be difficult under severe and threatening circumstances. To listen fully means to listen without judgment, without withdrawal, without denial, and without interference to the patient's hopes. To listen fully is to be present, with the patient, in facing death.

It is not possible within the limits of this entry to detail the implementation of each intervention given. Even experienced clinicians may not be skilled in every type of intervention listed here. A practical self-assessment model now exists to help clinicians gauge their readiness to provide chronic illness consultation and services (Belar et al., 2001) and postdoctoral continuing education programs in the areas listed here are available through state and national mental health associations.

6. *Face the personal impact of working with chronically ill adults.* Clinicians have their own idiosyncratic responses to the presence of disease and to patients' characterological reactions to disease. Entering into a therapeutic relationship with a chronically ill adult carries special challenges. Like everyone else, clinicians have deeply held personal attitudes toward bodily needs, functions, disfigurements, and pains and toward caretaking and dependency. They have personal fears about debilitation, decline, and death. Working with chronically ill patients often induces countertransference reactions in clinicians, which may be expressed as follows:

- Anxiety (e.g., exposure to death, failure, vulnerability, or loss may stimulate anxiety)
- Affect (e.g., anger may be a marker of frustration with the toll of disease or with patients who complain more than the clinician thinks is necessary; disgust or distaste may be evoked by the graphic details of illness)
- Defensive reactions (e.g., withdrawal, denial, moralizing, minimizing, or rescuing may occur if clinicians' anxieties or negative emotions become sufficiently aroused)

It is not always possible to resolve these issues in ideal ways, but it is realistic to identify and manage clinicians' personal responses that interfere with clinical care. Potential signs of difficulty include the following:

- Preoccupation with thoughts of the patient out of session
- Persistent intense feelings about the patient
- Depressive constellation of discouragement, fatigue, and pessimism
- Treatment impasse
- Feedback from patient, supervisor, colleagues, family, or friends regarding affects, anxieties, or reactions to the work

Psychological interventions in adult chronic illness have become increasingly important as the number of people with chronic conditions grows. The research literature on interactions among behavior, biology, and disease provides the basis for increasingly targeted psychological intervention strategies. The overview framework for these strategies includes obtaining sufficient medical information; assessing response to illness and psychological status; integrating psychological theory and the illness; considering pathways, outcomes, and competing needs; offering a varied selection of interventions; and facing the personal impact of working with chronically ill adults.

References, Readings, and Internet Sites

Belar, C. D., Brown, R. A., Hersch, L. E., Hornyak, L. M., Rozensky, R. H., Sheridan, E. P., . . . Reed, G. W. (2001). Self-assessment in clinical health psychology: A model for ethical expansion of practice. *Professional Psychology: Research and Practice, 32*(2), 135–141.

Belar, C. D., & Deardorff, W. W. (1995). *Clinical health psychology in medical settings: A practitioner's guidebook.* Washington, DC: American Psychological Association.

Goodheart, C., & Lansing, M. (1997). *Treating people with chronic disease: A psychological guide.* Washington, DC: American Psychological Association.

HealthyPeople.gov. (2011). Retrieved January 2013, from healthypeople.gov

National Institutes of Health. (2011). Retrieved January 2013, from www.health.nih.gov/

Porter, R. S. (Ed.). (2011). *The Merck manual of diagnosis and therapy* (19th ed.). Rahway, NJ: Merck.

The Robert Wood Johnson Foundation. (2011). *Improving chronic illness care.* Retrieved January 2013, from www.improvingchronic-care.org/

Related Topics

Chapter 65, "Considerations in Treating People with Disabilities"

Chapter 86, "Helping Children Cope with Chronic Medical Illness"

72 LOCATING THE BEST RESEARCH EVIDENCE FOR EVIDENCE-BASED PRACTICE

Lauren A. Maggio and Marilyn L. Tinsley

Psychologists recognize that clinical practice should be predicated on the best available research integrated with the clinician's expertise within the context of patient characteristics, values, and culture (American Psychological Association, 2006). This chapter features resources designed to save busy practitioners time and effort in accessing and analyzing research articles, by providing expert analysis, synthesis, and filtering of research literature for evidence-based practice (EBP). We focus on online resources, some of which are free, as they tend to be the most current and easily accessible. Search tips are included in each description.

FILTERED RESOURCES

Filtered resources synthesize the available information on a topic. In other words, the literature review is made available to you and then translated into evidence-based clinical practices.

Cochrane Database of Systematic Reviews

The Cochrane Database of Systematic Reviews (CDSR) (www.thecochranelibrary.com), one of six databases that make up the Cochrane Library, is comprised of systematic reviews that identify and synthesize randomized controlled trials (RCTs) on a given health care topic. Each review is written by a team of experts and is peer reviewed. Reviews are updated quarterly to annually. Considered to be a "gold standard" of EBP in mental health, the CDSR includes reviews on developmental and psychosocial problems, learning problems, depression, anxiety, and schizophrenia, among many others. Cochrane reviews are divided into user-friendly sections, including implications for practice and research, authors' conclusions, and descriptions and analysis of the RCTs examined. Abstracts and plain-language summaries of Cochrane Reviews, which contain substantial and conclusive information, can be accessed freely through the Cochrane Library at www.thecochranelibrary.com and via PubMed. The full-text of CDSR reviews is available online by subscription.

Browse the CDSR by topic or search by title words, keywords, medical subject heading (MeSH) terms, and more. PubMed/Medline can also be searched for CDSR reviews.

Campbell Collaboration Reviews of Interventions and Policy Evaluations

Established in 2000, the Campbell Collaboration Library of Systematic Reviews (C2) (www.campbellcollaboration.org) creates and maintains systematic reviews focused on behavioral science evidence in the areas of "education, crime and justice, and social welfare." Topics include bullying, attention-deficit hyperactivity disorder, domestic violence, and more. C2 reviews feature expert meta-analyses of topics with extensive bibliographies, providing a convenient gateway into the literature. C2 reviewers are urged to update their reviews at least every 24 months. Access to the C2 Library is available freely online at www.campbellcollaboration.org and includes access to PDF versions of the full text of systematic reviews. Search by keyword or simply browse reviews by three subdivisions: education, crime and justice, and social welfare.

Database of Abstracts of Reviews of Effects

The Database of Abstracts of Reviews of Effects (DARE) (www.crd.york.ac.uk/crdweb), which is updated daily, is produced by the UK Centre for Reviews and Dissemination, which is both a part of the National Health Service and the University of York. The stated purpose of DARE is to assist busy practitioners in locating and assessing evidence from the literature. DARE currently contains over 9,000 structured abstracts that critically analyze systematic reviews pulled from major biomedical databases, select journals, and a wide range of other literature, plus summaries of Cochrane reviews and protocols and Campbell reviews. DARE reviews focus on investigating the cost-effectiveness and impact of various health and social care interventions, making it a relevant resource for mental health and addiction questions. A few DARE abstracts also analyze diagnostic systematic reviews. DARE reviewers provide a concise summary of the systematic review and a critical analysis of both the selected systematic review and the strengths and weaknesses of the studies it evaluates. This summary provides a direct link to the original review's citation in PubMed, also saving time.

DARE is currently available in full-text format without charge at www.crd.york.ac.uk/crdweb/. It is also available by subscription as part of the Cochrane Library (Wiley InterScience).

The CRD Web site provides free searching and free access to the DARE reviews. Quick Search, Advanced Search, and MeSH terms are all available. Note a subscription is necessary to retrieve full text from the CDSR and other subscription-based resources.

BMJ Clinical Evidence

BMJ Clinical Evidence (www.clinicalevidence.bmj.com) provides evidence for over 2,000 treatments and preventative interventions for more than 200 common health conditions, including mental health. A notable feature is the emphasis on benefit or harm of a particular intervention. Available by subscription at www.clinicalevidence.bmj.com, this resource is continuously updated.

One of the major advantages of using BMJ Clinical Evidence is that each disorder and intervention is presented as an easy-to-use comprehensive module. Clinicians or epidemiologists who have significant EBP experience author all of the modules. Each module contains a systematic review of the health condition, which succinctly summarizes the benefits or disadvantages of the various interventions. These systematic reviews are based on current RCTs, observational studies, and other systematic reviews.

Each webpage of BMJ Clinical Evidence features a standard search box in which OR is automatically inserted between all terms, and Boolean operators AND or NOT must be typed in and capitalized. For example, "anxiety AND hypnotism" retrieves articles containing both words; "anxiety hypnotism" retrieves items where either word appears. BMJ Clinical Evidence is also easily browsed by section or health condition.

Practice Guidelines

Multiple practice and treatment guidelines can be found through clearinghouse sites such as The National Guideline Clearinghouse (www.guideline.gov) and the UK-based National Institute for Health and Clinical Excellence (NICE) (guidance.nice.org.uk/). Both of these sites are searchable and provide access to or information about the full text of evidence-based practice guidelines. For mental health and addictions, for example, the National Guideline Clearinghouse features over 800 specific mental health guidelines from relevant professional organizations such as the American Academy of Child and Adolescent Psychiatry and the Substance Abuse and Mental Health Services Administration. In addition to the guidelines themselves, the Clearinghouse includes side-by-side comparison of guidelines selected during a search, expert commentaries, and guideline syntheses, in which multiple guidelines on a topic are compared and evaluated by an expert in the field.

Evidence-Based Journals

Journals specifically dedicated to facilitating EBP have become a recent trend in publishing. Examples include *Evidence-Based Complementary and Alternative Medicine, Evidence-Based Nursing, Journal of Family Practice,* and *Evidence-Based Mental Health.*

Evidence-Based Mental Health is a quarterly journal of structured abstracts that summarize and analyze mental health articles; these include original studies and review articles from over 50 international medical journals and the Cochrane Library. Each structured abstract summarizes an individual article and succinctly presents its methods, main results, and conclusions. A mental health expert also provides a short critical analysis of the main article and makes recommendations for its use in clinical practice. This value-added commentary can influence a practitioner's decision to pursue the original article for further examination.

Evidence-Based Mental Health is accessible by subscription in print or online at www.ebmh.bmj.com/. This resource is best accessed electronically for ease of browsing by journal issue or clinical topic. It is also possible to search by keyword or title word. To access these search options, click on "advanced search." This search assumes OR between search terms, but you can also use AND or NOT to narrow a search. Another use of this resource is to input the citation of an article to see whether it has been appraised by *Evidence-Based Mental Health.* Although this journal requires a subscription to view its latest content, materials published before 2006 are freely available to users who register at journals.bmj.com/cgi/register.

In addition to EBP journals, many other titles across a wide range of specialties include evidence sections, including meta-analyses of articles, systematic reviews, or an evidence-based approach to a particular topic. For example, the *American Journal of Psychiatry* includes a monthly series called "New Treatment in Psychiatry," which features a hypothetical clinical case that presents a common problem in patient care, summarizes the relevant literature, and includes expert recommendations for treatment and diagnosis. For another example, the journal *Psychiatric Services* often includes a column "Best Practices" that introduces a best practice based on research evidence and then provides commentary.

EVIDENCE-BASED PRACTICE WEB SITES

EBP search engines simultaneously present access to filtered and unfiltered resources. The freely available TRIP Database is an excellent example, because it quickly retrieves practice guidelines, Web sites, Cochrane reviews, and journal citations in a single search.

Turning Research into Practice

The Turning Research Into Practice (TRIP) database (www.tripdatabase.com) is updated monthly and contains evidence-based synopsis resources like *Clinical Evidence,* clinical guidelines, systematic reviews, core medical journals such as *The New England Journal of Medicine,* and links to "canned" searches in PubMed that allow users to run PubMed Clinical Queries designed for their research topic. Citations from certain subscription resources appear in TRIP, and it is still necessary to have subscription access to those titles in order to obtain the full text of documents. The TRIP Database is a commercial site featuring advertising, which raises the possibility of external influence by its advertisers, prominently including the pharmaceutical industry.

The TRIP Database is easy to use. The database automatically utilizes a synonym dictionary to include related terms (e.g., ADHD will be searched along with attention deficit hyperactivity disorder and several other synonyms). On the search results page, you can view the synonyms used in a search. Quotes are used to alert the system to search a phrase (e.g., "family therapy"). The TRIP Database displays the title, the source of the information, and its dates. In the right navigation bar you will find several key filters, including evidence-based synopses, guidelines (broken out by region), systematic reviews, e-textbooks, and clinical questions.

Substance Abuse and Mental Health Services Association Web site

Substance Abuse and Mental Health Services Association (SAMHSA) (www.samhsa.gov), a US government site, features extensive statistical data on the national and state levels and a wide variety of valuable reports, including Surgeon General Reports. Importantly, SAMHSA features the National Registry of Evidence-Based Programs and Practices (NREPP).

NREPP is a free database of research-sup ported mental health and substance abuse treatments available at www.nrepp.samhsa.gov/find.asp. This full-text database provides intervention summaries, which describe each intervention and its targeted outcomes, comments on the research which supports the intervention, reports the intervention's references, and identifies the individuals who developed the intervention. Two ratings are provided for each intervention: a quality-of-research rating and a readiness-for-dissemination rating. Currently this database contains 200 interventions, which can be quickly browsed by clicking "view all." NREPP features a user-friendly search by keyword, with the option of limiting to various topics, areas of interest, evaluations/study designs, or population groups.

FINDING RANDOMIZED CONTROLLED TRIALS AND SYSTEMATIC REVIEWS

You may have a clinical question that is not answered by any of the review resources mentioned earlier. PubMed provides efficient search tools for identifying particular RCTs and systematic reviews in the health sciences journal literature. Go to PubMed's Clinical Queries page (www.ncbi.nlm.nih.gov/pubmed/clinical) and enter keywords or MeSH terms in the search box. Select parameters, such as diagnosis or therapy, and click "Search." Lists of RCTs and systematic reviews appear in the left-hand and center columns. Click a title to view the abstract; access the complete article by clicking on the publisher's button. Some journals provide free access ("open access"), and some require subscription. See your institution's library for subscription information or to request an article via interlibrary loan.

AND MORE ASSISTANCE

This chapter has introduced you to a wide variety of popular online review and EBP resources for mental health, addictions, and health care. There will probably be times when you come up against a clinical question that is difficult to answer. Specialized searching methods or niche resources may be required. When this happens, your best bet is to contact a librarian, either at your local university or at your regional health care library.

References and Readings

APA Presidential Task Force on Evidence-Based Practice. (2006). Evidence-based practice in psychology. *American Psychologist, 61*(4), 271–285.

Berke, D. M., Rozell, C. A., Hogan, T. P., Norcross, J. C., & Karpiak, C. P. (2011). What clinical psychologists know about evidence-based practice: Familiarity with online resources and research methods. *Journal of Clinical Psychology, 67*, 329–339.

Falzon, L., Davidson, K. W., & Bruns, D. (2010). Evidence searching for evidence-based psychology practice.

Professional Psychology, Research and Practice, 41(8), 550–557.

Norcross, J. C., Hogan, T. P., & Koocher, G. P. (2008). *Clinician's guide to evidence-based practices: Mental health and the addictions*. New York: Oxford University Press.

Pagoto, S. L., Spring, B., Coups, E. J., Mulvaney, S., Coutu, M. F., & Ozakinci, G. (2007). Barriers and facilitators of evidence-based practice perceived by behavioral science health professionals. *Journal of Clinical Psychology, 63*, 695–705.

Spring, B. (2007). Evidence-based practice in clinical psychology: What it is, why it matters; what you need to know. *Journal of Clinical Psychology, 63*(7), 611–631.

Walker, B. B., & London, S. (2007). Novel tools and resources for evidence-based practice in psychology. *Journal of Clinical Psychology, 63*(7), 633–642.

Related Topics

Chapter 27, "Locating Information about Psychological Tests and Measures"

Chapter 30, "Compendium of Psychotherapy Treatment Manuals"

Chapter 31, "Compendium of Empirically Supported Treatments"

Chapter 32, "Compendium of Treatment Adaptations"

73 PREVENTING RELAPSE

Katie Witkiewitz

Lapses, defined as engaging in a previously problematic behavior following a successful behavior change, are the modal outcomes following treatment for addictive behaviors. Treatments have often focused on changing behavior, but not necessarily on maintaining positive changes over time. Individuals often left treatment programs without specific knowledge about how to maintain treatment gains. This situation led to a "revolving door" phenomenon, whereby many treatment completers returned to treatment following a relapse. Clearly, more emphasis needs to be placed on the problem of relapse and skills for preventing its occurrence.

Relapse prevention (RP) is a manualized intervention and a treatment strategy that focuses on the maintenance stage of change and the problem of relapse through an integration of behavioral skills training, cognitive interventions, and lifestyle change procedures (Marlatt & Gordon, 1985). Although initially developed for alcohol-use disorders, the principles of RP have been adapted to many other addictive and nonaddictive disorders.

The effectiveness of RP has been reasonably well established across disorders. Irvin and colleagues (1999) conducted a meta-analysis on the efficacy of RP techniques in the improvement of substance abuse and psychosocial outcomes. Twenty-six studies representing a sample of 9,504 participants were included in the review, which focused on alcohol use, smoking, polysubstance use, and cocaine use. The treatment effects demonstrated that RP was successful in reducing substance use and improving psychosocial adjustment.

An important question that was not addressed by that meta-analysis was whether RP is equally effective for all individuals, or whether certain RP skills may be more or less important for a specific gender, race, or ethnicity. In one study (Walton, Blow, & Booth, 2001), women and African Americans reported greater coping skills than men or Caucasians, respectively. Men were also more likely to have negative social influences and greater exposure to substances than women. Drink refusal skills training, which is often included in RP interventions, was more effective for African American clients than it was for non-Hispanic White clients (Witkiewitz, Villarroel, Hartzler, & Donovan, 2011).

In a narrative review of controlled clinical trials evaluating RP in the treatment of smoking, alcohol, and other drug use (Carroll, 1996), RP was found to be generally effective compared with no treatment and as good as other active treatments. One interesting finding was that some RP treatments sustained main effects for RP, suggesting that RP may provide continued improvement over a longer period of time (indicating a "delayed emergence effect"), whereas other treatments may be effective over only a shorter duration. This delayed emergence effect is consistent with the skills acquisition basis of the RP approach. As with learning any new skill, clients become more experienced in acquiring and performing the skill, leading to overall improvements in performance over time.

CLINICAL PRACTICE OF RELAPSE PREVENTION

RP teaches clients how to (1) reframe the relapse process; (2) identify high-risk situations for relapse; (3) learn how to cope with craving to engage in the addictive behavior; (4) reduce the harm of relapse by minimizing the negative consequences and learning from the experience; and (5) achieve greater lifestyle balance. Suggestions on how to implement these in clinical practice are described next.

Reframe Relapse as a Process

Begin by exploring the client's subjective associations with the term *relapse*. Relapse can be described as either an outcome—the dichotomous view that the person is either ill or well—or a process, encompassing any transgression in the cyclic process of behavior change (Witkiewitz & Marlatt, 2004). Many clients view relapse in dichotomous terms ("I was either able to maintain abstinence or not"). Alternatively, we can teach clients to use the term *lapse* to describe the first episode of the behavior after the commitment to abstinence. A lapse is a single event, a reemergence of a previous habit, which may or may not lead to a complete relapse. When a slip is defined as a lapse, it implies that if a corrective action can be taken, the outcome can still be considered positive (called a *prolapse*). Small setbacks can be described as opportunities for new learning and the reevaluation of coping strategies in high-risk situations, rather than indications of personal failure or a lack of motivation.

Clients often hold a belief that a single lapse indicates failure, whereas many clients who experience a lapse are likely to get back on track in the direction of positive change. It is important that clinicians provide an overview of the relapse process and encourage clients to consider a single lapse as part of that process. One analogy that is often helpful for clients is for the clinician to compare substance use lapses to another condition that can have setbacks. For example, the clinician might provide the example of an individual with diabetes, who is likely to experience a spike in high blood sugar due to poor dietary choices. A single increase in blood sugar (while potentially dangerous and severe) does not imply personal failure; rather it informs the individual that he or she needs to change behavior to control the blood sugar.

Identify High-Risk Situations

The initial component in RP is the identification of a client's unique profile of high-risk situations for relapse and evaluating the client's ability to cope with these high-risk situations. A high-risk situation is one in which the individual's sense of perceived control is threatened. High-risk situations can include environmental influences, an interpersonal interaction, or intrapersonal factors (such as affective states, cognitions, and physiological states). The procedures available to identify high-risk situations differ based on the readiness of the client and whether the client is engaged in the target behavior at the time of the assessment.

1. *Self-monitoring.* Ask the client to keep a continuous, daily record of the target behavior (what time the behavior began and ended, amount consumed, amount of money spent, etc.), along with a brief description of additional situational factors (where, who was present, doing what); events that may have occurred prior to the target behavior (what was happening, how you were feeling); amount consumed (be specific); and consequences associated with use (what happened afterward, how you felt, what you were thinking). Self-monitoring can also be used as an assessment device, to monitor urges to use, along with records of coping responses and whether the urge was followed by engaging in substance use. Psychological reactivity to self-monitoring can serve as an intervention strategy, since the client's awareness of the target behavior increases as the assessment continues and can lead to reductions in the monitored behavior.
2. *Autobiographies.* Have clients provide a descriptive narrative of the history and development of their problem. Ask the client how and why he or she initiated or first became involved with the problematic behavior; how the patterns of engaging in that behavior may have changed over time; and what people, places, and events are associated with it.
3. *Assessment tools.* Numerous self-report measures and observational techniques have been developed to help clinicians and their clients identify and prioritize their individual high-risk situations. These include the Inventory of Drug-Taking Situations (Annis, 1985) and the Identifying High-Risk Situations Inventory (Daley, 1986). Once high-risk situations are identified, it is helpful to assess the client's degree of self-confidence in his or her ability to resist urges and maintain abstinence in those situations.

In addition to these three strategies, the clinician can be extremely helpful to the client by conducting a functional analysis of previous high-risk situations. Specifically, it is often useful for the clinician to review with the client what makes a particular situation a high-risk situation for the client. For example, many clients who are abstaining from alcohol will acknowledge that going past their favorite bar is a high-risk situation. Yet a clinician has the opportunity to further explore *why* going past a favorite bar is a high-risk situation. The clinician can explore the client's perception of his or her potential cognitive, affective, and behavioral reactions to the high-risk situation, which can provide valuable information for coping skills training.

Learn to Cope with Urges to Use in High-Risk Situations

After the client and therapist identify potential high-risk situations, it is important for the therapist to evaluate existing coping skills and provide training in additional ways that a client might cope with urges and resist using substances in a high-risk situation. The assessment of cognitive, affective, and behavioral reactions to high-risk situations (described in the previous section) can provide guidance in identifying the client's coping skills deficits. For example, if the client states that going past a favorite bar is a high-risk situation because the bar makes him or her feel anxious and then think about how a drink would relieve the anxiety. Given this scenario, a clinician might focus on skills for coping with anxiety.

1. *Assess coping skills.* Any situation can be considered "high risk" if the person is incapable or unwilling to respond to that situation with an effective coping response. Therefore, it is critical that the clinician

focus on the assessment of a client's coping skills with regard to previous, or probable, high-risk situations.

2. *Teach effective coping behavior.* Following assessment, the clinician should teach the client how to respond to cues (that occur before or during a high-risk situation) by engaging in an alternative effective coping behavior. Coping skills can be behavioral (action or action), cognitive (planning, reminders of negative consequences, "urge surfing"), or a combination of cognitive and behavioral coping processes. The goal is to teach clients how to respond to early warning signs of relapse, such as the rationalization of making seemingly unimportant decisions that eventually lead to a lapse (e.g., maybe I should buy a bottle of vodka and keep it in the house, just in case guests drop by). RP combines practice in general problem-solving skills and specific coping responses. Skills training methods incorporate components of direct instruction, modeling and behavioral rehearsal and coaching, and therapist support and feedback. In those cases in which it is not practical to use new coping skills in real-life settings, the therapist can utilize imagery or role plays to represent high-risk situations.
3. *Teach "urge-surfing."* Urge-surfing is a metaphor for coping with the conditioned response to stimuli associated with an addictive behavior (coping with reactivity to cue exposure). It is based on the analogy that urges are like ocean waves, in that they have a specific course of action, with a given latency of onset, intensity, and duration. Remind clients that urges will arise, subside, and pass away on their own. In this technique, the client is taught to label internal sensations and cognitive preoccupations as an urge and to foster an attitude of detachment from that urge. The goal is to identify, accept, and "surf" the urge, keeping one's balance so as to not get wiped out by the temptation to give in.
4. *Develop a decisional matrix.* Clients who are on the verge of using may only selectively attend to the positive expectancies of use. Help clients develop a decisional matrix that summarizes both immediate and delayed negative consequences of engaging in the prohibited behavior. A reminder card (also referred to as an emergency card) is one way of listing both cognitive and behavioral techniques that can be used in the event a client has an urge to use.
5. *Train clients to be on the lookout for warning signs.* Clients can be taught to look for impending high-risk situations and to take preventive action at the earliest possible point. Depending on the situation and the client's self-efficacy, the recommended action might be to avoid the high-risk situation. However, not all high-risk situations can be identified in advance. Many situations arise suddenly without warning—for example, being with a supposed nonusing friend who offers drugs. In this type of situation, the individual must rely on previously acquired coping responses. Emphasize that the earlier one intervenes in the chain of events leading up to a high-risk situation and possible relapse, the easier it will be to prevent the lapse from occurring.

Minimize the Negative Consequences of a Lapse by Learning from the Experience

One of the key principles of relapse prevention is the recognition that lapses happen and that lapses do not need to be viewed as failure, but rather lapses can be viewed as an opportunity to learn about the client's reactions to high-risk situations and lapsing.

1. *Explain the abstinence violation effect (AVE).* The client's attributional response to a slip can further increase the probability of a full-blown relapse. Clients who view relapse as inevitable following the occurrence of a lapse are setting themselves up for an even larger transgression of behavior. This abstinence violation effect results from two cognitive-affective elements: cognitive dissonance (conflict and guilt) and a personal attributional effect (blaming oneself as the cause of the uncontrollable relapse). Clients should be instructed that a slip does not have to result in a major relapse and that

lapses provide an opportunity for corrective action. A lapse may turn out to be a valuable learning experience (prolapse) that raises consciousness and teaches the client information about possible high-risk situations and sources of stress or lifestyle imbalance.

2. *Conduct relapse debriefings.* One way to learn from lapses is through the use of relapse debriefings. Explore all aspects of the chain of events leading up to the relapse (or a particular temptation or lapse), including details concerning the high-risk situation, alternative coping responses, and inappropriate and appropriate cognitions.

The clinician, who is often viewed as the expert, can be immensely helpful to clients who believe a single lapse equals failure by inquiring about the client's assumptions and encouraging the client to consider viewing the lapse as a learning experience. In providing this corrective feedback for clients it is important for clinicians to take a nonjudgmental stance toward the client's lapse.

Achieve Lifestyle Balance

One of the most important, and often overlooked, tasks in RP is to intervene in the client's lifestyle to increase the client's capacity to deal with perceived hassles or responsibilities ("shoulds") and perceived pleasures or self-gratification ("wants"). A key goal for a lifestyle intervention is to provide alternative sources of reward and to replace the problem with other positive activities. Many activities that might be positive for a client may be experienced negatively at first; thus, the clinician must often provide some coaching and reinforce the idea that positive activities are highly beneficial with long-term positive effects. Some examples of positive activities include exercise, relaxation training, or meditation. Indeed, recent research has found that training in mindfulness meditation is particularly effective in preventing and minimizing relapse (Bowen, Chawla, & Marlatt, 2010).

In evaluating lifestyle balance, the clinician can conduct a thorough assessment of the client's preferences and previous success. Positive activities that have previously been paired with the problem might not be ideal activities. If a client can only identify positive activities that have been paired with substance use, then the clinician can brainstorm with the client about ways of engaging in the activity without using substances. Ideally the client and clinician should work to identify positive activities that are necessarily problem-free (e.g., running), easily accessible, and have few barriers to participation.

References and Readings

Annis, H. M. (1985). *Inventory of Drug-Taking Situations.* Toronto, ON: Addiction Research Foundation.

Bowen, S., Chawla, N., & Marlatt, G. A. (2010). *Mindfulness-based relapse prevention for addictive behaviors: A clinician's guide.* New York: Guilford Press.

Daley, D. (1986). *Relapse prevention workbook for recovering alcoholics and drug dependent persons.* Holmes Beach, FL: Learning Publications.

Irvin, J. E., Bowers, C. A., Dunn, M. E., & Wang, M. C. (1999). Efficacy of relapse prevention: A meta-analytic review. *Journal of Consulting and Clinical Psychology, 67,* 563–570.

Marlatt, G. A., & Gordon, J. R. (1985). *Relapse prevention: Maintenance strategies in the treatment of addictive behaviors.* New York: Guilford Press.

Walton, M. A., Blow, F. C, & Booth, B. M. (2001). Diversity in relapse prevention needs: Gender and race comparisons among substance abuse treatment patients. *American Journal of Drug and Alcohol Abuse, 27,* 225–240.

Witkiewitz, K., & Marlatt, G. A. (2004). Relapse prevention for alcohol and drug problems: That was Zen, this is Tao. *American Psychologist, 59,* 224–235.

Witkiewitz, K., Villarroel, N. A., Hartzler, B., & Donovan, D. M. (2011). Drinking outcomes following drink refusal skills training: Differential effects for African American and non-Hispanic white clients. *Psychology of Addictive Behaviors, 25,* 162–167.

Related Topics

Chapter 34, "Applying the Stages of Change"
Chapter 55, "Terminating Psychotherapy"
Chapter 66, "Practicing Harm Reduction"

PART IV

Couples, Family, and Group Treatment

74 RECRUITING, SELECTING, AND PREPARING PATIENTS FOR INTERPERSONAL GROUP PSYCHOTHERAPY

Victor J. Yalom

Although proper recruitment, selection, and preparation of members are key to the development of a successful psychotherapy group, these steps are frequently rushed or skipped, leading to a less-than-optimal group experience. The following principles are geared toward an interpersonally oriented process group, and they may need some modifications for other forms of group therapy (e.g., cognitive-behavioral therapy, psychoeducational groups).

The interactional or interpersonal approach assumes that patients' presenting symptoms and underlying difficulties are to a large extent the result of maladaptive patterns of interpersonal relationships. A major therapeutic factor in group psychotherapy occurs via interpersonal learning—that is, group members become more aware of and modify their maladaptive interpersonal behaviors and beliefs. Over a course of successful group treatment, patients consistently receive direct, honest feedback about the effects of their behavior on others—feedback of a quality they are unlikely to receive in a constructive and supportive manner anywhere else in their lives. Other important therapeutic factors in groups include feelings of support and belonging, catharsis, the instillation of hope, and the experience of altruism in helping other members. Note that in this model, the group itself becomes an *agent* of change, and not just a *setting* where the therapist directs therapeutic activity.

A basic assumption underlying the change process is that the group is a social microcosm: the types of relationships patients tend to form in their daily lives will eventually be re-created within the group itself. Because of this phenomenon, the most powerful and efficacious way to learn from these recapitulated relationships is to focus on them as they continuously recur during the course of therapy. This is referred to as the "here and now," because the focus is *here* (in the group) and *now* (interactions during the therapy session). Accordingly, past events or relationships outside the group are used primarily as jumping-off points, which then guide the here-and-now work in the group rather than remaining the central focus.

Tasks of the Group Therapist

Given that interpersonal learning is maximized in a group that operates largely in the here and now, what must the therapist do for this to occur?

1. The therapist actively assists patients in translating their presenting complaints into

interpersonal issues. For example, a patient who initially requests therapy because of a feeling of depression would be urged to explore the interpersonal context of her depression—for example, the depression might be triggered by feelings of rejection by a lover, with subsequent loneliness or humiliation. This initial reformulation of the problem must then be broadened so that it can be addressed in the group. With additional effort, the therapist might help the patient restate the complaint as, "I feel depressed when others don't give me the attention I want, and yet I am unable to state my needs directly." In this manner, the complaint has been transformed into one that can be addressed in the here and now of the therapy group: The patient can explore how she experiences similar feelings of rejection by other group members and yet has difficulty in letting them know what she wants from them. This reformulation of symptoms or complaints into interpersonal issues must occur initially in the group preparation (see later), and it should continue throughout the course of the group.

2. The therapist actively helps the group members to interact directly with each other and to share their observations and feelings about one another. During the initial session, it is common for the members to take turns talking about themselves, including their reasons for seeking therapy and the areas in which they would like to change. From the first meeting, the astute therapist will look for every opportunity to direct the interactions toward the here and now. For example, if a patient states that he is feeling anxious, a few probing questions may reveal that the patient invariably compares himself with others and usually concludes that they will look down on him because of his lack of education and sophistication. The therapist can bring this general concern into the here and now by asking, "Of the people in this group, which ones have you imagined are having critical thoughts of you?" Although the group members may initially resist the leap into the here and now, with time and reinforcement they will begin to engage with each other more spontaneously.
3. The experiential element of the group interactions is crucial, but on its own insufficient to induce personal change. To this end, the therapist helps group members to reflect upon the encounters they experience in the group, namely on the group's process rather than the content of the discussions. In the context of group therapy, whereas *content* consists of the actual words or topics discussed, *process* refers to the meaning that these conversations have in terms of the relationships between the group members. Thus, from a process orientation, the same utterance by a patient will have vastly different connotations depending on the manner in which it was delivered, the timing, and the context of the group discussion.

The therapist thus finds ways to help the group reflect on its own process. Again, this is an area where therapists must be very active, since group members themselves are unlikely to initiate this type of activity. Process comments can range from simple observations of specific incidents (e.g., "I noticed that when you said that, your fists were clenched") to more generalized interpretations (e.g., "You seem to instinctively challenge whatever the other men say in the group; I wonder if you feel the need to be competitive with them?"). Over the course of therapy, process comments serve to heighten patients' awareness of how their behavior appears to others in the group. Ultimately, patients become aware of how they determine the quality of the interpersonal world they live in. With this awareness comes the possibility for true behavior change, leading to more satisfying relationships.

Recruiting Group Members

Getting groups up and running can be the most challenging aspect of conducting group psychotherapy. Group leaders need to recruit an appropriate number of clients in a relatively short amount of time; if the group formation process is stretched out too long, some individuals may drop out before the group begins.

On the other hand, starting a group with fewer than five members is likely to be problematic. With anticipated absences and unanticipated dropouts, some meetings will have as few as two or three clients. These meetings lack the richness of exchanges and overall dynamism experienced in larger group sessions. Furthermore, they are likely to engender in the members (and the leader) fears about group survival, which are unproductive and distract from the therapeutic goals.

Thus, therapists need a steady referral base, or an ability to effectively market their groups; both of these can be challenging for solo private practitioners. Clearly, having a Web site is helpful for effective marketing, and having a subpage of your Web site dedicated to your group therapy offerings will make it much easier for clients and referring professionals to become aware of your services. It is also recommended that you or your Web designer become familiar with basic search engine optimization (SEO) techniques so your Web site will be properly listed in search engines. This is not as difficult as it sounds and is certainly worth the investment of a few hours of your time. Joining your local chapter of the American Group Psychotherapy Association or Psychology Association is a good way to network with other colleagues; this also offers you the opportunity to announce new and ongoing groups via association listservs. Running groups is in fact a way to distinguish yourself from other colleagues, as it is a treatment format that most private practitioners do not offer. Once you have opened your practice and sent out your initial announcements, many therapists do not know how to continue to market their practice; announcement of therapy groups is not only a good way to recruit new members, but it is also a way to keep yourself visible to your colleagues.

Often it is easier to publicize groups targeted to specific populations, such as incest survivors, teens with eating disorders, or recovering alcoholics. Another possibility is for therapists to team up as co-leaders, which allows them to draw patients from their combined practices, making it easier to fill groups and keep them filled as openings occur. This also has other advantages for the therapists, including complementing each other's clinical skills and combating the isolation of private practice.

Group practices, clinics, and managed care organizations present their own set of hurdles to developing successful group psychotherapy programs. Although they offer the advantage of having the large numbers of patients necessary for conducting multiple groups, they pose challenges in appropriately and tactfully funneling these patients to the group therapists. It is common to encounter resistance (conscious and unconscious) at every level of an organization—from intake workers to front-line therapists to administrators—to implementing a group program. Many clinicians still have limited knowledge and training regarding groups, and they view group psychotherapy suspiciously as a second-class form of treatment. Unfortunately, some large institutions that are successful in running large numbers of groups unwittingly encourage these beliefs by emphasizing to their staffs the importance of accommodating large patient populations rather than the particular treatment benefits of groups.

To overcome this resistance, each level of the organization can be retrained to think "group" as one of the treatment options for each patient. Telephone and in-person intake workers should think in interpersonal terms as they ask about presenting symptoms and should inform callers of available group treatments. If a client appears to be a good candidate for a group, he or she should be referred directly to the group leader, who can perform a more in-depth assessment.

Selecting Group Members

As groups focus largely on interpersonal functioning, a thorough interpersonal history should be taken. The screening interview should include an exploration of friendships from childhood onward, as well as a history of intimate and work relationships. For example, a client who has an easy time making friends but who experiences difficulties in intimate relationships will hold different goals from someone who is extremely socially isolated. Prudent screening and selection will lead to fewer premature dropouts, which are a significant risk in group therapy: Dropout rates of up to 50% are frequently reported. Dropouts not only receive less benefit from the treatment but also can be disruptive to the rest of the group.

General principles of group selection are as follows:

1. In order to maximize the potential for group cohesion, members should be relatively homogenous in terms of overall ego functioning and psychological mindedness. For example, it is inadvisable to place a patient who is psychotic or manic, or who has poor impulse control, into a group of high-functioning, professional adults.
2. For interpersonally oriented process groups, heterogeneity of symptoms or problem areas provides for a rich, diverse group. For example, if one group member has difficulty dealing with male authority figures, then the addition of a strong male member will provide more of an opportunity for those issues to be worked on. Obviously, for focal or symptom-focused groups (e.g., depression, eating disorders), by definition there should be some commonality of symptoms.
3. For coed groups, it is optimal to have a balance of male and female members; for example, if there are eight members in the group, then a four-four or five-three male-female ratio is ideal.
4. In practice, selection of group therapy members is in fact a process of *deselection* of inappropriate members, especially members who are likely to become group "deviants." Group deviants are unlikely to benefit from the group and may in fact be harmed by it—and also are likely to be disruptive to the group.
5. Attention must be given to whether prospective members are likely to attend the group reliably. As a rule of thumb, individuals who are likely to miss the group once every 6 weeks or more are not good candidates, as spotty attendance will diminish the benefits to them as well as be disruptive to the group.
6. If a prospective member is not appropriate for the group currently being offered, then every effort should be made to refer the person to another group that would be beneficial for the client.

Preparing Group Members

If the client appears to be a good fit, then the psychologist can spend some time preparing him or her for the group to increase acceptance of the referral and decrease the likelihood of early dropout. Both intake workers and therapists need to fully understand how groups work so they can intelligently discuss how the group will address the particular concerns of each client. Both selection and preparation can be conducted in a single session and should include:

1. A description of the format and structure of each group, and the group over time. For example, is the group open ended or time limited? Is there a check-in at the beginning of the group? How do the members typically interact? What is the role of the leader(s)? It is also helpful to provide some general information about the members of the group, such as their ages, professions, and problem areas.
2. An explanation of how the group will be helpful to the client in addressing his or her issues. This may include translating the presenting problems into interpersonal ones, as mentioned earlier. For example, if a young woman struggles with loneliness and depression, much of this may be exacerbated by relationship difficulties, which in turn exacerbate her negative self-image. The therapist can explain that the group is a place for her to get honest feedback about how others experience her, to learn what she may be doing that prevents her from developing more successful relationships, and to practice new interpersonal skills.
3. Addressing a patient's resistances and fears. If the client described earlier is anxious about joining the group, and convinced that the other members will not like him, it is helpful to assure him that such anxiety is quite normal. After explaining the here-and-now orientation of the group, and the concept of the group as a social microcosm, we let him

know we *want* him to experience *some* of the difficulties in the group that he has in his outside life. In other words, we want to see some of the behavior that leads to his having a difficult time connecting with others, because only by observing his interpersonal challenges can we give him accurate feedback that can help him change his behavior. (The analogy of taking a car in for repair can be useful: The mechanic must see the malfunction in order to correctly diagnose the problem.) So, in fact, it is useful to predict the difficulties he may experience in the group, and then outline how he is likely to tackle and overcome these through the course of group therapy. This may also serve to diminish—but not entirely eliminate—the common anticipatory anxiety regarding the group experience.

References and Readings

Bernard, H., Burlingame, G., Flores, P., Greene, L., Joyce, A., Kobos, J. C., Feirman, D. (2008). Clinical practice guidelines for group psychotherapy. *International Journal of Group Psychotherapy, 58*, 455–542.

Burlingame, G. M., Strauss, B., Joyce, A., MacNair-Semands, R., MacKenzie, R., Ogrodniczuk, J., & Taylor, S. (2005). *American Group Psychotherapy Association's CORE battery—revised*. New York: American Group Psychotherapy Association.

Leszcz, M., & Kobos, J. C. (2008). Evidence-based group psychotherapy: Using AGPA's practice guidelines to enhance clinical effectiveness. *Journal of Psychology: In Session, 64*, 1238–1260.

Ormont, L. (2003). *Group psychotherapy*. New York: Jason Aronson.

Rutan, J. S., & Stone, W. N. (2007). *Psychodynamic group psychotherapy* (4th ed.). New York: Guilford Press.

Sadock, H., & Kaplan, B. (Eds.). (1993). *Comprehensive group psychotherapy* (3rd ed.). Baltimore, MD: Williams & Wilkins.

Wilfley, D. E., MacKenzie, K. R., Ayers, V. E., Welch, R. R., & Weissman, M. M. (2000). *Interpersonal psychotherapy for groups*. New York: Basic Books.

Yalom, I. D., & Leszcz, M. (2005). *The theory and practice of group psychotherapy* (5th ed.). New York: Basic Books.

Related Topics

Chapter 59, "Selecting a Treatment Format"
Chapter 79, "Conducting Psychoeducational Groups"

75 CONDUCTING PARENT MANAGEMENT TRAINING

Melanie M. Nelson and Sheila M. Eyberg

Several evidence-based treatments for child disruptive behavior are variations on parent management training (PMT; Eyberg, Nelson, & Boggs, 2008). These programs are designed to teach parents skills for managing their child's behavior effectively, decreasing the child's unwanted behaviors, and increasing the child's incompatible, prosocial behaviors.

Parent training programs have been implemented in children with a range of diagnoses and have targeted populations at risk due to poor parenting as well.

As the PMT field has grown, strategies such as role playing, video modeling, and therapist coaching have been added to teach new parenting skills more effectively, and several treatment formats have been examined. PMT has been administered individually, in group format, in clinics, in schools, and in homes by professionals and paraprofessionals. PMT has also been used in conjunction with other approaches for managing disruptive behaviors, including medications, teacher training in behavior management, and child therapy groups. To reduce children's comorbid disorders, functional impairments, or family disruptions, PMT has been combined with other treatments, including exposure and response prevention strategies for anxiety and fears, social skills training, academic tutoring, and supportive counseling for parents. The goal of all PMT variations is ultimately the child's optimal behavioral, social, and emotional health.

ASSESSMENT

Careful child and family assessment is necessary in PMT to determine immediate treatment goals and evaluate treatment progress. Most PMT programs require assessment before treatment begins, and several recommend assessment periodically throughout treatment or at every session. Clinicians typically conduct a clinical interview and administer a broad-band screening instrument (e.g., Child Behavior Checklist or Behavior Assessment System for Children) to identify the scope of the child's behavior problems, and then evaluate identified areas of concern in more depth. Multiple informants and methods of measurement are used in this process. For treatment planning, parent functioning is often assessed as well. The specific methods and instruments depend on factors such as the settings in which the problem behaviors occur and the age of the child, and they are selected at the clinician's discretion. For preschoolers, the most commonly used methods are parent rating scales and behavioral observations of the parent–child interaction. With school-age children, parent and teacher rating scales are most common. At middle-school age (12–14 years), teacher-report scales are prominent, with youth self-report frequently used as well. For older adolescents, both parent- and self-report instruments are common, and at this age official records become an important part of assessment of conduct-disordered behaviors (Eyberg et al., 2008).

PARENT SKILLS: ENCOURAGING POSITIVE CHILD BEHAVIOR

Once the initial assessment is complete, PMT may begin by teaching parents strategies for maintaining or increasing positive child behaviors. Skills that parents are taught include:

- Implementing a short daily playtime during which parents provide children with consistent positive feedback. Parents are generally instructed to follow the child's lead in play and praise the child's appropriate behavior (e.g., "Thank you for putting the crayons away after you finished coloring").
- Creating a positive home environment by ensuring children's safety, providing engaging toys and activities, and establishing consistent rules and routines. Noticing and praising children's positive behaviors (e.g., cooperation, social skills, persistence, problem solving) throughout the day are further ways to create a positive environment in the home. Ignoring minor annoying misbehaviors and resuming positive attention when the child re-engages in desirable behaviors.
- Using incentive programs or point charts to monitor and reward positive behaviors.
- Setting realistic expectations for children's behavior through psychoeducation around child development and behavior problems. For children with conditions that may put them at higher risk for behavior problems, such as attention-deficit/hyperactivity disorder, parents may be educated about how

the child's diagnosis affects his or her development and behavior.
- Helping their child develop problem-solving or negotiation skills through incidental or directed teaching and practice opportunities.

PARENT SKILLS: CONSISTENT CONSEQUENCES FOR MISBEHAVIOR

In PMT, parents are also instructed in how to apply consistent and developmentally appropriate consequences for misbehavior. Specific skills vary depending on the child's developmental level, but they may include the following:

- Redirection or distraction, typically reserved for children with a receptive language level below 2½ years of age.
- Time-out from positive reinforcement, usually implemented with children ages 2–6 years. This strategy has been associated with the greatest effect sizes in PMT research.
- Removal of privileges or logical consequences, most appropriate for school-age children.
- Behavior charts, also for school-age children who can benefit from delayed consequences.
- Token economies, often implemented with 10- to 12-year-old children.
- Problem-solving strategies, best for older school-age children and adolescents.

STRATEGIES FOR TEACHING PARENTS

PMT programs vary in how they teach parents to implement these skills. The best method for a particular family may depend on the therapist's aptitude, the treatment setting, or the parent's preference. However, a meta-analysis of the research literature found that the largest treatment effects were associated with providing parents with immediate feedback as they interacted with their child (Kaminski, Valle, Filene, & Boyle, 2008). Strategies for teaching parents new skills include:

- Direct instruction, a didactic approach that describes each skill to parents, its implementation, and its rationale.
- Modeling, or demonstrating the skill with the target child or another individual, with the goal of showing parents how they might implement the skill with their own child in a similar situation.
- Role playing to engage parents in practicing new skills in a contrived setting, allowing the clinician to provide feedback and encourage problem solving.
- Discussing parents' experiences in using the skill to elucidate parent-perceived difficulties and promote parent problem solving.
- Video modeling to enable parents to observe more realistic parenting situations and discuss how they could implement the skills in similar situations with their child.
- Using bug-in-the-ear technology to cue and give immediate feedback to parents on their use of the skills as they interact with their child.

PARENT MANAGEMENT TRAINING PROGRAMS

Several manualized PMT programs have demonstrated efficacy in reducing children's disruptive behavior (Eyberg et al., 2008). These include the following:

- Helping the Noncompliant Child (HNC) is a secondary prevention program for noncompliant children (ages 3–8 years) and their parents. The program incorporates modeling, role playing, and in-vivo feedback to help parents change how they interact with their child.
- Incredible Years (IY) Parent Program is designed for parents of children between birth and age 12, is delivered in a group format, and incorporates video modeling strategies for parent discussion, as well as role play. Children usually are seen separately in a child-focused group.
- Parent-Child Interaction Therapy (PCIT) treats disruptive behavioral disorders in 2- to 7-year-olds seen with their parents. Parents are coached via bug-in-the-ear technology in the use of authoritative parenting strategies as they play with their child.

- Parent Management Training Oregon Model (PMTO) teaches parents of disruptive children (ages 3 to 12) to monitor their child's behaviors and then implement appropriate behavior modification techniques.
- The Positive Parenting Program (Triple P) offers a range of parenting interventions for children ages 0 to 17, ranging from public health applications for all families, to intensive treatment for children with severe behavior problems and their parents.
- Problem-Solving Skills Training and Parent Management Training is a program developed for children up to age 13 that combines PMT with training in problem-solving skills for children. In this model, PMT is implemented through modeling and role playing as the parent learns to observe and reinforce positive behaviors (e.g., using social praise, token economy, or point charts), shape children's behaviors, and apply consistent consequences for negative behaviors.

SPECIAL CONSIDERATIONS

The evidence available for each PMT program may be limited by its intended population and research samples. When selecting a program, clinicians need to consider the population for which a treatment was designed and for which efficacy has been demonstrated. Many PMT programs have shown efficacy in varied ethnic and cultural populations, diagnostic groups (e.g., hyperactivity, abuse and neglect, mental retardation, anxiety), and settings (e.g., home, school, clinic, hospital).

References and Readings

Eyberg, S. M., Nelson, M. M., & Boggs, S. R. (2008). Evidence-based psychosocial treatments for children and adolescents with disruptive behavior. *Journal of Clinical Child and Adolescent Psychology, 37*, 215–237.

Kaminski, J. W., Valle, L. A., Filene, J. H., & Boyle, C. L. (2008). A meta-analytic review of components associated with parent training program effectiveness. *Journal of Abnormal Child Psychology, 36*, 567–589.

Kazdin, A. E. (2008). *The Kazdin method for parenting the defiant child: With no pills, no therapy, no contest of wills.* Boston, MA: Houghton Mifflin.

McMahon, R. J., & Forehand, R. L. (2003). *Helping the noncompliant child: Family-based treatment for oppositional behavior* (2nd ed.). New York: Guilford Press.

McNeil, C. B., & Hembree-Kigin, T. L. (2010). *Parent-child interaction therapy* (2nd ed.). New York: Springer.

The Incredible Years. (2012). *Parents, teachers, children training series.* Retrieved January 2013, from www.incredibleyears.com

Triple P Positive Parenting Program. (n.d.). Retrieved January 2013, from www.triplep.net

Weisz, J. R., & Kazdin, A. E. (2010). *Evidence-based psychotherapies for children and adolescents* (2nd ed.). New York: Guilford Press.

Related Topics

Chapter 31, "Compendium of Empirically Supported Treatments"

Chapter 81, "Treating Bullying Behaviors among Youth"

Chapter 85, "Treating the Behaviorally Disordered Child"

76 CONDUCTING COUPLE AND FAMILY THERAPY

Jay L. Lebow

The following guidelines stem from a review of the couple and family therapy (CFT) literature, research assessing CFT, and from clinical experience. The goal of this chapter is to suggest evidence-based guidelines for improving the process and outcomes of CFT.

1. *Develop a systemic perspective.* A system consists of interacting components; in a family, these include such subsystems as couple, sibling, and individual. Individuals do not function in a vacuum but continually influence one another through feedback.
2. *Always consider context in attempting to understand couples and families.* Behavior that appears to make little sense often emerges as far more understandable when the surrounding conditions are understood. For example, a child's school phobia or a spouse's depression frequently becomes more intelligible when its meaning in the life of the family system is recognized.
3. *Understand multiple perspectives.* The therapist should grasp and communicate understanding of the respective viewpoints of various family members, which may vary considerably.
4. *Examine potential circular pathways of causality that may maintain problems.* The therapist should understand ways in which family members are influenced within circular pathways in which the behavior, thoughts, and feelings of one person promote those of another, which in turn promote those of the first person. Although not all causal pathways are circular, and even among circular causal chains the participation of family members may not be coequal, such cycles frequently block problem resolution. For example, parents' angry and punitive behavior may both lead to and flow from the acting-out behavior of a child. Regardless of where the cycle begins, the punitive behavior by the parents leads to more acting out by the child, which, in turn, leads to more parental punitive behavior.
5. *Respect the diversity of family forms.* Families assume many forms, including single parent, remarried, and gay and lesbian. The therapist should become knowledgeable about typical life across this range of forms and, along with the families, should develop therapeutic goals that honor the family's form and culture.
6. *Understand the special ethical considerations of couple and family therapy, particularly concerning confidentiality.* Couple and family therapists face special ethical dilemmas, such as deciding which individuals are to be considered clients and who is entitled to confidentiality of communication. All individuals who attend conjoint sessions become clients and should retain the same rights. In couple

and family therapy, confidentiality should be broken only with agreement of all participants, except in those circumstances in which legal duty to report or warn takes precedence. The therapist should articulate a clear position about confidentiality for confidential communication in and outside of sessions, as well as for when participants vary across sessions.

7. *Begin assessment and intervention with the first phone call.* Couple and family therapies require more effort before the first session on the part of the therapist than do other therapies. Active efforts before the first session to engage family members who are clearly important to the problem or its solution substantially increase participation in therapy and thereby impact on treatment outcome.
8. *Determine early in treatment and clarify who will be included in treatment.* There are a variety of methods in family therapy, ranging from some that include multiple generations to others that include only a few or even one member of the family. Who is and who is not part of the therapy always needs to be clearly designated in the therapy contract with clients and understood by the clients. In general, it is easier to include members of the family earlier in treatment, rather than later, by which time alliances are well set. Involving fathers as well as mothers (who tend more readily to make themselves available) in the treatment of children promotes better outcomes.
9. *Begin with an emphasis on engagement and alliance building.* The therapist builds an alliance with each member of the family, with each subsystem, and with the family as a whole. Techniques such as eliciting input from each family member, joining with each around some aspect of the problem, and assimilating and adapting to the culture of the family help build such alliances. Pay particular attention to the alliance with those member(s) of the family who have most say in whether the therapy will continue. Alliances with the therapist and between family members about the therapy predicts outcome regardless of the form of couple or family therapy. Split alliances where some family members support treatment and others do not are associated with poor outcomes.
10. *Assess through history gathering and observing interaction.* Assessment should have multiple foci, including the family system, its subsystems, and individuals. Assessment typically is intermingled with treatment, rather than a distinct phase. The intervention strategy should be grounded in the assessment.
11. *Understand that certain difficulties in family life are grossly underreported.* Family violence, sexual abuse, infidelity, alcoholism, and drug abuse, among other problems, are typically reported at much lower frequencies than they occur. Inquire about them in a standard noninvasive way; questionnaires or individual interviews are most useful for learning about underreported behaviors.
12. *Understand each client's expectations and how well they are satisfied.* Family members bring a range of expectations about such issues as money, sex, and intimacy. These expectations are manifested at several levels ranging from expectations about behavior to expectations about object relations. Relationship satisfaction is often the product of unmet expectations. Help family members articulate and negotiate their expectations.
13. *Compile a genogram to understand how family of origin factors affect the system.* Elaborating on who is in the extended family, what the key experiences have been in the life of the family, and repetitive issues across the generations increases mutual understanding, promotes the working through of experiences, and potentially sets the stage for exploring individual and interactive patterns.
14. *Remember that couple and family therapy is usually brief.* Families typically are only willing to engage in therapies of under 10 sessions. Accordingly keep most family therapy focused.

15. *Promote solutions, a focus on coping, and a view of family health.* Families respond far better to a focus on creating solutions. Reframe behavior in a form that can be more positively understood. Stress the normal developmental aspects of what the couple or family is experiencing.
16. *Negotiate clear goals for treatment.* Family life presents endless possible goals, and participants often begin with varying agendas. Negotiating an agreed set of goals for therapy is an essential task early in treatment. Goals may be added or modified as therapy progresses.
17. *Establish control of sessions in a collaborative context.* Therapists in couple and family therapy must intervene actively to move clients from habitual patterns. For example, the therapist must be able to interrupt habitual patterns of destructive arguing in couples.
18. *Develop a clear plan.* Couple and family therapy is innately complex and typically has multiple foci. A clear road map mitigates the dangers of losing focus. This road map may require revision as treatment progresses.
19. *Employ individual, couple, family, and macrosystemic interventions in the context of the treatment.* Empirical support is strongest for approaches that combine intervention with the whole family with other intervention strategies. Treatment of severe mental illness almost invariably should include the use of medication; treatment of adolescent disorders focuses on school and peer systems; and treatment of depression should include "individual" intervention that addresses the depression.
20. *Teach empathy, communication, fair fighting, contingency management, and other relational skills when such skills are inadequately developed.* Many couples and family members lack the requisite skills to perform essential conjoint tasks. Instruction, modeling, in-session practice, and homework can help family members master these skills.
21. *Suggest tasks that fit with the families' stage of change and have a high likelihood of being carried out successfully.* Suggestions that are not followed are likely to increase client reactivity and resistance. For example, repeatedly proposing communication exercises to a family that is not ready to utilize them is likely to retard progress.
22. *Develop contracts between family members that are mutually satisfying.* Couples and families who are dissatisfied with their relationships typically have much lower rates of positive exchange and higher rates of coercion. Negotiating positive quid pro quo exchanges leads to more satisfying relationships.
23. *Promote clear family structure.* Flexible yet clear boundaries, stable yet not rigid patterns of alliance, and an age-appropriate distribution of power promote family health.
24. *Understand the personal narratives of family members and promote the development of a positive understanding of the narratives of other family members.* The stories created by family members often carry with them the seeds of difficulties. Examining these narratives and helping create new ones that frame motives and behaviors in a more positive way promote more harmonious family life and problem resolution.
25. *Help individuals to take responsibility for their own behavior.* Blame leads to endless cycles of misunderstanding and alienation. Helping clients assume an "I" stance about their own behavior helps break such cycles.
26. *Promote the expression of underlying softer affect that lies behind anger and criticism.* Individuals often express defensive reactions rather than feelings such as sadness or fear. Exploring such underlying feelings in a safe environment promotes empathic connection. For example, uncovering the sad affect that lies behind anger expressed toward a spouse in couple therapy can alter typical dysfunctional patterns of conflict.
27. *See couples with relationship distress conjointly.* Conjoint couples therapy is

the only demonstrated effective form of treatment for couple relationship problems. Although spouses who are unhappy with their relationships frequently seek individual therapy, there is no evidence that this helps the couple relationship and some evidence that it has a deleterious effect.

28. *Focus a major part of treatment on conjoint couple therapy when there is coexisting relationship difficulty along with depression in an individual.* Individual treatment of depression does not appear to impact on the relationship problems, and the presence of relationship difficulties predicts poor prognosis over time for depression.
29. *Recognize and target Gottman's four signs of severe relationship difficulty: criticism, contempt, defensiveness, and stonewalling.* Clients presenting such patterns should be warned of their high risk for worsening levels of marital distress and for divorce. When present, initial work should center directly on developing alternative patterns of relating. Couples are unlikely to benefit from treatment unless these signs change.
30. *In divorcing and remarried systems, promote good-enough communication to allow for co-parenting.* Help families understand the typical stresses and coping strategies in divorce. Refer for mediation if substantial conflicts arise between divorcing parents.
31. *Utilize psychoeducational interventions when dealing with severe mental illness.* Families in which there is severe individual dysfunction often fail to understand the origins of disorders and feel blamed when encountering psychotherapists. An educative stance that teaches about the disorder and about typical family processes is enormously helpful in gaining cooperation and reducing symptoms and recidivism. Reducing expressed emotion (i.e., highly emotional critical affect) appears to have particularly great value in the context of severe mental illness. Treatment that increases emotional arousal and conflict in these families is contraindicated.
32. *In disorganized families, promote stabilizing rituals.* In particular, families with members with alcohol and substance use disorders fare much better when they maintain such rituals as a regular dinner hour.
33. *In family violence and abuse, protect safety first.* At times, couples and families present in situations where contact is dangerous. The ethical obligation must be first to safety and then to other goals of therapy.
34. *In oppositional children and in adolescent conduct disorder, utilize family therapy as part of a multisystemic approach that also addresses other relevant systems.* The relevant social system in these cases does not stop at the boundary of the family but extends into various other domains, including school, peer, and legal systems.
35. *Assess the impact of treatment on each individual, each subsystem, and the system as a whole, as well as on the presenting problem.* Outcome in family systems is complex, including many stakeholders and numerous foci, such as the presenting problem, individual functioning, and family functioning. Tracking such outcomes and the treatment alliance over the course of treatment is helpful in improving treatment outcomes.
36. *Promote the maintenance of change.* All treatment effects appear to wane over time. Promote maintenance of change through follow-up sessions, tasks, and through the family's continuing homework, and self-monitoring of their processes after treatment.
37. *Be aware of the meanings of gender and culture in therapy.* The therapist's work should be informed by an understanding of the impact of gender and culture. Therapist gender and culture also affect treatment process, regardless of therapist behavior.
38. *Utilize couple and family therapies to engage difficult-to-engage cases.* There is considerable evidence that many difficult-to-engage clients, such as those

with substance use disorders and oppositional and delinquent adolescents, are more easily engaged with couple and family therapy. Specifically, engaging another member of the family system who recognizes the problem first can dramatically increase the rates of engagement and retention of individuals with these difficulties in treatment.

39. *Expect treatment to have an impact.* Couple and family therapies have been demonstrated to be effective in 75% of cases and have been shown to have effect sizes much like those of individual therapy.
40. *Become knowledgeable about the many evidence-based treatments in couple and family therapy.* Evidence-based couple therapies include emotion-focused, cognitive-behavioral, and integrative behavioral couple therapy as well as specific variations of these models targeted at problems such as substance abuse and depression. Evidence-based family therapies include multidimensional family therapy, multisystemic therapy, brief strategic therapy, and functional family therapy (all targeted at acting out adolescent problems), several psychoeducational methods targeted at bipolar disorder and schizophrenia, and the Maudsley approach for treatment for eating disorders. Draw from the wide array of these strategies for intervention.

References and Readings

Gurman, A. S. (Ed.). (2008). *Clinical handbook of couple therapy* (4th ed.) New York: Guilford Press.

Lebow, J. L. (Ed.). (2005) *Handbook of clinical family therapy*. New York: Wiley.

Lebow, J. L. (Ed.). (2013). *Family process*. Retrieved January 2013, from the Wiley Web site: www.wiley.com/bw/journal.asp?ref=0014–7370

Pinsof, W., & Lebow, J. L. (Eds.). (2005). *Family psychology: The science of the art*. New York: Oxford University Press.

Snyder, D. K., Castellani, A. M., & Whisman, M. A. (2006). Current status and future directions in couple therapy. *Annual Review of Psychology, 57*, 317–344.

Snyder, D. K., Heyman, R. E., & Haynes, S. N. (2005). Evidence-based approaches to assessing couple distress. *Psychological Assessment, 17*(3), 288–307.

Sprenkle, D. H. (Ed.). (2002). *Effectiveness research in marriage and family therapy.* Washington, DC: AAMFT Press.

Sprenkle, D. H., Davis, S. D., & Lebow, J. L. (2009). *Common factors in couple and family therapy*. New York: Guilford Press.

Stanton, M. & Bray, J. (Eds.). (2009). *Blackwell handbook of family psychology*. Hoboken, NJ: Wiley-Blackwell.

Related Topics

Chapter 59, "Selecting a Treatment Format"
Chapter 77, "Treating High-Conflict Couples"
Chapter 78, "Treating Partner Infidelity"
Chapter 80, "Using Genograms in Assessment and Therapy"

77 TREATING HIGH-CONFLICT COUPLES

Susan Heitler

In high-conflict couples the frequency and/or intensity with which the partners express anger interferes with their ability to sustain a healthy loving relationship. The following clinical methods, drawn from the research literature and clinical experience, enhance safety in treatment and at home, and improve the probability of positive psychotherapy outcomes.

SETUP FOR TREATMENT

1. *Arrange the chairs to encourage dialogue flow between the couple and to maximize your ability to intervene quickly.* To encourage spouses to talk with each other rather than through you (the therapist), place three chairs in an equilateral triangle (no side-by-side sitting as on a couch). Rollers on the therapist's chair are useful. When tensions rise, roll the chair between the couple to block dialogue flow or next to one spouse for calming individually focused interventions.

2. *Record treatment sessions.* Bring a recorder or encourage clients to bring one. Include consent-to-record forms in clients' initial paperwork; check that both spouses have signed before beginning to record. Explain that the recordings are for them only; you will not keep a copy. Assign listening as homework; repetition enhances learning. Recordings are contraindicated, however, if divorce proceedings are imminent, lest one spouse use them against the other.

3. *Explain your confidentiality policies.* My rules for talking about secrets are as follows: (a) I am not free to disclose anything said in a couple session, or that we even had a session, to anyone not present at the session; (b) when I meet with one spouse individually, I am not free to disclose what was said by one spouse to the other, or even that we met for a session; (c) confidentiality binds me, not them, so after individual sessions they can choose whether and what to share with the other; and (d) when there is danger to self or others the rules flip. I then am required to report.

4. *Establish a one-therapist treatment policy.* Multiple therapists (e.g., for individual and couple treatment components) may make treatment unsafe and undermine progress. I require that couples in treatment with me take a break from individual work with other therapists. I conduct individual and couple sessions as needed, integrating the work from both formats. Most sessions are with the couple; individual sessions break through impasses. The one exception is when special expertise is needed, such as referral for medication (Heitler, 2001).

Why this policy? Multiple therapists leave each with partial information. For instance, in a rare situation in which I allowed one spouse to continue in treatment with her individual psychotherapist, the individual therapist taught our mutual client "assertiveness training."

When the wife tried out her new skills at home, the shocked husband knocked her down a staircase. The individual therapist, not being in a format where she could prepare the husband to receive his wife's new behavior, had inadvertently created a dangerous situation.

DIAGNOSIS

1. *Delineate goals.* Ask the partners to discuss with each other what they have come to treatment to accomplish. This question simultaneously sets goals and enables you to observe their capacity for insight and collaborative dialogue. At the outset of each session determine goals similarly for that particular hour. Observe and address skill deficits such as speaking in *don't wants* instead of *would likes* or responding with negations such as *but*.

2. Obtain a threefold diagnostic picture.

- Identify individuals' symptoms (depression, anxiety, anger, or character pathologies).
- Generate a laundry list of conflicts about which the couple argues.
- Note communication and conflict resolution skill deficits.

3. *Detail the couple's anger and argument patterns.*

- Ask what tends to trigger fights, their frequency and duration, highest levels of escalation, how fights end, how the spouses recover, how each feels about the arguments, and whether drugs or alcohol are involved. Bear in mind the tendency of people with anger problems to minimize and deny rages, emotional abuse, and physical violence.
- Note externalizing (blame, criticism, accusations), lack of insight or responsibility taking, and controlling behavior (telling the other what to do, controlling finances and friends, etc). These habits suggest abusive patterns, undermine the credibility of a client's self-reports, and suggest that individual sessions may need to precede couple work.
- Assume that high-conflict individuals typically have overlapping clinical patterns. For example, an abusive individual may show paranoid, borderline and narcissistic tendencies, hot-reactor quickness to anger, bipolar or sociopathic indicators, and/or alcohol or drug use.
- Verify your data by meeting privately with each partner, asking the partner or spouse to wait outside of your office for a few minutes. Ask direct questions using explicit words like "shouts," "curses you," or "hits you" to make it easier for spouses to admit to what is actually happening. "What is the worst your partner does when angry?" "How do you respond?"; "...the worst you do?" "What is your partner's response?"
- Reflect back to clients that "I only get mad because *s/he...*" signals non-responsibility-taking for anger.

4. *Note contraindications for couple treatment sessions.*

- Unwillingness to agree that violence is out of bounds, at home or in session
- Poor impulse control or other signs that psychotherapy may be unsafe
- Reprisals after sessions for comments by the partner that the abuser disliked
- A paranoid stance characterized by a fixed ideational system about the other, rejection of nonconfirmatory data, externalizing, and projection
- Drug or alcohol abuse
- Hyperfocus on the other and controlling behaviors that suggest verbal, emotional, or physical abuse

Address these symptoms in individual therapy prior to and/or simultaneously with couple treatment. Offer simultaneous individual therapy for the healthier partner to enhance coping skills and prevent depression. Add couple treatment later.

5. *Make safety arrangements.* The vast majority of high-conflict couples spontaneously exit before physical violence is likely. However, if there is any risk of physical violence, remove guns from the home, prepare escape options for the victim partner, and build awareness in both of the increase in danger with alcohol and drug use. Clarify the danger of even "minor" violence (e.g., a small push can cause a serious head injury). Encourage a temporary separation, a double-domicile living arrangement for the couple, or a safe house if violence risk is high.

TREATMENT

1. *Aim to accomplish three main strands of treatment.*

- *Ameliorate symptoms.* Anger, anxiety and depression. Arguments. Narcissistic, borderline, hysteric, paranoid, abusive, and/or bipolar features.
- *Guide win-win resolutions of conflicts.* In the process, note, explore, and rectify negative impacts from problematic earlier relationships (Lewis, 1997).
- *Coach collaborative communication and conflict resolution skills,* teaching spouses how to address their differences calmly. People with histories of excessive anger need to aim for zero anger or fights, as small spats can be like a little alcohol for an alcoholic.

2. *Ensure safety.* Early in treatment, teach disengagement/self-soothing/reengagement routines to prevent hurtful fights and violence escalations (see Table 77.1). Practice these routines in the session. Inquire intermittently about the couple's experiences with their exit routines to ensure their plan is fully effective.

3. *Initiate a collaborative perspective.* Block attempts to change the partner; teach each partner to focus instead on what he or she could do differently. Clarify each partner's contributions to the negative interaction cycles, and what each can do toward creating positive interaction cycles.

At the same time, if one partner is abusive, then his or her individual pathology may be the starting point for most of the conflict. While most high-conflict couples have a takes-two-to-tango dynamic, some high-conflict couples are more like a *bank robber and bank teller*. Explain this dynamic in a kindly but clear way, blaming the pathology (e.g., the volcanos inside you that erupt so quickly), not the person.

TABLE 77.1. Levels of Anger Escalation

Level 5: Violence against people: grabbing, pushing, choking, shaking, hitting, sexual aggression, punching, burning, use of weapons such as a knife.
Level 4: Violence against things: slamming doors, throwing things, hitting walls. Shaking a fist in a threatening manner.
Level 3: Verbal violence: blaming, criticism, sarcasm, name calling, lecturing, shouting, accusing, issuing intimidating threats. Harangues that build a case to justify anger.
Level 2: Bickering, repeating the same points multiple times, talking louder, talking faster, getting snippy, critical, or defensive; feeling adversarial, desiring to win, proving who's right.
Level 1: Low-level anger feelings such as irritation, frustration, emotional overload, upset expressed in normal voice tones and I-messages. "I feel frustrated. My concern is...."

4. *Develop face-saving explanations for the couples' conflicts.*

- Identify external or developmental stresses that may have overloaded the system (e.g., arrival of children, illness, financial setbacks).
- Explain the role of insufficient communication and conflict resolution skills.
- Identify the anger, dialogue, and conflict resolution models in each spouse's family of origin to clarify where each participant learned his or her patterns. Compassionately explore parents' histories.

5. *Intervene immediately at first departures from collaborative interaction.* Interrupt the dialogue with a question or comment; restart it by prompting cooperative skills. If anger rises, ask the healthier spouse to step out for a few moments. Talk quietly to calm the angry spouse. Explore his or her concerns before inviting the partner back. If an angry spouse threatens to leave a session, praise the departure impulse, inviting a return when he or she feels calmer.

6. *Gradually introduce and practice the four communication skill sets that enable couples to sustain a harmonious relationship.*

- Emotional self-regulation (ability to stay calm without anger outbursts)
- Positivity (expression of appreciation, agreement, affection, good humor)
- Collaborative communication (talking, listening, and dialogue skills)
- Win-win conflict resolution (for healing past conflicts and making shared decisions for upcoming actions)

Most high-conflict couples fit the adage "if they knew better they would do better." At the same time, high-intensity emotions can overpower the ability to utilize new communication and conflict resolution skills. Therapists need therefore to prevent emotional eruptions by teaching exit routines.

7. *Address symptom removal.* Insufficient conflict resolution skills create and maintain psychopathology. To remove symptoms, readdress conflicts with healthier dialogue and conflict resolution patterns.

- *Anger* settles conflicts by domination.
- *Anxiety* and *tension* signify that conflicts are hovering unaddressed.
- *Depression* emerges when conflicts are settled with one partner giving up.
- *Addictive* and other *obsessive-compulsive disorders* (including eating disorders and hypochondria) indicate escape from conflicts by means of distraction.

8. *Teach about anger.* Teach the physiological, cognitive, and other changes caused by anger arousal (e.g., high arousal decreases ability to take in new information, to think flexibly and to create new solutions). Like physical pain, angry feelings indicate problems. Angry actions however seldom effectively ameliorate them. Clarify that people yell to get heard; yet the louder they yell the less their partner is likely to digest their message.

9. *Resolve current disputes.* Psychotherapists can guide a three-step movement from conflict to resolution on couples' divisive conflicts as follows:

Step 1: Express initial positions, ensuring that both spouses speak up and both listen to the other.
Step 2: Explore underlying concerns, listing all of both spouses' concerns as one shared list.
Step 3: Design a plan of action, a solution set responsive to all the concerns of both spouses.

10. *Teach the four Ss of conflict resolution* (Heitler, 1997):

- *Specifics* lead to resolution; generalities breed misunderstandings. "We spend too much" is less helpful than "We spent $2,000 over our budget this month."
- *Short segments.* In healthy dialogue, participants take turns talking, avoiding long monologues. Listeners can respond only to one point; further data beyond one point per talk time gets lost. When partners ramble or lecture, suggest a *three-sentence max* rule.
- *Symmetry* of air time creates a sense of equal power and equal voice.
- *Summaries* consolidate understanding and propel solution building.

11. *Direct information flow.* In general, have spouses talk with each other, not to you. Redirect spouses who talk to you by looking at the listener rather than the speaker or by using hand gestures. In the following specific situations, however, it is helpful to have spouses talk to you to:

- Lower emotional intensities when anger is escalating
- Resolve conflicts early in treatment when the couple's skills are too insufficient
- Accelerate resolution of a conflict when the session time is running short

12. *Identify core concerns.* Heated emotions indicate strongly felt concerns, for example, "I hate not being heard!" or "I feel neglected!"

These repeated sources of emotion are usually transference issues or core conflictual relationship themes (Luborsky, Crits-Christoph, & Mellon, 1986). Find the sources of these excessively emotional reactions in prior life experiences by conducting a depth dive (Heitler, 1993). While you conduct a depth dive with one individual, the spouse hopefully can listen, holding his or her comments for the discussion afterward. That way you can explore one partner's sensitive conflicts and simultaneously build compassionate understanding in the other.

Spouses' core concerns will tend to interlock in negative circular interactions. For instance, her thought "I can't seem to please him" and resultant depressive withdrawal may trigger his "I never get the affection I want" and angry complaining stance. His angry complaints in turn retrigger her depressive withdrawal. Replace negative cycles with positive ones; for example, he expresses more frequent appreciation, and she more frequently hugs and cuddles with him. Practice the new patterns, both in sessions and as homework.

13. *Allow only healthy interactions.*

- *Prevent poor skills by prompting.* Offer sentence starters to insure safe talking. For example: "I felt (one word) when you...." Or "My concern is...." Or "I would like to... (not I would like you to, or I don't like)..." Prompt open-ended questions with, "Good questions begin with how or what." Prompt digestive listening responses by asking, "What did you agree with in what your spouse just said?"
- *Intervene immediately to request redo's* to modify slippages, such as blaming, criticizing, you-statements, sarcasm, defensiveness, or raised voices. The client can do the redo, or the therapist can offer to translate.
- *Request flips:* Flip *don't likes* to *would likes.* Flip *you make me feel* to *I feel.* Flip *I would like you to*...to *I would like to.* Flip *but* to *and at the same time*...On the listening side, immediate intervention when listening skills are insufficient also is vital.
- *Request that the listener first digest, and then add.* If a spouse negates what she or he heard ("*But*...") or continues on with his or her own thoughts without picking up on what was just said; request a re-do.
- *Translate provocative comments into collaborative formats.* For instance, roll your chair close to the speaker to translate an accusatory "You don't do your part in keeping up the house" to "I feel like I'm doing more than my share."
- *Repeat frequently the basic communication mantras.* The most popular include "Talk about yourself, or ask about the other; no talking about the other." "What's right or useful in what your partner just said?" or "Good questions begin with *how* or *what.*"
- *Set up practice drills to consolidate new skills.* Assign reading or Web-based homework exercise; for example, from PowerOfTwoMarriage.com.
- *Catch misplaced locus of focus.* Abusive individuals monitor their partner, telling them what to think and do. Teach them to be "self-centered." (See Table 77.2.)

14. *Learn after mistakes.* Teach the couple that after upsets the goal is to look insightfully at one's own part, apologize, and learn to how to prevent similar upsets in the future (not to punish the other).

15. *Teach positivity.* Encourage and practice expressing appreciation, affection, agreement,

TABLE 77.2. Time-Out Routines for Emotional Safety at Home

Initiate time-outs when you
- Feel too upset or negative to talk constructively.
- Sense that the other is too emotional to dialogue constructively.

To initiate a time-out
- Use a nonverbal signal, such as sports signals. Go to separate spaces without discussion.
- No door slamming or parting comments. Never block the other from leaving or pursue the other when he or she disengages.
- Instead of thinking about the other, focus on soothing yourself or on a distraction.

Reengage after regaining normal humor. Talk first about a safe topic. Then resume the tough subject.

enthusiasm, and gratitude to replace the prior criticism and argument. End sessions by summarizing accomplishments.

References and Readings

Heitler, S. (1993). *From conflict to resolution*. New York: Norton.

Heitler, S. (1995). *The angry couple: Conflict-focused treatment*. New York: Newbridge.

Heitler, S. (1997). *The power of two*. Oakland, CA: New Harbinger.

Heitler, S. (2001). Combined individual/marital therapy: A conflict resolution framework and ethical considerations. *Journal of Psychotherapy Integration, 11*, 349–383.

Intimate Partner Abuse and Relationship Violence. (n.d.). Retrieved from www.apa.org/pi/iparv.pdf

Lewis, J. M. (1997). *Marriage as a search for healing*. New York: Brunner/Mazel.

Luborsky, L., Crits-Christoph, P., & Mellon, J. (1986). Advent of objective measures of the transference concept. *Journal of Consulting and Clinical Psychology, 54*, 39–47.

Related Topics

Chapter 42, "Assessing and Treating Anger as a Clinical Problem"

Chapter 76, "Conducting Couple and Family Therapy"

Chapter 78, "Treatment of Partner Infidelity"

78 TREATING PARTNER INFIDELITY

Don-David Lusterman

Estimates of extramarital sex (EMS) vary widely. Glass and Wright (1995) report that 44% of husbands and 25% of wives had at least one extramarital experience. They found a correlation between extramarital involvement (EMI) and low marital satisfaction. A large sample study (N = 1,200) conducted annually over a 5-year period (Smith, 1006) reported a roughly 15% incidence, including 21% of men and 12% of women. An update in 2006, re-edited in 2010, reported similar findings, despite many changes in sexual behavior and sexual exploration. All the studies cited find that men engage in EMS more frequently than women.

The discovery of EMI becomes traumatic for partners, their children, families, and friends. Although a better term today might be "extrarelational infidelity," we will maintain EMI for consistency.

DEFINITION

Infidelity is the breaking of trust. While often thought of as sexual misconduct, it may also include nonsexual but secret relationships. The most distinguishing characteristic of all types of infidelity is secrecy. Most discoverers report that deceit is the most traumatic element of discovery. Thus, if a couple agrees that extramarital sex is acceptable, no infidelity has occurred. A negative answer to the therapist's question "Could you discuss your actions comfortably with your partner?" helps the patient to understand the relationship between deceit and infidelity. A wife's discovery that her husband has been involved in a "computer romance" might prove as shocking to her as the discovery that he had been involved in a sexual adventure. If a partner in a foursome becomes secretly involved with another member of the foursome, it becomes an infidelity. The violation of intimacy boundaries may be much more crucial than that of sexual boundaries; an intense and secretive platonic relationship may be more threatening than a sexual relationship.

TYPES OF INFIDELITY

Glass and Wright (1992) use three categories: *primarily sexual, primarily emotional,* and *combined-type.* Careful questioning of the involved partner is best done during a conjoint session with the discovering partner. Using these criteria, the therapist may facilitate a conversation that enables the couple and the therapist to arrive at a collaborative hypothesis about the nature of the infidelity. It also permits the therapist to examine conflicts about the infidelity. The discovered person may deny the affair, much to the chagrin of his or her partner. The therapist may at first respectfully explore each idea.

Most often the offending partner comes to accept that, at least given the definition of infidelity, his or her behavior may have been unfaithful. It is at this point that other aspects of the infidelity may become apparent. Is the person a philanderer? Is the person exploring his or her gender identity? Philanderers engage in frequent and brief encounters. They avoid emotional intimacy and seek power over the other person. Many show strong narcissistic features and are best diagnosed as personality disorder, not otherwise specified (NOS). If the therapist feels comfortable with providing both individual and conjoint treatment and can guarantee confidentiality in all individual sessions clearly to both partners, they will generally accept such treatment. Once the patients feel convinced of the therapist's assurances (often through testing the therapist's adherence), there are important advantages. Patients in this context are more willing to reveal hidden thoughts and actions, and the therapist has an opportunity to better understand the ecosystemic context. Other issues may also require combined treatment. These include infidelity that results from a patient's drive to explore his or her gender identity, and those that involve important cultural and ethnic differences. Even if there is no such intense issue, it is important to have at least occasional individual meetings. Often matters examined individually subsequently enable patients to converse with their partners autonomously.

DISCOVERY

EMI is a systemic phenomenon, involving the discoverer and the discovered, and, if it takes the form of an affair, the third party as well. Children, families of origin, and friends are also often affected. Partners in "good" relationships rate as most important "trust in each other that includes fidelity, integrity and feeling 'safe,' and 'permanent commitment to the marriage'" (Kaslow & Hammerschmidt, 1992). The discovery of infidelity shatters these assumptions, producing great trauma (Janoff-Bulman, 1992). The discoverer feels betrayed, and the discovered person is often ashamed and fearful of the discoverer's rageful reaction.

THE INITIAL SESSION

The discoverer often exhibits a rapid succession of conflicting emotions and behaviors. At one moment he or she may be sobbing and at another, ready to strike at the offending mate. The discovered partner may be by turns apologetic, defensive, and angry. The discovered person may deny the infidelity despite copious proof. Admission is often accompanied by the demand that there be no further discussion about it. The therapist's first responsibility is to indicate that avoiding the topic, while it may provide some momentary relief for the discovered party, will in the end cause more problems. The therapeutic approach, while sensitive to the affective issues, must also include a psychoeducational element. Couples and individuals alike find that clear information brings a degree of relief and often helps to restore or initiate improved communication.

THERAPEUTIC GROUND RULES

The couple should be told that the purpose of the therapy is to help them change their relationship. With work, they will be moving toward a better marriage or a better divorce. In a better divorce, both accept mature responsibility for the failure of the marriage. This lays the groundwork for an amicable settlement that is in the best interests of their children, and it also permits them to leave the marriage with new insights about future relationships. A better marriage is characterized by open and honest communication about both positive and negative issues.

CONFIDENTIALITY

Although it is crucial to establish a relationship with the couple, it is equally important that the therapist schedule a session to meet each member of the couple alone. Not all authorities view confidentiality the same way (for other perspectives, see Glass & Wright, 1995; and Pittman, 1989). I believe that holding individual sessions enables the therapist to see whether there are issues that one or the other is not yet ready to reveal in conjoint sessions. Individual sessions also enable the therapist to know whether the affair or other extramarital and secret sexual activity is still going on. The therapist prepares the couple for individual sessions by assuring each partner that anything discussed in such meetings is confidential. While nothing will be divulged to the other partner, the information obtained will enable the therapist to organize a treatment plan.

Making this contract with the couple provides the therapist with the freedom to decide whether subsequent sessions should be held with each individual, with the couple, or as some mix of individual and couples work. In some instances only one partner enters therapy. It may be the person who has just discovered the partner's infidelity, or it may be the affair-involved partner who cannot stop but is conflicted about it. A systemically oriented therapist will inform the person that it is probable that the partner will be included in the therapy at some point. It is very important to inform the affair-involved person that at no time will conjoint therapy include the third party. The involved person who decides to confess the infidelity to the partner should be strongly cautioned not to do so in the therapist's office. Should that occur the person's partner may experience it as a collusion between the partner and the therapist. This seriously compromises treatment. For that reason, it is wise to offer some coaching to the person who will be admitting an infidelity. Only after the person has acted on this responsibility should conjoint therapy be undertaken.

MORATORIUM

It is crucial that the therapist press the involved partner to declare a moratorium on the affair. Failing that, the involved person should be helped to disclose the affair to his or her partner. Until such time, the other partner should also be seen individually, so that both partners' perceptions of the marriage can be examined. Seeing the couple individually may greatly increase anxiety. Each may wonder what the partner is sharing with the therapist and why it may take more than one solo visit. This tension helps to break the impasse of denial and brings them back to therapy to work more directly on the marital or divorce issues.

TRUST BUILDING

Many discoverers consider themselves "victims." In such a case, it is wise for the therapist to begin by accepting this perceptual frame. Only when the discoverer feels fully supported is it possible to examine the predisposing factors that often play a role in infidelity.

SEQUELAE OF VICTIMHOOD

When the discoverer experiences himself or herself as the victim, the therapist must validate these feelings and provide the couple with information about the nature of trauma. Many discoverers report or evidence the following symptoms:

- Difficulty staying or falling asleep
- Irritability or outbursts of anger
- Difficulty concentrating
- Hypervigilance
- Exaggerated startle response
- Physiological reactivity upon exposure to events that symbolize or resemble an aspect of the traumatic event (e.g., being unable to watch a TV show or movie about infidelity)

The discoverer's responses are best reframed as a *normal*, nonpathological response to the shock of discovery (Glass & Wright, 1995; Lusterman, 1995). The therapist should make clear to both partners that these intrusive recollections and obsessive searching for more details or for evidence that the infidelity continues (when the mate has denied it) are all part of a posttraumatic stress reaction. Working together, the couple can alleviate and even overcome this trauma. The therapist should explain to the discovered mate that he or she can play a crucial role in helping the discoverer, who needs to hear nondefensive answers to his or her questions. This process is crucial to the restoration of trust. If the offending party blocks this process, recovery is slowed.

Dealing with the trauma is the first order of business. The discoverer still needs to express grief, shock, and anger directly to the partner and requires clear and honest responses. Several sessions may pass during which the therapist has the illusion that the couple is beyond the posttraumatic phase, only to discover that a fight has broken out between sessions because the discoverer, once again, *feels* that the partner is lying, withholding, and/or unable to empathize with the discoverer's pain. These posttraumatic episodes may be triggered by the discovery of old evidence, hang-up telephone calls, and even a movie that is too much a reminder. The partner's ability both to admit the deception and express remorse is necessary for the restoration of communication. In its absence, the prognosis for a good recovery from trauma is poor.

There are situations in which an appropriate and timely reaction to infidelity did not occur. An affair may have happened during the courtship or early in marriage, and only came into the discoverer's awareness many years later. The discoverer's long-delayed reaction usually takes on a strongly obsessive and very angry quality. Since it is so long "after the fact," the discovered partner is often unable to perceive any justification for the discoverer's intense reaction. It is the therapist's task to indicate that this is a genuine delayed posttraumatic reaction. Patients often accept the metaphor that the suppressed information has functioned as a time bomb in the marriage. Therapy will be most successful if the therapist treats the newly acknowledged infidelity as if it had just occurred.

JEALOUSY

It is an error to label normal reactive jealousy following the affair as if it were a personality problem. Treating it as such is a frequent cause of premature termination of therapy. In rare instances, the discoverer *is* obsessively jealous, despite honest reassurance. If careful examination reveals a history of pathological jealousy predating the marriage, this problem may require separate treatment for the pathologically jealous mate, in conjunction with the marital therapy. Pathological jealousy is best seen as an aspect of a paranoid personality disorder.

PREDISPOSING FACTORS

Once the couple has negotiated the hurdle of discovery, it is then possible to begin a review of the prediscovery phase of the marriage. During this process, the therapist helps the couple to move beyond the issue of perceived victimhood and on to an examination of factors within the marriage that may have contributed to the affair. Such factors generally include low self-disclosure and consequent poor problem solving. During this phase the therapist must be alert to posttraumatic episodes. These can be precipitated by such things as the discovery of old evidence, hang-up telephone calls or stalking by the third party. The therapist must halt the examination of predisposing factors and immediately address the posttraumatic issues. Once the posttraumatic response is ameliorated, it is possible to complete the exploration of prior relationship issues. This usually readies the couple for traditional marital therapy, with a focus on honest communication.

TERMINATION

Couples are ready for termination when they have examined the context and meaning of the infidelity and have resolved that they can either proceed to a healthier relationship or move toward divorce. A better marriage includes an improvement in mutual empathy and joint responsibility. When the discoverer accepts some responsibility for prior relationship problems, the idea of victimhood has lost its power. The understanding that both parties played a role in the marriage generally leads to a more amicable divorce.

Because the discoverer remains vulnerable to a possible recurrence, it is important to discuss with both partners the importance of a detection mechanism. The offending mate is reminded that, should the discoverer need reassurance, it must be patiently given. Both are reminded that they have spoken about such difficult issues that chances are they will be able now to stay focused on the quality of their relationship. They have not "recovered" and returned to their prior, affair-ready situation, but achieved an improved relationship. Most agree that there will probably not be another infidelity, but they may decide that the marriage is not working and arrive mutually at the conclusion that it is best ended. Both are asked to agree that in all likelihood a recurrence would require a divorce.

BIBLIOTHERAPY

As part of a psychoeducational approach, suggested readings can be helpful. The readings by Janoff-Bulman, Lusterman, Pittman, and Vaughan listed at the end of this chapter have been found to be of value. It is often effective to ask the couple to buy two copies of the book. Each should be asked to read a chapter and they then talk together about what they have read. A number of Web sites also provide an opportunity to receive information and participate in a bulletin board and chat line. These are best discovered by the couple through a computer search.

References and Readings

Glass, S., & Wright, T. (1995). Reconstructing marriages after the trauma of infidelity. In K. Halford & H. Markman (Eds.), *Clinical handbook of marriage and couple interventions* (pp. 471–503). New York: Wiley.

Janoff-Bulman, R. (1992). *Shattered assumptions: Towards a new psychology of trauma*. New York: Free Press.

Kaslow, F., & Hammerschmidt, H. (1992). Long-term "good marriages": The seemingly essential ingredients. *Journal of Couples Therapy, 3*(2/3), 15–38.

Lusterman, D-D.(1989). Marriage at the turning point. *Family Networker, 13*, 44–51.

Lusterman, D-D. (1995). Treating marital infidelity. In R. Mikesell, D-D Lusterman, & S. McDaniel (Eds.), *Integrating family therapy: Handbook of family psychology and systems theory* (pp. 259–269). Washington, DC: American Psychological Association.

Pittman, F. (1989). *Private lies: Infidelity and the betrayal of intimacy*. New York: Norton

Smith, T. (2006). *American sexual behavior: Trends, socio-demographic differences, and risk behavior*. Chicago, IL: National Opinion Research Center, University of Chicago.

Vaughan, P. (1989). *The monogamy myth*. New York: Newmarket Press.

Related Topics

Chapter 76, "Conducting Couple and Family Therapy"

Chapter 77, "Treating High-Conflict Couples"

79 CONDUCTING PSYCHOEDUCATIONAL GROUPS

Gary M. Burlingame and Sean Woodland

The Association of Specialists in Group Work (1991) identified psychoeducational groups (PEGs) as a distinct type of group treatment, distinguishing it from psychotherapy and activity groups. A cardinal feature of PEGs is the focus on developing members' cognitive, affective, or behavioral knowledge and skills through a structured and sequenced set of group interventions . In particular, group psychoeducation separates itself from other types of group treatments by its primary focus on education.

The wide range of extant PEG models is partially reflected by the diversity of settings, populations (e.g., psychiatric, medically ill, well), and professions that rely upon this group format. A growing number of models are being developed to respond to survivors of natural and human-made disasters. An equally impressive number of PEGs can be found in medical settings, such as patients with terminal (e.g., oncology) or chronic (e.g., cardiology, pain) medical conditions that have dual needs for education regarding the disease and its treatment, as well as support for psychosocial sequalae.

There is a dearth of independent reviews regarding the effectiveness of PEGs. Rather, evidence for their effectiveness is found in single studies or reviews of specific behavioral or medical conditions that rely upon PEGs for treatment delivery. While evidence exists for their effectiveness with specific populations (e.g., bipolar disorder and breast cancer; cf. Burlingame, Strauss, & Joyce, 2013), it should be emphasized that the outcomes measured often relate to educational objectives and behavioral compliance (e.g., health strategies) instead of symptom reduction or remission. Herewith are 10 recommendations from our clinical experience and the research literature on improving the process and outcomes of PEGs.

SUCCESS FACTORS

Careful examination of diverse PEG protocols found in the literature leads to three emergent organizing process components: a didactic presentation, an experiential exercise, and discussion. The interplay of these three processes lead to 10 characteristics associated with successful PEGs:

1. *Specify learning goal and related objectives.* Patient education is the primary aim or outcome; thus, PEGs should have clearly defined educational goals. For instance, a typical goal of a symptom management PEG is to teach the patient about the probable etiology of the disease attendant symptoms, and practices that are likely to hinder or assist in recovery from or management of these symptoms (e.g., medication, lifestyle, behaviors). To achieve these three educational goals, one must have operational

clarity for each learning objective. Ideally, learning objectives for symptoms, etiologies, and treatments would organize the flow of educational material to be presented over the course of the PEG. At minimum, written goals, objectives, and material should be available for each PEG session.

2. *Incorporate pedagogical methods that enhance patient learning.* Because patient education is paramount, PEG leaders are sensitive to different styles of learning and incorporate teaching methods to address each. Leaders are advised to provide a framework where the "big picture" of the PEG (learning goal) is initially presented and then linked to session objectives, thus establishing a learning gestalt for the entire PEG. Sensitivity to "how" members learn will lead to objectives being ordered hierarchically. For instance, Brown (2011) suggests a hierarchy where facts are initially presented followed by application, which then leads to an analysis and synthesis of knowledge. Periodic evaluation of knowledge acquisition is recommended to provide both member and leader with feedback on understanding and topics that may lack clarity.
3. *Use structured exercises to increase skill acquisition and experiential learning.* By definition, most PEGs require active participation or experiential learning, which also increases member retention. To achieve this, one needs to involve members in structured learning exercises. These exercises can range from the completion of a simple self-report instrument that is tied to a learning objective (e.g., assessment of symptoms) to activities that require members to use a principle or practice a skill learned during the didactic phase of the group. This experiential learning allows members to receive feedback on their skill acquisition from the leader or other members. Successful structured exercises must have a direct link to objectives stated in the didactic presentation.
4. *Apply material through discussion.* A frequent comment heard from leaders of unsuccessful PEGs is that members see it as an "academic" exercise having no personal meaning and often passively sit throughout group sessions. A process to counteract this tendency is to include structured exercises that invite member involvement and disclosure. This can take the form of spontaneous interaction regarding the topic under consideration to having members participate in a structured exercise that analyzes, applies, and synthesizes their personal experiences with the material just presented. Material that has personal meaning leads to longer retention and is more likely to be used after the group ends. Thus, PEG leaders are encouraged to plan for personal exchange and discussion between members in the latter portion of each session.
5. *Focus on careful patient selection.* Leaders should select members who are well matched to the educational goals of the group. The content and exercises used in the PEG should be calibrated with the educational and motivation level of the patient. For example, if a commercially available PEG manual is used, the content and homework will often need to be modified to match the specific needs of a patient population. Other patient factors to consider include readiness to change and level of anxiety, both of which can interfere with the learning objectives of PEGs.
6. *Design the structure to fit the function.* PEGs are time-limited interventions ranging from 1 to 12 sessions that take place over a defined time period. Group size also varies ranging from 5 to 100 members depending upon the primary goal of the group. PEGs with a remedial focus (i.e., overcoming a specific deficit) are typically smaller (fewer than 15 members), while preventative groups represent the larger end of the spectrum. The amount of time focused on didactic, experiential, and discussion systematically varies by underlying theoretical orientation and size of the PEG. Cognitive models devote more time to the didactic component, while existential and process models put greater emphasis on the experiential and discussion.

7. *Incorporate evidence-based properties from other group treatments.* PEGs, like all group treatments, are affected by group dynamic and therapeutic properties that have been studied for decades. An understanding and appreciation of *group dynamics*, for example, can assist in developing a group environment that is conducive to learning. There is some evidence that closed groups pass through predictable stages of development, which, in turn, change the interactive climate and responsiveness of members. Knowledge of such may assist in selecting stage-appropriate activities and discussion topics. The group climate, for another example, has been empirically linked to the successful group outcomes (Burlingame, McClendon, & Alonso, 2011). Use of empirically grounded principles to manage group climate can assist PEG leaders in creating an environment most conducive to patient learning. Short self-report measures of such (e.g., Group Climate Questionnaire; MacKenzie, 1983) when used periodically throughout the course of a group can provide invaluable information on the groups environment.
8. *Manage problem members.* Troublesome member roles emerge in group treatment, irrespective of the type or theoretical orientation guiding the group. For instance, problematic member roles range from the overparticipating to the underparticipating member, as well as those who engage in disruptive socializing conduct. It behooves the PEG leader to become familiar with the group therapy literature, which describes interventions to counteract such behaviors (Yalom & Leszcz, 2005).
9. *Attend to ethical issues.* A PEG leader should be aware of the ethical underpinnings behind group work. The public nature of group treatment imposes a unique ethical responsibility upon the leader. Examples include allowing freedom of exit, orienting the client regarding the nature of the group, avoiding imposing the leader's values, developing goals with member consultation, and addressing a member's premature termination from group. The foremost issue in most members' minds is that of privacy. While PEGs have lower levels of member disclosure, clarity on this point is essential for the leader to address at the beginning of the group and periodically thereafter (see www.agpa.org/guidelines/ethicalpractice.html for Ethical Standard suggestions).
10. *Train leaders in two dimensions.* A successful PEG leader must master two dimensions of knowledge and skill. The first reflects competencies specific to conducting a psychoeducational group treatment. These were briefly outlined earlier and are more completely delineated by professional association standards (e.g., ASGW) and in recent texts (Brown, 2011; Coyne, Wilson, & Ward, 1997). The second reflects competencies associated with the subject matter of the PEG. For instance, leaders conducting PEGs that focus on prevention (e.g., HIV) or remediation (e.g., anger management) are expected to develop content mastery associated with a specific topic or psychiatric disorder. These skills often require specialized training.

STEPS IN CONDUCTING PSYCHOEDUCATIONAL GROUPS

The literature suggests six steps to form and run a PEG:

1. *State a purpose.* A clear statement of purpose describes why the group is being conducted and how clients may benefit. The purpose is most often identified by the name of the group, but the group leader should explicitly identify the individual and collective goals of the group, and these should be reiterated throughout the course of the PEG.
2. *Establish goals.* Specific goals should be calibrated by key member factors such as cognitive impairment and readiness to change. For example, a goal for a psychiatric PEG typically includes understanding symptoms, their triggers, and ways to cope when triggers manifest themselves. The group leader

can establish goals that provide a realistic "road map" for each.

3. *Set objectives.* Objectives are action-oriented interventions that operationalize a goal. Using the aforementioned PEG as an example, objectives would include having members identify their own symptoms, articulate the relationship between these symptoms and their personal triggers, and identify personalized methods to cope with symptom triggers. This sequence would describe the hierarchal progression of class content, beginning with facts, and then move to in-session application and ending with synthesis and application of new knowledge.
4. *Select content.* Each objective is operationalized by selecting content to support the didactic goal and should be tied to relevant literature that is engaging and matches the skills and abilities of the client. This is a time-consuming task that undoubtedly explains the growing popularity of commercially available PEGs that are regularly updated by content experts.
5. *Design experiential activities.* Exercises should match the emotional intensity of the content being presented and be informed by the stage of group treatment. For instance, activities that involve more affectively laden self-disclosure should be reserved for the middle stages of the group. Likewise, experiential activities involving a low level of emotional intensity are more appropriate in the early and late stages of the PEG.
6. *Evaluate.* All PEGs should evaluate for content mastery and skill acquisition and other important outcomes (e.g., symptom reduction). In the absence of such information, the leader cannot determine the success of the PEG.

References and Readings

Association for Specialists in Group Work. (1991). Association for Specialists in Group Work: Professional standards for training of group workers. *Journal of Specialists in Group Work, 17*, 12–19.

Brown, N. W. (2011). *Psychoeducational groups* (3rd ed.). New York: Routledge.

Burlingame, G., McClendon, D., & Alonso, J (2011). Cohesion in group psychotherapy. In J. C. Norcross (Ed.), *Psychotherapy relationships that work* (2nd ed., pp. 110–131). New York: Oxford University Press.

Burlingame, G., Strauss, B., & Joyce, A (2013). Change mechanisms and effectiveness of small group treatments. In M. J. Lambert (Ed.), *Bergin & Garfield's handbook of psychotherapy and behavior change* (pp. 640–689). New York: Wiley.

Coyne, R. K., Wilson, F. R., & Ward, D. E. (1997). *Comprehensive group work: What it means and how to teach it.* Alexandria, VA: American Counseling Association.

Furr, S. R. (2000). Structuring the group experience: A format for designing psychoeducational groups. *Journal for Specialists in Group Work, 25*(1), 29–49.

Jones, K. D., & Robinson, E. H., III. (2000). Psychoeducational groups: A model for choosing topics and exercises appropriate to group stage. *Journal for Specialists in Group Work, 25*(4), 356–365.

MacKenzie, K. R. (1983). The clinical application of group measure. In R. R. Dies & K. R. MacKenzie (Eds.), *Advances in group psychotherapy: Integrating research and practice* (pp. 159–170). New York: International Universities Press.

Rindner, E. C. (2000). Group process-psychoeducation model for psychiatric clients and their families. *Journal of Psychosocial Nursing and Mental Health Issues, 38*(9), 34–41.

Yalom, I. D., & Leszcz, M. (2005). *The theory and practice of group psychotherapy* (5th ed.). New York: Basic Books.

Related Topic

Chapter 74, "Recruiting, Selecting, and Preparing Patients for Interpersonal Group Psychotherapy"

80 USING GENOGRAMS IN ASSESSMENT AND THERAPY

Sueli S. Petry and Monica McGoldrick

The *genogram* is a practical, visual tool for assessment of family patterns and context, as well as a therapeutic intervention in itself. Genograms allow clinicians to quickly conceptualize the individual's context within the growing diversity of family forms and patterns in our society. Using the genogram to collect historical and contextual assessment information is a collaborative, client-centered therapeutic process. By its nature, the process involves the telling of stories and emphasizes respect for the client's perspective, while encouraging multiple views and possible outcomes. While the genogram has been used for decades, it is a tool in progress, and clinicians use it for assessment of functioning, relational patterns, ethnicity, spirituality, migration, class, other socioeconomic factors, and for therapeutic interventions such as the creative play therapy genogram (McGoldrick, 2011; McGoldrick, Carter, & Garcia-Preto, 2011; McGoldrick, Gerson, & Petry, 2008; McGoldrick, Giordano, & Garcia-Preto, 2005; McGoldrick & Hardy, 2008; Petry, 2011).

Gathering genogram information should be seen as an integral part of a comprehensive, clinical assessment. There is no quantitative measurement scale by which the clinician can use a genogram in a cookbook fashion to make clinical predictions. Rather, the genogram is a subjective, interpretive tool that enables clinicians to generate tentative hypotheses for further evaluation in a family assessment. Typically, the genogram is constructed from information gathered during the first session and revised as new information becomes available. Thus, the initial assessment forms the basis for treatment. Of course, we cannot compartmentalize assessment and treatment. Each interaction with the family informs the assessment and thus influences the next intervention.

We include on the genogram the nuclear and extended family members, as well as significant nonblood "kin" who have ever lived with or played a major role in the family's life. We also note significant events and problems on the genogram. Current behavior and problems of family members can be traced on the genogram from multiple perspectives. The index person (the IP, or person with the problem or symptom) may be viewed in the context of various subsystems, such as siblings, triangles, and reciprocal relationships, or in relation to the broader community, social institutions (schools, courts, etc.), and sociocultural context.

The genogram usually includes cultural and demographic information about at least three generations of family members, as well as nodal and critical events in the family's history, particularly as related to family changes (migration, loss, and the life cycle) (Figs. 80.1 and 80.2). When family members are questioned about the present situation in relation to the themes, myths, rules, and emotionally

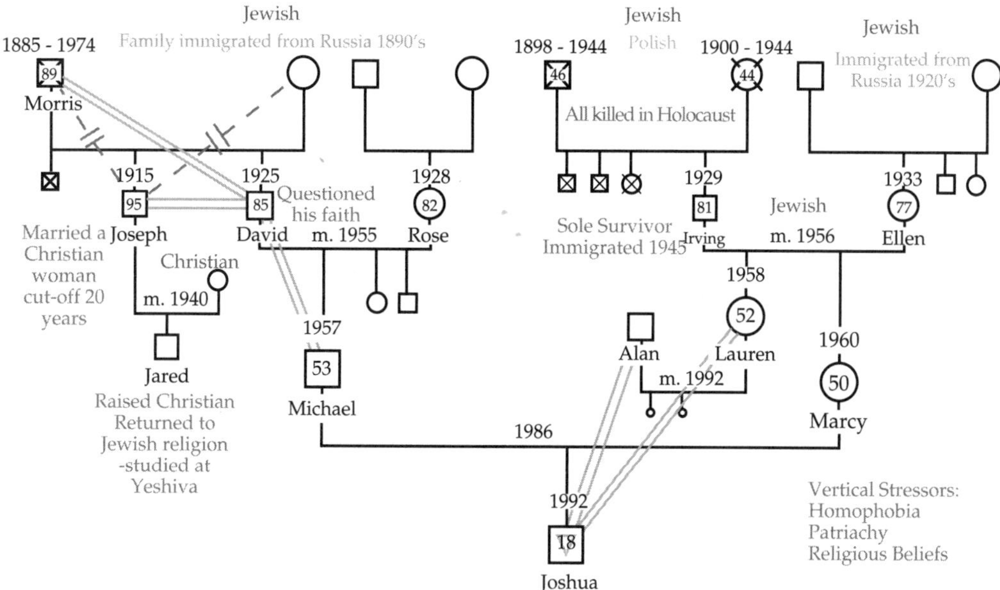

FIGURE 80.1. Joshua's Family Genogram.

charged issues of previous generations, repetitive patterns become clear.

Joshua's family genogram created with the computer program GenoPro (Fig. 80.1) illustrates a family struggling with their son's coming out and their religious belief that homosexuality is a sin, as it is considered in nearly all organized religions due to the rigid constructs of sexuality created by patriarchy (Petry, 2011). The genogram encouraged a dialogue that helped this family to see multiple possibilities and outcomes.

THE FAMILY INFORMATION NET

The process of gathering family information can be thought of as casting out an information net in larger and larger circles to capture relevant information about the family and its broader context. The net spreads out in a number of different directions:

- From the presenting problem to the larger context of the problem
- From the immediate household to the extended family and broader social systems
- From the present family situation to a chronology of historical family events
- From easy nonthreatening queries to difficult, anxiety-provoking questions
- From obvious facts to judgments about functioning and relationships to hypothesized family patterns

The IP usually comes with specific problems, which are the clinician's starting point. At the outset, the IP is told that some basic information about the family is needed to fully understand the problem. Such information usually grows naturally out of exploring the presenting problem and its impact on the immediate household. The clinician asks the name, age, gender, and occupation of each person in the household in order to sketch the immediate family structure. Other revealing information is elicited through inquiring about the problem. This is also a good time to inquire about previous efforts to get help for the problem, including previous treatment, therapists, hospitalizations, and the current referring person.

Next the clinician spreads the information net into the current family situation. This

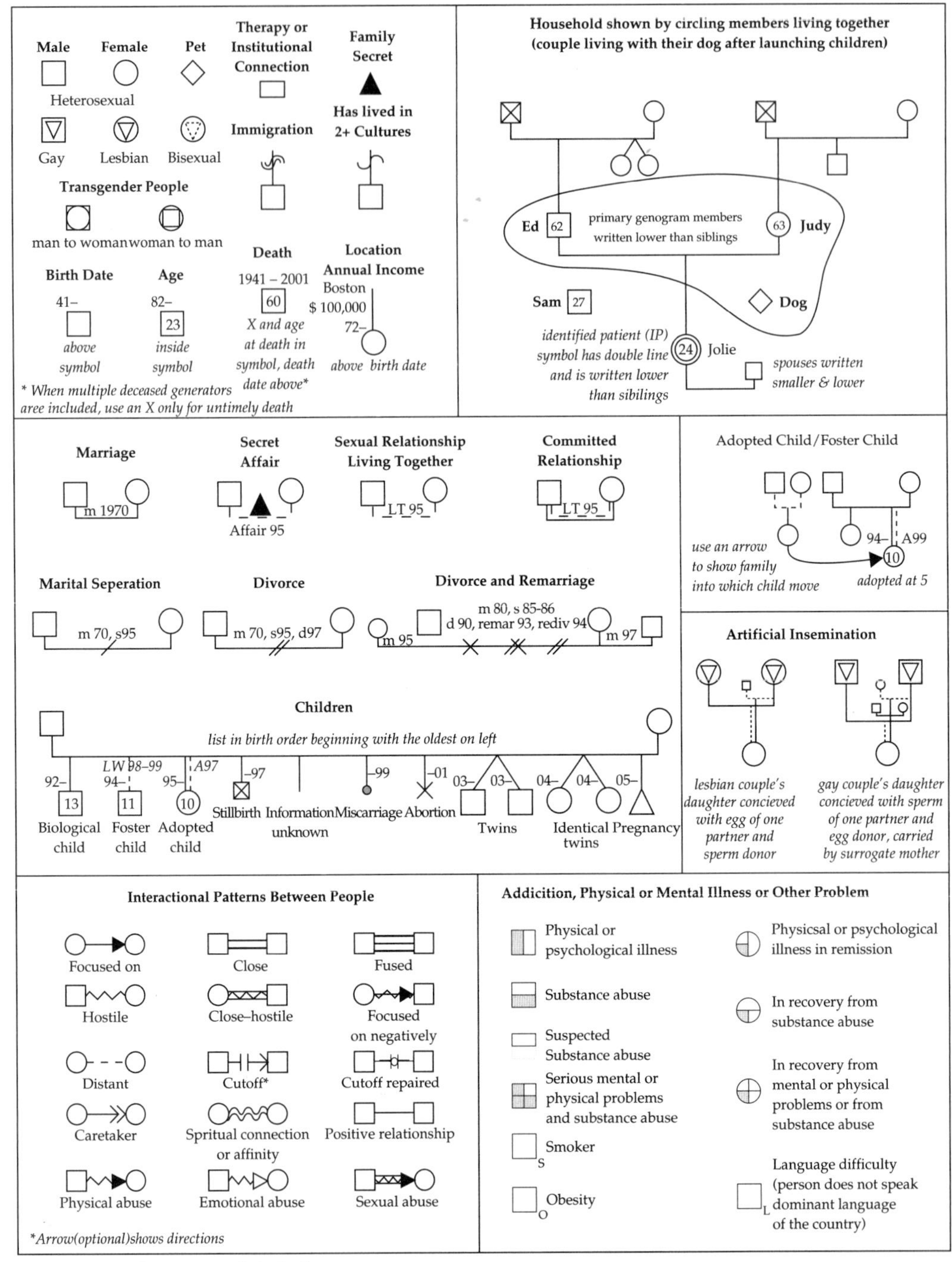

FIGURE 80.2. Genogram Symbols.

line of questioning usually follows naturally from questions about the problem and who is involved:

- What has been happening recently in your family?
- Have there been any recent changes in the family (e.g., people coming or leaving, illnesses, job problems)?

It is important to inquire about recent life cycle transitions as well as anticipated changes in the family situation (especially exits and entrances of family members—births, marriages, divorces, deaths, or the departure of family members).

The clinician looks for an opportunity to explore the wider family context by asking about the extended family and cultural background of all the adults involved. The interviewer might move into this area by saying, "I would now like to ask you something about your background to help make sense of your present problem."

DEALING WITH A FAMILY'S RESISTANCE TO DOING A GENOGRAM

When family members react negatively to questions about the extended family or complain that such matters are irrelevant, it often makes sense to redirect the focus back to the immediate situation until the connections between the present situation and other family relationships or experiences can be established. Gentle persistence over time will usually result in obtaining the information and demonstrating its relevance to the family.

The clinician inquires about each side of the family separately beginning, for example, with the mother's side:

- Let's begin with your mother's family. Your mother was which one of how many children?
- When and where was she born?
- Is she alive? If not, when did she die? What was the cause of her death?
- If alive, where is she now? What does she do? How is her health?
- When and how did your mother meet your father? When did they marry?
- Had she been married before? If so, when? Did she have children by that marriage?
- Did they separate or divorce or did the spouse die? If so, when was that?

And so on. In like fashion, questions are asked about the father. Then the clinician might ask about each parent's family of origin (i.e., father, mother, and siblings). The goal is to get information about at least three or four generations, including grandparents, parents, aunts, uncles, siblings, spouses, and children of the IP.

ETHNIC AND CULTURAL HISTORY

It is essential to learn something about the family's socioeconomic, political, and cultural background in order to place presenting problems and current relationships in context. When the questioning expands to the extended family, it is a good point to begin exploring issues of ethnicity, since the birthplace of the grandparents has now been established. Exploring ethnicity and migration history helps establish the cultural context in which the family is operating and offers the therapist an opportunity to validate family attitudes and behaviors determined by such influences. It is important to learn what the family's cultural traditions are about problems, health care, and healing, and where the current family members stand in relation to those traditional values. It is also important to consider the family's cultural expectations about relationships with health care professionals, since this will set the tone for their clinical responses.

Furthermore, class background between family members or between family members and the health care professional may create discomfort, which will need to be attended to in the meeting. Questions to ascertain class assumptions pertain not just to the family's current income but also to cultural background, education, and social status within their community. Once the clinician has a clear picture of the ethnic and cultural factors influencing a family (and, it is hoped, keeping his or her own biases in check), it is possible to raise delicate questions geared to helping families identify any behaviors that—while culturally sanctioned—may be keeping them stuck, such as traditional gender roles (see McGoldrick et al., 2005).

DIFFICULT QUESTIONS ABOUT INDIVIDUAL FUNCTIONING

Assessment of individual functioning may or may not involve much clinical judgment.

Alcohol abuse, chronic unemployment, and severe symptomatology are facts that directly indicate poor functioning. However, many family members may function well in some areas but not in others or may cover up their dysfunction. Often, it takes careful questioning to reveal the true level of functioning. A family member with a severe illness may show remarkable adaptive strengths and another may show fragility with little apparent stress. Questions about individual functioning may be difficult or painful for family members to answer and must be approached with sensitivity and tact. The family members should be warned that questions may be difficult and they should let the clinician know if there is an issue they would rather not discuss. The clinician will need to judge the degree of pressure to apply if the family resists questions that may be essential to dealing with the presenting problem.

Clinicians need to exercise extreme caution about when to ask questions that could put a family member in danger. For example, if violence is suspected, a wife should never be asked about her husband's behavior in his presence, since the question assumes she is free to respond, which may not be the case. It is the clinician's responsibility to take care that the questions do not put a client in jeopardy.

SETTING PRIORITIES FOR ORGANIZING GENOGRAM INFORMATION

One of the most difficult aspects of genogram assessment remains setting priorities for inclusion of family information on a genogram. Clinicians cannot follow every lead the genogram interview suggests. Awareness of basic genogram patterns can help the clinician set such priorities. As a rule of thumb, the data are scanned for the following:

- Repetitive symptoms, relationship, or functioning patterns across the family and over the generations. Repeated triangles, coalitions, cutoffs, patterns of conflict, overfunctioning, and underfunctioning are central to genogram interpretation.
- Coincidences of dates. For example, the death of one family member or anniversary of this death occurring at the same time as symptom onset in another, or the age at symptom onset coinciding with the age of problem development in another family member.
- The impact of change and untimely life cycle transitions: particularly changes in functioning and relationships that correspond with critical family life events and untimely life cycle transitions—for example, births, marriages, or deaths that occur "off schedule."

Awareness of possible patterns makes the clinician more sensitive to what is missing. Such missing information about important family members or events and discrepancies in the information offered frequently reflects charged emotional issues in the family. The clinician should take careful note of the connections family members make or fail to make to various events.

MAPPING THE GENOGRAMS OF THOSE WHO GROW UP IN MULTIPLE SETTINGS

Many children grow up in multiple settings because their parents divorce, die, remarry, migrate, or have other special circumstances that require the child to live for a while or even permanently in a different setting. Genograms are an exceptionally useful tool to track children's experiences through the life cycle, taking into account the multiple family and other institutional contexts to which they have belonged (McGoldrick et al., 2011). The more clearly the clinician tracks the actuality of this history, however complex, the better able he or she is to validate the child's actual experience and multiple forms of belonging. Such a map can begin to make order out of the at times chaotic placement changes a child must go through when sudden transitions or shifts in placement are necessary because of illness, trauma, or other loss. It can also help validate for a child the realities of his or her birth and life connections that vary from traditional norms.

Sometimes the only feasible way to clarify where children were raised is to take chronological notes on each child in a family and then transform them into a series of genograms that show the family context each child has grown up in. When the "functional" family is different from the biological or legal family, as when children are raised by a grandparent or in an informal adoptive family, it is useful to create a separate genogram to show the functional structure. Where children have lived as part of several families—biological, foster, and adoptive—separate genograms may help to depict the child's multiple families over time.

PLAY GENOGRAMS FOR INDIVIDUAL CHILD AND FAMILY THERAPY

The play genogram can be used with individual children, and with families, as an assessment tool and to facilitate therapeutic conversation. The basic genogram is drawn on a large sheet of easel paper. When working with individual children, clinicians invite the child to "choose a miniature that best shows your thoughts and feelings about everyone in the family, including yourself" and to place the miniature on the squares and circles on the easel paper. The clinician may give reluctant children examples of concrete and abstract choices to encourage the child to explore choices freely. When completed, the individual play genogram will have one miniature on each circle or square.

Some individuals may use more than one miniature to represent family members. This may reflect the complexity of a relationship or self-image. When working with children in foster care or other family situations where children have had multiple caretakers, it is helpful to construct a series of genograms on the same sheet of paper. Children may include friends, therapists, teachers, pets, or other important relationships, both past and present. This helps children to reference and prioritize their world

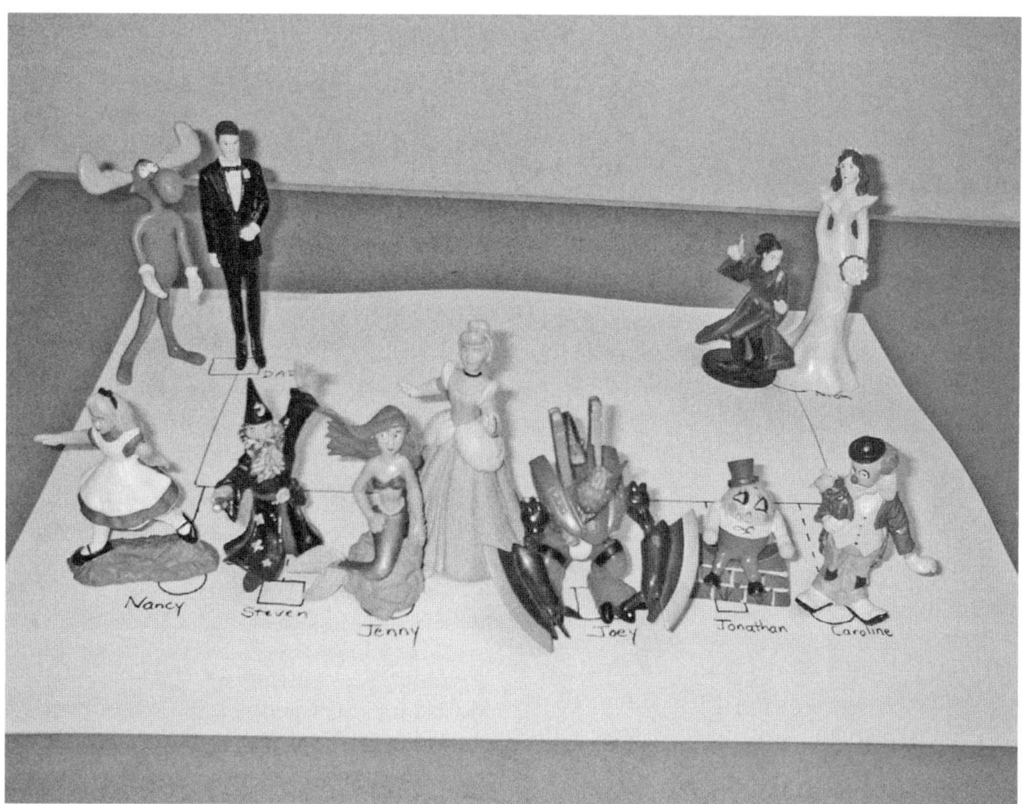

FIGURE 80.3. Play Genogram.

and gives the clinician a complex, yet easily scanned assessment. Figure 80.3 is an example of a play genogram with children in foster care. Jenny and Joey added foster siblings who had lived with them and talked about their feelings about each child who had come and gone. The play genogram helped the children process feelings of loss and quickly brought the clinician into their world.

The directives for the family play genogram are the same as for individuals: Clinicians help the family to construct a genogram of their immediate and extended family, then family members are asked to choose a miniature that best shows their thoughts and feelings about everyone in the family, including themselves. Clinicians observe the selection process for the type and level of interactions between family members. The interactions between family members will inform the clinician about the family's current relationship styles and patterns of relating. Encouraging family members to make their choices at the same time will yield a broader range of assessment information. Conflicts about specific miniatures are more likely to arise when the family is engaged in activity together, and as conflicts arise the clinician observes the family patterns of problem solving.

When everyone has made his or her choice, family members are encouraged to look at the family play genogram and to make comments and ask questions. Clinicians should not ask family members to explain why they chose a particular object. It is more useful to facilitate an open dialogue in which family members volunteer a broad range of information. The first person to speak tends to set the tone for the type of information that will be provided. Thus, the clinician should ask expansive questions in order to promote a more extensive dialogue, for example, "Can you tell me more about that?"

After the initial play genograms, the clinician may request a second level of activity by asking family members to choose a miniature that best represents their relationships with other family members; this yields other valuable information. Clinicians ask permission to take a photograph of the individual or family play genogram. The family may take the photograph home with them to facilitate additional conversation, or clinicians can keep the pictures to re-create play genograms at a later time for a continuation of the therapeutic dialogue. The play genogram technique is just one of the many ways that the genogram facilitates therapy.

The genogram, which is a highly condensed map of a rich and complex family, is an awesome lesson to anyone who is unable to see beyond the cutoffs that may occur in a family. We believe that no relationship is to be disregarded or discounted. All our relationships inform the wholeness of who we are and where we come from; more important, they can give us the possibility of making constructive, conscious choices about who we will choose to be in the future.

One of the most powerful aspects of genograms is the way in which they can steer us to the rich ongoing possibilities of complex kin relationships, which continue throughout life to be sources of connection and life support. It is not just our shared history that matters but also the spiritual power of our history of survival, as well as our current connections that strengthen us and can enrich our future. All our relationships inform the wholeness of who we are and where we came from, and more important, can give us the possibility of making constructive and conscious choices about who we will choose to become.

References, Readings, and Internet Sites

GenoPro. (2013). www.GenoPro.com

McGoldrick, M. (2011). *The genogram journey: Reconnecting with your family*. New York: Norton.

McGoldrick, M., Carter, B., & Garcia-Preto, N. (2011). *The expanded family life cycle: Individual, family and social perspectives* (4th ed.). Boston, MA: Allyn & Bacon.

McGoldrick, M., Gerson, R., & Petry, S. (2008). *Genograms: Assessment and intervention*. New York: W.W.Norton.

McGoldrick, M., Giordano, J. & Garcia Preto, N. (Eds.). (2005). *Ethnicity and family therapy* (3rd ed.). New York: Guilford Press.

McGoldrick, M., & Hardy, K.V. (Eds.). (2008). *Re-visioning family therapy: Race, culture and gender in clinical practice* (2nd ed.). New York: Guilford Press.

Petry, S. (2011). Spirituality and the family life cyle. In M. McGoldrick, B. Carter, & N. Garcia-Preto (Eds.), *The expanded family life cycle: Individual, family and social perspectives* (4th ed., pp. 133–148). Boston, MA: Allyn & Bacon.

Related Topics

Chapter 8, "Interviewing Children's Caregivers"
Chapter 76, "Conducting Couple and Family Therapy"

81 TREATING BULLYING BEHAVIORS AMONG YOUTH

Susan M. Swearer

Bullying is a complex set of behaviors that can cause great psychological distress in children, adolescents, and their adult caregivers. Bullying, by definition, is a subset of aggression that is characterized by intentional harmful behavior toward others. These behaviors are repetitive, and it is difficult for the person being bullied to defend himself or herself. Bullying behaviors comprise four areas: (1) verbal bullying, (2) physical bullying, (3) relational or social bullying, and (4) electronic bullying. Typically, there is overlap between these forms of bullying (i.e., someone who engages in verbal bullying is also likely to engage in electronic bullying). Regardless of the form the bullying might take, the consequences of being bullied can be disastrous and include school avoidance, somatic complaints, lower academic achievement, depression, anxiety, anger, and suicidal ideation and attempts.

Bullying also has detrimental outcomes for youth who are perpetrating bullying. A series of studies recently published in the *Journal of Aggression, Conflict, and Peace Research* have shown that youth who perpetrate bullying are at increased risk for delinquency, a correlation that is particularly strong for boys. Additionally, youth who bully others have higher rates of later mental health and adjustment problems and these difficulties persist into adulthood. Considering the connection between oppositional defiant disorder, conduct disorder, and antisocial personality disorder, this negative trajectory is not surprising and behooves psychologists to treat not only youth who are bullied but also youth who bully others.

Drawing on the comorbidity of depression and conduct disorder research, it is also important to recognize that youth who are bullied may also perpetrate bullying behavior. In fact, research has shown that youth who are bullied at home or who witness aggression at home are at increased risk for bullying others at school. So bullying is not a static conflict between *a bully* and *a victim*; in fact, we know that bullying is a complex dynamic, fueled by peer group dynamics, family dynamics, school climate, neighborhood climate, and societal factors. Effective interventions must address this complexity in order to effectively treat bullying among youth.

GENDER, RACE, AND DEMOGRAPHIC FACTORS

Both boys and girls engage in bullying behaviors. While some research has shown that boys are more likely to engage in physical bullying and girls are more likely to engage in relational or social bullying, these gender distinctions are influenced by the peer group, family, and school environments. The reality is that youth who bully will use the mechanisms (i.e., verbal, physical, relational/social, or electronic) whereby their behaviors will most likely be undetected by adults. Research by Sandra Graham and Jana Juvonen shows that bullying occurs across ethnicities and the most important predictor of being bullied is "ethnicity within a particular school context." That is, if a student is in the ethnic minority, regardless of his or her ethnicity, he or she will be at increased risk for being bullied. Other demographic factors such as socioeconomic status, rurality, urbanization, family composition, and domestic violence are other variables that contribute to victimization and bullying. One of the most important questions psychologists can ask about bullying with their clients is, "What are the conditions that allow the bullying to occur?" When psychologists can identify those conditions, then they can help their clients and families alter these conditions and reduce the likelihood that bullying will occur.

EFFECTIVE TREATMENT FOR YOUTH WHO ARE BULLIED

Much has been written about working with youth who are being bullied. This section will address basic approaches to working with youth and their families who are referred for being bullied. Typically, students who are bullied also experience co-occurring anxious and depressive symptomatology and psychologists should screen for depression and anxiety using standardized rating scales or clinical interviews that are appropriate for children. Psychologists should also ask questions about friendship groups, academic performance, family functioning, and extracurricular activities. The research is clear that protective factors such as friends, social support, academic engagement, and engagement in multiple activities serves as a buffer against the negative effects of being bullied.

Psychologists should follow treatment protocols for the treatment of depression and anxiety when clients present with internalizing symptomatology. Treatment should then include cognitive-behavioral approaches for the reduction of depressed and anxious mood and cognitive restructuring to address depressive and anxious cognitions. Depending upon the severity of the depression and/or anxiety, referral for pharmacological treatment may be warranted.

Psychologists need to obtain a release of information from their child client's parents in order to communicate with their client's teachers, school counselor, school administrators, and so on. The majority of bullying behavior takes place in school or involves the peer group at school or online. Best practices dictate that mental health professionals need to work with the adults in the child or adolescent's life in order to help ameliorate the bullying behavior. Questions psychologists can ask school personnel are as follows: Does my client have friends in school? Does my client play with others at recess? Does my client sit with other students at lunch? Does my client attend school consistently? What are my client's grades? Does my client seem happy and connected at school? What bullying prevention programs are in place at the school? What adults can my client talk with at school when he or she feels bullied? How does the school track or collect data on the bullying that may be occurring? It is very important that psychologists communicate with their client's school personnel in order to get a handle on the bullying that may be occurring (with parental/guardian permission). If parents do not consent to allow psychologists to communicate with their client's school, then psychologists should encourage the parents/guardians to communicate very closely with their child's teacher and school administrators.

It is also important to coordinate with school mental health professionals to see if there are group therapy options for clients who are being bullied. Research shows that group treatment for youth who are being bullied can be useful. When youth experience similar experiences such as being bullied, group therapy can be a positive therapeutic experience. Group therapy helps students realize that they are not alone and that other people are experiencing the same things they are. Group therapy can also help students think about various coping strategies and responses to being bullied.

EFFECTIVE TREATMENT FOR YOUTH WHO BULLY

While more has been written about working with youth who are being bullied, less has been written about working with youth who bully others. This section will address basic approaches to working with youth and their families who are referred for bullying behaviors. It is important for psychologists to remember that one criterion for a diagnosis of conduct disorder is "often bullies, threatens, or intimidates others" (APA, 2000). Thus, youth who bully others may display oppositional, defiant, aggressive, and coercive behaviors. Psychologists should assess their client's externalizing behaviors using standardized rating scales or clinical interviews that are appropriate for children. Results from these assessments will help guide treatment for youth who bully others.

It is important to recognize that there is no "profile" for students who bully others. Relatedly, when the secret service commissioned a report to look at the profile of the school shooters in the United States in the past two decades, what researchers found was that there is no "standard" profile for a school shooter. Some were from intact families; some were from single caregiver families. Some were loners; some were gregarious and social. Some played violent video games; some did not. A similar pattern holds for youth who bully others. There are a variety of risk factors that are related to whether youth will engage in bullying and these risk factors are determined by the social ecology in which youth reside. Therefore, individual risk factors (i.e., depression, anxiety, anger, impulsivity) will interact with peer risk factors (i.e., bullying as a normative behavior, alcohol and drug use, delinquency), which will interact with school risk factors (i.e., lack of effective prevention and intervention efforts, negative school climate, inconsistent discipline), which will interact with family risk factors (i.e., laissez-faire parenting, coercive family interactions, parental aggression, sibling aggression), which will interact with neighborhood risk factors (i.e., low supervision, high crime rate), which will interact with societal risk factors (i.e., intolerance, homophobia, sexism, racism), which will create the conditions under which an individual will be more likely to bully others.

Bullying among school-age youth is a behavior that requires adults and youth to work together to resolve these behaviors. Bullying behaviors transcend the school yard. They occur going to and from school, in the neighborhood, and in cyberspace. Therefore, bullying is a ubiquitous problem that requires coordinated solutions. Psychologists need to obtain a release of information from their child client's parents in order to communicate with their client's teachers, school counselor, school administrators, and so on. Questions psychologists can ask school personnel are as follows: Does my client have friends in school? Does my client play with others at recess? Does my client sit with other students at lunch? Does my client attend school consistently? What are my client's grades? Does my client seem happy and connected at school? What bullying prevention programs are in place at the school? What do adults say to my client when he or she is bullying others? How does the school track or collect data on the bullying that may be occurring? It is vital that psychologists communicate with their client's school personnel in order to get a handle on the bullying that may be occurring (with parental/guardian permission). If parents do not consent to allow psychologists to communicate with their client's school, then psychologists should encourage the parents/guardians to communicate very closely with their child's teacher and school administrators.

EFFECTIVE TREATMENT FOR YOUTH WHO ARE BULLIED AND WHO BULLY

Finally, it is critical that psychologists recognize the complexity of bullying behaviors and to understand that the research shows that about one-fourth of students involved in bullying are "bully-victims." These youth may be bullied at home or in the neighborhood and then, in turn, they bully at school. These youth are more likely to be in peer groups where bullying is an instrumental behavior used to gain social status, popularity, and group inclusion. Bully-victims have higher levels of depression and anxiety, and they are more likely to experience feelings of hopelessness and anger. It is critical that psychologists assess both bullying and victimization in their clients who are referred for problems with bullying. Bullying is a complex set of behaviors that rarely have a simple etiology and that rarely have a simple solution. Psychologists should be the mental health professionals who are leading our schools, families, and communities toward effective and lasting solutions for ameliorating bullying behaviors among school-age youth.

References and Readings

American Psychiatric Association. (2000). *Diagnostic and statistical manual of mental disorders* (4th ed., text rev.). Washington, DC: Author.

Espelage, D. L., & Swearer, S. M. (2008). Current perspectives on linking school bullying research to effective prevention strategies. In T. W. Miller (Ed.), *School violence and primary prevention* (pp. 335–353). New York: Springer.

Espelage, D. L., & Swearer, S. M. (2011). *Bullying in North American schools* (2nd ed.). New York: Routledge.

H. & H. Publishing. (2011). *Bully surveys*. Retrieved January 2013, from www.bullysurvey.com

Juvonen, J., & Graham, S. (2001). *Peer harassment in school: The plight of the vulnerable and victimized*. New York: Guilford Press.

Orpinas, P., & Horne, A. M. (2006). *Bullying prevention: Creating a positive school climate and developing social competence*. Washington, DC: American Psychological Association.

Pollack, W. S., & Swearer, S. M. (2011). Bullying. In G. P. Koocher & A. M. LaGreca (Eds.), *The parents' guide to psychological first aid: Helping children and adolescents cope with predictable life crises* (pp. 167–171). New York: Oxford University Press.

Swearer, S. M. (2013). *Target bullying: Best practices in prevention and intervention*. Retreived January 2013, from www.target-bully.com

Swearer, S. M., Espelage, D. L., Vaillancourt, T., & Hymel, S. (2010). What can be done about school bullying? Linking research to educational practice. *Educational Researcher, 39*, 38–47.

Ttofi, M. M., & Farrington, D. P. (Eds.). (2011). Health consequences of school bullying. *Journal of Aggression, Conflict, and Peach Research*, *3*(2), 57–121.

US Department of Health and Human Services. (2011). *Stop bullying*. Retrieved January 2013, from www.stopbullying.gov

Related Topic

Chapter 87, "Engaging the Reluctant Adolescent"

82 TREATING ENURESIS AND ENCOPRESIS

Patrick C. Friman

ENURESIS

Enuresis is the technical term used for chronic urinary incontinence that occurs after the conventional age at which toilet training is achieved. The International Classification of Diseases (ICD; World Health Organization, 2007) describes nonorganic enuresis as involuntary voiding of urine that is abnormal in relation to the individual's mental age and that is not a consequence of a lack of bladder control due to any neurological disorder, epileptic attacks, or structural abnormality of the urinary tract. The enuresis may or may not be associated with a more widespread emotional or behavioral disorder. For purposes of treatment one would look for repeated voiding of urine into clothing or bed that becomes a cause of significant distress or impairment to social, academic, or occupational functioning. The enuresis may be further classified into primary (in which the person has never achieved urinary continence) and secondary (in which incontinence develops after a period of continence) cases.

Nocturnal enuresis is, by a very wide margin, the most frequently presenting type. Prevalence estimates range as high as 25% of 6-year-old children and, although it is much less prevalent by the teenage years, as many as 8% of boys and 4% of girls are still enuretic at age 12.

Research (and speculation) has suggested several possible causes, but the one that stands out most in terms of supporting data is family history. The research shows that likelihood of enuresis mounts with the closeness and number of blood relatives with a history of the condition. Additionally, temporary delays in some physiological/anatomical characteristics are also correlated with enuresis. These include bone growth, secondary sexual characteristics, stature, and functional bladder capacity. Although most of the research on the relationship between deep sleep dynamics and enuresis suffers from design flaws, it yields some empirical support for the common parental observation that their enuretic children are abnormally difficult to waken. There is a long-standing tendency to attribute enuresis to psychological or character defects, but empirical support is conspicuously nonexistent. The initial enthusiasm for a model of enuresis involving deficiencies in antidiuretic hormone (ADH) has subsided due to the limited amount of supportive research and the limited success of treatments that increase ADH (e.g., DDAVP) (more on drug treatment later).

With the arrival of behavioral theory, the therapeutic approach to enuresis has become more benign psychologically and physically. Behavioral theory dispensed with psychopathological interpretations, favoring a skills deficit perspective instead, and behavioral treatment involved the conditioning of nocturnal urinary retention via the urine alarm. The urine alarm uses a moisture-sensitive switching system that activates an aversive stimulus (e.g., buzzer, bell, light, or vibrator) that conditions continence skills (e.g., waking and urinating, forestalling urination) via negative reinforcement. A large body of research shows that alarm-based treatment lasting from 5 to 12 weeks produces success in 65% to 75% of cases with a 6-month relapse rate of 15%–30% (Friman, 2008). Initial alarm treatments used only bed-based alarms, but pajama-based alarms have emerged as the universal preference. Currently the alarm is rarely used in isolation; it is typically accompanied by a range of other treatment components, resulting in treatment packages.

The treatment components most often combined with the alarm are retention control training (RCT), overlearning, Kegel exercises, cleanliness training, waking schedules, and reward systems. RCT requires children to drink extra fluids (e.g., 16 oz of water or juice) and delay urination as long as possible, thereby increasing the volume and decreasing the frequency of their routine urinations. Kegel exercises, initially developed for stress incontinence in women, involve manipulations of the muscles used to prematurely terminate urination. Waking schedules involve waking enuretic children and guiding them to the bathroom for urination. Early use of waking schedules typically required full awakening, often with sessions that occurred in the middle of the night, but present practice only requires conducting waking sessions just before the parent's normal bedtime. Overlearning, similar to RCT, requires that children drink extra fluids—but just prior to bedtime—and is used primarily to enhance the maintenance of treatment effects established by alarm-based means. Cleanliness training involves requiring children to attempt to return soiled beds, bed clothing, and pajamas to a presoiled state (e.g., taking sheets to laundry room for younger children or actually washing them for older children). Reward systems are used to enhance children's motivation to participate in treatment and usually involve rewards or incentives delivered on a nightly basis (e.g., one small reward for an accident-free night or day).

The oldest, best-known, and empirically supported treatment package is Dry Bed Training (DBT). Initially evaluated for use with a group of adults with profound mental retardation, DBT has been systematically replicated numerous times across child populations. In addition to the bed alarm, its initial composition included overlearning, intensive cleanliness (responsibility) training, intensive positive practice (of alternatives to wetting), hourly awakenings, close monitoring, and rewards for success. In subsequent iterations, the stringency of the waking schedule was reduced and retention control training was added. Similar programs were also developed, the best known and empirically supported of which is Full Spectrum Home Training. It includes the alarm, cleanliness training, retention control training, and overlearning.

The description of treatment options above pertain to nocturnal enuresis. There is much less research on diurnal enuresis, and it moderately supports scheduled toileting, incentives, and strategic use of the urine alarm.

An additional option for both nocturnal and diurnal enuresis involves medication. Unfortunately, the only two medications that have been shown to effectively reduce urinary accidents, imipramine (Tofranil) and desmopressin (DDAVP), are also accompanied by serious side effects. In fact, the United States Food and Drug Administration has recently disapproved of DDAVP for use in the treatment of enuresis (United States Food and Drug Administration, 2007) and since its emergence as a treatment, the use of imipramine has been all but discontinued. Whether imipramine will see resurgence seems unlikely given its problematic side effects. Thus, until or unless another viable medication is discovered, behavioral treatment is likely to become the dominant treatment method across medical and mental health providers.

ENCOPRESIS

Encopresis is a common, undertreated, and overinterpreted form of fecal incontinence. The ICD describes nonorganic encopresis as repeated, voluntary or involuntary passage of feces, in places not appropriate for that purpose in the individual's own sociocultural setting. The condition may represent an abnormal continuation of normal infantile incontinence, it may involve a loss of continence following the acquisition of bowel control, or it may involve the deliberate deposition of feces in inappropriate places despite normal physiological bowel control. The condition may occur as a monosymptomatic disorder, or it may form part of a wider disorder, especially an emotional disorder.

Failure to identify and treat encopresis can lead to multiple health-related problems. First, it can be caused by rare but serious medical conditions that, if left untreated, can have dire outcomes. Second, extended accumulation of fecal matter in the colon, which has a finite amount of space, can lead to severe abdominal pain, pathological distention, and possibly even bursting of the organ. Third, protracted encopresis can impair social acceptance and development. The primary reason for the social impairment is that soiling typically evokes more displeasure and disgust from peers, parents, and important others than other forms of incontinence and most other behavior problems. Children with encopresis are still frequently shamed, blamed, and punished for a condition that is almost totally beyond their control.

The definitions of encopresis typically list four criteria: (1) repeated passage of feces into inappropriate places whether involuntary or intentional; (2) at least one such event a month for at least 3 months; (3) chronological age of at least 4 years (or equivalent developmental level); and (4) the soiling is not due exclusively to the direct physiological effects of a substance or a general medical condition except through a mechanism involving constipation. Approximately 3% of the general pediatric population meets these criteria.

Two types have been described, primary in which the child has never had fecal continence, and secondary in which incontinence returns after at least 6 months of continence. Some sources also describe two subtypes, retentive encopresis in which constipation and overflow incontinence are present, and nonretentive encopresis in which they are absent.

Most cases (80%–90%) involve the retentive subtype with their primary cause of slow movement of fecal material through the colon (i.e., constipation), which, in turn, has multiple determinants such as genetics, stress, irregular eating habits, limited dietary fiber, elevated intake of highly processed foods, medications that decrease colonic motility, and ineffective toilet training. Any of these factors, singly or in combination, put the child at risk for reduced colonic motility, actual constipation, and corresponding uncomfortable or painful bowel movements. Uncomfortable or painful bowel movements, in turn, negatively reinforce toileting avoidance, which leads to fecal retention, leading to a regressive reciprocal cycle resulting in regular fecal accidents. When the constipation is severe or chronic, the child may develop fecal impaction, a large blockage composed of dehydrating fecal material, which can lead to "megacolon," the end result of which is dramatically reduced colonic motility. One unfortunate result occurs when liquid fecal matter seeps around the fecal mass producing "paradoxical diarrhea." Although such children actually have constipation, they appear to have diarrhea. Some parents attempt to treat this type of "diarrhea" with over-the counter antidiarrheal agents, which only worsen the problem.

Psychopathology and sexual abuse are two variables that clinicians have historically been prone to nominate as causes of encopresis. However, scientific studies have not supported that conclusion. A small number of studies have detected an increase in psychological problems in children with encopresis, but the increase is seldom clinically significant and is more likely the consequence of encopresis than a cause of it. Regarding the causal role of sex abuse, the available evidence is mostly anecdotal, and empirical attempts to buttress that evidence have been unsuccessful.

Just as the clinical presentation and causal picture differ between retentive and nonretentive subtypes, so too does the approach to their treatment. Treatment for the retentive type involves a multicomponent approach that includes colonic evacuation (initiated by health care professionals and transferred to parents on an as-needed basis), stool softeners, a consistent toileting schedule, dietary changes (e.g., increased meal time consistency and dietary fiber, decreased amounts of dairy products and highly processed foods), increased fluid intake, postural support on the toilet (so the child's feet are on a firm surface), incentives, and elimination of punitive responses to fecal accidents. The multicomponent approach has shown success in both well-controlled single-subject analyses and randomized clinical trials. It has also shown effectiveness when delivered by a psychotherapist in a group setting and by interactive electronic programs on the Internet. Unfortunately, the treatment picture for nonretentive encopresis is not nearly so optimistic. Presently no published reports of supportive randomized trials, quasi- experimental group studies, or even controlled case studies exist. In other words, no treatments have garnered empirical support. The tiny relevant literature is composed of a small number of case reports with loosely defined treatments that vary widely across these studies.

References and Readings

Christophersen, E. R., & Friman, P. C. (2010). *Encopresis and enuresis*. Cambridge, MA: Hogrefe.

Friman, P. C. (2008). Evidence-based therapies for enuresis and encopresis. In R. G. Steele, T. D. Elkin, & M. C. Roberts (Eds.), *Handbook of evidence-based therapies for children and adolescents* (pp. 301–323). New York: Springer.

McGrath, M. L., Mellon, M. W., & Murphy, L. (2000). Empirically supported treatments in pediatric psychology: Constipation and encopresis. *Journal of Pediatric Psychology, 25*, 225–254.

Mellon, M. W., & McGrath, M. L. (2000). Empirically supported treatments in pediatric psychology: Nocturnal enuresis. *Journal of Pediatric Psychology, 25*, 19–214.

Ritterband, L. M., Cox, D. J., Walker, L. S., Kovatchev, B., McKnight, L., Patel, K., … Sutphen, J. (2003). An Internet intervention as adjunctive therapy for pediatric encopresis. *Journal of Consulting and Clinical Psychology, 71*, 910–917.

US Food and Drug Administration. (2007). *Information for healthcare professionals: Desmopressin acetate (marketed as DDAVP nasal spray, DDAVP rhinal tube, DDAVP, DDVP, Minirin, and Stimate nasal spray)*. Retrieved February 4, 2008, from www.fda.gov/cder/drug/InfoSheets/HCP/desmopressinHCP.htm

World Health Organization. (2007). *International Classification of Diseases (ICD-10) F98.0 and F98.1 Nonorganic enuresis and encopresis*. Retrieved March 22, 2013 from: a www.who.int/classifications/icd/en/GRNBOOK.pdf

Related Topic

Chapter 85, "Principles of Treatment the Behaviorally Disordered Child"

83 TREATING VETERANS AND MILITARY FAMILIES

Marjan Ghahramanlou-Holloway and Jennifer L. Bakalar

To develop a solid treatment plan for veterans and their family members, a provider must first conduct a comprehensive psychological assessment of the individual(s) seeking services. In particular, providers must pay attention to unique military stressors as well as the onset or exacerbation of psychological symptoms following initiation and throughout military service (e.g., increased irritability and labile mood during postdeployment reintegration). The checklist that follows provides guidance on psychological assessment data that should be collected from veterans and/or military family members when they present for care. Providers must use clinical judgment and be mindful that assessment should not be limited to the items mentioned here.

- *Military service data*: branch of service, rank, years of service, time in grade, number and location of deployment(s), military promotion and/or legal problems, disciplinary actions, approximate discharge date, type of discharge, benefits coverage.
- *Relevant stressors during and/or following military service*: exposure to traumatic events and/or combat, sexual assault, harassment, frequent relocations, loss of rank due to demotion, legal problems such as Article 15 or other Uniform Code of Military Justice (UCMJ) violation, financial problems, interpersonal difficulties with superiors, relationship problems, intimate partner violence, dual military couple status, satisfaction with military career and current placement, medical injuries and pain, psychiatric diagnosis associated with service, loss, shame, survivor guilt, sexual orientation, sleep disruption, medical amputation, traumatic brain injury, exposure to toxic substances, reintegration and adjustment to civilian life, perceived support from local Veterans Administration medical setting and/or military resources, inpatient psychiatric hospitalization, history of suicide-related ideation and/or behaviors, perceived and actual barriers to care, stigma related to mental health and help seeking, concerns about continuity of care, homelessness.

TREATMENT CONSIDERATIONS

Veterans and military families face significant stressors, especially during times of high operational tempo, postdeployment reintegration, and following the transition back to civilian life. In addition to the fact that most military marriages and childbirths occur earlier in life than for civilians, these stressors can place a heavy burden on the individual and the family unit. Therefore, it is not surprising that empirical studies indicate that veterans and their families (e.g., spouses, parents, children) are at risk for psychiatric disorders, including mood, anxiety, sleep, eating, sexual, adjustment, and/or substance-use disorders (e.g., Mansfield et al., 2010). Additionally, emerging evidence suggests that such psychiatric disorders may be addressed by working directly with the veterans and/or their loved ones on family-related problems. While it is beyond the scope of this entry to review all of the clinical tools available for veterans and their families, the section below provides a brief summary of key areas of treatment conceptualization and planning. For more detailed information on Department of Veterans Affairs and Department of Defense Practice Guidelines, refer to www.healthquality.va.gov/.

Psychoeducation

One of the most important evidence-informed practices that we recommend for this population is psychoeducation because it is often the impetus for treatment engagement. In a recent report (Buchanan, Kemppainen, Smith, MacKain, & Cox, 2011) of veterans and their female spouses, two-thirds of the spouses surveyed reported that they did not receive any formal education about posttraumatic stress disorder (PTSD). Recent research (Gewirtz, Polusny, DeGarmo, Khaylis, & Erbes, 2010) indicates that in addition to the symptoms, causes, and treatments available for PTSD, it may be helpful for military family members to know that PTSD symptoms are associated with parenting challenges and this relationship is independent of the impact of the disorder on the military couple's adjustment. Furthermore, another illustrative example that highlights the importance of psychoeducation can be found in the 2010 Department of Defense Task Force Report on the Prevention of Suicide Among the Armed Forces. The task force found that military families generally do not receive much-needed education on suicide prevention and yet they are often the first individuals to detect signs of distress in their loved one. Psychologists can maximize the quality of the psychoeducation they provide by staying informed about the new scientific literature in the military mental health field and actively participating in continuing education opportunities (see offerings provided by the Center for Deployment Psychology at Uniformed Services University of the Health Sciences, http://deploymentpsych.org/).

Acceptance

Military-related stressors may have an immediate and/or gradual impact on veterans and their family members, underscoring the importance of personal acceptance and the ability to move forward despite difficulties. For instance, depression has been documented among military spouses (e.g., Verdeli et al., 2011) and the symptoms of depression may persist well after the veteran leaves the military. Deployment history appears to have a measurable impact on the elevation of depressive symptoms both during pregnancy and the postpartum period for military spouses (Smith, Munroe, Foglia, Nielsen, & Deering, 2010). Furthermore, depressive symptoms in military spouses may be exacerbated as a result of adjustment issues following separation, experiential avoidance by oneself and/or one's partner, and psychological and/or physical aggression within the relationship.

A recent study (Reddy, Meis, Erbes, Polusny, & Compton, 2011) indicated that experiential avoidance, which describes the attempt to suppress unwanted thoughts and emotions, is related to impaired relationship adjustment in both sexes. In men, experiential avoidance was also associated with increased perpetration of physical aggression in intimate relationships. Therefore, one evidence-informed clinical recommendation for veterans and their spouses in the context of couples therapy is to evaluate and monitor experiential avoidance. Specifically, patients should be encouraged to develop a nonjudgmental awareness of internal mental states, including cognitions and associated images and ways to move toward acceptance. In this case, principles of Acceptance and Commitment Therapy (ACT) may be used effectively to help couples move in the direction of achieving their life goals and upholding their values while decreasing reliance on experiential avoidance strategies. For training options, refer to http://contextualpsychology.org/.

Promoting Adaptive Coping

Not surprisingly, depressive symptoms and experiential avoidance can place the veteran and/or his or her family members at risk for problematic coping behaviors such as substance use or abuse. While different models of intervention should be considered, the "Screening, Brief Intervention, Referral to Treatment" (SBIRT) model provides a theoretical framework and programmatic structure for addressing substance-related disorders. Screening can be conducted using well-established self-report and/or interview measures (e.g., Alcohol Use Disorders Identification Test [AUDIT], Drug Abuse Screening Test [DAST]). Brief interventions may include motivational interviewing strategies to increase the patient's awareness of substance use and its consequences in order to move the individual toward the desire for behavioral change. For patients exhibiting severe risk, brief treatment focusing on problem solving, psychoeducation, and building coping strategies is recommended until a formal referral for specialized treatment can be made. Referral for specialized treatment follows brief intervention in order to match the individual's need to the appropriate level of care based on the initial screening. For more information on SBIRT, please refer to the following Substance Abuse and Mental Health Services Administration (SAMHSA) Web site: www.samhsa.gov/prevention/SBIRT/index.aspx.

Safety

While some veterans and their families never encounter situations concerning the safety of self and/or others, most have been exposed to threatening events. Patients who have been deployed at least once may have experienced combat-related trauma and/or exposure to other types of violent events (e.g., killing of civilians, seeing a buddy killed). For some families, intimate partner violence and/or child maltreatment may be significant familial stressors that may go unreported for some time due to concerns about military-specific consequences. Such violence may begin to manifest when the veteran is adjusting to military life and/or transitioning back to civilian life. Alcohol-related problems in combination with PTSD symptoms may exacerbate conflict in the family environment and lead to further safety concerns. Other safety concerns may involve suicide-related ideation and/or behaviors due to psychological difficulties, relationship problems, and a range of other stressors briefly noted in the assessment section earlier. Military sexual trauma is yet another stressor that will have a deleterious effect on an individual's perceptions of safety.

An empirically informed treatment recommendation is for providers to sensitively address any perceived and/or actual threats to the safety of the patient and his or her family. In cases requiring immediate assistance, the provider's role is to ensure that the veteran and/or his or her family members receive services in a timely manner to promote safety and prevent injury or death. For instance, safety planning is a clinical strategy that can be easily implemented. In collaboration and with the guidance of the provider, the identified patient outlines a detailed plan for how best to respond to future crisis events such as imminent suicide risk. For a sample clinician guide to safety planning with suicidal veterans and/or their family members, refer to www.returningveterans.org/sites/default/files/VA_SafetyPlan_quickguide.pdf).

Social Support

The military capitalizes on the value and strength of working as a team where service members always look out for each other; military training emphasizes effective teamwork. However, in reality, after reintegration into civilian life, many veterans experience a significant reduction in the size of their social support network. This loss, in addition to other losses (e.g., death of a peer, relationship termination), may result in loneliness, isolation, and/or feelings of emptiness and boredom, which can subsequently lead to onset and/or exacerbation of psychiatric symptoms. In his Interpersonal Psychological Theory of Suicide, Dr. Thomas Joiner, a prominent suicidologist, proposes that thwarted belongingness may be one of three important factors that precipitate suicide (along with capability for self-harm and a perception of being a burden to others). Joiner's Interpersonal Theory has been supported by recent published research that examined these constructs in military and veteran populations.

Therefore, one important evidence-informed treatment recommendation is to encourage patients to explore opportunities to bolster the breadth of their social support network in addition to fostering interactions with individual members of the network. Psychologists may note that some veterans and their family members simply do not have anyone within their circle to truly rely on due to factors such as frequent relocation and/or high turnover. Group therapy, referral to support groups, and/or encouragement to participate in community-based volunteer programs may promote a sense of connection and purpose. Additionally, veterans and their families may consciously or unconsciously contribute to conflict in their relationships, which may be partly or mostly related to stressors experienced over the course of service. Psychologists can teach effective communication and conflict resolution skills, which are necessary to resolve relationship conflict and to promote healthier relationships in the future.

Reducing Perceived Stigma and Barriers to Care

An open dialogue and empathic understanding of the unique concerns of veterans and their family members may serve as the foundation of support that psychologists should provide to this vulnerable population. Many veterans may view seeking treatment as a sign of personal failure and weakness. Psychologists are in a unique position to provide support and potentially shape cognitions (e.g., "I have served my country well and I now deserve to serve myself and my family.") that may increase help-seeking behaviors. For example, simply normalizing reactions and providing psychoeducation about symptoms and treatment options may help reduce perceived stigma. Integrative and collaborative clinical care efforts with primary care providers may be beneficial as well. Moreover, gender and cultural factors must be carefully considered in the context of psychological assessment and treatment delivery (e.g., review Ghahramanlou-Holloway, Cox, Fritz, & George, 2011 for treatment of military women and veterans). Finally, psychologists are encouraged to take a nondefensive stance and try to actively validate veterans' experiences and concerns associated with the delivery of care. In such cases, one genuinely caring provider can make a significant difference in minimizing attrition and maximizing treatment engagement, compliance, and follow-up.

Veterans and military families have sacrificed a great deal to perform their duties. Psychologists have an important role in helping veterans heal from the wounds of war and the possible negative experiences that were associated with and/or defined their military service. While most veterans and their families first present for services with complex issues (i.e., after waiting too long to seek help), none of the clinical challenges are expected to be insurmountable. Each psychologist's ethical responsibility is to acquire ongoing education and training in how to best serve this unique subset of the population.

References and Readings

Buchanan, C., Kemppainen, J., Smith, S., MacKain, S., & Cox, C. W. (2011). Awareness of posttraumatic stress disorder in veterans: A female spouse/intimate partner perspective. *Military Medicine*, *176*(7), 743–751.

Gewirtz, A. H., Polusny, M. A., DeGarmo, D. S., Khaylis, A., & Erbes, C. R. (2010). Posttraumatic stress symptoms among National Guard soldiers deployed to Iraq: Associations with parenting behaviors and couple adjustment. *Journal of Consulting and Clinical Psychology, 78*(5), 599–610.

Ghahramanlou-Holloway, M., Cox, D., Fritz, L., & George, B. (2011). An evidence informed guide for working with military women and veterans. *Professional Psychology: Research and Practice, 42*, 1–7.

Hall, L. (2008). *Counseling military families: What mental health professionals need to know.* New York: Routledge.

Mansfield, A. J., Kaufman, J. S., Marshall, S. W., Gaynes, B. N., Morrissey, J. P., & Engel, C. C. (2010). Deployment and the use of mental health services among U.S. Army wives. *New England Journal of Medicine, 362*(2), 101–109.

Reddy, M. K., Meis, L. A., Erbes, C. R., Polusny, M. A., & Compton, J. S. (2011). Associations among experiential avoidance, couple adjustment, and interpersonal aggression in returning Iraqi war veterans and their partners. *Journal of Clinical and Consulting Psychology, 79*(4), 515–520.

Smith, D. C., Munroe, M. L., Foglia, L. M., Nielsen, P. E., & Deering, S. H. (2010). Effects of deployment on depression screening scores in pregnancy at an army military treatment facility. *Obstetrics and Gynecology, 116*(3), 679–684.

Verdeli, H., Baily, C. Vousoura, E., Belser, A., Singla, D., & Manos, G. (2011). The case for treating depression in military spouses. *Journal of Family Psychology, 25*(4), 488–496.

Related Topics

Chapter 5, "Assessing Suicidal Risk"Chapter 36, "Treating and Managing Care of the Suicidal Patient"

Chapter 76, "Conducting Couple and Family Therapy"

84 ASSESSING AND TREATING AUTISM SPECTRUM DISORDERS

James A. Mulick and Courtney E. Rice

Autism spectrum disorders (ASDs) are neurodevelopmental disorders often characterized by significant developmental delays in language and communication skills, abnormalities in language when it does develop, significant impairment in reciprocal social behavior, a restricted and narrow repertoire of interests and behavior, ritualized and repetitive behavior patterns, and stereotyped, often socially disruptive behavior problems. Diagnosing an ASD is not a straightforward process. No single biological marker or laboratory test or procedure exists to identify children with an ASD. Although the diagnosis is primarily a behavioral one based upon a comprehensive history, direct observation, and standardized assessment, any psychologist conducting an assessment of a child suspected of meeting criteria for an ASD should also recommend that the child's family or caregivers seek medical evaluation to rule out specific known causes of expressed behaviors as well as formal speech/language, fine, and gross motor evaluation. Medical evaluation has been discussed in Filipek and colleagues (2000), and the more recent investigation of metabolic and genetic factors in etiology has been discussed in Zecavati and Spence (2009).

ASSESSING FOR AUTISM SPECTRUM DISORDERS

- *History and current concerns.* It is essential to administer a semistructured interview to obtain a comprehensive medical, developmental, and psychosocial history as well as to identify the family's current concerns. An evaluator should document birth and neonatal history, developmental milestones, and any developmental regression. When obtaining historical information, review communication, social and behavioral development, and current functioning within these three areas. There should be a discussion of the individual's play and leisure skills, especially noting the presence of any repetitive or restricted aspects of these characteristics as well as the level of adaptive functioning. Inquire about the presence of any of the following problems: self-injury, pica, feeding or sleeping disorders, seizures, excessive irritability, or extreme hyperactivity. Review all available records (e.g., medical, school, previous testing, intervention reports).
- *Child observation.* Create a context in which to observe the child's social communication behavior, play, and preferences. These observations should occur during the clinical interview with the family or caregiver and during direct testing. The use of a direct observational instrument, such as the *Autism Diagnostic Observation Schedule,* Second Edition (ADOS-2), is beneficial because it is designed to include multiple opportunities for social interaction and communication that elicit spontaneous behavior in standardized contexts. These conditions permit symptoms of ASD to be noted if they occur. It is considered a "gold standard" method of assessment in both research and clinical practice, and it can be used in clinical settings as long as the examiner has had appropriate training. Similarly, the *Childhood Autism Rating Scale-2* (CARS-2) is a structured observation instrument that is used to rate behavior during the evaluation process. The CARS-2 can also be used with parents and teachers to discover whether behaviors observed during assessment were consistent with child's behavior in other settings. The highly structured conditions associated with testing protocols can suppress patterns of behavior seen in autism during unstructured conditions.
- *Direct testing.* A comprehensive evaluation will consist of intellectual, language, academic, and adaptive behavior assessment. The level of intellectual functioning is negatively correlated with severity of autistic symptoms. Severe symptoms suppress the child's ability to acquire skills, to function adaptively, and conversely high intellectual functioning is one of the best predictors, in addition to good language functioning, of positive long-term outcome.

The results of psychometric testing are used to generate a profile of strengths and weaknesses, to facilitate educational planning, to determine eligibility for educational or publicly funded services, and to suggest prognosis. There are several commonly used tests for children with low mental age (e.g., those who are younger, nonverbal, or who have moderate to severe intellectual disability) such as the *Leiter International Performance Scales—Revised (Leiter-R),* the *Differential Abilities Scales-II,* the *Bayley Scales of Infant Development-III,* and the *Mullen Scales of Early Learning.* Higher functioning children are typically able to complete more standard measures of intellectual functioning (e.g., the *Wechsler Intelligence Scales for Children-IV, Stanford-Binet Intelligence Scale-5th edition*). Because major cognitive assessment batteries are based on spoken instructions and children with ASD often exhibit poor verbal comprehension, thorough assessment may require administration of a spoken-language-based measure like the Stanford-Binet *and* the Leiter-R for a complete picture.

There are a variety of instruments to assess language skills, which range from picture vocabulary tests to tests that assess receptive and expressive language abilities. A referral for a comprehensive speech and language evaluation is often helpful to generate specific recommendations for treatment. Children with adequate language abilities may still exhibit deficits in the social use of language. Evaluation of pragmatic communication is warranted to assess nonverbal behaviors, turn taking, and understanding inferences and figurative expressions.

Assessment of academic knowledge is helpful for the purposes of educational decision making. Look for academic strengths that may augment or mask other personal weaknesses. Include appropriate batteries that highlight both academic strengths and weaknesses to interpret the learning patterns they suggest and communicate that information to the family and school with appropriate recommendations. Younger children often show gaps in word knowledge or syntax that render understanding of group instruction in classroom settings difficult and detection of such deficiencies is important. In such cases augmentation of presentations with redundant visual cues, sequenced pictorial instructions, and diagrams should be provided.

Assessment of adaptive functioning should always accompany intellectual testing to determine whether a diagnosis of intellectual disability is merited. Use information gathered from adaptive behavior measures, such as the *Vineland Adaptive Behavior Scales-II,* to set appropriate treatment goals to further independence in activities of daily living and to determine how much supervision is required during these activities. The pattern most often observed in ASD is lower communication and socialization scores together with higher self-help scores and relatively intact motor skills.

- *Parent/teacher rating scales.* Use parent and teacher rating scales to assess behavioral characteristics of ASD (e.g., *Autism Spectrum Rating Scale, Social Communication Questionnaire, Social Responsiveness Scale*) that are present in the home and school environment. Additionally, other measures of more general behavioral and mental health functioning (e.g., *Child Behavior Checklist, Behavioral Assessment for Children-2, Aberrant Behavior Checklist, Conners-3, Conners Early Childhood*) should be a component of the assessment to aid in comorbid and differential diagnosis. Behavior problems in this population include social avoidance, compulsions, aggression, self-injury, stereotypy, and unusual or strong aversions or preferences for sensory stimulation.
- *Additional components.* Depending on the referral question, the goal of assessment, and practical constraints, comprehensive evaluation would most likely include an assessment of the family functioning (e.g., parenting stress), the family support network in place, and the evaluation of response to treatment. Once observations, direct testing, and report measures are complete, preliminary evaluation may reveal the need for additional data to answer questions arising during assessment. If no further information is required to complete the planned evaluation, full consideration of the findings and their implications should precede actually meeting with the family to discuss the results. It is helpful to prepare the written report in advance, with the stipulation that alterations or addenda may be required later for clarification or elaboration of points raised during the information-sharing session.
- *Conveying results.* The initial assessment leading to a diagnosis or classification of the child with an ASD is an anxiety-laden experience. The most important outcome of assessment and its interpretation, interventions in their own right, is the movement of the family and child toward effective ameliorative and preventative interventions and professional services. The practitioner must be familiar enough with the specific assessment tools used and general standards for psychological and educational testing to be able to discuss and explain them frankly, including their practical value and limitations, in everyday language. Candor and truthfulness are essential in presenting results and recommendations. Intended meaning cannot be taken for granted; rather, it must be explored through the use of requests for family reaction or exchange of interpretative views. Technical and diagnostic terms should be introduced and used appropriately, with explanation and qualification insofar as the degree of certainty

requires. Predictions that can be supported should be provided. Environmental conditions during the information-sharing session are important. Care should be taken to create a setting conducive to the exchange of complex and emotionally laden ideas. Evidence that the practitioner is busy or preoccupied will not be conducive to understanding and comfort. Discourse is often facilitated by opening the discussion with concrete recollections of events that occurred during the evaluation. Restating the family's primary concerns solicits their active participation, indicates caring, and conveys the impression that the purpose of the evaluation is to help. Time, however, is limited, so guiding the discussion away from repetition and following a planned format toward a natural summary and a request for feedback from the family. Scheduling follow-up sessions may sometimes be necessary as a result of apparent discomfort or clearly unresolved issues. It is useful to offer alternative sources of information, such as support and advocacy groups, information agencies, books, and credible Web sites.

TREATING AUTISM SPECTRUM DISORDERS

Historically ASDs have been a difficult set of disorders to treat. Children with ASD often function within the impaired range of general intellectual ability, failing to benefit from conventional social and educational therapy. Once a child has been diagnosed with an ASD, it is imperative to implement effective intervention services. Within the context of this book, it not feasible to delineate in detail the necessary components of comprehensive treatment for an individual with an ASD. Therefore, a series of broad guidelines will be provided. Practitioners should utilize the resources at the end of this section to gain further knowledge in this area.

- *Defining desirable outcomes.* Operationalizing long-term goals is a good and necessary place to start. These goals should reflect the parent's desires for his or her child, as well as determining some appropriate societal goals so that the individual's behavior conforms to some general social expectations. Institutional goals, typically within the context of education, will also be a part of this process. Practitioners must be able to articulate what type of educational setting is appropriate, the type of classroom that would be sufficient to learn and socialize in, and the type of instruction that would be optimal for learning skills. Short-term goals would consist of the child's readiness for learning, and specific cognitive and academic skills to acquire. Other factors such as practical life and work skill goals as well as behavior management gains should also be considered.
- *Early intensive behavioral intervention (EIBI).* An early intensive behavioral intervention (EIBI) program will greatly improve the outlook for most young children with autism by targeting the core behavioral deficits and excesses with individualized strategies. This comprehensive intervention, using the principles of applied behavior analysis (ABA), has become the standard psychological and educational treatment for children with ASDs. When delivered early, during the sensitive period for language acquisition and foundational aspects of brain organization from the preschool period up to about 7 or 8 years, recovery of delayed overall learning can occur. Intensive behavioral intervention is gradual, systematic, intensive, and errorless. An intensity of 25–40 hours per week of treatment is typically provided for at least 2 years. It involves one-on-one work with a therapist, addresses a broad range of skills, including cognitive (e.g., generalized imitation, discrimination, matching), language, adaptive behavior, and motor skills. Individualized instruction maintains attending and performance via immediacy, minimizes practicing errors, and can shape behavior via successive approximation. The goal is to maximize the intensity of instruction (i.e., the number of hours/days of treatment) to achieve an efficient accelerated rate

of acquisition and to displace the practice of autistic behavior. Competent clinicians will use a well-sequenced hierarchical curriculum to target behavioral deficits and symptomatic excesses. A well-developed program will address the following in the behavioral treatment of children with an ASD: the lack of responsiveness to people, the severe language impairment, the resistance to change, extreme inattention, little or no appropriate play, unusual reactions to normal environmental stimulation, self-stimulation, and uneven development.

- *Treating high-functioning autism/Asperger's disorder.* For children with this type of ASD profile, intensive behavioral intervention is typically not required. Children with HFA or Asperger's disorder would most likely benefit from classroom and school-based interventions that address the social and behavioral aspects of impairment. Targeted academic intervention focusing on time management skills, organization of materials, planning for short and long-term assignments, and any academic weaknesses (i.e., identified learning disability, difficulty with more abstract conceptual learning) should be components of treatment. Other aspects of intervention include social skill development, anger management, friendship finding, and counseling to address feelings of anxiety and/or depression, which are commonly comorbid in this population.
- *Parent training.* Remediation of language and social skill deficits must be maintained in the everyday environment if they are ever to become fluent and internalized. Parent or caregiver training in the basics of behavior change technology has become an essential component of the long-term success of treatment. Parents with a good understanding of the behavior principles such as reinforcement/punishment, extinction, motivating operations, errorless learning, prompting, shaping, chaining, and task analysis will be better equipped to intervene with their child. Modeling and coaching of techniques is essential when working with parents. Teaching parents the value of data collection during training, such as collecting antecedent-behavior-consequence (ABC) data, collecting discrete trial data, and completing a task analysis are all helpful. Parent-delivered interventions can enhance generalization of skills, efficiency of delivery, and increase self-efficacy.
- *Psychopharmacology.* There are no pharmacologic treatments for the core symptoms of autism spectrum disorders. Psychopharmacologic intervention is, however, useful in the amelioration of some commonly associated conditions. These conditions include irritability for which some of the atypical neuroleptics may be helpful, and impaired attention and concentration for which the psychostimulants may be helpful. Some of the serotonin reuptake inhibitors may sometimes be helpful for social anxiety or compulsions, and a number of drugs helpful for mood stabilization have also been proposed as useful.
- *Fad treatments.* All too often families become prey to purveyors of treatment fads, outright frauds, and unsubstantiated remedies. In general, any treatment promising quick, effortless, or unconventional approaches should be treated with skepticism. Long-standing behavioral characteristics are best remediated through the acquisition of new and more effective ways of behaving, and this is most directly achieved through behavior analytic interventions. Behavior changes in real time and as a result of systematic effort. It is the practitioner's responsibility to have sufficient awareness of the process of science and to assist the families in understanding what constitutes evidence-based treatment. Kay and Vyse (2005) suggest if talking and education are not enough to dissuade families from using unsupported treatments, a practitioner may suggest the family collect data to determine the value of the alternative treatment for their own child. If presented properly, the proposition of an empirical test can diffuse conflict and provide a shared goal for both the family and the practitioner.

References and Readings

Association for Science in Autism Treatment. (n.d.). Retrieved January 2013, from www.asatonline.org

Cambridge Center for Behavioral Studies. (n.d.). *Autism and ABA*. Retrieved from, www.behavior.org/autism/

Chawarska, K., Klin, A., & Volkmar, F. R. (2008). *Autism spectrum disorders in infants and toddlers: Diagnosis, assessment, and treatment.* New York: Guilford Press.

Eldevik, S., Hastings, R. P., Hughes, J. C., Jahr, E., Eikeseth, S., & Cross, S. (2009). Meta-Analysis of early intensive behavioral intervention for children with autism. *Journal of Clinical and Adolescent Psychiatry, 38*(3), 439–450.

Filipek, P. A., Accardo, P. J., Ashwal, S., Baranek, G. T., Cook, E. H., Jr., Dawson, G.,...Volkmar, F. R. (2000). Practice parameters: Screening and diagnosis of autism. Report of the quality standards subcommittee of the American Academy of Neurology and the Child Neurology Society. *Neurology, 55*, 468–479.

Goldstein S., Naglieri, J. A., & Ozonoff, S. (Eds.). (2009). *Assessment of autism spectrum disorders*. New York: Guilford Press.

Kay, S., & Vyse, S. (2005). Helping parents separate the wheat from the chaff: Putting autism treatments to the test. In J. Jacobson, R. M. Foxx, & J. A. & Mulick, (Eds.), *Controversial therapies for developmental disabilities: Fad, fashion, and science in professional practice* (pp. 265–277). New York: Erlbaum.

Mayville, E.A., & Mulick, J. A. (Eds.). (2011). *Behavioral foundations of effective autism treatment*. Cornwall-on-Hudson, NY: Sloan.

Organization for Autism Research. (2010). Retrieved January 2013, from www.researchautism.org//index.asp

Zecavati, N., & Spence, S. (2009). Neurometabolic disorders and dysfunction in autism spectrum disorders. *Current Neurology and Neuroscience Reports, 9*, 129–136.

Related Topic

Chapter 85, "Principles of Treatment with the Behaviorally Disordered Child"

PART V

Child and Adolescent Treatment

85 TREATING THE BEHAVIORALLY DISORDERED CHILD

Sheila M. Eyberg

Psychosocial treatments for children are changing rapidly in concert with the expanding pace of research in child psychopathology and intervention. Despite changes in procedures, timing, and even targets of treatment within the same disorder, there are basic principles of psychotherapy that remain the same over time. This chapter describes a set of principles of effective psychosocial treatment for children with disruptive behavior that are useful to review when preparing to treat these children. The scope of this chapter is limited to children between 2 and 12 years of age whose problems are related to attention-deficit/hyperactivity disorder or disruptive behavior disorders, including oppositional defiant disorder and conduct disorder. The challenges these children and their families present to treatment are considerable. The following seven principles are designed to maximize treatment effectiveness.

ESTABLISH RAPPORT

To conduct effective psychotherapy with a disruptive child, the psychologist must first establish an ambiance of safety and comfort for the child in the therapeutic situation. Disruptive children may express their initial apprehensions by resistance or defiance of the unfamiliar situation in which they may not be voluntarily involved. Providing a structure for the child at the outset will reduce the child's anxiety and help to encourage participation. With a young child, for example, reading together *A Child's First Book about Play Therapy* (Nemiroff & Annunziata, 1990) may provide the 4- to 7-year-old with age-appropriate information about what takes place in psychotherapy. Older children also require age-appropriate information about the purpose and process of therapy, presented in a positive but noncoercive atmosphere of understanding and acceptance. To establish a therapeutic alliance, it is necessary to convey respect for the child and avoid any suggestion of judgment, such as siding with a third person or prematurely suggesting change.

Certain communication techniques help establish and maintain rapport. The use of paraphrasing, for example, by using either reflective or summary statements, conveys genuine interest and concern for the child. Paraphrasing also increases the child's willingness to provide information, and it enables the psychologist to verify understanding of that information. Phrasing questions in ways that avoid leading (e.g., closed-ended questions) or blaming (e.g., "why" questions) helps the child feel at ease and increases the child's willingness to engage. With disruptive children, key strategies for managing behavior must be used as well. The psychologist must begin at the first encounter to provide age-appropriate praise for "positive opposites"—behaviors that are incompatible with the child's known problem behaviors. At the same time, it is important that the psychologist *not* inadvertently reinforce verbalizations of any unacceptable behavior known to be part of the child's problem constellation. That might include, for example, not responding to a statement suspected to be untrue when it is known that lying is one of the child's problem behaviors. In this example, by changing the subject and verifying the child's statement later before considering the response, the psychologist can move forward productively while maintaining respect for both self and child.

ADDRESS PARENT MOTIVATION

Parent motivation is critical to a child's therapy. It usually determines the child's participation in treatment if only because parents generally must provide the transportation. In many additional ways, however, parent motivation remains critical to the child's attendance and progress in treatment. Therapy is inconvenient for parents in terms of their time, schedules, routines, and pocketbook. It is even more inconvenient if the parents feel embarrassed, angry, guilty, or stressed by their child's behavior. The sense of inconvenience is heightened for parents if they lack confidence in the effectiveness of the treatment. It is at least as essential that the psychologist motivate the parents as the child.

Parental motivation is strengthened by understanding. Before treatment begins, the psychologist needs to meet with the parents alone to review assessment results. It is important to explain the nature and likely causes of the child's disorder (to the extent this is known) and emphasize that the disorder can be treated. The psychologist needs to describe the treatment and the expected outcomes clearly and then check the accuracy of the parents' recall. The psychologist must also review with the parents the potential barriers to treatment participation and help them reach workable solutions before leaving. By the end of this meeting, the parents should have an understanding of the child's disorder, how it will be treated and their own role in the child's treatment. They should have realistic and positive expectations for the likely outcomes of treatment, and they should express motivation and commitment to follow-through.

CONSIDER DEVELOPMENTAL LEVEL

Children are constantly undergoing biological, cognitive, social, and affective changes. Childhood is a disjointed period of development during which there are rapid shifts in what is deemed appropriate in children's thinking, feeling, and behaving. Typical expressions children use in therapy would characterize maladjustment in children older or younger but have no clinical significance at the child's present age. Psychologists who work with children must have strong academic grounding in child development and must remain up to date on the fads and trends at different ages by observing normal children with their parents and peers and by examining children's media and other sources for developmental information.

Along with children's general developmental progression, there is often inconsistency in their rate of development across the various developmental domains. A 12-year-old may have a developmental spurt in motor skills yet show immature emotional development. In psychotherapy, cognitive development is a critical domain because of the many therapeutic techniques that rely on specific levels of cognitive competency. Even psychologists' perceptions of children's intellectual functioning may be skewed based on a child's attractiveness or verbosity. Although treatments that include a substantial cognitive component are generally better suited to school-age children than preschoolers, there are exceptions at every age. Intellectual assessment can help prevent false starts in treatment.

USE ASSESSMENT TO GUIDE TREATMENT

In addition to cognitive functioning, children's emotional and behavioral functioning is important to assess when selecting and implementing treatment. Many rating scales with strong reliability and validity now exist for diagnostic screening and more detailed measurement of severity within identified problem domains. Drawing upon multiple sources of information using well-standardized measures of emotional and behavioral functioning not only provides the psychologist with dependable information on the best targets for efficient intervention but also provides baseline information for tracking change.

Rating scales measuring the primary targets of intervention may be administered regularly during treatment. Monitoring change in key symptoms and behaviors has several advantages. First, it can provide feedback to the psychologist on the effectiveness of the intervention approach and can signal when a change in approach may be needed. The ratings across time can also be graphed to provide feedback for parents to reinforce their participation, particularly if based on a parent's own ratings. Finally, ratings on standardized scales can show when targeted symptoms reach the non-problem range, indicating the need to review treatment goals and perhaps to begin preparation for termination.

MAINTAIN TREATMENT INTEGRITY

Integrity refers to the accuracy of application of the intended treatment. It can be challenging to maintain treatment integrity for a number of reasons. One reason is the inevitable "crisis" that children and families bring into treatment to obtain the psychologist's help. There are times when the psychologist must abandon the treatment plan and provide support and crisis intervention. However, when following empirically supported protocols, the psychologist must be mindful that although dealing with the crisis will set back progress toward the established goals, it is not wise to attempt including both "therapies" in the same session. A crisis session should be devoted to the crisis, and the established treatment plan can be resumed effectively in the next session. If a family has repeated crises, it is best to refer them to another therapist for crisis management so that the treatment of the child's disorder can be accomplished effectively.

Veering off the protocol of an evidence-based treatment, for any reason, is likely to be unproductive. These treatments are generally based on decades of research and testing of each component and its variations. Although it can be tempting to follow a hunch that some alternative procedure would work better for a particular child, a psychologist should resist doing so. After having experience with five to ten cases "by the book," psychologists will come to trust the treatment and become proficient in tailoring its components to the needs of each individual child.

ABIDE BY THE TREATMENT THEORY

Thoroughly understanding the theory that underlies a treatment is another critically important principle of psychotherapy. It is similar in ways to treatment integrity, but it is particularly pertinent to everything that occurs in the therapy session that is *not* written in the protocol. In every session, children present unique issues that psychologists must respond to. These are the times when the theory guides what is an "okay" or "not okay" response. Families become familiar with the theory guiding changes that occur by experiencing its application week after week. Without theoretical consistency in the psychologist's responses, the confusion transferred to the child and family not only affects treatment progress but also threatens the therapeutic relationship.

PLAN FOR TREATMENT GENERALIZATION

Generalization occurs when changes in the targeted behaviors lead to changes in nontargeted behaviors and in settings beyond the setting in which they are learned. For example, a psychologist might use parent-training sessions to target changes in child responses to parental commands. The child's new behaviors may then generalize to compliance with teachers. To ensure lasting treatment effects, it is important to program generalization explicitly to situations beyond the therapy room. Psychologists can include generalization practice of newly learned behaviors in real-life settings during the therapy hour, although this procedure may be impractical. It is more common for the psychologist to devote the child's last few sessions to teaching the parents how to reinforce the new behaviors at home and in public.

The principles presented in this chapter address the treatment of children with disruptive behaviors. These principles address elements important to effective treatment and include establishing a working alliance with the child and family, maintaining adherence to treatment theory and procedures, tailoring treatment to the child through careful assessment and monitoring of child progress, and programming generalization. The principles are broadly applicable to psychosocial treatments across theoretical orientation and targeted problem areas. They highlight attention to both the uniqueness of the child and family and the shared characteristics of children in treatment. By following these principles, psychologists treating children and families can heighten the likelihood of therapeutic success.

References and Readings

Boggs, S. R., & Eyberg, S. M. (2008). Positive attention. In W. O'Donohue & J.D. Fisher (Eds.), *Cognitive behavior therapy: Applying empirically supported techniques in your practice* (2nd ed., pp. 396–401). New York: Wiley.

Eyberg, S. M., Schuhmann, E., & Rey, J. (1998). Psychosocial treatment research with children and adolescents: Developmental issues. *Journal of Abnormal Child Psychology, 26,* 71–82.

Nemiroff, M. A., & Annunziata, J. (1990). *A child's first book about play therapy.* Washington, DC: American Psychological Association.

Querido, J., Eyberg, S. M., Kanfer, R., & Krahn, G. (2001). Process variables in the child clinical assessment interview. In C. E. Walker & M. C. Roberts (Eds.), *Handbook of clinical child psychology* (3rd ed., pp. 75–89). New York: Wiley.

Related Topics

Chapter 82, "Enuresis and Encopresis"

Chapter 84, "Assessing and Treating Autism Spectrum Disorders"

86 HELPING CHILDREN COPE WITH CHRONIC MEDICAL ILLNESS

Lauren Mednick

The term *chronic medical condition* refers to an enduring state of medical illness that requires ongoing management and has the potential to interfere with normal development and long-term functioning. Although chronic medical conditions differ in severity and chronicity, there are many commonalities related to the psychological impact on a patient (e.g., multiple doctors' visits, following a medical regimen, invasive medical procedures, feeling socially isolated). The ultimate goal in working with children diagnosed with chronic medical conditions is to help them manage the obstacles associated with their disease, while continuing to progress with normative developmental tasks. To this end, the majority of children diagnosed with chronic medical conditions tend to cope most effectively when they have the following characteristics:

- They are involved in their treatment and age-appropriate health-related discussions. This encourages an age-appropriate understanding of their medical condition, promotes developing a sense of control, and fosters age-appropriate responsibility for their care.
- They are encouraged to share their concerns related to their medical condition and treatment.
- They are supported in spending time with friends and engaging in normative age-appropriate activities.
- They are assisted in sharing information about their medical condition with their friends and family.
- They are aided in finding ways to meet other children with similar medical conditions (e.g., camps, events sponsored by specific illness foundations, one-to-one meeting facilitated by a clinician), which are aimed at decreasing feelings of social isolation.
- They are taught and encouraged to use coping and problem-solving skills to deal with difficulties related to their medical condition.

When a child is having significant problems adjusting to and coping with factors related to his or her medical illness, specific interventions can be implemented that take into account factors related to the child's particular medical condition and individual and family characteristics. In addition to helping them effectively cope with the general stress of having a chronic medical condition, problems frequently addressed as part of psychotherapy with these children and their families often include the following: increasing adherence to their medical regimen, managing chronic and acute pain, and receiving preparation for invasive medical procedures.

INCREASING ADHERENCE TO MEDICAL REGIMENS

Children with chronic medical illness must often complete many tasks related to caring for their condition (e.g., taking oral medications, sticking to a specific diet, attending medical appointments). Medical adherence involves an agreement between medical advice and the patient's actions in regard to his or her medical care. The term *adherence* is preferred over the term *compliance*, as it implies an active role with the patient working in collaboration with the provider, rather than a passive role with the patient following the commands of the provider. On average, research with various illness populations suggests that the prevalence of poor adherence to medical regimens in children with chronic medical conditions is 50% or more (Kahana, Drotar, & Frazier, 2008). Helping to improve adherence to medical regimens is critical to avoiding serious adverse consequences (e.g., symptom exacerbations, repeated hospitalizations, poor school attendance, disease related complications, and death).

Due to the complexity associated with management of many chronic medical conditions, it is essential to recognize that adherence is not a yes/no trait (either adherent or not), but rather occurs on a continuum in which adherence varies within (e.g., may take morning pills but often forgets nighttime pills) and between (e.g., always takes pills, but frequently misses injections) the various aspects of a child's medical regimen. Thus, in determining a child's level of adherence, it is important to evaluate his or her behavior concerning each aspect of the medical regimen. Furthermore, to develop an effective intervention aimed at improving adherence, it is necessary to identify the factors associated with why the child is having difficulty following the prescribed medical plan. Interventions that do not consider the specific barrier to adherence will have limited success (see Table 86.1 for common barriers and suggested interventions).

TABLE 86.1. Common Barriers to Adherence and Suggested Interventions

Barrier	Intervention
Lack of understanding concerning regimen implementation or importance	Provide age-appropriate education
Forgetfulness	Set alarms; use visual reminders
Inconvenience	Work with the medical team to change the regimen to fit better with the child's lifestyle
Inconsistent schedule of medication	Implement a reminder system (e.g., alarms); use a self-monitoring chart to document completion of tasks
Side effects of treatment	Find ways to help minimize or cope with the side effects
Length of treatment	Help the child find activities to do to during the treatment
Complicated regimen	Simplify regimen (with medical team); create a self-monitoring chart to document completion of each task
Social stigma	Engage the child in treatment aimed at improving self-esteem; encourage the child to meet other children with similar medical conditions
Poor supervision	Increase adult involvement and monitoring
Cultural or religious beliefs	Work with family to understand their beliefs and when possible work with the medical team to adapt treatments to fit within their values
Psychiatric illness	Treat underlying psychiatric illness
Family psychopathology	Work with caretakers to create an environment that is conducive to encouraging adherence (e.g., decreased conflict, increased communication)
Poor social support	Help the child/family find resources within their disease community

In general, effective interventions aimed at improving adherence usually do the following:

- Incorporate behavioral or multiple strategies (e.g., education, increased monitoring), as these have a more significant impact on improving adherence then educational interventions alone (Christophersen & Mortweet, 2001; Kahana et al., 2008)
- Include children and their parents in the development
- Start from where the child is at, gradually increasing goals, while working toward the ideal
- Need revision over time

Operant techniques also may be useful to increase a child's cooperation with adhering to his or her medical regimen (La Greca & Mackey, 2009). Reinforcement in the form of verbal praise, stickers, small toys, privileges, or other incentives may help to motivate a child to cooperate. Moreover, by pairing a positive outcome (e.g., sticker, toy) with an aversive stimuli (e.g., injection), the child develops a positive association with the aversive event, thereby increasing the likelihood of cooperation in the future. Some parents may have cultural or familial beliefs that make them uncomfortable with the idea of rewarding their child for cooperating with an expected, necessary task. It may be useful to help these parents think of the reward as a motivator. The goal of a motivator is not to "bribe" the child to cooperate, but rather to help create a positive association with adhering to the medical regimen. This concept is not so dissimilar from adults being motivated to go to work each day in order to earn a paycheck. Taking the medication for the child is like his or her work, and having an immediate, salient motivator may help the child to cooperate. As the child gets older and gains the cognitive capacity to understand that the long-term reward of adherence will be better health and potentially living a longer life, an external motivator will likely be unnecessary.

For young children, cooperation can be increased by turning taking medication into a fun activity. For example, parents can play a simple game with their child (e.g., Candyland) and every time the child takes a turn he or she must take a sip of his or her medicine. Another game to play is a race against time (e.g., presenting a sand timer and telling the child to try to finish medication before all of the sand is at the bottom), so he or she can have a prize. This method is particularly useful for young children, as they have not yet developed a good concept of time.

Finally, as children of all ages benefit from feeling "in control," providing children with choices regarding their medical regimen when appropriate will help to improve cooperation. For example, children can be asked, "Do you want to take the medicine now or in 5 minutes?" or "Do you want the shot in your right or left arm?" Open-ended questions are less effective than providing the child with two specific choices. Importantly, when giving a child two choices, parents/clinicians must be comfortable with whichever option the child chooses.

MANAGING CHRONIC AND ACUTE PAIN

Children with chronic medical conditions frequently experience pain from medical procedures (acute) and their medical condition (chronic). Psychological treatment with children experiencing pain aims to teach them a variety of behavioral coping strategies to manage their pain and distress. In addition, children are taught to understand how their thoughts and behavior can influence how they experience pain. Effectiveness of a particular strategy will vary depending on characteristics of the child (e.g., child's age/developmental level, interest), parent, and type of pain; however, the most effective interventions for acute procedural pain include distraction, multicomponent cognitive-behavioral therapy interventions, and hypnosis (Uman, Chambers, McGrath, & Kisely, 2006), and the most effective interventions aimed at reducing the severity and frequency of chronic pain include relaxation and cognitive-behavioral therapy (Eccleston, Palermo, Williams, Lewandowski, & Morley, 2009). Often psychological treatment with children experiencing pain will include teaching more than one coping strategy. Children should be encouraged to indicate which strategies they prefer and instructed to practice these interventions while not experiencing significant pain and distress, as this will increase the likelihood of the child successfully using the technique to manage his or her pain.

Distraction and relaxation are two commonly used strategies taught to children to help them cope with pain and distress. Distraction involves a purposeful refocusing of attention from the painful, distressing aspects of a situation to less threatening thoughts, objects, sights, or sounds. The efficacy of distraction varies across types of situations and depending on the nature of the chosen distraction technique. In general, multisensory, active distraction is most efficacious as long as the stimulus is one that will sufficiently interest the child and keep her or him actively engaged (Blount et al., 2009). To this end, distraction techniques should be adapted to the child's interest and age/developmental level. Rocking, patting, sucking on a pacifier, or playing with a toy with lights and sounds can help distract an infant. Toddlers respond well to blowing bubbles, party blowers, and interactive books. With older children and adolescents, effective distraction techniques include listening to music, playing video games, working on riddles, or watching movies/television shows. Prompts from adults are helpful to facilitate coping behavior and redirect their attention away from their pain for younger children. Distraction is a technique that is most useful with acute, short-term pain, but it can also be used to help children cope with chronic pain.

Relaxation is a form of conditioning in which a child is taught to induce a physiological state that is incompatible with pain and distress. It is the most common behavioral procedure used in a variety of treatment protocols (Christophersen & Mortweet, 2001; Spirito & Kazak, 2006). Through relaxation, children can regulate their emotional and physical responses to pain by learning to reduce physiological changes associated with stress and pain (i.e., heart rate, breathing, temperature, and muscle tension). Frequently used relaxation strategies include deep breathing, guided imagery, and progressive muscle relaxation.

Often the first step in teaching children to relax involves instructing them in how to engage in diaphragmatic breathing. Rather than shallow chest breathing, children are taught to take breaths from their diaphragm, which leads to a deeper state of relaxation by focused attention on their breathing. Older children can be aided in accomplishing this task by instructing them to put their hand on their stomach and watch it move up and down. For younger children, the imagery of blowing a balloon or slowly blowing a large bubble may help them master this technique. Bubbles, pinwheels, party blowers, or kazoos can help children practice deep breathing. Importantly, children with certain medical conditions, such as pulmonary diseases, may find this technique challenging. For these children, engaging in this exercise may inadvertently lead to increased stress and frustration rather than relaxation.

Guided imagery exercises utilize imagination and visualization to help children focus their concentration away from their pain experience. Children can be guided to imagine themselves in a peaceful, relaxing place (real or imaginary) that is incompatible with pain. Prior to starting this imagery exercise, it is helpful to have children draw a picture of their place and describe what they see, hear, taste, smell, and feel when there. Children with pain may also benefit from imagining their pain transforming in some way (e.g., melting into their stomach rather than stabbing; turning down with a pain dial). Although there are numerous CDs, books, and websites with relaxation scripts, tailoring the imagery to the characteristics associated with a specific child (e.g., age, interests, medical condition, temperament) will enhance effectiveness.

Progressive muscle relaxation (PMR) involves tensing and relaxing the various muscle groups in the body. This technique aims to teach children the difference between feeling tense and feeling relaxed. Many younger children are likely to enjoy PMR more than imagery-based relaxation because it allows them to stay physically active. To help young children understand how to tense specific muscle groups, imagery-based scripts have been created utilizing helpful analogies (e.g., pretend you have two lemons in your hand and you want to squeeze them to make lemonade). PMR exercises are not appropriate to use with children diagnosed with certain medical conditions, such as musculoskeletal diseases which limit controlled movement.

For all relaxation exercises it is helpful to do the following:

- Explain to the child the rationale for engaging in the exercise.
- Expect some resistance in the beginning.
- Have the child rate his or her level of pain/distress both before and after the exercise.
- Explain to the child that like with any newly learned skill, he or she will get better at relaxation through practice.
- Make the child a CD so that he or she can practice on his or her own.
- Assign a practice schedule and even consider working toward earning a small reward.

Additional psychological interventions commonly used with children experiencing pain that require further training include hypnosis, biofeedback, and Acceptance and Commitment Therapy (ACT).

PREPARATION FOR INVASIVE MEDICAL PROCEDURES

Children diagnosed with chronic medical conditions are often the recipients of invasive medical procedures. Effective psychological interventions that focus on helping these children and their parents cope with these challenging medical procedures provide them with an increased sense of control and mastery. This will in turn help to minimize the pain resulting from procedures as well as decrease levels of anxiety prior to and during procedures. Effective preparation for medical procedures includes providing information, modeling, play, and teaching of pain coping strategies mentioned earlier.

The provision of information regarding upcoming procedures promotes accurate expectations and may provide the child with a degree of exposure that reduces anxiety to the potentially frightening medical intervention (Blount et al., 2009). Effective pre-procedural information also should include the following:

- A developmentally appropriate verbal explanation of what the child will see, hear, feel, and smell during, before, and after the procedure. This should include a reminder to the child that he or she will eventually return home, as this is a frequently overlooked piece of procedural information that can help children more adaptively cope with the stress of the procedure.
- Minimally threatening, but accurate information. Children who are given information that turns out not to be true (e.g., "You will not feel a thing" when in fact the child is likely to experience some pain) are more likely to develop a distrustful relationship with the medical team that may negatively affect future interactions.
- Use of visual aids (e.g., books, pictures, models, videos)
- Time for the child to ask questions

When to prepare a child for an upcoming medical intervention requires thoughtful consideration. Preparation provided too far in advance of the procedure may allow the child too much time to worry, think, and fantasize about the event. Moreover, too long of a delay between preparation and the procedure, especially with young children, may prevent children from linking the two events. However, preparation provided too close to the procedure does not allow the child enough time to process the material, ask relevant questions, and practice coping skills. From a developmental perspective (Blount et al., 2009):

- Children younger than 6 years old usually do best if prepared 1–2 days prior to the procedure.
- Children 6 years and older should be prepared for procedures about 1 week in advance.
- Adolescents usually do best when they are included from the beginning in the decision-making process regarding the planned medical intervention.

Parents should be involved in the preparation activities, as providing information and support to parents is likely to reduce parental anxiety, with positive indirect benefits for their children. Moreover, although older children are more independent, younger children frequently require direct help from adults to understand information and utilize coping skills.

In addition to describing the medical procedure to the child through words, books with pictures and medical play can further be utilized for preparation. Children can be taught about the procedure by using the equipment in role plays with a doll or another person. Alternatively, the equipment can be used in a nondirective manner, simply allowing the child to explore and feel comfortable around the equipment. Medical play is a particularly useful activity with younger children who learn best by doing. In general, real medical equipment should be used as part of these preparation strategies; however, some children may find real equipment overly threatening and prefer toy replicas.

References and Readings

Blount, R. L., Zempsky, W. T., Jaaniste, T., Evans, S., Cohen, L. L., Devine, K. A., & Zeltzer, L. K. (2009). Management of pediatric pain and distress due to medical procedures. In M. C. Roberts & R. G. Steele (Eds.), *Handbook of pediatric psychology* (4th ed., pp. 171–188). New York: Guilford Press.

Christophersen, E. R., & Mortweet, S. L. (2001). *Treatment with children that works*. Washington, DC: American Psychological Association.

Eccleston, C., Palermo, T. M., Williams, A. C. D. C., Lewandowski, A., & Morley, S. (2009). Psychological therapies for the management of chronic and recurrent pain in children and adolescents (review). *Cochrane Database of Systematic Reviews, 12*, CD003968.

Kahana, S., Drotar, D., & Frazier, T. (2008). Meta-analysis of psychological interventions in promote adherence to treatment in pediatric chronic conditions. *Journal of Pediatric Psychology, 33*(6), 590–611.

La Greca, A. M., & Mackey, E. R. (2009). Adherence to pediatric treatment regimens. In M. C. Roberts & R. G. Steele (Eds.), *Handbook of pediatric psychology* (4th ed., pp. 130–152). New York: Guilford Press.

Spirito, A., & Kazak, A. E. (2006). *Effective and emerging treatments in pediatric psychology*. New York: Oxford University Press.

Uman, L. S., Chambers, C. T., McGrath, P. J., & Kisely, S. (2006). Psychological interventions for needle-related procedural pain and distress in children and adolescents (review). *Cochrane Database of Systematic Reviews, 4*, CD005179.

Related Topic

Chapter 71, "Helping Patients Cope With Chronic Medical Illness"

87 ENGAGING THE RELUCTANT ADOLESCENT

Alice K. Rubenstein

While the majority of adolescents have been bribed, forced, or prodded into entering treatment, the reluctant adolescent poses the greatest challenge for the psychotherapist. Many treatment-reluctant adolescents often have great difficulty owning and verbalizing their problems, and they do not see how talking to someone whom they have never met before and who knows nothing about them can help. Herewith are 20 research-informed and practice-tested strategies for engaging reluctant adolescents in mental health treatment.

ADOPT AN INTEGRATIVE FRAMEWORK

The majority of difficulties facing adolescents today are systemic, requiring an integrative approach in regard to both diagnosis and treatment. Treating adolescents requires systemic interventions with a focus on here-and-now problem solving. Adolescents who are reluctant to enter treatment often believe that we have nothing to offer them. They assume we will not understand them, that we will align with their parents and other authority figures against them, and that we have no clue about their lives. Therefore, from the moment of first interaction, it is critical to communicate your allegiance to the adolescent and to demonstrate that you can understand him or her.

AVOID TRADITIONAL MODELS

Traditional models, developed for working with children and adults, are frequently not effective. Adolescents are beyond the playroom, and most do not have the patience for the traditional "talk" therapies. Insight can come later. In treating reluctant adolescents, it is important to begin by focusing on *their* concerns in the present. As soon as possible, get the reluctant adolescents to believe that you can help with something that matters to them.

BEGIN WITH THE FIRST CONTACT

The initial phone contact provides the opportunity to begin assessing the presenting problem(s) and ascertaining the adolescent's appropriateness for the psychotherapist's skills and setting. Most often, initial contact is made by a parent and points to be covered include the following: the timing and content of feedback to the parents; the likely need for collateral contacts with the other systems and professionals who interact with the adolescent; the responsible parties for getting the adolescent to his or her appointments; payment and insurance coverage procedures; expectation of their support and involvement in the adolescent's treatment; and most important, the confidential nature of your sessions with the adolescent. While reluctant adolescents rarely initiate treatment, an adolescent who has been court-ordered to seek treatment might make the first contact. In those cases, it is most often both legally and financially necessary to gain parental permission for treatment.

SCHEDULE AN INITIAL MEETING WITH PARENTS

Parents are a critical resource for gathering diagnostic data. The decision to have an initial meeting with the parent(s) is based on a number of factors, including the age of the adolescent; the therapist's initial feel for the presenting problems; the parents' anxiety; and the therapist's style. Reluctant adolescents will often test a practitioner's trustworthiness by seeing how he or she handles confidentiality. The adolescent's confidentiality is best ensured by having the initial meeting with the parents prior to the first session with the adolescent. Except in unusual circumstances, any additional meetings with parents should take place in the presence of the adolescent or, if this is not possible, with the adolescent's full permission. In addition to gathering developmental and diagnostic information, the meeting with the parent(s) provides insight into parenting style and family dysfunction. It is helpful to have both parents attend this meeting, even in cases of separation or divorce. If a joint meeting is not possible, meet separately with each parent.

MAKE CONTACT WITH THE ADOLESCENT

In most cases, the parent(s) arrange the initial appointment for the adolescent; however, I recommend telephone confirmation directly with the adolescent. This direct contact not only communicates respect for the adolescent as a separate person but also provides data regarding the adolescent's resistance to treatment. If possible, try to leave no more than 10 days between the first three sessions.

CONDUCT INDIVIDUAL AND SYSTEMS ASSESSMENTS

When a psychotherapist is working with adolescents, two diagnostic assessments are being made simultaneously: the individual assessment of the adolescent as "patient" and an assessment of the adolescent's systems. Assessment is interwoven with the ongoing process of listening, supporting, confronting, and reframing. Systems assessment is accomplished by exploring the adolescent's experience of all the systems in which he or she interacts—for example, family, school, community—as well as accessing as much direct information as possible from and about these systems. This includes an assessment of relevant stressors, such as parent–adolescent conflicts; peer group relationships; school achievement, including possible learning disabilities; daily stressors, including home and work responsibilities; and stressful life events, including geographic relocation, divorce, and deaths. It usually takes three sessions to establish the rapport necessary to identify the major contributors to the reluctant adolescent's dysfunctional affect and behavior. Understanding the adolescent in developmental and systemic contexts is key to engagement.

EMPHASIZE THE FIRST SESSION

In their first few minutes of contact, adolescents usually determine whom they can and cannot trust. The first encounter with the treatment-reluctant adolescent must be handled carefully. If there is a parent in the waiting room, greet the adolescent first. Express appreciation directly to the adolescent for coming, especially since it may not have been his or her decision. Cover the limits and boundaries of confidentiality as soon as possible. Since in most instances you will have already met with the parent(s), share with the adolescent what you have been told about the "problem." Ask the adolescent whether he or she agrees or disagrees with what you have been told. Find out what he or she wants. Emphasize that you work for the *adolescent,* not for his or her parents, school, or the court. Be honest and do not be afraid to use humor.

REFER FOR PSYCHOLOGICAL TESTING

Standardized assessment methods are useful with this population, particularly if the therapist suspects intellectual, learning, or neurological problems. At the same time, it is important to move slowly and work with the reluctant adolescent to help him or her see how such an assessment can benefit him or her. Careful consideration must be given to who will conduct the testing, and the adolescent must be assured that all test results will be shared with him or her, preferably before they are shared with anyone else. No test results should be shared with a school or any agency without the adolescent's permission, unless legally required. In light of the complexity of forming a therapeutic alliance with an adolescent, many clinicians refer diagnostic testing to an outside resource.

ASSURE CONFIDENTIALITY

Confidentiality is essential in establishing and maintaining the integrity of a viable working relationship with any adolescent, but it is especially critical with the treatment-reluctant adolescent. The guidelines for confidentiality should be established at the time of initial contact with the parents and discussed with the adolescent at the beginning of treatment. Assuring confidentiality is the first step in gaining trust and empowering the treatment-reluctant adolescent. Explaining to parents the therapeutic value of confidentiality not only helps them to support the treatment process but also provides for developmentally appropriate separation between the adolescent and his or her parents.

Confidentially requires that the therapist not repeat anything the adolescent says (except for the legally mandated exceptions). The adolescent needs assurance that the therapist will not withhold any contact the therapist has with the adolescent's parents. Treatment-reluctant adolescents will often watch for any behavior on the part of the therapist that can be considered a violation of confidentiality. If the adolescent suggests such a violation has occurred, the therapist should immediately inquire why he or she believes that confidentiality has been compromised. The therapist should then either clarify what did or did not happen and, in either case, express concern for the adolescent's understandable feelings of betrayal, as well as offer an apology if something was said that made the adolescent feel that trust had been compromised. What is most important is not to allow this confrontation to be used as a justification to stop treatment.

Both the adolescent and his or her parents should be informed that confidentiality will be waived if the practitioner judges that the adolescent is in danger of harming him or herself. If this becomes necessary, it is best to tell the adolescent first. In keeping with the goal of empowerment, the adolescent should be encouraged to talk directly with his or her parents, possibly in a conjoint family session. In cases where there is suspected physical or sexual abuse, the adolescent must be informed that you are required by law to notify the appropriate agency.

INVOLVE PARENTS

In almost all cases, particularly with younger adolescents, therapeutic change necessitates parental involvement in the treatment process. In developing a treatment plan, the therapist includes both the adolescent's and their parents' perspectives. Working with treatment-reluctant adolescents requires balancing parental involvement with the adolescent patient's confidentiality. It is often necessary to wait for many weeks—until there is a solid therapeutic alliance—before directly addressing the parents' role in the adolescent's dysfunctional behavior. Having the adolescent directly involved in negotiations with his or her family system enhances empowerment. However, the treatment-reluctant adolescent may well refuse to be part of any such meeting, or the therapist's clinical judgment may suggest having separate meetings with parents before meeting with them together with the adolescent. If the adolescent does not attend the meeting, be sure to meet, call, or e-mail the adolescent soon after the meeting. What is most important is to assure the adolescent that the clinician has maintained his or her confidentiality during the meeting and share, as clinically indicated, what transpired at the meeting.

INVOLVE THE ADOLESCENT IN EXTERNAL CONTACTS

Try to involve adolescents in decisions regarding contact with their parents, teachers, and other adults or agencies. A signed release should be secured from the parents *and* the adolescent before any collateral contacts are made. This is particularly important in regard to medical and legal issues. In terms of the parents, this is a legal necessity; with the adolescent it is a therapeutic one. Whenever possible, work directly with the adolescent in the preparation of any court-ordered written report.

HANDLE PARENTAL CONTACT WITH CARE

The therapist should take phone calls from parents regarding their adolescents. The therapist may listen but should not offer any information that might compromise confidentiality. If there is a question about how the adolescent would feel about your sharing something with his or her parents, check with the adolescent first. You can call the parent(s) back. It is a lot more difficult to get the treatment-reluctant adolescent back if he or she believes you have violated his or her trust. The therapist is free to share with the adolescent all communications with the parents.

FIT THE THERAPIST AND OFFICE TO THE ADOLESCENT

If the adolescent is coming straight from school or work, then offer a snack or beverage. The therapist's attire should be casual, avoiding strong images of power and authority. Consider your office environment. Adolescents do not wish to be confronted with how learned we are. Shelves stacked with books and journals are often distancing. The physical environment should be comfortable and inviting.

CONSIDER MULTIPLE TREATMENT FORMATS

Group therapy or activity therapy can be an effective treatment for adolescents, particularly those with dual or multiple diagnoses, and in cases of substance abuse, depression, and oppositional disorders. Group psychotherapy makes use of peer confrontation and support, while providing for connection and belonging. As increased autonomy emerges as a primary struggle during adolescence, family therapy can help to mediate parent–adolescent conflicts, as well as foster effective communication through the process of separation and individuation. Treatment-reluctant adolescents are surprised and affirmed when the therapist confronts the parents with the fact that their sons or daughters' problems are not *all* their fault.

CULTIVATE EMPOWERMENT

Psychotherapy with adolescents requires a special kind of advocacy. It is a delicate balance between helping adolescents empower themselves while supporting, challenging, and directly intervening when needed. Focus on *what they need,* not why they were sent or ruminate about their helplessness. It is important to begin to set operational goals early on. Tangible things *they* want to be different. Help them to identify exchanges or trade-offs they can make with those in power—for example, a C average in exchange for being able to get a driving permit. It is often helpful to make a list. Their goals might include such things as a later curfew, increased spending money, having more friends, getting a job, doing better in school, eliminating substance abuse, reducing delinquent behaviors, and surviving in a dysfunctional system. Identify ways *they* can try to reach *their* goals by brainstorming with them. The process involves teaching and modeling how they can take control of their own life. Be careful not to take responsibility for their reaching their goals. It is *their* job, and then the success is *theirs.*

AVOID SPLITTING WITH THE SYSTEMS

Almost every adolescent who appears for treatment is struggling with one or more of the systems with which he or she interacts. While it is important for the psychotherapist to be supportive of the adolescent's feelings, it is equally important not to pair with the adolescent against all of these systems and to engage in institutional splitting. Adolescents want the support and approval of these systems, even if they are dysfunctional. Whenever possible, the adolescent should be encouraged and helped to figure out ways to meet his or her own needs while, at the same time, find ways to work with the systems with which he or she must interact.

MONITOR COUNTERTRANSFERENCE CAREFULLY

Maintain a therapeutic boundary between yourself and adolescent patients. Overidentification with the treatment-reluctant adolescent (or the judgmental parents) can damage the therapeutic relationship and interfere with productive change. Adolescents must learn how to navigate their own systems, regardless of the degree of dysfunction. Empowerment necessitates appropriate boundaries. Adolescents will not feel empowered unless they believe that *they* are primarily responsible for making positive changes in their lives.

INTERVENE OUTSIDE OF THE OFFICE

Since the world of the adolescent is significantly impacted by other systems, it is important to be willing to leave the office. This may include meetings with teachers, youth leaders, and probation officers. Always inform the adolescent that such a meeting has been requested or that you would like to hold such a meeting. Empower adolescent patients to take an active role in effecting change by encouraging them to attend. If they refuse, review with them what you will say at the meeting. In seeking to engage the reluctant adolescent, the therapist may determine that it is therapeutically appropriate to meet with the adolescent outside the office setting for one or more sessions. In any of these situations, do whatever is necessary to ensure his or her trust and connection.

BE FLEXIBLE AND AVAILABLE

Unlike adults, adolescents require a great deal more flexibility and availability in the course of treatment. They often require far more phone or e-mail contact, especially in a crisis. It is helpful to let adolescents know if and how they can reach you between sessions. In addition, the course of treatment with adolescents is likely to be more variable than it is with adults. Particularly with the reluctant adolescent, balance regular contact with offering some choice of when the next session should take place.

MODEL AN APPROPRIATE TERMINATION

The psychotherapy relationship is critical in an adolescent's life, and thus termination has special ramifications and opportunities. Emphasize an open-ended arrangement and the ability to reinitiate contact. Underscore the ongoing process of solving life problems. Reinforce the adolescent's successes and his or her acquired skills. Remind adolescents of any initial reluctance and tell them again how much you appreciate their willingness to give you a chance to work with them. Let them know that you have learned things from them that will help in your work with other adolescents. Discuss your position on posttherapy contacts, such as e-mailing, phone contact, social media, graduations, holiday cards, and weddings. Encourage adolescents to discuss their feelings about termination. Within a therapeutic context, share your own feelings about the termination. Model a healthy and mature farewell.

References and Readings

Benhke, S. H., & Warner, E. W. (2002). Confidentiality in the treatment of adolescents. *Monitor on Psychology, March*, 44–45.

Bromfield, R. (2007). *Doing child and adolescent psychotherapy: Adapting psychodynamic treatment to contemporary practice* (2nd ed.). New York: Wiley.

Holmbeck, G. N., & Kendall, P. C. (2002). Introduction to the special section on clinical adolescent psychology: Developmental psychopathology and treatment. *Journal of Consulting and Clinical Psychology, 70*, 3–5.

Kazdin, A. E. (1999). *Psychotherapy for children and adolescents: Directions for research and practice*. New York: Oxford University Press.

Rubenstein, A. (2003). (Ed.). Adolescent Psychotherapy. *In Session: Journal of Clinical Psychology, 59*(11).

Steinberg, L. (2002). Clinical adolescent psychology. What it is and what it needs to be. *Journal of Consulting and Clinical Psychology, 70*, 124–128.

Weisz, J. R., & Kazdin, A. E. (Eds.). (2010). *Evidence-based psychotherapies for children and adolescents* (2nd ed.) New York: Guilford Press.

Wintersteen, M. B., Mensinger, J. L., & Diamond, G. S. (2005). Do gender and racial differences between patient and therapist affect therapeutic alliance and treatment retention in adolescents. *Professional Psychology: Research and Practice, 36*, 400–408.

Related Topics

Chapter 39, "Treating Reluctant and Involuntary Clients"

Chapter 51, "Conducting Evaluations of Client Outcomes and Satisfactions"

Chapter 59, "Selecting a Treatment Format"

Chapter 76, "Conducting Couple and Family Therapy"

88 INTERVIEWING CHILDREN ABOUT SEXUAL ABUSE

Karen J. Saywitz and Joyce S. Dorado

Mandated by law to report suspicions of child abuse, practitioners face a dilemma. There is rarely physical evidence or an adult witness to verify a child's report. Hence, professionals rely heavily on children's statements to determine protection, liability, and treatment. When abuse is suspected, the interview goal is to elicit reliable and complete information without tainting children's reports. There is no legally sanctioned interview protocol free of trial ramifications. In fact, there is little expectation that a single protocol can emerge as useful for all ages, clinical conditions, levels of severity, and agency needs, given the developmental and individual differences among children, the variations among circumstances from case to case, and the varied responsibilities of the agencies involved. There is, however, a good deal of consensus on general guidelines derived from the existing research base—guidelines that we summarize herein.

KEY CONSIDERATIONS FOR EFFECTIVE INTERVIEWING

Reliability and Suggestibility of Children's Reports

To examine children's accuracy and determine how best to interview children, researchers have conducted both experimental studies comparing children's reports to staged events, fictitious events, and naturally occurring stressful events, such as injuries or emergency room visits, as well as field studies, including those where perpetrators videotape sexual assaults, inadvertently providing objective documentation against which to compare children's later reports. Despite limited completeness, what children report, when questioned without highly suggestive techniques, is quite accurate.

The most reliable information is obtained in response to open-ended questions that elicit free narratives. School-age children can provide such accounts, and follow-up questions can be used to elaborate, clarify, and justify information provided by the child. Children under 5 years of age depend on context cues and adult questions to help trigger and organize recall. They rarely provide more information than is asked for. Further information is forthcoming in response to specific questions that help focus children's attention on the topic at hand, trigger recall of detail, organize retrieval efforts, and overcome reluctance and anxiety.

Unfortunately, if questions are misleading, they have the potential to distort young children's reports. No witness is immune to the suggestions and biases of the interviewer, regardless of age. Yet young children, especially preschoolers, are a unique group. Very young children (3–4 years of age) are the most vulnerable to the effects of suggestive techniques. By 6–7 years of age, children's resistance to suggestion increases dramatically. By 10–11 years of age, there is another shift toward adult levels of suggestibility. Still, some 3-year-olds remain resistant in response to the most relentless interviewers, while some older children may acquiesce readily under certain conditions. Thus, interviewers must keep presumptions in check and avoid suggestive techniques as described later in this chapter while considering multiple explanations and sides of an issue.

Indicators of True and False Allegations

Thus far, researchers have not produced reliable and valid tests to detect false allegations. Many criteria thought to be indicative of false cases also appear in cases of genuine abuse. No single constellation of behaviors or symptoms is pathognomonic to child abuse, and many genuinely abused children, even those with sexually transmitted diseases, may show no measurable behavioral problems. Often children are referred for an interview because of behavioral changes, for example, nightmares or imitations of adult sexual activity. Although many reactions to trauma can accompany the onset of maltreatment (e.g., nightmares, personality change, fearfulness, anxiety), these occur more frequently in a population of nonabused children who are distressed for other reasons.

However, one indicator is unique to a history of sexual abuse or exposure: age-inconsistent sexual behavior and knowledge. Studies suggest that sexually abused children demonstrate significantly higher rates of sexualized behavior than normative and clinical (nonabused) samples. Still, nonabused children do engage in sexualized behaviors, albeit at a lower rate. While preschoolers are rarely aware of adult activities like genital, oral, and anal penetration, there is no definitive way to know when a child's age-inconsistent knowledge is a function of victimization or of exposure to pornography, crowded living conditions, and so forth.

Behavior changes indicate that further evaluation and investigation are necessary. Their occurrence cannot be used to determine the existence of maltreatment, nor can their absence be used to conclude that a child was not maltreated.

Consistency is often relied upon as an indicator of reliability. However, inconsistency across interviews is frequent, if not expected, among young children questioned by different adults, with different questions, in different settings, even when memories are largely accurate. In one study, children telling the truth about being touched were more inconsistent than children coached to lie about being touched.

Lack of detail is to be expected and cannot be used as an indicator of reliability. Children often perceive different aspects of an event to be salient and memorable. They can remember details that go unnoticed by adults and fail to report information that adults find crucial. Accurate recounts may not include unique details placing individual incidents in spatiotemporal context.

Interview Objectives

Before the interview begins, clarify the objectives for all parties and agencies involved. The objectives dictate many of the methodological choices the interviewer faces. Procedures that are legitimate for one purpose can have unintended ramifications when used for another.

Objectives vary. Interviews often are conducted to determine whether the findings are consistent with the occurrence of abuse. Other times, the goal is treatment planning, custody arrangements, home and school placement, visitation, or family reunification. Sometimes the purpose is a description of current functioning and differential diagnosis. Other times, the need for questioning can arise in the midst of therapy with an unanticipated need to assess imminent risk of danger.

Interviewer's Proper Role

When interviews have implications for legal decision making, the interviewer's role is one of a fact finder, objectively gathering details of legal relevance. Although supportive of the child's efforts, the interviewer remains neutral to the veracity of a child's statements and refrains from behaviors that could unduly influence a child's report. In contrast, the goal of a therapeutic interview is to effect change; there is no obligation to determine the reliability of the child's statements; hence, there is less demand to pursue alternative hypotheses or to word questions in the least suggestive fashion possible.

Interviewers should clearly define their role for themselves, the child, the family, and the court. Most professional organizations recommend that forensic interviews be conducted separately from clinical efforts, in separate sessions by separate individuals whenever possible. After determining whether suspicion of abuse is present, clinicians should consider referring investigative interviewing to specially trained forensic interviewers. Clinicians who remain involved in the case should carefully consider the clinical and forensic implications of invitations to expand and alter their role midstream.

Interviewers need to understand the limitations of the interview process as a means of proving that abuse occurred; be knowledgeable of relevant legal and ethical issues; and avoid dual relationships. When an interviewer is both the treating therapist and an evaluator who provides information to the police or court, competing demands can undermine confidentiality and therapeutic alliance, creating ethical dilemmas.

Interviewers should employ methods that provide the necessary substantiation for their conclusions. Psychological tests can provide useful information but do not provide proof of abuse or of a false allegation. Abuse is an event, not a diagnosis. A reliable and valid test to verify its occurrence does not exist.

GETTING STARTED

Preparation and Gathering of Background Information

- *Before questioning, coordinate with other agencies to reduce multiple interviews.* Verifying information by contacting collaterals is often necessary. Reports may be reviewed from schools, law enforcement agencies, pediatric records, child protective services, and prior court hearings.

Documentation

- Questions and responses should be documented verbatim whenever possible. Never paraphrase children's statements; use his or her words.
- Documentation of the following is optimal: description of abusive acts and alleged offender, age of child at each incident, first and most recent incidents, location(s), enticements, threats, elements of secrecy, and evidence of motive to fabricate. Also document indicia of reliability associated with the child's statement and behavior (e.g., age-appropriate use of terms, spontaneity, hurried speech, belief that disclosure leads to punishment).
- Document precautions taken to avoid contamination, consultation with colleagues, rationales for special techniques, and alternate hypotheses pursued.

Timing of Interviews

- *Interviews should be conducted as soon as possible, while memories are fresh and detailed.* In the field, however, practical, motivational, and emotional considerations affect the timing of interviews.
- *Repeated interviewing in and of itself is not necessarily detrimental to the quality of children's recall.* However, when misleading questions are used in multiple interviews, they have the potential to distort young children's statements.
- *Reducing the number of interviews is often advised.* Yet disclosure of genuine abuse is sometimes a process that occurs over time rather than a singular event. When several interviews are necessary, returning to the same interviewer is optimal.

Setting the Context and Atmosphere

- *Provide a private environment with minimal distractions.* Interview children alone to avoid undue influence on children's statements, unless there is good reason indicating support persons are necessary. Support persons if present should not have an obvious stake in the outcome of the case and should sit behind the child and refrain from advising the child.
- *Before questioning children about alleged abuse, interviewers can discuss the limits on confidentiality.* Also, children may need an outline of the forthcoming interview, as well as education about the flow of information through the investigative and judicial process. For example, to demystify the legal context and reduce uncertainty about interviewer intentions, explain the interviewer's job (to be sure children stay safe and healthy, to help children with problems, or to help a judge make the best plan for the whole family).
- *Provide a supportive, child-friendly, welcoming, nonthreatening atmosphere.* Social support in the form of eye contact, relaxed body posture, smiling, and warm intonation have been shown to help children to be more resistant to misleading questions without contaminating their accounts even over 1-year delays. Supportiveness should not include reinforcing specific content of children's statements.

ADAPTING THE INTERVIEW TO THE CHILD'S STAGE OF DEVELOPMENT

Avoid Miscommunication

- *Use language children can understand. Simplify language by using shorter sentences and words with fewer syllables.* The vocabulary and grammar of the question must match the child's stage of language development. Avoid compound sentences, embedded clauses, multiword verbs (e.g., might have been), pronouns, passive voice, and uncommon word usage. Use simple tenses (e.g., -ed, was), common terms, proper names, and active voice.

Avoid Misinterpretation

- *Avoid questions that require skills children have not yet mastered.* A child who has not yet learned to count cannot be asked how many times something happened. If he or she is, the answer must be weighed accordingly within a developmental framework. Potentially problematic topics include conventional systems of measurement (e.g., weight in pounds, height in feet, timing in minutes/hours), ethnicity labels, kinship terms, and relational terms (e.g., first, always, never, before, ever).
- *Use concrete, easily visualizable terms rather than abstract concepts.* Paint a picture with your words.

Take Precautions to Minimize Suggestibility

- *Avoid creating an accusatory atmosphere by referring to people in derogatory or accusatory terms* (e.g., "Tell me the bad things that the bad man did to you." "He wasn't supposed to do that; that was bad").
- *Avoid suggesting the interviewer is an infallible authority figure with "inside" knowledge of what happened gained from other sources* (e.g., "Well, that's not what your mom said"). Suggest the child is the expert on the event in question, not the adults. Avoid peer pressure, such as "Your sister already told me what happened."
- *Interviewers can be supportive of children's efforts (e.g., "Thanks for listening carefully") but should avoid reinforcing specific content that might shape children's responses.* Do not allow preconceived notions to be reinforced while other leads are ignored or devalued.
- *Respect children's denials.* Do not press children to imagine, visualize, or pretend about what might have happened.
- *Avoid suggestive question types that increase children's errors.* Statements followed by *requests for affirmation* (e.g., "He hurt you, didn't he?"), *insertions of negatives* (e.g., "Didn't he hurt you?"), *multiple choice,* and *suppositional questions.* In the latter, information is embedded into the question without giving the child the opportunity to affirm or deny the presumption (e.g., "When John hurt you, was your mother home?" "Did he hit you with his hand or a club?").

KEY STEPS FOR QUESTIONING CHILDREN

Establish Rapport through Nonsuggestive Means

- Take time to develop rapport in order to promote motivation, cooperation, openness, and honesty with unfamiliar adults in unfamiliar settings, especially when secrets, threats, embarrassments, and loyalties are involved. Convey that it is safe for children to tell as much or as little of what really happened as they feel comfortable.
- With sufficient patience and rapport, many children do report abuse when questioned carefully. Others are reluctant to discuss traumatic events with strangers. In one study, over half of the children with sexually transmitted diseases failed to disclose abuse in a clinical interview.
- Avoid pressuring reluctant children. The goal is to provide an opportunity for disclosure of genuine abuse without creating false report, especially if children have been threatened not to tell. Avoidance is a common childhood strategy for coping with anxiety-provoking topics and a hallmark of posttraumatic stress disorder. Ambivalence, shame, fear of retaliation, or loss of caretaker love is not uncommon.

Help Children Understand How Forensic Interviews are Different from Regular Conversations by Using Narrative Elaboration Practice

- *Before questioning about abuse, give children practice narrating past experiences unrelated to the target event.* In our studies we ask children to describe what they did that morning from the time they woke up until they came to our office.
- *Use open-ended requests for multiword responses. Model your expectation for independent verbalization by inviting children to elaborate with general prompts* (e.g., "Tell me more. You said you got up, what did you do first/next/last? Who else was there?"). This type of question/answer format will demonstrate that the interview is a joint effort in which children are to tell as much as possible in their own words—neither an interrogation with a barrage of leading questions nor a regular conversation in which adults support the conversation.
- *Refrain from filling in silence too quickly or asking detailed questions that can be answered yes or no.*

Set Ground Rules and Consider Explicit Instructions

- Instruct the child to tell only what really happened and everything she can remember, even the little things that she might not think are important, from the beginning to the end.
- Instruct the child to ask for clarification if she does not understand a question (e.g., "Tell me when you do not understand my words ... if you do not understand my question ... Say 'I don't know what you mean' or 'I don't get it.'")
- Instruct the child to say "I don't know" or "I don't remember" if she does not know the answer but to tell the answer when she knows the answer.
- Remind the child that the interviewer was not present at the alleged incident and instruct the child to correct the interviewer if the interviewer says something that is wrong or puts his guess into the question.
- Instruct the child to tell the truth and not to pretend or make up anything.

Provide an Opportunity for an Unbiased Spontaneous Statement

- For example, "I'd like to get to know you better. Is there something important we should talk about? Is there anything you want to tell me? ... think I should know to do my job better today? What made someone bring you here today?"
- *If a forensically relevant event is mentioned, help child elaborate in his or her own words with general prompts* (e.g., "And then what happened? Who else was there?"). Do not interrupt until description is complete.
- *Follow up with short, open-ended wh- questions* about participants, location, bodily sensations, conversations, objects, and timing with who, what, when, where, how, and why.
- *Double back to important, vague, or contradictory points for elaboration or clarification by restating the point and asking for clarification or justification* (e.g., "You said.... how did that happen?" "You said ... how did that feel?" "You said ... what makes you think so?").

If Necessary, Focus the Conversation on the Target Topic with Nonleading Questions

- *Start by focusing children's attention on general topics of relevance* such as alleged participants (e.g., caretakers, "Tell me about your family/babysitter"), locations (e.g., home, school, camp, "Tell me about your summer vacation"), injuries (e.g., "Tell me about the time you hurt your leg"), and so forth.
- *Ask children to list important people and events in their lives* (e.g., "Tell me the names of the people who are important to you") and *preferences and dislikes* (e.g., "Tell me about best/worst most/least favorite activities, people to babysit... to help you with a problem").

- *Children can be asked to describe a typical day in the household, sleeping arrangements, discipline, and supervision patterns; family rules for privacy and safety; histories of injuries; reasons the child gets upset, things that make him mad, and how he copes with problems inside and outside of the family* (e.g., "What would you do if you hurt yourself ... got into trouble at school or home").
- *Try roundabout, indirect ways of eliciting relevant information without leading questions.* For example, ask children who brought them to the interview and why (e.g., "My social worker because I can't be with my dad." *"Why?"* "Because of the way he touched me." *"Oh, what happened?"*).
- *Ask children to describe recent changes at home* (e.g., "My uncle had to leave after my mom got mad at him." *"What was she mad about?"* "What happened to me." *"What happened?"*).

If Legally Relevant Information is Raised, Explore the Topic with Open-Ended Prompts

- *Again, invite children to elaborate in their own words by following-up with "Wh" questions (Who? What? When? Where? How?)* (e.g., "What did you see/hear/do? You said Joan was there; what did she do? What else can you tell me about what she was doing/saying? Was anyone else there? Who?").
- *Use short answer and yes/no question judiciously.* Follow-up with requests for further explanation (e.g., "What makes you think so?") to be certain yes or no means what you think it means.
- *Rephrase yes/no questions into wh- questions when possible* (e.g., "Did he hit you?" becomes "What did he do with his hands?").

Help Children Elaborate the Details

- *Participants and other witnesses.* For example, "Who was there?" "What are their names?" "What did Nora look like?"
- *Actions* (including sexual or aggressive acts). For example, "You said Joan was there; what did she do?"
- *Locations.* For example, "Where did it happen?" "Tell me about the place." "What did it look like?" "Where was your babysitter when this happened?"
- *Conversations (including threats of coercion, secrecy, promises).* For example, "You said Joan was there; what did Joan say?" "What words did Joan use?" "What would happen if you did not do what the grown up told you to do?" "How do you know that would happen?"
- *Sensations* (including nature of injuries or pain). For example, "What did that feel like?" "Where did you hurt, which body part?" "Tell me how it felt...how he moved?" (e.g., hard/soft, fast/slow).
- *Timing of the events.* For example, "You said Mary was there; when did Mary come into the room?" "How old were you when it happened?" "How do you know you were 10?"
- *Objects* (including evidence of force, drugs, alcohol, lubricants, or pornography). For example, "What did he have in his hand?" "What did it look like?" "How did it work?" "What made him put it down?"
- *Context and conclusion* (including what happened right before or after alleged events). For example, "How did it begin/start? How did it end/turn out/stop?"
- *Nudity* (including bathing and toileting practices). For example, "What clothes was he wearing on his legs?"

Query Information from the Child First and from Other Sources Last

- Decisions about raising specific information not yet mentioned by the child are made on a case-by-case basis. Some questions may be justified when there is corroborating evidence to suggest a child may be in danger of further abuse and decisions of protection are paramount. The same questions may be controversial in cases where alleged perpetrators have no access to children and there is little evidence other than children's statements.

Take Time for Closure

- *Children may need time to regain composure and ask their own questions.* They can be praised for their effort and bravery but not for the content of their statements. Children need to know what will happen next to dispel misperceptions and reduce fears.

References and Readings

Goodman, G. S., & Melinder A. (2007). Child witness research and forensic interviews of young children: A review. *Legal and Criminological Psychology, 12,* pp. 1–19.

Lamb, M. E., Hershkowitz, I., Orbach, Y., & Esplin, P. W. (2008). *Tell me what happened: Structured investigative interviews of child victims and witnesses.* West Sussex, England: Wiley.

Pipe, M. E., Lamb, M., Orbach, Y., & Cederborg, A. C. (2007). *Child sexual abuse: Disclosure, delay and denial.* Mahwah, NJ: Erlbaum.

Sattler, J. (1998). *Clinical and forensic interviewing of children and families.* San Diego, CA: Jerome Sattler.

Saywitz, K., & Camparo, L. (2009). Contemporary child forensic interviewing. In B. L. Bottoms, C. J. Najdowski, & G. S. Goodman (Eds.), *Children as victims, witnesses and offenders: Psychological science* (pp. 102–127). New York: Guilford Press.

Saywitz, K., Lyon, T., & Goodman, G. (2011). Interviewing children. In J. Myers (Ed.), *Handbook of child maltreatment* (3rd ed., pp. 337–360). Thousand Oaks, CA: Sage.

Related Topic

Chapter 89, "Treatment of Child Sexual Abuse"

89 TREATING CHILD SEXUAL ABUSE

Kathryn Kuehnle and Mary Connell

Psychotherapeutic intervention is an important consideration when child sexual abuse has occurred; it almost seems to go without saying. However, for treatment to be appropriate and effective, an individualized approach is necessary. Treatment interventions must address each sexually abused child's developmental history within a family, community, and cultural context. Risk factors that are associated with heightened vulnerability for children to be sexually victimized, such as family chaos, alcoholism, and domestic violence, can also independently cause trauma and must be addressed in treatment plans. A continuum of treatment interventions and the role of the mental health professional during the process of investigation and judicial determination on the abuse status of the alleged victim must be identified. When a child is determined by the judiciary to have been sexually abused, evidenced-based treatment interventions for sexually abused children can then be identified and implemented. This chapter will address these subjects.

PREVALENCE AND RISK FACTORS

The National Survey of Children's Exposure to Violence is the most comprehensive nationwide survey of the incidence and prevalence of children's exposure to violence to date (Finkelhor, Turner, Ormrod, Hamby, & Kracke, 2009). Conducted in 2008, the survey measured the past-year and lifetime exposure to violence for children age 17 years and younger through telephonic interviews with the youths ages 10 to 17 years, and with adult caregivers of children age 9 years and younger. One in 16 children reported having been sexually abused within the past year of the interview, and nearly 1 in 10 reported sexual abuse over their lifetimes. Adolescents of both genders ages 14 to 17 were the most likely to be sexually victimized, with almost one in six reporting some form of sexual victimization in the preceding year. Most sexual abuse is not committed by biological fathers or mothers, although sexual abuse perpetrated by a parent is potentially one of the most psychologically traumatic forms of child sexual abuse (see Kuehnle & Connell, 2012).

Children are at increased risk for sexual victimization when they live in a home where parents' abilities to nurture and supervise are substantially compromised by violence, substance abuse, poverty, and single-parent status. Sex offenders target children who have family problems, lack supervision, and are in need of help. Incarcerated sex offenders reported the use of two primary methods to access children: infiltrating families and infiltrating child-centered jobs. The family infiltrator becomes acquainted with the family and offers different types of help. The child-centered job infiltrator chooses a profession that provides access to children. Incarcerated sex offenders also identified methods including seduction of their victims over time and the use of strategies such as giving special rewards or threatening to withdraw benefits such as special attention. Because of the power and status differences between perpetrators and victims, force is typically unnecessary although not absent in all cases (see Kuehnle & Connell, in press). Because a child victim's trauma and recovery are intertwined with the experience of sexual abuse and the child's own developmental history within a family, community, and cultural context, treatment interventions must address the aggregate of these intertwined factors.

SYMPTOMS AND MEDIATING FACTORS IN PSYCHOLOGICAL RECOVERY

Sexual abuse events interact with a complex matrix of factors, including the abuse characteristics, family dynamics, co-occurring forms of maltreatment, caretaker response to the abuse allegation, involvement in the legal system, and the premorbid personality of the victim. Longitudinal studies show that some symptoms and behaviors displayed by sexually abused children (e.g., posttraumatic stress symptoms and fearfulness) can diminish without therapy within a period of 1–2 years. Findings regarding spontaneous improvement of other symptoms and behaviors such as withdrawal, acting out, and depression are variable. Research indicates that one-quarter to one-third of child sexual abuse victims may show no signs or symptoms that are related to the abuse (see Kuehnle & Connell, in press). In comparison to symptomatic sexually abused children, asymptomatic children generally have more limited histories of abuse; the abuse to which they were subjected is less likely to have involved force, violence, or penetration; their abuser is less likely to have been a parent or primary caregiver; and they typically live in more supportive and higher functioning families. Although empirically derived findings are limited, some researchers propose the existence of subgroups of asymptomatic children to include those children who are resilient and dealing successfully with their abuse, those who suppress conflicts related to the abuse but remain distressed at another psychological level, and those who have a delayed onset of disturbance. Children who experience multiple forms of child maltreatment, such as sexual abuse and physical abuse and/or domestic violence, are at the greatest risk for long-term psychopathology and, for them, effective treatment may require the provision of different therapeutic interventions than therapy provided to children experiencing more limited histories of abuse.

Each child is a unique individual whose totality of experiences forms the child's personality. The impact of traumatic experiences of maltreatment on a particular child is not predictable, although estimates on increased risk for poor lifetime adjustment can be made. The specific impact of a potentially traumatic event depends on a number of factors, and trauma may affect children in diverse ways. Internal risk and resiliency factors such as personality characteristics and the personal interpretation of the abuse event (e.g., attributions, optimism, and positive reframing) are related to differences in the psychological impact of maltreatment experiences. External factors, such as family chaos versus family stability or the parents' responses following disclosure, also are associated with children's risk and resiliency. Levels of distress in sexually abused children, emotional and behavior problems, and speed of recovery are related to parental support and level of parent distress. Furthermore, characteristics of the abuse experience, such as timing, duration, frequency, severity, degree of threat, and relationship to the perpetrator are all associated with better or worse outcomes. Children abused and neglected by their parents or caretakers show greater vulnerability to long-term psychological problems. There is a growing body of research that indicates chronic maltreatment commencing in early childhood and continuing into adolescence has the most deleterious effect on the foundation of children's psychological development. A substantial number of maltreated children also experience more than one form of maltreatment. These multiply maltreated children generally lack the resiliency of less pervasively abused children and are at greater risk for maladjustment. There is evidence that children experiencing the combinations of abuse and neglect, multiple forms of abuse, or abuse with exposure to intimate partner violence have decreased odds of stable psychological functioning compared to children experiencing a single maltreatment form (see Kuehnle & Connell, 2011).

MENTAL HEALTH PROFESSIONALS' ROLES IN TREATMENT INTERVENTIONS

Determination of an alleged victim's sexual abuse status—that is, determining whether the suspected abuse occurred—is a complex process and cannot be based solely on a child's statement or the presence or absence of a particular behavior or pattern of symptoms without considering other collateral information. To minimize iatrogenic outcomes for children alleged to have been sexually abused, professionals involved in such cases should carefully establish and maintain professional role boundaries and take on only one role in a case. Potential roles may include investigative forensic interviewer, court appointed forensic evaluator, or therapist.

Mental health treatment providers may be called upon to provide psychotherapy during the investigative phase of allegations of child sexual abuse. They may be asked to provide interventions for children's symptomatic behaviors that are causally undetermined, to treat symptoms assumed to be associated with the experience of sexual abuse, or, problematically, to assist in obtaining evidence for criminal prosecution. Thus, there are a number of roles the therapist may play, including those roles supported by professional ethics and the legal context or those that lack such support.

Within the past decade, some professionals involved in the development of the child advocacy interview centers have advocated that for children with ambiguous disclosures, some form of further investigation, in a form resembling therapy, should be provided for five to seven sessions to allow for the disclosure of more salient information (Carnes, Nelson-Gardell, Wilson, & Orgassa, 2001). Although this approach may provide further opportunities for children to narrate forensically relevant information, there are also risks regarding the effects on children's memories. Well-designed research studies investigating the consequences of extending the information-gathering phase in therapy-like sessions have not been conducted. Currently, these extended information-gathering sessions are generally not conducted in a way that preserves the information-gathering process for later examination, such as the use of video or audio recording. Furthermore, there is no clear endpoint for "allegation facilitating" therapy, and such therapy may continue until an allegation is elicited, which may further confound the task of determining the veracity of the allegation. Possible but unknown effects of therapeutic advocacy, bias, and the absence of transparency are troubling, especially for children with allegations of sexual abuse that are untrue. The use of the term "therapy" for extended investigations may be a misnomer; in these cases, the therapist is acting as an investigator. When the therapist's clinical role bleeds into the role of the forensic interviewer, children who are exposed to ongoing questioning and probing are effectively denied needed therapeutic support or appropriate intervention (see Kuehnle & Connell, 2010).

The therapist's role is to design and implement treatment interventions based on empirical findings and effect change in the child's behavior, emotions, or cognitions, not to investigate abuse allegations. To avoid role confusion, the therapist should formally delineate the parameters of his or her role to the child's parent(s). The therapist should make clear to the parent(s) that the therapist's role is to provide treatment to the sexually abused child and is not to provide an evaluation to determine the veracity of a sexual abuse allegation.

CONTINUUM OF TREATMENT INTERVENTIONS

Prior to and following legal determination of their abuse status, many alleged victims may benefit from therapy or other interventions that are not abuse focused. These interventions may focus on alleviating children's symptoms of distress, such as anxiety and other emotional reactions. We argue that in many undetermined cases of alleged child sexual abuse, the therapist may be most helpful to children by addressing their stress, anxiety, frustration, worry, or other traumatic events, such as the exposure to community or family violence or loss of loved ones.

There are multiple pathways by which children alleged to have been sexually abused may suffer traumatic reactions other than or in addition to the experience of sexual abuse, including home and neighborhood violence, extreme poverty, domestic violence, and other forms of child abuse and neglect. Although research is robust in showing that child sexual abuse is a significant risk factor in children's development of mental health disorders and serious emotional and behavioral difficulties, these disorders are not specific to sexually abused children and are also observed in children experiencing other forms of maltreatment or traumatic events. Treatment interventions must address the unique circumstances, varied needs, vulnerabilities, and resiliency of each child alleged to have been sexually abused. The therapist should design a treatment plan that is appropriate for the unique child and the specific event(s) experienced. Although research cannot be conducted to address this issue, it is quite possible that therapy designed to treat sexually abused children may cause psychological harm when it is provided to non–sexually abused children. The therapist may ardently believe abuse has occurred based on the allegations that have been relayed to the therapist. If those allegations are false, treating the nonabused child as if they are true essentially teaches the child to misperceive reality and to develop the belief he or she is a victim.

FORMING THE TREATMENT PLAN: SUBSTANTIVE ISSUES

The likelihood of effective outcomes is aided when interventions are matched to specific problems through appropriate assessment. Treatment goals for sexually abused children must specify the therapeutic interventions and what aspects of these interventions (e.g., content of treatment) are specifically targeted to behavioral symptoms and/or pathological cognitions or emotions. While the content of treatment interventions should ideally be informed by science, research on this aspect of treatment is limited. For example, it is currently unknown whether expression of abuse memories is beneficial for all children, if repression of abuse memories is beneficial for some children, and whether the pursuit of traumatic memories prior to the development of coping strategies and reinforcement of internal resources may have iatrogenic effects or cause symptoms to appear. Children sometimes get progressively worse during treatment, possibly because the treatment is not suited to their needs or because there are important issues that are not being addressed. Ongoing assessment and revision of treatment planning is necessary to refine the intervention and tailor it to the child's needs.

Prior to designing and implementing interventions with sexually abused children, the mental health professional must also consider the larger environmental context regarding culture, religious, and racial/ethnic groups to which the child and his or her family belong. Values and beliefs about issues such as sexuality, nudity, personal privacy, family roles, and help seeking are all influenced by a family's cultural, religious, and racial/ethnic connections, and must be considered in treatment planning and intervention.

Several important conclusions are derived from research regarding treatment of specific symptoms and behavior problems, including that (1) children show differential responses to treatment with some showing greater treatment effects than others; (2) the psychological characteristics that distinguish sexually abused children who make significant improvement in treatment from children who make no improvement have not been identified; (3) sexual problems and externalizing behaviors (e.g., aggression, acting out) are more resistant to treatment compared to internalizing behaviors (e.g., depression, fearfulness); and (4) preschool children's externalizing symptoms may show greater positive treatment responses when the treatment intervention includes helping parents to manage the acting-out behaviors.

TREATMENT APPROACHES

Research on the treatment approaches for sexually abused children has progressed and criterion-based classification systems have been designed to identify best practice mental health interventions. The Kauffman Best Practice Project (Hensler, Wilson, & Sadler, 2004) identified the following nine criteria for examining a treatment protocol concerning its clinical efficacy and its transportability to common clinical settings:

1. The treatment has a sound theoretical basis in generally accepted psychological principles indicating that it would be effective in treating at least some problems known to be outcomes of child abuse.
2. The treatment is generally accepted in clinical practice as appropriate for use with abused children, their parents, and/or their families. A substantial clinical-anecdotal literature exists indicating the treatment's value with abused children, their parents, and/or their families from a variety of cultural and ethnic backgrounds.
4. There is no clinical or empirical evidence, or theoretical basis indicating that the treatment constitutes a substantial risk of harm to those receiving it, compared to its likely benefits.
5. The treatment has at least one randomized, controlled treatment outcome study indicating its efficacy with abused children and/or their families.
6. If multiple treatment outcome studies have been conducted, the overall weight of evidence supports the efficacy of the treatment.
7. The treatment has a book, manual, or other writings available to clinical professionals that specifies the components of the treatment protocol and describes how to conduct it.
8. The treatment can be delivered in common service delivery settings serving abused children and their families with a reasonable degree of treatment fidelity.
9. The treatment can be delivered by typical mental health professionals who have received a reasonable level of training and supervision in its use. (p. 7)

Three protocols were identified as best practice interventions and as having the greatest level of theoretical, clinical, and empirical support. One of these protocols, trauma-focused cognitive-behavioral therapy (TF-CBT), was identified as the best practice intervention for sexually abused children. The other two protocols, abuse-focused cognitive-behavioral therapy (AF-CBT) and parent–child interaction therapy (PCIT), were identified as best practice interventions for physically abused children and their abusive parents.

TF-CBT is an empirically supported intervention based on learning and cognitive theories. This intervention is designed to reduce children's negative emotional and behavioral responses, and correct maladaptive beliefs and attributions related to the abusive experiences. It is also designed to provide skills to nonoffending parents to help them cope effectively with their own emotional distress and effectively respond to their abused children. When primary presenting problems include significant behavior and conduct problems that existed prior to the trauma, interventions directed at these preexisting problems need to precede the provision of TF-CBT. Dialectical-behavior therapy may be most effective prior to providing TF-CBT to adolescents with a history of running away, cutting themselves, or engaging in other parasuicidal behavior. The gradual exposure component of TF-CBT may be contraindicated for children who are acutely suicidal or substance dependent.

Abuse-specific therapy or elements of this therapy may be inappropriate with specific subgroups of victims. For example, some elements of abuse-specific therapy (e.g., encouragement of expression of abuse-related feelings) are inappropriate when sexual abuse remains unsubstantiated. Additionally, elements of abuse-specific therapy that include exposure to other victims' abuse histories may be inappropriate for preschool children and children who are cognitively impaired, diagnosed with pervasive developmental disorder, or have significant mental illness in which perceptions are distorted and thinking processes are disturbed.

The treatment outcome literature supports the efficacy of behavioral and cognitive-behavioral interventions, but because of the paucity of treatment outcome research, the effectiveness of other theoretically based and structured treatment models cannot be ruled out. As noted by Hensler and colleagues (2004), many, if not most, providers of services to sexually abused children are still largely ignorant of the best practice interventions for sexually abused children or ignore evidence-based practice because they view therapy as more an art than a science. Insurance companies and state agencies paying for therapeutic interventions provided to sexually abused children do not require mental health practitioners to substantiate the efficacy of the treatment they provide. In the field of child sexual abuse, there is a schism between best practice and everyday practice. Each day, children receive a wide variety of therapeutic interventions of which distressingly few are demonstrated to be scientifically efficacious.

References and Readings

Carnes, C. N., Nelson-Gardell, D., Wilson, C., & Orgassa, U. C. (2001). Extended forensic evaluation when sexual abuse is suspected: A multisite field study. *Child Maltreatment, 6,* 230–242.

Finkelhor, D. (2008). *Childhood victimization: violence, crime, and abuse in the lives of young people*. New York: Oxford University Press.

Finkelhor, D., Turner, H., Ormrod, R., Hamby, S., & Kracke, K. (2009). *Children's exposure to violence: A comprehensive national survey*. Juvenile Justice Bulletin: National Survey of Children's Exposure to Violence, Office of Justice Programs, Department of Justice Office of Juvenile Justice and Delinquency Prevention. Retrieved July 19, 2012, from https://www.ncjrs.gov/pdffiles1/ojjdp/227744.pdf

Hensler, D., Wilson, C., & Sadler, B. L. (2004). *Closing the quality chasm in child acuse treatment: Identifying and disseminating best practices. The findings of the Kauffman best practices project to help children heal from child abuse.* Retrieved July 22, 2012 from, www.chadwickcenter.org/Documents/Kaufman%20Report/ChildHosp-NCTAbrochure.pdf

Kuehnle, K., & Connell, M. (2010). Child sexual abuse suspicions: Treatment considerations during investigation. *Journal of Child Sexual Abuse, 19*(5), 554–571.

Kuehnle, K., & Connell, M. (2011).Managing children's emotional and clinical needs. In M. Lamb, D. La Rooy, C. Katz, & L. Malloy (Eds.) *Children's testimony: A handbook of psychological research and forensic practice* (2nd ed., pp. 179–198). Hoboken, NJ: Wiley.

Kuehnle, K., & Connell, M. (2012). Child sexual abuse evaluations. In I. B. Weiner (Series Ed.) & R. Otto (Vol. Ed.), *Handbook of Psychology: Vol. 11. Forensic Psychology* (2nd ed., pp.579–614). Hoboken, NJ: Wiley & Sons.

US Department of Health and Human Services, Administration for Children and Families, Administration on Children, Youth and Families, Children's Bureau. (2010). *Child maltreatment 2009*. Retrieved January 2013, from www.acf.hhs.gov/programs/cb/resource/child-maltreatment-2009

Related Topics

Chapter 61, "Working with Patients Who Have Been Sexually Abused by Previous Therapists and Clergy"

Chapter 88, "Interviewing Children about Sexual Abuse"

PART VI
Biology and Pharmacotherapy

90 ADULT PSYCHOPHARMACOLOGY

Christine Blasey, Joseph K. Belanoff,
Charles DeBattista, and Alan F. Schatzberg

GENERAL GUIDANCE

Make the appropriate diagnosis but especially identify the target symptoms (see Table 90.1). Ideally, one would like to see the patient in a drug-free state for 1–2 weeks, although this is not always possible. Target symptoms are critical. Past history of medication response is quite predictive of current response. Family history of drug response is often helpful in making a medication choice.

MAJOR DEPRESSION

Major depression is a common and debilitating illness (lifetime prevalence of approximately 16%). Success rates for psychopharmacological interventions are approximately 60%–70%.

- *Bupropion.* Bupropion is a norepinephrine and dopamine reuptake inhibitor. Since introduced in the United States in 1989, it has proved to be an effective, safe (and underutilized) antidepressant. Response and remission rates are comparable to the selective serotonin reuptake inhibitors. Initially, the introduction of buproprion had been delayed after the occurrence of seizures in patients with bulimia.
- *Mirtazapine.* Mirtazapine enhances both noradrenergic and serotonergic transmission. Side effects include weight gain and sedation but few sexual side effects.
- *Monoamine oxidase inhibitors (MAOIs).* MAOIs are probably underutilized because of concern about tyramine-induced hypertensive crisis (extreme high blood pressure brought on by eating certain foods, including aged cheese, aged meat, and red wine, while using an MAOI).
- *Selective serotonin reuptake inhibitors (SSRIs).* The release of fluoxetine in 1988 greatly expanded the number of patients with major depression treated pharmacologically. The SSRIs are virtually never lethal in overdose, and their side-effect profiles are relatively benign.
- *Trazodone.* Trazodone is an inhibitor of serotonin reuptake, an agonist at some serotonin receptors, and an antagonist at others. It is also an alpha-adrenergic blocker and an antihistamine, so common side effects include orthostatic hypotension and sedation. Although the primary indication for trazodone is major depression, it is quite effective in low doses (50–100 mg) as a hypnotic.
- *Tricyclic antidepressants (TCAs).* TCAs have demonstrated proven efficacy in major depression but can produce side effects, ranging from the annoying (dry mouth) to the dangerous (arrhythmia). Desipramine and nortriptyline are least likely to produce

TABLE 90.1. Adult Psychopharmacology

Indication	Class	Drug Name	Daily Dosage	Blood Level
Major depression	MAOI	Phenelzine (Nardil)	45–75 mg	
	MAOI	Tranylcypromine (Parnate)	30–50 mg	
	NRI	Buoropion (Wellbutrin)	300–450 mg (divided)	
	NRI	Bupropion (Alpenzin)	174–522 mg	
	SARI	Trazodone (Oleptro)	150–375 mg or XR 75–225 mg	
	SNRI	Venlafaxine (Effexor)	75–375 mg	
	SNRI	Duloxetine (Cymbalta)	20–60 mg	
	SNRI	Desvenlafaxine (Pristiq)	50–100 mg	
	SSRI	Fluoxetine (Prozac)	20–80 mg	
	SSRI	Sertraline (Zoloft)	50–200 mg	
	SSRI	Paroxetine (Paxil)	20–50 mg	
	SSRI	Fluvoxamine (Luvox)	50–300 mg	
	SSRI	Citalopram (Celexa)	20–40 mg	
	SSRI	Escitalopram (Lexapro)	10–20 mg	
	TCA	Imipramine (Tofranil)	150–300 mg	150–300 μg/ml
	TCA	Desipramine (Norpramin)	150–300 mg	150–300 μg/ml
	TCA	Amitriptyline (Elavil)	150–300 mg	100–250 μg/ml
	TCA	Nortriptyline (Pamelor)	50–150 mg	50–150 μg/ml
	Other	Mirtazapine (Remeron)	15–45 mg	
Antidepressant augmentation		Lithium	600–1,800 mg	0.5–0.8 mEq/L
		Aripriprozole (Ability)	2–20 mg	
		L-triodothyramine	25–50 mcg	
Atypical depression	MAOI	Phenelzine (Nardil)	45–75 mg	
Psychotic depression		ECT and Combination Therapy (Antipsychotic/ Antidepressant)		
Dysthymia	SSRI	SSRI		
Bipolar disorder		Lithium	900–2,000 mg	0.8–1.2 mEq/L*
	Anticonvulsant	Carbamazepine (Tegretol)	400–1,600 mg	6–10 μg/ml
	Anticonvulsant	Divalproex sodium (Depakote)	750–2,250 mg (divided)	50–100 μg/ml
	SGA	Risperidone (Risperdal)	1–3 mg	
	SGA	Aripriprazole (Abilify)	2–30 mg	
	SGA	Lamotrigine (Lamictal)	25–400 mg	
	SGA	Asenapine (Saphris)	10–20 mg	
	SGA	Olanzapine (Zyprexa)	5–15 mg	
	SGA	Ziprasidone (Geodon)	80–160 mg	
	SGA	Quetiapine (Seroquel)	100–800 mg	
	SGA	Asenapine (Saphris)	20 mg	
Schizophrenia	Low-potency antipsychotic	Chlorpromazine (Thorazine)	300–800 mg	
	High-potency antipsychotic	Haloperidol (Haldol)	3–10 mg	
	SGA	Risperidone (Risperdal)	1–8 mg	
	SGA	Clozapine (Clozaril)	300–900 mg	
	SGA	Olanzapine (Zyprexa)	5–20 mg	
	SGA	Quetiapine (Seroquel)	50–400 mg	
	SGA	Ziprasidone (Geodon)	40–160 mg	
	SGA	Aripiprazole (Abilify)	10–15 mg	
	SGA	Iloperidone (Fanapt)	12–24 mg	
	SGA	Asenapine (Saphris)	10–20 mg	
	SGA	Palperidone (Invega)	3–12 mg	
	SGA	Lurasidone (Latuda)	40–80 mg	

(continued)

TABLE 90.1. Adult Psychopharmacology (*continued*)

Indication	Class	Drug Name	Daily Dosage	Blood Level
Panic disorder	Benzodiazepine	Alprazolam (Xanax)	1–6 mg	
	Benzodiazepine	Clonazepam (Klonopin)	0.5–4 mg	
	SSRI	Fluoxetine (Prozac)	20–60 mg	
	SSRI	Sertraline (Zoloft)	50–200 mg	
	SSRI	Paroxetine (Paxil)	10–60 mg	
	SSRI	Venlafaxine (Effexor) XR	75–225 mg	
Generalized anxiety disorder	SSRI	Paroxetine (Paxil)	12.5–37.5 mg	
	SSRI	Venlafaxine (Effexor) XR	75–225 mg	
	SSRI	Sertraline (Zoloft)	50–200 mg	
	Other	Buspirone (BuSpar)	15–30 mg (divided)	
Obsessive-compulsive disorder	SSRI	Fluvoxamine (Luvox)	100–350 mg	
	SSRI	Fluoxetine (Prozac)	20–60 mg	
	SSRI	Paroxetine (Paxil)	20–60 mg	
	SSRI	Sertraline (Zoloft)	25–200 mg	
	TCA	Clomipramine (Anafranil)	150–250 mg	
Social anxiety disorder	SNRI	Venlafaxine (Effexor) XR	75–225 mg	
	SSRI	Paroxetine (Paxil) CR	12.5–37.5 mg	
	SSRI	Sertraline (Zoloft)	25–200 mg	
Body dysmorphic disorder	SSRI	SSRI		
Insomnia	Antihistamine	Diphenhydramine	25–50 mg	
	GABA modulator	(Benadryl)	5–10 mg	
	GABA modulator	Zolpidem (Ambien)	5–20 mg	
	GABA modulator	Zaleplon (Sonata)	2–3 mg	
	Melatonin receptor agonist	Eszopiclone (Lunesta)	8 mg	
		Ramelteon (Rozerem)		
	SARI	Trazodone (Oleptro)	50–100 mg	
Narcolepsy	Psychostimulant	Modafanil (Provigil)	200 mg	
		GHB (Xyrem)	6–9 g	
		Dextroamphetamine (Dexedrine)	10–40 mg	
	TCA	Protriptyline (Vivactil)	10–40 mg	
Schizotypal personality disorder	Antipsychotic	Haloperidol (Haldol)	3 mg	
Borderline personality disorder	Antipsychotic	Loxapine (Loxitane)	5–25 mg	
	Anticonvulsant	Valproic Acid (Depakote)	750 mg	
	SSRI	Fluoxetine (Prozac)	20–60 mg	
Avoidant personality disorder	MAOI	Phenelzine (Nardil)	45–60 mg	
	SSRI	Fluoxetine (Prozac)	10–40 mg	
Alcohol withdrawal	Benzodiazepine	Chlordiazepoxide (Librium)	25–100 mg Q 6 h	
	Benzodiazepine	Lorazepam (Ativan)	1 mg Q 1 hr PRN pulse > 110, BP > 150/100	
	Vitamin	Thiamine	100 mg 1–3×QD	
	Vitamin	Folic acid	1 mg QD	
	Vitamin	Multivitamin	1 tablet QD	
Heroin withdrawal	Opioid	Methadone	5 mg Q 4 h as needed on first day then decrease by 5 mg QD until 0	
	Opioid agonist/ antagonist	Buprenorphine and Natoxone (Suboxone)	16/4 mg	
Relapse prevention		Disulfiram (Antabuse)	500 mg QD for 2 weeks then 250 Q D (1st dose at least 12 h after last ETOH use)	
	Opioid agonist	Naltrexone (ReVia)	25 mg QD for 1–2 days then 50 mg (1st dose at least 7–10 days after last opioid use)	

(*continued*)

TABLE 90.1. Adult Psychopharmacology (*continued*)

Indication	Class	Drug Name	Daily Dosage	Blood Level
Bulimia nervosa	SSRI	Fluoxetine (Prozac)	40–60 mg	
Alzheimer's dementia	Anticholinesterase	Tacrine (Cognex)	Start at 40 mg and raise by 40 mg every 6 weeks up to 110 mg	
	Anticholinesterase	Donezepil (Aricept)	5 mg	
	Anticholinesterase	Galantamine (Razadyne)	4–24 mg	
	Anticholinesterase	Rivagistigmine (Exelon)	3–12 mg	
	NMDA receptor antagonist	Memantine (Namenda)	5–20 mg	

*Levels ≥1.5 mEq/L may be toxic, and levels ≥ 2.5 mEq/L may be fatal.
MAOI, monoamine oxidase inhibitors; NRI, norepinephrine reuptake inhibitor; SARI, serotonin antagonist and reuptake inhibitor; SGA, second-generation antipsychotic; SNRI, serotonin–norepinephrine reuptake inhibitor; SSRI, selective serotonin reuptake inhibitor; TCA, tricyclic antidepressant.

sedation, postural hypotension, and anticholinergic side effects.

- *Venlaflaxine and duloxetine.* Venlafaxine is a nonspecific reuptake inhibitor. Unlike the TCAs, venlafaxine does not block cholinergic, histaminergic, or adrenergic receptors, so its side-effect profile is relatively benign. Duloxetine is an effective, approved treatment of major depression, generalized anxiety disorder, and fibromyalgia.
- *Electroconvulsive therapy (ECT).* When depression is accompanied by delusions or is very severe, ECT is the treatment of choice.
- *Adjunct therapy.* If a patient's depression has been nonresponsive to a 6-week course of antidepressants at appropriate dosages, adjunct therapy with either lithium or thyroid hormone is an alternative.
- *Atypical depression (hyperphagia, hypersomnia, leaden paralysis, rejection sensitivity, mood reactivity).* MAOIs have demonstrated superior efficacy compared with TCAs in treating this variation of major depression.
- *Psychotic (delusional) depression.* Antidepressant medication alone is usually ineffective. The combination of an antidepressant and an antipsychotic is effective in some patients. ECT is probably the most effective treatment.
- *Dysthymia.* For many years the prognosis for individuals with dysthymia was poor. There is now increasing evidence that long-term use of antidepressants, particularly SSRIs, is quite effective in improving dysthymia and perhaps in preventing declines into major depression.

BIPOLAR DISORDER

The most effective acute treatment for manic psychotic agitation (virtually always administered in the emergency room) is an antipsychotic medication (e.g., haloperidol) combined with a benzodiazepine (e.g., lorazepam). Shortly thereafter, sometimes following a negative toxicology screen, a mood-stabilizing agent must be started.

- *Lithium.* Lithium remains the gold standard for the treatment of bipolar disorder. Seventy to eighty percent of acutely manic patients respond to lithium, but it often takes 1–3 weeks for a full response.
- *Carbamazepine.* Primarily used as an anticonvulsant, carbamazepine also has been shown to be quite effective in treating bipolar disorder.
- *Valproic acid.* Valproate (primarily used now in divalproex sodium form) has been granted FDA approval for the treatment of bipolar disorder. It appears that valproate may be especially effective in the treatment of rapid-cycling bipolar disorder and mixed

manic-depressive states. Because there are many drug–drug interactions with valproic acid, the prescribing physician must be made aware of all medication changes (including over-the-counter drugs).

- *Other anticonvulsants.* Lamotrigine is currently being studied for the treatment of bipolar disorder. Other anticonvulsants used for bipolar disorder include tiagabine, oxcarbazepine, gabapentin, and levetiracetam, although none of these are currently approved by the FDA for use in bipolar disorder.
- *Second-generation antipsychotic medications.* These medications have been commonly used to treat schizophrenia. Their mechanism of action is described in the subsequent section on schizophrenia treatment. More recently, these types of antipsychotic medications are being prescribed for the treatment of bipolar disorder. In 2006, quetiapine became the first atypical antipsychotic to also receive FDA approval for the treatment of bipolar depressive episodes. Quetiapine also relieves the symptoms of severe manic episodes. Risperidone and ziprasidone are other second-generation antipsychotics that may be prescribed for controlling manic or mixed episodes. In 2009, the FDA approved asenapine for schizophrenia and bipolar disorder in adults. Other commonly used second-generation antipsychotics include olanzapine and aripiprazole. Olanzapine, when given with an antidepressant medication, may help relieve symptoms of severe mania or psychosis. Olanzapine is also available in an injectable form, which quickly treats agitation associated with a manic or mixed episode. Olanzapine can be used for maintenance treatment of bipolar disorder as well. However, studies show that people taking olanzapine typically gain significant weight and may experience other metabolic side effects that can increase their risk for diabetes and heart disease. Aripiprazole is approved for treatment of a manic or mixed episode. Aripiprazole is also used for maintenance treatment after of bipolar disorder. As with olanzapine, aripiprazole also can be injected for urgent treatment of symptoms of manic or mixed episodes of bipolar disorder.

SCHIZOPHRENIA

Antipsychotic medication is often divided into two groups, first generation and second generation. Both groups are effective in treating the symptoms of schizophrenia, but they differ in terms of their side-effect profile. All first-generation antipsychotics are dopamine-2 receptor blockers. Second-generation antipsychotics are less prominent dopamine-2 receptor blockers, and they tend to block many other receptors, particularly serotonin-2 receptors.

First-Generation Antipsychotics: Dopamine Receptor Antagonists (D2 Receptors)

All traditional antipsychotic medications work essentially the same way and have the same side-effect profile. Medications such as chlorpromazine with a relatively low affinity for D2 receptors ("low potency") require a higher dose, and medications with a relatively high affinity for D2 receptors such as haloperidol ("high potency") require a lower dose. The dopamine receptor antagonists are effective in the short and long term; they reduce current symptoms (e.g., hallucinations, delusions, and agitation) and can prevent future relapses. These medications have adverse effects, including sedation, tardive dyskinesia, and severe agitation. The low-potency medicines may also have cardiac and orthostatic hypotensive side effects and may lower the seizure threshold.

Second-Generation Antipsychotics: Dopamine/Serotonin Receptor Antagonists

Aripiprazole, asenapine, clozapine, iloperidone, olanzapine, risperidone, quetiapine, and ziprasidone are all less likely than the first-generation antipsychotics to cause motoric side effects. However, the second-generation antipsychotics are associated with weight gain and metabolic problems. The second-generation antipsychotics may be more effective than the first generation in treating the negative symptoms (e.g., emotional withdrawal) and cognitive deficits of schizophrenia.

ANXIETY DISORDERS

Biological theories of anxiety disorders have pointed to problems in the norepinephrine, serotonin, and gamma-aminobutyric acid neurotransmitter systems. As a consequence, a wide variety of medications has been tried with varying success.

- *Panic disorder.* Antidepressants should be considered the first line of pharmacotherapy for patients with panic disorder. Benzodiazepines have also been shown to be effective in treating panic disorder but have a number of disadvantages over antidepressants. They often produce sedation, increase the effects of alcohol, produce dys-coordination, and are associated with dependence and withdrawal. Patients can have *severe* panic attacks while withdrawing from benzodiazapines. Response rates to the antidepressants paroxetine and sertraline are superior to benzodiazepines, although they work less rapidly.
- *Generalized anxiety disorder (GAD).* The SNRI venlafaxine is an effective approved treatment for GAD. Other antidepressants have also been shown to be effective. Benzodiazepines have been frequently used to treat patients with GAD. They are effective in the short run for symptom relief. However, for all of the reasons listed earlier, their longer term use is problematic. Buspirone, a serotonin partial agonist, has been shown to be as effective as benzodiazepines in patients with GAD.
- *Social anxiety disorder.* The SNRI venlafaxine is an effective approved treatment for social anxiety disorder. Antidepressants are effective for reducing symptoms and disability from social anxiety disorder. The SSRIs paroxetine and sertraline are approved, effective treatments for social anxiety disorder. Alprazolam and phenelzine have been reported to produce improvement in symptoms of social anxiety disorder. Beta-blockers have helped reduce physical manifestations of performance anxiety (in events like public speaking) but are not particularly effective with social anxiety.
- *Obsessive-compulsive disorder (OCD).* OCD is both relatively common and quite responsive to pharmacotherapy. All of the SSRIs have been shown to be effective in reducing the symptoms of OCD. Fluvoxamine, clomipramine, fluoxetine, paroxetine, and sertraline are FDA-approved treatments of OCD. Clomipramine, a nonspecific (but very serotonergically potent) reuptake inhibitor, has been best studied and is often effective.

SLEEP DISORDERS

- *Insomnia.* Insomnia is a common symptom in many psychiatric illnesses, particularly major depression. Insomnia often resolves as the depressive episode resolves. However, when insomnia is particularly distressing to the patient, low doses of trazodone or diphenhydramine are often effective in improving sleep. Patients suffering from insomnia can benefit from hypnotic effects of benzodiazepines or from nonbenzodiazepine agonists, which include zolpidem, zaleplon, and triazolam. The benzodiazepine agonists are less likely to cause rebound insomnia or tolerance. Because insomnia may be a symptom of a physical or psychiatric disorder, hypnotics should not be used for more than 7 to 10 days without a thorough evaluation as to the cause of the insomnia.
- *Narcolepsy.* Psychostimulants (i.e., amphetamines) have long been accepted as valuable treatment for the daytime sleepiness seen in narcolepsy. Stimulants do not prevent the cataplexy that some narcoleptic patients experience, but either TCAs or SSRIs in combination with stimulants may be helpful. Modafinil has proven efficacy in maintaining wakefulness in patients with narcolepsy. In 2002, the FDA approved gamma-hydroxybutyric acid

(GHB) for the treatment of narcolepsy with cataplexy.

PERSONALITY DISORDERS

Despite the fact that pharmacotherapy has increasingly gained acceptance as a treatment option for severe personality disorders, there are few well-controlled studies that document pharmacological efficacy. In addition, many specific personality disorders have not been studied pharmacologically at all. Those that have include the following:

- *Schizotypal personality disorder.* It appears that schizotypal personality disorder has a genetic association with schizophrenia, so it is not surprising that there is some evidence for improvement with low-dose antipsychotic medication.
- *Borderline personality disorder (BPD).* SSRIs seem to help in BPD, particularly with impulsive aggression and affective instability. Low-dose antipsychotic medication is often effective in improving hostility and cognitive perceptual disturbances. Anticonvulsants, particularly valproic acid, seem to improve behavioral dyscontrol; benzodiazepines and noradrenergic antidepressants often seem to make behavioral dyscontrol worse.
- *Avoidant personality disorder.* There are no double-blind placebo-controlled studies, but there is evidence that MAOIs, SSRIs, beta-adrenergic receptor antagonists, and benzodiazepines may be useful in combination with psychotherapy.

PSYCHOACTIVE SUBSTANCE ABUSE AND WITHDRAWAL

- *Intoxication.* Most treatment for serious intoxication is focused on physiological support (controlling blood pressure, heart rate, respiration, etc.). The psychosis seen in amphetamine and cocaine intoxication may be treated with standard antipsychotics, often in combination with benzodiazepines (which help with agitation).
- *Withdrawal.* Withdrawal from alcohol, benzodiazepines, and barbiturates is similar and is potentially life-threatening. All of these withdrawals are best pharmacologically treated with benzodiazepines. Lorazepam (Ativan) is recommended for patients with significant liver disease because its metabolism is less impaired in advanced liver disease. Methadone and clonidine are used in opiate withdrawal.
- *Relapse prevention.* The prevalence of substance abuse disorders, particularly alcohol abuse and dependence, has sparked interest in pharmacological methods to help prevent relapse. Disulfiram (Antabuse) has been tried for many years, although its popularity has certainly declined. Naltrexone, a synthetic opioid antagonist, is used in the treatment of alcoholism and narcotic dependence. Naltrexone aids abstinence by blocking the "high" caused by narcotics. Suboxone (Buprenorphine) is effectively used for opioid withdrawal and relapse prevention.

SOMATOFORM DISORDERS

Most of the somatoform disorders are ineffectively treated with current medication, and, unfortunately, psychoactive medication therapies are probably overused significantly. The one exception is body dysmorphic disorder, where the effective use of serotonergic agents (particularly SSRIs) has dramatically improved the prognosis for affected patients.

EATING DISORDERS

- *Anorexia nervosa.* Unfortunately, there is no shining star of pharmacological treatment for this life-threatening illness. Antipsychotic medication has not worked, and cyproheptadine, amitriptyline, and fluoxetine have had limited success.

- *Bulimia nervosa.* Antidepressants work very well in the treatment of bulimia apart from their ability to elevate mood.

IMPULSE-CONTROL DISORDERS

Among the impulse-control disorders, intermittent explosive disorder and trichotillomania are most often treated pharmacologically.

- *Intermittent explosive disorder.* Anticonvulsants are used most often, although the results are mixed. Benzodiazepines often make matters worse, with more behavioral dyscontrol. There is increasing case evidence that buspirone (often in higher doses than used in generalized anxiety disorder) may be effective.
- *Trichotillomania.* New pharmacological studies are taking place with both serotonergic antidepressants and the anticonvulsant valproic acid.

References, Readings, and Internet Sites

Baldwin, D., Bobes, J., Stein, D. J., Scharwachter, I., & Faure, M. (1999). Paroxetine in social phobia/social anxiety disorder. Randomised, double-blind, placebo-controlled study. Paroxetine Study Group. *British Journal of Psychiatry, 175*(2), 120–126.

Fournier, J. C., DeRubeis, R. J., Hollon, S. D. Dimidjian, S., Jay, D.,. Amsterdam, J. D., ... Fawcett, J. (2010). Antidepressant drug effects and depression severity. *Journal of the American Medical Association, 303*(1), 47–53.

Kane, J. M., & Correll, C. U. (2010). Pharmacologic treatment of schizophrenia. *Dialogues in Clinical Neuroscience, 12*(3), 345–357.

Katzman, M. A. (2009). Current considerations in the treatment of generalized anxiety disorder. *CNS Drugs, 23*(2), 103–120.

Koran, L. M., Hanna, G. L., Hollander, E., Nestadt, G., Simpson, H. B., & American Psychiatric Association. (2007). Practice guideline for the treatment of patients with obsessive–compulsive disorder. *American Journal of Psychiatry, 164*(7 Suppl), 5–53.

PDR Network. (2012). *Physician's desk reference.* Montvale, MJ: Author.

Rush, J., Trivedi, M. H., Wisniewski, S. R., Stewart, J. W., Nierenberg, A. A., Thase, M. E., ... Fava, M. (2006). Bupropion-SR, sertraline, or venlafaxine-XR after failure of SSRIs for depression. *New England Journal of Medicine, 354*(12), 1231–1242.

Sadock, B., Sadock, V., & Sussman, N. (2006). *Pocket handbook of psychiatric drug treatment* (4th ed.). Philadelphia, PA: Lippincott Williams & Wilkins.

Schatzberg, A. F., Cole, J., & DeBattista, C. (2010). *Manual of clinical psychopharmacology.* Washington, DC: American Psychiatric Publishing.

US Food and Drug Administration. (2012). *Drug interactions: What you should know.* Retrieved January 2013, www.fda.gov/Drugs/ResourcesForYou/ucm163354.htm

Related Topics

Chapter 91, "Understanding Side Effects and Warnings in Psychopharmacology"
Chapter 92, "Pediatric Psychopharmacology"
Chapter 94, "Herbal Treatments for Psychological Disorders"

91 UNDERSTANDING SIDE EFFECTS AND WARNINGS IN PSYCHOPHARMACOLOGY

Elaine Orabona Foster and Ruth Roa-Navarrete

Therapists prescribing psychopharmacologic agents must stay abreast of the ever-growing body of information regarding the use of psychotropic medications, their side effects, their interactions with other drugs, and associated risks. This chapter reviews the common set of variables that must be considered for the safe and effective practice of pharmacotherapy. This review is not exhaustive; rather, it highlights collected information from clinical assessments that can affect the interactions between drug and patient. By understanding these interactions, one can modify treatment regimens in a safe and effective manner based on the unique needs of the patient.

- *Age:* Physiological changes occur with advancing age, causing the elderly to metabolize drugs at a slower rate. Children, on the other hand, are characteristically more rapid metabolizers, but other pharmacokinetic factors also come to bear. This is one reason why the common axiom, "start low and go slow" pertains to both the young and the elderly.
- *Sex:* Significant differences in drug absorption, distribution, metabolism, and excretion have been found between men and women. Women metabolize drugs differently during menstrual cycle phases, pregnancy/lactation, and menopause. Certain severe side effects are more common among women (torsade de pointe, a fatal ventricular arrhythmia, and tardive dyskinesia [TD]). Psychotropics can have physical and behavioral teratogenic effects on the developing fetus and newborn. Some mood stabilizers may lead to abnormal cognitive development of children exposed in utero. Therefore, all women of childbearing age must be counseled about the risks as well as benefits of psychotropics and encouraged to avoid all but essential medications during pregnancy. When medication is unavoidable, serotonin-specific reuptake inhibitors (SSRIs) have typically been first-line medications, although there are current concerns regarding cardiac, pulmonary, and other neonatal effects.
- *Ethnicity:* Ethnic groups differ in their expression of genes that allow metabolism of various drugs. The cytochrome P450 enzymes responsible for the metabolism of most psychotropic medications are 1AD, 2D6, and 3A3/4. Knowledge of genetic differences known as "polymorphisms" can help guide pharmacotherapy when individuals who are "fast" or "slow" metabolizers show either subtherapeutic response or excessive side effects or toxicity in the context of therapeutic doses.

- *Symptoms:* A thorough assessment will assist with establishing targets for treatment and monitoring. Side effects may play an important role in the selection of pharmacotherapy (e.g., sedation for a patient with dyssomnia). Choosing a medication must also include pertinent negatives such as the absence of a history of mania, since antidepressants can precipitate a manic "switch" for those with a predisposition for bipolar disorder.
- *Past psychiatric history:* Look for previous psychotropic medication use and benefit, or lack thereof, to include family psychiatric history and response to psychotropic medications. Suicide history and current risk profile will suggest whether it is safe to utilize medications with narrow versus broad therapeutic windows.
- *Past medical history:* Medical illness and concomitant drug use—even over-the-counter medication, homeopathic remedies, or folk remedies—can affect the pharmacokinetics and pharmacodynamics of psychotropic medications. Some combinations can be monitored with relative safety, while others are absolutely contraindicated, such as a monoamine oxidase inhibitor (MAOI) and meperidine or dextromethorphan.
- *Habits:* Regular alcohol use can either speed up or slow down the metabolism of psychotropic medications, depending on the stage of liver damage. Also, alcohol withdrawal can lower seizure thresholds, which means drugs that also lower these thresholds (e.g., bupropion, tricyclics [TCAs], and low-potency antipsychotics) should be avoided in those with alcohol dependence and history of seizure. Tobacco and caffeine can also induce the metabolism of various drugs and must be considered during pharmacotherapy. Illicit drugs can cause a patient to appear depressed, psychotic, and/or anxious. These must always be considered because of their influence on diagnostic and treatment decisions.
- *Laboratory studies:* The most common laboratory studies for psychiatric patients include complete blood count (CBC) with platelets; blood chemistries (typically include liver, kidney function indicators, electrolytes, and blood glucose level); thyroid function tests (TFTs); lipid profile; tests for sexually transmitted diseases; urinalysis with toxicology screen; blood alcohol level; and, when indicated, drug serum levels. For women of child-bearing age, a pregnancy test (HCG) should be included. Some of these studies will assist with differential diagnoses, but they can also provide baselines for the introduction of new medications that can affect various systems. For example, many atypical antipsychotics are associated with weight and the metabolic syndrome; therefore, lipid panels should be checked regularly over the course of pharmacotherapy with these agents.

ANTIDEPRESSANTS

All antidepressants (ADs) and several other psychotropic classes carry a black box warning regarding the increased risk of suicidal thinking and behavior, especially in young adults ages 18 to 24 years during initial treatment. Patient and caregiver education, in addition to close follow-up and monitoring, is indicated when beginning, changing, or discontinuing treatment with an AD.

- *TCAs:* All the TCAs cause varying degrees of anticholinergic effects (e.g., dry mouth, urinary retention, constipation, blurred vision); antihistaminic effects such as sedation and weight gain; orthostatic hypotension from alpha-1 receptor blockade; sexual dysfunction; and the potential for cardiotoxicity. In fact, cardiac conduction problems are a significant contraindication to treatment with TCAs.
- *MAOIs:* Because of potentially lethal interactions and overdose effects, MAOIs are not used as first-line drugs. A lethal hypertensive crisis can occur when these drugs are mixed with sympathomimetics or foods containing tyramine (a natural by-product of the fermentation process), such as cheeses, wines, beers, chopped liver, fava beans, and chocolate. L-dopa and TCAs can also cause excessive elevations in blood pressure that can result in myocardial

infarction and stroke. Signs and symptoms of hypertensive crisis include severe headache, excessive sweating, dilated pupils, and cardiac conduction problems. MAOIs are also contraindicated with SSRIs (requiring a careful discontinuation/switch schedule), serotonin precursors (e.g., Tryptophan), and some narcotic analgesics because of potential serotonin syndrome, characterized by rapid heart rate, hypertension, neuromuscular irritability, fever, and even coma, convulsions, and sometimes death. These drugs can cause postural hypotension, sexual dysfunction, weight gain, and symptoms similar to those produced by muscarinic blockage (i.e., anticholinergic side effects). A transdermal form of the MAOI selegiline (Eldepryl, Emsam) was designed to eliminate the dietary interactions associated with the oral formulation. The main side effect encountered was skin rash.

- *SSRIs:* Common side effects include activation (sometimes experienced as anxiety), headache, nausea, vomiting, diarrhea, sexual dysfunction (mainly delayed ejaculation/orgasm), and occasional asthenia. Both activation and sexual dysfunction should be closely monitored as they are often associated with early discontinuation and/or noncompliance. SSRIs may cause either insomnia or sedation with no apparent predictability. Serotonin syndrome may occur at normal SSRI doses in combination with other serotonergic drugs like the triptans commonly prescribed for migraine headaches (e.g., zolmitriptan). SSRIs have also been implicated in acute hyponatremia associated with syndrome of inappropriate secretion of antidiuretic hormone (SIADH). Acute-onset hyponatremia may present with behavioral changes and delirium and may be followed by neurologic morbidity and death. More recently, these medications have been associated with decreased bone mineral density.
- *Trazodone (Desyrel) and Nefazodone (Serzone):* Both of these drugs can cause sedation, postural hypotension, nausea, and vomiting. Trazodone has a greater potential for sedation (therefore, it is commonly used as a sleep aid), cardiac arrhythmias, and priapism (a sustained, painful engorgement of the penis or clitoris). Nefazodone's labeling carries a black box warning concerning hepatoxicity with the potential for encephalopathy and hepatic coma. Patients who show symptoms such as anorexia, fatigue, malaise, abdominal pain, discolored stools, dark urine, jaundice, ascites, nausea, and vomiting should discontinue the drug immediately. Because of this concern, Nefazodone is now rarely used as a first-line agent.
- *Serotonin-norepinephrine reuptake inhibitors (SNRIs):* Venlafaxine and duloxetine's side effects are similar to the SSRIs' in addition to sweating, constipation, sedation, and dizziness. These drugs are associated with a mild to moderate, transient, dose-dependent increase in diastolic blood pressure. Therefore, patients with hypertension should be monitored closely upon initiation of treatment and before dose increases. Duloxetine is contraindicated for patients with hepatic impairment.
- *Bupropion (Wellbutrin, Zyban):* Bupropion shows various advantages over the SSRIs in that it does not have anticholinergic, postural hypotension, conduction arrhythmias, sexual dysfunction, or significant drug interaction effects. Side effects include activation and anorexia. In rare cases, bupropion has been associated with psychotic symptoms and seizure in doses over 450 mg per day. Patients with a history of eating disorders, seizure, and alcohol dependence with significant withdrawal symptoms should not take this drug.
- *Mirtazapine (Remeron):* A tetracyclic agent that has been associated with inverse, dose-dependent sedation (i.e., sedation is reduced with doses above 15 mg) and significant weight gain. Adverse drug effects include exfoliative dermatitis, neutropenia (1.5% risk), and agranulocytosis (.1%). Avoid in the immunocompromised, and monitor complete blood counts at baseline, annually and with signs/symptoms of infection. Other side effects include hyperlipidemia and hypercholesterolemia (over 20% above upper normal cholesterol levels).

SELECT MOOD STABILIZERS

- *Lithium (Eskalith, Lithonate, Lithane):* Lithium's side-effect profile includes nausea, vomiting, diarrhea, abdominal pain, sedation, tremor, muscular weakness, increased thirst and urination, swelling due to excessive fluid in body tissues, weight gain, dry mouth, and dermatological reactions. Because of its narrow therapeutic index, lithium can easily result in toxic effects (at serum levels above 1.5 mmol/L, with severe adverse effects occur as low as 2.0 mmol/L and above). Signs of toxicity include sluggishness, impaired gait, slurred speech, tinnitus, abdominal distress, tremor, electrocardiogram abnormalities, low blood pressure, seizures, shock, delirium, and coma. Chronic use can result in leukocytosis, hypothyroidism/goiter, weight gain, acne, and cardiac conduction changes.
- *Carbamazepine (Tegretol):* Associated with a number of rarely occurring toxicities, which include hepatitis, blood dyscrasias such as agranulocytosis and aplastic anemia, and exfoliative dermatitis with higher risk for certain Asian populations. As a result, the FDA requires genetic testing at baseline. Incidents of leukopenia, thrombocytopenia, elevated liver enzymes, and dermatological reactions are typically reversible. Initial signs of toxicity include dizziness, blurred or double vision, sedation, and ataxia. Carbamazepine is a potent inducer of hepatic enzymes, speeding up metabolism and therefore reducing the levels of several drugs, including antipsychotics, valproate, TCAs, benzodiazepines, and hormonal contraceptives, which may result in unintended pregnancy. Therapeutic drug monitoring is recommended.
- *Valproic acid (Depakote):* Initial common side effects include gastrointestinal effects, sedation, and tremor. With chronic use, there can be mild impairment of cognitive function, alopecia, and weight gain. Hematological effects include those seen commonly (e.g., thrombocytopenia, platelet dysfunction) and uncommonly (bleeding tendency). Hepatic effects can range from benign increase of liver enzymes to rare hepatitis/hepatic failure.
- *Lamotrigine (Lamictal):* In order of decreasing frequency, the most common side effects are dizziness, tremor, somnolence, headache, rash, nausea, and insomnia. Rash can be a serious adverse event leading to drug discontinuation. The lamotrigine-based cutaneous reactions include measles-like rash, hives, and angioedema, as well as more serious rashes such as Stevens Johnson syndrome. The rate of serious rash requiring hospitalization and discontinuation of treatment is 3 in 1,000 and usually occurs within 1 to 2 months of initiation of treatment.
- *Topiramate (Topamax):* This medication has few drug interactions based on its predominately renal excretion. Side effects include parasthesias, headache, fatigue, somnolence, and weight loss. Because of the weight-loss side effect, this medication is often used for patients who do not comply with treatment on other mood stabilizers because of weight gain, especially young females. This medication may also decrease the serum concentration of oral contraceptives which can result in unintended pregnancy.

ANXIOLYTICS

- *Benzodiazepines:* The common side effects are sedation and fatigue. Ataxia, slurred speech, and memory (usually anterograde amnesia) and cognitive function impairment may occur. Behavioral disinhibition in the form of rage, aggression, impulse dyscontrol, and euphoria has been reported. All benzodiazepines can cause depression and when mixed with other central nervous system depressants, including alcohol, can result in respiratory depression/arrest.
- *Buspirone (Buspar):* This drug does not tend to produce sedation but can be initially activating. Side effects can include headache and gastrointestinal distress. It is preferable to benzodiazepines in its side-effect profile since it shows virtually no cognitive and motor impairment, disinhibition, potentiation with

alcohol, or risk of dependence. Also, despite being serotonergic, it does not typically produce sexual dysfunction.

ANTIPSYCHOTICS

- *First-generation antipsychotics (FGAs):* Primary side effects include sedation, weight gain, anticholinergic effects, and extrapyramidal symptoms (EPSs). EPSs (mostly associated with high-potency agents) include Parkinsonian symptoms (rigidity, bradykinesia, and resting tremor), akathisia (internal restlessness), acute dystonias (muscle contractions/spasms [e.g., ocular gyric crisis]), and tardive dyskinesia. Some antipsychotics can also lower the seizure threshold, usually in a dose-dependent fashion. Hyperprolactinemia can cause galactorrhea with all of the conventional agents and the atypical agent, risperidone. Prolonged elevations of prolactin may reduce bone mineral density and thereby increase the risk of fractures. Thioridazine has been associated with an increased risk of sudden death secondary to torsades de pointes, hypertension, and ischemic heart disease. Its use is contraindicated with the antidepressant sertraline because of the latter's potent 2D6 inhibition. Some FGAs carry an increased risk of phlebitis or embolism. All antipsychotic medications carry a black-box warning related to increased risk of death in elderly patients with dementia-related psychosis. Careful evaluation of risk versus benefits is warranted before initiating therapy.
- *Second-generation antipsychotics (SGAs):* These agents show similar side effect profiles including dose-dependent EPSs for olanzapine, risperidone, and ziprasidone. The risk for TD is lower with SGAs, and lowest for Clozapine, but with all SGAs, monitoring for TD should occur at baseline and yearly for the duration of treatment. Most SGAs are associated with metabolic syndrome, including impairment of glycemic control, and hyperlipidemia. Weight gain is a troublesome side effect of both the FGAs and SGAs and can interfere with treatment compliance. Other side effects include decreased libido, sexual dysfunction, prolactin elevations (dose dependent), temperature dysregulation, photosensitivity, and photoallergic skin reactions. Neuroleptic malignant syndrome may also occur with this class of agents.

OTHER SPECIFIC SIDE EFFECTS

- *Clozapine:* Because of the risk of agranulocytosis, clozapine should only be used after treatment failure with other antipsychotics. Weekly blood monitoring is required for the first 6 months of treatment, and then every other week for the duration of treatment. Agranulocytosis mortality is high if the drug is not discontinued and condition immediately treated. Clozapine has the lowest risk of TD to date and is even used to treat this condition when caused by other antipsychotics. Other significant side effects include seizures, orthostatic hypotension, hypersalivation, tachycardia, constipation, hyperthermia, neutropenia, and eosinophilia.
- *Olanzapine:* Olanzapine's major side effects include dose-dependent EPSs, agitation, insomnia, nervousness, hostility, constipation, and dry mouth.
- *Risperidone:* Although risperidone has a lower incidence of EPS, at higher doses, its EPS profile approximates the traditional neuroleptics. Other side effects include postural hypotension, cognitive impairment, asthenia, constipation, nausea, dyspepsia, tachycardia, headache, fatigue, dizziness, galactorrhea, and "burning sensations."
- *Ziprasidone:* This drug tends to prolong the QT interval on an electrocardiogram, which can potentially result in torsades de pointes. The package insert states that it should be prescribed only after other agents have been tried. Conservative treatment suggests routine electrocardiogram monitoring for patients treated with ziprasidone. Holter monitoring is advisable for patients on ziprasidone who complain of dizziness, palpitations, or syncope. This drug should not be

used in combination with medications that prolong the QT interval (e.g., TCAs). Rash and orthostatic hypotension can occur. It is less likely to cause weight gain than the other SGAs.

- *Quetiapine:* The package insert notes that with chronic use this drug may result in ocular lens changes. Slit lamp examinations are recommended at baseline and every 6 months. This warning was based on animal studies and has not been reported in postmarketing studies. Ocular assessments may, therefore, be based more on malpractice concerns than on empirical pharmacological science, especially since individuals with schizophrenia often have other risk factors, such as smoking and diabetes and therefore greater risk for ocular lens changes. Dose-dependent reductions in total T4 and Free T4 levels have also been observed.

ACKNOWLEDGMENTS

The opinions contained herein are the private views of the authors and should not be construed as the official policy or position of the U.S. government, the Department of Defense, or the Department of the Air Force.

References and Readings

Hahn, R. K., Albers, L. J., & Reist, C. (2009). *Current clinical strategies: Psychiatry 2010 edition.* Irvine, CA: Current Clinical Strategies.

Janicak, G., Marder, S. R., & Pavuluri, M. N. (2010). *Principles and practice of psychopharmacotherapy* (5th ed.). Baltimore, MD: Lippincott Williams & Wilkins.

Maxmen, J. S., Kennedy, S. H., & McIntyre. (2008). *Psychotropic drugs fast facts* (4th ed.). New York: Norton.

Ng, F., Mammen, O. K., Wilting, I., Sachs, G. S., Ferrier, I. N., Cassidy F., Beaulieu, S., Yathan, L. S. & Berk, M. (2009). The International Society for Bipolar Disorders (ISBD) consensus guidelines for the safety monitoring of bipolar disorder treatments. *Bipolar Disorders, 11,* 559–595.

Nicolas, J-M., Espie, P., & Molimard, M. (2009). Gender and interindividual variability in pharmacokinetics. *Drug Metabolism Reviews, 41*(3), 408–421.

Preston, J., & Johnson, J. (2011). *Clinical psychopharmacology made ridiculously simple* (7th ed.). Miami, FL: MedMaster.

Virani, A. S., Bezchilibenyk-Butler, K. Z., & Jeffrics, J. J. (Eds.). (2009). *Clinical handbook of psychotropic drugs.* Toronto, ON: Hogrefe & Huber.

Related Topics

Chapter 90, "Adult Psychopharmacology"
Chapter 92, "Pediatric Psychopharmacology"

92 PEDIATRIC PSYCHOPHARMACOLOGY

Colleen A. Ryan and Michael L. Trieu

Psychopharmacological treatment is indicated for children and adolescents suffering moderate to severe psychiatric symptoms and/or exhibiting only partial response to psychotherapeutic interventions. Potential risks and benefits, alternative treatments (including no treatment), side effect profile, and severity of symptoms must be carefully considered in collaboration with parents/guardians in determining the choice of psychotropic medication. This chapter briefly reviews child and adolescent psychiatric disorders and available medication treatments.

DEPRESSIVE DISORDERS

Selective serotonin reuptake inhibitors (SSRIs), including fluoxetine, citalopram, escitalopram, sertraline, and fluvoxamine, are first-line medications used to treat juvenile depression (see Table 92.1). SSRIs have been found to be most useful in managing depressive symptoms when used in combination with cognitive-behavioral therapy. Relative to placebo, antidepressants are efficacious for pediatric depression, although effects are generally modest. The most significant treatment effects have been found for fluoxetine, sertraline, and citalopram. Venlafaxine, a dual noradrenergic and serotonergic agent, is an effective second-line intervention for adolescent depression and requires careful down-titration if discontinued. Tricyclic antidepressants (imipramine, amitriptyline, and nortriptyline) have been found to have no greater efficacy over placebo in treatment of depression in youths. An alternative antidepressant, bupropion, is unstudied as a monotherapy in juvenile depression but has shown some benefit in the treatment of comorbid depression and attention-deficit hyperactivity disorder (ADHD).

Frequent assessment should occur during acute treatment to assess emergence of medication-associated suicidal adverse events (SAEs) or other side effects, such as gastrointestinal and sleep disturbance. Side effects are often dose dependent and subside with time. The SSRI black box warning provides guidelines related to monitoring pediatric patients for SAEs. It recommends weekly mental status examinations (MSEs) by a licensed clinician for the first month of treatment, biweekly MSEs the following month, and monitoring as deemed appropriate by the patient's provider thereafter. SAEs include suicidal ideation, suicidal behaviors, and suicide attempts. To date, there have been no incidences of suicide completion in published trials with antidepressants treating juvenile depressive disorders. Compared to placebo, risk of SAEs with antidepressant use is low across treatment indications. Most SAEs were noted to occur early in the course of treatment, possibly induced by SSRI side effects and/or medication discontinuation symptoms. A 2012 reanalysis of randomized controlled trials with

TABLE 92.1. Medication Uses and Cautions

Medication	Target Symptoms & *FDA approval (pediatric age range)	Dosage Range	Side Effects (SE)	Medical Monitoring
Selective Serotonin Reuptake Inhibitors (SSRIs)				
Fluoxetine (Prozac)	Depression (8–17)*, OCD (7–17)*, Anxiety	5–60 mg/d	Restlessness, GI symptoms, headaches, sweating, sleep/ appetite changes, impaired sexual functioning, "behavioral activation", suicidal adverse events	
Fluvoxamine (Luvox)	Depression, OCD (8–17)*, Anxiety	25–300 mg/d		
Sertraline (Zoloft)	Depression, OCD (6–17)*, Anxiety	25–200 mg/d		
Citalopram (Celexa)	Depression, OCD, Anxiety	5–40 mg/d		
Escitalopram (Lexapro)	Depression (12–17)*, OCD, Anxiety	5–20 mg/d		
Paroxetine (Paxil)	Paroxetine use is generally avoided in youth	5–60 mg/d		
Non-SSRI Antidepressants				
Venlafaxine (Effexor)	Depression, Anxiety	12.5–375 mg	See SSRI SE; hypertension	Routine blood pressure (BP) checks
Bupropion (Wellbutrin)	Depression with ADHD	75–450 mg/d	See SSRI SE; Seizure risk with eating disorder patients	
Clomipramine (Anafranil)	OCD (10–17)*	25–200 mg/d	Dry mouth, constipation, dizziness, sedation, arrhythmias, lethality with overdose	Serum levels 150–300ng/ml; monitor ECG, BP, pulse
Mood Stabilizers				
Lithium Carbonate (Eskalith)	BPD (acute mania/mixed, maintenance, 12–17)*, depression	600 to 1800mg/d in divided doses	Sedation, thirst, GI symptoms, tremor, wt gain, hypothyroidism, headache, cognitive impairment, increased urination, ECG changes, seizures, ataxia, fetal cardiac defects	Serum levels 0.8–1.5mEq/L acute mania; 0.6–1.2mEq/L maintenance; monitor ECG, renal function, thyroid test, wt
Valproate (Depakote)	Acute mania/mixed	15–60mg/kg/day	Sedation, dizziness, blurred vision, ataxia, GI symptoms, wt gain, hair loss, tremor, liver damage, PCOS, pancreatitis, fetal neural tube defects	Serum levels 50–125mcg/ml; monitor CBC, PLTs, LFTs, wt

(continued)

TABLE 92.1. Medication Uses and Cautions (*continued*)

Medication	Target Symptoms & *FDA approval (pediatric age range)	Dosage Range	Side Effects (SE)	Medical Monitoring
Lamotrigine (Lamictal)	BPD depression	25–400mg/d	Stevens-Johns Syndrome (SJS) especially with rapid dose titration, rash, GI symptoms, headache	
Carbamazepine (Tegretol)	Acute mania/mixed	400–1200mg/d in divided doses	Sedation, aplastic anemia, agranulocytosis, ataxia, rash (SJS)	Serum levels 8–12mcg/ml; monitor CBC, ECG, LFTs, wt
Anti-Hypertensive Medication				
Clonidine (Catapres)	Hyperactivity, hyperarousal, insomnia, agitation, tics	0.025mg–0.4mg/d, often 3 to 4 divided doses	Sedation, dizziness, hypotension, rebound hypertension	BP, Pulse
Guanfacine (Tenex)	See clonidine	0.5mg to 4mg/d, often in 2 to 3 divided doses	Sedation, hypotension	
Propranolol	Hyperarousal, agitation, akasthisia	20–160mg/d, often in divided doses	Bradycardia, hypotension, syncope, depression	
Atypical Antipsychotics				
Risperidone (Risperdal)	Acute mania/ mixed (10–17)*, Schizophrenia (13–17) *, Irritability (autism, 5–16)*, tics	0.25 mg-6 mg/d	Neuromotor SE (parkinsonism, dystonia, akasthisia), wt gain, sedation, elevated prolactin level (galactorrhea, amenorrhea, sexual dysfunction), ECG abnormalities, metabolic syndrome, NMS	Wt, BP, Pulse, fasting glucose and lipids, ECG
Aripiprazole (Abilify)	Acute mania/mixed, maintenance (10–17)*, Schizophrenia (13–17) *, Irritability (autism, 6–17)*	2–30 mg/d		
Olanzapine (Zyprexa)	Acute mania/ mixed (13–17)*, Schizophrenia (13–17)*, agitation	2.5–20 mg/d		
Quetiapine (Seroquel)	Acute mania/ mixed (10–17) *, Schizophrenia (13–17) *, agitation	25–800 mg/d	See SE above, excessive salivation, seizures (risk increases with increasing dose), hypotension, agranulocytosis, myocarditis, cardiomyopathy	Wt, BP, Pulse, fasting glucose and lipids, ECG, Baseline EEG
Ziprasidone (Geodon)	Mania, Psychosis, Agitation	20–160 mg/d with food		
Clozapine (Clozaril)	Psychosis, agitation	12.5–900 mg/d		
Long Acting Stimulants				
Methylphenidate (Concerta)	Inattention, Hyperactivity, Impulsivity, ADHD (6–17)*	18–108 mg/d	Insomnia, headache, GI symptoms, increased BP, decreased appetite, weight loss, anxiety, motor tics, emotional lability	Ht, Wt, BP, Pulse
Dexmethylphenidate (Focalin XR)	Inattention, Hyperactivity, Impulsivity, ADHD (6–17)*	5–50 mg/d		
Amphetamine combination (Adderall XR)	Inattention, Hyperactivity, Impulsivity, ADHD (6–17)*	5–60 mg/d		

(*continued*)

TABLE 92.1. Medication Uses and Cautions (*continued*)

Medication	Target Symptoms & *FDA approval (pediatric age range)	Dosage Range	Side Effects (SE)	Medical Monitoring
Dextro-amphetamine (Dexedrine Spansule)	Inattention, Hyperactivity, Impulsivity, ADHD (3–17)*	5-60mg/d		
Methylphen-idate Transdermal System (Daytrana)	Inattention, Hyperactivity, Impulsivity, ADHD (6–17)*	10–30 mg/9 h patch		
Lis-Dexamphet-amine (Vyvanse)	Inattention, Hyperactivity, Impulsivity, ADHD (6–17)*	20–70 mg/d		
Intermediate Acting Stimulants				
Methyl-phenidate (Metadate ER, Metadate CD, Methylin ER, Ritalin LA, Ritalin SR)	Inattention, Hyperactivity, Impulsivity, ADHD (6–17)*	10–100 mg/d	Insomnia, headache, GI symptoms, increased BP, decreased appetite, weight loss, anxiety, motor tics, emotional lability	Ht, Wt, BP, Pulse
Short Acting Stimulant				
Dexamethyl-phenidate (Focalin)	Inattention, Hyperactivity, Impulsivity, ADHD (6–17)*	2.5–50 mg/d	Insomnia, headache, GI symptoms, increased BP, decreased appetite, weight loss, anxiety, motor tics, emotional lability	Ht, Wt, BP, Pulse
Methylphen-idate (Ritalin, Methylin)	Inattention, Hyperactivity, Impulsivity, ADHD (6–17)*	5–100 mg/d		
Amphet-amine combination	Inattention, Hyperactivity, Impulsivity, ADHD (3–17)*	2.5–60 mg/d		
Dextro-amphetamine (Dexedrine)	Inattention, Hyperactivity, Impulsivity, ADHD (3–17)*	2.5–60 mg/d		
Selective Norepinephrine Reuptake Inhibitor				
Atomoxetine (Strattera)	Inattention, Hyperactivity, Impulsivity, ADHD (6–17)* with co-morbid anxiety	10–100 mg/d	Dry mouth, GI symptoms, insomnia, decreased appetite, somnolence, sexual side effects, BP and pulse increase	Ht, Wt, BP, Pulse

ADHD, attention-deficit/hyperactivity disorder; BP, blood pressure; BPD, bipolar disorder; CBC, complete blook count; ECG, electrocardiogram; GI, gastrointestinal; LFT, liver function tests; MDD, major depressive disorder; OCD, obsessive-compulsive disorder; PLT, platelets; PTSD, posttraumatic stress disorder.

fluoxetine for depression showed no evidence of increased suicide risk in youths receiving this medication. Approximately 3%–8% of youths exhibit "behavioral activation"—impulsivity, irritability, agitation, or silliness—with antidepressant medication. Behavioral activation should be differentiated from mania/hypomania in bipolar disorder and medication-induced manic conversion.

Adjunctive antipsychotic medications are used to treat youths with severe symptoms of depression, including profound neurovegetative signs/symptoms and/or psychotic features. Lithium and thyroid hormone may be helpful when given with antidepressant therapy in cases of treatment-resistant pediatric depression. Electroconvulsive therapy (ECT) is an alternative treatment that should be considered for adolescents who are severely disabled by their depressive symptoms and have been unresponsive or only partially responsive to psychopharmacotherapy.

OBSESSIVE-COMPULSIVE DISORDER

SSRIs are first-line medications recommended in the treatment of pediatric obsessive-compulsive disorder (OCD; see Table 92.1). Relative to placebo, SSRIs have been shown to be moderately efficacious for pediatric OCD, with all SSRIs comparably effective. Due to its side effect profile, clomipramine, a tricyclic antidepressant, is reserved as a second-line monotherapy or as an SSRI augmentation agent in pediatric OCD. In some studies, clomipramine has shown superior efficacy to SSRI treatment. Antipsychotics (risperidone, haloperidol) are used as an augmentation therapy for treatment-resistant OCD, with approximately one-third of treatment-refractory OCD patients exhibiting treatment response in adult OCD studies. Psychopharmacotherapy is often an imperative treatment in moderate to severe OCD, in order to alleviate symptom-related distress and allow patients to participate in necessary cognitive-behavioral therapy. Medication may also treat comorbid depressive disorders often seen in moderate to severe cases of childhood OCD.

NON–OBSESSIVE COMPULSIVE DISORDER ANXIETY DISORDERS

Non-OCD pediatric anxiety disorders include generalized anxiety disorder (GAD), social phobia (SoP), posttraumatic stress disorder (PTSD), separation anxiety disorder (SAD), selective mutism (SM), specific phobia (SP), and panic disorder (PD). SSRIs are first-line pharmacologic agents used in juvenile anxiety disorders (see Table 92.1). Despite lack of FDA indications for non-OCD pediatric anxiety disorders, multiple studies support the use of SSRI monotherapy for SAD, GAD, and SoP, with moderate-to-large effect sizes and demonstrated efficacy in placebo-controlled trials. In adults, randomized controlled trials, case reports, and open trials support SSRI use in PTSD, with sertraline FDA approved for adult PTSD. SSRI therapy in juvenile PTSD is relatively unstudied, with one study revealing no difference between SSRI and placebo. Smaller studies have yielded some positive results in SSRI treatment of selective mutism in youths. Adult data and open clinical trials in children suggest SSRI use for youths with PD, starting at relatively low doses to reduce the risk of symptom exacerbation early in treatment. Pharmacological treatment studies of SPs are sparse but some suggest SSRI usefulness. Benzodiazepine (alprazolam, lorazepam, and clonazepam) efficacy in acute adult anxiety disorders has been documented. The pediatric data, however, do not consistently support benzodiazepine use, with side effect burden (sedation, disinhibition with irritability and aggression, risk of abuse) often outweighing risk. Clonidine and propranolol have been used in adult PTSD to treat hyperarousal, impulsivity, nightmares, and intrusive thoughts. Antipsychotics are sometimes used in pediatric PTSD to target persistent and overgeneralized anxiety. Some adult randomized controlled trials and open-label trials support the use of tricyclic antidepressants, non-SSRI antidepressants, and monoamine oxidase inhibitors in adult anxiety disorders, although use in the pediatric population is restricted based on sparse pediatric data and high side effect burden.

TABLE 92.2. Medication Uses by Condition

A. Behavior Disorders		
Attention-deficit hyperactivity disorder (ADHD)	Inattentiveness, impulsivity hyperactivity 50% may continue to manifest the disorder into adulthood Associated with mood, conduct, and anxiety disorders	Stimulants (use of extended release preparations; for uncomplicated ADHD; careful in patients with tics) Atomoxetine (nonstimulant, useful in anxiety comorbidity) Tricyclic antidepressants: desipramine, nortriptyline, imipramine (second line for non-responders) Clonidine (good for preschoolers, severe hyperactivity, aggression, ADHD + tics; nonresponders): guanfacine (Tenex)—generally used if clonidine too sedating Bupropion (second line for nonresponders, useful in mood lability/depression) Combined pharmacotherapy for treatment resistant or co-morbid cases
Conduct disorder (CD)/ Oppositional defiant disorder (ODD)	Persistent and pervasive patterns of aggressive and antisocial behaviors Often associated with other disorders such as ADHD and depression	No specific pharmacotherapy available for core disorder Behavioral/Family Therapy For ADHD (see above), complex combinations (i.e., clonidine and stimulants) For agitation and aggression: Clonidine or Tenex Beta blockers (i.e., propranolol) Mood stabilizers (i.e., Lithium, Carbamezapine, Valproate) Atypical antipsychotics (e.g., risperidone) Other Axis I disorders (i.e., ADHD, MDD, pyschosis, anxiety): treat the underlying disorder
B. Mood Disorders		
Major depressive disorder (MDD)	Sad or irritable mood and associated vegetative symptoms occurring together for a period of time Similar to the adult disorders with age-specific associated features	Selective Serotonin reuptake inhibitors (SSRIs): fluoxetine, sertraline, fluvoxamine, (es)citalopram Bupropion, venlafaxine Antidepressants and antipsychotics when psychosis develops Adjunct strategies for Tx refractory (Lithium, T3, ECT)
Bipolar disorder depressed	Same as depression	Mood stabilizers (Lithium, Carbamezapine, Valproate, Lamotrigine) Combined with MDD Tx Consider bupropion, short-acting SSRIs Atypical Antipsychotics (quetiapine)
Bipolar disorder manic	Pervasive and/or severely irritable/ angry mood Elevated or expansive mood More frequent psychotic symptoms in juvenile mania	Atypical antipsychotics (for acute mania first line; e.g., risperidone, quetiapine, olanzapine, ziprasidone, aripiprazole) Mood stabilizers (Lithium: first line) Mood stabilizers and antipsychotics if marked mania or mood lability or psychosis For Tx refractory: two mood stabilizers (lithium and valproate) Mood stabilizers and adjunct antipsychotics Mood stabilizers and high potency benzodiazepine

(*continued*)

TABLE 92.2. Medication Uses by Condition (*continued*)

Bipolar disorder mixed	Mixed depressed and manic symptoms Chronic course Most common presentation of juvenile bipolar disorder Usually very severe clinical picture	Mood stabilizers and atypical antipsychotics Mood stabilizers/antipsychotics and antidepressants (bupropion) Mood stabilizers and benzodiazepines
C. Anxiety Disorders		
Childhood anxiety disorders		
Non OCD Anxiety Disorders such as Generalized Anxiety Disorder, Separation Anxiety Disorder, Social Phobia, and Panic Disorder	Excessive or unrealistic worry about future events Excessive anxiety on separation from caretakers or familial surroundings. Recurrent discrete periods of intense fear (panic attacks) Frequent comorbidity	Selective serotonin reuptake inhibitors (SSRIs) Benzodiazepine (acute treatment) Clonidine, guanfacine, propranolol: hyperarousal in PTSD Combined pharmacotherapy for refractory or comorbid patients
Obsessive compulsive disorder	Recurrent, severe, and distressing obsessions and/or compulsions Often associated with Tourette's disorder, ADHD, mood and anxiety disorders	SSRIs Clomipramine Adjunctive Treatment: antipsychotics Combined pharmacotherapy for Tx refractory or comorbid patients (i.e., MDD, ADHD)
D. Other Disorders		
Psychotic disorders	Delusions and hallucinations Loose associations Paranoia often present Often associated with mood disorders	Atypical antipsychotics (SGAs) Traditional antipsychotics (FGAs) (risk for tardive dyskinesia) High potency BZDs for agitation For treatment-resistant cases: Antipsychotics and mood stabilizers Antipsychotics and benzodiazepines Clozapine
Tourette's disorder	Multiple motor and one or more vocal tic Frequently associated with OCD and ADHD	Clonidine or Tenex Antipsychotics (high potency FGA: Haldol, Pimozide) or SGA (risperidone) Combined pharmacotherapy for treatment resistant or comorbid cases
Enuresis	Bed wetting	ddAVP (Vasopressin) Tricyclic antidepressants (imipramine)
E. Developmental Disorders		
Pervasive developmental disorders	Qualitative impairment in social interactions, acquisition of, language, and motor skills Stereotypies and self-stimulating behaviors often present It can be global, or in specific or multiple areas	No specific pharmacotherapy for the core disorder For repetitive behaviors, serotonin-specific reuptake inhibitors (SSRIs) Pharmacotherapy of complications: Aggression, irritability, and self-abuse: Atypical antipsychotics (risperidone, aripiprazole) Clonidine, Guanfacine Other Axis I disorders (i.e., ADHD, MDD, psychosis, anxiety): treat the underlying disorder as in individuals

Abbreviations. ADHD = attention-deficit/hyperactivity disorder; OCD = obsessive-compulsive disorder; MDD = major depressive disorder; CD = conduct disorder; MR = mental retardation; TCAs = tricyclic antidepressants; MAOIs = monozmine oxidase inhibitors; SSRIs = serotonin-specific reuptake inhibitors; DDAVP = desmopresin; BZDs = benzodiazepines; Tx = treatment; Dx = diagnosis.

PSYCHOTIC DISORDERS

Psychosis may present in youths suffering from a primary psychotic disorder, such as early onset schizophrenia, or in those experiencing psychotic features accompanying major depressive disorder or bipolar I disorder. It may also present in the context of substance intoxication (ecstasy, amphetamines) or as an acute reaction to witnessing/experiencing a traumatic event. The psychiatric, developmental, social, and family history of the youth must be carefully factored when assessing for psychotic illness. Timing, duration, and severity of symptoms, as well as any evidence of a decline in functioning of the youth, are carefully taken into consideration when determining severity of psychotic symptoms and management strategies. Antipsychotics (also referred to as neuroleptics) are the primary treatment for pediatric psychotic disorders, in combination with psychotherapeutic interventions focused on recovery, relapse prevention, and social and family functioning.

In the treatment of psychosis, second-generation antipsychotics (SGAs), also known as atypical antipsychotics, have been found to have efficacy equal to first-generation antipsychotics (FGAs). SGAs are generally better tolerated than FGAs and are recommended as the first-line treatment for pediatric psychotic disorders. Because of varying receptor selectivity, it is postulated that SGAs appear more useful than FGAs in treating both the positive (hallucinations, delusions) and negative symptoms (amotivation) of psychotic illness. All produce improvement in psychotic symptoms by their D2 dopamine receptor-blocking action. Common short-term adverse effects of antipsychotics are motor restlessness or spasms, Parkinsonism, dry mouth, and significant weight gain. Motor side effects may be treated, prevented, or managed with the anticholinergic medication benztropine or diphenhydramine (Benadryl). Long-term administration of antipsychotics may be associated with abnormal involuntary motor movements called tardive dyskinesia (TD). Metabolic syndrome, including weight gain, is a serious adverse effect found with SGAs and FGAs and must be monitored routinely. Due to the potential side effects of antipsychotics, initial and interval monitoring of vital signs, weight, liver function, and lipid profile, as well as electrocardiogram (ECG), is warranted. Antipsychotics also carry a risk of serious side effects such as dystonic reactions (painful muscle spasm most frequently involving muscles in the neck though rarely muscles impairing breathing), akathisia (restlessness), cardiac disturbances such as QTc prolongation with possible torsades de pointes, and neuroleptic malignant syndrome (a potentially fatal condition). They can also lower the seizure threshold, though little data are available about this in the child and adolescent population. FGAs are more likely to cause neuroleptic malignant syndrome and dystonic reactions. Youths and elders are more susceptible to developing neurological side effects, particularly young males. FGAs are generally not prescribed to manage psychotic illness in youths until after at least one failed trial of SGAs.

In children and adolescents, SGAs risperidone, quetiapine, olanzapine, ziprasidone, aripiprazole, and clozapine are used to treat psychosis, severe mood lability, such as in mania, and aggression. Risperidone is the best studied SGA in the pediatric population and is noted to have fewer neurological side effects than high-potency D2 dopamine receptor-blocking FGAs (such as haloperidol) at therapeutic doses. Clozapine (Clozaril) is a low-potency D2 blocking agent that is used in treatment refractory pediatric patients, particularly those with negative symptoms or in those who have developed tardive dyskinesia. Clozapine has a relatively high incidence of dose-related seizures and bone marrow suppression, making weekly to biweekly white blood counts mandatory and its use limited, despite its demonstrated effectiveness in early-onset schizophrenia refractory to treatment with other first-line agents. There are a variety of FGAs that are classified based on their potency (strength) and, because of long-term adverse effects such as tardive dyskinesia (TD), are considered second-line agents for the treatment of psychosis. The most frequently used and best studied FGA is the high-potency

D2 dopamine receptor-blocking haloperidol. Low-potency agents include chlorpromazine and thioridazine and intermediate-potency agents include trifluoperazine and perphenazine. The low-potency agents are more likely to cause hypotension, tachycardia, and sedation, while the high-potency agents may cause muscle spasms. ECT is used as an adjunctive treatment, which should be considered for those pediatric patients severely disabled from severe psychosis who are unresponsive or only partially responsive to adequate trials of antipsychotics.

BIPOLAR DISORDER

A distinct episode of mood change with concurrent alterations in cognition and behavior, following strict *DSM-IV* criteria for bipolar disorder (BPD) in adults, is needed before assigning BPD in youth. Mood stabilizers and/or antipsychotics, in conjunction with psychotherapeutic interventions focused on relapse prevention, recovery, and social and family functioning, are the primary treatment for pediatric BPD. FDA-approved medications are recommended first-line agents in juvenile BPD (see Table 92.1). Lithium is an FDA-approved mood stabilizer used in pediatric BPD. Much of the data supporting the use of lithium in acute and maintenance treatment of BPD are derived from the adult literature, with some open-label studies supporting lithium use in acute depression associated with adolescent BPD. Due to its narrow therapeutic index and high frequency of side effects, frequent follow-up during initial dose titration is necessary to ensure safe and therapeutic serum concentrations. Side effects of lithium include tremor, gastrointestinal disturbances, frequent thirst and urination, acne, and weight gain. Serious adverse effects, particularly in lithium-induced toxicity, include acute mental status change associated with confusion, muscle spasms, moderate to severe tremor, and, in severe cases, coma with kidney failure and death. Risk for toxicity can increase with dehydration and medications that reduce kidney clearance of lithium (e.g., ibuprofen). Antiepileptic medications (AEDs), including valproate, lamotrigine, and carbamazepine, are frequently prescribed therapies for BPD in children and adolescents. To date, no AED has FDA approval for use in juvenile BPD. Valproate and extended-release carbamazepine have FDA approval for acute treatment in adult BPD. Studies involving valproate as a monotherapy for BPD in youths are mixed. A few open-label studies support valproate use in juvenile BPD while one randomized controlled trial does not. Valproate is used with caution in females of reproductive age due to associated risks of polycystic ovarian syndrome and teratogenic defects. Lamotrigine is FDA approved for maintenance therapy in adult BPD and has reported benefit in depressive symptoms associated with BPD, with relatively few side effects. Rapid dose titration of lamotrigine has been associated with Stevens-Johnson syndrome, a potentially lethal allergic reaction characterized by rash and skin lesions. Other AEDs, including topiramate (Topamax) and oxcarbazepine (Trileptal), have minimal evidence supporting their use in adult and juvenile BPD. SGAs risperidone, quetiapine, olanzapine, and aripiprazole have FDA approval for use in BPD youths. Ziprasidone is FDA approved for treatment of acute BPD in adults only. SGAs have been shown to be superior to placebo in treatment of pediatric BPD, with no significant differences in efficacy between different FDA-approved SGAs. FGAs are generally not used as a first-line BPD agent. For severely impaired (refusal to eat/drink, neglect of self care), catatonic, pregnant, or medication nonresponsive or medication contraindicated BPD patients, ECT is a viable treatment option.

EATING DISORDERS

Medication should not be used as the primary treatment for anorexia nervosa (AN). SSRIs have shown no promise in treating core AN symptoms. SGAs such as olanzapine have increased weight gain, decreased obsessions, and reduced agitation in some AN case studies. Medications are often used to target comorbid psychiatric disorders in AN. Fluoxetine is FDA approved for adult bulimia nervosa (BN), reducing core BN symptoms. Higher SSRI doses may be indicated when treating BN patients. Buproprion is contraindicated in those with eating disorders due to increased seizure risk.

ATTENTION-DEFICIT/HYPERACTIVITY DISORDER

Attention-deficit/hyperactivity disorder (ADHD) may affect approximately 7% of school-age children and persists into adolescence and adulthood in approximately 50% of cases. Effective pharmacological treatment of ADHD dramatically improves the child and family's quality of life as well as reduces the risk for substance abuse in approximately 50% of patients. The pharmacological management of ADHD includes the use of agents that affect dopaminergic and noradrenergic neurotransmission—namely stimulants, antidepressants, and antihypertensives. Stimulants are the first-line treatment for ADHD, including the methylphenidate (Ritalin, Ritalin LA, Concerta) or dexmethylphenidate (Focalin, Focalin XR) compounds, and the amphetamine (Adderall, Adderall XR) or dextroamphetamine (Dexedrine) compounds. Stimulants have been shown to be effective in a majority of youths with ADHD and symptoms respond almost immediately and are individually dose dependent with improvements in cognition and behavior. The most commonly reported short-term side effects associated with the stimulants are appetite suppression, sleep disturbances, and abdominal pain. Long-term side effects remain controversial, with mixed literature indicating some association with motor tic development and effects on height/weight. Atomoxetine (Straterra) is a highly specific nonstimulant agent prescribed second line for children and adults with ADHD who have not responded favorably to the stimulant classes and/or have struggled significantly with side effects. One major drawback is that atomoxetine can take 2–6 weeks to achieve relief from symptoms. An antihypertensive agent, alpha-agonist clonidine, has been used increasingly for the treatment of ADHD, particularly in younger children and those with hyperactivity and aggressive, externalizing behaviors. Clonidine is a short-acting agent and may be used adjunctively with the stimulants and antidepressants. Short-term adverse effects include sedation (which tends to subside with continued treatment), dry mouth, depression, confusion, and ECG changes. Abrupt withdrawal of clonidine has been associated with rebound hypertension; thus, slow tapering is advised. Another antihypertensive agent used alone or adjunctively in the treatment of ADHD and externalizing behaviors associated with low frustration tolerability is guanfacine (Tenex). Guanfacine appears to be longer acting, less sedating, and more effective for attentional problems than clonidine and also comes in an extended-release form (Intuniv). In the past, tricyclic antidepressants (TCAs) were generally considered second-line drugs of choice because of a long duration of action, greater flexibility in dosage, and minimal risk of abuse or dependence. However, TCA use is limited due to potential cardiac side effects, need for ECG and serum level monitoring, and potential lethality in overdose. Thus, TCA use is scant in ADHD given other available effective treatment options. The antidepressant bupropion has been reported to be useful in the treatment of children with ADHD, particularly those with comorbid mood disorders, though it may provide no symptom control for several weeks.

TICS AND TOURETTE'S DISORDER

A tic is defined as a sudden, rapid, recurrent, nonrhythmic, stereotyped motor movement or vocalization that is experienced as irresistible, but it can be suppressed for varying lengths of time and is usually markedly diminished during sleep. Patients commonly have spontaneous symptom fluctuation regardless of medication use. Tourette's disorder is a childhood-onset neuropsychiatric disorder commonly associated with OCD, ADHD, and anxiety disorders; it consists of multiple motor and one or more phonic tics that have been present at some time in the illness, although not necessarily concurrently. Medication for tic reduction in youths is reserved for tics that cause marked distress or significant impairment in psychosocial functioning and for significant comorbid conditions. Clonidine and guanfacine are first-line agents in treating mild to moderate tic disorders. Sedation and low blood pressure are common side effects that require monitoring particularly when initiating treatment. The high-potency antipsychotics haloperidol (Haldol) and pimozide (Orap) and risperidone (Risperdal) are effective in reducing tics, but the potential neurological and metabolic side effects limit their use as first-line treatment. Children with tic disorders and comorbid diagnoses such as OCD, depressive disorders, or anxiety disorders may also benefit from an SSRI. Augmentation of an SSRI with an atypical antipsychotic medication is a consideration in patients with tic disorders and OCD who respond poorly to an SSRI alone. The presence of tics does not preclude the use of stimulants to address comorbid ADHD, though careful monitoring is required for possible tic exacerbation.

PERVASIVE DEVELOPMENTAL DISORDERS

Pharmacological treatment does not address core pervasive developmental disorder (PDD) symptoms; rather, medication is used to reduce dysfunctional behavior and treat comorbid mental health illness. SSRIs treat mood, anxiety, and compulsive and stereotypical behaviors. SGAs are used in youths with PDDs to target aggression, irritability, self-injurious behavior, hyperactivity, stereotypical behaviors, and temper outbursts. Specifically, risperidone and aripiprazole are FDA-approved treatments for irritability and behavioral dysregulation in children with autism spectrum disorders. Stimulants and the nonstimulant medication atomoxetine may reduce hyperactivity, distractibility, and impulsivity in PDD, albeit to a lesser degree than non-PDD youths. Clonidine and guanfacine target irritability, impulsivity, and hyperactivity in youths. Children with PDDs are often susceptible to medication side effects in a magnitude larger than typically developing youth.

PEDIATRIC AGITATION

Agitation consists of a psychological state (feeling of inner tension evident by pressured, loud, disorganized, or poverty of speech) and a motoric state (excessive motor activity evident by pacing, fidgeting, hand wringing, pulling of clothes, etc.), which can lead to aggression and placing the patient and others in danger. There are no published investigation trials comparing various medication options for treatment of agitation in children and adolescents. In a hospital setting, when behavioral interventions to assist with calming the agitated patient are unsuccessful or inappropriate due to level of dangerousness, the use of psychotropic medication is warranted to protect the patient and others. Goals of treatment for pediatric agitation with medication are to promote safety for the patient and environment, and to help the patient achieve a state of calmness. Classes of medication to be considered in the treatment of pediatric agitation include benzodiazepines, alpha-agonists, and antipsychotics. Patients should be given an option of taking oral medication first and should only be given medication IM (intramuscularly) or IV (intravenously) if necessary and clinically warranted (such as patients with severe agitation, dangerous to self and others, refusal of medication by mouth, delirium, impaired level of consciousness, etc.).

Due to high frequency of paradoxical responses in the pediatric patient, patients and guardians should be asked about any previous treatments with antihistamines and benzodiazepines. Benzodiazepines (e.g., Lorazepam) are commonly used to manage agitation. The main side effects are oversedation, disinhibition, and respiratory depression. One should be especially cautious in giving this medication to children with autism spectrum or pervasive developmental disorders, developmental delay, learning disorders, or other neurological disorders. If a primary anxiety disorder is suspected, one should first try a benzodiazepine medication for mild agitation. Clonidine should be considered in the mildly agitated patients who are already prescribed this medication and/or in those who carry a diagnosis of ADHD, a disruptive behavior disorder, and PDD.

FGAs and SGAs can be used in the treatment-naïve pediatric patient experiencing a severely agitated episode where there is imminent risk of harm to self and/or others. Haloperidol, risperidone, and olanzapine are most frequently used in cases of pediatric agitation utilizing antipsychotic therapy in the hospital setting. An advantage of haloperidol is that it can be given IV, though this type of dosing is associated with an increased risk of QTc prolongation and should be only administered in an intensive care unit setting with ECG monitoring. Risperidone can be given in oral tablet, liquid, and oral disintegrating (ODT) preparation; olanzapine is available in oral, ODT, and IM form. The advantage of olanzapine and risperidone is that they have a more favorable short-term side effect profile than haloperidol. Diphenhydramine can be administered with an antipsychotic medication to prevent some of the more serious side effects of the antipsychotic, but it should be used with caution. The most common side effects of diphenhydramine are anticholinergic side effects such as sedation, dry mouth, dizziness, constipation, urinary retention, dry skin, flushing, and exacerbation of reactive airway disease. Additionally, it can cause a paradoxical reaction, manifesting in increased agitation and disinhibition, particularly if administered alone.

References and Readings

American Academy of Child and Adolescent Psychiatry. (n.d.). *Practice parameters*. Retrieved January 2013, from aacap.org/cs/root/member_information/practice_information/practice_parameters/practice_parameters

Bloch, M. H., Landeros-Weisenberger, A., Kelmendi, B., Coric, V., Bracken, M. B., & Leckman, J. F. (2006). A systematic review: Antipsychotic augmentation with refractory obessive compulsive disorder. *Molecular Psychiatry, 11*(7), 622–632.

Bridge, J. A., Iyengar, S., Salary, C. B., Barbe, R. P., Birmaher, B., Pincus, H.A., ... Brent, D. A. (2007). Clinical response and risk for reported suicidal ideation and suicide attempts in pediatric antidepressant treatment: A meta-analysis of randomized controlled trials. *Journal of the American Medical Association, 297*, 1683–1696.

Fraguas, D., Correll, C. U., Merchán-Naranjo, J., Rapado-Castro, M., Parellada, M., Moreno C., & Arango, C. (2011). Efficacy and safety of second-generation antipsychotics in children and adolescents with psychotic and bipolar spectrum disorders: Comprehensive review of prospective head to head and placebo controlled comparisons. *European Psychopharmacology, 21*, 621–645.

Hilt, R. J., & Woodward, T. A. (2008). Agitation treatment for pediatric emergency patients. *Journal of the American Academy of Child and Adolescent Psychiatry, 47*(2), 132–138.

Kumra, S., Frazier, J., Jacobsen, L., McKenna, K., Gordon, C., Lenane, M., ... Rapoport, J. L. (1996). Childhood onset schizophrenia: A double blind clozapine-haloperidol comparison. *Archives of General Psychiatry, 53*, 1090–1097.

Martin, A., & Volkmar, F. M. (Eds.). (2007). *Lewis's child and adolescent psychiatry, a comprehensive textbook* (4th ed.). Baltimore, MD: Lippincott Williams & Wilkins.

Related Topics

Chapter 90, "Adult Psychopharmacology"

Chapter 91, "Understanding Side Effects and Warnings in Psychopharmacology"

93 COMMON DRUGS OF ABUSE AND THEIR EFFECTS

Christopher J. Correia and James G. Murphy

The Substance Abuse and Mental Health Services Administration's (SAMHSA, 2011) National Household Survey on Drug Abuse estimates that 21 million Americans, or 9% of the population, used an illicit drug during the previous month. Approximately 22.5 million (9%) met the *Diagnostic and Statistical Manual*, fourth edition (*DSM-IV*) diagnostic criteria for substance abuse or dependence, which are among the most common mental disorders. Because drug use afflicts individuals from every demographic group, and because drug-related problems are common in clinical settings, it is important for all mental health professionals to understand the common drugs of abuse.

Table 93.1 provides an overview of the common drugs abused—specifically, their slang names, routes of administration, acute effects, adverse effects, tolerance potential, and how they interact with other drugs. The table provides only general information on drug interactions; it is not an exhaustive list of potentially hazardous drug interactions.

Although prescription medications are generally safe when used as prescribed, when misused their subjective effects and addiction potential are similar to illicit drugs of abuse. For example, medications such as opioid analgesics (e.g., Oxycodone), methylphenidate (Ritalin), and benzodiazepines (e.g., Valium) can produce physiological and subjective effects that are similar to heroin, cocaine, and alcohol, respectively. Prescription drug misuse is especially common among young adults, individuals with other substance-abuse or mental health problems, and individuals who have been treated with prescription analgesics or sedatives for long periods (e.g., chronic pain or anxiety patients).

In the following sections, we outline several assessment considerations for these common drugs of abuse.

DRUG-USE PATTERNS

A drug-use assessment should begin with questions about lifetime and current use of drugs, with consideration of the base rate for the client's demographic group. Individuals are most likely to provide accurate information when they are asked about use of specific substances, including misuse of prescription drugs. In some settings, biological tests (e.g., breath, hair, saliva, urine) can be used to detect recent drug use. The validity of self-reports can be enhanced by asking about drug use in a nonjudgmental manner and by providing assurance of confidentiality. In the absence of legal or other repercussions (e.g., loss of child custody or employment)

TABLE 93.1. Common Drugs of Abuse: Summary of Routes of Administration, Effects, and Interactions

Drugs, Commercial and Slang Name	Routes of Administration	Acute Effects of Intoxication	Possible Adverse Effects	Tolerance and Dependence	Drug Interactions
Cannabinoids—Cannabis products such as marijuana and hashish contain THC, a chemical that produces mild sedative, euphoric, and hallucinogenic effects. Although there is no risk for overdose, regular use can result in tolerance, functional impairment, and mild withdrawal symptoms. The use of synthetic cannabis products may produce more severe side effects.					
Hashish: boom, hash, hash oil, hemp Marijuana: Marinol, pot, grass, weed, reefer, blunt Synthetic marijuana: K2, spice, herbal incense	Smoked via cigarette, pipe, or water filtered pipe (i.e., bong). Can also be administered orally.	Increased pulse and appetite, dry mouth, enhanced sensory perception, mild euphoria, relaxation, sedation, and psychomotor impairment. Possible dizziness, illusions, and hallucinations	Some users experience brief paranoid reactions and panic. Chronic use of smoked THC associated with pulmonary damage. Possible deficits in learning, cognition, and motivation. Possible precipitant of psychotic episode among those with latent potential. Possible immunosuppressant.	Tolerance occurs with repeated use. Withdrawal symptoms include restlessness, anxiety, depression, irritability/aggression, insomnia, tremor, and chills. Withdrawal does not pose medical risk. Although not well studied, there are reports that synthetic marijuana may produce more severe withdrawal symptoms.	May interact with heart and blood pressure medication, or with other drugs that suppress the immune system.
CNS depressants—These include alcohol, barbiturates, benzodiazepines, and other drugs that induce behavioral depression, sedation, and relief from anxiety. At high doses these drugs produce motor impairment, amnesia, unconsciousness, and potentially fatal respiratory depression. Chronic use of CNS depressants can produce physical dependence, including severe withdrawal symptoms.					
Alcohol Barbiturates: Amytal, Seconal, Phenobarbital, barbs, reds, yellows Benzodiazepines: Diazepam (Valium), Lorazepam (Ativan), Clonazepam (Klonopin), Alprazolam (Xanax), candy, downers, sleeping pills	Benzodiazepines and alcohol are orally administered.	Effects of CNS depressants can be context dependent and "biphasic." Euphoria and disinhibition are common at low to moderate doses. High doses produce clouded sensorium, sedation, impaired judgment and motor ability, amnesia/blackouts, affect lability, aggression, delusions, and hallucinations.	Dangerous levels of respiratory depression. Sedation, impaired judgment and cognitive performance, amnesia, and psychomotor impairment. These effects can increase risk for automobile accidents, falls, and high-risk behavior. High doses of	Tolerance occurs with long-term use. Withdrawal symptoms include agitation and increased anxiety, insomnia, muscle tension, and nausea with vomiting. Severe withdrawal symptoms include tremors and seizures (e.g.,	Can produce potentially lethal respiratory depression when taken in combination with other CNS depressants (e.g., alcohol), or with heroin or prescription analgesics.

		Benzodiazepines are intended for short-term relief of anxiety and insomnia; higher doses produce lightheadedness, vertigo, and muscle incoordination.	alcohol can lead to asphyxiation from vomiting. Chronic heavy use of alcohol can lead to irreversible liver damage, dementia, pancreatitis, gastritis, peptic ulcers, and cancers.	deliriums tremens), hallucinations, and psychotic symptoms. These symptoms can be fatal and often require medical attention.	
Dissociative anesthetics—These drugs are difficult to classify, as they produce a combination of stimulant, depressant, and hallucinogenic effects. They can also cause fatal overdoses resulting from seizures and coma. Ketamine is also referred to as a "club drug" because of its association with all-night dance parties (raves).					
Ketamine: cat, K, special K, vitamin K, date rape drug Phencyclidine: PCP, angel dust, boat, hog, love boat, peace pill, rocket fuel, sherms	Ketamine can be injected, snorted, or smoked. PCP can also be swallowed.	Dream-like disorientation, euphoria, and analgesia. Impaired motor functioning, slurred speech, and detachment from environment. Increased heart rate, blood pressure, and temperature.	PCP can cause potentially lethal seizures and coma. Possible acute and prolonged psychotic states, leading to bizarre or dangerous behaviors. Ketamine produces more extreme CNS depression, numbness, nausea and vomiting, amnesia, and dissociation.	Tolerance rises quickly, and chronic users will experience permanent tolerance after several months of use. These drugs do not appear to produce withdrawal symptoms or physical addiction.	Dangerous when used with other drugs that depress respiration. Psychological effects are unpredictable when taken with other drugs.
Entactogens—Drugs from this class produce both stimulant and mild hallucinogenic effects. They are sometimes referred to as "designer drugs" or as "club drugs" because of their association with all-night dance parties (raves).					
Methylenedioxyamphetamine: MDA Methylenedioxyethlylamphetamine: MDEA, Eve Methylenedioxymethamphetamine: MDMA, Ecstasy, X, XTC, Adam, lover's speed, peace, STP; Trail mix and sextasy used to denote combination of MDMA and Viagra (sildenafil citrate).	Usually swallowed in the form of a pill, although pure powder forms are sometimes injected, and tablets can be inserted into the anus.	MDMA produced mild hallucinogenic effects, increased tactile sensitivity, empathic feelings, mental alertness, and sympathetic nervous system stimulation. MDEA effects resemble those of MDMA, but without the empathic qualities. MDA produces stronger hallucinogenic effects	MDMA can be fatal when combined with high levels of physical activity, leading to hyperthermia, hypertension, and kidney failure. MDMA appears to lead to long-term changes in the serotonergic system, which may result in residual anxiety, depression, and cognitive impairment. Flashbacks following repeated use have been reported.	Tolerance develops, but there is no evidence of physical withdrawal. After-effects can include fatigue, depression, and anxiety.	Over-the-counter cold remedies and MAO inhibitors. MDMA and Viagra may cause dangerous changes in heart rate and blood pressure, and prolonged erection leading to permanent anatomical changes.

(*continued*)

TABLE 93.1. Common Drugs of Abuse: Summary of Routes of Administration, Effects, and Interactions (*continued*)

Hallucinogens—Hallucinogens produce altered states of perception and intense emotions that vary widely across individuals and occasions. Hallucinogens do not produce dependence, although use of these drugs can result in negative physical and psychological consequences.					
Dimethyltrypyamine: DMT, business man's trip Lysergic acid diethylamide: LSD, acid, blotter, cubes, microdot Mescaline: peyote, buttons, cactus Psilocybin: psychedelic or magic mushrooms shrooms	Oral administration is typical. LSD can also be absorbed through mouth tissue; DMT and mescaline can be smoked.	Altered states of perception and bodily sensations, intense emotions, detachment from self and environment, and, for some users, feelings of insight with mystical or religious significance. Mescaline also has some amphetamine-like effects.	Psychological symptoms such as emotional lability, panic, and paranoia can lead to bizarre or dangerous behavior. Persisting mental disorders, including panic attacks and psychosis, after use in those with latent potential. Hallucinogenic persisting perception disorder (flashbacks).	Tolerance builds up rapidly but fades after a few days. Hallucinogens do not produce withdrawal and are not physically addictive.	Mescaline can be dangerous when used in combination with other stimulants. Effects are more unpredictable when taken with other drugs.
Inhalants—The drugs in this category have little in common in terms of chemical structure, pharmacology, or behavioral effects. They are all taken by inhalation, however, and thus are often considered as a group.					
Anesthetics: nitrous oxide Solvents: paint thinner, glue, correction fluid, marker pens Gases: butane, propane Aerosols: paint, hair spray Nitrites: "poppers" from heart medications	Inhalation	Rapid onset of sedation, euphoria, and disinhibition. Acute effects can include loss of consciousness, blackout, muscle weakness, impaired coordination, and slurred speech. Nitrates dilate blood vessels and produce sensation of heat and excitement believed to enhance sexual pleasure.	Use of inhalants can lead to lack of oxygen, ischemia of heart tissue, life-threatening cardiac arrhythmias, cardiac collapse, peripheral nerve damage, liver or kidney damage, and suffocation. Regular use can produce irreversible brain and peripheral nerve damage.	Tolerance and withdrawal are possible with prolonged use of nitrates. Tolerance to nitrous oxide is possible but unlikely with recreational use. Little is known about the tolerance and withdrawal profile of other inhalants.	Interactions with other drugs with depressant effects, including cold medicines, opiates, alcohol, barbiturates, and benzodiazepines are especially dangerous. Nitrates and Viagra can lead to fatal changes in blood pressure.

Opioid analgesics—These drugs bind to the opioid receptors and block the transmission of pain messages to the brain. They also produce euphoria, drowsiness, and potentially fatal respiratory depression. Chronic use can produce physical dependence, including severe withdrawal symptoms.					
Heroin: black tar, smack, junk, dope Prescription analgesics: Morphine, Codeine, Demerol, Oxycodone, Oxycontin, Percocet, Vicodin	Heroin is injected, smoked, and used intranasally. Oral medications are misused by crushing tablet and snorting or injecting.	Analgesia, euphoria, sedation, reduced anxiety, tranquility, respiratory depression, and cough suppression	Respiratory depression can be fatal at high doses, or when regular users use in novel environments. Other side effects include nausea, vomiting, constipation and intestinal cramping, severe itching, and asthma-like symptoms. HIV, Hepatitis C, and bacterial infections are spread through injecting.	Tolerance occurs with prolonged use. Withdrawal symptoms include craving, sweating, anxiety, depression, irritability, fever, chills, vomiting, diarrhea, and pain. Compulsive use to avoid withdrawal is common.	Interactions with CNS depressants such as alcohol or benzodiazepines can cause potentially fatal respiratory depression.
Stimulants—These drugs produce sympathetic nervous system stimulation, which leads to increased heart rate and blood pressure, and an increase in purposeful movement. Additional effects include euphoria, increased alertness, and increased energy.					
Amphetamines: Adderall, Dexedrine, bennies, speed Cocaine: coke, blow, crack Methamphetamine: crank, crystal fire, ice, meth, speed methylenedioxypyrovalerone, more commonly referred to as "bath salts" and sold with names like Aura, Ivory Wave, Loco-Motion, and Vanilla Sky Methylphenidate: Ritalin, vitamin R, Nicotine Chew, cigars, cigarettes, smokeless tobacco, snuff, spit tobacco	Injected, smoked, and snorted. Stimulant medication can be swallowed, or crushed and then snorted or injected.	Feelings of euphoria, increased energy, mental alertness, and rapid speech. Signs of sympathetic nervous system stimulation, including increased heart rate, blood pressure, temperature, and both purposeful and compulsive movements.	Rapid or irregular heartbeat, heart failure, respiratory failure, strokes, seizures, headaches, abdominal pain, and nausea. With prolonged exposure to high doses, a psychotic state of hostility and paranoia can emerge that is similar to acute paranoid schizophrenia. Specific effects of prolonged exposure to nicotine products include chronic lung disease, cardiovascular disease, stroke, and cancer.	Tolerance builds quickly. Users typically experience fatigue and dysphoria after intoxication. Withdrawal symptoms are rarely dangerous but include fatigue, anxiety, sleeplessness, irritability, anhedonia, and depression.	Over-the-counter decongestants, MAO inhibitors, medications that raise heart rate or that increase sensitivity to seizures.

for reporting drug use, self-reports of drug use are generally consistent with collateral reports and biological tests (Tucker, Murphy, & Kertesz, 2010).

After gathering information about recent drug use, assess quantity and frequency of use over time. Drug-use patterns are generally quite variable, and information on contextual factors associated with periods of abstinence or increased use can be useful for treatment planning. Changes in substance use are often preceded by changes in other life areas, including employment, relationships, and physical health. Since many abused drugs are not sold in standard quantities, money spent on drugs and hours/days spent under the influence are useful proxies for drug amount. It is also crucial to gather information on route of administration, since this has implications for drug potency, abuse potential, and HIV/hepatitis C risk. In general, snorting, smoking, and injecting drugs are associated with increased potency and abuse potential relative to oral ingestion. For example, prescribed drugs such as Oxycontin or Ritalin are often crushed and either snorted or injected for a more potent and addicting high.

RISKS AND NEGATIVE CONSEQUENCES

Regular drug use is associated with significant social, interpersonal, legal, health, and occupational impairment. Substance abusers typically present for treatment because of substance-related impairment, such as marital or health problems, rather than substance use itself. Thus, clinicians need to discuss drug-related negative consequences and query about the presence of symptoms of drug dependence, such as increasing tolerance, withdrawal symptoms, and compulsive use.

It is especially important to carefully assess risk for immediate harm resulting from drug use. High-risk behaviors such as sharing injection needles, driving while intoxicated, risky sexual behavior, and taking dangerous drug combinations should be an immediate treatment priority.

COMORBIDITY

Substance-use disorders occur among those with other *DSM-IV* disorders at elevated rates, relative to the general population. In fact, 37% of alcohol abusers and 53% of drug abusers meet criteria for an additional mental disorder (Reiger et al., 1990). Stated differently, 29% of persons with a mental disorder were comorbid for a substance-use disorder. Persons with more severe mental illness are the greatest risk; 47% of persons with schizophrenia and 56% of persons with bipolar disorder have a lifetime diagnosis of substance abuse or dependence. Substance abusers with another psychiatric diagnosis tend to experience more psychosocial and physical health impairment compared to those without a comorbid diagnosis.

References and Readings

Julien, R. M. (2004). *A primer of drug action* (10th ed.). New York: Worth.

National Institute on Drug Abuse. (2011). Drugs of abuse. Retrieved February 2013, from www.drugabuse.gov/drugpages.

National Institute on Drug Abuse. (2011). Screening tools for tobacco, alcohol and other drug use. Retrieved 2011 from www.nida.nih.gov/nidamed/screening/

Reiger, D. A., Farmer, M. E., Rae, D. S., Locke, B. Z., Keith, S. J., Judd, L. L., & Goodwin, F. K. (1990). Comorbidity of mental disorders with alcohol and other drug abuse: Results from the Epidemiological Catchment Area (ECA) study. *Journal of the American Medical Association, 21*, 2511–2518.

Substance Abuse and Mental Health Services Administration. (2011). *Results from the 2009 National Household Survey on Drug Abuse: Volume I. Summary of National Findings* (DHHS Publication No. SMA 10–3856). Rockville, MD: US Department of Health and Human Services.

The Vaults of Erowid. (2011). *Psychoactive vaults: Plant and chemical library*. Retrieved February 2013, from www.erowid.org/psychoactives

Tucker, J. A., Murphy, J. G., & Kertesz, S. G. (2010). Substance Use Disorders. In M. H. Anthony, & D. H. Barlow (Eds.). *Handbook of Assessment and Treatment Planning* (2nd ed.). New York: Guilford Press.

Related Topics

Chapter 1, "Lifetime Prevalence of Mental Disorders in the General Population"
Chapter 7, "Identifying and Assessing Alcohol, Drug, and Tobacco Use Disorders"
Chapter 91, "Understanding Side Effects and Warnings in Psychopharmacology"
Chapter 98, "Dietary Supplements and Psychological Functioning"

94 HERBAL TREATMENTS FOR PSYCHOLOGICAL DISORDERS

Paula J. Biedenharn and Brian A. Kiernan

Used in parts of the world for thousands of years, herbal medicines continue to grow in popularity in the United States. Herbal medicines are the most commonly used type of complementary and alternative medicines (CAMs). Also known as botanicals or phytomedicines, herbal treatments number in the hundreds, with St. John's wort, ginkgo, and ginseng among the most commonly used (Fetrow & Avila, 2004). In the United States, these herbs were used by an estimated 1 in 5 adults or 38 million people in a 2007 study (NCCAM, 2010). In addition to being used for physical health problems, these herbs are often used by those seeking relief from emotional illnesses. While many tout the efficacy of these herbal treatments for psychological disorders such as depression, there are several concerns about herbal treatments that warrant a cautious approach.

CAUTIONS FOR HERBAL TREATMENTS

First, many important medications started as herbal treatments, including warfarin (sweet clover), capsaicin (red pepper), and Taxol (Pacific yew tree) (Fetrow & Avila, 2004). Therefore, it seems plausible that some phytomedicines will be found useful for the treatment of psychological symptoms. However, additional research is needed to confirm both the safety and the effectiveness of these herbs. Given that herbs often contain thousands of phytochemicals, identifying the active ingredient can be difficult and users may be unknowingly consuming ineffective or possibly toxic substances (Lakhan & Vieira, 2010).

Second, there are considerable variations in product strength for herbal medications, making accurate, consistent dosages difficult (McCabe, 2002). Because herbal CAMs are considered dietary supplements (1994 Dietary Supplement Health and Education Act), they are not regulated by the U.S. Food and Drug Administration (FDA) and therefore are not standardized. Illustrating this problem, one analysis of St. John's wort products found variations in hyperforin, believed to be the active ingredient in this herb, from 0% to 3.26% in samples from various manufacturers.

Third, many herbal medicines have side effects and the potential for drug interactions, particularly when taken with certain prescription as well as nonprescribed over-the-counter medications (McCabe, 2002; NCCAM, 2010). Since consumers can purchase these herbs at grocery stores and convenience markets, they tend to see herbal medicines as safe, natural substances, not as drugs. This is further complicated by the fact that product dosages may not be consistent, products may be adulterated or contaminated by the production process and the assumed product may not even be contained in the herb purchased (NCCAM, 2010). An added concern is the fact that patients typically do not report the use of herbal medicines to their physicians and many physicians fail to ask about usage (Hammerness et al., 2003). Therefore, psychologists should encourage their patients to report all herbal treatments to their primary care physicians.

Perhaps the most significant problem is the tremendous lack of scientifically rigorous experiments testing the efficacy of herbal products. While traditional pharmaceuticals are subjected to multiple, large-scale, double-blind studies prior to approval, the evaluation of an herb's efficacy is the result of primarily anecdotal evidence and case studies (McCabe, 2002). While randomized controlled trials of many herbal treatments are under way, the current lack of scientific evidence for efficacy and safety undermines the use of herbal treatments.

Nonetheless, with many people seeking alternatives to prescription medications and with the continuing rise of interest in "natural" products, herbal use is not likely to diminish. Therefore, a working knowledge of these herbal medicines is becoming essential for psychologists, as many clients are likely to be using these herbal treatments or may be interested in trying them (Hammerness et al., 2003). The following is a brief review of the most commonly used herbal medicines for psychological disorders. Table 94.1 provides a summary of these herbal treatments and basic parameters for their usage.

ST. JOHN'S WORT

St. John's wort (*Hypericum perforatum*), a common roadside weed with yellow flowers, has been used for thousands of years to treat a wide variety of health problems. Today it is most commonly used for the treatment of depression (Hammerness et al., 2003) and is even prescribed for children and adolescents in Europe (Kapalka, 2010).

Overall, St. John's wort has been studied extensively and has been found to be as effective as some prescription drugs for mild to moderate depression (Kapalka, 2010). Recent meta-analyses (Linde, Berner, & Kriston, 2009; Rahimi, Nikfar, & Abdollahi, 2008) have confirmed that St. John's wort works better than placebo and equal to selective serotonin reuptake inhibitors (SSRIs) and tricyclic antidepressants (TCAs). Rahimi, Nikfar, and Abdollahi (2008) noted that while there was no difference in adverse reactions for St. John's wort versus SSRIs, withdrawal rates were higher for those taking SSRIs due to side effects. At this time, St. John's wort appears to be less effective for more severe cases of depression (Medline Plus, 2011). Although St. John's wort has also been examined for effects on anxiety, obsessive-compulsive disorder, attention-deficit/hyperactivity disorder (ADHD), and seasonal affective disorder, not enough data are available to confirm efficacy (Hammerness et al., 2003; Medline Plus, 2011).

While a popular herb worldwide and considered safe when taken short term, St. John's wort does have side effects and potentially serious drug interactions, though side effects tend to be lower than those of other antidepressants (Hammerness et al., 2003). Side effects commonly include gastrointestinal upset, restlessness, sedation, dizziness, dry mouth, headaches, and skin reactions. Because photosensitivity is common, people taking St. John's wort should use sunscreen (McCabe, 2002). Use is not recommended during pregnancy or while breast-feeding, and there is some concern that it may interfere with the ability to conceive a child. In addition, St. John's wort might worsen ADHD and bipolar disorder and might bring out psychosis in schizophrenics (Medline Plus, 2011).

The list of potential interactions between St. John's wort and prescription medications continues to grow (Medline Plus, 2011). In particular, St. John's wort interferes with the protease inhibitors used to treat HIV (such as indinavir) and with the most common antirejection drug used after transplant surgery (cyclosporine), causing reduced blood levels of these crucial medications (McCabe, 2002). Acting as a weak monoamine oxidase inhibitor (MAOI), St. John's wort adds to the effect of prescription MAOIs, SSRIs, and TCAs—potentially leading to serotonin syndrome or a hypertensive crisis. St. John's wort can also cause increased anxiety when taken with flagyl. Theoretically, drugs such as warfarin (Coumadin) and oral contraceptives, statin anticholesterol drugs, and anticonvulsant drugs may all have decreased blood levels when St. John's wort is taken (McCabe, 2002).

GINKGO BILOBA

Ginkgo biloba is derived from the leaves of a commonly cultivated, ancient tree. It is among the most commonly prescribed herbs in Europe. In Germany, ginkgo is used to treat vascular disorders as well as dementia patients. Healthy young and older adults take ginkgo to improve short-term memory, and ginkgo is also used to counteract the sexual dysfunction that often accompanies the use of SSRIs (Fetrow & Avila, 2004).

Recent research has contradicted the previously held conviction of ginkgo's efficacy in the treatment of dementia. Birks and Grimley Evans' (2009) meta-analysis found inconsistent results for the effect of ginkgo on cognition, activities of daily living, and mood in cognitively impaired adults and dementia patients. The Ginkgo Evaluation of Memory study (DeKosky et al., 2008) followed 3,000 adults over the age of 75 who took 240 mg of Ginkgo EGb-761 daily over the course of several years. Results indicate that ginkgo was ineffective in preventing or delaying the onset of dementia or Alzheimer's disease. In addition, no memory improvement was found in a study that followed healthy adults who took ginkgo for 6 weeks. Ginkgo is presently being studied for use with multiple sclerosis, ADHD, and the short-term memory loss that follows electroconvulsive therapy for depression (NCCAM, 2010).

Side effects from ginkgo include anxiety, insomnia, headache, and gastrointestinal distress. More seriously, ginkgo may be a possible teratogen, may cause mania at high dosage, and may cause serious bleeding due to its anticoagulant effect (McCabe, 2002). Ginkgo may interact with anticoagulants, antiplatelets, and oral hypoglycemic medications.

GINSENG

Considered the most widely used herb worldwide, ginseng comes in many types, including Chinese, Korean, Japanese, Siberian, and American. The most studied variety is panax ginseng, which is considered the "true ginseng" (Spinella, 2001, p. 167). Ginseng may be white or red depending on the preparation of the plant's rhizome (which may alter the pharmacological effect) and is expensive to produce and purchase. Panax ginseng is used for improving thinking, concentration, and work efficiency; physical stamina; and athletic endurance and has been used to improve and minimize the effects of dementia (Geng et al., 2010).

While there are few rigorous randomized controlled trials of ginseng, a recent meta-analysis (Geng et al., 2010) found that ginseng may improve cognition, memory, and performance in healthy subjects, but there is little evidence that ginseng helps people with dementia or cognitive impairment. Further research is warranted.

Common side effects for ginseng include insomnia, nervousness, headaches, hypertension, diarrhea, and vaginal bleeding (Fetrow & Avila, 2004). At normal doses, ginseng has little toxicity; however, manic symptoms have been reported at high doses (Spinella, 2001). Drug interactions may occur when ginseng is taken with oral contraceptives, steroids, antidepressants, antipsychotics, and anticoagulants. Also, ginseng is contraindicated for patients with diabetes, hypertension, hypotension, and cardiovascular disease.

Use is not recommended during pregnancy and ginseng may be unsafe for infants and children. It also should not be used for those with autoimmune conditions and bleeding disorders. Use has been linked to sleep problems and agitation in people with schizophrenia. Ginseng can affect heart rhythm and blood pressure on the first day of use (but not thereafter) and therefore should be used with caution in heart disease patients (Medline Plus, 2011).

KAVA

A native plant of the South Pacific Islands, kava (*Piper methysticum*) is a derivative of the rhizome of a pepper plant (Spinella, 2001). Used ceremonially or recreationally by Micronesian and Polynesian cultures, kava causes a mild euphoria at normal doses and is known for having relaxation, sleep, analgesic, and anticonvulsant effects. In the West, it is most commonly used for anxiety and insomnia.

Recently, Lakhan and Vieira's (2010) review of randomized controlled trial studies found that kava significantly reduces anxiety symptoms in patients with generalized anxiety disorder (GAD) and other anxiety-related disorders. In addition, kava may be effective for anxiety in women going through menopause and may help reduce symptoms of benzodiazepine withdrawal. However, it does not seem to help with insomnia, stress, ADHD, psychosis, or depression withdrawal (Medline Plus, 2011).

Numbness of the mouth and tongue is a common side effect of kava use, as are mild gastrointestinal upset, allergic skin reactions, and visual disturbances (McCabe, 2002). Anecdotal reports suggest kava may add to the depressant effect of alcohol and may aggravate underlying depressant states in some individuals. Another problem is that the strength of kava extracts can vary tremendously, as strength is dependent on what part of the plant is processed. The most serious concern about kava is that fact that it is a drug of abuse in the South Pacific and Australia, undoubtedly for its euphoric effects. Recently, kava was banned in Switzerland, Germany, and Canada due to reported cases of liver damage and even some deaths from kava use. However, Lakhan and Vieira (2010) found no liver issues in their meta-analysis of recent studies and assert that liver toxicity is a rare side effect.

VALERIAN

Valerian (*Valeriana officinalis*) is a small plant with pink-white flowers. With use dating back at least a thousand years, the plant's roots or rhizomes are the source of this herbal preparation. Used as a muscle relaxant, digestive aid, and anticonvulsant in Europe (Fetrow & Avila, 2004), it is most commonly used for the treatment of anxiety and insomnia (Spinella, 2001).

Empirical research on valerian is limited. Placebo-controlled studies are particularly difficult due to the strong, distinctive, unpleasant odor of this herb (McCabe, 2002). Although some studies reported that valerian improved sleep, a recent meta-analysis by Fernandez-San-Martin and colleagues (2010) found that valerian improved subjective reports of greater sleep quality, but its effectiveness was not quantitatively confirmed (for example, there was no difference in time to fall asleep). Lakhan and Vieira's (2010) review suggests that valerian may significantly reduce anxiety disorder symptoms.

There seems to be little risk of side effects or drug interactions with valerian; however, patients should be cautioned that the use of alcohol, benzodiazepines, and other sedatives should be avoided when taking valerian as it may cause excessive sleepiness (Medline Plus, 2011). Only overdose or chronic use produces symptoms such as nausea, headache, and blurred vision. However, use is contraindicated for those with active liver disease as anecdotal reports suggest hepatotoxicity (Fetrow & Avila, 2004).

PASSIONFLOWER

Passionflower (*passiflora incarnata*) is a perennial climbing vine whose colorful flowers are dried for use as a mild sedative. It has been used to treat anxiety all over the world (Lakhan & Vieira, 2010) and is approved to treat nervousness and insomnia in Germany (Kapalka, 2010).

Research on the efficacy of passionflower is promising. In their meta-analysis, Lakhan and

Vieira (2010) found no difference in effectiveness between passionflower and benzodiazepine in treating GAD. In addition, those taking passionflower reported low job performance impairment, but those taking benzodiazepines reported faster symptom relief. These authors assert that while more research is needed, passionflower holds potential for the treatment of anxiety disorders.

RHODIOLA (GOLDEN ROOT)

Rhodiola (*Rhodiola rosea*) is a perennial plant that has been used for years in Russia, Scandinavia, and Iceland. The roots of the plant (also referred to as Golden Root) are ground to make a general tonic used for improved sexual potency, enhanced mood, and improved energy (Bystritsky, Kerwin, & Feusner, 2008). Rhodiola may demonstrate anxiolytic properties and may be a successful adjuvant therapy to standard SSRI treatment for depression. It has been found to reduce the most common side effects of SSRIs, including poor memory, weight gain, and sexual dysfunction (Iovienio, Dalton, Fava, & Mischoulon, 2011). Kapalka (2010) suggests that Golden Root has possible efficacy in treating symptoms of ADHD. It is presumed safe with no adverse reactions and no prescription drug interactions.

LAVENDER

Lavender (*Lavandula angustifolia*) is a perennial with small purple flowers. The oil from these flowers has become popular in aromatherapy as a treatment for anxiety, restlessness, insomnia, and depression (NCCAM, 2010). There is little scientific evidence for lavender's effectiveness. Studies have found mixed results for the effect of lavender on anxiety. Lavender has been tried as a means to reduce agitation in dementia patients with mixed results (Medline Plus, 2011). Adding lavender oil to a daily bath may produce small improvements in mood; and adding lavender to a vaporizer overnight might help with mild insomnia. Lavender is being examined as a treatment for mild to moderate depression.

Lavender is considered safe for topical use but can cause skin irritation. Lavender oil can be poisonous if taken by mouth, and lavender teas and extracts taken by mouth may cause headache, appetite change, and constipation. Use of lavender while taking sedative medications may increase drowsiness (NCCAM, 2010).

RAUWOLFIA (INDIAN SNAKEROOT)

Rauwolfia (*Rauwolfia serpentina*) is a shrub in the milkweed family (also known as Indian Snakeroot). The roots of this plant are ground into a powder that has been used as an antipsychotic medication and tranquilizer for thousands of years. Adverse side effects (primarily depression) and interactions have limited its use (Spinella, 2001). While used in Western medicine since the 1950s to treat psychosis, prescription medications are more frequently used due to their success at treating symptoms with fewer side effects. However, rauwolfia is still sometimes used as an adjunct to prescription antipsychotics (Kapalka, 2010; Spinella, 2001).

CANNABIS

The flowers and leaves of the marijuana plant (*cannabis sativa* or *cannabis indica*) have been utilized for medicinal purposes for thousands of years. Today, marijuana is the most frequently used illegal drug in the United States, Europe, and other parts of the world (Crippa et al., 2009). Over the last few years, several states (starting with California in 1996) have legalized the medicinal use of cannabis. While most states have approved its use for physical conditions, many individuals are also prescribed cannabis for psychological conditions. In addition, there appear to be many individuals who are "self-medicating" with cannabis. A recent review (Bricker et al., 2007) revealed that 22%–29% of adults with anxiety and 17%–40% of adults with depression are treating themselves with

TABLE 94.1. Herbal Interventions and Parameters for Use

Herbal Treatment	Indications	Dosage	Contraindications	Interactions	Side Effects	Notes
St. John's wort	Depression	Adults, 300 mg (@.3% hypercin) tid	Pregnancy, breastfeeding, sensitivities to plant	Alcohol, cold/flu remedies	Photosensitivity, GI distress, dyssomnia, dizziness	Efficacy equal to TCAs and SSRIs and over placebo generally recognized; not universally accepted
Ginkgo biloba	Dementias	120 to 240 mg daily in 2–3 doses	Pregnancy, use in children, sensitivity to plant	Anticoagulants/antiplatelets, oral hypoglycemics	GI distress, headache, nausea, hematlogic issues	Efficacy potentially based on vasoactivity of compound
Ginseng	Well-being/performance	200 to 600 mg extract daily in 1–2 doses	Pregnancy, breastfeeding, sensitivities to plant, cardiovascular issues	Anticoagulants/antiplatelets, oral hypoglycemics, insulin, MAOIs	Cardiovascular issues, GI distress, headache, dyssomnia, agitation, dermatologic issues	Ginseng syndrome can occur when used with other stimulants (coffee/tea) existence is debated
Kava	Anxiety	Based on *kavapyrone* content; usually 70 to 240 mg of *kavapyrone* daily	Pregnancy, use in children, administration with psychotropic drugs	Alcohol, use of with benzodiazepines may cause coma, digoxin	CNS effects, hypertension, GI distress, decreased platelets, metabolic dysfunction, respiratory issues, kava-dermatopathy syndrome	Reports of hepatic failure secondary to kava use, with mixed evidence. Risk in use with any psychotropic medication may limit its use in most patients
Valerian	Anxiety, dyssomnia	400 to 900 mg of standardized extract (0.8% *valerinic* acid) 30 min to 1 hr before bed; tinctures 3 to 5 ml several times daily	Pregnancy, breastfeeding, hepatic dysfunction, sensitivity to plant	Alcohol, CNS depressants (risk of additive effects)	Headache, excitibality, insomnia, cardiac dysfunction, blurred vision, hepatoxicity, nausea	Reports indicate decreased sleep latency without hangover effects. Standardization of herb differs with manufacturing process, purity of medication may also vary with manufacturer

Passion flower	Anxiety	.25 to 2g dried herb 3 times daily; tincture .5 to 4 ml 3–4 times daily; liquid extract .5 to 1 ml 3 times daily	Pregnancy, breastfeeding, sensitivity to plant	Anticoagulants/ antiplatelets, MAOIs, other CNS depressants	CNS depression, altered LOC, hypersensitivity vasculitis	Limited and mixed data on efficacy. Research focused on intervention in multiple issues, complicating overall review of specific efficacy
Lavender	Anxiety, dyssomnia, depression	Essential oil added to bath may improve mood, added to vaporizer may aid in insomnia	Pregnancy, breastfeeding	Sedatives, barbituates	Constipation, contact dermatitis, CNS & respiratory depression, nausea	Limited data on overall efficacy for any indication
Rauwolfia	Anxiety	600 mg of rauwolfia or 6 mg of reserpine per day	Active peptic ulcer disease, ulcerative colitis, history of breast cancer, pregnancy	Antihypertensives, nitrates, barbituates, CNS depressants, cardiac glycosides, levodopa, NSAIDs, tricyclic antidepressants, sympathomimectics	Depression, hallucinations, SI, parkinsonian symptoms, bradycardia, nasal congestion, GI distress, metabolic issues	Multiple interactions and side effects make use difficult to manage and reserved for experienced prescribing professionals
Rhodiola	Anxiety, enhanced mood and energy	50 to 100 mg 2 or 3 times per day	None known	Presumed safe	No adverse effects	Very limited data on efficacy

CNS, central nervous system; GI, gastrointestinal; LOC, level of consciousness; MAOIs, monoamine oxidase inhibitors; NSAIDs, nonsteroidal anti-inflammatory drugs; SSRIs, selective serotonin reuptake inhibitors; TCAs, tricyclic antidepressants.

marijuana. The available research (Crippa et al., 2009) indicates that cannabis has a complex relationship with anxiety. For inexperienced users, a large dose of delta-9-tetrahydrocannabinol (the active ingredient in cannabis) can actually induce fear and anxiety—sometimes to the point of panic or phobic attacks. However, regular users report that marijuana reduces their anxiety, which serves as a primary motivation for continued use. Additional studies are needed as the classification of marijuana as a Schedule 1 controlled substance has greatly limited research on its efficacy.

OTHER HERBS AND APPLICATIONS

Far less information is available on most of the other herbal treatments used for psychological concerns. Chamomile and skullcap have been used for their sedative properties. Ginger has been used to augment antidepressant medications and counteract negative side effects of prescription drugs (Spinella, 2001). Black cohosh is used to ease menopausal symptoms. Evening primrose oil has been tested on hyperactive children with mixed results and with the risk of producing temporal lope epilepsy (Fetrow & Avila, 2004). The Chinese herb yokukansan is being examined as a treatment for Parkinson's disease. The use of various herbs in combination with prescription medications continues to be examined as well.

References and Readings

Birks, J. & Grimley Evans, J. (2009). Ginkgo biloba for cognitive impairment and dementia. *Cochrane Database of Systematic Reviews, 1,* doi: 10.1002/14651858.CD003120.pub3.

Bricker, J. B., Russo, J., Stein, M., Sherbourne, C., Craske, M., Schraufnagel, T. J., & Roy-Byrne, P. (2007). Does occasional cannabis use impact anxiety and depression treatment outcomes? Results from a randomized effectiveness trial. *Depression and Anxiety, 24,* 392–398.

Bystritsky, A., Kerwin, L., & Feusner, J. D. (2008). A pilot study of rhodiola rosea (Rhodax®) for generalized anxiety disorder (GAD). *Journal of Complementary and Alternative Medicine, 14,* 175–180.

Crippa, J. A., Zuardi, A. W., Martin-Santos, R., Bhattacharyya, S., Atakan, Z., Maguire, P., & Fusar-Poli, P. (2009). Cannabis and anxiety: A critical review of the evidence. *Human Psychopharmacology, 24,* 515–523.

DeKosky, S. T., Williamson, J. D., Fitzpatrick, A. L., Kronmal, R. A., Ives, D. G., Saxton, J. A., Furber, C. D. (2008). Ginkgo biloba for prevention of dementia: A randomized controlled trial. *Journal of the American Medical Association, 300*(19), 2253–2262.

Fernandez-San-Martin, M. I., Masa-Font, R., Palacios-Soler, L., Sancho-Gomez, P., Calbo-Caldentey, C., & Flores-Mateo, G. (2010). Effectiveness of Valerian on insomnia: A meta-analysis of randomized placebo-controlled trials. *Sleep Medicine, 11,* 505–511.

Fetrow, C. W., & Avila, J. R. (2004). *Professional's handbook of complementary and alternative medicines.* Philadelphia, PA: Lippincott, Williams & Wilkins.

Geng, J., Dong. J., Ni, H., Lee, M. S., Wu, T., Jiang, K.,... Malouf, R. (2010). Ginseng for cognition. *Cochrane Database of Systematic Reviews, 12,* doi: 10.1002/14651858.CD007769.pub2.

Hammerness, P., Basch, E., Ulbright, C., Barrette, E., Foppa, I., Basch, S.,... Ernst, E. (2003). St. John's wort: A systematic review of adverse effects and drug interactions for the consultation psychiatrist. *Psychosomatics, 44,* 271–282.

Iovieno, N., Dalton, E. D., Fava, M., & Mischoulon, D. (2011). Second-tier natural antidepressants: Review and critique. *Journal of Affective Disorders, 130,* 343–357.

Kapalka, G. M. (2010). *Nutritional and herbal therapies for children and adolescents.* Burlington, MA: Academic Press.

Lakhan, S. E., & Vieira, K.F. (2010). Nutritional and herbal supplements for anxiety and anxiety-related disorders: Systematic review. *Nutrition Journal, 9,* 42.

Linde, K., Berner, M. M., & Kriston, L. (2009). St. John's wort for major depression. *Cochrane Database of Systematic Reviews, 4,* doi: 10.1002/14651858.CD000448.pub3.

McCabe, S. (2002). Complementary herbal and alternative drugs in clinical practice. *Perspectives in Psychiatric Care, 38,* 98–107.

Medline Plus. (2011). *Herbs and supplements.* Retrieved August 12, 2011 from www.nlm.nih.gov/medlineplus/druginfo/herb_All.html

National Center for Complementary and Alternative Medicine. (2010). *Herbs at a glance: A quick guide to herbal supplements*. Retrieved August 12, 2011 from nccam.nih.gov/health/NIH_Herbs_at_a_Glance.pdf

Rahimi, R., Nikfar, S., & Abdollahi, M. (2008). Efficacy and tolerability of Hypericum perforatum in major depressive disorder in comparison with selective serontonin reuptake inhibitors: A meta-analysis. *Progress in Neuro-Psychopharmacology and Biological Psychiatry, 33*, 118–127.

Spinella, M. (2001). *The psychopharmacology of herbal medicine: Plant drugs that alter mind, brain, and behavior*. Cambridge, MA: MIT Press.

Related Topics

Chapter 90, "Adult Psychopharmacology"
Chapter 91, "Understanding Side Effects and Warnings in Psychopharmacology"
Chapter 98, "Dietary Supplements and Psychological Functioning"

95 MEDICAL CONDITIONS THAT MAY PRESENT AS PSYCHOLOGICAL DISORDERS

William J. Reed

Medical illnesses frequently present with psychological problems that affect, behavior, mood, thought processes, memory, emotions, motor activity and performance, and learning. Of course, the contrary is often true when psychological or psychiatric disorders present with physiological dysfunction. Many medical disorders may present with psychological symptoms, cognitive disturbances, or both. Often these symptoms are the direct result of a disease process, such as the anxiety and mania caused by the overproduction of thyroid hormone or the schizophreniform picture of central nervous system involvement with systemic lupus. What may not be as readily appreciated is how frequently psychological disorders present with signs or symptoms of physiological dysfunction, such as the rapid heart rate and shortness of breath accompanying a panic attack. Patient amplification of symptoms frequently produces somatic complaints out of proportion to the objective medical findings as well as occasional diagnostic confusion (Broom, 2000). It is also well documented that the duration of physical complaints coupled with the side effects of medication may contribute to the presentation of both physical disease and psychological illness.

A wide variety of medical conditions can present as psychological disorders in everyday clinical practice. As many as 10%–20% of all pediatric and adolescent medical complaints may be "psychosomatic" or "somatic" in origin, that is, presenting as a conversion reaction without identifiable alterations in organic function (Gold & Friedman, 1995). Both terms are probably incorrect descriptions since they suggest that disease cannot exist in the absence of recognizable pathological change such as "functional" gastrointestinal disease (Barsky & Burus, 1999). And because of conventional medical training, many clinicians and psychologists frequently struggle with the notion that a "physiologic" cause must necessarily exist for every symptom complaint. The dualistic model that created an artificial distinction between organic (medical) illness and psychological (or psychiatric) illness is long been outdated since the role of the neurotransmitters in human disease was discovered.

There is very little evidence to suggest that mind (psyche) and body function (soma) differ psycho-neuro-immunologically, endocrinologically, or psycho-physiologically (Ryan, 1998). Clinicians should recognize the contribution of both the mind and the body (psychophysiology) as a continuum, especially when:

- A disease process or disorder persists unexplained (genetic mullerian duct anomalies presenting as enuresis).
- There is poor patient compliance (recurrent abdominal pain with child abuse or neglect).
- There is deterioration in the school performance of an adolescent (the illicit use of prescribed medications or the abuse of illicit drugs).
- There is withdrawal from social or peer activities (avoidant behaviors vs. neurological regression).
- There is clinical evidence of significant mood change and/or disruptive behaviors.

The combination of a complete medical history and physical examination coupled with a psychological evaluation and judicious laboratory testing usually separates the ongoing pathological processes and those conditions that mimic either psychological or physiological disease. The following is an attempt to list those entities seen most often in a pediatric and adolescent medicine practice.

MEDICAL CONDITIONS THAT MAY PRESENT AS ATTENTION-DEFICIT/HYPERACTIVITY AND DISRUPTIVE DISORDERS

- Absence seizures
- Attention-deficit/hyperactivity disorders
- Allergic tension fatigue (allergic diatheses)
- Atopic dermatitis (chronic itching)
- Anxiety disorders
- Asperger syndrome
- Bipolar disorders
- Child abuse and neglect
- Complex and simple partial seizures
- Conduct disorders
- Cyclothymia
- Disordered sleep, including obstructive sleep apnea
- Fetal alcohol syndrome and effect
- Frontal lobe disorders
- Genetic syndromes (Down, Turner, Williams, Fragile X, and many others)
- Heavy metal toxicity (see above), especially lead
- Hearing disorders
- Hyperkinesia with/without developmental delays
- Intellectual deficits
- Landau-Kleffner syndrome
- Learning disorders, specifically reading disorders
- Dysphoric dysregulation of mood
- Mania
- Medication side effects (see elsewhere)
    - Xanthines (caffeine, theophylline, theobromine)
    - Barbiturates
    - Inhalants (albuterol, Xopenex, huffing substances)
- Neurocysticerosis
- Nonverbal learning disorders
- Obsessive-compulsive disorder
- Oppositional defiant disorder
- Pervasive developmental disorders (autism spectrum)
- Posttraumatic stress (acute and chronic)
- Reactivation seen in antidepressant-treated depression
- Substance abuse (marijuana, stimulants, PCP, designer drugs, others)

- Thyrotoxicosis (Grave's disease, Hashimoto's thyroiditis)
- Tourette syndrome and other tic disorders

MEDICAL CONDITIONS THAT MAY PRESENT AS ANXIETY (AND PANIC ATTACKS)

- Akathisia from antipsychotic medications
- Cardiovascular
  - Angina
  - Cardiac arrhythmias
  - Congestive heart failure
  - Hypertension
  - Mitral valve prolapse (Barlow's syndrome)
  - Myocardial infarction
  - Pulmonary embolism
- Subclavian steal syndrome
- Chronic illness
- Deficiencies
  - Calcium
  - Magnesium
  - Potassium
  - Niacin
- Vitamin B12
- Diet effects, caffeine, nicotine, illicit substance abuse
- Drug use or withdrawal (alcohol, amphetamines)
  - Endocrine
  - Carcinoid syndrome
  - Cushing's disease
  - Hyperthyroidism
  - Hypoglycemia
  - Pheochromocytoma
- Menopause
- Gastroesophageal reflux
- Hyperhidrosis
- Lack of exercise
- Learning disorders
- Medications and withdrawal
  - Anticholinergics
  - Antihistamines
  - Barbiturates
  - Bronchodilators
  - Calcium channel blockers
  - Corticosteroids
  - Digitalis
  - Neuroleptics
  - Phenothiazines
- Theophylline
- Neurological
  - Delirium
  - Labyrinthitis
  - Multiple sclerosis
  - Partial complex seizures
  - Post concussion
- Vestibular dysfunction
- Nummular eczema (neurodermatitis circumscripta)
- Premenstrual dysphoria syndrome
- Recreational drugs
- Respiratory
  - Asthma
  - Chronic obstructive pulmonary disease (and emphysema)
  - Hyperventilation syndrome
  - Hypoxia
  - Pulmonary embolism
- Urticaria

MEDICAL CONDITIONS THAT MAY PRESENT AS CHRONIC PELVIC PAIN IN FEMALES

- Dysmenorrhea (secondary)
- Dyspareunia (painful intercourse)
- Endometriosis
- Functional gastrointestinal disorders
- Mullerian duct anomalies
- Mittleschmerz un lust
- Ovarian disorders
- Pregnancy
- Pseudocyesis
- Sexual abuse or sexual assault
- Surgical adhesions (e.g., Ashner's syndrome)

MEDICAL CONDITIONS THAT MAY PRESENT AS DEMENTIA

- AIDS-associated CNS infections
- Alzheimer's disease
- Creuztfeld-Jakob disease
- Head trauma

- Hepatolenticular degeneration (Wilson's disease)
- Huntington's disease
- Hydrocephalus ex vacuo
- Neimann Pick disease
- Neurosyphilis
- Parkinson's disease
- Post anoxia
- SSPE of Dawson (measles)
- Substance abuse
- Vascular thrombosis and embolism

MEDICAL CONDITIONS THAT MAY PRESENT AS DEPRESSION

- Acne vulgaris
- AIDS
- Cancer-pancreatic
- Collagen diseases
  - Fibromyalgia syndrome
  - Juvenile rheumatoid arthritis
  - Mixed connective tissue disease
  - Sjogren's syndrome
  - Systemic lupus erythematosis
- Cystic fibrosis
- Endocrine disorders
  - Diabetes mellitus
  - Hyperparathyroidism
  - Hyperthyroidism
  - Hypopituitarism
  - Hypothyroidism
- Infections
  - AIDS
  - Encephalitis
  - Hepatitis
  - Influenza
  - Pneumonia
  - Syphilis
- Insulin-dependent diabetes mellitus
- Leukemia
- Medications
  - Antihypertensives
  - Barbiturates
  - Benzodiazepines
  - Clonidine
  - Corticosteroids
  - Digitalis
  - Guanfacine
  - Oral contraceptives
- Medication-induced personality changes
- Migraine headaches
- Neurologic disorders
  - Cerebrovascular accidents
  - Epilepsy
  - Multiple sclerosis
  - Subarachnoid hemorrhage
  - Wilson's disease
- Neurosympathetic dystrophy
- Psoriasis
- Sleep disorders
- Substance related, substance dependent and abusive
- Verrucae vulgaria

MEDICAL CONDITIONS THAT MAY PRESENT AS FAILURE TO THRIVE OR WEIGHT LOSS

- Achalasia (e.g., trypanosomiasis)
- Aganglionic megacolon (Hirschsprung's)
- Anorexia
- Attachment disorders
- Bartter syndrome
- Celiac disease
- Cerebral damage from hypoxia and hemorrhage
- Child neglect and abuse
- Chronic anemias
- Chronic hypoxemia
- Chronic protein malnutrition
- Congenital anomalies and developmental feeding problems
- Congenital infections
  - AIDS
  - Cytomegalovirus
  - Histoplasmosis
  - Rubella
  - Toxoplasmosis
  - Tuberculosis
- Cystic fibrosis
- Dwarfing syndromes
  - Leprechaunism
  - LeJeune's asphyxiating syndrome
- Diencephalic syndromes
- Endocrine disorders
- Fetal alcohol syndrome
- Hypocalorism
- Idiopathic hypercalcemia
- Inborn errors of metabolism

- Leigh syndrome
- Metabolic storage diseases
- Newborn narcotic withdrawal
- Protein losing enteropathy
- Protein losing nephropathy
- Rumination
- Schwachman-Diamond syndrome (pancreatic achylia)
- Severe gastroesophageal reflux

MEDICAL CONDITIONS THAT MAY PRESENT AS FATIGUE AND MALAISE

- Allergic tension fatigue
- Cardiovascular disease
  - Arteriovenous fistula
  - Congenital heart disease
  - Congestive heart failure
  - Hypertrophic cardiomyopathy
  - Persistent pulmonary hypertension
  - Takayasu's temporal arteritis
- Collagen diseases
  - Dermatomyositis
  - Mixed connective tissue disorder
  - Polymyositis
  - Rheumatoid arthritis
  - Sjogren's syndrome
  - Systemic lupus erythematosus
- Chronic fatigue syndrome
- Chronic renal diseases
- Endocrine disorders
- Ehlers Danlos syndrome
- Familial hypokalemic periodic paralysis
- Fibromyalgia
- Gastrointestinal
  - Chronic liver disease
  - Inflammatory bowel disease
- Genitourinary
  - Glomerulonephritis
  - Pregnancy
  - Pyelonephritis
- Hematological disorders
  - Anemia
  - Leukemia
  - Lymphoma
  - Polycythemia
- Infections (common)
  - AIDS
  - Epstein-Barr (infectious mononucleosis)
  - Coccidiomycosis
  - Cytomegalovirus
  - Histoplasmosis
  - Lyme disease (chronic)
  - Sarcoidosis
  - Subclinical hepatitides (B, C)
  - Tuberculosis
  - Wegener's granulomatosis
- Lymphoid hyperplasia (Down's syndrome)
- Medications
  - Illicit (e.g., Blue Tuesday's from amphetamines)
  - Over the counter
  - Prescription
- Myasthenia gravis
- Muscular dystrophy
- Narcolepsy
- Orthostatic edema
- Obstructive sleep apnea
- (Modified with permission from Cavanaugh, 2002)

MEDICAL CONDITIONS THAT MAY PRESENT AS MEMORY LOSS AND DELIRIUM

- Alcohol dependence
- Alzheimer's disease
- Anoxia
- Carbon monoxide poisoning
- Carcinoid syndrome
- Cerebrovascular disorders
- Electroconvulsive therapy
- Head trauma (postconcussion)
- Heavy metal toxicity
- Hypercarbia
- Hypoglycemia
- Infections
  - Herpes encephalitis
  - HIV
  - Koru
  - Malaria
  - Neurocysticerosis
  - Neurosyphilis
  - Rabies encephalitis
  - Subacute sclerosing panencephalitis of Dawson
- Keane-Sayres disease
- Kluver-Bucy disease

- Medications
  - Benzodiazepines
  - Diltiazem
  - Thiopental
  - Others
- Multiple sclerosis
- Organic solvents
- Postoperative
- Seizures
- Sexual abuse facilitating drugs
  - Gamma hydroxybutyrate (GHB)
  - Flunazitram
  - Beta lactone
  - Gamma butyrate
  - 3–4 methylenedioxy provalerone (MDPV)
  - 4-methyl-methcatherone
- Sheehan's syndrome of postpartum CNS hemorrhage
- Substance abuse
- Metabolic
- Postoperative
- Substance abuse/withdrawal
- Vitamin B12, B6 deficiency

MEDICAL CONDITIONS THAT MAY PRESENT AS PSYCHOSIS

- Addison's disease (hypocortisolism)
- Cardiovascular disease strokes
- Cushing's disease (hypercortisolism)
- Central nervous system infections
- CNS neoplasms
- CNS trauma
- Folate deficiency
- HIV and AIDS
- Homocysteinuria
- Hepatic failure/encephalopathy
- Hyperthyroidism
- Hyperparathyroidism
- Hyponatremia
- Hyperparathyroidism
- Hypothyroidism
- Huntington's disease
- Klinefelter syndrome
- Medication-induced catatonia
- Multiple sclerosis
- Pancreatitis
- Porphyria
- Renal failure
- Systemic lupus erythematosus
- Temporal lobe seizures
- Traumatic brain injury
- Vitamin B deficiencies
- Wilson's disease
- Substance-induced (intoxication or withdrawal)

MEDICAL CONDITIONS THAT MAY PRESENT AS SLEEP DISORDERS

Hypersomnia

- Attention-deficit/hyperactivity disorder
- Autism spectrum disorders
- Bipolar disorder
- Chronic fatigue syndrome
- Cranial irradiation
- Depression
- Drug/medication use
- Inadequate sleep
- Intrathecal chemotherapy
- Klein Levin syndrome (with hyperphagia in males)
- Narcolepsy
- Neurodevelopmental delays
- Nocturnal hypoventilation
- Poisoning and child abuse
- Postencephalitic sequelae
- Posttraumatic head injury
- Sleep reversals
- Upper airway resistance and sleep apnea

Developmental Dyssomnias/Parasomnias

- Arousal disorders (non-REM)
  - Bruxism
  - Head banging
  - Night terrors
  - Paroxysmal nocturnal enuresis
  - Somnambulism
- Benign neonatal sleep myoclonus (Lennox Gastaut)
- Bruxism
- Circadian rhythm disorders
  - Primary latency phase disorder
  - Zeitgebers (night shift)
- Enuresis

- Head banging
- Nightmares
- Night terrors
- Nighttime body rocking
- Narcolepsy
- REM disorders
    - Nightmares
    - Seizures
- Obstructive sleep apnea
- Resistance to sleep
- Restless legs syndrome
- Somnambulism
- Somniloquy
- Trained night crying
- Trained night feeding
- Ultradian disorders
    - Seasonal affective disorder
- Vulnerable child

References and Readings

Barsky, A. J., & Burus, J. F. (1999). Functional somatic syndromes. *Annals of Internal Medicine, 130,* 910–921.

Broom, B. C. (2000). Medicine and story: A novel clinical panorama arising from a unitary mind/body approach to physical illness. *Advances in Mind-Body Medicine, 16,* 161–207.

Cavanaugh, R. M. (2002). Evaluating adolescents with fatigue: Ever get tired of it? *Pediatric Review, 23,* 337–348.

Gold, M. A., & Friedman, S. B. (1995). Conversion reactions in adolescents. *Pediatric Annals, 24,* 296–306.

Morris, M. (1998). *Pediatric diagnosis: Interpretation of symptoms and signs in children and adolescents* (6th ed.). Philadelphia, PA: W. B. Saunders.

Morrison, J. (1997). *When psychological problems mask medical disorders.* New York: Guilford Press.

Ryan, N. D. (1998). Psychoneuroendocrinology of children and adolescents. *Psychiatry Clinics of North America, 21,* 435–441.

Wood, B. L. (2001). Biobehavioral continuum of psychologically and physically manifested disease to explain the false dichotomy of organic v. psychological illness. *Child and Adolescent Psychiatric Clinics of North America, 7,* 543–562.

Related Topic

Chapter 9, "Evaluating the Medical Components of Childhood Developmental and Behavioral Disorders"

96 NORMAL MEDICAL LABORATORY VALUES AND MEASUREMENT CONVERSIONS

Gerald P. Koocher

Although the measurement conversion data provided here are standard, note that normal biological and chemical values differ across hospitals and laboratories as a function of the methods, reagents, and equipment used. The data presented here represent an overview compiled from several sources and should not be regarded as absolute (see Tables 96.1–96.6).

TABLE 96.1. Temperature Conversions: Fahrenheit = $\frac{9}{5}$ (Centigrade) + 32; Centigrade = $\frac{5}{9}$ (Fahrenheit − 32)

Fahrenheit	Centigrade
95.0	35.0
96.8	36.0
98.6	37.0
100.0	37.8
100.4	38.0
101.0	38.3
102.0	38.9
102.2	39.0
103.0	39.4
104.0	40.0

TABLE 96.2. Units of Measurement Conversions

1 kg = 2.204 lb
22 lb = 10 kg
1 lb = 16 oz = 0.454 kg or 454 g
1 oz = 29.57 ml
1 tsp = 5 ml
1 tbsp = 15 ml
1 in = 2.54 cm
1 cm = 0.394 in
1 ft = 30.48 cm
1 yd = 91.44 cm
1 m = 1.093 yd
1 m = 3.28 ft
1 mile = 1,669.3 m
1 km = 1,093.6 yd

TABLE 96.3. Prefixes Denoting Decimal Factors

Prefix	Factor	Prefix	Factor
mega	10^6	milli	10^{-3}
kilo	10^3	micro	10^{-6}
hecto	10^2	nano	10^{-9}
deka	10^1	pico	10^{-12}
deci	10^{-1}	femto	10^{-15}
centi	10^{-2}		

TABLE 96.4. Normal Resting Respiratory and Heart Rates

Age	Respiratory Rate	Heart Rate
Neonate	30–50	92–180
1–2 years	22–30	100–150
2–12 years	16–24	65–120
Adolescent–adult	12–20	55–110

TABLE 96.5. Normal Lab Values

Chemistries	Adult Values	Pediatric Values		
Sodium	134–146 mEq/L	Term, 132–142 mEq/L Child, 135–146 mEq/L		
Potassium	3.5–5.1 mEq/L	Term, 3.8–6.1 mEq/L >1 month, 3.5–5.1 mEq/L		
Chloride	92–109 mEq/L	95–108 mEq/L		
Bicarbonate	24–31 mEq/L			
BUN (blood urea nitrogen)	8–25 mg/dl	5–25 mg/dl		
Creatinine	<1.5 mg/dl	0.7–1.7 mg/dl		
Glucose	55–115 mg/dl	Term, 32–100 mg/dl >2 weeks, 60–110 mg/dl		
Calcium	8.0–10.5 mg/dl	Term, 7.2–12.0 mg/dl >1 year, 7.8–11.0 mg/dl		
Phosphorus	2.6–4.6 mg/dl			
Uric acid	2.4–7.5 mg/dl	3.0–7.0 mg/dl		
Total protein	5.6–8.4 g/dl			
Albumin	3.4–5.4 g/dl	3.8–5.6 g/dl		
Total bilirubin	0.2–1.5 mg/dl	Total Bilirubin	Premature	Term
		1 day	<8–9	<6
		2 days	<12	<9
		1 week	<15	<10
		2–4 weeks	<10–12	<10
Direct bilirubin	0.0–0.3 mg/dl	<0.2 mg/dl		
SGOT, AST (serum glutamic oxaloacetate, aminotransferase)	0–40 U/L	Term, 25–125 U/L Infant, 20–60 U/L Child, 10–40 U/L		
SGPT, ALT (alanine aminotransferase, serum glutamic pyruvate transaminase)	0–40 U/L			
LDH (lactic dehydrogenase)	50–240 U/L	Term, 150–600 U/L <1 year, 140–350 U/L Child, 140–280 U/L		
CK (creatine kinase)	5–200 U/L			
CK MB (CK-myocardial band)	<3%–5%			
Cholesterol	<200 mg/dl			
LDL cholesterol (low-density lipoprotein)	<130 mg/dl			
HDL cholesterol (high-density lipoprotein)	>35–40 mg/dl			
Triglycerides	30–135 mg/dl			
Amylase	60–180 U/L			
Lipase	4–25 U/L			
Magnesium	1.6–3.0 mg/dl	1.5–2.1 mg/dl		
GGTP (gamma-glutamyl transpeptidase)	10–50 U/L			
PSA (prostate-specific antigen)	<4.0 ng/ml			
Osmolarity	274–296 mOsm/kg	274–296 mOsm/kg		
Iron	50–160 µg/dl			
TIBC (total iron-binding capacity)	240–425 µg/dl			
Iron% sat	20%–55%			
Ferritin	30–250 ng/ml			
Anion gap	8–12 mEq/L			
Vitamin B_{12}	200–1,000 pg/ml			
Folate	5–12 ng/ml			
Ammonia	<45 µg/dl			
Lactate	4–16 mg/dl			
Aluminum	4–10 µg/L			
Copper	90–200 µg/dl			
Zinc	50–150 µg/dl			
APF (alpha-fetoprotein)	<25 ng/ml			

(continued)

TABLE 96.5. Normal Lab Values (*continued*)

Chemistries	Adult Values	Pediatric Values
CEA (carcinoembryonic antigen)	<2.5 ng/ml	
CEA, smoker	<5.0 ng/ml	
Hematology		
Hgb (hemoglobin)	Males, 14–18 g/dl Females, 12–16 g/dl	Term, 13–20 g/dl 1–4 days, 14–22 g/dl 2 weeks, 13–20 g/dl 1 month, 11–18 g/dl 2 months, 10–15 g/dl 6 months, 10–14 g/dl 1 year, 10–13 g/dl 2–8 years, 11–14 g/dl
Hematocrit	Males, 40%–52% Females, 37%–47%	Term, 40%–58% 1–4 days, 45%–60% 2 weeks, 40%–58% 1 month, 32%–54% 2 months, 28%–44% 6 months, 30%–42% 1 year, 32%–40% 2–8 years, 33%–40%
RBC (red blood cell [density])	Males, 4.8–6.0 × 10^6/ mm^3 Females, 4.1–5.5 × 10^6/ mm^3	
MCV (mean corpuscular volume)	Males, 80–90 fl Females, 80–100 fl	
MCH (mean corpuscular hemoglobin)	27–32 pg	
MCHC (mean corpuscular hemoglobin concentration)	32%–36%	
Hgb A_{1c} (hemoglobin A_{1c})	3%–5%	
WBC (white blood cells)	5,000–10,000/µl	Term, 8–30 (10^3/mm^3) 1–3 days, 9–32 (10^3/mm^3) 2–4 weeks, 4–20 (10^3/mm^3) 2 months, 5–20 (10^3/mm^3) 6 months, 6–18 (10^3/mm^3) 1 year, 5–18 (10^3/mm^3) 2–8 years, 5–15 (10^3/mm^3)
Segs	40%–60%	
Bands	0–5%	
Lymph	20%–40%	
Mono	4%–8%	
Eos	1%–3%	
Baso	0–1%	
Platelets	150–400 × 10^3/µl	150–357 × 10^3/µl
Haptoglobin	100–250 mg/dl	
ESR (eosinophil sed rate)	Males, <10 mm/hr Females, <20 mm/hr	
Retic count	0.5%–2.0%	Term, 3%–8% 2 days, 2%–4% 1 month, 0.3%–1.6% 6 years, 0.5%–1.3%
PT (prothrombin time)	11–13 s	11–14 s
PTT (partial prothrombin time)	25–35 s	21–35 s
Bleeding time	<5–6 min	

(*continued*)

TABLE 96.5. Normal Lab Values (*continued*)

Chemistries	Adult Values	Pediatric Values
Thrombin time	10–14 s	
Fibrinogen	200–400 mg/dl	
Lymphocyte (differential)		
Total T, CD3	60%–87%	
Total T/mm^3	630–3,170	
B cell	1%–25%	
Suppr, CD8	10%–40%	
Suppr/mm^3	240–1,200	
Helper, CD4	30%–50%	
Helper/mm^3	390–1,770	
H:S, CD4/CD8	0.8–3.0	
ABGs (arterial blood gases)		
pH	7.35–7.45	Birth, 7.32–7.45 1 day, 7.27–7.44 2 days, 7.36–7.44 1 month, 7.35–7.45
$PaCO_2$	35–45 mmHg	Birth, 25–45 mmHg >2 months, 30–45 mmHg
PaO_2	80–100 mmHg	Birth, 65–80 mmHg Infant, 70–100 mmHg Child, 85–105 mmHg
HCO_3	22–28 mEq/L	
O_2, saturation, artery	95%–98%	
O_2, saturation, vein	60%–85%	
Endocrinology		
T4 RIA (thyroxine radioiodine uptake)	5.0–12.0 µg/dl	
T3 uptake (thyrotropin)	22%–36%	
Free T4 (thyroxine)	0.8–2.2 ng/dl	
T3 (thyrotropin)	75–200 ng/dl	
TSH (thyroid-stimulating hormone)	0.3–5.0 µIU/ml	
Aldosterone, supine	3–12 ng/dl	
Aldosterone, upright	5–25 ng/dl	
Calcitonin	<75 pg/ml	
Cortisol	6–24 µg/dl, A.M. 2–10 µg/dl, P.M.	
Gastrin	0–200 pg/ml	
Growth hormone	1–10 ng/ml	
Pepsinogen	25–100 mg/ml	
Prolactin	Males, 0–5 ng/ml Females, 0–20 ng/ml	
PTH (parathyroid homone)	10–60 pg/ml	
BHCG (beta human chorionic gonadotropin, nonpregnant)	<5 mlU/ml	
0–2 weeks	0–250 mlU/ml	
2–4 weeks	100–5,000 mlU/ml	
1–2 months	4,000–200,000 mlU/ml	
2–3 months	8,000–100,000 mlU/ml	
2nd trimester	4,000–75,000 mlU/ml	
3rd trimester	1,000–50,000 mlU/ml	
Urine		
Albumin	20–100 mg/day	
Amylase	<20 U/hr	
Calcium	<300 mg/day	
Creatinine	0.75–1.5 g/day	
Creatinine clearance	80–140 ml/min	
Glucose	<300 mg/day	

(*continued*)

TABLE 96.5. Normal Lab Values (*continued*)

Chemistries	Adult Values	Pediatric Values
Osmolarity	250–1,000 mOsm/L	
Phosphorous	0.5–1.3 g/day	
Potassium	25–115 mEq/day	
Protein	10–200 mg/day	
Sodium	50–250 mEq/day	
Total volume	720–1,800 ml/day	
Urea nitrogen	10–20 g/day	
Uric acid	50–700 mg/day	
Specific gravity	1.002–1.030	
Cerebral spinal fluid		
Protein	10–45 mg/dl	Preterm, 60–150 mg/dl Newborn, 20–170 mg/dl >1 year, 5–45 mg/dl
Glucose	40–80 mg/dl	Preterm, 24–75 mg/dl Newborn, 34–119 mg/dl >1 year, 40–80 mg/dl
Pressure	60–180 mmH_2O	Newborn, 70–120 mmH_2O Child, 70–180 mmH_2O
Leukocytes, total	<5/mm^3	
Leukocites, differential		
Lymph	60%–75%	
Mono	25%–50%	
Neutro	1%–3%	
Cell count	0–5 lymphs/HPF	Preterm, 0–25 WBC/mm^3; <35% polys Newborn, 0–25 WBC/mm^3; <35% polys >2–4 weeks, 0–5 WBC/mm^3; 0% polys
Toxicology		
Ethanol		
Normal	<0.005% (5 mg/dl)	
Intoxicated	0.1%–0.4%	
Stuporous	0.4%–0.5%	
Coma	>0.5%	
Mercury, urine	<100 µg/24 hr, normal	
CoHgb (carbon monoxide hemoglobin)		
Nonsmokers	0–2.5%	
Smokers	2%–5%	
Toxic	>20%	
Lead	0–40 µg/dl, normal	
Lead, urine	<100 µg/24 hr, normal	

TABLE 96.6. Pediatric Normal Values (Subject to Individual Patient's Circumstances)

Values	Preterm	Term	3 Months	6 Months	9 Months	1 Year	1–1.5 Years	2 Years
Weight in kilograms	<3	3–4	5–6	7	8–9	10	11	12
Pulse rate	130–160	120–150	120–140	120–140	120–140	120–140	110–135	110–130
Blood pressure (systolic)	45–60	60–70	60–100	65–120	70–120	70–120	70–125	75–125
Respiratory rate	40–60	30–60	30–50	25–35	23–33	20–30	20–30	20–28
Weight in kilograms	14–15	16–17	18	20	24–25	30–32	40	45
Pulse rate	100–120	95–115	90–110	90–110	80–100	75–95	70–90	60–90
Blood pressure (systolic)	75–125	80–125	80–125	85–120	90–120	90–125	95–130	110–130
Respiratory rate	20–28	20–28	20–25	20–25	16–24	16–24	16–24	15–20

When interpreting specific results, contact personnel at the lab in question to ascertain their normal ranges for the test in question.

References and Readings

Expert Consult. (n.d.). Retrieved from www.expert-consult.com

Fleisher, G. R., & Ludwig, S. (Eds.). (2010). *Textbook of pediatric emergency medicine*. Philadelphia, PA: Lippincott Williams & Wilkins.

Kliegman, R. M., Stanton, B. F., St. Geme, J. W., Schor, N. F., & Behrman, R. E. (Eds.) (2011). *Nelson textbook of pediatrics* (19th ed.). Philadelphia, PA: Saunders.

Longo, D. L., Fauci, A. S., Kasper, S. L., Jameson, J. L., & Loscalzo, J. (Eds.). (2012). *Harrison's online internal medicine* (18th ed.). Retrieved February 2013, from the Access Medicine Web sitwww.accessmedicine.com/public/learnmore_hol.aspx

Related Topics

Chapter 97, "Use of Height and Weight Assessment Tools"

Chapter 129, "Common Clinical Abbreviations and Symbols"

97 USE OF HEIGHT AND WEIGHT ASSESSMENT TOOLS

Nancie H. Herbold and Sari Edelstein

In the past, to determine whether an individual was over- or underweight, clinicians consulted the Metropolitan Life Insurance Weight for Height Tables. These tables considered sex and frame size to determine desirable weight associated with greater life expectancy. Today, the preferred method for assessing body weight is the use of body mass index (BMI). Body mass index is more closely related to body fat content than the Metropolitan Tables. To determine BMI for either a man or a woman, body weight in kilograms is divided by height in meters squared.

$$\text{BMI} = \frac{\text{Weight(kg)}}{\text{Height(m)}^2}$$

$$\text{BMI} = \frac{\text{Weight(lbs)}}{\text{Height (inches)}^2} \times 703$$

For ease, Table 97.1 is provided to make the BMI calculation unnecessary. To use the table, find the appropriate height in the left-hand column. Move across to a given weight; pounds have been rounded. The number at the top of the column is the BMI for that height and weight, corresponding designations for normal, overweight, obese, and extremely obese BMI levels.

BMI is a tool for assessing body weight, but it is not without its limitations. For example, BMI does not totally differentiate between weight that is muscle and weight that is fat. Therefore, an athlete in good physical shape may have a high BMI but not high body fat. (Table 97.2 can be utilized for athletic individuals.)

INTERPRETATION

Both BMI, shown in Table 97.1, and waist circumference (WC), shown in Table 97.2, can be useful measures for determining obesity. According to the National Institutes of Health, a high WC is

TABLE 97.1. Body Mass Index Table

	Normal						Overweight					Obese										Extreme Obesity														
BMI	19	20	21	22	23	24	25	26	27	28	29	30	31	32	33	34	35	36	37	38	39	40	41	42	43	44	45	46	47	48	49	50	51	52	53	54
Height (inches)	Body weight (pounds)																																			
58	91	96	100	105	110	115	119	124	129	134	138	143	148	153	158	162	167	172	177	181	186	191	196	201	205	210	215	220	224	229	234	239	244	248	253	258
59	94	99	104	109	114	119	124	128	133	138	143	148	153	158	163	168	173	178	183	188	193	198	203	208	212	217	222	227	232	237	242	247	252	257	262	267
60	97	102	107	112	118	123	128	133	138	143	148	153	158	163	168	174	179	184	189	194	199	204	209	215	220	225	230	235	240	245	250	255	261	266	271	276
61	100	106	111	116	122	127	132	137	143	148	153	158	164	169	174	180	185	190	195	201	206	211	217	222	227	232	238	243	248	254	259	264	269	275	280	285
62	104	109	115	120	126	131	136	142	147	153	158	164	169	175	180	186	191	196	202	207	213	218	224	229	235	240	246	251	256	262	267	273	278	284	289	295
63	107	113	118	124	130	135	141	146	152	158	164	169	175	180	186	191	197	203	208	214	220	225	231	237	242	248	254	259	265	270	278	282	287	293	299	304
64	110	116	122	128	134	140	145	151	157	163	169	174	180	186	192	197	204	209	215	221	227	232	238	244	250	256	262	267	273	279	285	291	296	302	308	314
65	114	120	126	132	138	144	150	156	162	168	174	180	186	192	198	204	210	216	222	228	234	240	246	252	258	264	270	276	282	288	294	300	306	312	318	324
66	118	124	130	136	142	148	155	161	167	173	179	186	192	198	204	210	216	223	229	235	241	247	253	260	266	272	278	284	291	297	303	309	315	322	328	334
67	121	127	134	140	146	153	159	166	172	178	185	191	198	204	211	217	223	230	236	242	249	255	261	268	274	280	287	293	299	306	312	319	325	331	338	344
68	125	131	138	144	151	158	164	171	177	184	190	197	203	210	216	223	230	236	243	249	256	262	269	276	282	289	295	302	308	315	322	328	335	341	348	354
69	128	135	142	149	155	162	169	176	182	189	196	203	209	216	223	230	236	243	250	257	263	270	277	284	291	297	304	311	318	324	331	338	345	351	358	365
70	132	139	146	153	160	167	174	181	188	195	202	209	216	222	229	236	243	250	257	264	271	278	285	292	299	306	313	320	327	334	341	348	355	362	369	376
71	136	143	150	157	165	172	179	186	193	200	208	215	222	229	236	243	250	257	265	272	279	286	293	301	308	315	322	329	338	343	351	358	365	372	379	386
72	140	147	154	162	169	177	184	191	199	206	213	221	228	235	242	250	258	265	272	279	287	294	302	309	316	324	331	338	346	353	361	368	375	383	390	397
73	144	151	159	166	174	182	189	197	204	212	219	227	235	242	250	257	265	272	280	288	295	302	310	318	325	333	340	348	355	363	371	378	386	393	401	408
74	148	155	163	171	179	186	194	202	210	218	225	233	241	249	256	264	272	280	287	295	303	311	319	326	334	342	350	358	365	373	381	389	396	404	412	420
75	152	160	168	176	184	192	200	208	216	224	232	240	248	256	264	272	279	287	295	303	311	319	327	335	343	351	359	367	375	383	391	399	407	415	423	431
76	156	164	172	180	189	197	205	213	221	230	238	246	254	263	271	279	287	295	304	312	320	328	336	344	353	361	369	377	385	394	402	410	418	426	435	443

Source: National Institute of Health, 2003. Adapted from Clinical guidelines on identification, evaluation, and treatment of overweight and obesity in adults: The evidence report. Retrieved 2011 from www.nhlbi.nih.gov/guidelines/obesity/ob_gdlns.pdf

TABLE 97.2. Classification of Overweight and Obesity by Body Mass Index (BMI), Waist Circumference, and Associated Disease Risks

	BMI (kg/m^2)	Obesity Class	Disease Risk[a] Relative to Normal Men 102 cm (40 in) or Less Women 88 cm (35 in) or Less	Weight and Waist Circumference Men > 102 cm (40 in) Women > 88 cm (35 in)
Underweight	<18.5		—	—
Normal	18.5–24.9		—	—
Overweight	25.0–29.9		Increased	High
Obesity	30.0–34.9	I	High	Very high
	35.0–39.9	II	Very high	Very high
Extreme obesity	40.0+[b]	III	Extremely high	Extremely high

[a]Disease risk for type 2 diabetes, hypertension, and cardiovascular disease.
[b]Increased waist circumference can also be a marker for increased risk even in persons of normal weight.
Note: Divide weight in pounds by 2.2 to get kilograms.
Source: National Institutes of Health, 2011.

associated with an increased risk for Type 2 diabetes, hypertension, and cardiovascular disease when BMI is between 25 and 34.9. A BMI greater than 25 is considered overweight, and a BMI greater than 30 is considered obese. Additionally, WC can be useful for those people categorized as normal or overweight in terms of BMI. For example, an athlete with increased muscle mass may have a BMI greater than 25. Changes in WC over time can indicate an increase or decrease in abdominal fat. Increased abdominal fat is associated with an increased risk of heart disease. To use Table 97.2 for athletic individuals, convert the weight in pounds by dividing by a factor of 2.2 to equal the weight in kilograms.

WAIST CIRCUMFERENCE

To determine your WC, locate your waist and measure the circumference. The tape measure should be snug, but it should not cause compressions on the skin. Table 97.2 should be helpful in determining the possible risks associated with your BMI and WC.

References and Readings

Center for Disease Control and Prevention. National Center for Chronic Disease Prevention and Health Promotion. Division of Nutrition and Physical Activity. (2011). *BMI: Body Mass Index*. Retireved February 2013, from www.cdc.gov/healthyweight/assessing/bmi/index.html. (see also www.cdc.gov/nccdphp/dnpa/bmi/calc-bmi.htm)

National Institutes of Health. National Heart, Lung, and Blood Institute. (2011). *Aim for a healthy weight*. Retrieved February 2013, from www.nhlbi.nih.gov/guidelines/obesity/bmi_tbl.htm

National Institutes of Health. National Heart, Lung, and Blood Institute. (2011). *Nutrition curriculum guide for training physician*. Retrieved February 2013, from www.nhlbi.nih.gov/funding/training/naa/curr_gde.pdf

Related Topics

Chapter 96, "Normal Medical Laboratory Values and Measurement Conversions"

Chapter 129, "Common Clinical Abbreviations and Symbols"

98 DIETARY SUPPLEMENTS AND PSYCHOLOGICAL FUNCTIONING

Sari Edelstein and Nancie H. Herbold

Psychological disorders and substance abuse can be associated with nutritional deficiencies. The origin of these nutritional deficiencies can be due to undereating, overeating, or abnormal eating patterns (Table 98.1) or as a side effect of alcohol, drugs (Table 98.2), and medication use (Table 98.3). This chapter identifies the criteria for nutrient supplementation, the recommended amount of supplementation, and the signs of both nutrient deficiency and toxicity. The dosage values given in the tables represent the Recommended Dietary Allowance and Adequate Intake levels set by the National Academy of Sciences. These levels were intended to be necessary in the daily diet of healthy adults. Some nutrient supplementation may be contraindicated due to other chronic illness or medications the patient may be sustaining. When the practitioner suspects a deficiency or toxicity, confirmation laboratory values should be made along with consideration of other illness and medication use.

TABLE 98.1. Dietary Supplements

Diagnosis	Nutrient Deficiency Symptoms	RDA/AI Supplementation and Dosage[a]	Toxicity Symptoms	Food Sources
Anorexia nervosa	Osteomalacia, osteoporosis	Calcium, 1,000 mg/day	Excessive bone calcification	Milk, cheese, turnip, mustard greens, kale, broccoli
Bulimia	Glossitis; megablastic anemia	Folate, 400 µg/day	None known	Liver, green leafy vegetables, legumes, broccoli, nuts
Bulimia nervosa	Anemia, poor wound healing	Zinc, 12–15 mg/day	None known	Meat, liver, eggs, seafood
Anxiety	Muscle weakness, poor appetite, fatigue, Korsakoff's psychosis	Thiamine Males: 1.2 mg/day Females: 1.1 mg/day	None known	Pork, whole grains
	Skin and mouth lesions	Niacin Males: 16 mg/day Females: 14 mg/day	Flushing, tingling, nausea, dizziness	Lean meats, poultry, peanuts, fish, organ meats

(*continued*)

TABLE 98.1. Dietary Supplements (*continued*)

	Oral lesions	Vitamin B6, 1.3 mg/day	Numbness, ataxia, bone pain, muscle weakness	Red meats, liver, whole grains, potatoes, corn, green vegetables
	Pernicious anemia, possible depression, anorexia	Vitamin B12, 2.4 µg/day	None known	Meats, milk products, egg
	Glossitis, megablastic anemia	Folate, 400 µg/day	None known	Liver, green leafy vegetables, legumes, broccoli, nuts
	Anemia, poor wound healing	Zinc, 12–15 mg/day	None known	Meat, liver, eggs, seafood
	Muscle tremors, irritability, tetany, hyperhypoflexia	Magnesium Males: 420 mg/day Females: 320 mg/day	Increased calcium secretion	Whole grains, nuts, dried beans, peas
	Myalgia, muscle tenderness, fragile red blood cells	Selenium Males: 70 µg/day Females: 55 µg/day	Nausea, abdominal pain, diarrhea, fatigue	Meat, eggs, milk, whole grains, seafood, garlic
Depression	Skin and mouth lesions, depressive psychosis	Niacin Males: 16 mg/day Females: 14 mg/day	Flushing, tingling, nausea, dizziness	Lean meats, poultry, peanuts, fish, organ meats
	Oral lesions	Vitamin B6, 1.3 mg/day	Numbness, ataxia bone pain, muscle weakness	Red meats, liver, whole grains, potatoes, corn, green vegetables
	Glossitis, megablastic anemia	Folate, 400 µg/day	None known	Liver, green leafy vegetables, legumes, broccoli, nuts
	Bleeding gums, loose teeth, pinpoint hemorrhages	Vitamin C Males: 90 mg/day Female: 75 mg/day	GI upset, kidney stones, excess iron absorption	Citrus fruit, tomatoes, potatoes, brussels sprouts, broccoli, strawberries
	Muscle tremors, irritability, tetany, hyperhypoflexia	Magnesium Males: 420 mg/day Females: 320 mg/day	Increased calcium secretion	Whole grains, nuts, dried beans, peas
	Poor iron absorption, neutropenia, bone demineralization	Copper, 2.0 mg/day	Wilson's disease, liver cirrhosis, neurological deterioration	Liver, kidney, shellfish, nuts, raisins, chocolate
Schizophrenia	Skin and mouth lesions, depressive psychosis	Niacin Males: 16 mg/day Females: 14 mg/day	Flushing, tingling, nausea, dizziness	Lean meats, poultry, peanuts, fish, organ meats
	Muscle tremors, irritability, tetany hyperhypoflexia	Magnesium Males: 420 mg/day Females: 320 mg/day	Increased calcium secretion	Whole grains, nuts, dried beans, peas
	Bleeding gums, loose teeth, pinpoint hemorrhages	Vitamin C Males: 90 mg/day Females: 75 mg/day	GI upset, kidney stones, excess iron absorption	Citrus fruit, tomatoes, potatoes, brussels sprouts, broccoli, strawberries
Organic brain syndromes	Pernicious anemia, possible depression, anorexia	Vitamin B12, 2.4 µg/day	None known	Meats, milk products, egg
	Osteomalcia	Vitamin D, 5 µg/day	Hypercalcemia nausea, vomiting, polydipsia, polyuria	Fish, liver, eggs, fortified milk

(*continued*)

TABLE 98.1. Dietary Supplements (*continued*)

Diagnosis	Nutrient Deficiency Symptoms	RDA/AI Supplementation and Dosage[a]	Toxicity Symptoms	Food Sources
	Myalgia, muscle tenderness, fragile red blood cells	Selenium Males: 70 µg/day Females: 55 µg/day	Nausea, abdominal pain, diarrhea, fatigue	Meat, eggs, milk, whole grains, seafood, garlic
	Anemia, poor wound healing	Zinc, 12–15 mg/day	None known	Meat, liver, eggs, seafood

[a]Institute of Medicine, 2004.

TABLE 98.2. Nutritional Supplementation for Substance Abuse

Diagnosis	Nutrient Deficiency Symptoms	Recommended Dietary Supplementation and Dosage	Toxicity Symptoms
Folic acid deficiency	Glossitis, megablastic anemia	Folate, 400 µg/day	None known
Thiamine deficiency	Muscle weakness, poor appetite, fatigue, depression; Korsakoff's psychosis	Thiamine Males: 1.2 mg/day Females: 1.1 mg/day	None known
Vitamin B12 deficiency	Pernicious anemia, possible depression, anorexia	Vitamin B12, 2.4 µg/day	None known
Vitamin B6 deficiency	Oral lesions	Vitamin B6, 1.3 mg/day	Numbness, ataxia, bone pain, muscle weakness
Vitamin A deficiency	Dry eyes, gradual loss of vision, hyperkeratosis of skin	Vitamin A Males: 900 mg/day Females: 700 mg/day	Fatigue, vertigo, night sweats, lesions on lips and skin, abdominal pain, vomiting, jaundice
Zinc deficiency	Anemia, poor wound healing	Zinc, 12–15 mg/day	None known
Copper deficiency	Poor iron absorption, neutropenia, bone demineralization	Copper, 2.0 mg/day	Wilson's disease, liver cirrhosis, neurological deterioration

Source: Institute of Medicine, 2004..

TABLE 98.3. Medications and Their Nutritional Effects

Medication	Nutritional Effect	Recommendation
Alprazolam (Xanax)	Increased or decreased appetite, anorexia, increased or decreased weight, increased salivation, dry mouth, nausea, vomiting, constipation	Take with food or water, limit caffeine, avoid alcohol, caution with some herbal products (kava)
Amantadine HCL (Symmetrel)	Anorexia, dry mouth, nausea, constipation	Avoid alcohol
Amitriptyline (Elavil)	Dry mouth, nausea, vomiting, anorexia, taste changes, epigastric distress, diarrhea, constipation, paralytic ileus	Take with food, increase fiber may decrease drug effect. Limit caffeine, avoid alcohol, avoid St. John's wort, avoid SAM-e, avoid yohimbe.
Bupropion (Wellbutrin)	Anorexia, decreased weight, increased appetite, increased weight, dry mouth, stomatitis, dyspepsia, nausea, diarrhea, vomiting, constipationw	Take with food, avoid alcohol, avoid St. John's wort. Possible anemia.

(*continued*)

TABLE 98.3. Medications and Their Nutritional Effects (*continued*)

Benztropine mesylate (Cogentin)	Dry mouth, nausea, vomiting, epigastric distress, constipation	Take with food, avoid alcohol
Carbamazepine (Tegretol)	Anorexia, dry mouth, decreased appetite, stomatitis, glossitis, nausea, vomiting, abdominal pain, constipation, diarrhea	Take with food, avoid alcohol, avoid psyllium seed, aplastic anemia, caution with grapefruit juice
Clonazepam (Klonopin)	Dry/sore mouth, constipation, abdominal cramps, gastritis, changes in appetite, nausea, anorexia, diarrhea, increased salivation	Take with food, limit caffeine, avoid alcohol, caution with some herbal products
Clozapine (Clozaril)	Increased appetite, increased weight, anorexia, dry mouth, increased salivation, nausea, vomiting, dyspepsia, severe constipation, diarrhea	Take with food, limit caffeine, avoid alcohol, avoid St. John's wort. Nutmeg may reduce effectiveness of drug therapy
Diazepam (Valium)	Occasional nausea and vomiting, diarrhea, constipation	Contraindicated for people with soy protein sensitivity. Take with food, avoid caffeine, avoid alcohol, avoid kava.
Fluoxetine (Prozac)	Anorexia, decreased weight, dry mouth, taste changes, dyspepsia, nausea, vomiting, diarrhea, constipation	Take in A.M. with meals. No tryptophan supplements. Avoid alcohol, avoid St. John's wort. Caution with diabetes—hypoglycemia
Haloperidol (Haldol)	Increase appetite, increase weight, anorexia, dry mouth, increased salivation, dyspepsia, nausea, vomiting, constipation, diarrhea	Take with food, avoid alcohol
Lorazepam (Ativan)	Occasional dry mouth, nausea, constipation	Take with food, avoid caffeine, avoid alcohol
Levodopa (Dopar, Larodopa)	Dry mouth, bitter taste, nausea, vomiting, anorexia, constipation, diarrhea, abdominal pain, excessive salivation, increased or decreased weight, epigastric distress	May take with low protein food or juice, not with high-protein food
Lithium carbonate	Decreased appetite, increased thirst, metallic taste, dry mouth, nausea, vomiting, diarrhea, transient hyperglycemia	Take with foods, avoid caffeine, avoid alcohol, avoid psyllium seed since it may inhibit absorption
Nortriptyline (Pamelor)	Increased or decreased appetite, dry mouth, nausea, vomiting, constipation	Take with food, avoid caffeine, avoid alcohol, avoid St. John's wort
Paroxetine (Paxil)	Decreased appetite, increased or decreased weight, dry mouth, taste changes, nausea, dyspepsia, constipation, diarrhea	Take with food, avoid St. John's wort, avoid SAM-e, avoid yohimbe
Phenelzine sulfate (Nardil)	Possible B6 deficiency, increased appetite, increased weight	Avoid foods high in tyramine and tryptophan such as cheese, yogurt, pickled, fermented, and smoked foods. Limit caffeine, avoid tryptophan supplements, may need B6 supplement, avoid St. John's wort, avoid alcohol. Caution with diabetes as it may decrease serum glucose.
Phenobarbital (Phenobarbital)	Nausea, vomiting, constipation	Increase vitamin D and calcium intake. Limit xanthine/caffeine, avoid alcohol. May need vitamin D, vitamin B12, and folate supplement with long-term use.

(*continued*)

TABLE 98.3. Medications and Their Nutritional Effects (*continued*)

Medication	Nutritional Effect	Recommendation
Phenytoin (Dilantin)	Taste changes, dysphagia, nausea, vomiting, constipation	Take with food or milk, avoid alcohol, caution with diabetes as it may increase serum glucose. Folate supplement needed. May need Vitamin D supplement.
Risperidone (Risperdal)	Increased appetite, increased weight, increased or decreased salivation, nausea, vomiting, dyspepsia, constipation, diarrhea, abdominal pain	Take with food, avoid alcohol
Sertraline HCL (Zoloft)	Increased or decreased appetite, dry mouth, nausea, vomiting, diarrhea, constipation, dyspepsia	Take with food, avoid alcohol, anemia
Trifluoperazine (Stelazine)	Dry mouth, constipation, nausea, increased weight	Avoid alcohol, avoid kava, avoid St. John's wort, avoid yohimbe
Valproic acid (Depakene)	Anorexia, increased or decreased weight, increased appetite, nausea, vomiting, indigestion, cramps, gastroenteritis, diarrhea, constipation	Take with food, avoid alcohol. Do not take with milk. Do not take syrup in carbonated beverages as it may cause mouth/throat irritation or unpleasant taste.
Venlafaxine (Effexor)	Anorexia, increased or decreased weight, increased appetite, dry mouth, taste changes, nausea, vomiting, constipation, diarrhea, dyspepsia	Take with food, avoid St. John's wort, avoid alcohol

Source: Food and Nutrition Board, 2002; Food and Nutrition Board, 2004.

References and Readings

Augmentation strategies for depression. options include psychotherapy, drugs, and dietary supplements. (2010). *The Harvard Mental Health Letter/from Harvard Medical School, 27*(6), 1–3.

Beydoun, M. A., Shroff, M. R., Beydoun, H. A., & Zonderman, A. B. (2010). Serum folate, vitamin B-12, and homocysteine and their association with depressive symptoms among U.S. adults. *Psychosomatic Medicine, 72*(9), 862–873.

Institute of Medicine of the National Academies. (2004). Dietary supplements: A framework for evaluating safety. Retrieved February 2013, from iom.edu/Activities/Nutrition/SafetyDietSupp.aspx

Johannessen, B., Skagestad, I., & Bergkaasa, A. M. (2011). Food as medicine in psychiatric care: Which profession should be responsible for imparting knowledge and use of omega-3 fatty acids in psychiatry. *Complementary Therapies in Clinical Practice, 17*(2), 107–112.

Lakhan, S. E., & Vieira, K. F. (2010). Nutritional and herbal supplements for anxiety and anxiety-related disorders: Systematic review. *Nutrition Journal, 9*, 42–42.

Ng, R. C., Hirata, C. K., Yeung, W., Haller, E., & Finley, P. R. (2010). Pharmacologic treatment for postpartum depression: A systematic review. *Pharmacotherapy, 30*(9), 928–941.

Roman, M. W., & Bembry, F. H. (2011). L-methylfolate (deplin®): A new medical food therapy as adjunctive treatment for depression. *Issues in Mental Health Nursing, 32*(2), 142–143.

Smoliner, C., Norman, K., Wagner, K., Hartig, W., Lochs, H., & Pirlich, M. (2009). Malnutrition and depression in the institutionalised elderly. *British Journal of Nutrition, 102*(11), 1663–1667.

Related Topics

Chapter 91, "Understanding Side Effects and Warnings in Psychopharmacology"

Chapter 94, "Herbal Treatments for Psychological Disorders"

PART VII
Self-Help Resources

99 RECOMMENDED SELF-HELP BOOKS, AUTOBIOGRAPHIES, AND FILMS

John C. Norcross and Linda F. Campbell

Self-help resources for behavioral disorders and life challenges have proliferated in recent years. The use or recommendation of self-help books (bibliotherapy), autobiographies, and films (cinematherapy) as adjuncts to psychotherapy have correspondingly increased. Across mental health disciplines, nearly 70% of practitioners suggest self-help books to clients (Adams & Pitre, 2000). Among clinical and counseling psychologists, 85% recommended self-help books, 79% self-help groups, 54% movies, and 28% autobiographies to their patients in the past year (Norcross et al., 2013).

Self-help resources can offer multiple therapeutic benefits in a cost-effective manner. They educate the public about disorders and treatments; provide phenomenological accounts of those challenges in everyday terms; enhance identification and empathy; generate hope and insight; offer concrete advice and techniques; explain treatment strategies; and summarize research findings. Such resources can do so for a fraction of the cost of conventional psychotherapy and at higher levels of access and privacy than formal treatment. Moreover, those self-help materials that have undergone empirical testing generally show positive results with few negative outcomes (e.g., Mains & Scogin, 2003; Menchola, Arkowitz, & Burke, 2007).

The rub is that less than 5% of published self-help materials have been scientifically evaluated for safety or efficacy. We do not know which resources are effective as stand-alone therapies and which disorders prove amenable to self-help alone.

At the same time, the public and practitioners routinely confront questions of which self-help resource to recommend or purchase. Toward this end, we and our colleagues have sought to establish an expert consensus on the value of self-help materials (Norcross et al., 2013). Although expert consensus cannot substitute for controlled research, it definitely ranks as superior to individual preferences, marketing claims, and best-seller lists. Until and if such controlled research comes along, we believe our surveys constitute useful guides for those choosing to embrace and prescribe self-help.

In this chapter, we identify the top 50 self-help books, 50 autobiographies, and 50 films for particular mental disorders and life challenges. These top-rated self-help resources are listed under their respective disorders or challenges; the numbers in parentheses represent their ranking within self-help genre, where 1 is the most highly rated. These resources emerged as the consensual picks in our 12 national surveys of licensed psychologists over the past 20 years and are extracted from the fourth edition of

Self-Help That Works (Norcross et al., 2013; previously entitled the *Authoritative Guide to Self-Help Resources in Mental Health*). Readers can find methodological details and cautions there, but in a nutshell, nearly 5,000 psychologists rated self-help resources with which they were sufficiently familiar on a 5-point scale where +2 was "extremely good or outstanding" and −2 was "extremely bad" for a particular disorder or challenge. To be eligible for the following top-50 lists, a self-help book, autobiography, or film had to be rated by a minimum of 20 psychologists.

Recommending an effective self-help resource requires timing and clinical sensitivity (Norcross, 2006). Practitioners can become familiar with the respective books or films so they can explain the therapeutic process to patients and can ensure the messages are consonant with treatment itself. Practitioners can also attend to clients' values, preferences, and culture and prescribe accordingly. Clients suffering from debilitating disorders should be cautioned against relying on self-help by itself and warned not to overgeneralize or overidentify with recommended resources (Hesley & Hesley, 2001).

Identifying an expert consensus on self-help has distinct advantages over routine practice. Self-help books, autobiographies, and movies offer potentially powerful and cost-effective means to disseminate treatment methods, increase mental health awareness, generate inspiration, and stimulate self-reflection. We long for the day when controlled research is routinely conducted on the effectiveness of self-help materials, but until then, expert consensus can guide the public and professionals in selecting meritorious self-help that accurately portrays mental health disorders, credible treatments, and hopeful outcomes.

ABUSE

The Courage to Heal by Bass and Davis (book 13)
A Man Named Dave by Pelzer (autobiography 9)
The Lost Boy by Pelzer (autobiography 11)
The Color Purple (film 29)

ADULT DEVELOPMENT

Tuesdays With Morrie by Albom (autobiography 3)
The Trip to the Bountiful (film 11)
The Doctor (film 24)
It's a Wonderful Life (film 35)

AGING

The Virtues of Aging by Carter (autobiography 26)
The Fountain of Age by Friedan (autobiography 50)
On Golden Pond (film 6)

ANGER

The Anger Control Workbook by McKay and Rogers (book 32)
The Dance of Anger by Lerner (book 40)

ANXIETY DISORDERS

The Anxiety and Phobia Workbook by Bourne (book 7)
Mastery of Your Anxiety and Panic III by Craske and Barlow (book 12)
Mastering Your Fears and Phobias Workbook by Antony et al. (book 22)
The Panic Attack Recovery Book by Swede and Jaffe (autobiography 25)

ASSERTIVENESS

Your Perfect Right by Alberti and Emmons (book 46)
The Assertive Woman by Phelps and Austin (book 50)

ATTENTION-DEFICIT/HYPERACTIVITY DISORDER

Taking Charge of Adult ADHD by Barkley (book 5)

Taking Charge of ADHD by Barkley (book 38)
ADHD Handbook for Families by Weingartner (autobiography 29)
The Little Monster by Jergen (autobiography 37)
Parenting a Child with ADHD by Boyles and Contadino (autobiography 45)

AUTISM AND ASPERGER'S

Emergence by Grandin and Scariano (autobiography 6)
Born on a Blue Day by Tammet (autobiography 39)
Temple Grandin (film 1)
What's Eating Gilbert Grape? (film 36)

BIPOLAR DISORDER

An Unquiet Mind by Jamison (autobiography 13)
Skywriting by Pauley (autobiography 33)
A Brilliant Madness by Duke and Hochman (autobiography 38)

BORDERLINE AND NARCISSISTIC PERSONALITY DISORDERS

Skills Training Manual for Treating Borderline Personality Disorder by Linehan (book 2)
The Drama of the Gifted Child by Miller (book 34)
Girl, Interrupted by Kaysen (autobiography 27)
The Great Santini (film 34)
Sunset Boulevard (film 40)

CHILD DEVELOPMENT AND PARENTING

Your Defiant Child by Barkley and Benton (book 10)
The Explosive Child by Greene (book 18)
What to Expect: The Toddler Years by Eisenberg et al. (book 19)
Toddlers and Parents by Brazelton (book 45)
Searching for Bobby Fischer (film 44)

CHRONIC PAIN

Managing Pain Before It Manages You by Caudill and Benson (book 14)

DEATH AND GRIEVING

The Grief Recovery Handbook by James and Cherry (book 21)
How to Survive the Loss of a Love by Colgrove et al. (book 36)
Letting Go by Schwartz (autobiography 1)
A Grief Observed by Lewis (autobiography 4)
Death Be Not Proud by Gunther (autobiography 7)
The Year of Magical Thinking by Didion (autobiography 14)
The Wheel of Life by Kübler-Ross and Gold (autobiography 17)
Motherless Daughter by Edleman (autobiography 19)
After the Death of a Child by Finkbeiner (autobiography 23)
Corrina, Corrina (film 21)
The Bucket List (film 39)
Steel Magnolias (film 50)

DEMENTIA AND ALZHEIMER'S

The 36-Hour Day by Mace and Rabins (book 9)
Elegy for Iris by Bayley (autobiography 5)
Iris (film 2)
Away From Her (film 8)
The Notebook (film 17)

DEPRESSION

Feeling Good by Burns (book 16)
Mind Over Mood by Greenberger and Padesky (book 28)
The Feeling Good Handbook by Burns (book 43)

Darkness Visible by Styron (autobiography 20)
The Noonday Demon by Solomon (autobiography 22)
Undercurrents by Manning (autobiography 31)
On the Edge of Darkness by Cronkite (autobiography 42)
Leaves From Many Seasons by Mowrer (autobiography 44)
Down Came the Rain by Shields (autobiography 49)
A Woman Under the Influence (film 31)

DIVORCE

Dinosaurs Divorce by Brown and Brown (book 29)
Boys and Girls Book About Divorce by Gardner (book 39)
The Squid and the Whale (film 10)
Kramer vs. Kramer (film 28)

EATING DISORDERS

Breaking Free From Compulsive Eating by Roth (autobiography 2)
Feeding the Hungry Heart by Roth (autobiography 18)
Am I Still Visible? by Heater (autobiography 35)
Diary of a Fat Housewife by Green (autobiography 48)
Karen Carpenter Story (film 26)
Best Little Girl in the World (film 45)

FAMILIES AND STEPFAMILIES

The Joy Luck Club (film 9)
Life as a House (film 19)
Family Man (film 30)
Terms of Endearment (film 42)

GAY, LESBIAN, AND BISEXUAL ISSUES

Milk (film 3)
Angels in America (film 16)
Brokeback Mountain (film 33)

INFANT DEVELOPMENT AND PARENTING

Infants and Mothers by Brazelton (book 20)
What Every Baby Knows by Brazelton (book 25)
What to Expect the First Year by Eisenberg et al. (book 26)
Dr. Spock's Baby and Child Care by Spock and Parker (book 27)
To Listen to a Child by Brazelton (book 37)

LOVE AND MARRIAGE

Why Marriages Succeed or Fail by Gottman and Silver (book 6)
The Seven Principles for Making Marriages Work by Gottman and Silver (book 17)
Love Is Never Enough by Beck (book 47)
The Kids Are All Right (film 47)

MEN'S ISSUES

Real Boys by Pollack (book 44)
I Never Sang for My Father (film 5)
Billy Elliot (film 7)
October Sky (film 22)

OBSESSIVE-COMPULSIVE DISORDER

Mastery of Obsessive-Compulsive Disorder by Kozak and Foa (book 41)
S.T.O.P. Obsessing by Foa and Wilson (book 48)

POSTTRAUMATIC STRESS DISORDER

Trauma and Recovery by Herman (book 30)
In the Valley of Elah (film 13)
The Accused (film 41)

PREGNANCY

What to Expect When You're Expecting by Eisenberg et al. (book 8)
The Complete Book of Pregnancy and Childbirth by Kitzinger (book 33)

SCHIZOPHRENIA

The Center Cannot Hold by Saks (autobiography 12)
The Soloist by Lopez (autobiography 16)
I Never Promised You a Rose Garden by Greenberg (autobiography 21)
Out of the Depths by Boisen (autobiography 24)
Too Much Anger, Too Many Tears by Gotkin and Gotkin (autobiography 30)
Welcome, Silence by North (autobiography 40)
The Soloist (film 12)
A Beautiful Mind (film 23)
Bird (film 49)

SELF-MANAGEMENT AND SELF-ENHANCEMENT

Get out of Your Mind and Into Your Life by Hayes and Smith (book 35)
The Happiness Project by Rubin (autobiography 34)
Children of a Lesser God (film 25)

SEXUALITY

For Yourself by Barbach (book 1)
Becoming Orgasmic by Heiman and LoPiccolo (book 3)
For Each Other by Barbach (book 4)
Torch Song Trilogy (film 37)

STRESS MANAGEMENT AND RELAXATION

The Relaxation and Stress Reduction Workbook by Davis et al. (book 15)
Wherever You Go, There You Are by Kabat-Zinn (book 23)
The Stress and Relaxation Handbook by Madders (book 49)

SUBSTANCE ABUSE

Broken Cord by Dorris (autobiography 10)
Beautiful Boy by Sheff (autobiography 28)
Getting Better: Inside AA by Robertson (autobiography 32)
A Drinking Life by Hamill (autobiography 41)
Go Ask Alice by Anonymous (autobiography 43)
Codependent No More by Beattie (autobiography 46)
Drinking: A Love Story by Knapp (autobiography 47)
The Lost Weekend (film 14)
Days of Wine and Roses (film 15)
Requiem for a Dream (film 20)
The Fighter (film 27)
My Name Is Bill W. (film 38)
Clean and Sober (film 46)

SUICIDE

Night Falls Fast by Jamison (autobiography 8)
Ordinary People (film 4)

TEENAGERS

"Get out of My Life but First Could You Drive Me and Cheryl to the Mall?" by Wolf (book 24)
Reviving Ophelia by Pipher (book 31)
Stand by Me (film 18)
Dead Poets Society (film 32)

WOMEN'S ISSUES

The New Our Bodies, Ourselves by Boston Women's Collective (book 11)
The Second Shift by Hochschild (book 42)
Heart of a Woman by Angelou (autobiography 15)
Deborah, Golda, and Me by Pogrebin (autobiography 36)
Fried Green Tomatoes (film 43)
A League of Their Own (film 48)

References and Readings

Adams, S. J., & Pitre, N. L. (2000). Who uses bibliotherapy and why? A survey from an underserviced area. *Canadian Journal of Psychiatry, 45*, 645–650.

Hesley, J. W., & Hesley, K. G. (2001). *Rent two films and let's talk in the morning: Using popular movies in psychotherapy* (2nd ed.). New York: Wiley.

Mains, J. A., & Scogin, F. R. (2003). The effectiveness of self-administered treatments: A practice-friendly review of the research. *Journal of Clinical Psychology, 59,* 237–246.

Menchola, M., Arkowitz, H. S., & Burke, B. L. (2007). Efficacy of self-administered treatments for depression and anxiety. *Professional Psychology: Research and Practice, 38,* 421–429.

Norcross, J. C. (2006). Integrating self-help into psychotherapy: 16 practical suggestions. *Professional Psychology: Research and Practice, 37,* 683–693.

Norcross, J. C., Campbell, L. M., Grohol, J. M., Santrock, J. W., Selagea, F., & Sommer, R. (2013). *Self-help that works* (4th ed.). New York: Oxford University Press.

Watkins, P. L., & Clum, G. A. (Eds.). (2008). *Handbook of self-help therapies.* New York: Routledge.

Wedding, D., Boyd, M. A., & Niemiec, R. M. (2010). *Movies and mental illness: Using films to understand psychopathology* (3rd ed.). Cambridge, MA: Hogrefe.

Related Topics

Chapter 100, "Recommended Homework during Psychotherapy with Couples and Individuals"

Chapter 101, "Recommended Self-Help Internet Resources for Patients"

Chapter 102, "Recommended Online Computer-Assisted Treatments"

100 RECOMMENDED HOMEWORK DURING PSYCHOTHERAPY WITH COUPLES AND INDIVIDUALS

Arthur E. Jongsma, Jr.

The use of homework has been shown to strengthen the psychotherapy process and to improve treatment outcomes (Kazantzis, Whittington, & Dattilio, 2010). With the advent of managed care, which often requires shorter and fewer treatment sessions, therapists assign between-session homework to help maximize the effectiveness of briefer treatment. Homework is an extension of the treatment process, provides continuity, and allows the client to work between sessions on goals. Homework can also be a tool for more fully engaging the client in the treatment process. Assignments place more responsibility on the client to resolve his or her presenting problems, counteracting the expectations that some clients may experience that it is the therapist alone who can cure him or her. For some, it even may bring a sense of self-empowerment.

Another benefit of homework is that these assignments give the client the opportunity to implement and evaluate insights or coping behaviors that have been discussed in therapy sessions. Practice often heightens awareness of various issues. Furthermore, homework increases the expectation for the client to follow through with *making* changes rather than just *talking* about change. Exercises require participation, which creates a sense that the client is taking active steps toward change. Homework also allows the client to try new behaviors, bringing these experiences back to the next session for processing. Modifications can then be made to the client's thoughts, feelings, or behaviors as the homework is processed in the therapy session. Additionally, using assignments that call for their participation homework increases the involvement of family members and significant others in the client's treatment.

Three homework assignments have been adapted from *The Adult Psychotherapy Homework Planner* (Jongsma, 2006) for couples and three for an individual client. The three recommendations for couples focus on attending to meeting the partner's needs and desires in the relationship, identifying changes each partner can make to improve the relationship, and teaching the importance of clarifying parenting expectations in behavioral language and rewarding a child's rule-keeping behavior. The three recommended homework assignments for individual clients target anger management, behavioral activation for depression treatment, and exposure techniques for the treatment of phobic fear. Some assignments need the therapist to guide the client in completing the exercise while others can be completed independently by the client during the week between appointments.

HOW CAN WE MEET EACH OTHER'S NEEDS AND DESIRES?

Suggestions for Processing With the Client

This assignment has two parts—one to be completed by each of the partners within the relationship. It is recommended that each partner complete the homework independently and bring the results back for sharing and processing within a conjoint session. Take the opportunity to teach both partners the key concept that mutually satisfying relationships necessitate each partner being willing at times to sacrifice his or her own needs and desires and choose to meet the needs and desires of the partner. Also teach the partners that each of them should take personal responsibility for reasonable satisfaction of some needs outside of the relationship.

Meeting Each Other's Needs

A successful and healthy intimate relationship requires that each partner invest some of his or her time and energy into satisfying the needs and desires of his or her partner. When relational needs are not being met satisfactorily, the relationship is in serious trouble and eventually may break. However, all needs cannot be met by one partner. Each must take some responsibility for satisfying needs apart from the relationship. This exercise helps you identify and clarify your needs as well as the needs of your partner.

Partner One Perspective

1. List the needs and desires that you expect the relationship to meet.

a.

b.

c.

d.

2. List your partner's needs and desires (as you understand them) that he or she expects the relationship to meet.

a.

b.

c.

d.

3. List what you are willing to do to meet your partner's needs and desires.

a.

b.

c.

d.

4. List what you expect your partner to do to meet your needs and desires.

a.

b.

c.

d.

5. How have you let your partner down in meeting his or her needs and desires?

a.

b.

c.

d.

6. How has your partner let you down in not meeting your needs and desires?

a.

b.

c.

d.

7. What could you do to get some of your needs met outside of the relationship, by yourself or with the help of others?

a.

b.

c.

d.

8. Describe three times in which you feel that you have sacrificed your own needs and desires to meet the needs and desires of your partner instead.

a.

b.

c.

9. List at least three enjoyable and rewarding activities that you feel would help you and your partner satisfy each other's need for social contact.

a.

b.

c.

Repeat these questions for the Partner Two Perspective

POSITIVE AND NEGATIVE CONTRIBUTIONS TO THE RELATIONSHIP: MINE AND YOURS

Suggestions for Processing with the Client

Copy this exercise and give one to each partner. Ask each partner to complete the exercise independently and to bring it to a subsequent conjoint session. Review each partner's list and attempt to clarify the language and to put the changes requested in positive terms. Clients generally indicate what they would like not to happen rather than what they would like to happen. Ask each client for a commitment to work on making the changes that are called for in his or her own behavior.

When conflicts predominate in a relationship, an exaggerated focus gets placed on the negative aspects of the partner. Defenses keep us from evaluating our own contributions to the conflict and from noticing the positive things that the partner does to enhance the relationship. We become so focused on the negative aspects and primarily see the partner as the cause of the failure of the relationship. This assignment attempts to put things in perspective by asking each partner to take an honest look at himself or herself as well as evaluating the partner's contribution to conflict. Additional balance is sought by attempting to have each partner list the positive things that are brought to the relationship by each partner.

Partner List

Complete each of the following four lists. In the first list, itemize those things that you do that contribute positively to the relationship. In the second list, itemize those things that your partner does that enhance the relationship. Third, list the things that you need to do to improve the relationship and make it stronger. Finally (and this is always the easiest part), list the things that you believe your partner needs to do to make the relationship better.

1. What I do to enhance the relationship:

a.

b.

c.

d.

e.

2. What does my partner do to enhance the relationship?

a.

b.

c.

d.

e.

3. Things I need to do to improve the relationship:

a.

b.

c.

d.

e.

4. What does my partner need to do to make the relationship better?

a.

b.

c.

d.

e.

Repeat these questions for Partner Two List.

USING REINFORCEMENT PRINCIPLES IN PARENTING

Suggestions for Processing with the Client

Parents find it difficult to express expectations in behaviorally specific language—so do therapists. We must patiently try to shape parents' behavior as we process the rules that they develop. Also, be careful to bring to light unspoken rules that are left unlisted, but actually are very important for harmony in the household. Use counseling sessions to review lists and to model or role play positive reinforcement of rule-keeping behavior. Watch out for negative consequences for rule breaking that are not "tied to the crime" and are too protracted.

Parenting Methods

Rules are best kept when there are as few as possible; they are stated clearly and in a positive direction; obedience is recognized by reward; and disobedience is either ignored (if a minor violation) or met with a consequence that is swiftly administered, brief, not harsh, focuses on the offensive behavior and not on the child, and is somehow related to the broken rule. This exercise helps you think about what your rules are for your child and what the consequences for his or her obedience and disobedience are.

Think about, discuss, and then write out the three most important rules of the household for your child. Write them concisely and clearly so there is no misunderstanding as to what is expected from the child. Also, be sure to write them in observable terms and in a positive direction. For example:

Example A

Bad rule: Johnny must stop causing so much trouble with his sister.*Better rule*: Johnny must keep his hands off his sister, talk to her softly and politely, and allow her to finish her TV program before asking to change the channel to his preference.

Example B

Bad rule: Johnny must take his schoolwork more seriously and be more responsible about homework assignments.*Better rule*: Johnny must attend all his classes promptly and regularly, complete and hand in each assignment on time, keep the rules of the classroom, reserve at least 1 hour per night for quiet study, and obtain no grade below C–.

Example C

Bad rule: Johnny must not explode in anger whenever he is told he may not do some activity or must stop some activity he is doing.*Better rule*: When Johnny is told what he may or may not do, he must accept the parental or teacher limits calmly and respectfully, carrying out the request within 30 seconds or less.

Three Most Important Rules

1. ______________________________

2. ______________________________

3. ______________________________

When rules are kept or reasonably obeyed, it is easy to take this behavior for granted and not acknowledge it. But when the goal is to build self-esteem, increase compliance, and reduce conflict with authority, then it is advisable to focus positive attention on obedience or compliance. Find ways to reward obedient behavior whenever and wherever it occurs. Rewards do not have to be elaborate, expensive, or even concrete. The reward can be as simple as "Thanks, I appreciate that" or an affectionate pat on the back. At times, it may be appropriate to stop and talk about how pleasant it is for everyone when rules are kept, respect is shown, and conflict is at a minimum. Finally, some rewards may be more concrete such as a small gift, a favorite meal, a special outing, a privilege granted, or an appreciative note left on his or her pillow.

Now list four ways that you could show positive recognition to your child for keeping the rules.

1. ______________________________
2. ______________________________
3. ______________________________
4. ______________________________

Obviously, rules are not going to be kept 100% of the time by any child. The difficult task for a parent is to decide how to respond to disobedience most effectively and reasonably. Two cardinal rules for punishment: First, do not react when and if your anger is not well controlled; postpone action but make it known that you are doing so. Second, keep your focus on the child's behavior that is out of bounds and do not disparage, name-call, swear at, or belittle the child; give consequences with an attitude of respect.

Consequences should be given as soon as reasonably possible after the disobedience—long delays before consequences reduce effectiveness significantly. Consequences should be brief and tied to the offensive behavior, if possible. Long and extended consequences breed resentment, cause hardship for the enforcers of the consequences, and are not any more effective than something more pointed and brief. Finally, be sure to be consistent in giving consequences; both parents have to work together. Misbehavior should not be overlooked one time and addressed the next nor should it be overlooked by one parent and punished by the other.

Now list two possible consequences for each of the Three Most Important Rules that you listed previously.

1a.

1b.

2a.

2b.

3a.

3b.

ALTERNATIVES TO DESTRUCTIVE ANGER

Suggestions for Processing with the Client

Clients often feel they responded to a frustrating situation in the only way possible. They fail to realize that they have choices and control over their behavior. You may want to review the alternatives to rage listed in the first section of the assignment to help the client understand the alternatives he or she could apply when dealing with frustration or anger. Review the client's journal material and suggest additional constructive ways to respond to frustrating or hurtful situations that prompt his or her mismanaged anger.

Anger Response Alternatives

Destructive anger can take many forms. Anger can be expressed in rage that is out of control, either verbally or physically. We also can express anger by snapping at someone or being unkindly critical. A third form that anger may take is that of cold, icy withdrawal that punishes the other person by shutting the person out, shunning the person, or refusing to acknowledge the person's attempts to relate to us. All of these reactions and many more can be destructive to the relationship and to our own feelings of self-esteem. Destructive expressions of anger often generate later feelings of guilt and shame.

This exercise is designed to briefly identify some *constructive* alternatives to destructive anger by giving a brief description of the positive alternative. The goal is for you to consider these alternatives as you seek to replace destructive anger with more constructive behaviors. You will be asked to keep a journal of situations in your daily life that provoked anger and then note how one or more of these constructive alternatives may have been applied to the situations.

Constructive Alternatives

a. *Assertiveness.* Speaking forthrightly in a manner that is very respectful of the other person's needs and rights and does not attack anyone so as to make him or her defensive.
b. *Tune out/cool down.* Recognize that the situation has become volatile and nonproductive and suggest withdrawal from the situation to give each party a chance to cool down and collect his or her thoughts and regain personal control.
c. *Relaxation.* Learn and implement relaxation skills to reduce stress and tension through the use of words that cue relaxation, deep breathing that releases tension, imagining relaxing scenes, or deep muscle relaxation procedures.
d. *Diversion.* When anger is felt to be building, find diversionary activities that stop the buildup and focus the mind on more enjoyable experiences.
e. *Physical exercise.* When anger and tension levels rise, physical exercise can be a wonderful way to release tension and expel energy as an alternative to losing control or exploding in rage.
f. *Problem-solving skills.* Identify or clarify the problem, brainstorm possible solutions, review the pros and cons of each alternative solution, select the best alternative for implementation, evaluate the outcome as to mutual satisfaction, and finally, adjust the solution if necessary to increase mutual satisfaction.
g. *Self-talk.* Take time to talk to yourself in calming, reasoned, and constructive sentences that move you toward anger control and away from hurtful expressions of anger.
h. *"I" messages.* Speak to the target of your anger, describing your feelings and needs rather than attacking, labeling, or describing the other person's behavior, motivations, or goals. Begin your sentences with "I feel…" or "I need.…"
i. *Other.* Describe your own or your counselor's alternative to rage.

____

____

____

____

Application to Daily Life

In the columns that follow, describe the date and time, the situation that prompted the angry response, the destructive response, and the alternative constructive response that might have been used. In the final row, instead of writing a full description of the alternative, you may simply enter the alphabetical indicator of the constructive alternative, A through I.

Entry 1 Day/Date and Time: ______ ______	Situation	
	Response	
	Alternative Response	

Repeat recording situations in this format as often as necessary.

IDENTIFY AND SCHEDULE PLEASANT ACTIVITIES

Suggestions for Processing with the Client

The client's depression may interfere with his or her ability to recall pleasant activities and he or she may censor many of these activities, feeling he or she does not have the energy for them. Encourage him or her to brainstorm freely. If it is necessary, this assignment can be done within the counseling session rather than relying on the reduced motivation of the depressed client to fulfill the requirements of the assignment. Perhaps the brainstorming and scheduling need to be done within the session and the homework is that of implementing the activity and recording its impact. It is recommended that the client monitor his or her mood before, during, and after the event to focus him or her on the positive effect that the event has on mood. Review and reinforce the client's success in improving his or her mood using the satisfying activities.

Pleasurable Activities

People who are depressed almost always withdraw from participation in activities that they once found satisfying, rewarding, pleasurable, or just plain fun. It is very important to break this cycle of withdrawal and to begin reinvesting in the activities of life, the relationships around you, and the things you do well. A starting point for this task of reinvestment or reinvolvement is to create an inventory of all those things that you found to be pleasant events in the past.

1. On the lines that follow, write down a description in only a few words of those activities that you found pleasurable and pleasant in the past. These enjoyable activities should include (1) positive social interactions (e.g., spending time with a good friend), (2) useful or productive activities (e.g., caring for your child, doing a job well), and (3) intrinsically pleasant activities (e.g., a meal at your favorite restaurant, listening to favorite music, taking a warm bath). During this brainstorming session, allow yourself to freely recall any pleasant and enjoyable activities without censoring them based on whether you think you have the energy for them or whether they are feasible. You may want to ask significant others to give input to your list, but please remember that this is your list of personal pleasant activities and must reflect events that you find enjoyable.

Positive Social Interactions	Intrinsically Pleasant	Useful Activities Activities
________	________	________
________	________	________
________	________	________
________	________	________
________	________	________
________	________	________
________	________	________
________	________	________
________	________	________
________	________	________
________	________	________

2. Now select from your list of pleasant events seven that you believe are most likely for you to engage in. In the seven lines, list those activities and then to the right of the activity, write a few words that describe what was positive about the activity or why you found it pleasant or enjoyable.

Most Likely Activities	Why Pleasant?
1) ________	________
2) ________	________
3) ________	________
4) ________	________
5) ________	________
6) ________	________
7) ________	________

3. On the following lines, schedule one pleasant activity per day to which you are committed. Include the time of the day and with whom you might share the activity.

Activity		When and with Whom
Day 1	________	________
Day 2	________	________
Day 3	________	________
Day 4	________	________

Day 5 __________ ____________________

Day 6 __________ ____________________

Day 7 __________ ____________________

4. On the following lines, record the activity engaged in and the degree of satisfaction on a scale of 1 (low) to 10 (high) that was felt during and after the engagement with the pleasant event. Also record the effect that the pleasant event had on your mood using a scale of 1 (no positive effect) to 10 (strong uplifting effect on mood).

Activity	Satisfaction	Effect on Mood
Day 1 _____	__________	__________
Day 2 _____	__________	__________
Day 3 _____	__________	__________
Day 4 _____	__________	__________
Day 5 _____	__________	__________
Day 6 _____	__________	__________
Day 7 _____	__________	__________

GRADUALLY REDUCING YOUR PHOBIC FEAR

Suggestions for Processing with the Client

Graduated exposure to a feared object or situation has proven to be a very successful approach to extinguishing a fear response. This assignment focuses the client on the phobic stimulus and its effect on his or her life. Then, the client must develop a gradual hierarchy of exposure steps to the feared stimulus. You probably will have to be directly involved in constructing this hierarchy with the client. As preparation for beginning the in vivo exposure to the feared stimulus, it is recommended that you teach the client some behavioral and cognitive anxiety-reduction skills, such as deep breathing, progressive relaxation, positive imagery, confidence-building self-talk, and so on. Monitor and reinforce his or her implementation of these skills as the exposure program progresses. Urge the patient to increase exposure as anxiety diminishes to the current step.

Overcoming Fears

Fears that are so strong that they control our behavior need to be faced and overcome. This exercise helps you do just that: Identify what your fear is; describe how it affects you; develop a plan to face it systematically; and, finally, actually take steps to face your fear and win.

1. It is important to clearly identify what you fear and how it affects you emotionally (e.g., feel nervous and tense), behaviorally (such as avoid contact and/or do not talk about the feared stimulus), and physically (for instance, heart pounds, forehead and palms sweat, stomachache, nausea). Describe what the feared object or situation is and then tell how it affects you.

Feared Object or Situation	Reaction to Feared Object or Situation
______________	Emotional reaction: _____
______________	______________
______________	Behavioral reaction: _____
______________	______________
______________	Physical reaction: _____
	______________

To overcome a fear, it must be faced in a gradual but systematic fashion. We call this *exposure*. When you practice exposure in the proper way, fear steadily diminishes until it does not control your behavior or affect you physically. The key to the process is to develop a plan for gradually increasing exposure to the feared object or situation. Once the plan is developed, you then expose yourself one step at a time to the feared object or situation. You do not take the next step in the gradual exposure plan until you are quite comfortable with the current level of exposure.

For example, if your fear is that of driving alone on the expressway during heavy traffic, you could design a plan as follows.

Step 1: Drive on the expressway for 5 minutes at a time of light traffic with a supportive person to give reassurance.

Step 2: Drive on the expressway for 5 minutes at a time of light traffic, alone.

Step 3: Drive on the expressway for 10 minutes at a time of light traffic, alone.

Step 4: Drive on the expressway for 15 minutes at a time of light traffic, alone.

Step 5: Drive on the expressway for 5 minutes at a time of heavy traffic, alone.

Step 6: Drive on the expressway for 15 minutes at a time of heavy traffic, alone.

Each next step is taken only after the fear is low or gone in the current step.

2. Now create a gradual exposure program to overcome your feared object or situation. The steps can increase the time you spend with the feared object or situation, increase your closeness to it, increase the size of the object, or a combination of these things. Use as many steps as you need. Your therapist is available to help you construct this plan, if necessary.

Step 1. ____________________
____
____

Step 2. ____________________
____
____

Step 3. ____________________
____
____

Step 4. ____________________
____
____

Step 5. ____________________
____
____

Step 6. ____________________
____
____

Now it's time for a gradual but steady exposure to your feared object or situation. Stay relaxed. Your therapist may teach you some deep breathing, muscle relaxation, and positive self-talk techniques that you can use to keep yourself relaxed. For each attempt at exposure, record the coping technique you used and rate your degree of fear on a scale of 1 to 100, with 100 representing total panic, the sweats, and heart-pounding shakes. The rating of 1 represents total calm, complete confidence, peace of mind, looseness, and relaxed feeling. When your rating is reduced to 10 or lower on a consistent basis for the exposure to a particular step, then it's time to consider moving on to the next step.

Exposure Steps	Coping Technique and Fear Rating
Step 1. ________	1st attempt: ________
____________	2nd attempt: ________
____________	3rd attempt: ________
Step 2. ________	1st attempt: ________
____________	2nd attempt: ________
____________	3rd attempt: ________
Step 3. ________	1st attempt: ________
____________	2nd attempt: ________
____________	3rd attempt: ________
Step 4. ________	1st attempt: ________
____________	2nd attempt: ________
____________	3rd attempt: ________
Step 5. ________	1st attempt: ________
____________	2nd attempt: ________
____________	3rd attempt: ________
Step 6. ________	1st attempt: ________
____________	2nd attempt: ________
____________	3rd attempt: ________

References and Readings

Bevilacqua, L. J., & Dattilio, F. M. (2010). *Family therapy homework planner* (2nd ed.). Hoboken, NJ: Wiley.

Finley, J. R., & Lenz, B. S. (2009). *Addiction treatment homework planner* (4th ed.). Hoboken, NJ: Wiley.

Jongsma, A. E. (2006). *Adult psychotherapy homework planner* (2nd ed.). Hoboken, NJ: Wiley.

Jongsma, A. E., Peterson, L. M., & McInnis, W. P. (2006). *Adolescent psychotherapy homework planner* (2nd ed.). Hoboken, NJ: Wiley.

Jongsma, A. E., Peterson, L. M., & McInnis, W. P. (2006). *Child psychotherapy homework planner* (2nd ed.). Hoboken, NJ: Wiley.

Kazantzis, N., Whittington, C., & Dattilio, F. (2010). Meta-analysis of homework effects in cognitive behavioral therapy: A replication and extension. *Clinical Psychology: Science and Practice, 17,* 144–156.

Schultheis, G. M., Alexander O'Hanlon, S., & O'Hanlon, B. (2010). *Couples therapy homework planner* (2nd ed.). Hoboken, NJ: Wiley.

Related Topics

101 RECOMMENDED SELF-HELP INTERNET RESOURCES FOR PATIENTS

John M. Grohol

There are millions of websites available today, and tens of thousands are available on psychological and mental health concerns. Here you will find a select guide to a few of these sites that prove among the most reliable and useful for patients with mental health concerns. These 23 sites not only offer a balanced perspective on mental health and psychological disorders but also provide unique resources and content in a user-friendly format to make them worth the effort. All the sites listed in alphabetical order are available at no charge to the consumer to access and use.

- *About Psychotherapy* (www.aboutpsychotherapy.com): A down-to-earth information resource that provides detailed descriptions of various types of psychotherapy by psychologist Bennett Pologe, PhD. Dozens of pages describe how psychotherapy works, why a person might consider therapy, when to stop, and what legitimate psychotherapy consists of. Like Franklin's Psychology Information Online, About Psychotherapy also provides articles about starting treatment and the differences between types of professionals and their degrees. Case studies help clearly illustrate specific examples of different treatments.
- *American Psychological Association* (www.apa.org/): The American Psychological Association (APA) offers a wide range of resources for both consumers and psychologists. Updated behavioral health care news, research briefings, access to research databases, and journal archives are just a few of the many resources visitors will find at the APA site. Consumers will find the APA HelpCenter at www.apa.org/helpcenter/ more oriented toward their educational needs.

- *Beacon* (beacon.anu.edu.au/): If you are serious about using an interactive self-help health application online, Beacon offers a peer-reviewed ratings directory of health and mental health interactive Web sites. Housed at the Centre for Mental Health Research at the Australian National University, a panel of health experts rate online self-help programs according to the available research evidence. Those that have multiple research studies demonstrating their effectiveness are rated more highly, while online programs that have little or no evidence are rated more poorly. The directory makes it easy to determine whether a consumer should invest his or her time with an online, interactive program. Free registration is required to access the directory.
- *BluePages* (bluepages.anu.edu.au): BluePages was created by The Centre for Mental Health Research at the Australian National University in 2001 to help people learn all about depression and related mood disorders. One of its most valuable components is its description of the wide variety of depression treatments available and rating them according to their scientific evidence support. For instance, they rate cognitive-behavioral therapy and antidepressants highly, while many lifestyle changes do not rate at all or rate poorly (such as listening to music, painkillers, or meditation).
- *Centre for Addiction and Mental Health* (www.camh.ca): Canada's largest psychiatric hospital runs an informative and helpful Web site that provides a wealth of information about mental disorders and addictions both in online form and in downloadable PDFs. In addition to traditional information, they also offer online tutorials on a wide range of mental health topics, as well as online courses (the latter for a fee). Public policy and information about their research programs round out the site.
- *Cognitive-Behavior Therapy Self-Help Resources* (www.get.gg/): This site, maintained by Carol Vivyan, RMN, RGN, offers visitors a wide range of articles about cognitive-behavioral therapy (CBT) techniques for mental health concerns, such as anxiety, depression, anger, and self-esteem. For instance, on the topic of automatic thoughts, the site has a dozen articles plus helpful worksheets that can be downloaded and printed out for everyday use. The site is a treasure trove of CBT information and resources, designed for self-help, patient use.
- *DrugDigest* (www.drugdigest.org/): DrugDigest is a noncommercial consumer health and drug information site that provides a searchable drug and herb database. The results are written in plain English, making it unlike most drug databases available on the Internet today. For each drug, the site provides what the medication is used for, how it works, what a person should know about taking it, common side effects and interactions, how it should be taken, and what to do if the person misses a dose. For more detailed and technical drug information, RxList (www.rxlist.com) or MedlinePlus (www.nlm.nih.gov/medlineplus/druginformation.html) is recommended.
- *Everyday Health* (www.everydayhealth.com/): This large, commercial general health Web site gives WebMD (www.webmd.com/) some much needed competition. Everyday Health makes it easy for a person to research any health topic—not just mental health concerns—and learn all there is to know about it. The symptom checker allows a person to enter in one's symptoms and receive a list of possible concerns, while the drug reference is easy to use and understand.
- *Healthfinder* (www.healthfinder.gov/): This excellent site, maintained by the US Department of Health and Human Services, is a health and wellness directory of government health Web sites as well as other, select Internet resources (such as from nonprofits). It is a good, objective source of sometimes-dated information that provides consumers with a way of orienting themselves to a particular health or mental health topic.
- *Helpguide.org* (www.helpguide.org/): This nonprofit resource offers a wealth of reliable information for consumers on mental health issues, typically providing everything a person would want to know about a disorder on a single page. Overseen by psychologist Jeanne Segal, PhD, the site also offers an

"emotional skills toolkit," designed to help improve a person's coping and relationship skills. Other topics covered by the extensive site include family, parenting, relationships, sleep, aging, and healthy living. Topics are often covered in one, easy-to-read page, making it ideal to print out and share with a family member or professional.

- *Mental Health America* (www.mentalhealthamerica.net/): Mental Health America, formerly known as the National Mental Health Association, publishes a consumer-oriented site that provides information on mental health concerns, advocacy and policy-making issues, a calendar of events, and links to supports groups as well as local community affiliates.
- *MeYou Health* (www.meyouhealth.com/): MeYou Health is home to the Daily Challenge, a community where members engage in simple, daily activities that are designed to help people improve their lives. The challenges are things people can do immediately, and they are meant to get people to make small changes in their behavior. Small behavioral changes are often more manageable and attainable than attempting larger goals, which can often disappoint. The site is designed around game theory, making it a fun, positive experience to engage in every day. Of particular interest, the emotional health area offers daily challenges centered on self-esteem, conflict management, improving communication, and self-empowerment. Free registration is required to access the service.
- *Mind* (www.mind.org.uk/): Mind is a registered charity in the United Kingdom that runs a very informative, up-to-date, and helpful Web site about general mental health conditions. While oriented toward a UK audience, the site is a reliable, easy-to-navigate resource that also provides links to dozens of related self-help organizations and resources.
- *MoodGYM* (moodgym.anu.edu.au/): Mood GYM is an online self-paced and self-tailored program designed to help a person with depression using proven cognitive-behavioral therapy and interpersonal therapy techniques and concepts. Offered at no charge, this comprehensive and engaging intervention was developed by Helen Christensen and her colleagues at the Centre for Mental Health Research at the Australian National University and now has over 400,000 registered users. Best of all, it is backed by research demonstrating its effectiveness (for example, Christensen et al., 2004). Free registration is required to use the program.
- *National Institute of Mental Health* (www.nimh.nih.gov/): The National Institute of Mental Health offers information and resources on mental health information to consumers. The site provides access to clinical trial opportunities, statistics on mental disorders, fact sheets, consumer-oriented brochures on common mental disorders and their treatments, research reports, national conference and event information, and behavioral science news.
- *Psych Central* (psychcentral.com/): Focused primarily on consumer mental health, Psych Central is a Web site that I founded and oversee. Its offerings include daily-updated mental health and psychology news; the Internet's most popular psychology blog, *World of Psychology;* and a mental health library with thousands of articles on topics ranging from depression, anxiety, and bipolar disorder, to psychotherapy, relationships, and parenting skills. The site also offers a thriving online self-help support community of over 180 mental health support groups, as well as dozens of consumer and professional bloggers who write about a wide range of mental health topics. Psych Central also provides access to its own psychotherapist directory, as well as a professional section with practice advice and research briefs.
- *Psychological Self-Help* (psychologicalself-help.org): This online self-help book, one of the first to be published on the Internet in 1996, delves into some practical techniques for individuals to use to try and help themselves with many emotional, relationship, and mental health issues. Offering 15 chapters of insight and handy techniques, psychologist Clay Tucker-Ladd, PhD, provides a

well-written but wordy volume that can be searched online.

- *Psychology Information Online* (www.psychologyinfo.com/): Donald J. Franklin, PhD, is a New Jersey psychologist who has put together this resource for consumers looking for more information about psychology. The site has articles that provide symptoms and descriptions for most psychological problems, as well as descriptions of various types of therapies available used to treat them. Articles about selecting a treatment provider and starting therapy are also available, as is a directory of psychologists.
- *Psychology Today* (www.psychologytoday.com/): One of the oldest consumer-oriented psychology magazines has a rich archive of thousands of articles online, dating back to 1992. While most of the material is of the "popular psychology" nature and often does not go into much depth, it does cover a broad range of issues that can act as a starting point for exploring a topic. In addition to one of the largest therapist directories available online, the site features many bloggers who write on a wide variety of mostly pop-psychology topics.
- *Psychotherapy Networker* (www.psychotherapynetworker.org/): While meant for psychotherapists, the Psychotherapy Networker's articles (which are reprints from its bimonthly print magazine) are so interesting, engaging, and well-written that patients enjoy them just as much. Popular topics include not only depression and anxiety but also couples, creativity, positive psychology, and mindfulness.
- *PubMed* (www.ncbi.nlm.nih.gov/pubmed): PubMed is the Internet-based search portal to MEDLINE, the renowned public medical research database. Maintained by the National Library of Medicine under the National Institutes of Health, it covers a vast amount of the social science literature and is a good, free alternative to proprietary research databases. Consumers may also find the National Library of Medicine's MEDLINEPlus (www.nlm.nih.gov/medlineplus/), a great place to start looking for general health and mental health information online. This information resource provides interactive tutorials, a medical encyclopedia and dictionary, updated health news, and a drug database, among other offerings.
- *ReachOut.com* (reachout.com/): ReachOut.com is a Web site focused on teenagers that provides fact sheets and information not only on common mental health concerns such as depression, anxiety, and eating issues but also other common adolescent concerns, such as drugs, alcohol, sexuality, school pressures, becoming independent, self-harm, and suicide. The site is designed to appeal to young adults and teens with the extensive use of videos and story-telling—making it relevant, engaging, and timely.
- *Tiny Buddha* (tinybuddha.com/): Tiny Buddha offers "simple wisdom for complex lives." What that means in practice is offering daily tips and techniques to help people in one of the site's eight focused categories: happiness and fun, meaning and passion, change and challenges, love and relationships, mindfulness and peace, letting go, healthy habits, and work fulfillment. Like some self-help resources, the advice at times may seem to be overly simplistic. But a person can take what he or she needs from the articles, while leaving what does not work or make sense.

References and Readings

Christensen, H., Griffiths, K. M., Korten, A. E., Brittliffe, K., & Groves, C. (2004). A comparison of changes in anxiety and depression symptoms of spontaneous users and trial participants of a cognitive behavior therapy website. *Journal of Medical Internet Research, 6*(4), e46.

Gackenbach, J. (1998). *Psychology and the Internet: Intrapersonal, interpersonal, and transpersonal implications*. New York: Academic Press.

Grohol, J. M. (2002). *The insider's guide to mental health resources online*. New York: Guilford Press.

McGuire, M., Stilborne, L., McAdams, M., & Hyatt, L. (2002). *The Internet handbook for writers, researchers, and journalists*. New York: Guilford Press.

Norcross, J. C., Campbell, L. M., Grohol, J. M., Santrock, J. W., Selagea, F., & Sommer, R.

(2013). *Self-help that works* (4th ed.). New York: Oxford University Press.

Winker, M. A., Flanagin, A., Chi-Lum, B., White, J., Andrews, K., Kennett, R. L.,...Musacchio, R. A. (2000). Guidelines for medical and health information sites on the internet. *Journal of the American Medical Association, 283*(12), 1600–1601.

Wootton, R., Yellowlees, P., & McLaren, P. (Eds.). (2003). *Telepsychiatry and e-mental health*. London: Royal Society of Medicine Press.

Related Topics

Chapter 99, "Recommended Self-Help Books, Autobiographies, and Films"

Chapter 102, "Recommended Online Computer-Assisted Treatments"

Chapter 134, "Optimizing the Use of Technology in Psychology with Best Practice Principles"

102 RECOMMENDED ONLINE COMPUTER-ASSISTED TREATMENTS

Luciano L'Abate

The exponential growth of computer-assisted online treatments means that in the future a great deal of health promotion, illness prevention, psychotherapy, and rehabilitation will be performed at a distance through computers, I-pads, and smart phone derivatives (L'Abate & Sweeney, 2011). *E-therapy* is a generic term referring to the delivery of mental health service to remote patients by using telecommunication technology (e.g., telephone, computer, video). This term has been referenced by many names: telehealth, online counseling, online therapy, telepsychiatry, telepsychology, telepsych, telepractice, behavioral telehealth, telemedicine, online psychoeducation, and mobile therapy (mHealth). Information about these programs increases daily, to the point that what was considered up to date a few years ago is now outdated (Gallego & Emmelkamp, 2011; Marks, Cavanagh, & Gega, 2007; Zwolinski & Zwolinski, 2009).

The pressing questions are how these treatments will be delivered and what kind of ethical and professional criteria will be used to evaluate them. For instance, are these treatments delivered through structured or unstructured programs? Do they possess research support for their safety and efficacy? What criteria, if any, are employed to accept or reject selection of potential patients/participants? How many online programs comply with professional and ethical requirements in the state in which they practice and apply the Health Insurance Portability and Accountability Act (HIPAA) requiring informed consent from participants?

Unstructured programs refer to any online approach that mimics what occurs in traditional psychotherapeutic practice. After a perfunctory interview about the reason for referral, participants talk and a professional responds. Apparently, a great percentage of online therapists do not collect identifying information because "Patients with a strong desire for anonymity might log off." Therefore, performing online psychotherapy without information about participants/patients should be considered a rogue practice that should be banned by most professional mental health associations. Even calling 911 requires giving basic information about the reason for the call and address of the caller.

Despite pressures to turn a profit, some telehealth service companies are poised for success without adhering to legal and ethical mandates. This is why recommending online therapy programs means also not recommending online therapy programs that do not live up to basic professional standards of practice. For instance, programs such as www.anxietyonline.org.au/ and www.onlinetherapyinstitute.com are not recommended because no pre-post-intervention evaluation seems required. Another program, www.therapion.com, is also not recommended, because in addition to no initial evaluation, credentials of faculty members are questionable. Furthermore, these unstructured programs do not have research-based support.

As of this writing, more than 50 online, unstructured psychotherapy programs have been found. However, professionals need to separate hype from reality as virtually all of these programs suffer from serious problems. To my knowledge, none of these programs advised potential participants that they would be evaluated objectively before being qualified and accepted for online treatment. Thus, none of them can be recommended.

In contrast to unstructured programs, structured online interventions for self-diagnosed conditions are recommended if they are supported by evidence to support their application. For example, Proshaska's ProChange (www.prochange.com), a structured and recommended approach, offers evidence-based programs on modifying smoking, alcohol consumption, domestic violence, credit card debt, and it has a new I-phone application for diabetes management. Another example of a disorder-specific program is www.NicotineFreedom.com. However, there is not sufficient research to support its use by other professionals except for its producer. Evidence for online use of workbooks or interactive practice exercises (L'Abate, 2011) produced a medium effect size (d = .44) for mental health and low (d = .25) for physical health (Smyth & L'Abate, 2001).

Several published resources can be accessed for lists of structured online programs. Marks, Cavanagh, and Gega's (2007) compendium probably remains the most authoritative source on online treatments because it includes extensive reviews of research. Their original list has been evaluated and brought up to date for qualified recommendation. Although most are supported by some research evidence, this does not mean that they can be recommended without caveats. Furthermore, recommendation does not imply in any way endorsement. The latter can be bestowed when there is irrefutable evidence to support any online intervention.

This chapter has been made easier by www.bcacon.anu.edu.au. If readers are serious about directing patients to interactive self-help treatments online, then Beacon offers a peer-reviewed ratings directory of health and mental health interactive Web sites. Housed at the Centre for Mental Health Research at the Australian National University, a panel of health experts rate online self-help programs according to the available research evidence. Programs that have multiple research studies demonstrating their effectiveness are rated more highly, while online programs that have little or no evidence are rated more poorly. The directory makes it easy to determine whether consumers should invest their time with an online program. Ratings range from one straight face for no evidence at the moment, a sad face for no evidence to suggest that the site does not work, all the way to five smiling faces that indicate complete approval. Free registration is required to access the directory.

The following list of 27 recommended computer-assisted therapy programs draws heavily from those compilations.

1. Childhood Sexual Abuse and Posttraumatic Stress Disorder: www.research.uky.edu/odyssey/spring03/puttingaway.html

This well-validated program allows participants to address past abuses and to learn to deal with them in more helpful and practical ways.

2. Alcoholism: www.collegedrinkerscheckup.com

The moderatedrinking.com app has been functional since 2009. Over 500 users have registered so far (not including those in the clinical trial). If readers like to take a look at the site, use username reviewer and password 111111. The cost is US $59 per year or $19.95 per month.

3. Balance: www.mhf.org.uk

CD-ROMs for general anxiety and mindfulness training. Available from the Mental Health Foundation at no cost.

4. Beating the Blues: www.ultrasis.com PC CP for depression.

Available commercially but price unavailable. This program is recommended by the UK National Institute of Health and Clinical Excellence (NICE). Other programs are available at this site, but no sufficient information is available to recommend them.

5. The Drinker's Checkup: www.drinkerscheckup.com and www.behaviortherapy.com/software.htm

This is an online, behavioral self-control program for problem drinking. It is included in SAMSHA's National Registry of Evidence-based Programs and Practices. Available for free in English and French.

6. *Mood Calmer*: www.ccbt.co.uk

CCBT joined with the Danish military to deliver online treatments to troops returning from active service. This self-help CCBT program is designed for people experiencing low mood and depression and takes 12 weeks to complete. These sites include other available programs, but their cost could not be evaluated.

7. *Captain's Log Cognitive System:* www.braintrain.com

A commercial computer program for cognitive training. Hands-on training software that may improve cognitive training, attention, self-control, listening skills, reasoning ability, and memory. No information on cost was available.

8. *Cope for Depression:* www.ccbt.co.uk

This commercial online program is part of a larger company that has thus far supported 66 projects for various interactive programs. No information on costs was available.

9. *Emotion Trainer:* www.emotiontrainer.co.uk/intro.htm

Another commercial program for young people with autism or Asperger's; it is designed to help them recognize and predict emotions in others. This is a multimedia program using real photographs and examples relevant to daily life, to gradually teach some of the skills underlying emotional understanding. License starts at $25 for one introductory program.

10. *Empowerment Solution for Permanent Weight Control:* www.empowerplan.com

This CD is available commercially, but it was impossible to log in without a username or password.

11. *FearFighter:* www.fearfighter.com

A computer program for phobias and panic is another CCBT Ltd. product. Research conducted on this method has shown that it may improve phobic participants as much as face-to-face therapy. FearFighter is also more readily available and more cost and time efficient. Like MoodCalmer, the program takes 9 to 12 weeks to complete. Costs are not available.

12. *Good Days Ahead*: www.mindstreet.com.

This multimedia program attempts to reduce depression and anxiety using videos, graphics, and stimulating self-help exercises. Cost is $69.00 Canadian dollars.

13. *Headstrong:* mrapoff@kumc.edu

A CD-ROM pain management program for recurrent headache in children. Not yet available for general use but available to researchers.

14. *Intherapy:* www.interapy.nl

An interesting online program for posttraumatic stress disorder, depression, and burnout. In Dutch language only as of this writing.

15. *MoodGym:* www.moodgym.anu.au

Online training to detect and prevent depression and anxiety. Available free. Sister Web sites at www.bluepages.anu.edu.au and blueboard.anu.edu.au/, which offer multiple online programs covering several clinical conditions, apparently available for free.

16. *OCFighter:* www.ccbt.co.uk

This is another commercial offering by CCBT Ltd. (see #6 and #11), but no information was available regarding cost.

17. *Overcoming Bulimia:* www.calipso.co.uk

This commercial CD-ROM is produced for health care professionals and for use with patients as self-help materials. See #18 for costs and more information.

18. *Overcoming Depression on the Internet:* www.calipso.co.uk

A CD-ROM with a single-user license is UK$100, while a CD-ROM for a multiuser license is UK$250. A set of clinical training CD-ROMs, including all the titles in the series, is available for UK$1,000. This package includes mood disorders, anxiety disorders, dementia, depression (with self-help patient workbook), schizophrenia, and paranoia disorders.

19. *Overcoming Depression 2:* www.calypso.co.uk

This CD-ROM extends the previous entry.

20. *Panic Program:* www.paniccenter.net

The broader site at www.evolutionhs.com/About.aspx provides online programs for alcohol, depression, smoking, and weight control under the direction of Peter Farvolden, PhD. Impossible to log in without user ID and password. No information about costs could be found.

21. *PositScience.com*

Although this is not an online treatment program in the traditional sense of dealing with disorders through words, programs sold by this company deal with memory, language, cognition, and brain functioning, visually and auditorily. It is recommended on the basis of its solid research. Drivesharp costs $89; BrainFitness (auditory) $395; Insight (Visual) $395; and the Total Training Package (Auditory and Visual) $690.

22. *QuitNet (QN):* www.quitnet.com

A free Internet stop-smoking program in both English and Spanish languages.

23. *Stop Smoking:* www.stopsmokingcenter.net

This program is free and competes well in presentation with the QuitNet in the previous item.

24. *Social phobia*: www.ecentreclinic.net

This online program is supported by eight studies on Internet based-self help under the direction of Nickolai Titov. This source has also conducted multiple trials on depression and generalized anxiety disorder. More information is available online.

25. *Stop Tabac:* www.stop-tabac.ch/en/welcome.html

In 1995 this program received the European Health Club Prize. Available for free.

26. *Teen Online Problem Solving (TOPS)*: research.cchmc.org/tops/Cincinnati

This program is structured into 16 sessions, with 10 "core" sessions providing problem solving, executive functioning, communication, and social skills training and 6 sessions addressing content related to the stressors experienced by individual participants. The intervention relies on the adolescent to change and monitor his or her own behavior with support from parents. Each online session includes audio clips of adolescents talking about their experience, video clips of adolescents and families modeling skills, and skills practice exercises. Each session also involves an online appointment with a therapist via video conference, to provide an opportunity to review exercises and address problems.

27. *Y-Can-Poop-Too:* ycanpooptoo.com

This online program addresses pediatric encopresis. A current national trial evaluating Internet Intervention contains three arms: Patient Education Website, U-Can-Poop-Too, and U-Can-Poop-Too plus support from staff members. However, previous trials support this approach.

In addition to these 27 online treatments recommended here, there are free, recommended paratherapeutic, preventive approaches. Five of these sites are: www.self-compassion.org, www.self-improvement.com, www.compassionatemind.co.uk, www.mindandlife.org, and www.maplink.com.au

References and Readings

Anthony, K., & Merz-Nagel, D-A. (2010). *Therapy online: A practical guide*. Thousand Oaks, CA: Sage.

Anthony, K., Merz-Nagel, D-A., & Goss, S. (2010). *The use of technology in mental health: Applications, ethics, and practice*. Springfield, IL: Thomas.

Barak, A., Hen, L., Boniel-Nissim, M., & Shapira, N. (2008). A comprehensive review and meta-analysis of the effectiveness of Internet-based psychotherapeutic interventions. *Journal of Technology in Human Services, 26*, 109–160.

Gallego, J. M., & Emmelkamp, P. M. G. (2011). Effectiveness of internet psychological treatments for mental health disorders. In L. L'Abate & D. A. Kaiser (Eds.), *Handbook of technology in psychology, psychiatry, and neurology*. New York: Nova.

L'Abate, L. (2011). *Sourcebook of interactive practice exercises in mental health*. New York: Springer-Science.

L'Abate, L., & Sweeney, L. G. (Eds.).(2011). *Research on writing approaches in mental health*. Bingley, England: Emerald.

Maheu, M. M., Pulier, M. L., Wilheim, F. H., McMenamin, J., & Brown-Connolly, N. (2005). *The mental health professional and the new technologies: A handbook for practice today*. Mahwah, NJ: Erlbaum.

Marks, I. M., Cavanagh, K., & Gega, L. (2007). *Hands-on help: Computer-aided psychotherapy*. New York: Psychology Press.

Richardsohn, K., Frueh, B. C., Grubaugh, A. L., Egede, L., & Elhal, J. D. (2009). Current directions in videoconferencing tele-mental health research. *Clinical Psychology: Science and Practice, 16*, 323–338.

Smyth, J. M., & L'Abate, L. (2001). A meta-analytic evaluation of workbook effectiveness in physical and mental health. In L. L'Abate (Ed.), *Distance writing and computer-assisted interventions in psychiatry and mental health* (pp. 77–90). Newport, CT: Ablex.

Zwolinski, R. M., & Zwolinski, C. R. (2009). *Therapy revolution: Find help, get better, and move on without wasting time money*. New York: Health Communications.

Related Topics

Chapter 99, "Recommended Self-Help Books, Autobiographies, and Films"

Chapter 100, "Recommended Homework during Psychotherapy with Couples and Individuals"

Chapter 101, "Recommended Self-Help Internet Resources for Patients"

Chapter 134, "Optimizing the Use of Technology in Psychology with Best Practice Principles"

PART VIII
Ethical and Legal Issues

103 ETHICAL PRINCIPLES OF PSYCHOLOGISTS AND CODE OF CONDUCT

American Psychological Association

CONTENTS

4. Privacy and Confidentiality

4.01 Maintaining Confidentiality
4.02 Discussing the Limits of Confidentiality
4.03 Recording
4.04 Minimizing Intrusions on Privacy
4.05 Disclosures
4.06 Consultations
4.07 Use of Confidential Information for Didactic or Other Purposes

5. Advertising and Other Public Statements

5.01 Avoidance of False or Deceptive Statements
5.02 Statements by Others
5.03 Descriptions of Workshops and Non-Degree-Granting Educational Programs
5.04 Media Presentations
5.05 Testimonials
5.06 In-Person Solicitation

6. Record Keeping and Fees

6.01 Documentation of Professional and Scientific Work and Maintenance of Records
6.02 Maintenance, Dissemination, and Disposal of Confidential Records of Professional and Scientific Work
6.03 Withholding Records for Nonpayment
6.04 Fees and Financial Arrangements
6.05 Barter with Clients/Patients
6.06 Accuracy in Reports to Payors and Funding Sources
6.07 Referrals and Fees

7. Education and Training

7.01 Design of Education and Training Programs
7.02 Descriptions of Education and Training Programs
7.03 Accuracy in Teaching
7.04 Student Disclosure of Personal Information
7.05 Mandatory Individual or Group Therapy
7.06 Assessing Student and Supervisee Performance
7.07 Sexual Relationships with Students and Supervisees

8. Research and Publication

8.01 Institutional Approval
8.02 Informed Consent to Research
8.03 Informed Consent for Recording Voices and Images in Research
8.04 Client/Patient, Student, and Subordinate Research Participants
8.05 Dispensing with Informed Consent for Research
8.06 Offering Inducements for Research Participation
8.07 Deception in Research
8.08 Debriefing
8.09 Humane Care and Use of Animals in Research
8.10 Reporting Research Results
8.11 Plagiarism
8.12 Publication Credit
8.13 Duplicate Publication of Data
8.14 Sharing Research Data for Verification
8.15 Reviewers

9. Assessment

9.01 Bases for Assessments
9.02 Use of Assessments
9.03 Informed Consent in Assessments
9.04 Release of Test Data
9.05 Test Construction
9.06 Interpreting Assessment Results
9.07 Assessment by Unqualified Persons
9.08 Obsolete Tests and Outdated Test Results
9.09 Test Scoring and Interpretation Services
9.10 Explaining Assessment Results
9.11 Maintaining Test Security

10. Therapy

10.01 Informed Consent to Therapy
10.02 Therapy Involving Couples or Families
10.03 Group Therapy
10.04 Providing Therapy to Those Served by Others
10.05 Sexual Intimacies with Current Therapy Clients/Patients
10.06 Sexual Intimacies with Relatives or Significant Others of Current Therapy Clients/Patients
10.07 Therapy with Former Sexual Partners
10.08 Sexual Intimacies with Former Therapy Clients/Patients
10.09 Interruption of Therapy
10.10 Terminating Therapy

2010 AMENDMENTS TO THE 2002 "ETHICAL PRINCIPLES OF PSYCHOLOGISTS AND CODE OF CONDUCT"

INTRODUCTION AND APPLICABILITY

The American Psychological Association's (APA's) Ethical Principles of Psychologists and Code of Conduct (hereinafter referred to as the Ethics Code) consists of an Introduction, a Preamble, five General Principles (A–E), and specific Ethical Standards. The Introduction discusses the intent, organization, procedural considerations, and scope of application of the Ethics Code. The Preamble and General Principles are aspirational goals to guide psychologists toward the highest ideals of psychology. Although the Preamble and General Principles are not themselves enforceable rules, they should be considered by psychologists in arriving at an ethical course of action. The Ethical Standards set forth enforceable rules for conduct as psychologists. Most of the Ethical Standards are written broadly, in order to apply to psychologists in varied roles, although the application of an Ethical Standard may vary depending on the context. The Ethical Standards are not exhaustive. The fact that a given conduct is not specifically addressed by an Ethical Standard does not mean that it is necessarily either ethical or unethical.

This Ethics Code applies only to psychologists' activities that are part of their scientific, educational, or professional roles as psychologists. Areas covered include but are not limited to the clinical, counseling, and school practice of psychology; research; teaching; supervision of trainees; public service; policy development; social intervention; development of assessment instruments; conducting assessments; educational counseling; organizational consulting; forensic activities; program design and evaluation; and administration. This Ethics Code applies to these activities across a variety of contexts, such as in person, postal, telephone, Internet, and other electronic transmissions. These activities shall be distinguished from the purely private conduct of psychologists, which is not within the purview of the Ethics Code.

Membership in the APA commits members and student affiliates to comply with the standards of the APA Ethics Code and to the rules and procedures used to enforce them. Lack of awareness or misunderstanding of an Ethical Standard is not itself a defense to a charge of unethical conduct.

The procedures for filing, investigating, and resolving complaints of unethical conduct are described in the current Rules and Procedures of the APA Ethics Committee. APA may impose sanctions on its members for violations of the standards of the Ethics Code, including termination of APA membership, and may notify other bodies and individuals of its actions. Actions that violate the standards of the Ethics Code may also lead to the imposition of sanctions on psychologists or students whether or not they are APA members by bodies other than APA, including state psychological associations, other professional groups, psychology boards, other state or federal agencies, and payors for health services. In addition, APA may take action against a member after his or her conviction of a felony, expulsion or suspension from an affiliated state psychological association, or suspension or loss of licensure. When the sanction to be imposed by APA is less than expulsion, the 2001 Rules and Procedures do not guarantee an opportunity for an in-person hearing, but generally provide that complaints will be resolved only on the basis of a submitted record.

The Ethics Code is intended to provide guidance for psychologists and standards of professional conduct that can be applied by the APA and by other bodies that choose to adopt them. The Ethics Code is not intended to be a basis of civil liability. Whether a psychologist has violated the Ethics Code standards does not by itself determine whether the psychologist is legally liable in a court action, whether a contract is enforceable, or whether other legal consequences occur.

The modifiers used in some of the standards of this Ethics Code (e.g., *reasonably, appropriate, potentially*) are included in the standards when they would (1) allow professional judgment on the part of psychologists, (2) eliminate injustice or inequality that would occur without the modifier, (3) ensure applicability across the broad range of activities conducted by psychologists, or (4) guard against a set of rigid rules that might be quickly outdated. As used in this Ethics Code, the term *reasonable* means the prevailing professional judgment of psychologists engaged in similar activities in similar circumstances, given the knowledge the psychologist had or should have had at the time.

In the process of making decisions regarding their professional behavior, psychologists must consider this Ethics Code in addition to applicable laws and psychology board regulations. In applying the Ethics Code to their professional work, psychologists may consider other materials and guidelines that have been adopted or endorsed by scientific and professional psychological organizations and the dictates of their own conscience, as well as consult with others within the field. If this Ethics Code establishes a higher standard of conduct than is required by law, psychologists must meet the higher ethical standard. If psychologists' ethical responsibilities conflict with law, regulations, or other governing legal authority, psychologists make known their commitment to this Ethics Code and take steps to resolve the conflict in a responsible manner in keeping with basic principles of human rights.

PREAMBLE

Psychologists are committed to increasing scientific and professional knowledge of behavior and people's understanding of themselves and others and to the use of such knowledge to improve the condition of individuals, organizations, and society. Psychologists respect and protect civil and human rights and the central importance of freedom of inquiry and expression in research, teaching, and publication. They strive to help the public in developing informed judgments and choices concerning human behavior. In doing so, they perform many roles, such as researcher, educator, diagnostician, therapist, supervisor, consultant, administrator, social interventionist, and expert witness. This Ethics Code provides a common set of principles and standards upon which psychologists build their professional and scientific work.

This Ethics Code is intended to provide specific standards to cover most situations encountered by psychologists. It has as its goals the welfare and protection of the individuals and groups with whom psychologists work and the education of members, students, and the public regarding ethical standards of the discipline.

The development of a dynamic set of ethical standards for psychologists' work-related conduct requires a personal commitment and lifelong effort to act ethically; to encourage ethical behavior by students, supervisees, employees, and colleagues; and to consult with others concerning ethical problems.

GENERAL PRINCIPLES

This section consists of General Principles. General Principles, as opposed to Ethical Standards, are aspirational in nature. Their intent is to guide and inspire psychologists toward the very highest ethical ideals of the profession. General Principles, in contrast to Ethical Standards, do not represent obligations and should not form the basis for imposing sanctions. Relying upon General Principles for either of these reasons distorts both their meaning and purpose.

Principle A: Beneficence and Nonmaleficence

Psychologists strive to benefit those with whom they work and take care to do no harm. In their professional actions, psychologists seek to safeguard the welfare and rights of those with whom they interact professionally and other affected persons, and the welfare of animal subjects of research. When conflicts occur among psychologists' obligations or concerns, they attempt to resolve these conflicts in a responsible fashion that avoids or minimizes harm. Because psychologists' scientific and professional judgments and actions may affect the lives of others, they are alert to and guard against personal, financial, social, organizational, or political factors that might lead to misuse of their influence. Psychologists strive to be aware of the possible effect of their own physical and mental health on their ability to help those with whom they work.

Principle B: Fidelity and Responsibility

Psychologists establish relationships of trust with those with whom they work. They are aware of their professional and scientific responsibilities to society and to the specific communities in which they work. Psychologists uphold professional standards of conduct, clarify their professional roles and obligations, accept appropriate responsibility for their behavior, and seek to manage conflicts of interest that could lead to exploitation or harm. Psychologists consult with, refer to, or cooperate with other professionals and institutions to the extent needed to serve the best interests of those with whom they work. They are concerned about the ethical compliance of their colleagues' scientific and professional conduct. Psychologists strive to contribute a portion of their professional time for little or no compensation or personal advantage.

Principle C: Integrity

Psychologists seek to promote accuracy, honesty, and truthfulness in the science, teaching, and practice of psychology. In these activities psychologists do not steal, cheat, or engage in fraud, subterfuge, or intentional misrepresentation of fact. Psychologists strive to keep their promises and to avoid unwise or unclear commitments. In situations in which deception may be ethically justifiable to maximize benefits and minimize harm, psychologists have a serious obligation to consider the need for, the possible consequences of, and their responsibility to correct any resulting mistrust or other harmful effects that arise from the use of such techniques.

Principle D: Justice

Psychologists recognize that fairness and justice entitle all persons to access to and benefit from the contributions of psychology and to equal quality in the processes, procedures, and services being conducted by psychologists. Psychologists exercise reasonable judgment and take precautions to ensure that their potential biases, the boundaries of their competence, and the limitations of their expertise do not lead to or condone unjust practices.

Principle E: Respect for People's Rights and Dignity

Psychologists respect the dignity and worth of all people, and the rights of individuals to privacy, confidentiality, and self-determination. Psychologists are aware that special safeguards may be necessary to protect the rights and welfare of persons or communities whose vulnerabilities impair autonomous decision making. Psychologists are aware of and respect cultural, individual, and role differences, including those based on age, gender, gender identity, race, ethnicity, culture, national origin, religion, sexual orientation, disability, language, and socioeconomic status, and consider these factors when working with members of such groups. Psychologists try to eliminate the effect on their work of biases based on those factors, and they do not knowingly participate in or condone activities of others based upon such prejudices.

ETHICAL STANDARDS

1. Resolving Ethical Issues

1.01 Misuse of Psychologists' Work

If psychologists learn of misuse or misrepresentation of their work, they take reasonable steps to correct or minimize the misuse or misrepresentation.

1.02 Conflicts Between Ethics and Law, Regulations, or Other Governing Legal Authority

If psychologists' ethical responsibilities conflict with law, regulations, or other governing legal authority, psychologists clarify the nature of the conflict, make known their commitment to the Ethics Code, and take reasonable steps to resolve the conflict consistent with the General Principles and Ethical Standards of the Ethics Code. Under no circumstances may this standard be used to justify or defend violating human rights.

1.03 Conflicts Between Ethics and Organizational Demands

If the demands of an organization with which psychologists are affiliated or for whom they are working are in conflict with this Ethics Code, psychologists clarify the nature of the conflict, make known their commitment to the Ethics Code, and take reasonable steps to resolve the conflict consistent with the General Principles and Ethical Standards of the Ethics Code. Under no circumstances may this standard be used to justify or defend violating human rights.

1.04 Informal Resolution of Ethical Violations

When psychologists believe that there may have been an ethical violation by another psychologist, they attempt to resolve the issue by bringing it to the attention of that individual, if an informal resolution appears appropriate and the intervention does not violate any confidentiality rights that may be involved. (See also Standards 1.02, Conflicts Between Ethics and Law, Regulations, or Other Governing Legal Authority, and 1.03, Conflicts Between Ethics and Organizational Demands.)

1.05 Reporting Ethical Violations

If an apparent ethical violation has substantially harmed or is likely to substantially harm a person or organization and is not appropriate for informal resolution under Standard 1.04, Informal Resolution of Ethical Violations, or is not resolved properly in that fashion, psychologists take further action appropriate to the situation. Such action might include referral to state or national committees on professional ethics, to state licensing boards, or to the appropriate institutional authorities. This standard does not apply when an intervention would violate confidentiality rights or when psychologists have been retained to review the work of another psychologist whose professional conduct is in question. (See also Standard 1.02, Conflicts Between Ethics and Law, Regulations, or Other Governing Legal Authority.)

1.06 Cooperating With Ethics committees

Psychologists cooperate in ethics investigations, proceedings, and resulting requirements of the APA or any affiliated state psychological association to which they belong. In doing so, they address any confidentiality issues. Failure to cooperate is itself an ethics violation. However, making a request for deferment of adjudication of an ethics complaint pending the outcome of litigation does not alone constitute noncooperation.

1.07 Improper Complaints

Psychologists do not file or encourage the filing of ethics complaints that are made with reckless disregard for or willful ignorance of facts that would disprove the allegation.

1.08 Unfair Discrimination Against Complainants and Respondents

Psychologists do not deny persons employment, advancement, admissions to academic or other programs, tenure, or promotion, based solely upon their having made or their being the subject of an ethics complaint. This does not preclude taking action based upon the outcome of such proceedings or considering other appropriate information.

2. Competence

2.01 Boundaries of Competence

(a) Psychologists provide services, teach, and conduct research with populations and in areas only within the boundaries of their competence, based on their education, training, supervised experience, consultation, study, or professional experience.

(b) Where scientific or professional knowledge in the discipline of psychology establishes that an understanding of factors associated with age, gender, gender identity, race, ethnicity, culture, national origin, religion, sexual orientation, disability, language, or socioeconomic status is essential for effective implementation of their services or research, psychologists have or obtain the training, experience, consultation, or supervision necessary to ensure the competence of their services, or they make appropriate referrals, except as provided in Standard 2.02, Providing Services in Emergencies.

(c) Psychologists planning to provide services, teach, or conduct research involving populations, areas, techniques, or technologies new to them undertake relevant education, training, supervised experience, consultation, or study.

(d) When psychologists are asked to provide services to individuals for whom appropriate mental health services are not available and for which psychologists have not obtained the competence necessary, psychologists with closely related prior training or experience may provide such services in order to ensure that services are not denied if they make a reasonable effort to obtain the competence required by using relevant research, training, consultation, or study.

(e) In those emerging areas in which generally recognized standards for preparatory training do not yet exist, psychologists nevertheless take reasonable steps to ensure the competence of their work and to protect clients/patients, students, supervisees, research participants, organizational clients, and others from harm.

(f) When assuming forensic roles, psychologists are or become reasonably familiar with the judicial or administrative rules governing their roles.

2.02 *Providing services in Emergencies*

In emergencies, when psychologists provide services to individuals for whom other mental health services are not available and for which psychologists have not obtained the necessary training, psychologists may provide such services in order to ensure that services are not denied. The services are discontinued as soon as the emergency has ended or appropriate services are available.

2.03 *Maintaining Competence*

Psychologists undertake ongoing efforts to develop and maintain their competence.

2.04 *Bases for scientific and Professional Judgments*

Psychologists' work is based upon established scientific and professional knowledge of the discipline. (See also Standards 2.01e, Boundaries of Competence, and 10.01b, Informed Consent to Therapy.)

2.05 *Delegation of Work to Others*

Psychologists who delegate work to employees, supervisees, or research or teaching assistants or who use the services of others, such as interpreters, take reasonable steps to (1) avoid delegating such work to persons who have a multiple relationship with those being served that would likely lead to exploitation or loss of objectivity; (2) authorize only those responsibilities that such persons can be expected to perform competently on the basis of their education, training, or experience, either independently or with the level of supervision being provided; and (3) see that such persons perform these services competently. (See also Standards 2.02, Providing Services in Emergencies; 3.05, Multiple Relationships; 4.01, Maintaining Confidentiality; 9.01, Bases for Assessments; 9.02, Use of Assessments; 9.03, Informed Consent in Assessments; and 9.07, Assessment by Unqualified Persons.)

2.06 *Personal Problems and Conflicts*

(a) Psychologists refrain from initiating an activity when they know or should know that there is a substantial likelihood that their personal problems will prevent them from performing their work-related activities in a competent manner.

(b) When psychologists become aware of personal problems that may interfere with their performing work-related duties adequately, they take appropriate measures, such as obtaining professional consultation or assistance, and determine whether they should limit, suspend, or terminate their work-related duties. (See also Standard 10.10, Terminating Therapy.)

3. Human Relations

3.01 Unfair Discrimination

In their work-related activities, psychologists do not engage in unfair discrimination based on age, gender, gender identity, race, ethnicity, culture, national origin, religion, sexual orientation, disability, socioeconomic status, or any basis proscribed by law.

3.02 Sexual Harassment

Psychologists do not engage in sexual harassment. Sexual harassment is sexual solicitation, physical advances, or verbal or nonverbal conduct that is sexual in nature, that occurs in connection with the psychologist's activities or roles as a psychologist, and that either (1) is unwelcome, is offensive, or creates a hostile workplace or educational environment, and the psychologist knows or is told this or (2) is sufficiently severe or intense to be abusive to a reasonable person in the context. Sexual harassment can consist of a single intense or severe act or of multiple persistent or pervasive acts. (See also Standard 1.08, Unfair Discrimination Against Complainants and Respondents.)

3.03 Other Harassment

Psychologists do not knowingly engage in behavior that is harassing or demeaning to persons with whom they interact in their work based on factors such as those persons' age, gender, gender identity, race, ethnicity, culture, national origin, religion, sexual orientation, disability, language, or socioeconomic status.

3.04 Avoiding Harm

Psychologists take reasonable steps to avoid harming their clients/patients, students, supervisees, research participants, organizational clients, and others with whom they work, and to minimize harm where it is foreseeable and unavoidable.

3.05 Multiple Relationships

(a) A multiple relationship occurs when a psychologist is in a professional role with a person and (1) at the same time is in another role with the same person, (2) at the same time is in a relationship with a person closely associated with or related to the person with whom the psychologist has the professional relationship, or (3) promises to enter into another relationship in the future with the person or a person closely associated with or related to the person.

A psychologist refrains from entering into a multiple relationship if the multiple relationship could reasonably be expected to impair the psychologist's objectivity, competence, or effectiveness in performing his or her functions as a psychologist, or otherwise risks exploitation or harm to the person with whom the professional relationship exists.

Multiple relationships that would not reasonably be expected to cause impairment or risk exploitation or harm are not unethical.

(b) If a psychologist finds that, due to unforeseen factors, a potentially harmful multiple relationship has arisen, the psychologist takes reasonable steps to resolve it with due regard for the best interests of the affected person and maximal compliance with the Ethics Code.

(c) When psychologists are required by law, institutional policy, or extraordinary circumstances to serve in more than one role in judicial or administrative proceedings, at the outset they clarify role expectations and the extent of confidentiality and thereafter as changes occur. (See also Standards 3.04, Avoiding Harm, and 3.07, Third-Party Requests for Services.)

3.06 Conflict of Interest

Psychologists refrain from taking on a professional role when personal, scientific, professional, legal, financial, or other interests or relationships could reasonably be expected to (1) impair their objectivity, competence, or effectiveness in performing their functions as psychologists or (2) expose the person or organization with whom the professional relationship exists to harm or exploitation.

3.07 *Third-Party Requests for Services*

When psychologists agree to provide services to a person or entity at the request of a third party, psychologists attempt to clarify at the outset of the service the nature of the relationship with all individuals or organizations involved. This clarification includes the role of the psychologist (e.g., therapist, consultant, diagnostician, or expert witness), an identification of who is the client, the probable uses of the services provided or the information obtained, and the fact that there may be limits to confidentiality. (See also Standards 3.05, Multiple Relationships, and 4.02, Discussing the Limits of Confidentiality.)

3.08 *Exploitative Relationships*

Psychologists do not exploit persons over whom they have supervisory, evaluative, or other authority such as clients/patients, students, supervisees, research participants, and employees. (See also Standards 3.05, Multiple Relationships; 6.04, Fees and Financial Arrangements; 6.05, Barter With Clients/ Patients; 7.07, Sexual Relationships With Students and Supervisees; 10.05, Sexual Intimacies With Current Therapy Clients/ Patients; 10.06, Sexual Intimacies With Relatives or Significant Others of Current Therapy Clients/ Patients; 10.07, Therapy With Former Sexual Partners; and 10.08, Sexual Intimacies With Former Therapy Clients/Patients.)

3.09 *Cooperation With Other Professionals*

When indicated and professionally appropriate, psychologists cooperate with other professionals in order to serve their clients/ patients effectively and appropriately. (See also Standard 4.05, Disclosures.)

3.10 *Informed Consent*

(a) When psychologists conduct research or provide assessment, therapy, counseling, or consulting services in person or via electronic transmission or other forms of communication, they obtain the informed consent of the individual or individuals using language that is reasonably understandable to that person or persons except when conducting such activities without consent is mandated by law or governmental regulation or as otherwise provided in this Ethics Code. (See also Standards 8.02, Informed Consent to Research; 9.03, Informed Consent in Assessments; and 10.01, Informed Consent to Therapy.)

(b) For persons who are legally incapable of giving informed consent, psychologists nevertheless (1) provide an appropriate explanation, (2) seek the individual's assent, (3) consider such persons' preferences and best interests, and (4) obtain appropriate permission from a legally authorized person, if such substitute consent is permitted or required by law. When consent by a legally authorized person is not permitted or required by law, psychologists take reasonable steps to protect the individual's rights and welfare.

(c) When psychological services are court ordered or otherwise mandated, psychologists inform the individual of the nature of the anticipated services, including whether the services are court ordered or mandated and any limits of confidentiality, before proceeding.

(d) Psychologists appropriately document written or oral consent, permission, and assent. (See also Standards 8.02, Informed Consent to Research; 9.03, Informed Consent in Assessments; and 10.01, Informed Consent to Therapy.)

3.11 *Psychological Services Delivered To or Through Organizations*

(a) Psychologists delivering services to or through organizations provide information beforehand to clients and when appropriate those directly affected by the services about (1) the nature and objectives of the services, (2) the intended recipients, (3) which of the individuals are clients, (4) the relationship the psychologist will have with each person and the organization, (5) the probable uses of services provided and information obtained, (6) who will have access to the information, and (7) limits of confidentiality. As soon as feasible, they provide information about the results and conclusions of such services to appropriate persons.

(b) If psychologists will be precluded by law or by organizational roles from providing such information to particular individuals or groups, they so inform those individuals or groups at the outset of the service.

3.12 Interruption of Psychological Services

Unless otherwise covered by contract, psychologists make reasonable efforts to plan for facilitating services in the event that psychological services are interrupted by factors such as the psychologist's illness, death, unavailability, relocation, or retirement or by the client's/patient's relocation or financial limitations. (See also Standard 6.02c, Maintenance, Dissemination, and Disposal of Confidential Records of Professional and Scientific Work.)

4. Privacy and Confidentiality

4.01 Maintaining Confidentiality

Psychologists have a primary obligation and take reasonable precautions to protect confidential information obtained through or stored in any medium, recognizing that the extent and limits of confidentiality may be regulated by law or established by institutional rules or professional or scientific relationship. (See also Standard 2.05, Delegation of Work to Others.)

4.02 Discussing the Limits of Confidentiality

(a) Psychologists discuss with persons (including, to the extent feasible, persons who are legally incapable of giving informed consent and their legal representatives) and organizations with whom they establish a scientific or professional relationship (1) the relevant limits of confidentiality and (2) the foreseeable uses of the information generated through their psychological activities. (See also Standard 3.10, Informed Consent.)

(b) Unless it is not feasible or is contraindicated, the discussion of confidentiality occurs at the outset of the relationship and thereafter as new circumstances may warrant.

(c) Psychologists who offer services, products, or information via electronic transmission inform clients/patients of the risks to privacy and limits of confidentiality.

4.03 Recording

Before recording the voices or images of individuals to whom they provide services, psychologists obtain permission from all such persons or their legal representatives. (See also Standards 8.03, Informed Consent for Recording Voices and Images in Research; 8.05, Dispensing With Informed Consent for Research; and 8.07, Deception in Research.)

4.04 Minimizing Intrusions on Privacy

(a) Psychologists include in written and oral reports and consultations, only information germane to the purpose for which the communication is made.

(b) Psychologists discuss confidential information obtained in their work only for appropriate scientific or professional purposes and only with persons clearly concerned with such matters.

4.05 Disclosures

(a) Psychologists may disclose confidential information with the appropriate consent of the organizational client, the individual client/patient, or another legally authorized person on behalf of the client/patient unless prohibited by law.

(b) Psychologists disclose confidential information without the consent of the individual only as mandated by law, or where permitted by law for a valid purpose such as to (1) provide needed professional services; (2) obtain appropriate professional consultations; (3) protect the client/patient, psychologist, or others from harm; or (4) obtain payment for services from a client/patient, in which instance disclosure is limited to the minimum that is necessary to achieve the purpose. (See also Standard 6.04e, Fees and Financial Arrangements.)

4.06 *Consultations*

When consulting with colleagues, (1) psychologists do not disclose confidential information that reasonably could lead to the identification of a client/patient, research participant, or other person or organization with whom they have a confidential relationship unless they have obtained the prior consent of the person or organization or the disclosure cannot be avoided, and (2) they disclose information only to the extent necessary to achieve the purposes of the consultation. (See also Standard 4.01, Maintaining Confidentiality.)

4.07 *Use of Confidential Information for Didactic or Other Purposes*

Psychologists do not disclose in their writings, lectures, or other public media, confidential, personally identifiable information concerning their clients/patients, students, research participants, organizational clients, or other recipients of their services that they obtained during the course of their work, unless (1) they take reasonable steps to disguise the person or organization, (2) the person or organization has consented in writing, or (3) there is legal authorization for doing so.

5. Advertising and Other Public Statements

5.01 *Avoidance of False or Deceptive Statements*

(a) Public statements include but are not limited to paid or unpaid advertising, product endorsements, grant applications, licensing applications, other credentialing applications, brochures, printed matter, directory listings, personal resumes or curricula vitae, or comments for use in media such as print or electronic transmission, statements in legal proceedings, lectures and public oral presentations, and published materials. Psychologists do not knowingly make public statements that are false, deceptive, or fraudulent concerning their research, practice, or other work activities or those of persons or organizations with which they are affiliated.

(b) Psychologists do not make false, deceptive, or fraudulent statements concerning (1) their training, experience, or competence; (2) their academic degrees; (3) their credentials; (4) their institutional or association affiliations; (5) their services; (6) the scientific or clinical basis for, or results or degree of success of, their services; (7) their fees; or (8) their publications or research findings.

(c) Psychologists claim degrees as credentials for their health services only if those degrees (1) were earned from a regionally accredited educational institution or (2) were the basis for psychology licensure by the state in which they practice.

5.02 *Statements by Others*

(a) Psychologists who engage others to create or place public statements that promote their professional practice, products, or activities retain professional responsibility for such statements.

(b) Psychologists do not compensate employees of press, radio, television, or other communication media in return for publicity in a news item. (See also Standard 1.01, Misuse of Psychologists' Work.)

(c) A paid advertisement relating to psychologists' activities must be identified or clearly recognizable as such.

5.03 *Descriptions of Workshops and Non-Degree-Granting Educational Programs*

To the degree to which they exercise control, psychologists responsible for announcements, catalogs, brochures, or advertisements describing workshops, seminars, or other non-degree-granting educational programs ensure that they accurately describe the audience for which the program is intended, the educational objectives, the presenters, and the fees involved.

5.04 Media Presentations

When psychologists provide public advice or comment via print, Internet, or other electronic transmission, they take precautions to ensure that statements (1) are based on their professional knowledge, training, or experience in accord with appropriate psychological literature and practice; (2) are otherwise consistent with this Ethics Code; and (3) do not indicate that a professional relationship has been established with the recipient. (See also Standard 2.04, Bases for Scientific and Professional Judgments.)

5.05 Testimonials

Psychologists do not solicit testimonials from current therapy clients/patients or other persons who because of their particular circumstances are vulnerable to undue influence.

5.06 In-Person Solicitation

Psychologists do not engage, directly or through agents, in uninvited in-person solicitation of business from actual or potential therapy clients/patients or other persons who because of their particular circumstances are vulnerable to undue influence. However, this prohibition does not preclude (1) attempting to implement appropriate collateral contacts for the purpose of benefiting an already engaged therapy client/patient or (2) providing disaster or community outreach services.

6. Record Keeping and Fees

6.01 Documentation of Professional and Scientific Work and Maintenance of Records

Psychologists create, and to the extent the records are under their control, maintain, disseminate, store, retain, and dispose of records and data relating to their professional and scientific work in order to (1) facilitate provision of services later by them or by other professionals, (2) allow for replication of research design and analyses, (3) meet institutional requirements, (4) ensure accuracy of billing and payments, and (5) ensure compliance with law. (See also Standard 4.01, Maintaining Confidentiality.)

6.02 Maintenance, Dissemination, and Disposal of Confidential Records of Professional and Scientific Work

(a) Psychologists maintain confidentiality in creating, storing, accessing, transferring, and disposing of records under their control, whether these are written, automated, or in any other medium. (See also Standards 4.01, Maintaining Confidentiality, and 6.01, Documentation of Professional and Scientific Work and Maintenance of Records.)

(b) If confidential information concerning recipients of psychological services is entered into databases or systems of records available to persons whose access has not been consented to by the recipient, psychologists use coding or other techniques to avoid the inclusion of personal identifiers.

(c) Psychologists make plans in advance to facilitate the appropriate transfer and to protect the confidentiality of records and data in the event of psychologists' withdrawal from positions or practice. (See also Standards 3.12, Interruption of Psychological Services, and 10.09, Interruption of Therapy.)

6.03 Withholding Records for Nonpayment

Psychologists may not withhold records under their control that are requested and needed for a client's/patient's emergency treatment solely because payment has not been received.

6.04 Fees and Financial Arrangements

(a) As early as is feasible in a professional or scientific relationship, psychologists and recipients of psychological services reach an agreement specifying compensation and billing arrangements.

(b) Psychologists' fee practices are consistent with law.

(c) Psychologists do not misrepresent their fees.

(d) If limitations to services can be anticipated because of limitations in financing, this is discussed with the recipient of services as early as is feasible. (See also Standards 10.09, Interruption of Therapy, and 10.10, Terminating Therapy.)

(e) If the recipient of services does not pay for services as agreed, and if psychologists intend to use collection agencies or legal measures to collect the fees, psychologists first inform the person that such measures will be taken and provide that person an opportunity to make prompt payment. (See also Standards 4.05, Disclosures; 6.03, Withholding Records for Nonpayment; and 10.01, Informed Consent to Therapy.)

6.05 *Barter with Clients/Patients*

Barter is the acceptance of goods, services, or other nonmonetary remuneration from clients/patients in return for psychological services. Psychologists may barter only if (1) it is not clinically contraindicated, and (2) the resulting arrangement is not exploitative. (See also Standards 3.05, Multiple Relationships, and 6.04, Fees and Financial Arrangements.)

6.06 *Accuracy in Reports to Payors and Funding Sources*

In their reports to payors for services or sources of research funding, psychologists take reasonable steps to ensure the accurate reporting of the nature of the service provided or research conducted, the fees, charges, or payments, and where applicable, the identity of the provider, the findings, and the diagnosis. (See also Standards 4.01, Maintaining Confidentiality; 4.04, Minimizing Intrusions on Privacy; and 4.05, Disclosures.)

6.07 *Referrals and Fees*

When psychologists pay, receive payment from, or divide fees with another professional, other than in an employer–employee relationship, the payment to each is based on the services provided (clinical, consultative, administrative, or other) and is not based on the referral itself. (See also Standard 3.09, Cooperation With Other Professionals.)

7. Education and Training

7.01 *Design of Education and Training Programs*

Psychologists responsible for education and training programs take reasonable steps to ensure that the programs are designed to provide the appropriate knowledge and proper experiences, and to meet the requirements for licensure, certification, or other goals for which claims are made by the program. (See also Standard 5.03, Descriptions of Workshops and Non-Degree-Granting Educational Programs.)

7.02 *Descriptions of Education and Training Programs*

Psychologists responsible for education and training programs take reasonable steps to ensure that there is a current and accurate description of the program content (including participation in required course- or program-related counseling, psychotherapy, experiential groups, consulting projects, or community service), training goals and objectives, stipends and benefits, and requirements that must be met for satisfactory completion of the program. This information must be made readily available to all interested parties.

7.03 *Accuracy in Teaching*

(a) Psychologists take reasonable steps to ensure that course syllabi are accurate regarding the subject matter to be covered, bases for evaluating progress, and the nature of course experiences. This standard does not preclude an instructor from modifying course content or requirements when the instructor considers it pedagogically necessary or desirable, so long as students are made aware of these modifications in a manner that enables them to fulfill course requirements. (See also Standard 5.01, Avoidance of False or Deceptive Statements.)

(b) When engaged in teaching or training, psychologists present psychological information accurately. (See also Standard 2.03, Maintaining Competence.)

7.04 *Student Disclosure of Personal Information*

Psychologists do not require students or supervisees to disclose personal information in course- or program-related activities, either orally or in writing, regarding sexual history, history of abuse and neglect, psychological treatment, and relationships with parents, peers, and spouses or significant others except if (1) the program or training facility has clearly identified this requirement in its admissions and program materials or (2) the information is necessary to evaluate or obtain assistance for students whose personal problems could reasonably be judged to be preventing them from performing their training- or professionally related activities in a competent manner or posing a threat to the students or others.

7.05 *Mandatory Individual or Group Therapy*

(a) When individual or group therapy is a program or course requirement, psychologists responsible for that program allow students in undergraduate and graduate programs the option of selecting such therapy from practitioners unaffiliated with the program. (See also Standard 7.02, Descriptions of Education and Training Programs.)

(b) Faculty who are or are likely to be responsible for evaluating students' academic performance do not themselves provide that therapy. (See also Standard 3.05, Multiple Relationships.)

7.06 *Assessing Student and Supervisee Performance*

(a) In academic and supervisory relationships, psychologists establish a timely and specific process for providing feedback to students and supervisees. Information regarding the process is provided to the student at the beginning of supervision.

(b) Psychologists evaluate students and supervisees on the basis of their actual performance on relevant and established program requirements.

7.07 *Sexual Relationships with Students and Supervisees*

Psychologists do not engage in sexual relationships with students or supervisees who are in their department, agency, or training center or over whom psychologists have or are likely to have evaluative authority. (See also Standard 3.05, Multiple Relationships.)

8. Research and Publication

8.01 *Institutional Approval*

When institutional approval is required, psychologists provide accurate information about their research proposals and obtain approval prior to conducting the research. They conduct the research in accordance with the approved research protocol.

8.02 *Informed Consent to Research*

(a) When obtaining informed consent as required in Standard 3.10, Informed Consent, psychologists inform participants about (1) the purpose of the research, expected duration, and procedures; (2) their right to decline to participate and to withdraw from the research once participation has begun; (3) the foreseeable consequences of declining or withdrawing; (4) reasonably foreseeable factors that may be expected to influence their willingness to participate such as potential risks, discomfort, or adverse effects; (5) any prospective research benefits; (6) limits of confidentiality; (7) incentives for participation; and (8) whom to contact for questions about the research and research participants' rights. They provide opportunity for the prospective participants to ask questions and receive answers. (See also Standards 8.03, Informed Consent for Recording Voices and Images in Research; 8.05, Dispensing With Informed Consent for Research; and 8.07, Deception in Research.)

(b) Psychologists conducting intervention research involving the use of experimental treatments clarify to participants at the outset of the research (1) the experimental nature of the treatment; (2) the services that will or will not be available to the control group(s) if appropriate; (3) the means by which assignment to treatment and control groups will be made; (4) available treatment alternatives if an individual does not wish to participate in the research or wishes to withdraw once a study has begun; and (5) compensation for or monetary costs of participating including, if appropriate, whether reimbursement from the participant or a third-party payor will be sought. (See also Standard 8.02a, Informed Consent to Research.)

8.03 *Informed Consent for Recording Voices and Images in Research*

Psychologists obtain informed consent from research participants prior to recording their voices or images for data collection unless (1) the research consists solely of naturalistic observations in public places, and it is not anticipated that the recording will be used in a manner that could cause personal identification or harm, or (2) the research design includes deception, and consent for the use of the recording is obtained during debriefing. (See also Standard 8.07, Deception in Research.)

8.04 *Client/Patient, Student, and Subordinate Research Participants*

(a) When psychologists conduct research with clients/patients, students, or subordinates as participants, psychologists take steps to protect the prospective participants from adverse consequences of declining or withdrawing from participation.

(b) When research participation is a course requirement or an opportunity for extra credit, the prospective participant is given the choice of equitable alternative activities.

8.05 *Dispensing with Informed Consent for Research*

Psychologists may dispense with informed consent only (1) where research would not reasonably be assumed to create distress or harm and involves (a) the study of normal educational practices, curricula, or classroom management methods conducted in educational settings; (b) only anonymous questionnaires, naturalistic observations, or archival research for which disclosure of responses would not place participants at risk of criminal or civil liability or damage their financial standing, employability, or reputation, and confidentiality is protected; or (c) the study of factors related to job or organization effectiveness conducted in organizational settings for which there is no risk to participants' employability, and confidentiality is protected or (2) where otherwise permitted by law or federal or institutional regulations.

8.06 *Offering Inducements for Research Participation*

(a) Psychologists make reasonable efforts to avoid offering excessive or inappropriate financial or other inducements for research participation when such inducements are likely to coerce participation.

(b) When offering professional services as an inducement for research participation, psychologists clarify the nature of the services, as well as the risks, obligations, and limitations. (See also Standard 6.05, Barter With Clients/Patients.)

8.07 *Deception in Research*

(a) Psychologists do not conduct a study involving deception unless they have determined that the use of deceptive techniques is justified by the study's significant prospective scientific, educational, or applied value and that effective nondeceptive alternative procedures are not feasible.

(b) Psychologists do not deceive prospective participants about research that is reasonably expected to cause physical pain or severe emotional distress.

(c) Psychologists explain any deception that is an integral feature of the design and conduct of an experiment to participants as early as is feasible, preferably at the conclusion of their participation, but no later than at the conclusion of the data collection, and permit participants to withdraw their data. (See also Standard 8.08, Debriefing.)

8.08 *Debriefing*

(a) Psychologists provide a prompt opportunity for participants to obtain appropriate information about the nature, results, and conclusions of the research, and they take reasonable steps to correct any misconceptions that participants may have of which the psychologists are aware.

(b) If scientific or humane values justify delaying or withholding this information, psychologists take reasonable measures to reduce the risk of harm.

(c) When psychologists become aware that research procedures have harmed a participant, they take reasonable steps to minimize the harm.

8.09 *Humane Care and Use of Animals in Research*

(a) Psychologists acquire, care for, use, and dispose of animals in compliance with current federal, state, and local laws and regulations, and with professional standards.

(b) Psychologists trained in research methods and experienced in the care of laboratory animals supervise all procedures involving animals and are responsible for ensuring appropriate consideration of their comfort, health, and humane treatment.

(c) Psychologists ensure that all individuals under their supervision who are using animals have received instruction in research methods and in the care, maintenance, and handling of the species being used, to the extent appropriate to their role. (See also Standard 2.05, Delegation of Work to Others.)

(d) Psychologists make reasonable efforts to minimize the discomfort, infection, illness, and pain of animal subjects. (e) Psychologists use a procedure subjecting animals

to pain, stress, or privation only when an alternative procedure is unavailable and the goal is justified by its prospective scientific, educational, or applied value.

(f) Psychologists perform surgical procedures under appropriate anesthesia and follow techniques to avoid infection and minimize pain during and after surgery.

(g) When it is appropriate that an animal's life be terminated, psychologists proceed rapidly, with an effort to minimize pain and in accordance with accepted procedures.

8.10 *Reporting Research Results*

(a) Psychologists do not fabricate data. (See also Standard 5.01a, Avoidance of False or Deceptive Statements.)

(b) If psychologists discover significant errors in their published data, they take reasonable steps to correct such errors in a correction, retraction, erratum, or other appropriate publication means.

8.11 *Plagiarism*

Psychologists do not present portions of another's work or data as their own, even if the other work or data source is cited occasionally.

8.12 *Publication Credit*

(a) Psychologists take responsibility and credit, including authorship credit, only for work they have actually performed or to which they have substantially contributed. (See also Standard 8.12b, Publication Credit.)

(b) Principal authorship and other publication credits accurately reflect the relative scientific or professional contributions of the individuals involved, regardless of their relative status. Mere possession of an institutional position, such as department chair, does not justify authorship credit. Minor contributions to the research or to the writing for publications are acknowledged appropriately, such as in footnotes or in an introductory statement.

(c) Except under exceptional circumstances, a student is listed as principal author on any multiple-authored article that is substantially based on the student's doctoral dissertation. Faculty advisors discuss publication credit with students as early as feasible and throughout the research and publication process as appropriate. (See also Standard 8.12b, Publication Credit.)

8.13 Duplicate Publication of Data

Psychologists do not publish, as original data, data that have been previously published. This does not preclude republishing data when they are accompanied by proper acknowledgment.

8.14 Sharing Research Data for Verification

(a) After research results are published, psychologists do not withhold the data on which their conclusions are based from other competent professionals who seek to verify the substantive claims through reanalysis and who intend to use such data only for that purpose, provided that the confidentiality of the participants can be protected and unless legal rights concerning proprietary data preclude their release. This does not preclude psychologists from requiring that such individuals or groups be responsible for costs associated with the provision of such information.

(b) Psychologists who request data from other psychologists to verify the substantive claims through reanalysis may use shared data only for the declared purpose. Requesting psychologists obtain prior written agreement for all other uses of the data.

8.15 Reviewers

Psychologists who review material submitted for presentation, publication, grant, or research proposal review respect the confidentiality of and the proprietary rights in such information of those who submitted it.

9. Assessment

9.01 Bases for Assessments

(a) Psychologists base the opinions contained in their recommendations, reports, and diagnostic or evaluative statements, including forensic testimony, on information and techniques sufficient to substantiate their findings. (See also Standard 2.04, Bases for Scientific and Professional Judgments.)

(b) Except as noted in 9.01c, psychologists provide opinions of the psychological characteristics of individuals only after they have conducted an examination of the individuals adequate to support their statements or conclusions. When, despite reasonable efforts, such an examination is not practical, psychologists document the efforts they made and the result of those efforts, clarify the probable impact of their limited information on the reliability and validity of their opinions, and appropriately limit the nature and extent of their conclusions or recommendations. (See also Standards 2.01, Boundaries of Competence, and 9.06, Interpreting Assessment Results.)

(c) When psychologists conduct a record review or provide consultation or supervision and an individual examination is not warranted or necessary for the opinion, psychologists explain this and the sources of information on which they based their conclusions and recommendations.

9.02 Use of Assessments

(a) Psychologists administer, adapt, score, interpret, or use assessment techniques, interviews, tests, or instruments in a manner and for purposes that are appropriate in light of the research on or evidence of the usefulness and proper application of the techniques.

(b) Psychologists use assessment instruments whose validity and reliability have been established for use with members of the population tested. When such validity or reliability has not been established, psychologists describe the strengths and limitations of test results and interpretation.

(c) Psychologists use assessment methods that are appropriate to an individual's language preference and competence, unless the use of an alternative language is relevant to the assessment issues.

9.03 *Informed Consent in Assessments*

(a) Psychologists obtain informed consent for assessments, evaluations, or diagnostic services, as described in Standard 3.10, Informed Consent, except when (1) testing is mandated by law or governmental regulations; (2) informed consent is implied because testing is conducted as a routine educational, institutional, or organizational activity (e.g., when participants voluntarily agree to assessment when applying for a job); or (3) one purpose of the testing is to evaluate decisional capacity. Informed consent includes an explanation of the nature and purpose of the assessment, fees, involvement of third parties, and limits of confidentiality and sufficient opportunity for the client/patient to ask questions and receive answers.

(b) Psychologists inform persons with questionable capacity to consent or for whom testing is mandated by law or governmental regulations about the nature and purpose of the proposed assessment services, using language that is reasonably understandable to the person being assessed.

(c) Psychologists using the services of an interpreter obtain informed consent from the client/patient to use that interpreter, ensure that confidentiality of test results and test security are maintained, and include in their recommendations, reports, and diagnostic or evaluative statements, including forensic testimony, discussion of any limitations on the data obtained. (See also Standards 2.05, Delegation of Work to Others; 4.01, Maintaining Confidentiality; 9.01, Bases for Assessments; 9.06, Interpreting Assessment Results; and 9.07, Assessment by Unqualified Persons.)

9.04 *Release of Test Data*

(a) The term *test data* refers to raw and scaled scores, client/patient responses to test questions or stimuli, and psychologists' notes and recordings concerning client/patient statements and behavior during an examination. Those portions of test materials that include client/patient responses are included in the definition of *test data*. Pursuant to a client/patient release, psychologists provide test data to the client/ patient or other persons identified in the release. Psychologists may refrain from releasing test data to protect a client/ patient or others from substantial harm or misuse or misrepresentation of the data or the test, recognizing that in many instances release of confidential information under these circumstances is regulated by law. (See also Standard 9.11, Maintaining Test Security.)

(b) In the absence of a client/patient release, psychologists provide test data only as required by law or court order.

9.05 *Test Construction*

Psychologists who develop tests and other assessment techniques use appropriate psychometric procedures and current scientific or professional knowledge for test design, standardization, validation, reduction or elimination of bias, and recommendations for use.

9.06 *Interpreting Assessment Results*

When interpreting assessment results, including automated interpretations, psychologists take into account the purpose of the assessment as well as the various test factors, test-taking abilities, and other characteristics of the person being assessed, such as situational, personal, linguistic, and cultural differences, that might affect psychologists' judgments or reduce the accuracy of their interpretations. They indicate any significant limitations of their interpretations. (See also Standards 2.01b and c, Boundaries of Competence, and 3.01, Unfair Discrimination.)

9.07 *Assessment by Unqualified Persons*

Psychologists do not promote the use of psychological assessment techniques by unqualified persons, except when such use is conducted for training purposes with appropriate supervision.

(See also Standard 2.05, Delegation of Work to Others.)

9.08 *Obsolete Tests and Outdated Test Results*

(a) Psychologists do not base their assessment or intervention decisions or recommendations on data or test results that are outdated for the current purpose.

(b) Psychologists do not base such decisions or recommendations on tests and measures that are obsolete and not useful for the current purpose.

9.09 *Test Scoring and Interpretation Services*

(a) Psychologists who offer assessment or scoring services to other professionals accurately describe the purpose, norms, validity, reliability, and applications of the procedures and any special qualifications applicable to their use.

(b) Psychologists select scoring and interpretation services (including automated services) on the basis of evidence of the validity of the program and procedures as well as on other appropriate considerations. (See also Standard 2.01b and c, Boundaries of Competence.)

(c) Psychologists retain responsibility for the appropriate application, interpretation, and use of assessment instruments, whether they score and interpret such tests themselves or use automated or other services.

9.10 *Explaining Assessment Results*

Regardless of whether the scoring and interpretation are done by psychologists, by employees or assistants, or by automated or other outside services, psychologists take reasonable steps to ensure that explanations of results are given to the individual or designated representative unless the nature of the relationship precludes provision of an explanation of results (such as in some organizational consulting, pre-employment or security screenings, and forensic evaluations), and this fact has been clearly explained to the person being assessed in advance.

9.11 *Maintaining Test Security*

The term *test materials* refers to manuals, instruments, protocols, and test questions or stimuli and does not include *test data* as defined in Standard 9.04, Release of Test Data. Psychologists make reasonable efforts to maintain the integrity and security of test materials and other assessment techniques consistent with law and contractual obligations, and in a manner that permits adherence to this Ethics Code.

10. Therapy

10.01 *Informed Consent to Therapy*

(a) When obtaining informed consent to therapy as required in Standard 3.10, Informed Consent, psychologists inform clients/patients as early as is feasible in the therapeutic relationship about the nature and anticipated course of therapy, fees, involvement of third parties, and limits of confidentiality and provide sufficient opportunity for the client/ patient to ask questions and receive answers. (See also Standards 4.02, Discussing the Limits of Confidentiality, and 6.04, Fees and Financial Arrangements.)

(b) When obtaining informed consent for treatment for which generally recognized techniques and procedures have not been established, psychologists inform their clients/ patients of the developing nature of the treatment, the potential risks involved, alternative treatments that may be available, and the voluntary nature of their participation. (See also Standards 2.01e, Boundaries of Competence, and 3.10, Informed Consent.)

(c) When the therapist is a trainee and the legal responsibility for the treatment provided resides with the supervisor, the client/patient, as part of the informed consent procedure, is informed that the therapist is in training and is being supervised and is given the name of the supervisor.

10.02 *Therapy Involving Couples or Families*

(a) When psychologists agree to provide services to several persons who have a relationship (such as spouses, significant others, or parents and children), they take reasonable steps to clarify at the outset (1) which of the individuals are clients/patients and (2) the relationship the psychologist will have with each person. This clarification includes the psychologist's role and the probable uses of the services provided or the information obtained. (See also Standard 4.02, Discussing the Limits of Confidentiality.)

(b) If it becomes apparent that psychologists may be called on to perform potentially conflicting roles (such as family therapist and then witness for one party in divorce proceedings), psychologists take reasonable steps to clarify and modify, or withdraw from, roles appropriately. (See also Standard 3.05c, Multiple Relationships.)

10.03 Group Therapy

When psychologists provide services to several persons in a group setting, they describe at the outset the roles and responsibilities of all parties and the limits of confidentiality.

10.04 Providing Therapy to Those Served by Others

In deciding whether to offer or provide services to those already receiving mental health services elsewhere, psychologists carefully consider the treatment issues and the potential client's/patient's welfare. Psychologists discuss these issues with the client/patient or another legally authorized person on behalf of the client/patient in order to minimize the risk of confusion and conflict, consult with the other service providers when appropriate, and proceed with caution and sensitivity to the therapeutic issues.

10.05 Sexual Intimacies with Current Therapy Clients/Patients

Psychologists do not engage in sexual intimacies with current therapy clients/patients.

10.06 Sexual Intimacies with Relatives or Significant Others of Current Therapy Clients/Patients

Psychologists do not engage in sexual intimacies with individuals they know to be close relatives, guardians, or significant others of current clients/patients. Psychologists do not terminate therapy to circumvent this standard.

10.07 Therapy with Former Sexual Partners

Psychologists do not accept as therapy clients/patients persons with whom they have engaged in sexual intimacies.

10.08 Sexual Intimacies with Former Therapy Clients/Patients

(a) Psychologists do not engage in sexual intimacies with former clients/patients for at least two years after cessation or termination of therapy.

(b) Psychologists do not engage in sexual intimacies with former clients/patients even after a two-year interval except in the most unusual circumstances. Psychologists who engage in such activity after the two years following cessation or termination of therapy and of having no sexual contact with the former client/patient bear the burden of demonstrating that there has been no exploitation, in light of all relevant factors, including (1) the amount of time that has passed since therapy terminated; (2) the nature, duration, and intensity of the therapy; (3) the circumstances of termination; (4) the client's/patient's personal history; (5) the client's/patient's current mental status; (6) the likelihood of adverse impact on the client/patient; and (7) any statements or actions made by the therapist during the course of therapy suggesting or inviting the possibility of a posttermination sexual or romantic relationship with the client/patient. (See also Standard 3.05, Multiple Relationships.)

10.09 Interruption of Therapy

When entering into employment or contractual relationships, psychologists make reasonable efforts to provide for orderly and appropriate resolution of responsibility for client/patient care in the event that the employment or contractual relationship ends, with paramount consideration given to the welfare of the client/patient. (See also Standard 3.12, Interruption of Psychological Services.)

10.10 Terminating Therapy

(a) Psychologists terminate therapy when it becomes reasonably clear that the client/patient no longer needs the service, is not likely to benefit, or is being harmed by continued service.

(b) Psychologists may terminate therapy when threatened or otherwise endangered by the client/patient or another person with whom the client/patient has a relationship.

(c) Except where precluded by the actions of clients/ patients or third-party payors, prior to termination psychologists provide pretermination counseling and suggest alternative service providers as appropriate.

The American Psychological Association's Council of Representatives adopted this version of the APA Ethics Code during its meeting on August 21, 2002. The Code became effective on June 1, 2003. The Council of Representatives amended this version of the Ethics Code on February 20, 2010. The amendments became effective on June 1, 2010 (see p. 15 of this pamphlet). Inquiries concerning the substance or interpretation of the APA Ethics Code should be addressed to the Director, Office of Ethics, American Psychological Association, 750 First Street, NE, Washington, DC 20002-4242. The Ethics Code and information regarding the Code can be found on the APA website, http://www.apa.org/ethics. The standards in this Ethics Code will be used to adjudicate complaints brought concerning alleged conduct occurring on or after the effective date. Complaints will be adjudicated on the basis of the version of the Ethics Code that was in effect at the time the conduct occurred.

The APA has previously published its Ethics Code as follows:

American Psychological Association. (1953). *Ethical standards of psychologists*. Washington, DC: Author.

American Psychological Association. (1959). Ethical standards of psychologists. *American Psychologist, 14*, 279–282.

American Psychological Association. (1963). Ethical standards of psychologists. *American Psychologist, 18*, 56–60.

American Psychological Association. (1968). Ethical standards of psychologists. *American Psychologist, 23*, 357–361.

American Psychological Association. (1977, March). Ethical standards of psychologists. *APA Monitor*, 22–23.

American Psychological Association. (1979). *Ethical standards of psychologists*. Washington, DC: Author.

American Psychological Association. (1981). Ethical principles of psychologists. *American Psychologist, 36*, 633–638.

American Psychological Association. (1990). Ethical principles of psychologists (Amended June 2, 1989). *American Psychologist, 45*, 390–395.

American Psychological Association. (1992). Ethical principles of psychologists and code of conduct. *American Psychologist, 47*, 1597–1611.

American Psychological Association. (2002). Ethical principles of psychologists and code of conduct. *American Psychologist, 57*, 1060–1073.

Request copies of the APA's Ethical Principles of Psychologists and Code of Conduct from the APA Order Department, 750 First Street, NE, Washington, DC 20002-4242, or phone (202) 336-5510.

RELATED TOPICS

Chapter 113, "Understanding Legal Terms of Special Interest in Mental Health Practice"

Chapter 125, "Prototype Mental Health Records"

Chapter 126, "Fulfilling Informed Consent Responsibilities"

Chapter 127, "Elements of Authorization Forms to Release or Request Client's Records"

2010 AMENDMENTS TO THE 2002 "ETHICAL PRINCIPLES OF PSYCHOLOGISTS AND CODE OF CONDUCT"

The American Psychological Association's Council of Representatives adopted the following amendments to the 2002 "Ethical Principles of Psychologists and Code of Conduct" at its February 2010 meeting. Changes are indicated by underlining for additions and striking through for deletions. A history of amending the Ethics Code is provided in the "Report of the Ethics Committee, 2009" in the July-August 2010 issue of the *American Psychologist* (Vol. 65, No. 5).

Original Language With Changes Marked

Introduction and Applicability

If psychologists' ethical responsibilities conflict with law, regulations, or other governing legal authority, psychologists make known their commitment to this Ethics Code and take steps to resolve the conflict in a responsible manner~~. If the conflict is unresolvable via such means, psychologists may adhere to the requirements of the law, regulations, or other governing authority~~ in keeping with basic principles of human rights.

1.02 Conflicts Between Ethics and Law, Regulations, or Other Governing Legal Authority

If psychologists' ethical responsibilities conflict with law, regulations, or other governing legal authority, psychologists clarify the nature of the conflict, make known their commitment to the Ethics Code, and take reasonable steps to resolve the conflict consistent with the General Principles and Ethical Standards of the Ethics Code. ~~If the conflict is unresolvable via such means, psychologists may adhere to the requirements of the law, regulations, or other governing legal authority.~~ Under no circumstances may this standard be used to justify or defend violating human rights.

1.03 Conflicts Between Ethics and Organizational Demands

If the demands of an organization with which psychologists are affiliated or for whom they are working are in conflict with this Ethics Code, psychologists clarify the nature of the conflict, make known their commitment to the Ethics Code, and ~~to the extent feasible, resolve the conflict in a way that permits adherence to the Ethics Code.~~ take reasonable steps to resolve the conflict consistent with the General Principles and Ethical Standards of the Ethics Code. Under no circumstances may this standard be used to justify or defend violating human rights.

104 DEALING WITH LICENSING BOARD AND ETHICS COMPLAINTS

Gerald P. Koocher and Patricia Keith-Spiegel

Receiving a formal inquiry or complaint letter from a licensing board or professional association's ethics committee invariably becomes one of the most stressful events in a psychologist's career. The actual incidence of actionable complaints against psychologists is relatively low. In 2010, for example, the American Psychological Association (APA) Ethics Committee received 176 inquiries, but it received only 64 actual complaint forms cases, amounting to less than 1 member per 1,000. During the same year a total of 18 members left APA by resignation or expulsion via some ethics enforcement action (APA, 2011). The number of psychologists disciplined by licensing boards is higher, in part because there are many more licensed psychologists nationally than APA members. The percentage disciplined by licensing boards is also low, but not readily known because some licensing board disciplinary actions are treated as confidential and not centrally reported.

Nonetheless, receiving a notification letter often feels like an attack or a personal affront from one's colleagues and does constitute a threat to one's professional practice. In such situations it is important to understand the system, know one's rights, and assure oneself of fair treatment. Keep in mind that "beating the system" is not the appropriate goal. Psychologists have previously agreed—voluntarily and with full informed consent—to enter a profession that has obligated itself to formal peer monitoring. All of us, as well as the public, gain advantage from this system. Psychologists initiated the legislation that created our licensing boards and professional association ethics committees. If the profession abandoned an active role in self-regulation, it would ultimately fall under regulation by outsiders with inadequate understanding of the history, practices, and scientific foundations of the profession.

We have seen a wide range of reactions from respondents to official inquiries and complaints. Some psychologists become so stressed that they appear to jeopardize their own health. Others become hostile or avoidant in ways that only serve to antagonize those charged with evaluating the complaint. Many seem able to retain a dignified approach to the charge, but all become anxious to get to the matter as soon as possible and gain a favorable resolution. Receiving an inquiry or formal notice of charges from any professional monitoring agent will not, of course, improve anyone's day. However, we offer some advice to consider in the event you ever find yourself in such a situation.

KNOW WHO YOU ARE DEALING WITH AND UNDERSTAND THE NATURE OF THE COMPLAINT AND THE POTENTIAL CONSEQUENCES BEFORE RESPONDING

- Are you dealing with a statutory licensing authority or a voluntary professional association? A professional association's most severe sanction is likely to be expulsion, but a licensing board has the authority to suspend or revoke a professional license. Action by either group may trigger action by the other because of mutual notification policies.
- Are you dealing with nonclinician investigators or professional colleagues? In some smaller states or provinces, the staff of the licensing board may consist of a nonpsychologist who lacks a fully professional understanding of the applicable ethics codes and regulations. Even when the investigator for a licensing board or ethics committee has training as a psychologist, the degree of experience and expertise can vary widely. In many cases additional clarification from others in authority may be warranted.
- Is the contact you received an informal inquiry or a formal charge? Sometimes licensing boards and ethics committees approach less serious allegations by asking the psychologist to respond before they decide whether to open a formal complaint. In such instances, however, "informal" does not mean "casual." Rather, such inquiries may be a sign that the panel has not yet concluded that the alleged conduct was serious enough to warrant drastic action or meets their definition of issuing a formal charge. Do not respond impulsively. Knee-jerk actions will more likely than not be counterproductive and complicate the process unnecessarily. The correct response should always be thoughtful and cautious.

UNDERSTAND THE PRECISE NATURE OF THE COMPLAINT AND RULES THAT APPLY TO RESPONSES AND ANY PROPOSED ACTIONS

- Have you been given a detailed and comprehensible rendition of the complaint made against you? You should not respond substantively to any complaint without a clear written explanation of the allegations. In many jurisdictions you may also be entitled to a written copy of the actual complaint made against you.
- Have you been provided with copies of the rules, procedures, or policies under which the panel operates? If you do not have this information, request it and review it carefully to determine where you fall in the time line of the investigatory process and what rights, options, and inquiries you have available before responding.
- Do not contact the complainant directly or indirectly. The matter is no longer subject to informal resolution. Any contact initiated by you may be viewed as an attempt at coercion or harassment.
- If the complaint involves a current or former client, make certain that the authorities have obtained and provided you with a waiver signed by the client authorizing you to disclose confidential information before responding to the charges. We know of instances where licensing boards initiated complaints based on third-party inquiries without such waivers and then asked the psychologists complained about to obtain release of information consent from their own clients. Such requests are inappropriate, because they put the psychologist in the uncomfortable and awkward position of asking someone to surrender confidentiality to serve the needs of another. The Federal HIPAA (Health Insurance Portability and Accountability Act) regulations prohibit the release of protected health information without such a signed release.
- Obtain consultation before responding. A colleague with prior experience serving on ethics panels or licensing boards is an ideal choice. Pay for an hour or two of professional time. Doing so establishes a confidential and possibly privileged relationship (depending on state law) with the consultant. Consultation with an attorney is also advised, especially if the matter involves an alleged legal offense, if the ethics committee does not appear to be following the rules and

procedures, or if the case might result in any public disciplinary action. Some professional liability insurance policies provide coverage for legal consultation in the event of a licensing board complaint. This insurance does not generally apply to professional association ethics complaints and may not be allowed in some jurisdictions. We recommend that you check your liability policy and secure such coverage if you do not already have it.

- If asked to provide unusual materials during the investigatory process, do not comply without first seeking legal consultation. We know of one state licensing authority that claimed the right to examine "samples of reports" from a psychologist's work with clients other than the ones involved in the complaint—a clear violation of the privacy rights of the affected clients. In another case, a licensing board insisted that a psychologist provide typed transcripts of substantial files of handwritten notes at his own expense.
- If offered a settlement, "consent decree," or any resolution short of full dismissal of the case against you, obtain additional professional and legal consultation. Even an apparently mild "reprimand" may result in difficulty in renewing liability insurance policies, gaining access to insurance provider panels, qualifying for hospital staff privileges, or being hired for some jobs. Any formal disciplinary action, even as mild as a reprimand, may result in reports to interstate monitoring agencies or professional associations. Agreeing to accept an ethics or licensing sanction may also compromise your legal defense, should the client file suit. If you have done something wrong, a penalty may be appropriate. However, you should be fully aware of the potential consequences before simply agreeing to the sanction.

ORGANIZE YOUR DEFENSE AND RESPONSE TO THE CHARGES CAREFULLY AND THOUGHTFULLY

- Assess the credibility of the charge. Compile and organize your records and the relevant chronology of events. Respond respectfully and fully to the questions or charges within the allotted time frame. Failure to cooperate with a duly constituted inquiry is in itself an ethical violation.
- Psychologists are expected to respond personally to the inquiry. It is appropriate to consult with colleagues or an attorney before responding, but a letter from your attorney alone (i.e., without a response over your signature) is often not sufficient and may also be regarded as inappropriate or evasive.
- Limit the scope of your response to focus on the content areas and issues that directly relate to the content of the official complaint letter. Do not ramble or introduce tangential issues.
- If you need more time to gather materials and respond, ask for it. Be sure to retain copies of everything you send in response to the inquiry.
- Do not take the position that the best defense is a thundering offense. This will polarize the proceedings and reduce the chances for a collegial solution.
- If you believe that you have been wrongly or erroneously charged, state your case clearly and provide any appropriate documentation.
- If the complaint accurately represents the events, but does not accurately interpret them, provide your own account and interpretation with as much documentation as you can.
- If you have committed the offense charged, document the events and start appropriate remediation actions immediately (e.g., seek professional supervision to deal with any areas of professional weakness, enter psychotherapy for any personal problems, or take other steps to demonstrate that you do not intend to allow the error to recur). Present information regarding any mitigating circumstances. It would probably also be wise to seek legal counsel at this point, if you have not already done so.
- If a charge or complaint is sustained and you are asked to accept disciplinary measures without a formal hearing, you may want to consider reviewing the potential

consequences of the measures with an attorney before making a decision.
- Know your rights of appeal.

TAKE STEPS TO SUPPORT YOURSELF EMOTIONALLY OVER WHAT IS LIKELY TO BE A STRESSFUL PROCESS EXTENDING OVER SEVERAL MONTHS

- Be patient. It is likely that you will have to wait for what will seem like a long while before the matter is resolved. It is perfectly acceptable to respectfully inquire regarding the status of the matter from time to time.
- If appropriate, confide in a colleague or therapist who will be emotionally supportive through the process. Your relationship with your therapist may be protected by privilege. We strongly suggest, however, that you refrain from discussing the charges against you with many others. Doing so may increase your own tension and likely produce an adverse impact as more and more individuals become aware of your situation and may possibly raise additional problems regarding confidentiality issues. In no instance should you identify the complainant to others, aside from the board or committee making the inquiry (after they produce a signed release) and your attorney.
- Take active, constructive steps to minimize your own anxiety and stress levels. If this matter is interfering with your ability to function, you might benefit from a professional counseling relationship in a privileged context.

References and Readings

American Psychological Association. (2011). Report of the Ethics Committee, 2010. *American Psychologist, 66*, 393–403.

Association of State and Provincial Psychology Boards. (n.d.). *Home page*. Retrieved December 2012, from www.asppb.org

Pope, K. S. (n.d.). *Psychology laws and licensing boards in Canada and the United States*. Retrieved December 2012, from www.kspope.com/licensing/index.php

Shapiro, D., Walker, L., Manosevitz, M., Peterson, M., & Williams, M. (2008). *Surviving a licensing board complaint: What to do, what not to do: Practical tips from the experts*. Phonex, AZ: Zeig, Tucker, & Theisen.

Woody, R. H. (2008). Obtaining legal counsel for child and family mental health practice. *American Journal of Family Therapy, 36*, 323–331.

Related Topics

Chapter 105, "Defending Against Legal (Malpractice and Licensing) Complaints"

Chapter 107, "Dealing with Subpoenas"

Chapter 120, "Essential Features of Professional Liability Insurance"

105 DEFENDING AGAINST LEGAL (MALPRACTICE AND LICENSING) COMPLAINTS

Robert Henley Woody

Modern mental health practices occur in a legal framework. Whether in an agency or independent practice, safeguards against threats of legal (malpractice or licensing) complaints are essential for quality care and risk management.

For malpractice cases, professional negligence theory holds that a legal cause of action (the basis for a complaint) requires that the plaintiff (complainant) prove that the defendant or respondent (practitioner) was the source of damage (i.e., the alleged injury was due to a preexisting condition) (Shapiro & Smith, 2011). However, investigations of licensing complaints often bypass the legal tenets of negligence, searching for any sort of possible wrongdoing, with or without injury, by the practitioner. Suffice it to say, legal complaints inflict substantial professional and personal damage to the psychologist (Woody, 2009).

By professional standards and ethics, the psychologist should maintain a reasonable treatment or service plan focused on benefits for the clients. Psychologists are not expected to kowtow to abusive or threatening clients, nor does the therapeutic relationship require that the psychologists allow inappropriate preferences from patients' service users to usurp their practitioner's legal rights. Being defensive is a positive, not a negative, condition, and this prepared stance benefits the client, the psychologist, and our society via strengthening professionalism for quality care. Consequently, every practitioner must acquire adequate knowledge and skills pertaining to the law through self-study, continuing professional education, and other authoritative means.

Just as services of an accountant may be necessary for bookkeeping and tax matters, reliance on an attorney is essential to mental health practitioners in this day and age. Since the law is unique to the particular jurisdiction(s) in which the psychological services are conducted, the attorney should be selected accordingly (see Chapter 132 in this volume). Investing in an attorney admitted to the state bar for the jurisdiction(s) in which the psychologist practices is a contemporary requisite business expense.

Avoiding errors requires crafting treatment, intervention, or service plans that are derived from the best available research scholarly information. In addition to the desirability of empiricism, the use of evidence-based interventions can ward off legal complaints.

Threat assessment involves investigative and operational activities that will detect potential danger, whether in the form of the client's noncompliance, illogical expectations, inappropriate demands, or threats of an ethics, malpractice, or licensing complaint (Bartol & Bartol, 2012). Given the nature of clients served by psychologists, it is not uncommon to encounter a lack of responsibility and a tendency to fault others for hardships in life. Before accepting a potential client, the practitioner should consider the risks that the client's characteristics may pose to self, others, *and* the practitioner. Bennett et al. (2006, p. 12) state:

> High-risk patients include those who are diagnosed with serious personality disorders, have complex PTSD or dissociative identity disorders, report recovered memories of abuse, have been abused as children, present a serious risk to harm themselves or others, are wealthy, or are involved in lawsuits or other legal disputes.... Patients with serious personality disorders, such as borderline or narcissistic personality disorders, present special risks for psychologists. The specific diagnosis is less important than the presence of special traits, such as a belief in one's entitlement to special treatment, a pattern of idealization and vilification of others, a pervasive inability to accept objective and constructive feedback, or the use of romantic seduction as a consistent strategy to express affection or closeness.

Clients who are prone to litigation (e.g., relevant to divorce and custody disputes) are often poor candidates for psychological services (Woody, 2007).

With the foregoing warning, the psychologist should investigate whether the would-be service user shows CONDEMNS traits:

C = COMPLAINS about his or her lot in life
O = OWNING responsibility for self is absent (e.g., blames someone else or bad luck for problems)
N = NARCISSISTIC thought processes or verbalizations
D = DEFENSIVE behavior in many interactions
E = EXECUTIVE functions are impaired (e.g., faulty planning and decision making)
M = MONEY is an obsession or constant worry, even if unrealistic
N = NONCOMPLIANT tendencies show up immediately
S = SUSPICIOUSNESS is a pattern

For defending against malpractice and licensing complaints, the psychologist should accept this sort of person only under conditions that will assure strict adherence to a reasonable treatment plan.

I have offered 20 defensive strategies that any mental health practitioner should maintain as a preventive approach or when faced with a complaint (Woody, 2000):

1. Maintain a healthy mindset.
2. Accept the adversarial nature of the complaint.
3. Recognize the adversaries.
4. Become defensive.
5. Be a warrior.
6. Adopt a long-range perspective.
7. Obtain legal counsel.
8. Trust and rely on an attorney.
9. Do not allow financial considerations to dominate decision making.
10. Formulate a factual and defensible explanation.
11. Trust no one but your attorney.
12. Avoid creating witnesses for the other side.
13. Learn to respond properly to discovery methods and during testimony.
14. Be modest in professional representations.
15. Implement a risk management system.
16. Define an appropriate standard of care.
17. Buttress your professional credentials.
18. Screen clients to eliminate undue risks.
19. Guard against a copy-cat complainant.
20. Develop a healthy personal-professional life.

As a specific action plan for defending against malpractice and licensing complaints, the mental health practitioner can:

- View modern agency or independent practice as necessitating risk management.
- Provide professional services in accord with an individualized evidence-based treatment plan and require strict and consistent adherence by the respective client.
- Consider a client whose resistance, transference, or noncompliance cannot be managed therapeutically to be high risk for a complaint.

- If a conflict or threat arises, conceptualize the client as a potential "party opponent" and tactfully terminate services (with no vacillation).
- Have an attorney identified in advance, and at the first "red flag," rely immediately and have the attorney deal with the potential or actual complaint.
- At the first indication of legal involvement or "red flag," rely fully on the attorney for dispute resolution.
- Avoid trying to control or "quarterback" the defense.

Some of these suggestions may seem to contradict the traditional tenets of the treatment alliance, but (regrettably) if the alliance is not working, these suggestions may be necessary in contemporary mental health services delivery.

References and Readings

American Psychological Association Presidential Task Force on Evidence-Based Practice. (2006). Evidence-based practice in psychology. *American Psychologist, 61*, 271–285.

Bartol, C. R., & Bartol, A. M. (2012). *Introduction to forensic psychology*. Thousand Oaks, CA: Sage.

Bennett, B. E., Bricklin, P. M., Harris, E., Knapp, S., VandeCreek, L., & Younggren, J. N. (2006). *Assessing and managing risk in psychological practice*. Rockville, MD: The Trust.

Shapiro, D. L., & Smith, S. R. (2011). *Malpractice in psychology: A practical resource for clinicians*. Washington, DC: American Psychological Association.

Woody, R. H. (1988). *Fifty ways to avoid malpractice: A guidebook for the mental health practitioner*. Sarasota, FL: Professional Resource Exchange

Woody, R. H. (2000). What to do upon receiving a complaint. In L. VandeCreek & T. L. Jackson (Eds.), *Innovations in clinical practice: A source book* (Vol. 18, pp. 213–229). Sarasota, FL: Professional Resource Press.

Woody, R. H. (2007). Avoiding expert testimony about family therapy. *American Journal of Family Therapy, 35*, 389–393.

Woody, R. H. (2009). Psychological injury from licensing complaints against mental health practitioners. *Personal Injury and Law, 2*, 1009–1113.

Related Topics

Chapter 104, "Dealing with Licensing Board and Ethics Complaints"

Chapter 106, " Minimizing Your Legal Liability Risk Following Adverse Events or Patient Threats"

Chapter 107, "Dealing with Subpoenas"

Chapter 120, "Understanding Professional Liability Insurance"

Chapter 132, " Selecting and Relying on an Attorney"

106 MINIMIZING YOUR LEGAL LIABILITY RISK FOLLOWING ADVERSE EVENTS OR PATIENT THREATS

Jeffrey N. Younggren

On the late afternoon of Friday, July 22, 2011, Mark Lawrence was fatally shot by a patient as he walked down the stairs of his Virginia home. Shortly after having murdered Dr. Lawrence, the patient, Barbara Newman, walked outside and committed suicide. Dr. Lawrence had told one of his colleagues the day before these events that this particular patient had begun blaming all of her problems on him. This colleague recommended that Dr. Lawrence get consultation from someone, if the patient was getting paranoid about him. However, this never happened (Wu & Castaneda, 2011).

Heather Ensworth was a psychologist practicing in Pasadena. Cynthia Mullvain was her patient from November 1982 until September 1984, at which time Dr. Ensworth terminated the treatment. Ms. Mullvain did not accept the termination well, so Dr. Ensworth saw her again to address the termination issues that appeared to remain between the two of them. Subsequently, a series of harassing incidents occurred, and Dr. Ensworth was again forced to terminate contact with Ms. Mullvain in May 1987. Dr. Ensworth obtained a restraining order against Ms. Mullvain. Ms. Mullvain did not dispute the evidence that Dr. Ensworth produced at the hearing on the matter, showing that Ms. Mullvain, among other things, followed Dr. Ensworth, circled around her office building, kept her house under surveillance, made numerous phone calls, and sent threatening letters to her, including one letter indicating that she was going to commit suicide in Dr. Ensworth's presence (*Ensworth v. Mullvain*, 1990).

Psychologists treat troubled people, and sometimes this leads to actual risk to the psychologist. The treatment of emotionally disturbed individuals can prove both unpredictable and dangerous for the patient and for those around them. Sometimes psychotherapists get caught up in their patient's difficulties, a circumstance that can prove dangerous. At other times patients actually focus their pathology onto their psychotherapist, something that is even more dangerous. Too often psychologists feel complacent about their personal and professional risk when treating impaired individuals. There are a number of reasons for this. Sometimes psychologists do not recognize how they too could become entangled in their patient's pathology, or they simply believe that it could never happen to them. Finally, some clinicians feel confused about the duties and obligations that confront them when adverse incidents occur or when patients misbehave or act out against them.

Some psychologists fail to understand that providing therapeutic services to another individual is fundamentally a business relationship that includes ethical obligations and legal responsibilities shared by *both* therapist and patient. To begin with, treating psychologists have a legal obligation to bring their expertise to the treatment setting and engage in conduct advancing the best interests of the client. When they contract to provide services to anyone, they implicitly agree that they will fulfill the ethical and legal requirements that go with assuming the care of another person in a professional capacity. When this occurs, the psychologist actually becomes a fiduciary to the patient, meaning that the patient trusts that the psychologist will operate in the patient's best interests. However, the fulfillment of this legal duty can become quite complex and confusing depending on the case, the setting, or the intervention. Consequently, different psychologists might discharge their responsibilities to the same person differently, given setting and/or theoretical orientation. Failure to fulfill a fiduciary obligation to a patient could result in legal action against the psychologist. Interestingly, most psychologists focus only on their obligations to treat and care for patients, regardless of what the patients do.

A second important aspect to the psychotherapy relationship involves patient responsibilities. Most psychologists seem out of touch with the reality that when patients enter psychotherapy they enter it taking on a series of obligations of their own. For example, patients are agreeing that they will be honest with the psychologist and that the psychologist will be compensated for their services. Other patient obligations include attending sessions, following the treatment plan, doing homework, complying with therapist requests (or resolving disagreements), and so on. These behaviors represent the patient's end of the business agreement, since they must be done in order for treatment to continue and for the patient to make progress. When problems in these areas occur, they must be addressed and resolved because failure to follow the psychologist's treatment plan may well impede progress.

The psychologist and the patient have other shared obligations when they choose to begin working together. These include a need to behave in a fashion that reflects respect for the importance of the alliance and to avoid conduct that violates the rights of the other person. Both psychologist and patient have obligations to be civil, to work to resolve impasses that might develop during therapy, and to communicate with each other in a clear fashion. Without these conditions, successful treatment is much more difficult to achieve.

Many psychologists fail to understand the importance of this second aspect of the therapeutic relationship. They do not understand the importance of patients fulfilling their responsibilities to the treatment dyad. They often avoid directly dealing with adverse incidents when they occur or with addressing patient/therapist conflict out of fear that doing so might damage the treatment alliance. In addition, psychologists sometimes feel concerned that confrontation and adversity in the treatment setting might seem unprofessional and, consequently, a violation of the standard of care. Regardless, when confronting adversity, some psychologists begin to make compromises that can increase the risk of professional sanction of some sort. Such behavior on the part of the psychologists frequently leads them to continue to treat individuals under less than optimal conditions because they either believe they can or that they must do so. Such practitioners fail to recognize that the standard of care requires them to address and resolve untoward events as they occur and *not continue treatment they consider compromised or suboptimal.* If these issues cannot be resolved with a patient, the correct step would involve terminating treatment and referring the patient to another professional who might better address the patient's needs. To continue psychotherapy under less than optimal conditions only exposes the psychologist to increased risk of some type of negative outcome. To quote the Hon. Steven Hjelt, an administrative law judge in California, on this very issue:

> There is a cold hard truth often ignored by the "helping" professions. It is this: sometimes YOU cannot "fix" or heal everyone...you cannot put Humpty Dumpty back together again. Perhaps someone else can, in which case it is incumbent to transition that patient to the person who better suits the patient's needs. Sometimes no one can "fix" or heal a patient;

> no one can put Humpty Dumpty back together again. If that be the case, you are engaged in acts of futility which translate into providing unnecessary treatment sessions. (Younggren, Fisher, Foote, & Hjelt, 2011, p. 168)

The following list of strategies, if implemented, will reduce the likelihood of an adverse incident in the treatment setting. These risk management strategies not only constitute good practice but also reduce the risk of losing a malpractice action or licensing board complaint.

SET CLEAR RULES AT THE BEGINNING OF TREATMENT

Review the rules of the psychotherapy relationship at the outset of treatment as part of an informed consent agreement that the patient reads and signs. This agreement forms the basis of a contract between patient and psychotherapist outlining the rules of the relationship, including what the therapist is willing to do, what the therapist must do, and what the therapist will not agree to do. Through the use of a comprehensive informed consent, psychologists clarify for the consumer the nature of the obligation that they are taking on and how they will fulfill that obligation.

A good informed consent document also outlines expectations regarding the patient's behavior. In this respect, it should clarify the importance of adhering to the proposed treatment plan or the need to resolve any disagreement the patient may have with the treatment plan before proceeding. The document also should outline the important role that trust and honesty play in therapy and the need for therapy to remain a place where both psychologist and patient can experience that trust. The form should also outline any financial obligations the patient has and how these will be fulfilled. It also addresses any limitations that could apply. For example, any service limitations created by managed care companies should be outlined and clarified at the beginning of therapy—including potential endpoints due to payment restrictions by the health insurer. This practice helps align the client's expectations with the realities of the client's health insurance and any related limitations. In addition, discussing an endpoint of treatment at the outset makes it clear to the patient that termination forms a part of the process of therapy.

The consent process should also include some discussion about privacy rights. In so doing the psychologist demonstrates a respect for the patient's privacy and explains how this also applies to limitations placed on other types of intrusions into each other's private lives.

While a comprehensive consent form helps assure that a practice is operating in a fashion consistent with ethics and law, no form will cover every possible difficulty. Since therapy is a dynamic process, unpredictable questions and problems will surface throughout therapy. Consequently, discussions about changes in the therapist–patient agreement need to occur throughout treatment with notations of these discussions included on the patient's chart.

MAINTAIN CONTROL OF THERAPY

Consider psychotherapy as a railroad transporting the patient from one point to another. While the patient determines where he or she wants to go, the psychologist serves as the engineer of the treatment locomotive. As applied directly to psychotherapy, the psychologist has the responsibility for what happens in treatment. Because the psychologist has a legal duty of care, he or she determines the treatment plan and the model for intervention and moves forward with the patient's consent and active participation. Do not misconstrue this as trivializing the patient's wishes or concerns at all times during treatment, but rather that the professionally based decisions dealing with the direction of psychotherapy rest squarely upon the shoulders of the person providing that treatment.

The patient's interests are important. However, the patient is not in a position to direct what the psychologist does as part of the treatment process. For example, if the therapist believes that obtaining treatment records from a prior therapist is necessary and the patient objects, the therapist who believes that the information might be helpful in treating the patient may make such access a condition of treatment. Having access to the records of previously treating professionals in order to better understand the patient's needs is a standard of care issue, and a patient cannot require a psychotherapist to violate the standard of care. Should such a problem occur, the therapist must discuss the reasons for needing the records with the patient in the context of trying to understand the patient's objection. The discussion may lead to the decision that such information is unnecessary, which is an acceptable resolution. The therapist should not however, allow the patient to unilaterally dictate how treatment should proceed in ways that create a condition of suboptimal psychotherapy.

IMMEDIATELY ADDRESS PATIENT BOUNDARY CROSSINGS AND UNACCEPTABLE CONDUCT

Given that patients vary widely in their emotional and behavioral struggles that at times could interfere with their decision making and adherence to therapy limits, it is not unusual for some patients to violate boundaries in a variety of ways during the course of treatment. When this occurs, the wise psychologist will address the violation immediately. In so doing the treating professional can better understand the motive for such behavior and educate the patient on the importance of maintaining appropriate limits. Such prompt action not only brings early resolution to the matter but also increases the probability that this type of behavior will resolve and not reoccur.

Frequently, psychologists avoid addressing boundary violations for fear that they will disrupt the treatment alliance or increase the boundary crossings by having paid attention to them. Ignoring such violations is a bad idea since the patient has engaged in behaviors inconsistent with good therapy that could damage the therapeutic alliance. Addressing boundary violations when they occur fulfills the therapist's obligation to maintain control of the therapy, and opening the matter for discussion fulfills informed consent requirements.

Note all boundary violations in the patient's chart, including a description of the behavior in question and how it was addressed. If the patient does not comply with the limit setting that the therapist seeks to implement, document that, too.

DO NOT FEAR TERMINATION

Probably no standards of professional practice seem more confusing and misdirected than those addressing patient termination and abandonment. Concerns about allegations of wrongful termination or abandonment have caused many psychotherapists to believe that no matter what a patient does, or no matter what circumstances occur during the treatment relationship, the psychologist continues to bear the duty of care for that patient. This assumption is really only half true. The psychologist does have a duty of care. However, clients also bear responsibilities to the treatment alliance, responsibilities that have direct impact on the direction of psychotherapy, including its termination, if necessary.

Thinking of therapy as a dynamic relationship that evolves based on the type of service, the location of the service, the nature of the treatment alliance, and the type of patient; it follows that appropriate termination also has dynamic aspects. In some instances, termination might simply consist of abruptly transferring a patient to another psychotherapist with no termination sessions needed. Under other circumstances, termination might occur over a protracted period of time. For example, a patient's threats against a therapist might necessitate immediate termination with no further sessions, while termination of a long-term psychodynamic case could call for an extensive and gradual termination reflecting respect for the nature of the alliance. In either case, the appropriate termination plan depends on aligning with circumstances of the individual case.

Another circumstance that warrants termination of treatment occurs when a psychologist has exhausted the treatment options he or she can offer a patient without further progress. When this occurs, termination and referral may become the only remaining option to advance the best interests of the patient. Even if the patient objects to a decision to terminate, such an objection does not make the decision wrong. Rather, the objection makes managing termination more complex. The psychologist must remember that he or she has a responsibility to act as a fiduciary in the treatment relationship and engage in acts focused on the patient's best interests even though the patient may not fully understand this or even agree with it. To continue to treat under these circumstances creates a circumstance of professional compromise and violates the standard of care (Davis, 2008; Gottlieb & Younggren, 2008).

Many psychologists fear that terminating treatment of someone against the person's wishes will result in an accusation of abandonment or wrongful termination. Yet not one case exists of such an action against a psychologist when termination has occurred coupled with referral and/or transfer of treatment responsibilities to another mental health professional (Gottlieb & Younggren, 2008). You have not legally abandoned your client when you have transferred or offered to transfer that individual into the care of another. In addition, a review of the existing case law fails to produce even one citation of a successful tort action taken against a mental health professional for damages secondary to wrongful termination. Most of the cases in this area have to do with a refusal to provide treatment to an individual to whom a duty was owed in a crisis or emergent circumstance.

DO NOT ACCEPT PATIENT MISBEHAVIOR AND THREATS

When dealing with patient misconduct, including situations when the therapist is threatened, psychologists should know that they usually bear no continued duty of care to such a client. The word "usually" is used here because some exceptions may exist. For example, if the threats come from highly impaired individuals, the degree of impairment must be taken into consideration since the threats may reflect the patient's pathology and not the patient's intent. However, that does not mean that a psychotherapist has any less likelihood of harm at the hands of highly impaired individuals. Remember that no psychotherapist has any professional obligation to accept increased levels of risk to his or her safety, welfare, and/or privacy when facing a threat from a patient. In that spirit, one can argue that when a patient makes a threat, the duty owed by the psychotherapist to that patient has ended. In essence, by making the threat the patient has effectively terminated the therapy.

MEMORIALIZE ALL PATIENT MISCONDUCT AND YOUR TERMINATION PLANS

Good record keeping will prove vital when an adverse event occurs or when dealing with patient misconduct. As patient therapist conflict and disagreement increase or as disruptive circumstances develop, the frequency and level of detail of record keeping should also increase. Such records not only memorialize the patient's conduct but also record how the psychologist deals with it. When confronted with a need to terminate any patient, the clinician should outline it in detail as part of the treatment record. This should include a description of the reasons for the termination, the thought processes that led to the decision, and a detailed outline of the actual plan. If the termination has adversarial elements, the details of the termination plan as outlined in the record can become a strong defense in the face of accusations of unprofessional conduct.

If termination becomes necessary because of the occurrence of an adverse event or the existence of a threat, correspondence to the patient should memorialize the plan. This letter should clearly describe the event or conduct on the part of the patient that forced a decision to terminate. The correspondence should also outline the client's subsequent treatment options. For example, and as appropriate, such a letter should include referral to the patient's health care insurance panel or to other professionals for continued assistance. Finally, this letter should discuss what professional acts the psychologist is willing and unwilling to fulfill. Remember, when terminating treatment of a patient under adversarial or adverse circumstance, no future clinical contacts should occur after termination.

CONSULT

Consultation remains one of the most important types of ethical and risk management practices. Along with record keeping and informed consent, consultation helps protect the psychologist from allegations that his or her conduct in terminating a patient violated the standard of care (Bennett et al., 2006).

Through consulting with colleagues and the memorialization of that consultation, psychologists establish the reasonableness of their conduct and its consistency with appropriate standards of care. Psychologists confronted with adverse incidents, including threats made by patients, should seek out consultation from a qualified attorney, an expert in ethics, or a risk management expert. In doing so and documenting that consultation, psychologists establish proof that they sought guidance in the matter to assist them in making a correct decision for the patient and for themselves.

Psychotherapy is not a one-way street. Engaging in a treatment alliance with a patient involves a business agreement wrapped around ethical and legal obligations and the psychologist's duty to care for another individual. That said, the patients who enter therapy also have responsibilities to the treatment alliance. When patients violate those obligations or when incidents occur that disrupt therapy, the psychologist's obligation to continue to treat that individual becomes modified. Psychologists should remember satisfied consumers do not file law suits or licensing board complaints. The existence of an adversarial relationship with a patient creates a serious risk to the psychologist, who then has a very brief period of time to either improve the relationship, fix the impasse, or to terminate the relationship and refer the patient. If that adversity leads to legal action taken against the psychologist, the existence of a comprehensive informed consent form, a detailed record, and evidence of consultation with others on the matter will become a strong defense against any allegations of professional misconduct.

References and Readings

Bennett, B. E., Bricklin, P. M., Harris, E., Knapp, S., Vandecreek, L., & Younggren, J. N. (2006). *Assessing and managing risk in psychological practice: An individualized approach*. Rockville, MD: The Trust.

Davis, D. (2008). *Terminating therapy: A professional guide to ending on a positive note*. Hoboken, NJ: Wiley.

Ensworth v. Mullvain, 224 Cal. App. 3d 1105, 274 Cal. Rptr. 447 (October 1990).

Wu, J. O., & Castaneda, R. (2011, July 23). Patient kills McLean psychiatrist before fatally shooting herself. *The Washington Post*. Retrieved August 2011, from www.washingtonpost.com/local/patient-kills-mclean-psychiatrist-before-fatally-shooting-herself/2011/07/23/gIQAs4-bmVI_story.html

Younggren, J. N., Fisher, M. A., Foote, W. E., & Hjelt, S. E. (2011). A legal and ethical review of patient responsibilities and psychotherapist duties. *Professional Psychology: Research and Practice, 42*(2), 160–168.

Younggren, J. N., & Gottlieb, M. C. (2008). Termination and abandonment: History, risk and risk management. *Professional Psychology: Research and Practice, 39*, 498–504.

Related Topics

Chapter 104, "Dealing with Licensing Board and Ethics Complaints"

Chapter 105, "Defending Against Legal (Malpractice and Licensing) Complaints"

Chapter 120, "Essential Features of Professional Liability Insurance"

107 DEALING WITH SUBPOENAS

Lindsay Childress-Beatty and Gerald P. Koocher

Receipt of a legal document commanding you to appear at a legal proceeding or turn over your records to attorneys, especially when unexpected, can be a very stressful experience. This brief guide can help you understand the nature and meaning of a subpoena and possibilities for response. However, law and procedures vary from jurisdiction to jurisdiction and psychologists work in a wide range of settings beyond solo private practice as a psychotherapist. The nature of the setting may dictate the procedure to follow in determining the response. It is always wise to consult with an attorney who is knowledgeable about your local jurisdiction and particular situation.

BOTTOM-LINE ADVICE

Neither ignore nor immediately respond to a subpoena. Determine whether the subpoena is valid, what is being requested, and whether your client has consented to the waiver of any privilege and the release of the information or records.

QUESTIONS ABOUT SUBPOENAS

What is a Subpoena or a Subpoena Duces Tecum?

A subpoena is a legal document requiring a person to produce documents, appear and give testimony at a deposition or trial, or both. From the Latin meaning "under penalty bring with you," a subpoena duces tecum requires the person to bring specified records, reports, tapes, documents, or other tangible evidence to court or a deposition. In many jurisdictions, a subpoena can be issued as a matter of routine by a court clerk at an attorney's request or even signed directly by the requesting attorney. The subpoena states the name of the court and issuing authority, the title of the legal action, and the time and place of testimony or production of documents. In many instances, even if the subpoena is not termed a "subpoena duces tecum," the requesting party may only be seeking records and will not actually require that the psychologist appear and give testimony. In addition, often the records specified in a subpoena or subpoena duces tecum can be produced to the requesting party by mail without actual attendance at court or the stated location. Normally, the original record or documents need not, and should not, be provided. A notarized or authenticated copy of the records as they are normally kept will generally suffice. An attorney can help you determine what to produce if your records are held electronically.

How Does a Court Order Differ from a Subpoena?

It is important to understand the difference between a subpoena and a court order. Unlike a subpoena, a court order is generally issued by a judge only after a hearing. The court decides what information or records are protected and what are not. The court order compels disclosure of even privileged information unless the order is appealed to a higher court.

Must I Comply with the Subpoena?

Failure to comply with a valid subpoena could lead to being held in contempt of court. However, simply because you have been served does not mean that the subpoena is valid, or that you must testify or produce all materials requested. Even if the subpoena is valid, it may be possible to limit or better define the request or negotiate an alternative response.

What Do I Do When Served?

The subpoena document should be accepted, and you should then consult legal counsel regarding applicable law and resulting legal obligations. Do not disclose any information concerning whether the subpoena actually involves someone whom you have treated. The setting in which you work may help determine your next step. For example, as the first step in determining how to respond, psychologists working in hospital settings may be required to inform and consult with the hospital's general counsel who may be involved throughout the process. On rare occasions, a subpoena may arrive at a clinician's office in the hands of a person seeking immediate access to records. Under such circumstances it is reasonable to inform the person: "I cannot disclose whether or not the person noted in the subpoena is now or ever was my client. If the person were my client, I could not provide any information without a signed release from that individual or a valid court order."

What Issues are Involved in Determining whether the Subpoena is Valid?

A subpoena may be invalid for a variety of reasons, including if it is not issued by the proper authority, is not properly "served," does not provide proper time frames for response, is issued outside the proper reach of the issuing authority, or causes an undue burden on the person required to respond. You will need to consult with your own attorney or possibly the relevant client's attorney regarding the validity of the subpoena. If the subpoena is invalid, a motion to quash the subpoena can be filed or in some instances the requesting attorney can simply be informed in writing that the subpoena is invalid and no response will be forthcoming.

What Should I Do if the Subpoena is Determined to Be Valid?

You will need to obtain your client's permission prior to releasing the documents or testifying. You should obtain this permission in writing even when written consent is not required by law. (If you are covered by HIPAA's Privacy Rule, specific requirements for the written authorization may apply, and it is not recommended that you simply rely on the assurances and documentation of the requestor that reasonable efforts have been made to provide notice to your client.) Contact your client and explain the situation, including what information or records would be released and the possibility of further release once you are required to testify or documents leave your hands. Ask for permission to talk with his or her attorney. Ask the client's attorney to move to modify or quash the subpoena, or work out any privilege issues and/or a more limited response with the opposing attorney. The involvement of the client's attorney helps to ensure that the client's legal interests have been fully considered.

What if I Am Worried about the Impact of the Release on My Client or Others?

Even if a signed release form is included, if you believe that the material may be clinically or legally damaging, discuss these issues with the client. It is not unreasonable for the clinician to personally confirm the client's wishes, especially if the content of the records is sensitive. You may also be able to negotiate to limit the information released such as by releasing more limited records or producing a summary report as a substitute for the records, or obtain an agreement to protect the records from further release. Consider any possible privilege or confidentiality issues related to others named in the records as well.

What Do I Do if Test Data or Test Materials are Requested?

If the subpoena is valid and the client consents to the release, test data (test information specific to a client such as raw and scaled scores, responses, and notes related to the client) that do not disclose any important information concerning the test itself may be released as part of the response to the subpoena. However, if a valid subpoena seeks actual test materials sold only to professionals (such as test kits, manuals, or test questions and protocols) or raw test data that are merged with test materials (e.g., individual client record forms also containing test questions or stimuli), additional consideration should be given to the release even if the client has consented. Many test publisher websites contain helpful information concerning test security as well as contact information for the test publisher's privacy officer or general counsel. One of these individuals can be an excellent resource for help in protecting the test materials. Consider obtaining a letter or other assistance and then speaking to the requestor and, if necessary, the court, concerning limiting the response or placing the information under a protective order that limits access and re-release. Another option after explaining the need to protect the test materials is to offer to provide the raw data to a qualified professional. However, in response to a court order, both raw test data and test kit materials would ultimately have to be produced if attempts to limit the court order fail.

What Do I Do if the Client Does Not Wish to Have the Records or Information Disclosed?

Without admitting that the subpoena actually involves someone whom you have treated, you may need to assert the client's privilege by informing the requestor, usually through an attorney, that the information is privileged and that you do not have consent to release documents or testify absent a legally recognized exception to that privilege. Again you may be able to work with the client's attorney to assert the client's legal privilege, quash the subpoena, or modify the subpoena. Keep in mind, however, that the client's attorney works for the client and you may need your own attorney if your interests begin to diverge from those of your client. Ultimately the psychologist may need to seek a ruling from the court concerning the release.

What if the Subpoena Requires My Actual Attendance and I Cannot Attend on the Specified Date?

Consider contacting the lawyer who issued the subpoena to explain your dilemma and ask that the date be changed. If the attorney refuses and the schedule is unreasonable (e.g., if you do not have time to cancel appointments or provide patient coverage), if appropriate, tell the attorney that you plan to contact the judge in the case in order to complain about the inadequate notice. This approach often stimulates increased flexibility by the attorney. If necessary and appropriate, do contact the judge and explain your scheduling problem. Except in unusual circumstances, the judge is likely to be accommodating.

References and Readings

American Psychological Association. (2002). Ethical principles of psychologists and code of conduct. *American Psychologist, 57,* 1048–1051.

American Psychological Association. (2007). Record keeping guidelines. *American Psychologist, 62,* 993–1004.

American Psychological Association Practice Organization. (2008). *How to deal with a subpoena.* Retrieved February 2013, from www.apapracticecentral.org/update/2008/12-17/subpoena.aspx

Campbell, L., Vasquez, M., Behnke, S., & Kinscherff, R. (2010). *APA ethics code commentary and case illustrations.* Washington, DC: American Psychological Association.

Committee on Legal Issues, American Psychological Association (2006). Strategies for private practitioners coping with subpoenas or compelled testimony for client records or test data. *Professional Psychology: Research and Practice, 37*, 215–222.
Committee on Psychological Tests and Assessment, American Psychological Association. (1996). Statement on disclosure of test data. *American Psychologist, 51*, 644–668.
Committee on Psychological Tests and Assessment, American Psychological Association. (2007). *Recent developments affecting the disclosure of test data and materials: Comments regarding the 1996 statement on the disclosure of test data.* Retrieved February 2013, from www.apa.org/science/programs/testing/test-disclosure-statement.pdf
Koocher, G. P., & Keith-Spiegel, P. C. (2008). *Ethics in psychology and the mental health professions: Standards and cases* (3rd ed.). New York: Oxford University Press.

Related Topics

Chapter 104, "Dealing with Licensing Board and Ethics Complaints"
Chapter 105, "Defending Against Legal (Malpractice and Licensing) Complaints"
Chapter 106, "Minimizing Your Legal Liability Risk Following Adverse Events or Patient Threats"
Chapter 127, "Elements of Authorization Forms to Release or Request Client's Records"
Chapter 128, "Understanding Fundamentals of the HIPAA Privacy Rule"

108 CONFRONTING AN UNETHICAL COLLEAGUE

Patricia Keith-Spiegel

The ethics code of the American Psychological Association (APA, 2010) actively deputizes psychologists to monitor peer conduct, although in a somewhat cautious and protective manner. Earlier versions of the code mandated that psychologists deal directly with ethics violations committed by colleagues as the first line of action. Only if an informal attempt proved unsuccessful should an ethics committee be contacted. Currently, and partly because of reported incidents of harassment and intimidation and the potential for violations of confidential information, the newer code offers the option of deciding the appropriateness of dealing with the matter directly. If an informal solution seems unlikely (for reasons left unspecified in the code), psychologists are mandated to take formal action—such as contacting a licensing board or ethics committee—so long as any confidentiality rights or conflicts can be resolved (Ethical Principles of Psychologists and Code of Conduct, Sections 1.04 and 1.05). The level of seriousness of the alleged behavior is not stated as a consideration, although Canter, Bennett, Jones, and Nagy (1994) and Keith-Spiegel, Sieber, and Koocher (2010) advise against attempting informal resolutions when the suspected violations are complex or very serious.

BARRIERS TO CONFRONTING UNETHICAL COLLEAGUES

O'Connor (n.d.) and Keith-Spiegel, Sieber, and Koocher (2010) have generated reasons that may result in reticence to approach a colleague behaving badly. These include the following:

- I don't want to be seen as disloyal to the individual or an organization.
- I want to protect my friends.
- I don't want to cause colleagues harm, especially if they are sympathetic (e.g., depressed or physically ill, or already facing intense personal stressors).
- I am concerned about the potential for retaliation or being labeled as a snitch.
- The suspected individual is very difficult or drug addicted or mentally ill.
- I want to avoid the stress that may result from speaking out, especially if the matter is moved to a formal forum, such as an ethics committee.
- The matter seems too minor to be concerned about.
- I think someone else will take care of it.
- I don't know what to do.

Although these reasons may feel safe and reasonable, the entire profession is tainted when others are harmed by psychologists. In addition, "moral distress" is a disquieting feeling that occurs when one knows what should be done but fails to act (Austin, Rankle, Kagan, Bergum, & Lemermeyer, 2005). Such feelings can last indefinitely, especially if harm results, and it could have been avoided had intervention been attempted.

IDEAS FOR CONFRONTING COLLEAGUES SUSPECTED OF ENGAGING IN UNETHICAL CONDUCT

1. The relevant ethical principle that applies to the suspected breach of professional ethics should first be identified. If no law, relevant policy, or ethics principle has been violated, then the matter may not be an ethical one. This conclusion is reached most often when a colleague has an offensive personal style or holds personal views that are generally unpopular or widely divergent from your own. You have the right, of course, to express your personal feelings to your colleague, but this should not be construed as engaging in a professional duty.

2. Assess the strength of the evidence that an ethical violation has been committed. Most ethical infractions are seldom committed openly before a host of dispassionate witnesses. With few exceptions, no tangible exhibits corroborate that an unethical event ever occurred. A starting point involves categorizing the source of your information into one of five types:

- clear, direct observation of a colleague engaging in unethical behavior;
- knowing or unknowing disclosure by a colleague that he or she has committed an ethical violation;
- direct observation of a colleague's suspicious but not clearly interpretable behavior;
- receipt of a credible secondhand report of unethical conduct from someone seeking out your assistance as a consultant or intervening party; or
- casual gossip about a colleague's unethical behavior.

3. If you did not observe the alleged infraction directly, how credible is the source of information? Can you imagine a reason that would explain why the person might have engaged in this action that would not constitute an ethical violation? That is, can you think of more than one reason the colleague might have acted that way? If the information came by casual gossip, proceed with considerable caution. If there is no way to obtain any sufficiently substantial or verifiable facts, you may choose to ignore the information or, as a professional courtesy to the colleague, inform your colleague of the "scuttlebutt." If the colleague is guilty of what the idle hearsay suggests, you may have had a salutary effect; however, we recognize that this will be effective only if you can reasonably anticipate the colleague's reaction in advance.

4. Get in close touch with your own motivations to engage in (or to avoid) a confrontation with a colleague. Psychologists who are (or see themselves as being) directly victimized by the conduct of a colleague appear to be more willing to get involved. In addition to any fears, anger, biases, or other emotional reactions, do you perceive that the colleague's alleged conduct—either as it stands or if it continues—may undermine the integrity of the profession or harm one or more of the consumers served by the colleague? If your answer is affirmative, then some form of proactive stance is warranted. However, if you recognize that your emotional involvement or vulnerability (e.g., the colleague is your supervisor or a very difficult individual) creates an extreme hazard that will likely preclude a satisfactory outcome, you may wish to consider passing the intervention task on to another party. In such cases, any confidentiality issues must first be settled.

5. What is your relationship with the suspected colleague? This will affect both the approach taken and how you interpret the situation. Those who observe or learn of possible unethical actions by other psychologists often know the alleged offenders personally. They could be good friends or disliked antagonists. They could be subordinates or supervisors. Reactions, depending on the relationships with those suspected of ethics violations, affect both the approach taken to deal with them and the attributes assigned to colleagues. If the colleague is disliked, courage to act may come more from the thrill of revenge rather than from genuine courage and conviction. If the colleague is a friend or acquaintance with whom there have been no previous problematic interactions, the meeting usually goes easier. You can express to your friend that your interest and involvement are based on caring and concern for his or her professional standing. The danger, of course, is that you may feel that you are risking an established, positive relationship. If your friend can be educated effectively by you, however, you may well have protected him or her from embarrassment or more public forms of censure. If the colleague is someone you do not know personally, the confrontation will be, by definition, more formal. An expression of concern and a willingness to work through the problem cooperatively may still be quite effective. If the colleague is someone you do know but dislike, your dilemma is more pronounced. If the information is known to others (or can be appropriately shared with others), you might consider asking someone who has a better relationship with this person to intercede or to accompany you. If that is not feasible and a careful assessment of your own motivations reveals a conclusion that the possible misconduct clearly requires intervention on its own merits, then you should take some form of action. It may still be possible to approach this individual yourself, and if you maintain a professional attitude, it may work out.

6. Consultation with a trusted and experienced colleague who has demonstrated a heightened sensitivity to ethical issues is strongly recommended, even if only to assure yourself that you are on the right track. Identities should not be shared if confidentiality issues pertain.

7. Make your final decision about confronting the colleague and how to best do it. Even though you are not responsible for rectifying the unethical behavior of another person, the application of a decision-making model may facilitate a positive educative function. You might well find yourself, at this point, tempted to engage in one of two covert activities as alternatives to confronting a colleague directly. The first is to pass the information along to other colleagues in an effort to warn them. Although informing others may provide a sense that duty has been fulfilled, it is far more likely that responsibility has only been diffused. Idle talk certainly cannot guarantee that an offending colleague or the public has been affected in any constructive way. Moreover, to the extent that the conduct was misjudged, you could be responsible for an injustice to a colleague that is, in itself, unethical. The second temptation is to engage in more direct but anonymous action, such as sending an unsigned note or relevant document (e.g., a copy of an ethics code with one or more sections circled in red). Constructive results, however, are hardly guaranteed. The recipient may not understand the intended message. Even if the information is absorbed, the reaction to an anonymous charge may be counterproductive. Also, the warning may instill a certain amount of paranoia that could result in additional negative consequences, such as adding suspiciousness to the colleague's character. Thus, although both of these covert actions seem proactive, we strongly recommend neither.

8. If you decide to go ahead with a direct meeting, schedule it in advance, although not in a menacing manner. Indicate to your colleague that you would like to speak privately and schedule a face-to-face meeting at his or her earliest convenience. A business setting would normally be more appropriate than a home or restaurant, even if the colleague is a friend. Handling such matters on the phone is not recommended unless geographic barriers preclude a direct meeting. Letters create a record, but they do not allow for back-and-forth interaction, which we believe to be conducive to a constructive exchange in matters of this sort. We do not recommend electronic communications for the same reason.

9. When entering into the confrontation phase, remain calm and self-confident. The colleague is likely to have an emotional reaction. Remain as nonthreatening as possible. I suggest non-inflammatory language such as expressing confusion and seeking clarification. It might go something like this: "The data reported in your article is not quite the same as what you showed me earlier. I am confused about that and wonder if you could help me understand it. Is there a problem here?" Or, "I met a young woman who, upon learning that I was a psychologist, told me that she was your client and that the two of you planned to start dating. I thought we should talk about it." Things are not always as they seem, and it would be wise at the onset to allow for an explanation rather than provoke unnecessary anxiety. For example, it is at least possible that it was the first data set that was recorded in error or that the young woman was briefly a client years earlier for services that did not qualify as traditional psychotherapy, such as short-term work on smoking cessation or other habit control. Such responses may not always render the matters moot, but the discussion would likely proceed far differently than with a more strident opening.

10. Set the tone for a constructive and educative session. Do not take the role of accuser, judge, jury, and penance dispenser. The session will probably progress best if you see yourself as having an alliance with the colleague—not in the usual sense of consensus and loyalty, but as facing a problem together.

11. Describe your ethical obligations, noting the ethics principle or policy that prompted your intervention. Rather than equivocating, state your concerns directly and present the evidence on which they are based.

12. Allow the colleague ample time to explain and defend in as much detail as he or she required. The colleague may be flustered and repetitive; be patient.

13. If the colleague becomes abusive or threatening, attempt to steer him or her to a more constructive state. Although many people need a chance to vent feelings, they often settle down if the confronting person remains steady and refrains from becoming abusive in return. If the negative reaction continues, it may be appropriate to say something calming, such as, "I see you are very upset right now, and I regret that we cannot explore this matter together in a way that would be satisfactory to both of us. I would like you to think about what I have presented, and if you would reconsider talking more about it, please contact me within a week." If a return call is not forthcoming, other forms of action must be considered. This could involve including another appropriate person or pressing formal charges to some duly constituted monitoring body. The suspected offender should be informed (in person or in a formal note) of your next step.

CONFIDENTIALITY AND SECONDHAND ISSUES

Occasionally, yet another person critical to the case is unavailable or unwilling to get involved or to be identified. These situations pose extremely frustrating predicaments. Approaching colleagues with charges issued by "unseen accusers" violates the essence of due process. Furthermore, alleged violators often know (or think they know) their accusers' identities anyway. When the alleged unethical behaviors are extremely serious, possibly putting yet others in harm's way, and when the fearful but otherwise credible individuals making the charges are adamant about remaining anonymous, psychologists may not feel comfortable ignoring the situation altogether. However, there may be nothing else that can be done. Sometimes the option to do nothing may not exist, as with state mandatory reporting laws. However, for other reporting situations where legal mandates do not apply, the current APA code of conduct leaves psychologists no options other than respecting confidentiality.

If you are intervening on behalf of another, you will first have to disclose why you are there and offer any other caveats. You might say something like, "I have no personal direct knowledge of what I want to discuss, but I have agreed to speak with you on behalf of two students." Your role in such instances may be to arrange another meeting with all the parties present and possibly serve as mediator during such a meeting.

If you are approached by a credible person who claims firsthand knowledge and is seeking assistance, we advise being as helpful as you can. Because we advise consulting with colleagues before taking any action, it is only fitting that you should be receptive when others approach you for assistance in working through ethical issues. Often you will be able to assist the person with a plan of action that will not include your direct involvement or offer a referral if the dilemma is not one about which you can confidently comment. If you do agree to become actively engaged, be sure that you have proper permission to reveal any relevant identities and that you have available all possible information.

DO INFORMAL INTERVENTIONS ACTUALLY WORK?

Numerous anecdotal accounts indicate that successful outcomes are always possible. Colleagues who commit ethical infractions may even express appreciation for a collegial resolution. Often enough they were not fully aware that their actions were proscribed against in the ethics code, occurring most often when the offense was relatively minor. Unfortunately, it is difficult to systematically study the success of informal interventions in clinical settings because violations usually occur behind closed doors. Exceptions are largely confined to plagiarism, inappropriate advertising, and observations of psychologists who are so distressed or mentally ill that their behavior is exhibited in settings outside of the therapy room. Psychologists may also be made aware of unethical behavior by previous clients, although intervention in such instances may prove more difficult.

Data collected about social science researchers reveal that the majority of observers of misconduct do confront their colleagues when they suspect or observe research wrongdoing, and positive solutions are common (Koocher & Keith-Spiegel, 2010).

Despite the paucity of clear data in clinical and counseling settings regarding the efficacy of peer monitoring, the responsibility still lies with individuals to act in a way that upholds professional values. If you are ever the recipient of a colleague's inquiry, be grateful for the warning about how you have been perceived and try to openly and honestly work toward the goal of settling the matter in a way that satisfies all those involved without necessitating a review by outside evaluators.

References and Readings

American Psychological Association. (2010). *Ethical principles of psychologists and code of conduct*. Washington, DC: Author.

Austin, W., Rankle, M., Kagan, L., Bergum, V. & Lemermeyer, G. (2005). To stay or to go, to speak or stay silent, to act or not act: Moral distress as experienced by psychologists. *Ethics and Behavior, 15*, 197–212.

Canter, M. B., Bennett, B. E., Jones, S. E., & Nagy T. F. (1994). *Ethics for psychologists: A commentary on the APA ethics code*. Washington, DC: American Psychological Association.

Keith-Spiegel, P., Sieber, J. E., & Koocher, G. P. (2010). *Responding to research wrongdoing: A user friendly guide*. Retrieved February 2013, from the Ethicsresearch.com Web site www.ethicsresearch.com/freeresources/rrwresearchwrongdoing.html

Koocher, G. P., & Keith-Spiegel, P. C. (2008). *Ethics in psychology: Professional standards and cases* (3rd ed.). New York: Oxford University Press.

Koocher, G. P., & Keith-Spiegel, P. (2010). Peers nip misconduct in the bud. *Nature, 466,* 438–440.

O'Connor, M. F. (n.d.). *Intervening with an impaired colleague.* Retrieved December 2011, from the APA Practice Central Web site www.apapracticecentral.org/ce/self-care/intervening.aspx

Related Topics

Chapter 103, "American Psychological Association's Ethical Principles"

Chapter 109, "Recognizing, Assisting, and Reporting the Impaired Psychologist"

Chapter 144, "Consulting on End-of-Life Decisions"

109 RECOGNIZING, ASSISTING, AND REPORTING THE IMPAIRED PSYCHOLOGIST

Gary R. Schoener

The term *impaired,* when applied to a psychologist or another health care professional, has historically been considered almost synonymous with alcoholism or substance abuse. This reflects the fact that one of the most common sources of impairment is drug or alcohol addiction. Most "impaired practitioner" programs in health professions, and even in the legal profession, focus on alcoholism and other substance abuse. Most of these programs also deal with other problems—for example, depression, marital difficulties, anxiety disorders, and sexual compulsivity—but today the focus remains on substance abuse.

As defined in psychology, *impairment* refers to objective change in a person's professional functioning. An impaired psychologist is one whose work-related performance has diminished in quality. This may be manifested in one or more of the following ways: work assignments are typically late or incomplete; conflict with colleagues has noticeably increased; clients, students, or families have registered complaints; or the amount of absenteeism and tardiness has markedly increased (Schwebel, Skorina, & Schoener, 1994). The American Psychological Association's (2006) monograph on *Advancing Colleague Assistance in Professional Psychology* lists a number of problems associated with and leading to impairment:

- Stress and burnout
- Financial stresses
- Family-of-origin conflicts
- Divorce and relationship difficulties
- Depression
- Suicide

- Substance and alcohol abuse
- Vicarious/secondary trauma

An important factor in the handling of impairment is the Americans with Disabilities Act (ADA; Bruyere & O'Keeffe, 1994). While prohibiting discrimination against individuals with disabilities, both mental and physical, the act requires employers to "make reasonable accommodations" to employees' disabilities. This affects the handling of the impaired professional in two ways. First, it provides an incentive to acknowledge disability rather than hide it; second, it directs the psychologist in the role of employer to make reasonable efforts to help someone dealing with a disability function on the job. Thus, the impaired or potentially impaired psychologist has reason to present his or her difficulties to an employer or supervisor in hopes of negotiating a helpful accommodation.

RESPONSIBILITY TO REPORT

Psychologists often have professional responsibilities with regard to clients, students, and others who may be affected by the practitioner's impairment. Where such individuals are at risk, there may be a duty to act quickly. In addition, reporting duties need to be carried out if you learn of possible child abuse or of anything else that must be reported to a state board or other regulatory authority.

First and foremost, never promise or agree to keep something confidential until you know what the impaired professional has to say and whether you can keep it confidential. As with clients, anyone with whom you consult about impairment needs to know the limits of the privacy of your discussions with them. All of the following reporting duties would be based on state laws or guidelines:

1. Reporting of abuse or neglect of a minor or of a vulnerable adult
2. Any reporting to a state board required by licensure statutes (e.g., Minnesota requires reporting of certain offenses unless they are communicated by the psychologist who is seeking help; the Province of Ontario requires reporting of any sexual contact with clients)
3. Any reporting duties based on your knowledge of dangers to others, such as potential dangers to clients
4. Duties to report impaired functioning of a staff member who works in the same facility as you do. Once a professional staff member knows of problems, the organization is considered to be "on notice" so that the failure to then act becomes negligent supervision.

In some states, colleague assistance or impaired practitioner programs have selected exemptions from reporting duties. If the intervention is part of a peer review process in a hospital, for example, it may be protected by law. It is important that you determine whether such an exemption might apply to your activities. They are typically limited to work by professional review committees or impaired practitioner programs. Those involved in subsequent treatment or rehabilitation should also note their responsibilities.

GUIDELINES FOR INTERVENTION

The APA Code of Ethics and general standards in professional practice, education, and research require that psychologists consult with colleagues who are at risk to engage in unethical practice. The practical issue of how and when to intervene depends on the following factors:

1. Your relationship with the colleague who is, or may be, impaired
2. Your professional status vis-à-vis the colleague—for example, a supervisor, professor, or administrator
3. Whether the colleague has come to you for assistance
4. The organizational or institutional setting in which you work and what policies, procedures, and departments exist to help with the situation

The 2002 Ethical Principles of Psychologists and Code of Conduct contain a section that cautions about inquiring about a student's personal adjustment. Section 7.04 reads:

> Student Disclosure of Personal Information. Psychologists do not require students or supervisees to disclose personal information in course- or program-related activities, either orally or in writing, regarding sexual history, history of abuse and neglect, psychological treatment, and relationships with parents, peers, and spouses or significant others except if (1) the program or training facility has clearly identified this requirement in its admissions and program materials or (2) the information is necessary to evaluate or obtain assistance for students whose personal problems could reasonably be judged to be preventing them from performing their training- or professionally related activities in a competent manner or posing a threat to the students or others.

Before acting, examine any organizational policies or guidelines concerning impaired staff. In larger organizations, human resources departments often play a role in such intervention. They may be consulted for advice or for direct assistance. Employee assistance programs also provide guidance that may be of help.

There also may be experts in your local community who can be of assistance. A number of state psychological associations have colleague assistance committees. The Practice Directorate at the APA has such information through staff of the Advisory Committee on Colleague Assistance. The APA effort, in fact, is focused on the creation of state committees to provide assistance to those seeking to intervene or obtain help for colleagues. If there are no readily identifiable local experts and there is no state committee, it is also possible to arrange for help with substance-abusing or alcoholic colleagues through Psychologists Helping Psychologists (PHP), a national organization founded in 1980. It can be contacted through Ann Stone at 703-243-4470 or AnnS@Erols.com.

Another possible resource is the colleague assistance committee of another health profession, such as medicine. These committees can be easily located by contacting the state professional organization. In addition, PHP is connected to International Doctors in Alcoholics Anonymous, which consists of professionals in many fields who are involved in Alcoholics Anonymous. Founded in 1949, IDAA has a yearly convention and can be contacted for resources through its Web site.

Several videotapes that focus on practitioner impairments may prove useful for staff orientation in an organization for assisting an individual professional. *The Journey Back*, produced by a public television station, is available from Video Finder (800-343-4727). Michael F. Myers, MD, has produced two films. *Physicians Living with Depression*, done under the auspices of the Committee on Physician Health, Illness, and Impairment, can be purchased from American Psychiatric Press. Another tape consists of Dr. Myers interviewing a physician who became impaired and had sexual contact with a patient. *Crossing the Boundary: Sexual Issues in the Doctor-Patient Relationship* can be ordered from Dr. Michael Myers at www.michaelfmyers.com or mmyers0609@aol.com

One of the fundamental questions in this area is the manner of intervention. Some circumstances permit a private talk with an impaired practitioner to start things moving, whereas in other cases a more active intervention is necessary. Whenever several professionals confront an impaired psychologist jointly, or involve others, such as family members, there is the potential for greater anger and defensiveness. However, in some circumstances, little else works. Three intervention options (Schwebel et al., 1994) are presented next.

Voluntary Intervention

In some situations, an impaired psychologist calls for help or approaches a colleague. It is essential to remember the importance of follow-through. The fact that a colleague comes in for help does not mean that he or she will take the next step. Sometimes receiving support reduces the person's motivation. Furthermore, it is important to have a competent diagnostician determine what sort of treatment is needed. Professionals often look healthier than they are, and as a result, inadequate treatment may be planned. In the case of professional misconduct, such as sex with clients, it is critical that someone with specialized experience do the assessment and treatment planning to avoid common pitfalls in such cases (Gabbard, 1995).

Confrontive Intervention

In this intervention, an employer or a colleague assistance committee receives a report that a psychologist has a significant problem and has not responded to suggestions that he or she seek help. An investigation is conducted to determine whether such a problem can be documented behaviorally and then a small team of professionals (or, in some instances, a work supervisor) confronts the psychologist with the evidence that has been gathered. A treatment referral has previously been identified, the psychologist is offered a plan of action, and peer pressure is used to try to bring about an agreement to receive help and follow-through.

Comprehensive Intervention

Comprehensive intervention is reserved for situations in which the psychologist's problem is severe, or getting worse, and he or she has not responded to input or suggestions that he or she seek help. It goes beyond the confrontive intervention in that the information-gathering process usually involves discussions with the psychologist's spouse or significant other, and an intervention team is organized that includes a number of key people in the psychologist's life. Prior to the intervention, this group meets and plans the intervention, including some role playing of possible scenarios. The eventual intervention is thus scripted beforehand. The psychologist is then told that if he or she does not enter and complete treatment, specific negative consequences will occur. This can involve job suspension, a report to a licensing body, or a spouse filing for divorce. This approach is coercive and intrusive, and it may bring about an angry response from the psychologist. It should be done with the aid of persons experienced in such work.

SUPPORT AND MONITORING

A major factor in the success of colleague assistance is the degree to which you can help the psychologist start the treatment process. Helping to arrange for work coverage, a medical leave, and identification of affordable treatment covered by insurance are all important. Many such practical problems can sabotage treatment efforts. When someone is in treatment for impairment, maintaining contact in a supportive fashion can be quite helpful. It is also important to monitor compliance, to the degree possible, in order to be able to confront those who attempt to quit before completion.

WORK REENTRY

The main goal of any intervention should be to facilitate a professional assessment and treatment plan for the psychologist. After that, it is important to consult with the assessor concerning job or practice limitations. When it seems that the treatment is completed, there should be an assessment of the situation, including a "return to work" assessment, which specifies things that would help prevent a recurrence and also reduce the risk of any misconduct or relapse.

With alcoholism there may be a requirement that the psychologist attend support groups and also a warning that the smell of alcohol on his or her breath may be sufficient cause for suspension. In the case of substance abuse, random urine testing may be required. It is also likely that more frequent supervisory meetings will be required at first in order to ensure that workload and duties are realistic given the recovery process.

REDUCING LEGAL RISKS

The more confrontive the intervention, the riskier it is. However, despite fears of retaliation for invasion of privacy, such cases appear to be quite rare. The most common mistakes with legal consequences are failures: to consult with human resources personnel; to plan the intervention within the personnel guidelines of a facility; and to review the Americans with Disabilities Act for its applicability to the situation. Psychologists need to be aware that when disputes arise within the family, especially in cases of family dissolution or divorce, well-intentioned helpers can find themselves pawns in intrafamilial power struggles. Thus, it is vital to carefully gather background data and to be clear on what basis you believe the psychologist has a problem.

References and Readings

Advisory Committee on Colleague Assistance. (2006). *Advancing colleague assistance in professional psychology*. CAP Monograph. Washington, DC: American Psychological Association.

Barnett, J. E., & Hillard, D. (2001). Psychologist distress and impairment: The availability, nature and use of colleague assistance programs for psychologists. *Professional Psychology: Research and Practice, 32*(2), 205–210.

Bruyere, S., & O'Keeffe, J. (1994). *Implications of the Americans with Disabilities Act for psychology*. Washington, DC: American Psychological Association.

Gabbard, G. (1995). Transference and countertransference in the psychotherapy of therapists charged with sexual misconduct. *Psychiatric Annals, 25*, 100–105.

Gonsiorek, J. (1995). Assessment and treatment of health care professionals and clergy who sexually exploit patients. In J. Gonsiorek (Ed.), *Breach of trust: Sexual exploitation by health care professionals and clergy* (pp. 225–234). Thousand Oaks, CA: Sage.

O'Connor, M. J. (2001). On the etiology and effective management of professional distress and impairment among psychologists. *Professional Psychology: Research and Practice, 32*(4), 345–350.

Schoener, G. R. (1995). Assessment of professionals who have engaged in boundary violations. *Psychiatric Annals, 25*, 95–99.

Schwebel, M., Skorina, J., & Schoener, G. (1994). *Assisting impaired psychologists: Program development for state psychological associations* (rev. ed.). Washington, DC: American Psychological Association.

Smith, P. L., & Moss. S. B. (2009). Psychologist impairment: What is it, how can it be prevented, and what can be done to address it? *Clinical Psychology: Science and Practice, 16*, 1–15.

Related Topics

Chapter 49, "Managing Sexual Feelings for Patients in Psychotherapy"

Chapter 103, "American Psychological Association's Ethical Principles"

Chapter 108, "Confronting an Unethical Colleague"

Chapter 144, "Psychotherapist Self-Care Checklist"

110 UNDERSTANDING SPECIAL EDUCATION LAW

Linda Wilmshurst

The Education for All Handicapped Children Act (EHA) began in 1975 with the passage of Public Law 94-142 that provided federally funded programs and services for children with disabilities 3 to 21 years of age. In 1990, the name changed to the Individuals with Disabilities Education Act (IDEA). The most recent version of IDEA, signed into law in

December 2004, became effective as of July 1, 2005. The US Department of Education (DOE) has responsibility for overseeing public school compliance with laws pertaining to issues of civil liberties (Americans with Disabilities Act Amendments Act of 2008, Section 504) and educational rights (IDEA, 2004). The Rehabilitation Act and IDEA (2004) are available on the DOE Web site, under the Department of Rehabilitation and Special Services (www2.ed.gov/policy/speced).

AMERICANS WITH DISABILITIES ACT AMENDMENTS ACT (2008) AND SECTION 504

ADAAA and Section 504 include civil rights laws that prohibit discrimination against individuals with disabilities. Under ADAAA, accommodations for public access and employment, such as access ramps and TTY text telephone, enable individuals to perform major life activities (performing manual tasks, seeing, hearing, speaking, breathing, learning, working, reading, and concentrating) and essential job functions (Wilmshurst, 2011). Students employed in community jobs are also covered under ADAAA.

Section 504 protects the rights of individuals with disabilities enrolled in programs and activities funded by the US Department of Education and ensures "free appropriate public education" (FAPE) for each student with a disability and educational opportunities equivalent to their nondisabled peers. Accommodations to the education program (a so-called 504 Plan) are developed by the school's 504 team (relevant school personnel, parent, and child). The 504 team reviews all available information to determine whether the child qualifies for assistance (Wilmshurst & Brue, 2010, p. 247). While any student who qualifies for special education services would also qualify under Section 504, not all students eligible under Section 504 would qualify for services under IDEA. Accommodations to the child's program are provided in the regular education class (e.g., FM audio system, note taker, extra time to complete tasks). Parents and guardians must provide permission for any assessments required to determine need, and they must be provided with appropriate information and timely notice of any significant changes planned for a child's program. If parents do not agree with the identification, evaluation, or placement decisions, the local education agency (LEA) must provide due process hearings.

CIVIL RIGHTS LAWS AND IDEA

The government does not provide direct financial funding to implement either of the civil rights laws; however, the state has fiscal responsibility for Section 504. Although schools may not use funds from IDEA to service children under Section 504, IDEA (2004) states that at the discretion of the school district, up to 15% of the funding for regular education can fund direct services or teaching training for students deemed "at risk" of requiring special education services in the future. While the antidiscrimination laws define a disability as any physical or mental impairment that impedes a major life activity, IDEA defines a disability as one of 13 categories that impede a child's ability to learn. Under IDEA (2004), a child with a disability will only qualify for special education services, if the disability impairs learning.

IDEA 2004

IDEA (2004) governs special education (individualized educational programs [IEPs]) and related services (e.g., speech and language pathology, counseling services, physical and occupational therapy) for children who meet criteria for one of thirteen categories of disabilities: autism, deaf-blindness, deafness, emotional disturbance, hearing impairment, mental retardation, multiple disabilities, orthopedic impairment, other health impairment, specific learning disability, speech or language impairment, traumatic brain injury, and visual impairment, including blindness. IDEA also provides discretionary funds for the state and school district to provide services for children ages 3 through 9 years (or any subset of ages within this minimum and maximum) for children considered at risk who demonstrate developmental delays.

Eligibility procedures, regulations, and services available for children between 3 and 21 years of age are discussed in *Part B* of IDEA (2001), and *Part C* for children under 3 years.

IDEA: Part C—The Infants and Toddlers with Disabilities Program (Birth to 2 Years)

IDEA (2004) provides financial funding for early intervention services to develop multidisciplinary and interagency systems to support the identification and evaluation of children with developmental delays or those at risk for potential developmental delay without such services. IDEA defines a developmental delay (Sec. 635) as 35% or more in one of the five developmental areas or 25% or more in two or more of the five developmental areas. The five different developmental areas include cognitive development (learning), physical development (motor skills), speech and language development (communication skills), social/emotional development, and adaptive functioning (Sec. 632).

Evaluations are conducted by a multidisciplinary team to determine a child's specific needs, at no cost to the parent. Although some services may not be fully funded, usually there is a sliding scale relative to income, or services may fall under Medicaid or other health insurance plans. Programs may be administered by the department of education or the health department.

Under IDEA (Sec. 636), an individualized family services plan (ISFP) will address the evaluation results and recommended services for the child and family, and will be reviewed annually with status reports available at 6-month intervals. Children involved in this program must, by their third birthday, have a plan (IEP or IFSP) implemented. As for the transition from the IFSP to the IEP, the service coordinator has responsibility for scheduling a conference and initiating the transition planning process with the school district.

IDEA 2004: Part B—Special Education Programs and Services for Preschool Children (Age 3 to 5 Years)

According to IDEA (2004), any child who has a disability must be provided with free special education services once he or she turns 3 years of age. Children become eligible for services if they meet three criteria: they have received an individual evaluation (as per the IDEA regulations); they have a disability in one of the thirteen areas, specified by IDEA; and the disability impedes the child's ability to learn (Wilmshurst & Brue, 2010, p. 236).

Preschool children (3 to 5 years of age) qualify for services, if they demonstrate risk through documentation of significant delays in one of the five developmental areas mentioned previously. As of the latest revision of IDEA (2004), older children (5 to 9 years of age) who demonstrate developmental delays may at the discretion of their local educational agency (LEA) also qualify for special education services, but this is not mandatory.

The possibility of expanding the age criteria for developmental delay under IDEA has met with considerable controversy. Proponents in favor cite the lack of reliability of standardized assessments in the early years, while opponents suggest early diagnosis could lead to overidentification of children eligible for special services (Wilmshurst & Brue, 2010, p. 237).

IDEA 2004: Part B—Special Education Programs and Services for School-Age Children

IDEA (2004) stipulates that every child (3 to 21 years of age) who has an identified disability (one of the thirteen categories mentioned earlier) that interferes with his or her ability to learn is legally entitled to a FAPE in the *least restrictive environment* (LRE). Identified children qualify to receive special education and related services from their third birthday, until either receipt of their high school diploma or the end of the school year culminating in their twenty-first birthday, whichever comes earlier.

Parents or teachers can request a comprehensive individual evaluation to determine whether their child qualifies for services under IDEA (Section 614), and the school district will conduct the evaluation, with parental consent, at no cost to the parent. The comprehensive evaluation may include individual assessments of intellectual and academic functioning, review of school reports and records, behavioral rating scales completed by parents and teachers, classroom observations, and interviews. Evaluations must take place in the language in which the child has the best proficiency. Under IDEA (2004), once parent permission is obtained, the school district must complete the assessment and convene an eligibility meeting, within 60 days. To qualify for services, the problems in learning must flow from a reason other than lack of appropriate instruction (in reading or mathematics) or limited English proficiency. If a parent refuses to give consent for evaluation, the school district may engage in due process or mediation; however, if a child is deemed eligible for special education services and parents decline, the district will not be considered in violation of the law for not providing FAPE or developing an IEP.

Procedural Safeguards

Parents must be provided with a copy of the *procedural safeguards* developed by their state educational agency, or school district, outlining the rights of children and their legal guardians. Procedural safeguards must be distributed, at the initial referral for evaluation, upon notification of educational meetings, at the annual IEP meeting, when a complaint is filed, and when a parent requests a copy. Each state has responsibility for producing procedural safeguards that must address issues of notice, consent, records, disciplinary hearings, and due process. Informed parental consent is required before an initial evaluation is conducted, before a child receives special education services, and for any reevaluation conducted while the child is receiving services. If parents do not agree with the evaluation conducted by the school district, they have the right to request an independent evaluation, at the public's expense. In this case, the school district can either conduct a due process hearing or grant the request. However, the school district may conduct a reevaluation without consent, if parents have failed to respond, despite repeated attempts.

Disciplinary issues are dealt with on a case-by-case basis. A student with a disability may be disciplined in the same manner as nondisabled peers for a period of up to 10 school days, including suspensions or alternative settings. If an alternate placement exceeds 10 days, and the behavior is not deemed a function of the disability, the child may then be disciplined in the same manner as nondisabled peers. If the violation is of a severe nature (causing bodily harm; involving drugs or weapons), the child may remain in an alternate educational setting for up to 45 school days without parental permission or a hearing. Parents have the right to appeal this decision.

Educational records must comply with the Family Educational Rights and Privacy Act of 1974 (FERPA), which ensures the rights of parents and students 18 years of age and older to access educational records and to protect the release of information contained in those records. For more information on procedural safeguards, readers are directed to Section 615 of the law (for children 3 to 21 years of age) or Section 639 (infants and toddlers).

IDEA and Issues in Classification

States differ on how they interpret classification and eligibility requirements under IDEA (2004). This can pose difficulties for children who transfer between states because a child may be eligible for services in one state yet not qualify for services in another state. In addition, a clinical practitioner may diagnose a child based on mental health nomenclature such as the current *Diagnostic and Statistical Manual* (*DSM*) of the American Psychiatric Association or the *International Classification of Diseases* (*ICD*) of the World Health Organization criteria, but if the disability does not meet educational criteria (e.g., impairs a child's ability to learn), the child may not qualify for services. Parents often find these discrepancies very frustrating. The problem becomes especially notable for the classification of disabilities that are not based on physical or sensory impairments, such as attention-deficit/hyperactivity disorder (ADHD), intellectual disabilities (formerly mental retardation), specific learning disabilities, and emotional disturbance. MacMillan and Reschly (1998) refer to the classification of these types of disabilities as "judgmental categories" because they rely more on judgment. Although the *DSM, ICD,* and IDEA represent categorical systems of classification (all or nothing), the systems differ on the nature and extent to which these categories are defined.

According to the *DSM* and American Association on Intellectual and Developmental Disabilities (AAIID, 2009), an *intellectual disability* manifests during the developmental period and is represented by an IQ score approximately two standard deviations below the mean (IQ of 70 or below), with accompanying deficits in at least one (AAIID) or two (*DSM*) areas of adaptive functioning. However, IDEA (2004) does not identify a cutoff score for IQ or specify the number of areas of adaptive functioning deficits required for this category, resulting in inconsistencies across states. In their study of eligibility requirements for intellectual disability across 50 states, Bergeron, Floyd, and Shands (2008) found an "upper cutoff ranging from a low of 69 to a high of 80 for initial evaluations, and a high of 85 for re-evaluations" (p. 130). The authors report that variations existed in "terms used to describe this exceptionality, the criteria used to identify an intellectual deficit, and the scores and criteria used to identify adaptive behavior deficiencies" (p. 131).

While an intellectual disability impacts overall cognitive functioning, an individual with a *specific learning disability* is likely to have average overall intelligence but encounter academic difficulties in specific areas such as reading (dyslexia), mathematics (dyscalculia), or written expression. IDEA (2004) defines a specific learning disability as "a disorder in one or more of the basic psychological processes" resulting in "an imperfect ability to think speak, read, write, spell or do mathematical calculations" (Federal Register, 2006: 300.8 (10), p. 46757). According to the *DSM*, a learning disorder is diagnosed when standardized assessments of achievement reveal performance levels substantially below intellectual expectations (discrepancy of more than two standard deviations between achievement and IQ). Up until the last reauthorization of IDEA, this "discrepancy criteria" (a significant difference between IQ and achievement) constituted the cardinal method of identifying a specific learning disability for educational purposes. However, under IDEA (2004) identification procedures (developed by each state) now *must not require* the use of a severe discrepancy between intellectual ability and achievement for determining whether a child has a specific learning disability. Instead, the state *must permit the use* of a process based on the child's response to scientific, research-based intervention and *may permit the use* of other alternative research-based procedures for determining whether a child has a specific learning disability (Federal Register, 300.307 (a), p. 46786). Critics have argued that this "response to intervention" (RTI) alternative is vague, wide open to interpretation, and changes the underlying manner in which learning disabilities have been conceptualized (Kavale, 2005). Proponents of RTI criticize the failure of states to adopt a consistent discrepancy formula (fluctuations from state to state between one and two standard deviations) and suggest the discrepancy criteria represent a failure-based model (Wilmshurst, 2011).

IDEA (2004) defines *emotional disturbance* as a long-lasting condition causing significant educational impairment that may be characterized by problems affecting the following: learning, relationships with peers and teachers, responding appropriately to normal circumstances, pervasive mood of unhappiness or depression, and tendencies to develop physical symptoms in response to personal problems or problems at school. The category includes schizophrenia, but it excludes children with social maladjustment, unless they also qualify as having an emotional disturbance. This category has met with criticism, since it does not distinguish between internalizing and externalizing disorders.

Prior to IDEA (2004), children with ADHD were able to receive accommodations under Section 504 of the Rehabilitation Act of 1973. Currently, children with ADHD can become eligible under the category of other health impairments, which are defined as "having limited strength, vitality or alertness, including a heightened alertness to environment stimuli, that results in limited alertness with respect to the educational environment" (IDEA, 2004). Other disabilities in the same category include acute health problems such as asthma, diabetes, epilepsy, a heart condition, hemophilia, lead poisoning, leukemia, and rheumatic fever. ADHD must adversely affect education and a child's ability to learn in order to warrant special education.

References and Readings

American Association on Intellectual and Developmental Disabilities. (2009). Intellectual disability: Definition, classification and systems of support (11th ed.). Washington, DC: Author.

Bergeron, R., Floyd, R. G., & Shands, E. I. (2008). States' eligibility guidelines for mental retardation: An update and consideration of part scores and unreliability of IQs. *Education and Training in Developmental Disabilities, 43*(1), 123–131.

Kavale, K. A. (2005). Identifying specific learning disability: Is response to intervention the answer. *Journal of Learning Disabilities, 38*, 553–562.

MacMillan, D., & Reschly, D. J. (1998). Over-representation of minority students. The case for greater specificity or reconsideration of the variables examined. *Journal of Special Education, 19*, 239–253.

Wilmshurst, L., & Brue, A. W. (2010). *The complete guide to special education* (2nd ed.). San Francisco, CA: Jossey-Bass.

Wilmshurst, L. (2011). *Child and adolescent psychopathology: A casebook* (2nd ed.). Thousand Oaks, CA: Sage.

PART IX
Forensic Practice

111 UNDERSTANDING INVOLUNTARY PSYCHIATRIC HOSPITALIZATION

Stuart A. Anfang and Paul S. Appelbaum

ADULTS

Criteria

The state's power to hospitalize involuntarily is based on a combination of two rationales: parens patriae (the state caring for those incapable of caring for themselves) and "police power" (the state's obligation to protect the public safety). Initially, the rationale for commitment was treatment oriented, hospitalizing mentally ill persons who were deemed to be in need of care. By the late 1960s and early 1970s, states moved to dangerousness-based criteria for civil commitment, permitting the involuntary hospitalization of only those patients who were dangerous to themselves or to others. By the end of the 1970s, every state had adopted dangerousness-based criteria for involuntary hospitalization, typically with judicial procedures and protections similar to criminal proceedings.

The dangerousness-based criteria vary across states, but they usually require (1) the presence of mental illness (in many states this does not include mental retardation, dementia, or substance abuse, in the absence of other psychiatric illness) and (2) dangerousness.

Dangerousness typically includes (a) danger to self (physical harm); (b) danger to others (physical harm, not usually psychological harm or harm to property); or (c) grave disability (severe inability to care for one's minimal survival needs in the community). There is variability across states regarding the definition of dangerousness—including how imminent or overt the risk of harm must be. Some court decisions and statutes require that involuntary hospitalization be the "least restrictive alternative" before allowing a commitment, raising a question of whether the state is obligated to create less restrictive alternatives, such as community residences. The creation of such alternatives may be required in some circumstances by the US Supreme Court's decision in *Olmstead v. L.C.* (1999), though such requirements may be limited by constraints on financial and programmatic resources.

In recent years, several states have broadened the definition of dangerousness, often expanding the "grave disability" standard to include the prospect of severe deterioration leading to predicted dangerousness. Other states have expanded their commitment criteria to include incompetence, disabling illness, or need for treatment. Future litigation may challenge the constitutionality of these statutes, which appear to move away from strict dangerousness criteria. Clinicians should be familiar with the statutory criteria in their jurisdictions, as well as the relevant regulations and court decisions (case law) regarding civil commitment.

Critiques of the dangerousness standard usually include one or more of three basic arguments: (1) the current system makes it difficult to obtain involuntary treatment for patients who are not overtly dangerous but are desperately in need of care; (2) dangerousness is notoriously difficult for clinicians to predict accurately; and (3) basing commitment on dangerousness, particularly dangerousness to others, alters the character of the mental health system, shifting its mission from providing treatment to a quasi-police function. A substantial literature exists documenting the difficulty that clinicians have in predicting future harm to self or others. Despite studies suggesting that predictive accuracy regarding violence to others is improved when structured assessment tools, such as the HCR-20 or the Violence Risk Assessment Guide (VRAG), are used, most clinicians continue to rely on clinical evaluation. An approach termed "structured professional judgment," which allows data from structured assessments to be taken into account in the clinical decision-making process—without superseding it—appears promising and may be more palatable to clinicians. Unfortunately, similarly well-validated tools for the assessment of dangerousness to self are lacking.

Despite considerable and often impassioned debate, the empirical data generally suggest that, in practice, more restrictive commitment criteria appear to have little impact on the qualitative and quantitative characteristics of the civilly committed population as a whole. The system generally appears to allow involuntary hospitalization for those mentally ill patients clearly in need of treatment, regardless of the precise criteria of the dangerousness-based standards. The "grave disability" standard—or the inability to provide for one's basic survival needs in the community—typically allows for such clinical flexibility.

Procedures

In most states, civil commitment procedures include many of the protections associated with criminal trials. These often encompass such safeguards as timely notice of the allegations that may result in commitment and of the respondent's due process rights, including the right to an attorney; the right to a prompt judicial hearing, sometimes including the right to jury trial; the right to remain silent when examined by a psychiatrist or at trial; and placing on the state the burden of proving that the respondent meets the commitment criteria. Jurisdictions differ in the standard of proof required, ranging from an intermediate "clear and convincing evidence" standard (the minimum constitutionally acceptable standard) to the more stringent "beyond a reasonable doubt" standard required for criminal prosecutions.

Nearly every state allows for emergency commitment based on a physician's or other mental health professional's certification of mental illness and dangerousness; this commitment can typically last from 48 hours to 10–14 days, with most statutes allowing 3–5 days, before requiring the scheduling of a judicial hearing for further commitment. Various jurisdictions also allow for emergency commitment based on a judge's order (bench commitment), the certification of a police officer, or approval of another designated official. All mental health clinicians who work with potentially dangerous patients should be familiar with the commitment procedures and mechanisms within their jurisdictions. Attorneys knowledgeable about mental health law can be an invaluable resource, as can forensically trained clinicians. Clinicians in all jurisdictions should be aware of the need to alert the patient to the limits of confidentiality—that clinical interview information may be disclosed in the judicial commitment hearing. Some states require such a warning and allow the patient the right to refuse to participate further.

In addition to describing the appropriate procedures and criteria, most state commitment statutes provide immunity to mental health clinicians who act in good faith when seeking to hospitalize a patient involuntarily. In all states, if the clinician can document a commitment decision based on appropriate clinical judgment within the professional standard of care, he or she can feel reasonably safe from malpractice liability for improper commitment (although actual verdicts will be based on the particular facts and circumstances of the situation). As with all complex and difficult clinical decisions, consultation with colleagues is often an important tool—both for guidance and for risk-management purposes.

Involuntary Outpatient Commitment

Over the past 25 years, involuntary outpatient commitment (IOC) has gained increasing attention as a possible alternative to inpatient commitment in systems with declining inpatient resources. The large majority of states (44 by 2010) have laws explicitly permitting some form of outpatient commitment, although there is considerable local and regional variation in criteria and procedures, and in how commonly the option is used.

The most recent recommendations from the American Psychiatric Association (see Gerbasi, Bonnie, & Binder, 2000) regarding statutory guidelines for IOC include evidence that a person (1) suffers from a severe mental illness; (2) is likely, without treatment, to suffer a relapse that would render the patient a danger to self or others or unable to care for self in the foreseeable future; (3) is unlikely to seek or comply with needed treatment; and (4) has a reasonable prospect of responding to the proposed treatment. Many state legislatures have included several of these provisions when writing their statutes.

Outpatient commitment laws and practices generally follow one of three basic patterns: (a) conditional release for involuntarily hospitalized patients; (b) "less restrictive" alternative to hospitalization for patients who meet inpatient commitment criteria; or (c) alternative for patients not meeting criteria for inpatient commitment, but at risk for severe decompensation without treatment. This last model, often called *preventive commitment* or *predicted deterioration*, has generated considerable debate because it is seen as a move further away from an "imminent dangerousness" standard toward a need-for-treatment approach.

Mental health clinicians should be familiar with the availability of IOC in their jurisdictions and with the range of possible options and resources. Even as state legislatures rush to write IOC statutes, considerable debate continues over the efficacy and utility of these outpatient commitment programs, with a limited but growing number of empirical studies. Studies suggest improved clinical outcomes for patients under IOC, including increased compliance with treatment, reduced rates of hospitalization and arrest, and less violence—provided that adequate resources for treatment and support are funded and available. However, merely enacting an IOC statute without providing sufficient, dedicated public mental health resources to support committed patients, has limited effect.

CHILDREN

Criteria and Procedures

Constitutional due process rights for children in the juvenile justice system were first recognized by the US Supreme Court in 1967 (In re *Gault*). Children were held to be entitled to due process protections similar to those of adults in criminal proceedings, including the right to counsel, the right to written notice of charges, the right to cross-examine witnesses, and the privilege against self-incrimination. But the momentum to apply adult-type protections to hospitalization of juveniles stalled when, in 1979, the US Supreme Court (*Parham v. JR*) upheld the right of a parent or guardian to admit a minor to a psychiatric hospital without a judicial hearing. In the 1980s, many commentators pointed to alarmingly high admission rates, especially in private for-profit psychiatric facilities, as evidence of a pattern in which troublesome juveniles without clear psychiatric illnesses were being hospitalized, often as an alternative to the juvenile justice system. As managed care transformed inpatient mental health care in the 1990s, this pattern decreased in frequency. Except in state facilities for severely ill children and adolescents, short-term hospitalization is the rule.

Given the relatively low constitutional "minimum" required under *Parham*, states have diverse approaches to the issue of child hospitalization. Involuntary civil commitment without the consent of a parent or guardian is rare and typically follows guidelines similar to those for adult civil commitment. More common is the "voluntary" hospitalization by a parent or guardian (including a state social service agency) without the consent of the minor. States range from the minimum of allowing a parent to admit a child without any administrative or judicial review to requiring a formal judicial hearing with specified due process protections for all admissions. Some states have more extensive regulations covering public psychiatric facilities and minors who are wards of the state. Typically, states require the presence of a mental illness needing treatment, the availability of such treatment through the hospital, and evidence that the hospital is the least restrictive setting available. The American Psychological Association and the American Academy of Child and Adolescent Psychiatry have issued suggested statutory guidelines.

Most states have provisions for the minor to appeal the hospitalization, requesting an adversarial judicial hearing. For adolescents between 13 and 18, states provide varying procedures, allowing minors of a certain age to sign in or out of a hospital voluntarily, without the approval of a parent or guardian. Mental health clinicians should be familiar with the statutory requirements and case law in their jurisdictions. Consultation with an attorney familiar with child mental health issues or a clinician with forensic expertise is helpful.

GENERAL CLINICAL ISSUES

- *Predicting dangerousness.* Clinicians should be familiar with relevant risk factors, base rates, and both external and internal factors that influence the potential for violence. They should be aware of the leading structured tools for dangerousness assessment and consider using them in appropriate cases. Risks, resources, and benefits must be balanced in a clinically sensitive and sophisticated decision process. Corroborative clinical data are invaluable.
- *Maintaining a therapeutic alliance with a patient coerced to receive care.* Patients should be involved in the decision process as much as possible. As treatment restores the patient's ability to assess his or her own functioning, the patient and clinician can aim to shape the experience into one that enhances the patient's responsibility, self-respect, and therapeutic rapport.
- *Resolving conflicts between legal mandates and ethical imperatives in the commitment setting.* Whereas legal standards suggest a rigidly defined set of criteria, ethical and clinical imperatives often encourage the clinician to err on the side of caution to protect the patient and others. Clinicians must be sensitive to both factors and strive for a balanced, thoughtful approach to decision making in cases of involuntary hospitalization.
- *When in doubt, consult.* Consultation with clinical colleagues can be valuable to establish and document a reasonable thought process and good faith efforts to meet the professional standard of care. Similarly, procedural questions/concerns may be discussed with a hospital lawyer or other attorney familiar with mental health law in that jurisdiction.

References and Readings

American Psychological Association. (1984). *A model act for the mental health treatment of minors*. Washington, DC: Author.

Anfang, S. A., & Appelbaum, P. S. (2006). Civil commitment—the American experience. *Israeli Journal of Psychiatry and Related Sciences, 43*, 209–218.

Appelbaum, P. S. (1994). *Almost a revolution: Mental health law and the limits of change*. New York: Oxford University Press.

Gerbasi, J. B., Bonnie, R. J., & Binder, R. L. (2000). Resource document on mandatory outpatient treatment. *Journal of the American Academy of Psychiatry and the Law, 28*, 127–144.

Melton, G. B., Petrila, J., Poythress, N. G., & Slobogin, C. (2007). *Psychological evaluations for the courts: A handbook for mental health professionals and lawyers* (3rd ed.). New York: Guilford Press.

Monahan, J., Steadman, H., Silver, E., Appelbaum, P. S., Robbins, P. C., Mulvey, E. P., Banks, S. (2001). *Rethinking risk assessment: The MacArthur Study of Mental Disorder and Violence*. New York: Oxford University Press.
Otto, R. K., & Douglas, K. S. (2010). *Handbook of violence risk assessment*. New York: Routledge.
Swartz, M. S. (2010). Special Section on Assisted Outpatient Treatment in New York State. *Psychiatric Services, 61*, 967–1000.

Related Topics

Chapter 103, "American Psychological Association's Ethical Principles"
Chapter 112, "Applying Standards for Use of Physical Restraint and Seclusion"

112 APPLYING STANDARDS FOR USE OF PHYSICAL RESTRAINT AND SECLUSION

Thomas Graf

Regulations and practice standards for the use of physical restraint and seclusion have been changing since 1998. The terms *restraint* and *seclusion* will be used interchangeably unless indicated. Providers now face more legal and financial accountability for injury from restraints. In 2008 the Center for Medicare and Medicaid Services (CMS) designated severe injury from restraint as medical error. Workforce turnover is higher in restraint-using facilities, which is another reason for creating work and treatment environments that actively reduce the need for restraint. Some patients will still require restraint, like actively psychotic and dangerous patients. However, federal legislation and standards for psychiatric facilities have increased patient protection from unnecessary restraint, in particular for children, youth, and the elderly. In the school setting, there have been similar regulations at the state level.

RECENT REGULATIONS AND CHANGES OF STANDARDS

Physical restraint has been an essential part in reducing safety risks in violent and self-harming patients who are in psychiatric care. Restraints can be human (such as a therapeutic or protective hold), can use mechanical devices (e.g., wrist restraint, jacket vest, or papoose), or consist of sedating drugs. Restraint has not only been used for reducing imminent risk for harm to self or others but also for control, convenience, and retaliation. For an overview of changes in laws and regulations in regard to restraint and seclusion, see also Luna (2001). In 1987, the Nursing Home Reform Act was passed. Since then, freedom from unwarranted restraint has been one of the rights monitored in the oversight of care facilities for the elderly and mentally disabled adult. However, there was no federal or state monitoring of serious injury and death as a result of restraint, especially in psychiatric inpatient or residential treatment. In 1998, the Hartford Courant released a five-part investigative report. It documented the alarming number of restraint-related deaths that occurred in psychiatric treatment facilities across the United States (Weiss, Megan, Blint, & Altimari, 1998). The newspaper conducted a 50-state survey in mental health facilities, mental retardation facilities, and group homes and documented at least 142 deaths during the preceding decade, mostly through asphyxiation. This contributed to Congress passing the Children's Health Act in October 1999, which legislated restrictions in the use of restraint in residential treatment and all psychiatric facilities that received federal or state funds like Medicaid (Children's Health Act, 2000). In children and adolescents, only personal restraint is permitted, and only in emergency situations to ensure the immediate physical safety of the resident or others. Both the use of chemical and mechanical restraint is prohibited. Use of restraint in correctional and educational settings, including schools, wilderness camps, or prisons, has not been regulated on the federal level. State laws have been passed that regulated school district use of restraints. Most school districts now have a restraint policy, which typically stipulates that restraint is used only if there is imminent danger to self or others, alternative and less restrictive containment has been tried but failed, staff is trained in safe restraint, and a physician has ordered the use of mechanical, medication, or physical restraint. Most school districts post those on their Web sites, like the Cambridge Public School District.

The Joint Commission on Accreditation of Healthcare Organizations (JCAHO) issues practice standards for health and psychiatric care facilities. In 1999, JCAHO issued restrictive and protective guidelines in regard to restraint and seclusion of patients of all ages. Implementation and documentation of compliance with JCAHO standards is necessary for all accredited organizations, thus leading to changes in practice.

In 2001, the Centers for Medicare & Medicaid Services (CMS) released their interim final rule regarding restraint and seclusion (Interim Final Rule, 2001). This regulation applies to patients under the age of 21 years who receive inpatient or residential psychiatric treatment. In contrast, JCAHO standards apply to any accredited medical setting in which emotional or behavioral problems require use of restraint, and they apply to patients of all ages.

CMS STANDARDS

Injury and death from restraint has been included in a list of "Never Events" by CMS (Substance Abuse and Mental Health Administration, 2011). CMS and most insurers are no longer going to pay treatments related to serious disability acquired during hospitalizations. One of the 28 "Never Events" is related to use of restraint or bedrails. Institutions also risk increased liability premiums and exclusion from insurances with such events.

What follows is a summary of the CMS standards in regard to restraint (Interim Final Rule, 2001). Exempt conditions of physical containment are also discussed.

- The restraint and seclusion policy of a facility must be posted. Upon admission to a facility, the patient's guardian must review the policy and indicate consent by signature.
- Restraint and seclusion can only be used to ensure the patient's safety or the safety of others during an emergency safety situation. Imminent danger must be present.
- Restraint must end when the emergency safety situation is over.
- The least restrictive intervention should be used. Only a licensed independent practitioner (LIP; i.e., physician, nurse practitioner, or physician assistant, depending on state law) may give the order for carrying out restraint or seclusion.

A LIP must perform a face-to-face evaluation of the patient no more than 1 hour after the restraint or seclusion is initiated. Ongoing monitoring of physical and psychological condition is required and must be documented. After removal from restraint, immediate examination by an LIP is required. The patient's legal guardian must be notified of the situation that led to the use of restraint or seclusion as soon as possible. Two debriefing sessions must be conducted after the use of restraint or seclusion. One of them is between the patient and the staff involved, and one is only for the staff involved.

- All deaths have to be reported to the regional CMS office.
- All staff must have appropriate training in the use of nonphysical interventions, the safe use of restraint, identification of factors that lead to emergency situations, and CPR. Documentation of each staff member's training must be maintained and available for review by a state survey agency.

The following holding situations are not regarded as physical restraint or requiring a physician order:

- Briefly holding without undue force a patient for the purpose of comforting him or her.
- Holding a patient's hand or arm to safely escort him or her.

JCAHO DEFINITIONS AND STANDARDS

The JCAHO's regulation regarding restraint for behavioral health reasons applies whether the patient is in a behavioral health care (psychiatric hospital or residential treatment) or a general hospital setting. For example, if a patient on a postsurgical unit is restrained because he or she tries to assault another patient, the behavioral health standard applies (TX.7.1 – TX.7.4, JCAHO, 2002).

A second set of regulations applies to restraint or seclusion used for medical/surgical care reasons. That restraint aims at directly supporting medical healing, such as preventing a patient from trying to walk on an injured leg or preventing the removal of an IV or feeding tube. (TX.7.5, JCAHO, 2002). I will not elaborate on the medical/surgical care standards as they are primarily relevant for nurses and physicians. Furthermore, there are more detailed standards regarding the medical assessment of patients during the process of restraint which are also not reviewed. See Orhon (2002) for a review of restraint standards from a nursing perspective. Orhon (2002) also compares JCAHO and CMS standards from a general perspective.

- Restraint is defined as the direct application of physical force to a person, with or without the individual's permission, with the purpose of restricting freedom of movement (JCAHO, 2002).
- Seclusion is defined as the involuntary confinement of a person in a locked room. It is less restrictive than physical restraints because it allows an individual to move about.
- Patients in restraint and/or seclusion require continuous personal monitoring through observation and have to be assessed every 15 minutes for injury, health, psychological status, and readiness for the restraint or seclusion to be discontinued. A patient in a physical hold must have a second staff person observe the patient.
- The time limitations for an order for restraint or seclusion are as follows: 4 hours for patients 18 years and older, 2 hours for children 9 to 17 years, and 1 hour for children under 9 years.
- The JCAHO also requires prompt notification of the patient's family or guardian when restraint or seclusion is initiated. Extended episodes of restraint or seclusion (more than 12 hours) or multiple episodes (two or more in 24 hours) require notification of the organization's clinical leadership.
- The JCAHO's standard for long-term care and assisted living in adults includes the right to a restraint-free environment. Past deaths in long-term care during or after restraint were associated with mechanical and chemical restraints, used for long periods of time and without monitoring of patients' well-being (United States General Accounting Office, 1999). The restraint standards aim at increasing dignity and independence in the long-term care population.

EXCEPTIONS TO THE APPLICABILITY OF THE BEHAVIORAL HEALTH CARE RESTRAINT AND SECLUSION STANDARDS

The JCAHO standards for restraint and seclusion (2002) do not apply to the following:

- The use of restraint associated with acute and postoperative medical or surgical care
- Holding or physically redirecting a child, without the child's permission, for 30 minutes or less—staff involved in holding has to be trained in physical restraint and seclusion.
- Time-out, which consists of removing a child from the immediate environment and restricting him or her to an unlocked quiet room for 30 minutes or less in order to regain self-control. The child or adolescent may not be physically prevented from leaving the time-out area. These restrictions have to be consistent with the unit's rules and the patient's treatment plan.
- To forensic restrictions and restrictions imposed by correction authorities for security purposes. However, use of restraint in the clinical care of a patient under forensic or correction restrictions is not surveyed under these standards.
- The use of protective equipment such as helmets
- Physical escorts—the use of restraint with patients who are severely developmentally delayed and receive treatment through formal behavior management programs that target intractable, severely self-injurious, or injurious behaviors

COMPARING CMS AND JCAHO STANDARDS

CMS requires continuous in-person monitoring only when patients are concurrently in restraint, whereas JCAHO requires continuous monitoring. The CMS rule of face-to-face evaluation by an LIP within 1 hour of initiation of restraint or seclusion is more stringent than the JCAHO rule of within 4 hours. However, the JCAHO requires organizations to comply with the CMS rule because organizations must meet federal and state regulations in order to meet JCAHO's requirements.

Compared to the CMS standards, the JCAHO standards are more specific, also in defining situations exempt from restraint and seclusion standards. This writer is not qualified to give legal advice about which standards may take precedent and a qualified attorney should be consulted if more clarification is needed. Furthermore, the reviewed CMS and JCAHO standards were current as of July 2011, but changes should be monitored as they are announced by CMS and JCAHO.

STAFF TRAINING

The JCAHO "Standard TX 7.1.2—Staff Training and Competence" (2002) outlined requirements for competence and training of staff who conduct seclusion or restraint. These standards also comply with CMS standards. Direct care staff should be trained in and understand the following:

- The underlying causes of threatening behaviors exhibited by the patients they serve
- Aggressive behavior that is related to a patient's medical condition and not related to his or her emotional condition, for example, threatening behavior that may result from delirium in fevers or from hypoglycemia
- How their own behaviors can affect the behaviors of the patients they serve
- The use of de-escalation, mediation, self-protection, and techniques, such as time-out
- Recognize signs of physical distress in patients who are being held, restrained, or secluded
- Competence in the safe use of restraint, including physical holding techniques, take-down procedures, and the application and removal of mechanical restraints

Staff-initiated physical contact is the most frequent precursor to patient restraint. Direct care staff must be able to de-escalate potentially aggressive patients without touch, as well as apply physical control strategies safely.

Both JCAHO and CMS require training documentation.

CLINICAL APPLICATION OF RESTRAINT AND SECLUSION

The reviewed seclusion and restraint standards have been mandated to protect patients' physical and mental integrity. However, effective reduction of restraint also depends on correct diagnosis and treatment of a patient's condition as it contributes to aggression against self or/and others. Luiselli, Bastien, and Putnam (1998) identified contextual variables associated with restraint and seclusion on a child and adolescent psychiatric inpatient unit. They found that staff-initiated physical contact often (34% of instances) precipitated restraint or seclusion and occurred in the context of patients refusing to leave or enter the quiet room. They recommended the use of closed-door seclusion time-out to reduce the avoidance and repeated leaving which precipitated the restraints. Another finding was that mechanical restraints occurred for long periods of time, in the absence of clear release criteria. Luiselli et al. point out that "contingent procedures such as time-out and physical holding are most effective when they are of brief duration and include a differential release criterion. These guidelines ensure that the person who receives time-out learns to end the procedure rapidly by ceasing negative behaviors and achieving a more relaxed state" (p. 153). Luiselli et al. recommended that occurrence of restraint can be reduced through identification of patient-specific triggers. CMS and the JCAHO recommended that to be part of direct care staff competence. However, Luiselli et al. emphasize linking diagnosis to treatment in a formal treatment plan, to assess the nature, contexts, and consequences of challenging behaviors, and to identify how restraint can reduce aggression under specific circumstances. A behavioral assessment is one way to determine a patient's condition as it contributes to injurious behavior, which lends itself well to determine the effectiveness of restraint procedures. The use of restraints in the treatment of retractable, self-injurious behaviors in the developmentally delayed is exempt from JCAHO's restraint and seclusion standards. However, even there, an individualized treatment plan is ethically imperative, in that restraints should be used effectively to reduce the future need for restraints. Fisher, Piazza, Bowman, Hanley, and Adelinis (1997) describe the effective use of restraint fading to control injurious and self-injurious behaviors in such a manner in three profoundly mentally retarded individuals.

References and Readings

Children's Health Act, Public Law No. 106-310, § 3207, 114 Stat. 1178 (2000).

Fisher, W. W., Piazza, C. C., Bowman, L., Hanley, G., & Adelinis, J. D. (1997). Direct and collateral effects of restraints and restraint fading. *Journal of Applied Behavior Analysis, 30*(1), 105–120.

Interim Final Rule, Use of Restraint and Seclusion in Psychiatric Residential Treatment Facilities Providing Inpatient Psychiatric Services to Individuals Under Age 21, 42 C.F.R. § 441 and 483. (2001). Retrieved March 2003, from www.access.gpo.gov/su_docs/aces/aces140.html

Joint Commission on Accreditation of Healthcare Organizations. (2002). *Comprehensive accreditation manual for hospitals: The official handbook*. Oakbrook Terrace, IL: Author.

Luiselli, J., Bastien, J., & Putnam, R. (1998). Behavioral assessment and analysis of mechanical restraint utilization on a psychiatric, child and adolescent inpatient setting. *Behavioral Interventions, 13*(3), 147–155.

Luna, J. (2001). *Limiting the use of physical restraint and seclusion in psychiatric residential treatment facilities for patients under 21*. Retrieved March 2003, from University of Houston, Law Center Web site. www.law.uh.edu/healthlawperspectives/Mental/010829Limiting.html

Orhon, A. J. (2002). *Of human bondage: Alternatives to restraint*. Retrieved March 5, 2003 from Nurses Learning Network Web Site 216.155.28.162/nurse/courses/nurseweek/nw0187/c1/index.htm

Substance Abuse and Mental Health Services Administration (SAMSHA). (2011). *The business case for preventing and reducing restraint and seclusion use*. HHS Publication No. (SMA)

11-4632. Rockville, MD: Substance Abuse and Mental Health Services Administration.

US General Accounting Office. (1999, September). *Mental health: Improper restraint or seclusion use places people at risk.* Retrieved March 2003, from www.gao.gov/archive/1999/he99176.pdf

Weiss, E., Megan, K., Blint, D., & Altimari, D. (1998, October 11–15). Deadly restraint: An investigative report. *The Hartford Courant* .

Related Topics

Chapter 103, "American Psychological Association's Ethical Principles"

Chapter 106, "Minimizing Your Legal Liability Risk Following Adverse Events or Patient Threats"

Chapter 111, "Understanding Involuntary Psychiatric Hospitalization: Adults and Children"

113 UNDERSTANDING LEGAL TERMS OF SPECIAL INTEREST IN MENTAL HEALTH PRACTICE

Gerald P. Koocher

A list of legal terms holding special interest for mental health practitioners follows, but first I focus on three commonly confused terms: *privacy, confidentiality,* and *privilege.* At least part of the confusion is related to the fact that in particular situations these terms may have narrow legal meanings quite distinct from broader traditional meanings attached by mental health practitioners. The distinctions between these three oft-confused terms can prove critical to understanding a variety of ethical and legal problems.

- *Privacy* (a constitutional guaranty and personal value addressed in the Fourth, Fifth, and Fourteenth Amendments to the US Constitution) refers to the right of individuals to decide about how much of their thoughts, feelings, or personal information should be shared with others. Privacy has often been considered essential to ensure human dignity and freedom of self-determination and to preclude unreasonable governmental intrusions into individuals' lives.
- *Confidentiality* refers to a general standard of professional conduct that obliges one not to discuss information about a client with anyone else, absent proper authorization. Confidentiality may also be based in statutes (i.e., laws enacted by legislatures such as HIPAA), regulations (i.e., rules promulgated by the executive branch of government), or case law (i.e., interpretations of laws by the courts). When cited as an ethical principle, confidentiality implies an explicit contract or promise not to reveal anything about a client, except under certain circumstances agreed to by both parties.
- *Privilege* (or privileged communication) is a legal term describing certain specific types of relationships that enjoy protection from disclosure in legal proceedings. Privilege is

granted by law and belongs to the client in the relationship. Normal court rules provide that anything relative and material to the issue at hand can and should be admitted as evidence. Where privilege exists, however, the client is protected from having the covered communications revealed without explicit permission. If the client waives this privilege, the psychologist may be compelled to testify on the nature and specifics of the material discussed. The client is usually not permitted to waive privilege selectively. In most courts, once a waiver is given, it covers all of the relevant privileged material.

An important point: *Privilege is not automatic.* Traditionally, privilege has been extended to attorney–client, husband–wife, physician–patient, and priest–penitent relationships. Some jurisdictions now extend privilege to psychologist–client or psychotherapist–client relationships, but the actual laws vary widely, and it is incumbent on each psychologist to know the statutes in force for his or her practice. In 1996, the US Supreme Court took up this issue based on conflicting rulings in different federal appellate court districts in the case of *Jaffe v. Redmond* and upheld privilege between a psychotherapist/social worker and her client.

GENERAL LEGAL TERMINOLOGY

Abandonment: Unilateral termination of a psychotherapist–patient relationship by the psychotherapist without the patient's consent at a time when the patient requires continuing mental health care and without the psychologist's making arrangements for appropriate continuation and follow-up care.

Affidavit: Sworn statement that is usually written.

Agency: Relationship between persons in which one party authorizes the other to act for or represent that party.

Allegation: Statement that a party expects to be able to prove.

Answer: Defendant's written response to a complaint.

Appeal: Process by which a decision of a lower court is brought for review before a court of higher jurisdiction. The party bringing the appeal is the *appellant*. The party against whom the appeal is taken is the *appellee*.

Assault: Intentional and unauthorized act of placing another in apprehension of immediate bodily harm.

Battery: Intentional and unauthorized touching of a person, directly or indirectly without consent. For example, a surgical procedure performed upon a person without express or implied consent constitutes a battery.

Causation: Existence of a connection between the act or omission of the defendant and the injury suffered by the plaintiff. In a suit for negligence, the issue of causation usually requires proof that the plaintiff's harm resulted proximately from the negligence of the defendant.

Cause of action: Set of facts that give rise to a legal right to redress at law.

Civil action: Action invoking a judicial trial either at law or in equity, which is not criminal in nature.

Common law: Body of rules and principles based on Anglo-Saxon law, derived from usage and customs, and developed from court decisions based on such law. It is distinguished from statutes enacted by legislatures and all other types of law.

Complaint: Initiatory pleading on the part of the plaintiff in filing a civil lawsuit. Its purpose is to give the defendant notice of the general alleged fact constituting the cause of action.

Consent: Voluntary act by which one person agrees to allow another person to do something. *Express consent* is that directly and unequivocally given, either orally or in writing. *Implied consent* is that manifested by signs, actions, or facts or by inaction and silence, which raises a presumption that the consent has been given. It may be implied from conduct (implied-in-fact), for example, when someone rolls up his or her sleeve and extends an arm for vein puncture, or by the circumstances (implied-in-law), for example, in the case of an unconscious person in an emergency situation.

Contributory negligence or comparative negligence: Affirmative defense to a successful action against a defendant where the plaintiff's concurrent negligence contributed to his or her own injury, even though the defendant's actions may also have been responsible for the injury.

Damages: Money receivable through judicial order by a plaintiff sustaining harm, impairment, or loss to his or her person or property as the result of the accidental, intentional, or negligent act of another. *Compensatory damages* are intended to compensate the injured party for the injury sustained and nothing more. *Special damages* are the actual out-of-pocket losses incurred by the plaintiff, such as psychotherapy expenses and lost earnings, and are a part of the *compensatory damages. Nominal damages* are awarded to demonstrate that a legally cognizable wrong has been committed. *Punitive damages* are awarded to punish a defendant who has acted maliciously or in reckless disregard of the plaintiff's rights. (Some states do not allow punitive damages except in actions for wrongful death of the plaintiff's decedent.)

Defamation: Willful and malicious communication, either written (libel) or spoken (slander), that is false; injures the reputation or character of another.

Defendant: Person against whom a civil or criminal action is brought.

Deposition: Testimony of a witness or party taken before trial, consisting of an oral, sworn, out-of-court statement.

Directed verdict: Verdict for the defendant that a jury returns as directed by the judge, usually based on the inadequacy of the evidence presented by the plaintiff as a matter of law.

Discovery: Pretrial activities of the parties to litigation to learn of evidence known to the opposing party or various witnesses and therefore to minimize surprises at the time of trial.

Due process: Course of legal proceedings according to those rules and principles that have been established in systems of jurisprudence for the enforcement and protection of private rights. It often means simply a fair hearing.

Expert witness: Person who has special training, knowledge, skill, or experience in an area relevant to resolution of the legal dispute and who is allowed to offer an opinion as testimony in court.

Fraud: Intentionally misleading another person in a manner that causes legal injury to that person.

Guardian: Person appointed by a court to manage the affairs and protect the interests of another who is adjudged incompetent by reason of age, physical status, or mental status and is thereby unable to manage his or her own affairs.

Guardian ad litem: Person appointed as a guardian for a particular purpose, interval, or matter. Functioning in this role may involve undertaking investigations and issuing reports to the court (e.g., as in child custody matters). The court order appointing the guardian ad litem should specify the nature of the role and duties.

Hypothetical question: Form of question put to a witness, usually an expert witness, in which things that counsel claims are or will be proved are stated as a factual supposition and the witness is asked to respond, state, or explain the conclusion based on the assumptions and questions.

Immunity: In civil law, protection given certain individuals (personal immunity) or groups (institutional immunity) that may shield them from liability for certain acts or legal relationships. Ordinarily, the individual may still be sued, because immunity can be raised only as an affirmative defense to the complaint, that is, after a lawsuit has been filed.

Incompetency: Inability of a person to manage his or her own affairs because of mental or physical infirmities. If this status or condition is legally determined, a guardian will usually be appointed to manage the person's affairs.

Indemnity: Agreement whereby a party guarantees reimbursement for possible losses.

Independent contractor: Person who agrees with a party to undertake the performance of a task for which the person is not expected to be under the direct supervision or control of the party. Ordinarily this arrangement and relationship shield the party from liability for negligent acts of the independent contractor that occurred during the performance of the work. For example, a psychological consultant is an independent contractor for whose negligent acts the attending psychologist is not liable.

Informed consent: Patient's voluntary agreement to accept treatment based on an awareness of the nature of his or her disease, the material risks and benefits of the proposed treatment, the alternative treatments and risks, and the choice of no treatment at all.

Injunction: Court order commanding a person or entity to perform or to refrain from performing a certain act or otherwise be found in contempt of court.

Interrogatories: Written questions propounded by one party to another before trial as part of the pretrial discovery procedures.

Intestate: One who dies leaving no valid will.

Invasion of privacy: Violation of a person's right to be left alone and free from unwarranted publicity and intrusions.

Joint and several liability: Several persons who share the liability for the plaintiff's injury can be found liable individually or together.

Libel: Defamation of a person's reputation or character by any type of publication, including pictures or written word.

Malice: Performance of a wrongful act without just cause or excuse, with an intent to inflict an injury or under such circumstances that the law will imply an evil intent.

Malicious prosecution: Countersuit by the original defendant to collect damages that have resulted to the original defendant from a civil suit filed maliciously and without probable cause. Ordinarily, such prosecution (what is it?) may not be brought until the initial suit against the original defendant has been judicially decided in favor of the defendant.

Malpractice: Professional negligence. Failure to meet a professional standard or care resulting in harm to another. Failure to provide generally acceptable psychological care and treatment.

Negligence: Legal cause of action involving the failure to exercise the degree of diligence and care that a reasonably and ordinarily prudent person would exercise under the same or similar circumstances; the result is the breach of a legal duty which proximately causes an injury which the law recognizes as deserving of compensation. The standard of care of a defendant psychologist in a malpractice case is not that of the reasonable and ordinarily prudent person (such as an automobile operator) but that of the average qualified psychologist practicing in the same area of specialization or general practice as that of the defendant psychologist.

Opinion evidence: Type of evidence that a witness gives based on his or her special training or background rather than on his or her personal knowledge of the facts in issue. Generally if the issue involves specialized knowledge, only the opinions of experts are admissible as evidence.

Pain and suffering: Element of "compensatory" nonpecuniary damages that allows recovery for the mental anguish and/or physical pain endured by the plaintiff as a result of injury for which the plaintiff seeks redress.

Perjury: Willful giving of false testimony under oath.

Plaintiff: Party who files or initiates a civil lawsuit seeking relief or compensation for damages or other legal relief.

Pleadings: Technical means by which parties to a dispute frame the issue for the court. The plaintiff's complaint is followed by the defendant's answer, and subsequent papers are filed as needed.

Prima facie case: Complaint that apparently contains all the necessary legal elements for a recognized cause of action and will suffice until contradicted and overcome by other evidence.

Prima facie evidence: Such evidence as is sufficient to establish the fact; if not rebutted, it becomes conclusive of the fact.

Probate court: Court having jurisdiction over the estates of deceased persons and persons under guardianship.

Proximate causation: Essential element in a legal cause of action for negligence; that is, it must be shown that the alleged negligent act proximately caused the injury for which legal damages are sought. The dominant and responsible cause necessarily sets other causes in operation. It represents a natural and continuous sequence, unbroken by any intervening cause.

Proximate cause: Act of commission or omission that through an uninterrupted sequence of events directly results in an injury that otherwise would not have occurred or else becomes a substantial factor in causing an injury.

Publication: Oral or written act that makes defamatory material available to persons other than the person defamed.

Reasonable medical certainty (or reasonable psychological certainty): As used in personal injury lawsuits, a term implying more than mere conjecture, possibility, consistency with, or speculation; similar to a probability, more likely than not 50.1%, but an overwhelming likelihood or scientific certainty is not required.

Release: Statement signed by a person relinquishing a right or claim against another person or persons usually for a payment or other valuable consideration.

Respondeat superior: "Let the master answer." A doctrine of vicarious or derivative liability in which the employer (master) is liable for the legal consequences of the breach of duties by an employee (servant) that the master owes to others, if the breach of duty occurs while the servant is engaged in work within the scope of his or her employment. For example, a hospital is liable for the negligent acts of a psychologist it employs if the acts occurred while the psychologist was working within his or her job description.

Settlement: Agreement made between the parties to a lawsuit, which resolves their legal dispute.

Slander: Method of oral defamation in which the false and malicious words are published by speaking or uttering in the presence of another person, other than the person slandered, which prejudices another person's reputation and character.

Standard of care: Measure against which a defendant's conduct is compared. The required standard in a professional negligence or psychological malpractice case is the standard of the average qualified practitioner in the same area of specialization.

Statute of limitations: Statutes that specify the permissible time interval between the occurrence giving rise to a civil cause of action and the actual filing of the lawsuit. Thus, failure to file the suit within the prescribed time limits may become an affirmative defense to the action. In malpractice actions, a typical statute of limitations might be 3 years from the date the cause of action accrues, but the measuring time for bringing the suit does not begin to run until the party claiming injury first discovers or should reasonably have discovered that he or she was injured and that the defendant was the one who caused the injury. Furthermore, if the injured party is a minor, additional extensions may be provided. Practitioners should check their own state laws for applicable details.

Stipulations: An agreement entered into between opposing counsel in a pending action.

Subpoena: Court document requiring a person to appear to give testimony at a deposition or in court.

Subpoena duces tecum: Subpoena that requires a person to personally bring to the court proceeding a specified document or property in his or her possession or under his or her control.

Summary judgment: Pre-verdict judgment rendered by the court in response to a motion by a plaintiff or a defendant, who claims that the absence of factual dispute on one or more issues eliminates those issues from further consideration.

Summons: Process served on a defendant in a civil action to secure his or her appearance in the action.

Tort: Civil wrong in which a person has breached a duty to another, which requires proof of the following: that a legal duty was owed to the plaintiff by the defendant; that the defendant breached the duty; and that the plaintiff was injured as a proximate cause of action, such as negligence.

Vicarious liability: Derivative or secondary liability predicated not upon direct fault but by virtue of the defendant's relationship to the actual wrongdoer, in which the former is presumed to hold a position of responsibility and control over the latter.

Waiver: Intentional and volitional renunciation of a known claim or right or a failure to avail oneself of a possible advantage to be derived from another's act. For example, a waiver might allow a person to testify to information that would ordinarily be protected as a privileged communication.

Wanton: Conduct that by its grossly negligent, malicious, or reckless nature evinces a disregard for the consequences or for the rights or safety of others.

Willful: Term descriptive of conduct that encompasses the continuum from intentional to reckless.

References and Readings

Law.com. (n.d.). *Legal dictionary*. Retrieved February 2013, from dictionary.law.com/

Jaffe v. Redmond, 116 S. Ct., 64 L.W 4490 (June 13, 1996).

The 'Lectric Law Library. (2012). *Free legal definitions*. Retrieved January 2013, from www.lectlaw.com/def.htm

Nolo. (2013). *Nolo's free dictionary of law terms and legal definitions*. Retrieved February 2013, from www.nolo.com/dictionary/

US Courts. (n.d.). *Glossary*. Retrieved February 2013, from www.uscourts.gov/Common/Glossary.aspx

Related Topics

Chapter 103, "American Psychological Association's Ethical Principles"

Chapter 110, "Understanding Special Education Law"

114 APPLYING THE DUTY TO PROTECT AND WARN

James L. Werth, Jr. and Jennifer Stroup

At some point in their careers, psychologists may be faced with a situation where they have to decide whether a client is a potential danger to someone else. To know how to proceed, these types of cases require the psychologist to accurately understand the American Psychological Association (APA, 2010) ethics code, the laws and regulations and court cases applicable in her or his jurisdiction, and the client's intent and ability to actually put someone else's well-being at risk (Werth, Welfel, & Benjamin, 2009). Unfortunately, many psychologists believe they know these things but are incorrect in their interpretations (Pabian, Welfel, & Beebe, 2009). This chapter highlights key considerations and provides additional resources. The chapter will not discuss possible harm to self because different issues apply in these cases.

APA ETHICS CODE

Many psychologists appear to believe that the APA (2010) ethics code requires that confidentiality be broken if the therapist believes the client may be at risk of harming himself or herself or someone else. However, this is inaccurate. The relevant portion of the ethics code is found in Standard 4—Privacy and Confidentiality, specifically number 4.05 (Disclosures):

(b) Psychologists disclose confidential information without the consent of the individual only as mandated by law, or where permitted by law for a valid purpose such as to…(3) protect the client/patient, psychologist, or others from harm.

This section is interpreted as *permitting but not requiring* the psychologist to break confidentiality if the professional believes that the client may harm others. Because the section refers to the law, the code cannot be interpreted in isolation. However, the key point is that the APA ethics code itself does not mandate that confidentiality be broken.

We want to note that other professions have different language in their codes so psychologists working on multidisciplinary teams may find themselves collaborating with professionals who do have an ethical obligation to take some action if a client or patient is believed to be a possible harm to self or others. The course of action to be taken in these situations needs to be discussed in order to minimize the likelihood that any member of the team may feel caught between ethical requirements and team treatment planning.

TARASOFF V. REGENTS OF THE UNIVERSITY OF CALIFORNIA (1976)

Perhaps the most famous, and yet misunderstood, case associated with mental health care is *Tarasoff*. Because of the common misinterpretations, we encourage readers to read the actual 1976 case itself, which can be found online. We believe that most of the confusion results from the fact that there were two *Tarasoff* cases, one decided in 1974 and then reheard and redecided in 1976 (Werth et al., 2009). The key difference between the two cases is that the California Supreme Court held in the first one that therapists have a "duty to warn," whereas in the second case the Court modified the ruling to indicate that there was a "duty to protect." The ruling of the 1976 case overrides the earlier decision so the final ruling of *Tarasoff* (1976, p. 340) was that:

When a therapist determines, or pursuant to the standards of his profession should determine, that his patient presents a serious danger of violence to another, he incurs an obligation to use reasonable care to protect the intended victim against such danger. The discharge of this duty may require the therapist to take one or more of various steps, depending upon the nature of the case. Thus it may call for him to warn the intended victim or others likely to apprise the victim of the danger, to notify the police, or to take whatever other steps are reasonably necessary under the circumstances.

The justices clearly indicated that warning was but one of many possible ways that the therapist could intervene. This is important because if the psychologist believes that she has a *duty to warn*, then she will break confidentiality; however, if the psychologist understands that she has a *duty to protect*, then she can consider other options such as, but not limited to, hospitalization, increasing session frequency, adding other modalities such as family therapy, and referring to a psychiatrist. We emphasize this point because it is the foundation for the interpretation of subsequent cases in other states and resulting state statutes.

STATE LAWS AND CASES AND REGULATIONS

There is wide variation in the laws passed by state legislatures or the ways that state courts have ruled in cases involving potential harm to others as well as how psychology licensure boards have written regulations (Werth et al., 2009). As a result, we can only provide a broad overview of the issues here and otherwise refer the reader to her or his own state statutes and case law and regulations. State psychological associations can be good resources for information on requirements within the state, local psychologist-experts available for consultation, and attorneys who are familiar with mental health law in the state.

When examining case decisions or laws or regulations, psychologists will want to ensure they understand the key aspects and implications of the material. Because of our familiarity with the statute, we use Virginia as an example. However, we add that we are not attorneys and our commentary here should not be construed as legal advice. Rather, we are intending merely to highlight carefully how a psychologist may want to read a statute and the types of things that may need to be explored with a legal consultant.

The relevant Virginia law is § 54.1-2400.1. Mental health service providers; duty to protect third parties; immunity. Part A is a set of definitions. Although definitions are very important when attempting to interpret statutes (consider the example of how the definition of "child abuse" or "child neglect" can influence whether a report is made), we skip this section here for the sake of space. Section B is included in its entirety.

> B. A mental health service provider has a duty to take precautions to protect third parties from violent behavior or other serious harm only when the client has orally, in writing, or via sign language, communicated to the provider a specific and immediate threat to cause serious bodily injury or death to an identified or readily identifiable person or persons, if the provider reasonably believes, or should believe according to the standards of his profession, that the client has the intent and ability to carry out that threat immediately or imminently. If the third party is a child, in addition to taking precautions to protect the child from the behaviors in the above types of threats, the provider also has a duty to take precautions to protect the child if the client threatens to engage in behaviors that would constitute physical abuse or sexual abuse as defined in § 18.2-67.10. The duty to protect does not attach unless the threat has been communicated to the provider by the threatening client while the provider is engaged in his professional duties.

The first thing to note is that both the title of the statute and the first line of Section B specifically state that there is a "duty to protect" not a "duty to warn." Section C of the statute identifies those actions that would meet the protection requirement. We return to Section C shortly.

Section B continues by specifying that the client herself or himself must be the one making the statements to the therapist. This is not the case in every state, where reports by significant others of the client may be enough to warrant intervention. Note also that the communication can come via voice or writing or sign language. This has significant implications in this era of electronic communication where therapists may receive e-mails or text messages in addition to phone or video messages. Receiving information through any of these mechanisms could be enough to trigger intervention, which highlights how important it is to include information about non-face-to-face communication in informed consent documents—a point to which we return at the end of this entry.

Next, there is the requirement that the threat be "specific and immediate." The statute does not define "specific" but does indicate that the threat would involve "serious bodily injury or death," which means that in Virginia, the threat would not need to be that the client wants to "kill" someone but would include a larger number of actions, including beating up or hitting with a car. Furthermore, the potential victim needs to be "identified or readily identifiable," meaning that the client would not need to give a specific name but could say "my boss" and this person would be identifiable through the initial paperwork where the client indicates her or his employer. In some states, a readily identifiable person could include someone who lives in a home or works in a building, so threats to structures may also warrant intervention. In terms of "immediate," the statute itself does not provide a timeframe; however, there is a reference to the child abuse statute and in that law "immediate" is defined as within 24 hours. Thus, one possibility (but by no means the only one) is that an "immediate" threat of harm is an action that will take place within 24 hours.

The statute continues by focusing on whether "the provider reasonably believes, or should believe according to the standards of his profession, that the client has the intent and ability to carry out that threat immediately or imminently." The issue of whether the provider believes or should believe refers to the professional standards. This can be interpreted as the standards of care for working with potentially dangerous individuals. The issue at hand is the ability to conduct an assessment of the risk for harm. There are instruments in the literature available for this, and there are lists of risk factors that should be considered when doing these assessments and we refer the reader to other sources for more information (see Werth et al., 2009). The key point is that psychologists need to know how to conduct these types of assessments and have consultants available, because consulting with others demonstrates that one is attempting to live up to the standards of the profession instead of relying on one's own knowledge. According to the statute, this assessment needs to consider both the client's intent and ability. One without the other is not sufficient, so the therapist must examine both factors and if both are present, then the duty to protect applies; however, if only one but not the other exists, then the statute does not apply even though some intervention may be warranted. We covered the immediate threat component in the preceding paragraph.

The final sentence is, as far as we can tell, idiosyncratic to Virginia. We are aware of no other statute that specifies the duty to protect only applies when the therapist is officially working. The statute does not specify what constitutes "professional duties," but we could envision a case being made that if a psychologist is checking work e-mails, even over the weekend, then he or she is engaged in professional duties. On the other hand, running into a client while grocery shopping would not be part of one's professional duties, but if a client says he plans on killing his wife when he gets home, we would find it difficult to defend a decision not to do something merely because the psychologist was not working and therefore the duty to protect statute did not apply.

With this analysis of Section B complete, we move to Section C, which specifies how the professional meets the duty to protect.

C. The duty set forth in subsection B is discharged by a mental health service provider who takes one or more of the following actions:

1. Seeks involuntary admission of the client under Article 16 (§ 16.1-335 et seq.) of Chapter 11 of Title 16.1 or Chapter 8 (§ 37.2-800 et seq.) of Title 37.2.

2. Makes reasonable attempts to warn the potential victims or the parent or guardian of the potential victim if the potential victim is under the age of 18.

3. Makes reasonable efforts to notify a law-enforcement official having jurisdiction in the client's or potential victim's place of residence or place of work, or place of work of the parent or guardian if the potential victim is under age 18, or both.

4. Takes steps reasonably available to the provider to prevent the client from using physical violence or other means of harm to others until the appropriate law-enforcement agency can be summoned and takes custody of the client.

5. Provides therapy or counseling to the client or patient in the session in which the threat has been communicated until the mental health service provider reasonably believes that the client no longer has the intent or the ability to carry out the threat.

The reader should first note that the introduction to the list says "takes *one or more* of the following actions" [emphasis added]. With this type of language, we believe it prudent for the therapist to consider all of the options provided and document why the ones that were implemented were selected and why each of the others was rejected. Otherwise, an argument could be made that if the therapist had done one of the other things, the bad result would not have happened.

It is very helpful to the psychologist that the legislature has listed the options because, as we will see later, Section D of the statute indicates that professionals cannot be held civilly liable for "Failing to take precautions other than those enumerated in subsection C to protect a potential third party victim from the client's violent behavior." Thus, as long as the psychologist demonstrates how she or he considered the applicability of the five listed interventions, others cannot claim that the harm would have been avoided if some other intervention had been attempted. The first three options—involuntary hospitalization, notifying the potential victim or guardians, and notifying law enforcement where the potential victim/guardians lives or works—are fairly common. Other states may include different types of hospitalization or include law enforcement where the potentially violent client lives or works; therefore, psychologists need to look at the requirements in their own state statutes.

The other two options provided may or may not be present in other areas. The fourth one seems to indicate that the therapist could keep talking to the client in her or his office or on the phone or via technology until law enforcement arrive to take the person into custody. The inclusion of the word "reasonably" means that the psychologist does not need to put herself or himself at risk or physically restrain the client from leaving the therapist's presence.

The fifth one specifies that the psychologist can intervene in the session during which the threat is communicated until either the intent or ability of the client is eliminated. This would appear to mean that if the therapist intended to solely rely on this option, she or he may have to extend the length of the session until legitimately satisfied that the client no longer had intent or ability. Establishing a treatment plan designed to reduce intent or ability would not be satisfactory (whereas in other states the development of a plan may be enough). The definition of "session" is ambiguous in this era of electronic communication, so it is unclear whether texting back and forth would be considered a session.

Finally, Section D specifies that providers cannot be held civilly liable for:

1. Breaching confidentiality with the limited purpose of protecting third parties by communicating the threats described in subsection B made by his clients to potential third party victims or law-enforcement agencies or by taking any of the actions specified in subsection C.

2. Failing to predict, in the absence of a threat described in subsection B, that the client would cause the third party serious physical harm.

3. Failing to take precautions other than those enumerated in subsection C to protect a potential third party victim from the client's violent behavior.

Thus, as long as psychologists act within the parameters outlined in the statute, they are protected from civil suits. However, note that included within Section D as well as in Section B is the idea of living up to the standard of care in terms of assessing for risk.

INFORMED CONSENT

Earlier we alluded to the importance of informed consent. Most discussions of ethical and legal issues highlight the importance of a good informed consent document, initial discussion at the outset of therapy, and seeing informed consent as a process that requires ongoing consideration instead of being restricted to the beginning of the first session. The other piece that must be emphasized is that this informed consent document and discussion must accurately reflect the ethics code, laws, regulations, and other limitations imposed by the therapist or agency. Thus, for a psychologist in Virginia, it would be inaccurate to indicate in writing or in a verbal review of the document that "As a psychologist, my ethics code and state law requires me to break confidentiality if you tell me you are going to kill a specific person." Not only is this inaccurate as far as the APA (2010) ethics code is concerned, it also is an inaccurate summary of state law. A client who heard this, without further elaboration, would not be able to give truly informed consent to participate in therapy that involved discussion of possible violence because she or he has not been fully informed about what situations might lead to the breaking of confidentiality or what other interventions might be attempted and under what circumstances when a threat to others emerged.

Psychologists need to be able to accurately assess to what extent clients are a potential threat to others and know when these threats warrant intervention based on state-specific laws, court cases, and regulations. Significant misunderstanding of ethical, legal, and regulatory obligations exists and places psychologists at risk of not properly informing clients of limitations of confidentiality and improperly intervening when a threat is detected.

References and Readings

American Psychological Association. (2010). *Ethical principles of psychologists and code of conduct*. Retrieved February 2013, from www.apa.org/ethics/code/index.aspx

Code of Virginia. (2010). § 54.1-2400.1. Mental health service providers; duty to protect third parties; immunity. Retrieved February 2013, from leg1.state.va.us/cgi-bin/legp504.exe?000+cod+54.1-2400.1

Pabian, Y. L., Welfel, E., & Beebe, R. S. (2009). Psychologists' knowledge of their states' laws pertaining to Tarasoff-type situations. *Professional Psychology: Research and Practice, 40*, 8–14.

Tarasoff v. Regents of the University of California, 13 Cal.3d 117, 529 P.2d 553 (1974), vacated 17 Cal.3d 425, 551 P.2d 334 (1976).

Werth, J. L., Jr., Welfel, E. R., & Benjamin, G. A. H. (Eds.). (2009). *The duty to protect: Ethical, legal, and professional considerations for mental health professionals*. Washington, DC: American Psychological Association.

Related Topics

Chapter 103, "American Psychological Association's Ethical Principles"

Chapter 106, "Minimizing Your Legal Liability Risk Following Adverse Events or Patient Threats"

Chapter 128, "Understanding Fundamentals of the HIPAA Privacy Rule"

115 PREPARING AND GIVING EXPERT TESTIMONY

Stanley L. Brodsky and Tess M.S. Neal

FACTS ABOUT TESTIFYING

Effective witnesses are familiar with expected trial procedures and the dynamics of testifying. Witnesses with little or no experience need preparation before testifying (see Table 115.1). Inexperienced expert witnesses may not know that (1) at most times experts do not testify, (2) most testimony is routine, (3) clothing choice and appearance beyond a conventional threshold is largely irrelevant, (4) the best preparation does not take place immediately before the trial, and (5) it is not about winning (Brodsky, 2004).

1. Although experts are often filled with anticipatory anxiety, most cases never reach the trial stage. Most civil cases settle and most criminal cases are plea bargained before trial.
2. Most testifying experiences of expert witnesses are unremarkable, without harsh cross-examinations or vigorous attacks on the expert.
3. The appearance and clothing of lucid and persuasive experts fades into the background and has a modest impact on perceivers' evaluations of the expert. We recommend

that experts dress professionally but comfortably and naturally.

4. Ongoing study and learning is the best method to prepare for testifying. Cramming just before the trial is not an effective way to prepare.
5. Being concerned about "winning" is problematic, because expert witnesses are hired to provide an objective opinion. Testimony should be the same regardless of retaining party. The psychological facts of a case are independent of referral source.

PREPARE RESPONSIBLY

Before testifying, ensure that your knowledge is current in psychological conceptualizations, assessment practices, and relevant professional issues. Preparation and realistic knowledge are the natural allies of good testimony.

TABLE 115.1. The Courtroom-Oriented and the Courtroom-Unfamiliar Expert Witness

Stage	Courtroom Oriented	Courtroom Unfamiliar
Pretrial		
Training	Forensic psychology graduate programs or post-docs, legal-medical institutes, or other training centers. Sometimes self-taught	No relevant training
Point of entry of witness into proceeding	Early in proceedings; pretrial conferences with emphasis on appropriate questions to elicit evaluation-related content	Late entry; minimal or no pretrial conferences with attorney; minimal preparation with attorney on techniques for eliciting forensic opinions
Knowledge of law, evidence, and privilege	Usually aware; occasionally more aware than the lawyer in the trial	Sometimes aware or minimally informed
Record keeping	Thorough; organized to anticipate cross-examination; exact as to dates, times, places, detail, prior hospital records	Often is variable, imprecise; omits or uncertain of dates, times
Reaction to subpoena	Minimal emotional reaction; reviews records, calls lawyer, determines basis of subpoena and information desired	Distress and anxiety; no conferences unless requested by lawyer; unaware of legal position
On the witness stand		
Written report	Clear, concise, equivocal when necessary; avoids legal conclusions but answers questions raised	Technical language, poorly understood by lay audiences; often does not answer legal questions
Target of testimony	Jury or judge	Lawyer or mental health colleagues
Language	Spoken English	Professional terminology
Purpose of testimony	Teaching; may advocate for findings	Nonpersuasive presentation of clinical information
Testimony process	Steady; consistent; aware of "traps"; concedes minor points easily	May be badly manipulated; stubborn; backed into corner
Reaction to cross-examination	Acceptance as routine procedure	Resentment, anger, confusion
Posttrial		
Reaction after court findings, especially to distortion of opinion and loss of case by retaining counsel	Acceptance; learns; reappears in court	Nonacceptance; alienated; reacts by future avoidance
Results of court adjudication	More consistent with expressed view of witness	Less consistent with expressed view, particular in cases with opposing testimony
Fees	Higher, based on actual time spent in evaluation, reporting, and courtroom time	Variable, generally low or occasionally unrealistically high

Source: This table has been modified substantially from the original version by Brodsky and Robey (1973) and the revision by Brodsky (1991).

FAMILIARIZE YOURSELF WITH THE COURTROOM ENVIRONMENT

New or relatively inexperienced expert witnesses who are anxious about testifying can work to reduce anxiety before taking the stand. Become familiar with the physical space of the courtroom in which you will testify—sit in the empty courtroom alone, observe witnesses in other trials, or ask the judge hearing the case for a waiver of the rule that excludes a witness from observing earlier testimony. Feeling comfortable in the setting will improve performance (Brodsky, 1991, 2004).

DEPOSITIONS

Besides the stated purpose of discovery by opposing counsel of facts and findings, depositions serve two additional and sometimes nonobvious purposes. They inform both sides so that evidence may be weighed that would influence settlement discussions. Depositions also allow witnesses to learn the lines of inquiry that may be pursued in the trial. The following is a piece of specific advice for testifying in depositions: If you don't know, don't discuss. Much more than in live trials, witnesses in depositions sometimes babble on and speculate well beyond their knowledge, competence, and findings.

UNDERSTAND THE LEGAL CONTEXT

The legal rules of evidence and procedure profoundly affect acceptability of testimony (American Psychology-Law Society, 2012; Committee on Ethical Guidelines for Forensic Psychologists, 1991). Read one of the psychology and law texts on this subject. We recommend the book by Melton, Petrila, Poythress, and Slobogin (2007). An important issue in forensic work is whether psychological experts should answer the ultimate legal question the court has under consideration (e.g., is the defendant competent to stand trial, was the defendant sane at the time of the offense). Although there is some debate in the field, most forensic psychological scholars as well as the *Specialty Guidelines for Forensic Psychology* (American Psychology-Law Society, 2012) conclude expert opinions that offer ultimate conclusions, especially about mental state at time of offense, are not proper. This conclusion rests on the fact that psychological observations, inferences, and conclusions are distinct from legal facts, opinions, and conclusions. We recommend experts become familiar with "the ultimate issue issue" (see Melton et al., 2007) and, furthermore, that experts do not testify to the ultimate legal issue, except in cases of involuntary commitments and certain other situations. Instead, we suggest testifying about findings and conclusions based soundly in psychological science and allow the trier-of-fact to extrapolate how those psychological findings apply to the ultimate legal issue at question.

TESTIFY ONLY WITHIN THE SCOPE OF REASONABLE AND ACCEPTED SCIENTIFIC KNOWLEDGE

Experts are bound to this standard by the US Supreme Court *Daubert* decision. Research results should be used in an impartial manner in the face of adversarial pulls of attorneys. It is not unethical to disagree with other experts about readings or applications of knowledge. It is unethical to relinquish the role of neutral expert in favor of highly selective gleaning of knowledge (Sales & Shuman, 2005).

STAY CLEARLY WITHIN THE BOUNDARIES OF YOUR OWN PROFESSIONAL EXPERTISE

This mandate from the APA Code of Ethics (Knapp, 2011) means that practitioners with expertise only in psychology of adults do not assess children or testify about child psychology and vice-versa. In the same sense, one should not consider observation of other witnesses' behavior on the stand to be remotely equivalent to findings from conventional psychological assessments.

CREDENTIALS

Skilled opposing counsel can always find something you have not accomplished, written, or mastered. Admit all nonaccomplishments in a matter-of-fact way. It is okay.

EXPERIENCE

The legal system uses breadth, depth, and duration of experience as part of credentialing expert witnesses. Clinicians should be aware that, by itself, clinical experience is at best modestly related to accuracy of diagnostic judgments. Early studies and reviews indicated no relation between clinical skills and experience (see e.g., Garb, 1989), while a more recent meta-analysis indicated about a 13% improvement in diagnostic accuracy with experience (Spengler et al., 2009).

CREDIBILITY

An implicit goal of witnesses is to be credible and believed. People believe witnesses who are likable and confident. To the extent possible, given the nature of the setting, allow the likable aspects of who you are to be visible, and confidently present your findings and conclusions.

USE EFFECTIVE VERBAL LANGUAGE

Tell a compelling story with your testimony and present your message in a sensible and approachable way. Avoid exaggeration, unfamiliar words, dramatic and emotional words, a monotone voice, and overqualifying what you say. Instead, be calm and poised, talk slowly enough to allow your message to be processed, vary the format of your answers, and personalize your testimony by using personal pronouns (e.g., "I" and "we"). Treat the jurors as interested lay acquaintances rather than colleagues (Brodsky, 2004).

USE NARRATIVE STATEMENTS WHEN POSSIBLE

Persuasive witnesses use smoothly flowing statements and make the testimony come alive by creating a meaningful story about the defendant or litigant. Narrative answers tell a compelling story, as opposed to fragmented answers, which are shorter and more broken and thus more difficult to follow. Good attorneys will allow for narrative answers on direct examination, and good attorneys will try to prevent narrative answers on cross-examination. Look for opportunities to provide narrative answers during both direct and cross-examination (Brodsky, 1991, 2004).

USE EFFECTIVE NONVERBAL LANGUAGE

Nonverbal language accounts for more of the variance in person perception than verbal language. Eye contact is one of the most important nonverbal communication tools at your disposal. It is natural to look at the person(s) with whom you are speaking—which is most often the attorney during testimony; however, looking at the jury and judge is also important during narrative answers. What is hard is avoiding being captured in eye contact solely with the cross-examining attorney. Look for opportunities to provide narrative answers, and make sure to look at the jury as you answer (Brodsky, 1991, 2004).

ADMIT IGNORANCE

Some expert witnesses present themselves as omniscient and infallible in their fields. Do not do this. Instead, state "I don't know" in response to queries when you truly do not know the answer.

DATA THAT DO NOT SUPPORT YOUR CONCLUSIONS

Excessively partisan witnesses attempt to deny existing information they have gathered that contradicts their conclusions. Conscientious and responsible witnesses freely and without defensiveness acknowledge and discuss contradicting information.

HANDLING CROSS-EXAMINATION ATTACKS AND BULLYING

One way to prepare for the possibility of a tough cross-examination experience is to understand cross-examination techniques through the eyes of the attorney. Chastisement, cornering, and bullying are techniques some attorneys use to intimidate or discredit the witness (Brodsky, 2004). Good witnesses retain control by using simple, reflective answers. Do not try to be equally aggressive or loud to match the style of the cross-examining attorney. These responses diminish credibility and the appearance of impartiality. Instead, attempt to present yourself in the opposite way; that is, if the attorney demands an immediate and unreasonable response, answer in a careful and reasoned way. If the attorney is loud and insistent, reply with quiet, measured, and assured responses (Brodsky, 2004). Maintaining professional poise and effectively handling personal attacks and bullying during cross-examination takes practice, which you can do by yourself in front of a mirror or with a colleague. Videotaping your practice and critically examining your responses are also good ways to prepare yourself for the possibility of a tough cross-examination.

USE EVALUATIONS AND TESTIMONY AS STIMULI TO LEARN

Evaluators and witnesses are typically so caught up in "doing" that they are not open to conceptualizing cases and testimony as learning experiences. We suggest asking, "What additional validated measures might I administer that are directly related to these forensic issues? What else should I read or what sort of courses should I take to be better prepared? What have I learned about my own needs for professional and scholarly growth?"

References and Readings

American Psychology-Law Society. (2012). *Specialty guidelines for forensic psychologists.* Retrieved January 2012, from: www.ap-ls.org/aboutpsychlaw/SpecialtyGuidelines.php

Brodsky, S. L. (1991). *Testifying in court: Guidelines and maxims for the expert witness.* Washington, DC: American Psychological Association.

Brodsky, S. L. (2004). *Coping with cross-examination and other pathways to effective testimony.* Washington, DC: American Psychological Association.

Committee on Ethical Guidelines for Forensic Psychologists. (1991). Specialty guidelines for forensic psychologists. *Law and Human Behavior, 15,* 655–665.

Garb, H. N. (1989). Clinical judgment, clinical training, and professional experience. *Psychological Bulletin, 105,* 387–396.

Knapp, S. J. (Ed.). (2011). *APA handbook of ethics in psychology* (Vols. 1–2). Washington, DC: American Psychological Association.

Melton, G., Petrila, J., Poythress, N. G., & Slobogin, C. (2007). *Psychological evaluation for the courts: A handbook for mental health professionals and lawyers* (3rd ed.). New York: Guilford Press.

Sales, B. D., & Shuman, D. W. (2005). *Experts in court: Reconciling law, science, and professional knowledge.* Washington, DC: American Psychological Association.

Spengler, P. M., White, M. J., Ægisdóttir, S., Maugherman, A. S., Anderson, L. A., Cook, R. S., ... Rush, J. D. (2009). The meta-analysis of clinical judgment project: Effects of experience on diagnostic accuracy. *Counseling Psychologist, 37*(3), 350–399.

Related Topics

Chapter 113, "Understanding Legal Terms of Special Interest in Mental Health Practice"

Chapter 116, "Evaluation of Competence to Stand Trial"

Chapter 117, "Conducting a Child Custody Evaluation"

116 EVALUATING COMPETENCE TO STAND TRIAL

Carla A. Lourenco

A defendant's competence to stand trial (CST) may be questioned by the judge, prosecution, or defense at any stage of the legal proceedings, from time of arraignment to the end of trial and sentencing. It is determined by a set of legal standards, based on established case law, and therefore varies across jurisdictions. In general, CST takes into consideration a defendant's mental status and his or her ability to meaningfully participate in all relevant legal proceedings. A defendant's psychiatric diagnosis or cognitive condition (e.g., developmental disability) is only important insofar as it provides a label for the set of symptoms that may adversely impact his or her competence-related abilities. It should be emphasized that CST is based on a defendant's *present* mental status and functional abilities. A given defendant's CST status may change over time, depending on various factors (e.g., compliance with psychiatric medications, substance abuse, head injury). As such, a defendant adjudicated CST on charges in the past may become incompetent in the future, and vice versa.

The US Supreme Court established the standard used by all states for CST in *Dusky v. United States* (1960). Many states have adopted the *Dusky* standard verbatim, while others have slightly revised or expanded upon it. As such, evaluators must ensure that they are familiar with the standard used in the state in which they plan to do these evaluations.

EVALUATING COMPETENCE TO STAND TRIAL

The general criteria that determine CST include (a) awareness and understanding of one's charges and associated allegations, basic verdicts, and potential dispositions, (b) awareness and understanding of the roles of key trial participants and relevant legal proceedings, (c) ability to consult rationally with one's attorney and assist in the preparation of one's own defense, and (d) ability to make relevant and well-reasoned decisions about one's case. During a CST evaluation, the evaluator must assess each of these areas, which is accomplished through the gathering of data by various means and from various sources. These typically include (a) a clinical interview of the defendant, (b) review of the defendant's medical/mental health records, and (c) interviews of collateral sources, such as the defendant's family members and treatment providers. In addition, evaluators may utilize psychological and forensic assessment instruments to assist in their evaluation of psychopathology, cognitive impairments, and relevant forensic matters. These procedures are discussed next.

Clinical Interview

This involves gathering information about the defendant's psychosocial history, including developmental and educational background, previous employment, past mental health symptoms and treatment, and medical history (with a focus on conditions that may affect one's mental status, e.g., traumatic brain injury). This also includes an assessment of the defendant's current mental status and symptomatology.

Review of Medical/Mental Health Records

Although the defendant's current mental status is most relevant, as CST is based on one's *present* functional abilities, information regarding the defendant's medical and mental health history helps to inform the evaluation. This proves particularly useful in cases in which the defendant is uncooperative with the evaluation and/or there is concern that the defendant may be attempting to feign or exaggerate symptoms for purposes of malingering.

Interviews of Collateral Sources

As with review of health records, information collected from individuals familiar with the defendant and his or her medical/mental health history can also help to inform the evaluation, particularly in cases in which there are limited available data.

Use of Psychological and Forensic Assessment Instruments

Psychological assessment instruments may be useful in helping to identify psychopathology and cognitive deficits that may impact the defendant's mental status. These may include personality measures (e.g., Minnesota Multiphasic Personality Inventory-2 or -RF) and tests of cognitive functioning (e.g., the Wechsler intelligence and/or memory scales). Again, these data alone will not determine a defendant's CST, but they can help to inform the evaluation.

There are a variety of forensic assessment instruments that can assist in the assessment of CST. Such instruments provide structure for the evaluator as well as empirical support for the evaluator's subsequent opinions. One of the most recently developed CST instruments includes the Evaluation of Competency to Stand Trial-Revised (ECST-R; Rogers, Tillbrook, & Sewell, 2004), which is based on the *Dusky* standard. It employs a semistructured and structured interview format, designed to assess CST generally, as well as screen for attempts to exaggerate CST deficits. The MacArthur Competence Assessment Tool-Criminal Adjudication (MacCAT-CA; Hoge, Bonnie, Poythress, & Monahan, 1999; Poythress et al., 1999) is another well-known CST assessment instrument. It also employs a semistructured and structured interview format that assesses a defendant's understanding, reasoning, and appreciation abilities. When evaluating a defendant with a history of intellectual disability, the Competence Assessment for Standing Trial for Defendants with Mental Retardation (CAST*MR; Everington & Luckasson, 1992) can be particularly useful. It is comprised of 50 multiple-choice items and additional open-ended questions that are read aloud to the defendant and designed to assess the *Dusky* standard.

It should be emphasized that these forensic assessment instruments were developed to assist in the evaluation of CST, and their results alone do not determine whether a defendant is competent or incompetent to stand trial; rather, one must interpret these data within the context of all available information, obtained via the procedures discussed earlier.

Malingering (i.e., deliberate attempts to feign or exaggerate symptoms for secondary gain) must always be considered when evaluating forensic populations. A number of measures have been developed to evaluate respondents' attempts to feign or exaggerate psychiatric symptoms and/or cognitive impairment, which are often used by forensic evaluators to assist in the evaluation of CST. The Structured Inventory of Malingered Symptomatology (SIMS; Widows & Smith, 2005) is a self-report measure designed to screen for a range of malingered psychiatric and cognitive symptoms that is relatively brief and easy to score. The Structured Interview of Reported Symptoms (SIRS; Rogers, Bagby, & Dickens, 1992) was also designed to assess malingering of psychiatric impairment, with a focus on psychotic symptomatology, and utilizes a structured interview format. In contrast, the Test of Memory Malingering (TOMM; Tombaugh, 1996) was developed to discriminate between individuals suffering from genuine memory impairment and those intentionally feigning memory deficits; it is an item recognition test which employs a forced-choice format.

PREPARING A WRITTEN REPORT

Referrals for CST evaluations may come directly from the court in the form of a court-ordered (statute-driven) evaluation of a defendant before the court on criminal charges, or from a prosecutor or defense attorney seeking an independent (private) evaluation of a defendant whom they are prosecuting or defending, respectively. Therefore, once the CST assessment has been completed, the forensic evaluator will need to consider the referral source and his or her role before preparing a report.

Court-Ordered Evaluations

In a court-ordered evaluation, the "client" is the court, and the evaluator is expected to submit a written report to the court. Although the format of these reports can vary, they typically include (a) a summary of the defendant's criminal charges and underlying allegations, (b) the standard that will be used for determining CST, (c) notification of the limits of confidentiality provided to the defendant at the start of the interview, (d) the sources of information that were used in completing the evaluation, (e) the defendant's relevant history, (f) a description of the defendant's current mental status and symptomatology, (g) the results of assessment instruments that were administered, (h) data describing the defendant's abilities and deficits associated with CST, and (i) the evaluator's opinion regarding the defendant's CST, including the cause of any deficits and potential for restoration. The report will be shared with the judge, prosecutor, and defense attorney. In some cases, the court may want the evaluator to provide testimony regarding the contents of the report at a future hearing and will typically subpoena the evaluator to court to provide such testimony.

Defendants adjudicated incompetent to stand trial on the basis of mental illness may be subject to a period of involuntary psychiatric hospitalization (civil commitment) for "competency restoration." The commitment period, typically dictated by statue and therefore time limited, serves two goals; the defendant receives treatment for his or her psychiatric symptoms (e.g., paranoid delusions), which in turn, may resolve his or her competence-related deficits (e.g., paranoid delusions about the criminal charges). The evaluator should address the likelihood that the defendant's competency may be restored within the statutory limitation in the report to the court.

Independent Evaluations

In an independent or private evaluation, the "client" is whichever party has retained the evaluator (typically the defense attorney) and the evaluator will therefore discuss his or her opinion regarding the defendant's CST with this party directly. Depending on whether this party chooses to use the evaluator's findings during future legal proceedings, the evaluator may be asked to prepare a written report that will be entered as evidence in court. This decision is made at the discretion of the party, based on whether the evaluation supports the legal strategy that he or she intends to pursue. The retaining party may also ask the evaluator to testify at a later date.

References and Readings

Dusky v. United States, 362 U.S. 402 (1960).

Everington, C. T., & Luckasson, R. (1992). *Competence assessment for standing trial for defendants with mental retardation.* Worthington, OH: IDS Publishing.

Poythress, N.G., Nicholson, R. A., Otto, R. K., Edens, J. F., Bonnie, R. J., Monahan, J., & Hoge, S. K. (1999). *The MacArthur Competence Assessment Tool-Criminal Adjudication.* Odessa, FL: Psychological Assessment Resources.

Rogers, R., Bagby, R. M., & Dickens, S. E. (1992). *Structured Interview of Reported Symptoms (SIRS) and professional manual.* Odessa, FL: Psychological Assessment Resources.

Rogers, R., Tillbrook, C. E., & Sewell, K. W. (2004). *Evaluation of Competency to Stand Trial-Revised professional manual.* Lutz, FL: Psychological Assessment Resources.

Tombaugh, T. N. (1996). *Test of Memory Malingering (TOMM) manual.* Toronto, ON: The Psychological Corporation.

Widows, M. R., & Smith, G. P. (2005). *Structured Inventory of Malingered Symptomatology professional manual.* Lutz, FL: Psychological Assessment Resources

Related Topic

Chapter 115, "Preparing and Giving Expert Testimony"

117 CONDUCTING A CHILD CUSTODY EVALUATION

Robin M. Deutsch

This chapter describes a recommended process for conducting a child custody evaluation. Evaluating the needs of children and families in custody disputes is complicated, and it requires specialized knowledge and experience. In this chapter the word *parties* will be used, as custody evaluations may be ordered or stipulated to by grandparents, de facto parents, or guardians.

THE ROLE OF THE EVALUATOR

The mental health evaluator is generally appointed by the court to gather and report factual data and form clinical opinions, when possible and appropriate, for the court to use as evidence to render custody and parenting decisions when parents are in dispute about the care of and responsibilities for their children. In some states, each parent hires his or her own evaluator, and in other jurisdictions evaluators are hired with a private consent agreement. It is incumbent on the evaluator to know the laws, standards, and rules governing custody evaluations in the jurisdiction in which he or she practices. One of the first steps in conducting a custody evaluation is being clear about your client. Generally, in most jurisdictions, the court is your client and you report directly to the court. However in some jurisdictions the parents and their lawyers, or a parent and lawyer, are the clients. Important psychological knowledge for a custody evaluator to have includes the following:

- Psychological and developmental needs of children and the impact of temperament, physical, learning, and emotional needs on children and parenting
- Reliable and valid interviewing techniques for children and adults

- Research on risk and protective factors predicting child and adolescent outcomes
- Family dynamics, including impact of relationship dissolution on parents and children, sexual orientation, sibling relationships, and presence of significant others, including extended family
- Effects of interparental conflict on parents and children
- Contribution of personality disorders, mental illness, substance abuse on parenting and co-parenting
- Understanding the types of domestic violence, and the identification of and effects of intimate partner violence on relationships, parenting and the current evaluation process and context
- Effects of child maltreatment/trauma on the psychological needs of children
- Significance of religion and culture on parenting and the lives of the parties

There are a few cardinal rules that guide the custody evaluation process:

- Having an understanding of the legal rights of the parties to the evaluation and of individuals who may be affected by the evaluation process, including the report
- Maintaining an attitude of respect toward all family members, collateral contacts, attorneys, and others with whom the evaluator deals throughout the custody evaluation process
- Avoiding role shifts, such as providing therapeutic intervention, mediation, or consultation in the process
- Maintaining a system of record keeping that is consistent with rules and laws of the jurisdiction in which you practice
- Being familiar with sources of ethical and professional guidance relevant to conducting a child custody evaluation (APA ethical principles of psychologists and code of conduct, 2002; APA guidelines for child custody evaluations in family law proceedings, 2009; AFCC model standards for custody evaluations, 2006; APA guidelines on multicultural education, training, research, practice, and organizational change for psychologists, 2003)

STEPS IN STRUCTURING A COMPREHENSIVE CUSTODY EVALUATION

Prior to beginning the evaluation, the custody evaluator secures court orders or consent agreements and reviews their role, the purpose of the evaluation, and the areas of focus. It is incumbent upon the custody evaluator to determine whether he or she has the requisite training and experience as an evaluator in general, and in the areas of evaluation defined by the court order or consent agreement. If the evaluator has had minimal experience, supervision or consultation with an experienced professional is recommended (AFCC, 2007).

The custody evaluator may write to the attorneys, informing them of receipt of appointment and requesting contact information for the parties, and the relevant record, including affidavits, motions, court orders, and evaluations. If the parties are pro se (without attorney representation), the evaluator contacts the parties directly or obtains contact information from the court.

The evaluator begins the evaluation by providing written information about policies, procedures, and fees, including a request for a retainer to cover the anticipated costs of the evaluation, unless the court is paying for the service. A custody evaluation is not a health service and the evaluator cannot complete a claim for health insurance reimbursement. The next step is to review court orders and schedule appointments with each of the parties.

The scope of the evaluation is determined by the court order or consent agreement. At times other issues arise in the midst of a custody evaluation, for example, allegations of abuse or wish to relocate. To broaden the scope of the evaluation, the evaluator will seek the approval of the court or the agreement of the parties and their attorneys.

First contacts with all parties, including collateral contacts, begin with a warning about the nonconfidentiality of the process, in that the evaluator will write a report to the court that may be read by the judge, attorneys, or both parties. In addition, during the process there is no confidentiality between the parties as the evaluator will question each party to obtain information and understand disclosures and areas of concern expressed by anyone who is a party to the evaluation.

Data gathering must use a fair and balanced process with diverse, reliable, and valid methods. Using diverse sources of data assists the exploration and analysis of multiple and divergent hypotheses and claims. To the extent possible, alternating meetings and spending similar amounts of time with each party and in observational interviews helps to maintain neutrality and avoid partiality. There may be reasons why time spent appears unbalanced, and the evaluator should document that in notes and the report. To allow a response, the evaluator brings to the attention of both parties any allegations or concerns that may form the basis for opinion.

The evaluation consists of meetings with each party, with each child, any other adult who performs a caretaking role and/or lives in the residence with the children, parent–child observations and/or home visits, interviews with relevant collateral contacts, especially professionals involved with the children and parents, and review of relevant records.

Psychological testing may be used as an additional source of data. If formal assessment instruments are used, the evaluator should consider the reliability and validity of the instruments and the admissibility of the particular instrument in the court. The testing can be referred to another psychologist who has training and experience in the interpretation of psychological testing in a forensic setting if the evaluator is not experienced or trained in the administration of formal assessment instruments. Psychological testing is one of many sources of data and should only be interpreted in the context of other sources of data, and not as a sole source of information to make conclusions about the child or party.

Careful documentation of each interview, whether face to face or telephonic, is essential and may be subpoenaed for deposition or trial.

AREAS FOR EVALUATION

Unless otherwise ordered by the court, it is the capacities of each parent, needs of the children, the parent-child relationship and ability of each parent to meet the child's needs that are central to any evaluation and form the basis for the parenting plan. One significant consideration is the status quo or current and historical parenting plan. Protecting the child's continuity of relationships and attachments is a prime consideration (ALI, 2002). That being said, when parents separate, the child will generally never again have the same level and extent of contact with both parents.

The evaluation of each party includes the concerns raised by each of the parties, including facts relevant to the parenting of the children, parenting history, and family history. The child's developmental, physical, psychological, educational, and social needs require careful evaluation and will be considered in the context of a parent's ability to meet those needs, while protecting or building the parent–child relationship. A child's stated wishes and preferences should be considered in the context of the child's developmental maturity and his or her ability to express his or her wishes independently. Sibling relationships should also be assessed and considered in the context of parenting capacities and responsibilities and different developmental needs and relationships.

Parent–child observations may be done in the home or office, though if there is any question about appropriate home life, the home visit is important. The purpose of the parent–child observation is to sample parenting skills and abilities, including attunement to the needs of the child, developmentally appropriate expectations for the child, and ability to communicate with and manage behavior of children effectively. Generally the evaluator does not have the opportunity to observe the child under stress, so any conclusions made about the parent-child relationship should take that into consideration. Parent–child observations are not conducted when there is a verifiable threat to the child's physical or psychological safety.

While in-person interviews with each party are necessary to the evaluation, telephonic interviews are often used for interviewing collateral contacts and to receive additional information from the parties. Information from collateral sources can provide confirming or disconfirming data about critical issues raised in the evaluation. The evaluator must weigh the reliability of the collateral data with a focus on the professional contacts, for example, teachers, medical doctors, psychotherapists, and records, including previous evaluations, social service, medical, hospital, school, employment, police and court, criminal offender record information (CORI and CARI), and e-mail correspondence.

WRITTEN REPORT: FACTS AND OPINIONS

The report presents the sources of information, including dates and durations of contacts, data collected and organized by person, observations, and interpretation and opinions. Separation of facts and opinions is critical. Opinions must be based upon facts or data obtained in the evaluation. Evaluators identify limitations in data collection and incomplete, unreliable, or missing data. They identify alternative hypotheses with risks and benefits, supported by the relevant facts relating to both parties and the children. Specific information, including time frames, may be helpful when making recommendations for parenting access and responsibilities and treatment.

Considerations for recommendations:

- References to research can inform recommendations.
- Offering alternative hypotheses and predictions about future functioning of the child under different access scenarios may be useful.
- For young children or in cases of child maltreatment, domestic violence, mental illness, or substance abuse, the recommendation may offer a progressive plan for increasing contact between a parent and child based on benchmarks.
- If making treatment recommendations, be specific about to whom, for what, and what kind.

LIMITATIONS

Limitations of custody evaluations include the following:

- Limitations of existing social science research
- Limitations on evaluator's abilities to make reliable predictions about the future
- Variation in experience and expertise of evaluators
- Variation in experience and interests of judges

The custody evaluator retains all materials gathered and created during the evaluation until 3 years after the youngest child in the family reaches the age of majority, or the period of time required by legal, regulatory, and institutional requirements.

References and Readings

American Law Institute. (2002). *Principles of the law of family dissolution: Analysis and recommendations.* Newark, NJ: LexisNexis

American Psychological Association. (2002). Ethical principles of psychologists and code of conduct. *American Psychologist, 57,* 1060–1073.

American Psychological Association. (2003). Guidelines on multicultural education, training, research, practice, and organizational change for psychologists. *American Psychologist, 58,* 377–402.

American Psychological Association. (2007). Record keeping guidelines. *American Psychologist, 62,* 993–1004.

American Psychological Association. (2010). Guidelines for child custody evaluations in family law proceedings. *American Psychologist, 65,* 863–867.

Association of Family and Conciliation courts. (2007). Model standards of practice for child custody evaluations. *Family court Review, 45,* 70–91.

Related Topics

Chapter 103, "American Psychological Association's Ethical Principles"

Chapter 104, "Dealing with Licensing Board and Ethics Complaints"

Chapter 105, "Defending Against Legal (Malpractice and Licensing) Complaints"

118 ASSESSING AND RESPONDING TO AGGRESSIVE AND THREATENING CLIENTS

Leon VandeCreek

Dangerous clients pose a special challenge to psychotherapists. If, on the one hand, the therapist underestimates the client's threats and harm comes to a third party, the therapist may feel that more should have been done to protect the innocent victim, and the victim, or survivors, may initiate a lawsuit. On the other hand, if the therapist incorrectly believes that harm is imminent and acts to warn a potential victim, the client may feel betrayed and the therapeutic relationship may be threatened. Even worse, the client may drop out of therapy and lose faith in therapists, thereby ending any preventive role that therapy may have had in preventing violence.

The American Psychological Association's (APA) "Ethical Principles of Psychologists and Code of Conduct" (2002) permits psychologists to breach confidentiality if it is necessary to protect the client or others from harm. The option of breaching confidentiality, permitted by the ethics code, may protect the psychologist from charges of ethical violations, but the psychologist must still exercise judgment about when to breach confidentiality or when to engage in other strategies that may reduce the potential for violence.

Decision making with dangerous clients is made more precarious by the increased possibility of legal liability. Prior to the 1976 California Supreme Court decision of *Tarasoff v. Regents of the University of California*, psychotherapists did not have to contend with legal repercussions surrounding confidentiality in their management of dangerous clients. The *Tarasoff* ruling, and that of other courts and legislation that followed the lead of *Tarasoff*, however, has created a "duty to protect" doctrine that psychologists believe applies to them even if their states have not formally endorsed the doctrine through legislation or court decisions (Werth, Welfel, Benjamin, & Sales, 2009). Consequently, psychologists must now consider clinical issues in the context of both ethical and legal constraints. Fortunately, courts recognize that psychotherapists cannot predict dangerousness with complete accuracy. Instead, the courts consider whether the psychologist used acceptable professional judgment in completing an assessment of dangerousness and in developing and implementing the treatment plan (Benjamin, Kent, & Sirikantraporn, 2009; VandeCreek & Knapp, 2000).

One of the difficulties that therapists face, however, when managing dangerous clients is that no standard of care has been established. The recent practice of specifying empirically supported treatments for a variety of mental health conditions has not yet been applied to the diagnosis and treatment of clients who pose a danger to others

(VandeCreek & Knapp, 2000). A recent study (Pabian, Welfel, & Beebe, 2007) found that about 75% of psychologists were misinformed about their legal duties with dangerous clients. When faced with dangerous clients, psychologists can consider many options, including hospitalizing the client, strengthening the therapeutic alliance, managing the client's environment, and breaking confidentiality. Truscott, Evans, and Mansell (1995) presented a model for decision making when working with dangerous clients. Their model is presented here.

The model proposes that clients who pose a threat of violence be thought of as occupying one of four cells in a 2 × 2, Violence Risk × Therapeutic Alliance Strength table. Interventions can be selected to strengthen the alliance and reduce the violence risk. The model is presented in Figure 118.1.

The authors suggest that, whenever possible, psychologists should work to strengthen and maintain the therapeutic alliance because the alliance is the backbone of most interventions. If the alliance is weak, the psychologist has a reduced chance of effectiveness with the client, especially when risk of violence is high. The model suggests that when the alliance is strong, the psychologist can focus on violence management, and if the risk of violence increases, therapy should be intensified and the client's environment more carefully managed. On the other hand, if the alliance is weak and the risk of violence is high, the psychologist should attempt to strengthen the alliance and/or involve significant others in treatment and consider hospitalization. Breaking confidentiality, then, should occur only in the context of a weak alliance and high violence potential.

To implement this model, or any other decision-making model, when working with potentially dangerous clients, psychologists must make assessments of violence potential. The legal test in predicting violence is one of "reasonable foreseeability." That is, would other psychologists with a similar client make a similar assessment and draw a similar conclusion? Aspects of client diversity must be included in the calculus. Liability is more likely to be imposed if the psychologist failed to follow appropriate procedures in reaching a decision and in implementing the decision than if an incorrect prediction was made. Thorough records are imperative to document decision making about dangerous clients.

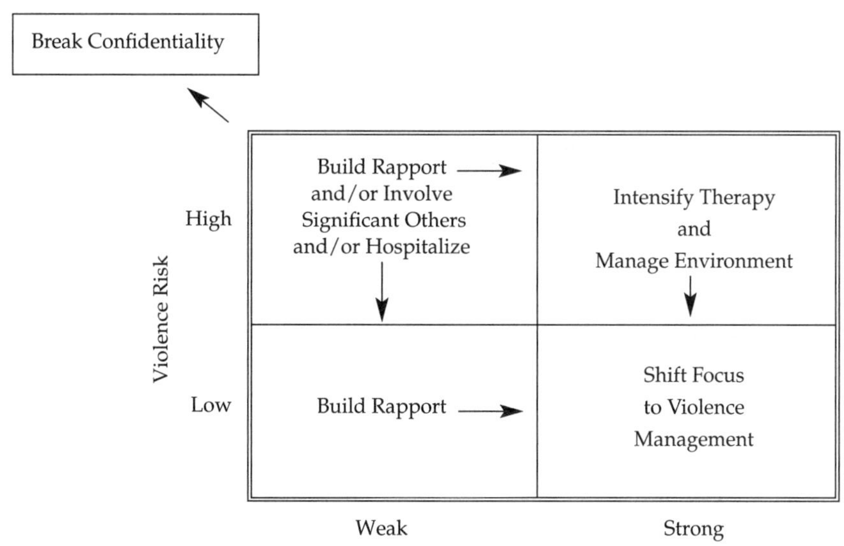

FIGURE 118.1. Decision Making with Dangerous Clients. (*Source*: Truscott, Evans, & Mansell (1995). Reprinted with permission from the American Psychological Association.)

The following variables should be considered when reviewing a client's potential for violence. Individual characteristics include the following:

- *History of violence.* This is the single best predictor of violent behavior. The age at which the first offense occurred is also an important variable. Individuals who commit their first violent offense prior to adolescence are more likely to engage in violent behaviors throughout their lifetime.
- *Clinical risk factors.* A diagnosis of substance abuse or dependence is probably the second most important factor. Persons with mental illness who believe that they are being threatened by others are also more likely to resort to violence.
- *Demographic variables.* Non-White persons in their late teens and early 20s with low IQ and education are most likely to engage in violent behaviors. Unstable residential and work histories increase the risk. Until recently, men were believed to pose more risks of violence than women, but research now suggests that clinicians, at least those working with more disturbed client populations, should not consider client sex to be a baseline risk factor (Otto, 2000).

Situational characteristics include the following:

- *Availability of potential victim(s).* Most violent crimes occur between people who know each other.
- *Access to weapons.* Persons with martial arts training or combat experience, and those who possess great physical strength are capable of inflicting greater harm.
- *Stressors.* Daily stressors such as relationship and financial problems can reduce a person's frustration tolerance.

Psychotherapists can assess the quality of their management of dangerous clients by asking the following questions:

1. Am I aware of state and federal laws and agency policies?
2. Have I done a thorough evaluation of the dangerousness of the client and have I updated it recently?
3. When clients have presented a threat of harm, have I modified my treatment plan to address the increased risk, such as by increasing the frequency of sessions, addressing anger in psychotherapy, incorporating other parties into treatment, asking the client to release weapons, and reviewing requirements of relevant duty-to-protect statutes?
4. Have I consulted with a knowledgeable colleague?
5. Have I carefully documented my clinical judgment and treatment and my consultations?

References and Readings

American Psychological Association. (2002). Ethical principles of psychologists and code of conduct. *American Psychologist, 57,* 1060–1073.

Benjamin, G. A. H., Kent, L., & Sirikantraporn, S. (2009). A review of duty-to-protect statutes, cases, and procedures for positive practice. In J. L. Werth, Jr., E. R. Welfel, & G. A. H. Benjamin (Eds.), *The duty to protect: Ethical, legal, and professional considerations for mental health professionals* (pp. 9–28). Washington, DC: American Psychological Association.

Otto, R. K. (2000). Assessing and managing violence risk in outpatient settings. *Journal of Clinical Psychology, 56,* 1239–1262.

Pabian, Y. L., Welfel, E. R., & Beebe, R. (2007, August). *Psychologists' knowledge and application of state laws in* Tarasoff*-type situations.* Paper presented at the 115th Annual Convention of the American Psychological Association, San Francisco, CA.

Tarasoff v. Regents of the University of California, 17 Cal. 3d 425, 551 P2d 334 (1976).

Truscott, D., Evans, J., & Mansell, S. (1995). Outpatient psychotherapy with dangerous clients: A model for clinical decision making. *Professional Psychology: Research and Practice, 26,* 484–490.

VandeCreek, L., & Knapp, S. (2000). Risk management and life-threatening patient behavior. *Journal of Clinical Psychology, 56,* 1335–1351.

Werth, J. L., Jr., Welfel, E. R., Benjamin, G. A. H., & Sales, B. D. (2009). Practice and policy responses to the duty to protect. In J. L. Werth, E. R. Jr., Welfel, & G. A. H. Benjamin (Eds.). *The duty to protect: Ethical, legal, and professional considerations for mental health professionals* (pp. 249–261). Washington, DC: American Psychological Association.

Related Topics

Chapter 39, "Treating Reluctant and Involuntary Clients"

Chapter 106, "Minimizing Your Legal Liability Risk Following Adverse Events or Patient Threats"

Chapter 128, "Understanding Fundamentals of the HIPAA Privacy Rule"

PART X
Financial and Insurance Matters

119 HANDLING MONEY MATTERS AND GIFTS IN PSYCHOLOGICAL PRACTICE

Jeffrey E. Barnett and Allison J. Shale

Fees, financial arrangements, and other money matters, along with the issue of gifts from clients, constitute important boundary issues in the professional relationship that require careful forethought and application by psychologists due to the significant potential for how they may impact both the treatment relationship and treatment outcomes. Boundaries are typically thought of as the ground rules of the professional relationship. In addition to fees, financial relationships, and gifts, examples of other boundaries present in psychologists' professional relationships include self-disclosure, touch, personal space, time, and location. At times, each will have relevance for the professional relationship and will require the practitioner's attention consistent with the client's best interests. Failure to manage these boundaries appropriately may result in harm to the client and to the professional relationship or in charges of unethical and/or illegal practices. We recommend addressing these issues openly with clients and considering decisions about boundaries thoughtfully since each client's individual circumstances and needs may result in different actions on the psychologist's part. Widely accepted general standards applying to managing these boundaries, including fees, exist in the American Psychological Association's *Ethical Principles of Psychologists and Code of Conduct* (APA, 2010). We advise psychologists to become familiar with these standards.

GETTING COMFORTABLE WITH MONEY AND BEING A BUSINESS PERSON

Most psychologists enter this profession, at least in part, out of a desire to help others. In general, psychologists are caring and compassionate individuals who seek to make a positive difference in the lives of others. Additionally, practicing psychologists provide services of value to others for which they receive compensation. As such, practicing psychologists operate or work in businesses. Most psychologists have little training in the business aspects of the profession and may feel ill equipped to manage this aspect of their work, both practically and emotionally.

All psychologists must become comfortable with their role as business persons. In this role, psychologists must directly address money issues and overcome any discomfort that they may have, including feelings of guilt associated with charging and collecting fees from clients for the services they provide. While they provide a caring, compassionate, and emotionally supportive relationship to clients, psychologists simultaneously provide professional services and they must be comfortable with the business and financial aspects of this relationship. It is essential that psychologists not see the roles of compassionate helper and business person as contradictory because both roles will prove important for the client's success. For example, failure to collect agreed-upon fees for professional services provided will likely result in business failure, and thus an inability to help future clients, as well as possibly leading to a clinical failure to respect and consistently apply agreed-upon boundaries.

INFORMED CONSENT

The issues of fees and financial arrangements should be addressed with each client at the outset of treatment. Clients have the right to know the cost of services to be provided and should understand all expectations of them. We suggest that in addition to a general informed consent agreement, psychologists have a specific financial agreement with each client, or with the financially responsible party if the client is a minor whose parent is paying for treatment. Similarly, when a third party, such as a court or an employer, makes requests for professional services, one should clarify financial responsibility at the outset.

The psychologist should ensure that the client (or the other responsible party) fully understands all services to be provided and the accompanying fees. While most clients will naturally expect to pay a specific fee for each 50-minute psychotherapy session, they may not anticipate fees for other services that may incur a charge and these should be specified in the financial agreement as well. Examples include fees charged for telephone consultations in between in-person sessions, e-mail correspondence, written reports, and the like. Nothing requires psychologists to charge for these additional services, but if one does, this requires clarification in advance. Because of the importance of the relationship between the psychologist and the client for successful treatment outcomes, psychologists do not want to engage in actions that may jeopardize it. This relationship, which is founded in large part on trust, can be promoted through open and direct discussions of fees and related financial arrangements. It is important to ensure that clients have reasonable and realistic expectations for the professional relationship, to include all fees charged, when and how payment is due, and all related expectations.

In discussions of financial policies with clients, include whether the psychologist requires payment at the time services are rendered or if the client will be billed for fees owed at some specific interval, such as monthly. Clients should also understand what form of payment is expected of them. Psychologists will also want to clarify all policies with regard to fees charged for returned checks, missed appointments, and cancellations. Many psychologists require 24 hours notice or they will bill for the appointment time. Such practices can qualify as ethical as long as the client has previously agreed to this policy as part of the informed consent process. Explaining the reasons for such policies to clients, such as psychologists reserving a specific time for each client that cannot easily be reassigned to another, will prove helpful. For those who accept automatic credit card payment from clients, including any information about charges for missed appointments or similar fees in the informed consent agreement will avoid later misunderstandings.

Because each psychologist's time is valuable and failure to earn compensation for their time will not yield a sustainable business model, take care in implementing the policy mentioned earlier. While it is an important policy to have in place, exercising good judgment in when to apply it will prove helpful. For example, one may see a big difference between a client who lands in the emergency room following an automobile accident and clients who acknowledge forgetting to enter the appointment date and time on their calendars. When a client fails to pay agreed-upon fees, one may feel tempted to utilize a collections agency or take legal action through a small claims court. Psychologists should exercise extreme caution when considering this, as it may feel antagonistic to the client and it may precipitate the filing of an ethics complaint or malpractice suit. Instead, include in the financial agreement a maximum allowable outstanding balance, such as the fees for three sessions, and specify the actions to follow should the outstanding balance reach that point (e.g., meeting less frequently until the balance is paid, referring the client elsewhere, etc.).

SETTING AND CHANGING FEES

Each psychologist must appropriately value the professional services that he or she provides. Factors to consider when setting fees include the number of years one has been in practice, particular skills and areas of expertise one has, the uniqueness of the services one offers, what others with similar expertise charge for their services, and prevailing community standards to include what the local population can likely afford. One may research what other professionals offering similar services charge, but ultimately each psychologist must decide on his or her own fees. This has business implications (charging too much may result in few clients; charging too little may result in low income) as well as clinical implications (the ability to offer services to those in need). Each psychologist must decide on the appropriate balance between promoting one's business and providing needed services to one's community that are accessible financially.

The APA Ethics Code (APA, 2010) makes it clear that psychologists should not exploit those that they provide professional services to and this includes financial exploitation. An example of possible financial exploitation would be charging one fee initially and then dramatically increase it after the client becomes dependent on the psychologist. Yet each psychologist has the right to increase fees over time to maintain a viable business. As expenses increase over time, an increase in fees will be needed; however, the manner in which one increases fees has important ethical implications. We recommend that any anticipated increases in fees be addressed in the initial financial agreement as part of the informed consent process. Thus, one might note that the fee charged will increase by $15 each January 1. Or one can give clients notice before increasing fees, if one has not discussed an annual increase on a specified date previously. One should give sufficient notice for clients to have time to make alternative treatment arrangements in the event they find themselves unable to continue due to financial limitations.

ALTERNATIVE PAYMENT ARRANGEMENTS

At times, clients may seek services they cannot afford. This may occur with prospective clients seeking treatment or with current clients who experience changes in their ability to pay for continued treatment. This may occur when a client loses his or her job or health insurance, when other expenses such as medical care for an ill family member occur, and in numerous other situations. We recommend that psychologists stay mindful of the possibility of such events arising during the course of treatment and have a written policy for payment alternatives in the financial agreement.

When an ongoing client experiences financial hardship, the psychologist has a number of options to consider. These include referring the client to a clinic or practice that charges a lower fee, lowering one's own fee, meeting with the client less frequently, providing services to the client pro bono, or engaging in barter with the client. We address each of these topics next.

A sliding fee scale involves charging clients based on their ability to pay. Psychologists willing to use this approach should include how they determine clients' fees in their written policy. This may include requiring documentation such as a client's recent tax returns or copies of recent pay stubs. The written policy should specify how the fee may change based on different income levels. One may advertise the availability of this fee structure to all clients or only share this information with those who inquire about it or display such a need.

The APA Ethics Code (APA, 2010) encourages providing professional services pro bono as part of each psychologist's responsibility to promote access to needed care for those who might not otherwise be able to receive it. Each psychologist will need to determine how many billable hours he or she can donate to pro bono services and still maintain a viable business. But one hopes that each psychologist will donate some portion of his or her time to those in need consistent with ethical principles of our profession.

In some communities and under some circumstances psychologists may engage in the practice of barter, the exchange of goods or services by the client for the psychologist's professional services. Ethical standards make it clear that barter with clients in not necessarily unethical, but that bartering for services requires great care. We recommend fully discussing the possible use of barter with those clients interested in using it, including potential benefits, potential risks, and available alternatives before making a decision to use it. If barter is used, establishing the value of the goods or services to be exchanged up front will prevent problems later. It may prove to be easier to agree on the value of goods than on the value of services. Yet, in doing so, it is important to ensure that clients are not exploited and that fair value is agreed upon. Each party's satisfaction with the arrangement will require monitoring and open discussion throughout the course of the arrangement to ensure that the bartering does not adversely impact the client, the psychologist, or the success of the professional relationship.

INSURANCE AND MANAGED CARE

Many clients will wish to utilize their insurance coverage to help pay for the psychological services they receive. Potential clients will want to know whether the psychologist's services will be covered under their insurance and what their financial responsibility will be. It is important to ensure that potential clients understand whether the psychologist participates in their insurance plan before initiating services (and before incurring any fees). One does not want clients to assume that their insurance plan will cover the fees charged, only to find out when a claim is rejected that they are responsible for the fees.

For those psychologists who do participate in a client's insurance plan it is vital that all benefits and potential limits to coverage be clarified and confirmed from the outset. Clients may assume that certain services or levels of service are covered by their insurance when in fact this is not the case. Verifying each client's insurance coverage from the outset helps the psychologist and client to agree on a realistic treatment plan based on the client's financial resources and insurance coverage. It would not be appropriate to develop a treatment plan that will likely take 50 or more sessions to complete when the client's insurance only provides coverage for 12 sessions each year and the client cannot afford to pay out of pocket.

Some insurers require each client's treatment plan undergo a utilization review process. The goal of this process for insurers is to lower costs and ensure that unneeded services are not provided. At times, utilization review personnel may exert pressure on the psychologist to limit the professional services provided in an effort to reduce costs to the insurer. Psychologists' ethical obligations require that they make clinically sound treatment decisions, not fiscally motivated decisions based on the insurer's needs. Similarly, psychologists should exercise caution about conflict of interest situations that would promote such fiscally motivated treatment decisions. For example, fear that failure to keep costs to the insurer low might result in being dropped from a provider panel should not drive decisions about client needs.

GIFTS FROM CLIENTS

As with other boundaries, psychologists should exercise a thoughtful approach to offers of gifts from clients. While it is important to act consistently with one's theoretical orientation, each client should be considered individually. Issues to consider include the client's motivation for offering the psychologist a gift (e.g., an expression of thanks vs. an effort to influence the psychologist), the circumstances of the gesture (e.g., at a holiday time vs. when asking for a report to the court), and the type and value of the gift (e.g., artwork made by a child vs. an expensive car). It is also important to consider cultural and other diversity factors that may shed light on the meaning of the gesture and how declining or accepting would likely impact the client and the treatment relationship. Finally, one should consider how accepting the gift would impact the psychologist and what the psychologist's motivations are for making this decision. If accepting the gift would likely adversely impact the psychologist's objectivity and judgment, great caution is recommended.

Open discussions of such issues with a client may prove helpful when it is unclear if the psychologist should accept or reject the gift or if the psychologist feels uncertain about any of the issues raised earlier. Furthermore, in such situations, consultation with experienced colleagues may prove helpful. But, at times, having such discussions and exploring the client's motivations may be countertherapeutic. A gift of homemade cookies during the winter holidays may represent an expression of appreciation that contains no hidden motivations and no potential for impacting the psychologist's objectivity or judgment. In such circumstances, questioning the meaning or rejecting the gift may damage the treatment relationship.

When dealing with finances, fees, and gifts, psychologists should do the following:

Utilize the informed consent process to discuss financial expectations and responsibilities, ensuring their understanding of fees and any planned increases to prevent clients from feeling exploited.

Remain aware of one's own financial needs and intentions and how clients may perceive your actions.

Consider each client's background and culture, among other diversity factors, when establishing financial expectations and when responding to gift gestures.

Anticipate potential limitations to client finances and be flexible in response, choosing the treatment and payment options best suited to the client's situation.

Ensure clients understand any limitations to insurance coverage for services to be provided, set treatment goals consistent with insurance coverage, and ensure that all treatment decisions are made with the client's best interests in mind.

When presented with gifts from clients, evaluate the nature of the gift, any cultural factors relevant, and how your decision may impact future therapeutic progress.

References and Readings

American Psychological Association. (2010). *Ethical principles of psychologists and code of conduct.* Retrieved February 2013, from www.apa.org/ethics

Barnett, J. E., & Walfish, S. (2011). *Billing and collecting for your mental health practice: Effective strategies and ethical practice.* Washington, DC: APA Books.

Haber, S., Rodino, E., & Lipner, I. (2001). *Saying good-bye to manage care.* New York: Springer.

Hunt, H. A. (2005). *Essentials of private practice: Streamlining costs, procedures, and policies for less stress.* New York: W. W. Norton.

Knapp, S., & VandeCreek, L. (2008). The ethics of advertising, billing, and finances in psychotherapy. *Journal of Clinical Psychology, 64,* 613–625.

Related Topic

Chapter 22, "Interpreting Clinical Scale Scores on the MMPI-2"

120 UNDERSTANDING PROFESSIONAL LIABILITY INSURANCE

Bruce E. Bennett

THE RELATIONSHIP BETWEEN RISK AND INSURANCE

Risk management essentially involves the transfer of financial obligations from one party to another.

- A significant feature of managed care arrangements is that some of the risk for payment of claims is shifted from the payer to the provider.
- In clinical practice, a missed diagnosis or improper treatment that damages a patient may result in a malpractice suit against the practitioner.
- Fortunately the psychologist can shift the risk for the potential financial loss to another party by purchasing professional liability insurance.

WHO NEEDS PROFESSIONAL LIABILITY COVERAGE?

Ideally, risk management would lead to the total elimination or avoidance of activities that could lead to harm, damage, or other negative consequences. In practice, the risk of damage or harm to a client or other entity receiving professional services can only be minimized. Even the most ethical and skilled practitioners have been subject to malpractice suits. It is important that psychologists recognize there is always the possibility of a negative outcome associated with the delivery of professional services.

- The risk of real or perceived damage or harm is not limited to psychologists who deliver health care services.
- Psychologists working for or consulting with business or governmental agencies, industrial organizational psychologists, academic and research psychologists, and school psychologists also are vulnerable to litigation for any harm or injury that may result from their services. For example, a psychologist who uses psychological tests for employee selection, retention, or promotion may be sued for any negative outcome based on the evaluation. A student who feels harassed or is dissatisfied with a grade or evaluation may sue his or her psychology professor or supervisor.
- The delivery of psychological services is never without risk.
- Any psychologist who provides professional services without adequate professional liability insurance has assumed the entire risk for any financial losses, including legal expenses to defend the practitioner and any damages awarded.

POLICY TYPE

Insurance is a written contract between the insured and the insurance carrier. For the premium received, the insurance carrier agrees to both defend the psychologist (i.e., pay the legal expenses associated with defending a claim) and indemnify the psychologist (i.e., pay for any cash settlements or damages awarded by a jury subject to any policy limitations). Two basic types of professional liability coverage are available: occurrence coverage and claims-made coverage.

- *Occurrence coverage:* An occurrence policy covers any incident that happens while the policy is in force—regardless of when the claim is filed. In an occurrence policy the claim will be covered according to the terms and conditions of the policy in force at the time the alleged malpractice occurred. A psychologist who terminates an occurrence policy (e.g., due to retirement, leave of absence, or changing to another policy type or another carrier) would be covered for any claim filed in the future based on any alleged malpractice during the policy period. There would be no need to purchase additional insurance.
- *Claims-made coverage:* A claims-made policy covers any incident that happens after the policy is in force. The claim, however, must be reported while the policy is in force. All claims-made policies have a *retroactive date*—the day that continuous coverage under the claims-made policy begins. To be covered under a claims-made policy, the incident must have occurred after the *retroactive date* and the claim filed before the policy is terminated. Claims filed after coverage ends will be covered only if the practitioner has purchased an *extended reporting period,* commonly referred to as "tail coverage." In a claims-made policy, the claim will be covered according to the terms and conditions of the policy in force at the time the claim is filed.

FACTORS AFFECTING POLICY PRICE

The majority of psychologists today purchase claims-made insurance with coverage levels at $1 million/$3 million (i.e., a maximum of $1 million in coverage for a single incident and up to $3 million aggregate coverage for all claims filed in the year). The range of coverage available extends from $200,000/$200,000 up to $2 million/$4 million.

- The premium for an occurrence policy is higher than the premium for a claims-made policy because coverage in an occurrence policy is provided for all future claims that resulted from alleged malpractice during the policy period. Occurrence premiums remain relatively stable over time, changing primarily as a function of losses in the program, increases in legal expenses, and general inflation.
- Premiums for a claims-made policy are lower during the first few years because coverage is provided only for claims filed during the coverage period. For example, first-year premiums need only cover the claims filed during the first year. Second-year premiums are set to cover the claims filed during the first and second year. As the policy matures the premiums will continue to increase.
- The differential in cost between an occurrence and a claims-made policy will generally exceed the price of the tail coverage necessary to terminate the claims-made policy. The psychologist can save considerable money by purchasing claims-made coverage.
- Independent of policy type, premiums will increase as a function of losses, inflation, and market fluctuations; as the policy limits increase; as the scope of coverage increases; and as benefits and enhancements are added to the policy.
- Premiums for practitioners are higher in some states than in others.
- Premiums are generally lower in policies that exclude certain types of activities, services, or service settings (e.g., custody evaluations, coaching, parent coordinating, certain types of forensic activities, and working in a correctional setting).
- Some policies include the cost of defending a malpractice suit within the policy limits, thus reducing the amount available

for payment of damages by the amount of the legal expenses. When the policy limits are reduced by defense cost, the policy price should be lower. Because of the high cost of defense, however, psychologists are encouraged to avoid this restriction.

READ YOUR POLICY AND UNDERSTAND HOW IT WORKS

It is important that psychologists be familiar with the terms, conditions, and exclusions in their professional liability policy.

Policy Conditions

Insurance policies contain a number of conditions that the insured must meet in order to keep the policy in force.

- The policy may require that the insured immediately report a suit or threat of suit to the carrier and that the insured cooperate with the carrier in the defense of a claim against the insured.
- The policy may prohibit the insured from assuming any obligations, incurring any costs, or settling any claims without the company's written consent. These and other conditions are included in the policy to protect the carrier from additional unnecessary expenses that may result from the practitioner's inappropriate actions.
- If the psychologist violates policy provisions, the insurance company may attempt to restrict or deny coverage for a specific claim. In the extreme, the carrier may sue the psychologist to rescind the policy, thus attempting to avoid all coverage for any claim.
- If the carrier determines that the psychologist is a bad risk for coverage, the policy may be terminated or not renewed.

Policy Limitations or Exclusions

In addition to specific conditions regarding coverage, professional liability insurance policies place limitations on, or exclude, coverage for specific activities.

- Psychologists' professional liability insurance generally will not cover claims against the insured for business relationships with current or former clients or as an owner or operator of a hospital or other overnight facility. These functions involve business and managerial decisions rather than the delivery of professional services. Facilities such as hospitals will need "directors and officers" and "errors and omissions" coverage.
- The policy may exclude claims of dishonest, criminal, or fraudulent acts by the psychologist. Insurance is not sold to protect dishonest or criminal behavior.
- A malpractice suit may allege that the psychologist's services and conduct were intended to injure the plaintiff. Intentional and willful acts are generally excluded from coverage.
- If a claim alleges acts or services that are excluded from coverage, the carrier will issue a "reservation of rights" letter to the defendant. This letter generally provides that the carrier will defend the case but may not have responsibility to pay for any damages awarded for the noncovered acts.

Special Provisions Related to Sexual Misconduct Claims

Historically, approximately half of the losses in the psychologists' professional liability program were due to sexual misconduct claims. Small wonder, then, that many insurance carriers have imposed specific limitations on such claims. The carriers, noting that sexual misconduct is unethical and that an increasing number of states have criminalized sexual relations between therapist and patient, are not willing to assume the liability for associated losses. Put differently, the company shifts the risks associated with such behaviors to the practitioner, keeping the premiums charged to ethical practitioners lower.

- Some carriers cap the amount the policy will pay for sexual misconduct claims, including both defense and indemnification costs.
- Other carriers will fully defend a sexual misconduct claim but exclude any payments for damages.

An insurance carrier may control for potential future losses by terminating or not renewing the policy of a psychologist who has been found guilty of sexual misconduct by a licensing board or ethics committee, even if no malpractice suit has been filed. Psychologists dropped by one carrier will have difficulty finding another carrier willing to offer coverage.

Ethical practitioners should be concerned with how the policy will respond to a frivolous claim alleging sexual misconduct.

- A policy that contains a blanket exclusion for therapist–patient sex may not even provide a legal defense. It is important that the policy defend claims alleging malpractice, regardless of the claim's merit.
- Some policies cap the carrier's liability in sexual misconduct cases at a fixed dollar amount. Under these terms, if a frivolous case is settled, the psychologist may be required to pay that part of the settlement that is in excess of the capped amount.
- A policy that will not pay damages but will defend multiple claims for sexual misconduct may, in fact, provide the best protection for a frivolous claim. The legal costs of going to trial can be very high, for both plaintiff and defendant. If the case is frivolous or weak, the plaintiff, or plaintiff's attorney, may wish to negotiate a settlement. Generally, insurance carriers will attempt to settle a case for an amount that is less than the cost of defense. If such a settlement is reached, the carrier will make the payment.

CHANGING POLICY TYPES OR INSURANCE CARRIERS

When changing policy types or changing carriers, be careful to avoid gaps in coverage.

- *Occurrence coverage to claims-made coverage.* To avoid any gap in coverage when moving from an occurrence policy to a claims-made policy, the retroactive date of the claims-made policy must be the same as or earlier than the termination date of the occurrence policy.
- *Claims-made coverage to occurrence coverage.* To avoid any gap in coverage when moving from a claims-made policy to an occurrence policy, the psychologist must (a) purchase the *extended reporting period* or the "tail coverage" for the terminated claims-made policy and (b) purchase occurrence coverage with a date that is the same or earlier than the termination date of the claims-made policy. If the tail coverage is not purchased, any claims filed after the claims-made policy is terminated will not be covered. Because of the general long reporting period for psychological malpractice claims, the insured is advised to purchase the longest tail coverage possible. The cost for indefinite tail coverage is usually 175% of the final year's premium.
- *Occurrence coverage to occurrence coverage by a different carrier.* To avoid any gap in coverage when moving from an occurrence policy to an occurrence policy from another carrier, the policy date of the new coverage should be the same as or earlier than the termination date of the terminated policy.
- *Claims-made coverage to claims-made coverage by a different carrier.* The psychologist who desires to change claims-made carriers has two choices. (a) Purchase the tail coverage on the old claims-made policy and purchase the first-year step rates on the new claims-made policy using the same renewal date as the old policy. If tail coverage is purchased on the old policy, the previous carrier will cover all claims generated under the terminated policy. The new carrier will cover claims resulting from alleged malpractice occurring after the effective date of the new policy. (b) Drop the old claims-made policy and purchase the new claims-made policy using the same retroactive date as the old policy. If the practitioner drops the old policy and purchases the new policy at the next step rate (e.g., if the current policy is at the fourth-year step rate, the new policy will be at the fifth-year step rate), all claims will then be covered by the new carrier. Purchasing the new claims-made policy at the next step rate will generally be more cost-effective in the short run. In addition, if the new carrier has a better reputation for

handling claims, the practitioner should follow this latter strategy.

- In addition to cost and dates of coverage, when changing from one carrier to another, it is essential to compare policy features to assure that the scope of coverage is not reduced.

COVERAGE FOR PSYCHOLOGISTS EMPLOYED IN GROUP SETTINGS

Psychologists employed in group or corporate practices, in schools or academic settings, or in agency settings (e.g., mental health centers, hospitals, or other government agencies) need to determine whether they are adequately covered for the services they perform in that setting. If not, they should purchase their own personal liability insurance. The following issues should be considered:

- Does the employer/group (e.g., group or corporate practice, mental health center, hospital, corporation, government agency, school, academic institution) have professional liability insurance?
- Does the insurance list both the group and the employee as a named insured under the policy?
- Are the levels of coverage adequate to cover any losses against the group and its employees?
- Do all members in the group share the aggregate limit of coverage, or does each member have his or her own aggregate limit? It is strongly recommended that each member of a group practice have his or her own aggregate limit.
- Does the policy require the carrier to defend and indemnify an employee who is sued for malpractice if the employee is not a named insured under the policy?
- Will the group policy cover an employee for services rendered outside the group setting?
- Do local, state, or federal statutes provide good-faith immunity for employees working in certain government settings? If a jury determines that the psychologist actually acted in bad faith (e.g., acted in a way to intentionally harm the plaintiff), the immunity statute may be voided, and the psychologist could then be responsible for payment of all costs.
- Regardless of the workplace setting, psychologists should avoid an uninsured risk. If the practitioner renders professional services outside the group setting (e.g., part-time consulting, supervision, teaching, or private practice), it is always recommended that individual coverage be in place.
- Psychologists serving as independent contractors for a group should have individual coverage. Group policies will cover a suit brought against the group as a result of the wrongdoing of an independent contractor, but they will not cover the independent contractor.
- If a group is uninsured, it is possible that the group may refuse to defend or indemnify a psychologist-employee named in a malpractice suit. The group may attempt to defend itself by asserting that the psychologist-employee acted outside the scope of the employment contract and that the group has no duty to defend the alleged wrongdoing. In effect, the group might join the plaintiff against the psychologist-employee.
- Whereas an uninsured agency or organization may have resources to defend a claim, it may be unable to pay damages. Uninsured psychologists employed by such agencies who are named as codefendants in the case may have to contribute to any damages awarded.
- If a group or agency does not have professional liability coverage, or if a psychologist-employee determines that the coverage available is not adequate, serious consideration should be given to purchasing individual coverage.

SETTLEMENT VERSUS TRIAL

Very few malpractice suits go to trial. Insurance carriers know that the most cost-effective resolution of this type of litigation is to settle the case. On the other hand, psychologists who do not believe they are guilty of malpractice usually want to go to trial, even if an appeal to the US Supreme Court is necessary.

- Regardless of the "innocence" of the practitioner, there is always the possibility that a jury will award large damages. The psychologist would be personally responsible for any damages that exceed the policy limits.
- No one can predict how a jury will respond, even to a claim that has no merit.
- The plaintiff may want to settle the case if the allegations of malpractice will be difficult to prove, if the evidence indicates that the case is not clear-cut, or if the damages are not significant.
- The defendant may wish to settle to avoid painful depositions, prolonged litigation, potential embarrassment in the public arena, and the loss of income due to time away from the practice.
- The net effect is that both the plaintiff and the defendant may have strong incentives to seek a settlement rather than go to trial.
- Most frivolous cases are dismissed or settled for small amounts. Fortunately frivolous cases are generally transparent; if so, they may not have a significant impact on the psychologist's insurability.
- On the other hand, a large settlement is often interpreted as an indication of the seriousness of the charges and resulting damages.

THE PSYCHOLOGIST'S ROLE IN CASE SETTLEMENT

Most insurance policies (e.g., auto or homeowner's insurance) permit the insurance company to settle a claim without the consent of the insured. One professional liability policy contained a provision that required the written consent of the insured to settle a claim; if an insured refused to settle, the carrier was forced to take the case to trial. Although this provision may seem beneficial to the insured individual, the result is that almost all cases go to trial, at great expense to all practitioners insured under the program.

The major psychologists' professional liability policies provide a compromise between these two extreme positions. In the course of litigation, the attorneys for the plaintiff and defendant may discuss settlement as an option to trial. Even if the attorneys representing the plaintiff and defendant reach agreement on a proposed settlement, the carrier cannot settle the case without the written consent of the insured. However, if the insured refuses to accept the settlement proposal, the carrier's ultimate liability will be capped at the amount of the proposed settlement. If a jury awards damages in excess of the capped amount, the psychologist, not the carrier, will have to pay the difference.

PROFESSIONAL LIABILITY INSURANCE IS FOR THE LONG TERM

Over time, the insurance industry tends to go through market cycles, fluctuating between "soft" and "hard" markets. Competition is a key factor in a soft market: The return on investments is high, and insurance carriers attempt to increase their cash flow by offering new products or by decreasing premiums on current products to capture competitors' business. In a hard market, when the economy is not doing well, rates usually increase dramatically, and some companies may go out of business.

Malpractice suits against psychologists tend to be filed long after the alleged negligence or misconduct occurred. The premiums collected today must provide coverage for a possible claim against the psychologist in the future, sometimes years later. If current rates are too low, the carrier may not be able to provide the protection when needed. Moving from a soft to a hard market when premiums have been artificially low could result in large rate increases, modifications in the scope of coverage, or a decision by the carrier to drop this line of coverage. Psychologists are advised to view the purchase of professional liability insurance as an investment in the future. Put differently, a cheap policy may come with a high price.

ADMITTED VERSUS SURPLUS LINES CARRIERS

Most insurance carriers are "admitted," that is, approved by the state insurance commissioner to do business in that state. Admitted carriers are required to participate in consumer protection programs in the state. If an admitted carrier cannot meet its obligations to cover losses, state insurance funds may be available to protect the insureds. Some carriers, however, offer policies on a *nonadmitted* basis, commonly referred to as "surplus lines coverage." Such policies will clearly state that insured psychologists are not protected by state-authorized consumer protection programs.

- Surplus lines coverage may be available for practitioners who are otherwise uninsurable because of a history of previous claims. Such policies are usually very expensive and may restrict available limits of liability.
- Other carriers may offer surplus lines coverage in markets where coverage is not readily available (e.g., in hard markets when carriers fail or stop offering this type of coverage).

WHERE TO PURCHASE PROFESSIONAL LIABILITY INSURANCE

The diligent psychologist will approach the subject of professional liability insurance as an important business decision, both to protect the psychologist's assets and to provide the comfort and security needed to function in a professional capacity.

Policy features, strength and stability of the carrier, price, special enhancements, and representation of the psychologist's interests with the carrier are important aspects of any purchasing decision. The majority of practitioners purchase professional liability insurance from programs endorsed or sponsored by their national professional association. The American Psychological Association Insurance Trust has endorsed or sponsored comprehensive and cost-effective professional liability insurance for more than 37 years, during both soft and hard markets, including times when some carriers dropped psychology as a line of coverage. The current Trust-sponsored professional liability insurance program was developed by psychologists for psychologists. The Trust serves as an ombudsperson for practitioners, representing their interests on all aspects of coverage and price.

References and Readings

Bennett, B. E., Bricklin, P. M., Harris, E., Knapp, S., VandeCreek, L., & Younggren, J. N. (2007). *Assessing and managing risk in psychological practice: An individualized approach.* Bethesda, MD: APA Insurance Trust.

Koocher, G. P., & Keith-Spiegel, P. C. (2008). *Ethics in psychology and the mental health professions: Professional standards and cases* (3rd ed.). New York: Oxford University Press.

Woody, R. H. (1988). *Protecting your mental health practice: How to minimize legal and financial risk.* San Francisco, CA: Jossey-Bass.

Wright, R. H. (1981). Psychologists and professional liability (malpractice) insurance: A retrospective review. *American Psychologist, 36,* 1485–1493.

Related Topics

Chapter 105, "Defending Against Legal (Malpractice and Licensing) Complaints"

Chapter 106, "Minimizing Your Legal Liability Risk Following Adverse Events or Patient Threats"

121 MANAGING YOUR MANAGED CARE CONTRACTS

Gerald P. Koocher

When practitioners sign contracts with insurance companies or other third parties (such as managed care organizations [MCOs]) for payment of their services, we accept a set of legal obligations. Failure to fully grasp the nature of such agreements or failure to observe contractual obligations can create significant legal problems. Although focused on MCOs, the comments herein apply equally to any third-party payer with whom practitioners sign services contracts.

CONSIDERING A CONTRACT

- Review any MCO contract thoroughly before signing. Do not assume that all health professional service contracts are alike. Read every contract carefully.
- Make sure you understand what the terms mean and that you are willing and able to meet them before you sign a contract.
- Seek modification of any terms with which you do not agree, although you may not have much leverage. Practitioners sometimes believe they can modify a contractual provision that they find objectionable by striking through it and signing their initials. However, that perspective may not be shared by companies that expect acceptance of a provider contract in its entirety.
- When in doubt about any contractual terms or desired modifications, consult with your state psychological association or an attorney. Many state associations have close familiarity with insurance or managed care contracts operating in their states or can suggest knowledgeable lawyers.

AFTER SIGNING ON

- Make sure to keep a copy of your contract readily accessible. Reviewing the contract when questions or problems arise may provide easy citations that resolve the matter quickly. A common example involves timely notice provisions regarding changes in fees.
- Keep track of any revisions or amendments to the contract. These may come as separate sheets with a notice letter, but they should be filed together with the easily accessible copy of the original contract.
- Keep copies of any policy statements, manuals, fee schedules, or other documents referenced by the contract. This might include any documentation for determining medical necessity, treatment exclusions, and so on.

IN THE EVENT PROBLEMS ARISE

- *Understand which regulatory agencies directly address your MCO's operations in your practice jurisdiction.* This could include a state insurance commissioner or similar state agency responsible for overseeing contracts issued by MCOs. Whenever you send a complaint letter to the MCO, consider sending a copy to the state insurance commissioner or agency as well.

- *Understand the issue of "no-cause termination" from an MCO Provider Panel.* When considering whether to sign a provider contract, recognize distinction between "for-cause" and "no-cause" terminations. Contracts will typically list provisions in the contract as constituting grounds for terminating the provider "for cause" if he or she does—or fails to do—these items. Be prepared to fully abide by such provisions. Some contracts have so-called no-cause termination clauses. These allow an MCO to terminate a contract without giving any reason for doing so, usually following a notice period. Typically, such no-cause terminations typically get implemented when a company determines that it no longer has a business interest to continue the contract. It is difficult to fight a no-cause termination because it leaves no "due process" appeal from the MCO decision. Some states have found no-cause termination clauses contrary to public policy and have legislation prohibiting such provisions in provider contracts.
- *Continuity of care.* Practitioners should understand in advance whether they have a contractual obligation to continue providing services to patients covered by the MCO for a specified period of time (for example, 90 days) after their relationship with the company has terminated, or at least until the patient is transitioned safely to another health professional's care.
- *Record access.* Record retention policies are addressed elsewhere in this volume, but some MCO contracts may include retention requirements more onerous than professional standards or state law would suggest. If you sign an agreement to abide by the MCO's standards, you must follow them. If you keep psychotherapy notes as defined by the Health Insurance Portability and Accountability Act (HIPAA), in addition to a standard clinical record, a health insurer cannot demand to review such notes.
- *Retrospective audits.* Many contracts give the MCO the right to audit a practitioner's records for quality control purposes or fraud and abuse detection. In some instances, companies have gone beyond what their contract or state law allows when conducting retrospective audits. In some cases audits resulted in practitioners being told to refund monies to an MCO because of alleged deficiencies in recordkeeping. If you face a retrospective audit that you consider excessive, check your contract and provider manual, as well as relevant state laws, to determine whether the company seeks to go beyond what the contract or law allows.
- *Prompt payment laws and related contract provisions.* Many states have statutes or regulations requiring MCOs to pay within a designated period of time after receiving "clean claims" that contain all the information needed to process that claim. Check your state laws regarding prompt payment and make sure that your contract's payment provisions match state law requirements.
- *Clauses governing changes to contract terms.* Contractual provisions on payment rate changes or other modifications to contract terms specify how the MCO can change terms of the provider contract. Typically, contracts may specify that the company can make unilateral contract changes—that is, on its own without the provider's agreement—or that changes must be agreed to by the MCO and the health professional. Before signing a contract you should understand what provisions of the contract an MCO may change on its own, and the amount of notice required. Some contracts allow the practitioner to object to a proposed change, but doing so may constitute an automatic resignation from the provider panel.

References and Readings

Albizu-García, C. E., Ríos, R., Juarbe, D., & Alegría, M. (2004). Provider turnover in public sector managed mental health care. *Journal of Behavioral Health Services and Research, 31*, 255–265.

APA Practice Central. (2005). *A matter of law: Managing your managed care contracts*. Retrieved February 2013, from http://www.apapracticecentral.org/business/legal/professional/secure/managed-care-contract.aspx

DeBlasio, S. L. (2008). *Managed care contracts—key provisions for providers*. Retrieved February 2013, from http://corporate.findlaw.com/law-library/managed-care-contracts-key-provisions-for-providers.html

Keagy, B. & Thomas M. (Eds.). (2012). Essetials of Physician Practice Management. New York: Wiley.

Zuvekas, S. H., Rupp, A., & Norquist, G. (2007). Cost shifting under managed behavioral health care. *Psychiatric Services, 58*, 100–108.

Related Topics

Chapter 122, "Setting Fees for Psychological Services"

Chapter 123, "Navigating Adverse Managed Care Decisions"

122 SETTING FEES FOR PSYCHOLOGICAL SERVICES

Kavita J. Shah and John C. Norcross

This chapter integrates empirical research and clinical experience in assisting psychologists to determine how to set their fees for psychotherapy and psychological testing.

PSYCHOTHERAPY FEES

Probably the most systematic study of psychotherapy fees is that undertaken by the Ridgewood Financial Institute every 2 or 3 years and published in *Psychotherapy Finances*. Since 1979, this nationwide survey of private practice mental health clinicians has covered individual and group therapy fees, psychological testing fees, regional variations in fees, managed-care allowances, and practice expenses, among other elements of the financial profile of psychotherapy practice. (Subscriptions for monthly issues of *Psychotherapy Finances* can be directed to 1-800-869-8450 or purchased through its Web site.)

The most recent survey, conducted in 2006, encompassed 1,011 licensed mental health professionals, principally psychologists ($n = 394$) and social workers ($n = 333$). Table 122.1 presents the usual and customary fees charged by psychologists and social workers for an initial evaluation, a 50-minute individual session, a family/marital session, and a group therapy session.

Table 122.2 presents another type of psychotherapy fee: that actually paid to or received by psychologists and social workers. The numbers are presented separately for three types of fees: direct pay, managed care, and indemnity insurance.

From 1979, when the first *Psychotherapy Finances* survey was conducted, median fees had constantly risen for independent practitioners. Starting in the mid-1990s, however, there

TABLE 122.1. Usual and Customary Fees of US Psychologists and Social Workers

Type of Service	Psychologists	Social Workers
Initial evaluation	$150	$110
Individual session (45–60 minutes)	$125	$100
Family/martial session (50 minutes)	$125	$100
Group therapy	$50	$40

Source: January 2006 Psychotherapy Finances.

TABLE 122.2. Psychologists' Median Received Fees for Individual and Group Therapy Sessions

	Direct Pay	Managed Care	Indemnity Insurance
Individual therapy	$50	$75	$110
Group therapy	$50	$40	$50

Source: October 2006 Psychotherapy Finances.

was a definite downward pressure on fees. Most psychotherapists reported that their usual and customary fees had either remained the same (thus actually decreasing when adjusted for inflation) or eroded by an average of $5. In fact, the consumer price index (CPI) is climbing faster than psychotherapy fees are rising.

In several respects, the results substantiate the obvious economics: Providing psychotherapy to managed-care patients yields lower hourly reimbursements. Managed care exacts significant "costs" from the practitioner: a 25% fee reduction on average and the additional paperwork and administrative duties that such programs typically entail. Heavy reliance on managed-care fees concretely translates into decreased annual incomes for full-time practitioners.

PSYCHOLOGICAL TESTING FEES

The *Psychotherapy Finances* study also collects data on psychologists' fees for administering various psychological tests. The mean fees charged for psychological testing are presented in Table 122.3 for four types of patients: self-pay, Medicare, managed care, and indemnity insurance. As seen there, there are large discrepancies in testing fees between self-pay and managed-care patients in favor of the former.

Table 122.4 presents the 2009 maximum allowable reimbursement for psychotherapy and psychological therapy and psychological testing under Medicare, Medicaid, and selected health insurance plans in South Texas (Gasquoine, 2010). Although these numbers

TABLE 122.3. Mean Fees Charged by Psychologists for Psychological Tests

Test	Self-Pay	Medicare	Managed Care	Indemnity Insurance
Wechsler Adult Intelligence Scale III	$209	$151	$150	$200
Wechsler Intelligence Scale for Children III	$212	$157	$150	$200
Leiter International Performance Scale—Revised	$168	$132	$203	$160
Wechsler Memory Scale III	$182	$139	$150	$176
Minnesota Multiphasic Personality Inventory II (or MMPI-A)	$131	$106	$105	$121
Millon Clinical Multiaxial Inventory III	$127	$98	$100	$133
NEO Personality Inventory	$141	$100	$143	$140
Rorschach (Exner system)	$219	$118	$150	$194
Wechsler Individual Achievement Test	$159	$100	$126	$160
Wide Range Achievement Test III	$99	$67	$90	$96
Peabody Individual Achievement Test	$128	$75	$102	$119
Child Behavior Checklist	$82	$84	$68	$78
Dementia Rating Scale	$123	$96	$75	$107

Source: October 2006 Psychotherapy Finances.

TABLE 122.4. Maximum Allowable Reimbursement Rates in 2009 for Outpatient Psychological Practice Under Medicare/Medicaid and Selected Health Insurances in South Texas

Health Insurance Company	Reimbursement Rates	
	90806	96101
Medicare	$93.54	$84.40
Medicaid	$80.79	$125.00
Aetna	$76.00	$80.00
BlueCross BlueShield (Magellan)	$87.23	$83.42
CIGNA	$65.00	$75.00
Humana (Lifesynch)	$65.00	$100.00
MHNET Behavioral Health	$50.00	$50.00
United Behavioral Health	$70.00	$60.00

Note. 90806 = procedure code for 45–60 minutes of psychological therapy, and 96101 = procedure cost for psychological testing, interpretation, and report writing per hour.

Source: Gasquoine, 2010.

hail from only one section of the country, the figures are illuminating and consistent with those from other evidentiary sources.

CREATING A FEE STRUCTURE: THE MATH

Often the most taboo topic in psychotherapy is not sex but money. Little attention and training have been given to money matters. There are no professional rules in place and virtually no formal graduate training to guide professionals in setting a fee structure for their own practices. Many professionals believe the fee they set is not only the price of their services but also a reflection of their self-worth, education, and professional value. Creating a fee structure carries immense weight with it and thus requires multiple considerations.

Start by asking yourself four fundamental questions. One: what is the *demand* for my services, in general as a psychologist, and in particular for me? The greater the demand, the more elastic the fee. Two: what is the local *supply* or *competition* for the services I provide? The law of supply and demand operates imperfectly in health care, but it does influence fees. Three: what is the *prevailing fee* or *market value* of my services? Antitrust laws prohibit one from sharing or setting pricing information in a public forum; however; a practitioner can certainly examine the tables in this chapter and privately secure such information from individual colleagues. Four: what is the *level of affluence* and health insurance coverage of the typical patient in my geographic region? Fees in Manhattan are generally double that in the rural Midwest.

After asking these fundamental questions, you can work backward with your goal in mind (Sears, 2005). The goal is your monthly take-home income; the divider is how many hours you desire to work a month. This simple math helps you to calculate how much to charge per hour.

Say, your goal is $10,000 gross income per month. Beginning practitioners forget to differentiate between billable hours and total hours spent on a practice task. That $10,000 translates into $12,000 or $13,000 billed hours per month. Say, you are willing to spend 40 hours a week at the office, but 10 of those hours will probably be devoted to returning calls, missed appointments, peer consultations, and pro bono sessions. That leaves, for the sake of our example, 30 billable hours per week or 120 billable hours per month. Dividing your monthly billable goal of $12,500 by 120 hours yields $104 per hour charged. Of course, you will also need to factor in the overhead costs of the practice.

CREATING A FEE STRUCTURE: THE CHOICES

In one study (Newlin, Adolph, & Kreber, 2004), 75 psychologists completed surveys on how they set fees for their clients in private practice. Here are the 12 factors, in descending order of importance, exerting the strongest influence on practitioners' fees:

- Practitioner's education/qualifications
- Local competition
- Business experience
- Type of clientele you wish to serve
- Network with opposite-sex colleagues
- Network with same-sex colleagues
- Nonmonetary motivators

- Setting a minimum fee
- Self-image
- Other sources of family income
- Cost indices, for example, Consumer Price or Cost of Living Index
- Negotiating fees with prospective client

Four other factors were influential to at least one-third of the practitioners in the study. These were comparing their own fees to insurance reimbursement rates, considering the major source of patient referrals, feeling guilt about charging for help, and the motivating force of making money.

We would also like to add a couple of considerations, not mentioned in the study, that our colleagues take into account when setting their practice fees. One is specialization, which is related to demand and supply. Some specializations, such as forensic psychology, large business consultation, and clinical neuropsychology, seem to demand more money because of the limited supply of board-certified experts. The other consideration is the practitioner's personal values or a vision. Some very experienced and talented psychologists could demand much higher fees but choose to pursue their calling to assist economically or historically disadvantaged populations. Such decisions cut into profits but reward the heart.

Regardless of which factors you consider and the weights you afford them, creating a fee structure for psychological services constitutes a complex and foundational part of any practice. The recent evolution (or devolution) of health insurance and reimbursement rates complicates the task, but in the end, you, the practitioner, remain responsible for the decisions.

References and Readings

Gasquoine, P. G. (2010). Comparison of public/private health care insurance parameters for independent psychological practice. *Professional Psychology: Research and Practice, 41*(4), 319–324.

Newlin, C. M., Adolph, J. L., & Kreber, L. A. (2004). Factors that influence fee setting by male and female psychologists. *Professional Psychology: Research and Practice, 35*(5), 548–552.

Phelps, R., Eisman, E. J., & Kohout, J. (1998). Psychological practice and managed care: Results of the CAPP Practitioner Survey. *Professional Psychology: Research and Practice, 29*, 31–36.

Pingitore, D., Scheffler, R., Sentell, T., Haley, M., & Schwalm, D. (2001). Psychologist supply, managed care, and effects on income: Fault lines beneath California psychologists. *Professional Psychology: Research and Practice, 32*, 597–606.

Psychotherapy Finances. (n.d.). *Home page*. Retrieved February 2013, from www.psyfin.com/

Sears, M. (2005, November 12). The matters of fees: How to decide what to charge and how to increase fees when it's time. *The National Psychologist*. Retrieved August 2012 from www.professionalpracticemanagement.com/files/61322851.pdf

Williams, S., Kohout, J. L., & Wicherski, M. (2000). Salary changes among independent psychologists by gender and experience. *Psychiatric Services, 51*, 1111.

Williams, S., Wicherski, M., & Kohout, J. L. (2010). *2009 salaries in psychology*. Washington, DC: American Psychological Association.

Related Topics

Chapter 119, "Handling Money Matters and Gifts in Psychological Practice"

Chapter 121, "Managing Your Managed Care Contracts"

123 NAVIGATING ADVERSE MANAGED CARE DECISIONS

Katherine C. Nordal and Shirley Ann Higuchi

This chapter provides strategies for navigating adverse managed care and insurance company determinations. (For ease of reference, we will use the terms "managed care company" or "company" to refer broadly to managed care companies and health insurers.)

PREVENTIVE MEASURES

You can avoid many problems with managed care by understanding the company's policies and procedures before you provide services and before you submit claims.

Before providing services, you should review your provider contract (if you have one), the company's provider manual, and the provider section of the company Web site for provider updates from the company. Look for pre-authorization or pre-certification requirements (which require you to obtain company approval before you provide services), procedures for submitting claims, recordkeeping requirements, and other restrictions that can impact reimbursements (i.e., requirements for timely submissions).

Before submitting claims, make sure that you are using the required forms and providing the requested information accurately. Claims are often rejected because of simple mistakes like missing or incorrect diagnosis and procedure codes or patient and provider information.

You should also have a system for tracking whether your claims are being fully and promptly paid. Having a good billing service or utilizing billing software can reduce the burden of obtaining authorizations, submitting and tracking claims, and resolving disputes with managed care companies when they do arise.

If certain companies make up a significant share of your practice. It may be helpful to identify a contact at the company who can help you resolve problems. Developing a rapport with that company representative.

Keeping good records is another important preventive measure. You should keep records of all your contracts, contract addenda, fee schedules, and provider updates organized for each insurer. It is also critical to keep your authorization and claims records complete and organized for each patient.

WHEN PROBLEMS DO ARISE: OVERALL STRATEGIC APPROACH

Despite the preventive measures outlined earlier, you should expect to encounter some adverse managed care determinations and other problems. Managed care companies process an enormous volume of claims and problems are inevitable. Moreover, the fundamental purpose of these companies is to "manage" care to reduce unnecessary or inappropriate care and to reduce costs. However, in some cases, the company may be trying to cut costs regardless of what is appropriate. The authors have observed that a company will often ignore the requirements stated in its own provider contracts. Also a company might ignore what patients have been promised in their benefits booklets and other marketing material.

NAVIGATING DENIALS

Your overall approach to navigating denials should be to start as politely as is appropriate and then increase your assertiveness as necessary to resolve the problem. For significant problems that you cannot promptly resolve, your goal is to find the available leverage to increase your bargaining position against the large managed care company.

It is important to be persistent. The saying "the squeaky wheel gets the grease" is very applicable to managed care. Some companies seem to have the view that if they deny most requests the first or second time, most providers will become frustrated and give up. This leaves a much smaller group of persistent providers to deal with. You should be one of those providers.

The best starting point is often a cordial phone call. This is particularly appropriate if you have an established relationship with a company representative. The problem may be a simple mistake or misunderstanding on your part or the company's part. Starting confrontationally may trigger an equally confrontational, and unhelpful, response from an overworked company representative. If your initial cordial attempts do not resolve your problem, do not hesitate to escalate to written communications by e-mail or certified letter. This will create a paper trail that will be helpful if you need to take the issue higher up within the company or to an outside entity.

You should also determine whether the adverse decision is one that is subject to the company's appeal procedures, as is the case for most denials of patient care. If so, inform yourself about the appeal procedures and the deadlines for filing an appeal. Appeals can be cumbersome and sometimes involve two or three levels (if your appeal is denied at the lower level), but this can be the best vehicle for responding to denials, particularly where detailed information about a particular patient is central to the dispute.

If an appeal is not available or advisable (for example, a patient urgently needs care and there is no expedited appeals process) and your initial efforts did not resolve your issue, escalate by applying leverage. Some companies are more responsive when you demonstrate that you know how to enlist help from outside entities such as professional associations, government agencies and others who can help put pressure on insurance companies in resolving persistent problems. Consider copying your next e-mail or letter to the following:

1. The national, state, and local psychological associations to which you belong
2. Your insurance commissioner
3. Your state attorney general or other agency concerned with protecting consumers (if the issue has an impact on patients)
4. Federal enforcement authorities (if you believe the company violated HIPAA, the federal parity law, or other federal law)
5. Your state or federal legislator

These entities may be able to provide you with guidance or advocacy support. Your national, state, or local psychological association can be an important resource, particularly if your issue is one with a broad impact on other psychologists and their patients. On adverse decisions affecting many psychologists, there is often strength in numbers. A managed care company is more likely to act on a complaint from a state or local psychological association than one from an individual psychologist. A listing of the state psychological associations and their contact information can be found at www.apapracticecentral.org/advocacy/state/associations.aspx.

If your initial company contact is not helpful, do not hesitate to elevate your problem to the next level. Ask for contact information for the person's supervisor. That person may be more knowledgeable about company policies or have greater authority than a lower level "front line" employee has.

WHEN PROBLEMS DO ARISE: SPECIFIC POINTERS

Clarify the Company's Decision and its Justification

An important threshold step is to verify exactly what the company's adverse decision is and the justification for the decision. If either is uncertain, ask the company for clarification.

Start by reviewing the denial letter, explanation of benefits, or other communications from the company that state or relate to the adverse decision. Determine whether the cited reason makes sense in light of the policy provisions, policies, criteria, statutes, or regulations that the company cites. If the company cites internal policies or other documents that you do not have, ask to see them.

The general trend is toward greater transparency by managed care companies about their policies. In fact, the Office of Legal and Regulatory Affairs of the American Psychological Association Practice Organization has been successful with several state psychological associations in improving transparency of managed care and insurance company operations.[1] The interim final regulations implementing the federal mental health parity law require that the companies subject to parity make available to providers and patients any medical necessity criteria used to deny care.

Be Clear and Concise

Company employees typically handle large volumes of information and do not have time to read a lengthy or rambling description of your problem. Your communications should be as succinct as possible.

Start with a clear, simple statement of the problem and what action you want from the company to fix it. Also, provide a brief factual background and argument explaining why the company's decision was wrong. Briefly cite any applicable contract provisions by citing the provider contract or other materials that relate to coverage, payment, and limitations. In addition, certain states may have favorable laws (like a "prompt payment law") that can help your case. Again this is where contacting your state psychological association is extremely helpful, since they will be familiar with state laws in your jurisdiction.

Where further detail is necessary or helpful to your argument, you can "layer" your communication by providing that additional detail in an appendix or later section of the communication. This makes the additional information available if the company representative needs it, without cluttering your communication.

Direct Your Request to the Right Company

Some managed care issues are made more confusing by the managed care practice of having different companies involved in contracting with the psychologist, authorizing care, processing claims, and paying them. This may leave the psychologist unsure as to which company should address the problem. In the case of adverse managed care decisions, however, it is usually clear which company has announced that decision. If there is any uncertainty, you can direct your communications to all companies that might be involved and let the companies sort out who is responsible. If your problem is with the behavioral health carve out company (or some other company that is essentially performing services on behalf of the main health insurer), you may want to copy your complaint to the main insurer. That is the company ultimately responsible for providing quality care to their insureds, and it may be the only company subject to state or federal insurance regulation.

[1] For example, the April 2004 settlement with CIGNA in the class action *In re Managed Care Litigation* (US District Court, S.D. Florida) contained several provisions that made the company's policies and procedures more transparent to providers. Similar provisions were contained in the August 2006 settlement with Humana in the same case. In both settlements, the APA Practice Organization collaborated with the Florida Psychological Association.

RESPONDING TO PARTICULAR TYPES OF ADVERSE DECISIONS

Medical Necessity and Patient Privacy

Managed care determinations that mental health treatment is not medically necessary have always been one of the most common managed care problems for psychologists. This issue has become more prominent, however, since the federal mental health parity legislation took away companies' ability to rely on annual limits on care (e.g., 20 or 40 outpatient therapy sessions per year). With annual limits no longer available as a tool for containing costs, many managed care companies have placed greater emphasis on medical necessity criteria.

Before considering strategies for responding to an adverse medical necessity determination, it is important to understand the company's definition of medical necessity, how it applies the definition to mental health care, and its strategy for managing medical necessity determinations. Most companies use a medical necessity definition that has the same basic provisions, focusing on treatment that is necessary, appropriate, and effective for treating a mental health condition or relieving its symptoms. Obtain the company's medical necessity definition and any guidance on how it is applied to the type of mental health care you are providing (e.g., outpatient therapy for moderate depression).

Many companies have an "up and out" view of how medical necessity applies to the course of treatment. They expect that there will be a treatment plan aimed at improving the patient's symptoms attributable to the mental health diagnosis and improving his or her functioning to the point that treatment can be reduced and then terminated. Some companies expect that the treatment plan will set goals for the level of improvement that will trigger a reduction or termination of care. Generally, companies consider coverage for long-term treatment to be the exception rather than the rule; and something they only accept in rather severe cases.

As far as strategies for managing medical necessity, some managed care companies scrutinize all care for medical necessity at a particular point, for example by considering medical necessity for therapy after 10 or 12 sessions or reviewing all psychological or neuropsychological testing for medical necessity in advance. Other companies "manage the outliers." They recognize that most mental health care takes place within certain parameters and they focus their medical necessity scrutiny on cases where treatment has taken place over what the company considers a long time period at a high level of care, considering the patient's diagnosis, symptoms, and risks.

The challenge in fighting medical necessity determinations is often providing sufficient information to justify further care without providing more than the minimum necessary information about the patient to the managed care company. For instance, some psychologists will attempt to protect the patient's privacy by providing a milder diagnosis than the psychologist really believes is actually appropriate. The diagnosis may be of particular concern when the patient is likely to become involved in litigation or apply for a military or government position that will cause his or her mental health records to be voluntarily or involuntarily released. The milder diagnosis, however, is likely to make the managed care company approve less care than the patient actually needs for his or her condition.

Another privacy dilemma concerns the amount of detail about the patient you should provide in order to support your position that the assessment or treatment that you have requested or provided is medically necessary. For this issue, it is important to understand privacy protections under HIPAA. Under the HIPAA Privacy Rule, companies may only request the "minimum necessary" patient information to carry out the intended purpose of the request. Psychologists and managed care companies, however, often had very different interpretations about how much sensitive patient information was necessary for determining medical necessity. This rule was revised by the Health Information Technology for Economic and Clinical Health (HITECH) Act to place this decision in the hands of the party releasing this information. Contrary to expectations, however, the federal government did not provide guidance on how this revision would be implemented when it issued the January 2013 regulations to finalize the HITECH changes to HIPAA. For example, it did not provide more specific guidance on how you should make the "minimum necessary" determination. Absent further guidance, you should strive to provide only basic information that justifies further treatment without unnecessarily revealing information to the company.

The HIPAA Privacy Rule draws a brighter line for those psychologists who choose to maintain separate psychotherapy notes: You may only release them with the patient's authorization and the managed care company may not coerce the release of those notes by withholding payment or refusing to authorize care unless the patient authorizes their release. Thus, the company is only entitled to that basic information, such as a diagnosis and a summary of symptoms and the treatment plan, which is excluded from psychotherapy notes protection. This basic information (sometimes called the "clinical record" and analogous to "progress notes") is the type of information designed to be shared with others in the health care arena, treating professionals and insurers. By contrast, the detailed and unprocessed psychotherapy notes are meant for the psychologist's own use in treating the patient.

While companies have generally respected the prohibition on seeking or coercing release of psychotherapy notes, some companies have asked during telephone medical necessity reviews for the detailed, sensitive information that would typically be protected within psychotherapy notes. If you keep psychotherapy notes and are faced with such a request, argue that this is an attempt to circumvent psychotherapy notes protection under the law.

Remember that where you are seeking to uphold your patient's privacy rights under HIPAA, the US Department of Health and Human Services' (HHS) Office of Civil Rights (which enforces HIPAA) may be an important source of leverage (www.hhs.gov/ocr/).

Adverse Actions Regarding Your Reimbursement Rate

If you are in-network and have a contract with the managed care company, look to the payment provisions and payment schedule in your provider contract.

If the issue is that the company has reduced its reimbursement rate, review the provision of the provider contract regarding changes to the contract. Most provider contracts allow the company to make changes to the contract, including the reimbursement rate, after a certain amount of written notice—typically 60 or 90 days. So make sure that the company is following the terms of the contract regarding notice requirements. Most provider contracts also state that you must either accept the change or terminate your contract, but companies are sometimes willing to forego a rate cut with respect to psychologists who have a unique value to the network. A provider can document that he or she has a practice specialty in demand or that they are one of the few psychologists in their geographic area. These strategies can all be utilized in your communication with the company. Further strategies for responding to reimbursement rate cuts and negotiating with insurers are found in *Responding to Rate Cuts* in the reference materials.

If you do not have a contract with the company, your reimbursement rate is typically determined by the managed care company's contract with the employer and/or policyholder; this is typically considered "out of network coverage." Managed care companies generally do not reimburse psychologists at their full private pay rate. Prior to 2009, many companies based out-of-network rates on a percentage of the "usual, customary and reasonable" (UCR) rate as determined by the "Ingenix" database. However, settlements in a number of Ingenix cases (which alleged that the flawed database improperly suppressed UCR rates) have caused companies to shift to other methods for determining out-of-network rates, such as using a percentage of Medicare rates.

A special consideration for fee disputes is that if you discuss the rate issue with other psychologists who are your economic competitors, or conduct advocacy with those competitors, you must be mindful of antitrust concerns. What may seem like a natural discussion of what the rate should be, or the effects of a rate cut, could be perceived by antitrust enforcement agencies as evidence of unlawful price fixing or boycotts. (See antitrust resources in reference list for further information.) Concerns about perceived price fixing and boycotts often occur when a provider along with a group of economic competitors attempt to advocate a reimbursement rate. While there is still strength in numbers when tackling fee issues, advocating privately on your own is often wiser since you will not trigger antitrust risks.

ACKNOWLEDGMENTS

Special thanks to Alan Nessman and Ieshia Haynie for their contributions.

References and Readings

American Psychological Association. Practice Organization (n.d.). *Practice central: Resources for practicing psychologists*. Retrieved February 2013, from www.apapracticecentral.org

Appelbaum, P. S. (1993). Legal liability and managed care. *American Psychologist, 48*(3), 251–257.

Bruce W. Clark, B. W. (1995). Negotiating successful managed care contracts. *Healthcare Financial Management, 49*(8), 26–30.

Gray, B. H., & Field, M .J. (Eds.). (1990). *Controlling costs and changing patient care: The role of utilization management*. Washington, DC: National Academy Press.

Higuchi, S. A., & Hinnefeld, B. J. (1998). *Practicing in the new mental health marketplace: Ethic, legal, and moral issues*. Washington, DC: American Psychological Association.

Hummel, J. R. The managed care contract: The blueprint for monitoring agreements. *Healthcare Financial Management, 55*(6), 49–50.

See www.apapracticecentral.org/reimbursement/maximize/index.aspx for guidance on disputes with managed care companies.

See www.apapracticecentral.org/reimbursement/billing/index.aspx for guidance on billing and claims disputes.

See www.apapracticecentral.org/business/hipaa/index.aspx for HIPAA guidance.

See www.apapracticecentral.org/advocacy/index.aspx for information on the HITECH Act, mental health parity and litigation against managed care companies.

Related Topics

Chapter 105, "Defending Against Legal (Malpractice and Licensing) Complaints"

Chapter 121, "Managing Your Managed Care Contracts"

Chapter 128, "UNDERSTANDING FUNDAMENTALS OF THE HIPAA PRIVACY RULE"

PART XI
Practice Management

124 MAKING GOOD REFERRALS

Steven Walfish and Jeffrey Zimmerman

In clinical practice you are routinely asked, or placed in a position, to make referrals on behalf of your clients. You are also asked to make referrals for potential clients who may call you for services but for whom you are not the appropriate match to meet their clinical needs. You may be asked to provide referrals as a courtesy to other professionals with whom you work, who may be seeking resources for one of their clients. For example, a physician who routinely refers clients to you may have a patient in her office that is in need of admission to a residential substance abuse treatment center to address his cocaine addiction. Since the physician has confidence in your professional judgment, she may ask for recommendations on where she may refer her patient.

Making appropriate referrals is a professional service and courtesy that psychologists provide to their clients, referral sources, and the community at large. Clients come to psychologists to address their mental health needs. However, such needs and problems rarely occur in a vacuum and may be complicated by complex biological, psychosocial, or judicial components.

REFERRALS ARE PART OF EXCELLENT CUSTOMER SERVICE

Walfish and Barnett (2009) suggest that those clinicians with the best customer service practices will likely be the most successful in private practice. Making excellent and appropriate referrals, and having the ability to connect clients to these resources, enhances a clinical practice and adds value to the services provided.

For example, if a client needs to be hospitalized because he or she is suicidal, you are providing the client a service and a convenience by being able to call a psychiatrist with whom you have a working relationship. You can explain the situation and ask the psychiatrist whether he or she would be willing to admit the client to a hospital where the psychiatrist has privileges. If the psychiatrist says, "Yes," then he or she will facilitate the admission. He or she may also be able to arrange for you to see the client while in the hospital, if this is desired. The psychiatrist should also refer the client back to you upon discharge (if clinically appropriate), along with providing a formal or informal discharge summary. Without that professional referral relationship, the client might be placed in the position of going to the emergency room of a local hospital, waiting to be seen and evaluated, and then admitted by the psychiatrist on call, with whom you do not likely have a working relationship. This process may take many hours and the client will not have the same continuity of care.

WHAT TYPE OF PROFESSIONALS TO HAVE IN YOUR REFERRAL NETWORK

While you may see clients in your practice for depression, anxiety, marital conflict, or parenting problems, in order to be most effective you need to be linked to other professionals who may complement the services you provide and be helpful to your clients. At a minimum, we think it important that psychologists develop working relationships with the following types of professionals:

- *Physicians.* Family practice, internal medicine, pediatrics, neurology, psychiatry, addictionology
- *Attorneys.* Family law, personal injury, employment law, workers compensation, Social Security disability, criminal defense
- *Financial professionals.* Certified public accountant, certified financial planner, consumer credit counseling service
- *Facilities.* Psychiatric hospitals, substance abuse treatment centers
- *Low-fee services options.* Social service agencies, community mental health clinics, university training clinics

AVOID CONFLICTS OF INTEREST

Principle 3.06 of the *Ethical Principles of Psychologists and Code of Conduct* (APA, 2010) states, "Psychologists refrain from taking on a professional role when personal, scientific, professional, legal, financial, or other interests or relationships could reasonably be expected to impair their objectivity, competence, or effectiveness in performing their functions as psychologists." Barnett and Walfish (2011) argue that it is important that referrals should not be motivated by possible financial gain for the referring practitioner but be based solely on the client's clinical and financial needs and interests.

Clinicians making referrals on behalf of clients need to consider any potential conflicts of interest that may be present that interfere with making an objective recommendation. For example, there have been cases where clinicians receive either direct payment for making referrals to a substance abuse treatment center or are hired as consultants to the program with the specific expectation (written or unwritten) that they will send all of their clients to that specific treatment program. This is a blatant example of conflict of interest. Others may be more subtle. Do you refer your client to psychiatrist Dr. Smith rather than psychiatrist Dr. Jones for a medication evaluation because Dr. Smith has referred ten of his clients to you for psychotherapy and Dr. Jones has referred only two or none at all? This may be especially problematic when Dr. Jones has a specialty area that would better suit your client's needs than Dr. Smith.

Another subtle example of conflict of interest may be found in group practices where owners of the practice have a financial interest in assuring that the clinicians renting space and services from them have their caseloads maximized. In this way the clinicians are happy and the incomes of the owners may be assured and even increased if their practice's associates are paying a percentage of monies collected to the practice for overhead. The more collected, the more the owners earn. While it may be fine to refer within one's group practice, the key point is that the referral being made has to be in the best interest of the client. At times it may be more beneficial for a client to see a clinician in another practice who specializes in the presenting problem of the client.

WHEN TO REFER TO OTHER MENTAL HEALTH PROFESSIONALS

Private practitioners like to keep their schedules filled. If no service is delivered, then no income is generated. This can lead to a tendency, whether consciously or unconsciously, to overfill one's schedule. It is important that clinicians develop for themselves an internal threshold of number of clients they may see each week and still deliver effective and ethical services. This threshold will vary from clinician to clinician. For some practitioners a full practice may be 25 clients per week, while for others it may be over 30 or even 40. There will be individual differences in determining this threshold with some variables, including theoretical orientation, diagnosis of most clients treated, physical and emotional stamina, amount of administrative time needed to see the client (e.g., writing of chart notes, completion of disability forms, correspondence with referral sources, filling out treatment planning requests from managed care companies), and need for income. As one colleague once commented to us about a psychologist who saw 55 hours per week in his practice, "I wouldn't mind being the 20th client that he saw that week, but I certainly wouldn't want to the 50th!" Once your threshold is reached, it is important to refer to colleagues. This will increase the likelihood that you do not make a clinical mistake (perhaps as a function of fatigue) or cross an ethical boundary.

It is also important to refer, when the presenting problem of the client falls outside of your own area of expertise. Standard 2.01 of the APA Ethics Code states, "Psychologists provide services, teach, and conduct research with populations and in areas only within the boundaries of their competence, based on their education, training, supervised experience, consultation, study, or professional experience." For example, because a psychologist may be skilled in psychological assessment, he or she may not be skilled in all applications where an evaluation may be requested. For example, evaluations for attention-deficit disorder/attention-deficit/hyperactivity disorder, learning disabilities, or clearance for bariatric surgery or implant of a spinal cord stimulator require specialized knowledge and experience. It is important that if you are referred a client for such an evaluation and you have little or no experience in the area, that you seek out consultation and supervision or refer the client to a specialist in that area.

It is important to refer when there may be a conflict of interest in the case (e.g., seeing both a husband and wife for individual psychotherapy) or when asked to be placed in a dual role (e.g., being both an evaluating psychologist and a treating psychologist in a forensic case, or being asked to do couple's work with a referral source and his or her partner).

When it appears that the client is not benefiting from psychotherapy, it is important that he or she be referred to another clinician. We are not talking about clients where the purpose of psychotherapy is palliative care, maintenance of gains previously made in treatment, or reducing the likelihood of hospitalization. Standard 10.10 of the APA Ethics Code states, "Psychologists terminate therapy when it becomes reasonably clear that the client/patient no longer needs the service, is not likely to benefit, or is being harmed by continued service." Naturally, this termination and transfer of care is not done impulsively but in consultation with the client. However, if the client's goals are symptom reduction and psychotherapy is not resulting in symptom reduction, the client may be better served by another clinician.

OBTAIN PROPER RELEASE

Making a referral with the best of intentions does not relieve the psychologist of the responsibility to obtain appropriate release(s) of information. While HIPAA may allow for the release of information between health care professionals in certain circumstances, HIPAA is the minimum expectation. That is, state and provincial regulations may have stricter requirements when a release of information is required. For example, a psychologist refers a child for psychotherapy to another clinician for academic/intellectual assessment. The parents of the child follow through and schedule an appointment with the evaluator, who then telephones the referring psychologist to obtain relevant background information. State regulations may require a signed release for the referring psychologist to indeed have this discussion with the evaluator. This becomes more complicated if the parents are divorced with joint custody and one parent favors the evaluation and the other does not (Zimmerman et al., 2009). Be sure to check your local statutes regarding confidentiality to make sure you are in compliance with state law.

WHEN POSSIBLE, PAVE THE WAY

With written permission it can be extremely useful to call the professional you are referring to, in advance of the client being seen. It can serve to make sure there is availability for the referral to be accepted and that the referral is indeed an appropriate one. It can help assure that not only is the client referred, but that the client is actually seen by the specialist. The knowledge that you called can be reassuring to clients and give them a sense that they are well cared for by their psychologist. It can even serve as an opportunity for some soft marketing to build your relationship with that professional. Most important, speaking to the professional you are referring to can help make sure there is clarity about the clinical reason for the referral and what specific services or information you are seeking in requesting the consultation. It can also help avoid the confusion that can occur by having the client try to represent the reason for the referral. Speaking directly with the professional also provides you the opportunity to arrange for a clear understanding of what additional information you may need, in return, subsequent to the client being seen.

DO NOT OVERSELL OR OVERPROMISE

Even when the psychologist making the referral has an excellent long-standing relationship with the professional to whom the client is being referred, the referral relationship may not go well for the client. Setting overly high expectations for the client can heighten the likelihood of disappointment. This in turn can also then impact one's own relationship with the client, as who you refer to may be viewed as a reflection of your professional judgment. In addition, if expectations are too high, there may be a missed opportunity for the client to gain maximum benefit from the referral. It is best to be clear about the potential benefits of the referral, and at the same time set realistic expectations about the process and outcome of the referral (e.g., time to be seen, information to be gathered, skills to be learned). It is often best to even give more than one name to clients, allowing them ample opportunity to screen the experts and use who they believe may be most helpful.

RESPECT COLLATERAL RELATIONSHIPS

This is an often neglected aspect of making a referral, especially by early-career psychologists. Before making a referral, it is important to consider who else is involved in the case. Who referred the client to you? Who else may consider the client "my client or patient"? Because of this, after you have seen the client, do not refer the client to another professional without first consulting with the professional who made the initial referral to you. As a psychologist, you are often part of a larger system of care where other professionals may see themselves as the hub of the wheel responsible for the overall care of the client. The client's primary care physician may be in this role, as can a guardian ad litem for a child under his or her auspices, or an attorney involved in a divorce or personal injury case. It can be crucially important to discuss in advance the possibility of a referral with school personnel, physicians, attorneys, and other professionals involved in the case (making sure of course that the appropriate releases are in place). These professionals may feel the need to have a say in the referral decision-making process. Furthermore, it may be critically important that they have a good working relationship with the professional to whom the referral is going. Discussing referral options will help avoid undermining of the referral and instead maximize the likelihood of a successful outcome. From a clinical standpoint, imagine making a referral to a psychiatrist with whom you have a good working relationship, but with whom the client's primary care physician has an awful working relationship. This is probably not in anyone's best interest. A short call in advance to the primary care physician asking his or her preferences in psychiatrists can make sure the referral can work both clinically and in terms of the overall system of care.

If the psychologist making the referral does not have a strong working relationship with the professional receiving the referral, checking with other providers on the case may yield helpful information about community resources that may be a best fit for that particular client. Similarly, ignoring a professional relationship that another professional has with that client may lead to a fracture in one's own professional relationships. In short, the key is to view the referral as an intervention being made in a larger system of care and not just as a prescriptive recommendation between you and the client.

FINDING REFERRALS OUTSIDE OF YOUR AREA

At times it becomes necessary to make a referral elsewhere. A client may be moving or have a family member in another state (or country) who needs psychological services. You may have a friend or relative who consults with you about obtaining professional services for his or her own care.

There are some relatively easy methods for finding such leads. Professional associations (both state and national) often have directories of professionals that specify specialty areas. Most state psychological associations have a portal on their Web sites where one can search for a psychologist. This is also true on the Web site for the American Psychological Association (http://www.apa.org), as well as the National Register of Health Service Providers in Psychology (http://www.nationalregister.org). Professional LISTSERVs are often excellent sources, as one can reach professionals from around the country to obtain recommendations. If the client is already living in the area, he or she can consult with a primary care physician about local resources.

BE SENSITIVE TO FINANCIAL ISSUES

Standard 6.01(d) of the APA Ethics Code points to the need for the psychologist to anticipate possible limitations in services due to limitations in available funds for clients to pay for services. These considerations should be taken into account when referring a client to other clinicians or treatment programs. For example, if you know that a client must utilize her insurance to pay for services, it would not be a reasonable or an effective referral if the recommended clinician is only an out-of-network provider. Similarly, you do not want to refer such a client to an expensive day treatment or residential treatment center if she is uninsured. The referral should take into consideration the financial circumstances of the client.

Overall, making appropriate referrals can be a key factor to enhancing clinical outcomes, being seen as a resource to clients and other professionals and to building one's practice.

References and Readings

American Psychological Association. (2010). *Ethical principles of psychologists and code of conduct.* Retrieved February 2013, from http://www.apa.org/ethics/code/index.aspx

Barnett, J., & Walfish, S. (2011). *Billing and collecting for your mental health practice: Effective strategies and ethical practice.* Washington, DC: APA Books

Walfish, S., & Barnett, J. (2009). *Financial success in mental health practice.* Washington, DC: APA Books.

Zimmerman, J., Hess, A. K., McGarrah, N., Benjamin, G. A. H., Ally, G. A., Gollan, J. K., & Kaser-Boyd, N. (2009). Ethical issues in divorce and child custody cases: Navigating through the minefield. *Professional Psychology: Research and Practice, 40,* 539–549.

Related Topic

Chapter 142, "Cultivating Relationships and Coordinating Care With Other Health Professionals"

125 PROTOTYPE MENTAL HEALTH RECORDS

Gerald P. Koocher

This chapter describes a recommended style and content for mental health practitioners' clinical case records covering specific content domains and other important issues in record keeping aside from content. Not all of the content information described here will be necessary for every record, nor would one expect to complete a full record as described here during the first few sessions with a new client. By the end of several sessions, however, a good-quality clinical record will reflect all of the relevant points summarized herein.

GENERAL REGULATORY ISSUES

Depending on the nature of the records (i.e., business records, health records, or educational records), a range of state and federal laws may apply, including regulations of the Internal Revenue Service (IRS) and requirements of the Health Insurance Portability and Accountability Act (HIPAA) or Family Educational Rights and Privacy Act (FERPA). Web site links at the end of this chapter will guide readers to specific regulatory policies of the IRS and for HIPAA- and FERPA-covered entities.

CONTENT ISSUES

- *Identifying information.* Name, record or file number (if any), address, telephone number, sex, birth date, marital status, next of kin (or parent/guardian), school or employment status, and billing and financial information.
- *First contact.* Date of initial client contact and referral source.
- *Legal notifications.* HIPAA requires that clients be given specific notifications regarding privacy and other matters (discussed elsewhere in this volume) at the initiation of the professional relationship. Some states have parallel or more extensive requirements, and the APA Code of Conduct specifically requires psychologists to notify clients about the limits of confidentiality at the outset of the professional relationship. Such notice will generally cover limitations on confidentiality, including mandated reporting obligations (e.g., child, dependent persons, or elder abuse and neglect) that apply in the practice jurisdiction. Provision of this notice, ideally by means of a signed notice form, should be noted in the record.
- *Notification of fees and billing policies.* Document notification of fees, fee increases, any fee agreements, and billing practices if these are not already covered in other notices given to the client at the beginning of the professional relationship. Note any special circumstances such as sliding-fee agreements, retainers, plans to bill for missed appointments, barter transactions, or special fees in a manner that reflects the client's understanding and agreement in advance of incurring charges.

- *Relevant history and risk factors.* Take a detailed social, medical, educational, and vocational history. This need not necessarily be done in the very first session and need not be exhaustive. The more serious the problem, the more history you should take. Get enough information to formulate a diagnosis and an initial treatment plan. Be sure to ask: "What is the most impulsive or violent thing you have ever done?" and "Have you thought of hurting yourself or anyone else recently?" Seek records of prior treatment based on the nature of the client (e.g., the more complex the case, the more completely one should review prior data). Always ask for permission to contact prior therapists and consider refusing to treat clients who decline such permission without giving good reason (e.g., sexual abuse by former therapist).
- *Medical or health status.* Collect information on the client's medical status (i.e., When was his or her last physical exam? Does the client have a personal physician? Are there any pending medical problems or conditions?). This is especially important if the client has physical complaints or psychological problems that might be attributable to organic pathology.
- *Medication profile.* Collect information on all medications or drugs used, past and present, including licit (e.g., prescribed medications, alcohol, tobacco, and over-the-counter drugs) and illicit substances. Also note any consideration, recommendation, or referral for medication made by you or others over the course of your work with the client.
- *Why is the client in your office?* Include a full description of the nature of the client's condition, including the reason(s) for referral and presenting symptoms or problems. Be sure to ask clients what brought them for help at this point in time and record the reasons.
- *Current status.* Include a comprehensive functional assessment (including a mental status examination) and note any changes or alterations that occur over the course of treatment.
- *Diagnostic impression.* Include a clinical impression and diagnostic formulation using the most current *DSM* or *ICD* model. Do not underdiagnose to protect the patient. If you believe it is absolutely necessary to use a "nonstigmatizing" diagnosis as opposed to some other diagnostic label, use the R/O (rule-out) model by listing diagnoses with the notation "R/O," indicating that you will rule each "in" or "out" based on data that emerge over the subsequent sessions. Your diagnosis must also be consistent with the case history and facts (e.g., do not use "adjustment reaction" to describe a paranoid hallucinating client with a history of prior psychiatric hospital admissions).
- *Treatment plan.* Develop a treatment plan with long- and short-term goals and a proposed schedule of therapeutic activities. The plan should be updated every 4 to 6 months and modified as needed.
- *Progress notes.* Note progress toward achievement of therapeutic goals. Use clear, precise, observable facts (e.g., I observed; patient reported; patient agreed that ...). As you write, imagine the patient and his or her attorney looking over your shoulder as they review the record with litigation in mind. Avoid theoretical speculation or reports of unconscious content. Do not include humorous or sarcastic personal reflections or observations. Your record should always demonstrate that you are a serious, concerned, dedicated professional. If you must keep theoretical or speculative notes (e.g., impressionistic narratives for review with a supervisor), use a separate "working notes" format, but recognize that these records may be subject to subpoena in legal proceedings.
- *Service documentation.* Include documentation of each visit, noting the client's response to treatment. In hospitals or large agencies, each entry should be dated and signed or initialed by the therapist, with the service provider's name printed or typed in legible form. It is not necessary to sign each entry in one's private (i.e., noninstitutional) case files, since it is reasonable to assume that you wrote what is in your own private practice files.

- *Document follow-up and correspondence.* Include documentation of follow-up for referrals or missed appointment, especially with clients who may be dangerous or seriously ill. Retain copies of all reminders, notices, or correspondence (including telephone messages and e-mail) sent to or on behalf of clients, and note substantive telephone conversations in the record.
- *Obtain consent.* Include copies of consent forms for any information released to other parties, or for other forms of recording (e.g., consent to record interviews).
- *Termination.* Include a discharge or termination summary note for all clients. In cases of planned termination, be certain that case notes prior to the end of care reflect planning and progress toward this end.

NONCONTENT ISSUES

- *Control of records.* Psychologists should maintain (in their own practice) or support (in institutional practice) a system that protects the adequate control over and confidentiality of records. Clear procedures should be in place to preserve client confidentiality and to release records only with proper consent. The specific medium used (e.g., paper, magnetic, optical) may require special considerations to assure utility, confidentiality, and durability. For example, a locked file cabinet may suffice for paper records, but digital records will require secure c4omputing environments, encryption, and appropriate backup. Practitioners must assure that they have taken reasonable steps to assure the security of patient records and should review their practices in that regard regularly as record keeping and storage technologies evolve.
- *Multiple-client therapies.* When treating families or conducting group therapy, records should be kept in a manner that allows for the preservation of each individual's confidentiality in the event that a release form arrives for the records of only one party.
- *Adequate supervisory oversight.* Psychologists have responsibility for construction and control of their records and the obligation to assure that the people they supervise, whether administrative support staff, clinical staff, or trainees, also exercise appropriate practices.
- *Retention of records.* Psychologists must remain aware of and observe all federal and state laws that govern record retention. In the absence of clear regulatory guidance under law, the American Psychological Association (2007) recommends maintaining complete records for 7 years after the last client contact for adults and for 3 years after any child clients reach age 18. Many practitioners store electronic files or paper case summaries for longer periods. All records, active or inactive, should be stored in a safe manner, with limited access appropriate to the practice or institution.
- *Outdated records.* Outdated, obsolete, or invalid data should be managed in a way that assures no adverse effects will result from its release. Records may be culled regularly so long as this is consistent with legal obligations. Records to be disposed of should be handled in a confidential and appropriate manner. Never alter or remove items from a record that has been subpoenaed or is otherwise subject to legal proceedings.
- *Death or incapacity.* Psychologists need to make arrangements for proper management or disposal of clinical records in the event of their death or incapacity. This would include identifying potential custodians and providing information on accessing the records (e.g., keys and passwords). Ideally, this can be accomplished with a professional will as described in Chapter 127.

References and Readings

American Psychological Association. (2007). Record keeping guidelines. *American Psychologist, 62,* 993–1004.

Internal Revenue Service. (2012). *How long should I keep records?* Retrieved February 2013, from www.irs.gov/businesses/small/article/0,,id=98513,00.html

Koocher, C. P., & Keith-Spiegel, P. C. (2008). *Ethics in psychology: Professional standards and cases* (3rd ed.). New York: Oxford University Press.

US Department of Education. (2012). *Family educational rights and privacy act*. Retrieved February 2013, from www2.ed.gov/policy/gen/guid/fpco/ferpa/index.html

US Department of Health and Human Services. (n.d.). *Understanding health information privacy*. Retrieved February 2013, from www.hhs.gov/ocr/privacy/hipaa/understanding/index.html

Related Topics

Chapter 127, "Elements of Authorization Forms to Release or Request Client's Records"

Chapter 128, "Understanding Fundamentals of the HIPAA Privacy Rule"

126 FULFILLING INFORMED CONSENT RESPONSIBILITIES

Kenneth S. Pope

Informed consent is a basic right and useful process that goes beyond the signing of forms and other formalities at the start of psychological treatment.

AVOID MISCONCEPTIONS

The first and often hardest step in providing truly informed consent is setting aside misconceptions that consent is a burdensome formality, a wasteful technicality to be gotten out of the way. Sokol (2009, p. 3224) wrote:

> So what is the most redoubtable obstacle to valid consent? It is the still prevalent attitude that obtaining consent is a necessary chore, a ... hurdle to jump over. Too often "consenting" a patient is reduced to the mechanistic imparting of information from clinician to patient or, worse still, the mere signing of a consent form, rather than the two-way, meaningful conversation between clinician and patient it should be. If we can change this mindset and view obtaining consent as an ethical duty first and foremost, one that is central to respecting the autonomy and dignity of patients, then we will have taken a major step towards first-class consent.

This process of "meaningful conversation" enables psychotherapist and patient to work together in a way acceptable to both. In the words of the Canadian Psychological Association's (CPA) Ethics Code, "informed consent is the result of a process of reaching an agreement to work collaboratively, rather than of simply having a consent form signed."

Informed consent takes the form of negotiation: "While most therapists recognize that negotiation can clear up clients' misconceptions, fewer recognize that negotiation is also a vehicle for clearing up the *therapist's* misconceptions. An open dialogue can make the therapist aware of features of the case that depart from both the therapist's model and his or her previous experience, and thus it serves as a corrective to the representativeness and availability biases" (O'Neill, 1998, p. 176).

KEEP UP WITH THE LAW

A second step in ensuring informed consent is keeping up with the legal standards. Informed consent often requires that the patient be competent to give or withhold consent to assessment or treatment, possess adequate knowledge to make an informed choice, and freely make an independent decision. However, different states, provinces, and other legal jurisdictions define and interpret these principles differently. Some impose additional requirements. Psychologists must keep abreast of the constantly evolving legislation and case law relevant to informed consent.

Legal standards governing confidentiality and privilege—those areas in which therapists may or must take steps that would reveal confidential information—warrant special care in informed consent for assessment and treatment. For example, depending on the jurisdiction, health care practitioners may be authorized or required to report child or elder abuse, threatened violence, or suspected terrorist activity. Only if therapists know these standards can they convey them to patients; only if patients know these exceptions to confidentiality and privilege can they consider how these standards affect the assessment or therapy, and make an informed decision about whether to consent. For a patient to learn about these exceptions only *after* saying something that triggers a report to an agency or third party represents a violation of the practitioner's ethical duty to provide adequate consent.

KEEP UP WITH ETHICAL AND PROFESSIONAL STANDARDS

In providing informed consent, psychologists must also take into account relevant ethical and professional standards. The CPA Code of Ethics (2000), for example, uses the word "consent" 50 times. The Web page "Informed Consent in Psychotherapy & Counseling: Forms, Standards & Guidelines, & References" (kspope.com/consent/index.php) provides links to and excerpts from the standards and guidelines of 19 professional associations, including the American Group Psychotherapy Association, American Psychoanalytic Association, American Psychological Association, British Association for Counselling & Psychotherapy, Canadian Psychological Association, European Federation of Psychologists' Associations, and the Psychological Society of Ireland.

KEEP UP WITH RELEVANT RESEARCH

Maintaining awareness of research in three areas is key to providing informed consent:

- Research focusing on the consent process itself illuminates how the process can affect therapy. Studies tend to suggest that a well-conducted consent process can produce a variety of benefits, such as decreased patient anxiety, increased adherence to the treatment plan, and enhanced therapeutic alliance (Beahrs & Gutheil, 2001; Pinals, 2009; Pope & Vasquez, 2011).
- Research relevant to treatments enables clinicians to provide patients with accurate, up-to-date information about those treatments' short- and long-term effectiveness, their potential risks or downsides, the degree to which they rest on a solid research base, and how they compare with alternative treatments.
- Decision-making research—especially regarding health issues—can inform the ways in which psychologists present information to patients. For example, one landmark study (McNeil et al., 1982) demonstrated that patients considering outcome data for surgery and radiation treatments for cancer made significantly different choices when faced with the *same* data depending on whether those data were presented in terms of survival or mortality (i.e., the percentage of patients in each treatment group who survived at each stage vs. the percentage who died at each stage). Our patients' decisions about whether to consent to psychological services and what sort of therapeutic approaches to try can exert profound effects on their lives, and we have a responsibility to present the information they need to make

those decisions in ways that are informed by research.

CONSIDER CONTEXTS

Practitioners must tailor the consent process to specific contexts such as culture, number of patients, parents or guardians of minor clients, setting, and changing circumstances. Examples:

- A therapist from the majority culture might start working with a patient who has recently immigrated. The degree of acculturation can influence (a) the desire for independent decision making, (b) ways of relating within cultural contexts, and (c) how psychological disorders, authority, and so on are viewed (Wang, 2009).
- Therapies involving more than one client present special issues in ensuring that patients understand the ground rules. Will the therapist keep material from one patient secret from his or her partner in couples therapy? If a patient in family therapy waives privilege in a court proceeding, will it result in the disclosure of information about other family members? If a former patient authorizes both a subsequent treating therapist and an insurance company to receive all records relating to group therapy, will any information about other group members be included?
- Attending to the limited rights of minor clients and responsibilities to parents or guardians presents special challenges. What legal and ethical rights, if any, does a minor possess in regard to informed consent or assent? Can a practitioner present information relevant to consent or assent at the appropriate developmental level? Do parents or guardians understand and agree to any limitations to their learning from the therapist what the minor client tells the therapist and what the therapist says to the client? The context changes significantly depending on whether the minor client is younger (e.g., 6 years) or older (e.g., 15 years).
- Settings are a third context warranting special attention. If treatment occurs in a military setting, does the patient understand the special limits of confidentiality? If the therapy is provided by interns or other trainees, does the patient understand whether the intern possesses a doctorate, is licensed, will be supervised, and will no longer be available at the end of the internship? If the treatment is court-ordered or takes places in a prison setting, does the patient understand what reports might be filed and how these may affect the patient's prospects?
- Changing circumstances illustrate why therapists must remain alert to consent issues throughout the course of therapy. A patient seeking one-session hypnosis for performance anxiety about presenting an annual report may end up wanting additional sessions with the same therapist to explore career options that would be more fulfilling. A 10-session course of behavior therapy for agoraphobia may suddenly shift when the patient reveals being battered and terrorized by a spouse and now feeling hopeless and suicidal.

TAKE INVENTORY

Psychotherapy is a complex, evolving endeavor shared by two (or more) unique individuals. Set scripts and inflexible steps to informed consent do not work, but considering the questions in the following inventory can help to identify aspects that need attention. Some items may not be relevant in some situations, and some may need adapting.

- Are you up on the legislation and case law governing informed consent in your jurisdiction?
- Are you up on the relevant ethical standards and professional guidelines?
- Are you up on the research enabling you to handle consent efficiently and effectively?
- Are there any language or cultural circumstances that might interfere with meaningful conversation and clear understanding?
- Is this patient competent to provide informed consent?
- What factors, if any, might affect the patient's freedom to give or withhold truly voluntary consent?

- Does the patient understand the treatment approach you suggest, the intended benefits, risks, and alternative approaches?
- If the treatment involves more than one patient (e.g., couple, family, group therapy), do the patients understand the ground rules and how the presence of others may affect the treatment?
- Does the patient understand whether you are licensed to practice independently?
- Does the patient understand whether you will be supervised and/or whether there may be others who will be discussing his or her treatment?
- Does the patient understand who besides you and the patient will have access to the patient's records?
- Does the patient understand limitations to confidentiality and privilege?
- If you use any forms as part of your consent process, are they clear, direct, free of jargon, and readable by those without advanced degrees in linguistics?
- If you imagine yourself in the role of this particular patient, is there anything else you might want to know at this point that might influence your decision about whether to give or withhold informed consent?

References and Readings

Beahrs, J. O., & Gutheil, T. G. (2001). Informed consent in psychotherapy. *American Journal of Psychiatry, 158*, 4–10.

Canadian Psychological Association. (2000). *Canadian code of ethics for psychologists* (3rd ed.). Ottawa, QB: Author.

McNeil, B., Pauker, S. G., Sox, H. C., & Tversky, A. (1982). On the elucidation of preferences for alternative therapies. *New England Journal of Medicine, 306*, 1259–1262.

O'Neill, P. (1998). *Negotiating consent in psychotherapy*. New York: New York University Press.

Pinals, D. (2009). Informed consent: Is your patient competent to refuse treatment? *Current Psychiatry, 8*(4), 33–43.

Pope, K. S., & Vasquez, M. J. T. (2011) *Ethics in psychotherapy and counseling: A practical guide* (4th ed.). New York: Wiley.

Sokol, D. K. (2009). Informed consent is more than a patient's signature. *British Medical Journal*, 339. doi: 10.1136/bmj.b3224.

Wang, C. (2009, August). *Managing informed consent and confidentiality in multicultural contexts*. Paper presented at the Annual Meeting of the American Psychological Association, Toronto, Ontario. Retrieved February 2013, from psycnet.apa.org/psycextra/606622009–001.pdf

Related Topics

Chapter 103, "American Psychological Association's Ethical Principles"

Chapter 127, "Elements of Authorization Forms to Release or Request Client's Records"

Chapter 128, "Understanding Fundamentals of the HIPAA Privacy Rule"

127 ELEMENTS OF AUTHORIZATION FORMS TO RELEASE OR REQUEST CLIENT'S RECORDS

Edward Zuckerman

The contents and formats of releases of information (also called authorizations, requests for records, releases) are based on federal and state statutes and laws like the Health Insurance Portability and Accountability Act (HIPAA), ethical codes of the helping professions, regulations and decisions of licensing boards, and local case law (court decisions) about privacy and consent. Each psychologist should construct a release of information (ROI) from the topics listed here tailored to location, clientele, and purposes. In choosing the exact wording, bear these factors in mind:

- *Client's reading skill.* Online resources can estimate the educational levels required to understand office forms.
- *"Plain English."* That is required by statue and our ethics, as is making available translations.
- *Choices of party.* Do you want to speak as "Dr. Smith" or "I/we" or "The Smith Clinic"? Do you address "clients" or "you or your child"?

ELEMENTS OF A RELEASE OF INFORMATION

To be legally valid, an ROI must address all of the following topics:

1. An accurately informative title such as "Patient Authorization for Use and Disclosure of Protected Health Information." These are the HIPAA terms. What is done with the PHI (Protected Health Information) in your office is "use"; releasing it to other organizations or covered entities is "disclosure."

2. Identifying information about the client:

Complete name:

Other names such as aliases and maiden names:

Because names are not unique it is advisable to also ask for birthdate and Social Security number.

Sex:

Current and complete address:

Parent/guardian (where applicable) and address of parent/guardian:

3. The specific intended recipient of the records.

Name, position, affiliation, function.

Full address:

Telephone and fax numbers are advantageous.

If the requester is unfamiliar or the purposes of the ROI are unclear, then "verify the requester's identity and official capacity" before proceeding (Stromberg et al., 1988, p. 394).

4. The source of the records, either the name or general designation of the program.

If you are the one to release the records, then provide your identifying information and address here or by referring to your letterhead.

If you will charge for sending records, show your federal tax identification number or Social Security number or you will waste a lot of time on the phone when requesters want to pay you.

5. The desired interchange, which can be indicated in several ways. One way is a simple format arranging the above as "From" the source or releaser and "To" the recipient of the records. Another way is to provide a single space and precede it by text such as "By signing, I authorize the practice listed on this letterhead to use and/or disclose the indicated protected health information to ____" or [ ] Obtain from: [ ] Release to:

5. The purpose of the request. Why is this information sought and exactly how will it be used? A variety of purposes are listed from which a checklist can be constructed.

The information will be used or disclosed for the following purpose(s):

[ ] Continuation/Coordination of care or treatment/Changing or adding providers

[ ] Consultation

[ ] Disability certification

[ ] Insurance claim/Application

[ ] Attorney inquiry/Legal matter

[ ] Other: (specify):

If disclosure is requested by the patient, the purpose may be listed as "at the request of the individual." A possibly protective addition is: "In consideration of this consent, I hereby release the source of the records from any and all liability arising therefrom."

6. The contents or nature of the information to be disclosed. I recommend the following language: "I hereby authorize the source named above to send, as promptly as possible, the records marked by an X in the boxes below. The items not to be released have a line drawn through them. Page numbers are indicated where appropriate."

[ ] Inpatient or outpatient treatment records for physical and/or psychological, psychiatric, or emotional illness or drug or alcohol abuse with date(s) of admission/treatment.

Admission and discharge summaries. Treatment recommendations and plans, recovery plans, aftercare plans.

[ ] Psychological evaluation(s) or testing records, and behavioral observations or checklists completed by any staff member or by the patient.

Psychological/Educational/Achievement/Vocational and other test results.

Academic or educational records.

Reports of teachers' observations.

[ ] Psychiatric evaluations, reports, or treatment notes and summaries.

[ ] Social histories, assessments with diagnoses, prognoses, recommendations, and all similar documents.

Developmental history.

[ ] Information about how the patient's condition affects or has affected his or her ability to complete tasks, activities of daily living, or ability to work.

Workshop reports and other vocational evaluations and reports.

Case management records.

A release that authorizes you to "release and disclose all information and to discuss anything pertaining to this client and the client's progress" appears to be illegally vague and broad, and may be prohibited by HIPAA regulations concerning the "minimal necessary" disclosure rules (see Section 164.502 of the HIPAA Act).

Some information is considered more sensitive and requires a more specific release. Consider adding: "HIV-related information and drug and alcohol information contained in these records will be released under this consent unless indicated here: _ [ ] Do not release."

When the records are extensive they can be limited with this: "Dates of treatment covered by this release: [ ] All prior episodes of care. Limited to the following dates/programs: ____"

For ease of communication, this caveat can be added: "I authorize the source and recipient named above to speak by telephone about history, diagnoses, treatment and similar information."

7. When, how, or on what condition upon which the consent will expire if not revoked earlier. ROIs must give enough time to allow for verifying the validity of the request and processing the paperwork. Sixty days is common but, if HIPAA applies, a 30-day extension can be sought. Alternately: "It shall be valid no longer than is reasonably necessary to meet the purposes stated above, and not to exceed 1 year." ROIs must have time limits because records may change over time as new information is added and so they should be re-requested.

Ethical and legal principles do not permit withholding records needed for immediate or emergency care or as required by law solely because payment for them or previous services has not been made.

8. The client must be told of his or her right to revoke, in writing, an ROI. Describe the means for doing so and the exceptions to such revocation. "I hereby revoke this consent effective ________. I understand that this revocation has no effect on information released prior to the date of this revocation."

9. Electronic records have risks of loss of confidentiality different from those of paper records. If you plan to use electronic records, then you might include this language: "The designated information about me/my child [ ] may [ ] may not be transmitted by fax, electronic mail, or other electronic file transfer mechanisms."

10. Who may see these records. HIPAA allows sharing of PHI among all treaters and consultants without any release (beyond the consent signed with the NPP), but state laws are usually more restrictive. Thus, clarify who has access and, if any might cause difficulties, get an ROI signed.

Re-disclosure is a foreseeable risk and must also be addressed. Consider adding: "Although applicable law may prohibit re-disclosure of these records, I understand that if the person or organization that receives this information is not a health care provider or health insurer the information may no longer be protected by federal or state privacy regulations." Also consider adding that "Federal rules restrict any use of the information to criminally investigate or prosecute any alcohol or drug abuse client."

11. A statement that the client does not have to agree to and sign the authorization. This HIPAA rule is designed to prevent nontreating covered entities (CEs), such as insurers, from requiring ("conditioning") the release to them of more information than is present in the routine progress notes ("the Clinical Record" in HIPAA terms) before they agree to pay for services.

Presumably all clients would agree to your use of their PHI. You can, of course, treat them without their agreement to release your records to someone else. However, caution suggests that you not treat a client who denies you access to get others' records, for both therapeutic and risk management reasons. "I understand that I do not have to sign this authorization in order to receive treatment from this practice. In fact, I have the right to refuse to sign this authorization."

12. An indication that you will be paid directly or indirectly for this release, if that is true. This pertains to the marketing restrictions created by HIPAA and rarely if ever applies to psychotherapists. "This office [ ] will [ ] will not receive payment or other remuneration from a third party in exchange for using or disclosing the/your PHI."

13. The fact that you will change a reasonable fee when releasing records. "This office charges for the cost of retrieving, reproducing, and mailing records, according to the amounts allowed by law, and payment is required before releasing the records."

14. Clients have the right, under HIPAA, to access their records. HIPAA does not define "access" but indicates that any mutually agreeable format is acceptable so reading them, having them read, perusing, or obtaining a copy is possible. "I have had access to my records and am satisfied that I know what they contain."

15. How the information in the records can be corrected or amended. Along with access comes the right to correct errors and make qualifications of what is contained in your records and to have those changes accompany the records. Consider using the language, "I have reviewed the contents of my records and have made written amendments to them which will be included in the records whenever they are released after this time."

16. Clients have the right to a copy of their records. "I understand that I have the right (granted by HIPAA) to inspect and copy any of the information I request/authorize for release."

17. Clients have the right to a copy of the ROI. Make two copies of the ROI: one for the client if he or she wants it and, if not, keep that in your files and one for your own files. The original goes to the source of the records requested. When releasing records, make a single copy for the client, if accepted. "I understand that I have the right to receive a copy of this form upon my request."

18. The ROI must be consensual: informed, voluntary, and executed by a competent client.

For fuller comprehension, your release-of-records form should be available for the client to read; anything the client does not understand must be explained at his or her level of comprehension, and in his or her native language if necessary. "I affirm that everything in this form that was not clear to me has been explained."

This may seem obvious, but the client must believe that it is in his or her long-term best interest to release the records. Voluntary consent requires attending to and explaining what decision(s) will be based on it and what repercussions would follow from granting or withholding permission. You can then add, "This clinician and I have explored the likely consequences of waiving the privilege of confidentiality about these records. The information to be obtained or disclosed was fully explained to me and this consent is given on my own free will."

As to competency, consider adding a statement like "I, a licensed psychologist, have discussed the issues above with the patient and/or his or her parent or guardian. My observations of behavior and responses give me no reason to believe that this person is not fully competent to give informed and willing consent." Then provide space for signature of the psychologist, printed name of the psychologist, and date.

19. Signatures. A signature is not consent but the public acknowledgement of consent. In the simplest case, the signature of the client, the printed name of the client, and the date will suffice.

Because records change, the patient's signature must usually be given within 90 days of the time an ROI is received, but local legal and professional contexts may alter this.

Substitute or surrogate consent is required for a minor, for someone adjudicated incompetent, or for a dead person. In one of those instances, add:

Signature of parent/ guardian/legal representative/judge   Printed name Relationship   Date

In family therapy, the "family" or "couple" cannot have legal confidentiality; only individual members have this privilege. Thus, you will have to clarify and negotiate rules for release with each adult family member. Ideally, you have specified in your introductory materials that all members must sign a release.

If there is joint legal custody, then either parent can have access to the records.

When the client consents (perhaps orally) but cannot create a legitimate signature, witnessing is required. "I witnessed that this client understood the nature of this ROI and freely gave his or her consent, but was physically unable to provide a signature."

20. Do not comply with a request to release your records if the release form sent to you is faulty, such as missing some of the necessary contents listed earlier. Should there be a legal, ethical, or clinical problem, responsibility cannot be assigned to the requesting party.

Finally. many health care practitioners provide a cover letter accompanying a request or release of information. Many topics can and probably should be addressed in such a letter. For example, the letter could include the cost for collecting, copying, and mailing the records and how and to whom this is to be paid. Perhaps add a certifying note that the records released are copies of the entire clinic record or all records requested, or that no records were found or that the records are incomplete and will be forwarded when complete.

References and Readings

Stromberg, C. D. (1988). *The psychologist's legal handbook.* Washington, DC: National Register of Health Service Providers in Psychology.

Zuckerman, E. (2008). *The paper office* (4th ed.). New York: Guilford Press.

The educational level required and reading difficulty of your documents can be assessed at anyof these sites: /www.addedbytes.com/lab/readability-score/, juicystudio.com/services/ and readability.php.

Related Topics

Chapter 107, "Dealing with Subpoenas"
Chapter 128, "Understanding Fundamentals of the HIPAA Privacy Rule"

128 UNDERSTANDING FUNDAMENTALS OF THE HIPAA PRIVACY RULE

Alan C. Nessman

The Privacy Rule under the Health Insurance Portability and Accountability Act of 1996 (HIPAA), promulgated by the Department of Health and Human Services (HHS), went into effect in April 2003. The Privacy Rule sets standards for when and how to disclose patient information to third parties. It also defines patients' rights to access and control their own health information.

The Privacy Rule is distinguishable from the HIPAA Security Rule in several respects. While the Privacy Rule focuses on *intentional* disclosures of patient information, the Security Rule (which went into effect in 2005) focuses on managing the risk that patient information will *unintentionally* or maliciously become disclosed, altered, or destroyed. The Security Rule is also distinct in that it applies only to *electronic* protected health information (PHI), while the Privacy Rule applies to all forms of health information (paper, electronic, and oral). Thus, the Security Rule applies primarily to mental health practitioners who transmit or store patient information electronically.

Some aspects of the Privacy Rule were, or will eventually be, modified by The HIPAA Final Omnibus Rule (Final Rule) regulations issued in January 2013. The Final Rule has a September 23, 2013. The Rule was the latest of a series of regulations issued under the regulations under the Health Information Technology for Economic and Clinical Health (HITECH) Act of February 2009. Further information on the Final Rule changes and how to comply with them is available on the second Web site listed in the references and resources section at the end of this chapter. That Web site, as well as the others listed, provides more detailed information regarding the Privacy Rule and compliance with the rule.

The Privacy Rule, or at least the issues around it, will likely change further as the health care world increasingly adopts electronic health records and systems allowing for a freer exchange of health information. This will affect the operation of the Rule in ways not contemplated when it first became effective in 2003.

WHO MUST COMPLY?

HIPAA and the Privacy Rule apply to "covered entities," a category that includes health plans, health care clearinghouses, and certain health care providers. The Final Rule also makes "business associates" directly regulated under HIPAA, as described later in this chapter.

Most mental health practitioners who become covered entities do so by (1) electronically transmitting (2) protected health information (PHI) (3) in connection with insurance claims or other third-party reimbursement. The key terms, *PHI* and *electronic transmission*, are discussed later. Many practitioners forget the third requirement and do not realize that electronic submissions of PHI that are *not* associated with a claim or third-party reimbursement will not make them a covered entity. For example, e-mailing records to another practitioner for a consultation will not trigger the need to comply with HIPAA and the Privacy Rule.

Protected health information (PHI) is an important term, not only because it defines which providers are covered entities but also because it defines the type of health information to which the Privacy Rule applies. Because of the way the Privacy Rule broadly defines PHI, most information in a patient's file constitutes PHI. The key elements of the PHI definition include the following:

- Information that relates to (a) the past, present, or future physical or mental health condition of a patient; (b) providing health care to a patient; or (c) the past, present, or future payment for the patient's health care
- Information that identifies the patient or could reasonably be used to identify the patient

Under this broad definition, patient contact information and patient lists are considered PHI.

The most common form of electronic transmission for mental health practitioners occurs via the Internet (e.g., e-mail or transactions on an insurance company Web site). Paper faxes (i.e., by inserting paper into a fax machine and sending) do not qualify as electronic submissions. However, computer-generated faxes (i.e., when transmitting a document already in electronic form by fax directly from a computer) do constitute electronic submissions.

If someone acting on behalf of the practitioner, such as a billing service, electronically submits PHI (in connection with a specified transaction), this makes the practitioner a covered entity subject to HIPAA.

Once a practitioner becomes a covered entity, the Privacy Rule applies to all of the PHI in his or her practice. The Privacy Rule does not permit an individual practitioner to segregate that part of his or her practice to which the Privacy Rule applies.

Some mental health practitioners still seek to avoid HIPAA and the electronic world, but this will become increasingly difficult to continue as electronic submissions become more ubiquitous. Even for those practitioners not technically covered, the Privacy Rule may well become a standard of care for protecting patient privacy, in terms of licensing board complaints or lawsuits. Finally, some practitioners who do meet the definition of covered entity have not bothered to become Privacy Rule compliant. Ignoring the rule in this way is strongly discouraged in light of enforcement provisions discussed later in this chapter.

PREEMPTION ANALYSIS—STATE-SPECIFIC INFORMATION

The Privacy Rule establishes a national floor of privacy protection and rights for patients. Accordingly, the Privacy Rule will not preempt state law provisions that provide higher levels of privacy protections to patients in terms of shielding their PHI from third parties. Additionally, state laws that allow patients greater access to, or control over, their PHI will not be preempted. Conversely, provisions of the Privacy Rule that give patients greater privacy protection or greater access to their records will preempt the corresponding provisions of state law. Note, however, that the Privacy Rule specifically does not preempt certain types of state laws, such as laws giving or denying parents access to their children's records, regardless of whether they provide greater privacy protection. The key result of these complicated preemptions: Practitioners must remain aware of how disclosing and protecting PHI flows from a mixture of Privacy Rule and state privacy law provisions.

CONSENT AND AUTHORIZATION

The two types of patient permission to release PHI are consent and authorization. Consent is a general prospective agreement signed by the patient, typically at the start of treatment or when the patient applies for health insurance. The patient agrees to a variety of types of releases that might become necessary in the future (e.g., disclosures to insurers and to other treating providers). Authorization, by contrast, includes a detailed form that the patient signs at the time of, or just before, a particular disclosure. It describes in detail what information will be released to whom, for what purposes, during what timeframe, and under what conditions.

An important principle of the Privacy Rule is that routine releases within the health care system for treatment and payment purposes should be carried on relatively freely, without the delay and burden of having to obtain patient authorization for each release. The same principle applies to releases for the broader category of "health care operations," which includes an array of administrative and quality control functions, such as audits.

State consent laws apply to releases of PHI (other than psychotherapy notes) for these treatment, payment, and health care operations purposes. In other words, the mental health practitioner simply needs to have whatever consent state law requires before releasing PHI. (In a number of jurisdictions, like California and the District of Columbia, an authorization is necessary for most releases of PHI.)

The Privacy Rule requires mental health practitioners to obtain written authorization for any use or disclosure of patient information not for the purpose of treatment, payment, or health care operations. An authorization is also required for releasing psychotherapy notes, as described later.

MINIMUM NECESSARY

The Privacy Rule requires practitioners to make reasonable efforts to limit the amount of patient information they release to the "minimum necessary" to accomplish the intended purpose of a disclosure. The "minimum necessary" standard does not apply to (1) disclosures made to other health care providers for treatment purposes; (2) disclosures permitted by a written authorization; and (3) disclosures required by law.

The original Privacy Rule did not state who decided exactly what this vague "minimum necessary" standard meant. Thus, for example, mental health practitioners often disagreed with insurance companies over the scope of information necessary for the company to determine whether care for a patient qualified as medically necessary. The HITECH Act specified that minimum necessary would now be determined from the perspective of the party disclosing the information. In most situations, that disclosing party will be the practitioner. The Final Rule, however, does not provide further guidance on this change.

PSYCHOTHERAPY NOTES

The Privacy Rule allows, but does not require, mental health practitioners to give heightened protection to certain sensitive patient information. Psychotherapy notes receive several forms of increased protection. First, with limited exceptions, practitioners must obtain a written authorization for any disclosure of psychotherapy notes. That authorization must be separate from any other authorization for releasing PHI. Second, health plans and third-party payers may not condition treatment, payment, enrollment, or eligibility for benefits on obtaining information in psychotherapy notes. For example, a health insurer cannot tell a patient that he or she will only authorize further therapy sessions if the patient signs an authorization to release psychotherapy notes about his or her treatment. Finally, the Privacy Rule does not give patients the right to access their psychotherapy notes, but in the majority of states preemption rules grant patients broad access to psychotherapy notes.

Psychotherapy notes are (1) notes by a mental health professional; (2) documenting or analyzing the contents of conversation during a private counseling session (including group, joint, or family counseling sessions); (3) kept separated from the rest of the patient's mental health record.

Specifically excluded from the definition are (a) any summary of the following items: diagnosis, functional status, the treatment plan, symptoms, prognosis, and progress to date; (b) the modalities and frequencies of treatment furnished; (c) results of clinical tests; (d) counseling session start and stop times; and (e) medication prescription and monitoring.

The special protection accorded to psychotherapy notes flows from their content, which typically includes highly sensitive communications whose confidentiality is essential to successful psychotherapy, and that these notes are intended as the therapist's private notes for his or her own use. They contain details not needed by others in the health care delivery system such as third-party payers and other health care professionals. By contrast, the items excluded from psychotherapy notes protection include basic elements of the separate "clinical record" appropriate for sharing with other treating providers and health insurers.

As required by the HITECH Act, HHS has considered whether to give similar heightened protection to psychological test data. The Final Rule does not address test data and at the time of this writing there has been no update from HHS regarding this issue. Thus, it is unclear whether HHS will decide to provide additional protection for test data.

BUSINESS ASSOCIATES

A "business associate" is an organization or person outside of the mental health practitioner's practice to whom the practitioner sends PHI (or provides access to PHI) so that the outside entity can provide services to the practitioner. Examples include accountants, lawyers, billing services, collection agencies, and computer repair services. Other health care providers are not considered business associates.

Under the original Privacy Rule, business associates were beyond the regulatory reach of HIPAA (which previously governed only actors in the health care arena such as health care providers and insurers). The Rule required covered entities to have "business associate agreements" with these entities. These agreements contractually obligated the business associates to protect the privacy of PHI they handled and obligated them not to make any releases of PHI that violate the Privacy Rule. However, the HITECH Act made business associates directly regulated under the Privacy Rule. While this would seem to make the business associate agreements unnecessary, the Final Rule still requires that providers enter into business associate agreements with their business associates.

BREACH NOTIFICATION

One other major Final Rule change affecting mental health practitioners is known as the breach notification rule. This rule may require the practitioner to give timely notice to his or her patients if or when a "breach" involving the PHI occurs. A breach is defined as (1) the acquisition, access, use or disclosure of PHI; (2) that violates the Privacy Rule; and (3) involving PHI that has not been "secured" by HHS-approved encryption (or other technologies that make the PHI unusable to unauthorized users). Upon learning of a breach, a practitioner must conduct a 4-point risk assessment. If that assessment fails to establish a low probability that unsecured PHI has been compromised, the practitioner must give a specified notice of the breach to patients whose PHI is implicated and to HHS. Further information on this rule is available at the second Web site listed in the References for this chapter.

ADMINISTRATIVE REQUIREMENTS

The key administrative requirements under the Privacy Rule involve (1) designating a "privacy officer" within the practice responsible for developing, implementing, and overseeing written privacy policies and procedures (a contact person should also be designated for receiving and documenting complaints from patients); (2) training employees (if any) in the practice's written privacy policies and procedures so that each member may carry out his or her respective functions; (3) taking reasonable steps to safeguard all PHI from those who do not need or are not permitted access; and (4) providing patients with information about their privacy rights and explaining how their personal information may be used, as described in the next section.

NOTICE OF PRIVACY PRACTICES

The Privacy Rule requires mental health practitioners in direct treatment relationships with patients to give a Notice of Privacy Practices to each patient by the date of first service delivery and to make a good-faith effort to obtain each patient's written acknowledgment of receipt of the notice. The notice must contain specific core elements, including each patient's rights in relation to his or her health information and the practitioner's duties to patients. The Final Rule added further statements that must be included in the Notice, if they are applicable to the practitioner. Practitioners are required to abide by the terms of their current privacy notice. Additionally, practitioners who maintain an office must also post the notice in the office in a clear and prominent location. In practice, the HIPAA privacy notice has become a piece of required paperwork that most patients never read.

INCIDENTAL DISCLOSURES

Mental health practitioners are not required to eliminate all risks of "incidental uses and disclosures" of their patients' information. Any use or disclosure of patient information "incident to" another permitted use or disclosure is permitted so long as "reasonable safeguards" to protect patient information have been adopted by the practitioner. An example of a permitted incidental disclosure might occur when an individual in the practitioner's waiting room accidentally overhears a confidential conversation between another patient and the doctor.

SCALABILITY OF THE PRIVACY RULE

To ease the burden of compliance, the Privacy Rule requirements are "scalable" to apply to the various types and sizes of practices. The scalability of the Privacy Rule allows for flexibility in the practice's internal written policies and procedures. For instance, the privacy officer in a solo practitioner's practice will, in most instances, be the solo practitioner; the privacy official in a large group practice may be a receptionist, the office manager, a practitioner, or if the practice is large enough, a full-time employee solely dedicated to HIPAA compliance.

ENFORCEMENT

HHS has responsibility for enforcement of the Privacy Rule. In response to complaints about lax HIPAA enforcement, the Final Rule Act increased enforcement in several key respects. For example, it creates a system of tiered civil penalties based in part on the willfulness of the covered entity's violation. In cases of "willful neglect," the maximum penalty is $1.5 million per violation. In addition, the government must consider letting individuals affected by the violation share in civil penalties, which would create whistleblower type incentives for reporting violations. Finally, HHS is required to conduct periodic audits of covered entities and business associates, rather than relying primarily on complaints to find violations, as it had done prior to HITECH.

DISCLAIMER

This chapter is not intended to provide legal advice or to give full details regarding HIPAA, the Privacy Rule or the Final Rule. It is likely that HHS will provide further clarification regarding the Final Rule. For information on relevant updates, see the second Web site listed in the references. Rather it provides an overview of basic aspects of, and some common issues under, the Privacy Rule. Legal and regulatory issues are complex and highly fact specific and require legal expertise that cannot be provided by any single book. The information in this chapter should not be used as a substitute for obtaining personal legal advice and consultation prior to making decisions regarding individual circumstances.

References and Readings

American Psychological Association Insurance Trust. (n.d.). *Health Insurance Portability and Accountability Act*. Retrieved February 2013, from www.apait.org/apait/resources/hipaa/

American Psychological Association Practice Organization. (n.d.). *Practice central: Business of practice*. Retrieved February 2013, from www.apapracticecentral.org/business/hipaa/index.aspx

US Department of Health and Human Services. (n.d.). *Health information privacy*. Retrieved February 2013, from www.hhs.gov/ocr/hipaa

Related Topic

Chapter 127, "Elements of Authorization Forms to Release or Request Client's Records"

129 COMMON CLINICAL ABBREVIATIONS AND SYMBOLS

John C. Norcross and Brian A. Zaboski

ā	before
AA	Alcoholics Anonymous
A&B	apnea and bradycardia
AAV	AIDS-associated virus
A-B-C	antecedent, behavior, consequence
abd	abduction; abdomen
ABG	arterial blood gas
a.c.	before meals
ad lib	as desired
ADA	Americans with Disabilities Act
ADHD	attention-deficit/hyperactivity disorder
ADLs	activities of daily living
adm	admission
ADSA	Attention Deficit Scale for Adults
ADTP	alcohol and drug treatment program
aero, aero Rx	aerosol inhalation equipment, treatment
AF	auricular fibrillation
A/G	albumin-globulin ratio
AHCPR	Agency for Health Care Policy and Research
AIDS	acquired immune deficiency/immunodeficiency syndrome
AK	above knee
A&O	alert and oriented
alb	albumin
alks, p'tase	alkaline phosphatase
ALL	allergy
AMA	against medical advice; American Medical Association
amb	ambulatory
anes	anesthesia

angio	angiogram
ANS	anesthesia
ant.	anterior
AODM	adult-onset diabetes mellitus
Ao DT	descending aorta
AP	anteroposterior
AP & Lat	anteroposterior and lateral
APA	American Psychological Association; American Psychiatric Association
≈	approximate
AQ	achievement quotient
ARC	AIDS-related complex
art mon	arterial pressure monitor
ARV	AIDS-related virus
AS	aortic stenosis; left ear
ASA	aspirin
AsAo	ascending aorta
ASD	atrial septal defect
ASL	American Sign Language
ASPD	Antisocial personality disorder
@	at
A2	aortic second sound
AU	both ears
AV	arteriovenous
AVC	atrioventricular canal
AVPD	avoidant personality disorder
AVVR	atrioventricular valve regurgitation
AWOL	away without official leave
AX	angle jerk
b	born
Bab	Babinski
bact	bacteria
BBS	bilateral breath sounds
BC/BS	BlueCross/BlueShield
BD	birth defect
BDD	body dysmorphic disorder
BDI	Beck Depression Inventory
BE	barium enema
b.i.d.	twice a day
BJM	bones, joints, muscles
BK	below knee
BM	bowel movement
BMT	bone marrow transplant
BP	blood pressure
BPD	borderline personality disorder
BS	bowel sound
B/S	breath sounds
BSC	behavioral specialist consultant
BUN	blood urea nitrogen
$\bar{c}$	with
C	centigrade
C&S	culture and sensitivity
C&Y	children and youth
ca	calcium; chronological age
CA	cancer, carcinoma
CAM	cardiac medical
cap	capsule
CAS	cardiac surgery
CAVC	complete atrioventricular canal
CBC	complete blood count
CBG	capillary blood gas
CBT	cognitive-behavioral therapy
c.	monitor cardiac monitor
cc	cubic centimeter
CC	chief complaint
CDC	Centers for Disease Control and Prevention
CDI	Children's Depression Inventory
CF	cystic fibrosis
Δ	change
CHD	congenital heart disease
□	check
chol	cholesterol
Cl	chloride
cldy	cloudy
cm	centimeter
CNS	central nervous system
c/o, CO	complaint of
CO_2	carbon dioxide
coarc	coarctation
COD	co-occurring disorders
COI	conflict of interest
conj	conjunctive
conv	convergence
CP	cerebral palsy
CPAP	continuous positive airway pressure
CPC	clinicopathological conference
CPR	cardiopulmonary resuscitation
CPT	chest physiotherapy
CRC	clinical research
C/S	cesarean section
CSF	cerebrospinal fluid
CT	chest tube
CT, CT scan, CAT	computerized tomography
CVA	cerebrovascular accident

CVL	central venous line
CVP	central venous pressure
CVS	clean-voided specimen
CXR	chest X-ray
CYS	cystic fibrosis
D&C	dilation and curettage
DAT	diet as tolerated
d/c	discontinue
D/C	discharge
↓	decrease
DD	dual diagnosis
DHHS	Department of Health and Human Services
DID	dissociative identity disorder
dil	dilute
DOA	dead on arrival
DOB	date of birth
DOC	doctor on call
DOE	dyspnea on exertion; date of evaluation
DOPP	duration of positive pressure
DNR	do not resuscitate
DP	dorsalis pedis
DPT	diphtheria, pertussis, tetanus
DS	Down syndrome
D/S	dextrose and saline
DSM-IV	*Diagnostic and Statistical Manual of Mental Disorders*, fourth edition
DTR	deep tendon reflex
DTV	due to void
D/W	dextrose and water
DX, Dx, dx	diagnosis
EAP	employee assistance program
EBP	evidence-based practice
ECG, EKG	electrocardiogram
ECHO	enterocytopathogenic human orphan viruses
ECMO	extracorporeal membrane oxygenation
ECT	electroconvulsive treatment
EDC	endocrine
EEG	electroencephalogram
e.g.	for example
EMDR	eye movement desensitization and reprocessing
EMV	expired minute volume
ENT	ears, nose, throat; otolaryngology

EOM	extraocular movement
eos	eosinophils
ER	emergency room
ERG	electroretinogram
ESR	erythrocyte sedimentation rate
ETOH	alcohol
ETT	endotracheal tube
eve	evening
ext	extension
extrem	extremities
EYE	ophthalmology
f	frequency
f/b	followed by
F	Fahrenheit; father
FAS	fetal alcohol syndrome
FBA	Functional Behavioral Assessment
FBS	fasting blood sugar
FDA	Food and Drug Administration
♀	female
FFP	fresh frozen plasma
FH	family history
FIO_2	fractional inspired oxygen
flex	flexion
FOO	family of origin
for. bend	forward bending
FP	family physician
FTT	failure to thrive
f/u	follow up
FUO	fever of unknown origin
g, gm	gram
GAD	generalized anxiety disorder
GAF	Global Assessment of Functioning
GB	series gallbladder series
GC	gonorrhea
g/dl	grams per hundred millimeters
GF&R	grunting, flaring, and retracting
GI	gastrointestinal
GIS	gastroenterology
GNS	general surgery
gr	grain
GSR	galvanic skin response
gtt	drops
GTT	glucose tolerance test
gyn	gynecology
h	hour
H	husband
HA	headache

HC head circumference
HCT hematocrit
HEENT head, eyes, ears, nose, throat
HEM hematology
Hgb hemoglobin
HI homicidal ideation
HIPAA Health Insurance Portability and Accountability Act of 1996
HIV human immunodeficiency virus
HLHS hypoplastic left heart syndrome
HMO health maintenance organization
HO_2 humidified oxygen
HPF high-power field
HR heart rate
HRT hormone replacement therapy
h.s. at bedtime
ht height
HTN hypertension
Hx history

IA intra-arterial
I&D incision and drainage
I&O intake and output
I&R information and referral
ICP intracranial pressure
ICU intensive care unit
IDS infectious diseases
i.e. that is, namely
IJ internal jugular vein
IL intralipid
IM intramuscular
imp impression
↑ increase (elevated)
in rot in rotation
inv inversion
IOFB intraocular foreign body
IOM Institute of Medicine
IP inpatient
IQ intelligence quotient
IT intrathecal
IV intravenous
IVC inferior vena cava
IVH intraventricular hemorrhage
IVP intravenous push

JCAHO Joint Commission on the Accreditation of Healthcare Organizations
JD juvenile delinquent
JT jejunostomy tube

K potassium
kg kilogram
KJ knee jerk
KUB kidney, ureter, bladder
kV kilovolt

L left
LA left atrium
lab laboratory
L&A light and accommodation
LAO left anterior oblique
LAP left atrial pressure
lat. bend lateral bending
LBP low back pain
LCSW licensed clinical social worker
LFT liver function test
LL lower lid
LLE left lower extremity
LLL left lower lobe
LLQ left lower quadrant
L/min liters per minute
LMP last menstrual period
LOA leave of absence
LP lumbar puncture
LPA left pulmonary artery
LTG long-term goal
LTM long-term memory
LUE left upper extremity
LUL left upper lobe
LUQ left upper quadrant
LV left ventricular
lymphs lymphocytes
lytes electrolytes

m meter
M mother
♂ male
M&T myringotomy and tubes
MAP mean arterial pressure
MAPI Millon Adolescent Personality Inventory
MCL midclavicular line
MCMI-III Millon Clinical Multiaxial Inventory-III
MDD Major Depressive Disorder
med medicine
mEq milliequivalent (per liter, mEq/L)
mets metastasis

mg	milligram
Mg	magnesium
mg/dl	milligrams per hundred milliliters
MHC	mental health center
MI	myocardial infarction
ml	milliliter (preferred over cc)
ML	middle lobe
M&M	morbidity and mortality
MMPI	Minnesota Multiphasic Personality Inventory
Mn	manganese
mod	moderate
mono	monocyte infectious; mononucleosis
MR	mental retardation
MRI	magnetic resonance imaging
MS	multiple sclerosis
MSE	mental status examination
MVA	motor vehicle accident
Na	sodium
NAD	no apparent distress
NAMI	National Alliance for the Mentally Ill
neb, htd neb	nebulizer, heated nebulizer
NEC	necrotizing enterocolitis
NEO	neonatology
neph	nephrotomy
NG	nasogastric
NICU	newborn intensive care unit
NIDA	National Institute on Drug Abuse
NIH	National Institutes of Health
NIMH	National Institute of Mental Health
NKA	no known allergies
NKDA	no known drug allergies
nl	normal
NLS	neurology
NMJ	neuromuscular joint
NOS	not otherwise specified
NP	nasopharyngeal
NPO	nothing by mouth
NRC	normal retinal correspondence
N/S	normal saline
NSF	National Science Foundation
NSS	neurosurgery
NT	nasotracheal
NTA	nothing to add
N_2	nitrogen
N_2O	nitrous oxide
N/V	nausea and vomiting
NVD	normal vaginal delivery
N/V/D	nausea, vomiting, diarrhea
O&P	ova and parasites, stool
obs	obstetrics or obstetrical
OBS	organic brain syndrome
occ	occasionally
OCD	obsessive-compulsive disorder
OD	right eye
ODD	oppositional defiant disorder
odont	odontectomies
OFS	orbitofrontal syndrome
OHID	oxygen tent
OM	otitis media
1:1	one to one
OOB	out of breath; out of bed
OOP	out on pass
op	operation
OP	oropharyngeal
OPD	outpatient department
OR	operating room
ORL	otorhinolaryngology (ENT)
orth, ORT	orthopedics
OS	left eye
OT	occupational therapy
OTC	over-the-counter
O_2	oxygen
O_2sat	oxygen saturation
OU	both eyes
$\bar{p}$	after
P	phosphorous
PA	posteroanterior; pulmonary artery
PA cath	pulmonary artery catheter
P&A	percussion and auscultation
P&V	percussion and vibration
PAP	pulmonary artery pressure
Pap	Papanicolaou smear
p.c.	after meals
PCA	patient-controlled analgesia
PCO_2	partial carbon dioxide pressure
PDD	pervasive developmental disorder
PE	physical examination
ped, pedi, peds	pediatrics
PEEP	positive end-expiratory pressure

PERLA	pupils equal, reactive to light and accommodation
PF	plantar flexion
PFC	persistent fetal circulation
PFO	patent foramen ovale
PFT	pulmonary function test
pg	per gastric
pH	hydrogen ion concentration
PH	past history
PHP	posthospital plans
PI	present illness
PID	pelvic inflammatory disease
PIE	pulmonary interstitial emphysema
PIV	peripheral intravenous
PKU	phenylketonuria
PLS	plastics
plts	platelets
PMH	past medical history
PMS	premenstrual syndrome
PNP	psychiatric nurse practitioner
p.o.	by mouth
PO_2	partial pressure oxygen
PPD	purified protein derivative
PPH	persistent pulmonary hypertension
PPOs	preferred provider organizations
p.r.	per rectum
PRBC	packed red blood cells
premie	premature
prep	preparation
p.r.n.	as needed
prot	protein (total protein preferred)
PS	pulmonic stenosis; pulmonary stenosis
psi	pounds per square inch
PSP	phenolsulfonphthalein
psy; psych	psychiatry; psychology
pt	patient
PT	physical therapy; prothrombin time
PTMDF	pupils, tension, media, disk, fundus
PTSD	posttraumatic stress disorder
PUL	pulmonary
PVC	premature ventricular contraction
PWS	Prader-Willi syndrome
q	every
q.a.m.	every morning
q.d.	every day
q4h	every 4 hours
q.h.	every hour
q.h.s.	every night
q.i.d.	four times a day
q.n.s.	quantity not sufficient
q.o.d.	every other day
QR	quiet room
qs	quantity sufficient
q2h	every 2 hours
q3h	every 3 hours
R	right
RA	right atrium
RAO	right anterior oblique
RBC	red blood cell; red blood count
RD	radial deviation
RDS	respiratory distress syndrome
re	regarding
REBT	rational-emotive behavior therapy
REN	renal/dialysis
Rh+, Rh–	rhesus blood factor
RHD	rheumatic heart disease
RLE	right lower extremity
RLL	right lower lobe
RLQ	right lower quadrant
RML	right middle lobe
RN	registered nurse
R/O	rule out
RPA	right pulmonary artery
RR	respiratory rate
RRE	round, regular, and equal
RT	respiratory therapy; reaction time
RTC	return to clinic; residential treatment center
RTH	radiation therapy
RTO	return to office
RUE	right upper extremity
RUL	right upper lobe
RUQ	right upper quadrant
RV	right ventricle or ventricular
Rx	treatment; treatment with medication
$\overline{s}$	without
S	suction
SAD	seasonal affective disorder
SAE	serious adverse event
SC, SQ, Subq	subcutaneous

SCA	subclavian artery
SD	systematic desensitization
sed. rate	erythrocyte sedimentation rate
SG	specific gravity
SH	social history; serum hepatitis
SI	suicidal ideation
SIB	self-injurious behavior
SIDS	sudden infant death syndrome
SLR	straight leg raising
SOB	shortness of breath
sol	solution
SMR	severe mental retardation
SP	special precautions
S/P	status post
SPA	serum protein analysis
SS	signs and symptoms
SSRI	selective serotonin reuptake inhibitor
S.T.	speech therapy
STAT	immediately and only once
STG	short-term goals
stm	short-term memory
strep	streptococcus
sub AS	subaortic stenosis
surg	surgery or surgical
SV	single ventricle
SVC	superior vena cava
SW	social worker
sx	symptoms
SZ	schizophrenia
Sz	seizure
TA	tricuspid atresia
tab	tablet
T&A	tonsillectomy and adenoidectomy
T&C	type and crossmatch
T&H	type and hold
TAT	Thematic Apperception Test
TB	tuberculosis
TBA	to be announced
tbsp	tablespoon
TCA	tricyclic antidepressant
TCO_2	total (calculated) carbon dioxide
TENS	transcutaneous electrical nerve stimulator
TF, TOF	tetralogy of Fallot
TGA	transposition of great arteries
TGV	transposition of great vessels

t.i.d.	three times a day
TLC	tender loving care
TM	tympanic membrane
TP	total protein
TPR	temperature, pulse, and respiration
Tq	tourniquet
TSH	thyroid stimulating hormone
tsp	teaspoon
Tsp	tablespoon
TSS	therapeutic staff support
TT	tracheostomy tube
TTX	tumor therapy
TV	tidal volume
2	secondary to
TX, Tx	treatment
U	unit
UA	urinalysis
UDT	undescended testicles
UGI	upper gastrointestinal series
umb(i)	umbilical
ung	ointment
UO	urinary output
ureth	urethral
URI	upper respiratory infection
uro, urol	urology or urological
US	ultrasound
UTI	urinary tract infection
V, VA	volt; vision or visual acuity
VA	Department of Veterans Affairs
vag	vagina or vaginal
VAMC	Veterans Administration Medical Center
VC	vital capacity
VCO_2	carbon dioxide production
VD	venereal disease
VDRL	Venereal Disease Research Laboratory
vert	vertebrae (D. vert: dorsal; L. vert: lumbar)
VF	volar flexion; vocal fremitus
vit	vitamin when followed by specific letter (e.g., vit A)
VO_2	oxygen consumption
VS	vital signs
Vx	vertex

W	wife
WAIS-III	Wechsler Adult Intelligence Scale-Third Edition
WB	whole blood
WBC	white blood cell; white blood count
WD	well developed
WDWN	well developed, well nourished
WFL	within functional limits
WHO	World Health Organization
WISC-III	Wechsler Intelligence Scale for Children-III
wk	week
WMS	Wechsler Memory Scale
WN	well nourished
WNL	within normal limits
WRAT	Wide Range Achievement Test
wt	weight
w/u	workup
y.o.	years old

Related Topics

Chapter 96, "Normal Medical Laboratory Values and Measurement Conversions"
Chapter 125, "Prototype Mental Health Records"

130 CREATING A PROFESSIONAL LIVING WILL FOR PSYCHOLOGISTS

Stephen A. Ragusea

Every life is different from any that has gone before it, and so is every death.

The uniqueness of each of us extends even to the way we die.

—Nuland, 1995 (p. 1)

The idea of having a professional living will or advanced directive was unheard of 20 years ago, but the document's importance is undeniable and professionals are increasingly making provision for the unexpected end of their professional practices.

On rare occasions, reality breaks through our merciful denial and we all consider our own demise. Yes, the last great adventure beckons to us; even psychologists die. Most of us like to think that we will pass away quietly in old age, peacefully sleeping in our own beds and, perhaps, surrounded by loved ones. But what if the path goes off in a different, surprising direction? What if we die suddenly, unexpectedly?

We have probably made provision for the end of our personal lives. We bought life insurance; we have a last will and testament, even a living will perhaps, to advise our family about when and how to "pull the plug." Our personal matters are in order. But what have we done about the end of our professional lives?

For most of us, if we consider the subject at all, we imagine that our professional practices have long since been terminated and we have spent our final wonder years in blissful retirement on Golden Pond. While this projected outcome may be accurate for some of us, it is not the finality that awaits all of us. There are many variations.

In fact, psychologists in the full blossom of their careers sometimes die suddenly. Accidents happen. Murder happens. So does suicide.

When this occurs, what is the impact on the psychologist's patients? Who tells them the terrible news? Who helps forcibly terminated patients deal with a kind of abandonment they never imagined? And who manages the financial accounts, the records, the managed care contracts, the myriad business details? This is a professional issue that gets scant attention by most clinical psychologists.

The American Psychological Association's current Ethical Principles of Psychologists and Code of Conduct (APA, 2002) directly addresses the most basic of the issues discussed herein. For example, there are applicable statements in Standards 4.08 and 6.02(c)). Standard 4.08 requires that "psychologists make reasonable efforts to plan for facilitating services in the event that psychological services are interrupted by factors such as the psychologist's illness, death, unavailability." Standard 6.02(c)) stipulates, "Psychologists make plans in advance to facilitate the appropriate transfer and to protect the confidentiality of records and data in the event of psychologists' withdrawal from positions or practice."

How then is a responsible psychologist to make provision for his or her patients "in the event that psychological services are interrupted" by events such as sudden death, disappearance, or disability? Surprisingly little has been written in the psychological literature addressing these issues.

Kahn (1999) suggests that psychologists identify a licensed colleague who will be willing to serve as a professional executor and that the addresses of the psychologist's professional organizations be provided, along with identifying data of all patients requiring notification. Dr. Kahn also believes that certain specific instructions should be provided to help guide the professional executor, some of which are included in the document provided herein.

What follows is a proposed model, which endeavors to deal appropriately with the end-of-life issues unique to those of a clinical psychologist. I have entitled the document *Professional Executor Instructions* because that term seems to most clearly describe the purpose of the document. A lawyer might describe this as a subtype of a commonly utilized legal document called a limited power of attorney. In any case, the document is designed to function as a professional living will for psychologists and it is written in plain language, deliberately avoiding the arcane jargon sometimes associated with legal documents.

Individual psychologists are encouraged to copy, adapt, and utilize this offering, as they deem appropriate. A few details of the provided model are based upon Florida law and will require some modification in other locations. Although several attorneys in different states have found this specific format acceptable, it would be wise for any user to have his or her final draft examined by local legal counsel.

Professional Executor Instructions
For the Disposition of the Practice of
Chris A. Person, PsyD
In the Event of Death, Disappearance, or Disability
January 1, 2008

A. My Professional Executors are as follows:
The Psychology Staff, Child, Adult & Family Psychological Center (C.A.F.P.C.)
777 Elm Street, Suite 218, Everywhere, Florida 24680 (123) 456-7890

B. My Attorney is currently:
Diane Covan, Esquire
1601 Pennsylvania Avenue, Everywhere, Florida 2468 (123) 654-0987

C. My Accountant is currently:
C. J. Wagner, CPA
1 Park Place, Everywhere, Florida 24680 (123) 222-4816

D. General information:
1. My office is located at 777 Elm Street, Suite 218, Everywhere, Florida 24680.

2. The keys to my office and file cabinets are located on my personal key ring. Keys to all office files are held by the C.A.F.P.C. clerical staff.

3. My closed client files are stored in the locked filing cabinets in the basement of my home.

4. My open client files are kept in the filing cabinets at C.A.F.P.C.

5. My billing files and records are at the C.A.F.P.C. office.

6. My psychology license, malpractice insur ance policy, and managed care contracts are at the C.A.F.P.C. office.

7. All client-related materials must be handled only by my Professional Executors as named above.

8. C.A.F.P.C. Psychologists will assist in any therapeutic issues which may need to be addressed with my clients. Billing issues, insurance, and other administrative details already handled by C.A.F.P.C. clerical staff or C.A.F.P.C. officers will continue to be handled by them.

9. My appointment book, which is confidential, is normally kept in my personal briefcase. Clerical staff may contact clients to cancel appointments, but if there is a need for discussion with clients regarding my being disabled or deceased, my Professional Executors will handle client contact and follow-up.

10. Patient records, including notes and reports may be found on my personal computer located at my home. The security password for accessing that data is, "Bronx." The electronic records contained therein should be treated in a similar manner to the written materials in my file cabinets.

E. *Specific instructions to my Professional Executors:*

1. In the event of a serious illness such as when I am unable to work for more than 2 weeks but can communicate effectively, please contact me as soon as I am able to communicate about how to proceed. Whatever I communicate to you at that time will take precedence over this document.

2. In the event of my death, disappearance, or in the event of temporary or permanent decisional incapacitation as determined by a licensed psychologist or physician, my Professional Executors should take the following steps. First, telephone all scheduled clients and notify them of my current circumstances.

Assess their psychological vulnerability and need for ongoing psychological intervention, via recent therapy notes and your telephone conversation. Make professional referrals as appropriate. If the client is willing to accept a referral, please obtain the client's written permission to release his/her name and records to the designated therapist. Please make an effort to match each client with a provider who is approved by, or is on the panel of, the client's insurance or managed care company. Please offer clients at least one face-to-face therapy session, individual or group format, with yourself or another professional therapist that you designate, to process the event of my death or incapacitation. If possible, please make generous allowances for any client's inability to pay for this session, or for insurance coverage if that session is denied.

3. Copies of referred client's records should be forwarded to their new therapists, if the therapists so request. All remaining records should be maintained in a safe, confidential place for the minimum number of years currently required by state and federal law. Please dispose of all records not required by such laws to be maintained, in a manner, which destroys completely all identifying client information, such as shredding.

4. Please defer to my spouse, and the executor of my estate, Pat Person, regarding any financial decisions to be made regarding payment of any of my outstanding bills, and client bill collections. In the event of the concurrent incapacitation or death of my spouse, please refer these decisions to the executor of my personal estate. If there is a clinical component to these client based financial decisions, please review the file and share minimum pertinent information necessary so the executor may make an informed decision.

5. Please notify, in writing, all managed health care companies, hospitals, and other professional organizations with which I am affiliated of my circumstances. Also notify my state Board of Psychology.

6. If any further information or an update of legal requirements for the care of records is required, please contact my state psychological association or the Office of Ethics at the American Psychological Association.

7. There are three copies of these Professional Executor instructions. The first is located with my other important personal papers in my safe deposit box. The clerical staff at C.A.F.P.C holds the second. The third is on file with my attorney.

8. Please bill my estate for the cost of professional time and any other reasonable expenses that may be incurred as the result of executing these instructions.

9. This Professional Living Will is established in and shall be governed by the laws of my state. I intend that this power of attorney be universally recognized and admissible in any jurisdiction.

F. *Legal Notice:*

An appropriate notice regarding my practice may be published in the newspaper. In this regard, the following rules of the Florida Board of Psychology should be followed unless the Board has changed the rules since the signing of this document.

Disposition of Records Upon Termination or Relocation of

Psychological Practice

1. When a licensed psychologist terminates practice or relocates practice and is no longer available to service users in the practice area, the licensed psychologist shall provide notice of such termination or relocation of practice. Such notice shall be published in the newspaper of greatest circulation in the county from which the licensed psychologist is relocating or, in the case of termination of practice, in each county where the licensed psychologist has practiced. Such notice shall be published weekly for 4 consecutive weeks. The notice shall contain the date of termination or relocation of practice and an address at which the psychological records of the service users may be obtained by them, their legal representatives, or licensed mental health professionals designated by service users in writing, to receive the service user's records.

2. The executor, administrator, personal representative or survivor of a deceased licensed psychologist shall ensure the retention of psychological records in existence upon the death of the psychologist for a period of at least 2 years and 2 months from the date of the licensed psychologist's death. Within 1 month of the death, the executor, administrator, personal representative or survivor of the deceased licensed psychologist shall cause notice to be published in the newspaper of greatest general circulation in each county where the licensed psychologist practiced. Such notice shall be published weekly for 4 consecutive weeks and shall advise of the licensed psychologist's death. Such notice shall also state the address from which service users, their legal representative, or licensed mental health professionals designated by the service user in writing, may obtain the services user's psychological records. A copy of such notice shall be mailed to the administrative office of the Board of Psychology. At the conclusion of 24 months from the date of the licensed psychologist's death, the executor shall cause a notice to be published in the newspaper of greatest circulation in each county where the deceased psychologist practiced. Such notice shall advise that the psychological records still in the possession or under the control of the executor will be destroyed on a date specified which may not be any sooner than 1 month from the last day of the last week of the publication of the notice. Such notice shall also be published once a week for 4 consecutive weeks. Thereafter, on the date specified in the notice, the executor shall destroy unclaimed psychological records.

______________________ Psychologist Signature	______________________ Date
______________________ Witness Signature	______________________ Date
______________________ Notary Signature	______________________ Date

References and Readings

American Psychological Association. (2002). Ethical principles of psychologists and code of conduct. *American Psychologist, 57*(12), 1060–1073.

Kahn, F. (1999, April). Ending a clinical practice—in the event of disability, retirement or death. *The California Psychologist, 31*(4), 32–33.

Nuland, S. (1995). *How we die: Reflections on life's final chapter.* New York: Alfred A. Knopf.

VandeCreek, L., & Jackson, T. L. (Eds.). (2002). *Innovations in clinical practice: A source book* (Vol. 20). Sarasota, FL: Professional Resource Press.

Related Topic

Chapter 144, "Psychotherapist Self-Care Checklist"

131 UNDERSTANDING STATISTICS IN THE RESEARCH LITERATURE

William F. Chaplin and Niketa Kumar

One of the foundational components of graduate training in all areas of psychology is quantitative methods. Ideally this training prepares practicing applied psychologists to sensibly and thoughtfully interpret the statistical findings of a study. Proper interpretation of statistical information regarding evaluation of treatments, assessments, and risk factors is critical for sound clinical practice. The reality, however, is that many applied psychologists have long since forgotten their statistics courses, often with a substantial feeling of relief that they will not have to cross paths with a standard deviation, correlation coefficient, or *p*-value again. At best, the research literature is understood by reading summaries of results found in Abstracts and Discussion sections. The actual results are skipped.

Unfortunately, abstracts and discussions contain the authors' interpretations of their results, and generally authors tell the best story they can about their findings. It is not that the Discussion contains outright fabrications, but it tends to contain the best "spin," or story, that the authors can tell. Within nearly all empirical research there is a difference between the results and what someone thinks about the results. It is in the Results section that we learn what was actually found, and so that is where a clear understanding of the results, as opposed to the author's interpretation of the results, is obtained. The purpose of this chapter is to provide some guidance and examples for how to read Results sections in the empirical clinical literature. To provide some background, we begin with a discussion of recent developments in statistics and how these developments have impacted modern data analysis.

STATISTICS THEN AND NOW

The first author of this paper will have turned 60 when this chapter is published (or perhaps be even older if he keeps ignoring the editors' deadlines). When he was learning statistics roughly 40 years ago, many of the analyses were still done by hand or with the assistance of very limited statistical software on very slow computers. The standard inferential analysis was the Analysis of Variance (ANOVA), the modal experimental design was probably the 2 × 2 between-subjects factorial, and the outcome variable was a single, normally distributed, continuous variable. For those who studied individual differences, the computation of Pearson product moment correlations between two variables was the standard, and statistical inference was pretty much universally based on the null hypothesis test accompanied by the $p < .05$ ritual. The good news was that for those who found studying statistics an unpleasant chore, there was not that much to learn. The bad news was that the types of hypotheses that could be tested were severely limited and could not remotely capture the complexity of the multivariate and longitudinal nature of development, change in life, and for that matter psychotherapy. Moreover, the approach to statistical inference was not remotely applicable to the everyday or professional inferences that were made in applied settings. So the attitude of practicing clinical psychologists of the generations surrounding that of the first author's that their statistical training had little relevance to their work was to some extent justified.

Times have changed. The second author will have turned 25 when this paper is published. Extremely powerful computers have always been a part of her life and the available statistical software can now model extraordinarily complex phenomena and test meaningful hypotheses about multivariate and longitudinal data which are at the heart of clinical practice (and life). There is no longer a standard way to analyze data, nor is there a modal research design. We have slowly come to recognize that the null hypothesis test is not only inapplicable to clinical inference, but it is pretty much a wretched model for statistical or any other type of inference as well. For example, Bayesian models that show how inferences should change in light of new information not only capture more realistically what happens during scientific research but are directly relevant as models of clinical and even everyday inferential processes. Multiple regression/correlation analysis provides, in the words of the late Jack Cohen, a "general data analytic system" that seamlessly incorporates categorical (e.g., treatment) and continuous (e.g., individual differences) variables in the same analysis and allows for the testing of hypotheses about how treatments have different effects for different types of individuals. The extension of univariate multiple regression to repeated measures through mixed effects regression analysis allows for the estimation of models of how individuals, not just averages of individuals, change over time and allows us to see how these changes are impacted by treatments, individual characteristics, and the combination of the two. We have techniques such as logistic regression and survival models for handling categorical and other types of non-normal outcome variables that are more representative of what is seen and done in the clinic. And through structural equation modeling we are no longer held hostage by "operational definitions" (where we had to ridiculously pretend that a measure of, say, depression, was depression) and instead can explicitly analyze latent constructs where we recognize that measures are imperfect representations of the complex phenomena we are investigating.

The good news is that statistics and statistical models are now far more relevant and useful in applied data analytic situations. They have supported the expansion of psychology from a primary focus on the laboratory-based experimental study of college undergraduates to the examination of more naturalistic processes and treatments in applied contexts on populations who are underserved. The bad news is that there is now much more to learn. The second author of this chapter is now required to take three semesters of "statistics" courses in our clinical program. In the remainder of this chapter we present a few key topics and some additional resources with the goal of empowering readers to become more sophisticated as they read the modern behavioral science literature.

STATISTICAL SIGNIFICANCE AND INFERENCE: WHAT IS A *P* (PROBABILITY)-VALUE, ANYWAY?

For much of its history the evaluation of research results in the psychological and medical literature was based on a single standard: whether the statistical test was "significant at the .05 level." The somewhat arbitrary cutoff of .05, applied to the null hypothesis *test*, represented near universal practice and it was essentially impossible to publish results that did not use this approach and meet this standard. However, as far back as the 1950s the voices of a few individuals, such as Rozeboom, Bakan, and Meehl, were raised in protest against this standard. The essence of the protest was that the null hypothesis *test* was based on the evaluation of a model that was a priori known to be strictly false. This was recognized in the old adage, "You cannot prove the null hypothesis." If the investigator had the resources (large enough samples) to reject the false model, then he or she could claim that he or she had found something important, or at least "significant." The test was, and is, vacuous. However, it had the appealing virtues of being easily applied and objective.

Because the null hypothesis test cannot be interpreted sensibly, it is not surprising that it has primarily become a ritual. When we asked students and colleagues what a *p*-value means, typical responses ranged from "if its less than .05 it is significant," "it is the probability that your hypothesis is supported," to "it means you can publish your results." None of these responses answer the question; instead they refer to the consequences or particular interpretations applied to a *p*-value. However, the value of *p* that is obtained from a psychological test has a precise and sensible interpretation. Indeed, the *p*-value for a particular test can be thought of as a descriptive sample statistic just like a mean or correlation. Specifically, when applied to the null hypothesis, *p* is the probability of obtaining a particular result (such as a mean difference) under the condition that the null hypothesis is true. For example, in a study that compares two treatments one might see the following: The difference between the control and treatment groups on their mean depression scores was 2.5 (12.5 versus 10), $p = .023$. The value .023 means that in this sample (with the stated number of participants and the obtained standard deviation) the probability of observing sample means of 12.5 and 10 in the control and treatment groups, respectively, is .023 *if the true difference was zero*, that is, the null hypothesis is exactly true.

So, when confronted with *p*-values and statistical significance in the research literature, how might we sensibly rather than ritualistically use this information?

Look at the Confidence Intervals

p-values refer to the data (not the hypothesis) under the assumption that the hypothesis is true. The null hypothesis (no difference or relation) is a reasonable model to consider. It just should not be the only model to consider. When we are told the data we observe are unlikely (say $p < .05$) under the null model, we should immediately think: "But how likely are the data under a *different* model," such as treatment reduces depression by a clinically meaningful amount (say 5 points). The process becomes far more sensible when we test multiple models. Fortunately, including (as is now required for results sections by most journals) 95% confidence intervals around the sample results allows readers to immediately see the entire range of values that are reasonably likely and unlikely. So when we see that the obtained mean difference is 2.5 and that the 95% confidence interval is 2.5 ± 2.4 (that is, from .1 to 4.9), we see that 0 (null hypothesis) is outside the interval and so statistically significant, but so is our minimal clinically meaningful difference of 5. Testing multiple models allows us to reach the more sophisticated conclusion that although the observed treatment effect is statistically significant (reject the null hypothesis), that effect is also statistically significantly lower than the minimal clinically meaningful effect, meaning that the treatment may not have a strong enough effect to warrant using it in practice. This valuable information cannot be found solely through null hypothesis testing.

Look at the Sample Size (N)

p-values are sample statistics and so depend on the characteristics of the sample, including the N. Indeed, the test statistics (such as the t-test) that we use to obtain the *p*-values come from multiplying an effect size and the sample size. That is, statistical tests can all be generically written as

$$\text{effect size} \times \text{sample size}.$$

The implication of this is that very large samples can turn very small effects into statistically significant ones. This is important to psychologists as psychological treatments (such as life style interventions) are often evaluated in low-resource environments, whereas pharmacological effects (e.g., lipid-lowering drugs) are often evaluated in high-resource environments ("Big Pharma"). If all we focus on is statistical significance, very small effects of drugs may be significant in a sample of 10,000, whereas a reasonably large effect of a behavioral intervention may not be significant in a smaller sample of 100. We are not arguing in favor of small samples. Indeed, larger samples are better because they contain more information and so, all other aspects of the study being equal, should give us more confidence in the findings (that is, the effect sizes). Our caution here is that large samples can have a misleading inflationary effect on the statistical significance of those findings. Fortunately, scientific journals now generally require that effect sizes of results be reported independently of statistical significance so readers can separate the influence of the sample size from the influence of the effect size on the *p*-values. However, this information, as with confidence intervals, may only be available in the Results section and not in the Abstract or Discussion. You should be very suspicious of articles that report only the statistical significance of the findings and not the findings themselves.

Think Replication

There are many examples in the literature of treatments and risk factors that were found to be promising and important in an initial study but later found to be ineffective and trivial. The most dramatic recent example was the apparent link between childhood vaccines and autism. The importance of this link, if true, would have enormous implications, so efforts to replicate the finding on large data sets were undertaken. None of these new studies could support the link, and it eventually came to light that the data in the initial study were falsified to support the author's testimony as an expert witness in a lawsuit filed against a vaccine manufacturer. However, as psychologists we know the power of first impressions, so it is perhaps not surprising that many parents continue to fear vaccinating their children, with the very sad result that babies are dying of easily preventable diseases such as whooping cough. As we read the scientific literature, it is important to recognize that statistical significance is not the arbiter of scientific acceptability, treatment effectiveness, or risk: *Replication* is. One of the most important developments in science has been the increase in systematic quantitative reviews ("meta-analysis") of the literature. These reviews provide us with estimates of the average effects of treatments, risks, and protective factors across multiple studies, including those that failed to replicate an effect. Thus, meta-analyses allow us to make informed treatment decisions and free us from the seduction of a single dramatic finding. These reviews also help solve the problem of small sample sizes in studies of underserved populations or expensive and complex treatments by aggregating the findings (effect sizes) across a number of small studies to give us more confidence in the nature of the effect. The link to the Cochrane Collaboration at the end of this chapter provides more information about these methods and access to the results of systematic reviews of medical and behavioral studies.

EFFECTIVE SIZES: ABSOLUTE EFFECTS ARE IN GENERAL PREFERABLE TO RELATIVE ONES

Providing effect sizes is a major improvement toward making the results of research transparent. However, effect sizes can be reported in many different ways, some of which may be vague or misleading. In addition, authors, reviewers, and readers have tended to substitute more or less arbitrary guidelines or rules for interpreting effect sizes (similar to the p <. 05 rule for interpreting p-values) with the result that the clinical meaning of an effect may be obscured.

In this section we consider the issue of standardized and unstandardized effects for continuous outcomes and the issue of absolute versus relative odds for categorical ones.

Continuous Outcomes: Standardized versus Unstandardized Effect Sizes

Many outcomes in the behavioral sciences are, or can be sensibly treated as, continuous. Often measures of these outcomes have a natural interpretation. Attending college versus not increases average annual income by $20,000, motivational interviewing versus usual care increases medication adherence from 60% to 80%, for each therapy session scores on a symptom checklist decrease by .50 of a symptom, and so on. All of these results are expressed in unstandardized units and can be easily understood and explained to policy makers, clients, and fellow scientists. By unstandardized units we mean in the original (e.g., raw score) units of measurements, such as dollars, percentages, and symptom counts.

In contrast, consider the use of standardized effect sizes in these contexts. A standardized effect size (e.g., z-scored) is one that expresses the effect sizes in units that have nothing to do with the original measures. The two most common standardized effect sizes are Cohen's d, which expresses a mean difference between groups as a z-score and the correlation coefficient r. In standardized terms we might see the above summaries written as: "Attending college versus not increases average annual income, Cohen's d = .70, motivational interviewing versus usual care increases medication adherence, Cohen's d = .45, for each therapy session scores on a symptom checklist decrease, r = –.10." This summary is far less transparent than the one based on unstandardized effect sizes. Indeed, to make these standardized values interpretable, arbitrary interpretive rules are invoked so that authors can call an effect small, medium, and large for values of d equal to .30, .50, and .80 and values or r equal to .10, .30, and .50, respectively. These rules are generally attributed to Jack Cohen, who provided them only after he was forced to by the editors of his papers on effect sizes. He confided to a number of people that he always regretted doing so. He regretted doing so because he recognized that effect sizes must always be interpreted in context; sometimes a conventionally small effect is important and sometimes a conventionally large effect is not.

Standardized effect sizes do serve the important purpose of allowing us to compare effect sizes from measures in different metrics to each other and to aggregate results from studies using different outcome measures in systematic quantitative reviews. So generally one should prefer standardized effect sizes (e.g., d and r) for comparisons across studies and variables and unstandardized effect sizes (e.g., means, mean differences, and unstandardized regression coefficients) when interpreting them. When authors claim in discussion sections that their effects are "large" or "moderate," we should be deeply suspicious and consider the context.

Categorical Outcomes: Absolute versus Relative Risks

As psychology has developed into a more applied field, the importance of dichotomous outcomes has increased. Intervention and prevention must typically be invoked on an all-or-none basis so even if an underlying disorder (e.g., posttraumatic stress disorder) is continuous, it must often be treated as present or absent. When outcome measures are dichotomous, the common standardized effect sizes are odds ratios, or relative risks. However, these effect sizes present results for each group or decision relative to the other group or decision. Thus, they often suffer from the same lack of transparency for treatment decisions as the continuous standardized effect size indices. This issue is clearly and compellingly discussed in the monograph by Gigerenzer et al. listed at the end of this chapter who argue strongly for presenting risk in absolute terms just as we have argued for using unstandardized effect sizes with continuous variables. If readers follow up this brief presentation by reading one more paper, we recommend this one. Next we provide an example to illustrate the issue:

If you were a woman in the United Kingdom in 1996, your doctor may have advised that third-generation oral contraceptive pills increased the relative risk of life-threatening blood clots in the legs or lungs (thrombosis) twofold, or by 100%. When presented this way, understandably, many women feared taking oral contraceptives and discontinued their usage. This led to an estimated 13,000 additional abortions and just as many extra births in the next year, as well as all the psychological consequences these decisions entail. A far different picture emerges if the information is presented in terms of absolute risk. Here you would have been told that a study found that 1 in every 7,000 women who took a second-generation oral contraceptive pill had a thrombosis, and that this number increased to 2 in 7,000 in women taking third-generation pills. The relative risk is twice as much, 2 in 7,000 versus 1 in 7,000, but the absolute risk of taking the pill was only .0003. That is, 3 out of 10,000 women taking the pill would have thrombosis. We suspect that if the data were presented as an absolute risk, far fewer women would have stopped taking oral contraceptives and far fewer unplanned births and abortions would have occurred.

The critical point here is that when effect sizes are presented in relative terms such as odds ratios or risk ratios, the effect is magnified compared to the absolute risk to the individual. In this regard it is interesting that when treatments are advertised, companies tend to report benefit in terms of relative odds and adverse effects in terms of absolute ones. As psychologists, we know that how information is presented can have a dramatic effect on how people act upon it, and as psychologists we should try not to be fooled so easily.

References and Readings

The Cochrane Collaboration. (2006). *Home page.* Retrieved February 2013, from www.cochrane.org.

Cohen, J. (1990). Things I have learned (so far). *American Psychologist, 45,* 1304–1312.

Cohen, J. (1994). The earth is round (p < .05). *American Psychologist, 49,* 997–1003.

Gigerenzer, G., Gaissmaier, W., Kurz-Milcke, E., Schwartz, L. M., & Woloshin, S. (2008). Helping doctors and patients make sense of health statistics. *Psychological Science in the Public Interest, 8,* 53–96.

Schmidt, F. L. (1996). Statistical significance testing and cumulative knowledge in psychology: Implications for training researchers. *Psychological Methods, 1,* 115–129.

Wilkinson, L., & Task Force on Statistical Inference. (1998). Statistical methods in psychology journals: Guidelines and explanations. *American Psychologist, 54,* 594–604.

Related Topic

Chapter 26, "Interpreting Test Scores and Their Percentile Equivalents"

132 SELECTING AND RELYING ON AN ATTORNEY

Robert Henley Woody

With the 1970s advent of licensing and third-party payments, control and regulation by members of the profession of psychology (e.g., ethics committees) decreased and governmental regulation increased. The specter of discipline being imposed by a state licensing board created an irrefutable need for the practitioner to rely on legal counsel to establish quality care and manage risks. Similarly, clients' increased opportunity to file licensing complaints and, indeed, malpractice lawsuits, puts risk management front and center in modern professionalism.

SELF-REPRESENTATION IS FOOLISH

An iconic article by Wright (1981) emphasized that psychologists are prone to think that they can resolve legal problems with psychological tactics, and he urged reliance on an attorney. When faced with a legal issue, some mental health practitioners are prone to incredulity. Depending on the situation, they reason that their intelligence and savvy about psychology will allow them to take care of the legal matter (e.g., without knowledge of the legal ramifications, they draft their own contract or form a business entity online) or if there is a complaint, attempt to talk it out (often resulting in admissions against their own interests).

A frequently quoted proverb admonishes, "He who is his own lawyer has a fool for a client." This assertion has proven to be true over and over. Due to emotions and bias plaguing self-representation, it is common for an attorney who is a party to a legal action to hire an attorney for representation. Certainly a mental health professional should not attempt self-representation.

YOU GET WHAT YOU PAY FOR

In business, expense versus income is always a consideration. The more competitive marketplace (e.g., declining revenues) for practitioners requires prudent budgeting. Paying for an attorney can be a significant cost, but in this day and age, it is an undeniable component of the "cost of doing business." Whether it is a client or patient choosing a psychologist or the latter selecting an attorney, cost should not override quality.

The old adage "you get what you pay for" offers sound guidance for selecting any professional service. Heeding the advice of a friendly layperson is cheaper than paying for psychological service, just as asking an attorney "a quick question" in an informal social setting is cheaper than a formal consultation; however, in both cases, the quality of response is apt to be minimal.

In choosing a licensed psychologist, the service user gains protection against incompetence or nefarious motives. Similarly, retaining a licensed attorney safeguards that accurate information will be provided.

DO NOT ACCEPT LEGAL ADVICE FROM AN UNQUALIFIED PERSON

Mental health practitioners should not accept legal advice from a nonattorney or an attorney who is not admitted to practice law in the jurisdiction in which the mental health professional practices. In selecting an attorney, there are two "red-flag" scenarios.

First, some mental health professionals, especially within the ranks of forensic psychology, may be tempted to dispense legal advice in response to queries from colleagues. Another old adage merits repeating: A little knowledge is a dangerous thing. Having served as a forensic expert does not prepare any psychologist to integrate comprehensive knowledge of law into analysis of legal issues.

Second, when an attorney who has not been admitted to the bar of the given jurisdiction (in which the mental health professional practices) gives a legal opinion about a particular case or situation, it may well constitute the unauthorized practice of law (UPL). This would be similar to the unlicensed practice of psychology (e.g., a licensed psychologist in State A going into State B without a license to provide professional services); this act is potentially subject to prosecution.

One forensic psychologist advised another one about how to deal with discovery (subpoena, deposition, etc.) in a case. When deposed, an attorney of record asked why the psychologist took a certain action; upon learning that the source of legal advice was a nonattorney, the attorney reported the first forensic psychologist to the state bar association, which issued a "cease and desist" demand, making clear that unless honored, there would be prosecution of the forensic psychologist who gave legal advice.

Caveat: A psychologist should not give any legal advice, be it in a personal contact or, for example, on a LISTSERV. The fact that a LISTSERV is sponsored by a professional association offers no exemption from the UPL risk.

BE WARY OF AN ATTORNEY EMPLOYED TO OFFER LEGAL ADVICE FROM A PROFESSIONAL ASSOCIATION OR INSURANCE COMPANY

Every state jurisdiction uses bar examinations to confirm an attorney's knowledge relevant to the laws of the particular state (and federal) jurisdiction. Sales, Miller, and Hall (2005) note: "Each state enacts its own laws, and wide variation exists in the way a topic is handled across jurisdictions" (pp. 4–5). Struggling to gain and retain more members and subscribers, increasingly state and national professional associations and malpractice carriers provide "free legal counsel."

The problem with this service is simple. Although the "free legal counsel" on the phone may well be from a highly qualified attorney admitted to the bar in State A, he or she is not admitted in States B, C, and so on. Although there are commonalities between state jurisdictions, there are also significant, often subtle, distinctions which, for legal quality, should be interfaced with the idiosyncratic considerations of the given judicial system.

"Hot-line" attorneys often try to accommodate the fact that they are not qualified in numerous jurisdictions (i.e., not admitted to practice in the practitioner's state) by couching their responses in generalities; this leaves the mental health practitioner-caller to make nonlegal assumptions that are not based on comprehensive legal knowledge. Here again, the practitioner is operating with less than comprehensive or competent legal counsel.

ESCHEW FREE LEGAL COUNSEL

Relevant to the aforementioned caution, some attorneys, perhaps with the blessing of a state professional association to "benefit our members" (i.e., increase and retain our dues-paying membership), will arrange for a local attorney to offer "free legal consultation." Although potentially of benefit, such an attorney is likely trying to attract clients who will pay for future services (beyond the initial consultation). Since the service is based on financial benefits for the professional association, not the mental health practitioner per se, there is no assurance that this limited free consultation offers quality service.

EVALUATE AN ATTORNEY'S PAST RECORD

History tends to support a prediction for the future. State and local bar associations commonly maintain a referral service. Although "specialization" is not a good indicator of quality, any state-level certification program is useful. Also, bar associations will not recommend an attorney who does not have a clean record of practice. Of course, raising specific questions with the bar association can aid in the verification of competency.

The practitioner seeking a referral will want an attorney with knowledge of the particular legal issues, not necessarily a background in mental health services. For example, when asking a bar association for referrals for a malpractice issue or professional negligence, the basic issue is whether an attorney does defense work. For ethics complaints, being knowledgeable about professional standards and the unique nature of professional associations would be helpful. For a licensing complaint, an attorney needs to be competent in administrative or regulatory law.

Perhaps the best means for selecting an attorney is to ask colleagues for the names of attorneys from whom they have received counsel. With no disrespect to forensic psychologists, some of these specialists might harbor conscious or unconscious bias about an attorney since they may prefer attorneys who provide their referrals. Therefore, it might be wise to seek names of attorneys from mental health practitioners with no potential vested interest in promoting any attorney.

SUCCESSFUL PRACTICE REQUIRES LEGAL

Information Beyond Client Management Per Se

Possibly because of the cost issue, some mental health practitioners are prone to delay obtaining legal counsel until a problem arises, although legal service could enhance the possibility of developing a successful practice. For example, avoiding contracts, such as between associated practitioners, is foolish.

In the decades that have passed since Wright's (1981) warnings, the legal dimension of mental health practice has not lessened; if anything, the need for at attorney now extends to such areas as creating a legal entity (e.g., incorporating), employment contracts, noncompetition agreements, compliance with governmental dictates (e.g., the Health Insurance Portability and Accountability Act), collection of overdue accounts, responding to legal process (e.g., dealing with a subpoena or court order), unifying professional ethics with legal proscriptions and prescriptions, enforcing personal privacy rights, and so on.

RISK MANAGEMENT STRATEGIES

The present-day economics of mental health practice could lead to lackadaisical acceptance of high-risk service users. The needs and criteria for selecting and relying on an attorney are influenced by many issues. Increased risks are associated with the following: providing direct service to clients who have a known penchant for litigation, decreased community mental health services, a growing distrust of health care providers, the demands and restrictions imposed by third-party payment sources, the highly competitive mental health service marketplace (i.e., economic conditions), and as mentioned, the increase in governmental control (which is likely to be profoundly determinative in a national health care system). Said simply, practice success and professional survival require quality care, risk management, and qualified legal counsel (Barnett & Henshaw, 2003; Walfish & Barnett, 2009).

References and Readings

Barnett, J. E., & Henshaw E. A. (2003). Training to begin a private practice. In M. Prinstein & M. Patterson (Eds.), *The portable mentor: Expert guide to a successful career in psychology* (pp. 145–156). New York: Kluwer Academic/Plenum.

Sales, B. D., Miller, M. O., & Hall, S. H. (2005). *Laws affecting clinical practice*. Washington, DC: American Psychological Association.

Walfish, S., & Barnett, J. E. (2009). *Financial success in mental health practice*. Washington, DC: American Psychological Association.

Woody, R. H. (2008). Obtaining legal counsel for child and family mental health services. *American Journal of Family Therapy, 36*(4), 323–331.

Woody, R. H. (2009). Psychological injury from licensing complaints against mental health practitioners. *Psychological Injury and Law, 2*(2), 109–113.

Wright, R. H. (1981). What to do until the malpractice lawyer comes: A survivor's manual. *American Psychologist, 36*(12), 1535–1541.

Related Topics

Chapter 104, "Dealing with Licensing Board and Ethics Complaints"

Chapter 105, "Defending Against Legal (Malpractice and Licensing) Complaints"

Chapter 144, "Psychotherapist Self-Care Checklist"

133 MANAGING REAL-TIME TELEPSYCHOLOGY PRACTICE

Eve-Lynn Nelson and Teresa A. Lillis

Telepsychology or real-time videoconferencing for clinical purposes addresses gaps in accessible psychological services, particularly in rural communities. Videoconferencing allows the client and the psychologist to talk with each other and observe nonverbal behavior in real time, approximating the relationship developed in onsite therapy. The visual component in videoconferencing creates a social presence that promotes familiarity, connectedness, and comfort discussing complex topics.

In the absence of national telepsychology-specific guidelines, psychologists rely on the American Psychological Association's ethics code (2002) that "In those emerging areas in which generally recognized standards for preparatory training do not yet exist, psychologists nevertheless take reasonable steps to ensure the competence of their work and to protect clients, students, research participants, and others from harm." The core ethical principle *to protect the client* remains paramount with services over videoconferencing. Attention must be given to clinical, administrative, and technical components of the telepsychology service.

Psychologists considering telepsychology services should first complete a needs assessment within the community to determine perceived interest and availability of such psychological services. This assessment should include candid discussions and meetings across key constituents, including consumers and their families, local mental health professionals, primary care providers, consumer advocates, and other community leaders likely to be affected by telemedicine initiation. Telepsychology works best when seen as complementing or adding to the community's local care.

The needs assessment should also clarify *who* the telepsychology service will serve. The choice of who will be seen depends on client/parents' preferences, developmental and diagnostic considerations, personnel and other resources at the distant site, and the psychologist's comfort. Telepsychology may be especially suited for younger populations who are often already comfortable and accepting of the technology medium, but there are no data suggesting exclusion based on age. Anecdotally, adolescent clients, in particular, may respond well to the personal space and feeling of control allowed by the televideo system. With telepsychology's extended reach comes the responsibility of the psychologist to follow all professional standards of cultural competence across ethnicities, languages, genders, religions, sexual preferences, geographies, and other competence areas, including an understanding of the impact of rural culture on the clinical presentation.

Psychologists follow legislative and regulatory requirements at the local, state, and national level when providing services by videoconferencing. Most states require that psychologists are licensed in the state where the client receives service, but psychologists should review state-specific guidelines with their licensure boards. Additionally, institutional requirements concerning credentialing at the client site should be reviewed. Psychologists new to telepsychology should shadow existing providers and be encouraged to seek mentoring from practicing telemental health professionals.

Technological advances in personal computer-based videoconferencing systems have made inexpensive, user-friendly, reliable videoconferencing more available. With videoconferencing services, the psychologist and distant site must assess the availability of (1) modern, well-functioning televideo equipment; (2) encrypted videoconferencing software; (3) secure clinical space for the equipment setup; and (4) consistent high-speed connectivity. For telepsychology consultations, serious consideration should be given to privacy and security. Most guidelines recommend use of point-to-point encrypted software, with transparent company information about transmission and encryption protocols. Sites sometimes must run an additional network line to support the additional bandwidth requirements associated with televideo services. It is important to discuss payment for equipment, software, and connectivity when establishing the televideo clinic and with ongoing services.

Technicians should support psychologists with strategies to maximize the quality of the videoconferencing encounter. Current videoconferencing speeds have decreased the pixilation/tiling associated with earlier videoconferencing, rendering fewer technical difficulties over time. Important consideration should be given to camera angle, monitor selection, and positioning in order to better facilitate communication. Proper lighting is also important in order for psychologists to clearly see facial expressions and affective responses. Psychologists are encouraged to check in with clients to make sure clients can see and hear psychologists as anticipated. While the technology has the ability to record sessions, the psychologist should discuss with clients that sessions are not videotaped or archived in any way without client knowledge and consent.

Ultimately, the purpose of the psychology clinic should drive the selection of the technology. It is easy to be drawn into the marketing buzz and enthusiasm for the newest technologies; however, the best fit for the outreach purpose may render those technologies less useful, depending on the needs assessment. Similar to other equipment purchases, psychologists should dialogue not only with technology vendors but also with peers who have used the technology as well as telehealth resource centers.

As with establishing any new clinic, it is essential to consider the target population and client characteristics that will affect clinic volume and financial viability (e.g., insurance status, transportation availability, etc.). The psychologist as well as the distant site administrative and clinical staff must discuss the site's commitment to allow personnel time and space to complete televideo encounters over time. In addition, a written protocol should be established by the psychologist and the client site. This protocol should be revised over time in order to most effectively guide the telepsychology service before, during, and after the telepsychology consult. Key protocol components are described in the next sections.

REFERRAL AND SCHEDULING

Identify psychologist office personnel responsible for scheduling across the client sites (e.g., clinics, hospitals, schools, home, etc.). This person is responsible for coordinating the psychologist's schedule, the client site schedule, and room availability. As in the face-to-face setting, obtain the referral for the new client and determine whether the client meets the insurance requirements consistent with the practice. Send the client the same paperwork as in the face-to-face setting, often including (a) psychology intake form; (b) registration form, including insurer information; (c) consent form, including telemedicine-specific language; (d) HIPAA-related Notice of Privacy Protection (NPP); (e) previous medical history and documentation; (f) requested lab or other tests prior to the telemedicine encounter; and (g) any other information requested by the telemental health team specific to the consult (e.g., school records/testing, etc.). Best practices related to the transmission of health-related information are followed and the client's designated medical record is maintained by the psychologist.

PRE-SESSION

Both the psychologist room and the client room are treated as confidential clinical space. Good lighting and quiet, safe, client-friendly space is crucial. The room needs to be large enough to accommodate the client, family, and other relevant community participants (e.g., case managers, teachers, etc.). Test connections are made with new sites. The Picture in Picture feature is often utilized at both the psychologist and client sites. A technician supports the psychologist's and the client's equipment to ensure best videoconferencing practices (e.g., that the microphone is not muted, that the camera is focused on the psychologist, that microphones are placed away from the monitor's speakers, and that the client is aware of any other individuals in the room). The psychologist utilizes the zoom and scan capabilities of the camera if necessary to complete the examination components. Backup plans are in place in the event of technology failure, most often contacting the client site by telephone and discussing appropriate follow-up.

CLIENT SITE

Telepsychology procedures should establish who is expected to attend the appointment (client, family members, case managers, other community members) and who is expected to coordinate the appointment at the distant site (school nurse, clinic nurse, other clinic personnel, etc.). Telepsychology consults, other than in the home setting, most often include a telepsychology coordinator to assist during the consult. The coordinator at the client site facilitates the telepsychology session and often serves as the service "champion." Psychologists must carefully consider the risks and benefits related to inclusion of a coordinator for their specific clinical purpose. Psychologists often work with coordinators in order to have assistance with the technology, support for the client, and immediate help in the event of safety or other emergent concerns.

TELEPSYCHOLOGY SESSION

Most often, telepsychology sessions approximate all key components of face-to-face sessions both at intake and follow-up visits. The psychologist introduces the client to the telepsychology setting, including a developmentally appropriate explanation of how the technology works. Often, families have utilized videoconferencing for informal communication with family and friends, and it is important to describe the additional security utilized for clinical consultations. Videoconferencing etiquette includes rapport-building strategies and simple adaptations, such as the client showing a photo over televideo or faxing a picture drawn during the session to the therapist. Some programs have utilized innovative solutions such as an online whiteboard, but lower cost measures include mailing common materials/books. Creativity and flexibility before, during, and after the televideo visit facilitate relationship building just as in the onsite setting. The psychologist has full discretion to advise the client/family to be seen in person related to any questions/needs. As in the onsite setting, the psychologist asks a series of questions to gain more information about the client, the current presenting concern, and the relevant history. The psychologist observes the client throughout the session and notes behavior as well as physical presentation (e.g., gait, tics, affect). The zoom feature of the telemedicine camera can assist with this and allow unobtrusive close-up observation of such features. The psychologist completes the same documentation as onsite clinics, including the use of electronic health records when appropriate.

POST-SESSION

The psychologist and coordinator collaborate to assist the client in understanding and following treatment recommendations and referral suggestions.

The psychologist schedules follow-up appointments based on standard of care practices for the particular diagnosis or concern. The psychologist completes the same releases of information with the client and follows up with the referring provider. If the psychologist is billing for the encounter, the same CPT codes are utilized with the telemedicine (GT) modifier included. The same protocol as onsite visits is utilized for between-session needs of the client/family.

Across telemental health clinics, clients tend to present with the same concerns as seen in traditional clinic settings. No presentation or diagnostic category has been excluded from mental health services over televideo. Due to the fact that clients presenting to telepsychology clinics may have had no previous access to mental health specialists, there may have been significant delays to treatment that may contribute to increased comorbidity and severity of presentations seen through the telepsychology service.

Psychologists should also consider the sustainability of the telepsychology service over time. The initial costs associated with starting telepsychology include equipment and software costs, connectivity/line charges, installation costs, costs of remodeling or adding space, personnel costs associated with telemedicine training, and costs with adding staff to assist with telemedicine or with changing workflow to meet telemedicine responsibilities. Notably, costs decrease over time as client volume increases. Psychologists have used varied initial funding for televideo implementation, including institutional seed money, community and foundational support, state grants, federal funding, billing reimbursement, and contractual agreements. Approximately a half dozen states have legislative requiring that telemedicine services be reimbursed as onsite benefits. A growing number of third-party insurers reimburse telemedicine services, including Medicare, the majority of state Medicaid policies, and many private insurers. Many, but not all, billing codes are covered over televideo, with the addition of a telemedicine GT modifier to the billing code. Some client sites are eligible for Medicare/Medicaid's originating site fees related to the coordinator assistance. Another option is contractual agreements to cover both psychologist time as well as related costs (e.g., line charges, office management, etc.).

Telepsychology services to primary care settings are anticipated to increase with national and state initiatives around the patient-centered medical home. The medical home model promotes increased coordination and communication between primary care and psychologists. Telepsychology is one strategy to increase access to psychologists in primary care settings. As in other telepsychology settings spanning systems of care, team building and good communication skills remain crucial for a successful delivery of service. New telepsychology models are emerging, including videoconferencing directly to the client's home. A range of technologies are used for home-based services and psychologists should consider the risks/benefits of the videoconferencing technology, including security and reliability. While access is increased, there is less control over the client's environment. Psychologists providing service to the home should continue to consider key telepsychology components, including (1) informed consent for telepsychology service; (2) protocols concerning the expected process, including key components discussed in other videoconferencing settings earlier (e.g., scheduling, follow-up, secure environment, backup plans in the event that the technology fails to the home, etc.); and (3) safety plans in the event the client reports suicidal, homicidal, or other safety concerns. Telepsychology services to the home are generally out of pocket. Mobile technologies (e.g., smartphones, tablets, etc.) with video capabilities expand accessibility further, but consideration must be given to the new benefits and risks for the client.

In sum, telepsychology's utility lies in its ability to connect with individuals in need of psychological services who live in rural or underserved communities. Psychologists considering utilizing this technology should complete a needs assessment at both a community and clinic level in order to address the feasibility of acquiring and using the technology as well as the demand for it. Psychologists who acquire this technology should use it in accordance with APA ethical standards for best practice and develop a working protocol in order to minimize the potential for misuse or error. Additionally, psychologists should be aware that successful telepsychology services are, by and large, a product of a team of professional working together to deliver the service (i.e., technical support, clinical coordinators at both sites, etc.). Furthermore, though telepsychology is often reimbursed to the same degree as in-person psychotherapy, psychologists should weigh the financial burden of implementing this service. Overall, telepsychology offers psychologists new ways of connecting with underserved populations; however, psychologists must be aware of the unique planning and implementations steps this technology demands in order for successful delivery of services.

References and Readings

American Psychological Association. (2002). Ethical principles of psychologists and code of conduct. *American Psychologist, 57*, 1060–1073.

Federal Telehealth Resource Centers. (n.d.). *Home page*. Retrieved September 2011, from www.telehealthresourcecenters.org

Grady, B., Myers, K. M., Nelson, E. L., Belz, N., Bennett, L., Carnahan, L.,...Voyles, D. (2011). Evidence-based practice for telemental health. *Telemed Journal and e-Health, 17*(2), 131–148.

Koocher, G. P. (2007). Twenty-first century ethical challenges for psychology. *American Psychologist, 62*(5), 375–384.

Myers, K., & Cain, S. (2008). Practice parameter for telepsychiatry with children and adolescents. *Journal of the American Academy of Child and Adolescent Psychiatry, 47*(12), 1468–1483.

Reed, G. M., McLaughlin, C. J., & Milholland, K. (2000). Ten interdisciplinary principles for professional practice in telehealth: Implications for psychology. *Professional Psychology: Research and Practice, 31*(2), 170–178.

Richardson, L. K., Frueh, B. C., Grubaugh, A. L., Egede, L., & Elhai, J. D. (2009). Current directions in videoconferencing tele-mental health research. *Clinical Psychology, 16*(3), 323–338.

Shore, J. H., & Manson, S. M. (2005). A developmental model for rural telepsychiatry. *Psychiatric Services, 56*(8), 976–980.

Related Topics

Chapter 134, "Optimizing the Use of Technology in Psychology with Best Practice Principles"

Chapter 135, "Practicing in the Era of Social Media"

134 OPTIMIZING THE USE OF TECHNOLOGY IN PSYCHOLOGY WITH BEST PRACTICE PRINCIPLES

Marlene M. Maheu, Joseph McMenamin, and Myron L. Pulier

This chapter is designed to educate and stimulate debate and research into ethical, legal, and professional issues for delivering clinical services using the Internet and other psychotechnologies. Of the 7 billion people on our planet, approximately 2 billion are Internet users, and more than 5.6 billion use mobile phones. The use of various types of technology in our own ranks is also widespread. For instance, an American Psychological Association survey indicated that 47% of psychologists in the study reported delivering "direct health services" via e-mail, with 22% doing so "once a week or more" (2010).

THE ONLINE CLINICAL PRACTICE MANAGEMENT MODEL

Despite the plethora of available empirical support for telepsychology (Maheu, Pulier, Wilhelm, McMenamin, & Brown-Connolly, 2004), telepsychology best practice guidelines lack readily available specificity. Psychologists seeking training for using 21st-century practice tools currently witness a dearth of psychotechnology-specific graduate and post-graduate training opportunities. The Online Clinical Practice Management (OCPM) model was proposed by the above authors as an early framework for training and making well-informed telepsychology decisions while minimizing risks. The model identifies seven core steps: professional training, referrals, client/patient education, applicable law, clinical assessment, direct care, and reimbursement. This chapter is focused on outlining currently relevant and technology-specific telepsychology guidelines and related training in two areas: applicable law and direct care.

"Online clinical practice" refers to the use of any technology to deliver therapeutic services across geographic distance, whether via a direct video link (e.g., telepsychology or telepsychiatry) or over a network such as the Internet (e.g., online therapy). The OCPM model is applicable for diagnostic procedures, psychotherapy, supervision, and case management. Relevant psychotechnologies include traditional telephone, Internet telephone (audio), video, e-mail, chat room, instant messaging, and mobile text messaging or "texting."

BEST PRACTICES RELATED TO APPLICABLE LAW: CONSENT AGREEMENT

- Identify requirements for consent in every jurisdiction in which you practice.

- Recognize that consent is a process, not a document, and that requirements vary among states. Talk over the client/patient consent agreement with client/patient and provide a written confirmation, both in plain language.
- Identify services that you are unwilling or unable to provide at a distance. If your client/patient condition is such that she may be incapable of giving appropriate informed consent to distance care, confine your services to those you can offer in person or refer to a local practitioner. Make sure your client/patient is over 18, or obtain written parental consent to treat a minor. If you judge your youthful patient to be unable or unwilling to take appropriate privacy precautions, decline to offer distance care, even if the parent consents.
- Describe the equipment and the nature and the purpose of services to be delivered. Describe how services delivered via technology differ from services delivered in person. Describe relevant advantages and pitfalls of providing services through technology as compared with the analogous risks and benefits of in-person care. Acknowledge that some of the risks and benefits may not have been identified yet. Once they are, update your consent process to reflect such new knowledge.
- Describe how deficiencies or breakdowns in electronic equipment or connectivity could interfere with diagnosis and treatment and provide a plan for dealing with this. Make provision for delayed receipt or nonreceipt of e-mail, problems with servers, or unannounced changes in the schedule of e-mail communications. Mention how easily human error could lead to messages reaching the wrong address. Document vacation arrangements, average response time, and topics not appropriate for discussion via technology. Provide any other relevant information that pertains to your specific use of technology.
- Obtain an agreement from your client/patient that your text-based communications, audio recordings, or video recordings will not be forwarded to others without the client/patient and your consent. Inform client/patient of who will have access to e-mail addresses, phone numbers, or any other contact information.
- Tell the client/patient who else might contact the client/patient on your behalf. Do not forward e-mail and other text-based communications from client/patient to others without client/patient consent. Take precautions to be aware of "message threads" contained within e-mail. Describe the specific roles of any consultant or local referring practitioner and who will have ultimate authority over the client/patient treatment.
- Document your social media policies, identifying which specific technologies you currently use (i.e., Facebook, LinkedIn, Yelp).
- Describe how client/patient may refuse to participate or withdraw from technology-based procedures, as well as foreseeable consequences of such decisions.
- Discuss whether client/patient information, including test data and results, will be collected and recorded and how long they will be stored. Describe who will have control and access to the stored information.
- Keep secured, password-protected, and encrypted records of e-mail, text messaging, telephone, and video-based work. Store records securely and allow for authenticated retrieval. Keep an accessible backup of all electronic records. Follow proper disposal procedures for these records. Encrypt for storage anything that can compromise client/patient privacy. When developing your consent document, and in any written communications, avoid using the phrase "standard of care." Consider including the following in your consent document and discussion:
  - "A consensus on proper use of this technology has not yet emerged."
  - "Research into the risks, benefits, and proper use of these procedures is incomplete."
- Consider creating, at or near the foot of the document, blanks for the client/patient initials beside each of the following items:
  - "I understand all the information presented here."
  - "I have had ample opportunity to ask questions, and all my questions have been answered to my satisfaction in terms I understand."

- "As of the time of my signature, all blanks on this form have been filled in."
- Provide written procedures for various types of follow-up when the client/patient does not appear for remote consultation. Document the extent of your involvement with emergency support and how crisis intervention can be limited if local resources are not adequately accessed. Clearly outline the conditions under which psychological services may be terminated.

LICENSURE

- Describe the limits of your license. For example, if you do not have needed licensure, you will not be commenting on blood work or prescribing medication.
- Verify the legality of delivering services to residents of foreign states or countries where you may not be licensed by checking with authorities in your state(s) of licensure, those foreign region(s), or by consulting with knowledgeable counsel. Know and follow relevant requirements (e.g., *Tarasoff*, mandatory abuse reporting, record keeping).

PROFESSIONAL LIABILITY

- Determine how a clinician–client/patient relationship is established and terminated in your jurisdiction as well as the jurisdictions of all your patients. Identify legal definitions of malpractice in your geographic and specialty areas. Obtain liability insurance with adequate limits from a solvent carrier, identifying your specific work as covered. If you practice over state or national borders, inform your malpractice carrier and obtain its written agreement to cover you in these regions.
- Provide client/patient with a compliance statement for HIPAA, HITECH, and any local or state requirements and how you have chosen to comply with such requirements in using any of the psychotechnologies.
- Bar use of regular technology in emergencies. Establish alternate methods to deal with emergencies. Have contact with the client/patient local emergency support systems before treatment, so you know who your support team is in the client/patient local community. Obtain the name, address, and contact information of a local relative or friend, or a medical practitioner who knows the client/patient. Discuss the conditions under which you will contact these individuals. Speak with local police and hospital staff to better understand the community; conduct distant community site visits when appropriate; and so on. If you search for information on your client/patient (i.e., Google, Bing), inform them of the frequency and reasons for searches.
- Document consultation with any other professionals as well as details of any Internet searches you have conducted about a client/patient, including your rationale(s).
- Consider allowing the client/patient to prohibit identifiable health information or images of video from appearing in any electronic medium.

BEST PRACTICES RELATED TO DIRECT CARE

- Limit services to those permitted in the jurisdiction and to your areas of licensure and competence. Work within the limits of your licensure, education, training, supervised experience, and appropriate professional experience with technology. For instance, obtain appropriate training to initially understand video or e-mail-based service delivery and enhance your skills in the use of these technologies. Evaluate and document scientific research that examines the treatment issues related to disorders (i.e., treatment protocols) before offering services to the public. Subject to clinical judgment, identify and follow treatment and practice guidelines for your profession and stay abreast of updates.
- Define at-risk populations and, if you plan to serve them, develop specialized services (i.e., intake, backup, emergency services). Refer clients with a condition that poses a serious risk—or see them in-person until their conditions are stabilized.

- Be aware of limits to how using specific technologies is supported by research or contra-indicated for a particular situation. Issues deserving particular attention include suicide, distortions of reality, sexual abuse, and violent behavior, especially when contact between psychologist and client/patient is mediated via a technology without emergency support access or support from information technology (IT) specialists. Learn the specific technologies and Web sites that can be used with specific populations when they are available (i.e., electronic games for children, adaptive devices for elderly or disabled client/patient).
- Value safety of the client/patient above all else. Err on the side of caution, particularly when considering services lacking empirical support. Require your client/patient, at each session, to identify anyone other than himself who is present in the room, and document the response. Cover safety basics as needed (i.e., asking the client/patient about the use of drugs and alcohol, and the presence of firearms, children, or elderly persons in the home when treating violent client/patient).
- Describe the limits of confidentiality, particularly how security is limited by the security of the particular technology chosen. Security limitations include system breakdown, viewing of messages by authorized (e.g., Internet service provider system administrator) and unauthorized persons, and the potential access to supposedly deleted messages where backup records have been made.
- Until better technology is readily available, in situations where authentication of the identity of the client/patient is required, take steps to do so, such as requiring an initial in-person screening; only accepting referrals from professionals who have met intended client/patient in-person, or when such traditional procedures are impractical, through a video-conferenced session using high-bandwidth connections, good lighting, and high-resolution cameras before providing services online. Obtain copies of other essential identifying information for authentication (e.g., driver's license, insurance card, electronic thumb print). Provide the patient with a means of authenticating your identity as well.
- Only offer services to client/patient for whom you can demonstrate cultural, linguistic, and other relevant competence to serve.
- Provide adequate technical support when providing Internet services, such as psychological testing, self-help modules, or online therapeutic programs.
- Avoid working with client/patient anonymously. Among other concerns, anonymity precludes the cautious and thorough reporting of abuse, homicidality, and suicidality when needed.
- Keep records of all exchanges with client/patient, including e-mail, chat room discussions, text-messages, telephone conversations, and video sessions. Document connectivity breakdown times and topics being discussed at those times. Be able to reach client/patient in an emergency. Consider keeping a non-digital, printed copy of each patient's phone number and contact information.
- If you choose to use text messaging, restrict yourself to text-messaging services that comply with the most stringent of all involved state or federal security and privacy laws (HIPAA). Also, be aware that texted messages may be stored elsewhere than on the owner's cell phone or other handheld device. For example, the *Google Voice* service can automatically transcribe and copy messages to a *Gmail* account, where security may be inadequate. Safeguard text messages securely so that they can be printed or saved for clinical records. Services are available to record text messages from smartphones. Applications are also available to forward text messages to your encrypted e-mail address on Blackberries and Windows Mobile devices for future access. Use such screen shots to send information to an encrypted e-mail address as an attachment to be saved for future archival purposes. With psychotechnologies, misunderstandings can arise easily and may be less likely to be recognized and corrected in voice, video, and text communications.
- In e-mail or *any other* text-based psychotechnology, avoid casual forms of speech,

slang, unorthodox spelling, grammatical errors, and the like; treat the text message as a professional communication similar to a formal consult. Keep in mind that anything you write may be copied (out of context) by the patient and sent to other people who could pass it along to yet others. While people may take with a grain of salt a patient's anecdotes about you, such apparently verbatim quotes will be seen as the unvarnished truth by many readers, including adversaries in legal proceedings.
- Manage your personal boundaries when using telecommunication technologies. Only show a professional background when videoconferencing. Monitor your personal information on the Internet. Take needed measures to remove inappropriate content; stay abreast of automatic changes in privacy settings on social networking Web sites; do not "friend" client/patient; understand how revealing personal information in blogs, forums, or other online venues may interfere with your therapeutic relationships. Remember, too, that for a litigation adversary, ill-considered content may be an invaluable source of damning evidence.
- On your Web site, include a statement regarding licensing of your content, royalty interests, and funding (e.g., advertisers). Include a cautious, carefully drafted statement of the purpose of your content or service, dates of original content posting and latest updates, editorial processes, and how to contact the Web site manager. Any Web sites supporting client/patient interaction should describe reliability and security of the technology (confidentiality). Your Web site should carry a statement describing the handling of personal client/patient information, your name, and your physical address.
- When devices (e.g., computers, PDAs, smartphones, etc.) are repaired, maintained, discarded, or recycled, follow accepted professional procedures. For example, devices to be discarded should be reliably cleansed of any client/patient information and stored records of texting communications. Conducting a simple "delete" will not suffice. Document how you removed confidential information from each device so discarded or recycled. Demand that any device-related cleaning service you use certify the effectiveness of its method.

References and Readings

American Psychological Association. (2002). *Ethical principles of psychologists and code of conduct.* Retrieved October 2002, from www.apa.org/ethics/code2002.pdf

American Telemedicine Association. (2013). *Practice Guidelines for Video-based Online Mental Health Services.* Retrieved May 2013, from http://www.americantelemed.org/practice/standards/ata-standards-guidelines

Maheu, M., Pulier, M., Wilhelm, F. H., McMenamin, J. P., & Brown-Connolly, N. (2004). *The mental health professional and the new technologies: A handbook for practice today*. Mahwah, NJ: Erlbaum.

Michalski, D., Mulvey, T., & Kohout, J. (2010). *2008 APA Survey of psychology health service providers.* Washington, DC: American Psychological Association. Center for Workforce Studies.

Nicholson, I. (2011). Demonstrating the relevance of the Canadian code of ethics for psychologists to the ever-sharper cutting edge of technology. *Canadian Psychology, 53*(3), 215–224.

Related Topics

Chapter 133, "Managing Real-Time Telepsychology Practice"

Chapter 135, "Practicing in the Era of Social Media"

135 PRACTICING IN THE ERA OF SOCIAL MEDIA

Jeffrey E. Barnett and Keely Kolmes

Social networking sites are becoming a ubiquitous aspect of life for both psychologists and consumers of professional services. Social media sites provide a means for interacting and sharing information with others via the Internet. Examples include Facebook, MySpace, LinkedIn, and Twitter, and many others. Social media permit individuals to share information with others in ways never before possible. These social media have significantly impacted how many individuals form, develop, and maintain relationships in their day-to-day lives.

Social media sites such as Facebook and MySpace allow users to create free accounts that enable them to post and share material online that includes personal information, photographs, videos, and links to other Web sites. Participants may also communicate with others by posting messages that others may respond to and by participating in blogs (online journals which may also allow comments by other users on issues relevant to a particular topic). Those who create an account grant access to other individuals by designating these individuals "friend," "contact," or "follower" status, permitting access to their posted material. While these sites offer a range of security settings that users may adjust to prevent unauthorized access to materials they post online, "friend" status generally permits greater access to material posted on one's online profile. For example, photos, news stories, or Wall comments can be accessed that would remain otherwise hidden to those who do not have friend or contact status.

WIDELY USED SOCIAL NETWORKING SITES

Founded in 2004, Facebook had over 175 million users in 2009 but has quickly grown to be the most widely used social networking site worldwide. There are now over 845 million active monthly users who post over 2.7 billion "comments" and "likes" on the site each day. Over 161 million of the active users are from the United States and 60% of all web users are reported to be active users of Facebook (ITProPortal.com, 2013). Users on Facebook share status updates, photos, videos, and news items and also comment on other users' "Walls." More recently, Facebook has partnered with other sites such as Youtube and *The New York Times* so that users have the ability to notify friends on Facebook of other online content viewed and "liked" on these Web sites.

LinkedIn is similar in format to social networking sites such as Facebook, but it is designed as a forum for professionals to share information with each other and to develop an online professional networking community. Many individuals use LinkedIn to make professional contacts, to seek employment, to recommend other professionals, and to grow their businesses. Some individuals also connect socially on LinkedIn with their friends. Many users are also now connecting their LinkedIn updates to sites such as Twitter, integrating and sending this content to multiple sites. LinkedIn has over 100 million active users with reportedly more than 1 million new users joining each week (LinkedIn, 2011).

Twitter is a communications platform that utilizes SMS text messaging on cell phones and other electronic devices that enable users to share brief messages of up to 140 characters in length (called Tweets) with users in their online network. Those in their network, called "Followers," automatically have access to the archive of tweets posted by that individual. Twitter offers individuals the ability to quickly share information with others, Direct Message (DM) users who follow them, and to easily keep in touch. Founded in 2006, Twitter is presently the third most widely used social networking site and continues to grow rapidly (Barnett, 2010).

PERSONAL VERSUS PROFESSIONAL USE OF SOCIAL MEDIA

Increasingly, psychologists and consumers of psychological services will each utilize social media as important ways to communicate, share information, and conduct relationships with individuals in their personal lives. While teenagers and young adults may have comprised a large percentage of social media's initial users, social networking sites are now used by millions of individuals across the life span. It is highly likely that many individuals who seek professional assistance from psychologists, and psychologists themselves, will maintain an online presence and actively use one or more social networking sites in their personal lives.

Before posting or sharing personal information via social networking sites, psychologists should exercise some forethought and caution. It is important to consider the possible effects or impact on clients should they access personal materials posted by a psychologist. Not all materials shared with friends and family would be appropriate for clients to access. Examples to consider include the following:

- Having clients view photos of you on your recent vacation, such as of you lying on the beach in your bathing suit. What if the client is struggling financially and the photos clearly show you at a very expensive resort?
- How might a client who is dealing with fertility issues in treatment be impacted by viewing photos of you joyously holding your new child or grandchild?
- If a client's spouse recently died and she is all alone, could that client be adversely affected by viewing photos of you spending a holiday surrounded by a large and apparently very happy extended family?

In considering these and similar questions, psychologists should exercise caution when making decisions about what they should post online and who should have access to it. While each individual has the right to post online whatever they wish, psychologists have a responsibility to consider the potential impact on clients who access these materials. They also have a responsibility with clients to only act in ways that are consistent with their clinical needs and interests. This makes granting clients unrestricted access to one's personal social media profile a significant ethical concern.

When utilizing social media such as Facebook and MySpace, it is important to first research and carefully consider the privacy policies of these sites and to ensure that the appropriate security settings are used so that unauthorized and unintended access to one's profile is prevented. Yet even when using the highest security settings, those that only permit a preapproved subset of "friends" to access one's online materials and communications, it is important to remember that "friends" can share or repost materials from your profiles onto theirs. Once information leaves your pages or profiles, you lose control over who may access it. Another important consideration is that messages exchanged between therapists and clients on these sites are not secure and may become a part of the legal record.

"FRIEND" REQUESTS FROM CLIENTS

Frequently, clients will search social networking sites they belong to in order to see who they know who may have a profile on that site.

Those who share cultural affiliations with their psychologist, such as ethnicity, sexual orientation, religion, or disability status, may find themselves more likely to have other friends and contacts in common on these sites. As a result, they may then send their psychologist a "friend" request. This is an online message used to request "friend" status. Friend status would permit the client greater access to your online profile, as well as minimally indicating a visible connection to you online. As a result of this connection, depending upon your privacy settings, the client may view more of your online information and the materials you have posted, as well as communicate with you online in this new online "friend" role. This new access may also permit the client to interact with others in your life who also post or comment on the content shared on your profile page. Such friend requests create a number of challenges for psychologists. These challenges include issues about confidentiality, boundary issues, and multiple relationships. Patients who gain access to your network of friends and contacts may come to discover the identities of others who have been or are currently in your care. In addition, they may attempt to establish relationships with those in your network. This can potentially compromise client confidentiality and create various other boundary dilemmas.

A number of relevant boundary issues must be considered before accepting a friend request from a client. The first is to consider how being "friends" will impact and alter the professional relationship. Most psychologists would not typically serve as a client's psychotherapist while simultaneously engaging in a social relationship or friendship with the client. Most clients understand that their psychologist is not their friend. Typically clients will not initiate a social relationship with their psychologist by inviting their psychologist to lunch, to go shopping together, and so on. Furthermore, most psychologists would not introduce their clients to their friends or family or encourage these individuals to engage and interact with one another. Yet, in the online world, communicating and sharing information with others through social media sites is done so frequently that many individuals may not even consider it as a multiple-relationship issue. They may simply just consider it a normal part of all relationships.

Psychologists, on the other hand, trained in the ethics of boundaries and multiple relationships, understand the need to generally limit contact with clients to our professional interactions. Engaging in intimate sharing from our personal lives holds great risk for adversely impacting the professional relationship because it erodes professional boundaries and jeopardizes the psychologist's objectivity and judgment. Furthermore, such sharing can alter the professional relationship for the client, creating expectations for increased mutuality of sharing and possibly even contact outside of therapy.

One option for psychologists who participate in social networking sites to consider is to have two separate profiles: one that is professional and one that is personal. The professional profile would include practice-related information such as announcements about recent publications or scheduled workshops. Photographs of one's office, of the psychologist, and of office staff could be included. Clients would be granted access to this profile or page. The personal profile, however, would not include any practice-related information, would only include information and materials from one's personal life, and would be accessed only by those with whom the psychologist has a personal relationship.

SELF-DISCLOSURE

One important boundary in all professional relationships is self-disclosure, the sharing of personal information with a client. Zur (2009) highlights several types of self-disclosure that may occur. These include deliberate self-disclosure such as when a psychotherapist shares a personal experience with a client to assist the client in dealing with a difficult issue, but it should be motivated by and relevant to the client's treatment needs; unavoidable self-disclosure may include client observations of a psychologist's age, gender, ethnoracial identity, visible disability, and for those who wear a wedding ring, one's marital status;

and accidental self-disclosure, which can occur when a client sees a psychologist with his or her family in a social or public setting.

Psychologists participating in social media must consider how their online sharing constitutes a form of self-disclosure for those clients who may access the psychologist's online profile and materials. Should clients be granted access to a psychologist's personal information online that the psychologist would not ordinarily share with clients in person? For example, if a psychologist would not bring a family photo album to work to share with clients in session, how could giving these clients access to such material online be considered ethical and appropriate? Psychologists must also keep each client's best interests in mind and consider the possible impact of inclusion in the psychologist's personal life on the client clinically.

INTEGRATING SOCIAL MEDIA INTO TREATMENT

Granting clients "friend" status creates an online secondary relationship with all the sharing of personal information mentioned earlier. While it can be seen as inimical to an appropriate therapeutic relationship, there may be times when clients want to share their online materials with their psychologist. Rather than "friending" and accessing the client's materials independently, it is recommended that the review of the client's online materials be done as part of the treatment relationship. Thus, the client could log in to a computer in the psychologist's office (the client can bring his or her laptop computer to the session, use the psychologist's, or access this material with his or her smartphone) and then together, client and psychologist could review the materials. This would be most appropriate when a client wishes to share his or her writings, artwork, photography, and the like, with the psychologist. Viewing them together in session helps keep appropriate clinical boundaries in place and enables the psychologist to process reactions to sharing with the client as they occur, helping to integrate the viewing of the online materials into the client's ongoing treatment.

Various social media may also be effectively and appropriately used for providing treatment. There are a range of software applications (apps) and social media platforms online that are well suited for integration into ongoing treatment. Some apps allow clients to track their mood and chart automatic thoughts; others give them the ability to gain social support for new, preferred habits and behaviors. Psychologists should educate themselves about these applications on an ongoing basis (new ones are continually developed) and consider their use as an adjunct to in-person treatment. They should also discuss with their clients the privacy implications of sharing this data with others. An example is Mood 24/7 (available at https://www.mood247.com/), an online application that sends registered users periodic prearranged text message reminders and allows clients to submit mood ratings to this site using text messaging on their cell phone. The site then records and tracks the ratings, which can be accessed by the client and the psychologist. For clients struggling with depression or bipolar disorder, for example, having access to changes in mood ratings in real time can be a great enhancement to ongoing in-person treatment.

ESTABLISHING A SOCIAL MEDIA POLICY

Based on all of the issues addressed earlier and in keeping with the requirement that each psychologist engage in a comprehensive informed consent process beginning at the outset of the professional relationship, it is recommended that each psychologist who has an online presence develop and share with each client a social media policy. As is highlighted by Kolmes (2010), each client should be informed of the psychologist's use of e-mail, blogging, and social media, how various platforms may be utilized in treatment, the psychologist's "friending" policies, and whether (or when) the psychologist uses search engines to supplement assessment or treatment. A sample social media policy that may be downloaded, modified to fit one's particular social media practices, and then used in one's practice is available online at drkkolmes.com/for-clinicians/social-media-policy/

Psychologists utilizing social media should do the following:

- Consider establishing separate profiles for personal or professional use.
- Understand the privacy settings of various social networking sites they use.
- Be mindful about what personal content they share on sites, understanding that others may share or forward this information.
- Consider the confidentiality and boundary risks inherent in accepting clients' friend requests.
- Carefully consider whether they wish to allow comments by others to be posted on any professional blogs they maintain.
- Develop a social media policy for their practice and share this with all clients.

References and Readings

Barnett, J. E. (2010). Psychology's brave new world: Psychotherapy in the digital age. *Independent Practitioner, 30*(3), 149–152.

ITPortal.com. (2013). Facebook releases usage statistics: 845 million users, 2.7 billion daily likes and comments. Retrieved April 25, 2013 from http://www.itproportal.com/2012/02/02/facebook-releases-usage-statistics-845-million-users-27-billion-daily-likes-and-comments/

Kolmes, K. (2010). Developing my private practice social media policy. *Independent Practitioner, 30*(3), 140–143.

LinkedIn. (2011). *About LinkedIn.* Retrieved February 2013, from press.linkedin.com/about/

Recupero, P. R. (2006). Legal concerns for psychiatrists who maintain websites. *Psychiatric Services, 57*(4), 450–425.

Younggren, J. N. (2010). To tweet or not to tweet, that is the question. *The Clinical Psychologist, 63*(2), 18–19.

Zur, O. (2009). Psychotherapist self-disclosure and transparency in the internet age. *Professional Psychology: Research and Practice, 40,* 22–26.

Related Topics

Chapter 133, "Managing Real-Time Telepsychology Practice"

Chapter 134, "Optimizing the Use of Technology in Psychology with Best Practice Principles"

136 FINDING, EVALUATING, AND USING SMARTPHONE APPLICATIONS

Marlene M. Maheu, Myron L. Pulier, and Sylvain Roy

"Apps" (applications) are programs that extend the function of smartphones (e.g., iPhone, Blackberry), "pad" or "tablet PCs" (e.g., iPad), and wireless medical devices collectively referred to as "mHealth" or "mobile health care." The rapidly increasing selection of apps can enhance the practice of psychology by connecting client/patient to clinicians wherever they may be, such as linking one party's device to the other's (computer, mobile devices, Web site, etc.); delivering both consumer and professional education; facilitating office management and billing functions; or expediting research. More specific examples of daily functions easily served by apps already include sending flash reminders, delivering self-help and support, running therapeutic protocols, and collecting information, including symptom reports and psycho-physiological data.

FINDING APPS

Research psychologists are at the forefront of developing safe, secure, and effective apps for mental health consumers. Usability testing is one cornerstone of responsible app development. Many professionals are also concerned about the differences between self-help apps and those designed to send and protect clinically relevant data. One of the primary concerns is how to securely store and transmit patient data, including protected health information (PHI). Therefore, another cornerstone of app development for app vendors, device manufacturers, and carrier services, as well as app selection by psychologists rightfully involves compliance with federal law. Examples of relevant law include mobile app development guidelines published by the US Federal Drug Administration (FDA) and the Health Insurance Portability and Accountability Act (HIPAA). Since most apps are free or available for less than $4.00, it is generally unwise to install apps from other sources unless supplied by a source known to be reliable. Smartphones and tablet computers are especially vulnerable to security breaches.

Apps obtained through the official online "store" of an operating system vendor such as the Android Market, AppStore, BlackBerry App World, or Windows Phone Marketplace (see Table 136.1) have passed through several layers of vetting. Such apps are far less likely to harbor "malware" that leads to identity theft; a virus that potentially steals sensitive information; or other technical compromises of PHI. Health-related information brings a high price on the black market, so clinicians should be cautious in selecting apps to recommend or use with patients.

In making recommendations to client/patient, clinicians must also consider incompatibilities between apps (which may come in different versions) and "operating systems" (new versions can also introduce incompatibilities). Operating systems are built into a smartphone or tablet PC as the underlying architecture enables various app functions. Prominent operating systems include Android from Google, Apple's IOS, Blackberry, and Windows Phone. While standardization is the goal, not all apps can yet share their data across devices with different operating systems ("interoperability"). For instance, iPhone apps may not run on iPads or Samsung Galaxy tablets.

Table 136.1 lists online resources for discovering, learning about, and downloading apps

TABLE 136.1. Online Leads to Psychology-Relevant Apps

Name	URL[1]
Android Market[2]	market.android.com
AppStore[3]	itunes.apple.com
BlackBerry App World	blackberry.com/AppWorld
Windows Phone Marketplace[2]	microsoft.com/WindowsPhone
Telehealth Institute Blog[4]	Telehealth.org
Technology for Psychologists[5]	sylvainroy.blogspot.com
The Psych Files	thepsychfiles.com
amazon.com	amazon.com[6]
cnet	cnet.com
eWeek	eweek.com
Macworld	macworld.com
PCWorld	pcworld.com
148 Apps	148apps.com
AppCraver	appcraver.com
Appdictions	appdictions.com
Appolicious	appvee.com
AppSafari	appsafari.com
AppShouter	appshouter.com
Apptism	apptism.com
AppVee	appvee.com
FreshApps	freshapps.com
iusethis	iphone.iusethis.com
iPhone App Café	iphoneappcafe.com
iPhone Apps Finder	iphoneappsfinder.com
iPhoneAppPodcast	iphoneapppodcast.com
iPhone App Review	iphoneappreview.com
iPhoneApp Reviews	iphoneapp-reviews.com
iPhone Medical Apps	iphonemedicalapps.com

1. It may be necessary to preface the URL with "www." and to search for "psychology" within the Web site.
2. Click "Apps."
3. Requires iTunes installation. Click "iTunes" at the top of the screen, then "App Store."
4. Produced by the authors of this chapter.
5. Blog owner Sylvain Roy contributed to writing this chapter.
6. Search for "Apps for Android" and "psychology."

relevant to clinical psychology. Sources listed are not necessarily vetted.

EVALUATING AND USING APPS FOR GENERAL OR SPECIALIZED PSYCHOLOGY PRACTICE

As there is no standard taxonomy for psychology-relevant apps, a practitioner must comb through listings or read articles to discover what to use in practice or to recommend to patients. Because new apps are appearing daily (tens of thousands are available), any printed listing would be obsolete even before this book is published. Accordingly, Table 136.2 offers a glimpse of broad categories and kinds of apps within each category that may be worth reviewing.

TABLE 136.2. Clinical Psychology App Categories, With Examples

Diagnosis and Clinical Decision Support
Depression by Doctot (assessment tools)
The Concise Cognitive Screen Exam
ICD-9 (coding aid)
DSM-V (coding aid)
STATworkUP (clinical decision support)
Therapy Adjunct
Mobile Mood Diary (CBT journal)
EMDR for Clinicians (timed stimuli, etc.)
Self-Help (may integrate with professional care)
mym3 (depression, anxiety screening)
Live Happy (mood-boosting suggestions)
Mobile Therapy (automated CBT therapy)
Your Child's Social Health (screening)
Migraine Tracker (track occurrence, severity)
Fear of Spiders Treatment (desensitization)
Professional Education
meStudying: AP Psychology (practice questions)
3D Brain (interactive viewing of anatomy)
Genetics and Birth Defect
Psychiatry on Call 2011
Practice Productivity
Dragon Dictation (speech transcription)
TeamViewer HD (control office computer)
Medicare Eligibility (benefit checker)
Google Translate (multiple languages)
Keynote (PowerPoint-like presentations)

Note: Copy the app name into a search engine to find a description and a download site.

MAP/MAP: EVALUATING MOBILE APPS IN CLINICAL PSYCHOLOGY

A practitioner should evaluate an app before deploying or recommending it. We here propose an approach we call the MAP/MAP (Maheu and Pulier mHealth App Perspective) for rating an app along six dimensions before recommending it. This instrument's validity and reliability have not been assessed. MAP/MAP ratings assigned by a clinician should take into account relevance for a particular practice, clientele, and the quality of alternative apps.

Values that may be assigned to each dimension are as follows: F (unacceptable, not to be used or recommended), P (poor), G (good), E (excellent), or N (not rated or not relevant). Scoring considerations for each MAP/MAP dimension are as follows.

APPLICABILITY

Does the app's set of features adequately cover the range of tasks required to satisfy an actual clinical or practice need? Answers to this question, including description of desirable features and how well they work, may be sought in the evaluations and users' comments posted on the World Wide Web and the online "stores" where one purchases and downloads apps. Such comments may describe creative uses, suggestions for improvements, missing features, and comparisons with other apps that could accomplish the task at hand.

It is unethical to use or recommend an app where there has been "pirating" (illegal copying to evade due payment), plagiarism, or copyright infringement (e.g., unauthorized exploitation of Rorschach images or of *DSM* codes and descriptions of psychiatric disorders). These conditions would be indicated with an F rating on the Applicability dimension.

VALIDITY

Does scientific evidence support the concept upon which the app is based? For example, is a cognitive-behavioral therapy (CBT) app implemented in accordance with CBT literature? Does the app's hardware allow the underlying concept to be implemented adequately? For example, although research supports using phototherapy to adjust the sleep-wake cycle and alleviate seasonal affective disorder, a smartphone may be intrinsically unable to muster sufficient luminosity or to deliver a scientifically validated distribution of wavelengths. Therefore, an app that purports to directly deliver phototherapy without an additional theoretical rationale would be rated F on the Validity dimension. Where this or some other dimension is inapplicable (e.g., Validity is irrelevant for a simple arithmetic calculator app), an N rating should be given.

EFFECTIVENESS

Rather than attempt too many functions, a good app accomplishes a specific, defined mission without crashes, error messages, or complications. The effectiveness of an app is essentially the probability of the user attaining desired goals with it.

There are several approaches for assessing this dimension. Efficacy studies that provide empirical validation of an app are only beginning to appear, but they will become more plentiful. A clinician may ask colleagues for their opinion, for example, in online discussion forums. Review articles in online magazines and anecdotes and numerical ratings posted by users at the Web site from which the app may be purchased and downloaded are usually useful although not completely reliable. In any case, a clinician should try the app out experimentally before deploying it in practice or recommending it to patients.

USABILITY

This complex category includes interface clutter; obviousness or familiarity of controls (buttons, text entry fields); tolerance for suboptimal eye-thumb coordination; steepness of learning curve; ease of navigation; ability to recognize, undo, or recover from error and to retreat to a previous screen without penalty; response latency; start-up and shut-down speed; and ability to perform offline. An app also needs to meet workflow requirements and ultimately to save time for the user. Finally, apps should not quickly drain the battery of their host device nor lose vital data if their operation is suddenly interrupted when the user turns the device off or it runs out of power.

INTEROPERABILITY

This dimension refers to the extent to which an app on one device can share data with other apps and/or other devices. Sharing can be with the same app on another machine, or it can involve copying data from a patient's smartphone to a program on a clinician's computer or transmitting it to a Web site that interprets the data. Interoperability also refers to a clinician's ability to have various patients use essentially the same app on devices with differing operating systems.

Another aspect of interoperability involves such matters as accepting security assurances generated by some other app. This brings us to the 800-pound gorilla in the room, namely security.

SECURITY

Security considerations include maintaining privacy; making sure that data are not lost, diverted, or altered by an unauthorized agent; and validating that it is actually the patient and the clinician who are communicating rather than an impersonator.

Apps can weaken the security of a user's data in many ways. An app designed to interact with a client/patient might ("interoperably"...see earlier) automatically enter the client/patient name and contact information in the phone/address book app, where it becomes available when the device is used by a clinician's spouse, children, or friends, or if it falls into the hands of strangers. Personal information might be intercepted while being transmitted wirelessly over WiFi or a cellular network. Firesheep, for example, is an extension for a Firefox browser that can "sniff" personal information, particularly when transmitted over a public WiFi service, such as those in a Starbucks or an airport waiting area.

A lost or stolen mobile device may contain sensitive data about a clinician's entire patient load, current and past. If a patient telephones a clinician's smartphone or the clinician calls the patient's mobile phone, the device may loudly announce the name of the caller for everyone in the vicinity to hear. Alerts that illuminate the phone and that circumvent password protection to display medical appointments, symptom checklists, and the like might be triggered at inopportune times, exposing information to anyone who is nearby, such as a patient's employer or child.

Available protection includes data encryption and password functionalities, which should be more elaborate than just letting a user select any password at all. Ordinary encryption methods (including the "WEP" option that many people use on their WiFi units) are easily undone. A secure app will not only employ a "strong" encryption technique but will even conceal the URL (the address of any device with which it communicates) before sending any messages out. Professionals choosing to recommend or use apps will do well to stay current with technology by learning about apps and their appropriate use. While technology can enhance client/patient care and improve professional workflow, it also can wreak havoc when misused. The single most important differentiating factor between these two divergent outcomes is the technical acumen of the professional.

References and Readings

De Leo, G., Brivio, E., & Sautter, S. W. (2011). Supporting autobiographical memory in patients with Alzheimer's disease using smart phones. *Applied Neuropsychology, 18*(1), 69–76.

Koocher, G. P., & Keith-Spegel, P. (2008). *Ethics in psychology and the mental health professions: Standards and cases* (3rd ed.). New York: Oxford University Press.

Maheu, M. M., Pulier, M. L., Wilhelm, F. H., McMenamin, J., & Brown-Connolly, N. (2004). *The mental health professional and the new technologies: A handbook for practice today.* Mahwah, NJ: Erlbaum.

Nicholson, I. R. (2011). New technology, old issues: Demonstrating the relevance of the Canadian code of ethics for psychologists to the ever-sharper cutting edge of technology. *Canadian Psychology, 52*(3), 215–224.

Richards, M. M. (2009). Electronic medical records: Confidentiality issues in the time of HIPAA. *Professional Psychology: Research and Practice, 40*, 550–556.

Svoboda, E., Richards, B., Polsinelli, A., & Guger, S. (2010). A theory-driven training programme in the use of emerging commercial technology: Application to an adolescent with severe memory impairment. *Neuropsychological Rehabilitation, 20*(4), 562–586.

Wu, R. C., Morra, D., Quan, S., Lai, S., Zanjani, S., Abrams, H., & Rossos, P. G. (2010). The use of smartphones for clinical communication on internal medicine wards. *Journal of Hospital Medicine, 5*, 553–559.

Related Topics

Chapter 101, "Recommended Self-Help Internet Resources for Patients"

Chapter 102, "Recommended Online Computer-Assisted Treatments"

PART XII

Prevention, Consultation, and Supervision

137 HELPING PEOPLE COPE WITH DISASTERS

Eric M. Vernberg and Erin P. Hambrick

Psychologists are well positioned to promote the use of evidence-based approaches to help people cope with disasters. This chapter provides an overview of these approaches as presented in the *Psychological First Aid Field Operations Guide* (Brymer et al., 2006).

Almost every community in the United States has a disaster response plan in place, yet the emphasis on mental health aspects of disasters varies greatly. Participation in planning activities is a necessity for psychologists who want to be involved in disaster mental health response because teams rather than individual providers carry out disaster responses. Understandably, emergency management personnel have difficulty processing offers to provide mental health assistance in the aftermath of a disaster and prefer to rely instead on relationships developed earlier. Disasters, especially those receiving intense media coverage, often draw a tremendous number of offers of help from a broad range of mental health service providers. The American Psychological Association maintains a Disaster Response Network (DRN) for psychologists who wish to engage in disaster preparedness and recovery activities (www.apa.org/practice/programs/drn/index.aspx).

The National Child Traumatic Stress Network and the National Centers for PTSD supported the development of the *Psychological First aid Field Operations Guide* (PFA Guide) to provide an evidence-informed modular approach for children, adolescents, and adults in the immediate aftermath of disasters and/or crises. The principles, objectives, and techniques of PFA are designed to meet four basic standards:

1. Consistent with research evidence on risk and resilience following trauma
2. Applicable and practical in field settings
3. Appropriate for levels across the life span
4. Culturally informed and deliverable in a flexible manner

Intervention strategies of PFA are grouped into eight modules called *core actions.* Within each core action, PFA offers a variety of specific recommendations for working with disaster survivors, depending on the individualized needs of the survivors and the context in which services are offered. The rationale for each core action rests on theory and research on stress, coping, and resilience in the aftermath of extreme events. Five basic principles that have received broad empirical support for facilitating positive adaptation following trauma guided the selection of PFA strategies and techniques: (a) promoting a sense of safety, (b) promoting calming, (c) promoting sense of self- and community efficacy, (d) promoting connectedness, and (e) instilling hope (Hobfoll et al., 2007; Vernberg et al., 2008).

CONTACT AND ENGAGEMENT

The goals of this core action are to respond to and initiate contacts in a nonintrusive, compassionate, and helpful manner; maintain a calm presence; and be sensitive to cultural norms in preparing to interact with survivors. Exposure to highly traumatic events induces a sense of disconnection from normal human experience. Initial contact with a survivor by a PFA provider is intended to begin a process of re-engaging in social contacts that are respectful, predictable, and familiar.

SAFETY AND COMFORT

This core action includes strategies to enhance a survivor's immediate and ongoing safety, help provide both physical and emotional comfort, and decrease physiological hyperarousal. This includes providing and clarifying risk-related information; giving information about the current disaster response and available services; and protecting survivors from unnecessary exposure to additional traumatic events and trauma reminders. The section also addresses high-risk circumstances, such as when children are separated from parents/caregivers, when a family member is missing or has died, and when death notification or body identification is necessary. Specific strategies are presented to address spiritual and practical issues that typically arise in circumstances where there has been a death of a loved one, including appropriate referral to a religious professional.

STABILIZATION

Most individuals affected by disasters will *not* require stabilization; however, the PFA Guide provides strategies to help calm and orient emotionally overwhelmed children and adults when necessary. "Grounding techniques" are offered to help individuals who are having difficulty managing overwhelming emotions. These consist of reality reminders, which bring individuals to the relative safety of the present time and promote calming. They can reduce trauma-related anxiety that can generalize to many situations, as well as reduce high arousal, numbing, or emotionality. These interventions seek to prevent the possible negative outcomes of overwhelming anxiety or dissociation, which has been shown to interfere with sleep, eating, hydration, decision making, and performance of life tasks, and to lead to panic attacks, dissociation, posttraumatic stress disorder, depression, anxiety, and somatic problems, if prolonged.

INFORMATION GATHERING

Information gathering to identify immediate needs and concerns is the foundation for all other PFA core actions. Once the PFA provider gathers information about the survivor's current needs, the PFA Guide includes specific courses of action that can be pursued in relation to information obtained. Categories included in the information-gathering section are based on empirically based pre-, peri-, and post-event risk factors. It is not recommended to apply these factors in a prescriptive fashion, but rather to use them as guideposts for the following:

1. *Identifying problems that require immediate attention.* These include concerns about immediate post-disaster circumstances and ongoing threat; separations from or concerns about the safety of loved ones; acute physical health and mental health needs, including access to medication; thoughts about causing harm to self or others; extreme feelings of guilt and shame.
2. *Monitoring "high-risk" individuals for future interventions.* Key pre-, peri-, and post-event risk factor categories are given to identify potential at-risk individuals and families who may warrant monitoring over time, including those with prior alcohol or drug abuse; prior exposure to trauma or death of loved ones; prolonged or intense exposure to trauma during the disaster; and history of mental health problems.
3. *Identifying target risk and resilience factors that can be addressed through other PFA modules.* Risk factors related to social

support and ongoing post-event stresses, for example, predict the development of long-term problems. These can be mediated by identifying existing strengths and resources that can be used to address current adversities.

Note: In clarifying disaster-related traumatic experiences, PFA providers should avoid asking for in-depth description of traumatic experiences because this may provoke unnecessary additional distress. Individuals should *not* be pressed to disclose details of any trauma or loss. If individuals are anxious to talk about their experiences, explain that what would be most helpful is to get some *basic* information to assist with current needs, and that the opportunity to discuss their experiences can be arranged.

PRACTICAL ASSISTANCE

This core action describes strategies to help children and adults identify their most immediate needs or problems, clarify these, discuss an action plan, and provide assistance in acting to address the need. Sense of self and collective efficacy are personal resources that are likely to be diminished by mass trauma. The loss of a sense of efficacy can be alleviated by a PFA provider's assistance in helping individuals to obtain practical, personal, and environmental resources that help reverse the downward spiral toward feelings of being overwhelmed and unable to cope.

CONNECTION WITH SOCIAL SUPPORTS

The aim of this core action is to assist children, adolescents, and adults in enhancing their access to primary support persons or other sources of support by helping them understand how they can seek or give support. Promoting social connectedness has many benefits, including providing opportunities for a range of social support activities such as practical problem solving, emotional understanding, and acceptance; sharing and normalization of traumatic experiences; and mutual instruction about coping. PFA also includes information to address problems among family members that may stem from differences in the type and magnitude of exposure to trauma, loss, and subsequent adversities, or differences between family members' personal reactions to trauma and loss reminders.

INFORMATION ON COPING

The aim of this core action is to provide psychoeducation to survivors about stress reactions and coping to reduce distress and promote adaptive functioning. To facilitate this goal, the PFA Guide includes basic information about stress reactions and strategies for talking with children, adolescents, and adults about physical, behavioral, and emotional reactions. Information on adaptive and maladaptive coping is described, along with brief relaxation techniques that can be used in acute post-disaster settings. A section that focuses on families is included, with information on the need to establish routines and for family members to be understanding and tolerant of differences in trauma reactions. There is also information about anger management, addressing highly negative emotions (e.g., guilt, shame), sleep problems, and acute problems with alcohol and substance use. Providing information on coping seeks to promote both a sense of self-efficacy and of hope.

LINKAGE WITH COLLABORATIVE SERVICES

This core action links survivors with available services needed at the time and in the future. This includes using appropriate referral procedures and resources, and promoting continuity of services. Linking individuals with collaborative services increases a sense of hope that additional resources are available to an individual following the initial phase of a disaster. Because many individuals are unlikely to seek mental health services on their own following disasters, PFA seeks to increase the possibility of help seeking by offering early assistance that is practical and immediately helpful. This may give a positive view of mental health services in general, as well as educating individuals about when to seek help, de-stigmatizing help seeking, and providing information and individual assistance on how to connect to services available in the community.

APPENDICES AND HANDOUTS

A number of handouts are included in the PFA Guide that provide information for children, adolescents, adults, and parents/caregivers about common reactions after disasters; seeking and giving support; positive and negative coping strategies; tips on assisting children at the infant/toddler, preschool, school-age, and adolescent levels; basic relaxation techniques; alcohol use and abuse after disasters; and self-care strategies for providers implementing the PFA protocol. Even in situations where it is not feasible to pass out handouts to survivors, these handouts can serve as talking points for PFA providers.

COMMON MENTAL HEALTH PROBLEMS AFTER DISASTERS

Mental health issues related to long-term adaptation following disasters begin to fit more traditional approaches to clinical assessment and treatment. People exposed to disasters often experience increased psychological distress, but many demonstrate resilience and maintain a trajectory of healthy functioning. Severe levels of these problems are typically observed in a minority of exposed individuals (Bonanno, Brewin, Kaniasty, & LaGreca, 2010).

Anxiety, Depression, and Somatic Complaints

The most consistent mental health problems found in studies of disaster survivors are symptoms of anxiety (including posttraumatic stress disorder), depression, and somatic symptoms.

Substance Abuse

Although widely believed to be affected by disasters, increases in substance abuse problems among disaster survivors have been reported less consistently than the anxiety/depression/somatic complaint symptoms described earlier. The topic needs further study, as some studies have found increases in alcohol use (and other substances, such as tranquilizers) among disaster-exposed populations in the United States and others have not.

Aggression and Anger

Problems with anger and aggression appear to be linked to disasters, although there is less evidence for this than for anxiety, depression, and somatic complaints. A number of studies have found anger and irritability to be higher in disaster-exposed populations than in non-exposed comparison groups, and there is some suggestion that these problems may be quite persistent over time. There is surprisingly little research documenting increases in actual aggression after disasters.

AGE AND ECONOMIC CONSIDERATIONS

Age is related to disaster response in numerous ways, and children and the elderly are typically viewed as "special populations" in the disaster literature. Children and some of the elderly are similar in their greater dependence on others to meet basic needs for food, clothing, and shelter. Impairment in individuals or systems that meet these dependency demands places both groups at risk for mental health disturbance, and possibly for physical danger.

Children and Adolescents

Children of different ages have different types of difficulties related to disasters. *Infants and toddlers* are often very sensitive to disruptions in caretaking and may show increases in feeding problems, irritability, and sleep problems. These behavioral problems in turn place increased demands on caretakers, who may themselves be highly distressed by a disaster.

Preschool children are beginning to use language in relatively sophisticated ways but are very limited in their understanding of disaster-related events. This limited understanding often leads to fears that may seem unwarranted to older children and adults (e.g., extreme fears during thunderstorms that occur after a flood or tornado). These fears may lead to dramatic reactions to relatively harmless post-disaster events.

School-age children understand the physical environment much better than preschoolers but may be very preoccupied by the loss of possessions or pets or by memories of traumatic events. Elementary school-age children also are often able to recognize distress in their caretakers and may be quite worried about the safety and security of their families. Children of this age can do relatively little to help actively in the recovery process, which may increase feelings of isolation and helplessness. Children over 8 years old generally are competent reporters of psychiatric symptoms (especially internalizing symptoms) when given appropriate measures. Children typically report more post-disaster symptoms than others (e.g., parents, teachers) report for them. Relying solely on parent or teacher reports to identify post-disaster mental health problems in school-age children is almost certain to underestimate these problems.

Adolescents are more competent to help with recovery and are less dependent than younger children. At the same time, adolescents may engage in greater risk-taking behaviors after disasters. Adolescents may also have intense feelings of being cheated out of expected experiences (e.g., athletic and social events that are cancelled or postponed) after disasters.

Young and Middle-Aged Adults

There is some evidence of differences in disaster-related distress between young adults (18–40 years) and middle-aged adults (40–65 years), with the latter group typically faring worse. Middle-aged adults are more likely than other age cohorts to have responsibility for children and elderly parents during and after disasters, and this increased responsibility may contribute to psychological distress.

Older Adults

Health status (including mental health) and competence to perform tasks of daily living are also important aspects in determining post-disaster needs of the elderly. Sensory changes accompanying aging are important to consider. Hearing and vision problems may make it more difficult for the elderly to obtain information regarding disaster relief efforts or to provide information to others. Noisy, crowded settings (such as disaster shelters or Disaster Assistance Centers) may be particularly problematic because it becomes increasingly difficult with age to filter out competing noises during conversations. Decreased sense of smell and taste tend to make the elderly prefer foods with more flavor, and elders may respond to bland food provided through disaster relief by adding salt (which aggravates hypertension) or reducing food intake (which may result in malnutrition). The relationship between cognitive functioning and physical health becomes increasingly strong during late adulthood, and declines in physical health due to poor nutrition or disruptions in medications may contribute to significant mental health problems, including confusion, disorientation, and depression. Similarly, loss of social support and disruptions in routines following disasters may produce poor health behaviors, leading to increased dysfunction. Sudden changes in living arrangements are difficult for older adults, especially those with cognitive, physical, or sensory impairments. Many elderly also attach a strong stigma to the use of mental health services, and substantial efforts may be required to make such service acceptable. Some older adults who are aware of their diminished capabilities may fear that they will be placed in nursing homes or other restrictive settings if their difficulties become known to relief workers. It is important to communicate that mental health workers are attempting to help the elderly live as independently as possible and that they may help garner the resources and support needed for this to occur.

ECONOMIC CONSIDERATIONS

Education and financial status may influence recovery from disasters and even levels of exposure to traumatic experiences during disasters. Education may influence an individual's ability to cope with the demands for documentation and careful completion of applications for disaster assistance. Education is also linked to skills in seeking information regarding resources. Financial status exerts multiple possible influences on post-disaster functioning. In terms of increased exposure to traumatic experiences during disasters, housing built of less durable materials (e.g., mobile homes) in less desirable locations (e.g., flood-prone land) is more likely to be damaged by disasters in the first place. This places poorer individuals, on average, at greater risk for loss of personal possessions and exposure to life-threatening circumstances. Following disasters, individuals with few financial resources (including personal property insurance) may find it virtually impossible to repair or replace lost belongings. Even for poorer families with some insurance, months of waiting may be required before claims are settled, placing extreme financial pressures on those with few financial reserves. Many lower paying, lower occupational-status jobs offer little in the way of paid personal leave or scheduling flexibility. This may further complicate post-disaster recovery by making it difficult for individuals to find the time to pursue aid or repairs.

References and Readings

Bonanno, G. A., Brewin, C. R., Kaniasty, K., & LaGreca, A. M. (2010). Weighing the costs of disaster: Consequences, risks, and resilience in individuals, families, and communities. *Psychological Science in the Public Interest, 11*(1), 1–49.

Brymer, M., Layne, C., Jacobs, A., Pynoos, R., Ruzek, J., Steinberg, A., and final authors. (2006) *Psychological first aid field operations guide* (2nd ed.). Los Angeles, CA: National Child Traumatic Stress Network and National Center for PTSD.

Hobfoll, S. E., Watson, P. E., Bell, C. C., Bryant, R. A., Brymer, M. J., Friedman, M. J., & Ursano, R. J. (2007). Five essential elements of immediate and mid-term mass trauma intervention: Empirical evidence. *Psychiatry: Interpersonal and Biological Processes, 70,* 283–315.

Vernberg, E. M., Steinberg, A. M., Jacobs, A. K., Brymer, M. J., Watson, P. J., Osofsky, J. D., & Ruzek, J. I. (2008). Innovations in disaster mental health: Psychological first aid. *Professional Psychology, Research, and Practice, 39*(4), 381–388.

Related Topic

Chapter 145, "Conducting Evidence-Based Prevention"

138 ESTABLISHING A CONSULTATION AGREEMENT

Len Sperry

THE FOCUS OF CONSULTATION

Consultation can be focused in at least four ways:

- *Client-centered consultation.* The goal is to aid the client, such as with executive consultation or executive coaching.
- *Consultee-centered case consultation.* The goal is to enhance the consultee's skills; for example, a psychologist meets with a group of line supervisors to study their understanding of and recognition of substance dependence in the workplace.
- *Program-centered administrative consultation.* The goal is to diagnose and resolve the consultee's difficulty in dealing with administrative problems. A common example is assisting LAP personnel to develop a corporation-wide depression awareness program.
- *Consultee-centered administrative consultation.* The goal is to diagnose and resolve the consultee's difficulty in dealing with administrative problems, such as functioning as a consultation-liaison psychologist to a weight management program at a community hospital.

TYPES OF INTERVENTION

It is useful to distinguish two types of consultant interventions: organizational interventions and clinical-organizational interventions (in contrast to clinical interventions). Traditionally, clinicians were thought to provide clinical interventions, such as individual, family, marital, or group therapy, whereas organizational consultants were more likely to provide individual, team, and organizational interventions, such as executive coaching, team building, and reengineering. Whereas traditional forms of organizational consultation require considerable skill and experience, there are a number of clinical-organizational interventions that mental health clinicians can competently provide corporations, schools, health care agencies and organizations, community groups, and government agencies. The following is a listing of commonly provided clinical-organizational interventions:

- Hiring, discipline, and termination consultation
- Work-focused psychotherapy
- Outplacement counseling and consultation
- Stress-disability and fitness-for-duty consultation
- Dual-career couples counseling and consultation
- Conflict resolution consultation with work teams
- Conflict resolution in a family business
- Crisis intervention consultation
- Consulting on resistance to planned change efforts

- Downsizing and merger syndrome consultation
- Mental health policy consultation
- Violence prevention and antibullying/mobbing consultation

ASSESSING THE REQUEST FOR CONSULTATION

Irrespective of the type of consultation offered, the process begins with a request from a prospective client. These requests can include a workshop on stress management, a violence prevention policy, team conflict resolution, stress-disability evaluation, or strategic planning, to name a few. The request is usually made by phone or face to face. How the clinician-consultant handles the request can greatly impact not only whether a consultation contract is offered but also the outcome of the intervention itself. Just as in psychotherapy, the first 5 minutes of the prospective consultant and client relationship is critical.

An accurate assessment of client need should be accomplished very early in the consultation process. This assessment should address the following questions:

- *What is the context of the consultation request?* Specifically, what is the client requesting? For example, if a hospital administrator phones a clinician asking whether he or she can "do something about employee morale," what is the administrator really asking for help with? As in psychotherapy, the initial presenting problem is often not the client's reason for seeking consultation. Consultation requests may be disguised because of lack of understanding of the consultation request, embarrassment, misperception of the basic problem, or even deceit. So the consultant would inquire about what is meant by "morale" and, specifically, by whom, where in the organization, and how it is being manifested and what effects it is having on productivity and communication between management and employees.
- *Why now?* As in psychotherapy, the answer to this question can be extremely revealing. Consultations are often requested only after the agency or organization has attempted to deal with its difficulty for a period of time without requesting outside help. What efforts were tried, and to what extent were they successful? In the "morale" example, it is critical to know what efforts the administrator has made and why these efforts have not worked as well as expected.
- *How will the consultation be framed?* Today, a distinction is increasingly made between the traditional form of consulting, called task based, and the recent approach to consulting, called value based. In task-based consulting the purpose is perform specifics tasks such as leadership training or coaching to create deliverables. The focus is largely tactical. In value-based consulting the purpose is to improve the client's situation organizationally, professionally, and personally. The focus is much more strategic. Even though the same or similar consulting activities may be involved in both, in value-based consulting the incentive is on specific activities that will make a real difference. In short, the emphasis is on achieving results rather than providing deliverables (Czerniawska, 2002). The way the consultation is framed will influence both delivery and fee. Because the value-based consultant frames his or her efforts in achieving results, the fee is based on outcomes rather than on billable hours or per diem rates (Weiss, 2008).
- *What is the client's readiness to change?* The likelihood that the client is willing to make changes to resolve the problem must also be assessed. Because the client and personnel resources are involved, it is essential that the clinician-consultant determine the client's willingness to allocate such resources. If it emerges that the hospital's problem is widespread and the administrator will authorize only two or three workshops on "team building," it may well be that the client's readiness is insufficient. Extended inquiry and discussion may be required before an appropriate level of readiness is achieved.
- *Can I competently provide the requested consultation?* The prospective consultant needs to ask himself or herself whether he or

she has sufficient content knowledge, technical and interpersonal skills, and experience to undertake this consultation. For fairly straightforward requests, such as presenting a lecture on stress management or providing a disability evaluation, both of which require specific technical expertise, the question may be easily answered. When process *plus* technical expertise is required, the question of competence is more complex.

- *Can I ethically perform this consultation?* Potential conflict of interest and dual roles must be considered by the consultant. Obviously, if the clinician is providing or has provided marital therapy to the hospital administrator, he or she probably should not be directly involved in consultation.

RESPONDING TO THE CONSULTATION REQUEST

The clinician-consultant now is in a position to respond to the service request. As in psychotherapy, the clinician-consultant first responds to the manifest content of the request by expressing awareness of the need and/or discomfort of the client organization. Next, the clinician-consultant proposes a plan for meeting the request. This may involve a face-to-face meeting—or a series of meetings—to discuss a plan of action for more complex consultations, or it may require only a brief phone meeting for straightforward consultations such as a workshop presentation.

DRAFTING A CONSULTATION AGREEMENT OR CONTRACT

Usually, a letter of agreement or a formal consulting contract will finalize these discussions. Although most consultants routinely draft a written contract, some do not. The written document of agreement becomes a contract if a consideration is stated (i.e., the provision of specified consultation for a given fee) and both parties sign the document (Block, 2011). Typically, the document should contain the specified service to be performed, the time frame, travel and lodging expenses, cost of assessment and/or intervention materials, and the consulting fee, which may include preparation time.

ESTABLISHING A CONSULTING FEE

Information on fees charged by consulting psychologists is difficult to come by since there is no such national survey data. Yet such data are regularly tracked for nonpsychology consultants. Overall, the figure indicates that about 60% of consultants generate revenues between $50,000 to $150,000 per year, while another 30% generate revenues between $150,000 and $300,000 per year. The fee a clinician-consultant charges a client can be established either on a project or a fixed-fee basis or on a time basis, in which the increments can be hours or days. Circumscribed activities or projects, such as presenting a stress management workshop or conducting a fitness-for-duty evaluation, are usually billed as a fixed fee, whereas facilitating team development or organizational restructuring is usually billed as day rate, called a *per diem.* Some consulting activities, such as critical incident stress debriefing (CISD) or facilitating a strategic planning retreat, may be charged on a project or a per diem basis depending on local or regional customs. Generally speaking, government contracts require fixed-fee agreement. For complex consulting activities, consultants tend not to use fixed-fee rates for projects with which they have little experience. As noted earlier, consultants who practice value-based consulting are more likely to negotiate a fee based on results achieved rather than on billable hours or days (Weiss, 2008).

Calculating Utilization Rate

Billable hours refers to the number of working hours the consultant bills the client. Experienced, full-time consultants do not actually consult full time. They have down time in which they may devote up to 20% of their time marketing their services to secure new consulting arrangements. Obviously, this time is nonbillable. *Utilization rate* refers to the percentage of total working hours the client can be billed. The utilization rate is the number of billable hours divided by the number of total working hours available. For instance, if a clinician-consultant plans to consult 12 hours per week and actually bills for 6 hours per week, the utilization rate is 50%. Obviously, the higher the utilization rate, the greater one's compensation. Utilization rate indicates how much consulting time clients are directly paying for, as compared with the time the consultant must absorb as overhead.

Calculating Billable Rate

The "rule of three" or "3 × rule" is used by consultants to calculate their billing rate (Biech, 2007). The rule assumes that a consultant should generate overhead and benefits that should equal base salary, while also producing a profit equal to base salary. For example, suppose a clinician-consultant works half-time as a clinician at a college counseling center and develops a half-time consulting practice. If he or she specifies a half-time base consulting salary as $50,000 a year, the total revenues of $150,000 should be estimated. This is derived from $50,000 base salary, plus $50,000 for overhead plus benefits and $50,000 for profit. The billing rate is estimated by dividing total revenue by yearly billable hours. For example, $150,000 is divided by 1,000 hours (based on 200 hours/year as full-time work). The minimum hourly billing rate is thus $150 per hour, and the minimum billing rate would be $1,200 per day. A corollary of the rule of three is that the more hours billed, the less one needs to charge to maintain profit levels, whereas the fewer the hours billed, the more that must be charged to maintain a reasonable profit level. Biech (2007) provides some useful tables for calculating fees.

Other Ways of Establishing a Billing Rate

A second way of setting a billing rate is based on the usual and customary fees in a geographic region. Usually, there is a typical daily rate for psychologists in particular metropolitan areas. For example, while $1,500 may be the norm in some midwestern cities, the rate in large northeastern cities may be $2,000–3,000 per day. Finding out the billing rates of three or four clinician-consultants should reveal the usual and customary rate for a given community. A third way of establishing fee arrangements is to consider the client's circumstances. Schools and community organizations may have limited funds for consultation, whereas defense attorneys may have unlimited funds for expert testimony. The beginning clinician-consultant also may be willing to offer a low-cost consultation fee to one or more clients in return for gaining experience and receiving a positive reference from that client.

COMPLETION OF CONSULTATION SERVICES RENDERED

Following completion of the consultation services rendered, it is customary to send or deliver the bill for payment. If a report of the consultation was specified in the agreement, the report is also sent. Following payment, it is customary to send a follow-up thank-you note.

MARKETING/SOLICITING FUTURE CONSULTATIONS

Experienced consultants usually do not view termination of consultation services rendered as termination of the consultation relationship. Successful consultations often result in other consultation requests from the same client. These clients tend to communicate their satisfaction with a consultant to their professional colleagues and friends. Since word-of-mouth advertising is the consultant's most effective marketing strategy, it behooves the consultant to make his or her initial consultations as successful as possible. Consultants may also seek written permission to mention the names of clients of their most successful consultations in written materials—such as brochures—or in verbal conversation with prospective clients.

References and Readings

Biech, E. (2007). *The business of consulting* (2nd ed.). New York: Wiley.

Block, P. (2011). *Flawless consulting* (3rd ed.). New York: Wiley.

Czerniawska, F. (2002). *Value based consulting*. New York: Palgrave Macmillan.

Weiss, A. (2008). *Value based fees* (2nd ed.). New York: Wiley.

Related Topics

Chapter 121, "Managing Your Managed Care Contracts"

Chapter 126, "Fulfilling Informed Consent Responsibilities"

139 INTERACTING WITH THE MEDIA

Lilli Friedland and Florence Kaslow

Media psychology developed as a formal field to address the ethical and professional concerns of "on-air" TV and radio psychologists and those being interviewed by journalists. Currently, media psychology encompasses a much broader array of activities (Luskin & Friedland, 1998). Although professional standards and ethics are the same whether psychologists use the newer technologies or the traditional media, consumer and professional protection parameters have not yet been developed (e.g., to whom would the consumer make a complaint given that some licensing boards and mental health professions may not yet have promulgated standards for these modalities, and where these standards exist, they may differ across states).

PUBLICITY BY AND ABOUT PSYCHOLOGISTS

Public statements encompass but are not limited to paid or unpaid advertising of professional services, product endorsements, printed materials, comments used in print or electronic transmission, statements in legal proceedings, lectures and public presentations, published materials, or "online" communications (such as blogs, webinars). The psychologist is responsible for the content provided in any marketing brochure or public relations information. Most public relations, publishing, marketing, and media personnel are not familiar with psychologists' ethical or professional standards and therefore may exaggerate claims or slant information to represent a particular point of view. As psychologists cannot usually control the information released by media personnel, they are urged to routinely offer a document describing their training and expertise to media personnel and publicists. Similarly, if the psychologist refers to research, the sources should be cited according to APA guidelines and sent to the media personnel, even though the research may not be directly used.

ON-AIR MEDIA PSYCHOLOGY

There are helpful steps that psychologists can take when receiving a request asking for an interview or information: (a) If one is not an expert on the requested subject matter and there is insufficient time to acquire the requisite information, the psychologist should decline the interview and recommend an expert. (b) If there is insufficient time to locate a subject matter expert, the psychologist who was approached can offer to conduct a literature search quickly. The most significant findings and conclusions should be written, including citations, and submitted to the interviewer. Experienced media psychologists have noted that media personnel rarely refer to the research, yet the information given sometimes incorporates the overall findings in the reports.

Frequently, media psychologists are asked to comment on a mode of therapy or an individual psychologist. Psychologists should indicate that they are commenting about the general psychological issues or processes posed rather than a particular treatment given for a specific person's symptoms or behaviors. Sometimes media psychologists are asked to opine about a particular individual, a psychotherapist or a well-known person. In this context, a psychologist should not diagnose or assess an individual with whom he or she has not professionally interacted. If there is a professional relationship, the psychologist cannot comment, as it violates the client's confidentiality. Some psychologists are asked to agree about a statement or give an example of a public figure whose behavior is illustrative of a particular psychological problem. The circumspect professional does not do so because this does not fall within the realm of psychologists' competencies and ethics.

Whenever psychologists work with media personnel, *nothing is "off the record" or "confidential" for them;* informal comments and expressions are often used in the final product. It is essential to maintain one's professional stance and composure until one is out of range of all recording or reproduction equipment (Koocher, Norcross, & Hill, 2001).

It is neither appropriate nor ethical to compensate any member of the media in return for publicity or for being showcased. There is a distinction between advertisements (i.e., using an actor to speak about a product or service) and an infomercial (i.e., the situation in which an individual endorses and gives a testimonial about the particular service or product). Some infomercials are camouflaged as news programs. When psychologists are being paid for their services, this should be transparent, if relevant. If the professional is known as a psychologist, she or he can be seen as endorsing the product/service. Any information provided by the psychologist should be based on current research, practice, and ethical standards.

To consumers, the psychologist is seen as representing the profession; therefore, the information imparted must be accurate and current. Psychologists need to be aware of the real and potential effects on viewers of the media activities in which they participate: Is the psychologist seen as endorsing or condemning a behavior, attitude, or an individual? Is the psychologist's stance a subjective one (based upon personal values or opinions) or an objective one (based upon research and prevailing community practice standards)? The positions stated should be objective and verifiable. In determining how to respond to media inquiries, the following questions should be asked:

- What is the type of information requested? What is the context in which it will be used?
- What type of psychological expertise is necessary to provide what is requested? Does the psychologist have expertise in this area? If not, is there another psychologist with the requisite knowledge to recommend? Will a literature search on the topic suffice?
- What is the time frame for the interview or information? Is it sufficient for the psychologist to develop a cogent presentation?

If asked to participate on air, every effort should be made by psychologists to determine the media personnel's sources, integrity, and previous history of types of guests and experts.

- Observe whether the host habitually interrupts the guest experts.
- Determine the source for the story idea (a current headline or a standing topic).
- Determine whether the host has a particular viewpoint that the show wants to substantiate, although current psychological knowledge does not confirm that position. If it will be a live program, become acquainted with the type of questions asked.
- Be aware of the audience and gear the presentation to their level of interest and understanding. For example, if it is a woman's television show, use examples aimed at the type of women who watch that program.
- Note the manner that the host queries the experts. Does the host try to get experts to give definitive opinions or one-word answers to complex issues?

Develop a vision of the information about the subject.

- Media personnel usually want simple, definitive answers to clear 30-second "sound bites." Psychologists need to be trained or practice giving brief, yet accurate information.
- The format of "real-time" programs is such that hosts control the focus.
- Experienced media psychologists find that planning, rehearsing, and delivering the three to five most salient facts on the subject yield the most successful presentations.
- The psychologist should offer the "talking points" he or she developed to the journalist.
- The psychologists should alert media personnel of potential harm or need for referrals for program guests, audience, or staff if she or he becomes aware an intervention is warranted.

If the program or media personnel have a history of seeking sensationalism or being demeaning to guests, it is wise to refuse to be involved, no matter how tempting the invitation.

Media personnel sometimes request psychologists to bring guests, preferably one of his or her past or present clients. Even if the client were to give informed consent after having discussed the potential emotional effects of participating, the psychologist should not agree to take part if this is an essential condition for the media involvement (APA Ethical Principles, 2002). Psychologists should attempt to educate members of the media to the possible dual relationships (i.e., some patients are apt to say "yes" to please their therapist and this implied inducement can have negative long-term effects on guests when brought in by their treating professional). Additional issues exist if the client is a minor. The impact on clients of being "Telling all" on TV or other media can have a dire impact that may not necessarily surface for a long time (McCall, 1990).

Experienced media psychologists know the key to the successful media interview is to make the points, not necessarily answering the questions posed (APA, 2002). Therefore, if psychologists are asked questions that do not address information they deem essential on this subject, they can bring up their talking points by using bridges such as "the real issue..." or "the three issues involved are..." (Friedland & Kaslow, 2005).

PRINT MEDIA

All of the principles cited earlier also apply when a reporter or writer contacts a psychologist. When contacted by a print journalist, the following procedures are suggested:

- Only give an interview if you are knowledgeable about a topic/breaking story.
- If the journalist stresses the immediacy of his or her deadline, try to be cooperative, but do not participate in the interview if you are not well prepared. It is their deadline, not yours.
- If accepting a request, ask for a minimum of half an hour to organize your thoughts.
- Ask the reporter to send you the article *before* it is submitted to go to press to review for accuracy. Many reporters will do so, if time permits.
- Ask the author to arrange for a copy of the article to be sent. This does not always happen.
- Keep comments short, straightforward, succinct, pithy, and free of jargon.

THE NEWER TECHNOLOGIES: GENERAL CONSIDERATIONS

The newer technologies are part of the expanding tools of the trade and psychologists need to learn their limitations and advantages. In using the newer technologies the psychologist may work outside the customary benchmarked practices of the profession. The wise psychologist will substantiate the underlying scientific assumptions when professionally involved in these new areas. Clarification of expectations (such as *not* being available 24/7) should be stated on Web site and intake/contract forms. Unless one is using secure/encrypted devices, texting, e-mailing, and postings are not secure and should not be used to convey any confidential data. If the device is not secure/encrypted, the client must be informed. It is recommended that the risks and benefits of using these technologies are included in the Informed Consent. It is essential to have backup plans in place and inform the client prior to using it in case there are problems using the technology. Before employing the newer technologies psychologists should consult with respected peers and/or ethics committees, documenting the process, safeguards, and procedures (APA, 2002; Kutner, 1997).

The newer technologies enable interactions and communications between individuals and groups both locally and globally; therefore, psychologists need to consider a specific client's language, ethnicity, and culture. Different licensing/credentialing requirements may apply, so it is essential to determine the standards of care required in the location of the client (which may change if the person moves, goes to school, or is on vacation). Information given to the media should be appropriate to the geographic/cultural area where the story will be disseminated.

It is essential to know whether the devices (e.g., computer, phone) are owned by the business for whom the client works. If that is the case, the employer has legal access to the device and its contents. Care must also be taken to ensure that if the psychologist's devices are lost or stolen that (a) there is a backup for all the information and (b) that there are strong passwords. Psychologists are advised to consult their professional (malpractice) liability insurance policy to ensure that the planned services are covered. It is advised to consult with one's own attorney to review documents.

PSYCHOLOGICAL INTERVENTIONS AND INFORMATION GIVEN OUT USING NEWER TECHNOLOGIES

In an effort to educate the public, some psychologists have conducted or shown "live" or recorded therapy sessions on television, videos, webinars, or other forms of media. Ethically psychologists cannot work with current clients/patients in such a manner (and even working with former patients is questionable); therefore, it is advised that actors be used. The psychologist should be cautious to ensure that the characters portrayed do not resemble specific patients/clients.

Telehealth

The definition of the "therapeutic relationship" has undergone reexamination in part due to the use of the newer media technologies. Using these media raises issues of (a) verifying client's identity; (b) awareness of the licensing regulations governing the psychologist (can he or she practice across jurisdictions if a client lives elsewhere?); (c) sensitivity to different ethnic or cultural populations, (d) authentication of informed consent and fee arrangements; and (e) understanding the risks to privacy and limits to confidentiality. Though patients must sign HIPAA (Health Insurance Portability and Accountability Act) forms to ensure they give their permission for their psychologist to share their personal information with other professionals or institutions, the confidentiality of their information is not necessarily ensured when using electronic tools. Recently huge confidential databases for defense contractors, media companies, health insurers, hospitals, and providers have been "hacked." Even with strong security protection measures in place their data systems were compromised. Data, including client identification, progress notes, supervision, and billing, were breached. Psychologists are urged to inform potential clients/patients about these concerns and take all reasonable precautions to protect the clients. Whenever there is a question, consultation with peers is advised, as well as documenting the process with careful notes. Guidelines for telehealth have been recommended (Barnett & Zur, n.d.):

- Provide online services only after completing an informed consent form covering essential information that every client needs to know prior to entering a professional relationship. Specify the limits of confidentiality in the online environment.
- Verify that each client has the legal authority to consent to treatment or consultation and establish identity of client.
- Document all online services in the same manner that in-person services are documented.
- Use appropriate safeguards such as virus and firewall protection, passwords, and encryption.
- Get authorization prior to services if the psychologist bills for a video or phone session.
- Obtain needed training prior to providing actual services.

"Virtual communities" such as chat groups and online communities are ongoing entities on the Internet. These modalities serve as sources of support, gaming, education, and information. Ethical implications need to be considered by a psychologist prior to participating as a professional in "group therapy" or as an expert consultant online with individuals he or she has not met. The psychologist has no idea whom he or she is "treating" and if that individual is participating using his or her real identity and truthful symptoms.

Testing (forensic, clinical, consulting, or educational) using the newer technologies presents the problem of ensuring the test conditions are similar to those when the tests are given in a person-to-person setting and that the designated individual takes and completes the testing.

ONE-WAY COMMUNICATION

Blogging

Blogging and micro-blogging are tools used by many people, including psychologists, to share spontaneous information, hypothesis-in-the-making (e.g., information not yet validated by a peer-reviewed process), research, or links that the psychologist's or organization's website wishes to circulate. Journalists frequently retrieve information from blogs and thus the psychologists should keep the "science/practitioner" perspective when deciding information to be posted. When in doubt, psychologists should request consultation or supervision.

RSS Feeds

RSS (i.e., Rich Site Summary) is a format used to deliver regularly changing Web content. When using such information-dissemination tools, it is essential to ensure that data are referenced appropriately and ethically (some professional organizations and/or journals do not allow full articles to be distributed online even by the authors). Psychologists should check and receive permission, preferably in writing, for articles on RSS feeds from the authorizing service.

Digital or Virtual Worlds

A digital or virtual world is an interactive simulated environment accessed by multiple users interfacing online. Individuals participate in virtual worlds (Second Life, Whyville, Sims Online, World of Warcraft, Active Worlds Educational Universe, Mokitown, Everquest, America's Army, etc.) to learn strategies, play games, role-play new identities, and for enjoyment. Avatars and virtual worlds are used effectively for organizational consulting, psychological treatment, educational learning, and assessment.

Video-postings on sites such as YouTube, FaceBook, and LinkedIn enable people to share both personal and professional information. Psychologists should cautiously present their information in a relatively simple format as different viewers may interpret what is portrayed quite differently.

TWO-WAY, INTERACTIVE MEDIA INTERACTIONS

Video-Conferencing

Video-conferencing has become a frequent communication modality for some psychologists, agencies, medical schools, and firms. Psychologists use this modality for giving information, for psychotherapy, supervision, testifying, consulting, or testing. To date, there are few video systems that keep information confidential by being highly encrypted or HIPAA compliant. All parties, including clients, should be told whether any recordings will be made using this technology prior to use.

Social Media

Social media such as FaceBook, Twitter, Google +, and LinkedIn, are primary modes of communication and connection. People reveal varying amounts of personal information on these social media sites, which each have different privacy settings. These settings can change without adequate warning to users. Some consumers have felt their privacy compromised at times and therefore psychologists need to be cautious and not assume that their own personal information will be concealed from clients. Some psychologists use social media for business purposes only as a way of disseminating information to the media, possible referral sources, and the public. Under these circumstances, posting only relevant professional data is advised. Psychologists need to keep in mind that "tagging" or facial recognition can occur.

The dynamics of using social media (e.g., quick responding, indicating one's current location, personal lists and photos of friends and/or family, etc.) inherently discourage the thoughtful interactions for which psychologists pride themselves. It is urged that psychologists realize that personal information may be shared by clients, patients, referral sources, or media personnel and interfere with professional relationships (Kaslow, Patterson, & Gottlieb, 2011).

As psychologists will increasingly be using the newer technologies as tools in their practice, it is essential to always refer to ethical standards and accepted practice.

References and Readings

American Psychological Association. (2002). *Ethical principles of psychologists and code of conduct.* Washington, DC: Author.

Barnett, J., & Zur, O. (n.d.). *Guidelines for telehealth, e-therapy, online therapy: Do's and don'ts for ethical practice.* Retrieved from www.zurinstitute.com/telehealthguidelines.html

Friedland, L., & Kaslow, F. (2005). Guide to Interacting With the Media. In Koocher, G.P., Norcross, J.C., & Hill, S.S. (Eds.). *Psychologists' desk reference.* New York: Oxford University Press.

Kaslow, F. W., Patterson, T., & Gottlieb, M. (2011). Ethical dilemmas in psychologists accessing internet data: Is it justified? *Professional Psychology: Research and Practice, 42*(2), 105–112.

Koocher, G. P., Norcross, J. C., & Hill, S. S. (Eds.). (2001). *Psychologists' desk reference.* New York: Oxford University Press.

Kutner, L. (1997). New roles for psychologists in the mass media. In D. Kirschner & S. Kirschner (Eds.), *Perspectives on psychology and the media* (pp. 173–192). Washington, DC: APA.

Luskin, B. J., & Friedland, L. (1998). *Task force report: Media psychology and the new technologies.* Division of Media Psychology, American Psychological Association. Retrieved from www.apadiv46.org/arttaskforcereport.html

McCall, R. (1990). Ethical considerations of psychologists working in the media. In C. B. Fisher & W. W. Tryon (Eds.), *Ethics in applied developmental psychology: Emerging issues in an emerging field* (pp. 163–185). Norwood, NJ: Ablex.

Related Topic

Chapter 126, "Fulfilling Informed Consent Responsibilities"

140 CONDUCTING EFFECTIVE CLINICAL SUPERVISION

Nicholas Ladany

The following pan-theoretical recommendations for conducting effective clinical supervision are derived from research evidence, theoretical literature, and clinical experience.

1. *Emphasize and readily attend to the supervisory relationship.* The supervisory working alliance is the likely foundation for the effectiveness of all supervision. Bordin (1983) conceptualized the working alliance as consisting of a mutual agreement on the (a) goals and (b) tasks of supervision, and (c) an emotional bond between the supervisor and supervisee. The strength of the supervisory alliance has been empirically shown to predict positive supervision process and outcome.

2. *Apply models of supervision, as opposed to generalizing models of psychotherapy to supervision.* Three supervision-based models have been identified as comprehensive and empirically supported: the Critical Events Model of Supervision (Ladany, Friedlander, & Nelson, 2005), the Integrative Developmental Model (e.g., Stoltenberg & McNeill, 2010), and the Systems Approach to Supervision (Holloway, 1995). Although most models of supervision have a developmental component, this preference seems more heuristically useful than empirically supported. It seems supervisors like to think developmentally but act from a skills-based approach.

3. *Attend to supervision's own unique dynamics.* The art and science of conducting supervision is different from the art and science of conducting psychotherapy in at least three ways. First, it is intended to be primarily educative. Supervision occurs with the inherent assumption that the supervisee is there to become more adept at psychotherapy skills. Second, supervision is evaluative. A critical role for the supervisor is to evaluate the supervisee on these predefined skills. Third, supervision is typically (especially pre-licensure and outside the United States) involuntary for the supervisee. In many instances, the supervisee has little choice in whether, or from whom, he or she receives supervision. These three conditions create different dynamics than does psychotherapy, and as such, supervision should be viewed through a supervision, rather than a psychotherapy, lens.

4. *Engage in role induction and contracting with all supervisees.* In role induction and contracting, supervisors provide supervisees with explicit parameters of supervision work. Although it may be reasonably assumed that more advanced supervisees are aware of what transpires in supervision, it is frequently the case that supervisees' experiences do not consist of typical experiences. Therefore, supervisors should engage in role induction and contracting that includes supervisor disclosures about educational, training, and clinical experience; theoretical approach to supervision and therapy; confidentiality limits; supervision parameters that include meeting time, length of time, place, fee arrangements, contact and crisis information, and use of taping; and supervisee expectations such as informed consent, who is primarily responsible for initiating the supervisory discourse, supervisee disclosure, note taking, supervisee's use of self in supervision, supervisory goals, and supervisor evaluation.

5. *Tend to administrative responsibilities.* Supervisors must fulfill a variety of administrative responsibilities that include maintaining records of supervision, keeping abreast of all clients supervised, ensuring clients are aware of the supervisee's and supervisor's status, signing off on supervisee notes, using due diligence in selecting supervisees, and ensuring that supervisees with rigid interpersonal difficulties are prevented from continuing to work with clients. In addition, the supervisory work has a legal dimension that varies by jurisdiction; supervisors are reminded to familiarize themselves with those laws and rules.

6. *Supervision should not be psychotherapy for the supervisee.* Although it can be legitimately argued that part of supervision is to help the supervisee explore how her or his reactions may influence the therapy work, supervision is not a place solely for therapeutic change in the supervisee. Supervision should focus on supervisee interpersonal dynamics inasmuch as they relate to work with the client. Additional thorough attention should be provided by a personal psychotherapist outside of supervision.

7. *Understand micro- to macro-level supervisor skills.* Supervisor skills can be conceptualized along three levels: nonverbal skills (e.g., facial expressions, head nods), verbal response modes (e.g., reflection of feelings, restatements, self-disclosure), and strategies. Strategies combine nonverbal skills and verbal response modes into more complex behaviors such as focusing on the supervisory alliance, normalizing the supervisee's experience, focusing on countertransference, attending to multicultural competence, observing parallel process, focusing on skill and knowledge, focusing on the therapeutic process, exploring the supervisee's feelings, focusing on the supervisee's interpersonal dynamics, assessing ethical awareness, evaluating theoretical knowledge, assessing research knowledge, and discussing cases. The supervisor must decide when and how much, each of these competing demands must be attended.

8. *Attend to both supervisee-focused and client-focused outcomes.* Client outcome, while always alluded to as important, has been examined in only a handful of empirical investigations, and a clear link between supervision and client outcome has not been established. Conversely, supervisee-based outcomes have been clearly identified in the research. These include strengthening the supervisory relationship; enhancing supervisee conceptualization skills, therapy knowledge, multicultural awareness, self-efficacy, tolerance of ambiguity, awareness of countertransference, awareness of parallel process, and therapy skills; decreasing supervisee anxiety; and facilitating the development of supervisee self-evaluation. Supervisors should flexibly approach the supervisee with a mix of collegial, interpersonally sensitive, and task-oriented styles in order facilitate these positive outcomes.

9. *Recognize the importance of covert processes.* Although supervisee self-disclosure and, at least to some extent, supervisor self-disclosure are implicit assumptions in most clinical supervision, it is likely that what is left unsaid is critical to the supervisor work. Some typical supervisee nondisclosures include negative reactions to the supervisor, clinical mistakes, sexual attraction toward a client, and negative reactions to a client. Some typical supervisor nondisclosures include negative reactions to the supervisees' therapy and supervision work, supervisor self-efficacy, and sexual issues in supervision. Hence, it behooves supervisors to consider what may not be said in supervision, as well as ways of conducting supervision to minimize important nondisclosures.

10. *Keep abreast of ethical and legal issues that influence the practice of supervision.* Supervisors accept two types of liability: first, direct liability when supervisors are found responsible for specific actions that cause harm to a client; and second, vicarious liability when supervisors are found responsible for actions of supervisees. Along with liability for supervisees' clients, supervisors also need to be concerned with malpractice where the supervisee is harmed.

11. *Evaluate supervisees consistently and objectively.* Bernard and Goodyear (2009), not completely facetiously, postulate that there may be as many evaluation instruments as there are training sites. With this lack of consistency, supervisor evaluation has been a problematic enterprise. Supervisors should consider, and communicate to the supervisee, the components of supervisee work that are under scrutiny. These components will frequently entail mode of therapy (e.g., individual, group, family), domain of supervisee behaviors (e.g., therapy, supervision, professional), competence area (e.g., therapy techniques, theoretical conceptualization, assessment), method (supervisee self-report, case notes, audiotape, videotape, live supervision), proportion of caseload (all clients, subgroup of clients), segment of experience (e.g., a specific session, or a segment of a session), time period (early, middle, or late in client treatment as well as early, middle, or late in training experience), evaluator (e.g., supervisor, clients), level of expected proficiency (e.g., demonstrated skill, comparison to cohort group), and feedback (e.g., quantitative vs. qualitative). No single evaluation can account for all of these components; however, having a clear set of parameters will enhance the effectiveness of supervisor's evaluation.

12. *Set clear goals and provide both summative and formative feedback.* Supervisor evaluation consists of both goal-setting and feedback (summative and formative). Effective goal-setting consists of goals that are explicit, specific, feasibly reached, related to identified tasks, clarified early, and mutually agreed upon. To be effective in giving feedback, the supervisor should provide it in a way that is systematic, timely, clearly understood, positively and negatively balanced, and reciprocal.

13. *Enhance your own multicultural competence in order to enhance supervisee multicultural competence.* As multicultural training has become an integral part of many training programs, so too has the situation in which supervisees are more knowledgeable about multicultural issues than are supervisors. To avoid becoming part of these "regressive" relationships, supervisors need to keep current on the evolving content of multicultural therapy. Multicultural (e.g., gender, race, ethnicity, sexual orientation, disability, socioeconomic status) competence in supervision consists of knowledge, self-awareness, and skills (Inman & Ladany, in press). Hence, supervisors need to develop multicultural competence in order to be adept in assessing supervisees along similar psychotherapy-based dimensions.

14. *Consider group supervision and peer supervision as adjuncts to individual supervision.* Group supervision, consisting of a leader and typically three to six supervisees, offers an educative experience whereby supervisees can experience the benefit of group work (e.g., universality) along with skill development. Additionally, peer supervision is one avenue through which supervisees may disclose more readily their challenges and receive supplemental guidance.

15. *Secure training in clinical supervision.* The majority of psychotherapy supervisors did not complete formal training in supervision themselves nor does any mental health organization currently require supervisor training. It seems likely that the lack of supervisor training may be responsible for many of the unmet challenges that supervisors face. Hence, systematic and comprehensive supervisor training is recommended for those who engage in supervision.

References and Readings

American Psychological AssociationDivision of Counseling Psychology, Section on Supervision and Training. (2013). *Supervision and training resources.*RetrievedMarch2013fromfromwww.div17.org/sections/supervision-and-training

Bernard, J. M., & Goodyear, R. K. (2009). *Fundamentals of clinical supervision* (4th ed.). Boston, MA: Allyn & Bacon.

Bordin, E. S. (1983). A working alliance based model of supervision. *The Counseling Psychologist, 11,* 35–41.

Falvey, J. E. (2002). *Managing clinical supervision: Ethical practices and legal risk management.* Pacific Grove, CA: Brooks/Cole.

Holloway, E. L. (1995). *Clinical supervision: A systems approach*. Thousand Oaks, CA: Sage.

Inman, A. G., & Ladany, N. (in press). Multicultural competencies in psychotherapy supervision. In F. T. L. Leong (Ed.), *APA handbook of multicultural psychology* (Vol. 2). Washington, DC: American Psychological Association.

Ladany, N., Friedlander, M. L., & Nelson, M. L. (2005). *Critical events in psychotherapy supervision: An interpersonal approach*. Washington, DC: American Psychological Association.

Ladany, N., & Bradley, L. J. (Eds.). (2010). *Counselor supervision* (4th ed.). New York: Routledge.

Ladany, N., & Inman, A. G. (2013). Training and supervision. In E. M. Altmaier and J. C. Hansen (Eds.), *The Oxford handbook of counseling psychology*. New York: Oxford University Press.

Stoltenberg, C. D., & McNeill, B. W. (2010). *IDM Supervision: An integrative developmental model for supervising counselors and therapists* (3rd ed.). New York: Taylor & Francis.

Related Topic

Chapter 141, "Responsibilities and Liabilities in Supervision"

141 RESPONSIBILITIES AND LIABILITIES IN SUPERVISION

Carol A. Falender and Edward P. Shafranske

Clinical supervision is now recognized as a separate practice that requires specific competencies distinct from general clinical practice. This has transformed the practice of supervision beyond mere replication through osmosis of the supervision one may have experienced when he or she was a supervisee. The following overview will help supervisors identify responsibilities and implement a competency-based program of supervision, applying metatheoretical approaches and evolving clinical practice and evidence (Falender & Shafranske, 2007; Farber & Kaslow, 2010).

1. *Establishing the supervisory relationship*. Regardless of theoretical orientation, the respectful, collaborative interaction with the supervisee, referred to as a supervisory alliance, is an essential component. A strong supervisory alliance is associated with supervision satisfaction, enhanced supervisee disclosure, including disclosure of countertransference, and effective evaluation. Creating an emotional climate of support, safety, and integrity is associated with supervisee comfort disclosing personal responses and raising difficult issues or clinical errors.

2. *Implementing supervisee self-assessment and identification of components of competence in a strength-based approach*. Using a supervisee self-assessment (Benchmarks, Fouad et al., 2009 or retrieve from www.apa.org/ed/graduate/competency.html) as a platform to develop collaborative goals and specific tasks to achieve by the supervisee through supervision. The process provides the supervisor and supervisee with data to construct the goals and tasks that serve as the structure for supervisee development of competence and assists in the creation of an emotional connection between supervisor and supervisee. This document should attend to the specific knowledge, skills, and value/

attitude components that are assembled to form clinical competencies, and augment the document with components of the local practice setting that supervisees are expected to master (e.g., suicide risk assessment, infant assessment, etc.). Competencies such as delineated in Benchmarks are criterion-referenced standards that have been consensually agreed upon by the profession articulating performance at various levels of training (i.e., readiness for practicum, readiness for internship, and readiness for entry to practice). A supervisory task is to assist the supervisee to build upon strengths to expand skills, knowledge, and performance.

3. *Addressing the power differential.* A power differential exists in supervision as the supervisor has the power and responsibility to evaluate, provide feedback to the graduate school and licensing board, protect the client, and serve as a gatekeeper to the profession generally. Discussing power and committing to and providing transparency in feedback and evaluation (e.g., keeping no evaluative surprises from the supervisee) provide for a respectful process with the supervisee.

4. *Spelling out supervisor and setting expectations.* Supervisees prefer clarity of supervisor expectations. These include expectations for duration, type of information the supervisee prepares for the supervision session (verbal report, completed charting, audio or video recordings, evidence-based treatments, proposed case conceptualization), criteria and procedures to contact a supervisor in emergencies and crises, theoretical orientation of supervision and clinical practice, expectation that exploration of the impact of personal factors and countertransference will be part of supervision, and value placed on identification and management of strains and ruptures in the supervisory process.

5. *Implementing educationally and contextually sound practices to foster supervisee learning and development.* As a significant role of the supervisor is educational, good practice should foster acquisition of knowledge and skills by instruction, modeling, reflection, and mutual problem solving. Important components include seeking feedback about the effectiveness of supervision processes and interventions, tailoring supervision interventions to be contextually appropriate and to facilitate learning, and monitoring the implementation and effects of the clinical recommendations and directions given to supervisees. Building on the recognition of the strengths and talents of the supervisee, supervision encourages self-efficacy (Falender & Shafranske, 2004) and increasingly accurate self-assessment of competencies.

6. *Infusing diversity.* Focus on diversity among client, supervisee, and supervisor and corresponding worldviews, attitudes for treatment planning, and impact throughout supervision and treatment. Describing and discussing multiple identities of the supervisor, supervisee, and clients assists with integration of diversity into all aspects of the supervisory relationship and client assessment and treatment. That is, consider the equation of multiple diversity dimensions (gender, age, socioeconomic status, race, ethnicity, sexual orientation, gender identity, religion and spirituality, disability, etc.) and resultant worldviews. Worldview refers to the intersection of traditional and nontraditional belief structures, and attitudes toward the importance of present, future, or past orientation; time; relationship with nature; and living in harmony with nature, family, and community. Supervisees may be more highly trained in diversity than supervisors requiring supervisors to ensure continuing competence in diversity and multiculturally competent assessment, case conceptualization, and intervention strategies.

7. *Prioritizing timely and specific processes for feedback and evaluation.* Providing ongoing accurate performance feedback and evaluation are ethical standards of education and training. Not providing these is an ethical infraction that frequently occurs in supervision. The supervisor is responsible for providing evaluation criteria and measures as well as criteria for successful completion of the training sequence. Description and provision of transparency requires the supervisor to identify any area of concern in which the supervisee is not meeting performance criteria for his or her level of training, and give feedback to the supervisee immediately to ensure the supervisee is informed and can collaboratively establish a process to achieve the performance criteria. Specific, targeted behavioral feedback, linked to supervisee self-assessment, is ideally given in every supervision session and feedback is solicited from the supervisee at very regular intervals regarding how well supervision is meeting supervisee needs.

8. *Identifying strains and ruptures to the supervisory relationship and implementing processes for repair.* Strains are a normative part of clinical supervision but often go unrecognized. If the supervisee who was actively engaged in the process becomes less forthcoming, withdrawn, or less receptive, it is useful to review when the change in behavior occurred, mutually identify the strain or rupture, and engage in a reflective process to explore its cause and take responsibility as is appropriate. Supervisors need to be mindful of the impact of the power differential on the supervisee's inclination to fully participate in such a process and must take steps to reestablish trust.

9. *Maintaining competence in ethical and legal standards.* The supervisor is responsible for ensuring that supervisees are knowledgeable about the state and federal laws, decisions, and statutes as they apply to clinical practice and supervision (e.g., duty to warn) and ethical codes and standards. As regulations vary in amount and type of supervision and hours of supervised professional experience required for licensure, supervisors ensure supervisee awareness of the state regulations regarding supervision and perform their obligations in completing and submitting documentation as required.

10. *Constructing a supervision contract.* Formalizing expectations and goals in a contract between supervisee and supervisor provides additional clarity and includes the parameters for the training sequence as well as other informed consent items such as the expectation that value is placed on personal reflection and self-assessment, including personal exploration in supervision regarding the impacts of personal factors (i.e., beliefs, attitudes, values, worldview on the treatment process) as well as management of countertransference or unusual reactivity to client presentation, distinctions between supervision and psychotherapy, and possible referral for psychotherapy should supervisee response or behavior require attention that is beyond purview of supervisor and is interfering with the clinical work or the supervisory relationship.

11. *Modeling self-assessment and limits of competence.* The supervisor models and engages the trainee in ongoing self-assessment and development of metacompetence or self-awareness of what one knows and what one does not know. Supervisor self-disclosure about limits of competence and need for consultation or other resources models self-assessment and ethical practice.

13. *Attending to personal factors and countertransference.* The supervisor provides an orientation to personal factors and establishes the expectation that the supervisee's emotional responses and reactions will be examined in supervision. Attention is placed on the distinctions between supervisee *responsiveness,* in which emotional arousal leads to empathy and appropriate therapeutic action, and *reactivity,* which indicates therapist overarousal and conflict. Supervisors assist supervisees to identify the manifestations of such reactions as countertransference phenomena, including deviations from normal practice, unusual emotional reactions, and idiosyncratic patterns of response. Such reactions may be more frequent when supervisees are exposed to vicarious trauma and when working with patients with severe character disorders. The supervisor assists in the management of countertransference by exploring the triggers of the reactions and helping the supervisee to reestablish empathic engagement and to use his or her reactions to better understand the client. Attention is placed on addressing counterproductive actions that may have threatened the therapeutic alliance. The supervisor has particular responsibility for monitoring the supervisee's ability to effectively manage sexual attraction and arousal.

14. *Assessing client and supervisee outcomes.* Incorporating client self-report on treatment outcomes in supervision is associated with treatment gains. Supervisee ratings of supervision satisfaction are an important outcome tool.

15. *Identifying contextual factors and setting specific boundary crossings.* Supervisee placements vary in policy and normative practice. Identifying what constitutes acceptable practice (e.g., accepting tea or food from a client when conducting in-home treatment) is a supervisory responsibility.

16. *Considering and balancing the multiple roles of the supervisor.* Roles include advocating for supervisees, facilitating learning, evaluating, and gatekeeping for the profession. Supervisors advocate for and support supervisees in present and future activities, evaluate their performance, and consider their suitability for the profession of psychology. Balancing these roles requires the supervisor to use ethical problem-solving frames, consultation with peers, and integrity in communication with supervisees.

SUPERVISOR LIABILITY

Supervisors have a responsibility to take reasonable steps to safeguard the client from inadequate or incompetent services. The supervisor should be sure that each client is informed that the therapist is a supervisee under the supervision of a particular individual or individuals. Two general legal doctrines govern clinical supervision: direct liability and respondeat superior.

Direct liability arises from negligent supervision, the supervisor's own negligent acts or omissions. Examples include failure to provide supervision or monitor client treatment process according to standards of care, or identifying an error in the supervisee's treatment but not addressing it. A direct link would need to be demonstrated between the supervisor's own supervisory actions and client injuries.

On the other hand, *respondeat superior* or *vicarious liability* refers to the doctrine that the "superior" or in other words one who occupies a position of authority or direct control over another (e.g., supervisor- supervisee) can be held legally liable for the damages of another suffered as a result of the negligence of the subordinate (Disney & Stephens, 1994) even if the "superior" or supervisor was not directly involved in providing the service. Thus, supervisors may be held liable for actions of supervisees with their supervisees, regardless of whether the supervisor breached a duty. Three elements must be established to hold the supervisor liable: (1) there must be an employer–employee relationship or control as demonstrated by such elements as power to select, dismiss, and direct the supervisee; (2) the act that injured the client must be within the scope of the supervisee's employment; and (3) the supervisee's client must prove injury. For the supervisor to be legally liable for supervisee's negligent act(s), the negligent act would have had to have been performed in the course and scope of the supervisory relationship and resulted in substandard care to the client. However, how to determine this may be complex.

Parties must voluntarily consent to enter into an arrangement in which the agent (supervisee) acts for the benefit of, and under the direction and control of, the supervisor. The supervisee must be acting on behalf of the supervisor, performing tasks within the scope of employment or training contract. The supervisor must possess general power to control and right to direct the means and methods of the supervisee's work.

The court would weigh factors such as the supervisor's power to control the supervisee (with a core faculty member having greater control than a volunteer site supervisor); the supervisee's duty to perform the act (a clearly defined approach to a problem versus a decision on whether the clients should divorce); the time, place, and purpose of the act (during a clinical session versus during a chance meeting in the community); the motivation of supervisee to perform the act (acting in best interests of the client versus acting for personal reasons); and whether the supervisor could have reasonably expected that the supervisee would commit the act (Disney & Stephens, 1994).

Another factor in determining vicarious liability is the type of financial arrangement, perhaps involving enterprise liability, where the institution or supervisor derives financial gain from the supervisee's work. In such cases, the institution or enterprise may be liable because it derives the financial gain.

The following are supervisor steps to provide responsible supervision and thus reduce risk.

1. Self-assess and gain competence in clinical supervision through continuing education, independent study, or supervision of supervision groups
2. Observe your supervisees at intervals (live observation or video). Much supervision is reliant on the supervisee's report of what ensued clinically. Video and live supervision are excellent techniques to approach the potential limitation caused by the metacompetence of supervisees, that is, the likelihood that the supervisee does not know what he or she does not know. Direct observation by a supervisor allows the supervisor to provide theoretical and cognitively complex constructions of client presentations, integrate context, and develop therapeutic interventions.
3. Monitor supervisees to be aware of their cases, risk factors, emergent issues, and clinical interventions.
4. Perform supervision with integrity and in adherence with ethical and legal standards.

References and Readings

Bernard, J. M., & Goodyear, R. K. (2009). *Fundamentals of clinical supervision* (4th ed.). Upper Saddle River, NJ: Pearson.

Disney, M., & Stephens, A. M. (1994). Legal issues in clinical supervision. Alexandria, VA US: American Counseling Association.

Falender, C. A., & Shafranske, E. P. (2004). *Clinical supervision: A competency-based approach.* Washington, DC: American Psychological Association.

Falender, C. A., & Shafranske, E. P. (2007). Competence in competency-based supervision practice: Construct and application. *Professional Psychology Research and Practice, 38*(3), 232–240.

Falender, C. A., & Shafranske, E. P. (Eds.). (2008). *Casebook for clinical supervision: A competency-based approach.* Washington, DC: American Psychological Association.

Farber, E. W., & Kaslow, N. J. (2010). Introduction to the special section: The role of supervision in ensuring the development of psychotherapy competencies across diverse theoretical perspectives. *Psychotherapy: Theory, Research, Practice, Training, 47*, 1–2.

Fouad, N. A., Grus, C. L., Hatcher, R. L., Kaslow, N. J., Hutchings, P. S., Madson, M. B., … Crossman, R. E. (2009). Competency benchmarks: A model for understanding and measuring competence in professional psychology across training levels. *Training and Education in Professional Psychology*, 3(4 Suppl), S5–S26.

Ladany, N., Friedlander, M. L., & Nelson, M. L. (2005). *Critical events in psychotherapy supervision: An interpersonal approach.* Washington, DC: American Psychological Association.

Related Topic

Chapter 140, "Conducting Effective Clinical Supervision"

142 CULTIVATING RELATIONSHIPS AND COORDINATING CARE WITH OTHER HEALTH PROFESSIONALS

John C. Linton

While aspirational in the past, interprofessional collaboration is now considered a core competency and best practice in professional psychology recognized by consensus conferences and endorsed by the American Psychological Association (APA). The federal government is funding interdisciplinary science and research through the National Academy of Sciences (www.nap.edu/catalog.php?record_id=11153), and the APA is working with the Interprofessional Professionalism Collaborative to designate specific behaviors in psychology to support the more general competencies (interprofessionalprofessionalism.weebly.com/index.html). Universities are building connections among departmental disciplines to develop centers that draw from multiple specialties, and psychology has sought recognition under Title VII (Health Professions Training) of the US Public Health Service Act to have predoctoral and postdoctoral trainees recognized under medical education provisions of Medicare, consistent with other medical residents.

No single discipline has sufficient knowledge and skills to provide superior care to patients. Integrated health care delivery systems in the private and public sector have emerged as the dominant theme of the 21st century, so psychologists must link with other health care providers to contribute to and influence the final configuration of this system. The alternative is for psychologists to be marginalized or left out entirely.

WHAT IS THE BENEFIT?

As a health care profession, psychology's target patient population has extended beyond those needing only mental health care. This expansion has led to an exponential increase in the knowledge required for psychologists to manage complex clinical situations, so collaboration with other health professionals toward a common goal is essential for psychologists to practice competently. And psychology has much to offer since a large portion of health care involves teaching patients about self-care and motivating them to do it.

All parties benefit from clinical and scientific collaboration by integrating expertise across disciplines and growing clinical information. Team members get to appreciate alternative perspectives, collegial support, and a division of labor by areas of professional knowledge. But to be successful, interprofessional partners must be dependable, flexible, able to share their proficiencies, and receive as well as give useful feedback to one another.

CULTIVATING RELATIONSHIPS

Other professionals do not instinctively recognize the potential value of behavioral science to their delivery of health care, so psychologists must take the initiative to collaborate. Who are the likely collaborators? The key is to cast a wide net and balance availability of collaborators with one's area of interest. If psychologists are drawn to a patient population or problem, then collaboration with others of like mind will be more rewarding than stretching to force an interest. But a passion for a topic of study and service will lead to teamwork only if there are others available for collaboration.

WHO ARE SOME POSSIBLE HEALTH CARE COLLABORATORS?

Family Physicians

Family systems medicine is an interdisciplinary field concerned with how illness affects families and families affect illness. Most mental health care now occurs in the medical system, and a large percentage of family medicine visits have behavioral components to them. Psychologists are experts at many of these such as coping with anxiety and depression, overcoming insomnia, and quitting tobacco. Psychologists can fill a practice from these referrals alone. They can function as independently practicing consultants off site who receive referrals from family physicians, as consultants located in a primary care group practice, or as employees in family medicine training programs not only treating patients but preparing trainees in communication skills and the value of understanding behavioral disorders in practice. The latter are typically staff or faculty positions that are advertised and applied for, whereas the others require more creativity.

Cultivating relationships with family physicians first requires understanding their worldview, which deviates from that of the average psychologist. Psychologists are used to predictably scheduled days with ample protected time for assessment and therapy that is sacred and uninterrupted. Family physicians see dozens of patients daily for brief visits of 10–15 minutes, and their days are filled with unpredictability and interruptions. Patients expect appointments with the psychologist to mirror that of primary care, to be seen quickly and to focus on brief and practical solutions to their problems. Referring physicians expect psychologists to see patients on little notice, and to report back quickly those aspects of the case they need to know. Psychologists can rarely think about a case in detail, develop a deep personal bond with patients, or produce comprehensive evaluations and detailed progress notes.

One must become a specialist at not specializing, a generalist providing integrated care and needing to know (among others) something about alcohol, back pain, cancer, depression, diabetes, domestic violence, eating disorders, fibromyalgia, grief, heart disease, menopause, obesity, stress, men, women, kids, adults, and the elderly. It is important to be focused and flexible, to develop a library of psychoeducational materials and a focus on prevention. The assessment endpoint is not a diagnosis, but a recommendation presented in a short, jargon-free report or a phone call. And because many referred patients do not keep their appointments with psychologists, one must also attend to the patient who is not in the office and document no shows; otherwise the referral source assumes they were seen and are under your care. Get used to curbside consultations or hallway handoffs, which can be uncomfortable because psychologists like to get all the facts before rendering an opinion, but if you withhold your opinion, physicians will stop asking. Referring family physicians expect prompt reports without signed patient releases. This is typical in family practice but can conflict with the requirements of the APA Ethical Code, as can discussion of patients in the hallway or making chart notes about sensitive matters. It is also crucial to remember that the family physician is the "customer" and continues to "own" the patient, and it is dangerous to get caught in power struggles between patients and their physicians, for example, excessively advocating for patients who complain about their medication regimens rather than supporting their discussing it with the physician.

To promote and nurture a collaborative relationship with a family medicine practice, it is necessary to make known one's availability for service. Gaining visibility can include offering to present topics of interest to local or regional family medicine conferences, or in larger practices to present to the medical staff during lunches. Scheduling brief meetings with individual family physicians at their sites to share your interest in working collaboratively on particular types of cases can open the door to regular referrals, and attention to the aforementioned suggestions can assure they continue. Also crucial is becoming familiar and cordial with the rest of the office staff, the secretaries, the nurses, and nursing assistants, since they often inform the physicians of your value and worth and can exert an influence on referrals. Patients ask support staff for assurance that their referral to a psychologist is appropriate and wise, and if the staff knows and respects a psychologist, such encouragement is forthcoming; if not, the patient may be quietly discouraged from following through.

Primary Care in the Schools

Psychologists can also provide services in concert with primary care physicians in school-based health centers. Frequently school counselors and school psychologists are overwhelmed with heavy caseloads and paperwork, and can serve as contacts that might support consultation from a non–school psychologist who is not on staff. Collaborative medical services in the schools make sense because that is where the children and adolescents are, and schools are often one of the few stable institutions in rural, impoverished, and underserved areas. The first school-based health centers established in the early 1970s provided only reproductive services to adolescents, but they now provide a range of services that go beyond students to meet the needs of their families as well. Services are often culturally sensitive, since schools often reflect the ethnicity or values of the local citizens more reliably than the clinic setting. Serious and chronic illnesses affect 6–12 million youngsters, they are absent from school more and have poorer school achievement, and treatments like radiation and medication can contribute to learning difficulties. Psychologists in school-based centers can focus not only on individual cases but affect family or classroom systems by consulting to providers and school staff about issues of disease course and treatment. Staff and students often need information about diagnoses and management, as well as support for coping with a child's disease.

Reimbursement can be complex since funding can come from a wide variety of federal, state, local, and private funds. Individual compensation can be difficult when working collaboratively with physicians, and diagnostic codes may not fit traditional psychiatric categories. Finally, ethical issues include informed consent, confidentiality, and competence, and the psychologist must be familiar with regulations of state health and education boards to assure compliance.

Pediatricians

In recent decades pediatrics has expanded its focus on the physical health of children to include their emotional, social, and educational health as well. But many pediatricians cope with considerable financial and time pressures, spending on average 14 minutes with each patient. They often possess insufficient knowledge and skills to manage developmental and psychosocial problems, and thus lack confidence in doing so. Some admit they are uncomfortable asking about family interactions, although parents often wish to share this information. In the collaborative model here, psychologists have similar options to working with family physicians, but the requisite knowledge base is narrower. They can work in one pediatrician's office or take referrals as independent specialists in a pediatric group practice or in their own private offices. With a dedicated consultant available pediatricians are more likely to screen for developmental problems or families in distress, and psychologists are better prepared to interact with schools and mental health centers, making collaboration mutually beneficial.

Adolescent Medicine

Physicians in adolescent medicine work on the cusp between pediatrics and adult internal medicine. In addition to the normal problems of adolescent health, such specialists are often the first to identify eating and weight-related problems in their patients. Overweight and obese adolescents typically have more medical and psychological problems than their normal weight peers, but most seek help for these problems rather than the eating disorders per se. Our modern, obesity-prone society promotes the default consumption of high-fat, high-calorie foods and faulty appetitive traits such as binge eating and loss of satiety responsiveness. At the other end of the spectrum, adolescents suffer with anorexia and bulimia nervosa, with associated severe medical and psychological complications. Although evidence-based interventions exist for the treatment of weight-related conditions, they are seldom used regularly in clinics. Those who wish to undertake the rigorous training necessary to become proficient in the treatment of eating spectrum disorders will find adolescent medicine collaborators who will gladly manage their patients medically if the psychologist will treat them behaviorally.

Internists

Internal medicine specialists deal with a variety of adult conditions that lend themselves to collaborative practice. The management of chronic pain is a prominent source of referral for psychological intervention. Psychologists can reduce the pain, increase functioning, and improve the quality of life of chronic pain patients by direct services as well as leading multidisciplinary teams. Pain center psychologists can assess patients, provide psychotherapy, educate patients in pain management skills training, provide social and family support services, support adherence, and assist in community reintegration. The interdisciplinary team often includes anesthesiology, physical medicine, social work, neurology, physical and occupational therapy, and nutrition. Because of the number of disciplines working toward a common goal, psychologists who understand communication, team dynamics and group process, operational goals, and evidence-based treatment outcomes are well suited to become team leaders.

Another example is the management of nonalcoholic fatty liver disease, which has the potential to progress to advanced liver failure and is associated with those patients with type II diabetes and metabolic syndrome. Psychologists instruct patients on lifestyle modification, dietary recommendations, self-monitoring, goal setting, stimulus control, cognitive restructuring, and problem solving. Some specialize in women's health, including pregnancy loss, perinatal depression, and life-threatening conditions such as cancer. Again, the key is to be visible, flexible, and available. Locate near an internal medicine practice, provide talks on behavioral health issues, or offer patient education materials on health psychology topics for the physician's facility, and be sure to build solid relationships with support staff.

Surgeons

Roughly 30,000 solid organ transplants are performed each year, but organs suitable for transplantation remain scarce. Psychological factors have an influence on postsurgical mortality and morbidity after transplant, so most transplant teams require a psychological evaluation to determine a potential recipient's suitability for receiving a transplant. This is a prime opportunity to coordinate care with surgeons, since psychologists assess patients for compliance, decisional capacity, and ability to work with a team; identify potential difficulties; educate patients and staff about specific issues; and in some cases provide follow-up patient care.

Bariatric surgery is a popular procedure spawned by the serious comorbidities associated with obesity. Although unclear, the literature suggests psychopathology is higher in super-obese patients, including depression, mood shifts, and even suicidality. The most common surgical procedures include gastric bypass or an adjustable gastric band. Potential patients must undergo psychological assessment before acceptance into candidacy for bariatric surgery. This is another opportunity for psychologists to join the bariatric team, to assess patients in advance of surgery, and in some cases to follow up with individual or group support and psychoeducation.

Reproductive Medicine: OB-GYN

There is a strong expectation in society that a married couple will have children. While psychological factors do not cause infertility per se, couples who are infertile for some time experience considerable stress. Those using reproductive assistance technologies undergo months or years of uncertainty and waiting, in addition to exhaustion of financial and emotional resources. One or the other partner may be overwhelmed, requiring the other to provide support. Normal coping skills can fail when facing infertility, and understanding these unique pressures can allow reproductive specialists to refer individuals and couples to psychologists for treatment.

Dentists

Coordinating patient care with dentists is a lesser known arrangement. Dental professional organizations and dental schools often seek speakers for workshops and conventions. Contact state dental associations to offer continuing education. Consult with dental schools, focusing on dental students under stress, or teach them about behavioral aspects of dentistry, communication skills, bioethics, and behavioral factors in facial pain or dental phobias. You can also contact individual dentists to offer consultation for their anxious or avoidant patients.

Exercise and Sport Psychology

Sports psychology is growing as professional and recreational athletes seek the services of psychologists, requiring collaboration with trainers, fitness consultants, and physical therapists. Research finds that focus and relaxation with goal setting are crucial to performance. Applied sport and exercise psychology includes instructing athletes, teams, coaches, fitness professionals, and other groups on the psychological aspects of their activities. Educational sports psychologists emphasize skills training, while clinical sports psychologists treat more significant problems such as substance abuse, eating disorders, and depression. Cultivating relationships requires an active knowledge of and interest in fitness and sports, as well as fundamental knowledge and skills in professional psychology.

References and Readings

Alexander, C. L., Arnkoff, D. B., & Glass, C. R. (2010). Bringing psychotherapy to primary care: Innovations and challenges. *Clinical Psychology: Science and Practice, 17,* 191–210.

Brown, K. S., & Folen, R. (2005). Psychologists as leaders of multidisciplinary chronic pain management teams: A model for health care delivery. *Professional Psychology: Research and Practice, 36,* 587–594.

Linton, J. C., & Shin, R. B. (2008) Bariatric surgery. In L. C. James & J. C. Linton (Eds.), *Obesity intervention for the lifespan* (pp. 115–127). New York: Springer.

Pidano, A. E., Kimmelblatt, C. A., & Neace, W. P. (2011). Behavioral health in the primary care setting: Needs, barriers and implications for psychologists. *Psychological Services, 8,* 151–165.

Wilfley, D. E., Vannucci, A., & Iacovino, J. (2010). The role of psychologists in the Identification and early intervention of eating and weight-related problems. *The Register Report, Fall,* 8–17.

Related Topic

Chapter 124, "Making Good Referrals"

143 CONSULTING ON END-OF-LIFE DECISIONS

James L. Werth, Jr. and Erica Whiting

Everyone dies. However, not everyone will die well and not everyone will be able to make his or her own end-of-life decisions. As a result, there are roles for psychologists and other mental health professionals when people are dying to assist the dying person, if she or he is conscious and able to interact with others; to assist loved ones who may be legally charged with making decisions or may be struggling with the fact that the person is dying; and to assist the health care professionals involved with the dying person and loved ones. We highlight each of these topics as they apply to adults who have at some point been legally competent to make their own decisions. Children and adolescents and individuals with developmental disabilities or other conditions that precluded their being able, legally, to make their own decisions are much more complicated and therefore not covered in this brief review. In addition, we do not address grief and loss after death or other associated topics such as futility and legal challenges to who is able to make decisions.

ASSISTING THE DYING PERSON

The circumstances surrounding the dying process can impact how the psychologist can help and what the emphasis may be (Qualls & Kasl-Godley, 2010). For example, an individual who was diagnosed with a potentially terminal condition many years ago that has progressed over time from being a chronic illness to the point where the person has a prognosis of 6 months or less to live is likely facing different issues from someone who has been healthy and was in an automobile accident from which she will not recover. Similarly, the dying person's culture could affect choices, including whether withholding or withdrawing treatment is an option or who makes decisions. The variables involved are significant and range from physical concerns such as pain, nausea, and lucidity to interpersonal ones such as quality and quantity of relationships with loved ones to intrapersonal issues such as previous experiences, fear, and goals.

The fact that there are so many different factors and issues that may affect individuals' end-of-life decisions and that each one may be important in influencing the dying person's quality of life and decision-making ability led the American Psychological Association's Working Group on Assisted Suicide and End-of-Life Decisions (APA, 2000) to develop a set of "Issues to Consider When Exploring End-of-Life Decisions" (see Appendix F). This outline begins with recommending that the psychologist examine her or his own beliefs regarding dying and end-of-life decisions and identify a consultant who can help the psychologist reduce the likelihood that her or his own issues, beliefs, and experiences are interfering with giving good service to the dying person. Next, the psychologist is advised to assess whether the dying person is mentally capable of making decisions or whether something may be interfering with capacity. If the person appears not to be capable, then involvement of the health care team and loved ones who are legally empowered to assist with decision making is crucial. However, if the person is able to make her or his own decisions, then the list of issues provides topics that could be explored with the dying individual, depending on the specific circumstances, including cultural issues and financial considerations. The involvement of significant others is included as is a special focus on the possibility that direct or indirect coercion may be influencing decision making. Furthermore, the use of psychological assessment instruments is briefly noted.

The APA's (2000) set of Issues to Consider provides the psychologist with a foundation for topics to explore in an effort to help the dying person make fully considered decisions while respecting the degree to which the person wants to involve others. One of the considerations is whether the dying individual wants to complete legal documents identifying (a) the types of treatment she or he would or would not want (i.e., a living will) and (b) who is legally empowered to make medical decisions if she or he becomes incapable of making decisions or who is empowered at present to receive and act on information because of cultural beliefs (i.e., a durable power of attorney for health care). Both of these documents have problems and neither should be relied upon in isolation or to solve all issues (Werth & Blevins, 2008). For example, the living will is often interpreted to only apply if the person is in exactly the condition specified in the document (e.g., reliant upon mechanical ventilation) and not if some other situation exists (e.g., the need for dialysis). Similarly, a power of attorney (POA) identifies who is legally permitted to make decisions but does not eliminate disagreements among loved ones (e.g., the person holding POA wanting to take action B but another loved one wanting to take action C). We turn to the issues associated with disagreements, and reducing their impact, in the next section. Ideally, the dying person and her or his loved ones will have engaged in conversations while the person is capable of expressing choices and before a crisis ensues and emotions are running high.

In summary, if a psychologist is working with a dying individual, we believe it would be helpful for the professional to review factors that may affect the person's quality of life and decision-making ability. Furthermore, assisting the person in taking steps that will maximize the likelihood that her or his wishes will be followed and that will make decision making easier on loved ones if they are called upon to step in if the dying person is unable to make decisions can be an important role.

ASSISTING LOVED ONES

A psychologist can be helpful to loved ones of a dying person in many ways. For the ease of discussion, we focus first on ways to assist while the dying person maintains the ability to make her or his own decisions and then on how to be helpful if the dying individual is unable to express her or his own decisions. As was the case earlier when talking about the dying person, the cultural beliefs and experiences of the loved ones can have important implications on how they handle the dying process and what they perceive their own roles to be. The ways in which the dying person's cultural beliefs and those of the loved ones intersect and how they may complement or contradict each other would be an important area for exploration by the psychologist.

Another area to be examined is how the loved one is interpreting or perceiving the dying person's condition and ensuring, to the degree possible and within the limits of confidentiality and scope of practice, that the significant other has the correct information on diagnosis and prognosis. Depending on the circumstances, the psychologist may be able to provide this information, may facilitate discussions among the dying person and loved ones, and/or may connect the loved one and members of the health care team.

A related issue is exploring the perceived role of the loved one in the caregiving of the dying person and encouraging dialogue among the parties to reduce the likelihood of miscommunication or misunderstanding. A related factor is how the loved one's beliefs and emotional experiences can influence interactions. For example, a loved one may believe that it is her or his responsibility to keep the person well and alive as long as possible and therefore hover around the dying person. If this is not what the dying person wants, then disagreements, hurt feelings, and broken relationships can result. On the other end of the spectrum, the loved one may be so afraid of being hurt if the dying person takes a turn for the worse or dies that she or he distances (physically and/or emotionally) from the dying person to protect herself or himself, leading to the dying person feeling abandoned. The value of open communication cannot be overstated in these situations.

An overarching consideration, whether the dying person is still capable of making her or his own decisions or is incapable of doing so, which will be considered later, is care for the caregiver and loved ones. Recognizing the pressure placed on caregivers, the American Psychological Association (2011) has developed a set of resources (the "Caregiver Briefcase for Psychologists") designed to help psychologists assist in promoting wellness among those caring for others. Caregivers may sacrifice themselves for the dying person and may need help in realizing that they have to care for themselves if they are going to be able to provide maximal help to the dying person. Furthermore, many caregivers get a sense of meaning and purpose out of helping their loved ones but, unfortunately, the dying person may perceive herself or himself as a burden on others, perhaps especially caregivers. Without good communication among these involved, the dying person may make decisions in an attempt to reduce perceived burden without realizing that this course of action actually creates more emotional difficulties for caregivers.

This being said, there are ways that dying individuals can reduce subsequent intrapersonal and interpersonal difficulties for loved ones. Psychologists can help facilitate discussions about what to do if the dying person is unable to make decisions for herself or himself, assist with the creation of legal documents that provide some direction for loved ones in terms of what to do and not do and who has primary responsibility for making these decisions and ensuring they are followed through. These discussions and documents will not eliminate problems and questions and ruptured relationships or guilt later, but they can provide a measure of reassurance for those tasked with the difficult decisions that may affect the manner and timing of death and perhaps even the perception of suffering by the dying person. It is not unusual for people not involved in the day-to-day life of the dying person to question decisions made and often people question their own decisions later, so having things in writing or audio or video can help reduce the problems among loved ones or within the person(s) who made the end-of-life decisions. To the extent that they have been involved before the death, psychologists also can be helpful in processing the decisions that were made, within the limits of confidentiality.

ASSISTING HEALTH CARE PROFESSIONALS

Psychologists can be helpful to the health care professionals who are working with dying persons. Everyone on the team has some emotional investment in their patients and other people who are in the lives of their patients. Thus, it is possible that the psychologist could be helpful with one or more members of a health care team who are having reactions to the death of a patient or the loved ones of a patient. Some health care professionals may become numb in order to protect themselves from the pain associated with watching people die difficult deaths or seeing significant others fight among themselves about how to proceed. To the extent that there are disagreements within the health care team about how to proceed in areas such as information sharing, courses of action, and involvement of others, there can be heightened tension and frustration in the team that can come out in many problematic ways.

Thus, one role for the psychologist is serving as a consultant to teams to help enhance individual and team functioning and decrease the chances of burnout.

Another role of the psychologist can be in helping the team work with people who have strong personalities, are culturally different from the team members, or are overwhelmed and frozen in the face of life-and-death decisions. Psychologists have the training to help people communicate and negotiate in difficult situations. Maintaining a focus on the ethical metaprinciples of respecting people, minimizing harm, maximizing benefits, acting in a just manner, and being honest can provide a useful framework for the psychologist.

ETHICAL AND LEGAL CONSIDERATIONS

When working in end-of-life situations, the psychologist must keep several ethical and legal considerations in mind (Kleespies, 2004). Certainly, the psychologist must be competent to provide services to dying persons, loved ones, and health care professionals or have competent consultants who are available to provide timely assistance. One of the aspects of competence is the ability to anticipate problems and either minimize the chances that such issues may develop or be prepared when they do come up. Many of these issues can relate to multiple relationships and/or confidentiality.

Psychologists often envision their role as being circumscribed in time and place—perhaps to a 50-minute session once a week that takes place in the therapist's office. When working with people who are dying, this traditional model may not be realistic. Often, people are too ill or tired to leave their homes or may have an exacerbation of their illness or condition and be hospitalized. The psychologist needs to be ready to make decisions about what is acceptable and possible when responding to these circumstances that are beyond the control of the client.

A related factor is how much and how to involve loved ones in the treatment. As we noted earlier, communication is a key issue when people are dying and end-of-life decisions are being made. The need to preserve confidentiality is not eliminated when a person is dying, but the possibility that a person may suddenly lose the ability to communicate needs to be anticipated and plans for how to handle exchange of information are important.

These and other factors illustrate the importance of the original informed consent agreement and the need to revisit informed consent and modify the original contract or include addenda as circumstances change. Given the fact that many people lose the ability to make their own decisions as the dying process progresses, it may make sense to have releases of information signed at or near the beginning of treatment, perhaps with some limitations on when the releases will be in force. A related issue is what information should be available for release after the person's death. If there is some concern about the release of information after death, this should be discussed and measures put in place prior to death. Along these same lines, issues associated with the dying person's ideas regarding the psychologist's involvement with any post-death rituals arise frequently and therefore warrant a proactive discussion to reduce confusion later.

Another issue that is discussed in the literature a fair amount is what the psychologist should do if the client discusses the possibility of hastening her or his own death through measures such as withholding or withdrawing treatment, taking an overdose of pills, or using other approaches such as a plastic bag and helium. There are complex ethical and legal considerations in such instances and guidance is available in the literature, but there is no replacement for an experienced consultant when these questions arise.

HYPOTHETICAL CASE EXAMPLE

John is a 62-year-old African American man who was a high school US history teacher and lived in a suburban area with his wife. Their son and one daughter lived many hours away with their own families but came home on holidays while the youngest daughter, who was single, remained close by and visited regularly. John prided himself on his rapport with students, the fact that he had several short stories and a few poems published, and his reputation as a well-respected speaker on topics such as what history can teach us about the present.

John had a family history of cancer and therefore was diligent in attending to his health and well-being. His wife, Veronica, had a breast cancer scare a few years ago so she, too, was vigilant about health issues. When John began having abdominal pain, he immediately saw his family physician, who referred him to an internist for further evaluation. An abdominal mass was found and John was scheduled for surgery. The surgeon found indications that the mass was cancerous and had metastasized. Further testing revealed that John did indeed have cancer that had spread beyond the original mass. John's wife and children were very supportive, but the family also felt overwhelmed by the news and what it meant.

John's younger sister is a social worker, so when she suggested that it would be helpful for him and his family to talk to a professional, which was also recommended by his oncologist, John agreed to talk to a psychologist covered by his health insurance whose name had been given to him by a coworker in whom John confided. Dr. Anderson was not a health psychologist but agreed to work with John with John's understanding that she would be consulting with a colleague who worked in a cancer unit. John and Dr. Anderson developed a solid therapeutic alliance and he was benefitting from their work together. However, John's physical health began declining and he began having significant pain. The powerful medication he needed to alleviate the pain interfered with his ability to think and communicate. After one of the appointments with the oncologist, John came in upset and angry, saying that the physician wanted him to give up trying and just die. Upon questioning John, and getting a release to talk with the physician, it appeared as if the physician had brought up the need for advance care planning and developing a living will, naming a power of attorney, and considering the possibility of hospice. John indicated that he would not abandon his family and wanted everything done to extend his life.

The progression of John's illness and the uncertainty associated with his condition was taking a toll on his wife and younger daughter, so he asked Dr. Anderson whether they could come into sessions as well. During the first family session, after John signed releases allowing Dr. Anderson to talk to both Veronica and Leah, Dr. Anderson asked whether they had talked about the physician's recommendations. Veronica and Leah said they agreed with John but admitted that the other two children disagreed and said that John should not force himself to suffer for their sakes. This disagreement was apparently straining the relationships between those who were present with John and the children who were out of town. As a result of these disagreements, John refused to sign releases allowing Dr. Anderson to talk to the other children.

Over the course of counseling with John and his family, a number of clinical, ethical, and legal issues are likely to continue to arise, including possible continued disagreements within the family, between the family and health care team, and perhaps between John and his family's decisions and Dr. Anderson's own beliefs. These likely events illustrate why Dr. Anderson needs to have a good consultant, be familiar with the issues involved, and be prepared to play many different roles as John's illness progresses.

References and Readings

American Psychological Association. (2011). *Caregiver briefcase for psychologists*. Retrieved February 2013, from www.apa.org/pi/about/publications/caregivers/index.aspx

American Psychological Association, Working Group on Assisted Suicide and End-of-Life Decisions. (2000). *Report to the Board of Directors*. Retrieved February 2013, from www.apa.org/pubs/info/reports/aseol.aspx

Kleespies, P. M. (2004). *Life and death decisions: Psychological and ethical considerations in end-of-life care*. Washington, DC: American Psychological Association.

Qualls, S. H., & Kasl-Godley, J. E. (2010). *End-of-life issues, grief, and bereavement: What clinicians need to know*. New York: Wiley.

Werth, J. L., Jr., & Blevins, D. (Eds.). (2008). *Decision-making near the end of life: Recent developments and future directions.* Philadelphia, PA: Routledge.

Related Topic

Chapter 48, "Practicing Psychotherapy with Older Adults"

144 PSYCHOTHERAPIST SELF-CARE CHECKLIST

John C. Norcross and James D. Guy, Jr.

Mental health professionals, by definition, study and modify human behavior. That is, we study and modify other humans. Psychological principles, methods, and research are rarely brought to bear on psychotherapists ourselves, with the probable exception of our unsolicited attempts to diagnose one another (Norcross, 2000). Although understandable and explicable on many levels, this paucity of systematic study on psychotherapists' self-care is unsettling indeed.

Our aims in this brief chapter are threefold: first, to remind busy practitioners of the personal and professional need to tend to their own psychological health; second, to provide evidence-based methods to nourish themselves; and third, to generate a positive message of self-renewal and growth.

The following list summarizes practitioner-recommended and research-informed methods of alleviating the distress of clinical work, or more optimistically, of replenishing the practitioner. Unfortunately, the research on psychotherapist self-care has not progressed to the point where controlled studies have been conducted. Nonetheless, the list presents a practical synthesis of clinical wisdom, research literature, and therapist experience on self-care methods from disparate theoretical traditions. The list is adapted from a more extensive catalogue of self-care activities published in our book *Leaving It at the Office* (Norcross & Guy, 2007), and it is divided into 12 broad strategies of self-care.

VALUING THE PERSON OF THE PSYCHOTHERAPIST

- Adhere to the ethical imperative of engaging in "self-care activities to maintain and promote your emotional, physical, mental, and spiritual well-being to best meet your professional responsibilities" (American Counseling Association).
- Ask your patients, if you have not done so recently, what has been most helpful in their psychotherapy. Take to heart their frequent compliments about your presence, affirmation, and support.
- Resist the pressures of managed care to define yourself as a nameless and disembodied "provider" of mental health services. Maintain your individual identity as a distinctive practitioner of psychological healing.

- Internalize the relational crux of the work. Yes, we conduct treatments to eradicate *DSM* disorders, but we also offer relationships that heal people.
- Assess your deep motives for becoming a psychotherapist beyond the altruism of "to help people." How are these motives facilitating or hindering your effective self-care?
- Prioritize your self-care: Put specific times in your schedule to sharpen the saw.
- Develop self-empathy: the capacity to notice, value, and respond to our own needs as generously as we attend to the needs of clients.
- Practice what you preach to your clients about nourishing the self: avail yourself (when applicable) of what you provide or recommend to clients with similar needs.
- Embrace an integrative mix of effective self-care strategies (as opposed to relying on a single theoretical orientation).
- Avoid concentration on a single self-care technique and promote cognitive and experiential growth on a broad front. Do you rely on only one or two self-care methods?
- Assess your own self-care, as you might a student's or a patient's—on a weekly or monthly basis.
- Track your self-care by maintaining a journal, calendar, or behavioral log of activity.
- Complete structured questionnaires on burnout and self-care periodically to facilitate your self-awareness and self-monitoring.
- Contract for some honest feedback from significant others about your work week, functioning, and self-care. Let others supplement and enhance your self-monitoring.
- Put your consequential self-care activities in your schedule/calendar first thing every month. Literally schedule your self-care.
- Alleviate the distress of conducting psychotherapy, to be sure, but also value and grow the person of the psychotherapist.

REFOCUSING ON THE REWARDS

- Recall that career satisfaction among psychotherapists is consistently high and rivals (or exceeds) that of other professionals.
- Remember your reasons for entering the profession in the first place as a means of refreshing your sense of calling and professional fulfillment.
- Build into your weekly schedule a concrete method to count your blessings, such as an imagery exercise or a gratitude journal.
- Attend to the profound satisfaction of helping others; vividly recall the life-transforming psychotherapies in which you were privileged to participate.
- Look for ways to create a greater sense of freedom and independence in your work.
- Variety and intellectual stimulation are indispensable. What can you do to increase their impact on your schedule and professional duties?
- Satisfaction from helping others is crucial, so be sure to include at least some clinical activities that demonstrate you are helping someone.
- Enjoy maintaining relationships with clients that span years, even decades, involving intermittent courses of treatment.
- Your work will ideally capitalize on both your natural and acquired abilities. Do what you do well.
- A sense of humor and the absurd is one of your most potent stress relievers. Practice.
- Be careful when applying your expertise to your family of origin...fools rush in where angels fear to tread.
- Self-monitor the quality of your friendships. Do they sustain you?
- Remember: you are actually self-employed, regardless of who you work for. Maintaining this perspective brings great freedom of choice.
- Clinical practice may not make you rich, but if it is your calling, it is a wonderful way to make a living.
- Bear in mind, particularly during your beleaguered moments, that there are typically many more benefits than hazards associated with the practice of psychotherapy.

RECOGNIZING THE HAZARDS

- Repeat the mantra "Psychotherapy is often a grueling and demanding calling" in order to establish realistic expectations.

- Affirm the universality of occupational hazards by sharing your stressors and distress with trusted colleagues.
- Identify the impact of clinical practice on you and your loved ones. All accounts indicate that clinical practice exacts a negative toll on the practitioner, particularly in the form of problematic anxiety, moderate depression, and emotional underinvolvement with family members.
- Consider the amount of physical isolation you experience each day. What steps can you take to create more opportunities for contact with other clinicians?
- Create variety in your day, such as intermingling psychotherapy sessions with supervision, consultations, study breaks, a trip to the gym, and so on.
- Invite family and friends to point out when you become too interpretive and "objective" when it would be healthier to be spontaneous and genuine.
- Know the actuarial data about the probability of a malpractice lawsuit or licensing complaint and thoughtfully consider high-risk aspects of your practice (e.g., involvement with borderline and narcissistic personality disorders, suicidal and violent patients, "recovered memory" cases, contested divorce cases).
- Calculate the possibility of patient violence in your office and take steps to enhance your personal safety accordingly.
- Take Coach John Wooden's advice and refuse to believe either your most idealizing or your most demeaning client—you are neither God nor the devil.
- Limit your exposure to traumatic images outside the therapy room by choosing movies, literature, and other entertainment carefully.
- Reevaluate your involvement with managed care, particularly its possible contribution to your experience of depletion and burnout. How might you restore some control in your work to enhance your sense of autonomy?
- Adopt a team approach in dealing with high-stress clinical situations; distribute the burden and lighten the individual load.
- Beware of inadvertent domestic violations of patient confidentiality, and limit the amount of client material you share with your significant others.
- Consider how you have managed the delicate balance between empathic connection and self-preserving distance in your clinical work. When you find yourself on one end of the pendulum, pursue balance.
- Reflect on the number of clients that you have said good-bye to over the years. What has been the cumulative impact of these terminations?
- Address your own limitations and needs in an open manner instead of playing competitive therapist games.
- Periodically reevaluate why you became a psychotherapist and why you continue to practice. Look for ways to work through those unhealthy motivations.
- Proactively discuss your professional and parental commitments within significant relationships.
- Accept some spillover from your professional life into your personal life as an inevitable cost of being human.
- Discuss with your spouse/partner the topics covered in this chapter. How does he or she perceive their impact on your relationship?
- Learn how to handle distracting intercurrent life events. Perhaps consult with a trusted and more experienced colleague.
- Implement proactive steps to reduce the low but real possibility of burnout.
- "Start where you are": Cultivate self-empathy regarding occupational hazards so that you can develop empathy for others.
- Tailor your self-care to your personality and context by disentangling transient, paradigmatic, and situational difficulties in your practice; each requires a different self-care plan.
- Reconcile and balance the hazards of psychotherapeutic practice with its rewards—"fountain of sorrow, fountain of life."
- Adopt the long perspective as a healing practitioner; most psychotherapists enjoy lengthy, successful careers and would elect to do it again.

MINDING THE BODY

- Mind your body as part of your self-care; do not become preoccupied with sophisticated self-care methods at the expense of your biobehavioral basics.
- Track the quality and length of your sleep. How many hours of sleep are you averaging each night, compared to what your body needs?
- Take your own advice: exercise regularly.
- Schedule minibreaks between sessions to self-massage your face, neck, and leg muscles; perhaps schedule regular massages to nourish yourself and relieve muscle tension.
- Stretch your muscles and reconnect to your body as antidotes to the sedentary nature of psychotherapy.
- Get moving during your workday: go for walks between sessions or during meals and avoid motionless sitting positions that reduce circulation and energy.
- Secure sufficient hydration during the day.
- Eat balanced, nutritious meals before, during, and after work; avoid the empty calories of comfort foods.
- Monitor your use of substances. Are you self-medicating with alcohol, tobacco, drugs, or food?
- Arrange for contact comfort and sexual gratification away from the office; it is your responsibility to meet your physical needs.

NURTURING RELATIONSHIPS

- Self-assess your peer support at the office. How does it fare? In one study of well-functioning psychologists (Coster & Schwebel, 1997), peer support emerged as the highest priority.
- Identify the three most nurturing people in your life. What can you do to increase the amount of support you receive from them?
- Insist on sufficient alone time. Do you know what to do with it when it's available?
- Pursue ongoing nurturance at the office with your clinical colleagues; take lunch, conversations, and walks with one another.
- Join or organize a peer support, supervision, or cuddle group.
- Participate in clinical teams and periodically conduct cotherapy to keep you fresh and vital.
- Seek nurturance from professionals in the community for both business assistance and collegial friendships.
- Develop arrangements for ongoing supervision or consultation. If it is unavailable or ineffective at your employment setting, then purchase it.
- Determine which clients "recharge your batteries" and brighten your day. Within the constraints of ethics and transference, structure your daily schedule and review your caseload to ensure that you see some of these patients on a daily basis.
- Identify the interpersonal gratifications you receive from favorite clients and what happens following termination with them.
- Name your most significant mentor during your career. How are your needs for mentoring being met today?
- Follow the evidence: The highest-rated career-sustaining behavior for psychotherapists is spending time with one's spouse/partner and friends.
- Try to include phone calls, lunches, and breaks in your workday several times each week to provide contact with family and friends.
- Maintain your old, civilian friends who keep you grounded in life outside of clinical work.
- Utilize your family-of-origin relationships to help you reality test and to confront your grandiosity.
- Beware if your friendships are becoming fewer in number or diminishing in significance over the years of professional practice. Take corrective action if necessary
- Take advantage of Colleague Assistance Plans, should practice troubles come your way.
- Something may be amiss if you are habitually giving out more nurturance than you are receiving. Seek a personal mentor or personal therapist to remedy the imbalance.
- When confronted with occupational stress, tend and befriend, rather than fight or flight.

SETTING BOUNDARIES

- Begin by understanding concretely your roles, responsibilities, and limitations as a psychotherapist; only then can you communicate and establish these boundaries with patients.
- Work under capacity (90%) so that emergencies, family demands, and self-care can be routinely accommodated.
- Be explicit with your clients about your professional expectations and limitations. Setting boundaries emerges in our research as the most frequent self-care strategy of mental health professionals.
- Secure goal consensus in a collaborative manner with patients early on in treatment to avoid subsequent boundary misunderstandings and confusion.
- Clearly delineate your policies regarding extra sessions, late appointments, extrasession telephone contacts, payment for services, and the like.
- Consider adopting an informed consent form as a written treatment contract.
- Establish a monitoring method to determine when a particular boundary has been crossed.
- Cultivate shared responsibility with patients for the change process and treatment outcome; avoid taking sole responsibility for psychotherapy.
- Craft your own professional bill of rights. What are your inalienable rights as a psychotherapist?
- Demand a livable wage and a "good enough" income.
- Set caseload boundaries: Maintain your caseload at an effective number for you and limit the number of at-risk patients at any one time.
- Minimize as possible your out-of-session exposure to emergencies and patient excursions into your personal time.
- Take protective measures to ensure your physical safety and that of your loved ones. Decline to treat certain clients, refuse to disclose personal data, prohibit clients from appearing uninvited at your home, and make your office secure.
- Customize treatment to individual patients, but limit your bending. Determine whether you are bending too far.
- Learn to say "no" to clients, referral sources, agencies, and administrators; become a responsible assertive therapist.
- Rebuff inappropriate incursions into your practice by managed care organizations and other entities that would compromise your integrity and ethics.
- Delegate nonclinical work to staff or external services; focus on doing what you uniquely are trained and interested in doing.
- Be clear about posttermination contacts with clients. Saying good-bye to clients properly requires explicit statements concerning how, when, and why treatment may resume in the future.
- Beware of avarice. Are you working long hours out of financial necessity or getting greedy?
- Bridge the gap between work hours and your loved ones by building in phone calls, personal visits, and short breaks.
- Demarcate the transition from work to non-work with regular rituals, such as music, exercise, change of clothes, or meditation.
- Transfer difficult patients—for an evaluation, a second opinion, or for treatment elsewhere—from a position of strength.
- Remember that your clients are not there to meet your needs; treatment relationships are not reciprocal.
- Define your relationships with colleagues with care. Transference influences these relationships, too.
- Let your hair down with family and friends. They want you to be genuine, spontaneous, and unprofessional.
- Establish an identity and life apart from your psychotherapist role. Don't get stale.
- Zealously protect your personal time with family and friends; work is work and home is home.
- Avoid friendships exclusively with clinical colleagues, as social gatherings may quickly deteriorate into work meetings.
- Embrace a mature synthesis of the dialectic between commitment to self and commitment to patients. It is possible to balance both with realistic boundaries.

RESTRUCTURING COGNITIONS

- Self-monitor your internal dialogue regarding your performance and your patients via thoughtful reflection, collecting data to dispute cognitive errors, or sharing with significant others.
- Compare your clinical and scholarly performance to same-aged peers in similar circumstances, not to authorities.
- Track your overly busy schedule and rate pleasure and mastery of activities to help you discover what changes need to be made.
- Self-treat the error of selective abstraction by determining actual successes and failures, accepting the inevitable limitations of your therapeutic skills, and distinguishing between case failures and yourself as a failure.
- Think through the transferential feelings directed to you; to whom are they aimed and to whom do they belong?
- Beware of absolutistic thinking: musturbation ("I must be...") and the tyranny of the shoulds ("I should have..."). They can affect you as much as your patients.
- Dispute the common fallacy that "good psychotherapy is equivalent to having all patients like us."
- Recall that the other side of caring consists of confrontation. Caring about others includes being honest and tough at times.
- Reassure yourself that the conditions in psychotherapy, as well as in life, are not always easy. This is unfortunate but not catastrophic.
- Remind yourself that you cannot cure every patient and that some patients will not succeed with you.
- Balance the amount of time you dwell on your successful cases and your frustrating cases.
- Redefine success as a process rather than an end result. Success includes your effort, and mini- or partial achievements, not simply the complete remission of patient symptoms.
- Assertively reduce unrealistic demands made on you: Do not take on more work than you need to or wrongly believe you are expected to do more.
- Recognize that your patients do not have to be as hard-working or persevering as you.
- Ask three critical questions—did that really occur? What are the probabilities? and What is the worst that could happen?—when you catastrophize about you and your clients.
- Catch yourself when assuming blame (i.e., personal causality) for events in clients' lives and consider alternate explanations.
- Calculate real probabilities when thinking about treatment outcomes. The worst happens only infrequently—to you or to your patients.
- Evaluate treatment success on a continuum to avoid dichotomous thinking; psychotherapy outcomes rarely fall on either extreme of a continuum.
- Use self-insight, empathy, anxiety management, and conceptualizing ability when experiencing countertransference reactions.
- Confront the ultimate psychotherapist fallacy: "I should not have emotional problems. After all, I am a therapist!" Yes, you are an expert on human behavior—but you're still nutty at times.
- Create realistic expectations for your self-care; avoid perfectionist tendencies toward eradicating your perfectionism.
- Offer yourself unconditional self-acceptance (USA) as a psychotherapist and as a person.

SUSTAINING HEALTHY ESCAPES

- Undertake a candid assessment of what purposes and significance overwork has for you. What really prevents you from engaging in healthy escapes?
- Perform an honest appraisal of *un*healthy escapes (e.g., substance abuse, isolation, sexual acting out) and determine whether the problem applies to you.
- Make relaxation part of your workday; it improves your energy, empathy, and attention.
- Take vital breaks between patients and between clinical responsibilities.
- Maintain your sense of humor; it is a career-sustaining behavior.

- Join your colleagues and staff for get-togethers in the office and spontaneous escapes from it.
- Include phone calls, lunches, and breaks in your workday several times each week to provide contact with friends and family.
- Practice balance: Over 80% of therapists routinely engage in reading or a hobby, take pleasure trips or vacations, and attend artistic events and movies as part of their self-care patterns (Mahoney, 1997).
- Schedule a weekly Shabbat—a regular day of rest and respite from the week's demands.
- Monitor your vacation time. Is it less than you as a psychotherapist would recommend to patients in similarly stressful occupations?
- Follow Freud's example: Every year take several weeks away from the office, and stay largely out of contact.
- Create adventure and other diversions away from the office. Is play a steady staple of your emotional diet?
- "Chop wood, carry water": Participate in concrete physical activities with a clearly visible and obvious outcome to counterbalance your psychotherapeutic work.
- Balance your socialization and alone time; determine how much restorative solitude you require.
- Take personal retreats that enable you to distance yourself geographically, emotionally, and interpersonally.
- Lengthen retreats into periodic clinical sabbaticals devoid of psychotherapy responsibilities.
- Reject ordinary thinking and adopt a more observational stance: Meditate.
- Try new and exciting activities for the first time: river rafting, camping, snorkeling, deep sea fishing, and the like.
- Avoid wishful thinking and self-blame in contemplating self-care; instead, pursue action-oriented strategies.
- Make a contract with yourself to integrate healthy escapes into your routine. Monitor and chart your progress.
- Ask yourself once a year (perhaps on your birthday), "How do I play?"

CREATING A FLOURISHING ENVIRONMENT

- Avoid falling prey to American individualism and the fundamental attribution error: Harness the power of your work environment to flourish.
- Conduct an environmental audit of your work space for comfort and appeal.
- Improve your work environment by providing pleasure in your furniture, aesthetics in your décor, and replenishment in your cupboard.
- Increase sensory awareness: using vision, hearing, touch, and olfaction counterbalances the cognitive and affective work of psychotherapy.
- Take protective measures to ensure your safety and that of your practice environment.
- Give yourself time between patients, 10 minutes to breathe, relax, make notes, review notes, return calls, and process what has happened during the preceding 50 minutes.
- Determine whether your clinical talents and interpersonal interests are poorly invested in paperwork. If so, consider a computer, a clerical assistant, a billing service, or other alternatives.
- Delegate, defer, and simplify the business aspects of your clinical position.
- Build behavioral boundaries to temporarily separate yourself from the clinical world by means of routines and time.
- Increase supports and reduce constraints to keep high-demand institutional jobs bearable and rewarding.
- Search for ways to create greater freedom and independence in your work.
- Beware of false interventions and short-term fixes in dysfunctional institutions; treat the systemic roots, not just the acute symptoms.
- Create a self-care village in a workaholic world by advocating for self-care as a means of improving productivity and outcomes.
- Assist your colleagues and administrators in acknowledging the occupational hazards and in offering group support, Me-Time, and other replenishment opportunities.

- Cultivate a self-care ethos in clinical training by improving the selection of students, broadening the training goals, increasing the availability of personal therapy, modeling the commitment to personal development, and encouraging research on psychotherapist self-care.
- Begin self-care at the top: Insist that your professional associations include self-care in their ethics, accreditation standards, publications, conferences, and continuing education.

UNDERGOING PERSONAL THERAPY

- Heed the evidence: Personal therapy is an emotionally vital and professionally nourishing experience central to self-care.
- Give yourself 50 minutes of time every few weeks in a holding environment; practice what you preach about the value of psychotherapy.
- Confront your resistances for not pursuing personal therapy. Are these "good reasons"—or convenient rationalizations to avoid accepting the patient role?
- Take seriously Freud's recommendation that every therapist should periodically—at intervals of 5 years or so—reenter psychotherapy *without shame* as a form of continued education. Do you heed his sage advice? Do you struggle with the shame?
- Beware the illusion that mental health professionals do not experience a need for personal therapy once they are in practice. More than half of psychotherapists do receive personal treatment following completion of formal training.
- Seek family therapy and family-of-origin work as well; do not limit yourself to individual therapy.
- Supplement personal therapy with regular self-analysis.
- Consider an annual satisfaction checkup with a valued mentor, trusted colleague, or former therapist.
- Pursue other personal development activities in addition to personal therapy. These might include the creative arts, Buddhist training, meditation seminars, dream work, or self-help groups.

CULTIVATING SPRITUALITY AND MISSION

- Identify and then resonate to your abiding mission in life. What mission do you want written on your tombstone (epitaph)?
- Embrace your sense of calling to be a clinician. What are the spiritual antecedents to your career choice?
- Cultivate awe and wonder at the human spirit; it will enable you to pull hope from hell.
- Invoke and augment your clients' spirituality to enrich their experience of psychotherapy.
- Connect to the spiritual sources of your hope and optimism regarding human behavior. If you have lost your enduring sense of caring and concern for others, get help.
- Assess periodically your belief in the potential for personality change, a prerequisite for good clinical practice.
- Take 10–15 minutes and write a stream of consciousness letter to your God, Nature, Spirit, or a higher power. What did you learn or relearn about your connection to spirituality?
- Evaluate the integration of spirituality and personal growth in your own life. How are you doing? What are you doing to promote such a synthesis?
- Confront squarely your own yearnings for a sense of transcendence and meaning.
- Create a hope-protecting philosophy of life that will help inoculate you from the despair of your clients.
- Cherish and practice your *Tikkun* (healing and repairing the world).
- Pursue the ultimate questions and find meaning in your personal life so that practicing psychotherapy does not become the ultimate meaning for you.
- Become a citizen-therapist by merging your vocation with social activism.
- Let your life speak—manifest your values and vocation in daily life.

FOSTERING CREATIVITY AND GROWTH

- Strive for adaptiveness and openness to challenges—the defining characteristics of passionately committed psychotherapists.
- Upload your creativity through innovative treatments, valuable metaphors, therapeutic irony, and novel methods.
- Diversify, diversify, diversify. Involvement in diverse professional activities balances your workload and expresses the full array of your skills.
- Mix up your therapy days: individual, couples, group, and family formats; younger and older patients; talk therapy and action therapy. What else can you do to increase variety and novelty in your schedule?
- Imagine periodically your future possible selves as a psychotherapist and then set sail in that direction.
- Embrace continuing education as *kaizen*—continuous improvement and lifelong learning.
- Attend clinical conferences, read literature, and form study groups to access the life springs of a committed professional. Do you feel you are just getting continuing education hours or refining and expanding your skills?
- Engage actively with professional organizations to shape our collective mission and to keep yourself involved.
- Create your own personal mission statement to sharpen your focus and prioritize your activities.
- Convert the skillful attitude of self-care into concrete behavior—lest your soul be lost to the demons.
- Invest in interdisciplinary movements to investigate and remediate the cries of the world.
- Be gentle with yourself—shed the heavy burden of expectations about personal perfection that psychotherapists carry.
- Expect a lifetime of struggle for awareness and growth; self-renewal is a process of creativity and growth.

References and Readings

Baker, E. K. (2003). *Caring for ourselves: A therapist's guide to personal and professional well-being.* Washington, DC: American Psychological Association.

Coster, J. S., & Schwebel, M. (1997). Well-functioning in professional psychologists. *Professional Psychology: Research and Practice, 28,* 5–13.

Geller, D. D., Norcross, J. C., & Orlinsky D. E. (Eds.). (2005). *The psychotherapist's own psychotherapy: Patient and clinician perspectives.* New York: Oxford University Press.

Guy, J. D. (1987). *The personal life of the therapist.* New York: Wiley.

Kottler, J. A. (1999). *The therapist's workbook: Self-assessment, self-care, and self-improvement exercises for mental health professionals.* San Francisco, CA: Jossey-Bass.

Mahoney, M. J. (1997). Psychotherapists' personal problems and self-care patterns. *Professional Psychology: Research and Practice, 28,* 14–16.

Norcross, J. C. (2000). Psychotherapist self-care: Practitioner-tested, research-informed strategies. *Professional Psychology: Research and Practice, 31,* 710–713.

Norcross, J. C., & Guy, J. D. (2007). *Leaving it at the office: Psychotherapist self-care.* New York: Guilford Press.

Related Topics

Chapter 130, "Creating a Professional Living Will for Psychologists"

Chapter 132, "Selecting and Relying on an Attorney"

145 CONDUCTING EVIDENCE-BASED PREVENTION

Sha'Kema M. Blackmon and Elizabeth M. Vera

Broadly speaking, prevention refers to a set of interventions intended to reduce suffering, ameliorate risk factors, foster well-being, and promote social justice (Hage, Romano, Coyne, Kenny, Matthews, Schwartz, & Waldo, 2007). Historically examined through a public health lens, prevention was traditionally conceptualized as being primary, secondary, or tertiary. Primary prevention includes prevention of a particular disorder with an asymptomatic population. Secondary prevention involves decreasing the number of existing disorders in an "at-risk" population, while tertiary prevention involves remediation or preventing relapse in a population that is already symptomatic (Conyne, 2004).

Using a synthesized definition of prevention, Conyne (2004, p. 25) asserts that there is no longer a need to classify prevention into three subcategories, defining it as "a goal for both everyday life and for service delivery, through which people become empowered to interact effectively and appropriately within varying levels of systems (micro, meso, exo, and macro) and in settings (individual, family, school, community, work). Prevention application can yield a reduction in the occurrence of new cases of a problem, in the duration and severity of incipient problems, and it can promote strengths and optimal human functioning."

Prevention efforts have been targeted at a wide array of problems such as mental illness, substance abuse/addiction, suicide, alcohol, divorce, cigarette smoking, illiteracy, violence in schools, and "problems in living" (Conyne, 2004).

Evidence-based prevention, inclusive of Conyne's definition of prevention, addresses the prevention of problems with the added distinction of incorporating theoretical and empirical research into the design of an intervention while measuring the success or outcomes of an implemented prevention program. While it is important that prevention programming be evidence-based, it is equally essential that prevention programming be culturally sensitive. Cultural sensitivity can be understood as developing prevention programming that is responsive to the culture(s) of the intended recipients of the prevention services. Culturally sensitive interventions can occur at two levels: surface structure and deep structure. Surface structure involves exterior modifications such as changes in the language of a brochure. In contrast, deep structure involves examining the heart and soul of an intervention to address "cultural, social, historical, environmental, and psychologic" factors relevant to the prevention target group(s) (Resnicow, Soler, Braithwaite, Ahlualia, & Butler, 2000). For instance, developing an HIV/AIDS prevention program might involve addressing concerns related to racial identity or gay lesbian identity development. The use of surface and deep structure adaptations is likely to yield the most effective culturally sensitive program because presentation and authenticity are addressed.

Two primary reasons exist for engaging in evidenced-based culturally sensitive prevention. First, not all preventive interventions will work for all individuals in need because of cultural, developmental, social, and ecological variability. For instance, a culturally relevant violence prevention program was effective for ethnically diverse youth under 12 years but ineffective for youth over 12 years; beyond age there were racial group differences in terms of the reduction of violence (Rodney, Johnson, & Srivastava, 2005). In the *Keeping it R.E.A.L.* prevention program, outcome measures revealed that for Native American youth, the program was ineffective, resulting in increased drug use, whereas the program had been previously successful with a group of Black, Latino, and White adolescents (Dixon et al., 2007). While the program was primarily designed for ethnic minority adolescents, it did not translate well when implemented with Native Americans because of varying contextual factors. The take-home message of such findings is that prevention is not a "one size fits all" undertaking (Roosa, Dumka, Gonzales, & Knight, 2002).

Second, evidence-based, culturally sensitive prevention is important for customer satisfaction. Customer satisfaction has been found to be an important factor for parents attending prevention programming (Coard, Foy-Watson, Zimmer, & Wallace, 2007). Prevention is similar to advertising in that preventionists[1] must know their constituents and adapt to their needs. Satisfied participants are more likely to return for programming which reduces attrition, especially when there are other factors in participants' lives that take precedence over participating in prevention services (e.g., work and childcare obligations).

SUGGESTIONS FOR CONDUCTING EVIDENCE-BASED, CULTURALLY RELEVANT PREVENTION

A primary component to be considered before designing any type of prevention activity is determining one's level of investment in engaging in prevention. Prevention is very different from psychotherapy and is a much less straightforward process that involves interacting with constituents at many different levels, some of whom may not initially see the value of what preventionists may try to offer. Next, preventionists must determine whether they have the skills to effectively engage in prevention. These skills include multicultural competence, advocacy skills, counseling skills (i.e., individual and group), clinical supervision skills, organizational and leadership skills, and research skills (Hage et al., 2007).

Once deciding to design such prevention programs, it is important for preventionists to consider the following suggestions during each step of the process. These steps can be categorized into four areas: program development, participant management, community building, and evidence-based factors. Program development entails becoming knowledgeable about issues relevant to the initiation of the program. Roosa and colleagues (2002) first suggest that preventionists research the cultural values (i.e., predominant cultural values, acculturation, and enculturation practices) of the population that the prevention program is aimed at with the intended purpose of integrating culture across the prevention process. This can best be achieved by reviewing literature for the target prevention group and identifying successful programming efforts and gaps in the literature. A review of the literature could be followed by an exploratory formative focus group (Resnicow et al., 2000) or needs assessment. A formative focus group involves understanding the beliefs and attitudes of community members. A needs assessment serves the purpose of determining what the general needs in a community may be or understanding needs in regard to a specific prevention issue.

In the area of participant management, establishing credibility, motivation, and change are important factors to be attended to (Roosa et al., 2002). Establishing credibility involves displaying attitudes and behaviors that enable participants and community members to believe that the prevention team has an investment in helping the community.

[1] The term *preventionists* is used to describe individuals interested in engaging in prevention services.

Credibility is established through knowledge of the community (Reese & Vera, 2007), genuineness, humility, and an internalized interest in those receiving the intervention and the surrounding community. The ongoing and end result of establishing credibility is that the prevention program is valued by the community; credibility can be established by volunteering for community programs and having a historical understanding of previous prevention programming efforts so that the current effort avoids the pitfalls of the past (Reese & Vera, 2007). Motivation consists of helping participants to develop and maintain an investment in the prevention service with the goal of helping participants complete the program. Change refers to being responsive to participants' cultural experiences; change is important for the reduction of resistance during the prevention implementation process. Therefore, if a specific practice integrated into a prevention program is at odds with participants' world view or values then it is important for preventionists to change the program so that it is more in line with participants' needs. Change further speaks to the need for formative evaluation and focus groups. Exploratory focus groups can be used to understand cultural content as well as pretest materials and content to be used in prevention programming (Resnicow et al., 2000) to avoid future resistance. Including community members early on and throughout the process can insure that the prevention program will be socially just (Reese & Vera, 2007).

Evidence-based prevention programming also involves having research skills relevant to prevention, in particular program evaluation and measurement equivalence (Roosa et al., 2002). Preventionists must select measures that translate across groups. That is, whatever measure is chosen, the measure should function in similar ways if given to two different groups of participants receiving the same prevention service. Preventionists may want to consider pilot testing measures before the implementation of a prevention program to be sure of measurement equivalence.

Community factors are activities related to community relations on the part of the preventionists. Maintenance of a community relationship involves taking the time to develop an initial connection with participants, community leaders, and local resources; making efforts to maintain the connection to the community; and conducting follow-up booster sessions to reinforce positive effects of the program (Roosa et al., 2002).

ADAPTING AN EXISTING EVIDENCE-BASED PREVENTION PROGRAM

While many of the strategies for creating evidence-based prevention programs apply to adapting prevention programs, there are some notable and important points unique to the adaptation process. This section will utilize the example of the *Black Parenting Strengths and Strategies Project (BPSSP)* (Coard et al., 2007) as a model for how to appropriately and successfully adapt a prevention program. The overall purpose in highlighting this program as a model is to document the steps that were taken rather than thoroughly describing the program, although some description will be provided for context. A thorough review of this program is strongly recommended to understand the full context of these recommendations.

The BPSSP is an intervention program designed to reduce early development and conduct problems among low-income African American children by providing preventive intervention services to parents (Coard et al., 2007). The BPSSP is a secondary prevention program that focuses on early intervention with African American parents with the goal of impacting the long-term health and development of children. The BPSSP was adapted from a prevention program previously established to be successful with ethnically diverse parents. Adaptation of the program for African American parents resulted in increases in content of parental racial socialization (i.e., racial/cultural messages about what it means to be a person of color and how to negotiate oppression) and positive parenting as well as addressing a reduction in harsh discipline. Attendance for the intervention was high, customer satisfaction was found to be positive, and the program was successful in achieving its overall goals.

In reviewing the work of the BPSSP team, there are several steps they took in adapting their program; some of these steps reflect Roosa and colleagues' (2002) framework for conducting prevention. First, they were clear in the goals for the prevention program and the adaptation that followed. Second, they selected an empirically supported program that was flexible and amenable to adaptation. Third, they examined the original program for its strengths and weaknesses in regard to its possible use with African American parents. Fourth, they considered what could be added to the standard existing program. This included the addition of a strong African American cultural component with a deep consideration of culture throughout the process of adaptation and service delivery. Fifth, they modified the content of the program. For instance, discussions specifically focused on topics such as promoting academic achievement and dealing with events that are common for African American children. Sixth, they tailored the delivery of the services to reflect habits and mannerisms common to African American culture. They utilized collective values and activities such as storytelling, role playing, and humor. Seventh, a strong investment was made in maintaining fidelity to the original program. This was done in part by actively consulting with the original developers of the program and providing supervision for group facilitators.

Eighth, selection and training of group leaders was also important. The BPSSP team utilized group facilitators who were members of the participants' ethnic group. This component is strongly tied to adaptation and delivery of service. Individuals that are members of the same ethnic group are more likely to have an understanding of expected cultural behaviors. Though cultural matching is a beneficial feature to have in such interventions, it is not always possible. In the event that this is not possible, then it is important for preventionists who are of a different racial or cultural group to be as multiculturally competent as possible. Collaborating with knowledgeable individuals in the community may help those who are not a member of participants' racial or cultural group understand some of the cultural nuances associated with implementing the prevention program.

Ninth, attrition and maintenance of attendance were addressed by providing reimbursement for participation, maintaining community contacts by sending reminders, birthday cards, or calling to check in, and staying active in the community where participants resided. Finally, a unique aspect of the BPSSP team's approach was thorough documentation of their process in a peer-reviewed journal. Understanding how they went about their process is essential for the development of future evidence-based, culturally sensitive prevention programming.

Conducting evidence-based prevention programming that is culturally sensitive is a difficult but necessary task. We submit that the best means of developing evidence-based, culturally sensitive prevention programming is best achieved through preventionists examining themselves as well as the content and process of prevention programs to ensure that such prevention programs will be well received and valued within the community.

References and Readings

Coard, S. I., Foy-Watson, S., Zimmer, C., & Wallace, A. (2007). Considering culturally relevant parenting practices in intervention development and adaptation. *The Counseling Psychologist, 35*(6), 797–820.

Conyne, R. K. (2004). *Preventive counseling: Helping people to become empowered in systems and settings.* New York: Brunner-Routledge.

Dixon, A. L., Yabiku, S. T., Okamoto, S. K., Tann, S. S., Marsglia, F. F., Kulis, S., & Burke, A. M. (2007). The efficacy of multicultural prevention intervention among urban American Indian youth in the southwest U.S. *Journal of Primary Prevention, 28*(6), 547–568.

Hage, S. M., Romano, J. L., Conyne, R. K., Kenny, M., Matthews, C., Schwartz, J. P., & Waldo, M. (2007). Best practice guidelines on prevention practice, research, training, and social advocacy for psychologists. *The Counseling Psychologist, 35*(4), 493–566.

Reese, L. E., & Vera, E. M. (2007). Culturally relevant prevention: The scientific and practical considerations of community-based programs. *The Counseling Psychologist, 35*(6), 763–778.

Resnicow, K., Soler, R., Braithwaite, R., Ahlualia, J. S., & Butler, J. (2000). Culturally sensitivity in substance use prevention. *Journal of Community Psychology, 28*(3), 271–290.

Rodney, L. W., Johnson, D. L., & Srivastava. (2005). Impact of culturally relevant violence prevention models on school-age youth. *Journal of Primary Prevention, 26*(5), 439–454.

Roosa, M. W., Dumka, L. E., Gonzales, N. A., & Knight, G. P. (2002). Cultural/ethnic issues and the prevention scientist in the 21st century. *Prevention and Treatment, 5,* doi: 10.1037/1522-3736.5.1.55a

Related Topic

Chapter 137, "Helping People Cope with Disasters"

INDEX

"f" indicates material in figures. "n" indicates material in footnotes. "t" indicates material in tables.